ALSO BY GARY J. BASS

The Blood Telegram: Nixon, Kissinger, and a Forgotten Genocide

Freedom's Battle: The Origins of Humanitarian Intervention

Stay the Hand of Vengeance: The Politics of War Crimes Tribunals

JUDGMENT AT TOKYO

JUDGMENT AT TOKYO

World War II on Trial and the
Making of Modern Asia

GARY J. BASS

ALFRED A. KNOPF   NEW YORK 2023

Library of Congress Cataloging-in-Publication Data
Names: Bass, Gary J., author.
Title: Judgment at Tokyo : World War II on trial and
the making of modern Asia / Gary J. Bass.
Description: New York : Alfred A. Knopf, 2023. |
Includes bibliographical references and index.
Identifiers: LCCN 2022061519 | ISBN 9781101947104
(hardcover) | ISBN 9781101947111 (ebook)
Subjects: LCSH: Tokyo Trial, Tokyo, Japan, 1946–1948. | International
Military Tribunal for the Far East. | War crime trials—Japan—History—
20th century. | World War, 1939–1945—Campaigns—Pacific Area—Atrocities.
Classification: LCC KZ1181 .B37 2023 | DDC 341.6/90268—dc23/eng/20230712
LC record available at https://lccn.loc.gov/2022061519

Jacket image: Tojo Hideki, former Japanese prime minister
and army minister, at the International Military Tribunal for the Far East,
Tokyo, Japan / Alpha Stock / Alamy
Jacket design by Chip Kidd
Maps by Mapping Specialists, LTD

Manufactured in the United States of America
2nd Printing

For Miriam

Where do murderers go, man! Who's to doom, when the judge himself is dragged to the bar?

—Herman Melville, *Moby-Dick*

CONTENTS

Part II: Catharsis

Part III: Nemesis

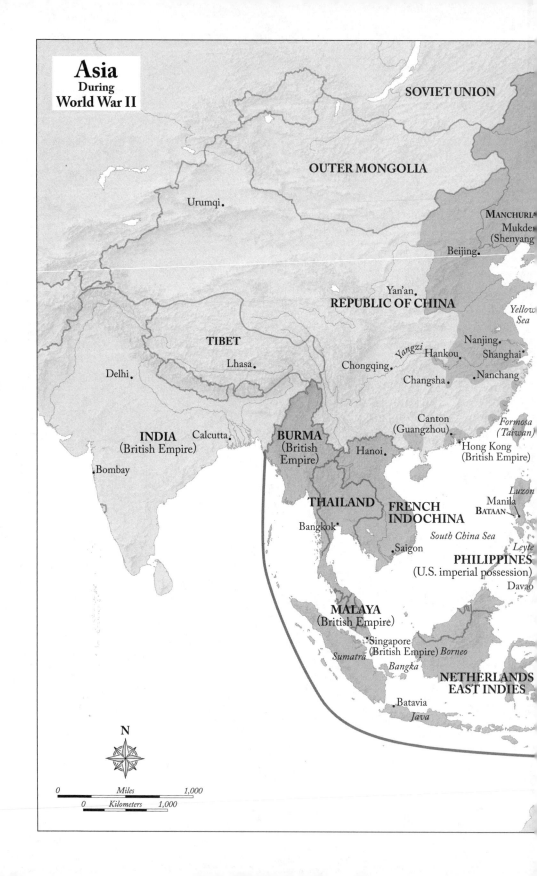

Asia
During
World War II

SOVIET UNION

OUTER MONGOLIA

Urumqi.

MANCHURIA
Mukden
(Shenyang)

Beijing.

Yan'an.
REPUBLIC OF CHINA

Yellow
Sea

TIBET

Lhasa.

Nanjing.
Yangzi Hankou. Shanghai
Chongqing. Nanchang
Changsha.

Delhi.

Canton
(Guangzhou).

*Formosa
(Taiwan)*

INDIA
(British Empire)

Calcutta.

BURMA
(British
Empire)

Hanoi.

Hong Kong
(British Empire)

.Bombay

THAILAND FRENCH
INDOCHINA

Luzon
Manila
BATAAN

Bangkok.

South China Sea

Saigon

Leyte
PHILIPPINES
(U.S. imperial possession)

Davao

MALAYA
(British Empire)

.Singapore
(British Empire) *Borneo*

Sumatra

Bangka

NETHERLANDS
EAST INDIES

Batavia
Java

N

0   Miles   1,000

0   Kilometers   1,000

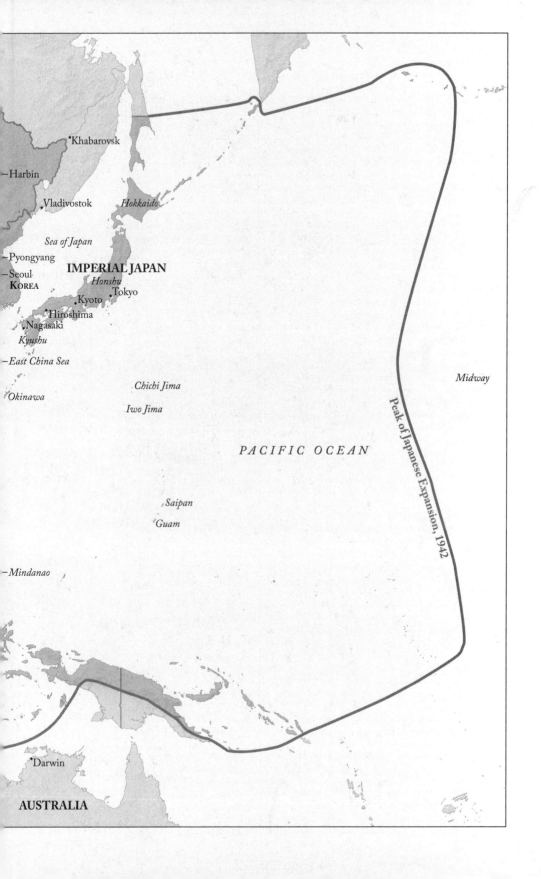

Khabarovsk

Harbin

Vladivostok   *Hokkaido*

Sea of Japan

Pyongyang

Seoul
KOREA   *Honshu*
IMPERIAL JAPAN
Kyoto Tokyo
Hiroshima
Nagasaki
Kyushu

East China Sea

Okinawa

Chichi Jima

Iwo Jima

Midway

PACIFIC OCEAN

Peak of Japanese Expansion, 1942

Saipan

Guam

Mindanao

Darwin

AUSTRALIA

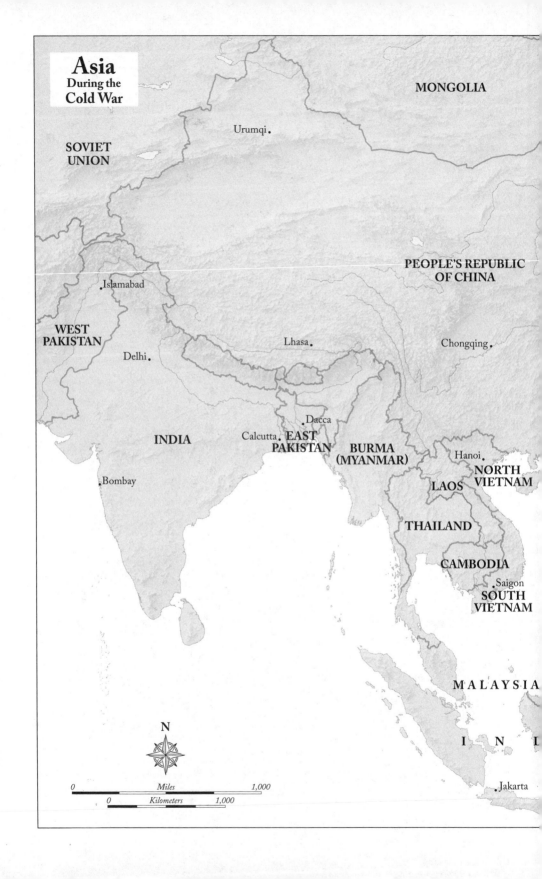

Asia
During the
Cold War

MONGOLIA

Urumqi.

SOVIET
UNION

PEOPLE'S REPUBLIC
OF CHINA

.Islamabad

Chongqing.

WEST
PAKISTAN

Lhasa.

Delhi.

.Dacca

Calcutta. EAST
PAKISTAN

INDIA

BURMA
(MYANMAR)

Hanoi.

NORTH
VIETNAM

.Bombay

LAOS

THAILAND

CAMBODIA

.Saigon
SOUTH
VIETNAM

MALAYSIA

N

I   N   I

0   Miles   1,000
0   Kilometers   1,000

.Jakarta

JUDGMENT
AT TOKYO

Introduction

TOJO HIDEKI HEARD THE soldiers coming for him. At his simple cottage in Tokyo's suburbs, on September 11, 1945, he was making no attempt to hide. With his fastidiously cropped mustache, bald head, round tortoiseshell glasses, and the assertive bearing of a career general, the prime minister of Imperial Japan during much of World War II was unmistakable. His grotesquely caricatured features—eyes slanted, teeth sharpened, fingernails pointy—had been a staple of American propaganda encouraging war bonds, routinely paired with Adolf Hitler and Benito Mussolini.

It was just over a month since the detonation of the two atomic bombs, and less than a month since Japan had at last surrendered. The victorious Allied armies were in the early, uncertain days of their occupation of Japan. One of their first tasks was to round up suspected Japanese war criminals.

Tojo was perfectly aware that U.S. troops knew where to find him. The day before, an American wire reporter had had little difficulty locating him at home. When asked who was responsible for starting the war, the prime minister whose cabinet had ordered the attack on Pearl Harbor was unrepentant. "You are the victors and you are able to name him now," he replied serenely. "But historians 500 or 1,000 years from now may judge differently."[1]

A small, nervous group of U.S. soldiers arrived at the cottage. At first Tojo refused to talk to them, and then, dressed casually in an open-collared white shirt, slid open a window to demand their credentials. For some unbearably tense minutes, they were stalled by a servant, until their patience wore out. "Tell this yellow bastard we've waited long enough," snapped the U.S. major in charge.

Soon after, the Americans heard a muffled gunshot from inside.

Startled, the soldiers kicked down the door. They burst into the house to find Tojo standing upright, reeling slightly. In his right hand was a smoking Colt .32-caliber pistol. His left hand was clutched to his chest, red blood streaming through his white shirt. He had made the efficient choice of a gun to kill himself, and an American-made one at that, instead of availing himself of any one of the three ceremonial Japanese swords in the room. The leading U.S. major, in the sights of the lurching pistol, screamed, "Don't shoot!" and Tojo let his gun fall with a clatter. Knees buckling, he crumpled into an easy chair. His eyes drooped and he strained to breathe, sweating, coughing, moaning in agony.[2]

Expert at dealing out death, Tojo botched his own. The bullet only grazed his heart, exiting his back at the left shoulder blade. American soldiers—one of them a Japanese American from the Bronx—bustled him out of the cottage and into a car, and raced him toward an American military hospital at Yokohama, south of central Tokyo.

They drove through a shattered, charred landscape. Six months ago, as many as a hundred thousand people in Tokyo had been, in the words of a U.S. general leading a massive incendiary bombardment, "scorched and boiled and baked to death" in a single night.[3] The city's rivers had boiled and liquefied glass had rained. The stench of burning flesh had been so intense that U.S. B-29 bomber pilots several thousand feet above had gagged.[4]

What was left was a vast city of ashes. Much of Japan's sprawling capital had been built with wood houses; those humble homes were now fine cinders. Tokyo was reduced to a series of shanties, endless rows of little shacks cobbled together from whatever scraps of metal or stone had survived the unnatural flames. The gloom was broken only by the occasional flower planted by the dispossessed residents of these huts, or a curtain hung over a makeshift window. Scoured by fire, sturdier buildings like factories were a mangled mess of steel girders. There were colossal piles of rubble strewn around trashed streets. Tokyo was dark, filthy, and collapsing. It reeked. With every kind of infrastructure systematically wrecked by the bombings, there were urgent shortages of every kind: electricity, heat, food, water. The despairing residents were left burned, broken, scarred, bereaved, unwashed, ill-clothed, and underfed.[5]

Tojo flickered between life and death. At the Yokohama hospital, a U.S. Army surgeon was unimpressed by the dire chest wound; he had seen hundreds of them. Lying on a simple cot, his shirt and trousers drenched in his own blood, the former prime minister grimaced in pain, groaning as he drew breath. Japanese and American doctors stitched him up and gave him plasma infusions. American soldiers watched his agonies with cool indifference; one shrugged that Tojo had earned himself a Purple Heart. Pulling through, he grew strong enough to lament that death was taking so long; he had meant to finish himself off with a single shot, he explained, rather than risking the delay of ritual disembowelment. He had chosen not to shoot himself in the head, he whispered to an interpreter, so that people could recognize his features and know that he was dead.

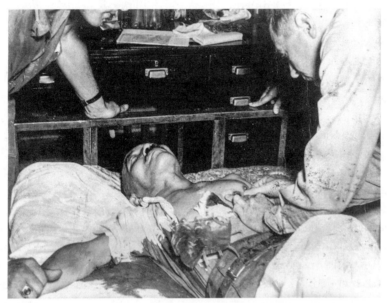

Tojo Hideki lies soaked in blood after shooting himself while American doctors try to save him on September 11, 1945.

Neither the fact of defeat, nor the devastation of his country, nor a fresh bullet hole through his chest were enough to make him question the rightness of his cause. "The Greater East Asia War was a justified and righteous war," waged by Japan to free its Asian neighbors from the oppressive grip of European colonialism, he declared in what he hoped would be his deathbed statement. He expressed his regrets to the Japanese nation and "all the races of the Greater Asiatic powers," although not to the Allied countries against which his cabinet had gone to war. Given the ruin all around him, he was not inclined to apologize to the bombers.

"I would not like to be judged in front of a conqueror's court," Tojo said. "I wait for the righteous judgment of history."[6]

·   ·   ·

This book is about that conqueror's court and the judgment of history. For two and a half years after his failed suicide, Tojo and twenty-seven other top Japanese wartime leaders were prosecuted by the Allies as war criminals—a trial that is the Asian counterpart to the more famous international war crimes tribunal at Nuremberg.

The Tokyo trial was a monumental accounting for the personal fates of Tojo and the other powerful Japanese defendants, who were viewed not just as defeated foes to be neutralized but as criminals accused of aggression and atrocity. Its unfolding drew in a host of household names, including Harry Truman, Emperor Hirohito, Chiang Kai-shek, Jawaharlal Nehru, Douglas MacArthur, and more, as well as lesser-known figures whose richly multifaceted life stories encompass much of their countries' modern histories: Mei Ruao, the cerebral, purposeful Chinese judge hoping to restore his war-torn country; Togo Shigenori, the peace-minded Japanese foreign minister who had struggled to prevent Pearl Harbor yet wound up on trial as a Class A war criminal; and Radhabinod Pal, the erudite Indian judge who is today a national icon in Japan for writing a blistering dissent that acquitted Tojo and all the defendants while denouncing the court itself as illegitimate.

It was, as the judges liked to call it, the "biggest trial of the world."[7] In a vast, echoing courtroom illuminated with sweltering klieg lights, the black-robed judges listened to the anguished testimony of Chinese survivors of the Nanjing massacre; heard nightmarish accounts of how British and Australian prisoners of war were worked to death in Thailand and Burma; recoiled at gruesome stories of Filipino civilians who had been bayoneted, beaten, tortured, and raped; eavesdropped on the secret plans being devised for aggression at Pearl Harbor; and gawped at the disgraced last Qing emperor of China, Puyi, who wound up as a star witness. As the Chinese judge wrote, "In my opinion, the Tokyo Trial, like the Nuremberg Trial, should also be considered as 'the greatest thing that comes out from this World War,' to borrow a phrase of President Truman."[8]

World War II was a war of atrocity, both in Europe and Asia. It is commonplace in wartime to denounce the bestial immorality of the enemy, but in the Pacific War the question of war crimes was fundamental. The war was defined in Allied minds by Japanese-inflicted horrors: the death march of Filipino and American prisoners of war at Bataan, the captive Australians who perished while building the Burma–Thailand railway, the sack of Manila.[9] More Australians died from being imprisoned by the Japanese than from combat against them.[10] The Chinese, who had endured more from Japan than any country in fourteen years of war, remembered the devastating bombing of Chongqing, countless villages set ablaze, a renewed opium trade, and mass executions and mass rape—as many as twenty thousand cases of rape during the first month of the Japanese occupation in Nanjing alone.[11] More than a million Filipinos were killed or wounded by their Japanese occupiers.[12] For the Americans, the war itself was a crime against peace, the poisonous result of an illegal sneak attack on Pearl Harbor. In the registers of war crimes assembled by U.S. investigators, over and over they listed "Cannibalism": some Japanese officers had believed they gained strength from eating the livers of American prisoners of war.[13]

While the defeated Japanese would have no opportunity to put the victors on trial, their government had spurred on its soldiers and motivated the home front with tales of Allied barbarism. The Japanese people were warned, wrongly, of the terrors and mass rapes that would be inflicted by demonic American occupiers. They recoiled at the dehumanizing Allied custom of collecting Japanese skulls and bones as souvenirs. And they were traumatized by the firebombing of scores of their cities and towns, culminating in the incineration of Tokyo and finally the atomic bombings of Hiroshima and Nagasaki.[14]

The Tokyo trial is the paramount historical event in Asia's efforts to grapple with this terrible legacy. As its Australian chief judge wrote privately, "The Tokyo and Nuernberg War Criminals Trials are undoubtedly the greatest in all history; that cannot be contested."[15] Spectators peered into the innermost workings of governments and the souls of people under the most extreme circumstances. They heard the telling and retelling of the fateful decisions for war through the contradictory perspectives of Allied prosecutors, defense lawyers, and individual Japanese defendants— a kind of *Rashomon* for World War II.[16] "The naivete I possessed at the time of leaving the homeland has long since disappeared," wrote a Japanese soldier in the Philippines in his diary, which was read aloud as evidence to a hushed auditorium. He admitted killing over a hundred guerrillas and Filipino civilians during a particularly violent campaign there. "Now I am a hardened killer and my sword is always stained with blood. Although it is for my country's sake, it is sheer brutality. May God forgive me! May my mother forgive me!"[17] From the Japanese island stronghold of Chichi Jima, the court heard a formal order to kill and eat an American prisoner of war: "The Battalion wants to eat the flesh of the American Aviator, Lieutenant (junior grade) Hall."[18] (Nine U.S. fliers bailed out during bombing raids at Chichi Jima. Eight of them were captured by Japanese troops and killed, with several of them partially eaten in early 1945. The ninth, who managed to escape, was a Navy pilot named George H. W. Bush.)[19] The mesmerizing experience of the Tokyo trial was, as the Dutch judge privately wrote, "the situation in which one, every day, in the corridor meets the Emperor of China and says: 'Hello, how are you this morning.' I thought in former days that only in fairy tales do you meet the Emperor of China. And, still, I am not quite sure if that opinion was wrong."[20]

As law, the Tokyo trial had grand ambitions to establish international principles for a safer postwar world—a revived international law that outlawed aggression and atrocity. It sought to reestablish the battered authority of the old international laws of armed combat, such as the illegality of killing innocent civilians or abusing prisoners of war. It insisted that powerful persons had to face individual judgment for war crimes committed under their commands, rather than claiming immunity as generals and cabinet ministers.[21] And like Nuremberg, it made a revolutionary attempt to enshrine aggressive war as the cardinal international crime, the one war crime that led to all the others.[22] These legal aspirations were often frustrating to nonlawyers, with MacArthur complaining that the trial's impending judgment "is like blowing up a ton of dynamite—one cannot possibly foresee what might happen."[23]

Beyond its legal significance, beyond the courtroom spectacular, the Tokyo trial was a political event. It was a measure of Asia's colonial past and a prelude of its Cold War future. The forging of a new Asia required military, political, economic, and territorial arrangements, but also a moral reckoning with the war and its causes. The Chinese judge hoped that the court's judgment would establish a historical record that would leave no room for future distortions of the truth.[24] "This trial is of a special importance for the whole world," the Dutch judge mused, "not only for the facts proven, or the kind of judgment delivered. It is more or less the touchstone for the possibility of organized international justice."[25]

This book is an attempt to tell the story of the Tokyo trial in the round, not just the drama in the grand courtroom but also its milieu in postwar Asia broadly. With prosecutors and judges drawn from eleven different Allied countries—including important Asia-Pacific powers such as China, India, the Philippines, and Australia—the Tokyo trial was a sweeping panorama of the making of postwar Asia.[26] Despite the might of the United States, this book is both an American history and an international history. In its creation, its workings, and its aftermath, the Tokyo trial was a simulacrum of the tremendous military and political changes that shaped modern Asia, today the most strategically important region in the world.[27] The unfolding of the trial in the pivotal years from 1946 to 1948 encompassed the founding of a new order in Japan, Communist revolutionary triumphs in the Chinese Civil War, the struggle for decolonization in India and elsewhere, and the onset of the Cold War.

These epic proceedings were meant to break from wartime hatreds to peacetime reconstruction. But the postwar peace was not so easily mastered. Instead of the tidy morality play that the United States wanted blaming Tojo and a small clique of militarists, the trial laid bare the underlying tensions of postwar Asia. Rather than solidifying the unity of the wartime Allies, the trial split them. The judges from China, India, the United States, the Soviet Union, Britain, France, Australia, and the Netherlands were frequently at each other's throats. The trial reveals some of the reasons why a liberal international order has not emerged in Asia, despite the wishes of some American strategists.[28] The divisions among the Allies were not just about American dominance or Soviet ambitions but a splintering in multiple directions.

Far from marking a new ascendancy of American-supported liberal democracy in Asia, the Tokyo trial played out against a chaotic background of rising anticolonial nationalism in India, Indonesia, Vietnam, and elsewhere, and Communist revolutionary victories in China. The war had finished off the Japanese Empire, but millions of people across postwar Asia were still left to contend with poverty, malnourishment, illiteracy, corruption, and tyranny—as well as repressive European empires seeking to return to old habits.[29] "America's war had cut blindly across the course of the greatest revolution in the history of mankind," wrote Theodore White, *Time*'s leading war correspondent, "the revolution of Asia."[30] Asian countries were whipsawed by the early days of the confrontation between the American and Soviet goliaths. Having done everything in their power to destroy Japan, the Americans now sought to rebuild it as a crucial bulwark against the Soviet Union and the Communist insurgents on the cusp of power in China. All these currents would undermine the tribunal and call into question its legacy.

For the American occupiers, the punishment of war criminals was an important element in their effort to draw the teeth of Japanese militarism. The edict from MacArthur, the supreme commander of the Allied powers, establishing the court was portentously numbered as General Orders No. 1.[31] The United States was obviously first among unequals, having crushed the Japanese with a seemingly limitless arsenal of industry and technology. Yet with so many Allied countries prosecuting and judging, it was a unique opportunity for an international moral and legal reckoning.

The internationalism of the Tokyo trial is central to its significance.[32] Combined, the eleven Allied governments represented a majority of the human race.[33] While Nuremberg did not have a judge for the Jews or the Poles, Tokyo had three Asian judges—from China, India, and the Philippines—who were in a position to speak for some of the Asian victims. (In a glaring omission, there were no Korean or Taiwanese judges, since the court began its study of Japanese imperialism after their annexations.)[34] Although the Americans skewed the trial toward aggression at Pearl Harbor, MacArthur rapidly lost patience with the tribunal, allowing it to be steered by the other Allied governments. Influenced by such Asia-Pacific powers as China and the Philippines, as well as Australia, it would compile a massive ledger of Japan's assault on China, its crimes against humanity from Indonesia to the Philippines, and its use of sexual violence as a weapon of war. Some of the most fascinating deliberations came from the Chinese and Indian judges, who were diametrically opposed in their evaluations of the war, as well as the judge from the Philippines. Because of these remarkable Chinese, Indian, and Filipino judges, the Tokyo trial featured at least a measure of Asian justice after an Asian war.

For the victorious Allied countries, the justice of their cause was clear. But for many Japanese living in rubble, and other skeptics throughout Asia, the Tokyo court's pretensions looked dubious. The high moral purpose of the tribunal was obviously undermined by the totalitarianism of the Soviet Union, whose forces in Manchuria killed or let perish as many as a quarter million captive Japanese prisoners *after* Japan's surrender in August 1945—yet which sent a Red Army major general to Tokyo as its judge, whose impeccable Stalinist qualifications included working on the Moscow purge trials. On top of that came tenacious European colonialism in today's independent states of India, Vietnam, Indonesia, and more. The court's repute was undermined by the United States' atomic bombing of Japanese civilians in Hiroshima and Nagasaki, the firebombing of Tokyo and dozens of other cities, and the awful civilian death tolls from combat on Saipan and Okinawa. "I suppose if I had lost the war, I would have been tried as a war criminal," later said Curtis LeMay, the U.S. general who targeted Tokyo and sixty-six other Japanese cities for obliteration from above. "Fortunately, we were on the winning side."[35] In a White House meeting alone with Harry Truman, Henry Stimson, the U.S. secretary of war, confessed his anxieties about the aerial bombardment of Japan: "I did not want to have the United States get the reputation of outdoing Hitler in atrocities."[36]

The Tokyo trial misfired and fizzled. Unlike Nuremberg, whose verdict has over the decades taken on an almost sacred status in democratic Germany and its neighbors, Tokyo is an ongoing source of bitter controversy across East Asia today. While Japanese leaders have repeatedly apologized for the crimes of World War II, there is no Japanese equivalent to the near-universal national repentance and grief that are at the core of current German politics and society.[37] Compared to the emotional, detailed, self-reflective statements of remorse from Willy Brandt, Richard von Weizsäcker, and Angela Merkel, Japan's official apologies are pallid and vague.[38] If German lawmakers today were to utter some of the opinions about World War II routinely expressed by Japanese politicians—some of these atrocities never happened, the other side was just as bad, the historical record is unclear, we have nothing to apologize for—they would be publicly anathematized, ostracized, and possibly indicted.[39] Far from marking an end to nationalist grievances, the Tokyo trial remains an occasion for patriotic quarrels across the most strategic and powerful region in the world.

Compared to the pacified and united Western Europe that emerged in the years after Nuremberg, postwar Asia stands out for its dangerous disorder.[40] It is impossible to understand East Asia's tensions today without considering what is ominously referred to as the "history issue" left from World War II.[41] South Korean nationalists rage against an officially pacifist Japan that is hardly poised to return to its old imperialist ways.[42] Xi Jinping, the paramount leader of China, pursues territorial disputes with Japan while remonstrating endlessly about World War II: "Chinese people who have made such a great sacrifice will not waver in protecting a history written in sacrifice and blood."[43] Seventy years after the war ended, according to a Pew survey, three quarters of Chinese saw the Japanese as violent, while just 10 percent of Chinese believe that Japan has adequately apologized for its wartime behavior.[44] When conservative Japanese politicians such as Abe Shinzo and Koizumi Junichiro have paid their respects to the war dead at the Shinto shrine in central Tokyo that honors Tojo and thirteen other Class A war criminals, Chinese patriots explode with state-sanctioned rage. It is only by understanding the reverberations of World War II in East Asia that one can begin to make sense of the otherwise baffling spectacle of a peace-loving democracy losing the moral high ground to a nationalistic Communist dictatorship.

The spectacular proceedings of the Tokyo trial remain an obsession in Japanese, Chinese, and Korean politics, as well as in many of their neighbors. Its judgment, which remains a foundation of the international law of war, has been internalized into the domestic political life of Japan, China, South Korea, and other Asian countries, but rarely in the ways that the American occupiers wanted.[45] Even Vladimir Putin, who in any sensible world would be in The Hague, has said that Japan's efforts to "glorify and exonerate war criminals and their henchmen are an outrageous flouting of the Nuremberg and Tokyo trials."[46]

Many Japanese, including much of the country's dominant conservative party and a long run of nationalistic prime ministers, scorn the Tokyo judgment as "victors' justice" and view many of the defendants as misguided patriots; they venerate the lengthy dissent by the Indian judge as the true moral verdict.[47] Kishi Nobusuke, who was jailed as a Class A war crimes suspect but went on to become prime minister of Japan, later wrote that the Tokyo trial "was in essence a unilateral, arbitrary sanctioning of a vanquished nation by victorious nations."[48] In South Korea, which was not yet independent during most of the trial, the verdict is a bedrock of popular resentment of Japan's imperial oppression.[49] Perhaps most important, China's Communist rulers promote blood-soaked wartime memories to put Japan on the defensive, create common ground with Koreans and other victims of Imperial Japan, undermine the authority of American power in Asia, and use past Chinese sacrifices to justify the present-day bluster of a rising great power.[50] In a 2014 speech, Xi extolled the Tokyo trial, as well as China's own military tribunals for lower-level Japanese war criminals: "The righteous nature of the trials is unshakeable and unassailable!"[51]

While the Nuremberg trial has come to symbolize a grand moment of moral clarity, the Tokyo trial is engrossing precisely because it remains so controversial. Nuremberg is exalted by lawyers and human rights activists as the template for recent efforts at international justice from Bosnia to Rwanda to the permanent International Criminal Court, while Tokyo is seen as an embarrassment best forgotten. The suffering of Asians gets little attention in the United States and Western Europe. If Nuremberg stands as a metaphor for ethical purity, then Tokyo represents a dive into murk. It calls into question a triumphalist view of World War II. In Japan in particular but across Asia, there are vexing doubts about the legitimacy of almost every aspect of the trial: its inception, its functioning, its verdicts, and its legacy. Because it was defined by the limits of Allied power, marked Allied hypocrisy, and the uncertainty of its outcome, the story of Tokyo is a far less heroic subject than Nuremberg—one that perhaps makes a more fitting World War II history for today, a time when American power is waning, its moral influence sharply diminished, and its democracy in crisis.[52]

Given how thoroughly peaceful and democratic Japan became, it is puzzling that the Tokyo trial, which provided the most detailed denunciation of Japan's war-making past, has gained so little regard among Japanese—in contrast to Germany, where Nuremberg has become more of a watchword for entrenched postwar ideals of pacifism and human rights. This was not because the Japanese couldn't understand the trial, as some cultural relativists have contended. Rather, this limited impact was more the result of politics: the stubbornness of right-wing Japanese leaders who, regaining their authority during the early Cold War, worked to undermine the trial; a willful ignorance about atrocities committed far away from the home islands (which suggests that the court might have done better to concentrate more time on detailing such enormities); and the terrible suffering of Japanese civilians in the American strategic bombing of their cities, which made it hard to accept the right of their conquerors to sit in judgment.

Today the Tokyo trial's flawed attempt to find justice has never been more important. Asia, which could once be arrogantly dismissed by American and European policymakers as the periphery, has become the core of world politics and power. Since now it would be impossible to imagine assembling eleven feuding countries to render collective judgment on World War II, the Tokyo trial—warped and skewed as it was— stands out as a crucial lost opportunity to put relations between Japan and its neighbors on a more normal footing, encouraging deeper self-reflection among Japanese while giving the victims a greater sense of redress, thereby setting East Asia's future on a more hopeful track.

This is a long book, necessarily so. It seeks to document the inner workings of the Tokyo trial, its law and its politics, and its long shadow. The trial alone was an enormous undertaking, lasting two and a half years, with 4,335 pieces of evidence, 419 witnesses testifying in court, 779 witnesses giving evidence in affidavits, and a court transcript of 49,858 pages.[53] This book seeks to fix that trial in a wider Asian and global history—not just embedded in the transformation of Japan but also in anticolonial nationalism in India and other Asian countries, the revolution in China, and the onset of the Cold War.

The book is meant to allow readers to make up their own minds about how the trial worked and what it meant. Readers will surely draw their own conclusions; this is, after all, a book about verdicts. Still, the reality of this period is rarely satisfying for the nationalists and partisans who dominate the rhetoric about the war in Japan, China, the United States, and elsewhere. And it is too easy to dismiss the Tokyo trial in the light of what we now know but which the participants did not; if Mei Ruao or Douglas MacArthur had somehow been shown a crystal ball which revealed what Japan would look like today, they might have fainted with relief.

My telling of the history does have its own core concerns. Widening the story to encompass not just Americans and Japanese but the rest of Asia, there are three main themes developed throughout these pages. The Tokyo trial is best understood as the product of a clash of armies, a clash of empires, and a clash of ideals.

I. A CLASH OF ARMIES

In most every conversation in Japan about the Tokyo trial, the first comment is that it was victors' justice. "I believe that it was a trial done by the victors to the defeated," says Santo Akiko, a nationalistic member of the House of Councillors, who met me at her Diet office seventy years after the end of the war. Her point is obviously true in several ways: there were no charges for the American bombardment of Japanese cities, conventional or atomic; there were eleven Allied judges and no Japanese; the court's proceedings were shot through with the wartime resentments and bigotries of the victorious nations.

More profoundly, Japanese complaints of victors' justice are right to point to Allied military power over their defeated foes. The Tokyo trial was both an act of war-making and peacemaking. The proper starting point for understanding the Tokyo trial is not the elevated principles of international law but the bloody realities of the final months of World War II. For all the grandiose legal trappings, it relied on the force of Allied arms to make good its promises of justice.

Yet the objection of victors' justice can understate the extent of Japanese power and agency in the end of the war and the postwar period, and exaggerates how much the Allies were masters of events. In fact, the unfolding of the trial was driven by three distinct but interlocking conflicts: the end of World War II, the Chinese Civil War between Nationalists and revolutionary Communists, and the early years of the Cold War.

First, the distinctive nature of Allied victory—sweeping and decisive by any historical standard, but less complete than what was imposed on Germany—had enduring consequences for the occupation and the postwar Japanese understanding of the war. Victory in World War II was secured at a horrendous cost: a total war fought from China to the Pacific islands to Japan itself, with nearly three million Japanese deaths.[54] Yet the Allies' defeat of Japan fell short of the unconditional surrender that they had demanded.

Early in 1945, Franklin Delano Roosevelt's administration grimly accepted that the Germans would "fight to a finish," which would allow the conquerors a chance to root out Nazi barbarism once and for all.

Soviet, American, British, and other Allied troops seized territory all the way to Berlin.[55] But the Truman administration did not want to endure a second fight to the finish in Japan. Despite a devastating Allied siege and bombing campaign that laid waste to its cities and towns, Japan still had an army of some four million troops to defend the country.[56] Senior U.S. leaders feared that an invasion of Japan's home islands would be bloodier than the recent pitched combat for Iwo Jima and Okinawa, and quite likely worse than the invasion of Germany itself. Truman instead chose to end the Pacific War with an implicit negotiation: a brutal arrangement, brought about by firebombing, blockade, advancing armies, and atomic bombs, but a negotiation all the same.

After two atom bombs and the Soviet Union's late entry into the war, the Truman administration decided to induce Japan to surrender by sparing Emperor Hirohito from overthrow or prosecution as a war criminal. If the emperor was to be toppled or put on trial, the Americans worried, the Japanese might well fight on even after Hiroshima and Nagasaki, bitterly resisting the ground invasion that Truman had ordered to follow. Despite Hirohito's involvement in much of his government's deliberations for expansion across Asia and the attack on Pearl Harbor, despite the formally paramount position of the emperor in the Japanese constitution and military chain of command, despite the stated Allied policy of unconditional surrender, the war ended with Hirohito staying in the Imperial Palace while his underlings were hauled into the dock. It was at his command that the Japanese laid down their weapons, and it was with his acquiescence that the United States occupied their home islands.[57]

Truman's choice, as understandable as it was, would cast a decades-long shadow over the rehabilitation of Japan.[58] The country was painfully induced to yield, not vanquished outright; its peaceful occupation would rely on a measure of goodwill from the Japanese authorities. Without such official cooperation, the Americans feared popular resistance and an endless occupation of some seventy million people.

Yet when the emperor escaped punishment for going along with the wartime militarists, it was hard to see how ordinary Japanese who had in their own much smaller way done the same could feel guilty.[59] Much of Japan's conservative establishment—including many who had helped the ultras or submitted to them—would be allowed back into public life as early as the 1950s, free to put forward their own nationalistic view of the war, defending some of the wartime deeds of Japanese troops, and questioning the legitimacy of the Tokyo trial.[60] The emperor's enduring presence on the throne and the revival of conservative elites around him permanently muddied postwar debates about Japan's culpability, making possible a view that Japan had fought a patriotic and perhaps legitimate war.[61]

Second, the Tokyo trial unfolded against the backdrop of the Chinese Civil War. Unlike at Nuremberg, where there was no official Jewish representation, the Tokyo bench reserved a seat for China, an important country which had been a foremost victim of Axis crimes against humanity. This offered a momentous chance for a verdict of international justice for the Chinese, who had suffered at the hands of the Japanese.

But here too justice was at the mercy of war—in this case, the Chinese Civil War. Mei Ruao, appointed by the Republic of China under Chiang Kai-shek, was representing a government that was about to be wiped out. Although China sent some remarkably talented officials to Tokyo, the prosecution of Japanese war criminals became a lower priority for Chiang than the mortal threat of the civil war at home. China hardly fits neatly within an accusation of victors' justice: soon after Chiang was counted among the victors of World War II, he would be the loser of the Chinese Civil War.[62]

Finally, the Tokyo tribunal has to be understood as part of the onset of the Cold War.[63] As the Allied judges were arriving in Tokyo, Winston Churchill was giving his speech in Fulton, Missouri, warning of "an iron curtain" descending across Europe; while the judges were deliberating about their verdict, the Berlin Airlift was under way. As the trial progressed, Americans increasingly voiced a fierce anti-Communism that was not wholly out of line with that of many of the Japanese accused. In American eyes, the Soviet Union went from a wartime partner to a global enemy, while China went from an ally and cause célèbre to an untrustworthy country rotten with Communism.

The Cold War brought an imperative to fortify Japan against the spread of revolutionary Communism into Asia, spearheaded by Mao Zedong, then friendly to the Soviet Union. As the Tokyo trial was nearing its end, George Kennan, the senior State Department official and grand strategist who masterminded the Cold War doctrine of containment, paid a high-profile visit to MacArthur to exhort him to build up the Japanese state as a fortress against the Soviet threat. This would necessitate halting the purges of militarists, ending the prosecutions of lower-ranked war criminals, forgoing a second round of trials of senior leaders, and even paroling and rehabilitating Class A war crimes suspects. At least as much as in West Germany, Americans found themselves reliant on conservative ruling classes implicated in the war years.[64] Shigemitsu Mamoru, a comparatively blameless foreign minister who would be convicted by the Tokyo tribunal and sentenced to seven years in jail, would become Japan's foreign minister in 1954. Kishi Nobusuke, an important ruler in Japanese-controlled Manchuria and a minister in Tojo's cabinet, spent more than three years in Sugamo Prison as a Class A war crimes suspect; he was released without being charged, and went on to become prime minister in 1957, laying some of the crucial foundations of a more autonomous alliance with the United States.[65] His grandson, Abe Shinzo, became a staunchly nationalist prime minister of Japan, seeking to amend the country's pacifist constitution in order to resist growing Chinese power. As one of modern Japan's most influential prime ministers—who after stepping down was shockingly assassinated in July 2022—he declared that "the biggest issue for Japan is truly escaping the postwar regime."[66]

II. A Clash of Empires

For Japanese rightists, one aspect of the Tokyo trial stands out as a bright spot amid darkness: the dissenting opinion written by the brilliant Indian judge, Radhabinod Pal. Today Pal is honored at the Yasukuni war shrine, where visitors leave flowers at a monument to him in a prime location near the fiercely nationalist-themed museum. Japanese conservatives tend to refer to it not as a solo dissent but as a judgment, suggesting that it is the real verdict of the trial. Pal's opinion is a powerful expression of the anticolonialism sweeping India and beyond. It has been repurposed by Japanese conservatives as a demonstration that the nations in the Greater East Asia Co-Prosperity Sphere were actually grateful to the Japanese, treating them not as invaders but as fellow Asians fighting to free Asian peoples from European imperialism.[67]

At every turn, the Tokyo trial was bedeviled by the question of empire. Most of its judges were from colonial powers who were resented across Asia, particularly the Soviet Union, Britain, France, and the Netherlands, as well as the United States with its stake in Hawaii and the Philippines. Britain's influence on the bench was magnified by its empire, which brought the inclusion of white, pro-British judges from Australia, Canada, and New Zealand—even though there were no judges from the brutalized peoples of Korea, Indonesia, Vietnam, or Singapore. All told, European imperialist powers of various kinds were allocated seven out of eleven judgeships at Tokyo. Even the belated addition of the judges from India and the Philippines was an afterthought done more as a courtesy to the British and Americans than to the Indians and Filipinos.

Many of the deepest fissures on display in the courtroom were about empire, while in the backroom deliberations of the judges, British and Soviet imperialists locked horns with Chinese and Indian anticolonialists.[68] This tacit, structural acquiescence with European imperialism did much to tarnish the legitimacy of the Tokyo tribunal. When the mostly white faces on the tribunal gave their eventual verdict, read aloud by the Australian chief judge, it sounded less like the voice of universal justice and more like that of familiar masters.[69]

While Nuremberg concentrated on aggression against sovereign states in the core of Europe, Tokyo had to contend with attacks on colonized lands in Asia. Much of Japan's war effort had been directed against British, French, Dutch, and American colonies, which looked less like a clear-cut case of foreign conquest and more like a clash of empire against empire.[70] While calling for freedom in Europe, the British Empire controlled almost four hundred million people in India, Burma, Ceylon, and Malaya; the Dutch held more than seventy-five million souls in what today is Indonesia.[71] What did aggression mean when the territories being seized were not self-governing countries but exploited imperial possessions?

For many people across Asia, the Tokyo trial's pretensions of justice were badly undermined by the shadow of empire. "The Japanese defended the action of Japan in this Asian land and in the world, to liberate Asia and to change the world," recalled the Dutch judge. "And they had a case, in this respect."[72] In postwar Europe, the United States and its allies trumpeted the principles of the Atlantic Charter, aiming both to resist Soviet aggression and build up a liberal order in the West.[73] Yet in Asia, the same project of defending Britain, France, or Holland meant retrenching their colonial empires.[74] The Japanese defendants were pilloried for building their own empire by the Soviet Union, Britain, France, and Holland, who were seeking to reestablish control over their own imperial possessions.

Despite Japanese nationalists' complaints today about American victors' justice, the court was to a surprising degree driven by the British Empire. As the U.S. chief prosecutor faltered, it was the British associate prosecutor who took over much of his brief behind the scenes. On the bench, the reliable core of the majority was the trio of British Commonwealth judges from Britain, Canada, and New Zealand, a tightly coordinated faction that drove the court's deliberations and final judgment. On two separate occasions the British government secretly sought to grab direct control: asking that the hapless American chief prosecutor be sacked and replaced by the British associate prosecutor, and pressing to remove the Australian chief judge and install one of its own bloc instead. These efforts were only thwarted by furious rebuffs from MacArthur himself.

Empire was a problem for the Japanese defendants too. Japan was certainly an imperial power, but had come late to its empire. By the time that Meiji Japan seized Korea and Taiwan, Victorian Britain was already at the zenith of its domination in India and beyond. In many ways, Japan emulated its European predecessors, complete with a kind of Yamato *mission civilisatrice*; but in other important respects, Japan was an imperial power that had taken on an anticolonial viewpoint.[75]

Yet millions of Asians—from Korea to Taiwan to Burma to the Philippines—had found their new Japanese overlords, desperate to extract resources for the war effort, to be even more cruel and exploitative than the Europeans. It is only by overlooking the reality of Japanese repression of Chinese, Koreans, Filipinos, and Indonesians that the war can be redefined as East against West. No less an anticolonialist than Jawaharlal Nehru, who had struggled for India's freedom from the British Empire while also resisting Imperial Japan, secretly scorned Pal's verdict: "In this judgment wild and sweeping statements have been made with many of which we do not agree at all."[76]

During the Tokyo trial, Japanese anxieties about American imperialism were anything but theoretical. Of course, Americans prefer to think of the United States as an anticolonial power since 1776, and there was a substantial measure of anticolonialism in American political thought and foreign policy during World War II and the postwar era.[77] Yet the face of the United States that most Asians saw throughout this era was that of another colonial power expanding into the region.[78]

In China, the United States had joined with European empires in imposing resented "unequal treaties" and claiming rights of extraterritoriality, under which Americans would be prosecuted by U.S. authorities rather than Chinese. Chinese nationalists had long fumed at an American arrogance manifested in the 1844 Treaty of Wangxia (copying the British example of taking extraterritorial rights in China), the 1858 Treaty of Tianjin (where the United States joined with Britain, France, and Russia in opening up more treaty ports), and the 1901 Boxer peace protocol (where the United States joined all the major European empires and Japan in imposing indemnities while posting troops to guard their legations in Beijing).[79] In the Philippines and Guam, the United States replaced Spain to become an imperial overlord after 1898.[80] To quash Filipinos fighting for independence, the Americans had waged a remarkably brutal colonial war from 1899 to 1902: executing prisoners, destroying villages, deporting civilians into disease-infested camps, systematically torturing rebels.[81] By the time that Japan attacked Hawaii and the Philippines in December 1941, the United States ruled the fifth-largest empire in the world by population, with almost nineteen million souls living in its overseas territories.[82]

MacArthur wielded power that any colonial potentate would envy. Yet the Americans proved contradictory as overlords. The United States reclaimed its colonized Pacific islands, while Hawaii was eventually made a state of the union. The Philippines, the largest U.S. colony, was set free in 1946 on the resonant day of July 4. Japan was soon restored to self-governance, as were the parts of Germany, Austria, and Korea under American control; the only near-annexation of territory seized from Japan was Micronesia, administered for decades by the United States as a United Nations trust territory. Instead of direct imperial control, the United States would opt for a more indistinct hegemony, resting on a global network of alliances, trade deals, and overseas bases from Guam to Guantánamo.[83]

The history of empire is always a history of racism. European and American imperialism was predicated on a belief in the inferiority of Asians. In 1903, W. E. B. Du Bois warned of "the recent course of the United States toward weaker and darker peoples in the West Indies, Hawaii, and the Philippines."[84] For many Japanese, the Tokyo tribunal was not merely unjust but racist: a white man's court, sitting in bigoted judgment. On this account, the trial was more a demonstration of white supremacy than of justice—part and parcel of a racist sensibility that had fueled the European colonization of much of Asia and then allowed the United States to pitilessly firebomb Japanese civilians and use two atomic bombs on them.[85] In his dissent, Pal, the Indian judge, argued that Western racism had driven Japanese leaders to protect "their race by inculcating their racial superiority in the youthful mind."[86]

Race and racism tended to lurk in the background of the court's daily proceedings; while American reporters might sneer at the "little brown-skinned" defendants, the judges knew not to say such things aloud.[87] Only in Pal's dissent was it made a central subject. Yet it is impossible to tell the story of the Tokyo trial without racism as a recurrent theme.

The Pacific War, as the historian John Dower has powerfully shown, was fueled by racist hatreds. In 1923, Franklin Roosevelt had argued against allowing Japanese to enjoy the same citizenship and property rights as whites: "So far as Americans are concerned, it must be admitted that, as a whole, they honestly believe—and in this belief they are at one with the people of Australasia and Canada—that the mingling of white with oriental blood on an extensive scale is harmful to our future citizenship."[88] During World War II, dehumanizing American propaganda treated the Japanese as primitive, simian, backward, childlike, insane, and mentally deficient, ultimately a subhuman race that deserved no quarter. Paradoxically, Japanese were also sometimes seen as eerily superhuman for their military victories after Pearl Harbor.[89] By the end of the war, American hatreds were so intense that the U.S. war secretary had to urge Truman to disavow the annihilation of the Japanese as a race. That is why the Potsdam Declaration, laying out the terms for Japan's unconditional surrender just before the atomic bombs fell, menacingly states, "We do not intend that the Japanese shall be enslaved as a race or destroyed as a nation."[90]

Since the Meiji era, Japanese nationalists and imperialists had advocated Asian racial solidarity against the whites. Japanese civilization was held up as superior to the corrupt, materialistic, greedy West. There were obvious racial overtones in the claims of many of Japan's pan-Asianist thinkers, believing that the Japanese had a special mission to protect similar if inferior races. Japan's pan-Asianist aspirations were often couched in racial terms, and its ambitions rested on a sense that the Yamato race was superior to lesser Asian races. Japanese imperialists were all too often convinced of their supremacy over Chinese, Indians, Indonesians, Malays, Burmese, and other peoples stigmatized as corrupt, primitive, or lazy.[91] During the war, Japanese leaders told their people that they were a distinctively pure race, while their American and European enemies were depicted as supernatural monsters and vicious demons.[92]

Although Mei and Pal locked horns over the guilt of the Japanese defendants, the Chinese and Indian judges shared a common contempt for European colonialism. Fuming at the British Empire in his diary, Mei was disgusted by "the nonsense of these imperialist white supremacists."[93] Oddly, Japanese conservatives today fixate on the Indian judge's dissent as an authentic Asian voice while ignoring the angry denunciations that came from the Chinese and Filipino judges, who had a no less authentic claim to speak for the Asian wartime experience.

All these racial anxieties and stereotypes, which were hardly less present on the Allied side than the Japanese, formed a crucial part of the Tokyo trial. In his dissent, Pal warned that the Allied judges might hold a "bias created by racial or political factors," which "may indeed operate even unconsciously."[94] For many Japanese nationalists, the Tokyo trial is still seen as just another sanctimonious, hypocritical chapter in the molding of a white man's world.

III. A CLASH OF IDEALS

The end of World War II brought a moment of idealism, however brief and imperfect. When Nazi Germany surrendered, Truman declared, "We must work to bind up the wounds of a suffering world—to build an abiding peace, a peace rooted in justice and in law."[95] Such legal aspirations would be carried by new forms of world organization and international cooperation. Instead of punishing war crimes with retaliation, as was the international legal practice in the eighteenth and early nineteenth centuries, the Allies would use criminal law.[96] *The New York Times* editorialized that "these proceedings at Tokyo should establish for the entire Orient the same principles confirmed at the Nuremberg trial. . . . [T]hey should knit into the whole body of human thought the fact that aggressive war is a criminal plot against mankind."[97]

Despite widespread American hatred for the Japanese as a race, the Allied occupation aimed not to destroy or plunder Japan but to rebuild it as a harmless democracy. Japan, along with West Germany, became an extremely rare success of imposed democracy. Exceptional in many ways—an advanced industrial economy, a skilled workforce, a powerful bureaucratic state, a history of cabinet government and democracy in the Taisho period, the shock of ruinous defeat—Japan stands in contrast to the United States' generally dismal record at gunpoint democratization in such countries as Nicaragua, Haiti, the Dominican Republic, Iraq, and Afghanistan.[98] MacArthur promulgated sweeping policies to liberalize Japanese society, promoting a new constitution which enshrined pacifism and human rights, empowering labor and enfranchising women, and breaking the power of militarists and war criminals.[99]

In that sense, at least, the Tokyo tribunal was an Asian manifestation of the heady postwar idealism that produced the United Nations in 1945, the Universal Declaration of Human Rights in 1948, and Truman's inaugural address in 1949 promoting democracy as the remedy to recent "unprecedented and brutal attacks on the rights of man."[100] In a major speech to Latin American leaders in Rio de Janeiro in 1947, Truman declared, "The attainment of worldwide respect for essential human rights is synonymous with the attainment of world peace."[101] Such ideals had considerable appeal in Japan. In the autumn of 1944, Togo Shigenori, the former Japanese foreign minister who had struggled to prevent the war, argued that "it was necessary that the Japanese take a fresh start from the concept of respect for human rights."[102] These aspirations formed part of a great global wave of democratization and liberalization—from Brazil to Turkey to Botswana—that would crest into the early 1960s.[103]

Of course, the Americans did not democratize Japan; the Japanese did that for themselves. In the phrase of the great historian John Dower, they embraced defeat—coming to reject their old militaristic rulers. Still, to rebuild Japan as a peace-loving, rights-respecting democracy, its criminal leadership had to be ousted and discredited. The Tokyo trial gave the Japanese themselves a formal opportunity to spurn the extremists who had brought their country to ruin.

The procedure of a trial may address a paradox highlighted by Dower. He has shown the Pacific War as a merciless conflict fueled by racist hatreds. Yet as he notes, much of this wartime hatred seemed to evaporate swiftly, with the defeated Japanese and the victorious Americans working together in a surprisingly constructive way.[104] As human rights advocates today argue, one virtue of war crimes tribunals is that they undermine accusations of collective guilt. Instead of lumping all Japanese together as subhuman savages, as was done throughout the war, the Tokyo court indicted specific leaders rather than the entire nation.

The Tokyo trial sought to use international law to instill its fundamental ideals in the Japanese people: that aggressive war was not a legitimate act of statecraft but the paramount international crime; that the laws of war were sacrosanct, thereby calling attention to the systematic atrocities against civilians in China, the Philippines, and elsewhere; and that ministers and generals should be prosecuted as individuals for war crimes, rather than being allowed to claim they had been acting as agents of the state. As the Nuremberg judgment noted, "the very essence of the Charter is that individuals have international duties which transcend the national obligations of obedience imposed by the individual State."[105] In the end, the judges at Tokyo were actually more apt to convict for crimes against peace than their counterparts at Nuremberg.[106]

The fact that there was a trial at all was remarkable.[107] The vengeful American, Chinese, and Australian peoples would overwhelmingly have preferred to summarily execute their Japanese foes. In December 1944, a Gallup poll found that one-third of Americans wanted to destroy Japan as a political entity and 13 percent wanted to kill *all* Japanese people. While 88 percent of Americans wanted to punish the Japanese militarists, only 4 percent of those seeking punishment wanted to use international law, instead suggesting "Turn them over to the Chinese" or "Take them to Pearl Harbor and sink them."[108] As a realistic example of the rougher vengeance that might have been meted out, look at what MacArthur did to General Yamashita Tomoyuki, his adversary in the Philippines: swiftly condemned in a military commission with piffling rules of procedure that didn't fill up seven pages, dispatched to the gallows by a panel of five U.S.

generals with no judicial experience. Instead of an international trial for the top Japanese leaders, MacArthur wanted a tribunal made up entirely of Americans to swiftly convict Tojo and his cabinet only for attacking Pearl Harbor.[109]

A commitment to a fair trial would be painful: the prosecutors needed evidence of the facts of Japanese aggression and atrocities, which often they could not get. The Japanese government had burned as much incriminating paperwork as it could, while the beleaguered Chinese were too busy fighting for their national survival to do an adequate job of gathering evidence of their ordeal. Nevertheless the Allies chose an odd kind of legalistic conscience. The other Allies demanded their say, and Truman overruled MacArthur.[110] Instead of just prosecuting Pearl Harbor, the sprawling indictment was kludged together from the particular grievances of the eleven Allied powers. The trial was given more legitimacy by its eleven judges, most of whom had a way of behaving like judges. They brought clashing perspectives, some of them with radically different evaluations of what the war had been about. With eleven judges, no one country could readily dominate the judgment, and the influence of the Soviet Union was diluted far more than at Nuremberg, much to the Soviets' frustration.

Despite all its limitations, the trial—covered daily by the Japanese press, albeit under MacArthur's censorship—revealed pivotal facts to the Japanese public that had been covered up by their wartime government: the horrific sacking of Nanjing and Manila, the abuse of Allied prisoners of war, the mass rape of civilian women. Somewhat less effectively, the trial shined a harsh light on such calamitous decisions as invading China and attacking the United States. Taken together, this fresh look at wartime history bolstered a Japanese repudiation of militarism.

"It was a rather fair trial," concluded the Dutch judge, a skeptical jurist who wrote a thoughtful dissent.[111] The judges would have to explain their reasoning in convicting or clearing the accused. The accused would be given some version of due process and legal procedure. They would be allowed to make their own case, arguing that Japan had been forced into war as an act of self-defense. The Japanese were provided with talented American defense lawyers, often in Army uniform; they were among the only people in the courtroom to really depart from their national scripts, giving a remarkable, full-throated representation to their Japanese clients. At the end, after the sentences were announced, the Supreme Court of the United States decided to hear sensational oral arguments about the legitimacy of the trial. And it was a core Allied conceit that both Nuremberg and Tokyo represented judicial independence, with freethinking judges ruling on the facts and the law rather than doing the partisan bidding of a president or prime minister.

So much for the ideals: the messy reality fell far short.

When the Allies were planning the Tokyo trial, it was not fanciful for New Dealers and progressives to hope that a radically different world was possible; by the time it ended, it was. While legal principles certainly had an impact on policy, the Allied powers had much more on their minds than that: a war to win and then a peace to secure. They dared not so alienate the Japanese as to make the Allied occupation untenable. When those strategic demands clashed with justice, the latter gave way.

The heyday of those reforming New Dealers was brief. At some of the most important junctures, the policy debate in Washington was won by conservatives who sought to advance U.S. national security or build up postwar hegemony, not instill lofty principles of international law. Realpolitik-minded conservatives such as Henry Stimson, Joseph Grew, and George Kennan prevailed in balking at a ground invasion of Japan, softening the ultimate terms of Japanese surrender to protect the monarchy, using the emperor and his circle to legitimize the occupation, and reversing away from liberalizing Japan to building it up as a Cold War bulwark. This was particularly remarkable since the first two men were Republicans in a partisan Democratic administration. The strategic imperatives in defeating, occupying, and remaking Japan were so overwhelming that even as staunch a New Dealer as Truman yielded to realpolitik.

The same kind of disenchantment extended into the trial itself. The defense lawyers—and subsequent generations of Japanese nationalists—argued that an Allied court was inherently unfair. After all, since the seventeenth century, it has been an elemental legal principle in the United States and Europe that individuals ought not to be judges in their own cases.[112] John Locke argued that it was unjust for self-serving men to be "Judges in their own Case," because "he who was unjust as to do his Brother an Injury, will scarce be so just as to condemn himself for it."[113] James Madison wrote, "No man is allowed to be a judge in his own cause, because his interest would certainly bias his judgment, and, not improbably, corrupt his integrity."[114] It does not inspire confidence that two of the judges—Mei and Delfin Jaranilla of the Philippines—were themselves victims of the Japanese military, in the bombing of Chongqing and the

Bataan death march, respectively. Yet after World War II, there was no viable option of neutral countries creating an impartial tribunal that stood above the hatreds and strategic interests of the war-making powers. Perhaps the Tokyo court could have included a Japanese judge, as MacArthur at one point proposed, but this would not have materially changed its verdict. Even if it is hard to see what the international alternatives were, the general objection from Locke and Madison is a powerful one.

On top of that, the Tokyo judges routinely failed to live up to the ideals of their legal mandate. Most spectacularly, at the start of the trial, when the defense lawyers offered a spirited challenge to the court's very jurisdiction, the judges had a furious debate among themselves—but were unable to agree on a reply. They sank into an embarrassing silence, not giving an explanation of their own jurisdiction until they delivered their verdict two and a half years later. Small wonder that many Japanese came to think that all the fancy talk about law was eyewash.

On the core ideal of judicial independence, most of the Allied governments fell short. Worst was the Soviet Union, whose Stalinist commissar on the bench enforced the party line at every turn. Mei kept in close contact with his patrons in China, doing the government's bidding as best he could within the court's legal constraints. Sir William Webb, the Australian chief judge, privately worked closely with MacArthur, and publicly offered spontaneous orations about the rectitude of the Allied cause. For most of the other judges, with the U.S. judge as an obvious case in point, their will was fused with that of their governments. After long years of total war, they needed no coaching or coercion to tell them which side they were supposed to be on. The British, Canadian, and New Zealand judges who dominated the court majority did not require direct orders from home; their mindset was synchronized throughout.

To be fair, even formally independent judges truckle to their elected leaders in wartime. During World War II, the Supreme Court of the United States was not so much politicized as it was militarized. When asked to approve curfews and detentions of Japanese Americans, and then the internment of Japanese Americans in the notorious *Korematsu* case in 1944, the Supreme Court rolled over. The Court—seven of whose nine members had been appointed by Roosevelt—did so again in early 1946 to uphold the shoddy U.S. military commission that condemned Yamashita to death.[115] It briefly seemed ready to tackle hard questions about the legitimacy of the Tokyo trial, agreeing to hear oral arguments before the hanging of seven convicted men. Yet then it ducked away, declaring that U.S. courts had no jurisdiction to review the judgments and sentences of an international tribunal, even one set up largely by the United States.[116]

Still, there were several judges at Tokyo who proved their integrity under law. While the Australian and Philippine members wrote concurring opinions voicing their concerns, the judges who did the most to vindicate the legitimacy of the court were the dissenting Indian, Dutch, and French members—precisely because they drove their home governments to distraction. The conscientious Dutch judge, who was secretly overseen by his government, defied it to follow his understanding of international law. Most strikingly, the newly independent Indian government did not muzzle Pal as he wrote his monumental dissent acquitting Tojo and all the defendants—even though Indian officials were privately mortified and Nehru, India's founding prime minister, was secretly appalled at Pal's opinion.

Such judicial independence was a mixed blessing. Taken together, the onslaught of conflicting opinions—the dissents, the squabbling concurrences, the Supreme Court's zigzag decision to hear oral arguments—would badly undermine the legitimacy of the judgment. The Nuremberg judgment, despite a sole dissent from the Soviet judge for not being harsh enough, never had to face anything like this. How could the Japanese embrace a judgment that so many judges from different Allied countries doubted?

As for the legal ideals pioneered by the court, these too were sapped. The doctrinal arguments for the illegality of aggressive war were flimsy, as the erudite dissents of the Indian and Dutch judges showed. When the defendants maintained they had acted in self-defense, the trial bogged down in the hoary historical claims and counterclaims of European and Japanese imperialists.[117] Even if the law itself had been impeccable, it would be naïve to imagine that an international legal regime alone could have outlawed aggressive war, particularly in a divided, seething Asia. At best it was possible to imagine an international law—perhaps backed up by powerful states—that could have stigmatized aggression, raising the costs of resorting to force and delegitimizing those states that did.[118] Yet the ancient necessities of a dangerous, anarchic world kept states prone to using violence, resulting soon enough in major wars in Korea and Vietnam.

That left an attenuated vision of international law, limited to outlawing conventional war crimes and crimes against humanity while demanding individual criminal responsibility.[119] This too was enfeebled. The principle of individual accountability, which has seen a resurgence since the 1990s, was dramatically undercut by the impunity of Emperor Hirohito. There were men convicted at Tokyo who had been less powerful and more antiwar than he. As for crimes against humanity, the trial did honor the

A U.S. intelligence photograph of Tokyo in rubble, September 1945

suffering of Chinese and other Asian civilians, and the recounting of the horrors in Nanjing had a considerable impact on the Japanese public. Yet the prosecutors and judges were so fixated on aggressive war that more conventional war crimes were given short shrift.[120]

Finally, the ideals of the Tokyo trial were an invitation to complaints of hypocrisy. Why should the Japanese be on trial for killing civilians when the Americans had dropped incendiaries and atomic bombs on Japanese cities? The Truman administration made a macabre decision not to prosecute General Ishii Shiro, the notorious chief of Unit 731, Japan's secret biological weapons operation in northern China, whose ghastly expertise might prove useful in the coming contest with the Soviet Union. As for the Soviet Union, it was obviously guilty of aggression, crimes against humanity, and war crimes during World War II. While the trial unfolded, the Soviet Union was imposing totalitarian rule over the eight European countries occupied entirely or partially by the Red Army, creating secret police and pumping out radio propaganda, consolidating control over the Baltic states seized under its secret pact with Nazi Germany.[121] The Soviets' shocking cruelty toward Japanese prisoners in Manchuria—which is properly remembered by Japanese conservatives today and too easily forgotten in the United States and elsewhere—hardly qualified them to sit in judgment.

Of course, it is scarcely surprising that Truman, Winston Churchill, or Joseph Stalin were not thrown into the dock alongside Tojo. There are few people in democratic Germany who would discount Nuremberg for the same reasons. The real point is that the victorious powers made little effort to scrutinize their own wartime conduct, nor to subject themselves to the same legal standards that they had championed at Tokyo and Nuremberg. No senior American leaders have really feared prosecution for war crimes in the long decades since, despite an abundance of violations of the laws of war in Vietnam, Cambodia, Iraq, Afghanistan, and elsewhere.[122] When the next international war crimes tribunal was created, for the former Yugoslavia in 1993, the United States, China, and Russia all made sure that their own leaders and officers would be safeguarded from prosecution. Today the United States, China, and Russia all oppose the International Criminal Court.

Nor have Americans engaged in any serious national reckoning with the firebombing of Japanese cities and the use of the atomic bombs. It was not until 2016 that a sitting president of the United States dared to visit Hiroshima, and the United States still has not made an apology for the unprecedented use of atomic weapons.[123] The victors were too quick to forget what Justice Robert Jackson said in his opening address at Nuremberg: "We must never forget that the record on which we judge these defendants today is the record on which history will judge us tomorrow. To pass these defendants a poisoned chalice is to put it to our own lips as well."[124]

PART I

GENESIS

CHAPTER 1

Nuremberg to Tokyo

ON APRIL 9, 1942, American and Filipino troops on Bataan surrendered to their Japanese adversaries. Defeated after a stubborn defense of the steamy, verdant peninsula on the core Philippine island of Luzon, the men had no idea what to expect. Still, as one American officer remembered, many of them were inwardly relieved: at least the fear of death in combat was over.

A ragged group of Filipinos and Americans gathered at an airfield at the southern tip of the Bataan Peninsula, across the bay from Manila. A few Japanese pilots in Zero fighters amused themselves by diving at the assembled Americans as if to strafe them, but without shooting. Flanked by Japanese guards, who prodded them with rifles, some seventy-six thousand Filipino and American prisoners of war were marched northward under a scorching tropical sun. They were bound for prison camps some sixty-five miles away.

Many of them were already sick with malaria and dysentery from the previous months of jungle warfare. Their steps faltered, legs and feet aching, knees buckling. By the first afternoon of the march, some men were already collapsing. "We were simply physical wrecks from the outset," one American survivor recalled. As he walked, he could hear the sound of rifle fire. The Japanese dealt out blows with rifle butts, open hands, or booted feet. When a disoriented prisoner wandered off, a Japanese guard shot him. Another Japanese soldier gripped a steel bar with both hands and smashed an American directly in the face. "I could tell by the force and sound of the blow that he crushed the prisoner's skull," remembered an American soldier. "He fell without a sound."

At a rare water break, when the men panicked and shoved each other, the Japanese guards clubbed them into order. "Our pain-racked bodies, sunburned and dirty from dust and sweat, could hardly endure much more of this endless torture," an American survivor remembered. As the prisoners marched the length of the peninsula for five to ten days, the nights and days blurred, ending with a ride in airless, stinking boxcars to a prison camp.

American soldiers on the Bataan death march, with their hands tied behind their backs, April 1942

By a standard estimate, some two thousand five hundred Filipinos and five hundred Americans died on the Bataan death march. When the prisoners crumpled, they were left by the side of the highway. The men stumbled past corpses lying in the ditches, their bodies bloating in the relentless heat. At one point, the Americans were dumbfounded by the sight of a corpse squashed flat, evidently by being run over by a tank. It was desiccated from days in the baking sun, just a few inches thick, but the human form was still apparent.[1]

As these troops were among the first to understand, this was no ordinary war. More than a clash of armies and industrialized societies on an unprecedented scale, Americans saw the Pacific War as a moral contest against a depraved power in Japan. Reports of Japanese atrocities stiffened the Allies' resolve to demand an unconditional surrender. The Japanese were widely hated among Americans as a savage, fanatical, and treacherous race, reviled as "yellow monkeys."[2]

The foundational offense in American eyes was aggression at Pearl Harbor, as well as attacks against the Philippines and British-held Malaya, Singapore, and Hong Kong on the same day.[3] In his fireside chat two days after Pearl Harbor, Franklin Delano Roosevelt pledged to punish "the perpetrators of these crimes."[4]

Throughout the war, U.S. officials fumed at Japanese abuse of American prisoners of war, although fearing that public statements might prompt even harsher Japanese reprisals.[5] While Japan had not ratified the Geneva Convention of 1929 on prisoners of war, the Roosevelt administration extracted a Japanese pledge to apply its provisions to American soldiers and civilians in Japanese hands. But this soon proved chimerical, triggering scores of protests from the State Department. After the Japanese hastily executed three captured American airmen who, under daredevil Lieutenant Colonel James Doolittle, had launched an air raid on Tokyo and other Japanese cities in April 1942, Roosevelt vowed that "the American Government will hold personally and officially responsible for these diabolical crimes all of those officers of the Japanese Government who have participated therein and will in due course bring those officers to justice."[6] (Although five airmen had their sentences commuted, they were assaulted and tortured, with one dying of illness and malnutrition.)[7] In 1943, General George Marshall, the U.S. Army chief of staff, secretly warned of the "storm of bitterness" coming when the American public learned of "the brutalities and savagery displayed by the Japanese towards our prisoners."[8]

For some in the U.S. military, Japanese cruelty became a grotesque alibi to justify the worst acts carried out by the Americans in the latter years of the war. It is no surprise that under the rules of war promoted by the United States, the outlawry of aerial bombardment of cities was conspicuously absent.[9] If ever questioned about the incendiary bombing of dozens of Japanese cities in 1944–45, American leaders were quick to invoke Pearl Harbor or Bataan. The commanding U.S. general at Okinawa rationalized to his wife the killing of civilians: "If we were not doing it here they would be doing it in our country and with their characteristic barbarous savagery."[10]

Roosevelt himself believed that Japan was a profoundly dishonorable enemy. When the president was briefed about a notorious German war crime against Americans—an SS regiment had machine-gunned some seventy defenseless American prisoners of war in Belgium during the

Battle of the Bulge—he said, "Well, it will only serve to make our troops feel towards the Germans as they already have learned to feel about the Japs."[11]

Perhaps the most remarkable fact about the Tokyo trial is that it happened at all. Today the moral authority of Nuremberg so dominates our thinking that it seems unimaginable that the victorious Allies would not have put the defeated Axis leaders on trial. In fact, the Allied peoples overwhelmingly preferred a simpler way of dealing with Japan's leaders: just kill them.

Polls barely capture the vengeful rage of wartime public opinion. In July 1942, a Gallup poll found that 2 percent of American respondents wanted the Nazi leaders to get a court-martial, and only 1 percent wanted that for Adolf Hitler. But 39 percent wanted him to be hanged or shot, 23 percent wanted him in jail or a lunatic asylum, 6 percent were for exile, 5 percent for treating him as the Nazis had treated others, and 3 percent for slow torture.[12] In October 1944, when Britons were asked how Hitler, Heinrich Himmler, and Hermann Göring should be punished, 53 percent wanted them executed, 25 percent were for exile, and 22 percent preferred other punishments—which, as Gallup noted, meant "mostly torture."[13] While there are no reliable polls of Chinese public opinion toward the Japanese, a song of Chinese guerrilla units gives the flavor of it:

> Ten years of insults, we now have our revenge;
> Ten years of shame, we now have washed clean:
> Those who scolded us, we now will flay their skins;
> Those who hit us, we now will pull out their veins. . . .
> Those who burned our houses
> Will now have nowhere to bury their bodies;
> Those who raped our girls
> Will now have their wives as widows.[14]

Americans were even angrier at the Japanese than at the Germans. Fully a third of Americans wanted Japan destroyed as a political entity, 28 percent wanted it supervised and controlled, and just 8 percent wanted it rehabilitated—while 13 percent wanted to "[k]ill all Japanese people." Nine out of ten Americans thought that the Japanese warlords should be punished, but just 4 percent said that these Japanese should be treated justly or handled under international law—the option of the Tokyo tribunal. Asked by pollsters how to punish the Japanese, Americans proved balefully imaginative:

> "We should string them up and cut little pieces off them—one piece at a time."
> "Torture them to a slow and awful death."
> "Put them in a tank and suffocate them."
> "Kill them, but be sure to torture them first, the way they have tortured our boys."
> "Let them have it wholesale; get rid of every one of them."
> "Take them to Pearl Harbor and sink them."
> "Put them in Siberia and let them freeze to death."
> "Turn them over to the Chinese."
> "Put them in foxholes and fire bombs and grenades at them."
> "Kill them like rats."[15]

Fueled by these popular passions, the New Dealers running the Roosevelt and Truman administrations were not inclined to bother with war crimes trials. In failing health, visibly exhausted and gray, Roosevelt scorned the notion that "the German people as a whole are not responsible for what has taken place—that only a few Nazi leaders are responsible. That unfortunately is not based on fact. The German people as a whole must have it driven home to them that the whole nation has been engaged in a lawless conspiracy against the decencies of modern civilization."[16] He was no less harsh toward Japan. "It is amazing how many people are beginning to get soft in the future terms [for] the Germans and the Japs," he wrote.[17] Cordell Hull, the secretary of state, favored summary executions: "I would take Hitler and Mussolini and Tojo and their arch accomplices and bring them before a drumhead court-martial. And at sunrise on the following day there would occur an historic incident."[18]

Don't Let's Be Beastly to the Germans

The prime mover for a softer treatment of postwar Germany and Japan was Henry Stimson, the U.S. war secretary. He would dominate the White House's momentous decisions to quietly soften the ultimate terms of surrender in Japan and to create international war crimes tribunals at Nuremberg and Tokyo.

He was the odd man out in the Roosevelt and Truman war cabinets: a lonely Republican. Wary of Democratic idealists, his seventy-eight years had pushed him to a frosty view of power politics.[19] With a neat white mustache, graying hair severely parted, and bags under his eyes not hidden by his rimless round spectacles, speaking in a reedy voice, he was every inch a patrician lawyer. A colonel in World War I, he had served as secretary of war under William Howard Taft, as well as governor general of the Philippines and secretary of state under Herbert Hoover.[20] Like most gentlemen of his social background then, he was confident of white superiority over Haitians, Malays, African Americans, Jews, and Japanese.[21] Although more preoccupied with Germany's threat to Europe, "the continent of the white race," he saw Japan's aggression against China as a dangerous assault on a law-governed world.[22]

In several ways, Stimson was a strange candidate to propose legal punishment for war criminals. Most obviously, to Japanese living in their firebombed cities, the U.S. war secretary was in no position to call anyone a war criminal.[23] Furthermore, Stimson was comfortably indifferent about some Axis atrocities: opposing letting Jewish refugees into the United States as late as 1944, while his War Department refused to destroy the infrastructure of extermination.[24] He had insisted that military resources not be devoted to bombing the gas chambers at Auschwitz—although his War Department was prepared to limit its war effort by sparing German medieval architecture at Rothenberg, and he personally intervened to spare the shrines of Kyoto.[25] Finally, his legal sensibilities had been distinctly absent when his War Department had led the forcible internment of more than a hundred thousand U.S. citizens on the West Coast because they were of Japanese descent—even though Stimson privately understood that such persecution based on "racial characteristics" made "an awful hole in our constitutional system."[26]

After Stalingrad and Midway, Stimson began preparing for possible war crimes trials of Japanese, primarily for aggression and abusing U.S. prisoners of war.[27] Soon before D-Day, the U.S. Army found shocking photographs taken from the body of a dead Japanese soldier: Japanese troops in New Guinea swinging swords high over gaunt Australians, blindfolded and kneeling, about to have their heads chopped off.[28] Shaken, Stimson noted in his diary these "horrible pictures of the way the Japanese are treating our poor Air Force boys when they get hold of them."[29]

It was not until after D-Day, with Allied troops rolling toward Berlin, that the United States decided its policies for remaking postwar Germany and Japan.

The decision for Nuremberg—which would necessitate a parallel war crimes court at Tokyo—was a hasty, disorderly one. In August 1944, Stimson began by telling Roosevelt that Nazi Germany would have to be disarmed, its industries controlled, and its children reeducated for decades to come. Still, he feared partitioning or deindustrializing Germany, a sweeping project that he thought impossible without terrible consequences for the German population. Perhaps the most loaded question was how to handle German war criminals, which Stimson noted bluntly: "Policy vs. liquidation of Hitler and his gang."[30]

The simplest solution was the first one on everyone's minds: shooting them. The case for swift executions was made by one of Roosevelt's closest confidants, his old friend Henry Morgenthau Jr., the treasury secretary. In an administration that did little to stop the Holocaust, Morgenthau had clashed repeatedly with an unmoved Stimson and his apathetic War Department about rescuing Jewish refugees. Stimson, with a standard measure of social antisemitism common to his rarefied clubs, routinely commented in his diary about how disagreeably Jewish his cabinet rival was, noting that he was, "not unnaturally, very bitter."[31] Determined to ensure that Germany would not be able to fight another war, Morgenthau feared that trials would allow Nazis to evade punishment through legal technicalities, as well as letting them give final speeches to the German people justifying their racist ideology.[32]

On September 5, the treasury secretary sent the president what would become known as the Morgenthau Plan: a punitive blueprint for the complete demilitarization of Germany, political decentralization, internationalization of the Ruhr, reparations, and reeducation. It stipulated that the "arch criminals of this war whose obvious guilt has generally been recognized by the United Nations"—meaning the Allies—should be identified by a general, and then "put to death forthwith by firing squads" of Allied soldiers.[33] In one Treasury Department meeting, the senior staff considered shooting about two thousand five hundred Germans.[34]

Stimson was at first open to such executions. He noted, "Our officers must have the protection of definite instructions if shooting required"—ironically, promoting the defense of superior orders that would be famously undercut at Nuremberg and Tokyo.[35] But he quickly developed misgivings. He had been horrified to learn that, at the Tehran conference in November 1943, Joseph Stalin had proposed killing at least fifty or a hundred thousand Germans—vastly larger than anything contemplated at the Treasury.[36] Reminding Roosevelt of Stalin's pledge for "the liquidation of 50,000 German officers," Stimson warned him that the Soviets would use "methods . . . in the liquidation of the military clique which the United States would not like to participate in directly."[37] He urged Roosevelt to stay away from murderous Soviet forces charging into Germany: "Let her do the dirty work but don't father it."[38]

Stimson's doubts soon crystallized into advocacy for a milder treatment of postwar Germany. He feared that the Roosevelt team's bitterness could spark another war.[39] To offset his more generous attitude toward the German nation, he proposed war crimes trials for individual Germans: "It is primarily by the thorough apprehension, investigation, and trial of all the Nazi leaders and instruments of the Nazi system of terrorism, such as the Gestapo, with punishment delivered as promptly, swiftly, and severely as possible, that we can demonstrate the abhorrence which the world has for such a system and bring home to the German people our determination to extirpate it and all its fruits forever."[40]

The New Dealers rallied for tough punishment. Stimson found Cordell Hull "as bitter as Morgenthau against the Germans." Hull and Morgenthau aimed to incapacitate the industrial heartland of the Ruhr and the Saar, while Harry Hopkins, Roosevelt's trusted adviser on foreign policy, wanted to ban the making of steel.[41] Meeting with Stimson, Roosevelt himself "showed some interest in radical treatment of the Gestapo."[42] In another White House meeting, the president looked directly at Stimson while suggesting that the Germans could live on "soup from soup kitchens" to drive home to them their national defeat. Stimson, in a strained attempt at folksiness, countered that destroying the Saar-Ruhr region's industries was like burning down a whole house in order to roast a pig.[43]

Brooding in his vast office in the Pentagon, Stimson was heartened by two American institutions that were supposed to be fixated on following rules: the Army and the Supreme Court. First he consulted with General George Marshall, who agreed with him that the Germans should get fair trials. Stimson noted with satisfaction, "Army officers have a better respect for the law in those matters than civilians . . . who are anxious to go ahead and chop everybody's head off without trial or hearing."[44]

Next Stimson took encouragement from Felix Frankfurter, the Supreme Court justice. For all the justice's awesome power and manifest brilliance, Stimson knew him first as an obsequiously loyal protégé and friend. (Despite his distaste for Jews, he made an exception for Frankfurter, whom he found sufficiently assimilated as to be socially inoffensive.)[45] The justice was an adoring old friend of Roosevelt who maintained a merry correspondence with the president, and a stalwart advocate of his war policies.[46]

As Stimson knew, the Supreme Court had endorsed some of the most shocking actions justified as part of the war effort. Nineteen years before

Pearl Harbor, the Court had held that a Japanese was "clearly of a race which is not Caucasian" and therefore could not become a citizen of the United States.[47] In 1943, the Court, stuffed with Roosevelt loyalists, had upheld a curfew against Japanese Americans, which had resulted in the summary detention and internment of some 120,000 people of Japanese heritage, most of them citizens of the United States.[48] In the case of Fred Korematsu, a young Japanese American welder from California who had been deported to a detention camp in Utah, the Court knew that he was a patriotic citizen who posed no danger.[49] Yet Justice Hugo Black, writing for the majority in the iniquitous *Korematsu* ruling in 1944, had upheld an exclusion order aimed at "all citizens of Japanese ancestry." Deferring to the presidency and Congress in wartime, he wrote that this U.S. citizen was "excluded because we are at war with the Japanese Empire, because the properly constituted military authorities feared an invasion of our West Coast and felt constrained to take proper security measures."[50] Although a dissenting Justice Robert Jackson had warned that "the Court for all time has validated the principle of racial discrimination in criminal procedure," Black never reconsidered his opinion. People were "rightly fearful of the Japanese in Los Angeles," he explained years later. "They all look alike to a person not a Jap."[51]

Most helpfully for Stimson, in a 1942 case with long echoes in Ameri-

Japanese Americans being deported to detention camps, Arcadia, California, April 5, 1942

can policy toward enemy combatants to this day, the Court had held that German saboteurs could constitutionally be tried by a U.S. military commission, deeming that a proper use of presidential power.[52] Writing to his fellow justices, Frankfurter had fumed at the saboteurs: "You damned scoundrels have a helluvacheek to ask for a writ that would take you out of the hands of the Military Commission and give you the right to be tried, if at all, in a federal district court. You are just, low-down, ordinary, enemy spies."[53]

Now Frankfurter offered Stimson just the legal authority he sought. When Stimson outlined Morgenthau's punitive plans, Frankfurter snorted with disdain. He backed Stimson's view that the Nazi war criminals must get the substance of a fair trial. As the gratified war secretary wrote in his diary, "Although a Jew like Morgenthau, he approached the subject with perfect detachment and great helpfulness."[54]

For a high-stakes White House meeting on September 9, Stimson wrote up a memorandum in which he made his fundamental case for what would become Nuremberg—and, by extension, the Tokyo trial.

Stimson proposed an international tribunal for the chief German leaders. He insisted on a "well-defined procedure" which embodied "at least the rudimentary aspects of the Bill of Rights," including the right to mount a defense. He hoped to build a historical record of the Nazi system. Relying on his talk with Frankfurter, he argued that the Supreme Court had provided the legal basis by upholding the laws of war—apparently referring to the German saboteurs case. While keen to punish crimes against U.S. prisoners of war, he believed that the Nazi regime could do as it pleased within Germany's borders so long as its atrocities were not related to the conduct of the war—allowing the extermination of German Jews. As he explained in a disturbing passage, international courts "would be without jurisdiction in precisely the same way that any foreign court would be without jurisdiction to try those who were guilty of, or condoned, lynching in our own country."[55]

This proposal was routed. As Stimson recalled, in the White House meeting, Morgenthau unleashed "a new diatribe on the subject of the Nazis," while Roosevelt again declared that the Germans should be fed from soup kitchens. Afterward, Stimson could barely hold himself together.[56] Soon after, he wrote in his diary, the president "pranced up" to Québec City for a summit with Winston Churchill.[57] (Whatever else Roosevelt may have done, he didn't prance.) Stimson moped in his diary that Morgenthau was "so biased by his Semitic grievances that he is really a very dangerous adviser to the President at this time."[58] He added, "It is Semitism gone wild for vengeance."[59]

Stimson chided Roosevelt that his punitive plans would betray the Atlantic Charter and the Declaration of Independence, even calling the Morgenthau Plan "just such a crime as the Germans themselves hoped to perpetrate upon their victims—it would be a crime against civilization itself."[60] At Québec, Roosevelt and Churchill initialed a paper formally agreeing to eliminate military industries in the Ruhr and the Saar. A despairing Stimson noted that "the President was very firm for shooting the Nazi leaders without trial."[61]

In defeat, Stimson or one of his War Department underlings apparently resorted to a timeworn Washington dark art: a leak. On September 24, *The New York Times* splashed a front-page Associated Press story about a split in the cabinet over postwar policy toward Germany, noting Stimson's opposition to the pastoralization of Germany.[62] The leak deftly did not mention the shooting of war criminals, which was popular with Americans, instead attacking deindustrialization, which most Americans rejected lest it spur German troops to fight harder.[63] The newspapers, Stimson noted with satisfaction, came out against Morgenthau, while Republicans scented a campaign issue.[64]

Just three days later, Roosevelt reversed himself with the casual ease of a master politician. He informed Stimson that he did not really want to pastoralize Germany after all.[65] A few days later at a conciliatory lunch at the White House, the president told him with a naughty grin, "Henry Morgenthau pulled a boner."[66] When Roosevelt tried to duck responsibility for the Morgenthau Plan, Stimson whipped out a copy of it and showed the president his own initials on it.[67] Stimson later bitterly wrote of overcoming "the zeal of the Jewish American statesman seeking for vengeance."[68]

AGGRESSION AND CONSPIRACY

Having chosen law over summary executions, Stimson busied himself with figuring out what exactly the law was.

Stimson and his War Department lawyers wanted these trials to build a voluminous documentary history of the evils of the enemy, which would make it impossible for subsequent generations to deny what had happened.[69] The war secretary planned for military tribunals run jointly by the Allies, which is what both Nuremberg and Tokyo would be, with "simply the skeleton of what we call the requisitional fair trial."[70]

He sought to use conspiracy charges, a distinctive bit of American federal and state law which drew on his own experience prosecuting monopolists as the U.S. attorney for the Southern District of New York. Suspects would be charged not just with specific war crimes but with participating in a criminal conspiracy; they could be held responsible for all acts performed by any person to carry out that conspiracy. Defense lawyers hate conspiracy charges for all the reasons that prosecutors love them: they make it much easier to convict defendants, and they treat the conspiracy itself as a separate crime on top of the actual crimes plotted.[71] The conspiracy charges would become one of the most peculiar elements of the prosecutions at Nuremberg and Tokyo, foreign not just to the Japanese legal system but to those of the other Allies as well.[72]

Both Nuremberg and Tokyo would be trials primarily for punishing Axis aggression.[73] Although Nuremberg is usually remembered as a trial for the Holocaust, crimes against humanity took a tertiary place there, behind the prosecution of aggressive war and conventional war crimes— leaving it to Israel and West Germany to deal out their own justice for the Holocaust in later years, most dramatically at the 1961 trial of Adolf Eichmann in Jerusalem.[74] There is an ancient tradition in political philosophy that treats military aggression as a fundamental wrong, but the United States was driven by the Japanese surprise strike on Pearl Harbor and Nazi Germany's subsequent declaration of war.[75] Roosevelt wrote, "The charges against the top Nazis should include an indictment for waging aggressive warfare, in violation of the Kellogg Pact"—the Kellogg-Briand Pact of 1928, signed by both Germany and Japan, which renounced war as an instrument of national policy.[76] Stimson eventually folded in atrocities against civilians as a part of Nazi Germany's drive for war.[77]

As with Germany, so with Japan. Having loftily promised trials for the German warlords, the United States could hardly refuse the same for the Japanese. Through the narrow, hard-won victory of Stimson's legalism over Morgenthau's righteous vengeance, the United States was now placed on a different path toward the Axis countries it would soon be occupying. In Japan, too, Stimson would call for a more lenient kind of peace, softening another core demand of Roosevelt and his New Dealers: Japan's unconditional surrender. This would have sweeping consequences for the fate of Japan's rulers and the rehabilitation of the country.

In the morning of April 12, 1945, Stimson was in yet another Pentagon meeting about prosecuting Nazi war criminals. Later that afternoon, he was called to the White House to be told that Roosevelt was dead.[78]

CHAPTER 2

Unconditional Surrender

THE PRESIDENCY FELL ON Harry Truman at a desperate, final hour. On April 12, 1945, with American troops still battling in both Europe and Asia, the vice president was urgently summoned to the White House. He was ushered into Eleanor Roosevelt's study on the second floor, where she draped her arm around his shoulder and told him, "The President is dead." He had no inkling that Franklin Delano Roosevelt had suffered a sudden cerebral hemorrhage in Warm Springs, Georgia. Stunned, Truman asked what he could do. She replied, "What can we do for you?"[1]

Roosevelt had known how much his vice president had to learn about the wider world. "Harry is a fine man, intelligent, able, and has integrity," he had once written privately. "He doesn't know much about foreign affairs, but he's learning fast." Truman, about to make decisions that would alter the destiny of millions of Asians, had never set foot in Japan, China, India, or anywhere else in Asia.[2] Only a day before, he had been grumbling about the uselessness of the vice presidency.[3]

Mournfully sworn in as president by the chief justice of the Supreme Court on a Bible snatched from a White House bookcase, having just witnessed the secretary of state in tears, Truman found himself commander in chief of armies at war. He was shocked as "the weight of the Government had fallen on my shoulders. I did not know what reaction the country would have to the death of a man whom they all practically worshipped." On that sorrowful first day, Truman could not shake the deferential habit of referring to Roosevelt as the president.[4] He looked gray and drawn.[5]

Truman, painfully aware of his ignorance, fretted about how the military would respond to him and was overawed at the prospect of contending with the hardened leaders in Moscow and London. "I knew the President had a great many meetings with Churchill and Stalin," he wrote in his diary. "I was not familiar with any of these things and it was really something to think about but I decided the best thing was to go home and get as much rest as possible and face the music."[6]

His underlings were even less sure that their new chief was up to the task. Henry Stimson, who would play a pivotal role in some of Truman's most important decisions about Japan, was already a wreck. Exhausted from overwork, leery of irritating Roosevelt with his outspoken opinions, the war secretary meant to quit his post as soon as the bullets stopped flying. Old and grouchy, suffering from a heart condition, he privately admitted to struggling with depression.[7]

At the White House, while waiting to be sworn in as president, Truman took his new war secretary aside and told him that he meant to continue the war as Roosevelt had conducted it.[8] Stimson, stricken by the death of a man he had come to see as a friend and as the best war president in American history, grieved for the loss of Roosevelt's vision in the coming crucial months. In his diary, he fretted, "No one knows what the new President's views are—at least I don't."[9] Truman seemed pleasant enough but "it was very clear that he knew little of the task into which he was stepping."[10]

As Truman swore his oath of office, American troops were moving across the Elbe, racing Soviet divisions toward Berlin. The United States was in the early days of its massive Okinawa campaign, with Japanese kamikazes attacking U.S. forces and sinking a destroyer that day.[11] As a Japanese colonel on Okinawa wrote, the "glorious news" of Roosevelt's death put the staff officers there into ecstasies, raising hopes that Japan could win the war after all.[12] The novice president swiftly set about meeting with his foreign policy advisers, admirals and generals, and the secretaries of state and war.[13] "We discussed Stalin, Churchill, de Gaulle, Cairo, Casablanca, Tehran and Yalta," wrote Truman wryly in his diary. "That is about all."[14]

With Truman listening intently, Stimson and the military chiefs briefed him on the European and Pacific theaters. The president struck the war secretary as "anxious to learn and to do his best," but was struggling with information that could only be mastered by "long previous familiarity." Afterward, in the car back to the Pentagon, General George Marshall, the chief of staff of the army, told Stimson, "We shall not know what he is really like until the pressure begins to be felt."[15]

Taking the train up to Hyde Park, in upstate New York, for Roosevelt's burial, the new president was shaken by the national grief. The somber ceremony had a wartime feeling: a military procession, a twenty-one-gun salute, Roosevelt's casket escorted by cadets from nearby West Point and borne by soldiers and sailors to the grave.[16] Seeing men and women, young and old, weeping in the streets, Truman was riveted by an "old Negro woman sitting down on curb with apron up . . . crying like she had lost her son." He told a pack of reporters "if they ever prayed, which I very much doubted, that they had better pray for me now."[17]

"It is a very, very hard position to fall into as I did," Truman wrote. "If there ever was a man who was forced to be President, I'm that man."[18] When Truman's mother was asked about her son becoming president, she gave what he considered "a jewel" of an answer: "I can't really be glad he's President because I am sorry President Roosevelt is dead. If he had been voted in, I would be out waving a flag, but it doesn't seem right to be very happy or to wave any flags now. Harry will get along all right."[19]

"Tokyo Rocks Under the Weight of Our Bombs"

Truman took an immediate dislike to much of being president: the constant glare of publicity, the sycophantic hangers-on, the profound isolation. "I'm always so lonesome when my family leaves," he wrote in his diary.[20] He hated living in the White House ("the great white jail"), which turned out to be vast, creaky, and spooky: "The damned place is haunted sure as shootin'."[21] His eyes strained from too much reading, with a hidden catch lurking in every memorandum.[22] And he was disconcerted by the adulation of power: "It is a most amazing spectacle, this worship of high office."[23]

While not versed in international relations, Truman was shrewd and diligent. He had a long-standing bookish interest in military history, from Napoléon Bonaparte's memoirs to studies of the Civil War, and drew on his tour fighting as an artillery officer in World War I.[24] He had discovered in the sludge of northern France that machine gun bullets whizzing overhead sounded like a swarm of bees, and was lucky to survive when a German shell exploded within fifteen feet of him.[25] In the major offensive in the Meuse-Argonne in the final weeks of the war, he advanced his battery with German artillery crashing down all around him, which left some of his men wounded or suffering from shell shock, although not him.[26] When German shells landed near one of his positions, they churned up chunks of French and German corpses left from a previous battle. He was, he confided in his wife, glad he wasn't afraid of ghosts.[27]

The neophyte wartime president initially meant to continue Roosevelt's uncompromising fight against Japan. Truman had long been committed to total victory, writing to his wife in 1942: "We must take this one to its conclusion and *dictate* terms from Berlin and Tokyo."[28] As the tide of battle seemed at last to be turning in 1943, at the Casablanca conference, Roosevelt had committed to a policy of unconditional surrender, vowing punishment for the guilty Axis leaders. Rather than leaving residual seeds of militarism as after World War I, Roosevelt sought a complete destruction of fascism and authoritarianism, making way for peaceful democracies.[29] Now in Truman's first major speech, a broadcast national address to a joint session of Congress on April 16, he too embraced unconditional surrender.[30]

Honoring Roosevelt's legacy, he quickly dashed any German or Japanese hopes that his new administration might soften his predecessor's conditions: "Our demand has been, and it remains—Unconditional Surrender! We will not traffic with the breakers of the peace on the terms of the peace." Only a month after the firebombing of the Japanese capital, Truman thundered, "Tokyo rocks under the weight of our bombs."

In this defining debut speech, Truman firmly committed himself to punishing Axis war criminals: "the laws of God and of man have been violated and the guilty must not go unpunished. Nothing shall shake our determination to punish the war criminals even though we must pursue them to the ends of the earth." He championed the nascent United Nations: "without such organization, the rights of man on earth cannot be protected." Invoking "fundamental rights" of freedom, he placed his trust in law: "Real security will be found only in law and in justice."[31]

Truman inherited the decision to put Nazi leaders on trial. Since his watchword at first was continuing Roosevelt's policies, by default he extended legal justice to the punishment of Japanese war criminals as well.

Truman held a plainspoken legalism. As he wrote privately, "We have a stern duty to teach the German people the hard lesson that they must change their ways before they can be received back into the family of peaceful, civilized nations."[32] He wanted trials for Filipinos who had collaborated with the Japanese occupiers, although insisting that the Philippines, about to become independent, handle the process itself.[33] Appalled at Japanese abuse of American prisoners of war, he personally made sure General Douglas MacArthur handled it properly: "What I am anxious to do is to be sure that these Japanese, where they deserve it, are tried."[34]

Truman frequently used the idiom of criminal justice to refer to Axis leaders as well as the German public, condemning "the crimes of the gangsters whom they placed in power and whom they wholeheartedly approved and obediently followed."[35] The new president saw law as a more pure alternative to the coarse politicking he knew all too well, although fearing that courts could be corrupted.[36] He reflexively used legalistic language to explain the war, contending that there would "be no peace until tyranny had been outlawed."[37] He would later call the "fair trial" at Nuremberg "one of the greatest things that has come out of this war."[38]

The president's respect for law was buttressed by his personnel. Truman was particularly fond of Samuel Rosenman, the savvy White House counsel whom Roosevelt had charged with setting up the Nuremberg trials, privately calling him "one of the ablest in Washington, keen mind, a lucid pen, a loyal Roosevelt man and an equally loyal Truman man."[39] Truman revered Robert Jackson, the Supreme Court justice whom he picked to be chief prosecutor at the international military tribunal at Nuremberg for the major German war criminals. "Made a great contribution to International Law," the president would write privately. "One good man."[40]

In the cabinet, Truman almost immediately clashed with Henry Morgenthau, who without Roosevelt's protections was driven to resign early in July.[41] This removed the administration's foremost advocate of summary executions for Axis war criminals, while Stimson would remain as war secretary throughout the crucial decisions about Japan's surrender and the punishment of its leadership.

When Stimson briefed Truman on a British initiative to execute the top Nazi leaders without trial, he was relieved to find that the president strongly supported war crimes trials instead.[42] Stimson exhorted Truman for "the trial of war criminals. They should be punished and, they being punished, the rest of the country should be rehabilitated." More unrestrained vengeance, he explained to the new president, sprang from "the problem of our Jewish people here," warning about Morgenthau and one of Roosevelt's advisers, Bernard Baruch, who was Jewish. As Stimson wrote in his diary, Truman "said they were all alike—they couldn't keep from meddling with it."[43]

The new president loudly praised Nuremberg. "I believe the effect will be very great on future wars—at least I hope it will help to prevent them," he wrote.[44] He applauded the trial for documenting the deaths of six million Jews: "That crime will be answered in justice."[45] He wrote proudly that "[a]n undisputed gain coming out of Nurnberg is the formal recognition that there are crimes against humanity," and that "I hope we have established for all time the proposition that aggressive war is criminal and will be so treated."[46]

Truman committed himself to a worldwide "peace of free men" based on human rights. As he declared in a Rio de Janeiro speech to Latin American leaders in 1947, his country believed "that there are basic human rights which all men everywhere should enjoy," which could only be secured "when the threat of war has been ended forever."[47] In his inaugural address in 1949, he would champion democracy as the corrective to "unprecedented and brutal attacks on the rights of man."[48]

OKINAWA

In the long years since Pearl Harbor, American forces had battled from rock to reef across the Pacific. Now they were mounting what would be, except for the D-Day landings, the largest amphibious assault of the war.[49] By seizing the large island of Okinawa, southwest of Japan, the Americans would secure important airfields, allowing an intensification of the bombing campaign and providing a base for conquering Japan's home islands.[50]

In order to "contribute our utmost to the final decisive battle of Japan proper," as a leading Japanese colonel wrote, the Japanese planned a defensive fight of bitter attrition.[51] The Americans assembling had already seen far too much combat, their eyes left with a "vacant hollow look," as one Marine noted.[52] "This is expected to be the costliest amphibious campaign of the war," said a U.S. lieutenant in a briefing, as the troops groaned. "We will be hitting an island about 350 miles from the Japs' home islands, so you can expect them to fight with more determination than ever."[53]

To the Americans' surprise when they landed, the Japanese had withdrawn into the interior; the small farm plots struck one of the Marines as beautiful, like a patchwork quilt. They passed Okinawan civilians, mostly old men, women, and children, bewildered and terrified of the Americans, who were sent to internment camps at the rear.[54] But as the Americans pressed ahead, the Japanese troops unleashed a ferocious defense from positions in the hills and limestone caves. "The beautiful, peaceful countryside of the Amekudai plateau," wrote a Japanese officer, "was now steeped in the blood of thousands of soldiers—Japanese and American." Soaked in mud and sweat, he composed a poem: "On the night where the moon shone beautifully over Shuri hill,/ I think of death, as I throw grenades."[55]

The terrors intensified over weeks of the most intense fighting endured yet by Americans in the Pacific.[56] Okinawa's civilians were cut down by bombardment, caught in crossfires, or, having been indoctrinated by the Japanese military that the Americans would torture and rape them, committed suicide in droves.[57] "It is pitiful to see what modern weapons do to civilian communities harboring enemy defenses," a U.S. general wrote to his wife, "but is necessary to shoot the enemy out of whatever positions they hold."[58] Wounded Japanese troops killed themselves with hand grenades, satchel charges, or cyanide, shouting, "Long live the Emperor!"[59] When Japanese artillery struck a muddy ridge, it blasted up not just soil but parts of dead Japanese soldiers who had been buried there. American Marines slipping in the mire found themselves covered in fat maggots, shaking them off, vomiting. These obscenities reduced the most battle-hardened Americans to screaming and madness. A Marine veteran of Okinawa later wrote, "to me the war was insanity."[60]

In eighty-two days of fighting to take Okinawa, 12,510 Americans perished. Some 70,000 Japanese troops died, as did as many as 100,000 Okinawan civilians.[61] A Japanese colonel there shuddered at the prospect of future sacrifices, perhaps the loss of millions of Japanese lives rather than a surrender. "We will have the decisive battle on Japan proper," Japanese military headquarters instructed its officers. "Okinawa is merely a front-line action."[62]

VICTORY IN EUROPE

The pressure on Japan intensified as Nazi Germany neared defeat, which would leave Japan facing the Allies alone. With German forces buckling under the combined advances of Soviet, American, and British troops, Truman would not compromise on peace terms. "The German idea, of course, was to split the three great powers and perhaps make things easier for themselves," he explained to Eleanor Roosevelt, but he insisted on "complete unconditional surrender on all fronts."[63]

Truman had a secret reason to expect that Japan might be pounded into defeat. Early in the Okinawa campaign, on April 25, Stimson informed a shocked Truman that within four months, the United States would have "the most terrible weapon ever known in human history, one bomb of which could destroy a whole city." These atomic weapons were so dangerous that "modern civilization might be completely destroyed."[64] For Stimson, though, the atomic bomb offered a way out of a bloody invasion of Japan's home islands.[65] As he later explained, he sought "a tremendous shock which would carry convincing proof of our power to destroy the Empire."[66]

After the deaths of Adolf Hitler and Benito Mussolini, Truman said bluntly: "the two principal war criminals will not have to come to trial; and I am very happy they are out of the way."[67] A few days later, on May 8, flanked in the Oval Office by cabinet members, congressional leaders, U.S. and British military chiefs, and his wife and daughter, Truman announced that German officials had signed an unconditional surrender.[68]

Victory in Europe freed the Allies to concentrate all their firepower on Japan.[69] "It was nonsense to continue the war in this corner of the Pacific after our only real ally had collapsed," wrote a clear-eyed Japanese colonel.[70] Truman declared, "The West is free, but the East is still in bondage to the treacherous tyranny of the Japanese." He restated the United States' commitment to unconditional surrender, reiterated by Roosevelt in the Cairo Declaration in 1943—a stern document which called for punishing Japan's aggression, stripping it of its island conquests since World War I, freeing colonized Korea, and returning Manchuria and Formosa (Taiwan) to China.[71] To the White House press corps gathered in the Oval Office, Truman emphasized that "we are only half through."[72]

The president warned the Japanese public that "the striking power and intensity of our blows will steadily increase," bringing "utter destruction" to the country's industrial and military capacities. "Our blows will not cease until the Japanese military and naval forces lay down their arms in *unconditional surrender*," he said. In a chilling measure of American wartime rage, Truman had to reassure the Japanese that they would not be annihilated: "Unconditional surrender does not mean the extermination or enslavement of the Japanese people."[73] Still, he tempered his harsh threats with legalism, hoping for "a peace rooted in justice and in law."[74]

Victorious in London, Winston Churchill concluded his BBC radio broadcast by reminding his war-weary citizens that "beyond all lurks Japan, harassed and failing but still a people of a hundred millions, for whose warriors death has few terrors." Britain would force this "evil power" to pay for "their odious treachery and cruelty." He exhorted, "Forward, unflinching, unswerving, indomitable, till the whole task is done and the whole world is safe and clean."[75]

"A Fight to the Finish"

Truman now faced a stark decision: should he soften the terms of peace to encourage Japan to quit the fight? He could swerve by offering to safeguard the emperor—a new policy whose most prominent supporter would be Stimson, the one Republican member of the cabinet, inspired in part by Herbert Hoover.

Stimson had a long history with Japan, from bright days to the bleak present. Visiting in 1928 during its first general election under universal male suffrage, he had been impressed with a liberalizing Japan's efforts soon after the Taisho era to be "a good citizen of the world."[76] But as Hoover's secretary of state in 1931, he had denounced Japan's conquest of the northeastern Chinese provinces that made up Manchuria.[77] He became a stern foe of Japanese aggression, seeing it as a threat to a peaceful, legalized world order under the League of Nations.[78]

In Germany, the Roosevelt administration had carried its commitment to unconditional surrender all the way through a bloody ground invasion to a ruinous end in the rubble of Berlin. Roosevelt and Stimson had agreed that there could be no "so-called negotiated peace" with Nazi barbarism, grimly accepting "a fight to the finish"—which the war secretary called "a long horrible contest where we needed all the manpower that we could summon."[79] Stimson had exhorted his Pentagon commanders that there could be no negotiated peace in Europe or Asia: "There is *no common ground* between civilization and barbarism. It must be war to a finish."[80]

But he grew alarmed as determined Japanese forces fought long after the tide of the war had turned against them.[81] Hoping to avoid a second bloody fight to the finish, he sought to avoid an invasion of Japan's home islands: on the one hand, breaking Japan's will with atomic weapons; on the other, offering concessions which might entice it to yield. After the slaughter on Okinawa, he expected much worse in the fight for the home islands. He wrote in his diary, "Fortunately the actual invasion will not take place until after my secret is out"—meaning the atomic bomb.[82]

He was spurred to action by a "rather dramatic and radical" paper by Hoover—one of the most discredited men in the country as far as the New Dealers were concerned, but an old friend whose acumen Stimson admired.[83] The former president urged him to drop demands for unconditional surrender in order to avoid the casualties from what Stimson repeatedly called "a fight to a finish."[84]

The war secretary helped to broker his old boss a meeting with his current boss, marking Hoover's first return to the White House in a dozen years—to the outrage of some of Truman's Democratic staffers.[85] Back in the Oval Office, a confident Hoover lectured Truman about bolstering Japan as a counterweight to the Soviet Union (Russians "had the characteristics of Asiatics"), which meant ending the war promptly. While he sought Japan's total disarmament for decades, as well as trials for those who had violated the laws of war, he suggested stating that the United States did not wish to exterminate the Japanese people or destroy their form of government. The former president left convinced that the current one was merely being nice and would ignore him.[86]

Not so. Truman gradually abandoned the policy of Franklin Roosevelt in order to adopt that of Herbert Hoover. Truman open-mindedly asked Hoover to send him a memorandum on Japan.[87] By issuing a declaration demanding peace, Hoover wrote, they could save the lives of as many as a million American boys and avoid "the impossible task" of creating a new Japanese government. Hoover emphasized the "desire of the Japanese to preserve the Mikado who is the spiritual head of the nation."[88]

The same day as Hoover's visit, the administration's foremost expert on Japan also urged Truman to reconsider the terms for surrender.

Joseph Grew, the undersecretary of state, had been the ambassador in Tokyo for a decade before being expelled after Pearl Harbor. A conservative Republican appointed to his post in Japan by Hoover, he was a starchy Bostonian with aquiline eyebrows and a trimmed mustache.[89] Unlike the neophyte Truman, he had stridden the streets of the cities being firebombed and mingled with the Japanese leadership. "Japan has needed no Hitler," he once wrote. "Her militarists are an oligarchy of Hitlers."[90] He had chatted about good golfing spots with Emperor Hirohito, who, clad in his military uniform, had a singsong voice and a pleasant smile.[91] Grew was convinced that the emperor had been a peaceful influence over his belligerent government.[92]

Grew told Truman that the biggest obstacle to Japanese surrender was their fear that the monarchy would be destroyed. If the Japanese could not salvage the fundamentals of their political structure, this "fanatical people" might fight to the last man. After the war, the emperor could help legitimize a new leadership, although Grew was convinced that "the best that we can hope for in Japan is the development of a constitutional monarchy, experience having shown that democracy in Japan would never work."[93] According to Grew's account of the meeting, Truman encouragingly said that he had been thinking along the same lines.[94] The president instructed him to press his case with Stimson, Marshall, and other senior military chiefs.[95]

After a briefing in the White House projection room from the navy secretary, Truman noted, "Apparently a very detailed plan worked out with idea of invasion of Japan."[96] Despite that terrifying prospect, Truman trusted his fortune. "Luck always seems to be with me in games of chance and in politics," he wrote in his diary. "No one was ever luckier than I've been since becoming the Chief Executive and Commander in

Chief. Things have gone so well that I can't understand it—except to attribute it to God. He guides me, I think."[97]

"Outdoing Hitler in Atrocities"

Truman repeatedly boasted about the firebombing of Tokyo and dozens of other Japanese cities. "Substantial portions of Japan's key industrial centers have been levelled to the ground in a series of record incendiary raids," he announced. "What has already happened to Tokyo will happen to every Japanese city whose industries feed the Japanese war machine. I urge Japanese civilians to leave those cities if they wish to save their lives."[98] Other U.S. officials were contemplating more extreme steps. General Joseph Stilwell, the commander of U.S. Army ground forces, secretly suggested using gas against the Japanese military while invading the home islands.[99]

Despite the horrific toll on civilians, Stimson was a rarity among top-ranked U.S. civilian officials in expressing qualms about the firebombing of Japan's cities. He suggested to Truman that the Air Force stick to so-called precision bombing as used in Europe, and try to spare Japanese civilians as a show of "fair play and humanitarianism." The same standard should "be applied as far as possible to the use of any new weapons"—namely, atomic bombs.[100]

This vision of an antiseptic air campaign was fantastical. U.S. B-29s pounded not just Japan's big cities but also small and medium-sized ones, leaving no urban dwellers safe. Moving away from an attempt at high-altitude precision bombing of military and industrial targets, the Americans early in 1945 embarked on a ruinous program of low-altitude incendiary bombardment against cities whose civilian homes were mostly made of wood. After the firebombing of Tokyo on March 9–10, the B-29s brought fiery ruin to some sixty-six cities across the country: Nagoya, then Osaka, then Kobe, and then others, many of them pounded repeatedly.[101] Tokyo suffered two more big incendiary raids in May, one of which destroyed much of the western and northeastern parts of the capital, as well as burning the emperor's residence at the Imperial Palace.[102]

From June onward, the Allies escalated their air assaults while continuing to throttle the country with a blockade.[103] The firebombing of ordinary civilians became commonplace.[104] University students were eating locusts; children were made to dig up pine roots for fuel oil.[105] Terrified, more than eight million people fled into the countryside. Transportation and communications ground to a halt. More than half of the three large urban regions which comprised the backbone of Japan's economy—

the Tokyo-Kawasaki-Yokohama area, Osaka-Kobe, and Nagoya—were scorched to the point of total paralysis. According to one Japanese report, in those three areas alone, almost 120,000 people suffered violent and painful deaths by the end of June.[106] All told, the U.S. Strategic Bombing Survey would later reckon that some 210,000 Japanese died from the conventional air bombardment. The postwar Japanese government put the death toll at 205,685.[107]

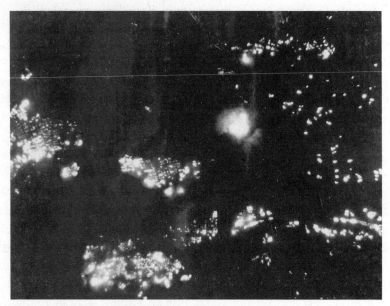

A U.S. intelligence photograph of Tokyo in flames from U.S. aerial bombardment, August 1945

Japan's government formally protested that the bombing of nonmilitary targets violated international law. In Tokyo, Nagoya, Osaka, Kobe, and other cities, the assault seemed "exclusively aimed at the wounding and killing of innocent civilians." The bombing reduced shrines, schools, hospitals, and residential neighborhoods to ashes, killing untold numbers of women, children, and the elderly. As with an earlier Japanese complaint about bombing civilians in Okinawa, the United States did not reply.[108]

In private, Stimson was startled by press reports showing that the firebombing of Tokyo had been far more destructive than the "precision bombing" he had been promised. But his air staffer explained that Japan's industries were widely scattered, leaving no way to destroy its war machine without killing civilians.[109] Stimson insisted that Kyoto, whose shrines had made a deep impression on him, be spared.[110]

The military emphasized the importance of incendiary strikes in destroying industrial targets in densely populated cities such as Tokyo,

Kobe, Osaka, Kawasaki, Nagoya, Amagasaki, Yawata, and more.[111] Stimson backed off relatively quickly. He later claimed that the destruction of the industrial capacity of some fifty-nine Japanese cities and the prospect of "utter desolation" of their homeland helped to break the will of Japan's leaders.[112]

On June 6, a year after D-Day, Stimson in a White House meeting confessed to Truman his anxiety about the "area bombing" of Japan, which he termed necessary because of its scattered manufacturing base. Stimson starkly told Truman, "I did not want to have the United States get the reputation of outdoing Hitler in atrocities."

Stimson had another pitiless consideration in mind. He noted, "I was a little fearful that before we could get ready the Air Force might have Japan so thoroughly bombed out that the new weapon"—the atomic bomb—"would not have a fair background to show its strength." Laughing, Truman said that he understood.[113]

THE SOVIET HAMMER

The Americans would not be smashing Japan alone. In November 1943 at the Tehran conference, Roosevelt had extracted from Stalin a commitment that once Nazi Germany was vanquished, the Soviet Union would join the war against Japan.[114] At the Yalta conference in February 1945, Stalin had agreed that the Soviet Union—despite having signed a neutrality pact with Japan in 1941—would be ready to attack Japan within three months after Germany's defeat.[115] Soviet troops had taken to greeting American soldiers by saying "when we meet in Tokyo."[116]

In return, Churchill and a frail Roosevelt had rewarded Stalin with the Japanese-owned Kuril Islands and the southern part of Sakhalin Island, as well as some territorial rights and naval bases in China's own lands in Manchuria.[117] Churchill privately warned Truman that an "iron curtain is drawn down" on the Soviets' eastern front in Europe, urging the president not to compromise the freedom of Central Europe.[118]

The wartime alliance between the United States and the Soviet Union deteriorated fast.[119] Truman, who as a senator had reckoned the Soviets "as untrustworthy as Hitler and Al Capone," found them prickly and suspicious.[120] He privately seethed at lying Soviet propaganda, while his administration sparred bitterly with Stalin over the Soviet vise grip on Poland.[121] "I'm not afraid of Russia," he wrote in his diary. "They've always been our friends and I can't see any reason why they shouldn't always be." But he quickly followed that by writing that "the dictatorship of the proletariat is no different from the Czar or Hitler."[122]

Truman dispatched his trusted envoy Harry Hopkins to Moscow, with instructions to "use a baseball bat if he thought that was proper approach to Mr. Stalin."[123] Sticking to his Yalta pledge with fearsome precision, Stalin told him that Soviet armies could strike by August 8. When Hopkins said that he hoped that the Russians would find Hitler's body, Stalin conspiratorially replied that Hitler might have fled to Japan by submarine.

Apparently aware that the Americans were toying with a conditional Japanese surrender, Stalin brusquely warned that the Japanese would like that in order to preserve their military for future aggressions. The Japanese, he believed, were so aggressive that they would never rest until exacting revenge for their impending defeat. Unconcerned at sacrificing yet more Soviet troops, he declared that this war could only happen once in a hundred years, and the Allies should take full advantage of it to "utterly defeat Japan" and thus secure fifty or sixty years of peace. He demanded the elimination of the Japanese monarchy, rather than bartering that for a surrender. Although he contemptuously dismissed Hirohito as a figurehead, he wanted to destroy the institution lest it one day be taken up by a more energetic leader.[124]

INVASION OR STRANGULATION

Truman moped in the White House, which he found old and creaky, "all the while listening to the ghosts walk up and down the hallway and even right here in the study." As he plaintively wrote to his wife, "The floors pop and the drapes move back and forth—I can just imagine old Andy and Teddy having an argument over Franklin." His mind turned unbidden to the most catastrophically failed presidents: "Or James Buchanan and Franklin Pierce deciding which was the more useless to the country. And when Millard Fillmore and Chester Arthur join in for place and show the din is almost unbearable. But I still get some work done."[125]

In the evenings, the haunted president would stop by the White House Map Room—the secret intelligence command center created by Roosevelt—to get a somber briefing about that day's losses: the ships sunk, the soldiers and sailors dead or injured.[126] In June, he confronted his most terrible choice. Although Japan had been defeated in the battles of Saipan, Luzon, Leyte, and Iwo Jima, and was losing Okinawa, it still fought on. "I have to decide Japanese strategy—shall we invade Japan proper or shall we bomb and blockade?" he wrote in his diary. "That is my hardest decision to date."[127]

It was clear that Japan would be defeated eventually. Neither its air force nor its industrial base was the equal of those of defeated Germany.

The Japanese navy, once formidable, was badly weakened and desperate for petroleum. In the pivotal year of 1943, the United States had built well more than five times as many aircraft as Japan.[128] In the first two months of combat on Okinawa, Japan had lost almost six times as many men as the Americans, with some sixty-one thousand Japanese killed.[129] During the devastating urban battle for Manila in February, the influential Prince Konoe Fumimaro had secretly urged Hirohito to end the war.[130] The Joint Chiefs of Staff, while seeing no evidence of Japan's abrupt collapse, were confident enough to order General Douglas MacArthur and Admiral Chester Nimitz to be ready to occupy Japan immediately in case of a sudden surrender.[131]

Still, nobody in Washington knew when or how Japan would finally yield. Japan still had over four million troops and could presumably muster many more in desperate defense of their homeland. Although the Japanese people were exhausted, their government's war plans called for massive new mobilizations, increased suicide attacks, and turning all able-bodied civilians, men and women alike, into a national guerrilla resistance.[132] To overcome that, the U.S. Army planned to deploy about seven million men to conquer Japan's home islands, somewhat smaller than the force of nine or ten million men that Roosevelt had been prepared to authorize for the final invasion of Germany.[133] After heavy losses at Saipan and Iwo Jima, with more deaths every day on Okinawa, Truman grimly noted "the increasing toughness of this war as our troops get closer to Tokyo."[134]

In an uncompromising speech about Japan, Truman told Congress that "there can be no peace in the world until the military power of Japan is destroyed—with the same completeness as was the power of the European dictators." But he was sobered by the mustering of national power required: sending millions of troops against an enemy fourteen thousand miles away; supplying six tons of equipment for every fighting man; deploying carrier-based air power in support of amphibious attacks. To rally a country sick of the war, Truman declared: "These are the same Japanese who perpetrated the infamous attack on Pearl Harbor three and one-half years ago; they are the same Japanese who ordered the death march from Bataan; they are the same Japanese who carried out the barbarous massacres in Manila."[135]

Hoover's proposal to soften the terms of Japan's surrender ricocheted across Washington. Grew wrote to Truman that sparing the emperor and preserving the throne were "irreducible Japanese terms."[136] On June 18, in a White House meeting, Grew exhorted the president to modify his demand for unconditional surrender, making an announcement when Okinawa fell.[137] Truman was genially noncommittal, saying that he liked the idea but had to wait until discussing it at the upcoming Potsdam summit with Stalin and Churchill.[138]

Later that day at the White House, Stimson and the Joint Chiefs of Staff briefed the president on the invasion of Japan. (Grew had cannily snuck in his own session beforehand.) In a momentous meeting, the generals proposed a massive conquest of the southwestern Japanese home island of Kyushu, as a staging area for eventually storming the main island of Honshu, where Tokyo sits. Truman was confronted with a daunting wall of military men unanimous in their advocacy.

George Marshall, General of the Army and army chief of staff, explained that they were already hitting Japan with everything they had: air bombardment and sea blockade in a "strategy of strangulation." Invading Kyushu was vital for "forcing capitulation by invasion of the Tokyo Plain." Marshall proposed storming Kyushu as early as November. By then, he said, the Japanese navy should be pounded into irrelevance, and "our air action will have smashed practically every industrial target worth hitting in Japan as well as destroying huge areas in the Jap cities." The invasion would be hard, he conceded, but no worse than the Normandy landing.

In the first month alone, Marshall anticipated some 31,000 American casualties, killed or wounded.[139] The bloodshed would be far worse for the Japanese, with the U.S. military calculating that in recent months, as many as twenty-two Japanese had died for every single American death—a total of more than three hundred thousand Japanese deaths in the past ten months. Less optimistically, the Navy's fleet admiral warned that U.S. casualties could be more like Okinawa, at about 35 percent. With a planned U.S. assault force of over seven hundred thousand, that would mean a quarter of a million American casualties—more if the Japanese raised additional troops to defend their homeland. Ultimately, some three hundred thousand Americans would die in World War II in total; this invasion could have added significantly to that number.[140]

Lest Truman blanch, Marshall lectured the novice president on his responsibilities: "It is a grim fact that there is not an easy, bloodless way to victory in war and it is the thankless task of the leaders to maintain their firm outward front which holds the resolution of their subordinates."

Truman, who knew from World War I what it was like to advance under artillery fire, was taken aback. He would later claim that Marshall told him that half a million Americans might die in a ground invasion.[141]

He worried about Japanese reinforcements to defend Kyushu—which were in fact already under way—and suggested deferring any decision about invading the main island of Honshu until the Soviets perhaps entered the war.[142] But none of the Joint Chiefs disagreed with Marshall, and Douglas MacArthur, the five-star Army general in the Pacific, had sent a telegram arguing that this invasion would ultimately save lives by avoiding pointless casualties in less important battles elsewhere in Asia.[143]

Stimson was wary. As he noted in his diary, Truman had asked him to speak on "the big political question" of whether there was "a liberal-minded section of the Japanese people with whom we can make proper terms."[144] While seeing no alternative to invading Kyushu, the war secretary said that he wanted to encourage the "large submerged class" of Japanese who did not support the war. But even those war-weary Japanese would surely resist tenaciously when attacked on their own soil. Truman sharply asked him if the invasion of Japan by white men would not unite the Japanese. Stimson agreed that it would.

Only one military man favored concessions to induce Japan to quit. William Leahy, the Navy fleet admiral who served as the White House intermediary to the armed services, argued strenuously against squandering American lives to force an unconditional Japanese surrender. Although he accepted an invasion of Kyushu, Leahy later noted that he saw no justification for conquering "an already thoroughly defeated Japan."[145]

Truman grimly said that he had wanted this meeting in the hope of "preventing an Okinawa from one end of Japan to the other." Obviously sobered, the president offered no decision yet on conquering Honshu, but ordered the military to go ahead with the planned invasion of Kyushu in November.[146]

The next day, he wrote to his wife that he wished he could turn his job over to Dwight Eisenhower right now.[147]

CHAPTER 3

"Prompt and Utter Destruction"

Henry Stimson was desperate to avoid the looming land invasion of Japan.[1] He wrote in his diary that "it would be deplorable if we have to go through the military program with all its stubborn fighting to a finish."[2] Instead he wanted to give Japan a final warning, which if unheeded would bring intensified bombing and "an attack of S-1"—code for the atomic bomb.[3]

On June 21, 1945, U.S. forces took Okinawa at last.[4] Truman, with a kind of folksy brutality, called his trophy "the base from which we will make it more 'pleasant' for the Japanese in Japan."[5] Striking from newly constructed airfields on Okinawa—and other bases in Iwo Jima, the Marianas, and the Philippines—the Joint Chiefs of Staff would intensify the aerial devastation of Japan, preparing for the ground assault on Kyushu in November. After that would come the decisive invasion of Honshu, the industrial core of Japan, scheduled to start in March 1946.[6]

The conquest of Kyushu would have been horrific for ordinary Japanese. The Japanese military had ordered the creation of village-level units to direct guerrilla warfare, while the cabinet set up a corps to enlist all men from the ages of fifteen to sixty and all women from seventeen to forty. Despite some plans for evacuation away from the front, millions of civilians could have been dragooned into supporting combat operations or fighting themselves, wielding spears or bayonets. The American invaders, not flush with sympathy for the Japanese, would likely have done poorly at distinguishing between those who were fighting and those who were harmless. If Soviet armies had moved into northern Japan, they would have slaughtered countless Japanese. The vast numbers of civilian deaths at Okinawa could have appeared in retrospect as merely a prelude to horrors on a national scale.[7]

Meeting with senior Navy and State Department officials, Stimson pressed for getting Japan to surrender by giving a warning "after she had been sufficiently pounded possibly with S-1."[8] Bracing for opposition from New Dealers who wanted to completely remake postwar Japan, Stimson lined up the endorsements of Joseph Grew and James Forrestal, the navy secretary.[9] He locked himself away at his posh country estate on Long Island for a few days to prepare to sway Truman.[10]

On July 2, Stimson forcefully made his case at the White House, urging the president to offer the Japanese a final chance to surrender before storming Kyushu.[11] As rough as the combat had been on Iwo Jima and Okinawa, Stimson argued in a powerful memorandum, the campaign for the home islands would be far worse. "The Japanese are highly patriotic and certainly susceptible to calls for fanatical resistance to repel an invasion," he warned. "Once started in actual invasion, we shall in my opinion have to go through with an even more bitter finish fight than in Germany." The Japanese would fight to the death in "fanatical despair." Reinforcing Truman's fears of a race war, Stimson warned that "the attempt to exterminate her armies and her population by gunfire or other means will tend to produce a fusion of race solidity and antipathy which had no analogy in the case of Germany."

He lectured Truman, who had never set foot in Japan, that despite what American newspapers said, "Japan is not a nation composed wholly of mad fanatics of an entirely different mentality from ours." The Japanese, he wrote with a perplexing blend of respect and condescension, were intelligent and could see reason: "I think she has within her population enough liberal leaders (although now submerged by the terrorists) to be depended upon for her reconstruction as a responsible member of the family of nations."

Stimson urged an ultimatum to Japan to surrender. Japan would lose its empire, be occupied and demilitarized; its militarist leaders would be permanently destroyed. Yet the United States should make a "disavowal of any attempt to extirpate the Japanese as a race or to destroy them as a nation" and promise them a future after occupation: a rebuilt economy, self-rule under a peaceful and representative government. Crucially, he proposed that the new political system would maintain "a constitutional monarchy under her present dynasty."[12]

The American public would have loathed Stimson's proposal to spare the emperor. Much of Congress wanted Hirohito on trial for war crimes, such as the Democratic senator from Tennessee who growled, "Damn the Emperor—he's a war criminal and I'd like to see him hung up by his toes."[13] Americans despised Hirohito, although polls found that only half of the public could name him, with about 5 percent believing that Tojo Hideki was the emperor, and others under the impression the monarch was named Hari-Kari. In a Gallup poll in June, 70 percent of Americans wanted harsh punishment for the emperor: a third of respondents wanted to execute him, 17 percent thought he should be put on trial, 11 percent preferred life imprisonment, and 9 percent favored exile. A meager 3 percent wanted to use him as a puppet to run Japan—the option that Stimson was promoting.[14]

Truman was impressed by Stimson's memorandum. In their White House meeting, the Republican war secretary also urged the president not to treat postwar Germany too harshly, in contrast to the vindictiveness of most New Dealers. Faced with this call for leniency against the two leading Axis powers, the president struck Stimson as "a man who is trying hard to keep his balance." Truman agreed that the Nazi war criminals should be punished and the rest of the country rehabilitated. He seemed to be won over about Japan's surrender, which Stimson thought was one of the most important issues the war secretary had ever faced. "I have to meet and overcome the zeal of the soldier," he wrote in his diary afterward. "I have to meet the feeling of war passion and hysteria which seizes hold of a nation like ours in the prosecution of such a bitter war."[15]

In a draft of the Allied declaration to be issued at the imminent conference at Potsdam, Grew proposed an explicit pledge that Japan could keep "a constitutional monarchy under the present dynasty" as part of a peaceful, representative government.[16] Yet prominent New Dealers lashed back against the effort to spare the throne.[17]

Truman had inherited a stern plan for the emperor from Franklin Delano Roosevelt's administration. Fearing frenzied resistance if the United States scrapped the monarchy outright, the plan was instead to apprehend Hirohito and the imperial family, remove him from the Imperial Palace, and keep him in seclusion. The occupation forces would make limited use of Hirohito's authority while leaving his ultimate future in doubt, hoping that a free Japanese people would eventually abolish the monarchy.[18]

Stimson grumbled in his diary, "Harry Hopkins is a strong anti-Emperor man in spite of his usual good sense and so are Archibald MacLeish and Dean Acheson—three very extraordinary men to take such a position."[19] Hopkins had been Roosevelt's closest confidant on foreign policy, with his opinion suggesting the position that Roosevelt himself might have taken had he lived.[20]

Acheson, then the assistant secretary of state, saw retaining the throne as a fatal eleventh-hour abandonment of the pledge to fundamentally reshape Japan. He scorned Hirohito as a weak, untrustworthy figure who had yielded to the military's drive for war.[21] In a fiery State Department meeting, he argued that the monarchy was a feudal anachronism ideal for manipulation by Japanese reactionaries.[22] When Grew claimed that Hirohito was not responsible for the war, Acheson shot back that Japanese militarists must believe the emperor was vital to their war efforts if they were so insistent on keeping him.[23]

The poet Archibald MacLeish, an erudite former Librarian of Congress then running the War Department's propaganda office, argued that it was worth sending more American troops in order to dethrone Hirohito. Although MacLeish had spent only a few months studying about Japan, he argued that a cult of emperor worship allowed militarists and industrialists to maintain their sway over the people: "The lives already spent will have been sacrificed in vain, and lives will be lost again in the future in a new war, if the throne is employed in the future as it has been employed in the past by the Japanese Jingos and industrial expansionists."[24]

The most prominent hard-liner was James Byrnes, a Roosevelt insider who had recently become secretary of state but nursed larger political ambitions. Truman privately scorned him as "a conversational pig" and "my able and conniving Secretary of State. My but he has a keen mind!"[25] Byrnes advocated stern punishment of war criminals: "It would take some of joy out of war if the men who started one, instead of a halo around the head, got a rope around the neck."[26] He was egged on by his courtly State Department predecessor, Cordell Hull, who warned by telephone that keeping the monarchy would look like the "appeasement of Japan," abandoning Roosevelt's stance of unconditional surrender. He exhorted that the emperor and the ruling class must be stripped of their privileges and put under the law like everybody else.[27] Soon after, he told Byrnes that nobody knew if retaining the emperor would really help to end the war, while warning that "the Japs would be encouraged."[28] Byrnes opposed any pledge that Japan could keep its dynasty.[29]

Stimson and Grew got some support from the U.S. military. Admiral William Leahy, the point person between the White House and the military, wanted to spare the emperor and hoped that he would be useful in bringing peace.[30] He later wrote, "We were certain that the Mikado could stop the war with a royal word."[31] And the Joint Chiefs asked Truman not to do anything that would preclude using the emperor's authority to order Japanese forces deployed all across Asia to surrender.[32]

After rounds of ferment and discussion, despite Stimson's and Grew's best efforts to shout down the New Dealers, there would be no explicit American pledge to maintain the monarchy.

CARTHAGE TO POTSDAM

"How I hate this trip!" Truman wrote privately, bound for Europe for the first time since fighting in France in World War I.[33] On July 7, griping all the way, he sailed for an Allied summit at Potsdam, near Berlin, "to see Mr. Russia and Mr. Great Britain." He, Joseph Stalin, and Winston Churchill—replaced late in the conference by Clement Attlee—would plan the defeat of Japan and a postwar European order.[34] Bracing himself, he noted, "Since Julius Caesar such men as Charlemagne, Richelieu, Charles V, Francis I, the great King Henry IV of France, Frederick Barbarossa, to name a few, and Woodrow Wilson and Frank Roosevelt have had remedies and still couldn't solve the problem."[35]

The president found the conquered capital of the Thousand Year Reich scorched and blackened, littered with mutilated vehicles and weaponry, its grand buildings smashed to rubble or gouged by bullets and bombs. There were streams of people walking along the road with their belongings on their backs.[36] Driving unannounced into Berlin, flanked by anxious Secret Service men and military guards, he was preceded by a decoy car "to fool 'em if they wanted to do any target practice." In the city he "saw absolute ruin. Hitler's folly. . . . He had no morals and his people backed him up. Never did I see a more sorrowful sight, nor witness retribution to the nth degree." Truman mordantly wrote, "I thought of Carthage, Baalbek, Jerusalem, Rome, Atlantis, Peking, Babylon, Nineveh; Scipio, Rameses II, Titus, Herman, Sherman, Jenghis Khan, Alexander, Darius the Great."

Boastful as Truman could be in speeches about the aerial bombardment of cities, the ground-level reality jerked him into an apocalyptic frame of mind. "I hope for some kind of peace—but I fear that machines are ahead of morals by some centuries." He added, "We are only termites on a planet and maybe when we bore too deeply into the planet there'll [be] a reckoning—who knows?"[37]

The dreaded summit conference convened at a grand Hohenzollern palace in Potsdam, a suburb which had not been flattened by Allied bombing. Arriving at a nearby estate dubbed the Berlin White House, Truman was nonplussed to discover it was a garish yellow and red, and had been pillaged by the Soviets, like the rest of the city: "not even a tin spoon left."[38] (It was also bugged.)[39] He galloped through the conference's agenda. "I'm not going to stay around this terrible place all summer just to listen to speeches," he wrote in his diary. "I'll go home to the Senate for that."[40]

"I was so scared," Truman admitted to his wife.[41] He found Churchill captivating, despite "a lot of hooey about how great my country is and how he loved Roosevelt and how he intended to love me etc. etc."[42] He initially warmed to Stalin, who, in an incongruously white military uniform, turned out to be slightly shorter than him. "I liked the little son of a bitch," Truman recalled, regretting trusting "the unconscionable Russian Dictator." He later called himself "an innocent idealist" at Potsdam, suckered by Stalin's worthless pledges.[43]

Here the Big Three met for what would be their last time as a common front. Truman and Churchill clashed with Stalin over Poland and the reconstruction of Germany, as the president grumbled privately about "the Bolsheviki land grab. . . . Russia helped herself to a slice of Poland."[44] In his diary, showing a keen awareness of how the Soviets were deploying secret police and violence in the lands occupied by the Red Army, he scorned Soviet Communism: "the Russian variety which isn't communism at all but just police government pure and simple. A few top hands just take clubs, pistols and concentration camps and rule the people on the lower levels."[45]

In public, the Big Three maintained a united stance against Japan.[46] Won over by Stimson, Truman wanted to issue an ultimatum giving the Japanese leaders one last chance to yield.[47] "I can deal with Stalin," he wrote in his diary after their first meeting, weathering a boozy series of Russian-style toasts at lunch. "He is honest—but smart as hell." Stalin repeated his pledge to attack Japan soon. Truman thought this might end the war a year sooner than expected. "He'll be in the Jap War on August 15th," the president noted privately. "Fini Japs when that comes about."[48]

Truman wrote to his wife, "I've gotten what I came for—Stalin goes to war August 15 with no strings on it."[49] Yet surely Stalin would try to extract a stiff price. American leaders feared that the Soviets would keep Manchuria and set up a pro-Soviet regime in Korea.[50] The Truman team particularly dreaded Soviet ambitions for Japan itself. As the Americans planned it, the British, Chinese, and Soviets might play support roles in the occupation of Japan but with the United States firmly in charge.[51]

On July 16 at a remote U.S. base in New Mexico, the Manhattan Project detonated its first nuclear explosion: the obliterating yellow-white light of eighty suns, a colossal ball of fire, which mushroomed and surged seven miles high. The flash was visible in Albuquerque, Santa Fe, and

Winston Churchill, Harry Truman, and Joseph Stalin at Potsdam, July–August 1945

towns as far as 180 miles away.[52] Apprised in Potsdam of the successful test, Truman was, as Stimson noted, "highly delighted."[53] Briefed on the fearsome power of atomic bombs, Truman seemed "tremendously pepped up by it," professing "an entirely new feeling of confidence."[54]

Truman suddenly had less need of the Red Army. The next day, Stimson handed Churchill a piece of paper with the message, "Babies satisfactorily born."[55] Stimson, expecting that the bomb would be used within weeks, wanted to notify Stalin so that he would not be blindsided.[56] With relief, the war secretary wrote in his diary, "with our new weapon we would not need the assistance of the Russians to conquer Japan."[57] The day after, Truman lunched with Churchill, noting in his diary: "Discussed Manhattan (it is a success). Decided to tell Stalin about it."[58]

Churchill, in a military uniform sporting a chestful of honors, was exhilarated. The British government had already agreed to the use of atomic bombs on Japan.[59] Shaken by accounts of Japanese troops on Okinawa blowing themselves up with hand grenades rather than surrendering, Churchill dreaded invading Japan's home islands with "the Japanese fighting to the death with Samurai devotion." As he later wrote, that nightmare prospect was replaced with "the vision—fair and bright it seemed—of the end of the whole war in one or two violent shocks." The brave Japanese, he thought, might "find in the apparition of this almost supernatural weapon an excuse which would save their honour and release them from their obligation of being killed to the last fighting man."[60]

For Churchill, the atomic bomb obviated the need to encourage a Soviet campaign for Manchuria, incurring debts to Stalin in the process.[61] The detonations would "avert a vast, indefinite butchery," saving Japanese lives as well as American and British ones. Using the same phrase he had used for the Dunkirk evacuation, Churchill called the atomic bomb "a miracle of deliverance."[62]

"In International Relations There Is No Mercy"

The morning after one of the firebombings of Tokyo, vast throngs of civilians, separated from their husbands, wives, or children, rushed to Ueno Station to flee to the countryside. Japan's foreign minister, Togo Shigenori, watched the terrified crowds in dismay.[63]

Togo had struggled to avoid this war. Thoughtful, candid, and urbane, he was a seasoned diplomat who had done postings in northeastern China, the United States, and Germany, most recently serving as ambassador to the Soviet Union. In contrast to the uniformed army officers dominating Japan's government, he wore elegant, wide-lapeled suits and big round glasses. A rare civilian official who dared speak up against generals and admirals, he believed in the peaceful resolution of disputes and the sanctity of treaties. His grandson Togo Kazuhiko, himself a successful Japanese diplomat, recalls that he believed that "you should never back away when you think you have a logical point." His other grandson, Togo Shigehiko, who wrote a biography of him, says, "He believes in always making his armament of logic."

At a time when Japanese nationalists extolled the supremacy of the pure-blooded Yamato race, Togo hailed from a Korean family that had been prospering in Japan for four centuries, long before the imperial annexation of Korea in 1910.[64] At birth his surname was Park, but that distinctively Korean name was changed to a Japanese one when he was five years old. He carefully kept his background to himself, not mentioning it to anyone at work. His grandson Togo Kazuhiko says there was scant anti-Korean bigotry in the government: "It was somewhere in their minds, but it was never expressed in the form of any discrimination."

Cosmopolitan in his personal affairs, Togo Shigenori had studied German literature at Tokyo Imperial University and had married an erudite German woman he had met while serving in Japan's embassy in Berlin after World War I. He studied Schiller; she adored Goethe. He saw himself as a man of peace who might integrate Western and Eastern civilizations. When he became Japan's ambassador to Nazi Germany in 1937, he was repelled by the stink of the Nazi upstarts, so different from the cultured Germany he had known. Opposing Japan's Axis alliance with Germany, he was forced out as ambassador in less than a year.[65]

Togo had bemoaned Japan's escalating militarism in an era when outspoken civilians risked getting assassinated. As foreign minister in late 1941, he had fought in vain to prevent the attack on Pearl Harbor. Returning now as foreign minister in the wreckage of that war, he hoped for peace at last. Aware that Japan would be defeated and its empire dismantled, he hoped only to maintain his country's industrial base and avoid reparations.[66] As he later wrote, "he who really desires peace must put his whole being into fighting for it. It is self-stultifying to act the bystander while events march by, then to speak up after all is over."[67]

Soon before the Allies assembled in Potsdam, Togo got an important boost from Hirohito himself. On June 22, the emperor joined with his government's top leaders in a formal meeting known as an imperial conference, the most important kind of Japanese government conclave. In an unprecedented intervention by the emperor, who had for years stood behind the war effort, he pressed them for a plan to end the war—marking the start of his direct efforts to halt the fighting.[68] Hirohito prodded his dilatory ministers to send an envoy to Moscow, hoping that the Soviet Union would intercede on Japan's behalf. Even the hard-liners agreed to seek Soviet mediation before a final battle to defend the homeland.[69]

The costs of delay had been unbearably high: as a Japanese historian reckons, the last year of stalemate meant the deaths of 1.5 million Japanese, some fifty thousand Americans, and vastly more Asians in Japan's empire.[70] Although lives were lost every hour, it took weeks of internal jockeying before Togo secretly sent the Soviets a letter directly from Hirohito with a peace overture.[71] Since U.S. intelligence had long ago cracked the Japanese code, Truman and senior U.S. officials in Potsdam promptly found out.[72]

Togo hoped that the Soviet Union, not yet at war with Japan, might mediate peace on less stringent terms.[73] In his appeal, Hirohito announced his "heart's desire to see the swift termination of the war." He proposed sending Prince Konoe Fumimaro, a prominent former prime minister who had recently warned him that the war was lost, as a special envoy to the Soviet Union.[74] Yet "as long as America and England insist on unconditional surrender, our country has no alternative but to see it through in an all-out effort for the sake of survival and the honor of the homeland."[75]

This was delusionary. Without being offered particulars which approximated unconditional surrender, the Allies were unlikely to relent. Anyway, relying on Stalin's tender mercies was fruitless, as some Japanese officials understood with painful clarity. There was no real chance that the Soviet tyrant would snub his advancing American and British allies— who had already secretly promised at Yalta to let the Soviets gnaw on the bones of Japan's empire—to mediate a more tolerable peace on Japan's behalf.[76]

The Japanese ambassador in Moscow, knowing his posting all too well, understood that Stalin's closed-door meetings at Yalta and Potsdam would hatch a Soviet attack on Japan.[77] Pressing his government to contemplate an almost unconditional surrender as American bombing intensified, he asked if there was "any meaning" in "sacrificing the lives of hundreds of thousands of conscripts and millions of other innocent residents of cities and metropolitan areas? . . . [I]n international relations there is no mercy."[78]

As Truman noted, Stalin promptly informed Churchill about a "telegram from Jap Emperor asking for peace," which the Americans had already intercepted.[79] Stimson told Truman that the time was right to warn Japan to quit the war or suffer "the full force of our newer weapons."[80] Churchill, who had for months questioned the need for unconditional surrender, urged Truman to soften his terms in order to save British and American lives. Churchill suggested sparing the Japanese their military honor and giving "some assurance of their national existence." Truman retorted that after Pearl Harbor, he did not think the Japanese had any military honor. Churchill calmly replied that they were willing to die in huge numbers for something. Truman softened, talking of his awful responsibility for the loss of so much American blood. The prime minister later wrote, "I felt there would be no rigid insistence upon 'unconditional surrender,' apart from what was necessary for world peace and future security and for the punishment of a guilty and treacherous deed."[81]

Hirohito's call for peace was enfeebled by its lack of specific peace terms.[82] The Soviets curtly sent back a noncommittal reply, which pleased Truman.[83] Togo Shigenori's hopes for peace were undercut by an unyielding Japanese message driven by the army faction in Tokyo, which the Americans intercepted.[84] Shackled by the military hard-liners' refusal to entertain tough concessions, Togo was left taking an official line that could hardly satisfy the Allies. He stated that Japan would end the war if the United States and Britain would "recognize Japan's honor and existence," but cautioned that "if the enemy insists on unconditional surrender to the very end, then our country and His Majesty would unanimously resolve to fight a war of resistance to the bitter end."[85]

To the Japanese ambassador in Moscow, the obstinacy in Tokyo was madness. Breaking decorum, he sent a cable so blunt that he thought it "a great crime to dare to make such statements." Facing unrelenting bombing and an imminent ground invasion, he recoiled at guerrilla warfare: "Do you think that the Emperor's safety can be secured by the sacrifice of seventy million citizens?" He urged painful concessions in order to save hundreds of thousands of lives, seeking only to preserve the fundamentals of Japan's government and secure "the survival of our race."[86]

The hard-line Japanese cable "depressed me terribly," Byrnes later wrote. "It meant using the atomic bomb; it probably meant Russia's entry into the war."[87]

"Believe Japs will fold up before Russia comes in," Truman wrote confidently in his diary. "I am sure they will when Manhattan appears over their homeland."[88] On July 20, he ceremoniously raised a United States flag over Berlin: the same one which had been flying at the White House on the day of Pearl Harbor. It had already been flown in North Africa, Rome, and Paris. "Will be raised over Tokyo," he vowed to himself.[89]

The Potsdam Declaration

While Truman, Churchill, and Stalin plotted in Potsdam, Chiang Kaishek was off in the mountains outside China's wartime provisional capital in Chongqing.[90] Distrusted by the Americans and despised by Churchill, the generalissimo was already bitterly familiar with being excluded from the most important Allied councils.[91] Drafting an ultimatum to Japan, a U.S. official scribbled an afterthought: "Should China be asked?"[92]

Truman sent along a completed declaration from Potsdam and perfunctorily asked "the Generalissimo to inform us without delay of his concurrence."[93] When Chiang did not immediately reply, Truman haughtily warned that he and Churchill would issue their proclamation without him.[94] When Chiang finally responded, he only asked to inflate his title from generalissimo to president of the Republic of China, a bit of puffery meant to bolster his shaky domestic standing.[95] Truman jotted in the change by hand, moving Chiang's name ahead of Churchill's.[96]

Stimson pressed Truman to have the Allied declaration include a reassurance to "the Japanese on the continuance of their dynasty," which could be "just the thing that would make or mar their acceptance." He faced stiff resistance from Byrnes, who was against giving Japan a warning to quit the war, let alone promising to retain the imperial system.[97] In the end, Truman and Byrnes cut out the promise to maintain the dynasty.[98] Both Stimson and Grew would later claim that, had the United States vowed the continued existence of a constitutional monarchy, Japan might have capitulated without the use of the atomic bombs.[99]

Informed by Truman on July 24 about a new American "weapon of unusual destructive force," Stalin coolly replied that he hoped good use was made of it against Japan.[100] Well briefed by Soviet spies, he seemed to grasp that Truman meant an atomic bomb, although it was uncertain how clearly he understood the full importance of the weapon.[101]

The next day, Truman noted in his diary a fact which had been manifest enough to him for weeks now: he would drop atomic bombs on Japan. "This weapon is to be used against Japan between now and August 10th"—which would preempt Stalin's entry into the war. "We have discovered the most terrible bomb in the history of the world," he wrote in his diary. "It may be the fire destruction prophesied in the Euphrates Valley Era, after Noah and his fabulous Ark."[102]

Among Truman's advisers, there was little real question of not using the atomic bomb. Although General Douglas MacArthur would later say that their use was "completely unnecessary from a military point of view," he was off in Manila, not informed of the existence of the weapons until just before they were used.[103] General Dwight Eisenhower was almost alone among the senior military leaders in opposing the atomic bombings.[104] He said he was gripped with depression and "grave misgivings" at the United States causing such horrible destruction. With Japan nearly defeated, he argued that the atomic bomb was "completely unnecessary" to save American lives and that the world would be shocked if it was used on people who were trying to surrender without losing too much face.[105] This was such apostasy that Eisenhower's stance infuriated Stimson and startled other military chiefs.[106]

Like almost all of Truman's team, Stimson favored using the bomb. He did sentimentally rule out annihilating Kyoto, with Truman agreeing not to vaporize that ancient center of Japanese civilization.[107] Stimson's mind was already on the postwar: "the bitterness which would be caused by such a wanton act might make it impossible during the long post-war period to reconcile the Japanese to us in that area rather than to the Russians."[108]

The lives of innocent Japanese civilians got less consideration. Stimson had cautioned against concentrating on a civilian area as a target, but had refused to give advance warning to the inhabitants and had favored hitting an important war plant employing many workers and closely surrounded by their houses. He wanted the bomb to make "a profound psychological impression on as many of the inhabitants as possible." That obviously meant killing vast numbers of civilians.[109]

The American public agreed wholeheartedly with Truman. In a Gallup poll immediately after the bombings of Hiroshima and Nagasaki, fully 85 percent supported the use of the atomic bombs, with just 10 percent against.[110]

Truman himself was shaken by the startling power of the New Mexico test. He carefully enumerated the details of its Armageddon impact, relieved that neither Hitler nor Stalin had discovered such a weapon. Eerily, he tried to deny to himself the massive killing of civilians that he was ordering. "I have told the Sec[retary] of War, Mr. Stimson, to use it so that military objectives and soldiers and sailors are the target and not women and children," he wrote in his diary. "Even if the Japs are savages, ruthless, merciless and fanatic, we as the leader of the world for the common welfare cannot drop this terrible bomb on the old capital"—Kyoto—"or the new"—Tokyo.

It is impossible to square Truman's clear understanding of what the bomb did with any private conceit that he could somehow use it without slaughtering civilians. "He & I are in accord," Truman wrote about Stimson. "The target will be a purely military one and we will issue a warning statement asking the Japs to surrender and save lives. I'm sure they will not do that, but we will have given them the chance." By writing "the Japs," his standard slur, he cruelly blurred the line between the leadership and the civilians who would surely die. He concluded, "It seems to be the most terrible thing ever discovered, but it can be made the most useful."[111]

Togo Shigenori still hoped that the United States might settle for terms short of unconditional surrender, perhaps offering a peace based on the idealistic terms of the Atlantic Charter.[112]

On July 26, the United States, Britain, and China issued their Potsdam Declaration—one of the most brutal statements ever pronounced by any democratic government, but by the standards of the total war in the Pacific, a slight softening of the U.S. position.[113] (The Soviet Union, not yet in the war, did not formally join.) Some on Truman's team saw the declaration as comparative restraint, hinting that Japan's government would not be completely destroyed.[114]

While offering a last chance to end the war, the declaration warned that the Allies had "necessarily laid waste to the lands, the industry and the method of life of the whole German people. The full application of our military power, backed by our resolve, *will* mean the inevitable and complete destruction of the Japanese armed forces and just as inevitably the devastation of the Japanese homeland."

The Allies demanded complete disarmament, the permanent removal of expansionist Japanese leaders who had sought "world conquest," and the disbanding of the empire, including Korea. The home islands would be temporarily occupied until these goals were realized and the country had a peaceful, responsible government "in accordance with the freely expressed will of the Japanese people." A new postwar government should allow the revival of Japanese democratic tendencies and the establishment of "fundamental human rights" including freedom of speech, religion, and thought.

The emperor was never mentioned, leaving his future in doubt. A constrained monarchy could coexist with democratic government, but the Allies made no guarantees. To his indignation, MacArthur only found out about the Potsdam terms when hearing them on the radio, but he too would have advocated an assurance that the Japanese could keep their emperor.[115]

The Potsdam Declaration insisted on the punishment of vast numbers of Japanese at all ranks for war crimes, which, as a British official coolly noted, "rather implied the elimination of Military clique."[116] This demand was voiced with undisguised menace: "We do not intend that the Japanese shall be enslaved as a race or destroyed as a nation, but stern justice shall be meted out to all war criminals, including those who have visited cruelties upon our prisoners."

It is only by the benchmarks of World War II that a disavowal of racial enslavement or national destruction can be taken as comparative leniency. In words distributed as widely as possible to the Japanese public, blasted out in Japanese by shortwave radio transmitters, the Allies finished by demanding "the unconditional surrender" of all Japanese armed forces.[117] The declaration's last sentence, a harbinger of atomic bombs, never mentioned the new technology of mass death: "The alternative for Japan is prompt and utter destruction."[118]

CHAPTER 4

Atomic Fire

HARSH AS THE POTSDAM Declaration was, many Allied officials thought it did not go far enough. Dean Acheson, the U.S. assistant secretary of state, worried that it was a risky "invitation to negotiate" which would leave Japan's overlords in control after the war inconclusively ended.[1] Cordell Hull stewed that the declaration allowed "the continuance of the Japanese Government as such."[2] Despite its battlefield sacrifices and the suffering of its prisoners of war, Australia was barely consulted; its cabinet learned the declaration's content from reading the newspapers. Australia's foreign minister indignantly declared that his country would not subscribe to such terms of surrender, more lenient than those imposed on Nazi Germany.[3]

Togo Shigenori, Japan's foreign minister, grasped at the declaration as a precious chance to end the war. Yet the decisive voices were those of the Japanese military, who would not accept demobilization and disarmament by the Allies, nor an occupation of Japan, nor Allied trials for Japanese war criminals.[4] Japan's hard-liners were alarmed by the Allies' tough stance toward Nazi war criminals. The army minister and the chiefs of staff of the army and navy pressed the hesitant prime minister, Suzuki Kantaro, to spurn the Potsdam Declaration. Suzuki was an elderly retired admiral, hard of hearing, reluctantly plunged back into politics.[5] He knew the risks of defying the army; he had been shot and nearly killed by a military fanatic back in 1936.[6] On July 28, 1945, the prime minister announced at a press conference that his government found no important value in the Potsdam Declaration, and would "ignore" it and fight on to the bitter end—tantamount to a rejection.[7]

Harry Truman took it badly.[8] "When we asked them to surrender at

Potsdam, they gave us a very snotty answer," he later said. "They didn't ask about the Emperor. I said, if they don't surrender, they would be completely, totally destroyed. They told me to go to hell, words to that effect."[9]

Hiroshima, August 6.

On that warm morning, dawning clear and bright, there was an air raid warning, as usual, followed by the all-clear, as usual. In the compact, leafy city, the sight and sound of incoming U.S. B-29 bombers was familiar enough. Hiroshima had been occasionally struck by B-29s, although not as badly as some bigger Japanese cities.[10] This bomber faced no Japanese fighter planes or flak.[11] People carried on with their morning routines: most industrial workers were already at their factories, other laborers were on their way to work, and schoolchildren were toiling in the open as part of a national effort to move valuables out of the cities to the countryside.

Nestled beneath low surrounding hills in southwestern Honshu, Hiroshima lies on the delta of the Ota River, jutting into the bay, which might have contained ordinary fires. It was then Japan's seventh-largest city, with modest homes made of wood, either one or two stories tall, clustered together. The industrial buildings were not much more sturdy, with makeshift construction and inadequate joints.[12]

At 8:15 a.m., about forty-five minutes after the all-clear, there was a brilliant yellow light—garish and bright, reminding one observer of the magnesium flash of a camera.[13] People directly underneath the explosion were immediately charred to dark brown or black, dying after minutes or hours at most.[14] Inokuchi Takeshi, a fourteen-year-old student working in a factory about a mile away from the hypocenter, remembers a dazzling flash of orange light. He was knocked down by the force of the blast. He managed to crawl into another room, pitch-black and stiflingly hot, where he passed out. When he came to, he could hear the shrieking and labored breathing of over a hundred other students trapped in the rubble of the burning building, calling for help, crying out to their mothers. With the factory in flames, a sea of red surrounding him, Inokuchi jumped from a window down to the riverbank. He landed on scraps left over from demolition work, with nails sticking up, which agonizingly pierced through his boots into his feet. When he wiped his face with a handkerchief, it came away covered with blood. In agony, he realized that there were shards of glass and other materials stuck in his head and face.

His eyes injured by the flash, he could see only dimly. All around him, the city was a burning, smoking ruin, with buildings, bridges, and trees on fire. One survivor wrote, "Where the city stood, there is a gigantic burned-out sear." Another eyewitness recalls the stench of burned hair. People were covered in blood and had burns all over their bodies. Buildings had collapsed everywhere, leaving so much rubble that it was hard to tell where the roads had been. Outside Inokuchi's factory, a crew of hundreds of workers had been exposed to the blast. Many were unconscious, some screaming out for water. "Their skin on their backs was all peeled away and hanging down at the waist, and the sinews were stripped away," Inokuchi remembers seven decades later with undimmed horror. "The faces of the people were burned so that they didn't look like human faces." Like many *hibakusha,* people who suffered atomic bombing, he recalls: "Those people looked more like ghosts than human beings."[15]

As a major report by the United States Strategic Bombing Survey clinically noted, Hiroshima suffered "an unprecedented casualty rate." Far from just hitting the military headquarters or the industry contributing to Japan's war effort, the atomic blast leveled almost the entire city, followed by a firestorm leaving well over four square miles almost completely burned down.[16] This report estimated that seventy or eighty thousand people had been killed, with about as many wounded. Hiroshima's immediate death toll was roughly equivalent to the March 9–10 firebombing of Tokyo, even though the American incendiaries had burned down an area about four times larger.[17] By the end of the year, as radiation sickness set in, some one hundred and forty thousand people had died, according to a Japanese survey.[18] Less than 10 percent of those killed on August 6 were military personnel.[19]

"Big bomb dropped on Hiroshima," Henry Stimson notified Truman in a terse note. "First reports indicate complete success which was even more conspicuous than earlier test."[20]

Truman had fled Berlin on August 2, relieved to be out of "that awful city." He got the news about Hiroshima in the Atlantic aboard the USS *Augusta,* a Navy cruiser which had fought in the Normandy landing and now served as the president's flagship.[21] Delighted, he told the ship's cheering crew.[22] "This is the greatest thing in history," he said. "It's time for us to get home."[23]

The president publicly justified the atomic bombing as retribution: "The Japanese began the war from the air at Pearl Harbor. They have been repaid many fold." He described an almost cosmic requital: "The force from which the sun draws its power has been loosed against those who brought war to the Far East." Complaining that Japan's leaders had rejected the Potsdam Declaration, he warned them to surrender or suffer "a rain of ruin from the air, the like of which has never been seen on this earth."[24]

Straining to portray Hiroshima as a strictly military target, the White House described the city only as "an important Japanese Army base" or a strategic and industrial "Army city."[25] In his memoirs, Truman claimed that he had chosen a military target in accordance with the laws of war—which was either disingenuous or deluded.[26] In fact, the teams choosing targets had wanted a military installation or factory surrounded by homes that would be destroyed, in order to break the Japanese will to fight.[27] Admiral William Leahy, Truman's liaison to the military, admitted that "the destruction of civilian life had been terrific."[28] The city did include a significant military headquarters, but as the U.S. Strategic Bombing Survey noted, most of the industries, on the city's perimeter, suffered only slight damage, while the devastated central areas were largely commercial or residential.[29]

Japan's government formally protested the atomic bomb as "an inhuman weapon" which massacred women, children, and the elderly without discrimination, violating the basic principles of international humanitarian law. It was worse than gas or other banned weapons of war. The Americans had already bombed civilians across most of Japan "in complete defiance of the essential principles of humanitarian laws, as well as international law. They now use this new bomb, having an uncontrollable and cruel effect much greater than any other arms or projectiles ever used to date. This constitutes a new crime against humanity and civilization."[30] The United States never replied to Japan's protest.[31]

Even Joseph Stalin was jolted: "War is barbaric, but using the A-bomb is a superbarbarity."[32] Leahy, a career Navy man, would become convinced that "this barbarous weapon" had been "of no material assistance" against Japan, which was already about to surrender due to conventional bombing and blockade. He recoiled at winning a war by killing women and children, and later wrote that "we had adopted an ethical standard common to the barbarians of the Dark Ages."[33]

Japan's next shock was a Soviet attack, which dashed any illusions that Stalin would graciously mediate Japan's way out of the war.

Impeccable about the formalities, the Soviet foreign minister, Vyacheslav Molotov, read aloud a formal declaration of war to the Japanese ambassador in Moscow, in effect as of August 9. Truman hastily called reporters into the Oval Office to shout, to applause and laughter, *"Russia has declared war on Japan! That is all!"*[34] The Red Army stormed into Japanese-controlled Manchuria, pressing southward toward the Korean Peninsula and the Japanese home islands.[35] To justify their late entry into the Pacific War, the Soviets noted that Japan had rejected the Potsdam Declaration and that the Soviets had obligations to their Allies; the 1941 neutrality pact with Japan went unmentioned.[36]

Japan, already desperate, had to fight on another front. The emperor told his closest adviser that "it is necessary to study and decide on the termination of the war."[37]

On August 8, Stimson briefed Truman, showing him a photograph of the "total destruction" of Hiroshima and explaining the blast radius. The war secretary was gratified by the effectiveness of the atomic bomb and gave no sign in his diary of remorse. The president spoke of the "terrible responsibility" placed on himself. In terms condescending to the Japanese, Stimson pressed for generous peace overtures now: "When you punish your dog you don't keep souring on him all day after the punishment is over. . . . In the same way with Japan. They naturally are a smiling people and we have to get on those terms with them."[38]

In private, Truman seemed troubled by what he had done. When a Georgia senator urged him to use more atomic bombs, he replied, "I know that Japan is a terribly cruel and uncivilized nation in warfare, but I can't bring myself to believe that, because they are beasts, we should ourselves act in the same manner. For myself, I certainly regret the necessity of wiping out whole populations because of the 'pigheadedness' of the leaders of a nation and . . . I am not going to do it unless it is absolutely necessary." Although his goal was to save American lives, he professed "a humane feeling for the women and children in Japan."[39]

Japan still had not surrendered. Whatever his personal qualms, Truman did not call off future atomic bombings and remained unflinching in public. "Our warning went unheeded, our terms were rejected," the president declared in a radio broadcast after reaching port in Virginia. "[T]he Japanese have seen what our atomic bomb can do. They can foresee what it will do in the future." He vowed to continue using the bomb until Japan surrendered. Again he claimed that the United States had tried to avoid killing civilians by targeting Hiroshima, which he misrepresented as being simply "a military base," while warning that future attacks would hit war industries and devastate civilians. He invoked Japan's war crimes as if every fisherman, housewife, or schoolchild in Hiroshima had been masterminding aggression or beating detainees: "We have used it against those who attacked us without warning at Pearl Harbor, against those who have starved and beaten and executed American prisoners of war, against those who have abandoned all pretense of obeying international laws of warfare."[40]

The same kind of retributive rationalization came to William Laurence, a science reporter for *The New York Times* who was secretly on the payroll of the Manhattan Project, aboard a U.S. B-29 Superfortress winging its way toward Nagasaki.[41] Lulled by the whirling airplane motors, the secret propagandist sank into a reverie, feeling like a solitary traveler in some interplanetary space. "Somewhere beyond these vast mountains of white clouds ahead of me there lies Japan, the land of our enemy," he wrote. "In about four hours from now one of its cities, making weapons of war for use against us, will be wiped off the map by the greatest weapon ever made by man." Having witnessed the New Mexico test, he knew that tens of thousands of people would be killed.

"Does one feel any pity or compassion for the poor devils about to die?" he wrote. "Not when one thinks of Pearl Harbor and of the Death March on Bataan."[42]

Below it was a partially cloudy day in Nagasaki, in the farthest southwestern reach of Kyushu. It is a harbor town lying in two river basins, much smaller than Hiroshima, built of the same small wooden houses.

Just three days after Hiroshima's inferno, Nagasaki's residents were little better prepared. They did not know that their city had been made a target at the last minute. Despite five bombing raids in the past year, the town was mostly intact. There was an air raid alert that morning, which was canceled soon after to considerable public relief. When incoming enemy planes were spotted, the air raid signal did not sound until minutes after the bomb was dropped. Although the city had underground tunnels serving as shelters, only about four hundred people were in them.[43]

Soon after 11 a.m. there was an intense flash. A giant ball of fire rose from the scorched earth, shooting up like a pillar. Laurence called it "a living thing, a new species of being, born right before our incredulous eyes." To him, it looked like a totem pole, with grotesque faces scowling out. Then it sprouted a monstrous mushroom cloud, which seemed "even more alive than the pillar, seething and boiling in a white fury of creamy foam, sizzling upward."[44]

The detonation again reminded people of magnesium, followed by hazy white smoke. There was a hideous roaring noise and an unearthly blast of force and searing heat. For over half a mile around, humans and animals were killed from "a force beyond imagination," in the stunned words of a Japanese report. People were burned beyond recognition, charred black, or crushed by collapsing buildings. Wooden homes were destroyed by the blast and flame; reinforced concrete buildings were gutted by fire or had their sides smashed in; railroad stations were wiped out; steel bent like jelly.

The scorched landscape of Nagasaki, about two months after the United States dropped an atomic bomb there on August 9, 1945

Nagasaki's uneven terrain limited the worst damage to the Urakami valley, over which the bomb detonated. The U.S. Strategic Bombing Survey reckoned the damage as somewhat less shattering than in Hiroshima: under two square miles completely destroyed, and between thirty-five and forty thousand killed, with about as many wounded. The civilian neighborhoods were devastated. As the report coolly noted, "many of these people undoubtedly died several times over, theoretically, since each was subjected to several injuries any one of which would have been fatal." At first, they perished of burns or from being crushed by debris, but within a week, people were dying mysterious deaths from radiation sickness: hair loss, bloody diarrhea, loss of white blood cells, fatal fevers. As authorities in Nagasaki noted, their city had suddenly become "a graveyard with not a tombstone standing."[45]

EVERY WAR MUST END

Late at night on August 9, the Japanese inner circle assembled in a basement air raid shelter at the Imperial Palace. In the thick, humid summer air, the leaders sweated into their suits and uniforms.

Night and day, Japan's rulers were pounded by American bombs. They found out about the annihilation of Nagasaki during their protracted discussions earlier that day, and had no idea when the next atomic bomb might fall. Yet the army leadership was still hoping for a decisive battle in the Japanese homeland which could force the Americans to offer peace terms. After two protracted cabinet meetings earlier that day, the six members of the inner circle remained stubbornly stalemated.

The peace camp was boldly led by Togo Shigenori, the foreign minister. He and the prime minister, sometimes joined by the navy minister, Admiral Yonai Mitsumasa, wanted to accept the Potsdam Declaration—with a stipulation that this would not prejudice the emperor's status. (They proposed no demands for the humane treatment of Japanese civilians under occupation.) Their proviso about the emperor meant something broader than the Truman team understood, aiming to preserve the *kokutai.*[46] As Togo's grandson Togo Kazuhiko explains, "*Kokutai* literally means national polity. Abstractly it means something most important to construct the essence of Japan. In reality, it meant the imperial system, which includes the emperor." For conservative leaders, preserving the *kokutai* was vital to forestall domestic upheaval or leftist revolution.[47] Even at this dark hour, all six leaders insisted on maintaining the monarchy.

Half went further. The powerful army minister and the army and navy chiefs of staff insisted on three more surrender conditions: Japanese troops abroad would withdraw and demobilize themselves voluntarily; Japan would handle its war criminals; and there would be no occupation of Japanese territory.[48] These terms would almost certainly be rejected by the Allies.

To break the impasse, Suzuki Kantaro, the prime minister, called an imperial conference, the highest-level meeting of government in the presence of the emperor. Ordinarily the monarch did not decide the outcome, deferring to his advisers. Yet if Hirohito ruled decisively between the two deadlocked factions, that might dissuade the military from a putsch against the peace camp.[49]

With the emperor listening, Togo argued that Japan had little leverage to dictate conditions. Although the imperial house was nonnegotiable, he said, the three extra conditions proposed by the military would mean more futile deaths. He uncomfortably admitted there were many precedents for war criminals being judged by foreigners, and said that there was no alternative but to turn them over. This meant that every neck in the room except the emperor's could wind up snapped by a rope.

The army minister contended that they should fight on even if Japan's hundred million people had to die side by side in combat. Unsubtly hinting at a military coup, he warned that his troops stationed abroad might not be willing to quit unconditionally. He said that many people at home wanted to fight to the end, so a surrender might spark a civil war.

Baron Hiranuma Kiichiro, a reactionary former prime minister attending as president of the privy council, demanded defending the *kokutai* and the imperial house even if the whole nation had to perish. While Togo's proposal upheld the emperor's status under Japan's national law, Hiranuma argued that the monarch's rule came from a higher authority than domestic laws. He was the one who came up with the phrase which would ultimately be sent back to the Allies: nothing should prejudice "the prerogatives of His Majesty as a sovereign ruler."

As the bitter debates stretched into the desolate early-morning hours of August 10, the prime minister asked the emperor to give his sacred decision.

It was after 2 a.m. The room went silent. Seated at the head of the table, Hirohito leaned forward. In his distinctively high-pitched voice, the emperor spoke haltingly but decisively.

He agreed, he said, with Togo. The foundations of the nation's survival were the imperial house, the people, and the national territory; they risked losing everything by continuing a hopeless war. He saw no chance of victory over enemies with such technological power. Hirohito did not suggest giving up himself or his throne to save his people. Mollifying the military—which could lash out at him or Togo—Hirohito said that he found it unbearable to see his loyal warriors disarmed and handed over to the Allies as war criminals. But, he said, they would have to "bear the unbearable" in order to save the people from disaster. With his hand sheathed in a white glove, Hirohito wiped away tears.

That, the prime minister declared, should be the government's decision. The assembled officials wept. Everyone stood and bowed formally as the emperor slowly exited. His subordinates held a hasty cabinet meeting to give legal force to the monarch's will. Hirohito sent word that, if the army or navy proved recalcitrant, he would personally tell them it was his will to end the war.[50]

"We Told 'Em We'd Tell 'Em How to Keep Him"

Truman awakened early on August 10, eager for victory. He wrote in his diary that he received the "Jap offer to surrender" that morning.[51]

The Japanese government sent him—as well as Britain, China, and the Soviet Union—a note through the Swiss and Swedish governments.[52] At

7:33 a.m., Japan made a public broadcast in English. The emperor, the broadcast noted, sought to end hostilities in the hopes of "saving mankind from the calamities" of further warfare. The Japanese government would accept the entirety of the Potsdam Declaration, but only "with the understanding that the said declaration does not comprise any demand which prejudices the prerogatives of His Majesty as a sovereign ruler."[53]

Even after two atomic bombs and a Soviet onslaught, facing a ground invasion of the home islands, this was not quite an unconditional surrender. This proposal kept in place not just the emperor but his sovereign rule—the fundamentals of the *kokutai*.

This Japanese decision had been painful to the limit, but even so, might not pass muster in Washington. In his diary, Stimson blamed Truman and the State Department for removing from his draft of the Potsdam Declaration an offer to Japan to keep its monarchy, railing against "uninformed agitation against the Emperor in this country mostly by people who know no more about Japan than has been given them by Gilbert and Sullivan's 'Mikado.'"

Truman hastily gathered an anxious gaggle of his top advisers—including Stimson, Leahy, and James Byrnes—in the Oval Office. Stimson urged accepting Japan's terms, but Byrnes, the secretary of state, recoiled at retaining the emperor after all the public demands for unconditional surrender from the Roosevelt and Truman administrations. "Of course during three years of a bitter war there have been bitter statements made about the Emperor," Stimson wrote in his diary. "Now they come to plague us."[54]

Stimson pragmatically argued that the emperor's paramount authority, placed under Allied command, would be necessary anyway to get the Japanese armies scattered across Asia to surrender. This would "save us from a score of bloody Iwo Jimas and Okinawas all over China and the New Netherlands."[55] Similarly, Leahy, who feared that some of the president's aides wanted to execute the emperor, wanted to utilize him. As he later wrote, "I had no feelings about little Hirohito, but was convinced that it would be necessary to use him in effecting the surrender."[56]

Byrnes shot back that since the Japanese were desperate to yield, this was no time for them to dictate conditions.[57] Always politically shrewd, he warned that accepting Japan's terms would result in "the crucifixion of the President."[58]

Truman ordered the secretary of state to write up a reply to Japan, as a mob of frenzied reporters gathered outside. Leaving Byrnes to work on a response to Japan, Stimson returned to the Pentagon. As he told his deputy John McCloy there, he needed to end the war before the Soviets got too far: "I felt it was of great importance to get the homeland into our hands before the Russians could put in any substantial claim to occupy and help rule it."

Byrnes made no explicit pledge that the imperial system would endure, nor that Hirohito would remain. Instead, he put the imperial house under the thumb of a military potentate who would undoubtedly be a U.S. general: "the authority of the Emperor and the Japanese Government to rule the state shall be subject to the Supreme Commander of the Allied powers who will take such steps as he deems proper to effectuate the surrender terms." To Stimson's satisfaction, this locked out Soviet influence.[59]

The other American terms were straightforwardly stringent. Hirohito and the Japanese high command would have to sign the surrender terms personally, order their forces to stop fighting, and carry out any order from the Allied supreme commander. Allied prisoners of war would be set free. Allied troops would occupy Japan until the goals of the Potsdam Declaration were achieved. In the end, the Truman administration allowed retaining the monarchy if the Japanese people wanted it: "The ultimate form of government of Japan shall, in accordance with the Potsdam declaration, be established by the freely expressed will of the Japanese people."[60]

Truman was satisfied; Stimson was delighted.[61] For the exhausted war secretary, keen to leave the government after a heart attack, the compromise was "pretty wise and careful."[62] "They wanted to make a condition precedent to the surrender," the president wrote in his diary, as if talking himself into what he had done. "Our terms are 'unconditional.' They wanted to keep the Emperor. We told 'em we'd tell 'em how to keep him, but we'd make the terms."[63]

As a "humane thing," Stimson proposed an immediate halt to the bombing of Japan, but this was flatly rejected on the ungenerous grounds that the U.S. government had not yet received an official surrender.[64] When a Presbyterian minister deplored the indiscriminate destruction of the atomic bombs, Truman harshly invoked Japan's war crimes: "Nobody is more disturbed over the use of Atomic bombs than I am but I was greatly disturbed over the unwarranted attack by the Japanese on Pearl Harbor and their murder of our prisoners of war. The only language they seem to understand is the one we have been using to bombard them. When you have to deal with a beast you have to treat him as a beast."[65]

He did, however, order that a third atomic bomb not be dropped without his command. It was too horrible, he told his cabinet, to wipe out another hundred thousand people, and he did not like the idea of killing "all those kids."[66]

. . .

The other Allied governments were sharply divided about retaining the monarchy.[67]

In London, Clement Attlee, the new British prime minister, and Ernest Bevin, his foreign secretary, agreed to the U.S. proposal in just a few hours. Although a progressive trade unionist, Bevin believed that constitutional monarchies could be useful; he thought that the ouster of Kaiser Wilhelm II had created an opening for Adolf Hitler.[68] Already heavily committed in occupying Germany, the Labour government feared that dethroning the emperor "might lead Japanese to adopt a suicidal policy." The British had a colonial motive for utilizing the emperor: his authority would be crucial to get Japanese troops in the far reaches of the British Empire to lay down their arms. The British suggested that Hirohito be spared the humiliation of signing the surrender himself.[69]

Australia's government publicly declared that maintaining the prerogatives of the emperor was utterly unacceptable, while privately urging Britain to keep open the possibility of trying the emperor for war crimes.[70] The British Foreign Office was aghast. Determined not to leave their autonomous dominion under any foolish misapprehensions, the British waited for several days to reply, making clear how little Australia's opinions mattered in London, let alone Washington or Moscow.[71] The British privately warned the Australians that "it would be a capital political error to indict him as a war criminal. We desire to limit commitment in manpower and other resources by using Imperial Throne as an instrument for the control of the Japanese people."[72]

Chiang Kai-shek, reached in Chongqing after his morning prayers, grudgingly agreed to the American terms, but asked that Hirohito and the Japanese high command sign the surrender. The emperor, he noted in his diary, should be kept under the new Allied supreme commander, with Japan's government determined by the free will of the people—something which he had been demanding for many years.[73]

The Soviet foreign minister, Vyacheslav Molotov, cannily said that since Japan had not made an unconditional surrender, the Soviets would continue their offensive in Manchuria.[74] Under American pressure, Molotov accepted the draft reply, but requested a say in choosing the Allied supreme commander running occupied Japan. The U.S. ambassador in Moscow, Averell Harriman, flatly refused to give the Soviets a veto. Molotov suggested putting a U.S. general and a Soviet general jointly in charge. That was unthinkable, Harriman retorted; the supreme commander had to be an American. After a furious quarrel, the ambassador stalked off. Soon after he got a call informing him that Stalin only wanted to be consulted about the makeup of the Allied occupation command.[75]

Following the British suggestion, the United States backed off from having Hirohito sign the surrender, although insisting that he command the Japanese military to lay down their arms.[76] Chiang, rebuffed again, grudgingly acquiesced.[77] The disunited Allies sent back a united response.

With every hour that passed, people died in aerial bombing and combat. Between August 10 and the end of the war on August 15, the United States likely killed some fifteen thousand Japanese.[78] "We are all on edge waiting for the Japs to answer," Truman wrote privately. "Have had a hell of a day."[79]

Truman would later bluntly say that Hirohito "was told that he would not be tried as a war criminal and that he would be retained as emperor."[80] Yet the actual nuanced note, too clever by half, left Japanese officialdom puzzling at the enigmatic Americans. What did it mean for the kokutai that Japan's government would be established by the free will of its people? Even Togo and the peace faction fretted at the absence of a guarantee of the imperial system. Marquis Kido Koichi, the emperor's closest adviser, urged the hard-line army minister to accept the Allied note: "We must abide by the wishes of His Majesty." Once again, the inner circle deadlocked, with a looming prospect of a military overthrow of the peace camp.[81]

After multiple coup attempts and assassinations, the advocates of peace had every reason to be terrified of military extremists.[82] Across Tokyo, posters menaced, "Kill Lord Keeper of the Privy Seal Kido!"[83] A group of young officers revealed their plans for a putsch to the army minister, who neither endorsed their plot nor actively tried to halt them.[84]

It would take a second intervention by the emperor—who had decided to swallow the American note—to wrench Japan out of its war. To the shock of palace officials, U.S. B-29s dropped leaflets over Japan's major cities revealing to everyone Japan's secret offer to surrender and the response from the Allies.[85] Fearing public chaos, revolution, or a military coup, Kido raced to warn the emperor, and professed himself filled with awe at Hirohito's determination for peace. In the morning on August 14, the emperor convened his senior military chiefs, told them that they could not match the atomic bombs and Soviet invasion, and asked them—all but commanding them—to end the war. When asked about the kokutai, he replied that the Allies had guaranteed the survival of the imperial house.[86]

Dressed formally in a marshal's uniform with decorous white gloves, Hirohito gathered his government's leaders for the last time in the war, crammed into a small room. The army minister and both the army and navy chiefs thought that the American reply was insufficient, leaving open the possibility of fighting on. Hirohito, apparently persuaded that the nuanced phrases devised by Byrnes would preserve the monarchy, declared that the Allied note was "acceptable." He told the military that it was difficult for him to "deliver so many of my trusted servants into the hands of the Allied authorities by whom they will be accused of being war criminals." But he could not endure letting his people suffer more, with tens or hundreds of thousands more deaths: "The whole nation would be reduced to ashes."

In an extraordinary step, the emperor said that he himself would broadcast the news to the nation in an imperial rescript. Gazing at his recalcitrant army and navy ministers, he asked them to convince soldiers to accept his choice for peace. In the cramped room, people wept and bowed. The emperor himself shed tears afterward as he recounted the events to Kido, who could not even lift his head.[87] At last, the Japanese cabinet could make its surrender.[88]

Without Hirohito's assent, many in the military might have defied a government decision to surrender.[89] Even after the emperor's two direct interventions for peace, some army leaders contemplated a putsch in order to keep fighting. There were underground assassination plots against the prime minister and Kido. The army minister, deeply torn, seriously considered a coup, but refrained—although he did not turn in a coterie of junior officers who were planning a revolt. Rather than hear the emperor's surrender broadcast, he sliced open his own throat and abdomen.

That night, August 14–15, those officers launched their coup. One of the young putschists shot dead a general and another officer who stood in their way. The officers swept into the Imperial Palace, trying in vain for several tense hours to find the phonograph recording of the emperor's surrender message, ready for broadcast. Jerked awake, Kido hid himself, then raced back to his office to shred crucial documents and throw them in the toilet, before finally taking shelter in the vault. After some indelibly frightening hours with the emperor locked behind iron shutters in his residence, the insurrectionists could not find the record, and the army quelled the mutiny. The two lead plotters committed suicide in front of the palace.[90]

In Washington, on August 14, around 4 p.m., Byrnes was in his office at the Executive Office Building, chatting with the visiting Duke of Windsor, when his telephone rang: Japan had accepted the Allied demand for surrender. The secretary of state raced next door to the White House, bursting into the Oval Office to tell Truman.[91]

The emperor had proclaimed his acceptance of the Potsdam Declaration, and said that he would command his military forces to cease fighting and surrender their weapons—at last bringing World War II to an end.[92]

Harry Truman announces the surrender of Japan to reporters crowded into the Oval Office, the White House, August 1945.

Truman called a throng of electrified reporters into the Oval Office, had the doors locked, and flanked himself with Byrnes, Leahy, Cordell Hull, and a crush of other officials. He spoke at 7 p.m. sharp, glaringly illuminated by klieg lights. Standing solemnly behind his Oval Office desk, in a dark double-breasted suit with a silver-blue striped tie, reading slowly off a single sheet of paper, the president announced "the unconditional surrender of Japan." The doors were unlocked and the reporters dashed out to flash the news to the world.

Jubilant crowds gathered outside chanting, "We want Truman! We want Truman!" Half a million people flooded the streets of the capital, dancing and cheering. As exuberant celebrations exploded in Washington and across the country, car horns blaring and bells ringing, Truman went to the White House residence and telephoned his elderly mother in Missouri to tell her what had happened.[93]

"Not Necessarily to Japan's Advantage"

All across Asia, Allied officers shifted from killing Japanese to accepting their surrenders.[94] Battle lines hardened into political demarcations.[95] General Joseph Stilwell, then drilling troops to storm Kyushu, wrote, "I am so thankful we don't have to throw Ben"—his youngest son who had just turned eighteen—"into the pot that I don't care what they do with the God damn emperor."[96]

Stimson wryly wrote that he could now resume the vacation which was "interrupted by a few events this week."[97] He crowed that Hirohito's word was being obeyed by Japan's armies "thereby saving tremendous loss of life" from a ground invasion.[98] His work done, the elderly war secretary could with relief tender his resignation to Truman.[99]

On August 15, Japanese radio suddenly proclaimed that the emperor would address his subjects at noon. People rigged up speakers in office buildings, schools, and farms, and at midday the country fell eerily silent as people crowded around their radios. At the front, soldiers strained to hear their fate; some expected a defiant call to resist the invaders. Many subjects bowed at the startling sound of the royal voice, "the voice of the crane," never before heard across the nation, as the radio broadcast the phonograph recording of Hirohito reading the imperial rescript of surrender.[100]

Hirohito's voice was thin, his tone somber. "His voice was slow and restrained, with a distinctive intonation," remembers a woman who had survived firebombing in Tokyo. His verbiage was elliptical at best, verging on cryptic. He justified the war without apology: Japan had declared war upon the United States and Britain for its own self-preservation, striving for the "emancipation of East Asia." He made no mention of the terrors inflicted upon the Chinese and other Asian peoples, nor the abuse of Allied prisoners of war. He expressed regrets only to the collaborationist regimes which had been Japan's partners in domination.

Despite the nation's best efforts, he said, the conflict had "developed not necessarily to Japan's advantage"—one of the grandest euphemisms in military history. The enemy had used "a new and most cruel bomb" which had killed many innocent people; if Japan fought on, it would mean not just the country's obliteration but "the total extinction of human civilization." He warned his subjects against civil strife, reassuring them that Japan had been able to "safeguard and maintain the structure of the Imperial State." Mourning the nation's wartime sacrifices, he turned to "enduring the unendurable."[101]

For Hirohito's subjects, straining to understand his classical dialect, this brief address was startling and confusing: the icon of war and sacrifice had suddenly become a champion of surrender. There was defiance, resignation, relief. In the capital, people marched to the Imperial Palace to bow, or assembled at the Yasukuni war shrine to honor the fighters who would never come home.[102] Listening at a military factory, a firebombing survivor in Yokohama could barely hear, but stunned people around her said that they had lost the war. In Nagasaki, a young woman who a few days earlier had been briefly knocked unconscious by the atomic blast and shockwave was too busy burning corpses to listen.

U.S. military intelligence feared that Hirohito might abdicate after surrendering.[103] He did no such thing. On August 16 at 4 p.m., he ordered the military to end hostilities immediately. To ensure that his will was followed, he sent members of the imperial family out to remote Japanese forces in Manchuria, China, and Indochina.[104]

In a special directive, Truman designated General Douglas MacArthur—the only five-star General of the Army available at the moment—as the supreme commander for the Allied powers. "From the moment of surrender, the authority of the Emperor and Japanese Government to rule the state will be subject to you," Truman ordered him. The emperor would have to issue a signed proclamation authorizing his underlings to sign an official instrument of surrender.[105]

Rather than shooting their way across Kyushu and Honshu, occupying Allied soldiers entered Japan through careful coordination with the Japanese authorities. On behalf of his defeated government, Togo Shigenori exhorted the Allies to limit their troops to the minimum number, station them as inconspicuously as possible, and keep them out of Tokyo altogether. He suggested that millions of Japanese soldiers be allowed to disarm themselves voluntarily under the command of the emperor.[106] Unimpressed, Byrnes replied that MacArthur would tell the Japanese how to carry out their surrender.[107]

Proclaiming that its wartime contributions were second only to those of the United States, Australia marked victory over Japan with renewed public complaints that it had not been consulted about the surrender terms. On the day of the emperor's broadcast, Australia's foreign minister declared that Hirohito might be a war criminal to be tried.[108]

As the Americans took over, they barely smothered their own rage for revenge. The Pacific fleet command ordered its officers that even though "the Japanese are still the same nation which initiated the war by a treacherous attack on the Pacific fleet and which has subjected our brothers in arms who became prisoners to torture[,] starvation and murder," it was nevertheless unbecoming for U.S. Navy officers to hurl "insulting epithets" at "the Japanese as a race or as individuals. Neither familiarity and open forgiveness nor abuse and vituperation should be permitted."[109]

For the Soviet Union, the mere fact of Japan's surrender was no reason to stop fighting. Having not fought during most of the Pacific War, the Soviets now kept on shooting during the peace. Thundering down from Manchuria, Soviet troops moved into northern Korea and menaced the northern Japanese home island, Hokkaido.

Stalin sought a Soviet occupation of northern Hokkaido, informing Truman that "Russian public opinion would be seriously offended if the Russian troops would not have an occupation region in some part of the Japanese proper territory."[110] Here was a bill coming due for the Soviet entry into the war, going well beyond what Stalin had been promised at Yalta. This could have ultimately left Japan sliced into American and Soviet zones, as would happen in Germany and Korea. But Truman brusquely refused, frostily informing Stalin that the Japanese in all the home islands, including Hokkaido, were to surrender to MacArthur only. He did allow Stalin to grab all the Kuril Islands, including the southern Kurils (known to Japanese as the Northern Territories)—resented to this day by Japanese in a festering territorial dispute with Russia.[111] Stung, Stalin huffily wrote that "I and my colleagues did not expect such an answer from you," but backed off from his Hokkaido plans.[112]

Two days after they surrendered, the Japanese military urgently complained to MacArthur that the Soviets were continuing their offensive in Manchuria, making it hard for the Japanese to follow the imperial order to yield. Worried that the Soviet assault was endangering a "bloodless surrender," MacArthur pressed the Soviet high command, although without replying to the Japanese.[113]

Stalin did not take his orders from MacArthur. While admitting that four hundred thousand Japanese had already been captured by his forces, Stalin claimed that some ostensibly surrendering Japanese troops in Manchuria had treacherously attacked the Red Army—who then killed or wounded forty thousand Japanese.[114] This kind of brutality would mark the Soviet foray—particularly the cruelty with which Japanese prisoners, two-thirds of them civilians, were treated by the Soviets. To this day, Japanese mourn their dead who perished in staggering numbers in Soviet captivity after the Manchuria campaign: more than a quarter million confirmed dead, and some ninety-three thousand more lost and presumed dead.[115]

By the time the Red Army finally stopped fighting on September 5—well after Japan had surrendered—the Soviet Union would have secured the prizes promised under the Yalta agreement, including southern Sakhalin and the Kurils.[116] Helpless, the Japanese government complained that the Soviets in Sakhalin were looting and were raping girls as young as fifteen years old, shooting those who resisted.[117] In Korea, the Soviets seized everything north of the thirty-eighth parallel, laying the foundations for today's Stalinist regime in North Korea.[118]

Japanese troops were deployed from the Philippines to Korea, Thailand to Singapore, Malaya to Java.[119] Some of their officers cried out to fight on, while Admiral Chester Nimitz and other top U.S. military leaders worried that the Japanese military would take matters into its own hands.[120] The head of U.S. Army intelligence warned that Japan's armies were large, well armed, well disciplined, and undefeated.[121]

There were thousands of spectacular suicides by tearful soldiers, unable to believe that they had lost or unwilling to face an American future. But while these gory extravaganzas commanded more attention, the actual numbers of mutinous soldiers were decidedly small for a vast army. Despite all the regimented bluster about fighting to the death, countless civilians who had fled their burned-out cities were privately overjoyed to have long years tacked back onto their life spans. Soldiers who knew perfectly well the hopelessness of their positions were willing to stand down.[122]

For all that, surrender was particularly difficult in China, where as many as a million Japanese troops could face retaliation from the furious Chinese.[123] General Okamura Yasuji, the chief of Japanese army forces in China, angrily told the army minister, "The surrendering of several million troops without fighting is without parallel in military history of the world."[124] He grudgingly issued a cease-fire two days after the emperor's broadcast.[125] In numerous places in China, Japanese troops refused to yield, threatened to use poison gas, or vowed to fight to the end and then commit suicide.[126] Hirohito himself appealed to MacArthur for help.[127]

Chiang Kai-shek urged magnanimity in his radio victory statement to his people on August 15. Although he mentioned Jesus specifically, this was not just Christian charity; he was reaching out to Mao Zedong to try to bring the Communist forces under national control, and hoped that postwar Japan could be a bulwark against Communism. While declaring victory over "the enemy's imperialistic designs on China," he urged his soldiers not to take revenge on surrendering Japanese troops: "We have always said that the violent militarism of Japan is our enemy, not the people of Japan." He ruled out vengeance against "the innocent people of Japan. We can only pity them because they have been so sadly deceived and misled, and hope that they will break away from the wrong doing and crimes of their nation."[128]

In India, the Philippines, Indochina, and other colonized lands, the end of the war meant the renewal of the struggle against Western imperialism.[129] France was desperate to reestablish its position in Indochina—which today is the independent countries of Vietnam, Cambodia, and Laos. With the Truman administration quietly refusing to assist in the reconquest, Charles de Gaulle was irritated by what he saw as Truman's simplistic fixations on democracy and independence.[130] Visiting the White House, the Free French leader warned Truman that granting independence too quickly to colonized Asians and Africans would unleash xenophobia, poverty, and anarchy among "peoples still primitive." When Truman said that his administration would not oppose the return of the French army and authority in Indochina, de Gaulle haughtily replied that France had no need to ask permission.[131]

To de Gaulle's embarrassment, France had done little to drive the Japanese out of Indochina, with two French divisions still preparing to deploy when the atom bombs dropped. After the Japanese occupation of Indochina, the general was appalled to find nothing left of France's authority in its colonial possessions, including Cambodia and Laos. France deployed some seventy thousand troops to Indochina, a show of force which de Gaulle candidly admitted was meant to overcome its recent humiliations. With Vietnamese Communists and nationalists agitating for independence, de Gaulle darkly speculated that the nascent Vietminh were being egged on by Japanese troops. As Ho Chi Minh formed a government in Tonkin, the populace throughout Indochina was obviously hostile to the French. When French troops returned to Saigon in September, there were riots against their presence, while the expeditionary corps struggled to retake Cambodia.[132]

Much the same was true for Holland. Two days after Japan surrendered, Indonesian nationalists on Java and Sumatra proclaimed the independence of a new Republic. The Dutch government, returning from exile in London to restore its prewar empire, did not grasp the scale of the

Indonesian revolution. Many of the Indonesian insurgents showed their Japanese influence: young men wearing bandannas, in simple trousers made of sacking, armed with curved Japanese-style swords. In public, the Dutch sometimes liked to claim that they only wanted to get a stable Indonesian government on its feet. The Republic, the Dutch insisted, was incapable of becoming a self-governing state fit for independence; its leaders, including the young Sukarno, were dismissed as nothing more than Japanese collaborators. Complaining of aggression from the Republic on Java and Sumatra, the Dutch launched what they preposterously termed two major "police actions" aimed at restoring law and order, helped by British troops. Indonesian nationalists would fight on for years against this revival of Dutch colonialism.[133]

In Southeast Asia, Japanese forces were to surrender unconditionally to the British, under Admiral Lord Louis "Dickie" Mountbatten, the Allied commander there.[134] Yet far from the bombed-out cities of Japan's home islands, and fearing Allied prosecution as war criminals, some Japanese commanders there were inclined to fight on. It took a personal order from Hirohito carried by an imperial prince to get the general in charge in Malaya to quit.[135] In Burma, British forces were badly outnumbered by hundreds of thousands of defiant Japanese. Mountbatten huffily noted that their attitude was that "their armies are undefeated but have been ordered by Emperor to surrender."[136] These Japanese were so confrontational that a senior British diplomat in Rangoon wrote, "I began to wonder whether we or the Japanese had won the war." As this official noted, the Japanese there "do not consider that they have been defeated and say so quite openly. Their attitude is that as a result of the atomic bomb, the Emperor has ordered them to lay down their arms, and they must obey the Emperor, though they do not quite know why." He added, "We have, I think, a very difficult time ahead."[137]

CHAPTER 5

Supreme Commander

IN THE BLAZING AFTERNOON sunlight of August 30, 1945, General Douglas MacArthur descended toward a Japanese airfield which shimmered with heat. His C-54 transport airplane was named *Bataan*. Since his defeat in the Philippines and the subsequent death march of his captured troops, it had been his aggrieved custom to give all his personal planes that name.[1]

On paper, MacArthur was landing in a country he ruled with absolute authority as the supreme commander for the Allied powers.[2] That was not how it felt as the plane made its descent. Atsugi airfield, near Yokohama, was known to the Americans as a training base for kamikaze pilots. His officers warned him that they would be landing amid some three hundred thousand Japanese soldiers in the vicinity; the C-54 carried a few dozen passengers at most.

The nervous Americans could see antiaircraft guns below which could have blasted them out of the sky. Once on the ground, it would be easy enough to shoot MacArthur and his small party, or to poison his next steak dinner. His officers lectured him that Japan had started the war with a sneak attack and might mark its ending with an assassination. Although MacArthur claimed to trust in Japanese chivalry, he and the Allied occupiers were arriving stoked with rage, badly outnumbered, and keenly hoping for Japanese cooperation.

The *Bataan* almost grazed the treetops before landing. There were a few other U.S. airplanes already there, although not enough to mount any real defense. MacArthur stepped out sporting Ray-Ban sunglasses and with his corncob pipe clenched in his jaw, which conveniently identified him for any moderately well-informed sharpshooter. He paused for the waiting photographers—with MacArthur, there were always photographers—and then his small crew scrambled into a ragtag procession of battered vehicles, MacArthur in an aged Lincoln car. When a fire engine started up with a bang, some of the Americans flinched.

As they drove, they were astonished to find some thirty thousand armed Japanese troops flanking both sides of the road to Yokohama with their backs turned to the occupiers. Some of the Americans thought it was deference. Others found it quietly sinister.[3]

Neither the best nor the most important American commander of the war, MacArthur was unparalleled at contriving his celebrity. His own wife addressed him as "General." Theatrical and petty, histrionic and grandiose, self-regarding and self-promoting, he was at least nearly as brave and intelligent as he thought he was. He was haunted by memories of being driven from his beloved Philippines by a Japanese assault accompanying the strike at Pearl Harbor.

The Philippines had been a crucial early objective for Japan: the largest American colony, which could block the sea lanes to the vital oil and other natural resources in the Netherlands East Indies (now Indonesia) and Malaya. At the start of the war, MacArthur had interned Japanese men, women, and children in Manila and Davao, making some of them dig trenches in a possible violation of the Geneva Convention.[4] As skillful Japanese soldiers had stormed the main Philippine island of Luzon and swiftly captured Manila, Filipino and American troops had retreated to the jungle peninsula of Bataan. MacArthur mostly holed up nearby on Corregidor, a fearsomely fortified island ("the Rock") just south of the peninsula, rarely showing his face on Bataan. This had led some of his famished, sickly, unsheltered, and demoralized troops to compose a ballad set to the tune of "The Battle Hymn of the Republic": "Dugout Doug MacArthur lies ashaking on the Rock / Safe from all the bombers and from any sudden shock."[5] The nickname would dog him forever.[6]

Corregidor had soon come under fierce Japanese shelling, which MacArthur had endured with cool bravery, accompanied by his wife and their four-year-old son. (In the family tradition, he was named, egregiously, Arthur.) The island had become, as one soldier put it, "a sunburned, God-cursed land, where bombs and shells made life a Hell, with death on every hand." Then to MacArthur's fury, Franklin Delano Roosevelt had ordered him to depart Corregidor. He had set off in one of four rickety little patrol boats, dodging Japanese warships across the squalling waves to reach a safe island, and then flying to security in Australia. He had dramatically told a crowd of Australians, "I came through and I shall return."

One of the tormented Americans taken prisoner after MacArthur's departure was not impressed: "Our leader has vanished like last summer's rose. / 'Gone to get help,' he would have us suppose."[7] Enraged by the death march of his Bataan soldiers, MacArthur had pressed for a decisive campaign to take back the Philippines, while other generals worried that he was driven more by emotion than strategy.[8]

In October 1944, MacArthur's troops had swept into the Philippines with a vengeful fury. He had come ashore on Leyte, wading through deep water in a carefully choreographed moment for a crowd of snapping photographers, with artillery and small-arms fire in the background. "People of the Philippines, I have returned!" he had exulted to the broadcasting cameras. "By the grace of Almighty God, our forces stand again on Philippine soil!"

"The guidance of Divine God points the way," he had exhorted Filipinos, treating the war as a Christian campaign. For all his vanity, MacArthur had been unflinching under repeated Japanese bombings. When one of his military aides had urged him to go no further while under Japanese fire, MacArthur had grinned and suggested that the officer return to their ship for ice cream.[9] He had insisted on trying to be among the first into Manila—a city that was flattened in the final battles.[10]

On September 2, World War II formally ended at a ceremony on the quarterdeck of the USS *Missouri*, a hulking, battered flagship anchored off Yokohama in the calm waters of Tokyo Bay. It was joined by a daunting armada of over two hundred Allied warships, meant to drive home to the Japanese their defeat.[11] None of the symbolism was subtle: the choice of the *Missouri* was a nod to Truman's home state; one of the flags pointedly displayed aboard was the one used by Commodore Matthew Perry's flagship when his American fleet had in 1853–54 forced Japan open to the world.[12] For a senior U.S. Army officer at the ceremony, General Joseph Stilwell (nicknamed "Vinegar Joe"), as for many Americans, it was a sublime moment of revenge. "Hard, cruel, hateful mugs under excruciating humiliation as we stared at them," he wrote in his diary. "Lots of fun."[13]

The small Japanese delegation of nine stiff, stony-faced men arrived wearing olive military dress uniforms, a light summer suit, or courtly black top coats and hats with white gloves. To Theodore White, *Time*'s leading Pacific War correspondent, they seemed dressed for a funeral, perhaps for their empire or even their nation.[14] One of the Japanese delegates later wrote, "were we not sorrowing men come to seek a tomb for a fallen empire?"[15] Their formal attire was a staid contrast to the surrounding throngs of ebullient Americans in casual open-collared khaki uniforms or British naval officers in shorts with knee-high socks, packed rows upon rows of them, hanging off the masts and gun turrets. Hundreds of reporters and photographers crammed the warship.[16] "Everybody just stood and stared at them," recalled Stilwell. "Terrible experience for those bastards. The downfall of Japan in complete disaster, and they had to stand and take it."[17]

MacArthur took center stage. For Theodore White, the general was conducting "an obsolete rite performed with primitive ceremony for a peace that had not come and a war that had not ended."[18] He made a brief, lofty, and surprisingly conciliatory speech urging a "higher dignity" both for victors and vanquished.[19] His hands and legs trembled from what one of his officers said was palsy, but his voice was firm.[20]

The parchment surrender documents were laid out for the Japanese on a large desk draped in dark cloth, incongruously prim atop the unadorned deck of a warship. The Imperial Palace had insisted that nobody of royal blood be made to sign them.[21] Instead Shigemitsu Mamoru, a bespectacled foreign minister—who had been hobbled by a bomb thrown by a Korean rebel in Shanghai—limped to the table with a cane, removed his top hat and his right-hand white glove, and signed on behalf of Emperor Hirohito and the Japanese government. Next General Umezu Yoshijiro, the hard-line chief of the army general staff, in his green uniform, bent over the table and reluctantly signed the instrument of surrender for the Japanese military.[22] On the other side of the table, MacArthur loomed over them.[23] "They stood stiffly and suffered," crowed Stilwell. "How we loved it."[24]

Joseph Stalin was even more vengeful. Flabbergasted by MacArthur's plans for a formal surrender ceremony, he warned that the Japanese were treacherous people with many "crazy cutthroats" left and suggested taking Japanese hostages just in case.[25]

"A million eyes seemed to beat on us with the million shafts of a rattling storm of arrows barbed with fire," recalled one of the Japanese delegates. "I felt them sink into my body with a sharp physical pain." The *Missouri* was daubed with little images of Japan's red-sun flag, which the American sailors called meatballs, each one celebrating a kill—a Japanese plane shot down or warship sunk. Counting them, he teared up.[26]

MacArthur rotated the documents around to face him on the table. His own thoughts, he later wrote, mixed sadness for the foxholes of Bataan

General Umezu Yoshijiro, the chief of the Japanese army general staff, signs the formal surrender aboard the USS *Missouri,* Tokyo Bay, September 2, 1945. General Douglas MacArthur stands by a microphone.

with overwhelming pride that "my own beloved country now leads the world."[27] He accepted the Japanese surrender as supreme commander. Behind him stood two gaunt, hollow-cheeked Allied generals who had just been freed from Japanese prison camps in Manchuria, where they had been repeatedly beaten: Lieutenant General Jonathan Wainwright, whom MacArthur had left behind in the Philippines to surrender, and Lieutenant General A. E. Percival, the British commander who had yielded at Singapore (and who struck an unsympathetic Stilwell as a "furtive, weak-chinned ferret looking sort of nut").[28] MacArthur had personally had them brought to Tokyo for the ceremony, and had been shocked to see how haggard Wainwright was, his uniform hanging off his wasted frame, his eyes sunken and cheeks pitted.[29] MacArthur used six pens; he handed the first pen back to Wainwright, and the second to Percival, as if unwriting their defeat at a stroke.[30]

While a parade of dignitaries signed for nine Allied powers, Stilwell winced at his side too: the Canadian had signed in the wrong place, the British was a "fat red dumpling," the Australian a "tub of guts," overall "a crew of caricatures in the eyes of the Japs. The human race was poorly represented."[31] When MacArthur declared the proceedings closed, wave after deafening wave of U.S. warplanes flew overhead to cap the belittlement of the Japanese with the largest fly-by in history, including four hundred of the B-29 bombers which had firebombed Japan's cities.[32]

Immediately after the broadcast from Tokyo Bay, Truman gave a radio address from the White House. "We shall not forget Pearl Harbor," the president said. "The Japanese militarists will not forget the U.S.S. *Missouri*."[33]

Yet even at this zenith of American triumphalism, there were signs of reconciliation toward some Japanese. Marquis Kido Koichi, the emperor's most powerful and trusted aide, wrote in his diary that he was "much relieved" by the emerging "liberal attitude of the U.S.A."[34] Emperor Hirohito was spared from the mortification of signing paperwork aboard the *Missouri,* allowed instead to issue a proclamation accepting the terms of the Potsdam Declaration and commanding his people to lay down their weapons.[35] As Truman stipulated, Hirohito and the Japanese government were responsible for carrying out the terms of the Potsdam Declaration, subject to the authority of the supreme commander.[36]

Shigemitsu returned that afternoon to the Imperial Palace for an audience with the anxious emperor.[37] The foreign minister's report to the throne was drafted in part by one of his most insightful diplomats, Kase Toshikazu, who aboard the *Missouri* was "struck and spellbound" by the "magnanimous tone" of MacArthur's speech. Soon after, Kase claimed that he had written in the imperial briefing that "were we the victors and imposed terms upon the vanquished foes, I wonder if we would have made such a great speech as that made by the Supreme Commander." According to this account, Hirohito concurred, praising MacArthur's "towering statesmanship, deep humanity, and far-sighted vision."[38]

"MR. PRIMA DONNA, BRASS HAT, FIVE STAR MACARTHUR"

Ever since he was nearly court-martialed three times as a headstrong junior officer, MacArthur had had trouble accepting higher authority.[39] After an ugly incident in 1932 when he violently evicted Great War veterans camped out in Washington petitioning for their bonuses, Roosevelt had privately called him "one of the two most dangerous men in the country," alongside the demagogue Huey Long.[40] Henry Stimson noted coolly that "his personality is so unpleasant" and that he had "affronted all the men of the Army and Navy with whom he has to work."[41]

Truman was only the latest of his unusually varied range of enemies. Years before the president spectacularly sacked MacArthur during the Korean War, he could not stand the man he in private repeatedly called Dugout Doug.[42] Late in World War II he groused about "what to do with Mr. Prima Donna, Brass Hat, Five Star MacArthur."

He hated the arrogance of the insubordinate officer who had challenged Roosevelt, imagining he would flout anyone: "Mac tells God right off." MacArthur was not "a real General and a fighting man" but "a play actor and a bunco man." He added, "It is a very great pity we have to have stuffed Shirts like that in key positions." The president seethed, "Don't see how a country can produce such men as Robert E. Lee, John J. Pershing, Eisenhower, & Bradley and at the same time produce Custers, Pattons, and MacArthurs." Truman regretted that Roosevelt had ordered MacArthur to escape Corregidor, spitefully writing that "I don't see why in Hell Roosevelt didn't . . . let MacArthur be a martyr" by forcing him to stay and surrender himself—which could have meant three ghastly and possibly fatal years in a Japanese prison camp in Manchuria.[43]

It was the least of Truman's complaints that MacArthur was angling to run for president against him. An influential Democratic senator warned Truman that he was "making a mistake in appointing Dugout Doug as Allied Commander in Chief to accept the Jap surrender. Said Doug would run against me in 1948 if I built him up." Truman calmly replied that "I didn't want to run in '48 and that Doug didn't bother me that way."[44]

From his first days in Japan, MacArthur bristled at oversight by the Truman administration. He griped to General George Marshall, the U.S. Army chief of staff, that direction from Washington "would exercise ten thousand miles away from the scene a degree of local control which would seriously hamper and perhaps prevent the successful execution of the mission for which I am held responsible."[45] He grumbled at public statements made by the Truman team which had not been cleared by him. Policy for ruling Japan, he thought, should be made at his General Headquarters in Tokyo, not in remote Washington.[46]

Wrong About Japan

There was an awful uncertainty as the first small detachments of Americans entered Tokyo, Yokohama, and other cities. The occupation had a substantial element of uncalled bluff. As one of MacArthur's advisers warned Truman, "the entire American occupying forces could have been wiped out overnight."[47]

In the final months of the war, the Japanese press had been thick with propaganda about guerrilla warfare. The whole population was to be armed; people would fight with bamboo spears; the armed forces would battle on from the central mountains.[48] Yet MacArthur professed himself unfazed, stating publicly that it would be impossible to arm Japanese civilians effectively for guerrilla resistance, and that at worst they would only be able to kill thousands of Americans.[49] With Japan's industries and economic base shattered by firebombing, the people were reduced to subsistence; the country was unable to wage modern war.[50] He found Japan's military chiefs "submissive and apparently sincere" in swiftly demobilizing their vast armies.[51] It would only be American ham-fistedness that could drive guerrilla bands into the mountains in resistance.[52]

MacArthur's unlimited powers were backed by limited manpower. Truman knew that exhausted Americans would balk at fresh military deployments.[53] The Allies might have provided more troops, but the United States refused to share its prize. Some three-quarters of the occupying soldiers were Americans, with everyone reporting to MacArthur.[54] This was meant above all to ward off Soviet ambitions, but also to prevent mischief from Britain or China.[55] "A divided command would be fatal," wrote MacArthur.[56]

American supremacy was paramount. While there had been no way to prevent the Soviet Union from seizing Central Europe and its eastern zone in Germany, the Americans had led the fight for Japan and now meant to rule it accordingly.[57] According to a top secret policy approved by Truman, there would be no division of Japan into zones run separately by different Allies, unlike in Germany and Korea. Japan would be ruled by a single American-dominated administration, with the United States "the controlling voice in the occupation authority of Japan Proper."[58]

MacArthur fretted over Soviet ambitions in nearby Korea and Manchuria, expecting a future clash between the United States and the Soviet Union.[59] He feared that the Soviets were planning to split Japan in two, as they were doing in Korea.[60] He warned about "underground Communist agitation," suspecting many Japanese liberals of actually being Communists.[61] In this, he was in accord with the Imperial Palace, where Kido was similarly frantic about Soviet ambitions.[62]

China had mooted a substantial force of some thirty thousand troops, but the Americans insisted that other Allied forces should be merely token-sized, with the smallest number of American troops always bigger than the combined total from other countries.[63] Still, the need for the racial symbolism of Chinese troops was urgent.[64] Cordell Hull, the previous secretary of state, had wanted a small presence of "other Asiatic peoples" in the occupation to "impress the Japanese that this had been not merely a white man's war against them."[65] The U.S. military was eager for participation from "Asiatic countries" in order to demonstrate that "the Pacific war is not a racial war."[66]

The Joint Chiefs of Staff wanted an army of two and a half million to control some seventy million Japanese, but MacArthur bullishly proposed a minimum of just two hundred thousand American troops.[67] After only a few days in Tokyo, MacArthur confidently informed Marshall that American troops could be returning home within a few months.[68]

When MacArthur bluffly asserted in public that the occupation forces could be down to two hundred thousand within six months, the White House and State Department recoiled. Truman, while promising not to keep American troops in Japan "a day longer than is necessary," said he could not forecast how the occupation would unfold.[69] Marshall scolded an uncharacteristically contrite MacArthur that his statement had set off an explosion in Congress and weakened the United States' position in Asia; he should not talk to the press without clearing it first.[70] Still, boxed in by MacArthur's statement, Truman had to hastily announce plans to get more than two million soldiers home by Christmas.[71]

In fact, long before the emperor's thin voice was heard from their radios, the Japanese people had had more than enough of war. Before the atomic bombings and the Soviet entry into the war, almost half of Japanese were certain that victory was impossible and a third had felt they could not go on with the war, according to the U.S. Strategic Bombing Survey.[72] "There will be no trouble in occupying Japan," predicted General Yamashita Tomoyuki, held by the Americans for war crimes in the Philippines. "The Japanese admire the Americans. The Japanese will like the Americans." Even after Hiroshima and Nagasaki? "Even after the atomic bombs."[73]

There were painfully apparent reasons for the Japanese to accept defeat. "The place is *ruined*," wrote Stilwell after driving through rainy Tokyo. "Completely gutted. Soul-satisfying sight." There were only stone, brick, and concrete structures standing, with everything else burned down, and shanties speckling the rust-colored landscape. Metal safes sat eerily alone: the stores that kept them had been incinerated around them. Despite the huge numbers of freshly demobilized Japanese soldiers, policemen blandly saluted the Americans, and the public seemed apathetic. "It is what a kick to stare at the arrogant, ugly brown-faced, buck-toothed, bowlegged bastards, and realize where this puts them."[74]

When MacArthur drove in from Yokohama to set up his new General Headquarters in the hulking Dai-Ichi Life Insurance Building in central Tokyo, he was stunned by "22 miles of devastation and vast piles of charred rubble."[75] Tokyo and its neighboring cities sprawled over 210 square miles; out of those, as the president of MIT, a physicist, reported to Truman after an official trip to survey the destruction, some 85 square miles were "nothing but a level ash heap." Out of nine million inhabitants, there were only two million still there.[76]

American stereotypes of the Japanese as mindless, death-seeking fanatics did not survive first contact with a battered, downcast people. Far from heading for the hills to commence guerrilla warfare, Japanese civilians heaped contempt on their soldiers in uniform.[77] There was virtually no sign of organized resistance. American troops disembarked, deployed, and moved about unimpeded and unassailed, to the relief of Truman and MacArthur, as well as Kido.[78] MacArthur boasted that the Japanese were totally docile, without a single clash with the Allied troops in the crucial first weeks of the occupation.[79] He was convinced that never in history had a people been so completely crushed as the Japanese were now.[80]

For their part, the Japanese were relieved to discover the falsity of wartime propaganda warning that the barbarian invaders would be murderers and rapists. MacArthur repeatedly admonished American troops that their self-restraint would determine the fate of the occupation.[81] Of course, the Allied occupation was often bungling and inept, and some American troops behaved horribly, running wild, stealing kimonos or watches.[82] "The U.S. Army is making a spectacle of itself," worried Stilwell.[83] Even if the foreign troops were not quite the ambassadors of goodwill that MacArthur fancied them, they were far from the demons promised by the Imperial Japanese authorities.

Truman sent MacArthur a directive outlining the transformation of Japan, which became the single most important blueprint for the Allied occupation.[84] The primary goal was to ensure that Japan would not threaten the world's peace again. Its empire was disbanded, including Formosa (Taiwan) and Korea.[85] Japan was suddenly stripped of its army, navy, air force, and secret police. Its vaunted general staff, the shadowy militarist organizations, and the ministries for the army, navy, and Greater East Asia were disbanded.[86] The Kempeitai, the dreaded military secret police, discharged thousands of its officers all across the country.[87] And suspected war criminals, particularly those who had abused Allied prisoners of war, would be arrested and tried.[88]

The most urgent task for the Allies was disarmament and demilitarization.[89] MacArthur did a fresh calculation showing that the Japanese Empire had just under seven million troops: some two and a half million now on the home islands, the remainder deployed from Manchuria to the Southwest Pacific.[90] The massive task of demobilizing all of them was left to Japan's army and navy chiefs, gathering up the wreckage of their war machine strewn across continental Asia and the Pacific islands. For a military which had for decades distinguished itself by its unwillingness to accept civilian command, there was an obvious risk of mutiny. Yet as MacArthur crowed, "it was the Japanese themselves who performed the task." General Headquarters noted with relief that Japan's army and navy "are now ready and willing to accede to the Emperor's desires for his people."[91]

The racist hatreds of American public opinion during the war, coupled with the New Dealers' demands for a revolutionary transformation of Japanese society, could easily have spelled a harsh peace. Yet driven by the imperative of maintaining a relatively light military presence, the occupation took a more generous form.

Despite MacArthur's personal bitterness over Bataan, he soon asserted himself as an opponent of what he called "a merciless peace." That got a frosty reception among the maximalist New Dealers at the State Department, as well as from Stalin and his foreign minister, Vyacheslav Molotov, who believed that the supreme commander had gone soft. MacArthur came to scorn "preconceived plans born in hate and dedicated to vengeance." Instead he meant to win the Japanese over to liberty and democracy.[92] "It was true that we intended to destroy Japan as a militarist power," he later explained. "It was true that we intended to impose penalties for past wrongs. . . . But we also felt that we could best accomplish our purpose by building a new kind of Japan, one that would give the Japanese people freedom and justice, and some kind of security."[93]

MacArthur's reign unfolded less along the retributive lines of the liberal New Dealers or the "China crowd" that dominated the State Department and more like that envisioned by Henry Stimson, Joseph Grew, and other conservative advocates of softening the terms of peace.[94] Stimson had cautioned Truman against remaking Japan as the United States planned to do for Germany. "I am afraid we would make a hash of it if we tried," he wrote. "The Japanese are an oriental people with an oriental mind and religion." Instead of fundamental transformation, the Republican war secretary preferred a restricted occupation "limited to that necessary to (*a*) impress the Japanese, and the orient as a whole, with the fact of Japanese defeat, (*b*) demilitarize the country, and (*c*) punish war criminals, including those responsible for the perfidy of Pearl Harbor."[95]

Fundamentally, the comparatively small American military presence would have momentous consequences for the future course of Japan's politics and society. It necessitated the continued cooperation of the conservative Japanese authorities and the imperial court, exerting substantial power even in defeat.[96] The authority of General Headquarters was layered on top of that of the Japanese government. With so few Allied troops, MacArthur's power, as a major directive from the Truman administration noted, was to be wielded "through Japanese governmental machinery and agencies, including the Emperor." The United States would use the Japanese state for American purposes whenever possible. As the Truman administration's directive bluntly stated, "The policy is to use the existing form of Government, not to support it."[97]

This meant a deepening dependence on the emperor and the reactionaries around him.[98] Stimson and Grew both argued that Hirohito's sanction would allow his subjects to accept orders from the Americans.[99] As one of MacArthur's civilian advisers explained to Truman, Japanese acquiescence in a foreign occupation stemmed from an inferiority complex and "the fact that the emperor had ordered their cooperation and hence they could give it without feeling of disgrace or disloyalty."[100] MacArthur, enraged at a heated press and radio campaign in the United States urging that the emperor be ousted or prosecuted, stated publicly that his policies were implemented "through the Emperor and the machinery of the imperial government."[101]

Hirohito's court was quick to demonstrate its usefulness. The emperor pressed for calm, trying to build confidence in the wobbly new postwar civilian government. While Hirohito still had no stomach for criticizing Japanese militarists in public, he expressed qualms about the "unrestrained" army in a letter to his eldest son and heir, Akihito, who would ultimately succeed him as emperor. "Our people believed too much in the empire and disdained Britain and the United States," he wrote. "Our military placed too much weight on the spiritual and forgot science."[102]

On September 4, the emperor made an extraordinary personal address to a special session of the Diet, exhorting his people to "win the confidence of the world" and build a peaceful country.[103] This speech, General Headquarters noted with relief, set the general tenor of the Japanese reaction to American occupation.[104] On Kido's advice, Hirohito had appointed Prince Higashikuni Naruhiko, who was married to a daughter of the Meiji Emperor, as a caretaker prime minister to handle demobilization and the arrival of the occupiers—even though the emperor secretly scorned his elder relative for his weak opinions.[105] Higashikuni, an army general and a member of the extended imperial house—the only person in the family ever to serve as prime minister—used his royal credibility to urge his country to accept the peace in the emperor's name.[106]

At the same time, Higashikuni promoted what would become a grand theme of the occupation era: rewriting history to exonerate Hirohito. All blame for the war would be heaped on the militarists, with the emperor incongruously cast as a brave advocate for peace. Rather than questioning the emperor's role in igniting an unwinnable war, Higashikuni instead stood before the Diet begging for his "imperial magnanimity to pardon our unpardonable stupidity and incompetence" in losing.[107] After absolving the emperor for starting the war, the prince credited its ending to the "gracious feeling of benevolence of His Majesty, who paved the way for the establishment of an eternal peace in order to save the people from hardships."[108]

Only a few days after the *Missouri* ceremony, both the American occupiers and the Japanese authorities converged on a common line: the imperial court, so useful for a peaceful occupation, was not to be blamed for the war.

"As Little Fitted for Self-Government in a Modern World as Any African Tribe"

How much freedom and democracy might be possible in the new Japan? The Americans, ignorant and discombobulated, could only guess.

The Truman administration's early directives sweepingly mandated "a non-militaristic and democratic Japan." Expunging Imperial Japan's laws restricting civil liberties, uprooting feudalism, the Japanese would be "encouraged to develop a desire for individual liberties and respect for fundamental human rights, particularly the freedoms of religion, assembly, speech, and the press."[109] Yet despite Japan's democratic experience in the Taisho period before the rise of militarism, nobody knew if these reforms could now endure. As MacArthur later wrote, "Japan had become the world's great laboratory for an experiment in the liberation of a people from totalitarian military rule and for the liberalization of government from within."[110]

Truman, with a soldier's distaste for prolonged deployments overseas, was predisposed to doubt that the United States could transform other countries. While Woodrow Wilson was electrifying crowds in Paris in 1919, the homesick young Truman, marooned in a dreary base near Verdun, had written, "I don't give a whoop (to put it mildly) whether there's a League of Nations or whether Russia has a Red government or a Purple one, and if the President of the Czecho-Slovaks wants to pry the throne from under the King of Bohemia, let him pry but send us home."[111]

As a neophyte president, he was muddled in his own views. "You know Americans are funny birds," he wrote in his diary soon after taking office. "They are always sticking their noses into somebody's business which isn't any of theirs. We send missionaries and political propagandists to China, Turkey, India and everywhere to tell those people how to live. Most of 'em know as much or more than we do."[112] Yet that skepticism wrestled with an idealistic faith in "a free Japan."[113] He took his cues from fellow Democrats at the State Department, who advocated a sweeping democratization of Japan. In the end, he often wound up passive about occupation policy, allowing MacArthur to seize the initiative.

Truman was in good company, at least, in knowing next to nothing about Japan. Most of the U.S. government's foremost experts analyzed the nation through a haze of stereotype and cliché. Even the optimists were condescendingly bigoted, such as the colonel who vouchsafed that the Japanese could adapt to American-style democracy: "The Japanese are essentially an imitative people. Like all Orientals, they have great respect for power."[114] Grew, the administration's preeminent Japan specialist, reached no more profundity than that the Japanese were like disciplined sheep or a swarm of bees following their queen.[115] "Any attempt to impose an outright democracy on the Japanese would result in political chaos and would simply leave the field wide open for would-be dictators to get control," he wrote confidently in the first days of the occupation. "One can't live in a country for ten years without knowing these things."[116]

The racial hatreds of the war extended into discussions of Japanese self-governance. "The reformation of Japan is basically a colonial problem," wrote a senior British official in Tokyo. "By the standards of modern democracy which the Allies are hoping to implant, the Japanese people are a hopelessly backward people with the typical slave mentality. They are as little fitted for self-government in a modern world as any African tribe, though much more dangerous." For this racist diagnosis he proposed a suitably imperial policy: "If we treat them as outlaws they will understand, and if we govern them thereafter by benevolent autocracy, which is the only form of government for which they are fitted, they may be led to fill a profitable, subservient rôle in a peaceful future Asia."[117]

Even when promoting democracy, MacArthur held profoundly patronizing views of the Japanese. To him they were still basically a pagan, feudal society some four centuries behind the West, more like ancient Sparta than any modern country.[118] He said privately early in the occupation that "the Japs" were an "Oriental" people with an inferiority complex that pushed them to "childish brutality" in war and slavish dependence in defeat.[119]

For a fervent conservative who let his name be touted as a Republican presidential candidate, MacArthur's agenda in Japan turned out in some respects to be surprisingly progressive: equal rights for women, civil liberties for all, land reform, empowerment of labor unions.[120] By his own account, he wanted to modernize the constitution, hold democratic elections, free political prisoners, liberate farmers, encourage workers, curb police, decentralize political power, and separate church and state. While he had no realistic choice but to embrace much of what the Truman administration was ordering, he declared himself appalled at what he saw as Japan's feudal lack of concern for the individual, and expressed disgust at the secret police, who had thrown some sixty thousand people in jail between 1937 and 1940 for seditious thoughts. "There was no such thing as civil rights," he wrote. "There were not even human rights."[121]

Distrustful of the Japanese ability to sustain free government, the Allies curtailed their new liberties at every step. Freedom of religion could not become a cloak for bellicose Shinto organizations; freedom of assembly could be overruled for the security of the Allied troops; freedom of speech was subject to intrusive censorship.[122] As an early directive from Washington dictated, the Japanese were only to get foreign news that was either official U.S. propaganda or authorized by General Headquarters. Japan's press could report inside the country so long as they gave no criticism of the occupation, no suggestion of the obvious discord among the big four Allied powers, and "[n]o praise or pity" for Japanese apprehended by the Allied authorities.[123]

MacArthur was left with the curse of getting what he wanted. For all his Christian convictions, was he really sure he knew what he was doing? Having studied the occupations of Alexander, Julius Caesar, and Napoléon Bonaparte, as well as his father's time as military governor of the Philippines and his own experience occupying part of the Rhineland after World War I, he concluded that no military occupation had ever succeeded. "[T]he disease of power" corrupted the occupiers and "bred a sort of race superiority." As he later recalled with uncharacteristic self-effacement, "my own doubts and fears still gripped me. You do not become overnight the chief magistrate of a great state without many qualms unless your own egotistical vanity has made you a fool or a knave."[124]

CHAPTER 6

Apprehensions

JAPAN AND ITS EMPIRE were suddenly treated as a massive crime scene. During the eerie interval waiting for the Allied armies to arrive, Japanese officials systematically incinerated documents for the war crimes trials that would surely follow—one of the grandest efforts at evidence-tampering in legal history.[1]

In June 1945, Foreign Ministry officials began burning secret documents in anticipation of an Allied ground invasion, expanding their efforts in August.[2] First to go up in flames were papers about China, then the Soviet Union, and then the Axis.[3] At the Imperial Palace, at around 4 a.m. on August 15 during the coup attempt, the emperor's top aide, Marquis Kido Koichi, rushed back to his room to tear up all important documents and throw them into the toilet.[4] Protecting the throne, the Army Ministry had the troops burn imperial rescripts or anything written by Emperor Hirohito.[5]

Such blazes went on across the country, sending up clouds of billowing smoke. A military police unit in southern Kyushu was secretly ordered to destroy documents about foreign affairs, counterintelligence, and coup attempts, although preserving such useful papers as a blacklist of leftists. Gasoline, they were advised, actually slowed the burning; better to use the natural draft of the fire.[6] In China, at a prisoner of war camp at Fengtai on the outskirts of Beijing, Japanese troops filled truck after truck with reports, ledgers, and photographs and dumped them into a firepit.[7] According to a U.S. report, the Japanese garrison at Nanjing burned its papers, obscuring for all time one of the worst atrocities of the war.[8] To this day, the official records of more than 70 percent of the

Japanese military units that stormed Nanjing have not been found or published.[9]

At a hidden site near Harbin in Manchuria, more than paper was obliterated. Japan had operated a secret biological warfare program run by the army's Unit 731, which had used helpless Chinese for fatal human experiments. Now the biowarriors destroyed some four hundred kilograms of dried anthrax, got rid of evidence about germ warfare attacks on several Chinese cities, and wrecked laboratories and centers in China, Burma, and Singapore.[10] Before Soviet troops reached Harbin, Unit 731 blew up its own headquarters. They permanently silenced all the remaining Chinese experimental subjects and workers, giving several hundred captives the choice of suicide by hanging or taking cyanide.[11]

Allied aerial bombardment had destroyed some official documents, such as papers lost when the Foreign Ministry was hit.[12] Japanese officials took care to sweepingly destroy documents about their maltreatment of Allied prisoners of war.[13] The Office of Strategic Services, the nascent U.S. intelligence agency, dropped commandos deep into Japanese-held territory in China and elsewhere both to find prisoners of war and prevent the destruction of evidence.[14] Frustrated, the Allied occupiers would demand that the Japanese government turn over a complete list of all documents about Allied prisoners of war which had been destroyed by the army and navy ministries, along with the names of the officials who directed the cover-up.[15]

All of this burning and shredding had dire consequences for justice. With many of the most incriminating orders consigned to the flames, Allied prosecutors would have to rely heavily on the doctrine of command responsibility: showing that war crimes were widespread or systematic, and that the accused leaders had known about them and had had the authority to stop them. Furthermore, the bonfires across Japan would undermine one of the signature achievements sought from war crimes trials: assembling a truthful, unassailable historical account. Much of that record was already ash and smoke.

Allied troops rolling into Japan and its empire were immediately confronted with fresh evidence of widespread abuse of prisoners of war—sick, desperately hungry, or visibly beaten.[16] In Singapore, a British diplomat reported, the liberated prisoners had "all too many ugly stories of atrocities and Japanese inhumanity."[17] On Hainan Island in China, four hundred

British and Dutch prisoners were found dying fast from malnutrition and illness.[18]

At a camp near Tokyo, a U.S. officer estimated that half of the inmates had been assaulted so badly they needed to be hospitalized.[19] At two other liberated camps, almost all of the seven hundred prisoners were suffering from malnutrition, 80 percent of them gravely so, with many requiring surgery. A camp near Yokohama, reported the United States' Third Fleet, resembled a "Gestapo center of worst sort."[20] Meeting with a group of freed American prisoners of war, an enraged Fleet Admiral William Halsey told them that the war had "ended too soon because there are too many Nips left."[21]

Soon after the war's end, Harry Truman loftily declared, "We all look forward to the day when law rather than force will be the arbiter of international relations."[22] Yet in an important directive from the Truman administration, MacArthur was ordered to arrest suspected war criminals fast, even before getting instructions about what charges would be brought against them. He was to detain the Japanese army and navy general staffs, the Imperial General Headquarters, all commissioned officers in the notorious Kempeitai, the important members of the various ultranationalist and terrorist organizations, all leaders of the government and the economy who had helped with Japan's aggression, and—without any hint of legal standards for an indictment—"[a]ll persons who you have reason to believe are war criminals."

Yet since the Allies were going to run their occupation largely through the Japanese government, they could not possibly arrest every person reasonably suspected of war crimes. The sheer scale of Axis criminality went far beyond the reach of any system of criminal justice. The result was an American war crimes policy seesawing between forbearance for many and wrath for some. The Truman administration concentrated on punishing Tojo Hideki and other army leaders. "By appropriate means you will make clear to all levels of the Japanese population the fact of their defeat," the Truman administration instructed MacArthur. "[O]nly when militarism has been eliminated from Japanese life and institutions will Japan be admitted to the family of nations."[23]

This would ultimately generate a version of recent history where all blame fell on a relatively small clique of senior military officers, avoiding uncomfortable questions about the complicity of civilian elites, mainstream conservatives, the Imperial Palace, and big business, as well as wider society. Such selective guilt was historically and morally dubious, but it had advantages for General Headquarters. It would help to delegitimize and sideline the coup-prone military officers who were most likely to threaten democracy; it would slake the American public's demand for vengeance; it would help the Japanese public disavow their wartime leadership and embrace a new constitutional order congenial to the United States. It matched neatly with MacArthur's personal fixation on the Japanese army. And it would speed Japan's rehabilitation on the world stage, letting it become an American ally in the Cold War.[24]

Given how widely the conservative establishment had served the cause of militarism, nobody knew the parameters of blame yet. In particular, the Truman administration had not ruled out the possibility of deposing the emperor, although directing MacArthur not to overthrow him without consulting with the Joint Chiefs of Staff first.[25] Several prominent members of the royal family might plausibly have faced investigation as possible war criminals, most notably Prince Asaka Yasuhiko, the emperor's uncle by marriage who as a lieutenant general had commanded Japanese troops in the horrific conquest of Nanjing, and perhaps even his brother Prince Chichibu, a career army officer who had fought in China. Court insiders kept a low profile, trying not to provoke the enemy.[26]

The most important royal courtier was Kido Koichi, who as lord keeper of the privy seal was the closest adviser to the emperor—and a possible target for arrest. He had been born at the center of power in Japan: his father had been the grand chamberlain to the future Taisho Emperor and his childhood friends included such swells as Prince Konoe Fumimaro, who grew up to become prime minister.[27] A devious and conservative mandarin, a master of court maneuverings, Kido was the kind of person who said "a free and frank exchange of views" when he meant a yelling match.[28] One postwar American report called him "that ever-cautious political litmus paper, Marquis Kido."[29] He routinely saw Hirohito for an hour a day.[30] Although a decade older than Hirohito, Kido was awestruck by the imperial house. Once when Hirohito prayed at the ancient Ise Shrine—much of which is sanctified to the sun goddess Amaterasu, the supposed ancestor of the royal line—Kido was overwhelmed at his privilege in attending the Shinto sacrament, reverential at the profundity of what the monarch must be thinking.[31]

Soon after the emperor's surrender broadcast, he confided to Kido that it would be "unbearable" to him to turn over the suspected war criminals to the Allies and that "he would rather bear all the responsibility himself, abdicating from the Throne." But Kido urged him to tough it out. Stepping down would not just end Hirohito's reign, he argued, but might ruin the legitimacy of his successors, resulting in a republican form of government. This royalist entreaty helped convince Hirohito to stay put.[32]

PRISONERS OF SUGAMO

As soon as MacArthur had enough troops in place, on September 11, he ordered the arrest of forty war criminals. Thousands more would follow to military stockades.[33]

The preeminent catch was General Tojo Hideki, with a fresh wound on his chest from his failed attempt at suicide by pistol. Also among the first group were the entire Pearl Harbor cabinet and top military officers including Lieutenant General Homma Masaharu, blamed for the Bataan death march.[34] Tojo and twenty others were first put in a refurbished prison camp on Omori Island in Tokyo, ridden of rats and bugs. In the autumn chill, they got the same thin blankets, albeit deloused, which had been given to American prisoners of war. They were fed a simple diet of rice and dried fish with American coffee and candy. Stripped of his military uniform, Tojo wore a simple white shirt and dark vest; his weight fell to just ninety-four pounds. He was shunned by most of the other prisoners, who ignored him with silent contempt when he tried to strike up a conversation at mealtime. He spent his solitary days in a tiny cubicle, writing and smoking cigarettes, awaiting his execution. "I want to be a good loser," he told an American photojournalist.[35]

Togo Shigenori was swept up for being foreign minister at the time of Pearl Harbor, although he had actually strenuously argued against war. Suffering from heart disease, he was at first placed under house arrest but later moved to Sugamo Prison in Tokyo.[36] In desperation, his wife, Edith Togo, tried to convince Allied investigators of his innocence: "This is a crime against humanity."[37]

Sugamo Prison was quickly filled up with more than a thousand suspected war criminals of various ranks. It was a grim network of squat, ugly, modern buildings of tan concrete, set behind forbidding twenty-foot walls and watchtowers in a quiet residential neighborhood. Constructed as a prison complex, it had been used to hold political prisoners, including alleged Communists, spies, or dissenters, and later Allied prisoners of war. Under the U.S. Eighth Army, the inmates could be thrown into solitary confinement as discipline; they were only allowed to write one letter a week; their mail was censored. Still, the colonel from Missouri who now ran the place liked to say that the accused men were not guilty until convicted, and even then were human beings.

The Japanese suspects were treated alike regardless of rank. Robbed of stature and dignity, generals and prime ministers and lords at Sugamo were thrown in with the ordinary men they had commanded. They got three simple meals a day, with fish, vegetables, and rice—better than

Tojo Hideki's mug shot at Sugamo
Prison, Tokyo, March 26, 1946

what many ordinary Japanese were eating. Each small cell had an electric light, straw floor mat for sleep, a table and chair, and a covered toilet. The grounds had trees and a vegetable garden. The defendants could exercise and were not required to work while awaiting trial; they had to bathe at least twice a week; and they were allowed Buddhist, Protestant, or Catholic services, although not Shinto. The Christian chaplain set up a library for the prisoners. The Buddhist priest said that compared to the camps that Japan had operated for Allied prisoners, Sugamo was "a window of heaven."[38] Yet outside the walls, the surrounding neighborhood was a wasteland of ashes from the firebombing.[39]

MacArthur was secretly authorized to go after a host of prime ministers, generals, admirals, cabinet ministers, diplomats, and propagandists.[40] Soon after, the Truman administration's war crimes office added more famous names who could be arrested at MacArthur's discretion, including such prominent civilian politicians as Hirota Koki, an elderly former prime minister and foreign minister, and Prince Konoe Fumimaro, the influential former prime minister who had close ties to the Imperial Palace.[41] The occupiers arrested lower-ranked Japanese, with MacArthur keen to punish the officers responsible for the execution of the captured American airmen of the Doolittle raid.[42]

The new Japanese government tried to preempt Allied justice by voting to create its own war crimes tribunal.[43] This proposal would almost certainly have been quashed by General Headquarters, but it was knifed first by Hirohito. The day after Tojo's arrest, he bluntly told the Japanese prime minister that "the so-called war criminal suspects were his most faithful subjects and had rendered valuable service to the nation," and that he did not have the heart to punish them in his name. Kido too was against this punishment of Japanese by Japanese. Hirohito instructed the prime minister to reconsider, while Kido demanded an explanation of the government's move. Within hours, the prime minister and his top ministers came before Hirohito to scuttle their own plan.[44]

Reliant on Japanese official goodwill, MacArthur wanted to delay some arrests, including Konoe, who had personally urged the supreme commander to maintain the imperial court and the *zaibatsu* conglomerates as stabilizing forces that could ward off Communism.[45] MacArthur reminded the Truman administration that he was using some of these Japanese officers to demobilize the armed forces.[46] Annoyed, Truman personally pressed MacArthur to swiftly start military trials following "the flexible procedure adopted in Europe."[47] On September 21, the Americans carried out a second wave of arrests, while the Japanese government turned over several senior suspects.[48]

When the Truman administration finally issued its working directive on what to do with the captured suspects, MacArthur found it exasperatingly broad and vague.[49]

The U.S. military was authorized to set up its own military commissions, or the supreme commander could create special international military courts alongside other Allied countries.[50] Even the loftiest defendants were to be detained "as befits ordinary criminals." As supreme commander, MacArthur could set the rules of procedure, review the verdicts, and reduce sentences.

The Japanese defendants could be charged with three kinds of war crimes, directly following those established for the imminent trials at Nuremberg. First, most importantly and controversially, there was the planning and waging of aggression, or participating in a conspiracy to do so. This meant nothing less than criminalizing aggressive war itself. As Truman declared days before the first arrests in Japan, "war must be abolished from the earth if the earth, as we know it, is to remain."[51] Driven by American wrath over Pearl Harbor, the outlawing of aggressive war would become the core charge at both Nuremberg and Tokyo, but one which international lawyers and Japanese conservatives have questioned to this day.

Second, least contentiously, there were violations of the laws and customs of war, covering a multitude of war crimes already fixed in international law: harming prisoners of war, murdering or abusing civilians, and destroying cities in ways not justified by military necessity.

Third, there were crimes against humanity, which were the least important for the Americans but which resonated deeply with Chinese, Filipinos, and other peoples who had suffered under Japanese rule. This meant murder, extermination, enslavement, deportation, or other inhumane acts against civilians, even before a war began. By including persecutions on political, racial, or religious grounds, it linked the supremacist claims of the Japanese Empire with the racial ideology of its Nazi German allies.[52]

THE EMPEROR AND THE GENERAL

By the end of September, the Americans held some seventy suspected war criminals, seized by the occupying U.S. Eighth Army or unceremoniously thrown into the stockades of the XI Corps at Yokohama. Among the generals, ministers, and Kempeitai chiefs was Kishi Nobusuke, a powerful official in Japanese-run Manchuria, who was jailed for serving as commerce and industry minister under Tojo in the Pearl Harbor cabinet.[53]

The Truman administration's directive ordered MacArthur to "take no action against the Emperor as a War Criminal" until getting special orders.[54] At the Imperial Palace, the suspense grew unbearable. Had the emperor escaped the dragnet for good? Or were the Allies gauging the Japanese public reaction to the arrests before booking the biggest name of all?

The court made a publicity barrage to clear Hirohito's name. With MacArthur's permission, Hirohito himself made the unprecedented step of being interviewed by two reporters, one with *The New York Times*. Since the Imperial Palace had been damaged in the firebombing, they met nearby in an improvised throne room in the Imperial Household Ministry on the palace grounds. His hands shaking slightly, his body twisting with nervousness, the emperor gave written responses to show himself as blameless and harmless. He lumped guilt onto Tojo, claiming to be surprised that he had used something as harmless as an imperial war rescript to launch an unannounced attack on the United States.[55]

In private, Hirohito took much the same line, telling Kido that he had thought "his heart would break" when he gave Tojo the imperial rescript declaring war on the United States. He claimed to have told Tojo that it would be "very regrettable to be antagonistic to the English royal family," as if there was a way to attack the British Empire without giving offense to the House of Windsor.[56]

Sending messages in *The New York Times* only went so far. To be secure on the throne, Hirohito needed to get guarantees from MacArthur in person. The two men faced an enduring dilemma in the annals of international justice: how to strike a deal for amnesty, as is commonly done at the end of inconclusive conflicts, as in South Africa or Chile, when neither side has an appetite for more fighting.[57] Since General Headquarters feared unrest, the contours of the bargain were clear: in exchange for Hirohito and conservative leaders supporting the occupation, MacArthur would spare the emperor, thereby curtailing future war crimes prosecutions. It would take a bizarrely elaborate courtship for the two grandees to cement their arrangement.

In MacArthur's account, his military staff wanted to summon the emperor to General Headquarters—which was just across the moat from the Imperial Palace grounds—as a show of American power. MacArthur refused, not wanting to offend the Japanese people or snub the emperor.[58] Instead he quietly let word out that he would like to meet, and the Imperial Palace secretly sent an invitation to call on the supreme commander anywhere and anytime, according to one of MacArthur's aides.[59] The supreme commander chose the U.S. embassy. "'Bout time he recognizes I'm in town," said MacArthur.

On September 27, the custom-made imperial limousine pulled up at the U.S. embassy bang on time at 10:30 a.m., followed by two cars of Imperial Palace staff. Informed that the emperor smoked, MacArthur stuffed a pack of Lucky Strike cigarettes in his pocket. Like the humiliated Japanese diplomats on the USS *Missouri,* the emperor showed up overdressed, wearing a black cutaway tailcoat, striped trousers, and top hat. In his retinue was an anxious Kido, aware that the Americans might soon arrest him as a war criminal. The emperor was met by a small group of gawping U.S. officers in simple uniforms, including MacArthur's military secretary, Brigadier General Bonner Fellers. Fellers saluted the monarch, while an American aide alarmed him by taking his top hat; Hirohito bowed and shook hands. As one of MacArthur's military officers later recalled, the supreme commander barreled over to the emperor, declaring, "You are very, very well-come, sir!" It was the first time that the American officer could recall hearing MacArthur call anyone "sir."

With Hirohito's hands still gripped by MacArthur's, the emperor bowed deeply, which left his hands awkwardly suspended above his head. Once they disentangled themselves, MacArthur loomed almost a head taller. He was older, bigger, and meatier than the living god. MacArthur was insouciantly underdressed, wearing pretty much what he always wore: a baggy khaki uniform with no medals, the collar open at the neck; he did at least skip the corncob pipe and sunglasses. To MacArthur, the emperor appeared obviously nervous, worn down by the stresses of the past months.

The general ushered the emperor into the grand drawing room. There was a photographer waiting; MacArthur would never let such an extravaganza pass without flashbulbs. The emperor stood stiffly, while a swaggering MacArthur casually stuffed his hands in his back pockets.[60] Then MacArthur closed the doors, leaving himself alone with the emperor and a royal interpreter. Outside their American and Japanese entourages made excruciating small talk about kabuki and duck hunts.

This was the first of eleven meetings between Hirohito and MacArthur, who developed an odd, secretive rapport. With only Hirohito, MacArthur, and the court interpreter in the drawing room, their conversation was kept strictly secret; only years later would the interpreter's notes surface.[61]

MacArthur's memoirs carefully burnished the legend of the peace-loving emperor.[62] Trying to ease the agony of humiliation, the general offered a soothing cigarette, which the monarch gratefully took with shaking hands. According to MacArthur, Hirohito declared, "I come to you, General MacArthur, to offer myself to the judgment of the powers you represent as the one to bear sole responsibility for every political and military decision made and action taken by my people in the conduct of war." MacArthur claimed this moved him to the marrow, particularly since he was sure the emperor was assuming guilt for deeds for which he was not responsible.[63] Yet Hirohito's statement is nowhere to be found in the interpreter's notes and lacks plausibility. If he accepted sole responsibility, then why had he just publicly fobbed guilt off onto Tojo? Why had he not simply abdicated the throne?

The Japanese transcript, not aimed at public consumption, was hidden for decades. More plausible than a self-serving memoir, it shows the bargain clearly. MacArthur decried hateful public opinion in the United States, Britain, China, and elsewhere—unsubtly assuring the emperor that he did not seek his neck. He praised the monarch for his "very heroic" decision to end a war that could have wiped out the country and cost millions of lives. Hirohito said, "I personally wanted to do everything I could to avoid" the Pacific War, "and what I find most regrettable about myself is that war was the result." MacArthur expressed his "fullest sympathy for Your Majesty's heartfelt desire to work toward peace," adding how difficult it was for a sole person to lead against the general sentiment—exonerating Hirohito while blaming everyone else. He reassured the monarch that the final judgment would have to come from future historians and public opinion after they were both dead, thereby implicitly undermining the Allies' authority to put war criminals on trial.

Holding up his part of the bargain, Hirohito would help to implement the Potsdam Declaration, whose terms included prosecuting war criminals. "I and the Japanese people fully understand the reality of defeat," the emperor said, pledging to build a peaceful Japan. MacArthur said how impressed he was that the government, military, and people followed an imperial decision to the letter, demonstrating an authority beyond that of leaders of other nations. The emperor said that he believed that MacArthur sought to bring peace, stability, and prosperity to Asia, and prayed for his success in doing so. Both men were relieved that the occupation had gone so smoothly. In a jarring note of insubordination against the president of the United States, the five-star general said that "there are authorities above me and I am no more than a forward agency of them. I wish that I myself were in the place of those authorities."

After MacArthur bluntly mentioned that "the devastation all around is so terrible that the old feeling of Tokyo is not there," the two men ended their meeting with another round of handshakes.[64] They had made their implicit pact. One of MacArthur's aides recalls him saying that he had a fatherly feeling toward the emperor, who was over two decades his junior. "I was born a Democrat," he said, "brought up a Republican, but for me to see a man once so high now brought down so low, grieves me."[65]

One record is not in dispute: the photograph of the two men. The American photographer had snapped three shots, two of which were discarded for unregal reasons: MacArthur had blinked at the flashbulb in one, and Hirohito's mouth was open in another. The third photo was published to great sensation, instantly becoming the defining image of the occupation. In palace photographs, the emperor was angled to make him appear taller than he was; here the supreme commander towered over him. Much of MacArthur's life had been devoted to demonstrating his dominance; he had now reached the zenith. Henry Luce's *Life* magazine spitefully used the photograph with the emperor's mouth open.[66]

The image of a massive American general overawing the emperor was too much for the caretaker Japanese government, which tried to block the newspapers from printing it. For once General Headquarters decried censorship, freeing the Japanese newspapers to print the photograph a day later.[67] The American press gloated at MacArthur casually lording it over "the little Japanese emperor," the "ex-god." *The New York Times* editorialized that "the whole present Japanese regime, including the god-Emperor, will ultimately have to go," while *The New York Herald Tribune* wrote, "Either Hirohito actively authorized and supported the militarist

The sensational photograph of Emperor Hirohito standing formally alongside a looming General Douglas MacArthur at the U.S. embassy in Tokyo, September 27, 1945

policy, in which case he is a greater war criminal than Tojo, or else he was simply a passive agent in the militarists' hands, in which case, however useful he is at the moment, he will ultimately have to go, like all other dangerous anachronisms."[68]

Hirohito came away from the meeting heartened. Two days later, he summoned Kido to complain about the American people's hatred of the emperor system. He wondered whether to ignore press broadsides or fight back by speaking privately to MacArthur—convinced, correctly, that the supreme commander would take his side. Kido assured Hirohito that these American journalistic indignities did not reflect the views of the U.S. government or MacArthur. The emperor decided to bottle up his feelings and stay silent, placing his trust in MacArthur.[69]

The Implicit Deal

Immediately after the meeting with Hirohito, MacArthur's team got to work protecting him. Nobody at General Headquarters seemed inclined to probe the paradoxical image of an emperor who was purportedly too weak to stop the outbreak of the Pacific War but strong enough to bring it to an end.

To the contrary, a U.S. military intelligence major was tasked with defending Hirohito from criminal guilt for Pearl Harbor. This major was blunt about the overarching "interest of peaceful occupation and rehabilitation of Japan, prevention of revolution and communism." The major contended that Hirohito, threatened by a militarist clique, had not acted of his own free will when he approved Japan's declaration of war against the United States. He urged a search for enough evidence of fraud or duress so that the emperor could not be convicted in a democratic court, in which case he recommended taking "positive action . . . to prevent indictment and prosecution of the Emperor as a war criminal."[70]

After doing some interviews at the Imperial Palace, Bonner Fellers, who had run MacArthur's psychological warfare branch, urged MacArthur to spare Hirohito from the wrath of the Truman administration and the Soviets. "Their Emperor is the living symbol of the race in whom lies the virtues of their ancestors," he contended. "Their abject homage to him amounts to a self abnegation sustained by a religious patriotism the depth of which is incomprehensible to Westerners." The Japanese, he argued, felt that their surrender "meant preservation of the State structure, which includes the Emperor"—a reference to the *kokutai*, the national polity. "By his order seven million soldiers laid down their arms," allowing "our bloodless invasion."

Fellers warned that if Hirohito was tried for war crimes, there would be a general uprising. Quashing such a revolt would require a large expeditionary force and a prolonged occupation over an alienated, hostile nation.[71] The occupation would become alarmingly dangerous: "Except in closely guarded areas the white man would not be free from assassination."[72]

MacArthur was easily won over. Yet a few days later, Truman declared publicly that it would be a "good plan" to allow the Japanese to determine Hirohito's fate through free elections.[73]

With such threats in mind, Fellers would proceed to skew the evidence to spare the emperor. In March 1946, he would meet at General Headquarters with Admiral Yonai Mitsumasa, the former navy minister who had voted for surrender at the end of the war. Warning that the Soviets wanted to prosecute Hirohito, Fellers told the admiral that "it would be most convenient if the Japanese side could prove to us that the emperor is completely blameless. . . . Tojo, in particular, should be made to bear all responsibility at his trial."[74]

·   ·   ·

While rounding up war crimes suspects, General Headquarters was freeing the Japanese to take control of their political destiny. These reforms remain outstanding in the history of imposed liberalization for their breadth and success, exceeded only by the parallel democratization project in West Germany.

On October 4, 1945, MacArthur issued what has become famous in Japan as the civil liberties directive: lifting restrictions on freedom of assembly and speech; emptying the jails of political prisoners, including many leftists and Communists; and sweeping away the secret police that had been used to stomp out dissent.[75] To be sure, the Allies still censored criticism of the occupation and secretly muzzled books and journalism about the atomic bombs.[76] Still, this directive brought dramatic changes in Japanese politics and society, unleashing the opinions of liberals, progressives, and Communists. Japan's partly unshackled journalists blasted the wartime leadership and State Shinto—the country's official religion since the Meiji era—in terms that previously would have been suicidal.[77] One Class A war crimes suspect in Sugamo Prison recalled, "The nation, which during the hey-day of the Tojo military regime blindly shouted '*Banzai* Tojo!' and lauded the militarists, began to hate and resent Tojo once the war ended."[78] Within a few months, the Communist Party held its first rally in twenty years in Tokyo, advocating the abolition of the monarchy.[79]

The partial freeing of the press was, General Headquarters thought, a particular boon in discrediting war criminals. Imperial Japanese censorship had assiduously kept the facts of Japan's atrocities away from the Japanese public, taking particular care to cover up the Nanjing massacre, while publicizing tales of British imperial cruelty. An analyst at General Headquarters expected that the Japanese would be revolted to learn how their soldiers had really behaved: "In this instance at least, the Japanese people need no 're-education' to enable them to draw the obvious conclusions." At the start of a Yokohama trial of a Japanese officer who had tortured Allied prisoners of war, a leading conservative newspaper wrote that the Japanese were "disgraced in the eyes of the world."[80]

This thunderbolt of a directive was soon followed by the resignation of the fragile caretaker cabinet of Prince Higashikuni Naruhiko. Here Hirohito and MacArthur's secret deal went to work. The emperor delighted the Allies by selecting a well-known liberal, Baron Shidehara Kijuro, as his new prime minister. "Whatever the motives back of this oriental mind," wrote a General Headquarters staffer, "all outward deeds point to a receptive Emperor who in turn has appointed a liberal minded Prime Minister with a wide experience in Western Manners and foreign affairs."[81] In return, MacArthur protected the royal house. Although a top State Department official in Tokyo suggested arresting Prince Higashikuni as a suspected war criminal, paving the way for prosecuting other royals, MacArthur apparently scuppered the proposal. The prince was never apprehended.[82]

On October 11, General Headquarters instructed Shidehara's government to write and implement a new liberal constitution, give the vote to Japanese women, encourage labor unions, and loosen the grip of the *zaibatsu*—the powerful family enterprises which had financed and built the industrial base of Japan's war machine.[83] The Meiji constitution would be replaced with one of the great, enduring freedom charters in the world. Along with the civil liberties directive, this October 11 order would allow as profound a transformation as that of any revolution—a major step toward the impressively free country which Japan has become.

Early in November, the dissolution of the *zaibatsu* began.[84] State Shinto, which the Americans saw as a government-sponsored xenophobic force for war, would be wiped away in December.[85] Soon after, the Diet passed a progressive new union law giving workers the right to strike and bargain collectively.[86]

The apprehension of war crimes suspects, for all its partiality and injustices, was part and parcel of this grand reform enterprise. With the institutional power of the most menacing nationalists and military officers broken, the Japanese people at last had a chance to shape their own future. At root, the triumph of Japanese democracy was achieved not by General Headquarters but by the Japanese people themselves. They were the ones who debated, organized, editorialized, mobilized, participated, and voted. They denounced their wartime chieftains as—in the assessment of one Japanese admiral—bloody-minded totalitarians, putschists, and fascists.[87] Having believed the worst about the Japanese people, General Headquarters sometimes sounded taken aback to see them as they were: "The press has been unshackled, the man on the street is not afraid to speak his mind, the government is breaking away from the old traditions, a new philosophy of education is developing, political status of Japanese subjects has been broadened, and the principles of democracy are beginning to make themselves felt throughout the land."[88]

Terrible Swift Sword

Indulgent toward Hirohito, MacArthur nursed grudges against two Japanese enemies: General Yamashita Tomoyuki, the commander in chief of Japanese forces in the Philippines at the end of the war, and Lieutenant

General Homma Masaharu, who had driven MacArthur from the Philippines early in the war and whose troops had corralled their American and Filipino prisoners in the Bataan death march. "I don't think it was such a tough march," Homma once said.[89] MacArthur was haunted by his abandonment of his troops on Corregidor: in rags, wasted and pale from exhaustion and terror. He said, "I shall always seem to see a vision of grim, gaunt, ghastly men, still unafraid."[90]

Although the two generals had the stature of major war criminals—Yamashita's chief of staff would wind up as one of the defendants at the Tokyo trial—MacArthur would not let the frippery of an international tribunal impede his vengeance. Instead he gave them speedy U.S. military trials in Manila ending in slipshod convictions, which for him were a possible model for how to handle Tojo.[91]

Yamashita was a worldly and nationalistic soldier, widely seen as Japan's finest general in the Pacific.[92] He was a big, beefy man, his hair buzzed close to his scalp, with a dour expression.[93] His greatest conquest was the British stronghold of Singapore, which he had taken with an unexpected knockout strike through the dense jungles of the Malay Peninsula—a tactical coup so astonishing that some of the British nastily speculated that the Japanese had swung from tree to tree.[94] At the end of the war, his troops had cruelly fought the Filipino guerrillas, culminating in a devastating battle for Manila. From shelling and urban combat, the city was largely reduced to rubble in three weeks, damaged almost as thoroughly as Warsaw, with as many as a hundred thousand residents killed.[95] MacArthur, entering what one of his closest aides called "the dead city," was stunned: "The Manila I knew is gone."[96] He seethed at the "Tiger of Malaya," taking Yamashita's sword and sending it to West Point, his alma mater, as a memento.[97]

On September 24, MacArthur issued orders for the creation of military commissions to try accused Japanese offenders in the Philippines, with Homma and Yamashita singled out for immediate indictment. Not prepared to risk the constraints of a standard U.S. military court, MacArthur laid down regulations of rudimentary criminal procedure that took up just seven pages. These were a prosecutor's dream: swift trials, loose evidentiary rules, no appeals to anyone but the U.S. military.[98]

At such a tribunal in Manila, five U.S. generals swiftly convicted Homma for the deaths of prisoners in the Bataan death march.[99] Yamashita posed a more complex challenge: he was accused not of ordering war crimes but of unlawfully allowing his troops to commit atrocities in the Philippines in the final months of the war.[100] He got only a few days of hasty consultation with his U.S. military defense lawyers before the start of the United States' first war crimes trials for the Pacific War. A prison officer asked, "So you're the guys that have to defend these monkeys, are you?"[101]

On October 8, Yamashita was arraigned in the stately palace which had belonged to the U.S. high commissioner. Its ballroom had been repurposed as a simple military courtroom, with a view of the wreckage of Intramuros, the old walled city destroyed in the fighting. Throngs of furious Filipinos jeered at him.[102] MacArthur handpicked the five U.S. generals serving as judges, none with any judicial experience.[103] In a courtroom where almost everyone—judges, prosecutors, defense counsel, and other officials—wore the same light U.S. Army uniforms, Yamashita stuck out in his darker green Japanese army uniform, his chest covered with campaign ribbons. In vain, his lawyers asked for the charges to be dropped since his actions did not violate the laws of war. Yamashita loudly pleaded not guilty, saying that he could no more be convicted than Truman or MacArthur could be if U.S. soldiers committed atrocities: "How can I be convicted of crimes I didn't even know about?"[104]

The trial began on October 29, lasting for seven weeks, until December 5. Under fierce klieg lights for motion picture cameras, Yamashita sat stone-faced as U.S. prosecutors presented a horrific list of atrocities committed by Japanese troops under his command. Rather than proving that Yamashita had ordered or connived at these deeds, the prosecution produced almost three hundred witnesses to describe horrors: massacres at a psychiatric hospital, burning an urban neighborhood and killing the inhabitants, tortures including the "water cure," widespread rapes, slaughtering priests, even stabbing babies.[105] At one point, a sobbing Chinese woman, whose family and baby had been killed, charged at an impassive Yamashita, yelling in Chinese, "Kill that Jap."[106] A tearful, scarred eleven-year-old Filipina girl testified about how both her parents were bayoneted to death and she was stabbed repeatedly.[107]

Yamashita's able defense lawyers argued that, while formally in charge, he had been cut off from his far-flung troops across the archipelago. He had not permitted any atrocities, nor known about them.[108] Reluctantly testifying, Yamashita's eyes glinted under the floodlights, his voice confidently booming. Without proper communications, he calmly testified, all his efforts were devoted to coordinating the fight. "I found myself completely out of touch with the situation."[109] He claimed not to have known anything about abuses of civilians or prisoners of war, which strained credulity: tens of thousands of Filipino civilians had been killed over seven months in dozens of incidents across the country.[110]

Still in the racist habit of comparing the Japanese to monsters and monkeys, *Time* reported that "he looked like an ogre—a squat, shaven-headed simian figure in a green uniform."[111] A typical cartoon in *Stars and Stripes*, reprinted in *The New York Times*, showed a bucktoothed, slant-eyed Yamashita holding a baseball bat dripping with blood, saying, "Tennis game over, we shake hands now."[112] As one of Yamashita's defense lawyers later noted, Americans and Filipinos saw all Japanese officers as "'Samurai fanatics,' 'Greater East Asia exponents,' 'Empire Imperialists,' etc., whose hands dripped with the blood of helpless and innocent women and children."[113]

On the gloomy, cloudy day of December 7—four years since Pearl Harbor, timing which was hard to accept as coincidence—the five U.S. generals pronounced that if there were widespread war crimes and no effective efforts by a commander to expose and control them, then "a commander may be held responsible, even criminally liable, for the lawless acts of his troops."[114] As his interpreter whispered to Yamashita the long-expected condemnation—death by hanging, not even the military respect of a firing squad—he nodded curtly, his face impassive and his mouth puckering. In the streets of Manila, joyful crowds shouted, "Yamashita will die!"[115]

That, MacArthur thought, was that. But Yamashita's dogged defense lawyers next approached the Supreme Court of the Philippines, only to be rebuffed; the Joint Chiefs had already sternly instructed the U.S. military commission that Philippine courts had no jurisdiction.[116] Next Yamashita's lawyers went to the Supreme Court of the United States, filing a motion for leave to seek a writ of habeas corpus and to challenge the jurisdiction and authority of the Manila military commission.[117] The chief justice called the solicitor general, who called the war secretary, who cabled MacArthur, suggesting that he accede to the Court's involvement. MacArthur exploded, huffily denying that the Supreme Court had jurisdiction. The war secretary made it an order, and MacArthur backed off.[118]

The Court was a faint hope. The justices, seven of whom had been appointed by Roosevelt and one by Truman, were conspicuously deferential to the president's authority to wage war.[119] The accusation that the justices were really politicians in robes cut a little closer to the bone than usual; only one of them, Wiley Rutledge, was best known as a judge, while the others included a former senator, an attorney general, and a governor. Chief Justice Harlan Fiske Stone privately worried that Japan could be a perpetual threat to peace and was anxious that "the white race" might be "wholly eliminated from the Far East."[120] In 1942, the Court had unanimously concluded that the trial of German saboteurs by a military commission, established by an executive order by Roosevelt, was lawful.[121] In *Hirabayashi* in 1943 and *Korematsu* in 1944, the justices had not restrained the wartime executive even when anti-Japanese bigotry against loyal U.S. citizens was written in public policy. One of the Court's titans, Justice Robert Jackson, was at Nuremberg as the U.S. chief prosecutor.

Yamashita's lawyers raced to write a Supreme Court brief in about a week. They argued that their client had not been charged with a violation of the laws of war, contending that a commander had never before been convicted for the crimes of his subordinates without evidence of his participation. The Manila tribunal's procedures had been so lax that they deprived Yamashita of a fair trial, which his lawyers claimed was guaranteed to anyone held by the U.S. government under the Fifth Amendment, which provides due process to criminal defendants. Even a foreign soldier "has fundamental human rights which inhere in him simply because he is a person."[122]

When the Court heard oral arguments in early January 1946, Yamashita's defense counsel were dumbstruck to be standing alongside the solicitor general in a formal frock coat as the nine black-robed justices emerged from behind velvet curtains. One of his lawyers recalled his awe at "the world's highest apotheosis of reason and logic, this most carefully wrought human machine."[123]

Yet when the justices ruled on February 4, they gave no cause for worry to Truman or MacArthur. Stone wrote a patchwork decision that emphasized judicial restraint, particularly in military affairs. Since Congress had granted its authority to create military tribunals to the U.S. Army, the Manila court was lawful. Yet U.S. courts could not review the judgments of such military tribunals if they made a wrong decision on disputed facts; only the military could do that. Since only military authorities could review Yamashita's case, it was "unnecessary" for the Court to consider what the Fifth Amendment might require.[124] As for Yamashita's responsibility, Stone held that failing to control one's subordinates was indeed "a violation against the law of war." Since the laws of war would be pointless if officers did not restrain their troops, Stone boldly asserted that a commander had "an affirmative duty to take such measures as were within his power and appropriate in the circumstances to protect prisoners of war and the civilian population."[125]

Stone won over a comfortable majority, including Justice Felix Frankfurter, who had also joined the majority in *Korematsu*. Jackson took no part in the decisions. Only Wiley Rutledge and Frank Murphy wrote up scorching dissents. An unshaven Rutledge worked through the night twice, and later regretted not giving "as much hell in Yamashita as I wanted to."[126] He privately told Murphy, "You take the charge; I'll take the balance."[127]

The dissenters read from the bench in bitter tones. Rutledge argued that a military tribunal that violated the Fifth Amendment could have no jurisdiction to punish Yamashita. The Manila commission's procedure was so threadbare that it could only be upheld if "an enemy belligerent has no constitutional rights." At a time when the United States was championing international law, the justice argued that Yamashita's trial was a violation of the Geneva Convention of 1929, signed and ratified into U.S. law, which mandated that enemy prisoners of war could only be punished by the same procedures used for one's own troops.[128] The majority, he said, had never before ruled that any human being was beyond the Fifth Amendment's guarantee of a fair trial. "That door is dangerous to open," he said. "I will have no part in opening it."[129] He privately wrote, "I think the decision was the worst in the Court's history, not even barring Dred Scott."[130]

Murphy was a popular former governor general of the Philippines, who adored Filipinos and knew their wartime ordeal well. Yet he believed that the Bill of Rights must follow wherever the American flag went.[131] He argued simply that the Fifth Amendment applied to any person charged with a crime by the U.S. government, and the slipshod procedures of the Manila tribunal had trampled it. Denying Fifth Amendment rights to an enemy belligerent was "contrary to the whole philosophy of human rights which makes the Constitution the great living document that it is." The "immutable rights of the individual," including the kind of due process inscribed in the Fifth Amendment, "belong to every person in the world, victor or vanquished, whatever may be his race, color or beliefs."

While Stone held that U.S. courts had no jurisdiction over military tribunals, Murphy refused to be "confined by the traditional lines of review" for suspected criminals in military custody who had no access to the federal judiciary. Although the U.S. military tribunals were lawful, they could only charge suspects for violating the existing laws of war, and indicting Yamashita for failing to prevent crimes was without precedent. In essence, he wrote, the American military had fought to destroy Yamashita's control over his soldiers and then condemned him for not maintaining command of them. The vengeful indictment let the military tribunal "make the crime whatever it willed," which he witheringly called "a practice reminiscent of that pursued in certain less respected nations in recent years." Some future president of the United States and his military advisers, he warned, might be condemned by the Court's standard of command responsibility one day. The Court's precedent would be magnified infinitely, "for here we are dealing with the rights of man on an international level." He concluded by warning against "an uncurbed spirit of revenge and retribution, masked in formal legal procedure."[132]

Delighted at the Court's ruling, MacArthur rushed Yamashita to the gallows.[133] Quickly reviewing the general's dossier for clemency, he presented the novel doctrine of command responsibility as blandly unremarkable. "No new or retroactive principles of law, either national or international, are involved," he implausibly claimed.[134] Truman refused to issue a pardon.[135]

On February 23, Yamashita was hanged at a crude wooden scaffold in a small town south of Manila, wearing U.S. Army fatigues. He went to his death declaring that he had done his best to control his army, seemingly undaunted as he climbed the final thirteen steps to the gallows. His last words were, "I will pray for the Emperor's long life and his prosperity forever!"[136]

Homma followed soon, after a futile petition to the Supreme Court. To no avail, Rutledge and Murphy again dissented. Murphy decried the "obviously unconstitutional" procedures of the military trial, warning that what was done to despised enemies today could be done to others tomorrow: "Either we conduct such a trial as this in the noble spirit and atmosphere of our Constitution or we abandon all pretense to justice, let the ages slip away and descend to the level of revengeful blood purges."[137]

On April 3 in the same town near Manila, Homma was executed by a firing squad. "I am being executed for the Bataan incident," he said a few weeks before. "What I want to know is: who was responsible for the deaths of tens of thousands of innocent civilians at Hiroshima and Nagasaki? MacArthur or Truman?"[138]

Yamashita's hanging might have passed as harsh postwar vengeance if not for its wider legacies. His doom has been inscribed into the annals of national and international law, not just as the first time that the Supreme Court ruled on a convicted war criminal but as a landmark case in an international doctrine of command responsibility. That precedent has become a crucial part of the evolving law of international criminal tribunals to this day, even though one of the doctrine's legal advocates calls it "born in sin."[139]

TOKYO YEAR ZERO

Truman and MacArthur locked horns over the punishment of war criminals. For all his wrath over Bataan, MacArthur preferred swift vengeance against a small group of militarists. He quickly became skeptical of the vast scope of war crimes prosecutions that might satisfy Americans, Chinese, Filipinos, or Australians. When the Truman administration proudly suggested publishing its directive about prosecuting war criminals, MacArthur barked that such a humiliation would force him to resort to military rule.[140] The president backed off.[141]

After the first arrests in September and early October, a wary MacArthur largely stopped. His political adviser, encouraged by the meek response to the first wave of apprehensions, urged him to keep going while the Japanese public was disillusioned with their wartime leaders and had not yet turned their resentment against the Americans.[142] Yet MacArthur complained bitterly that he was acting under hazy guidance from Washington, apparently trying to slow-walk his orders. It would be indefensible, he believed, to arrest men on vague allegations of criminality only to find later that the Allies could not make a legal case against them. He testily asked the State Department for a precise list of war criminals to arrest.[143]

The Truman administration prodded MacArthur into action. Starting in November 1945, General Headquarters ordered the Japanese government to turn over hundreds of lower-ranked soldiers accused of atrocities against Allied prisoners of war.[144] MacArthur pressed to wrap up these trials as fast as possible.[145]

All the occupying Allied powers were authorized to set up their own national military tribunals for low-ranking war criminals.[146] The U.S. Eighth Army set up a streamlined military commission in Yokohama to try cases about abuse of American prisoners of war.[147] In Shanghai, another U.S. military commission gave the death penalty to five Japanese soldiers, including a major general, for strangling three captured U.S. airmen after parading them through the streets of Hankou.[148] In Manila, a U.S. tribunal sentenced to death the chief of the local Kempeitai for torturing and killing Filipinos.[149] During one of the trials at Yokohama, a Japanese witness reenacted the beheading of an American B-29 pilot from Colorado, demonstrating to the military judges how a sword was wetted with water and then brought chopping down on a human's bared neck.[150]

The Truman administration hounded MacArthur with more than seventy names of major war criminals accused of crimes against peace and other war crimes, including several men who would wind up as defendants at the Tokyo trial.[151] MacArthur restarted the arrests, ordering Japan's government to seize slews of senior wartime leaders, including General Matsui Iwane, the commander of the troops that had carried out the Nanjing massacre.[152] One former commander of Japan's renegade

Kwantung (Guandong) Army ritually disemboweled himself rather than face trial, but the others went quietly into prison.[153]

Two days later, these incarcerated Japanese leaders got a preview of their future from Nuremberg. Justice Robert Jackson delivered a magnificent opening address, excoriating twenty-four top leaders of Nazi Germany: from Hermann Göring, the powerful Reichsmarschall; to Rudolf Hess, Adolf Hitler's deputy; to Julius Streicher, the Jew-hating propagandist.[154] Jackson declared, "Civilization asks whether law is so laggard as to be utterly helpless to deal with crimes of this magnitude by criminals of this order of importance."[155]

The dragnet closed in on the Imperial Palace. Australia wanted the emperor prosecuted as a war criminal, and royal courtiers in Tokyo feared that China would do the same.[156] Rumors about the emperor's abdication became so prevalent that Hirohito himself let it be known that he was aware of the question.[157]

Prince Konoe Fumimaro, a prominent former prime minister who had close ancestral links to the royal family, made the blacklist in part because of his ties to the palace.[158] Awkwardly, he was the Imperial Palace's choice to draft a new constitution. Although Konoe had struggled to prevent Pearl Harbor and in early 1945 had secretly begged the emperor to end the war before the *kokutai* was destroyed by a leftist revolution, he was better known in Allied countries as the prime minister who had invaded China in 1937.[159]

The Truman administration was still actively considering putting the emperor on trial. For New Dealers who wanted to uproot Japan's wartime political system, the continuing success of the occupation should eventually render the emperor disposable. On November 30, the State, War, and Navy Departments ordered MacArthur to collect evidence, although discreetly. They secretly instructed him, "The US Government's position is that Hirohito is not immune from arrest, trial and punishment as a War Criminal."[160]

In December, General Headquarters issued more sweeping lists of names for the Japanese government to arrest. In addition to the usual assortment of generals, admirals, and ministers, this slate for the first time included a prince of the imperial family: the elderly Prince Nashimoto Morimasa, who was a field marshal.[161] Japanese newspapers rushed out special editions to cover the arrests, with sympathetic press coverage for the prince.[162] Although the prince would eventually be freed, his detention was a jolt for the nation—showing that the royal house might be targeted. Seeing a newspaper photograph of the prince with a blanket being brought to prison, Konoe, an ardent monarchist, exploded: "They have freedom of speech and freedom of press, and look how indiscreetly these newspapers use it! Does not the government do anything when an imperial prince is imprisoned? The way things are, the government would do nothing even if the Emperor were arrested!"[163]

Marquis Kido Koichi, Hirohito's closest adviser, realized that he was probably on the Allied lists—another step closer to indicting the emperor himself. In order to protect the monarch, he made preparations to resign as lord keeper of the privy seal.[164] Feeling his days shorten, he made a solemn pilgrimage southwestward from Tokyo to the Ise Shrine, in Mie Prefecture, to give thanks to the Shinto sun goddess Amaterasu—purportedly the direct ancestor of Hirohito.[165] He withdrew into himself, staying home, quietly reading books, going for walks. At last, on December 6, he was listening to the radio when he heard that his name was on a new list of a dozen senior Japanese to be arrested.[166] His old friend Konoe was also named, bringing the American investigations perilously deep inside the court. Kido wrote in his diary, "Since I was prepared for it, I heard the news with unconcern."[167]

In secret, Kido held an unmatched prize for the Allies: he had kept a diary since 1930, with each daily entry—almost six thousand of them—written on the same day or in a few cases a day later. He knew that the diary had plenty of passages that "might cause trouble for His Majesty." Should he burn it or use it for his own defense? As Kido later noted, some of Hirohito's loyalists wanted to assert that the emperor had known nothing about what the military had done during the war, covering up all documentation to the contrary. But such claims of complete royal ignorance were scarcely plausible, Kido reckoned, and the diary might show the emperor as a force for peace. In his last hours of freedom, "I wore myself out thinking about all these things." Encouraged by MacArthur's successful meeting with the emperor, Kido decided that his diary was "the only documentation that would win acceptance of the emperor system."[168]

Kido turned himself in voluntarily a few days later, arriving at Sugamo Prison in style in a black limousine bearing the imperial crest.[169] He stunned the Americans by informing them about his diary, which he turned over without protest. This vast tract of the innermost workings of the Japanese government would guide the prosecution throughout the Tokyo trial.[170] His fellow defendants were horrified to discover that their secret deliberations had been documented and turned over to the enemy.[171]

With the arrest of Prince Nashimoto and warrants out for Kido and Konoe, Japanese leaders had a sense of a process spinning out of control.

Where would this stop? Who was next? Would the emperor be thrown in jail?

In fact, General Headquarters had had enough. MacArthur's political adviser knew that senior Japanese politicians were so alarmed that they might stop cooperating with the occupiers. He urged the supreme commander to privately tell Shidehara, the prime minister, that the arrests of major war criminals were in general finished. MacArthur, who had not wanted to do the December round of arrests, needed no exhortations to stop.[172]

Konoe, seeing himself as a lonely peacemaker who had been reviled by Tojo Hideki, was stung to be labeled as a war criminal. His record was rich in complexities: despite his leading role in the invasion of China, he had resisted attacking the United States, only to be replaced as prime minister by Tojo, who loathed him.[173] Secluded now at his country villa in the wintry cold, he asked if international law allowed the victors to try the vanquished. He drank heavily. When his confidants urged him to use his own trial to defend the emperor, he replied bitterly that the Americans were not interested in proving guilt. He told a friend that General Headquarters was overrun with Jews who were seeking to destroy the imperial family, and that MacArthur's team seemed to be plotting a Communist takeover of Japan.[174]

In the early hours of December 16, the day that Konoe was supposed to turn himself in at the Omori prison camp, he drank potassium cyanide.

The spectacular suicide of one of the most prominent politicians in Japan hardened the resolve of MacArthur and others at General Headquarters against more arrests. Yet the Japanese issued their own judgments against their former prime minister. The liberal *Asahi Shimbun* condemned Konoe for not taking responsibility for the China war and not standing up against the militarists.[175] The *Mainichi Shimbun* scorched him for invading China and allying with Nazi Germany, while searchingly noting that Japan's people shared in that responsibility.[176]

In a hastily penciled suicide note left with his son, Konoe admitted "many political faults, for which I feel deep responsibility. But I never thought that I should be tried at an American court as a war criminal." Feeling responsible for the China quagmire, he wrote that he had strained to avoid war with the United States. General Headquarters censored out his stinging last words: "The excitement and exasperation resulting from the war, presumptuous overdoings of the victors, excess humiliation of the defeated, malicious calumnies, rumors and canards based on misunderstandings, etc.—all of them constitute the public opinion which, however, will sooner or later resume calmness and normality. And it will be at that very hour that a fair judgment based on justice be passed on my case at the Court of God."[177]

THE TRIAL THAT NEVER WAS

As the Allies prepared to prosecute the major war crimes suspects, MacArthur hoped to convict the convalescing Tojo before anyone in Washington could saddle him with an unwieldy international court. His preferred model was the U.S. military tribunal which had swiftly hanged Yamashita. On October 7, MacArthur asked the Truman administration to authorize him to proceed with the trial of Tojo.[178]

The White House yanked back hard on his leash. After all, Nuremberg, which was about to issue its indictment, was an international court; the United States wanted uniformity in Tokyo.[179] MacArthur was ordered not to do anything until after seeing John McCloy, the assistant secretary of war and a Stimson confidant, who was due in Tokyo in about ten days.[180] When McCloy arrived, MacArthur outlined his plan for a U.S. tribunal to swiftly try Tojo and his cabinet for the Pearl Harbor attack. McCloy told MacArthur to hold off, explaining that Truman was about to approve the appointment of a special U.S. prosecutor at an international tribunal which would handle Tojo.[181] Thwarted, MacArthur urged McCloy to reconsider.[182]

The Truman administration argued that an international trial would encompass the suffering of U.S. allies and would diffuse the responsibility for victors' justice.[183] The State Department sent MacArthur a new directive for an international court, guaranteed to appall him. The United States' clout would be diluted, equal to that of Britain, China, and the Soviet Union, with participation from France, Holland, Australia, Canada, and New Zealand. The Philippines, a nation which MacArthur adored, was excluded.[184] Fellers stoked MacArthur's suspicions, warning darkly of Soviet schemes and American Jewish influence, dyspeptically explaining that the Washington bureaucracy was more interested in punishing top Nazi war criminals despite complaints from the U.S. military that most offenses against Americans had been committed by the Japanese.[185]

MacArthur urgently pressed to proceed without further delay with a trial for Tojo and his cabinet members for Pearl Harbor. He proposed charging them with illegally attacking the United States without a declaration of war, "causing the murder of nationals of a country with which their nation was still at peace." This notion that the Americans killed at Pearl Harbor had been murdered would hang over the rest of the Tokyo trial. Although Tojo's cabinet had also struck the British and Dutch Empires at the same time as Pearl Harbor, MacArthur wrote, "I believe the commission for trial should be composed of United States personnel as the offense was solely against the United States."[186]

Boxing MacArthur in, Truman named a U.S. chief prosecutor for Japanese war criminals accused of the Class A offense of waging a war of aggression. At Nuremberg, all four Allied powers—the United States, the Soviet Union, Britain, and France—could name a chief prosecutor; at Tokyo, only the United States' man would be chief prosecutor, helped out by associate prosecutors from the other powers. Joseph Keenan, a former United States assistant attorney general in charge of the Justice Department's criminal division, was a Truman crony with nothing like the stature, intellect, or integrity of his opposite number at Nuremberg, Justice Robert Jackson of the Supreme Court.[187] Beefy in his wide-lapeled suits and polka-dot bow ties, with thick cheeks and pudgy fingers and his gray hair swept back, Keenan cut an imposing figure. But he proved to be a florid and ineffective operator, ignorant about Asia and suffering from an alcoholism that became the talk of the court.[188] The top British diplomat in Japan privately called him "an ambitious but inefficient and vulgar man," hectoring toward others, often visibly "very much the worse for drink."[189] Through this thoughtless choice, Truman squandered American influence over the Tokyo trial.[190]

Since MacArthur had thoroughly worn out the Joint Chiefs of Staff with his objections, the new secretary of war, Robert Patterson, informed him of Keenan's appointment, although officially he would be appointed by MacArthur and serve on his staff.[191] With increasing irritation, the Joint Chiefs lectured MacArthur that the United States' official position was that Tojo and other Class A war crimes suspects should face an international tribunal. He was, though, authorized to launch trials of suspects accused of conventional war crimes, known as Class B, or crimes against humanity, designated as Class C.[192]

With mounting anger, MacArthur claimed that he wanted to prosecute Tojo not for aggression but for conventional war crimes, treating him as a Class B war criminal. This was bunk. If the Americans at Pearl Harbor had been murdered, that could only be because the attack was illegitimate—in which case the real crime was aggression, a Class A offense. "I reaffirm my most earnest conviction that one of the gravest possible psychological mistakes will be made in not permitting the immediate trial of this group," he exhorted. "It is self evident that no international action can be obtained here in the near future. This case should beyond all doubt be the first trial in Japan."[193]

Finally, MacArthur had to be slapped down by Truman himself—twice, in fact, since the first cuff didn't do the job. The first presidential rap came through Patterson, who informed MacArthur that Truman himself had decided that the prosecution of major Japanese war criminals would be handled by Keenan at an international tribunal: "This, I feel certain, is the desire of the President and the Department of Justice."[194]

Given an order from the president of the United States, MacArthur ignored it. After a few days of stony silence, Patterson wrote back to ask frostily when he might be favored with a reply.[195] MacArthur protested against the "grave injustice" of snubbing his own war crimes office in General Headquarters: "I do not believe that either the President or the Department of Justice if they understood the facts in the case would contemplate such action."[196]

The second rebuke from Truman was delivered by McCloy. After his visit to Tokyo, the assistant secretary of war had made the rounds in Washington explaining MacArthur's case for an American trial of Tojo. Truman had been unyielding, he reported: "The State Department and the President adhere to the position that they wish to call upon the other powers to take part in the trial of Tojo and the Cabinet." As McCloy explained the president's thinking, "we have set out on a path of establishing *international* responsibility for the type of conspiracy which resulted in the attacks on Poland by Germany and on Pearl Harbor and the Malay by Japan." Joining with the Allies, Truman believed in a global vision of outlawing war.[197]

Unable to block Keenan, MacArthur instead moved to co-opt him. He got a weary Patterson to confirm that the chief prosecutor would be "an independent agency serving directly under my immediate command," promising him "the maximum latitude and support."[198] When Keenan arrived in Tokyo on December 6, MacArthur launched a charm offensive, buttering him up as a "delightful gentleman."[199]

MacArthur quickly found that Truman had chosen a fussy, ostentatious man without much backbone. Keenan sought to prove himself a team player at General Headquarters, hinting broadly that he would accommodate his work to the grander project of building a self-governing Japan.[200] Throughout the trial, Keenan would truckle to MacArthur, privately praising his "inspiring" work in guiding the Japanese to understand democracy.[201] Later, when MacArthur was planning his ill-starred run for president of the United States, Keenan would obligingly send him the dates of Republican primary elections from New York to South Dakota.[202]

Above all, MacArthur wanted to keep American control of the court. Keenan agreed, seeking a fast-moving court drawn up largely by the United States, with the other Allies invited to take it as it was.[203] The State Department proposed a bench of nine judges, representing the Allied countries which had signed the surrender aboard the *Missouri*. China, Britain, France, Holland, and Australia quickly joined up.[204] Instead of the swift, narrow American trial that MacArthur had wanted, the Truman administration had chosen a vast trial whose reach would span all the wartime controversies of Asia.

CHAPTER 7

"When the Emperor Violates the Law"

M EI RUAO WAS AN ideal person to build a new China. He was a brilliant scholar and jurist with an unlimited future. With a strong jaw and neatly slicked-back hair, he favored urbane Western-style suits and round spectacles. Embarrassed at his youth as he rose fast, he sported a mustache to appear older. For modernizers hoping to propel a vulnerable China forward, he was exactly the sort of citizen required: rooted in his national traditions, superbly educated, curious about the outside world. In an old black-and-white photo—in a Republic of China file moldering in an archive in the lush hinterlands of sprawling Taipei—his gaze at the camera is direct and serious, as if braced for what is to come. His life, and even his afterlife, would span China's harrowing twentieth century.

The vindication of China's wartime suffering fell to Mei as its judge at the Tokyo trial. The only non-Western nation in the first rank of Allied powers, China was the sole Asian government guaranteed to lead in the punishment of Japanese criminality.[1] In 1944, the Allies had set up a commission to gather evidence of Japanese war crimes, based in the wartime Nationalist Chinese capital of Chongqing.[2] China charged forward with its own prosecutions of lower-level Japanese war criminals.

After the arrests of major Japanese leaders, including General Matsui Iwane, who was notorious for commanding Japan's troops in China during the bloody crushing of Nanjing, General Douglas MacArthur widened the prosecution of war criminals into an international effort. On September 21, 1945, General Headquarters asked the Allies—especially the leading powers of China, the Soviet Union, and Britain—to propose suitable officials to staff the new international military tribunal, to be approved by MacArthur.[3]

Mei, a quicksilver young star of the Republic of China, would become a crucial figure at the Tokyo trial. More than anyone, he would ensure that the tribunal's verdicts and final judgment would weigh the suffering of Asians, rather than merely condemning aggression against the United States as MacArthur would have preferred. Balancing his personal and national fury with his responsibilities as an international judge, he would shrewdly rally his fellow judges to convict and hang the Japanese officials responsible for the slaughter in Nanjing and elsewhere in China. Yet as Mei toiled in Tokyo, his country was being torn apart by civil war between the Nationalists and Communists. Soon he would have to choose between them.

MEANS OF ASCENT

Mei Ruao was born in 1904 in a suburban village near the city of Nanchang in the humid southeastern province of Jiangxi. Like many peasants, he took his family name from that of his village. The son of a farmer, he grew up in modest circumstances but with overwhelming expectations. His father, who cared deeply about education, could barely scrape together enough money to send one of his nine children to school; as the eldest son, little Ruao was the elect. Driven by his father, he studied at the forward-looking Jiangxi Model Primary School, doing so well that at the age of twelve he won a coveted place at Tsinghua College in faraway Beijing.

Tsinghua (Qinghua), today China's premier university for engineering, was then more like an elite finishing school. With a regimented, military-style schedule, the school was a shock for a homesick boy from the provinces. He arrived amid revolutionary ferment, only a few years after the Republic of China swept away the decrepit Qing dynasty. Speaking a dialect, he struggled to learn the proper Mandarin required for higher learning. Worse, many of the classes were taught in English, which most of the students spoke, but which was completely unfamiliar to him. He rose at dawn to recite extra lessons near a lotus pond. With grueling effort, he excelled in his classes, became editor of the school newspaper, and founded a progressive organization along with several classmates who became early members of the Chinese Communist Party and prominent government leaders.[4]

"He was very strict with himself," remembers his son, Mei Xiaoao, a

Mei Ruao, the Chinese judge, outside the former Army Ministry where the Tokyo trial was being held

personable man with spiky gray hair who works as an editor at an official newspaper. "He wanted to achieve something." Tsinghua aimed to send its graduates to study in the United States, and in 1924, Mei Ruao for the first time left China to study at Stanford. He graduated magna cum laude and Phi Beta Kappa and followed that with a law degree from the University of Chicago in 1928.

There are few details available about his American years, but he had good reasons to be wary of the United States. Despite its protestations about the inalienable rights of all men, the United States had held extraterritorial rights in China like any other wolfish European empire. Chinese people had been explicitly barred by nationality from the United States in the Chinese Exclusion Act of 1882; that discriminatory law was then extended, remaining in effect well into World War II. In another racist law, the United States in 1917 banned immigration from anyone born in countries in an "Asiatic Barred Zone," except for Japanese and Filipinos.[5] Yet despite all that, Mei's American sojourn left him with an abiding fondness for the country, its constitutional system, and its people, whom he warmly admired as friendly, open, fair, well educated, democratic, scientific, and efficient, although sometimes childishly naïve.[6] The politically awkward fact of his American affections is blotted out of Chinese remembrances of him today.

Alongside school friends from Tsinghua who were also studying in the

United States, he agitated for revolution among other Chinese foreign students, as well as earnestly setting up a research group on the theories of Sun Yat-sen (Sun Yixian), the revolutionary Nationalist who led the founding of the Republic of China. After finishing up at Chicago, Mei broadened his horizons with a European grand tour of London, Paris, Berlin, and Moscow, bookishly auditing classes in universities there. By the time he returned to China in 1929 after almost five thrilling years abroad, he had grown into a confident and sophisticated young man, well read in national and international journals, fond of Chinese opera, dedicated to tai chi for exercise, kindly and gently humorous.[7]

Mei believed that China's government had solemn duties to its people. "I feel that politics in China has always been passive," he later wrote in his diary. "As long as no one is staging an uprising and attempting to overthrow the Emperor, then it's called a peaceful and prosperous time. As for the education and hygiene of the people, that was left to their own fortune and their own efforts."[8] Working to educate the nation, he launched himself on a splendid academic career as a law professor at Nankai University and then Wuhan University. He taught and published on everything from U.S. and British law to the Napoleonic Code to Soviet revolutionary tribunals, as well as the constitutional debates raging in the Republic of China.[9]

His guiding light was the rule of law, which he saw as crucial for the new China's progress. Mei expounded his philosophy of law in 1932 in a heartfelt article composed in hard-won, elegant English. Anticipating some of his thinking at the Tokyo trial, he laid out a theory of natural law and called for individual criminal responsibility. He argued for accountable, progressive government under law—an ideal which would cause him to run afoul first of the ruling Nationalists and eventually the Communists.

Mei argued that Chinese law was made up of two supplementary strands: *fa*, which he compared to positive law, dealing primarily with criminal justice; and *li*, typically applied to civil conduct, often taken to mean convention or moral discipline, but which he provocatively suggested was equivalent to natural law. He contended, "To a Chinese a violation of *li* was even more serious and more shameful than a violation of law." When natural law alone could not maintain a peaceful society, it had to be given coercive power through positive law—resulting in a comprehensive system of criminal law evolving through successive dynasties. Decades before the famous debate between Lon Fuller and H. L. A. Hart over legal positivism, Mei made a case for a fundamental moral foundation for legal order.[10]

Mei believed that Confucian philosophy built a rule of law which rested on both positive law and natural law. For him, the Confucian ideal was to transcend the need for law by using education and moral discipline to harmoniously resolve the divisive disputes that curdled into litigation or crime. The broader progress of society, he wrote, comprised "the great emphasis laid by the Chinese, both in theory and in practice, on the rule of law."

He asserted proudly that "the principle of Equality before the Law" was a leading feature of China's legal system since the early eighteenth century, although in practice potentates had often defied the law. "It was a popular maxim in China that 'when the emperor violates the law, he will be punished like a common citizen.' . . . This maxim was known to every Chinese and was deeply ingrained in the Chinese consciousness." Mei stood in the tradition of Mencius, who had written centuries ago that a tyrant could be punished as a common thief or a felon.[11]

Mei would be entirely consistent when he later argued in Tokyo that Emperor Hirohito should have joined his underlings in the dock.[12] Japanese prime ministers, including Tojo Hideki, would find their fate in the hands of the judge who had written: "The prime minister was subject to the same rule of law as an ordinary plowman."[13]

"Great Aspirations"

Mei rose as his country fell. As he was formulating his legal philosophy in September 1931, Japanese troops marched into Manchuria—eight years before Nazi Germany's invasion of Poland would begin World War II.[14]

China fought back with what Generalissimo Chiang Kai-shek, the austere and calculating Nationalist leader, called "a long war of attrition."[15] The most basic numbers are beyond comprehension. Some fourteen million Chinese would die in the war, with perhaps eighty million people displaced from their homes. Even controlling for the enormous size of China's population—then about four hundred million—the country's suffering was roughly proportional to that of the Soviet Union or Poland.[16] Some scholars put the toll at twenty to thirty million Chinese dead.[17]

In wartime, Mei's conspicuous talents attracted the attention of the Nationalist government. In 1934, despite some private misgivings, he joined the Kuomintang (Guomindang), the National People's Party led by Chiang. Groomed for greatness, he was sponsored for party membership by Sun Ke (also known as Sun Fo), a top government official who was the son of Sun Yat-sen. Mei's personnel file extolled his character: "Upright ideologies, great aspirations and bearings, capable and experienced, dignified and elegant presence, talkative, sociable, erudite, with much to offer in the subject of social sciences." This file cryptically added that his sole imperfection was "mediocre virtues."[18]

Basking in the patronage of the Nationalists, Mei taught American, British, and international law at the Central School of Politics, an elite academy training senior civil servants. He served the Ministry of Judicial Administration by training judges, was appointed legal adviser to the Interior Ministry, and was named editor of a journal of international politics which advocated resistance to Japanese aggression. He became a legislator in the Legislative Yuan in the capital city of Nanjing, eventually rising to be acting chair of its foreign affairs committee.[19]

As Mei explained in an influential Shanghai journal, he saw himself as part of a century-old reform movement which, since the searing experience of the first Opium War, held that China could only withstand the onslaught of British and Japanese imperialism by learning from Western civilization, particularly constitutional government. At a time when many were tempted by party dictatorship, he argued that German- or Italian-style fascism was unlikely to succeed in China. Instead, championing a Nationalist proposal to secure "the Fundamental Rights and Duties of the People," he argued that constitutional government would help make China "a full-fledged modern State" by establishing "the Rule of Law."[20]

In July 1937, after a clash between Chinese and Japanese troops at the centuries-old Marco Polo Bridge on the outskirts of Beijing, Imperial Japan launched a massive invasion of the rest of China.[21] For over four years, the Chinese would fight almost entirely alone, until the Japanese attack on Pearl Harbor brought the United States into the war. Its government was led through the war by Chiang, whom Martha Gellhorn, the American war reporter, found "immensely intelligent, gracious and I thought inhuman." His "will to power was a thing like stone; it was a solid separate object which you felt in the room."[22]

Despite Chiang's disdain for the "Japanese dwarfs," their military was far more modernized and better equipped, outfitted with armor, artillery, and bombers.[23] They swept into Beijing (then temporarily called Beiping), Tianjin, and the crucial port city of Shanghai. The battle for Shanghai, which drew global attention to Chinese resistance, was the bloodiest since Verdun or the Somme.[24] Victorious, the Japanese mostly maintained the French Concession there but, as the visiting British poet W. H. Auden and novelist Christopher Isherwood noted months afterward, reduced the Chinese neighborhoods to a "cratered and barren moon-landscape."[25] Weeks into the invasion, Japanese bombers began pounding the Nationalist capital at Nanjing, keeping it up for months. Chiang and his government were forced to flee westward. Chinese troops were ordered to abandon the capital. On December 13, in a thunder of artillery and machine guns, the great city fell.[26]

For a month, Japanese troops marauded through Nanjing in a campaign of massacre, rape, arson, and looting. Many Chinese soldiers, hoping to save their lives, gave up their weapons even before the Japanese entered the city; yet huge numbers of these unarmed men were rounded up and killed.[27] In practice, almost any Chinese man could become a target. Some Japanese soldiers, apparently confident that their deeds would meet with approval back home, sent snapshots to their loved ones of beaming Japanese troops alongside naked Chinese women, or of Japanese soldiers swinging swords at the necks of Chinese prisoners.[28] In the hospital, a little boy, perhaps seven years old, died from four bayonet wounds.[29] Sexual violence was shockingly pervasive.[30] As one Chinese doctor wrote, "Streets turned red, and corpses obstructed the currents of the river."[31]

The atrocities, although abated in scale, continued for half a year. This was neither a chaotic spree nor a berserker fury; Japanese officers boasted of their firm hand over their men, reinforced by prominent visits from senior officers, including General Matsui Iwane.[32] The early estimates by Western observers reckoned a death toll of forty thousand, and account-

Displaced Chinese civilians gathered to receive relief funding at the headquarters of the International Committee for the Nanking Safety Zone, set up by foreigners to shelter civilians from Japanese troops. The worst massacres were over, but killing still continued in Nanjing when this photograph was taken in February 1938.

ing based on burials soon pushed the number closer to two hundred thousand. Today the Chinese government promulgates an official figure of three hundred thousand dead, while Japanese extremists falsely deny that there was a massacre at all. Yet there is no serious doubt that Nanjing was one of the cardinal horrors of World War II.[33]

Japanese forces swept as far inland as Shanxi, Henan, and Hunan provinces, as well as parts of the south. Because Japan had a policy of treating the China campaign as an "incident" rather than a war, its troops treated captured Chinese not as prisoners of war entitled to lawful protection but as "bandits," with large numbers of them killed or harshly mistreated. Chinese civilians were rounded up and used for labor.[34] Rape was widespread and institutionalized across occupied China, with 280 "comfort stations" set up throughout the country for the sexual gratification of Japanese soldiers.[35] From January 1938, Japan refused to deal with the Nationalists, calling both for the extirpation of Chiang's government and the creation of a "new order" in Asia.[36] In 1941, Japan began a devastating counterinsurgency campaign against mostly Communist base areas, known as the "three alls" policy: kill all, burn all, loot all. To root out guerrillas real or imagined, villages were burned, crops torched, and countless men killed.[37]

For years, Chiang went so far as to accuse Japan of what today would be called genocide, warning that Japan "is bent upon the destruction of our country and the extermination of our race," or denouncing "the Japanese design to exterminate our race."[38] This overheated accusation would not make it into the indictment or judgment at the Tokyo trial. Still, demanding that "Japanese bandits" not go unpunished, he paved the way for war crimes trials by speaking of "the vital importance of . . . honoring treaties and international law."[39]

Some of the direst calamities of the war came from an infernal combination of Japanese assault and Chinese misgovernment.[40] To hold off Japanese troops, Chiang's government made a frantic and callous decision to blow open the dikes of the Yellow River in central China, unleashing a flood which spread disease and starvation that proved lethal for as many as half a million Chinese peasants.[41] Worst of all was a terrible famine in Henan province starting in 1942, sparked by new wartime taxes paid in grain.[42] The resulting starvation ultimately claimed some four million lives. "In the Henan famine area, people are starving, dogs and animals are eating corpses," wrote a shocked Chiang in his diary.[43]

China's ordeal won widespread Allied sympathy. Henry Luce, the son of American missionaries in China, used his clout as publisher of *Time* and *Life*—with a combined wartime circulation of some five million—to

extol China and Chiang.[44] The U.S. War Department got the director Frank Capra to devote one of the propaganda films in his *Why We
Fight* series to the Chinese resistance. His film, seen by some four million
Americans, glorified China as an ancient, peaceful, and freedom-loving
republic beset by the fanatical legions of Japan's god-emperor. It made an
appeal to American sensibilities that was literally Capraesque: blurring
Sun Yat-sen's ideals with those of George Washington and Abraham Lincoln.[45] W. H. Auden, having braved Japanese bombing raids on his tour
of Shanghai, Nanchang, and other cities in southern China, composed
elegiac sonnets: "maps can really point to places/ Where life is evil now./
Nanking. Dachau."[46]

Mei's parents and grandparents, like millions of other Chinese civilians, escaped into the interior. Soon before the Japanese stormed Nanjing,
Mei had to flee inland with the remainder of the Nationalist government.[47] He arrived at the wartime provisional capital at Chongqing, in the
humid, foggy mountains of Sichuan province. But this was no safe haven,
with the ill-defended city—swollen with desperate hordes of displaced
people—suffering some of the worst Japanese bombardment of the war.
From February 1938 to August 1943, concentrated bombing would claim
some twelve thousand Chinese lives, almost all of them civilians. The
Japanese used fragmentation and incendiary bombs, which blew people
to pieces and spread wildfires throughout the city. Residents lived in terror of air raid sirens and the drone of Japanese warplanes, shaken by the
ear-shattering crash of incoming Japanese bombs and Chinese antiaircraft
fire.[48]

"In Chongqing, there was terrible bombing," remembers Mei Ruao's
daughter, Mei Xiaokan, a successful lawyer. "They often had to flee to
shelters. So he hated the Japanese invasion." His son, Mei Xiaoao, notes
that his father did not like to talk about the war, but other relatives who
were with him in Chongqing had horrific memories. Refugees unaccustomed to the steamy Sichuan climate perished from infectious diseases.
People tried to hide from the bombers in caves bored into the rocky
cliffs.[49] "Many people died in the caves because there were too many
people and not enough oxygen," Mei Xiaoao says, in what seems to be a
cleaned-up version of a grimmer reality: people were sometimes trampled
in the stampede to reach shelter. "Some died because buildings fell on
them because of the bombing."

There was one wartime consolation in battered Chongqing: a friend
introduced Mei Ruao to a capable, perfectionist, studious young woman
from a small town. She had wanted to go to university, but as part of
a large family, had no chance to do so; she had managed to go to high

school in Shanghai. She was working as a bank teller; to meet her, Mei's friend sent him to pretend to open a bank account. They would later marry and then after the war have two children, setting a cerebral example for them. "He didn't push us to study," recalls Mei Xiaokan, "but he was reading all the time."

THE FOURTH POLICEMAN

After Pearl Harbor, *Life* provided its readers with a racist's guide on "how to tell Japs from the Chinese," so that Americans seeking to beat up Japanese Americans would be able to "distinguish friendly Chinese from enemy alien Japs." Luce's magazine contrasted a photograph of a glowering Tojo Hideki with one of a benevolent Chinese economics minister: "His complexion is parchment yellow, his face long and delicately boned, his nose more finely bridged." "Chinese wear rational calm of tolerant realists," *Life* explained. "Japs, like General Tojo, show humorless intensity of ruthless mystics."[50]

Finally entering World War II, the United States saw China as crucial to winning the war and then the postwar.[51] The vast, impoverished country proved to be a sinkhole for the Japanese invaders, who had poured in roughly a million troops with no end in sight. The Allied strategic nightmare was that a weary Chinese government would cut a separate peace with Japan or simply collapse; Japan could then turn its full power against the Americans. For four years after Pearl Harbor, it was China's desperate, dogged resistance that made it possible for the Allies to advance on other European and Pacific fronts.[52]

Envisioning the globe after the war was won, the Americans hoped to see a renewed China replace Japan as a dominant power in Asia. China—a non-European, non-white, anticolonialist country—would stand alongside the United States, Britain, and the Soviet Union as one of Franklin Delano Roosevelt's "four policemen" guaranteeing postwar order.[53] For Winston Churchill, an ardent enthusiast for the British Empire, that fixation on an anticolonialist China was "the great illusion."[54] Chiang himself recognized the wishfulness of American thinking. "China is the weakest of the four Allies," he noted, acidly assessing his partners. "It's as if a weak person has met a kidnapper, a hooligan, and a bully."[55]

The Americans supplied and trained China's ragtag armies, pouring in military and economic aid. In 1943, the Roosevelt administration signed a treaty relinquishing U.S. extraterritorial rights in China, while securing China a spot as one of the four great powers calling for a new world organization to undergird a postwar peace.[56] At the White House's urging,

Congress began to dismantle the laws barring Chinese immigration and naturalization, allowing a small quota of Chinese into the United States.[57]

Behind closed doors, the Roosevelt and Truman administrations were frustrated at Chiang's corrupt, ineffectual, and autocratic government, and its ill-trained and sometimes mutinous armies. Still, Chiang was invited to join Roosevelt and Churchill at the Cairo conference in late 1943, which laid out a vision for postwar Asia. His was conspicuously the only non-white face among the Allied chiefs. At an old Giza hotel with a view of the Pyramids, he pressed for a postwar liberation from European imperialism, winning genial support from Roosevelt and fuming opposition from Churchill.[58] The generalissimo secured Roosevelt's agreement that all lands seized by Japan from China should be returned, including Manchuria and Formosa (Taiwan).[59] After leaving Cairo, Chiang highlighted the Allied agreements for "the punishment of war criminals in the East and West."[60]

Throughout the war, China was the most anticolonialist voice among the Allies, frequently clashing with the British. Chiang rallied Asian peoples against Western and Japanese imperialism alike.[61] Soon after Pearl Harbor, he visited India to urge Jawaharlal Nehru and other freedom campaigners to join with China in building an anti-imperialist Asia.[62] He urged Roosevelt to get Britain and Holland to promise independence for their colonies, as the United States had already done for the Philippines—the only real way, Chiang argued, to secure the support of colonized Asians for the Allied war effort.[63]

In early 1944, Japan launched a vast new offensive to knock China out of the war.[64] By one plausible estimate, at least a hundred thousand, and probably a quarter of a million, Asian noncombatants were perishing every month in the final year of the war. Among them, a hundred thousand Chinese could have been dying monthly.[65]

RED STAR OVER CHINA

For Chiang Kai-shek, there were really two wars: against enemies foreign and domestic. In addition to the Japanese, his Nationalists were waging a bitter fight against the Chinese Communists, which was spiraling toward civil war.[66] The generalissimo denounced the Communists as subversive opportunists hijacking Sun Yat-sen's revolution, jackals claiming credit for the military achievements of Nationalist China's army, and fanatics promoting Soviet policies which had cost hundreds of thousands of Soviet lives and would claim millions of Chinese.[67]

For a decade, Chiang sought to wipe out "the Communist-bandits" before the Japanese threat forced him into a precarious truce in 1937.[68] To resist the Japanese, the Communists fought under the nominal authority of the Nationalists in an uneasy national effort.[69] Yet to the generalissimo, the Chinese Communists remained at least as much a menace as the Japanese or their Chinese collaborators.[70]

With Japan's invasion, Mao Zedong, previously only one of the prominent Communist leaders, established himself as paramount.[71] The Communists matched the Nationalists in excoriating the Japanese invaders.[72] In the years of the united front, Communist official media often recycled news articles about Japanese atrocities from the Nationalists' news agency.[73] The Communist mouthpiece, *Xinhua Daily*, joined in popularizing a story—notorious to this day in Chinese memory and taught in textbooks, despite widespread doubts about its veracity—that two sword-wielding Japanese lieutenants had engaged in a killing competition during the sack of Nanjing, won by the officer who killed 106 Chinese, one more than his rival.[74] After the fall of Nanjing, the two top Communist military chiefs, General Zhu De and General Peng Dehuai, wrote that the enemy "raped and looted, killed the young and able-bodied, and burnt flesh and bones to ashes."[75]

Mao rankled at having his revolutionary troops subordinated to Chiang as part of the national army. He pressed his supporters to abandon cooperation with the Nationalists, planning for a nationwide proletariat resistance against Japan.[76] By 1941, when the united front of Chiang and Mao essentially collapsed, the two main Communist military forces—the storied Eighth Route Army and the New Fourth Army—had grown to some four hundred and forty thousand troops.[77] The Communist slogan in Yan'an became "Struggle against Japan *and* Chiang Kai-shek."[78] By the middle of 1944, Communists and Nationalists were often more concerned with fighting each other than the Japanese.[79]

Chiang relied increasingly on brute coercion and failed to reach out for a wider Nationalist base.[80] Clear-eyed observers such as Theodore White of *Time* despaired of the Nationalists, repelled by their secret police and censorship, despite exhortations from his boss Henry Luce.[81] After Auden's visit to China, the poet decided that the country's future lay with Mao (although he would later regret that). He concluded, "It is, surely, the first maxim of *realpolitik* that, whatever one's ideological preferences, one must never back a certain loser."[82]

Mei sided with the loser.

Proud of the Nationalists for shaking off European imperialism, Mei declared his fealty to Sun Yat-sen's philosophy. Under the leadership of his powerful patron Sun Ke, the Legislative Yuan drafted a constitution, which Mei outspokenly defended in a public address in 1944—as Japan was waging its new offensive to drive China out of the war. His patriotic beliefs aligned with the domineering Nationalist party line. As his public profile grew under an authoritarian government, his oratory became flecked with the bromides of a Nationalist party hack.

Plenty of foreigners doubted that China could sustain democracy; the American war correspondent Martha Gellhorn sneered, "I felt that it was pure doom to be Chinese; no worse luck could befall a human being than to be born and live there."[83] Yet Mei presented China as one of the world's great democracies. Sun Yat-sen, he said, "aims to make China a state 'of the people, by the people and for the people'"—quoting from Abraham Lincoln at Gettysburg. He believed that rights were perfectly at home in China, not a foreign imposition alien to the country's cultural traditions or level of socioeconomic development.[84] He was proud of proposed constitutional rights to freedom of speech, the press, religion, association, migration, and more: "we have whatever Europe and America have. We have everything." Indeed, he thought that Chinese republicanism was more comprehensive: "Democracy in the West only pursues political equality, but the Three Principles of the People"—Sun Yat-sen's credo of nationalism *(minzu zhuyi)*, rights of the people *(minquan)*, and people's livelihood *(minsheng)*—"also demand international, interracial, political, and economic equality."[85]

This was overstated. Chiang Kai-shek, whose authoritarian instincts were obvious, believed that individualistic Western liberalism was against "the spirit of China's own civilization."[86] Like much of the Nationalist leadership, Mei had a paternalistic view of governing the unready masses.[87] He wrote that during a "period of political tutelage, our party stands in the position of a nanny, exercises political power on behalf of the people and trains people to use their political power. When the people are prepared, constitutional democracy will ensue. Our party will naturally stop practicing dictatorship and no longer stay in the position of a nanny." (That period of political tutelage would keep slipping forward year after year.)[88] Again he invoked the American example, although mangling and misattributing a quotation: "Recall that when the U.S. Constitution was just passed, Madison and Jefferson, the great politicians of that era, looked at each other with a sigh and said, 'We have a critical task for the future. Waste no time to educate our masters.' This line is highly applicable to us today."[89]

.   .   .

When peace came at last in August 1945, China's battered government struggled to establish control over Japanese-occupied areas, punish or pardon the colossal numbers of Chinese who had collaborated, get millions of refugees home, rebuild the cities and countryside, kick-start a ruined economy, build democracy and the rule of law, and heal a traumatized society.[90]

China's war crimes trials would draw a line between Japan's criminals and its blameless masses. During the war, Chiang had declared, "Much as we hate the Japanese militarists, we have no intention of harboring undying hatred for the innocent Japanese people."[91] By not insisting on too sweeping a purge of Japan, the Nationalists could maintain a functional Japanese state as a counterweight to China's Communists. After wiping out Japan's militarists, the generalissimo said, postwar government should be "left to the awakened and repentant Japanese people to decide for themselves."[92]

The Republic of China swept up Japanese soldiers, industrialists, expatriates, and what it termed *ronin*—masterless samurai—as suspected war criminals, thrown into detention camps. For the major leaders, China was glad to participate in an international court—what would become the Tokyo trial. For "ordinary war criminals," China set up military tribunals at the front. The accused Japanese would usually face five military judges—in uniform and wearing swords—and a military prosecutor, sometimes helped by two judicial officials from the local province. The accused could pick their defense lawyers; those who did not would be assigned public defenders. Their trial and punishment would proceed according to the Chinese military's criminal code and international law, including the Hague and Geneva conventions and an international ban on opium.[93]

China's most prominent court was a military tribunal in Nanjing, which hastily convicted and executed several Japanese officers for the massacre there. The audience yelled "Down with Japanese imperialism!" and "We want our blood debt paid in kind!"[94] The court estimated the death toll there at three hundred thousand—the official figure used today by Communist China.[95] Harmonizing with the Allies, the Republic of China treated the planning and waging of aggressive war as a crime against international treaties or guarantees, even incorporating the American concept of a criminal conspiracy. It swiftly adopted the category of crimes against humanity. Following the standard that would be established at Nuremberg, war criminals would not be exempted for following superior orders, doing their duty, or carrying out government policy. Japanese suspects were charged with a dizzying array of war crimes: murder, massacre, rape, torture, executing hostages, starving civilians, abducting women for forced prostitution, enslaving people, using poison gas, pushing opium, and bombarding hospitals. Those found guilty could face the death penalty or life imprisonment.[96]

In the end, though, Nationalist China would only manage to charge a tiny fraction of the Japanese troops who could have been indicted. When Japan surrendered, it left stranded some 1.2 million soldiers in Manchuria and 1.5 million in the rest of China. Yet the Nationalist government had to worry about getting these dangerous Japanese troops out of China—a task that would be delayed by a sweeping push for justice. Chinese courts would prosecute approximately 850 defendants for conventional war crimes and crimes against humanity. Of those defendants, 350 were acquitted, while 355 were sentenced and 149 were executed. (Most of these defendants were Japanese, but included 173 Taiwanese, as well as some Koreans—subject peoples of the Japanese Empire who had participated in its war.) This effort would come to an end in 1949 when the Communists swept the Nationalists from power. All told, despite the magnitude of Chinese suffering, the Americans and Australians each prosecuted more Japanese for war crimes or crimes against humanity. So did the British and Dutch, reasserting their colonial grasp in Asia. China handled a small portion of the total of 5,700 Japanese defendants charged in Allied national courts, and of the 984 of those who were executed.[97]

"Idiotic Virtue"

The Communist Party asserted that the war had been won thanks to its "leading role," belittling the Nationalists as bungling cowards or outright traitors.[98] Chiang's magnanimity toward Japan left the Communists an opening. Mao's underlings rebuked the Nationalists for moving too slowly to arrest and prosecute war criminals, accusing them of truckling to the Japanese.[99]

During most of the Japanese invasion, though, the Communists had been more circumspect. While angrily denouncing a villainous Japanese clique of warlords and *zaibatsu* bosses, that Communist line did not imply eagerness for war crimes trials.[100] The Communists shunned the international laws of war and had made few references to war crimes trials until after Nazi Germany's surrender.

The Chinese Communist Party saw the laws of war as a foolish constraint on its own revolutionary brand of warfighting.[101] Referring to a feudal warrior who had chivalrously refused to attack a vulnerable enemy force, Mao declared, "We are not Duke Xiang of Song and have no use for his idiotic virtue and morality."[102] In Zhu De's wartime writings, he only once condemned the Japanese for violating international law, warning in 1938 that Japan might be about to drop bacterial bombs in northern China—an apparent reference to Unit 731, the secretive Japanese army unit in Manchuria that had launched aerial attacks on some Chinese cities and was preparing for more.[103]

The revolutionaries did not bother with procedural justice in courts of law. Although Mao wanted to publicize Japanese atrocities to "capture the attention of the whole world to punish Japanese fascism," he said nothing about prosecutions.[104] In an important speech late in World War II, he excoriated "the double pressure" of the Japanese aggressors and the Nationalist government, but did not mention war crimes trials in remaking Japan.[105] The businesslike wartime records of Zhou Enlai, the redoubtable revolutionary leader who would become the first premier of the People's Republic of China, barely mention Japanese war crimes, except once instructing Communist cadres to highlight enemy atrocities to foreign journalists.[106] General Peng Dehuai, who would become China's commander in the Korean War, recounted gruesome tales of the Japanese disemboweling civilians, burning people alive with kerosene, and jabbing hooks into anuses: "Blood debt has to be compensated with blood!"[107]

The Chinese Communist Party's vision of postwar justice was heavy on revenge and short on legal procedure. The *Xinhua Daily* raged, "Inhuman perpetrators must suffer revenge! . . . The only way to eliminate fascist invaders is to thoroughly annihilate these war criminals!"[108] The Communists scorned Allied legal prosecutions of German war criminals as sluggish, demanding that all Japanese fascists and their Chinese collaborators immediately face severe punishment. They envisioned popular denunciation by the masses, as in Communist public trials for those who deviated from the party line: "Mobilize the people, give them all types of freedom, let them report and openly judge war criminals."[109]

When Japan surrendered, the Chinese Communists offered their own list of war criminals, which covered many of the same names as the Nationalists, including Tojo Hideki and General Doihara Kenji, who was loathed among the Chinese as an architect of the conquest of Manchuria.[110] Although Hirohito was not on their blacklist, the Communists demanded that he be deprived of power in order to eradicate fascism.[111] The Communists fixated on General Okamura Yasuji, who had "carried out the so-called Three-Alls policy (burn all, kill all, and loot all) against soldiers and civilians"—atrocities particularly resented by the Communists for their impact on their own guerrilla war effort.[112]

Believing that the roots of fascism lay in capitalist industry, Communists compiled a long list of *"zaibatsu* leaders and military supply capitalists" to be purged and punished, including chiefs of vast business enterprises such as Mitsubishi, Mitsui, and Sumitomo. One of those named was Kishi Nobusuke, who had served as a vice minister for industry in the Japanese puppet regime in Manchuria, known as Manchukuo—one of five men, including Tojo Hideki, who dominated Japanese-controlled Manchuria as it brutalized Chinese workers.[113] A slim, long-faced man with a weak chin, Kishi became a member of Tojo's cabinet at the time of Pearl Harbor and then vice minister of munitions. A Chinese Communist organ commented, "He was a giant figure in the enemy bureaucracy's radical faction and had close communication with the radical faction among young military officers."[114]

As the Allied occupation of Japan began, the Chinese Communist Party decried a "lenient" American attitude toward Japan—attacks which also discredited the Nationalists. The *Xinhua Daily* condemned the Americans for working with the Japanese authorities: "the punishment of war criminals cannot be carried out through a government composed of war criminals."[115] Since MacArthur was targeting Tojo's entire Pearl Harbor cabinet, the Communists demanded the same for the whole cabinet which had invaded China in 1937. The *Xinhua Daily* complained that the first American lists of war criminals only included Tojo's cabinet at the time of Pearl Harbor and army leaders responsible for the Bataan death march, while overlooking those Japanese responsible for aggression in Manchuria, Shanghai, and China: "None of the war criminals who, since the 9/18, 1/28 and 7/7 incidents, engaged in burning, looting, killing, raping, wanton bombing and torturing of civilians and prisoners of war to death in the Chinese battlefield are included."[116]

ALL THE WORLD'S A STAGE

Mei Ruao's appointment as China's judge at the Tokyo trial came about haphazardly, typical of the slapdash postwar functioning of the Republic of China. The Nationalist military quickly admitted that they could not readily find someone who was both proficient in law and had excellent English, instead proposing a thirty-five-year-old colonel with no legal training and a cavalry major whose grandest achievement appeared to be meeting Chiang Kai-shek.[117]

The military command asked, "Is familiarity with law a necessary qualification when we select this military officer?"[118] With exasperation, the Foreign Ministry replied that "proficiency in law should be a necessary qualification" for a war crimes tribunal. To its embarrassment, the Foreign Ministry could only come up with two names, rather than the five requested.[119]

The first name floated was Xiang Zhejun. From Hunan province, he had been educated at Tsinghua and then Yale College, where he had been president of the Yale Cosmopolitan Club, an idealistic group dedicated to resolving international disputes peacefully. He had graduated from George Washington University's law school—a rare Asian face in Washington during a time of ubiquitous American discrimination against Chinese. Returning home, he had risen to be chief prosecutor of Shanghai's high court. When the Japanese had stormed into Shanghai, he had fled to the countryside pretending to be a paper merchant, sheltering with his family in Hunan.[120]

The second name was Mei, an academic without any courtroom credentials.[121] Despite his glaring lack of practical judicial experience, Mei was backed by the Foreign Ministry, wanting names who were well known to American lawyers.[122] The Chinese government initially neither knew nor cared whether Mei or Xiang was meant to serve as prosecutor or judge. Both men were personally picked by Chiang Kai-shek himself.[123]

The Nationalist government could have been forgiven for not being sure whether legal qualifications mattered. V. K. Wellington Koo (Gu Weijun), a former prime minister and foreign minister now serving as ambassador to Britain, was mystified by the legal basis for the international war crimes tribunal. Frustrated that the United States had never convened a discussion on the court, Koo preferred an Asian equivalent to the London agreement—the deal signed by Britain, France, the Soviet Union, and the United States establishing the charter for Nuremberg. That would have given China a better chance to shape the court. "What law or jurisdiction applies to the international court proposed by the American government remains questionable," Koo noted. He presciently warned, "As for crimes against peace and humanity, whether the court has jurisdiction is likely to cause a chaotic debate."[124]

The Chinese government rushed Xiang Zhejun to Tokyo early in 1946, flying him from Shanghai on a U.S. cargo plane.[125] Yet Mei was reluctant to take the assignment. After the displacements of the war, his family was about to return to his hometown and he did not want to leave them again for another sojourn abroad. And he worried about his own lack of judicial experience.

China's vice foreign minister exhorted him, "There is no need to refuse again." He was summoned to Chongqing to talk to his mentor Sun Ke, the head of the Legislative Yuan.[126] As Mei later remembered it, Sun beseeched his reluctant protégé, "This opportunity arises only once in a thousand years, and it is not only interesting and valuable but also allows you to mark your name in history." Just half a year ago, Sun pointed out, areas near the provisional capital of Chongqing were falling to the Japanese; it had been hard to imagine feeling proud of themselves, as they did now. Mei replied philosophically that the rise and fall of nations was unpredictable, almost like a drama. Sun replied in a Shakespearean tone that the world was always a stage and history was nothing more than a series of dramas. "Since it is a drama," he asked, "why can't you play a role in this scene?" At last, Mei yielded and agreed to go to Tokyo.[127]

He raced to Shanghai, sped on to Tokyo on a U.S. transport plane swiftly approved by General Headquarters.[128] "Really," Mei wrote in his diary, "I have taken up a role, and this scene will start in no time."[129]

CHAPTER 8

The God That Failed

E MPEROR HIROHITO BEGAN THE cold, bleak new year of 1946 by declaring that he was not a living god after all.

Japan's cities were in ruins and the people were enduring wintertime food shortages and rampant unemployment. Leftists were demanding the abolition of the monarchy. At huge demonstrations near the Imperial Palace, hungry citizens had bellowed to their emperor, "What will you have for dinner?"[1] In Hirohito's first message to his desolate people since the surrender, he issued an imperial rescript lending his authority to sweeping political change. Democracy, this rescript claimed, far from being a foreign imposition, had been nurtured since the Meiji Emperor.[2] Referring to war guilt, Hirohito announced that he sought to "proceed unflinchingly towards elimination of misguided practices of the past."

Hirohito declared that his bond with his people was "not predicated on the false conception that the Emperor is divine, and that the Japanese people are superior to other races and fated to rule the world."[3] Privately he was more enigmatic about his divinity. Although admitting that his body was the same as any human, he refused an earlier draft which denied his lineal descent from the Shinto sun goddess Amaterasu. He had accepted his central role in the *kokutai:* "I thought that if the nation is viewed as a human body, the Emperor is the brain."[4] Still, at a stroke, his rescript put the Japanese on the same level as other nations and himself as an ordinary man.

This sensational declaration of humanity was tailored to preserve Hirohito from arrest as a war criminal.[5] The monarch, in uniform as the supreme commander of Japan's armed forces, had visited the Yasukuni war shrine twenty times to exalt the war dead.[6] Now his rescript's phrasing echoed General Douglas MacArthur's recent order disestablishing State Shinto, which the Allies had execrated as a militaristic cult exalting the Japanese people as divinely descended and ruled by a god-emperor.[7] American newspapers, spun by General Headquarters, gradually shifted to depicting the mortal emperor as penitent, submissive, and helpful.[8]

Being human exposed him to new kinds of public censure. A prominent Japanese poet, Miyoshi Tatsuji, called for Hirohito's abdication: "Your Highness, who is not a god, should, as a son of man, obey the logic of the world of mankind." The emperor should bear responsibility for losing the war. The poet accused Hirohito of severe negligence in failing to restrain the militarists, reminding him of the soldiers who had died screaming the emperor's praises on the battlefield.[9]

While Hirohito insulated himself, his subjects faced harsh and sometimes arbitrary punishment for their wartime deeds. In a sweeping purge, MacArthur aimed to remove from public office and economic power anyone who had advocated nationalism and aggression, influential members of ultranationalist organizations and terrorist groups, schoolteachers who had actively espoused militant nationalism, and those hostile to the occupation.[10] Starting with politicians, civil servants, and *zaibatsu* executives, the purge would in its first eighteen months ensnare almost seven thousand judges, businessmen, publishers, editors, and writers. Although its reach was less sweeping than its equivalent in postwar Germany, it brushed aside governors of prefectures, mayors of cities and towns, even heads of block associations. As many as one hundred twenty thousand teachers were either sacked or preemptively resigned. In a subsequent expansion of the purge in July 1947, more than one hundred fifty thousand officers in the army, navy, civil service, and secret police would be barred from public life.[11]

The purge was loathed among Japanese elites, who were never sure when the latest list might ambush them, with scant process available to clear their names. Plenty of those purged were indeed nationalist firebrands, but many were relatively innocuous. Japanese conservatives complained that the purges showed a Soviet-inspired grudge against financiers and tycoons. Despite promises of freedom of the press, nationalistic publishers and writers were sacked. Some Japanese leaders would later concede that the purges did mark a break with wartime hierarchies, bringing fresh generations into democratic public life. But the haphazard and ignorant screening dealt out countless injustices in every corner of Japanese life.[12]

THE USUAL SUSPECTS

The Japanese government worked with General Headquarters to promote a remarkably liberal new constitution: reducing the emperor to a symbolic status, enshrining democratization, guaranteeing "the fundamental human rights," renouncing war as a national right for all time, and abolishing the armed forces. Although MacArthur pronounced himself largely done with his reform edicts, he had one more piece of business.[13] On January 19, he made a special proclamation—showily numbered as General Orders No. 1—establishing the international war crimes tribunal that he had struggled to avoid.[14]

The Allied governments immediately began to squabble over which Japanese leaders would be the defendants at the Tokyo trial. Driving the selection, the Truman administration asked the Allied powers to submit their own lists of major war criminals, seeking a group big enough to satisfy American public opinion.[15]

The British, hoping for a streamlined trial, sent a modest list of eleven suspects, mostly military men already targeted by the Americans.[16] Although some Chinese officials had proposed more than a hundred suspects, Chiang Kai-shek sent just thirty-three names—figures notorious in China such as Field Marshal Hata Shunroku, General Doihara Kenji, and General Itagaki Seishiro.[17] Hirohito, useful in resisting Communism, was spared.[18] More alarmingly, the Australians submitted an expansive list of sixty-one names, complete with a lengthy report. In addition to army men such as Tojo Hideki and other army officers, Australia slated Marquis Kido Koichi, the lord keeper of the privy seal. Konoe Fumimaro's name was crossed out in red pencil after his suicide. The seventh name, listed coyly in alphabetical order, was Hirohito.[19]

The Australians held fast on the emperor, scorching him for authorizing an illegal war and allowing crimes against humanity: "[H]e was not at any time forced by duress to give his written approval. He could have refused to do so and supported his protests by abdication or hari-kari."[20] The British were perturbed, while MacArthur saw his worst fears about an uncontrollable international court coming true.[21]

MacArthur lashed back with his most forceful defense of the emperor. He told General Dwight Eisenhower, now the U.S. Army chief of staff, that there was no specific evidence against Hirohito. The monarch had automatically approved his advisers' decisions, MacArthur claimed, and would have been in real jeopardy if he had defied the dominant military clique. Following the analysis of Brigadier General Bonner Fellers,

MacArthur warned that indicting the emperor would cause a "tremendous convulsion" with awful repercussions. "He is a symbol which unites all Japanese. Destroy him and the nation will disintegrate." In prose that was purple even by MacArthur's standards, he direly warned that almost all Japanese venerated the emperor and believed that the Allies had committed to keep him on the throne:

> They will regard Allied action to the contrary as the greatest betrayal in their history and the hatreds and resentments engendered by this thought will unquestionably last for all measurable time. A vendetta for revenge will thereby be initiated whose cycle may well not be completed for centuries if ever.
>
> The whole of Japan can be expected, in my opinion, to resist the action either by passive or semi-active means. They are disarmed and therefore will represent no special menace to trained and equipped troops; but it is not inconceivable that all government agencies will break down, that civilized practices will largely cease, and a condition of underground chaos and disorder amounting to guerrilla warfare in the mountainous and outlying regions result. I believe all hope of introducing modern democratic methods would disappear and that when military control finally ceased some form of intense regimentation probably along Communistic lines would arise from the mutilated masses.

Such turmoil would make it essential to greatly increase the occupying forces, with MacArthur proposing at least a million troops stuck in Japan indefinitely. Having hyperventilated at length, MacArthur then posed as the obedient soldier deferring meekly to whatever deranged insanity the president might choose: "The decision as to whether the Emperor should be tried as a war criminal involves a policy determination upon such a high level that I would not feel it appropriate for me to make a recommendation."[22]

Truman, no fool, would have instantly understood where the buck would stop. With Americans profoundly weary of war, he risked conscripting and deploying troops to a Japan in flames, while MacArthur's team ensured that all blame was pinned on him.

Working quietly together, the Truman administration and the British government knifed the Australian proposal. Hirohito was spared, at least for now.[23]

THRONE OF BLOOD

Waiting anxiously for the Tokyo trial to begin, Hirohito faced loud calls for his neck in China, Australia, and the United States.[24] A palace intrigue showed that other royals wanted him gone: Prince Higashikuni Naruhiko said publicly that he had suggested that the emperor abdicate when the surrender was signed on the USS *Missouri*, or when Japan got a new constitution or signed a formal peace treaty with the Allies.[25] To rebuild his stature, Hirohito began making visits to schools, hospitals, and factories.[26]

Fearing being indicted, interrogated, or called as a witness at the Tokyo trial, Hirohito decided to prepare his own version of events. Over a series of five talks spread over three weeks, the emperor gave his secret testament to a small group of trusted aides to clear himself of war guilt.[27] The full chronicle would not see daylight until after Hirohito's death in 1989, when it was accidentally discovered in the papers of a court official and published by a prominent Japanese magazine.[28] These eight-hour monologues represent the most sensational testimony which never happened.

At 10:30 a.m. on Sunday, March 18, Emperor Hirohito convened five of his closest courtiers. Suffering from a cold, he had a bed brought into his library—or possibly an air raid shelter—on the Imperial Palace grounds. He lay propped up on white silk sheets, wearing exquisite white silk pajamas. An aide found him gloomy, even depressed, and wondered how to raise the sensitive subject of abdication.

The emperor delivered his first three monologues from his palace bed that week, and then gave two more in the seclusion of the Hayama imperial villa, south of Tokyo. He spoke without notes. In one session, he answered questions from his aides—the kinds of things likely to be asked by Allied interrogators. One palace official took notes, while the others listened raptly; the only interruptions came when the deputy grand chamberlain asked for clarifications.[29]

An aide prepared a partial English summary and slipped it to Bonner Fellers, who would almost certainly rush such a momentous document straight to MacArthur. It was guarded at General Headquarters as an explosive secret.[30] In it, the emperor claimed there would have been "terrible disorder" if he had blocked plans to attack the United States. "The trusted men around me would have been killed, I myself might have been killed or kidnapped. Actually I was virtually a prisoner and powerless."[31]

Supine, the emperor pointed the finger in every direction other than himself. Although the Meiji constitution formally gave him vast powers—including declaring war and commanding the army and navy—he presented himself as a modest constitutional monarch who kept a low profile, guiding his government through discreet nudges. He claimed to have directly imposed his will only twice: ordering the crushing of a military revolt in February 1936, and breaking the government's deadlock to surrender in August 1945. Still, his testament showed him wielding considerable authority: offering his opinions on critical decisions, maneuvering men toward or away from high office, and exercising his authority to make appointments, such as picking ministers and selecting the prime minister when a cabinet collapsed. He declared that "if government officials were misbehaving, that was my responsibility and I should apologize to the gods."

Although the emperor carefully avoided mentioning atrocities, he directly incriminated himself in one apparent war crime: the execution of captured U.S. airmen from the Doolittle air raid. In a compromise between Tojo Hideki and the general staff, the emperor had publicly commuted five of the eight death sentences to life imprisonment—but if Hirohito had had the authority to spare five lives, why not the other three? Although Japanese show trials had condemned the airmen for bombing civilians, the emperor judged them innocent: "in fact there seem to have been anti-aircraft guns and anti-aircraft machine guns at the place attacked by the aircraft, so I think the three men also were not responsible."[32]

Although Tojo was being positioned to shoulder all blame, the emperor guardedly praised his prime minister: "Tojo worked very hard and ordinarily thought very carefully about what he said; he had his good points." While admitting that Tojo overused the Kempeitai and had a reputation as "a tyrant," Hirohito explained that he had taken on too many ministries and did not have time to communicate with his subordinates. Despite the devastation all around the palace, the emperor continued to justify his own approval of the Pacific War, not just out of deference to Tojo's cabinet but as the right thing to do.

Appropriately enough, the emperor himself became the first Japanese leader to give his own testimonial about the outbreak of the war. Later his underlings—most prominently Tojo, Marquis Kido Koichi, and Togo Shigenori—would tell their own kaleidoscopic versions in court, all addressing the ominous, escalating steps: the conquest of Manchuria in 1931, the all-out invasion of the rest of China in July 1937, the Axis alliance with Nazi Germany in 1940, the seizure of southern French Indochina, and finally the debate over attacking the United States in late 1941.

Hirohito expansively argued that the underlying cause of the war was the racist unfairness of the peace treaty ending World War I. The Japanese had been indignant at enduring "yellow-white discrimination," manifested in such interwar affronts as the failure of a Japanese proposal for racial equality in the League of Nations and the barring of Asian immigrants from California. Such public outcry, he claimed, made it hard to restrain the military.[33]

After taking the throne in 1926 as army radicals were trying to grab Manchuria, he quickly learned to express his opinions but not veto policies.[34] The one big exception came in February 1936, when young army officers had led more than a thousand soldiers to attack the prime minister's residence, seize part of central Tokyo, and kill the home minister, the finance minister, and the lord keeper of the privy seal. This was so terrifying that Hirohito had given an order to bring the rebels under control.[35] Yet despite claiming that "I always called for the issuance of peace overtures while also threatening military action," he had done little to prevent the conquest of Manchuria and then the full-scale invasion of China. He blamed army hard-liners for the ensuing China quagmire, scorning the army minister, General Itagaki Seishiro, as "a complete military 'robot.'" Although he mentioned the fall of Nanjing, he said nothing about the atrocities there or elsewhere across China. Nor did he discuss the role at Nanjing of his own uncle Prince Asaka Yasuhiko, a lieutenant general in command of Japanese forces there during the massacre.

Hirohito presented himself as especially cautious about tangling with the Soviet Union, accusing the bellicose Itagaki of tricking him into approving an attack on Soviet troops near the Manchurian border in 1938. He blamed the Axis alliance with Nazi Germany and Italy on the army, claiming that he had rebuffed his brother Prince Chichibu, an army officer who was seen by militarists as their best voice inside the court—perhaps even a replacement for Hirohito.[36] Although Hirohito called the Axis alliance a disaster for Japan, he admitted that he "ultimately supported it. . . . I agreed to the alliance, half believing, half doubting it."

He pinned the seizure of southern French Indochina on the military, claiming that he had vainly urged Tojo to call off the invasion.[37] The resulting American oil embargo, he explained, was the real cause of the Pacific War: "The war between Japan and the U.S. can be seen as having started because of oil and ended because of oil."

He presented himself as struggling to avoid war with the obstinate United States. As tensions grew, the emperor had summoned his military chiefs and spent an hour asking them skeptical questions: if the army could not win in China, how could it do so fighting throughout the vast

Pacific? He recalled how, in an imperial conference on September 6, 1941, he had spoken up for diplomacy and read a *tanka* poem by the Meiji Emperor to show that he favored peace. Despite that, the "very troubling" imperial conference resolved for the first time to go to war if there was no diplomatic solution by mid-October, which Hirohito said left him "filled with anxiety. . . . With so few favoring peace, I found it very difficult."

Tojo Hideki (right), then army minister and a lieutenant general, bows to Emperor Hirohito at an imperial ceremony in Tokyo, October 21, 1940.

Hirohito scorned his peace-seeking prime minister, Prince Konoe Fumimaro, as lacking conviction and courage. When Konoe resigned after clashing with army hard-liners led by the bellicose Tojo Hideki, Hirohito had replaced him with Tojo himself. The emperor remained decidedly unrepentant about this calamitous choice. He had ruled out Prince Higashikuni Naruhiko, an army general who was married to a daughter of the Meiji Emperor, for fear that "the Imperial family would be responsible for starting a war." That left Tojo, and Hirohito liked the cut of his jib: "He had a good grasp of the mood within the army, so I thought that . . . this man would be able to keep the army under control and manage things smoothly."

Having installed one of the army's foremost hawks, the emperor had told Tojo to disregard the September 6 decision for war and seek a peaceful resolution. Although he claimed to have believed that Japan would probably lose the war, he laid no blame on Tojo for Pearl Harbor. Instead he faulted the Americans for their diplomatic obstinacy and oil embargo.

Despite later claims that the negotiations had been spoiled by a harsh note from Cordell Hull, the U.S. secretary of state, the emperor said that even before that note arrived, "[t]he opinion of the cabinet had already settled on war."[38]

Hirohito explained that if he had resisted a war, he would have been accused of surrendering to the United States too easily: "Public opinion would have seethed and there likely would have been a coup d'état."[39] When one of his younger brothers, who was a naval officer, urged him to prevent a war, he insisted that he was merely a constitutional monarch who had to respect the decisions of his government and military: "if I did not, Tojo would resign and a major coup d'état would occur, leaving extreme war supporters in control, so on the matter of stopping the war, I did not respond."

The emperor fatalistically accepted the final prewar imperial conference a few days before Pearl Harbor that set the date of the attack: "it would be meaningless to object, so I said nothing." He had paid little attention to a last personal appeal from Franklin Delano Roosevelt, which he had received as Japanese forces were about to strike. He claimed that he had wanted to respond but that Togo Shigenori, the foreign minister— who had fought hard against the war—had told him not to because two Japanese submarines had already been sunk near Hawaii. The emperor recalled that he had with a heavy heart approved an imperial rescript declaring war on the United States and the British Empire.

Hirohito professed that he had repeatedly denied military requests to issue imperial rescripts cheering on the war. Yet in fact, he had issued imperial rescripts in honor of the fights for Singapore, Burma, and the Coral Sea; before the war, he had put out rescripts in approval of withdrawing from the League of Nations and joining the Tripartite Pact. According to the diary of Kido Koichi, the first time that the Imperial Palace had balked at issuing an imperial rescript was in June 1942, after the momentous defeat at Midway.

The emperor admitted that even as Tojo's government grew unpopular, he had not tried to bring it down, fearing antagonizing the prime minister's supporters. "I sympathized with Tojo," said the emperor, "but I am not trying to make a special effort to defend him." Still, Hirohito was noticeably more enthusiastic about Tojo than about some of his other prime ministers.[40]

As the military turned to suicidal kamikaze attacks, Hirohito privately believed that the sacrifice of young lives was futile. Like Japan's military chiefs, he kept on gambling on the illusion of a decisive battle at Okinawa or elsewhere that would force the Americans to negotiate a favorable peace deal. "I wanted to hit the Americans hard at Leyte," he said, and despaired after the rout there: "I felt in my heart that the only path open to us was to sue for peace." He did not mention a harder truth: that these fanciful hopes of stalemating the Americans helped to prolong a losing war for fully a year, with more than a million Japanese and vastly more Asians perishing during that period.[41]

Seizing credit for ending the war, Hirohito downplayed the outspoken efforts of Togo Shigenori, saying that he and other doves wanted peace "but none of them would come forward and say it." In June 1945, Hirohito told his senior leaders to start reaching for peace, hoping that Soviet mediation could avert an unconditional surrender—a prospect dashed by Hiroshima and the Soviet assault.[42]

At last accepting the need for unconditional surrender, the emperor came to his second direct intervention in politics: ending the war. Recounting the climactic late-night imperial conference on August 9–10, 1945, Hirohito showed no embarrassment that even after the annihilation of Hiroshima and Nagasaki, his government was united to protect his throne as a surrender term. With the meeting deadlocked at 2 a.m., the emperor recalled, he saw no way to fight off an American ground invasion. He told the meeting that he agreed with Togo, allowing Japan to surrender at last.

His decision, he said, had been based first on his fear that "the Japanese people would perish if there was no change in the situation; I couldn't protect the people." Yet he had also feared that the invading Americans would quickly seize two of the three sacred treasures—a mirror and a sword, which, along with a jewel, comprised the imperial regalia symbolizing the divine origins of the royal line—held at the Ise Shrine southwest of Tokyo and the Atsuta Shrine in Nagoya. He said, "I thought I had to bring about peace, even at the sacrifice of myself."

He vividly recalled the bloody attempt to block the broadcast of his surrender message, with phone lines cut and the imperial library surrounded by rebelling soldiers. Luckily, steel doors on the windows had been shut against the air raids, so the insurrectionists did not figure out where he was. He remembered being saved by a brave officer who confronted the soldiers and made them stand down.

To the end, Hirohito expressed no regrets about Pearl Harbor: "approving the decision of the Tojo cabinet was something that I, as a constitutional monarch in a constitutional government, had to do." If Japan had not fought, it would have faced impossible demands from the Americans and would have run out of oil, leaving its fleet immobilized. Had he blocked the war, "The country would have fallen into severe civil strife, trusted people close to me would have been killed, and my own life could not have been guaranteed." In an overwrought conclusion, he suggested that Tojo would have attacked anyway in a savage war many times worse than what had happened: "In the end, it would have been impossible to stop the war, and I think Japan likely would have ceased to exist."[43]

In his white silk pajamas, Hirohito was right to worry about his future. A few days after he finished his last monologue, a U.S. military court convicted Japanese officers responsible for executing three of the Doolittle airmen, prompting the mother of one of the dead American fliers to call for Hirohito to be tried and executed.[44]

On the same day of his final monologue, the Chinese associate prosecutor reported to Mei Ruao that one of the prosecutors—presumably from Australia—had proposed charging the emperor as a war criminal, sparking a heated but inconclusive debate among the prosecutors. Mei found this "a political question," but argued that "from a purely legal perspective, I really can't see how the Emperor could take no responsibility for Japan's war of aggression. This question has been discussed in the private conversations of the judges, and many people hold the same opinion as me."[45]

This suggests that if the emperor had been indicted, he stood some chance of being convicted by the judges. He was lucky to have American protection. Soon after the emperor ended his monologues, MacArthur was secretly instructed by the Truman administration that his orders did not "authorize any action against the Emperor as a War Criminal."[46]

CHAPTER 9

The Imperial Hotel

MEI RUAO, THE CHINESE judge, was uneasy and vengeful as he landed in "the homeland of the enemies we have been fighting for the last eight years with sweat and blood." Driving in from Atsugi airfield on March 20, 1946, he was sobered by the bombed-out Tokyo landscape: "I finally understood the meaning of an old Chinese saying 'the houses are burnt to ground, and all that is left is the ruins.'" When a U.S. colonel whose house in Manila had been destroyed by the Japanese said that he was happy to see the debris, Mei replied that he felt the same way; his home in Nanjing had been burned down too. "The war criminals we are about to put on trial are responsible for all of this!" he wrote in his diary.[1]

Settling in for what he thought would be only a few months in Tokyo, he was underwhelmed by the Imperial Hotel, a weathered bungalow which could not compare with Shanghai's towers. Uncomfortable in his surroundings, he soothed himself by practicing tai chi.[2] Unable to enjoy his spacious three-room suite with a large balcony, he instead fretted at the expense while China risked going bankrupt. Even a defeated nation such as Japan was trying to find solutions but "we, as a victorious nation, supposedly 'one of the Big Four' victorious nations, are at our wit's end; it's very shameful."

The other judges, stuck together at the hotel, proved to be a convivial group.[3] Homesick and worried about his family, Mei relied on his new colleagues for companionship.[4] Drinking together at the hotel bar, they grew bluntly comfortable with each other, although Mei once collapsed from a single rum and Coke.[5] "The colleagues that each nation sent are all experienced, respectable judges," he wrote earnestly in his diary, "and so I must deal with this conscientiously and seriously, and cannot be careless at all."[6]

Mei knew nothing of how the judges had been chosen. All the Allied governments had proceeded according to the entrenched norms of their own domestic legal systems. Noticeably, the democracies had chosen leading lights from their own judiciaries. Although that tradition of judicial independence made it harder for liberal governments to overtly rig the court, even the democratic judges had absorbed their home countries' perspectives on the rights and wrongs of the war.

New Zealand had been the first to nominate a judge: Justice Erima Harvey Northcroft of its Supreme Court. White-haired and stately in pinstriped suits, he was calm and steady, a bellwether among the judges.[7] China had followed soon after by selecting Mei.[8]

Australia drove for control of the court by naming the formidable Sir William Webb as its judge. The chief justice of Queensland, he had been one of three judges comprising Australia's war crimes commission.[9] A determined man with a temper, he had endured a rough childhood— three of his brothers had died in infancy—and drew moral guidance from his Catholic faith.[10] Importantly, Webb was on good terms with MacArthur, who had supported his investigations into Japanese war crimes.[11] To put a non-American public face to the court, MacArthur picked him as the court's chief judge, known as the president.[12]

The British government deemed it "highly important for reasons of British prestige" that their delegation be no lesser in size or rank than the American party.[13] Britain chose a powerful judge: William, Lord Patrick, the lord justice of the High Court of Edinburgh. Austere and opinionated, he would take a domineering role throughout the trial, closely coordinating with the British government while leading a bloc of British Commonwealth judges.[14] Britain further tightened its grasp on the court by sending Arthur Comyns Carr, a brainy Oxford-educated lawyer, as its associate prosecutor.[15] A gangly man with a sharply intelligent gaze, he would become the dominant figure on the prosecution.[16] Faced with the British Empire's show of strength, Mei privately scorned the British as "imperialist white supremacists."[17]

Holland named a cerebral judge from the Court of Utrecht, Bernard Victor Röling (known as Bert), who was also a Utrecht law professor with a specialty in Indonesian law.[18] Imposingly tall, the youngest judge at just thirty-nine years old, his youthful looks were offset by gray hair.[19] He was shaken from experiencing the German occupation of Holland, with combat so near his house that he recalled "seeing the war in our garden."[20] He nursed doubts about lawyering: "It is stupid to have chosen in this world to look for what is right as I did, when it might have been possible to look for what is possible." Arriving in Tokyo, he already had murder and wicked kings on the brain: he was finishing a book about criminology and *Macbeth*.[21]

France's judge, Henri Bernard, had spent eighteen harrowing months during World War I in the front lines at the Aisne, in the second battle of the Somme, and in Italy. In a trial marked by disputes about imperialism, he had served the French Empire as a colonial magistrate in Togo, Senegal, and the French Congo. After Nazi Germany defeated France, he joined the Free French as a military prosecutor in the Congo and later in the Middle East and Austria.[22] Although his English was rusty, he refused to use a translator in Tokyo, struggling to follow debates in English. He became a marginal figure among the judges, annoying Mei with his "very odd and elusive" legal thinking. "He was born and raised in Paris," Mei once noted. "No wonder he is different."[23]

The Truman administration again made a fecklessly weak appointment. MacArthur had suggested as judge an unremarkable North Carolina politician and head of the American Bar Association, who should be easy to overawe.[24] Instead Truman chose a judge on Massachusetts' Supreme Judicial Court, John Higgins—a noticeable downtick from the U.S. judge at Nuremberg, the former U.S. attorney general Francis Biddle.[25] Joseph Keenan complained that he would be a "distinct embarrassment," proposing a former dean of Harvard Law School or a U.S. Court of Appeals judge.[26] Truman's attorney general dismissively told MacArthur that the president had made his decision.[27] He thereby squandered much of the United States' backroom clout in the maneuvering to come.

No sooner had the judges arrived in Tokyo that they realized how humiliatingly reliant they were on General Headquarters for everything from enforcing arrests to providing their housing. MacArthur cultivated the more pliable ones, and many kept up suspiciously chummy relationships with the occupying forces. Webb revealed a personal vanity and a love for creature comforts, securing the judges fancier suites at the Imperial Hotel and sedan cars with military chauffeurs appropriate to a U.S. general.[28]

The Australian chief judge faced an immediate test of his judicial independence when he heard that if there were disputes about interpreting the court's charter—which was modeled on Nuremberg—MacArthur would direct the tribunal to follow his own view. Webb exploded, telling MacArthur that only the judges could interpret the charter, and that he would resign if overruled.[29] MacArthur backed down, assuring Webb that he would respect the tribunal's independence.[30] Victorious, Webb cloyingly informed MacArthur that like all Australians he had "the most intense admiration and undying gratitude" for him.[31]

Over meals and drinks at the Imperial Hotel, Mei was impressed by the energetic and confident Webb, while Röling seemed sincere and an avid scholar.[32] He particularly liked Higgins, who told him that China and the United States were brother countries and that ordinary Americans loved China.[33] This fit with Mei's general fondness for the Americans in Tokyo, whom he found well educated and fair-minded, determined to rebuild Japan as a peaceful nation.[34] He was touched to find U.S. military officers well informed about China. He adored watching Hollywood movies and swigging Coca-Cola, bringing back syrupy-sweet memories of student days at Chicago and Stanford.[35] And he swooned when MacArthur sent him a personal note welcoming him, which he saw not as improper influence but a sign of the respect given to judges in a country under the rule of law.[36] In his diary, he reveled, "Who would have no time for a meal with General MacArthur?"[37]

Warm toward the Americans, Mei was frosty around the Soviets, angry that they still had troops in Manchuria. The strapping Soviet judge, Major General Ivan Michyevich Zaryanov, offended Mei—who had grown a beard to look more imposing—by saying that he looked no older than his early thirties, which sent the forty-two-year-old Chinese judge into a huff, fuming privately that Chinese were small and black-haired, thus looking young to Westerners.[38]

Mei was in good company in his distaste for Zaryanov. While it was impossible to exclude the Soviets, the Americans and British viewed them with barely concealed alarm.[39] As the Tokyo court was being assembled, George Kennan, the cerebral U.S. chargé d'affaires in Moscow, delivered what would become famous as his Long Telegram: an enduring warning that the Soviet Union, driven by an "instinctive Russian sense of insecurity" as well as Marxist dogma and an "atmosphere of oriental secretiveness and conspiracy," would strive to undermine the United States and other capitalist powers.[40] While the judges were flying into Tokyo, Winston Churchill—in a speech cleared by Truman and held on the president's home turf at a Missouri college—declared on March 5 that "an iron curtain has descended across the Continent." The Soviets, he warned, threatened Asia too.[41]

With the Soviet Union lodged in Manchuria and tightening its grasp on Poland and the Baltics, Truman regretted his eagerness to get the Soviets into the war against Japan, grumbling privately that they had been a headache ever since.[42] "Unless Russia is faced with an iron fist and strong language another war is in the making," he mused privately. "Only one language do they understand—'How many divisions have you?'" Recoiling at Soviet efforts to encroach on the American-led occupation, he insisted that "we should maintain complete control of Japan and the Pacific."[43]

The Soviet Union floated the creation of separate spheres of influence in Japan, but MacArthur was adamantly opposed to anything like the zones of occupation that would ultimately yield two German states. As a compromise, the Allies set up an unwieldy Far Eastern Commission based in Washington which nominally supervised MacArthur, made up of representatives of the eleven Allied countries which had fought Japan, including the Soviet Union. MacArthur was furious at Truman for allowing this elevation of Soviet influence, letting rumors spread that he was threatening to resign.[44]

Kennan had warned in his Long Telegram, "Russians will participate officially in international organizations where they see opportunity of extending Soviet power or of inhibiting or diluting power of others."[45] Sure enough, frozen out of the crucial decisions in remaking Japan, the Soviet Union took its grudging invitation to participate in the Tokyo trial as a Leninist chance to subvert American dominance.[46] The Soviets sent a massive delegation of sixty-three people, many with job titles so duplicative as to inspire suspicion that they were up to something else.[47] This Soviet host was supervised from Moscow by a commission of officials from Joseph Stalin's inner circle, led by Andrey Vyshinsky, the notorious chief prosecutor of the Moscow purge trials.[48]

At Nuremberg, Stalin had packed his delegation with prosecutors from those show trials; he did much the same for Tokyo.[49] Zaryanov had been a judge in the purge trials of Trotskyites and Bukharinites in the 1930s. He was a battlefront Red Army judge, a member of the Military Collegium of the Soviet Supreme Court, and a fully indoctrinated graduate of the Institute of Red Professors—the Soviet Communist Party's graduate-level school for revolutionary social science. While almost every other judge dressed in a suit and robes, he wore his Red Army uniform festooned with the Order of Lenin and the Order of the Red Star.[50] Burly and jovial in person, Zaryanov was not in any meaningful sense a judge but an enforcing officer of the Soviet state.[51] As Vladimir Lenin had once said, the dictatorship of the proletariat "is unrestricted by law."[52]

Following the party line from Moscow, Zaryanov paid scant attention to courtroom procedure. As at Nuremberg, the Soviets understood all the Tokyo defendants as guilty already; the tribunal would only measure that guilt and impose sentences.[53] As Mei noted grouchily, the Soviet judge did not understand a word of English, and his translator was not much better, making a mess of judicial meetings.[54] (This was unfair: Zaryanov knew "Bottoms up!")[55] The Chinese judge was suitably suspicious of Soviet jurisprudence: "It is said that he has lots of knowledge, but the legal understanding of the proletarian class differs from both the Common Law and Continental Law. Consequently, even though he talks at great length during meetings, the other judges consider him out of tune."[56]

"To Vent My Hatred"

Mei was fascinated and repelled by the Japanese: "I have no idea as to what they are really thinking in their hearts, what they feel about losing the war, what they think of Chinese people, and what is hiding behind those smiles."[57] Perfectly civil behavior struck him as sinister. When waitresses smiled and bowed, he wondered if it was a "honey trap."[58] When Japanese in Ueno Park showed no hostility as he and two Chinese generals emerged from his official car with a Chinese flag, he glowered that perhaps they were wallowing in self-pity or biding their time to exact revenge: "Our Allied friends should be careful."[59]

Although nominally an independent judge, Mei was fused to the Chinese government. He routinely went to bars and the movies with Xiang Zhejun, the Chinese associate prosecutor. He sent cables to his Foreign Ministry about his work, while informally advising Chinese officials in town about occupation policy.[60] He remained close with his patron Sun Ke, now the president of the Legislative Yuan, swapping noteworthy articles to read; Mei pointedly sent an article warning that Japan could revive its industrial capacities and dominate China.[61] Swigging Australian whiskey and Japanese sake in the absence of proper Chinese liquor, Mei and the close-knit group of Chinese in Tokyo spoke emotionally of their fear of Japan.[62]

To his indignation, he found defeated Japan better off than victorious China: industrialized, efficient, and crime-free, "not like us, whose livelihood is ravaged by the disaster of war year after year, with thieves and burglars running rampant."[63] The Japanese seemed to him better fed and better clothed than the average Chinese. He grew fixated on a barmy theory that newspaper reports of deprivation were somehow Japanese propaganda.[64]

Much as he liked the Americans, he abhorred their indulgence toward the Japanese.[65] He mused that "lenient American policies" had left the Japanese friendly toward the Americans, which he did not take as a good thing.[66] Strolling through downtown Ginza, he was indignant that Japanese shoppers acted nonchalantly around American soldiers "so one couldn't even tell who had defeated whom. Is this a success or failure of General MacArthur's policies? Let history be the judge!"[67]

Mei lay awake at night agonizing about his country's future. He was mortified to read English newspaper headlines about starving Chinese reduced to eating bark or about clashes between Communists and Nationalists.[68] He worried about relatives getting caught up in the fighting.[69] "Eight years of painful sacrifices had just succeeded in achieving a bit of international status," he wrote in his diary. "If we can't unite together and work hard at our development, the status that we currently have will vanish, too. This thought makes one shudder with fear."[70]

On March 29, in an incident that has become famous in China today, Chinese officials bought an elegant ornamented sword and held a small ceremony to dedicate it to Mei. He modestly said that fine swords were for heroes, but he was no hero. An official replied that Mei was representing four hundred and fifty million Chinese people and millions of Chinese killed in the war: what could be more heroic than coming to the invader's own capital to punish the evildoers? Fired up, Mei recalled traditional Chinese dramas where the official with the emperor's sword could swiftly execute criminals: "now it's the age of the rule of law and we have to hold trials before we can execute criminals, otherwise I would really like to execute a few of the war criminals first to vent my hatred!"[71]

The next day, he went for an aerial tour of Japan, arranged by Lieutenant General Robert Eichelberger for six of the judges, including Röling.[72] They soared over the ruined cities in Eichelberger's personal B-17 Flying Fortress, a term Mei found frightening—an imposing four-engined heavy bomber of the kind which had rained devastation on Japan. Circling over Yokohama and then Nagoya, Mei reckoned that about 80 percent of those cities had been bombed out. Kobe was worse. Kyoto, whose cultural riches had been spared by Henry Stimson, was the only city without visible destruction. Osaka, a sprawling metropolis which seemed as big as Chicago—where Mei had gone to law school—seemed about one-third destroyed. He was curious about one part of Nagoya that seemed unscathed, which a U.S. officer explained was a residential area. "From this we could sense humanitarianism in the American way of war as well as the accuracy of the pilots' bombing," Mei wrote in his diary. "I hope he wasn't making things up."

Finally the big bomber flew over Hiroshima. The judges chattered about what the radiation had done, entertaining themselves with a preposterous range of rumors: blind people regaining their eyesight, infertile women suddenly able to get pregnant, roosters laying eggs. "Seen from the air, Hiroshima looked like a land of rubble," Mei wrote in his diary. Large buildings had been flattened and the city was barren. Except for the skeletons of buildings, "it was all scorched earth and not a single tree or piece of grass was in sight. Who would think that an 'egg-sized' atomic bomb would have such power? If there were to be a third World War, I think humans might really be extinguished altogether."[73]

"Purged of All Sin"

The prosecution was backed up by massive Allied state power. It hardly evened the scales that the defendants did at least get serious, experienced Japanese and American lawyers.[74] Tojo Hideki, for instance, had two powerhouse Japanese lawyers: one was the former president of the Tokyo Bar Association, and the other had an erudition in Chinese, American, and European jurisprudence that would shame an Oxford don.[75]

Since the Japanese lawyers would be unfamiliar with a court that functioned more along American or British lines, the Japanese government suggested naming American and British defense lawyers to work alongside the Japanese lawyers. With the approval of the judges and MacArthur, the Judge Advocate General's Office found some twenty-five talented American lawyers, both military and civilian, to help defend all the accused.[76] Many defendants were enduringly grateful to their American lawyers. Marquis Kido Koichi marveled privately that the American counsel "genuinely took the side of the defendants." Thanks to their "strong sense of professionalism," he later wrote, "I believe the trial took a significant turn for the better."[77]

Some Japanese might have been included as more than defense counsel. Many Japanese wanted a role in judging their former masters. Newly emboldened liberals in the Diet had recently proposed that Japan form a court to prosecute its own war criminals, only to have conservatives and the prime minister, Shidehara Kijuro, reject that.[78] In February, Keenan floated the dramatic possibility of associating Japan with the Tokyo tribunal, although it is not clear if Truman or MacArthur had approved the initiative. The first U.S. draft indictment included the "Japanese Imperial Government" alongside the Allies charging the accused war criminals.[79]

To be sure, the Truman administration would only consider letting Japanese prosecute other Japanese, but not any crimes committed by the Allies. The Truman administration sternly instructed MacArthur that no Japanese courts would be allowed to have any kind of criminal jurisdiction over any Allied citizens. There would be no accounting for such grave matters as the firebombing of Japanese cities.[80]

The British mission in Tokyo warmed to the notion of a Japanese prosecutor or judge. A senior British diplomat wrote that this would show that "the trials are not merely the retribution by the victors against the vanquished."[81] There were excellent jurists who could have participated, such as Yokota Kisaburo, a future chief justice of Japan who had spoken out against the militarists and would become a loud supporter of the Tokyo trial.[82]

Yet policymakers in London balked. One senior British official scorned the Japanese as too "hopelessly backward" for an equal role in war crimes trials. "We are judging them by the rules of an adult's party to which they should never have been invited in the first place."[83] Britons whose relatives had suffered at Japanese hands would be incensed. The Foreign Office warned that including the Japanese would "give the impression that Japan is an innocent and in fact a wronged party. As soon as the trials are over we should be faced with argument that the guilty have been punished, that Japan has been purged of all sin, and that what remains is a population of seventy-five millions of entirely innocent people whom it would be our duty to help in every possible way."[84] The British government's top Japan expert, the scholar-diplomat Sir George Sansom, did not want to encourage the Japanese to claim they had been deceived by their leaders, nor to exculpate politicians who had seen their government choose a dangerous path but had chosen to keep silent or collaborate.[85]

The British resolved to fight Keenan's proposal. As at Nuremberg, the Tokyo court would be made up entirely of the victors.[86]

Japan Votes

On April 10, the day after Emperor Hirohito gave the last of his secret monologues, the Japanese people spoke for themselves in a historic national election, the first under occupation. Strolling downtown Tokyo on a glorious spring day, Mei was struck by the artistry of the campaign posters and slogans pasted all around, especially those of the Communist Party.[87]

Many Americans, having reviled the Japanese throughout the war as a diabolical and violent race, feared letting them vote. In an analysis endorsed by MacArthur, a General Headquarters staffer explained that "Jap psychology" was "fundamentally unlike that of any Western people." It was "impossible to predict Jap actions on the basis of Western logic."[88] General Headquarters worried that the long-entrenched reactionaries would triumph, creating a hard-line government which would be impossible to work with. The Far Eastern Commission had urged a postponement.[89] Others in Washington worried that Communists and leftists might prevail.[90] Mei scoffed at the notion that the Japanese were embracing real democracy: "The Japanese people, who have been long indoctrinated with fascist thought, must still be baffled by what an election means and the benefits it will bring."[91]

Not so. Some twenty-seven million people cast ballots; young people voted in droves. The women of Japan, enfranchised for the first time, proved heralds of a new society: two-thirds of them voted, showing their clout; they secured Diet seats for progressive women legislators advocating equality and birth control.[92] Countless old-time politicians and reactionaries were swept away or barred from running by the purge, replaced with fresh opinions in the Diet. MacArthur's team was satisfied with the outcome: a manageable conservative party took the most seats, forming a coalition government with another right-wing party, installing the English-speaking, conservative Yoshida Shigeru as prime minister. The election demonstrated the Japanese governing themselves without threatening their neighbors.[93]

"It was Lincoln who said the people are wiser than their rulers," said MacArthur. "The Japanese people provide no exception." The new Diet, he said, would "eliminate from public life those who were tainted with war guilt."[94]

Many Socialist and leftist candidates did quite well too, which caused considerable heartburn for the Truman administration.[95] Emboldened Japanese leftists organized mass meetings in a "Give Us Rice" campaign, aiming not just at food but also at revolutionary change to bring a truly democratic government.[96] Although General Headquarters officials complained that the "Jap Communist party" was "a well disciplined political instrument of Soviet policy," they hoped to embrace liberals and conservatives as stabilizing anti-Communist forces.[97] MacArthur emphasized that Japanese voters had rejected both rightist and leftist extremists.[98]

While the Americans breathed a sigh of relief, Mei found their embrace of Japanese democracy naïve.[99] He fumed, "Being generous is, of course, a virtue, but appeasement and fear are only cowardice."[100] Chinese officials in Tokyo told him that most of the new conservative parliamentarians were really "dogs of warlords and tycoons as well as opportunists. With some disguise and a democratic mask, they easily fooled the Americans."[101]

Two days after the election, MacArthur personally hosted Mei, some other judges, and the Chinese prosecutor for lunch at his residence at the U.S. embassy—part of his ongoing charm offensive aimed at the key players in the Tokyo trial.[102] Mei was beguiled by the general's fast-talking and outspoken wife, Jean MacArthur, who ardently praised Chinese cultural artifacts. MacArthur himself was even more dazzling: tall, sturdy, strong, politically expert, with a soldier's bearing. As a starstruck Mei swooned in his diary, "What's most impressive about him are his two shining eyes and his ability to make you feel that he has limitless sincerity and attraction when he shakes your hand or speaks to you."

Seated in a place of honor next to MacArthur for two hours, Mei got a full blast of the man as he orated without restraint and winked at his own undiplomatic style. MacArthur declared himself greatly interested in China and an avid admirer of Chiang Kai-shek, remembering China's contribution to the war. He spent much of lunch worrying that the world was rushing toward an atomic World War III which could destroy all mankind.

Ebullient after the election, MacArthur cheered its high voter turnout, the enfranchisement of women, and the fizzling of the Communists. Yet Mei inwardly bridled when instructed that the Chinese should be praised for accepting coexistence with Japan. He later glowered that "from General MacArthur's perspective, China's forgiving attitude is what he wants most and needs most. However, while being forgiving, we must also be vigilant! We should increase our vigilance towards Japan!"[103]

As they shook hands in farewell, an awed Mei recorded in his diary, "I felt the same heat and power I had felt when we first met. My impression of General MacArthur is that he is not only a military genius but also a great politician." But despite his memorable audience with the supreme commander, five stars and all, Mei still feared the occupation would turn out badly for China: "I still cannot determine whether General MacArthur's rule of Japan is an achievement or a sin."[104]

INDICTMENT

While the idle, irritated judges waited in mounting frustration, the prosecutors wrangled about a final decision on which Japanese to charge.[105] The prosecutors focused on the names of those who had attended the crucial imperial conferences preceding Pearl Harbor or featured prominently in Kido's essential diary.[106] Most of the likely candidates were detained in Sugamo Prison, but a few were, inconveniently, in Soviet custody. As an American prosecutor noted, the challenge was to assemble a slate of prominent defendants who represented all the phases of Japanese aggression, who embodied different parts of Japan's government, and who had so much evidence against them that they were almost certain to be convicted.[107]

Driven by the Americans, the initial lists from the Allied governments were painstakingly winnowed down. Most who remained were top military men, which spared many middle-ranked officers as well as civilians—business leaders, propagandists, judges, Shinto or Buddhist priests—who might have filled out a more expansive list. Lieutenant General Ishiwara Kanji, a Kwantung Army firebrand who had spearheaded the conquest of Manchuria, was surprisingly omitted.[108] So was General Ishii Shiro, who had run the sinister biowarfare program in occupied China known as Unit 731. No top leaders of the Kempeitai were accused. Nor were any of the corporate or financial leaders of the *zaibatsu* indicted, to the frustration of the Soviets.[109]

The prosecutors first agreed on thirteen defendants, starting with Tojo Hideki and including Hirota Koki, prime minister in 1936–37; General Itagaki Seishiro, a military leader of the invasion of China; and Togo Shigenori, the foreign minister who had in fact tried to prevent the attack on the United States, slated simply for being in Tojo's cabinet. But their first cut left out several prominent leaders who would later wind up in the final indictment, including the palace insider Kido and General Matsui Iwane, the commander of Japanese forces in central China during the Nanjing massacre.[110] Finally, when all seemed settled, the Soviet prosecutor apparently pressed for a few more names.[111] Shigemitsu Mamoru, a former foreign minister known in London as a voice for peace, was astonished to find himself indicted, in part due to Soviet and Chinese pressure.[112]

Despite hopes of indicting no more than fifteen people, the Allies wound up with twenty-eight Class A defendants.[113] In keeping with MacArthur's focus on uprooting Japanese militarism, the tribunal indicted sixteen military men and twelve civilians. The relative culpability of the various organs of Japanese government was neatly weighted: thirteen defendants were from the army, three from the navy, five from the Foreign Ministry, one finance minister, one propagandist, and just one from the Imperial Palace—Kido Koichi, of course, not the emperor. "They comprise ex-Prime Ministers, Foreign Ministers, Admirals, Generals, and other leaders of the nation," wrote Sir William Webb privately. "The charges against them are the gravest ever leveled at men."[114]

The British made sure that the indictment would justify their empire. When the British associate prosecutor gingerly asked if there should be a separate count in the indictment for aggression against India, Burma, and Malaya, the Foreign Office insisted on "a general allegation of making war against British Commonwealth of Nations." During the war, British officials had not even kept separate records on the victimization of Indians.[115] Japanese leaders would be booked not for attacking Burma, Malaya, or Singapore but for attacking the British Commonwealth. The indictment—and, years later, the judgment—was written to uphold the authority of the British Empire.[116]

Other empires secured the same prerogatives. Only India and the Philippines, on the verge of independence, would warrant their own counts in the indictment. The Indonesians would be spoken for by Dutchmen and the Vietnamese by Frenchmen, and the Koreans not at all.

Still, Mei was relieved when the prosecutors concluded their charges. "Thank God!" he wrote in his diary. "The machine may really be turned on."[117]

On April 29, the emperor's forty-fifth birthday, Keenan at last issued a vast indictment of those twenty-eight senior Japanese leaders—an overwhelming set of charges of aggression and atrocity across Asia.[118] The indictment was in large part the creation of the industrious British associate prosecutor, Arthur Comyns Carr—so much that it uses British spelling even for "Pearl Harbour."

In fifty-five harshly worded counts, these men were accused of forming a criminal conspiracy to plan or wage aggressive war against the United States, China, the British Commonwealth, the Soviet Union, Australia, Canada, France, Holland, New Zealand, India, and the Philippines, as well as Portugal and Thailand; of "murdering, maiming and ill-treating" prisoners of war and civilian detainees; and of perpetrating "mass murder, rape, pillage, brigandage, torture and other barbaric cruelties upon the helpless civilian populations of the over-run countries."[119]

The charges of conspiracy—central to Nuremberg as well—exported to Tokyo a concept in U.S. and British criminal law which was quite unfamiliar to Japan. Instead of having to prove an individual's specific involvement with a specific crime, the prosecutors only had to demonstrate that they were part of the conspiracy. The defendants in this criminal conspiracy were held "responsible for all acts performed by themselves or by any person in execution of such plan."[120]

The Japanese conspirators were presented as relentless: poisoning the minds of the Japanese people with ideas of racial superiority, seizing Manchuria in 1931, invading the rest of China in 1937, joining the Axis in September 1940, moving into French Indochina, attacking Pearl Harbor in 1941, and finally conquering the Philippines, Singapore, Hong Kong, Malaya, and the Netherlands East Indies. Alongside the aggressions of Nazi Germany and Italy, Japan's dominance over Asia would help ensure Axis supremacy over the entire world.[121]

The legal authority was provided by a long listing of treaties. For the Geneva and Hague conventions mandating decent treatment of prisoners of war, this was relatively straightforward. But for the novel concept of crimes against peace, the treaties were interpreted assertively, even brazenly. Those covenants included the Hague Convention III from 1907, which stipulated that Japan would not start hostilities without a declaration of war, a Nine-Power Treaty from 1922 committing to respect China's sovereignty, and the Covenant of the League of Nations, which pledged to protect the territorial integrity and political independence of its members. The most important was the idealistic Kellogg-Briand Pact of 1928 outlawing war, under which an internationalist Japanese government had formally renounced war as an instrument of national policy. But neither the Kellogg-Briand Pact nor the League Covenant made aggression a crime, let alone mandated individual criminal punishment for it.[122]

The indictment largely followed Nuremberg in its charges of crimes against peace, war crimes, and crimes against humanity. The indictment echoed Nuremberg's definition of crimes against humanity: "murder, extermination, enslavement, deportation, or other inhumane acts committed against any civilian population," as well as political or racial persecutions, even if committed before the war began, even if legal under a country's domestic law.[123] Because international law was still murky on the legality of aerial bombardment, which could have led to embarrassing scrutiny of the American firebombing of Japanese cities, the indictment conspicuously left out Japan's indiscriminate bombing of Chinese cities. While it did condemn "wantonly destroying cities, towns and villages beyond any reasonable justification of military necessity," it gave no mention of aerial bombing.[124]

More distinctive was a grouping of murder counts, an idea that came from MacArthur's plan for a swift trial for Tojo. This could sidestep cultural complexities; as the prosecution noted, murder was a crime in the law of every country.[125] The surprise attacks of December 1941—against American sailors at Pearl Harbor, members of the British armed forces in Hong Kong and Malaya, and Americans and Filipinos in the Philippines— were treated not just as a crime against peace but as murder.[126]

Capacious as it was, the indictment left out plenty. There was no mention of Korea, which had been part of the Japanese Empire before the war and did not yet have an independent government to join the Tokyo trial.

(Adding to the sting, the Allied powers were prosecuting some lower-level Korean and Taiwanese war criminals who had served as prison guards for Imperial Japan.)[127] Shockingly, there was only one mention of rape, and no defendants were indicted specifically for the sexual coercion of the women who were euphemistically called "comfort women."[128] And no one was indicted for Japan's top secret bioweapons program, with the United States and the Soviet Union eager to tap the grim knowledge of Unit 731.[129]

The indictment had considerable impact across Japan, giving a notable chance for citizens to excoriate their wartime leaders. One young woman studying at prestigious Meiji University blamed Tojo for starting the war and hoped that the trial would punish the war criminals for exploitation and enslavement of all the women of Japan.[130] The *Yomiuri* newspaper condemned Japanese imperialism for igniting the war, while urging that everyone responsible for the war be punished.[131] Another *Yomiuri* writer demanded that Japanese militarists be relentlessly tried so that Japanese youth would not believe that the war was in self-defense and that the war criminals were martyrs.[132]

Some Japanese reactions were more circumspect. Hatoyama Ichiro, a prominent conservative who was purged but would later go on to become prime minister, said, "Leaving Mr. Tojo aside as an exception, some of the others deserve sympathy." A right-wing Diet member urged defense lawyers and witnesses, "Please do not say that you 'hate to defend Tojo,' but do it openly and without flinching."[133]

American newspapers cheered the indictment, although many decried the omission of the emperor. "Has it been decided that he alone of the top Japanese had no part in the plan except that of a figurehead?" asked *The New York Times*. "Or has the decision been made that his help in expediting the occupation and the current reforms so overbalances the scales in his favor that he is not even to be named?"[134]

Like millions across Asia, Mei read the indictment with bitter familiarity. Chinese women and children would recognize these names, he thought. He was particularly incensed at two generals: Doihara Kenji was "an expert in stirring divisions and troubles in China, full of conspiracy and tricks," and Matsui Iwane, the commander whose troops committed the Nanjing massacre, "is an executioner whom the Chinese people will never forget." He wrote in his diary that "the Chinese people's hatred towards these names is deeply rooted." With the trial about to begin, he made no suggestion that these men were innocent until proven guilty: "The more I read, the more indignant I felt."[135]

PART II

CATHARSIS

CHAPTER 10

The Anatomy of the
Tokyo Trial

M EI RUAO, TAKING HIS place on the bench for the opening
day of the Tokyo trial, was exultant and enraged. "Today," he
wrote in his diary, "my ability to stand high at the judges' stage to punish
these evil culprits was paid for by the blood and flesh of millions and tens
of millions of our compatriots. I must be alert! I must be serious!"[1]

He and the other judges arrived early that morning of May 3, 1946, not
wanting to let any happenstance fumble their big moment. For a suitably
awe-inspiring courtroom, General Headquarters had spent almost two
months renovating a colossal auditorium at the former Army Ministry
on a hilltop in Ichigaya, a hulking structure just two miles from the
Imperial Palace in central Tokyo. (Joseph Keenan, the U.S. chief prosecutor, had considered using the Diet building but decided against that
particular insult to Japanese democracy.) The Army Ministry was chosen
in part because it was largely undamaged by American bombing; nearby
areas downhill had been devastated by B-29 raids. The symbolism of
repurposing this particular ministry was blatant—although few of the
assembling spectators would have realized that the emperor himself had
kept a resting room on the second floor, nor that the balcony had been
designed so that no commoner's eye level would be above that of the
monarch, nor that Tojo Hideki's old office was now a meeting room for
the Allied judges.[2]

The courtroom is grand and airy, with sweepingly high ceilings, a vast
space for a vast trial. When empty, it is dark and relatively cool even in
Tokyo's muggy springs and summers, with a pleasant smell of wood and
wood polish from over seven thousand decorative oak tiles.[3] One awed

Chinese official told Mei that no courtroom in the world could rival it, except for the Supreme Court of the United States.[4]

The judges had a raised bench on the eastern side of the courtroom, about twenty feet apart from the Japanese defendants. Military policemen stood watchfully behind the accused. The rest of the space, totaling over ten thousand square feet, was given over to rows of desks for the prosecutors and defense counsel, a host of translators and stenographers, and seating for visiting dignitaries. There was new wiring, heating, carpeting, and drapes, as well as sound-absorbing tiles on the ceiling and state-of-the-art headphones for live translation in Japanese and English. There was space to hang enormous maps, which one defense lawyer called "a Barnum-and-Bailey road show."[5] The judges and prosecutors, meant to encounter each other only in court, entered and exited through separate corridors; in fact they were routinely hobnobbing together after hours.[6]

Orchestrating the spectacle, General Headquarters had laid in abundant telephones and built about a hundred seats for Japanese and foreign journalists. There was a radio booth for broadcasters and three booths for motion pictures: one on the balcony, one near the defendants' box, and one at the southern end of the room. Headphones with switches gave either English or Japanese translation. For a public trial, there were more than two hundred seats for Japanese spectators.[7] Six big arrays of klieg lights were built into the ceiling, meant to be so bright that the photographers would not need to pop flashbulbs. It was warm already in Tokyo in May; when these batteries of klieg lights and spotlights were turned on, the courtroom quickly became uncomfortably hot and mercilessly bright.[8] "American youngsters love to play," Mei wrote in his diary. "Anything could be 'Hollywood-ized.'"[9] *Time* magazine had the same thought: "The klieg lights suggested a Hollywood premiere."[10]

It was a spring day, cloudy at first, with bright azaleas blooming on the green lawns outside the court.[11] As the judges donned their black robes, they heard that Tojo and twenty-five other defendants had already arrived from Sugamo Prison. Guarded by a convoy of military police jeeps, they were driven across the bombed-out city to court in a blue bus with the windows covered over.[12] The older defendants shuffled into the courtroom, gaunt, pallid, and weary. Forbidden to talk or smoke, they clutched copies of their indictments. "They looked like very ordinary, shrunken old men," noted General Douglas MacArthur's political adviser.[13] Tojo wore a drab green army uniform, stripped of his insignia and chestful of medals. An admiral had on his navy dress blues but without honors or rank. Togo Shigenori, the foreign minister who had tried to stop the attack on the United States, kept his expression so blank that an American reporter thought he would make a great poker player.[14] Two army defendants, being flown in that day from Thailand, were late; eventually the judges gave up and decided to include them in the afternoon session.[15]

The defendants on the bus from Sugamo Prison to the former Army Ministry to be arraigned on the first day of the Tokyo trial, May 3, 1946. All the windows are covered. Tojo Hideki sits in the second row on the left, while Marquis Kido Koichi has the aisle seat on the right side in the third row.

The judges lined up single-file backstage as a court marshal bellowed at the excited spectators for silence. The original plan had been to seat the judges according to the order in which their representatives had signed the surrender on the USS *Missouri*.[16] But Mei had insistently demanded a central position appropriate to China's wartime record. He secured a seat next to Sir William Webb, the chief judge, allowing him to whisper suggestions throughout. On Webb's other side was the United States judge. "This is a hard won position, the result of a fight with both open and secret means," Mei later boasted.[17] He explained to a Chinese reporter that this honor was "a result of our country's eight-year bloody resistance and not my personal achievement at all."[18]

As the stentorian marshal yelled for the packed audience to rise, the Chinese judge proudly strode in behind the stocky Webb.[19] Newsreel cameras hummed.[20] Flashbulbs crackled from all directions, seeming bright as the sun. Mei was struck by how huge the courtroom was and how high the stage was, making the judges' somber procession seem interminable. The galleries were packed, including Allied grandees and Lieutenant General Robert Eichelberger of the U.S. Eighth Army—but not MacArthur, who would never attend, believing that inappropriate for the supreme commander. The judges hovered behind their chairs as the rest of the black-robed queue arrived, before taking their seats, backed by their national flags. Then the prosecutors, staffers, and audience members deferentially took their seats. Japanese spectators—workers, students, and government officials, with some of the women in kimonos—looked on intently.[21]

From the rostrum, the marshal of the court formally announced, "The International Military Tribunal for the Far East is in session and is ready to hear any matter brought before it."[22] Webb, in his Queensland accent, began softly but with confidence: "There has been no more important criminal trial in all history." While the judges were only "a court of plain men" selected from high courts, the defendants had been "for more than a decade the leaders of Japan at the height of her power and prosperity." Pointing out the former premiers, ministers, and chiefs of staff arrayed before them, he sternly said, "the former high rank of the accused entitles them to no more consideration than would be extended to the humblest Japanese private or Korean guard." The accused sat stone-faced. He pledged, "To our great task we bring open minds both on the facts and on the law."[23]

While Webb orated, Mei—his mind by no means impartial—distractedly peered around at the scene below him, keen to inspect the accused but mindful that many hundreds of eyes were gazing at him. He remembered how not long ago, as Japanese troops advanced, it had seemed unimaginable that Chinese would ever feel national pride again. On his desk were photographs of the defendants arranged in the order of their seats. Dazzled by the klieg lights, he could only dimly make out Tojo and the chubby General Doihara Kenji. Slumped in their seats, the Japanese defendants kept stiff faces—pretending to be calm, he thought. "Those who faced me caused unlimited resentment and feelings in my heart," he wrote in his diary. "All of these people are old hands in the invasion of China, poisoning China for decades. Tens of millions of our fellow countrymen died in their hands, and consequently my resentment is my fellow countrymen's resentment."[24]

Bert Röling, the Dutch judge, inspected the accused men with only a little more sympathy. As he wrote to a friend, "They look tired and a bit desperate, since the Emperor forbade them committing hara-kiri, the only honourable way out. Emperor and people left them in the lurch, not because they started a war, but because they lost one."[25]

After the prosecutors and the defense lawyers rose to introduce themselves, it took many hours for prosecutors to read out the counts of the indictment, slowed because of Japanese translation. Under the brilliant lights, Keenan's face was, as an *Asahi Shimbun* reporter noted, "crimson itself," glaring at "the accused as the Capones of Japan."[26] The decorum of the day was punctured by one of the defendants, Okawa Shumei, a popular propagandist and putschist. Praying and tittering, he had either gone insane or, as Mei believed, was faking it. He suddenly smacked Tojo's bald head from behind and yelled that he would kill him. A guard pulled Okawa back. Tojo, startled at first, grinned in amusement. Babbling, Okawa was pulled from the court for psychiatric examination.[27]

With calm restored, Mei returned to inspecting balefully the defendants, concentrating on one of the late arrivals: General Itagaki Seishiro, a bald man with a mustache, whom he loathed as a leader of the invasion of China. "I could not help feeling full of anger once I saw this group, as if all of my compatriots' hatred had to be released from my chest!" he wrote in his diary. "Luckily, it was still early. It was just the beginning. Since these evil culprits are in the hands of the law, they could by no means escape serious punishment of justice."

At last the court adjourned. Not everyone was impressed by the extravaganza. The Soviet party line on state radio was that Emperor Hirohito and Japanese industrialists should join Tojo in the dock.[28] A *Time* correspondent jeered that the gala opening had looked like "a third-string road company of the Nurnberg show." The reporter wrote that Keenan, reminding him of the boozy comedian W. C. Fields, strained to handle "the *opéra bouffe* element which the West so often finds in the Japanese character." The Japanese accused, the correspondent taunted, were ill-behaved schoolboys indifferent to the gravity of the proceedings. If Nuremberg had evoked Wagner, *Time* wrote, Tokyo felt more like Gilbert and Sullivan.[29]

Yet returning to the Imperial Hotel, Mei was triumphant. "Today was the day when the machine was really set in motion," he wrote in his diary. "I felt a sense of joy that was hard to express in words."[30]

The next day, the prosecutors continued reading the lengthy indictment. Mei scrutinized each of the accused. "Their names and faces brought me many memories and much loathing," he wrote in his diary.

Without the trappings of power, the defendants looked like passengers on any Tokyo bus—a motley, undistinguished group who looked "no more than ordinary." Only Tojo kept his bearing, "almost motionless, like a sculpture." The elderly General Matsui Iwane, indicted for the Nanjing massacre, was "a poor creature as tame as a sheep." General Doihara Kenji tried to keep his composure but sometimes shuddered in apparent anxiety. The most pathetic was the sickly Matsuoka Yosuke, a hard-line foreign minister who, as Mei recalled sourly, had once called China nothing more than a geographical term. He was haggard, thin, and pale, with a messily untrimmed beard; his lawyer was trying to get him excused from the trial before he collapsed.

His rage at last abating, Mei subsided into a kind of racial empathy. These Japanese criminals, he reflected, resembled Chinese people. China and Japan shared the same national and cultural roots; it was only this gang which had abandoned their common destiny with their "absurd argument of national superiority." They were not just the enemies of China and the world, he thought, but also of the Japanese people. "I naturally felt national anger in my heart on the one hand, and could not help feeling sadness for our common race on the other," he reflected in his diary. "I hope that my effort to participate in this historical episode can be instrumental to the creation of a new principle of mutual respect, mutual understanding, coexistence and mutual prosperity among all nations!"[31]

In English alphabetical order, Webb asked each defendant to plead guilty or not guilty. When the first accused to rise, a general and former army minister, angrily bellowed in Japanese the beginnings of a statement denouncing the charges, Mei pressed Webb to stop him. The Australian chief judge snapped, "We want a plea, not a speech." Indignant, the general said that never in his life had he committed any of the atrocities charged against him. The others all rose in turn to declare themselves not guilty "like the flow of water," Mei noted. As the *Asahi Shimbun* reported, all the military defendants pleaded not guilty arrogantly and bluntly, while the civilians did likewise "in a reserved and weak-kneed tone."[32] Several of the generals and admirals sounded like they were angrily barking orders. With cameras swiveling to him as he rose, flashbulbs popping, Tojo Hideki spoke loudly but calmly: "On all counts I plead not guilty."[33]

Outside the courtroom, Tojo found himself the object of revulsion and derision. Ordinary Japanese heaped contempt on him. His family became pariahs, besieged by irate letters and threats from Japanese embittered by war, some of them urging his wife to commit suicide. His wife fled Tokyo for a farming life at her parents' remote home in Fukuoka, leaving it to Tojo's eldest daughter to bring him books, newspapers, and cigarettes in prison.[34]

Mei scornfully commented that Japanese newspapers were only lauding the court to push responsibility for the war onto "this group of evil culprits."[35] Yet the most influential newspapers were fulsome in support for the Tokyo trial. A writer for the liberal *Jiji Shimpo* praised the attempt to use justice to "root out war once and for all."[36] One *Asahi Shimbun* writer was disgusted by the "brazen and unscrupulous" denials of Tojo and the other defendants who had led Japan to defeat, preferring Okawa because he at least had the excuse of syphilitic derangement.[37]

"For Reasons to Be Given Later"

Mei inspected the Japanese lawyers with distaste. Although ordinarily a sucker for prestigious academic credentials, which they had in spades, he thought they looked mediocre. Tojo's lawyer, Kiyose Ichiro—a formidable former Diet member who would later become Japan's education minister and speaker of the House of Representatives—was gray-haired and bespectacled, his shirt collar sloppy, and struck Mei as "an old pedant."[38]

Even without the Chinese judge glaring at them, the Japanese and American defense counsel were badly outmatched. For some of them, the arraignment was their first chance to confer with clients on trial for their lives.[39] Understaffed and overworked, they were begging MacArthur for more resources, particularly more American lawyers.[40] They were divided among themselves about whether to try to exonerate their individual clients or mount a general defense of Japanese policy. Overwhelmed by Keenan's international prosecution section, which was backed up by General Headquarters, eight defense lawyers would soon resign in protest.[41] Several Japanese lawyers were unpaid and running short of food; unable to afford hotels in central Tokyo, they got home at 10 p.m. and left again at 4 a.m. Fearing a collapse of the defense, Webb had to get MacArthur to secure them a modest salary and hotel stipend from the Japanese government.[42]

Despite all these hindrances, the defense proved remarkably pugnacious. Tojo planned to make his defense a vindication of Japan's righteous war.[43] Taking copious notes, studying the indictment closely, he meant to be a combative defendant.[44] Kiyose alarmed Mei and several other judges by submitting that it was improper for Webb, a former Australian war crimes investigator, to serve as chief judge. The court grew tense. Keenan bristled. Annoyed, Webb asked the other judges to decide, adding that he would take no part in the determination "based on my alleged inability to sit because of the report on atrocities in New Guinea and elsewhere."[45]

As the judges retired to their meeting room, they worried that each one of them would be challenged in turn. They returned with a blunt ruling: they had been formally appointed by MacArthur and had no authority to remove themselves. This blocked any further challenges by the defense, who might reasonably have challenged Mei, Major General Ivan Zaryanov, or other judges, but it dodged the essential complaint about judges who were profoundly biased. "There was some commotion among the audience, who whispered to each other," Mei wrote in his diary. "They seemed to be expecting something."[46]

Unfazed as he stood at the lectern, Kiyose moved on to a vigorous attack on the basic legitimacy of the court. He calmly complained that crimes against peace and crimes against humanity had not been an established part of international law when the surrendering Japanese government accepted the Potsdam Declaration. Neither MacArthur nor the court had any authority to prosecute members of a government for their actions before the beginning of a war. More narrowly, the defense also pointed out that the indictment included acts, such as border battles with the Soviet Union in Manchuria, which happened years before the outbreak of full-scale war in Asia.[47]

The U.S. and Chinese judges wanted to swiftly dismiss this challenge.[48] Yet MacArthur and Keenan preferred to hear the defense out fully.[49] Mei unhappily braced himself for a "huge debate."[50]

On May 13 and 14, defense counsel stood before the court and told it that it was no real court at all. Kiyose and other defense lawyers, Japanese and American, offered a sweeping motion asking that the tribunal declare that it had no jurisdiction to adjudicate the indictment. The defense made forceful, interlocking arguments that the court itself was not properly constituted and that some of the offenses in its charter were not crimes: that war-making was an act of state for which there was no individual criminal responsibility; that the Potsdam Declaration and the *Missouri* surrender documents only provided for the prosecution of established war crimes, not newfound ones such as aggressive war; that the famous Kellogg-Briand Pact of 1928, which Japan had signed, had renounced war but had not made it a crime; that the tribunal's charter was nothing more than ex post facto law, belatedly declaring acts to be crimes which had not been criminal at the time they were committed (what lawyers condemn as *nullum crimen sine lege*); and that the accused could not get a fair trial in front of judges from the victor nations.[51] Kiyose suggested that Japan, unlike Germany, had actually made a negotiated surrender whose terms had to be honored by the Allies.[52] In newspaper articles, he took his case directly to the Japanese public, contending that the Allies could not prosecute newfangled crimes against peace or crimes against humanity—such as, in his example, the persecution of Jews in Germany.[53]

"The trial can neither be fair, legal, nor impartial," declared a U.S. captain serving as a defense lawyer. Major Ben Bruce Blakeney, an energetic young attorney from Oklahoma City with his dark hair neatly combed back, confidently said that he had as much right as the prosecution to "speak for America. We speak for American, . . . for Anglo-American, for democratic views of justice, of fair play. We speak for the proposition that observing legal forms, while ignoring the essence of legal principles, is the supreme atrocity against the law." Challenging the indictment's claim that the killing of American servicemembers at Pearl Harbor had been nothing more than murder, he startled the court by arguing that Harry Truman could equally well stand accused: "If the killing of Admiral Kidd"—Rear Admiral Isaac Kidd, who died on the USS *Arizona*—"by the bombing of Pearl Harbor is murder, we know the name of the very man whose hands loosed the atomic bomb on Hiroshima." He paused to let the audacious point sink in before continuing: "we know the chief of staff who planned that act, we know the chief of the responsible state."[54]

The Japanese defendants were pleasantly surprised to get such a robust defense. Togo Shigenori and Shigemitsu Mamoru looked pleased. Tojo, watching intently, took careful notes.[55]

Argued with skill and verve, these claims had considerable impact on the more open-minded judges. Röling was not sure that aggressive war was a crime.[56] Webb too was privately unconvinced that making war was an established crime, and seriously considered going forward only with a trial for more conventional war crimes instead.[57]

Rising to challenge the defense, Keenan got off to a disastrous start, both in style and substance. When the top U.S. prosecutor asked if the Allies were "totally impotent" to punish those responsible for spilling "deplorable and incalculable quantities of blood," a visibly annoyed Webb cut him off: "Mr. Chief Prosecutor, do you think those rhetorical phrases are fitting at this juncture?"

Keenan reddened. Some of the prosecutors wondered if he would have a stroke.[58] In a blur of mixed metaphors, he angrily asked "whether mankind will place itself in a straightjacket of legal precepts (which are without foundation or logic) by bowing to the force of such worm-wood legalisms?" When he quoted Franklin Delano Roosevelt and Joseph Stalin, an exasperated Webb cut him off and reprimanded him for making inflammatory statements.[59]

Mei, who thought Webb was being overemotional, tried to prevent the Australian chief judge from muzzling Keenan, who "lost a lot of face." Whatever the tension between Webb and Keenan, Mei wrote in his diary, this was not the place for such retaliation. As they sparred, Mei observed, Keenan's red face and red nose turned almost purple.[60]

Keenan argued that Japan had surrendered utterly without conditions as demanded in the Potsdam Declaration—overlooking that Japan had been allowed to keep its emperor.[61] He was bailed out by the British associate prosecutor, Arthur Comyns Carr, urbane and Oxford-educated, who provided real substance. There was nothing novel, the prosecutors argued, about seeing aggressive war as a crime. By signing the Kellogg-Briand Pact renouncing war, the Treaty of Versailles calling for the trial of Kaiser Wilhelm II, and other treaties, Japan had endorsed the illegality of aggressive war—which was already an established rule of international law before the war. As for Hiroshima and the firebombing of Japan, Keenan said, "we make no more apology for that than does a decent, innocent citizen walking home . . . employ the use of force to prevent his life being taken by an outlaw."[62]

Many of the judges were dismayed by Keenan's ripe performance. The chief prosecutor had been outshone by everyone else: the undaunted Kiyose; Comyns Carr, who spoke crisply and to the point; the forceful Blakeney, Harvard-educated and fluent in Japanese, who poked fun at Keenan's "flight of oratory, which I cannot emulate."[63] Mei, while annoyed at Comyns Carr's plummy British accent ("the anti-Britain tide inside my heart is very high these days"), was grudgingly impressed. "Keenan made a speech to the whole world," Mei wrote in his diary. "Comyns Carr's talk was a real argument justifying the tribunal."[64]

Webb was appalled that Keenan was relying on perorations about the awfulness of aggressive war to prove that it was a crime. War had always been horrible, Webb thought, but that did not mean it had always been illegal. He privately scoffed, "the whole of Mr. Keenan's argument based on the horrors of war produces no legal results, although its political effect is considerable."[65]

The courtroom clash impressed Japanese observers across the political spectrum, although newspaper editors were undoubtedly mindful of the censors at General Headquarters. One writer for the conservative *Yomiuri* marveled at the heated dueling. This journalist sided fully with Keenan, grieving for "the miserable loss of near relatives and homes and the hunger caused by the aggressive war planned and executed by this group of war criminals." Tojo and his henchmen "must definitely be held responsible" for massacring innocents all across Asia. In the new atomic age, the *Yomiuri* writer argued, "aggressive war is an enemy to peace, humanity and civilization"—an early sign of the pacifism that would take root in postwar Japan. "We must directly see and face the crimes committed by Tojo and his followers and straightforwardly recognize their crimes against peace, humanity and civilization and put the spirit of civilized trials into a concrete form so that it can shape a new international law."[66] Another *Yomiuri* writer, condemning Japan as guilty of the "war crime of aggression" from Manchuria to Pearl Harbor, was impressed that the victorious Allies allowed the defendants to make any defense they wanted in an open trial.[67]

Of course, disputing the tribunal's jurisdiction was an obvious opening gambit for any competent defense lawyer before a new court. It had happened at Nuremberg; it happens at the opening of almost every new international war crimes trial, challenging their shaky claims to judge the defendants before them. Yet astonishingly, the judges had no unified answer to this inevitable challenge. They disagreed bitterly both about the rationale for their jurisdiction and about whether aggressive war was really an international crime. Hinting at the can of worms that was about to be opened, the French judge, Henri Bernard, believed that "universal conscience" had long seen wars of aggression as subject to punishment, but did not believe that a handful of Allied leaders gathered at Potsdam had the authority to make international law for all nations.[68]

After a few days of consideration, the judges collectively punted, agreeing they would contrive their reasons eventually.[69] On May 17, Webb announced in court that the defense's jurisdiction motions were "dismissed for reasons to be given later"—an unsurprising outcome but with a shocking absence of any stated rationale.[70]

Meanwhile a fervent case for jurisdiction was made by someone with ample credibility: a future chief justice of Japan, Yokota Kisaburo. Then a liberal law professor at Tokyo Imperial University, he had bravely decried the invasion of Manchuria as illegal, facing public denunciations as a traitor and threats of assassination.[71] In a newspaper article vindicating the Tokyo trial, he proposed a broad interpretation of evolving international law. Yokota argued for individual liability for war crimes, while deriding the defense's "mechanical application" of the principle that there could be no punishment without preexisting law. The future chief justice even argued that killing in illegal warfare was murder.[72] In later months, he expanded his arguments into a book upholding the trial, arguing boldly that if actions were criminal in substance, legal formalities should not prevent their prosecution. He would even help with the official translation of the court's judgment into Japanese.[73]

The judges fell to bickering among themselves about their jurisdiction.[74] Webb proved unable to unify a majority to fulfill their promise to state their reasons. What seemed like a rather manageable task turned into a fracas which would last for more than two years. In the end, the judges would only deliver those "reasons to be given later" as part of the court's final verdict in November 1948. The entire Tokyo trial would be conducted without an explanation from the court of its own legitimacy.

STUMBLING OUT OF THE GATE

The tribunal adjourned, fixing a trial date of June 3. The defense lawyers protested that this left just one month to prepare, after the prosecutors had had eight to draw up the indictment.[75]

During the break, the U.S. judge abruptly quit. Realizing that the trial would take far longer than a few months, unswayed by an angry exhortation from the U.S. attorney general, he decided that he was needed back at the Superior Court of Massachusetts.[76] This was scandalous: how could the Japanese get a fair hearing from a court whose composition kept changing? Facing the embarrassment of a trial without a U.S. judge, MacArthur and Webb frantically sought a replacement.[77] Within two weeks, they chose Major General Myron Cramer, a Harvard Law graduate who had recently served as the U.S. judge advocate general.[78] He had helped to plan the Nuremberg trial, urging a "full-dress international trial of the ringleaders" to provide "convincing proof of guilt" to the world.[79]

Cramer rushed to Tokyo.[80] The oldest judge, he was an enthusiastic drinker, devoted to his wife, and prone to cheering loudly at ball games. Mei, always self-conscious about his height, was pleased to find that he was short. As the pair filed into court side by side, Mei noted, people joked that they made a good couple.[81] Nobody seemed aware that the new U.S. judge had in 1944 approved a thorough legal memorandum ripping apart the idea that aggression was a crime under international law.[82]

The governments of Britain and New Zealand formally complained to the United States about the impropriety of naming a new judge midstream.[83] When Cramer made his court debut, American defense lawyers immediately challenged their countryman and asked for a mistrial. As a general in the victorious U.S. Army, one American defense counsel argued, he could hardly be impartial toward the defeated foe. He had not been present to hear witnesses, listen to lawyers wrangling, and deliberate with the other judges. The Chinese associate prosecutor jumped in to emphasize that China particularly wanted to have an American judge on the bench. Despite private qualms, a majority of the judges agreed that Cramer could sit as the U.S. judge.[84]

In another embarrassment, the tribunal lost two defendants. Okawa Shumei, who had slapped Tojo, wound up in the psychiatric ward of Tokyo Imperial University Hospital, chattering incoherently in multiple languages.[85] General Headquarters spitefully let it be known that he would get treated for venereal disease.[86] Weakened from tuberculosis and heart disease from syphilis, believing that Jesus and Muhammad were visiting him, he later said that he had yearned for nine years to slap Tojo's bald head.[87] All charges against him would eventually be dropped on grounds of insanity.[88]

Matsuoka Yosuke, hospitalized, was found to be mortally ill. Having crafted the Axis alliance and led Japan's walkout from the League of Nations, he would soon die of tuberculosis, kidney disease, and other illnesses in an isolation ward at Tokyo Imperial University Hospital at the age of sixty-six.[89]

KEENAN MAKES HIS CASE

With the court reeling from these backstage disasters, Keenan on June 4 rose to open the prosecution's case. For many Japanese, this was the first time they heard a version of recent history that undercut the official wartime line.

It was a suitably gloomy and rainy day. Keenan, his plump face framed by round spectacles, strained for authority in a three-hour opening speech.[90] To the perplexity of Japanese spectators, he spoke facing the judges with his back to the defendants. His pompous vocabulary ("peradventure," "extinguishment," "advert") sent not only the translators reaching for a dictionary.

"This is no ordinary trial," he intoned, "for here we are waging a part of the determined battle of civilization to preserve the entire world from destruction." The accused, he said, had meant to destroy democracy and freedom. This paean to liberty was punctured by the presence of judges and associate prosecutors for the Soviet, British, French, and Dutch Empires. No less awkwardly, he tried to blame the devastation around the courtroom on the defendants, not the Allied bombers: "We need only . . . to take a few steps to the top of this building to see what they have brought upon their own people."

Since the judges had not explained the court's jurisdiction, Keenan took a stab himself. There was nothing novel about crimes against peace or crimes against humanity, he contended. Japan's militant leaders had known that they were violating their own treaty obligations. He argued that a litany of international agreements—the Treaty of Versailles, the unrealized Geneva Protocol for the Pacific Settlement of International Disputes, a 1927 resolution by the League of Nations Assembly, a Pan-

Allied judges in the courtroom in front of their eleven national flags. From left to right: Lord Patrick (Britain), Major General Myron Cramer (the United States), Sir William Webb (Australia), Mei Ruao (China), Major General Ivan Zaryanov (the Soviet Union). The civilian judges wear black robes, but the U.S. and Soviet judges are in their army uniforms. Based on the flag of British India, the photograph was taken between the arrival of Cramer in July 1946 and the independence of India in August 1947.

American Conference resolution in 1928, and above all the Kellogg-Briand Pact in 1928—had accumulated to make aggressive war an international crime.

To make it easier to condemn aggression as a war crime, the prosecution treated international law as something living and progressive, ultimately rooted in a higher natural law—an inherent sense of right and wrong among civilized peoples. Keenan even claimed that there had been punishment for aggressive war since "the prehistoric and primeval ages." International law, he noted, was based not just on treaties but on custom—consistent international practices of states carried out because of a sense of legal duty. As he claimed, "when many civilized nations have acted in voluntary concert on a matter of general welfare it becomes recognized as a principle of international law."

To sidestep complaints that alien Western laws were being imposed upon the Japanese, Keenan noted that murder was a crime in the Japanese penal code. The waging of aggressive war, he said, entailed the taking of human lives without legal justification, which—turning prehistoric again—"has been recognized from the dawn of history . . . as murder." This sweeping legal theory potentially meant that every Allied soldier killed in World War II had actually been murdered.

For Japanese audiences, Keenan's oration hit home with his recounting of recent history, offering a shockingly divergent view from what Japan's citizenry had heard through the long years of war. The address was heavily covered—and in some cases reprinted verbatim—by Japanese newspapers, and the full Japanese and English texts of the indictment were soon published and put on sale.[91] Keenan's tone became intense and he shook his hand like "a lion in all fury for the cause of justice," reported the influential *Jiji Shimpo*.[92]

He began with Japan's conquest of Manchuria in 1931, then the invasion of the rest of China in 1937. He described Japan's alliance with Adolf Hitler's Germany and Benito Mussolini's Italy as meant to stomp out democracy around the globe. According to Keenan, the Japanese leadership next fixed its ambitions on a Greater East Asia that included Indochina, Thailand, Burma, and Indonesia, and eventually even Australia, New Zealand, India, and Siberia. This would require war with the United States. Tojo's cabinet then treacherously struck "with deliberately criminal intent" in December 1941 against Pearl Harbor, the Philippines, and British-controlled Hong Kong. These were not just acts of aggression, he contended, but the murder of more than five thousand Allied nationals.

For a Japanese audience saturated with wartime propaganda, Keenan's horrifying tales—Australian prisoners being worked to death as slave labor building a railway through the Burmese and Thai jungles, Chinese civilians coerced to build military installations in Manchuria and then killed for secrecy, Australian nurses massacred off Sumatra—were fresh and shocking. So was the claim that the slaughters at Nanjing, Manila, and elsewhere were part of a systematic policy of atrocity warfare. Belying Imperial Japanese claims that its soldiers had fought honorably, Keenan contended that "identical measures were constantly employed throughout the areas of Japanese occupation to torture prisoners of war and civilians, such as the 'water-cure,' 'electric shock treatment,' hanging upside down, prying fingernails, and body beatings."[93]

Some of the accused generals remained nonchalant, but the oration struck home for Shigemitsu Mamoru, a pro-Western former foreign minister, who looked grave.[94] A *Yomiuri* reporter found the defendants' expressions "as dark as the rainy sky outside." At a mention of the destruction of the world's youth, Tojo, his glasses off, stared fixedly at the ceiling in what the reporter thought was either despair or humiliation.[95]

Many Japanese, especially the young, were impressed by this historical recital. "In the eyes of Prosecutor Keenan," wrote the *Asahi Shimbun*, "the Tokyo Trial is the battle-field of civilization."[96] The conservative *Yomiuri* noted the weighty feeling of the historic importance of the international trial.[97] The Jiji press agency was impressed that the trial charged officials for their wartime actions: "The human agents must be accountable, as Chief Prosecutor Keenan emphasized."[98]

Some progressive Japanese intellectuals even wondered what these atrocities meant about them as a race, painfully internalizing the American wartime view that the Japanese were a distinctively savage species.[99] One *Jiji Shimpo* writer, weeping "silent tears" at the indictment's listing of murder, torture, and enslavement, wondered how "the Japanese race was degraded into such a shameful and wretched mentality." The writer added that "we Japanese must thoroughly reflect upon our racial characteristics in connection with the trials now under way. . . . We must realize that it is the first requisite for the regeneration of the Japanese race to strive for the attainment of a far higher level of morality in full cognizance of their truly low standard of civilization."[100]

One Japanese spectator, a white-collar worker who was sick of war, was impressed that the accused were taking responsibility. A student at Waseda University arrived at the courthouse feeling somewhat sorry for the defendants, but came away convinced that the responsibility of the accused had to be uncovered.[101] And an economics student at Tokyo Imperial University hoped that the accused criminals would "reflect deeply upon themselves."[102]

THE EXCEPTION

Having boldly demanded individual criminal accountability regardless of rank, Keenan promptly made a whopping exception. On a visit to Washington, he told reporters that a decision had been made at "high political levels" not to try Hirohito as a war criminal, adding that it was his "official belief" that it would be "a distinct mistake to bring the Emperor to trial."[103] In Sugamo Prison, Marquis Kido Koichi exulted that "with this, my mission is complete."[104]

The other Allied prosecutors were stunned, as an alarmed Xiang Zhejun, the Chinese associate prosecutor, reported to the Chinese foreign minister. Comyns Carr wondered whether it was proper to continue his work as Britain's associate prosecutor. The Australian, Canadian, and New Zealand associate prosecutors fumed at Keenan for his embarrassing comment.[105]

In private, several of the judges, too, reckoned that Hirohito ought to be on trial. Like many Australians, Webb was convinced of the centrality of the emperor, informing his prime minister that "Kido and Tojo are in my opinion the two most important accused, the former as Lord Keeper of the Privy Seal and the latter as the Prime Minister when Pearl Harbor was attacked."[106] As Mei noted, Australia had consistently pressed to add the emperor to the list of major war criminals; Soviet state media called for prosecuting him; American newspapers called him Japan's foremost war criminal. In the Far Eastern Commission, the Soviet Union pressed for putting the emperor on trial, but the United States rallied most of the other Allied countries against that.[107] "I think although the Emperor escaped prosecution for political reasons this time," Mei wrote in his diary, "there will inevitably be a day when this old topic is discussed again. At least he cannot avoid the possibility of being called into the tribunal to provide evidence—this is just my own feeling and guess."[108]

As the Tokyo trial got under way, the U.S. policy of sanitizing Hirohito was given respectability by a series of patriotic Japanese, most notably Tojo, keen to protect their monarch. In the absence of a definitive documentary record or reliable memoirs, imperial loyalists could gloss up the emperor's pacifist credentials. Kase Toshikazu, an urbane, Amherst-educated Japanese diplomat who would later serve as Japan's ambassador to the United Nations (and whose niece is Yoko Ono) told General Headquarters that "without the firm guidance of the Emperor, termination of hostilities at that time was utterly impossible."[109] In another influential secret interrogation, the chief cabinet secretary described how the emperor had swayed the final wartime imperial conference with an emotional appeal.[110]

Around the same time, the blue-ribbon U.S. Strategic Bombing Survey, staffed by the likes of John Kenneth Galbraith and Paul Nitze (who had once called the Japanese "the most hateful of all people of earth"), reached similarly flattering conclusions about the role of the emperor in Japan's surrender.[111] They could not interrogate Hirohito himself, and MacArthur irately blocked them from meeting with Tojo.[112] This survey, which would dominate official U.S. thinking about postwar Japan, was based heavily on interviews with prominent royalists such as Kido Koichi, the emperor's inside man, who did their best to protect the throne.[113] Although the survey is best known for its conclusion that Japan would have soon collapsed even without the atomic bombings or a ground invasion, it also contended that the emperor's ultimate endorsement of surrender meant that the military could not effectively rebel.[114]

Thus both Japanese royalists and American occupiers burnished the image of the emperor as a peace-loving if passive figure.[115] Truman's secretary of state, James Byrnes, came to attribute much of the successful democratization of Japan to the decision to keep the institution of emperor and use it for carrying out MacArthur's policies.[116] Whatever the Tokyo trial might reveal, U.S. officials grew more convinced how useful the emperor could be in legitimizing a new constitutional order in Japan.[117]

CHAPTER 11

"Asia for the Asiatics"

RADHABINOD PAL ENTERED THE world in 1886 as a subject of Queen Victoria, Empress of India, in British-controlled Bengal.[1]

He grew up in hardscrabble, low-caste poverty in a small rural village in East Bengal, what is now Bangladesh. His father—a Hindu Vaishnavist dedicated to an austere piety—abandoned the boy when he was three years old, leaving his indomitable mother to raise him and his two sisters alone. He had to rely on charity during his school days. When he prospered in later life, he always remembered what it meant to be desperately poor, the terrifying precariousness of life on the edge of destitution. "He had a soft spot for the poor," remembers his daughter Smriti Kana Pal. "He always tried to help them."

Although obviously prodigiously bright, the little boy's extended family discouraged him from school, expecting a life of menial labor. His mother would have none of it. Driven by her, he got two degrees in mathematics at illustrious Presidency College in Calcutta, then went on to a Calcutta law college. In the legal profession, he found not just a way out of poverty but a calling.

His marriage was an arranged match, typical of that era, which blossomed into profound emotion and yielded fourteen children and a plethora of grandchildren. One of them, Satyabrata Pal—who became one of India's most eminent diplomats, serving as envoy to Pakistan and South Africa—remembers how deeply his grandfather loved and worshipped his intelligent and supportive wife, Nalinibala.[2]

"From the background that he came from," recalls Satyabrata Pal, "he'd become a completely unconventional man. He was a Hindu, but with none of the normal trappings of Hindu conservatism." Indifferent to caste or status, he ate with the servants and brought home dozens of students to feed them. His children and grandchildren fondly remember him as soft-spoken, polite, firm, and loving. At home he wore a dhoti and kurta, although he dressed in European-style suits for his professional work. Raised among Muslims in East Bengal, he was casually indifferent to communal prejudices, with plenty of Muslim friends and associates. He had no qualms about eating beef, and once, on a long trip to Geneva, duped his assistant, a strict Hindu vegetarian who was finding it impossible to nourish herself abroad, into having beef consommé. Tickled, he regaled his family with the tale for years.

Bengal became a center of the freedom struggle, although the British had long found the Bengalis particularly disagreeable subjects. In 1841, the historian and colonial administrator Thomas Babington Macaulay had unfavorably compared them to medieval Jews:

> The physical organization of the Bengalee is feeble even to effeminacy. He lives in a constant vapour bath. His pursuits are sedentary, his limbs delicate, his movements languid. . . . What the horns are to the buffalo, what the paw is to the tiger, what the sting is to the bee, what beauty, according to the old Greek song, is to women, deceit is to the Bengalee. Large promises, smooth excuses, elaborate tissues of circumstantial falsehood, chicanery, perjury, forgery, are the weapons, offensive and defensive, of the people of the Lower Ganges.[3]

To the last days of their exploitative rule, the British clung to that bigoted stereotype of Bengalis as talkative, radical, effeminate, and ungovernable.[4] The British Empire's governor of Bengal was exasperated by "the excitable nature of the people."[5]

Pal entered the law at a time when the profession attracted some of the most ardent opponents of British rule, most prominently Jawaharlal Nehru and M. K. Gandhi. Generations of Japanese nationalists have taken it for granted that he was a lionhearted foe of British imperialism and, as the *Asahi Shimbun* editorialized in 1966, "a follower of Gandhi."[6] Some Western legal scholars, too, place him in the great Gandhian tradition of anticolonial resistance.[7] In later years, he would complain that Western imperialism was "able to prostitute various colonial and semicolonial ruling classes to its own purposes."[8] Yet despite Pal's famous denunciations of European imperialism in his dissent at the Tokyo trial, there is little evidence of him challenging the British Empire in volatile Bengal. To the contrary, for the most part, he labored under the Raj while keeping his opinions to himself.

Although this deflates the image of him as a bold Gandhian hero, such compromises were common: vast numbers of Indian professionals and civil servants worked under the British while quietly harboring anticolonial views. After all, since the devastatingly bloody crushing of the 1857 rebellion and then the Jallianwala Bagh massacre in Amritsar in 1919, there were good reasons for Indians to fear what the British might do.[9] Some of Pal's work as a scholar, judge, and university chief was not necessarily in tension with the freedom struggle; even outspoken Indian activists understood the merits of the rule of law and the necessity of educating their children for self-governance. Still, none of his children or grandchildren—interviewed in Kolkata and Uttar Pradesh—remember him taking any part in the independence struggle, nor even talking about it. His grandson Satyabrata Pal says that nobody in the family knew of any such involvement. "He was not involved with any politics," says his granddaughter Ruby Pal.

Radhabinod Pal in his chambers at the
Tokyo trial, August 6, 1946

Rising fast, in 1921 he became an advocate in the High Court at Calcutta, and soon after started to teach law at Calcutta University, one of the finest universities in the land.[10] Delivering the prestigious Tagore Law

Lectures there, he offered an exhaustive history of primogeniture from ancient Egypt to Japan to British-ruled India. In 1932, he wrote an elegant academic book on Hindu law, admiring it as a source of authority since antiquity. Proud of India's legal traditions, he argued that "institutions resembling those prevailing in modern democracy did arise in ancient Indian Society." Yet his book provided a synthesis of Indian and British values, arguing that British ideals such as efficient administration, equality before law, and liberty would flourish in Indian culture.[11]

Pal believed that law, far from being purely a product of particular societies, was grounded in human reason, with common elements of social order across nations. He was fascinated, although unpersuaded, by Hindu sages who believed that law came from "divine reason" as understood by human beings. That would be close to a theory of natural law, in rough parallel to Mei Ruao's thinking along the same lines.[12] Yet the Indian scholar had something more forbearing in mind. Drawing on Hindu sources, Pal suggested that both the judge and the criminal—and the victor and the vanquished—were bound together by an ethical philosophy. He argued that law meant the rejection of indiscriminate revenge and hinted strongly that criminal justice could not be dispensed by the victims of a crime.[13]

It is a standard belief among Japanese conservatives today that Pal was the only judge in Tokyo competent in international law. "Judge Pal was the only expert on international law among the judges," says Fujioka Nobukatsu of the far-right Japan Society for History Textbook Reform. "From an expert's view, he made a judgment that Japan was innocent." This is nonsense. In fact, the best-prepared judges were Sir William Webb of Australia, Henri Bernard of France, and Myron Cramer of the United States, all of whom had worked on war crimes issues. In Pal's official biography for the Tokyo tribunal, his sole qualifications were membership in an international law association and once attending an international conference on comparative law in The Hague.[14] His legal expertise was in Hindu and Indian jurisprudence. As an advocate before the Calcutta High Court, he established his name by coauthoring a monumental treatise on income tax in British India, whose two hefty volumes weighed in at 2,351 pages.[15]

Steeped in Hindu legal scholarship, he proposed a kind of organic fit between Indian society and law. He wrote that the chief problem of legal thinkers had always been "how to make the legal order appear something fixed and settled and beyond question, while at the same time capable of adaptation to the exigencies of infinite and variable human demands." Yet he knew that there was a large legal literature driven by "a desire to hide the essentially political character of the question behind legal argument." He always feared that the powerful would "use the law as an instrument of domination."[16]

PAN-ASIANISM

Pal's scholarly writings show little curiosity about an object of widespread fascination among Bengali and Indian thinkers at the time: Japan.

For colonized Asians repressed by the armies, wealth, and technology of Western empires, Japan shone as an Asian power that withstood the arrogant white supremacists.[17] After the shock of being forced by the U.S. Navy to open to the outside world in 1853–54, Japan in the Meiji era had rehauled its government, economy, and military with breathtaking speed.[18] By 1894–95 it was strong enough to challenge China in a crushing war for domination over Korea, taking control over Taiwan.[19] Then in 1905, when Japan sank most of the Russian fleet in a spectacularly decisive battle in the Tsushima Strait, led by Admiral Togo Heihachiro, people across Asia were elated at this first modern triumph of an Asian power over a European empire.[20] Nehru, then fifteen years old and on his way to boarding school at Harrow, wrote to a relative, "Three Cheers for Togo."[21] Even Gandhi, then a youthful lawyer battling white supremacy in South Africa, wrote that when Japan's "brave heroes forced the Russians to bite the dust of the battle-field, the sun rose in the east. And it now shines on all the nations of Asia. The people of the East will never, never again submit to insult from the insolent whites."[22]

A few years after becoming the first Asian to win the Nobel Prize in Literature in 1913, Rabindranath Tagore, the great Bengali poet and educator, gave a lecture tour in Japan where he cheered the country for having "broken the spell under which we lay in torpor for ages, taking it to be the normal condition of certain races living in certain geographical limits."[23] A prominent Bengali revolutionary, Rashbehari Bose, fled to Japan and helped establish the Indian National Army to fight against the British (and, more enduringly, helped to popularize curry among the Japanese).[24]

In Japan, pan-Asianist thinkers developed their own reciprocal enchantment with India, although with only a hazy knowledge of the vast, varied subcontinent.[25] In 1933, a group of Japanese nationalists and foreign intellectuals, including Rashbehari Bose, founded the influential Greater Asia Association in Japan. Among its early members were Lieutenant General Matsui Iwane, who would command Japanese troops in the Nanjing massacre, and two future civilian prime ministers, Prince

Konoe Fumimaro and Hirota Koki.[26] Matsui declared that the white man's culture was alien for Asians, and Japan had a "divinely appointed mission" to lead the peoples of Asia.[27]

When Japan marched into Manchuria, the Greater Asia Association saluted the creation of the puppet state of Manchukuo as "a major miracle."[28] Matsui pledged to "extend to the 400 million people of China the same help and deep sympathy that we have given Manchuria," and then help all "the Asian peoples who share our race and stock." He vowed, "Even if our homeland should be burned to the ground, we cannot sacrifice justice."[29] As prime minister, Konoe elevated pan-Asianism into an official justification for the invasion of China in 1937. In a major radio address early in the war, he declared that Japan understood "China's racial aspiration and sentiment."[30]

Many Indians shuddered at Japan's conquests. Much as Tagore loved Japan's culture, he warned after the annexation of Korea, "She is hungry—she is munching Korea, she has fastened her teeth upon China and it will be an evil day for India when Japan will have her opportunity." During three tours of Japan, he rebuked audiences, "The new Japan is only an imitation of the West. This will ruin Japan."[31] Rebuffing an old Japanese friend who tried to enlist his pen to defend the invasion of China, Tagore admonished that "in launching a ravening war on Chinese humanity, with all the deadly methods learnt from the West, Japan is infringing every moral principle on which civilization is based. . . . You are building your conception of an Asia which would be raised on a tower of skulls."[32]

"A STRUGGLE BETWEEN RACES"

In January 1942, Japanese troops closed in on the British possession of Singapore, bombing the port city and naval base day and night. A few days before what Winston Churchill would call "the worst disaster and largest capitulation in British history," a Singaporean university student was shaken by the sight of tall Australian troops, despondent and scared; one of them offered the student his weapons. Early one morning, the student was jolted by an earthshaking explosion. The young man—named Lee Kuan Yew, who would become the strongman ruler of an independent Singapore—blurted, "That's the end of the British Empire!"[33]

Lee had always taken it for granted that the white British lived in superior houses in superior districts, had superior lifestyles, and ate superior food with meat and milk products. "The superior status of the British in government and society was simply a fact of life," he recalled. "After all, they were the greatest people in the world." Yet when Japanese troops stormed into Singapore, he was dazzled by the small, squat victors wearing split-toed canvas boots suitable for tropical treks, stinking in a way that Lee would never forget from months of slogging through the equatorial jungles.[34]

For millions of other Asians under the British, French, and Dutch Empires, it was equally thrilling to watch their imperial overlords get their comeuppance from Asians. Although British propaganda films mocked the Japanese as cross-eyed, bow-legged, inept cowards, people across Asia witnessed an audacious and effective fighting force. Japan put the lie to European claims of racial superiority with a spectacular series of battlefield victories in Hong Kong, the Netherlands East Indies, the Philippines, and elsewhere.

Imperial Japan portrayed itself as an army of liberation, driving out white and wicked European empires under the slogan "Asia for the Asiatics."[35] Emperor Hirohito took an active interest in cooperation with India.[36] "Britain's base of operations in the Far East is overthrown and annihilated," he declared in an imperial rescript celebrating the conquest of Singapore. "I deeply approve of this."[37] Rather than imposing a new empire, though, Japan claimed to be establishing a benevolent Greater East Asia Co-Prosperity Sphere. An influential Japanese colonel serving in Malaya would claim that Japan ultimately brought independence for India, Pakistan, Ceylon, Burma, Indochina, Indonesia, Malaya, and the Philippines. "Domination based on force must be overthrown by force," he argued.[38]

Japanese intellectuals promised a wholly new order from that of the ousted white supremacists: rejecting a rationalist, materialist, capitalist, and imperialist Western world for a soulful, holistic, and traditional Asian civilization unified under the divine rule of the emperor.[39] At a much publicized Greater East Asia Conference in Tokyo, the Burmese nationalist Ba Maw declared, "this is the time to think with our blood."[40] General Aung San, the foremost leader of Burma's independence (and the father of Aung San Suu Kyi), convinced that Japanese military help was imperative, visited Tokyo to be decorated by Hirohito.[41] In 1943, both Burma and the Philippines were formally given a token independence under the Japanese.[42] (Tojo Hideki, then prime minister, felt that Japan had to match or exceed the United States, which had already promised independence no later than July 4, 1946.)[43] In Indochina, where the Vichy French colonial rulers were shoved aside, the Japanese offered promises of "Asia for the Asians" and judo classes.[44] In the regions of China conquered by Japan, Wang Jingwei, formerly a leading patriotic revolutionary of the Republic of China, set up a collaborationist government. Based in sacked Nanjing, his regime lent credence to Japan's claims to speak for all of Asia.[45]

Japan's ideological appeals effectively rallied Asians against their colonial overlords.[46] A U.S. study of psychological warfare anxiously noted that Japan, with an insider mastery of "Oriental psychology," ruled the Philippines not just through repression but with appealing slogans of "universal brotherhood" and "Asia for the Asiatics."[47] No lesser expert on propaganda and colonialism than George Orwell worried that Indians and Burmese would accept the Japanese as liberators from British imperialism: "if you promise people what they want, they will always believe you."[48]

Japan's appeals posed a dire problem for Britain, which relied on the societies and economies of its global empire to wage World War II.[49] Yet after Nazi Germany invaded Poland, the British viceroy had not even consulted with Indian leaders before proclaiming on All India Radio that "India will make her contribution on the side of human freedom as against the rule of force." India became a crucial part of the Allied war effort; it fielded some 2.5 million troops, who would fight not just in relatively nearby Singapore, Hong Kong, and Burma but all across the Middle East and North Africa, even Italy. The Chinese government relied on India to keep open the Burma Road for supplies, rather than having to fly over the Himalayas (what the pilots called "the Hump"). Indian factories and farms kept the British war machine functioning. All of this meant acute hardships for Indians who had no say whatsoever in the decision to go to war. Gandhi, championing the Quit India movement in 1942, wrote that India's participation in the war "was purely a British act. If India were freed her first step would probably be to negotiate with Japan."[50]

The ideology of pan-Asianism offered the Japanese a unifying cause and motivated the troops.[51] In a widely circulated pamphlet for Japanese infantry fighting in Southeast Asia, the soldiers were assured that they would be welcomed as liberators. The pamphlet explained how "the English, the Americans, the Dutch, the Portuguese and others sailed into the Far East as if it were theirs by natural right, terrorized and subjugated the culturally backward native." Japan was fighting these white colonialists, according to the pamphlet, having already "rescued Manchuria from the ambitions of the Soviets, and set China free from the extortion of the Anglo-Americans. Her next great mission is to assist towards the independence of the Thais, the Annamese, and the Filipinos, and to bring the blessing of freedom to the natives of South Asia and the Indian people."

This was not mere anticolonialism but a race war. "The present war is a struggle between races," the pamphlet explained. They should fight with no mercy for Europeans, except of course for Germans and Italians. A hundred million Asians were "tyrannized by three hundred thousand whites." The "white invasion," grabbing the oil resources which Japan desperately needed, had only succeeded because the Asians "are lacking in any awareness of themselves as a group, as peoples of Asia." The pamphlet warned that "we have unthinkingly come to accept Europeans as superior and to despise the Chinese and the peoples of the South. This is like spitting in our own eyes. Bearing in mind that we Japanese, as an Eastern people, have ourselves for long been classed alongside the Chinese and the Indians as an inferior race, and treated as such, we must at the very least, here in Asia, beat these Westerners to submission, that they may change their arrogant and ill-mannered attitude."

Pan-Asianism only went so far. Japanese theorists had their own racial hierarchy, believing that the Yamato race should dominate lesser Asian breeds.[52] Many Japanese nationalists held prejudices that would have been perfectly at home over a gin and tonic at the Pegu Club in Rangoon. That infantry pamphlet patronized "the naturally lazy natives," noting with polite dismay that most of them were Muslims with fiercely held customs. The pamphlet singled out ethnic Chinese minorities across the region, who had long suffered discrimination, as corrupt European collaborators with "no racial or national consciousness, and no enthusiasms outside the making of money." It scorned tropical and malarial lands where "large populations of idlers" could "live in nakedness and . . . eat without working. What is more, after centuries of subjection to Europe and exploitation by the Chinese, these natives have reached a point of almost complete emasculation." Also, "native women are almost all infected with venereal disease."[53]

In private, many of Japan's leaders acted more out of strategic convenience than anticolonial principle. In a flash of candor about Japanese repression, Marquis Kido Koichi privately discussed with the emperor "the guiding principle for the subjugation of Greater East Asia."[54] Colonel Hashimoto Kingoro, a putschist army officer who wound up as a defendant at the Tokyo trial, argued that Japan should annex "those areas where the inhabiting races have no capacity for independence, or areas which are strategically important."[55] Hirohito's younger brother, Prince Mikasa, who fought in China, had no illusions about Wang Jingwei's collaborator government: "It cannot be said that Japan created that government out of a true wish to benefit China or to help the Chinese people form a unified state. Instead, it should be viewed as a kind of makeshift trick prompted by a desire to cover up Japan's policy of aggression."[56]

While reviling British, French, and Dutch imperialism, the Japanese government made an exception for the German variety. In 1941, Adolf Hitler personally informed Japan's foreign minister that "Germany . . . would satisfy her colonial demands in Africa."[57] Japan promised secretly that Germany's former colonies in the South Pacific would be kept by Japan or restored to Nazi Germany.[58] Most importantly, it was only with France and Holland conquered by Nazi Germany and Britain under bombardment that Japan could march across the European empires in Southeast and South Asia.[59] Outlining Hitler's plans to Kido, Tojo Hideki concentrated on undermining the British Empire. Once Nazi Germany had annihilated the Soviet military, he explained, it would attack British India and then if necessary invade the British isles.[60]

The cruelty of Japanese rule was apparent across Asia. In their brief occupation of Indonesia, the Japanese demonstrated for the first time the power of a militarized state, and taught Indonesian nationalist fighters the use of torture and collective punishment.[61] They trapped Indonesian women in sexual servitude for Japanese troops, raping and brutalizing them. They commandeered rice, contributing to a famine in 1944 that may well have killed more than two million people in Java alone.[62] In Singapore, the occupying Japanese treated Indians and Malays as racial inferiors, rounded up and killed thousands of ethnic Chinese, queued up for sex with subjugated Korean women at "comfort houses," and decapitated looters and exhibited their heads on bridges and roads as a warning. As Lee Kuan Yew recalled, the Japanese "soon demonstrated to their fellow Asiatics that they were more cruel, more brutal, more unjust and more vicious than the British."[63]

The Japanese soon alienated some of their strongest supporters. In Indonesia, Sukarno, the anti-Dutch independence leader who would become the country's first president, resented their use of water torture and decapitations, and complained to a Kempeitai officer about the Japanese habit of slapping Indonesians.[64] In Burma, Japanese troops desecrated monasteries, slapped civilians and monks, and shot suspected troublemakers. Ba Maw later admitted that the Japanese acted as arrogant colonizers with "racial pretensions," hoping to hold Burma as they had held Korea or Manchuria, fueled by an "outrageous master-race complex" among many Japanese.[65] Across Asia, the long-awaited liberation from cruel European empires curdled into a grim reality of repression, torture, and economic exploitation so severe that hundreds of thousands of Asian laborers died by the end of the war.[66]

Nevertheless, Japan's anticolonial stance widened a rift among the

Allies: China against the colonialists in Britain, France, and Holland, with the United States showing some sympathy for the anticolonialist camp. Chiang Kai-shek was stoutly opposed to Western imperialism, and Franklin Delano Roosevelt, although restrained in his criticism of his European allies, believed that Indian independence was inevitable and sought to loosen France's grip on Indochina. Chiang told a Chinese radio audience how impressed he was with Roosevelt's "firm determination to emancipate all the world's oppressed peoples."[67] In the Atlantic Charter, Roosevelt and Churchill's vision of what the war was for, they delighted Asian anticolonialists by promising "the right of all peoples to choose the form of government under which they will live," as well as "no territorial changes that do not accord with the freely expressed wishes of the peoples concerned."[68] Roosevelt, going further than a reticent Churchill, promised eventual independence to the Philippines and nudged the British and French to consider following suit for their colonies.[69] At the Tehran conference in 1943, he dressed down Churchill about the awful consequences of British and French colonialism.[70] He argued that it would violate the Atlantic Charter's pledge of self-determination for Britain and France to reconquer their imperial possessions after the war, and once breezily told reporters that Churchill "is mid-Victorian on all things like that."[71] At the Casablanca conference, he informed his son, "Don't think for a moment, Elliott, that Americans would be dying in the Pacific tonight if it hadn't been for the short-sighted greed of the French and the British and the Dutch."[72]

FAMINE AND WAR

The war came home fast in Bengal. With nearby Burma falling into Japanese hands, Japanese bombers struck at Calcutta and southeast Bengal.[73] As many as eight hundred thousand terrified people streamed out of Calcutta, about a third of the city's total population. There were rumors of an imminent Japanese invasion, a prospect welcomed by many Bengalis.[74] Alarmed by growing sympathy for Japan among Bengalis, the British colonial authorities rushed to spread propaganda about Japan's imperialism and atrocities in China, Malaya, and Burma, as well as censoring or harassing Indian newspapers which spread what the British considered antiwar propaganda.[75]

The war brought a grand opportunity for Indians seeking liberation.[76] The Indian National Congress, the foremost party struggling for freedom, proclaimed that Britain could not fight for democracy and liberty while denying the same to colonized Indians.[77] "What happens in India and China is of equal importance to America and Europe," Jawaharlal Nehru told a Bombay crowd in 1940. "War is indivisible now."[78]

The Indian National Congress had a nearly impossible balance to strike: not wanting to help the British Empire without trustworthy promises of liberty, while not wanting to let the Western powers fall to the Axis. Why win freedom from Britain only to be stuck under the hegemony of Japan? Nehru, who despised Nazism and militarism, had denounced Axis aggression in Manchuria, Abyssinia, and Czechoslovakia. If India was next, he wanted to wage a guerrilla war against the Japanese. "The Japanese may free India from the British yoke," wrote Gandhi, "but only to put in their own instead."[79]

The war and anticolonial ferment had little obvious impact on Pal's legal ascent. He joined the Calcutta High Court in January 1941, head-quartered in the British citadel of Fort William, sitting alongside British judges and subordinate to a British chief justice.[80] "At that time," recalls his son Pratip Bijoy Pal, "a judgeship was looked on as a dignified thing, very prestigious." His relative quiescence had worked for his career: this was a sufficiently important post that the Raj would not have given it to a known troublemaker.

While the streets were packed with the popular uprising of the Quit India campaign, Pal served the law in Fort William. He warmed to the fascinations of the job, writing densely argued rulings about everything from Hindu philosophical notions to Muslim religious institutions to drug dealers.[81] In a particularly rococo lawsuit which raised the mesmerizing question of whether a Hindu idol counted as a person in the eyes of the court, he conceded that idols could sue and be sued, but insisted that an idol's rights really depended on those of a human being.[82] Strikingly, for a judge whose fame would rest on a dissent, there is no record of him dissenting on the Calcutta High Court.

The inflationary financing of the war doubled, tripled, or quadrupled the price of such essential items as potatoes and milk—devastating for impoverished people across India. In the cities, British war expenditures drove up prices far beyond what the rural poor could afford. In Calcutta, the all-important cost of rice quadrupled, which amounted to a death sentence for the destitute. Worse, the Japanese occupation of Burma shut off rice imports from there. The result was a catastrophic famine in Bengal that caused some three million deaths from starvation or illness in 1943–44. In December 1943 alone, the Raj noted some 325,000 deaths.[83] Poor rural workers such as fishers, paddy huskers, or agricultural laborers were the most vulnerable. Everywhere there were skeletal people, their bones apparent, their eyes vacant. The starving were vulnerable to cholera and malaria. The dead rotted in the streets or rivers. One battle-hardened Indian soldier returning home from North Africa was haunted by the sight of "a baby barely two years old lying in the lap of his brother of about six, both so devitalised that they are not able even to move from the street corner."

The Raj botched its response at every point. British press censorship and propaganda impeded a proper government response.[84] The famine might have been mitigated by new imports, but shipping was being used for the war. As the viceroy privately admitted, India's problems were treated by the British "with neglect, even sometimes with hostility and contempt."[85] Winston Churchill, inclined to charge India for the cost of defending it from Japanese invasion, once said, "I hate Indians. They are a beastly people with a beastly religion."[86]

If Pal was radicalized into condemning the British Empire at its most predatory and incompetent, he certainly kept it out of his jurisprudence. His son Pratip Bijoy Pal, who was eight years old at the time, recalls that their family was wealthy enough not to be affected. "I remember lots of beggars on the streets," he says. During the famine, Pal ruled on a rent dispute which oddly turned on the local prices of staple food crops. It would have been a stretch, but he could have pointed out what the quadrupling of the cost of rice had meant to poor Bengalis; instead he donnishly cited *The Economist* and John Maynard Keynes, making no mention of the massive starvation from the British fleecing of Bengal.[87]

NETAJI'S WAR

While Pal toiled at Fort William, a very different sort of Bengali lawyer was fighting for Japanese assistance: Subhas Chandra Bose, a bold campaigner known popularly as Netaji (Revered Leader). He remains a national icon in India to this day, venerated as one of the champions of the freedom struggle, his statues freshly garlanded. Nelson Mandela spoke reverentially of him as a hero of militant anticolonialism, and Narendra Modi, the Hindu nationalist prime minister of India, routinely marks his birthday with accolades: "The valour of Netaji Subhas Chandra Bose makes every Indian proud."[88] Today he has become the favored founder of independent India for Modi's ruling Bharatiya Janata Party. The prime minister recently unveiled a gigantic statue of him—carved from black granite, uniformed and saluting—at India Gate, a monumental war memorial in Delhi, in the canopy where a graven King George V had once stood.

Bose's legend is strongest in West Bengal, where the bustling international airport in Kolkata (formerly Calcutta) is named after him. His face—sweet, babyish, balding, framed with round scholarly glasses—is plastered everywhere in the city today, as ubiquitous as those of Tagore and Mother Teresa. There is a handsome museum at his old family house in Kolkata, now called Netaji Bhavan, featuring a well-known photograph of him shaking hands with Hitler. In 2007, Abe Shinzo, Japan's nationalistic prime minister, toured Netaji Bhavan and its museum, declaring how respected Bose was in Japan.[89]

If Gandhi was India's prophet of idealistic nonviolence, Bose was its champion of calculated warfare.[90] Making a spectacular escape in 1941 after the British threw him in jail for the eleventh time, he headed for Berlin, convinced that only military force would achieve independence. Meeting Hitler's foreign minister, Joachim von Ribbentrop, he proposed sending Indian prisoners of war captured by Nazi Germany and Italy to fight alongside an Axis expeditionary force attacking British-ruled India. In the end, out of fifteen thousand Indian troops held by the Axis in 1943, only two thousand signed up; Germany sent them for police duties in occupied Holland and the Atlantic coastline.[91]

To the delight of Joseph Göbbels, the German propaganda minister, Bose began radio broadcasts from Berlin declaring that Axis military power would help free India, although he privately worried that Nazi Germany's invasions were scaring Indians.[92] In Bengal, Bose's many admirers circulated leaflets exhorting revolution against the British Empire and cooperation with Japan.[93] When Tojo Hideki, as prime minister, endorsed "India for the Indians," Bose gave a radio address lauding "the prophetic utterance of a far-seeing statesman." He pledged that India and Japan would "co-operate intimately" in building a new Asia.[94]

"Hitler and Japan must go to hell," Nehru countered. "I shall fight them to the end and this is my policy. I shall also fight Mr. Subhas Chandra Bose and his party along with Japan if he comes to India."[95]

In Berlin, Bose could not have overlooked the murderous racial ideology of his Nazi allies. While presumably unaware of all the details of the extermination of the Jews then escalating across Nazi Germany and German-occupied Europe, he could scarcely have avoided noticing the weekly antisemitic newsreels and newspaper propaganda, Hitler's speeches prophesying the annihilation of the Jews, nor the segregation and mass deportation of Jews from German cities.[96] Indicating some awareness of Axis cruelties, Bose exhorted Indians to ignore them: *The internal politics of Germany or Italy or Japan do not concern us—they are the concern of the people of those countries.*[97] In a radio address from Germany—which by then had attacked Belgium, Britain, Czechoslovakia, Denmark, France, Greece, Holland, Luxembourg, Norway, Poland, the Soviet Union, the United States, and Yugoslavia—he declared it a "moral tragedy" that "misguided people talk of aggression by Japan or Germany or Italy."[98]

Bose certainly understood that in Hitler's racial cosmology, Indians were a vile race who deserved domination by superior English blood.[99] When Bose pleaded his case personally to the Nazi dictator in May 1942, it went predictably badly. In a lengthy monologue, Hitler urged Bose to smash the British Empire with an Indian rebellion, while excoriating Nehru and Gandhi. Since German armies were otherwise engaged, he advised Bose to bank on Japan to bring the war to India. Bose pressed Hitler for moral and diplomatic support, yet elicited only a feeble lie from the Nazi tyrant distancing himself from the manifestly anti-Indian passages in *Mein Kampf*. Hitler ended their meeting by providing Bose with nothing more than a ride on a German submarine to Bangkok.[100]

Bose took that German U-boat halfway to Japan, where he switched to a Japanese submarine. In Tokyo, he met with Tojo and sat as an honored guest at a special session of the Diet where the prime minister pledged "everything possible" to help bring about India's independence.[101] Next he headed to Singapore, where Tojo helped set him up in 1943 as the supreme commander of a self-styled Indian National Army, kitted out in a khaki uniform with jodhpurs. Bose's troops were drawn from Indian prisoners of war taken when Singapore fell and from Indian expatriates in Malaya, Thailand, and Burma, eventually totaling over thirty thousand soldiers— with brigades named after Gandhi and Nehru, and troops who retained a habit of cheering for Gandhi as well as Bose.[102] Out of sixty-five thousand Indian troops held by the Japanese at Singapore, about twenty thousand joined Bose's force.[103]

Tojo personally reviewed these Indian National Army troops in Singapore, while Bose assured him of "our unshakeable determination to fight with you shoulder to shoulder."[104] In October 1943, Bose proclaimed himself the leader of an exile Indian government called Azad Hind (Free India).[105] He declared war on Britain and the United States, vowing to battle his way to India within months.[106] The next month he spoke for India at a ballyhooed Greater East Asia Conference in Tokyo, where he was hailed by Tojo and granted an audience at the Imperial Palace with Hirohito, who expressed his admiration for Bose's efforts to win India's independence. Bose proclaimed, "Only when our blood flows and mingles together in pursuit of the common cause will the unity—real, lasting unity—of Asia be created."[107]

Bose pressed Japan into trying to march through Burma to Bengal, hoping that his arrival would galvanize a revolt destroying the British Empire. This resulted in an embarrassing Japanese rout known as the Imphal campaign.[108] Yet on the day of Japan's surrender in World War II, Bose defiantly declared, "The roads to Delhi are many and Delhi still remains our goal."[109] He fled from Singapore to Saigon and then headed for the Soviet Union—foiled en route when he died in a sudden airplane crash off Taipei.[110]

Bose's legend grew after his death.[111] His dramatic demise has spawned a host of conspiracy theories, with commonplace Indian skepticism today that someone so uniquely threatening to the British Empire perished by convenient accident. "It's still not believed by ninety-nine percent of Indians that he died in a plane crash," says Jibananda Pal, the grandson-in-law of Radhabinod Pal.[112]

There are recurrent claims that Pal was a supporter of Bose, perhaps even a secret activist. Bert Röling, the Dutch judge in Tokyo who became a lifelong friend of Pal, would later claim that he had supported Bose. Röling recalled that Pal "had even been involved with the Indian Army that fought with the Japanese against the British. He was every inch an Asian." As Röling explained, Pal "really resented colonial relations. He had a strong feeling about what Europe did in Asia, conquering it a couple of hundred years ago, and then ruling and lording over it from so far away. That was his attitude. So this war of Japan to liberate Asia from the Europeans, the slogan 'Asia for the Asians,' really struck a chord with him."[113]

Yet there is scant evidence that Pal did anything to help Bose or his Indian National Army, which seems implausible given his long history of working with the Raj. There are no records of contact with Pal in Bose's well-organized papers at the Netaji Research Bureau in Kolkata, according to its archivists. Since the city's elite legal circles were small and clubby, it is quite possible that Pal knew the prominent lawyer Sarat Bose, the brother and confidant of Subhas Chandra Bose, another uncompromising anticolonial activist jailed by the British.[114] "My father was very much known to Sarat Bose," recalls Pratip Bijoy Pal. "They were always on good terms."

It is conceivable that Pal had some quiet sympathy with Subhas Chandra Bose and his cause. Indeed, as Pal's family points out, given the political mood in Bengal, it would be rather more surprising if he didn't. Still, his grandson Satyabrata Pal says firmly that it was nothing more than admiration, which was typical for Bengalis at that time. "It was more or less a given then that Bengalis felt that Netaji Bose was the way forward," he says.

However Pal's opinions about the British Empire were evolving, they did not prevent his continued cooperation. After his service on the Calcutta High Court, Pal was appointed the head of Calcutta University in 1944. He developed a good working relationship with the imperial governor of Bengal, a bluff Australian named Richard Casey who privately believed that Nehru was fomenting revolution and dictatorship. Casey would send in the British Army to put down demonstrations, although preferring truncheons to rifle fire. "I don't want to kill these poor misguided creatures," he wrote in his diary. "I only want to frighten them and so stop them doing the stupidities that the rabble-rousing politicians have driven them to."[115]

Pal met with Casey to discuss how to recruit Indians to work for the British authorities, and then brought the governor to campus to show off its physics department. The governor had Pal over for a posh dinner party with British lords and military chiefs, where the Bengali scholar enlightened the governor about the origins of an offshoot Hindu sect.[116]

As the agitation for independence escalated, Pal promoted dialogue. To defuse campus tensions, he brought Casey to meet quietly with some selected students and professors, none of whom had been told whom they would be meeting in order to avoid security problems. The students boldly asked the governor if they minded if they said *"Jai Hind"*—a phrase best known as the Indian National Army's slogan and Bose's rallying cry, to which Casey replied soothingly that it meant "Victory for India" and he was glad to join them in it. Pal said that it would make all the difference in the world to have more of this kind of meeting.[117]

In the final days of World War II, Pal spoke up for Indian independence, although he secretly allowed himself to be partially muzzled by the Raj. After seeing Pal's draft speech for the upcoming convocation at Calcutta University in July 1945, Casey summoned him. The imperial governor pointed out several "highly political references" which he could not accept quietly. If Pal did not amend his remarks, Casey threatened to reply to them from the podium. According to the governor's diary, Pal agreed to tone down his speech.

The convocation went forward without incident. In the grand Senate House, wearing an academic gown despite the soupy heat of a Calcutta summer, Pal gave a powerful speech which explicitly supported Indian independence but held back from the direct attacks that Casey had cautioned against. Freedom, Pal declared, was the essential prerequisite for attaining "the fundamental rights of man." He urged the graduates to help win "freedom for your motherland . . . in the genuine spirit of a crusader," although prudently adding that they should not be misled into a struggle "that is more harmful to your real interest or the national cause."[118]

Strikingly, in the same private meeting with Casey before the convocation, Pal tried to enlist the governor's help in repressing some of his fellow Indians. He spoke emotionally against a powerful faction of conservative Hindu chauvinists at the university, led by Syama Prasad Mookerjee. Pal's foe would go on to be a luminary of Hindu nationalists in India: a minister under Nehru, a founder of an important Hindu nationalist party that was a precursor to today's ruling Bharatiya Janata Party, hailed today as a hero by Narendra Modi himself.[119]

Mookerjee made a powerful foe for the more tolerant Pal: upper-caste, Cambridge-educated, a former chief of the university.[120] According to Casey's diary, Pal warned that Mookerjee and his group were "an uneasy and unpleasant influence in the University—which could not be eradicated in a brief period." He was doing his best to cope but it was not a pleasant situation.[121] Immediately after Pal's backroom denunciation, Casey warned the viceroy of India about Mookerjee's "malign influence" over the university. Casey cautioned the British viceroy and other nearby British governors that the university's administration was a stronghold for Mookerjee, who had stacked it with supporters and relatives "who so control the University's affairs that those who do not belong to his faction do not thrive."[122] Even as Pal emerged as a public anticolonialist, he saw Hindu nationalists as such a threat that he would secretly encourage the British Empire to suppress the forebears of India's current government.

THE ACCIDENTAL JURIST

When World War II ended, Indians doubted that this would spell the end of racial domination and imperialist exploitation.[123] Much of the Indian press recoiled at the annihilation of Hiroshima and Nagasaki, wondering how Germany and Japan could now be condemned for their atrocities.[124]

Since Pal's enduring fame would rest on his excoriation of Western colonialism, it is a jarringly odd fact that it was the British Empire that insisted on sending him to Tokyo in the first place. When the Americans first asked the Allies to designate judges and prosecutors for the Tokyo trial, they had invited Britain and its dominions of Australia, Canada, and New Zealand, but not India. Yet British and Indian officials, anticipating the imminent emergence of a self-governing India with some four hundred million people, demanded adding an Indian judge.[125]

General Douglas MacArthur, not wanting an international tribunal in the first place, hated to expand it further. To that end, the State Department conjured up a casuistic standard that the judges must come only from the nine countries which had signed the Japanese surrender on the USS *Missouri*. Thus neither India nor the Philippines would warrant a judge, deemed only important enough to send a single associate prosecutor apiece.[126]

British imperial authorities in London and Delhi were indignant.[127] British officials in Delhi fumed that it was "absurd" to shut out India because it had been excluded from the *Missouri* ceremony, not least because nobody seemed to know why it had been; India had been represented at Japanese surrender ceremonies in Singapore and Burma.[128] India certainly had as much of a claim as Australia or New Zealand.[129] Two and a half million Indian troops had sacrificed and fought from Burma to Sicily; twenty-four thousand Indian soldiers had died in the war; countless Indian prisoners of war had been abused by Japanese jailers.[130] "Neither France nor [the] Netherlands has as good a claim as India to nominate [a] judge," wrote Sir Girja Shankar Bajpai, the British-appointed Indian agent general in Washington.[131]

In Washington, the formidable Bajpai, who was also India's representative on the Far Eastern Commission, berated the Americans with the support of the British government.[132] India deserved "participation in the trial of Japanese war criminals on a footing of equality with the other powers who participated in the war against Japan." By demanding equality, he politely put the United States on notice that Indians would not brook racial discrimination. He argued that Indian soldiers and civilians in Southeast Asia and Burma had been abused by the Japanese, that Indian troops had helped to defeat the Japanese in Burma, and that India had plenty of eminent lawyers well trained in Western jurisprudence.[133] Bajpai, an Oxford graduate, explained wearily to the Raj that "in America, elementary facts about India belong to realm of unknown."[134]

The State Department concocted a new rationale: nine judges was already a lot. Better to keep the court as small as possible, ideally with only American, British, Chinese, and Soviet judges. Since India and the Philippines would have to be treated equally, adding two more judges would mean an unwieldy court of eleven.[135] Bajpai scoffed: why was eleven any more unwieldy than nine?[136] The British ambassador in Washington hectored the U.S. secretary of state, James Byrnes, finding him sympathetic but noncommittal.[137]

Britain took India's case to the Far Eastern Commission, which opened the door to Soviet mischief. The Soviets proposed adding their client state, the Mongolian People's Republic, alongside India and the Philippines—an idea that both the Americans and the British fiercely rejected.[138] Advocating for India, Bajpai explained privately that the British meant to put the Americans "in the wrong before world opinion."[139] Britain easily got its Commonwealth dominions of Canada, New Zealand, and Australia on side for adding India.[140] The Raj pointed out that India had "suffered as much as any nation at the hands of Japanese War Criminals," losing more prisoners of war than the French or the Dutch. The racial subtext was plain: the Allies were implicitly saying that white lives mattered more than those of Indians and Filipinos.[141]

Clearly understanding that accusation, the State Department conceded privately that it was "politically desirable to avoid being placed in position of discriminating against Asiatic Countries." The Americans dropped their opposition to an Indian judge but demanded a Philippine one as well.[142] All the Allied countries concurred.[143] After three months of opposition, MacArthur agreed to appoint an Indian judge.[144] He and Sir William Webb revised the tribunal's charter to add judges from India and the Philippines, urging the new members to race to Tokyo immediately.[145]

Victorious, the British realized that they did not actually have an Indian judge to send to Tokyo.

The ideal candidate, Indian civil servants concluded, would be a retired High Court judge, bringing stature without the inconvenience of pulling a working judge off the bench.[146] Pal wasn't their first or second choice, and probably not their fifth. First the British asked a former judge on the High Court of Bombay, who did not feel healthy enough, and then one from Allahabad, who dodged.[147] MacArthur badgered the Indians to get a judge to Tokyo by no later than April 20, 1946—which was just two days away. Worried about being permanently excluded if the trial started without an Indian judge, the Raj tried to nominate a judge within a week.[148]

Frantic, the Raj inquired whether any High Court judges in Bombay, Madras, Lahore, or Calcutta—retired or active—were willing to wing off on a moment's notice. The British would match the judge's current salary, plus 500 rupees monthly for incidentals, and cover airfare, board, and lodging for a caper that would purportedly be wrapped up in under six months.[149]

Radhabinod Pal jumped at the opportunity. Everything was wrapped up within four days. He outranked two temporary judges in Lahore who were interested, and cleanly beat out a distinguished High Court judge from Lahore, who was serving on the bench while Pal was retired. (It's not clear whether the British held it against the Lahore judge, who would go on to become the second chief justice of Pakistan, that he was Muslim.)[150]

Pal was not vetted for the judgeship. There was no time for the Raj to make even a cursory assessment of his competence or his political beliefs, let alone digest his voluminous paper trail. Had he been a prominent troublemaker, British officials would have recognized his name. Apparently all that the British knew was that Pal was a former High Court judge who had not made himself a conspicuous pest. That would do. On April 27, the Raj sent him a secret telegram naming him as India's judge on the Tokyo tribunal.[151] MacArthur rubber-stamped the appointment with no scrutiny.[152] Pal scrambled to grab a passport, airplane tickets, and vaccinations, flying out of Calcutta eight days later.[153]

By the time he arrived in Tokyo on May 14, the trial was already under way.[154] Gazing somberly through black-rimmed glasses, he wore a starchy collar with his robes in the manner of his home courts. On his first day in court, he heard Webb tersely declare that the defense's challenge to the court's jurisdiction was "dismissed for reasons to be given later"— something which could hardly have made a good first impression.[155]

While Pal's judicial robes showed him as an equal member of the bench, some observers marked him by the color of his skin. Although he was supposed to reside at the Imperial Hotel with all his colleagues, the Indian judge was conspicuously omitted from an edict from General Headquarters about British Commonwealth personnel which specified that the British, Australian, Canadian, and New Zealand judges could remain at the Imperial Hotel for the duration of the Tokyo trial. Only after those four white judges bluntly protested "this discrimination" was Pal was allowed to settle in.[156] Watching him in court, an Australian journalist described him as a "Hindu giant" and commented that "Judge Pal was a dignified statue of dark marble at the right-hand end of the lofty bench of 11 international judges."[157]

CHAPTER 12

The First Conquest

DELFIN JARANILLA HAD BEEN nearly sixty years old at Bataan. He was thin and unimposing, with a long white goatee. A colonel and the judge advocate general of the Philippine Army, he was inducted into the U.S. Army weeks after Pearl Harbor.[1] His Philippine Army unit was evacuated to the Bataan Peninsula for what he would bitterly remember as "my baptism by fire."

Although a crack shot with a rifle, Jaranilla's battlefront task was holding courts-martial for Filipino deserters, sentencing those convicted to go back to the front. When the defeated Filipinos and Americans finally surrendered in April 1942, he hoped for decent treatment as a senior officer.[2] Yet as he later remembered, "a bearded Jap" snatched away his shoes and other possessions, smashing him with a rifle. Before Jaranilla could regain his senses, the Japanese officer dragged him to join the Bataan march northward.

Barefoot, relying on a bamboo cane, the old man staggered along. "Those who fell on their knees were beaten and bayoneted by the merciless Japanese," he recalled. By the second day, hundreds of Filipinos had died from disease or beatings. Prisoners who could not walk "were murdered in cold-blood." Some who tried to escape were caught and beheaded. When Jaranilla tried to help a Filipino officer who had collapsed from exhaustion, he counted himself "lucky the Japs only kicked me."

"I was limping and could scarcely bear the pain," he remembered. He considered escaping but could barely walk. Hungry and enervated, he blacked out on the road. He survived because a Japanese officer let a Filipina nurse take him to a nearby hospital.

For months afterward, he was detained at a former Philippine Army camp, later transferred to Bilibid Prison in Manila, where hundreds of prisoners of war were crammed into a cell meant for twenty men. After eventually being released during the Japanese occupation of the Philippines, Jaranilla was so anti-Japanese that in 1943, when the collaborationist president of the Philippines was shot and nearly killed, he was questioned by the Kempeitai, who suspected the expert marksman.[3] In the final battle for Manila, his house was destroyed. The memory of Bataan would linger for the rest of his days, although with one consolation: he married the nurse who saved him.[4]

This was the man sent by the Philippines as its judge at the Tokyo trial. Jaranilla was the last of eleven to be chosen, alongside Radhabinod Pal of India. His appointment came in the waning days of American colonial rule, just a month before the Philippines became an independent country. He was hastily selected by Manuel Roxas, the aristocratic president of the Philippines.[5] Roxas himself was lucky not be in front of an Allied tribunal, rather than sending a judge to one; during the Japanese occupation, he had been part of the collaborationist government, prompting some members of the Roosevelt administration to call for him to hang. But he was sanitized by General Douglas MacArthur, who declared him a "great patriot" who had secretly spied for the resistance.[6] Unlike Roxas, Jaranilla had refused senior jobs in the pro-Japanese government, claiming that after Bataan he was too sick to work.[7]

Jaranilla's devotion to the United States ran deep. As a young boy in the city of Iloilo, he had learned English by chatting with American soldiers near his Catholic seminary, doing so well that the Philippine government sent him to high school in California. Then it was on to the University of Tennessee and law school at Georgetown in 1907.[8] Anti-Asian discrimination was ubiquitous in the United States; he once played a violin solo as a musical interlude during a Georgetown student debate about Japanese immigration where it was argued that the Japanese as a race were superior to the Chinese.[9] Returning to the Philippines, Jaranilla had worked his way up from court clerk to attorney general in 1925, serving under six American governors general.[10] In the final days of World War II, Jaranilla was appointed to the Supreme Court of the Philippines, before being sent to Tokyo.[11]

He shared wholeheartedly in the American view of the war.[12] He was an ardent admirer of MacArthur, reinforcing his view of himself as a Christian savior of the Philippines. Jaranilla wrote to MacArthur during the Tokyo trial, "With your long years of duty in the Philippines and with your brilliant victory over the enemy, you certainly have helped immeasurably the Filipino people in successfully attaining their coveted freedom."[13] When his wife had medical troubles, he was effusively grateful to MacArthur for helping to get her into a U.S. Army military hospital in Manila.[14] Proud of the Tokyo court, he argued that it would add more to international law than Nuremberg because of the wider range of legal traditions among the judges.[15]

Having personally endured Japanese war crimes, Jaranilla became a voice for the Asians who had suffered under Japanese conquest—particularly imperative since there was no Korean judge at Tokyo. He was consistently tough on the accused.[16] When confronted with procedural questions, his instinct was to speed the trial along.[17] He seethed at judges such as Bert Röling who took a more evenhanded approach.[18]

Mei Ruao liked him, finding him gregarious despite his ordeal at Bataan, often hosting boozy dinner parties.[19] Yet neither Jaranilla's friendliness nor his suffering earned him respect among the European judges. "The Filipino judge was totally Americanized," Röling said later. "He belonged to the ruling class in the Philippines which collaborated with the Americans. There was nothing Asian in his attitude at all."[20] The British judge, Lord Patrick, saw him as a vengeful idiot who had no business on the court. "The Phillipine [sic] judge, appointed at America's insistence, since we insisted that India must be represented, just doesn't understand," he wrote. "It is not lack of English, it is lack of gray matter with him." He jeered, "Only one thing is certain, that he will vote on some ground for conviction. 'Remember Bataan[.]' He was in the 'Death march of Bataan.'"[21]

As soon as the defense lawyers found out that Jaranilla had survived the Bataan death march, they filed a motion to remove him because of his "personal bias." (Somehow the defense counsel did not realize that Mei might also be biased from the bombing of Chongqing.) How could he possibly be an impartial judge of Japanese war crimes when he had experienced them firsthand?[22] Ducking a legitimate issue, the judges again declared that they had no authority to undo an appointment made by the supreme commander. On June 13, Jaranilla took his seat alongside the other Allied judges.[23]

Soon after, MacArthur invited Jaranilla to be his guest on the grandstand in Manila for a ceremony celebrating the independence of the Philippines on July 4. As Jaranilla wrote ebulliently to MacArthur, that resonant date would no longer only mark "the birth of the greatest American Republic in the world" but also the day that "the flag of the independent Republic of the Philippines was hoisted as a symbol of a true independent nation."[24]

MANCHURIA

Early in the prosecution's case, two gigantic screens were put up behind the Japanese defendants, displaying maps of Asia. In overlays added for every year since 1931, Japanese-controlled territory was marked in livid red. What started in 1931 with the invasion of Manchuria would by 1941 distend to include vast reaches of Southeast Asia and the Pacific Islands. Tojo Hideki and the other defendants grimly strained their necks to look behind them at their unfolding conquests.[25]

China, above all, was drowned in red. The prosecutors argued that the Axis drive for world domination had started in earnest with the Japanese seizure of Manchuria, China's three huge modern northeastern provinces.[26] Manchuria made a grand prize: an industrializing land as big as Britain and France put together, with massive economic potential, bordering Russia, temptingly close to Japanese-colonized Korea. The prosecution accused Japan of browbeating an unstable, fractious China into proffering special rights in Manchuria, ruling directly over the territories held by Japan's powerful colonial railroad company, the South Manchuria Railway. Next, Japanese extremists plotted a provocation in order to conquer the territory outright, hoping to use the prodigious resources of Manchuria and northern China to fortify the army and build up Japanese heavy industry in order to ward off the predatory United States.[27] The flashpoint was an explosion along a stretch of track of the South Manchuria Railway near the city of Mukden (Shenyang) on September 18, 1931, which the prosecution said had been staged by officers of Japan's renegade Kwantung Army. This so-called Mukden incident became a pretext for Japanese troops to attack a nearby Chinese base, which was quickly followed by an invasion by more than forty thousand Japanese soldiers. Japan nimbly conquered Manchuria while losing as few as three thousand troops, as well as five thousand wounded and over two thousand with frostbite.[28] Despite the Tokyo trial's narrative blaming only a small military clique, Japanese society had been widely swept with war fever. Instead of annexation, Japan in 1932 set up a puppet regime, styled as the independent state of Manchukuo (Manzhouguo), which inspired utopian dreams among Japanese imperialists. To lend Manchukuo legitimacy, Japan had installed as its nominal ruler Puyi, the last emperor of China's Qing dynasty, toppled as a young boy in the revolution that created the Republic of China.[29]

The next "incident" came in July 1937: a skirmish at the Marco Polo Bridge, outside of Beijing, which Japan took as a cue to march troops into

A long queue of Japanese waiting to watch their former leaders on trial, 1946

the Chinese mainland, seizing Shanghai and the Nationalist capital of Nanjing, soon occupying much of coastal China. Echoing the nineteenth-century Opium Wars with the British Empire, prosecutors accused Japan of using opium as a military weapon to undermine Chinese morale. From July 1937 to June 1941, according to an Imperial Japanese yearbook, over two million Chinese had been killed and almost four million Chinese troops had died, been wounded, or taken prisoner.[30]

Xiang Zhejun, the Chinese associate prosecutor, rose to his feet to debunk the Japanese official claim that these conflicts were merely a "Manchurian incident" and a "China incident," murky confrontations with blame on both sides, not rising to the level of war. Japan had taken "warlike actions" in Manchuria, he said, killing thousands of Chinese soldiers and civilians. Japan had "started a war at Marco Polo Bridge. . . . Later, Japan sent her soldiers all over China killing millions and millions of soldiers as well as children, women, and helpless civilians. . . . If that were not war, what is a war?" Bolstering Keenan, he added that the Tokyo trial was "not making new laws," but "simply embodies law and the principles already in existence."[31]

Starting its case in 1928 with the militarization of Japanese society, the Tokyo trial did not consider previous imperial conquests of Korea or Taiwan in the Meiji era. "We do not have the right to evaluate the merit of the annexation of Korea," wrote the French judge, Henri Bernard, noting that the judges repeatedly refused to rewind that far.[32] It was in

Manchuria, on the prosecution's account, that Japan committed itself to a ruinous drive for expansion, pursuing mirages of self-sufficiency and economic autarky through a widening series of conquests—next Southeast Asia, and finally in a desperate war against the French, British, and Dutch Empires and the United States.[33]

"They Wag Their Tails and Beg Our Sympathy"

As the Manchuria phase began in the Ichigaya courtroom, the Republic of China joined in the Allied reconstruction of a peaceful Japan. For China, this project had a terrifying urgency. As a Chinese diplomat in Tokyo warned, if "Japan returns to the old anti-democratic, anti-peace orbit, then it is our country that will bear the brunt."[34]

China urged the United States, the Soviet Union, and Britain to disarm Japan completely. Wang Shijie, China's foreign minister, told General George Marshall that only "the complete demilitarization of Japan" could eliminate the risk of renewed aggression.[35] Japan could not be allowed to rearm for at least three decades, until its people had embraced peace and democracy.[36] An influential Chinese general cautioned his government that Germany after World War I had been allowed to keep a small core of military forces, which it had expanded into an all-conquering army. Although not wanting to enslave or exploit the Japanese, "who are of the same race and culture as we are," this general warned that "Japan swallows the humiliation of American occupation and flatters America only to preserve its national power for revenge in the next great war."[37]

China's goal was to transform Japan to make it democratic and unthreatening. In one report approved by Guo Taiqi, a top diplomat and former Chinese foreign minister, the Chinese authorities sought to uproot what they saw as cultural sources of Japanese aggression in State Shinto, stamping out police powers used to enslave the minds of the people, implementing sweeping land reform, and remaking a school curriculum that had promoted national superiority.[38] That Chinese general argued for encouraging the defeated Japanese "to realize their hope for personal freedom and respect for human rights," because democracy would nurture peace.[39]

As the Manchuria phase was getting under way, a Chinese investigator working with the Allied prosecutors privately told his government, "The trial will expose the real face of Japan's aggressive war and brutality, thereby educating the Japanese nation to purge aggressive thoughts."[40] Yet Chinese officials fretted that the General Headquarters program had not eradicated the country's militarism. The Foreign Ministry's Asia political team wanted an extensive purge, while the Defense Ministry wanted to ban war movies and forbid Japanese from doing judo, kendo, or any Bushido-style sports.[41] Despite the purges, a Chinese official in Tokyo warned that "the aggressive spirit in Japanese politics and society is so prevalent and deep" that it would be hard to eradicate. Like many Chinese, this official wanted the Allied occupiers to get tougher: executing or dispossessing the most important militarists, sentencing the rest to prison or forced labor.[42]

China sought Japanese compensation for its wartime devastation, including pensions for the dead or injured. The total was an astonishing butcher's bill of 1,045,972,697,570,744 yuan, which comes out to roughly $87 billion—an enormous sum at the time, when, for comparison, the United States was helping to prop up postwar Britain with a loan of $3.75 billion.[43] The staggering scale of the losses was tallied with eerie bureaucratic specificity: more than 800,000 rifles, 63,000 machine guns, 5.7 million mortar shells, 3.6 million cannon shells, 1.3 million antiaircraft shells, almost 20 million grenades, 1.7 billion bullets, 267 hospitals, and more than 200,000 horses and mules. The Chinese air force had lost 1,813 fighters, interceptors, bombers, and other airplanes. The most painful losses could never be repaid: almost 3.4 million dead in the army and more than 14,000 in the air force.[44]

Chiang Kai-shek's government was cautious about abolishing the monarchy, even though Chinese officials believed that the emperor was deeply implicated in Japan's aggressions.[45] "Hirohito is responsible for war crimes committed during the Japanese war of aggression" in myriad ways, a Chinese diplomat argued. Under the Meiji constitution, he argued, the monarch was the head of the empire and wielded supreme command over the army and navy. The emperor's authority had been used to put Japan on a war footing and forge the Tripartite Pact with Nazi Germany and fascist Italy; he had authorized the invasion of Manchuria and the occupation of China; he had presided over the imperial conferences which deliberated about attacking the United States and the British Empire; he had issued imperial rescripts sanctioning Japan's withdrawal from the League of Nations, blessing the Tripartite Pact, honoring soldiers killed in battle, and declaring war on the United States and the British Empire.[46]

Many Chinese officials wanted to scrap the monarchy immediately, before rightists could use the throne to lead Japan into new wars.[47] The Foreign Ministry's Asia political staffers wanted to permanently abolish the imperial system; if that was not possible, the emperor should be demoted to a king and stripped of any privileges that could stand in the way of democracy.[48]

Yet despite that, China's government held back. When Australia put Hirohito on its list of war criminals, China's Foreign Ministry wanted to have the same policy as the United States, not expressing any strong opinions before finding out what MacArthur wanted.[49] In the end, China deferentially left the emperor off its list of war criminals.[50] Later, the Chinese government preferred to leave the fate of the emperor to the collective decision of the Allied powers. If the monarchy remained, the constitution should be democratized "to return the Emperor's power to the Japanese people."[51]

For all the talk of democracy, though, many Chinese officials worried about what direction a democratic Japan might take.[52] Chinese diplomats favored Japan's social democrats—at that time organized as the Japan Socialist Party—whose principles were similar to those of China's Nationalists, hoping to build them up and perhaps quietly take control of them.[53] But the other political parties, as a Chinese official in the Tokyo embassy wrote, were either violent leftists or rightists who had escaped punishment.[54] Chiang's government particularly dreaded the prospect that the Japanese Communists might win power, creating a government sympathetic to Mao Zedong.[55]

A Chinese war crimes investigator warned the Foreign Ministry that prosecutions had left the Japanese unrepentant: "I am deeply aware that they not only failed to wake up but deepened their contempt for our country."[56] A Chinese intelligence officer cautioned harshly that while the Japanese appeared submissive now, they were such a stubborn nation that they could rise again like the Germans: "We have to destroy Japan's national culture through collective control."[57] Using a common Chinese slur for the Japanese, he wrote, "The Wo"—the dwarfs—"are inherently ruthless and exceptionally tricky. After their defeat, they are like caged beasts. To survive, they wag their tails and beg our sympathy. To kill them is not benevolent on our side. It's better to assimilate and influence them with our morality so as to protect China from future scourges."[58]

THREE PRIME MINISTERS AND ONE GHOST

While Chinese officials fretted, the Allied prosecutors called the first of a long list of spectacular witnesses that would mark the Tokyo trial. Rather than foreigners hostile to Japan, though, the prosecutors relied heavily on the testimonials of centrist Japanese statesmen. The scene in Ichigaya often looked less like an international trial than a purely Japanese one, pitting liberal leaders against their hard-line successors. Civilian politicians who had been terrified to defy the swaggering generals and colonels were now able to slag them off without fear.

In the Manchuria phase, the high-profile witnesses included three Japanese prime ministers who unveiled the innermost disputes within their government—an unprecedented inside glimpse that helped to discredit the bellicose nationalists for much of the Japanese public.[59]

The first ex-premier was Baron Shidehara Kijuro, who until about a month ago had been prime minister supervising the country's demilitarization, and was now a minister in the government. He was renowned for his peaceful policies as foreign minister in the 1920s, at the end of the internationalist and liberalizing Taisho period, and for opposing the invasion of Manchuria. Handsome in a well-tailored suit, with a neat mustache and round spectacles, he stood out as a man of rank. At seventy-three years old, he walked slowly, but his mind was sharp. A Japanese newspaper reporter admired his adroit responses as befitting a senior statesman.[60] None of this earned him deference from Sir William Webb, who, when the former premier was asked to speak in his rather good English, snapped, "His English is impossible. Get him back into Japanese."[61]

Shidehara glowered stonily at the defendants.[62] As foreign minister in 1931, his conciliatory "Shidehara diplomacy" had envisioned a peaceful Asia built on interdependence between coexisting sovereign countries.[63] For that he had been reviled by several of the defendants now on trial, including General Doihara Kenji. Shidehara had tried in vain to get the headstrong Kwantung Army to withdraw from its Manchurian gains in 1931, as well as objecting bitterly to its scheme to enthrone Puyi, the last Qing emperor, as the royal figurehead of a Japanese-controlled regime in Manchuria. Shidehara had argued firmly that this was folly: the creation of an obviously artificial Manchukuo would only alienate the League of Nations; Puyi himself was an undemocratic anachronism; the Han Chinese in Manchuria would not embrace a Manchu emperor; and his installation would make it impossible to reach a peaceful resolution with China.[64]

Shidehara painted a terrifying picture of an army beyond civilian control. As often happened during the trial, he gave his main account through an affidavit, a time-saving measure adopted by the court, before facing cross-examination. Strikingly, he testified that the Japanese cabinet could not directly command the army. After all, under the constitution the army answered to the emperor, and the military could for all practical purposes sink a government by disapproving of its choice of army or navy ministers; at best, the cabinet could pass along its opinions about military policy through the army minister. He explained bluntly, "The Cabinet was not in a position to discipline either the army in Manchuria or any army anywhere." Soon before the invasion of Manchuria, he had tried to block "the military clique" from invading; when the cabinet had been unable to control the army, it had resigned.[65] Under a stern cross-examination that reminded a Japanese reporter of machine gun fire, he dropped another bombshell: Japan's troops in its colonial possession of Korea had, without the knowledge of the cabinet or the authority of the emperor, reinforced the Japanese forces in Manchuria.[66]

The next prime minister to testify was Baron Wakatsuki Reijiro, the centrist prime minister under whom Shidehara had served as foreign minister early in the Manchuria crisis, now a gaunt, white-haired octogenarian with a fading memory.[67] His statement and testimony reinforced the picture of an ungovernable military. His army minister, General Minami Jiro—now one of the defendants—had ignored the reluctant cabinet as Japanese troops plowed into Chinese territory. Day after day, Minami had reassured the helpless Wakatsuki that the troops would go no farther, and day after day they had advanced anyway.

Still, the elderly Wakatsuki wilted under cross-examination, often unable to remember details, with Minami's defense lawyer pressing him into conceding that his cabinet had accepted the Kwantung Army's claims that it was acting in self-defense against Chinese provocations.[68] Ridiculing the indictment, an American defense lawyer asked the former prime minister, "Do you know of any plan or conspiracy . . . to plan and wage wars of aggression, to conquer China and the Pacific Ocean, and eventually the world?" Wakatsuki had to reply, "I have never heard of anything of the kind."[69]

Tellingly, one former prime minister was not there to testify, his absence the starkest testament to the constant terror of coups and assassinations which had blighted the 1930s. Inukai Tsuyoshi, who had succeeded Wakatsuki as prime minister, had been gunned down by young military officers during the notorious coup attempt of May 1932. An advocate of cabinet government, he did not lack for bravery; he had refused to flee the prime minister's office, and after being shot repeatedly, he had said that he wanted to keep talking to the young officers.[70] Now, in the Army Ministry courtroom, Inukai's son, who had been his father's private secretary and had urged him to flee the assassins on that terrible day, emotionally claimed that his father had tried to pull back Japanese troops from Manchuria, which helped to mark him as an enemy to the ultranationalists.[71]

Inukai's son testified that his father had met with Hirohito himself seeking an imperial rescript ordering the army out of Manchuria but had been rebuffed. At this, Marquis Kido Koichi's lawyer leapt into action in defense of the emperor. Asked if he meant that the emperor was responsible for the army's failure to pull out of Manchuria, Inukai's son, who would later become justice minister, retreated, assuring the court that "His Majesty was a strong advocate of peace and had a very strong desire for an amicable settlement of the Manchurian Incident."

Webb, who kept Hirohito in his crosshairs throughout the trial, fumed. The next day, for the first time directly quizzing a witness, he pressed Inukai's son: if the emperor was such a lover of peace, why had he refused to issue that imperial rescript bringing the army to heel? Inukai's son uncomfortably explained that "it is the feeling of the Japanese to avoid bringing the name of our Emperor into this argument." Backtracking, he said that he was now unsure whether his father had directly asked for such an imperial rescript, or simply made his request known through Kido or other channels. Hirohito, he said, had given Inukai an audience and had expressed his hope for an end to the crisis and a lasting peace with China. Webb disdainfully cut the witness off, saying that the court had heard enough.[72]

Left unsaid was that Hirohito, despite his private misgivings that the Manchurian invasion was leaving Japan isolated, had in fact issued an imperial rescript in *support* of the Kwantung Army's adventurism. The emperor, who was officially in control of the ungovernable Kwantung Army, had on January 4, 1932—the fiftieth anniversary of the Meiji Emperor's famous Imperial Rescript to Soldiers and Sailors putting the military under the eternal command of the emperor—praised the Kwantung Army for fighting bravely in "self-defense" against Chinese "bandits."[73] In Kido's diary around the same time, the marquis had noted that the emperor's wish to rein in the Manchurian invasion had enraged the army, so much so that Kido and other civilian leaders had decided that Hirohito should not say anything more about Manchuria policy unless he absolutely had to.[74]

The third prime minister was Okada Keisuke, who had barely avoided assassination himself. A navy minister and then a member of the Supreme War Council during much of the Manchuria crisis, he had become prime minister in 1934. In the Army Ministry courtroom, Okada gave a statement that he had received numerous reports that the army was planning to stage an incident to give them a pretext to grab Manchuria. As navy minister, he had been briefed that the explosion along the South Manchuria

Railway "was plotted and arranged by the clique in the Kwantung Army."
He recalled the shock of the civilian government when Japanese troops in
Korea had "crossed the border and participated in this occupation without
any Imperial sanction." The Kwantung Army, he said, had been the real
power in Manchuria, outside the control of the government.[75]

Vividly showing the dangers of standing up to the military, Okada gave
a sworn statement about the major putsch attempt in February 1936, when
a score of officers and over a thousand troops "terrorized Tokyo for three
and a half days." They had seized his official residence as prime minister,
the Diet, police headquarters, and the Army Ministry—the very spot
where the trial was occurring. The radicals had killed his finance minister and several other senior officials with machine guns. He had barely
escaped. His brother-in-law, mistaken for him, had been shot dead. After
the slaughter, he and his cabinet had resigned under the shadow of the
army's dominance of the country.[76]

Not all the Japanese witnesses were so effective. Hoping to expose the
inner workings of Japan's government, the prosecution made the rash
decision to make use of Major General Tanaka Ryukichi, a former aide
to Tojo. A portly, round-faced, hard-eyed man who testified wearing
civilian suits, he was out to settle scores with Tojo and other old rivals.[77]
Hirohito had complained privately about Tanaka's bad reputation, saying that Tojo's own image had been tarnished by employing such a person.[78] When asked by a defense lawyer about his nickname "the monster,"
Tanaka gave a sinister laugh that was apparently meant to be jolly. Not
only did Tanaka prove unreliable, he would later testify for the defense as
well. For the Chinese, he was especially abhorrent as the commander of
Japan's North China Area Army, which under him in 1940 had developed
plans for crushing areas of Chinese guerrilla resistance.[79] Yet the general
was allowed to spend several days on the stand loudly testifying about
Japanese army plots, tarring Tojo as well as other army defendants.[80]

While personal testimony was important, the prosecution scored some
of its most palpable hits with internal Japanese documents. Throughout
the trial, the prosecution's leading piece of evidence was Kido's diary: a
massive record of the inside deliberations of the Japanese government and
court, fifteen volumes in full, running to over five thousand pages.[81] It
implicated not just its author but also many of the defendants, although
it showed more backstabbing and intrigue than a smoothly functioning
conspiracy. In September 1931, Kido had recorded that the army was so
determined in its Manchurian land grab that it might not obey orders
from the government.[82]

The prosecutors introduced damning telegrams from several Japanese consuls to Shidehara, revealing the split between Japanese moderates and the hotspurs on trial. The Japanese consul in Mukden had warned that the Kwantung Army was about to go on the offensive along the South Manchuria Railway. Other cables revealed Japanese military officials planning to create Manchukuo and install Puyi, the overthrown Qing emperor, with a formal declaration of independence meant to hoodwink the League of Nations. Doihara, nicknamed "Lawrence of Manchuria," was shown hard at work persuading Puyi to be Japan's instrument, while simultaneously figuring out how to pretend that Japan had nothing to do with the restored emperor. If any Chinese troops dared to challenge the puppet state, Doihara assured a nervous Puyi, who was terrified of assassins, the Kwantung Army would fight them off.[83]

In the cables, the accused convicted themselves with their own words. In one dispatch from January 1936, Hirota Koki, as foreign minister, outlined plans to encourage collaborator rule in north China under Japanese troops and the Kwantung Army. In August 1936, as prime minister in a government dominated by the military, Hirota's cabinet issued an important bellicose directive that "the fundamental national policy to be established by the Empire is to secure the position of the Empire on the East Asia Continent by dint of diplomatic policy and national defense . . . as well as to advance and develop the Empire toward the South Seas."[84]

Reminding the courtroom of how Japan's invasion had scotched the idealistic interwar hopes of the League of Nations, the prosecutors introduced a major League report that had been adopted by the world body's Assembly in 1933. (In his recent Imperial Palace monologues, Hirohito claimed that he had wanted to accept the report in its entirety but had feared opposing the cabinet, which wanted to reject it.)[85] The League had guardedly concluded that it "could not regard as self-defence" the military advances made by Japanese troops after the Mukden explosion. Despite Puyi's bombastic claims that he had been propelled to the throne by the will of the Manchurian masses, it had been perfectly apparent that Japan wielded the real political power in Manchukuo.[86] The League commission had stingingly concluded, "It is . . . indisputable that, without any declaration of war, a large part of Chinese territory has been forcibly seized and occupied by Japanese troops and that, in consequence of this operation, it has been separated from and declared independent of the rest of China."[87] In the end, only Japan had voted against the report at the League, with Matsuoka Yosuke storming out the door.[88]

THE MARSHALL MISSION

Of all the untutored Americans who could have benefited from the grand history lesson unfolding in the Ichigaya courtroom, Harry Truman took pride of place. His ill-preparedness particularly showed on Asia in general and China in particular. "I know very little about Chinese politics," the president privately wrote in early 1946. "The one thing I am interested in is to see a strong China with a Democratic form of Government friendly to us. It is our only salvation for a peaceful Pacific policy."[89] He remained uninformed about most of Asia, breezily falling back on ideology, myth, or bigoted stereotype, as he later admitted: "I thought India was pretty jammed with poor people and cows wandering around the streets, witch doctors and people sitting on hot coals and bathing in the Ganges and so on, but I did not realize that anyone thought it was important."[90]

He was, at least, painfully aware of his inadequacies: "This head of mine should have been bigger and better proportioned. There ought to have been more brain and a larger bump of ego or something to give me an idea that there can be a No. 1 man in the world." He remained glumly ill at ease with the job. "Well I'm here in the White House, the great white sepulcher of ambitions and reputations," he confided in an unmailed letter to his wife. "I feel like a last year's bird's nest which is on its second year."[91]

Truman began by supporting China's Nationalist government, although skeptical of Chiang Kai-shek and wary of getting pulled into China's internal quarrels. He thought that "Chiang's gov't fought side by side with us against our common enemy, that we have reason to believe that the so-called Commies in China not only did not help us but on occasion helped the Japs."[92] He publicly pledged to help the Chinese nation achieve "the democratic objectives established for it by Dr. Sun Yat-sen."[93]

Yet Truman soon grew alarmed by the brewing Chinese Civil War—so much that in late 1945 he sent no less than General George Marshall, who had been serving as U.S. Army chief of staff, to mediate between the Nationalists and Communists.[94] While professing faith in "a strong, united and democratic China," Truman pressed for a cease-fire between Nationalists and Communists and then a national conference to resolve the country's internal strife. He continued to recognize only the authority of Chiang's Nationalist government, but pledged not to send American troops to take sides in China's domestic struggle.[95] "We are all glad to welcome you back to trouble and strife," MacArthur cabled Marshall with wry congratulations on the impossible job.[96] As Marshall spent thirteen frustrating months in China, Truman despaired about his high-profile envoy's prospects. "Looks like Marshall will fail in China," he wrote to his wife.[97]

It is too easy to assume, with the clarity of hindsight, that Communist victory was inevitable. While the Nationalist government was hobbled by its long war against Japan, it would only fall through a series of blunders. It alienated crucial local chiefs, business leaders, and intellectuals. It relied on brute force rather than winning over skeptics in the cities and in the far-flung reaches of the vast country. Infuriated by Communist provocations in Manchuria, Chiang lashed back in 1946 with a military offensive that would prove to be more than his rickety state could stand.[98]

On the bench in Tokyo, Mei Ruao was mortified that American mediation was necessary. "It's inexcusable that our own affairs need foreign intervention," he wrote as he heard of Marshall's mission. "At the same time, what's even scarier is our economic crisis."[99] In the trial's early months, he glumly watched Marshall's mediation between the Nationalists and Communists.[100] He found it embarrassing and frightening to see the chaos in China, one of the war's victors. His country's unwinding made a miserable contrast with Japan, where MacArthur's friendly policies had "let Japan take many economic advantages and gradually get on the path toward rejuvenation."[101]

In a sign of the weakness of the Chinese state, the Manchurian case was presented not by the Chinese associate prosecutor but by Australian, American, and other prosecutors. The Chinese team seemed overmatched or irrelevant. Mei was preoccupied by China's declining status. "What a bad showing," he wrote in his diary.[102]

"Murder in Their Minds"

After the high drama of the opening days, the court settled into an uneasy routine. "To the foreigners in Tokyo," wrote a top Indian diplomat, K. P. S. Menon, "the trial had all the lure of a glittering social event. Men and women flocked to it, oblivious of the fact that great issues affecting human lives and international law were at stake. The Japanese accused behaved with the stoic dignity of tragic characters."[103]

Tojo followed the testimony keenly, his earphones almost always on, leaning forward as if to study an adversary.[104] When a defense lawyer complained about the conquerors passing judgment on the vanquished, Tojo suddenly raised his head.[105] While some of the generals retained their swagger, most defendants were ill at ease. As an *Asahi Shimbun* reporter noted, Kido Koichi's "violent turbulence of inward emotion" was revealed in his reddening ears.[106] Two former foreign ministers were distinctly uncomfortable: Shigemitsu Mamoru seemingly detached, staring at the floor, and Togo Shigenori taking notes with a pencil.[107]

As courtroom officials whispered that the proceedings could take nine months, Webb tried to find ways to speed it up: taking affidavits, reprimanding the lawyers for technicalities, snarling at defense counsel for asking questions which he found too long, upbraiding the translators. He did so with an all-encompassing rudeness that offended the accused, the prosecutors, the judges, and everyone else. When Japanese defense lawyers addressed the court politely, he brusquely urged them to eliminate "every unnecessary word."[108] He repeatedly exhorted the lawyers to get out the facts rather than dwell on fine evidentiary points, as would be done in a normal criminal trial.[109] At one point he cut off the testimony of a Japanese former cabinet minister: "That is enough; we have heard enough. We have heard some loquacious witnesses in this court, but none so loquacious as you."[110] Once when the defense counsel complained about the use of affidavits instead of courtroom testimony, he snapped, "No sermons here. The laws of evidence do not apply; you ought to know that by this time."[111] At another time, he shrugged off the gulfs among national legal systems: "There is no use in discussing the difference between the American system, the British system, the Dutch system, or the Russian system; we have no time for that here, nor would it lead us anywhere."[112]

Webb swiftly alienated his fellow judges. He was the only judge with a microphone; the others sat in silent annoyance or gossiped to their seatmates. "Our President was a dictator," recalled Röling.[113] Most significantly, the judges from Britain, Canada, and New Zealand united in frustration at Webb, a British bloc which would come to drive the court's majority. As the New Zealand judge, Erima Harvey Northcroft, wrote confidentially to his prime minister, Webb "has an unfortunate manner of expression, generally querulous, invariably argumentative and frequently injudicious." When the other judges scribbled notes to him, "he is often either, and sometimes both, hostile and unreceptive of our suggestions or incapable of understanding their purport or purpose."[114]

The animosity toward Webb became so intense that the polite Canadian judge, E. Stuart McDougall, tried to soothe him with a gentle chat. Webb was privately fuming at the British and Dutch judges.[115] The British judge tried to defuse Webb's entirely accurate impression that "the British Commonwealth Judges on the Tribunal are critical of and disappointed with your conduct of the proceedings of the Tribunal." Teeth clenched, the British judge assured Webb of his esteem and confidence.[116]

Ensconced at the Imperial Hotel with their room and board paid, the judges lived in luxury unimaginable to ordinary Japanese inhabitants of Tokyo's firebombed infrastructure.[117] Yet most of them wanted to go home. Mei, initially charmed by his colleagues, admitted in his diary that "it was quite boring to see the same judges day and night."[118] Others were ill at ease in the public spotlight, with the British judge appalled by the photographers: "these people, if a chance to get a sensational picture should arise, would trample their own mother underfoot in their rush."[119]

Wearing black judicial robes under glaring camera lights without air-conditioning, the judges wilted in the sweltering Tokyo summer heat. The Canadian justice, acclimatized to Montréal temperatures, was especially miserable.[120] Even Mei, who had endured the furnace heat of Chongqing, felt dizzy.[121] Webb adjourned the trial for a week in July because of the lack of air-conditioning, and considered decamping the court to a cooler city if too many people keeled over.[122] He wrote to General Headquarters, "Unless the members of the Tribunal, the prosecutors, or the accused are likely to collapse in any numbers, we must carry on."[123] At the stifling Imperial Hotel, Röling privately wrote that he was "living as a mild nudist in my hotel rooms, just sufficiently covered to prevent hurting the feelings of the Japanese angels who bring me iced tea or 'hotte cowee' (as they call it)."[124]

More profoundly, most of the judges were uneasy living in Japan. Röling was alternatively fascinated and disgusted by Japan. What he appreciated best was the women, privately pining after Japanese girls with "skins as peaches" and "eyes laughing in a mysterious manner." Like any prosaic tourist, he swooned for the cherry blossoms and—unlike the more politically obsessive Mei—was beguiled by the old conceit that they represented Japan's youthful warriors, "fiercely living for just a moment, giving all for being beautiful, sacrificing yourself in the flower of your life, leaving behind nothing more than an admired memory." Other than that, Röling found the country weird and unsettling. "I cannot understand this people," he wrote to a friend. Japan was a land "where the men are bowing and smiling with murder in their minds, well hidden."[125]

Furthermore, the judges understood how awkwardly their enterprise fit with the rest of the occupation. They were mostly foreign civilians in a scene dominated by U.S. soldiers. Among the military officers lodging at the Imperial Hotel, Röling admitted to "feeling as a civilian in this generals-hotel, between all those stars, a bit as a cloudy night."[126] Mei wrote in his diary that other countries were frustrated with American dominance and MacArthur's generous policy toward Japan.[127] Several of the judges would have shared the sentiments expressed by grouchy troops in the British Commonwealth Occupation Force (BCOF), headquartered at the Kure naval dockyards in southern Japan, who paid their disrespects to MacArthur with their version of the Lord's Prayer:

THE BCOF PRAYER

Our General which art in Tokyo,
Douglas be thy name,
Thy kingdom be off limits to BCOF troops,
Thy will be done in BCOF,
As it is done in Tokyo,
Give us this day our daily directive,
And forgive us for trespassing in the American Occupation Zone,
As we forgive postal for jettisoning our mail;
And lead us not into insanity,
But deliver us from Kure,
For thine is the kingdom and thou art almighty,
For the period of the occupation,
Sallaam.[128]

The Last Emperor

After the parade of Japanese prime ministers came an even more spectacular witness: Puyi, the last emperor of China's Qing dynasty, most recently the puppet emperor of Manchukuo.[129] His presence in the courtroom dazzled onlookers, even those repelled by his deeds. Newspapers across the world gobbled up coverage of the man they called Henry Puyi. (He had plucked the English appellation from a posh list of British royal names.) Röling privately marveled about "the situation in which one, every day, in the corridor meets the Emperor of China and says: 'Hello, how are you this morning.' I thought in former days that only in fairy tales do you meet the Emperor of China. And, still, I am not quite sure if that opinion was wrong."[130]

Puyi's fate had been a mystery since Soviet troops marched through Manchuria in the final days of World War II. Now the Soviets admitted that they had been holding him all along. The Soviets secretly meant to turn him over to China, but both the Chinese and Soviets quietly agreed that first he should serve his purpose as a witness at the Tokyo trial.[131] While he testified, the Soviets kept him locked up at their embassy there.[132]

Puyi looked gaunt as he emerged from a Soviet airplane at Atsugi airfield near Tokyo, escorted by Soviet secret police. At forty, the Son of Heaven looked decidedly common in round spectacles, a beret, and an ill-fitting suit, with an anxious expression on his face.[133] His old British tutor had once remembered the boy-emperor's dual nature: a bright child who might have made a progressive constitutional monarch, but also a keen admirer of Benito Mussolini, albeit aware that he was not cut from the same hard stuff.[134]

Puyi was sunk in the downtrodden gloom of a man who had lost his throne no fewer than three times: first as a five-year-old boy when the Qing dynasty was overthrown in the revolutionary fervor that inaugurated the Republic of China, then restored by one warlord and ousted by another, and now dragged off by the Soviets. As a connoisseur of defeat, the Soviet varietal did not agree with him. He still considered himself a superior being and inwardly lurched between feeling insulted and terrified.[135]

For those Japanese who had believed that Puyi had been a legitimate ruler in Manchukuo, his comeuppance in Tokyo was an awkward precedent: an emperor hauled before a war crimes tribunal. True, he was not on trial—although he would later be charged as a war criminal in Communist China—but this royal humiliation could not sit well with Japanese monarchists. His links to the Japanese throne went deep. Puyi had been thrilled when the Kwantung Army had sent him to Tokyo for a royal visit with Hirohito in 1935, meant to provide some respectability for the hireling. The emperor of Japan had greeted the emperor of Manchukuo at the train station, attended a banquet for him, and inspected a military parade alongside him. The two monarchs had worn similar medal-festooned dress military uniforms, boots, and caps. Puyi had visited a shrine to the Meiji Emperor and a military hospital treating Japanese soldiers wounded in Manchuria. On his return to his hinterlands palace in Changchun, Puyi had issued an imperial rescript declaring, "We and His Majesty the Emperor of Japan are of one spirit." Puyi had made a second trip to Tokyo in 1940, while he was adopting the Shinto worship of the sun goddess Amaterasu—the divine ancestor of Hirohito—as the official state religion of Manchukuo. This celestial merger had required a strained meeting with Hirohito, who had awkwardly said that he accepted the will of his Qing vassal in this matter.[136]

His Kwantung Army handlers had thrilled Puyi with visions of returning to the Forbidden City in Beijing in glory after the triumph of Japan's invincible forces. Daydreaming of his lost empire, his first thought was that he would need to find some imperial dragon robes. Stuck instead in remote Changchun, Puyi had ascended his ersatz throne on the cold, drizzly morning of March 1, 1934, with as much royal chintz—crimson carpets, silk curtains, a high-backed chair, minions performing the nine-fold bow—as could be mustered. Not long after, he was favored with a visit from Prince Chichibu, Hirohito's brother, bearing the emperor's congratulations and a lavish chrysanthemum medal. Yet his actual powers had been limited to having his household staffers flogged or beaten, in at least one case to death. For everything else, Puyi had taken his marching orders directly from the Kwantung Army, through a Japanese military attaché who wrote out his speeches in shaky Chinese, censored his mail, and told him where to go, whom to receive, what to tell his subjects, when to smile, and when to nod.[137]

As the war turned against Japan, Puyi was terrified: if his own troops did not kill him, the Soviets would. At farewell ceremonies to honor kamikazes sent off to die for their doomed empire, he was haunted by their ashen faces and the tears flowing down their youthful cheeks. He fled his grotty palace for the mountains. When told about Japan's surrender, he fell on his knees thanking heaven that the Americans would spare Hirohito—until being told that the same deal did not apply to him. Frantically trying to reach Japan, loaded up with as much jewelry as he could grab, he got as far as Mukden airport before being caught by Soviet troops wielding submachine guns. He was packed off to a chilly hotel in Khabarovsk repurposed as a detention center, where he spent his depressed days hoarding his remaining jewels and listlessly memorizing books about Leninism. It was, he thought, still better than being turned over to the Chinese.[138]

The galleries were packed as the emperor entered the Ichigaya courtroom on a steamy August day. Familiar with gawking crowds, Puyi was unfazed by the hubbub as he was marched to the witness box by Soviet guards. Thin and clad in a poorly fitting dark suit, his collar sometimes askew, he was nervous at first but grew confident. Pensively stroking his chin with his forefinger, leaning back in the witness box, he testified with regal authority.

The Allied prosecutors meant to use their royal witness to expose Japan's plan to conquer northeast China, with the Qing potentate confessing that he had been every inch the puppet that the newspapers said he was. By laying bare Japan's mastery over Manchukuo, the Allied prosecutors hoped to expose the other purportedly autonomous states that later became part of the Japanese colonial playbook in such places as East Hebei and Inner Mongolia, as well as discrediting the pro-Japanese authority in China led by Wang Jingwei. The prosecutors meant to brand all of them—as well as collaborationist governments in the Philippines, Burma, and elsewhere—as tools of Japanese aggression.[139]

Puyi was privately unrepentant as he was dragged back and forth between the Soviet embassy and the Ichigaya courtroom.[140] "I did not think that I bore any responsibility, I did not wonder what kind of ideology it was that caused my crimes, and I had never heard of the necessity of thought reform," he wrote years later, when he had restyled himself as a model citizen of Communist China, the final persona of his shape-shifting life.

His real peril now came from vengeful Soviets and Chinese, not a relatively docile panel of foreign judges. "I denounced Japanese war crimes with the greatest vehemence," he later wrote. "But I never spoke of my own crimes, for fear that I would be condemned myself." He later professed shame at his testimony, avoiding self-incrimination in order to protect himself from Chinese punishment.[141]

Joseph Keenan did the questioning of Puyi. Although the well-educated royal, his English rusty from disuse, had to speak through a clumsy Chinese translator, he still easily outmaneuvered the U.S. chief

A wary Joseph Keenan, the U.S. chief prosecutor, and a smiling Puyi, the former Qing emperor of China, Tokyo, August 1946

prosecutor. While the Japanese defendants glared daggers at him and the Chinese associate prosecutor repeatedly tried to shut him up, the Qing potentate nimbly presented himself as a helpless figurehead forced to serve the Japanese army or die.[142]

Puyi testified that he had only agreed to head a Manchurian regime when told that the Kwantung Army might kill him if he did not comply, although he would later admit that he had been working with Japan long before.[143] "On paper, in order to cheat people the world over, they"—the Japanese—"make Manchukuo look as if it is an independent state," he said. "But in actuality Manchukuo was being administered by the Kwantung Army." Manchuria had really been a Japanese colony, with himself effectively a prisoner in his palace: "In actuality, the Emperor has no rights and power whatsoever."[144]

As demonstrated by Puyi's deference to his Soviet captors, he now served new masters. When Keenan asked if he had seen evidence of Soviet designs on Manchuria, the Soviet prisoner gave the only reply possible: "The Soviet Nation had no aggressive plan against Manchuria."[145] This was too much for Röling, who was hostile to the Soviets throughout the trial. He correctly surmised that the Soviets had promised to turn the ex-emperor over to China for trial as a war criminal.[146]

In his most preposterous turn, the longtime Japanese instrument claimed to have been with the resistance all along. His young wife had comforted him by planning their revenge on the Japanese, he said, his voice raised with emotion, but they had poisoned her. (He would later write that he had no proof of that allegation and was playing up his grief to win sympathy.)[147] He testified that he had been biding his time in the hopes that the Chinese and Manchurians could one day strike back against the Japanese. "This was my ideal," he said, "and so I entered into the mouth of the tiger."

Webb interjected that fear of death did not excuse treason. "All this morning we have been listening to excuses by this man as to why he collaborated with the Japanese," the Australian chief judge snapped. "I think we have heard enough." Keenan, trying to protect his royal witness, irritably replied that he had not been aware than anyone other than the Japanese defendants were on trial. Webb barked back that Keenan would hear more if he wore his headphones.[148]

Puyi was not dissuaded. "In the Japanese plan they want to first enslave Manchuria and then China proper, and then East Asia, and then the whole world," he asserted without evidence, to groans of protest from defense lawyers. Accusing Japan of a kind of religious aggression, he said, "Deep in my heart I opposed absolutely the invasion of the Japa-

nese Shintoism"—a claim that called attention to how the promotion of
State Shinto became a part of Japanese colonization in Taiwan, Korea,
Singapore, Thailand, China, and elsewhere.[149] He made a spectacular
but unreliable claim that Hirohito, making Shinto the official religion of
Manchukuo, had given him a sacred sword and mirror, two of the three
articles of the imperial regalia which had been bestowed by the sun goddess Amaterasu to her divine line. Puyi claimed to have wept: "that was
the worst humiliation that I have ever faced."[150]

One of the sharpest defense lawyers, Major Ben Bruce Blakeney, had
previously written a withering profile of Puyi for *Life* magazine which
slagged him as "only a puppet, a prisoner in his empire, a pathetic, self-
effacing nonentity of an emperor, with an empire that is a fake."[151] Given
the unique opportunity to question his subject in the flesh, he conducted
a relentless cross-examination meant to show that Puyi had eagerly seized
the Japanese offer to restore him to gilded power. "Your first concern
again, then, was to save your own life, was it?" he asked scornfully. The
ex-emperor pounded the stand and waved his hands as he defended himself or evaded questions; offended by Blakeney's impertinence, he retorted,
"This is ridiculous." He parried so well that the lawyers suspected that his
English was better than he affected.

Blakeney pointed out that Puyi had long resented the Republic of
China, which had swept him from his throne, and suggested that he
had been eager to cooperate with Japan's Kwantung Army to get it back.
Puyi denied any such ambitions. The American defense lawyer bluntly
explained that the Qing emperor was now a Soviet prisoner held under
armed guard and was wanted for criminal prosecution in China. Since
Puyi had already testified under oath that he had distorted the truth when
menaced by the Japanese, Blakeney inquired, why would he not do the
same for the Soviets and Chinese? Asked if the Soviets had said what
they would do to him if he did not testify, again Puyi testily said, "This
is ridiculous." He was there, he lied, by his own free will.[152]

After Puyi completed ten days of testimony, Keenan wrote privately to
him in custody at the Soviet embassy to thank him for enduring a "very
severe ordeal" as a witness.[153] The Chinese associate prosecutor reported
to his government with satisfaction that Puyi had provided "cogent statements" about Japan's puppet government in Manchuria, as well as about
its military, political, economic, and religious aggression there.[154]

Puyi was not the only famous Japanese collaborator who might have
testified at the Tokyo trial. Subhas Chandra Bose and Wang Jingwei were

both dead, but several leading figures of Japan's pan-Asianist ambitions were under Allied lock and key. Ba Maw, an anti-British politician who had ruled a nominally independent Burma under Japanese domination, had been captured by the British and wound up in Sugamo Prison. Since his detention rankled with Burmese nationalists, the State Department, privately embarrassed, offloaded him back to Britain. The British did not want the headache of putting him on the witness stand in Tokyo, and instead pardoned him and flew him back to Burma.[155] The Philippine prosecutors had wanted to call José Laurel, the president of the Philippines under Japanese occupation, and Jorge Vargas, another prominent collaborationist. But after Puyi's impressive courtroom showing, other Allied prosecutors feared that they might exonerate themselves if given their day in court.[156] So Puyi alone wound up as the face of pan-Asianist collaboration.

He was packed off onto a special Soviet flight to Vladivostok, where the Soviets were supposed to send him to Mukden to face the avenging authorities of the Republic of China.[157] In the end, though, he was brought back to captivity in the Soviet Union, where he was waited upon by members of his family; since they dared not call him "Your Majesty," they instead discreetly called him "Above." After China's 1949 revolution brought Mao Zedong to power, the Soviets decided the time was right to turn Puyi over to a new Communist China.

In July 1950, he and other Manchurian collaborators were sent by train to China. Puyi was petrified. He dared not even hope for a painless death. His last years are chronicled in a memoir he wrote to please his final master in the Chinese Communist Party. He recounts being treated well, if gruffly, by the soldiers of the People's Liberation Army, as he was transported to a reeducation prison camp for a thousand Japanese and Manchurian war criminals at Fushun, in northeastern China. He was alarmed by the drab prison with its high, dark brick walls, watchtowers, and barbed wire.[158]

As an official Chinese state account of Fushun prison brags, as the prisoners "acquired highly internationalization-oriented peaceful transformation in this humanitarian Chinese prison, they began to introspect in the depth of the minds on their own war crimes, examine the ugliness of their souls."[159] Puyi's memoir of his reeducation is less enthusiastic but ultimately follows the Chinese Communist Party script. He was won over by good medical care and tasty pork buns; he steeped himself in books with titles like *Our New Democracy;* he learned to make his own bed, brush his own teeth, tie his own shoes. He slowly realized that other people were laughing at him.

After two months in Fushun, he was moved to a wretched jail cell in a former Manchukuo prison in Harbin. He passed several nervous years there, indoctrinated that the benevolent Communist Party believed that even war criminals could remold themselves into new men. He wrote, "One fact stood out clearly in my mind: the Communist Party used reason to win people over." Later he was sent back to Fushun to carry coal and study historical materialism. He was thrilled when, in 1959—in the depths of the terror-famine known as the Great Leap Forward—Mao himself allowed a special pardon for war criminals and enemies of the revolution. After ten years of reeducation, he stood with the Chinese people, their faces shining with joy in Maoist truth. At last, he wrote, his motherland had made him a man.[160]

CHAPTER 13

The Rape of Nanjing

T HE SHEER SCALE OF Japanese mayhem in China turned out, grotesquely, to be a boon for the Japanese defendants at the Tokyo trial. The Republic of China's debilitated government had been in no condition to gather evidence of war crimes, nor to mount adequate legal investigations. This became painfully apparent as the Allied prosecutors in Tokyo turned from Manchuria to Japan's invasion of the rest of China.

American prosecutors wanted to make Chinese suffering central to their charges of crimes against humanity—a novel offense defined as murder, extermination, enslavement, deportation, or other inhumane acts against a civilian population.[1] Yet in a quiet sign of lack of confidence in China's efforts, American staffers were put in charge of covering the evidence, politely but firmly urging China's foreign minister to dig up more material.[2] Chiang Kai-shek himself confided, "We heard that the General Headquarters doesn't think there is enough evidence about the enemy's atrocities in China."[3]

As Joseph Keenan flew to China to screen evidence, an anxious Chiang exhorted his government to brace for his visit and help the prosecution.[4] The Chinese did their best to charm the American chief prosecutor. The Chinese associate prosecutor, Xiang Zhejun, lavished him with hospitality in Shanghai, Beijing, and Chongqing.[5] Xiang and the Chinese foreign minister brokered a brief but symbolic meeting with Chiang himself in Chongqing.[6] In Shanghai, Keenan met with Chiang's wife, Soong Mei-ling, an important political figure in her own right, who merrily said that she would be glad to return with him to Tokyo as a stowaway.[7] Still, confirming Chiang's private fears, the evidence that the Chinese government presented to Keenan was of limited value: an official summary of Japanese war crimes in Manchuria, Chinese diplomatic messages to the Japanese embassy protesting the invasion of coastal China, and official Chinese overviews of Japan's atrocities and its spreading of opium in occupied China.[8]

Needing evidence that could stand up in court, Xiang pressed a range of Chinese ministries and offices for documentation of Japanese conspiracies to break international treaties, atrocities by Japanese troops, and acts meant to plunder and weaken China. With lawyerly precision, he sought lists of Japan's treaty violations, estimates of civilian deaths and destruction of public and private property from the Japanese invasion, and documents on the trafficking of narcotics.[9] Seeking documentation of Japanese atrocities against the ethnic Chinese diaspora in Hong Kong, Singapore, Hanoi, and elsewhere in Asia, he begged for firm evidence that the atrocities could be attributed to senior military and political figures.[10]

Overwhelmed by the war, the Nationalist government strained to help its Tokyo prosecutor. Chinese officials painstakingly pored through government archives.[11] At the Foreign Ministry, a few staffers urgently dug up the most important documents on a dizzying array of incidents: the invasion of Manchuria; assaults on Hebei and Chahar provinces; attacks on Shanghai; and the Marco Polo Bridge clash at the start of the full-scale invasion of China.[12] In Shanghai, a Chinese major general led a team of investigators collecting evidence of Japanese war crimes, helped by American transport planes.[13] Chinese diplomats in Indochina and Thailand took months carefully gathering accounts from people who had suffered atrocities, seen them personally, or had verifiable scars.[14] Yet a Chinese official cautioned that the forms they filled out "cannot present solid evidence."[15]

All too often, overworked Chinese bureaucrats worked less at fulfilling the prosecutors' requests than getting them off their desks.[16] The military had kept records about military losses, not civilian suffering; the Interior Ministry was still surveying the extent of the damage; the committee for compensation for wartime losses operated by the Executive Yuan, China's executive branch, was gathering information; Chinese diplomats in Singapore, Hanoi, and elsewhere found nothing useful.[17]

Without adequate documentation, China had to buttress its case with witnesses. One Chinese investigator fretted privately that too much was riding on such testimony. He cautioned that China's judicial authorities had not prepared the witnesses to testify, and that only one or two of the proposed witnesses were well-known figures: "The government has no clue about the backgrounds of the rest. It is a real shame that our side lacked initiative in appointing witnesses."[18] Another Chinese official warned that shaky testimony could "cause irreversible damage to our national prestige."[19]

Xiang was pleased to have corralled a relatively large number of witnesses, but worried about using the testimony of senior Nationalist officials. He doubted it was proper for Chinese leaders to travel far to "make statements repeatedly and stand questioning time and again." Xiang urged senior Chinese officials to come loaded with documents and to prepare systematically to understand the facts.[20] Yet as one Chinese general privately explained with embarrassment, "According to some reports, after the enemies occupied north China, their atrocious actions and drug policy became even more brutal. Because I was fighting along several lines, I am unable to present precise evidence. This is a shame."[21]

The Nationalists ignored some Japanese atrocities. Japan's notorious "kill all, burn all, loot all" campaign in 1941 had been directed largely against Communist base areas in northern China, and was noticeably neglected by the Nationalists. Despite the importance of the campaign and its obscene death toll, it would barely feature in the Tokyo trial.[22]

With the Tokyo trial under way, a Foreign Ministry investigator was morose. "We suffered for the longest period and lost the most, yet the evidence we could gather is less than anyone else's," he privately told his superiors. "Our country clearly lacks in the collection of important documents." China needed more diplomatic papers and testimonies from prominent figures. He had gathered sixty pieces of evidence from Guangxi to Wuhan to Shanghai, including photographs, letters, and Japanese soldiers' diaries and combat orders, but "[t]hese still do not feel enough. Our local authorities' lack of attention to evidence collection deeply surprised America."[23]

American prosecutors largely took over the China case in Tokyo. During the Manchuria phase, of the five officials from the prosecution section handling Manchuria, none were Chinese; two non-Chinese prosecutors joined Xiang and his assistant, Henry Chiu, to handle Japanese aggression against China; and five non-Chinese prosecutors dealt with crimes against humanity there, with only Xiang and Chiu from the country in question.[24] At its peak, the Chinese prosecution had, in addition to Xiang, just four secretaries and four legal advisers, a modest slice of the seventy-two total staffers.[25] A group of Allied prosecutors flew to Nanjing to collect photographs and statistical information about the massacres there, and to gather Chinese and foreign witnesses who could testify credibly.[26]

Mei Ruao lamented privately that "the evidence that we have to try the war criminals is simply insufficient." When fighting a legal case, he liked to say, the first thing was evidence, the second was evidence, and the third was still evidence.[27] The Chinese judge was embarrassed by his government's failure to marshal evidence, while Xiang was in agony. "We don't have much evidence and documents," Mei wrote in his diary. "In the future, can the Prosecution Section sufficiently substantiate these counts?" After fourteen years of warfare, "we should be able to provide much more evidence."[28]

To be sure, the Tokyo court could not get a complete evidentiary accounting of every substantial instance of Japanese killing of Chinese civilians; that would have taken many years. Yet it did get a compelling sampling about the massacres, rapes, and plunder in Nanjing, which showed distinct patterns of military conduct that strongly suggested an underlying method and the culpability of commanders. New Zealand's judge was persuaded that it was arguable that the abuse of prisoners and civilians in China was "the responsibility of General Matsui Iwane directly and of other defendants indirectly."[29] Despite Mei's anxieties, the courtroom testimony and sworn affidavits built a clear picture of the Japanese army's criminal behavior in Nanjing, which was echoed in many other places across China, although with less available evidence than for Nanjing.

In order to convict senior leaders, prosecutors sought proof of their personal responsibility for ordering or allowing crimes at Nanjing and elsewhere. Yet much of that evidence had been destroyed by Japanese officials in the last days of the war. The Japanese garrison at Nanjing had torched its papers, according to a U.S. report, while Japan's diplomatic records about China had been among the first to be burned.[30] Looking at the top of the chain of command, Chinese prosecutors yearned in vain for the orders given by commanders. At the bottom, the prosecution largely lacked access to such damning material as the battlefield diaries of Japanese troops, many of which recounted how they shot to death thousands of Chinese prisoners.[31] The lack of proper evidence about Japanese decisions was a boon to senior Japanese commanders at Nanjing, several of whom were never prosecuted.[32]

The Tokyo trial did not have documentation that has been recently used by a leading Japanese historian, Kasahara Tokushi, to show that Japanese divisional and regimental commanders ordered the execution of unarmed Chinese soldiers and did not discipline troops for atrocities against Chinese civilians. The Tokyo trial never knew that, as Kasahara has shown, General Matsui Iwane pressed for a swift assault on Nanjing in the hopes of forcing the surrender of China's government—a lacuna that allowed the general to present himself on trial as passive and doddering, rather than an active commander. A complete investigation, Kasahara suggests, could have implicated senior army officers, army leaders, and perhaps even Emperor Hirohito himself.[33]

The Tokyo trial did not have adequate evidence about Prince Asaka Yasuhiko, the emperor's elder uncle by marriage, who as a lieutenant general had been put in command of Japanese forces at Nanjing while the ailing Matsui was on the sidelines.[34] Although the prince had enjoyed an impressive army career, he was not particularly close with Hirohito, who privately called him "a war hard-liner until the very end."[35] Still, the prince's career got a boost after his bloody victory at Nanjing, with his name circulated for important army commands. According to the emperor's private monologues, the prince would maintain considerable influence among the members of the imperial family in military careers, including Prince Mikasa, the emperor's youngest brother. Prince Asaka would later be linked to an order to execute Chinese prisoners of war, but the Tokyo tribunal did not have any evidence of that allegation.[36]

In the end, the imperial prince in command of the troops who stormed Nanjing would never face charges of war crimes. When Allied interrogators asked Matsui if the prince was escaping responsibility for the Nanjing massacre because of his royal stature, Matsui leaped to the monarchy's defense. The prince, he said, had only taken command about ten days before. "[I]n view of the short time he was connected with this army I do not think he can be held responsible," Matsui said. "I would say that the Division Commanders are the responsible parties."[37] Prince Asaka would go on to play golf with the emperor.[38]

Compared to the detailed record of internal Japanese deliberations that would be introduced in the prosecution case for, say, the formation of the Axis or for Pearl Harbor, the Chinese case looked threadbare. The brute facts of Japanese aggression and massacre in China were clear enough, but thanks in part to the Japanese cover-up, the prosecutors could only mount a disappointingly thin case about the deliberations, orders, and intentions of the Japanese warlords in the dock.

To the Marco Polo Bridge

The basic facts of Japanese aggression were not in dispute. After a clash at the Marco Polo Bridge near Beijing on July 7, 1937, Japan had invaded China in force, capturing the Nationalist capital at Nanjing, and refusing to deal with Chiang Kai-shek's government.

The flashpoint was Beijing. With the Nationalist government based down south in Nanjing holding more control over southern China, the north was where Japan made its encroachments—posting troops, making demands, cutting deals with local warlords. In an awkward colonial arrangement, there had been Japanese troops legally posted on Chinese territory for decades. After foreign powers had crushed the Boxer Rebellion, China's tottering Qing dynasty had signed a protocol in 1901 allowing those foreign powers—including the United States and Britain, as well as Japan—to station deployments of their troops around Beijing to safeguard access to the sea and discourage riots against foreigners. One of a long series of despised "unequal treaties" signed under pressure from foreign imperialists, this protocol allowed Japan a toehold on the northern Chinese mainland.

The prosecutors made the ill-advised decision to begin with a microscopic dissection of the skirmish at the Marco Polo Bridge (known in Chinese as Lugouqiao), rather than telling the bigger strategic story of the massive invasion that followed. Worse, they left it to senior Nationalist officials who dutifully followed Chiang's party line to recount the outbreak of war on July 7. Xiang Zhejun, the Chinese associate prosecutor, privately fretted about the testimony of the main Chinese witness, Qin Dechun, a general and the mayor of Beijing, a sharp-eyed man with a tidy military mustache. Xiang urged him to prepare, and someone managed to get rid of some of the most cringe-inducing passages in his draft testimony.[39]

Xiang was right to worry. Bald and clad in his army uniform, Qin swayed back and forth in the witness box. The mayor, who as a general had served under Chiang, testified about Japanese plotting during the Marco Polo Bridge clash even though he had no inside knowledge of what the Japanese were thinking. This did nothing to establish guilt but did make the Chinese prosecution look cheapjack.[40] It was more convincing when a U.S. military official in Beijing at the time testified that the Chinese had shown no signs of aggressive intentions, while the Japanese had been provocative.[41]

The trouble had begun when the Japanese garrison stationed in Fengtai in the southwestern outskirts of Beijing had wanted to build a barracks and airfield, which would consolidate their sway over north China. As the mayor testified, China had harshly refused Japanese demands to pull Chinese troops out of the area.[42] Then in the evening of July 7, the Japanese commander, General Matsui Iwane, called the Chinese to say that there was a Japanese soldier missing and that gunshots had been fired by Chinese troops in nearby Wanping Fortress. He demanded that Japanese forces be allowed to enter and search the fortress. The Chinese refused.

According to the mayor, Japanese troops ringed Wanping Fortress and began firing machine guns. After fierce combat, the Japanese asked for a cease-fire, which Qin speculated was an excuse to get reinforcements from the Kwantung Army. A few days later, the fighting began again, with the Japanese shelling the fortress. While the Japanese demanded that China stand down or they would attack with large forces, the Chinese went on the offensive at Fengtai. Referring faithfully to Chiang, Qin said, "They never thought that, at the call of our supreme leader, all Chinese would rise and take up the War of Resistance on all fronts."[43]

In cross-examination, Qin was torn apart by the defense counsel—exactly as Xiang had feared. One American defense lawyer tarred the Chinese witness as a Nationalist partisan and then asked him if he had "one single fact" on which to base his accusation that his client, General Doihara Kenji, had instigated the conquest of Manchuria and north China. He did not. "General, sir," scolded the defense lawyer, "I have asked for facts in the courtroom."[44] Sir William Webb agreed: "the whole of his examination in chief consists of conclusions."[45]

The trial degenerated into a confusing, unproductive wrangling over which side was to blame for moving troops, skirmishing, and firing first around the Marco Polo Bridge. As a reporter for the *Yomiuri Shimbun* noted, the Chinese general steadfastly refused to be manipulated by the defense counsel and "testified persistently that responsibility lay only with Japan."[46] The Chinese Communist Party, keen to see the Nationalists stumble, was less impressed. A *Liberation Daily* editorial raged that Qin "was not only unable to raise powerful charges but also appeared timid in front of Doihara's arrogance, thereby putting up a strange show in which the war criminal tried the witness."[47]

This constricted lens on the Marco Polo Bridge obscured the more important strategic panorama. The clash had forced China's government into a terrible choice: accept Japan's new encroachment on the north or fight to resist against the superior might of a centralized, industrialized, battle-tested Japan. The crucial point was Japan's subsequent massive onslaught across China, helped along by its troop presence near Beijing.[48]

Instead of a comprehensive record of Japanese aggression and atrocity, the prosecution had to rely on whatever papers had been haphazardly spared from the flames lit by Japanese officials. The prosecution revealed a Japanese Foreign Ministry document which noted that just four days after the Marco Polo Bridge fighting, "the Imperial Government, at a cabinet meeting of 11 July, made an important determination and decided to take necessary steps in connection with the dispatching of troops to North China."[49] In January 1938, the Japanese government declared that it would no longer recognize the Nationalist government in China, seen as working with the Communists, instead seeking the establishment of a new government in China that would cooperate with the Japanese Empire and recognize Manchukuo.[50] Later that year, a diplomat preparing to brief Emperor Hirohito bluntly noted that Japan would continue to work for "the destruction of the Chiang Kai-shek Regime."[51] By the end of that year, after negotiations deadlocked, the Japanese prime minister, Prince Konoe Fumimaro, was openly calling for the Nationalist government to be completely wiped out.[52]

Taken together, this suggested an intentional Japanese invasion of China with the aim of compelling the destruction of the Nationalist government. But while this might condemn the Japanese government in general, the prosecution strained to offer the crucial evidence of internal deliberations—burned to ashes or ripped to pieces at the end of the war— that would prove the personal responsibility of individual defendants for these decisions.

There were only a few documents that specifically implicated the accused. Hirota Koki, who had been foreign minister during the invasion, was found in an October 1937 meeting with the prime minister and other senior ministers setting onerous demands on China, such as recognizing Manchukuo and forming an anti-Communist pact with Japan.[53] Several of the defendants, including Marquis Kido Koichi, had attended a meeting which voted unanimously to break off Japan's remaining ties with the League of Nations for its condemnations of Japan's war in China.[54] Most dramatically, a month before the Marco Polo Bridge incident, Tojo Hideki, then chief of staff of the Kwantung Army, had written, "I am convinced that if our military power permits it, we should deliver a blow first of all upon the Nanking regime to get rid of the menace at our back."[55] While this showed that Tojo had welcomed an attack on the Nationalist government in order to prepare for a possible clash with the Soviet Union, it did not show him ordering aggression.

"The Modern Dante's Inferno"

Now came a heart of darkness. The courtroom shuddered as the prosecutors came to the massacres and rapes at Nanjing. The most notorious event of the China war, the bloody fall of the Nationalist capital in December 1937 made the nucleus of the Chinese prosecution. People of all nationalities—not least the Japanese spectators in the visitors' galleries— sat stunned for days of grisly testimony from eyewitnesses in the doomed city. The defendants gazed fixedly at the floor.[56]

The cerebral judges, unsettled, coped in odd ways. During the testimony about Nanjing, Bert Röling, who sat next to Radhabinod Pal, wrote privately of his distracted friend, "When the proceedings are boring to us he recites poems in Bangali about love, timid love. It is one of the strangest contrasts—one ear is concerned with the Rape of Nanking and all the horrible things involved—the other hears a slow and dark voice, reciting what translated means: 'I shall come when you smile at me,' or 'When you are not with me no poem develops in my heart.'"[57]

The defendant most implicated by the charnel of Nanjing was General Matsui Iwane. During the war, an American friend had remembered him as a "little wisp of an old man," pleasant, well-meaning, thin, with a jerking palsy on his right arm and the right side of his face.[58] Now sixty-eight, wearing a civilian suit, he was not a well man: the doctors at Sugamo Prison worried about his clogged arteries and a heart disease from an old case of syphilis.[59] During the Nanjing testimony, he sat back impassively with his arms crossed, as if at an uncomfortable meeting of his staff officers.[60] A *Yomiuri Shimbun* reporter noted his hard countenance as he listened.[61]

In Nanjing and beyond, the prosecutors sought to demonstrate a systematic pattern of Japanese commanders breaking the laws of war, thus implicating the senior Japanese leaders in the dock. In particular, since the conflict in China was labeled as an incident rather than a war, Japanese military regulations had treated captured Chinese troops not as prisoners of war but as "bandits" unworthy of the protection of the laws of war—allowing them to be killed or abused in large numbers. The other Tokyo defendant most obviously implicated for the Nanjing massacre, General Muto Akira, who in 1937 had served under Matsui as adjutant to the chief of staff of the Japanese army in China, had confirmed this to Allied investigators, noting that it had been decided in 1938 that "because the Chinese conflict was officially known as an 'incident' . . . Chinese captives would not be regarded as prisoner of war."[62] To show that the atrocities were widespread and standardized, the testimony was both sickening and often repetitive: that unsettling mix of horror and monotony which is typical of war crimes trials.

After the debacle of Qin Dechun's testimony, the judges were more impressed with three non-Chinese eyewitnesses who had been working in Nanjing during the massacre: impeccably credentialed Americans, they were less easily accused of bias by defense counsel, and came from the same social milieu as many of the judges.[63] Awful as their testimony was to hear, it was as comprehensive as the prosecution needed. Calm and authoritative, they gave a harrowing survey of the Japanese army's cruelty.

The first was Robert Wilson, a Harvard-educated surgeon who now

The corpses of Chinese people killed by Japanese soldiers near a temple in Nanjing soon after the city fell in December 1937

lived in California, so pedigreed that even the gruff Webb treated him with deference. Almost forty years old, he was bald and wore round eyeglasses. Born in Nanjing, he had returned there after medical school, and was working at the University Hospital there when the city fell to the Japanese on December 13, 1937. Over the objections of defense lawyers, he impassively told what he had seen as the hospital filled up.

A middle-aged Chinese woman had all the muscles of her neck severed. A sixty-year-old man came in with a bayonet gash in his chest. One man, treated by Wilson for a bullet wound in the shoulder, said he had been part of a group of men taken to the Yangzi riverbank and shot, with their corpses dumped into the river; he had survived by playing dead and sneaking away later in the dark. A policeman suffering from a deep laceration was the sole survivor of another large group hauled outside the city wall to be machine-gunned; those who were still alive after that had been bayoneted. Another man had been badly burned over about two-thirds of his body and had a bullet through his jaw; as best as Wilson could tell, he had had gasoline dumped on him and set aflame. He died two days later.

To the court's horror, Wilson told of seeing an eight-year-old boy with a deep penetrating wound in his belly. A little girl of seven or eight had a badly injured arm; she told the surgeon that Japanese soldiers had killed her father and mother in front of her eyes.

Like many other eyewitnesses, the American surgeon described numerous instances of rape by Japanese soldiers. As confirmed by a medical exam, a fifteen-year-old girl had been raped, and later had to be treated for syphilis. During lunch one day at his home, Wilson's neighbors had rushed in to tell him that Japanese troops were raping women at their house. Racing to the scene, they found two Japanese soldiers raping two Chinese women. They took the traumatized women to the precarious safety of the University of Nanjing campus, where they joined a large group of refugees.[64]

Horrific as it was, Wilson's testimony was actually milder than what he had written in his personal family letters home at the time, which lends additional credibility to his testimony. His letters are packed with more examples of atrocities, beyond the ones in his courtroom statements. Wilson had recorded that he was in "the modern Dante's Inferno, written in huge letters with blood and rape. Murder by the wholesale and rape by the thousands of cases. There seems to be no stop to the ferocity, lust and atavism of the brutes."[65]

The second American eyewitness, Miner Searle Bates, was a missionary from Ohio with a Yale doctorate in Chinese history, sporting clear-framed spectacles and close-cropped hair. As a history professor at the University of Nanjing, he had dedicated himself to safeguarding Chinese from Japanese troops. He was a founding member of the International Committee for the Nanking Safety Zone, hastily established by a small group of foreigners in an attempt to provide a refuge where Chinese civilians could escape the fighting. "I, myself, observed a whole series of shootings of individual civilians without any provocation or apparent reason whatsoever," he said. There had been almost no resistance to the Japanese, he testified. One Chinese from his own house was killed. Two of his neighbors had objected when their wives were raped; for that, they were taken out and shot.

In the Safety Zone, Japanese troops did sweeps for men accused of being Chinese soldiers. Men were condemned to die for having calloused hands or marks from wearing a cap on their forehead. Bates admitted that there were some former soldiers among the refugees, but testified that the majority of those swept up were manual laborers with callouses on their hands from work. They were marched to the edges of the city and shot in droves.

His voice lowered as he told of hundreds of cases of rape among the thirty thousand refugees gathered at the university. Young girls and elderly women were not spared. On five separate occasions, he said, he had encountered soldiers in the act of rape and had pulled them away from the victims. His own letters, written at the time, recorded multiple cases of rape and abduction. Bates estimated some eight thousand rapes in the Safety Zone alone.

After doing his own investigations and checking for burials, Bates concluded that at least twelve thousand civilians had been killed inside the city walls—with many more civilians executed outside the city, as well as tens of thousands of former Chinese soldiers. The International Committee had arranged burials for at least thirty thousand of those soldiers, but more corpses had been carried off by the river or buried elsewhere: "The total spread of this killing was so extensive that no one can give a complete picture of it."

Bates carefully linked the rampaging troops to their commanders. Early on, he said, senior officers had seen their underlings murdering and raping but had not disciplined them. In a few cases, foreigners saw soldiers shooting or bayoneting a civilian, or raping; the soldiers got nothing worse than a quick reprimand or an order to give an extra salute. Later on, after foreigners complained to the Japanese embassy, they were assured that orders had been sent from Tokyo to restore order in Nanjing—which implied that the senior leadership knew about the atrocities and had control of the troops.[66]

When one of the defense lawyers contended that Bates had no idea who in Tokyo had gotten those telegrams from the Japanese embassy in Nanjing, he shot back that Joseph Grew, the longtime U.S. ambassador in Tokyo, had shown him telegrams that Grew had sent to Hirota Koki and other officials in Japan's Foreign Ministry.[67] Hirota jerked upright in his seat.[68]

Bates's testimony unnerved several other defendants. Matsui stared intently at the witness, flinching when his name was mentioned. Tojo Hideki, who usually took copious notes, did not take any.[69]

The final American eyewitness, Reverend John Magee, was a courtly, bespectacled, affable, Yale-educated Episcopal minister in Nanjing. He too had been a member of the International Committee for the Nanking Safety Zone.[70] He calmly testified that immediately after the city fell, Japanese soldiers began "the organized killing" of large numbers of men. "Soon there were bodies of men lying everywhere, and I passed columns of men being taken out to be killed." Out of a group of hundreds of Chinese men, he did not see any in army uniform. Survivors recounted that they had been marched to the banks of the Yangzi River and machine-gunned. After a few days, he came across piles of over three hundred corpses, many of them burned. He saw a Chinese man fleeing in terror from two Japanese soldiers, who shot him in the face at close range: "They were both laughing and talking as though nothing had happened. . . . [T]hey killed him with no more feeling than one taking a shot at a wild duck, and walked on."

Magee, a keen amateur photographer, had taken gruesome photographs and short films of Nanjing, including of women with slit throats or stab wounds.[71] Scores of women told him that they had been raped. One middle-aged widow said that she had been raped over a dozen times. In one house, he testified, he drove out three Japanese men from a woman's rooms. He then burst into another room where he found a Japanese soldier raping a Chinese woman, and chased the soldier out of the house. A few months later, he caught two Japanese soldiers in the bed of a fifteen-year-old girl and hectored them off. Afterward, the girl's father said that she had been raped; it was her fifth time.[72]

Just as powerfully, a series of Chinese survivors gave their own tales of horror from their fallen capital—although they were treated less cordially by the court than the Americans. Their terrible stories largely matched with those of the foreign witnesses, building a picture of systematic criminality.

Hsu Zhuanying, a sixty-two-year-old railway official, held a doctorate from the University of Illinois. Except for one secondhand story about rape told to him by a trusted boatman, almost all of his testimony drew from his own experience. He testified that Japanese troops had shot at everybody in sight. By the third day after the city fell, he saw corpses strewn all over, many of them mutilated. He lost count of the hundreds of dead. None were in uniform. Many were elderly or children. It took hundreds of Chinese laborers to bury all the accumulating corpses. Several times, he testified, he saw Japanese soldiers raping Chinese women and girls, some as young as thirteen. He visited one house where two teenagers had been raped and killed; he had photographs of the violated corpses as evidence.

In cross-examining Hsu, Matsui's lawyer suggested that Chinese troops had also raped and plundered—which would neither disprove nor justify Japanese war crimes in Nanjing. In a calmly effective rebuttal, Hsu evenhandedly conceded that there had been instances of pillaging by Chinese troops, but noted that the Japanese commanders had not tried to halt the atrocities in the long weeks after Nanjing fell. This pointed the finger at senior officers such as Matsui. Webb sharply added that the rape and murder of civilian women could never be legitimate reprisals, no matter what Chinese troops might have done elsewhere.[73]

Shang Deyi, a shopkeeper, testified about surviving a mass execution. Along with neighbors and relatives, he had been rounded up from the Safety Zone by Japanese troops. Tied together with rope, they were taken to the banks of the Yangzi River, joining about a thousand other men, apparently civilians, sitting in terror facing machine guns. After about an hour of mortal dread, a Japanese army officer arrived and ordered them all shot. Shang slumped to the ground and was covered by corpses. He passed out, later awakening and slipping away.[74]

One young man from Nanjing, Zhen Fubao, had seen some forty men dragged from the Safety Zone. Anyone with calloused hands was machine-gunned to death. He testified that he knew some of them and that they were civilians; one of the dead had been a policeman. That same day, he saw three Japanese troops rape a sixteen-year-old girl in a schoolhouse. In the building where he lived, he saw a Japanese soldier enter a neighboring apartment, drive out the men, and enter a room with a pregnant, married woman, and close the door; the soldier left about ten minutes later, with the woman weeping.[75]

Many Chinese survivors could not afford to come to Tokyo to testify, so the prosecution had to rely on some seventy sworn affidavits. These statements, read aloud by prosecutors, did not allow the judges to evaluate the credibility of the witnesses in person. Nor did they pack the same emotional punch as hearing people tell their own stories. The defense lawyers immediately protested: they would have no chance to cross-examine the witnesses. Still, Webb wanted to use affidavits to speed up the proceedings; he would allow hundreds more affidavits in other phases of the trial.[76]

In one affidavit, a Chinese rice merchant recalled watching men and women lined up on a riverbank and gunned down over the course of an hour. A young Chinese man had been held by Japanese troops who checked his hands and those of other terrified captive men; five had callouses and were promptly bayoneted to death. Another youthful Chinese man recalled the same frightening experience of having his hands checked by Japanese soldiers; a vendor had been found with callouses—from making noodles, not wielding a rifle—and shot to death. Other Chinese witnesses recalled how Japanese troops had killed four civilians, kicking one woman to death, using guns and bayonets for the others.[77]

Disconcertingly, it was only in these affidavits that the court heard from the female victims of sexual violence in what was widely called "the Rape of Nanking." None of the major witnesses, Chinese or otherwise, who appeared in the courtroom to tell their stories from Nanjing and elsewhere in China were women. There were no female voices heard in the proceedings about Nanjing; instead, the testimony from Chinese women was read aloud by men, mostly American men.

In an affidavit, the elderly Chinese dormitory director at a Christian women's college in Nanjing remembered trying to shelter more than ten thousand women and children refugees. For over a month, she testified,

Japanese troops would storm into the grounds nightly, ostensibly looking for soldiers but aiming to carry off girls. In one nighttime raid, eleven girls were taken; two were never heard from again, but nine of them returned to tell of their rape and abuse. One of those survivors "could not walk and she was terribly bruised and swollen and stated that she had been repeatedly raped and abused by four or five soldiers. She was a nervous wreck." Other soldiers tried to rape women on the grounds, and were driven off by the Chinese and American women who ran the college. Another widow recalled that three Japanese troops had ripped off her top and were about to rape her when her husband came to protect her. The Japanese soldiers kicked him to death in front of his baby and his toddler.[78]

Taken together, these overlapping accounts gave plausible indications of an organized, systematic onslaught. The Red Swastika Society, a Chinese philanthropic organization, had alone buried 43,071 people. In total, the chief prosecutor of the Nanjing district court had estimated approximately 260,000 dead.[79]

"THE FLAG OF THE RISING SUN IS FLOATING HIGH OVER NANKING"

Despite the overwhelming evidence of horrors at Nanjing, the prosecutors had less success proving that individual Japanese commanders had ordered or condoned these war crimes, due in part to the postwar destruction of evidence.

The International Committee for the Nanking Safety Zone had filed dozens of detailed protests with the Japanese embassy, urging the government to restrain the army.[80] The committee wrote, "We hope the Japanese Army will find some way to prevent soldiers from robbing, raping and killing the civilian population." The committee had only reported cases that they had been able to check carefully: civilians as innocuous as street sweepers and a blind barber killed; women raped at the University of Nanjing's library; husbands killed after their wives were raped; widespread looting and burning. The committee had assured the Japanese government that there were no disarmed Chinese soldiers among the refugees in the Safety Zone.[81] These reports were contemporaneous evidence of atrocities with distinct credibility: it would be dangerous and pointless to exhort the Japanese army about nonexistent outrages. More importantly, they made it impossible for the accused to claim that no senior leaders had known what was happening in Nanjing.

Matsui had made himself conspicuous as the senior commander. A few days after his troops entered the Chinese capital, he went there for a week, holding a military review and a memorial service for fallen soldiers.[82] He issued the proud statement of an officer in command of his forces: "the army took firm possession of Nanking and performed the triumphal entry yesterday." While expressing sympathy for the Chinese dead, he warned the Chinese people that his army would fight on until the Chinese government surrendered. He boasted, "Now the flag of the rising sun is floating high over Nanking, and the Imperial Way is shining in the southern parts of the Yangtze-Kiang."[83]

Under postwar questioning from Allied interrogators, Matsui had admitted to hearing about excesses by his troops "almost as soon as I entered Nanking." By the time he entered the city, he said, the corpses had been removed, although he saw a few dead Chinese soldiers near one gate. Japanese diplomats, he recalled, had informed him of abuses— suggesting that at least the gist of the complaints from the International Committee for the Nanking Safety Zone had passed through the Foreign Ministry back to him. Asked about the discipline of his troops in Nanjing, he conceded, "I considered the discipline excellent but the conduct and behavior was not. . . . I think there were some lawless elements in the army." He disapproved of his troops' "behavior towards the Chinese population and their acts generally." Yet he could only recall minimal disciplinary measures: a court-martial of an officer and perhaps three soldiers for the rape of Chinese in Nanjing. There may have been more punishments recorded in his diary, he said, but it had been burned when his house was destroyed by an Allied bombing raid.

When asked directly about atrocities, Matsui lurched into outright denial. Was there any blame for Prince Asaka Yasuhiko, Hirohito's uncle by marriage, who had led the troops into Nanjing? None. Had he made a report to his superiors about the behavior of his troops at Nanjing? "No, I was not asked to make a report." What about Chinese claims that several hundred thousand civilians had been killed? "That is absolutely untrue. There was no, absolutely no, grounds for such accusations. This I can state upon my honor."[84]

General Muto Akira, another defendant, who in 1937 had been working under Matsui, told Allied investigators that he had heard from that army's chief of staff about "incidents of stealing, killing, assault and rape." He recalled that Matsui had been enraged at these actions and chewed out his subordinates, and then issued an order to the military police to suppress such actions and arrest wrongdoers. Yet Muto claimed there had only been between ten and twenty such incidents. When pressed by incredulous Allied investigators, who told him that there had been thousands, he said that he could never believe that.[85]

Although Nanjing was the most notorious case, the prosecution meant to convict the accused for "the Japanese pattern of warfare."[86] All across China, villages had been devastated by aerial bombing or artillery bombardment, set on fire, with civilians shot dead.[87]

Beyond Nanjing, though, the evidence was far less comprehensive, often lacking corroboration or specifics. Nor did these statements show orders from commanders or link the war crimes to any of the defendants. This was the realization of Mei Ruao's fears about insufficient evidence gathered by the debilitated authorities of the Republic of China. In Nanjing, the prosecution put forward a compendium that could only be denied by fanatics; for the rest of China, while clearly there had been widespread horrors, the particulars were more debatable, sometimes unsuitable for conviction beyond a reasonable doubt.

The court heard scattershot affidavits from across China. Chinese witnesses testified about students in Beijing shot or tortured to death, women and girls raped in Hebei province, and killings and rapes in Changsha in Hunan province.[88] Also in Changsha, the prosecutors introduced an affidavit from a Japanese lance corporal, who said that Japanese troops had forced some two hundred Chinese prisoners of war to plunder rice and wheat, and had then hidden the theft by killing the Chinese with artillery.

Webb was wary of this sketchier evidence.[89] He was openly disdainful of the evidence about Hubei province in central China in 1943, and quickly ruled out two short affidavits by Chinese witnesses about the killing of civilians in Jiangsu province in 1937. "That is hardly evidence," he scoffed. "There are no details. What court could act on evidence like that?"[90]

One distinctive aspect of the China phase evoked the country's colonized past: charging Japan with spreading opium in order to enfeeble Chinese society. This summoned up excruciating memories of the British subjugation of the faltering Qing dynasty, most notoriously in the Opium War of 1839–42, still remembered today by Chinese nationalists as part of their "century of national humiliation."[91] Puyi, the last Qing emperor, testified that the Kwantung Army had distributed opium to break Chinese morale and health so that they could not resist the Japanese.[92] After the Japanese conquered Shanghai in 1937, they opened opium houses; heroin addicts there quickly became emaciated, filthy, and sick.[93] Wilson, the American surgeon, testified that he had never seen opium dens in Nanjing before the Japanese arrived; a year after the occupation, he counted twenty-one opium dens in about one mile of one of the city's main streets.[94]

Frustratingly for the Chinese prosecutors, a whole category of evidence would never be appraised: aerial bombardment. Japanese bombers had pounded cities and towns across China, most notoriously Chongqing. Nanjing had been battered repeatedly by Japanese bombers for half a year before it fell.[95] The prosecution had enterprisingly found a damning 1939 report by the Japanese army which bluntly advocated the aerial bombardment of Chinese civilians as a terrorizing way of warfare. Such bombing was meant to break the Chinese people's "very deep and keen racial consciousness and anti-Japanese feeling." As the war dragged on, the Chinese people would eventually turn against their own government: "what we expect of offensive operations against the interior is the mental terror they will create among the enemy forces and civilians rather than the material damage inflicted direct upon enemy personnel or equipment. We will wait and see them falling into nervous prostration in an excess of terror and madly starting anti-Chiang and pacifist movements."[96] Yet because such aerial bombardment was not then clearly forbidden by international law—and also perhaps because the Allies did not wish to invite discussions about their own bombing campaigns—this evidence would never feature in the Tokyo trial's judgment.

"Indelible Historic Sins"

The Japanese people recoiled in shock at the evidence from China. The wartime press had suppressed reporting about these enormities, so what was notorious around the world was largely unknown in Japan. Confronted with a radically different image of their army's behavior, ordinary Japanese widely took it to heart.

After Wilson's eyewitness testimony, the *Yomiuri Shimbun* ran devastating headlines about the Nanjing massacre: "Even Women and Children Machine-Gunned—Mountains of Dead Bodies Thrown into the River." As a Japanese reporter wrote, "The packed courtroom listened in silence to numerous examples of slaughter, assault, rape, and other horrors hard to face with open eyes."[97]

Appalled by the evidence, the *Yomiuri Shimbun* wrote a blistering editorial condemning "the evil of Japanese imperialism" and "cruelty unprecedented in the ten-plus centuries of Japanese-Chinese relations." The editorial demanded that "we must recognize the indelible historic sins of the military clique's barbarism, the most prominent incident of which was the Rape of Nanjing." Expressing "bitter regret," the editorial self-critically castigated jingoistic Japanese wartime reporters for accepting barbarism as an inevitable part of war: "We put a blindfold on our higher sense of humanity and deliberately rendered ourselves unable to plainly report what we saw." Far from a sacred war, Japan had waged a war of aggression; the rape of Nanjing alone left a sense of guilt that could never be expunged.[98]

According to a roundtable of Japanese reporters covering the Tokyo trial, the Japanese public was unimpressed by claims about the criminality of aggressive war but shocked by revelations about Nanjing. The Japanese public had been told that their troops had fought a chivalrous war, so the evidence of the Nanjing massacre was distressing.[99]

Wrenchingly, the testimonials about rape at Nanjing struck home with Japanese women in the spectators' galleries. One said that the trial confirmed rumors she had heard when she had visited Nanjing six months after its fall. An eighteen-year-old Japanese woman said, "I was convinced today . . . of the utter nonsense of the Japanese army's boast that the Japanese soldiers were the model of honor and discipline the world over."[100]

JUSTICE AND MERCY

During the testimony about Nanjing, the conservative prime minister, Yoshida Shigeru, expressed "our national gratitude" for Chiang Kai-shek's magnanimity to postwar Japan.[101] The Japanese press echoed that sentiment, noting that their country ought to be grateful for Chiang's generous postwar attitude, seeking democratic rebirth for Japan rather than retaliatory violence.[102]

This was more true than Yoshida realized. Just a few months after the Tokyo trial heard about atrocities in China, the Nationalist Chinese government was secretly looking for ways to back away from Japanese war crimes trials.

In October 1946, China's defense minister, General Bai Chongxi, a renowned strategist, gathered senior officials to lay down the line. He was the rare person who was even more fiercely anti-Communist than Chiang. After Nationalist troops had defeated the Chinese Communists in a recent clash in northeastern China, Bai had unsuccessfully urged Chiang to pursue and crush the Communist forces. That single-minded focus on wiping out the Chinese Communists was on full display in his lenient approach to Japanese war criminals. Like many Nationalists, he hoped that a rebuilt Japan could be a bulwark against Communism in Asia.[103]

Bai Chongxi explained that Chiang himself had declared that China's postwar policy toward Japan should be based on the spirit of "benevolence and tolerance . . . repaying good for evil." He praised MacArthur's emphasis on winning over the Japanese public as well as "our spirit of tolerance," and lauded Nuremberg as not merely punitive but also educational. He pointedly recalled going to a meeting with the generalissimo on how to deal with the top Japanese war criminals: although staffers from across the government had proposed more than a hundred names to prosecute, Chiang had approved only thirty or so. "We can sense his generosity and carefulness," Bai said, urging the officials to design policies that would be "lenient but not overly indulgent and mindful of both fairness and international friendliness."

Such leniency was apparent in China's national trials for lower-level Japanese war criminals. While wartime China had come up with a large number of cases—67,774 cases before the government's war crimes committee—only a small fraction of those had since come to trial. Out of 36,902 cases sent from the Foreign Ministry to the Allies' wartime investigation commission, the delegates there had whittled those down just to some two thousand international suspects. At home, according to a Defense Ministry staffer, the Nationalist government had already put 3,215 suspects on trial—almost all Japanese except for a few dozen Koreans and Taiwanese—and was now pursuing 1,575 more individuals, of whom 464 were still at large. Another Defense Ministry official noted that its bureau of military justice had reviewed just fifty cases in total, approving the death penalty for ten and imprisonment for seven, acquitting two, and freeing or retrying the rest. This was not a trivial effort, with military courts located in Nanjing, Shanghai, Guangzhou, Beijing, Taipei, and five other Chinese cities—but it was all a drop in the ocean compared to the number of Japanese troops who had actually committed war crimes.

This relative forbearance was not just a strategic decision to mend fences with Japan but a product of the inability of the weakened Chinese state. Without adequate investigations, one investigator angrily warned, "many people listed as war criminals cannot stand trial."[104] The minister of judicial administration sheepishly admitted that about two-thirds of all processed cases did not even have the names of the suspected criminals. In Guangzhou, for instance, the Chinese authorities had rounded up Japanese accused of being Kempeitai war criminals, but could find no evidence against 476 suspects and had to send them home to Japan. As a Defense Ministry official noted, few Chinese judges had studied international law, but if their courtroom actions were even slightly inappropriate, they would draw stern criticism from foreign governments. The evidence that had been collected was "mostly incomplete." The judges and staffers of the military courts were badly underpaid. Worse, many detainees lacked winter clothes and had gotten sick from cold and hunger, with some dying because of shortages of medicine and medical equipment: "War criminals should of course receive legal punishment, but it seems against humanity to let them die from coldness and hunger."

Some Chinese officials were furious at how their country was floundering in its pursuit of lower-level perpetrators.[105] Out of roughly one million Japanese prisoners of war in Chinese hands, a Chinese investigator wrote at another point, they had arrested fewer than two thousand suspected war criminals, most of them "unimportant, minor war criminals." The ones who really deserved punishment had long since fled home. Fewer than twenty had been sentenced. He privately complained that the Ministry of Judicial Administration still had not responded to one hundred and forty thousand accusations against alleged war criminals. China was failing, he warned, both at delivering legal justice and at awakening Japanese minds.[106]

Yet despite such misgivings, the government saw its limits. Bai and the other Nationalist functionaries agreed that "important war criminals involved in massive killings such as the Nanjing massacre should be dealt with strictly," but also resolved that "ordinary" Japanese war criminals should be treated "based on the principles of lenience and speediness." China should move quickly against the promising cases, but for those without evidence, "we should punish them without prosecution, release them, and send them back to Japan." While China would continue its pursuit of the worst malefactors, it could do little to bring lawful justice to the vast numbers of lower-ranked Japanese. Hobbled by years of hard war, challenged anew by revolution, eager to reassure its wavering allies, this was the best that the Chinese state could manage.

CHAPTER 14

Remember Pearl Harbor

THE WHITE-HOT CORE OF the American prosecution was the Japanese attack at Pearl Harbor. That bolt from the blue defined the Tokyo trial and made it a political necessity for the American victors. In his speech to Congress marking "a date which will live in infamy," Franklin Delano Roosevelt had vowed that Americans would never forget "this premeditated invasion."[1] If General Douglas MacArthur had had his druthers, Pearl Harbor alone would have been the totality of the trial—more than enough, in his mind, to hang Tojo Hideki and his cabinet.[2]

For months, a series of Allied prosecutors laid out a long chronicle leading to Japan's coordinated December 1941 attacks on Pearl Harbor, Guam, Wake Island, the Philippines, Malaya, Singapore, and Hong Kong. One Japanese newspaper editorialized that the trial was for the first time giving the Japanese a lesson in their true history.[3] Yet for all the prosecution's efforts to tell a straightforward tale of Japanese aggression, the road to Pearl Harbor emerged as considerably more twisty. The picture was complicated by rifts within the Axis alliance, the clash of empires as Imperial Japan sought to drive out Western colonizers in Asia, and the Soviet Union's embarrassing efforts to bill itself as one of the main victims of Japanese aggression. One American defense lawyer objected that the prosecution's bloated case on aggression against the United States and the British Empire was "glorifying the spirit and actions of the prosecuting nations."[4]

Japan's baneful decision to attack the United States, as well as the British and Dutch Empires, emerged from the prosecution's evidence as rather different from the Nazis' fixed ideological drive for racial purity and *Lebensraum* in the eastern reaches of Europe.[5] As presented in court, Pearl

Harbor unfolded largely as a staggeringly ill-considered act of desperate improvisation. Having committed itself to imperial expansion in China and Southeast Asia, Japan had been unsure how to cope with the backlash from the United States and its European allies; its attacks in December 1941 were meant to reap rewards from its colonial land grabs and to shock the Americans into negotiations on better terms. Japan's strike at Pearl Harbor was driven less by genocidal visions than by the prosaic reality that its navy was running out of oil.[6] If Japan had moderated its imperial aspirations, above all in China, it might even have avoided war with the United States.[7]

Despite the blunt warnings from the outspoken Togo Shigenori about the military-industrial might of the United States, Japan's ruinous decision coalesced from maddeningly cautious, elliptical conversations which ducked the hard debates when they were most vital. The empire's top men never reconciled their contradictory images of the United States as being simultaneously so relentlessly aggressive that Japan had no choice but to attack it but also so submissive that it would slink to the bargaining table once struck.[8] Nor did they explain how exactly a surprise attack would lead the American people back to gentlemanly negotiations, rather than into an all-out war that Japan was bound to lose.[9] The scale of the resulting blunder was immediately clear to a relieved Winston Churchill, who knew after Pearl Harbor that "the Japanese . . . would be ground to powder" by superior American production, and to Charles de Gaulle, who noted, "In this industrial war, nothing will be able to resist American power."[10]

The case of Pearl Harbor makes a more ordinary, applicable precedent for condemning aggressive war than what was revealed at Nuremberg. During the Cold War, Japan's decision to start a self-immolating war that it could not win—despite a prescient warning from Admiral Yamamoto Isoroku, himself a planner and advocate of the attack, that the Americans had the capacity to burn down Tokyo and other cities—would make a terrifying example of what it might look like if nuclear deterrence failed. For generations of nuclear strategists, Pearl Harbor was a preview of the end of the world.[11]

THE AXIS

By the time that the Tokyo trial began its phase on Japanese aggression, the parallel court at Nuremberg was hanging the condemned. Field Marshal Wilhelm Keitel had gone to the gallows bellowing *"Alles für Deutschland! Deutschland über Alles!"*; the antisemitic propagandist Julius

Streicher gibbered "Purim festival, 1946!"; and the slave labor chief Fritz Sauckel's last words were "God protect Germany and make Germany great again."[12] The mountain of documentation assembled at Nuremberg from the Nazi regime's files proved an asset for the Allied prosecutors at Tokyo, seeking to show how Japan had worked alongside Nazi Germany and Benito Mussolini's fascist Italy to wage wars of aggression.

For Adolf Hitler, Japan kept the Allies tied down in the Pacific, giving more opportunities to achieve racist utopias in Europe; fortified by Axis support, Japan was emboldened in its Asian conquests. Still, while the prosecution sought to portray a menacingly unified front for global aggression, its own trove of secret evidence revealed deep fissures in the Axis alliance: Japan urgently trying to fend off the Soviet Union and the United States, while Nazi Germany fixated on its racial war against what it called the "Judeo-Bolshevik" Soviet Union.[13]

The Japanese leadership had shown few compunctions about casting their lot with the Third Reich, although the evidence showed that Japanese leaders knew plenty about the Nazis' exterminatory obsessions. One of the Tokyo defendants, Major General Oshima Hiroshi, the dapper and fanatical ambassador to Nazi Germany, was delighted by an infamous speech by Hitler to the Reichstag in January 1939 in which he forewarned that a Jewish-instigated world war would result in "the annihilation of the Jewish race in Europe"—what he would boast of as his "prophecy."[14] The day after, Oshima told Heinrich Himmler, the head of the SS, that the genocidal speech had "pleased him very much, especially because it had been spiritually warranted in all its features."[15]

The seeds of the Axis partnership lay in a common antipathy to the Soviet Union.[16] In November 1936, with Hirota Koki as prime minister, Japan joined Germany in the Anti-Comintern Pact, officially against the Communist International but with a secret agreement pledging not to help the Soviet Union if it attacked either Germany or Japan.[17] Yet for the Nazis, their Japanese partnership was always an alliance of convenience with a lower race. In Mein Kampf, as the prosecutors did not mention, Hitler had scorned the "yellow Asiatic" Japanese as racial inferiors.[18]

The Nazis proved unreliable partners. The Japanese leadership was stunned when the Third Reich, in the middle of negotiating its Japanese alliance, cut a nonaggression deal with the Soviet Union in August 1939. To be sure, the pact between the totalitarian foreign ministers, Joachim von Ribbentrop and Vyacheslav Molotov, was only a tactical feint for Hitler's inexorable eastward drive for racial Lebensraum.[19] Yet for the Japanese, the Molotov-Ribbentrop Pact was a spectacular breach of shared anti-Soviet commitments.

Nevertheless, in September 1940, at a lavish ceremony in Berlin attended by a strutting Hitler and hosts of Nazi dignitaries, Japan signed a formal alliance with Nazi Germany and Italy: a Tripartite Pact pledging to come to the others' aid if attacked by any countries not already embroiled in the European or Chinese wars. In the pact, Germany and Italy accepted Japan's domination of Asia. As the prosecutors showed, Tojo Hideki, then army minister, tried to silence skeptics inside Japan's government by pointing out that Emperor Hirohito had graciously approved the draft treaty.[20] The Tripartite Pact was endorsed unanimously at a privy council meeting attended by Hirohito.[21] In an imperial rescript, the emperor declared himself "deeply pleased" by the Berlin pact, stating that Germany and Italy had "similar objects with the Empire" in restoring peace.[22]

Tojo Hideki (to the right of the microphone), then army minister, toasts the Axis alliance just signed between Nazi Germany and Imperial Japan, Tokyo, September 27, 1940.

Japanese extremists celebrated the Axis pact as a rejection of individualism, liberalism, and democracy, alien ideas imposed upon Asians by Western democratic powers, in favor of a virile Japanese totalitarianism uniting sovereign and subjects as an organic whole.[23] The prosecutors revealed that Matsuoka Yosuke, as Japan's foreign minister, had told Hitler that Japan needed to recover its collectivist traditions from "the liberalism, individualism and egoism introduced from the west." Japan's emperor system, Matsuoka explained, was "the Japanese version of a totalitarian state structure," although he wistfully informed Hitler that the "Japanese nation has not yet found its Fuehrer."[24] One of the Tokyo defendants, the former prime minister Baron Hiranuma Kiichiro, wrote to Hitler praising his efforts for "an international peace founded upon principles of justice."[25]

Soon after Nazi Germany's invasion of Poland in September 1939 ignited World War II, Hitler assured a senior Japanese official that Germany and Japan were both young, soldier nations, striving upward.[26] Tojo had fewer illusions about Japan's new allies; when American interrogators later asked him what reason there was to believe that Nazi Germany and fascist Italy would take a virtuous attitude to the new order in Europe, he burst out laughing.[27]

German victories in Europe, the prosecutors asserted, meant Japanese opportunities in Asia. Japanese leaders welcomed Nazi Germany's swift conquest of Holland in May 1940 as a chance to grab the Netherlands East Indies.[28] After the stunning German defeat of France in June 1940, Japan was emboldened to set its sights on French Indochina. With Britain under German bombardment, Thailand, which was independent but under British influence, looked vulnerable to Japanese browbeating or conquest.[29]

Surprised by Britain's stubborn resistance, Ribbentrop urged Oshima to smash its empire, busying British troops far away from the European theater: "The decisive blow would be an attack on Singapore, to eliminate England's key position in East Asia."[30] In March 1941, with the British still holding out despite the ongoing aerial bombardment of the Blitz, Hitler issued a directive ordering the Wehrmacht high command to help Japan conquer the stronghold of Singapore as soon as possible.[31]

In a meeting between Hitler and the belligerent Matsuoka—which the prosecution left in even though the former foreign minister had recently died in the hospital—the Nazi tyrant urged Japan to strike Singapore, absurdly claiming there was little risk "when Russia and Britain are eliminated and America is not yet prepared." Matsuoka pledged to overcome "timid politicians in Japan" to attack as soon as possible. He told Hitler that Japan would "sometimes have to lead with a strong hand the nations affected by this new order."[32] In a second meeting, Hitler promised that Germany would strike without delay if war broke out between Japan and the United States. When Matsuoka mentioned that Japan's military feared a long war against the Americans, Hitler proudly recalled his brazen remilitarization of the Rhineland in 1936: "Providence favored those who will not let dangers come to them, but will bravely face them."[33]

Days after Nazi Germany at last invaded the Soviet Union on June 22, 1941, Ribbentrop reversed himself completely, exhorting the Japanese to put off Singapore and instead immediately open up another front against the Soviet Union.[34] Yet anxious to lock down its flanks before fighting the Americans, Japan had just concluded a neutrality pact of its own with the Soviet Union. Japan dodged the German request, concentrating instead on the quagmire in China and preparing to attack southward against Singapore, French Indochina, and Thailand rather than adventure northward against the Soviet Union.[35]

Nazi Germany did come through for Japan in its war against the United States. Ribbentrop, urging Japan to strike, promised that Germany would join the war against the United States immediately. Hitler, he said, was determined that the Third Reich would not make a separate peace with the United States.[36] Mussolini, too, promised to declare war on the United States to help Japan. "I am one who is firmly convinced that Japan has every right to be the leader of the Great East Asia area," he said, while the interpreter trembled like a leaf.[37]

Hitler was pleased by Pearl Harbor. Four days later, Germany and Italy formally pledged to join Japan in waging "the war forced upon them by the United States of America and the British Empire," without making any separate peace deals.[38] Presenting Oshima with a golden medal in Berlin, Hitler declared, "You gave the right declaration of war!" Japan had negotiated as long as possible, the tyrant said, but when the other side was only interested in humiliation, one should strike as hard as possible and not waste time declaring war. Delighted by the sinking of the American fleet, Hitler said that the American troops, whose God was the dollar, could not last.

Even at war, the Axis could not agree on shared objectives. After taking Singapore, Oshima explained to Hitler, Japan would attack India; he urged Hitler to threaten India as well. Balking, Hitler said that he would first move on the Caucasus in the Soviet Union, and Iraq and Iran, and North Africa.[39] When Hitler urged Japan to join in his invasion of the Soviet Union in June 1941, the Japanese leadership balked, preserving its firepower for the United States.[40] In private, unbeknownst to the Allied prosecutors in Tokyo, Hitler remained repelled by his Axis partners in arms. "The Japanese are yellow-skinned and slit-eyed," Hitler told his secretary. "But they are fighting against the Americans and English, and so are useful to Germany."[41]

THE SCRAMBLE FOR ASIA

The Allied prosecutors angrily presented Japan's seizure of French, British, and Dutch colonies as an early phase of its campaign of illegal aggression. Japanese attacks on the imperial possessions of French Indochina, the Netherlands East Indies, British-held Singapore, Hong Kong, and Malaya, and the American-ruled Philippines were treated as little different from aggression on the mainlands of Britain, France, Holland, and the United States: criminal assaults on sovereignty and territorial integrity.[42]

Yet the European prosecution dared not consider that the rise of Japan could instead be seen as a new empire supplanting older ones. Allied prosecutors, while condemning Japanese encroachments against the French and Dutch in the twentieth century, were not about to ask how that was different from French and Dutch impositions on the Vietnamese and Indonesians in the nineteenth century.

Outside the courtroom, though, the Allies were badly divided over French colonial claims. The Free French had fought from the colonies and Charles de Gaulle was determined to revive France's imperial stature. Yet Chiang Kai-shek was stoutly anticolonialist and Roosevelt was wary of British, French, and Dutch imperialism. Chiang was crestfallen when Harry Truman recognized French postwar sovereignty over Indochina—a hasty decision that would haunt Americans and Vietnamese for decades.

Indochina, seized by France over the latter half of the nineteenth century, had been the pride of the French Empire. Encompassing present-day Vietnam, Cambodia, and Laos, it was the main French foothold in Asia and a leading producer of rubber and rice. During Japan's invasion of China, neighboring Indochina took on fresh importance as Japanese leaders sought to block the French from helping the Nationalist Chinese government.[43]

After France fell to Nazi Germany in June 1940, the Third Reich gave Japan a free hand in Indochina. The prosecutors revealed that a few days before Wehrmacht troops paraded down the Champs-Élysées in Paris before a triumphant Hitler, Shigemitsu Mamoru, then Japan's ambassador in London, wrote that "it is quite advantageous to make use of the European War to strengthen the position of Japan in East Asia."[44] With Vichy France clinging desperately to its colonies, the small French force in Indochina had to knuckle under to a series of Japanese demands. By September 1940, Japanese troops marched into northern Indochina, although with the formality of Vichy French sovereignty preserved. After Marquis Kido Koichi warned Emperor Hirohito that the United States and Britain might use Indochina to increase their "mischief making" in helping China, the monarch went along with the intervention.[45] In July 1941, Japan demanded to establish bases in southern Indochina and announced that its troops would storm in violently if necessary; Vichy France again acquiesced. Near the end of the war, in March 1945, Japan demanded total control of French troops in Indochina. This time Vichy refused and Japan seized Indochina. Despite a warning by de Gaulle that Japanese war criminals would be held accountable, the Japanese forces killed, tortured, and abused French and Indochinese prisoners of war and civilians.[46]

The prosecutors at Tokyo breezed past the awkward fact that if any French authority was being trampled in Indochina, it was that of Vichy France. This put the Allied prosecution in the dicey position of upholding the imperial territorial claims of German collaborators. Nobody mentioned that British troops had died fighting against Vichy France in Madagascar and Dakar.

The French case was interrupted by a farcical squabble about language. There was a Russian channel on the IBM simultaneous translation machine for the Soviet judge, Major General Ivan Zaryanov. When Joseph Keenan supported this Russian channel, the Chinese government jealously asked Mei Ruao to add Chinese.[47] Offended, the French foreign minister instructed the French judge to complain to Sir William Webb that French was the traditional language of diplomacy.[48] When Webb, in no position to curb the Soviets, shrugged this off, the French associate prosecutor delivered his case in French, although he spoke passable English.[49] Webb complained that this verged on contempt of court; the French prosecutor continued *en français*. Webb rose to his feet, and, followed by the rest of the judges, swept out of the courtroom, leaving the French prosecutor shouting to an empty bench that he would be heard.[50] After a day wasted, with Keenan and Webb glaring balefully at each other, the Australian judge let the prosecutor speak in French.[51]

Next came the Dutch associate prosecutor to defend "the territorial integrity of the Netherlands Indies." When Nazi Germany attacked Holland in May 1940, Japan saw its chance to seize the natural resources of Sumatra, Java, and the rest of the vast archipelago.[52]

The Dutch legal case was more tenuous because there was no treaty committing Japan to respect Dutch rule over the East Indies; the best that the Dutch could manage was a 1922 formal declaration by Japan that it would respect Dutch insular possessions in the Pacific. Still, it was well understood by the Dutch government that Japan needed the oil—millions of tons of it—and raw materials of the Indonesian archipelago for its war effort in China and for fueling the war machines of its Axis partners. Soon after conquering Holland, Hitler's regime secretly approved of Japan expanding southward into the Netherlands East Indies. Japanese troops duly landed in the Netherlands East Indies in the months after Pearl Harbor.

Further muddying the waters, it was actually the exile Dutch government in London that had declared war on Japan immediately after Pearl Harbor—rallying to their American and British allies, as well as girding for an assault on their imperial possessions in Indonesia. This allowed an American defense lawyer to argue that "it certainly is a fact that Japan never declared war on the Netherlands."[53]

The Dutch prosecution worked hard to expose the cruelty used during the three and a half years of Japanese occupation, concentrating on the populous island of Java. While many Indonesians had been inspired by Japan's pledges of liberation, the Dutch prosecutors emphasized how the Japanese imposed an autocratic government backed up by the Kempeitai, the dreaded Japanese military police. The local political parties were dissolved and political activity was banned. Hundreds of thousands of Indonesians were hauled off as forced labor for the Japanese military—many of them perishing from inadequate food, shelter, and medicine. The schools, initially shuttered, were reopened as incubators of anti-Western resentment, with mandatory teaching of the Japanese language and customs. The Muslim religious authorities were urged to declare a holy war against Western powers. Dutch residents were interned, including women and children. As several scholars of modern Indonesia have noted, the Japanese occupation introduced the country to a militarized, ideological state and taught the local nationalists techniques of torture and collective punishment, presaging later political violence there.[54]

The Dutch case undermined the claims of Tojo and other Japanese defendants to have been fighting a principled war against European colonialism. In 1943, when Japan had Burma and the Philippines officially made independent, the Indonesian archipelago was kept under direct Japanese control, lest wayward Indonesians interfere with the war effort. It was not until well after the tide of the war had turned that Japan pledged independence at some point in the future. Japan finally ordered preparations for independence in May 1945, which were still under way when World War II ended.[55]

However opportunistic Japan was in its support for Indonesian independence, the anticolonial passions there were undoubtedly real. Days after Japan surrendered, Indonesian nationalists led by Sukarno—who had collaborated with the Japanese—declared independence. As the Tokyo trial met, the Dutch, who returned in November 1945, were fighting a bitter, brutal campaign to regain control of the archipelago they claimed as their own. It was not until 1949 that the United States, disenchanted with the Dutch efforts, pressured Holland into accepting the creation of a new Indonesia.[56]

REMEMBER PORT ARTHUR

On top of the embarrassments of the French and Dutch presentations, the Tokyo trial had to hear from the Soviet prosecutors.

Joseph Stalin's regime was exactly the type of rogue aggressor that was supposed to be censured by international legal institutions. In late 1939, the moribund League of Nations had declared illegal the Soviet invasion of Finland and had ejected the Soviet Union.[57] Poles, Finns, Estonians, Latvians, and Lithuanians could have borne witness to Soviet aggression and atrocities; surviving Ukrainians could have told how Stalin's terror-famine had left some four million of them dead, while crushing their political elites and intelligentsia in order to extinguish their nationhood.[58] The Soviets, having breached their neutrality treaty with Japan, were still squatting in Manchuria, holding more than a million Japanese prisoners, as well as some seven hundred thousand in Siberia, according to Japan. The indignant Japanese government estimated that over a hundred thousand of its citizens had died in Soviet-held Manchuria in the last winter from cold, hunger, and epidemics.[59]

Yet in the Ichigaya courtroom, the Soviets grabbed for international respectability with both hands. They dispatched a small platoon of military prosecutors to Tokyo to fuse their cause with that of their chagrined wartime allies. These uniformed Red Army officers insistently presented their political system as a democracy alongside those of the Allies. In florid speeches stippled with the Bolshevik idiom of "Hitlerite aggression," "Hitlerite bandits," and "the Japanese imperialist clique," the Soviet prosecutors averred that the Soviet Union had been a preeminent victim of Japanese aggression.

Showing the Tokyo trial's importance to the Kremlin, the Soviet state press devoted half of its foreign news coverage to printing verbatim the lengthy speech of the Soviet associate prosecutor, Sergei Golunsky.[60] Attired in a Soviet military uniform, he had keenly intelligent eyes and a balding pate; he spoke with his hands clasped behind his back. No minor apparatchik, he was the right-hand man of Andrey Vyshinsky, the chief prosecutor of the Moscow purge trials, and would later become a Soviet judge on the International Court of Justice.[61]

Rewinding history all the way back to Russia's humiliating defeat by Japan in 1904–5, which began with a surprise Japanese strike on Port Arthur on the Liaodong Peninsula, he asserted, "The attack on Pearl

Harbor is an exact replica of the attack on Port Arthur." He denounced Axis total warfare as requiring a state built "to suppress by terror any protests in its own country" and decried their "secret police" and "concentration camps"—all of which, of course, described the Soviet state and its Gulag.[62]

At the Soviets' behest, the Tokyo indictment charged several of the Japanese defendants with aggression in two border battles: one in July and August 1938 at Lake Khasan, and another around the Khalkhin-Gol River in the spring and summer of 1939. Even as presented by the Soviets, these were far less consequential than Japan's attacks on China, the United States, or the British Empire. The Lake Khasan clash was a two-week border battle that went badly for Japan. While significant, it had not spread nor triggered a wider invasion, with the Japanese government balking; afterward, many Japanese leaders were deterred from any more northern adventures.[63]

The second battle, against the Soviet client state of Outer Mongolia, was important as a model Soviet victory. It had begun as yet another foray of Japan's out-of-control Kwantung Army, which escalated a clash over grazing Mongol cavalry into an incursion onto Mongolian territory. Since the Mongolian People's Republic had a mutual assistance pact with the Soviet Union, Japan was accused of deliberately launching an attack which would lead to fighting the Soviet Union. Yet for once the Japanese government, preoccupied with the China quagmire, had successfully overruled the Kwantung Army, refusing its request for a counteroffensive. The fighting ended with eight thousand Japanese dead and over nine thousand Soviets killed, but with a clear victory by the Red Army. For Stalin, it had been a gratifying chance to teach Japan a lesson.[64]

Many of the judges, particularly Bert Röling, were obviously stunned by the Soviet presentation, shoddily constructed for a Stalinist show trial. There would be more acquittals on these counts than any others. The Soviet allegations, complained an American defense counsel, were flimsy, speculative, argumentative, and inflammatory. The Japanese accused, he noted, were not on trial for Port Arthur, and a clash in Outer Mongolia was not an attack on the Soviet Union. Webb, although refusing to strike even the wilder Soviet statements from the record, instructed the judges to take notice only of the parts which were backed up by evidence.[65]

If the Soviets' prosecution was threadbare both as history and law, it squared neatly with Stalin's approach to the early Cold War. The state-controlled Soviet press bitterly complained that the roots of Japanese imperialism were not being properly expunged by the Americans. Soon after the Soviet prosecutors wrapped up their case in Tokyo, Averell Harriman, the aristocratic U.S. ambassador in Moscow, scoffed, "It is difficult to believe that Soviet General Staff and POLITBURO are lying awake nights worrying about recrudescence of Jap Imperialism and aggression." Their real concern, he explained, was that an American-dominated Japan might "some day be utilized by Western powers as springboard for attack on USSR. Japan as much as Eastern Europe is in Soviet zone of vital strategic interest."[66]

WAR WITHOUT MERCY

After these vexed preliminaries, the prosecutors turned to Japan's attacks on the United States and the British Empire. These were presented not as legitimate acts of statecraft but as premeditated crimes.

The prosecution pointed to an array of treaties and conventions in an attempt to demonstrate that international law had outlawed aggressive war in the years preceding Pearl Harbor. Japan had been party to the 1899 Hague Convention for the Pacific Settlement of International Disputes, which proposed using mediation before going to war; the Hague Convention III from 1907 which recognized the need for a declaration of war before commencing hostilities; and the Kellogg-Briand Pact of 1928. The Covenant of the League of Nations, which Japan had left in 1933 and which the United States had never joined, bound its members to respect the territorial integrity and political independence of League member states and to seek arbitration or an inquiry by the League before resorting to war. Under the Nine-Power Treaty of 1922, Japan had pledged to respect the sovereignty and independence of China.[67] Yet none of these treaties mandated criminal penalties for violating them.

The United States' wartime support for China had fundamentally soured its relationship with Japan.[68] The U.S. and British governments had complained repeatedly about individual American and British citizens in China getting shot or losing property in the Japanese invasion.[69] In a moment laden with racial tension, an American prosecutor from North Carolina accused Japan of a systematic plan "to drive all whites, in particular all Americans and British, out of China."[70]

As Japan and the United States drifted toward war in 1941, the two countries entered protracted talks. The Washington talks had deadlocked, above all, over Japan's ongoing war in China. With China in mind, Cordell Hull, Roosevelt's secretary of state, had in April insisted on four principles: the sovereignty and territorial integrity of all countries, noninterference in the internal affairs of other countries, equal commercial access, and not changing the status quo by force.[71] Japan had proposed to negotiate a withdrawal from China, but still insisted on the recognition of Manchukuo and stationing troops in north China—all but unacceptable for the Americans.[72]

As the prosecution showed, Tojo Hideki, then army minister, had urged the convening of an imperial conference on July 2. That momentous meeting approved a "Southern advance" against southern Indochina and Thailand. If it proved necessary for that southern drive, the conference fatefully agreed, "Japan will not hesitate to have a war with Britain and the United States."[73]

Yet the prosecution only had the conclusions from that crucial July 2 imperial conference, not the debates. Those records have since emerged, showing how the qualms of civilian politicians were shouted down by the military. The army chief of staff had argued that capturing southern Indochina was necessary to cut off American and British support for Nationalist China, while the navy chief of staff had urged "immediate steps to push steadily southward," undaunted by the prospect of clashing with the United States and the British Empire. While Prince Konoe Fumimaro, the more dovish prime minister, had argued for wrapping up the China war, Tojo had advocated using force to take over Western foreign settlements in Shanghai, Tianjin, and elsewhere in China, which he thought were hurting Japan's war effort.

The president of the privy council, whose role it was sometimes to ask questions on behalf of the emperor, had proposed a peaceful diplomatic approach in southern Indochina, warning that grabbing the French colony would almost certainly mean war with the United States and Britain. Soon after, Tojo had said he agreed, although it was not clear exactly which points he was endorsing.[74]

The Americans had suspended the Washington negotiations in the face of the imminent conquest of southern Indochina, while Japan rebuffed a proposal by Roosevelt to treat Indochina as a neutralized country, not bothering to give the president a reply.[75] In June 1941, Japan had been emboldened by Nazi Germany's invasion of the Soviet Union, which eased fears about a Soviet assault on Japanese-controlled Manchuria. Later in July, the Japanese had at last marched into southern Indochina.[76]

Roosevelt had lashed back on July 26 with a punishing executive order freezing Japanese assets. Britain and Holland followed suit. Within a few days, the State and Treasury Departments turned that into a near-total end to trade with Japan, with an embargo on oil exports. Japan's government was stunned. These tough American sanctions would become pivotal to the Japanese leaders' argument that they were acting in self-defense: that this embargo had lethally choked Japan, stifled its navy, and forced it to lash out at Pearl Harbor.

Shaken by the embargo, Konoe had asked to meet with Roosevelt. Pledging that Japan was not planning any further military advances, the prime minister had offered to pull troops out of Indochina as soon as the China war was resolved or a just peace was established in Asia. In reply, Roosevelt suggested preliminary talks first. The Japanese ambassador had sent along new proposals: asking the United States to lift the embargo and "suspend any military measures" in Asia, and pledging that Japan would not advance from Indochina and would not move southward without justification. That meant that Japan could keep Indochina and advance southward if it felt justified, and implied an end to American aid to China.

On September 6, Konoe's faltering government had convened a second fateful imperial conference, whose attendees included Tojo and several other defendants from the army and navy. Here the emperor had made his most dramatic effort to stop the war, making clear his own wariness by quoting an antiwar poem by the Meiji Emperor. This had slowed the plans for executing a southern advance, allowing a precious pause for further negotiations. Yet if there had been no diplomatic progress by mid-October, the imperial conference agreed to wage war swiftly against the United States, the British Empire, and the Dutch Empire.[77]

The prosecutors gave only a snippet of the Japanese deliberations in this pivotal meeting. Their full discussions, which are now available, showed a blunt refusal to make the concessions that would have averted war. With little debate, the imperial conference had settled on stiff demands in China: the United States would end all military, political, and economic aid to Nationalist China, while Japan would insist on stationing troops in China under an unspecified new agreement there. In return, Japan would refrain from using its bases in French Indochina for advancing on countries other than China, guarantee the neutrality of the Philippines, and withdraw from Indochina when "a just peace has been established in the Far East." Although the prosecutors emphasized that the United States saw the seizure of southern Indochina as an intolerable prelude to wider aggression in Southeast Asia, the Japanese leadership would only pull out of there once the China war was resolved, whenever that might be.

As Konoe had pointed out, the Japanese Empire's power risked lagging behind the United States and Britain, requiring Japan to "take the ultimate step" if diplomacy failed. The army chief of staff had pressed to strike before the Americans and British got any stronger. (He was not on trial at Tokyo because he had put four bullets in his chest after Japan surrendered.) The navy chief of staff, who was on trial, had argued that if diplomacy failed, it was better to "undertake aggressive military operations with determination" before the navy ran out of oil. Yet he presciently noted that "even if our Empire should win a decisive naval victory, we will not thereby be able to bring the war to a conclusion. We can anticipate that America will attempt to prolong the war, utilizing her impregnable position, her superior industrial power, and her abundant resources."

Before the conference, Hirohito had expressed his doubts to his military chiefs, asking with atypical bluntness how a war across the vast Pacific could be resolved in three months while the China war was still dragging on after years. In the imperial conference, the president of the privy council, speaking for the emperor, had urged diplomacy to avoid war, but without discussing the meaningful concessions in China or Indochina that might have given life to such efforts. In fact, rather than considering withdrawing troops from China, the briefing papers asserted that new offensive steps—occupying Hong Kong and closing resupply through Burma—would force the surrender of the Nationalist government. The president of the privy council warned of the danger that ultranationalists would assassinate those civilians who were less eager for war. It was against that backdrop that the emperor himself finally spoke—a moment famous in postwar Japan as showing the enlightened peacefulness of the monarch. His *tanka* poem by the Meiji Emperor clearly expressed unease: "All the seas in every quarter are as brothers to one another. Why, then, do the winds and waves of strife rage so turbulently throughout the world?"[78]

THE PLOT AGAINST AMERICA

Kido's diary, the prosecution's best evidence, showed that Konoe had privately feared the worst "if the Military insisted on starting a war on 15 October." Kido had argued that, since there was little chance of winning, it would be "inadvisable to declare war against the U.S.A. immediately." Instead he had wanted to wrap up the China campaign, possibly by using all of Japan's military forces in China in a major new offensive to take the strategic southern city of Kunming and the wartime provisional capital, Chongqing.

In his own notes, Konoe recorded that, days before the mid-October deadline, Tojo, the army minister, had said there was no hope of a diplomatic solution. The navy minister wanted to continue the negotiations rather than risk a war. Although the talks were deadlocked over the American insistence that Japan pull all its troops out of China, Tojo had flatly refused to withdraw from China, unwilling to squander the sacrifices made in that bloody four-year war. In a cabinet meeting, Tojo had argued that the United States really wanted to control Asia, and that one Japanese concession would only lead to another. The cabinet had deadlocked. Facing the fatal decision, Konoe had felt his flesh creeping.

He and his entire cabinet had resigned. In his resignation letter, Konoe had told the emperor that he could not "endure plunging the nation again into a titanic war the outcome of which cannot be forecast when even the China Incident has not yet been settled." This allowed a new government that could reconsider the decision to go to war.[79]

The emperor's choice of the next prime minister would be all-important. The prosecutors dramatically made public Konoe's resignation letter, in which he had warned the monarch that Tojo believed that "the time has come to open war against the United States."[80] A more dovish option would have been Prince Higashikuni Naruhiko, an army officer who was married to a daughter of the Meiji Emperor. But as Konoe's notes showed, Hirohito had balked at the prospect of a member of the imperial family either choosing peace and being defied by the army, or choosing war and risking the overthrow of the monarchy.[81]

Instead the emperor named Tojo Hideki as the prime minister. Although Kido had hoped to revise the decision for an imminent war, the lord keeper had nevertheless assiduously orchestrated the installation of the foremost hawk in power, allowing Tojo to stay on as army minister and remain on active military duty while running the government. The prosecutors blamed Kido for persuading Hirohito that empowering Tojo was worth the risk, hoping that an army man could keep a grip on the army. Yet the emperor clearly understood the risk he was taking, telling Kido, "As it is said you know,—'He who will not go into the tiger's den will not get the tiger cub.'" Still, the emperor had urged his new prime minister to disregard the imperial conference's previous decision to go to war in October if talks failed, striving instead to find a peaceful outcome.[82]

To the Allies, the ascent of Tojo looked like Japan sliding into military dictatorship in preparation for war.[83] Despite the popular American wartime image of Tojo as an unchecked dictator equivalent to Hitler or Mussolini, the new prime minister had continued Japan's consultative style of cabinet deliberation, pushing back the deadline for an attack into November. But Tojo himself remained firmly resolved on war. As he had told American interrogators after his arrest, "my opinion was that there remained practically no hope of a diplomatic break and I suggested that the time had come when we had better make up our minds for war."[84]

With Japan running out of oil, he believed his country would have to lash out now or be doomed to defeat later on.[85]

As the prosecutors made their case based on an incomplete documentary record, they did not realize how hard one of the defendants had worked to stop the rush to war. Sitting in the Ichigaya courtroom, Togo Shigenori, who had joined Tojo's cabinet as foreign minister, was lost in internal turmoil, torn between honor, pride, and self-pity. The mere fact of being foreign minister during Pearl Harbor had landed him in the dock. He privately seethed at the military for its folly in attacking the United States, and blamed it for losing the war with its rash offensives at Midway and elsewhere.[86]

The similarity of their family names was just about the only thing that the urbane, cosmopolitan Togo Shigenori had in common with the prime minister. He had only agreed to join the cabinet after Tojo Hideki assured him that he was prepared to make real concessions to make possible a deal with the United States—in particular, withdrawing troops from China. He would have been glad to back away from the Axis and saw the invasion of southern Indochina as a time bomb with a lit fuse, appalled by the government's failure to foresee the American oil embargo imposed afterward. As he wrote in his Sugamo Prison cell, "my purpose in entering the Cabinet was not to start a war, but to avert one."[87]

The facts of Togo's antiwar advocacy would surface years later in notes taken by army officials. At a meeting of senior leaders on October 30, Togo had infuriated the army by arguing that a prompt withdrawal from China would not bring economic ruin. As military leaders were heatedly objecting to mentioning a withdrawal from China even after twenty-five, fifty, or ninety-nine years, Togo had retorted that "it would be better to withdraw troops right away." While the military chorused that accepting the American terms would reduce the empire to a third-rate country, Togo had argued that everything would turn out better if Japan went along. As a scandalized army note-taker wrote, the foreign minister had forsaken reality: "he gave everyone a strange feeling."[88]

Togo's most dramatic effort came in a frenzied, bitter, seventeen-hour debate among top Japanese leaders that began on November 1. Unlike the stifling decorum of the imperial conferences, this meeting—an informal liaison conference between the government and the headstrong military—had been impassioned and direct. The full documentary record of this remarkable session would have shown the judges that Togo—helped by

Kaya Okinori, the finance minister, who was also on trial—had argued fiercely against attacking the United States.

Togo had begged for a last chance for negotiations, warning starkly that the fate of Japan, with 2,600 years of history, hung on this turning point. The finance minister had argued that there was no chance of victory. "This won't do," Togo had gruffly warned the intransigent military. "We can't engage in diplomacy, yet it's best not to go to war." He had said, "I . . . cannot believe that the American fleet would come and attack us. I don't believe there is any need to go to war now."

Despite that, he and the finance minister had been shouted down by the military leaders, contending loudly that Japan had to fight now or perish. At one point, when the army vice chief of staff had insisted on war by no later than November 30, even Tojo Hideki had found this preposterous, asking why negotiations could not go on for a single day more; they had finally agreed on midnight. When asked by the finance minister when Japan could go to war and win, a top admiral had screamed, "Now! The time for war will not come later!"

Togo Shigenori had recoiled at the "outrageous" prospect of "diplomatic trickery" to lull the Americans before an attack, telling the military that they must "give up the idea of going to war." Still, to avoid riling the army up too much, this time he had wanted to reduce the scope of the negotiations to Southeast Asia, leaving out the neuralgic issue of the China war: "We cannot allow the United States a voice in the China Question." That alone could have sunk the negotiations with the United States.

Bellowing at the foreign minister, the army leaders had angrily denounced his proposed withdrawal from southern Indochina as disastrous for Japan's national defense. Togo had heatedly argued back, threatening to block any decision for war—so much that the others feared that he would resign, causing the cabinet to fall. After debating through the night until about 2 a.m. on November 2, Togo had weighed resignation, while Kaya had caved and accepted the consensus. In the end, though, Togo had stayed in the cabinet in the name of national unity. He joined in the group's decision: they would offer two final diplomatic proposals to the Americans, and if those failed, then it would be war.

On November 5, Tojo Hideki and his government had assembled for an unusually fiery imperial conference held in front of Hirohito.[89] Once again, the prosecutors apparently only had the conclusions of this important imperial conference, not the records of what was said. The cabinet had resolved to wage war on the United States and Britain unless negotiations with the United States made a breakthrough soon, probably after late November. The prosecutors correctly noted who had been in the room—including Tojo and Togo, as well as several other defendants—but without understanding that Togo and Kaya had been opposed to war.[90]

In secret army records that the Tokyo court did not see, Tojo Hideki had declared that "we have come to the conclusion that we must now decide to go to war" in early December if negotiations failed. He explained that officially the war would be for the empire's "self-preservation and self-defense" and to "establish a New Order in Greater East Asia."

Against that, Togo Shigenori had made an eleventh-hour push for concessions to avert war, while Kaya warned of the financial difficulties. This time Togo had to make his case sound more palatable to the ascendant war faction, endorsing the Greater East Asia Co-Prosperity Sphere and speaking of Japan's "holy war" in China. Yet he starkly warned that Japan would face a ruinous encirclement by the United States, Britain, China, and Holland, plus possibly the Soviet Union. This bleak assessment had contrasted sharply with the army's confident assertions that they could carry on a protracted war so long as they held crucial military bases in Hong Kong, Manila, and Singapore, and the oil and natural resources of the Netherlands East Indies.

Togo managed to get the government to offer two last proposals to the Roosevelt administration. The first was more ambitious. As he explained to the imperial conference, it tried to give some concessions to the Americans' wishes to get Japanese troops out of China, and to step gingerly back from the Tripartite Pact with Nazi Germany and Italy. If that one flopped with the Americans, as Togo privately expected, he had a second fallback proposal which would essentially rewind to the situation before Japan seized southern Indochina: the United States would lift its oil embargo and Japan would pull its troops back into northern Indochina, pledging no further advances in the Southwest Pacific. That would still leave fundamental issues unresolved, especially the presence of Japanese troops in China, but would at least draw the two countries back from the brink of war.

Togo had explained to the seething army chiefs, "if we offer as many concessions as we can afford, and still the United States does not agree with us, then we will know that she intends to go to war, and at the same time our moral position will be made clear both at home and abroad." This time, he prudently had not dared to mention his own wish for pulling out of China: "the United States demands that we proclaim the withdrawal of all troops; but we cannot accept the demand."

Tojo Hideki had vehemently objected that the United States had not made any concessions. He had warned that the United States' call for respecting territorial integrity and sovereignty could wipe out Japan's gains in China and its puppet regime in Manchuria, and that when the Americans mandated noninterference in internal affairs, that could doom the collaborationist Chinese regime in Nanjing. He had refused to accept the U.S. demand not to change the status quo by force, especially in China or areas vital for Japan's national defense or for procuring resources. "The United States demands that we accept these principles," he said. "We cannot do so, because we carried out the Manchurian Incident and the China Incident in order to get rid of the yoke that is based on these principles." Having sent a force of a million men into China, costing over a hundred thousand Japanese dead and wounded, the grief of their bereaved families, and tens of billions of yen, he would not retreat without getting results for these sacrifices. He concluded, "We can expect an expansion of our country only by stationing troops."

The president of the privy council was wary of attacking the United States. He was one of the only Japanese leaders to consider how American public opinion would respond to a Japanese attack: "Their indignation against the Japanese will be stronger than their hatred of Hitler." Yet hoping for some initial victories, he had deemed it inevitable that Japan attack. Finally, in a remarkable peroration, he had cautioned that they might be entering into a catastrophic race war. The United States, Britain, and Germany, he had said, were "all of them countries whose population belongs to the white race." Although warring with each other now, "hatred of the yellow race" might unify them all in a race war against Japan.

Tojo had emptily reassured him, "I will be careful to avoid the war's becoming a racial war." Admitting some uneasiness about a protracted conflict, the prime minister had warned it would be worse for an embargoed Japan to wait for the United States to build up in the Pacific and expand its fleet. "Two years from now we will have no petroleum for military use," he had warned. "Ships will stop moving." Insistent on maintaining the empire, he had cautioned, "I fear that we would become a third-class nation after two or three years if we just sat tight." Concluding the imperial conference with its catastrophic decision, he assured the officials, "America may be enraged for a while, but later she will come to understand."[91]

Following Togo Shigenori's two linked proposals, the Japanese government had made its last offers to the United States. In the first proposal,

Japan had offered only that its forces in China would be moved to north-ern China and southern Hainan Island after a conjectured peace deal between Japan and China, and would not be withdrawn for at least two years, and perhaps as many as twenty-five years—what Tojo Hideki had privately admitted meant "close to being forever."[92] The Japanese Empire would be left to maintain garrisons in northern China to sustain Man-chukuo and the Japanese collaborator regime based in Nanjing, keeping up a sphere of influence that could allow a renewed drive for conquest in the future.[93]

Togo knew that the Americans would never swallow that. To postpone the hard question of pulling out of China, the foreign minister had man-aged to include a fallback offer for the Americans. This more modest proposal—presented to the United States on November 20—aimed only to rewind back to before Japan's seizure of southern Indochina.[94] Japan offered to pull its troops from southern Indochina back into the north, in exchange for the United States lifting the embargo and helping Japan get materials from the Netherlands East Indies. The proposal held out the prospect of a full Japanese withdrawal from Indochina after a peace deal there or an end to the war in China. Most consequentially, Japan appeared stuck to Tojo's line that, after four years of tremendous sacrifices in China, it could not just withdraw its troops.[95]

For the U.S. prosecution in the Ichigaya courtroom, the last wheezings of the negotiations were all but irrelevant. Togo's two diplomatic propos-als went further than the army wanted but still fell short of satisfying the United States.[96] Although the Roosevelt administration suggested reaching a temporary modus vivendi, that more modest goal too seemed out of reach.[97] On November 26, a massive Japanese task force of aircraft carriers, destroyers, and cruisers sailed to be ready to strike on an X-Day of December 8—although both Tojo Hideki and Togo Shigenori insisted that they did not know about the fleet's movement.[98] The day that those warships set off, an anxious Kido had met with Hirohito, who said that the talks with the United States had come to the worst, and that their decision for war should be carried out after a final consultation with a council made up of former prime ministers.[99]

That same day, November 26, Roosevelt's secretary of state, Cordell Hull, had given a tough offer to Japan. Notorious in Japan as "the Hull note," it has been treated by generations of Japanese nationalists as an out-rageous diktat that caused the war. In reality, in the months before Pearl Harbor, Roosevelt had shown his trademark flexibility. He had resisted British and Chinese calls for harshly confronting and deterring Japan, to the frustration of both Churchill and Chiang.[100] The Hull note had no deadline, potentially leaving the door open to renewed negotiations. The note certainly was tough: it demanded a legalistic respect for the sovereignty and territorial integrity of all nations, noninterference in the internal affairs of other countries, and equal commercial opportunity—all of those an abnegation of Japan's empire. Proposing an ambitious nonaggression pact between the United States, Japan, China, Britain, Holland, the Soviet Union, and Thailand, the note would wrench Japan out of the Tripartite Pact. On the core issue, the Hull note sternly insisted that Japan "withdraw all military, naval, air and police forces from China and from Indo-China," as well as abandoning both Manchukuo and the collaborationist government in Nanjing. In return, the United States would reopen trade and remove the freeze on Japanese funds.[101]

Togo Shigenori was stung, insulted both nationally and personally. Despondent, he told Japan's ambassador in Washington that it was impossible to negotiate on the basis of the "surprising and regrettable" Hull note.[102] Locked in Sugamo Prison after the war, Togo remembered his overpowering despair. "I had fought and worked unflaggingly until that moment; but I could feel no enthusiasm for the fight thereafter," he wrote. "I tried as it were to close my eyes and swallow the Hull Note whole, as the alternative to war, but it stuck in the craw." Gallingly, he had found the military hard-liners elated that the Hull note had demonstrated the futility of diplomacy: "Didn't we tell you so?"[103]

In the Ichigaya courtroom, American prosecutors blandly said that the Hull note was little different from Hull's four principles given in April. This was absurd. While the Hull note had followed those principles, it was clearly an escalation. Still, the Japanese leaders themselves had already largely given up on diplomacy in their imperial conference on November 5. Even before the Hull note knocked the legs out from under Togo, Japan's leaders had never accepted the painful compromises in Indochina and above all in China that would have gotten the United States to drop its oil embargo. They still had choices, although not good ones: to avoid war, they would have needed to make hard concessions and drop a deadline of their own making. Agonizing as that would have been, it would have averted a war whose consequences lay all around those leaders now.[104]

Buried among the prosecution's evidence was a smoking gun implicating Hirohito. On November 30, the emperor's younger brother, Prince Takamatsu, a naval officer, had warned the monarch that the navy was pessimistic about the imminent war. The anxious emperor had checked with the navy minister, the chief of the navy general staff, and Tojo Hideki. Yet according to Kido's diary, after being reassured by the navy, the emperor "ordered" Tojo "to act according to program."[105] This was a singularly explosive piece of evidence, the find of a lifetime: a private record from the emperor's closest aide that showed him personally ordering his prime minister to attack the United States. Nothing could be more inconvenient for General Headquarters. Yet the prosecutors read it into the record and then moved on without comment.

On December 1, at a somber final imperial conference, the Japanese government set X-Day for December 7, Pearl Harbor time. "Japan will declare war on the United States, Britain, and the Netherlands," the conference resolved. In addition to Tojo, Hirohito, and several of the defendants, one of the men in the room was Kishi Nobusuke, then Tojo's commerce and industry minister—a future prime minister and the grandfather of Abe Shinzo, an even more influential prime minister.[106]

Once again, the Allied prosecutors had no records of what was said in this last prewar imperial conference. Tojo had fumed against the Hull note, which he said meant unconditional Japanese withdrawal from China, abandonment of the pro-Japanese regime in Nanjing, and scuppering the Tripartite Pact. They could no longer delay: "our Empire has no alternative but to begin war against the United States, Great Britain, and the Netherlands." He had urged a crackdown at home on antiwar public opinion, singling out Communists, religious leaders, and "rebellious Koreans."

Togo Shigenori had at last joined the advocates for war. While he could have resigned to force a cabinet crisis, that would have been unlikely to derail the war at this late hour. Complaining about the Hull note, he had said that Japan could not agree to pull out of China and Indochina, sink the collaborationist Nanjing regime, and back out of the Tripartite Pact. He had despairingly said, "I believe that America's policy toward Japan has consistently been to thwart the establishment of a New Order in East Asia, which is our immutable policy." If the Japanese government had accepted the Hull note, he had warned, "the international position of our Empire would be reduced to a status lower than it was prior to the Manchurian Incident, and our very survival would inevitably be threatened."

Wrapping up, Tojo had declared that "our Empire stands at the threshold of glory or oblivion. We tremble with fear in the presence of His Majesty." Throughout this imperial conference, the emperor had nodded in agreement with various statements, displaying no signs of unease, awing his subjects with his apparently excellent mood.[107]

In Washington on the night of December 6, an anxious Roosevelt had made a final appeal for peace addressed personally to the emperor, urging peace in China and a Japanese withdrawal from Indochina. The president had reminded the emperor of their "sacred duty" to "prevent further death and destruction in the world."[108] (Unbeknownst to the Tokyo court, the president had bleakly quipped, "This son of man has just sent his final message to the Son of God.")[109]

Roosevelt's note had been delayed in Japanese bureaucracy for hours, arriving too late to matter, but U.S. prosecutors claimed that if it had been delivered promptly it "might have changed the course of history."[110] The accused Japanese fumed at this claim, which even Togo Shigenori called propaganda trying to prove Roosevelt's eagerness for peace but which contained nothing more substantive than a familiar call for a Japanese withdrawal from Indochina. While Roosevelt was in part stalling and trying to improve the optics of a war with the American public, he was reluctant to miss a last chance to avoid war.[111] "It's a good thing the telegram arrived late," Tojo Hideki had said jokingly, according to a memoir by Togo. "If it had come a day or two earlier we would have had more of a to-do."[112]

The U.S. prosecution did not emphasize what has since become clear: that the United States had cracked Japan's top secret diplomatic code.

The USS *Shaw* exploding under Japanese attack, Pearl Harbor, Hawaii, December 7, 1941

This helped to persuade the Roosevelt administration that Japan's government was not negotiating in good faith. The MAGIC cryptanalysis program had shown that Tojo's new cabinet was aggressive, that Japanese forces were massing, and that Japanese diplomats had faced deadlines for concluding their American negotiations for November 25, later bumped to November 29. Something might well be coming, but what and where? Roosevelt had refused when Harry Hopkins urged him to strike Japan first: "No, we can't do that. We are a democracy and a peaceful people. But we have a good record."[113]

It would have taken a rare clairvoyance for the Americans to sift signal from noise before, on December 7 at 7:55 a.m., the Japanese task force struck. Coordinating thousands of land- and carrier-based aircraft, surface craft and submarines, over a range of thousands of miles, Japan had unleashed a wave of surprise assaults across Asia. Japan hit not just at the U.S. fleet at Pearl Harbor but also bombed U.S. positions in Guam and Wake Island, attacked the Philippines and Malaya, bombed British strongholds in Singapore and Hong Kong, and marched into Thailand.[114] Launched from the Japanese aircraft carriers, hundreds of bombers and fighter planes managed to sink four U.S. battleships and severely damage four more, badly damaging several destroyers and cruisers, and wiping out scores of planes.

The prosecutors pointed out that despite Japan's ratified commitment under the Hague Convention III of 1907 that hostilities must not start before either a declaration of war or an ultimatum with a conditional declaration of war, Japan's ambassador had notified the United States of the attack about an hour after it had started.[115] The prosecutors conceded that Togo Shigenori had been concerned about breaking that Hague pledge; in contrast, top admirals had not even wanted to send a message. (Togo would later claim that Japan's stern note breaking off negotiations with the United States should count as the legal equivalent of a declaration of war.)[116] Churchill had formally complained that Japan's "flagrant aggression" in Malaya, Singapore, and Hong Kong without an ultimatum or a declaration of war was "a flagrant violation of international law."[117]

Hours after the Japanese strikes began, Hirohito had issued an imperial rescript: "We hereby declare war on the United States and the British Empire." The rescript—also signed by Tojo and his ministers, including Togo and Kishi—said that it was "far from Our wishes that Our Empire has now been brought to cross swords with America and Britain." Yet he cast the war as self-defense, claiming that the conflict was "truly unavoidable" because of the United States and Britain's support for

Nationalist China, their "inordinate ambition to dominate the Orient," and their economic sanctions "menacing gravely the existence of Our Empire." The rescript concluded: "Our Empire for its existence and self-defence has no other recourse but to appeal to arms and to crush every obstacle in its path."[118]

CHAPTER 15

The Narrow Road to
the Deep North

COLIN FLEMING BRIEN TOLD what it is like to have someone try to cut off your head.

An intelligent Australian private from Sydney, he had a strong jaw and a furrow between his brows which gave him a look of worry.[1] He was slender and his cheeks were hollow. In the Tokyo courtroom, he testified forcefully with a broad Australian accent.[2] He had been nineteen years old in February 1942 when, in the wilderness around Singapore, as part of an infantry battalion, he had been sliced up by Japanese shrapnel. Separated from his fellow troops, he bandaged his injuries as best he could. His wounds stank. His left hand would never recover. When found by Japanese troops several days later, semiconscious and weak, he offered no resistance as they took him to their headquarters at a Catholic convent in the outskirts of Singapore. One morning he was marched into the jungle by an armed Japanese officer.

Coming into a clearing, he saw a Japanese platoon arrayed in parade order and a shallow grave dug about two feet deep. There was a curved Japanese sword stuck into the earth next to the grave. He immediately knew that he was going to be killed, even before a Japanese officer told him that he was going to meet his God. His hands were tied behind his back, and he was sat down with his legs and feet sticking into the grave. A cloth was fastened over his eyes.

In the Tokyo courtroom, the young witness halted here, unable to find the words. "Go ahead," coaxed an Australian prosecutor.

He could feel his shirt being unbuttoned and pulled back to expose his neck. He thought: this is the end. He prayed. "My head was bent forward," he said, "and after a few seconds I felt a heavy, dull blow sensation on the back of my neck."

Somehow he was not killed by the impact of the sword. He slumped to the side, pretending to be dead, and then blacked out. When he eventually came to, he was at the bottom of the grave, with dirt thrown over him, covered in blood from a deep slash at the back of his neck. His hands were still tied behind him. After perhaps an hour, he finally dared to move. He managed to pull himself to the surface and lay there for the rest of the day. Over the night, he worked his hands free. (Australian doctors would later tell him that the flies teeming on his neck wound saved him from gangrene.) After three days, steeped in filth and blood, he dragged himself toward the city of Singapore, where he gave himself up at a police station. They turned him over to amazed Japanese troops, who brought him to a hospital. The Japanese either did not realize how he had gotten his distinctive wound or were not inclined to finish the botched execution. He spent the rest of the war in prison camps around Singapore.

Colin Fleming Brien, an Australian private who testified in Tokyo about surviving an attempted decapitation, Darwin, September 1945

The courtroom was hushed. Then the Australian prosecutor asked Brien to show his neck wound to the tribunal. "One of my colleagues questions whether this kind of thing is necessary," said Sir William Webb. "Personally, I think it is; but I will take the decision of all my colleagues." The judges conferred. "You may show your wound," said Webb. The Australian prosecutor told Brien to turn around and display his neck. As spectators cringed, he took off his coat. He pulled down the suspenders over his white shirt, then unbuttoned the top of his shirt and turned around. The silence deepened. The young man sat down as soon as he could. Webb called a recess.[3]

Brien's testimony was one small part of the prosecution's effort to wrap up its case by chronicling war crimes against Allied prisoners of war and civilians. Such retribution was specifically written into the Potsdam Declaration, which promised "stern justice" for "those who have visited cruelties upon our prisoners." The Bataan death march and the Burma–Thailand death railway were national rallying cries in Allied countries, but since information about such outrages had been strictly censored in wartime Japan, these revelations came as a shock to the Japanese public—a devastating blow to the military's claims to have fought an honorable war.[4]

There was no legal novelty to these charges, unlike the controversies swirling around the criminalization of aggressive war or the meaning of crimes against humanity. The legal tradition of protecting prisoners of war went back centuries. It had been instantiated in the landmark 1907 Hague Convention IV on land warfare, which mandated that prisoners of war be treated humanely and not worked excessively; Japan had ratified that convention in 1911.[5] Although Japan had not ratified the 1929 Geneva Convention on prisoners of war, it had promised the Allies to apply its terms *mutatis mutandis*—with changes to take account of different local circumstances and Japanese law—to American, Australian, British, Canadian, Dutch, and New Zealand troops in its custody.[6]

Any army would have strained with the task of using a relatively small number of guards to overawe the more than three hundred thousand Allied captives in custody by early 1943.[7] Yet from the start, Imperial Japan's treatment of Allied prisoners of war was marked by incompetence, inexperience, and severity. Despite its commitment to the Geneva Convention, its officers were not given the resources to abide by its strictures. Under tremendous logistical strain, sapped by incompetence and confusion, Japan put its military priorities far ahead of its commitments to prisoners under international law. Some of its troops were accustomed to fighting in China, where summary executions of "bandit" Chinese prisoners—seen as unworthy of the protection of the laws of war—were commonplace. At best, the Japanese military's attitude was an incompetent, ill-planned cruelty, although the Allied governments sought to prove that it was purposeful and systematic.[8]

In a wartime atmosphere of hatred, privation, and logistical chaos, few Japanese officers were keen to uphold the terms of the Geneva Convention, which were not inculcated among the officer corps. The Foreign Ministry was as impotent about the conduct of the war as it had been about its initiation. The Army Ministry, firmly in command of the treatment of enemy prisoners of war, indoctrinated its own troops that surrendering was a mark of dishonor. Some Japanese army officers were disgusted at Allied soldiers for being taken alive. Furthermore, the forced toil of Allied prisoners offered a tempting partial solution to a labor shortage caused by the manpower demands of the Japanese army and navy—a hole which was otherwise filled by recruiting millions of workers from across China, Taiwan, Korea, Indonesia, the Philippines, and elsewhere in Asia, often under duress.[9] And as always in the Pacific War, there was a racial stake. By establishing camps for Allied prisoners across China, Korea, Taiwan, Thailand, Malaya, the Philippines, and elsewhere, Imperial Japan often meant to humble its white captives and hearten Asian peoples.

The results were dire. Japan had captured huge numbers of Allied troops in its early victories: 50,016 Britons, some 37,000 Dutch, 21,726 Australians, and 21,580 Americans, plus others, for a total of 132,134 souls. Of those, the Tokyo trial, using distinctly conservative estimates, would conclude that 35,756 died in captivity: approximately 27 percent. One in three Australian and American prisoners perished. By contrast, just 4 percent of Western prisoners held by Germany and Italy died.[10]

The judges had no difficulty agreeing these were war crimes, with even the most vehement dissenters concurring. The harder question was whether these senior defendants were linked to the specific crimes of their subordinates. Some of the paperwork that might have established such links had been incinerated by the Japanese at the end of the war. There was plenty of evidence of war crimes, but much less documentation of an allegedly systematic policy that had been ordered or condoned by the accused.

During the grim months devoted to presenting the evidence of abuses against Allied prisoners of war, the New Zealand judge warned that he was not aware of "any basis for holding any of the defendants responsible for the wrongdoings of individual Japanese Officers and other ranks in charge of prisoners of war." If the tribunal wanted an enduring historical record of Japanese cruelties, he suggested, that could be provided by lesser courts prosecuting lower-ranked Japanese or by the reports of investigators.

The British judge, Lord Patrick, got him back into line by arguing that commanders of warring armies were responsible for making sure that their subordinates followed the laws of armed conflict. If the prosecution could show widespread war crimes in different theaters of the war, the court might infer a breach by commanders of carrying out their duties.[11] Thus the prosecutors worked to show a pattern of war crimes committed in similar ways all across Asia, so that the judges might conclude there was a government policy at work.[12]

THE DEATH RAILWAY

That emphasis on common methods of abuse meant a phase of the trial almost as distressing as the recounting of Chinese atrocities, for similar reasons. A series of prosecutors brought out horrifying, rhyming tales of cruelty toward prisoners of war, civilian internees, and populations under occupation across Asia: torture, beatings, overwork, hunger, deprivation, disease, rape. The scope of the atrocities—ranging across Singapore, Malaya, Burma, Thailand, Hong Kong, Taiwan, the Netherlands East Indies, Indochina, and more—was meant to prove that Japanese abuses were the result of a systematic, overarching policy, not a series of disconnected events or an uncontrolled rampage. The prosecutors did not explore the considerable variation in how the Japanese treated their prisoners across Asia, even though it was only for the Chinese that Japan had a clear policy of killing and abusing captive "bandits."[13] Still, the prosecution contended that such widespread enormities against Allied prisoners must have been committed either on the orders of commanding officers or at least with their knowledge and assent.

Worried about the length of the trial, Joseph Keenan infuriated the Commonwealth and Philippine prosecutors by asking if they could cut down their coverage of atrocities and abuses of prisoners of war. For the American chief prosecutor, the charges of aggression came first. Yet the Australians and Filipinos objected so bitterly that Keenan had to back down.[14] Following from that backstage maneuvering, it was the Commonwealth countries that dominated this phase. A long list of Australian, British, and Canadian witnesses recounted their ordeals.

The court heard searing testimony from a British colonel about what had happened after the surrender in Singapore in February 1942. There were about three thousand five hundred European citizens in Singapore, many of them women and children. They were thrown into a prison which had been constructed to house perhaps seven hundred inmates; there they stayed for over two years until being shipped to a nearby camp. Next the

British and Australian prisoners of war were marched out of Singapore, with the Indian troops separated and invited by Japanese officers to join the Indian National Army fighting against the British Empire. Those who refused were corralled into overcrowded labor camps, mostly on Singapore, to be abused and beaten. Chinese were treated worse: hundreds of them were machine-gunned outside Changi Prison in Singapore.[15]

In pouring rain with no sanitation, the British and Australian prisoners quickly caught dysentery. Out of some fifteen thousand men who passed through two camps by the end of 1942, more than three thousand had to be hospitalized. As the prisoners were put to hard labor, they were routinely beaten, often with rifle butts. When new Allied officers arrived, they brought fresh stories of bayoneting, assault, and torture, including the Kempeitai technique of near-drowning known as "the water treatment." A Japanese officer, asked how Japan would justify its treatment of prisoners after the war, replied, "A victorious Japan will not have to explain."[16] One Japanese major, told that sick prisoners would die without medical treatment, said, "It can't be helped; if they die, they die."[17]

For Australians, the most infamous horror was known as the death railway. After the devastating defeat at Midway, Tojo Hideki, then prime minister and army minister, had decided to put Allied prisoners of war to work to help the war effort, although this was prohibited by the Geneva Convention.[18] Starting around August 1942, the Japanese ordered a railway built across Thailand through Burma, meant to open up a front against eastern India and to challenge China's resupply through Burma. The railway needed to slice through dense, buggy, mountainous jungle.

Japan used forced labor from its Asian conquests—especially Burmese and Malays, as well as Javanese, Tamils, Indians, Chinese, and more—and roughly sixty thousand Allied prisoners of war, who ultimately constructed more than two hundred and fifty miles of track.[19] The Asians, many of them conscripted, were treated even worse than the Allied prisoners of war. It is not even clear how many of them there were, with one rough estimate of a total of two hundred thousand.[20] A British colonel estimated that some sixteen thousand Allied prisoners of war died, and between sixty thousand and one hundred fifty thousand Asians. The best accounts today show that Burmese and Malays died in numbers ten or twenty times greater than Allied soldiers.[21]

Dressed only in ragged shorts or makeshift sack kilts, almost none of them in boots, the hungry and sick Allied prisoners toiled from first light until after dark. They had to march two hundred miles in two and a half weeks. When the monsoons broke, many had nothing but banana leaves for shelter. Japanese or Korean guards lashed the prisoners with bamboo, swagger sticks, or wire. A thousand Britons died while building a single timber bridge across a river gorge.

Disease was the worst threat: cholera, malaria, typhus, dysentery, beri-beri, smallpox, diphtheria, often in combination. Wounds festered. The Asian conscripts were the first to perish from cholera, leaving the camps fouled with vomit and watery diarrhea and choked with flies. Even men with malaria were not excused from labor. Hundreds came down with tropical ulcers, reeking of putrefaction; in one camp, seventy Allied soldiers had their legs amputated, the surgeries performed in the open air under mosquito nets to keep flies out.[22]

After the British colonel, an Australian lieutenant colonel in the medical corps testified further about the death railway. He had been captured by Japanese troops in Sumatra in March 1942. Along with five hundred British prisoners of war, he was first sent to Burma, where, joined with a thousand more Australians, they were packed into a school building. In overcrowded and filthy conditions, amebic dysentery spread quickly. Stricken with fever and bloody diarrhea, their clothes soiled, men died of dehydration or bowel perforations.

He was sent to the Burma railway early in 1943, where work was well under way. Tending to two thousand sick prisoners of war, he found them dying in droves from amebic dysentery, malaria, partial blindness, burning feet, and diarrhea. Monsoon rain pounded through the huts and the men were barely clothed. At another camp, a Japanese doctor, told that the men were debilitated, replied, "They must finish the railway, and after that they will have a long rest." Korean guards beat the patients and sometimes the doctors. On a typical day, the Australian doctor would curette seventy or more ulcers of the leg and amputate nine or ten legs. In one camp along the line, in a makeshift bamboo lean-to, using a little cocaine as a spinal anesthetic, he sawed off a hundred and twenty legs. Of sixteen hundred men in one camp, three hundred and thirty died. As he testified, "The spectacle of the emaciated skeletons of men . . . many with rotting, gangrenous ulcers of the legs, emitting a nauseating stench, lying in their pain and misery, were such as I never wish to witness again."[23]

The prosecutors, while lacking evidence about Japanese decision-making, framed the death railway as an extreme example of a general pattern across Asia. One Australian brigadier testified about experiencing similar abuse—beatings, illness, filth—in three different camps in Java, Taiwan, and Manchuria. In response, the defense lawyers could do little but poke at the details or suggest that, since these war crimes had a specific geographical localization, they ought to be in front of Allied courts prosecuting conventional Class B war crimes.[24] The defense did not raise the considerable number of Allied prisoners who died when the Japanese ships carrying them were sunk by Allied warships, which would have complicated the picture of Japanese cruelty but without doing much to exonerate their clients.[25]

Demonstrating another kind of Japanese violation of the laws of war, a Canadian army chaplain from Québec City gave gut-wrenching testimony about a massacre in a hospital in Hong Kong—noteworthy for allegedly violating Japan's ratified commitments to the Hague Conventions of 1899 and 1907 and the Geneva Convention of 1929 for the sick and wounded in armies in the field. On Christmas morning in December 1941, the Canadian chaplain watched Japanese troops storm into St. Stephen's College hospital, where he was tending to wounded Allied troops. He testified that they bayoneted more than fifteen wounded men in their beds. Along with ninety other men, including staff and wounded soldiers, he was herded into a tiny room. On two occasions, Japanese troops entered to haul out an Allied soldier; both times he heard screams. When released from the room, he saw to his shock that roughly seventy injured British, Indian, and Canadian men had been bayoneted to death in their beds, and many more wounded. The two soldiers he had heard screaming had not just been killed but had had their ears, tongues, noses, and eyes flayed away from their faces. The chaplain helped cremate one hundred and seventy corpses.

Several nurses, who were British or Chinese, had been killed—one with her head nearly severed—despite being in nurse uniforms with Red Cross armbands. The surviving nurses said that they had been raped. (Later studies estimate that as many as ten thousand women and girls were raped in Hong Kong after its surrender.) His testimony was bolstered by an affidavit by a nurse at the hospital who recounted that she had been raped by three Japanese soldiers, and that two other nurses had also been raped.[26]

One of the most effective witnesses was an Australian army nurse, Sister Vivian Bullwinkel—one of the few women who testified at the Tokyo trial. In better times she had a toothy smile that brought out dimples; now her face was composed, and she wore her military uniform with her dark hair pulled neatly back under her hat. She spoke in a businesslike manner, one hand holding an earpiece. In February 1942, she testified, she and her fellow nursing sisters at an Australian hospital in Singapore had been evacuated southward on a small ship. It carried sixty-five nurses,

Sister Vivian Bullwinkel, an Australian army nurse, testifies about surviving a massacre in Indonesia, Tokyo, December 20, 1946.

about two hundred and fifty women and children, and a few elderly men. At sea three Japanese airplanes bombed the ship. As it sank, the lifeboats were machine-gunned by the Japanese planes. She jumped into the water and, with a dozen other nurses, swam desperately to a foundering lifeboat. They drifted for about eight hours before beaching on Bangka Island, off Sumatra in Indonesia. There they found other survivors, many wounded from Japanese strafing: between thirty and forty women and children, some fifty men, and ten more nursing sisters.

In the morning, the helpless group surrendered themselves. When about fifteen Japanese troops arrived, they marched the men away in groups. Bullwinkel heard gunshots. The Japanese returned, cleaning their rifles and bayonets. (Recently an Australian historian has argued that the Japanese troops raped the nurses at this point, although this was not included in the Tokyo trial testimony.)[27] Then the Japanese ordered the twenty-two surviving nurses to march into the sea. When the nurses were only a few yards in, the Japanese opened fire with a clatter of machine guns from behind. "I saw the girls fall one after the other," she testified in a matter-of-fact tone, "when I was hit." The bullet passed straight through her body at the waist, knocking her over.

The waves carried her to the beach, where Bullwinkel pretended to be dead. After ten or fifteen minutes, she dared to look up. The Japanese were gone. There were bodies strewn across the beach. She dragged herself into the jungle, where she passed out. After being fed by local villagers, she and a wounded British private hid out for several days, before giving themselves up to the Japanese. Too afraid to tell the Japanese of her bullet wound, she got no treatment for it, and was lucky to survive. She spent the rest of the war in a series of reeking, overcrowded camps, where as many as three-quarters of her fellow captives were sick from malaria and tropical fevers. She tended to them as best she could or dug their graves.

When Bullwinkel finished her testimony, the courtroom was silent. The defense made no attempt to cross-examine her. For once, Webb was deferential. "Well, you are a model witness, Sister Bullwinkel," he said. "You have given your evidence faultlessly."[28]

Bookending the wrenching testimony by Colin Fleming Brien, the prosecutors read aloud from the diary of a Japanese soldier which told from the Japanese perspective about the decapitation of an Australian prisoner. In New Guinea in March 1943, the Japanese were facing frequent bombings, but this twenty-three-year-old Australian Air Force flight lieutenant, blown out of the sky, was helpless. After being interrogated for several days, the Australian was given his last drink of water and put on a truck in twilight, accompanied by several Japanese officers carrying swords. The doomed young man gazed at the hills and the sea, lost in thought. The Japanese diarist averted his eyes in pity.

After disembarking at a bomb crater, the Japanese unit commander said, "We are now going to kill you." The prisoner was told that in accordance with Bushido, he would be killed with a Japanese sword, and gave him two or three minutes to prepare himself. The young man, subdued, his head bowed but brave in the face of death, said "One"—asking to be killed with one blow. Surrounded by guards, he was forced to his knees in the water in the bomb crater. "When I put myself in the prisoner's place," wrote the Japanese soldier, "and think that in one more minute it will be good-bye to this world, although the daily bombings have filled me with hate, ordinary human feelings make me pity him."

The unit commander unsheathed his sword, glittering in the fading light. He tapped the Australian's neck lightly with it, then raised the blade with both hands and slashed down. The Japanese diarist closed his eyes at the moment of killing: he heard a hissing noise as blood spurted. The body fell forward. The severed head rolled. Dark blood gushed. "All is over," wrote the Japanese soldier in his diary. "The head is dead white, like a doll. The savageness which I felt only a little while ago is gone, and now I feel nothing but the true compassion of Japanese Bushido. A senior corporal laughs loudly, 'Well, he will enter Nirvana now!'" Another Japanese flipped over the headless body and vengefully sliced open the belly. The mutilated young man was then hastily buried. "If I ever get back alive it will make a good story to tell," concluded the Japanese soldier, "so I have written it down."[29]

RACE WAR

There was a distinctively racial aspect to the abuse of Allied captives: Japanese authorities were keenly aware of the spectacle of putting white men to work. Although the Geneva Convention mandated that prisoners of war be protected "from insults and from public curiosity," there was some evidence that the Japanese military wanted to showcase its white prisoners in order to humiliate them—and by extension their nations and races.[30] While Japan banned newspaper accounts of these displays, the military was pleased by their effectiveness.

Imperial Japan sometimes treated its prisoners differently not by nationality but by skin color. In October 1942, the governor of Kanagawa Prefecture had noted that although the Japanese in the prefecture had once been pro-British or pro-American, they seemed "to realize with gratitude the glory of the Imperial Throne, seeing before their eyes English and American PWs at their labor." In March 1942, the chief of staff of the Japanese army in Korea got the Army Ministry to send two thousand "white prisoners of war," Americans and Britons, there because "it would be very effective in stamping out the respect and admiration of the Korean people for Britain and America, and also in establishing a strong faith in victory." General Itagaki Seishiro, one of the accused in Tokyo who was then commander in chief of Japan's army in Korea, explained in a letter to Tojo Hideki that interning American and British prisoners there should "make the Koreans realize positively the true might of our Empire as well as to contribute to psychological propaganda work for stamping out any ideas of worship of Europe and America which the greater part of Korea still retains at bottom."

In August 1942, the chief of staff of Japan's army in Korea crowed that the humiliation of Allied prisoners had been a grand success which would "contribute greatly toward ruling Korea." When a thousand British prisoners were marched through Seoul and Busan, some one hundred and twenty thousand Koreans and fifty-seven thousand Japanese had lined the streets to see them. The spectators "sneered at the disgraceful behavior" of the helpless, bedraggled British prisoners and concluded that it was "quite natural that an army so lacking in patriotism should be defeated by the Imperial Army, and realized afresh the victory gained by Imperial

Army." The spectacle "was very successful in driving all admiration for the British and Americans out of their minds."

One Japanese onlooker said, "Their spiritual state is pitiful. They feel no shame in being exposed to public show." The Japanese army gloated that Koreans had expressed newfound pride in being part of Japan's empire. As a Korean said, "When I saw young Korean soldiers, members of the Imperial Army, guarding the prisoners, I shed tears of joy." Another said, "It seems like a dream to see the British and Americans, who used to make light of us and thought us an inferior people, as prisoners." One Korean who had doubted Japanese propaganda about its victories was now reassured. "The war is being prolonged on their account," said one Korean onlooker. "They should be worked to death."[31]

BATAAN

While the British Commonwealth dominated this phase, there were several American witnesses who testified about deprivation, summary executions, and torture. U.S. prosecutors gave evidence that at strategic Wake Island in October 1943, Japanese troops shot to death ninety-six American prisoners of war whose hands were tied. Two Japanese admirals decapitated two more Americans.[32] The U.S. prosecution also complained about the Japanese sinking of the USS *Panay*, a gunboat destroyed near Nanjing soon before it fell.[33]

With the American public preoccupied with Japanese torture throughout the Pacific War, torture became a major theme for the United States at the Tokyo trial.[34] According to American testimony, at a captured U.S. airbase south of Manila, Japanese guards would force a hose down an American prisoner's throat, painfully distend his stomach with water, and then jump on his belly. Or they would tie a prisoner's hands behind his back and wrench his hands up between his shoulders with a rope thrown over a tree limb, leaving him to hang off the ground, usually pulling both arms out of their sockets. An American prisoner remembered being hung for twenty-four hours in that position under searing sun and then a deluge of rain, while being beaten with plaited rope and a pistol butt.[35]

One U.S. lieutenant colonel testified about abuse and torture at a jail in Iloilo City in the Philippines. He saw Filipinos—who were treated worse than the Americans—having their fingernails torn off, or being burned by hot coals under their chin or on the soles of their feet. He was beaten with bamboo poles and steel knuckles. In a bare, unfurnished room used as a torture chamber, he was beaten across the chest, ribs, and back with a bamboo pole and a two-by-four, until finally being knocked unconscious by a two-by-four blow to the head. These were not isolated incidents nor at the whims of soldiers, he said. He described the Japanese chain of command in operation, from enlisted men to a captain to a colonel.[36]

The low point for the Americans was the Bataan death march, with several American survivors testifying. Samuel Moody, a gruff U.S. Army staff sergeant from a working-class town in Massachusetts, testified bitterly that the roadside was littered with dead bodies—mostly Filipino or American soldiers, but also two Filipinas and some Filipino priests. He was burly in his uniform, his hair cropped close; below the walls of the witness box he threaded his fingers together in tension. "Many times I could look ahead and see my friends being stabbed and beaten," he said in a thick Massachusetts accent. One of his close friends had been stricken with dysentery and had fallen to the rear of the column, where he was bayoneted and beaten, later dying of his wounds. After a seven-day march along the Bataan Peninsula, he was put to a work detail in which thirty-seven men died. "I personally painted the crosses that we put on the graves," he told the hushed courtroom. "I put each man in the casket myself. There was 37 men."

Donald Ingle, a soldier from Illinois, had been forced to march at Bataan despite a wounded shoulder. He had seen sixteen men bayoneted to death. A U.S. Army chaplain, stricken with dysentery, had had to relieve his bowels by the side of the road; for that he was wounded with a bayonet. An American defense lawyer asked Ingle if he knew who was in charge of the march. "How could I?" snapped Ingle. The defense lawyer asked him if he was bitter. Ingle paused for a long moment. "Well, there are several thousand buddies that aren't here today that would be here if it weren't for that," he replied. "Use your own judgment."[37]

Of all the horrors faced by Americans, the most nauseating was cannibalism. There were scattered reports of Japanese eating the flesh of Allied prisoners of war in the Philippines and New Guinea, but the most sustained presentation—which left the court repulsed—was drawn from the testimony of Japanese officers facing a postwar U.S. Navy military tribunal.[38] Prosecutors read ghastly excerpts aloud.

In late 1944, nine U.S. fliers were shot down at Chichi Jima, an island stronghold in the ocean south of Japan. One of them, bleeding from a head wound and thinking about how American prisoners had been treated at Bataan, had the good fortune to be rescued by a U.S. submarine before his life raft drifted him onto the island. The other eight were captured and, in turn, executed.

In desperation to defend the island, the Japanese commander told his officers they would have to eat the flesh of fallen comrades and the "beastly" flesh of the enemy. A Japanese major testified that a group of Japanese officers, hungry for meat at a boozy party, had eaten human flesh from one of the American fliers while drinking sake. "Everyone present had a taste of it," the Japanese major recalled. "Of course, nobody relished the taste."

Several other times, this major had told the U.S. Navy tribunal, Japanese officers ate the livers of executed American prisoners. Human livers were thought to be a kind of medicine. This Japanese major testified that he had consumed human flesh at least three times, most recently a pill made of human liver given to him in Singapore. At Chichi Jima, this major had issued a punctilious order:

ORDER REGARDING EATING OF
FLESH OF AMERICAN FLYERS

   I The Battalion wants to eat the flesh of the American Aviator, Lieutenant (junior grade) Hall.
  II First Lieutenant Kanmuri see to the rationing of this flesh.
 III Cadet Sakabe (medical corps) attend the execution and have the liver and gall-bladder removed.[39]

The judges in Tokyo were not told the name of the one U.S. Navy flier, a lieutenant junior grade, who luckily escaped from Chichi Jima by submarine: George H. W. Bush. In 1989, as president of the United States, Bush would attend the funeral of Emperor Hirohito, where he politely declared himself moved by the pageantry.[40] On December 7, 1991, at a memorial service at Pearl Harbor, Bush would tell American and Japanese veterans, "I have no rancor in my heart for my former enemy."[41]

"REDUCED TO ASHES"

There was an especially vexed aspect to the U.S. prosecutors' case: some of these U.S. prisoners of war were executed on accusations of committing war crimes against Japanese civilians. Here the prosecution was indifferent to Japanese anguish at the firebombing of their cities and towns. Since aerial bombardment had not been definitively decreed a war crime, which let the U.S. bombers off the hook, the prosecution could make a one-sided case.

Japanese authorities began to put captured Allied airmen on trial as war criminals after the Doolittle raid in 1942. Later in the war, as the American bombing escalated, some downed U.S. airmen were summarily executed while others faced swift courts-martial for indiscriminately bombarding Japanese cities. These proceedings were minimal. In one court-martial in Osaka in July 1945, two U.S. airmen were asked only their names, their unit, and what cities they had struck—in this case, Tokyo, Osaka, and Kobe. One of the Americans admitted dropping bombs but said that he had "only obeyed his higher officers' orders." Both men were found guilty and sentenced to die by firing squad.

Others had not gotten even that kind of procedure. Many were, as a Japanese report noted, "disposed of" after it was "decided that these men were clearly guilty of inhuman and indiscriminate bombing." In Chiba Prefecture, a badly injured B-29 pilot was beheaded on the orders of a Japanese captain. As a Japanese report observed, after Fukuoka was "reduced to ashes" by firebombing in June 1945, the hostile feelings of the military, government, and populace intensified, leading to the summary execution of eight downed Allied airmen the next day.[42] After the atomic bombings of Hiroshima and Nagasaki, "the general feeling of animosity appears to have soared up to its zenith again": eight more airmen were killed. After the end of the war, a false rumor that U.S. forces were already landing caused chaos and "the weaker sex fleeing to places of refuge," which became a cue for the military to execute fifteen more captured airmen.

In Japan's central military district in June 1945, forty-one captured Allied airmen were killed without a trial, while two were given a court-martial before being executed. More captured Allied airmen were shot to death by firing squads in July and August 1945. A Japanese report commented that the intensification of U.S. firebombing of Japanese cities after March had "roused the indignation of the nation—especially towards the flight personnel—to an exceedingly high pitch." Explaining why Japan had given up on courts-martial after the firebombing of Tokyo, Nagoya, and other cities, the report observed that "the indiscriminate bombings by Allied aircraft became increasingly and ceaselessly violent and the people's spirit of vengeance reached its limit."

Soon after a big bombing raid on Nagoya on May 14, 1945—one of many aerial strikes that devastated this major city—the Japanese captured groups of downed Allied airmen. Under escalating bombardment, the Japanese ruled out courts-martial and chose to execute them instead. As an official Japanese report noted, "the damages caused by the indiscriminate bombing became gigantic, and the hostile feelings were reaching the limit. . . . [T]he area army decided that under the circumstances, sending these men to courts martial which are complicated and delaying, would not be consistent with the prevailing state of affairs." Twenty-seven Allied airmen were put to death in June and July.[43]

Webb, apparently feeling some bad conscience, blew up at the prosecution during an evasive discussion of the American bombardment of Tokyo and Osaka. "This is not a serious question," he snapped. "The prosecution cannot claim that the Americans did not bomb residential areas in the course of bombing Tokyo and Osaka."[44]

While the U.S. prosecutors were correct that prisoners accused of war crimes deserved a fair trial, that sidestepped the core Japanese claim: that the indiscriminate killing of civilians was a war crime, even if international law might be a step behind in its consideration of aerial warfare. In a jarring example of these two principles clashing, the prosecution complained about Allied prisoners who died by being bombed by the Allies. On the night of May 25, 1945, sixty-two Allied airmen detained in a Japanese army prison in Tokyo were burned to death in an air raid. An unmarked prisoner of war camp at Osaka was wiped out along with its surroundings in a B-29 raid in June 1945.[45] Still, if Allied prisoners of war were entitled to be spared from such destruction, why not Japanese civilians as well?

"A WARLIKE MASTER RACE"

As grim as the testimony about Commonwealth prisoners of war was, the nadir came with the prosecution's evidence about atrocities in the Philippines. Since Koreans had no representation at the Tokyo trial, this was a rare chance for Asians, rather than Westerners, to testify about their wartime ordeal. The intensity of this phase was matched only by the Chinese complaint about the Nanjing massacre several months earlier. A senior British diplomat called it part of a "month of horrors," with "most lurid" testimony.[46] "The atmosphere in the courtroom was cold and heavy," shuddered an American reporter, "like the air under a shroud."[47]

Filipinos were given few opportunities to speak for themselves during the Tokyo trial. The country only became independent of the United States on July 4, 1946, early in the proceedings. Its associate prosecutor was still on the payroll of the U.S. Department of the Army.[48] While Harry Truman had ordered that the newly sovereign republic should handle the trial of its own collaborators from the Japanese occupation, the Americans in Tokyo had not yet overcome their habits of condescension.[49] Unlike other colonized lands, aggression against the Philippines had warranted its own separate count in the indictment, but nevertheless that charge had been folded into the American presentation about Pearl Harbor.[50]

Delfin Jaranilla, the Philippine judge, was conspicuously absent, having voluntarily excused himself for this phase of the trial. He returned to Manila to visit his family, apparently preferring that his fellow judges handle this part without him.[51]

Before Pedro Lopez, the dapper associate prosecutor from the Philippines, could get to his feet, he was challenged by an American defense counsel, who argued humiliatingly that the new country had no standing in the Tokyo trial. The colonized Philippines had not been a party to the treaties that Japan was accused of breaking: "The Philippine Republic is only permitted to exercise the right of sovereignty as is granted under the Congress of the United States." Webb angrily overruled the defense counsel.

Lopez rose to deliver his case with zealous fervor. He spoke excellent English with a Filipino accent. Only forty years old, he had been an anti-Japanese guerrilla during the occupation, during which more than a million Filipinos were killed or wounded.[52] In a trial full of nightmarish presentations, his speech stood out. Webb, usually lenient to the prosecutors, said that his oration "exceeds the due limits of an opening statement, and to that extent will be disregarded by the tribunal."[53] Lopez repeatedly bookended violence against Chinese with that against Filipinos, seeking to show a systematic method from Nanjing to Manila—a consistent pattern across Asia of "wholesale murder, torture, and rape." Spotlighting Imperial Japan's claims of racial superiority over Chinese and Filipinos, he declared that Japanese authorities had meant "to produce a warlike master race dead set on world conquest."

As spectators flinched or left the courtroom in horror, he gave a litany of massacres.[54] His presentation was especially damning for General Muto Akira, who had been chief of staff to General Yamashita Tomoyuki in the Philippines. At St. Paul College in Manila, some eight hundred men, women, and children had been lured into an apparently safe hall and then killed by detonating grenades. Again and again, prosecutors introduced U.S. military reports of the killing of hundreds of civilians, with dozens of horrifying accounts of children and babies bayoneted to death. Entire villages were burned to the ground. According to an eyewitness, one forty-year-old Filipino man was crucified to the ground with six-inch nails driven through his wrists and the base of his skull—an apparent rebuke for an overwhelmingly Christian nation.[55] Describing the sack of Manila in February 1945, Lopez and a U.S. prosecutor provided horrific accounts

Pedro Cerono, a Filipino man who discovered eight skulls from a massacre several months earlier in Cagayan province, Luzon, the Philippines, November 23, 1945

of shooting, decapitation, torture, and rape—some of the worst atrocities of the Pacific War.[56] With grim precision, he noted that the U.S. War Department calculated that 131,028 Filipinos and Americans had been killed directly or through starvation—only counting civilians and captured soldiers who had died from murder, torture, starvation, or neglect.

Recounting the Bataan death march, Lopez estimated that sixteen thousand Filipinos had been "murdered and left in the dusty and bloody road to rot"—about six times the standard postwar statistic. Filipinos had died at worse rates than Americans. He reminded the courtroom of less well-known abuses, such as another forced march of hundreds of Filipino and American prisoners of war, on Mindanao on July 4, 1942, with many dead.[57]

He gave harrowing details of torture: pulling out tongues, fingernails, and toenails; electric shocks; cutting off ears and gouging eyes; and "the water cure, with several variations depending on the savage bent and imagination of the torturer." (Such water torture had been widely used in the Philippines by the conquering Americans after 1898, a fact Lopez did not mention.)[58] Fort Santiago, a magnificent old Spanish edifice, was turned into a torture chamber where "hundreds suffered slow and painful death in dark, foul and lice-infested cells" which, Lopez said with a gratuitous flourish, was worse than Dachau.

Describing sexual violence, the Philippine associate prosecutor's recital grew so distressing that, as the judges squirmed, he explained that "the crimes committed to my country and my people were so shocking, so brutal and so revolting that resort to euphemisms would only do violence to the truth." At several hotels in Manila during the final battle there, he described the rape of many Filipinas who were often killed afterward. Women had had their breasts slashed or sliced off. He told a sickening story of a pregnant woman in Manila with an eleven-month-old baby in her arms who was shot dead; the Japanese soldier heard the baby wailing, and came back to murder the infant with two shots.[59]

More than any other phase, this one allowed women to tell their stories in court. Wanda Werff, a twenty-five-year-old Filipina secretary working for the U.S. War Department in Manila, had survived two internment camps. In one crowded barracks, she testified, the inmates often went for four or five days without running water, and got one meager serving of rice or corn a day; they were not allowed to pick the bananas or coconuts growing nearby. The ravenous inmates scrounged for slugs, snails, cockroaches, and rats. She had weighed 152 pounds when she entered the camps; she left at eighty-eight pounds. She remembered how a young American man, digging for weeds near a perimeter fence, was executed for purportedly trying to escape.[60]

As the Japanese defendants stared grimly ahead, the prosecutors itemized instances of rape and sexual violence—so many that they implied a policy of allowing outrages against women.[61] In Davao City, an eyewitness had seen four Japanese soldiers select a terrified, weeping Filipina from an air raid shelter, drag her outside, tear her clothes off, force her to the ground, and take turns raping her. In a notorious episode during the last battle for Manila, according to a U.S. military report, Japanese forces detained scores of young Filipinas for several nights in three apartment buildings and a hotel, where they were raped repeatedly. Japanese troops said they felt entitled to seize a last worldly pleasure before dying in battle. In an affidavit, Easter Garcia Moras remembered praying and weeping as her sisters were dragged away to another room to be violated. When one of them eventually returned, she said she wanted to die. Moras was hauled away by Japanese marines, forced down onto a bare floor, and slapped until dazed. "I was raped between 12 and 15 times during that night," she testified in her affidavit. "I cannot remember exactly how many times. I was so tired and horror stricken that it became a living nightmare."[62]

.   .   .

In some of the most effective—and chilling—evidence of the entire Tokyo trial, the captured diaries of Japanese officers showed that they had been under orders to commit war crimes. A Japanese warrant officer wrote in 1944, "We are ordered to kill all the males we find." In another diary entry, he noted, "Our aim is to kill or wound all the men and collect information. Women who attempt to escape are to be killed. All in all, our aim is extinction of personnel." Another soldier wrote in early 1945 that all inhabitants of a town were killed: "Because 90% of the Filipinos are not pro-Japanese[,] Army Headquarters issued orders on the 10th to punish them. In various sectors we have killed several thousands (including young and old, men and women, and Chinese)."

Many of the Japanese executioners were distressed. A private first class noted in his diary, "Taking advantage of darkness, we went out to kill the natives. It was hard for me to kill them because they seemed to be good people. Frightful cries of the women and children were horrible. I myself stabbed and killed several persons." Another Japanese soldier remembered the beating of accused guerrillas, who were later shot or speared to death with bamboo lances: "It was pitiful, and I couldn't watch. . . . Indeed the Japanese Army does extreme things." One Japanese wrote in 1945 that he had killed more than a hundred Filipino guerrillas and natives: "The naivete I possessed at the time of leaving the homeland has long since disappeared. Now I am a hardened killer and my sword is always stained with blood. Although it is for my country's sake, it is sheer brutality. May God forgive me! May my mother forgive me!"

Other killers showed fewer qualms. In 1944, a Japanese soldier recorded bayoneting to death some thirty helpless Filipino guerrillas: "I noticed that some of them were small like children. They had no strength at all since they had not eaten for the last three days since their capture. . . . Their hands were tied behind their backs, and they stood in front of the holes"—graves dug for them—"with their heads bent slightly downward. It seemed that their minds were already made up that they would be killed, and they said nothing. Their hair was very bushy. I was irritated." Despite observing their helplessness, he joined in stabbing them one by one: "My turn was the second one. The moment I bayoneted the victim he cried 'Ah' and fell into the hole behind him. He was suffering but I had no emotion at all. That may be because I was so excited."[63]

The Philippines' evidence, in all its horror, stood out for its emphasis on Asian victims. The French and Dutch associate prosecutors gave evidence that concentrated more on French and Dutch people than on the Vietnamese or Indonesians. There were no Indonesians brought to Tokyo to testify, but the court heard from a series of Dutch survivors. Yet even a brief Dutch presentation, given at a fast clip, showed that Indonesians had faced terrible atrocities, evidently far worse than the Europeans.

Imperial Japan had used some 270,000 Indonesians, mostly from Java, as wartime forced labor.[64] The court heard affidavits from several Indonesians who had survived camps for Asians with far worse mortality than those for Europeans. The Japanese had euphemistically called these undernourished and hounded Indonesians the *romusha,* meaning laborers; the Tokyo tribunal condescendingly referred to them as "coolies." At one labor camp, the Indonesians were beaten and tortured, overworked, and exposed to disease; within a year, some five hundred prisoners died out of a total of seven hundred and fifty. At another camp, according to an Indonesian survivor, out of a group of five hundred, more than two hundred died.

The Kempeitai were prolific and inventive torturers of Indonesians, with specialists in electric current, kidney-beating, and what was called "the water test"—being slowly drowned with water poured through a towel drawn over the face. One Indonesian witness had seen one of his fellow workers killed by being wrapped in a mat which was set on fire. Another Indonesian saw a worker buried alive. The mayor of Semarang, in Central Java, gave an affidavit about being beaten by the Kempeitai until his shoulders were black-and-blue, kicked in the ribs and shins with heavy military boots, burned with cigarettes, and scorched with "applied electric current that made one bounce and dance like a frog, screaming until one fainted; all this in order to get the desired confessions."[65]

The French associate prosecutor, too, emphasized the ordeals of Europeans, recounting the torture of French captives and the rape of French women in Indochina.[66] Although the prosecutor did record the suffering of Vietnamese—a massacre in northern Indochina of both Vietnamese and French people, the beating of Vietnamese laborers, the forcing of Vietnamese women into prostitution—the priority went to the French. In one affidavit, a Frenchman jailed by the Japanese in Haiphong complained that he and his fellow Frenchmen had been thrown into a dungeon with "some verminous, scabious Annamites"—that is, Vietnamese—"who, in the course of a few days, covered us all with lice."[67]

The court heard scattered evidence of extreme cruelty toward other Asian peoples. Local Burmese laborers were sprayed in the eyes with disinfectant, poisoned, called subhuman and not worth consideration by a Japanese doctor. Husbands, wives, and children were separated from each other and sent to different work camps. Their ragged clothes were ridden with vermin. They were fed rice infested with weevils. Those with cholera were shoved into common graves and buried alive.[68] A Thai man swore to having been tortured horribly: cigarette burns, two days of electric current until his wrists and legs were charred, water forced into his belly, and a red-hot wire inserted into his penis.[69]

To preserve its public claims of pan-Asian solidarity, the Japanese government had maintained strict censorship about its use of Asians as slave labor. While Japan expurgated any reporting of its use of prisoners of war "for purposes other than common labor," it went further for Asians. A censorship directive banned "[a]ny reports indicating the capture of Orientals and the use of them for labor."[70]

CHAIN OF COMMAND

For all the hideous abundance of evidence of conventional war crimes, the prosecution had more difficulty linking these deeds to the defendants. Unlike in the Pearl Harbor phase, the prosecution was not dissecting incriminating meetings of senior Japanese officials. Nor could the prosecutors point to specific orders to kill or torture prisoners of war, which either did not exist or had been destroyed at the end of the war. Instead, the pointillistic presentation of crimes amounted to a vast pattern from which the judges could infer the guilt of the accused.[71] The Australian associate prosecutor argued that the numerous formal Allied complaints to the Japanese Foreign Ministry incriminated a dozen of the defendants: either they knew about these breaches of the laws of war and neglected to do anything to prevent them, or they failed to make a proper inquiry to find out if war crimes were going on.

The prosecutors carefully traced the chain of command to the top authorities in Tokyo.[72] General Doihara Kenji and General Itagaki Seishiro had commanded armies ruling Singapore; General Umezu Yoshijiro had been the commander of the Kwantung Army overseeing Manchukuo; and General Muto Akira had been director of the military affairs bureau responsible for prisoners of war.[73] That chain led upward to Tojo Hideki as army minister and prime minister, who had decided to use Allied prisoners as crucial labor for the war effort—and, as the Allied prosecutors did not note, to the emperor as the head of the empire and the commander of the army and navy under the Meiji constitution.[74]

There were sometimes more specific links. General Hata Shunroku had issued the order setting up the court-martial that executed three of the eight captive American airmen downed after the Doolittle air raid.[75] It was the general staff which had decided to use Allied prisoners to build the Burma–Thailand railway, thus incriminating several defendants, including Tojo and Admiral Nagano Osami.[76] And an Australian infantry captain testified to seeing Doihara make an inspection of a notorious camp in western Honshu where Australians were dying of malnutrition. After Doihara left, conditions did not improve. Webb asked the Australian captain if he recognized the general in the courtroom. "That is him there," he said, pointing at Doihara.[77]

One man high in this chain of command would never face judgment. On January 5, 1947, Nagano, who was sixty-eight years old, died of bronchial pneumonia, arterial sclerosis, and pulmonary tuberculosis, according to a U.S. autopsy. He had been spirited away from Sugamo Prison to a U.S. Eighth Army hospital a week before his death, but not in time to save him. With another suspect dead and one declared mad, that left twenty-five men out of twenty-eight accused.[78]

While the chain of command mostly pointed to army officers, it ensnared two foreign ministers. Togo Shigenori looked stricken. As foreign minister after Pearl Harbor, he was the one who had pledged in January 1942 that Japan would apply the provisions of the Geneva Convention *mutatis mutandis* to Allied prisoners of war.[79] At the Foreign Ministry, he had received scores of formal Allied complaints about executions, torture, and disease, passing them along to the army and navy. He later claimed that he had urged Tojo Hideki to make sure that there was more supervision of how prisoners of war were treated. He averred that the Foreign Ministry had known nothing about the Bataan march and the Burma–Thailand railway, while blaming the army for the execution of three captured American airmen from the Doolittle air raid.[80] Despite that, the prosecutors said that he must have known that the Army Ministry was not taking action to improve conditions.[81]

Shigemitsu Mamoru leaned forward and cupped his head in his hands during testimony about atrocities.[82] As foreign minister later in the war, he too had received and processed more Allied protests, as well as entreaties from the International Committee of the Red Cross about prisoners of war being abused in Burma and Thailand.[83] The prosecutors said that he must have been aware that the Army Ministry was not ameliorating the situation. Shigemitsu had sometimes been evasive, replying to the British during the construction of the death railway that prisoners of war in Thailand were equitably treated and that all sick prisoners had received proper treatment in hospitals, while forbidding permission to visit the festering camps.[84]

.   .   .

The prosecution worked hard to ensnare Tojo Hideki for conventional war crimes. Least effectively, the prosecutors again relied on Major General Tanaka Ryukichi, formerly chief of the military service bureau at the Army Ministry, still settling scores with Tojo and other adversaries.[85] He claimed to have seen Tojo, as army minister, in many meetings about the treatment of prisoners of war. According to Tanaka, in a meeting soon after the end of combat on Bataan, Tojo had decided that all prisoners of war would be used as forced labor, despite objections from a Japanese official that using officers for labor could violate the Geneva Convention.[86]

The defense slated Tanaka's motives and character. Under fierce cross-examination, he admitted that he was a leader of the Kempeitai, with the defense hinting that he was being offered immunity in exchange for his wobbly testimony. He acknowledged that he had gone to a hospital for mental illness after quitting the Army Ministry. Referring to his Kempeitai background, one defense lawyer asked him, "General, aren't you known by the people in Japan as 'The Monster'?" Over furious objections from the prosecution, Webb allowed the question. Tanaka conceded, "There are some people call me 'Monster.'"[87]

Far more convincing were Tojo's own directives as army minister—a rich trove of documentary evidence that had somehow escaped destruction. As these papers showed, he had kept well informed about how prisoners of war were being treated, in such granular detail as their effectiveness at working in factories or unloading coal.[88] Seeking to extract the maximum labor from Allied prisoners, his orders had all but begged Japanese army officers to overstep their formal restraints against abuse. There were so many of these damning documents that at several points Webb wearily asked if it was really necessary to read them out in court.[89]

In May 1942, Tojo had directed a Japanese army division that prisoners be put under "strict discipline as far as it does not contravene the law of humanity. It is necessary to take care not to be obsessed with a mistaken idea of humanitarianism or swayed by personal feelings." In another order, in June 1942, Tojo had instructed chiefs of prison camps in Japan, Korea, Manchukuo, and Formosa: "In Japan, we have our own ideology concerning prisoners-of-war, which should naturally make their treatment more or less different from that in Europe and America." While showing the "fair and just attitude of the Empire vividly," the labor of prisoners should be "fully utilized" for production and the war effort.

In another directive, in July 1942, Tojo told new chiefs of camps for prisoners of war in Southeast Asia that Japan had "a different conception of prisoners-of-war and consequently has different methods of treatment" than Americans or Europeans. While they had to abide by laws and regulations, they "must supervise them rigidly in so far as you do not become inhuman, and not let them remain idle even for a single day." Tojo had instructed the camp chiefs that "you must make the local people recognize the superiority of the Japanese people through the treatment of prisoners-of-war as well as make the local people conceive it as the greatest honor that they are able to collaborate with the Imperial Army in establishing the Greater East Asia Co-Prosperity Sphere."[90]

When interrogated by Allied investigators after the war, Tojo made no effort to deny his authority as army minister over Allied prisoners of war. "Yes," Tojo replied simply. "I was responsible for their treatment." He admitted that he had been familiar with the provisions of the Geneva and Hague Conventions about proper treatment of prisoners of war, and believed that they applied to Japan during the war. He said that he had ordered the creation of the ill-starred bureau overseeing Allied prisoners of war—while adding that no such office had been necessary for the China war, since Japan treated it as an "incident" rather than a proper war in which Chinese combatants deserved legal protections. He admitted that Allied protests had been taken up at the biweekly meetings of that bureau and had been routinely sent to him: "The War Minister received a stack of papers about a foot and a half high every day, and I suppose that was among them."

Tojo carefully insisted that the emperor had never been told about these Allied complaints: "No, he was not. I handled them on my own responsibility." Why was the emperor, as the commander of the armed forces, not informed? "I thought it was all right to handle them on my own responsibility," Tojo told the interrogators. "The Emperor was busy and had a great deal of work so I did this on my own. Consequently, the Emperor is not responsible in connection with this matter. I am responsible."

Yet when it came to war crimes, Tojo shifted from forthrightness to evasion. "Atrocities were not brought to my notice at all," he told incredulous Allied interrogators. "I am astounded at the truth regarding atrocities that is now being revealed in the newspapers. If the Japanese had followed the Emperor's instructions, these atrocities would never have happened." He had known about complaints about "food and so forth," but nothing worse.[91] "We did not even suspect that such things happened," he averred. "The Emperor especially, because of his benevolence, would have had a contrary feeling. Such acts are not permissible in Japan. The character of the Japanese people is such that they believe that neither Heaven nor Earth would permit such things. It will be too bad if people in the world believe that these inhumane acts are the result of Japanese character."

Tojo offered a series of excuses, many of which suggested how these war crimes might have been allowed. "The Japanese idea about being taken prisoner is different from that in Europe and America," he explained. "In Japan, it is regarded as a disgrace." (As nobody needed reminding, he had shot himself in the chest to avoid being taken prisoner by the American occupiers.) By disdaining Allied prisoners for being captured, he provided himself a possible criminal motive for ordering or allowing their abuse.

To justify the beating of foreigners, he said that slapping on the face was customary among less-educated Japanese families. Although it was formally forbidden in the armed forces, he admitted that it continued in practice. The habit ought to be stopped, he said, "but I don't think it is a crime. It is something that comes from custom." Even so, this argument would only have sufficed if the Japanese lower classes were in the habit of beating family members to death.

He said that he had supposed that Allied prisoners were treated the same as Japanese troops: "the conditions under which Japanese troops lived were bad and to that extent the treatment given to prisoners of war was bad too." Here again, the argument would only have passed muster if Japanese troops were beating and torturing each other to death. Japan had a lower standard of living, he said, so when Americans and Europeans were offered standard Japanese rations, they found them "very very unappetizing"—although Allied prisoners repeatedly testified that they got worse food than their Japanese captors.

Tojo was coy about the most infamous atrocities. Several months after the Bataan death march, he said, he had heard rumors that American prisoners of war had been forced to slog in the heat. He had brought up these rumors with the Japanese chief of staff in the Philippines on a visit there, but had accepted his subordinate's explanation that "the 'march' was due to the lack of transportation and there were no cases of atrocities." He let it go at that, presuming that there had been some kind of courts-martial but not following up with other senior officers: "I was acting as Prime Minister and War Minister and I was not able to attend to details of this sort." Anyway, he added, "Everyone thought that the Japanese character would not permit acts of an atrocious nature."[92]

Tojo made no effort to deny that he had authorized the labor of prisoners of war to build a railway with a military purpose, which could be a war crime, although he had claimed doing so was not criminal.[93] "I heard that prisoners had been mistreated by officers in the building of the railroad between Thai and Burma," he admitted, "that prisoners were made to work when they were sick, and, on the basis of this, I ordered a court martial." In his defense affidavit, he would add that he had also sent some surgeons and sacked a general in charge of railway construction.[94]

In addition, there had been "two or three cases" in China that came to his attention, but he was satisfied that the officers on the spot convened courts-martial, whose results were sent to him as army minister. In a few cases where he was not satisfied with the results, he sent them back for reconsideration.

In the one incident that directly implicated the emperor, Tojo defiantly took responsibility for the execution of captured Doolittle fliers. He called them war criminals executed lawfully after a proper military trial. That raid, he said, "was contrary to international law. It was not against troops but against non-combatants, primary school students, and so forth." He had ordered courts-martial for the U.S. airmen. (A 2003 study by researchers affiliated with Japan's Self-Defense Forces would conclude that some of the Doolittle fliers really had hit civilians.)[95] "This was the first time Japan had been bombed," he explained to his interrogators, "and it was a great shock. Public feeling ran very high. Now, of course, since the indiscriminate bombing of medium and small cities which were undefended and the use of the atom bomb, all things which are not permitted under international law, the tragic spectacle of this country today makes the first raid look like a very small thing, but it was a great shock to the people at the time." He admitted that he had issued an order for "severe punishment" of the American airmen, hoping to deter future air raids, although he admitted this was ex post facto law.

Tojo strained to exonerate Hirohito, who had commuted the death sentence of five of the eight American fliers sentenced to death. Not only did this display of power put the emperor atop the chain of command, it suggested that he had participated in the decision to execute three of the fliers. "The Emperor is not related at all to this problem," Tojo first told the interrogators. Then he contradicted himself, claiming that he had spared some of the fliers in deference to "the Emperor's benevolence." Tojo said that "because of his feelings, [I] wished to have only the minimum number of men executed." Having boxed himself in, Tojo had to admit: "This was discussed with the Emperor. . . . That one point was the Emperor's only relation to the thing."[96]

This ended a particularly grueling phase of the trial. The prosecution wrapped up its case with a sense of exhaustion. At last on January 24, 1947, one of the American prosecutors told the court, in a North Carolina accent that was a long way from home, "the prosecution will now rest."[97]

CHAPTER 16

Eleven Angry Men

ANYONE WOULD HAVE FOUND it hard listening for months to haunting testimony from Nanjing and Manila. The judges did so in a particularly odd frame of mind: discombobulated by their surreal, cloistered lives in Japan.

When not onstage under klieg lights, they were, as Mei Ruao noted, "a special and mysterious group."[1] Retreating immediately after court to the Imperial Hotel, they were an isolated and tight-lipped band. They drank together at the hotel bar, learning to swig sake and say *kanpai*, to toast *vashe zdorovye* with the Soviets and to your very good health with the English. Secluded from Japanese society, they flitted through an endless round of international ceremonies, diplomatic receptions, and expatriate parties in tuxedos—hosted one night by a French navy captain, another by the Indian political representative, a U.S. major general, the British associate prosecutor, or a senior Soviet official.[2] The Dutch judge, Bert Röling, privately wrote, "more or less we are living in a world apart, an international society which does as all international societies do."[3]

Even Röling, one of the most adaptable judges, whinged to a friend about "[t]his bloody country." Japanese music sounded to his homesick ears like "the mewing of a couple of not too vital cats in a moonlight"; the Japanese "apparently have no art of their own (the real art in this country comes from China)"; and "my very nature stands up against a mentality that expresses: 'What are you reading' with "What honorable reading' and 'I am going' with 'humbly going.'" Not going beyond blithely stereotypical impressions, he concluded, "I am quite prepared not to understand Japan, for east is east and west is west."[4]

He always fancied the women and slowly warmed to the whole people.

"I must confess that I like the Japanese better the more I learn them," he wrote. "There is something childish in them, and that is charming. As for the women, that childishness is regarded as their special virtue, I assume. . . . The men, on the contrary, served and spoiled by the women, are ugly looking, gloomy and discontent."[5] Although he remembered the hostility with which the Dutch had treated the occupying Germans, he found himself as an occupying foreigner being welcomed into Japanese homes. He played regularly in a string quartet with three Japanese.[6]

He still could not get past hackneyed images of an entire people, asserting that the Japanese had "a very deep feeling of inferiority" which made them "hide themselves and play up and invent stories about divinity." As he explained to a friend, "the Japs are the Germans and the Chinese as the English. Chinese have the inner sense of superiority (but they are losing that perhaps the last generation, so I hope the comparison stops there), and the Japs live on the opinion of the outer world and would be wonderful if they had not the need to show off."[7]

Seeing the Japanese through this haze of bigotry and cliché, the judges were at best, as Röling put it, uneasy spectators in an alien land. As he wrote, "You can walk here and be amazed by all the beautiful things you see. But, in the long run, you cannot get in touch with your surroundings. They are spiritually 'off limits.' And you go through it as a spectator, who does not share the game, and at least feels a bit lonely and unhappy."[8] Flummoxed by a changing Japanese society around them, the judges immersed themselves in the soothingly familiar realm of the law. If the country outside their hotel suites made no sense to them, they could still find solace in their professional acumen with treatise, doctrine, and interpretation. There, at least, they were still masters.

JURISDICTION

As the prosecution wrapped up its case, the judges still had not provided their "reasons to be given later" justifying the court's jurisdiction to charge the accused with aggressive war, crimes against humanity, and war crimes.[9] That turned out to mean much, much later. The judges secretly brawled through a long, bitter debate which would not be resolved until the end of the trial itself.

The judges had to confront two core issues. First, what gave their court jurisdiction over these individual defendants? Second, were the charges in its charter—particularly those of aggression and conspiracy—really crimes under international law? Wrangling over these fundamental questions, which they often blurred together under the shorthand rubric of jurisdiction, their angry infighting almost made the court collapse. At least three of the justices privately threatened to resign; two of them resolved to dissent; most of them were furious at Sir William Webb. Only the Soviet judge, who needed no legal arguments beyond the party line from Moscow, was satisfied with the chief judge's stance.[10] The judges proved obstinately uncooperative and politically tone-deaf. Locked in spirited intellectual combat, they failed to realize how awful it might look to even the most penitent Japanese for the Allied court to go for years without a public justification of its legitimacy. Some of their arguments, including their case for why aggressive war was a crime, were dubious on the merits. And their brawling left lingering wounds among them, presaging the eventual dissents from the court's final judgment.

"Our reasons for this judgment should have been promptly delivered," the British judge wrote confidentially. "The opinions of the waverers had not hardened into conviction."[11] Several other judges were equally frustrated at Webb. "A strong or even a sensible President would have cleared off the question of law at the time we heard the argument," fumed the New Zealand judge, Erima Harvey Northcroft.[12]

The judges were far more fractious than their home governments or General Headquarters realized. Unbeknownst to almost anyone in Tokyo, there was an official commission of four Dutch jurists in The Hague charged with controlling the idealistic Röling.[13] Yet he quickly slipped their leash, although without informing his overseers about his gnawing doubts.[14] "I wonder if international relations have developed to such a state that aggressive war can be regarded as a crime," he wrote skeptically. "Is the crime of war compatible with the national sovereignty as exists nowadays, is it consistent with the law of the jungle that seems to exist in the international society?"[15]

Röling's wayward leanings were bolstered with the arrival of the formidable Radhabinod Pal from Calcutta. The two men, who sat next to each other at the edge of the bench, became fast friends, gossiping and joking merrily. A few months after the Indian judge's arrival, Röling wrote fondly to a friend that "Justice Pal . . . is a poet in his heart."[16] He was also a maverick. According to several of the judges, the Indian judge had stepped off the airplane from Calcutta with his mind made up to dissent. "Nothing would change his views," growled the British judge, Lord Patrick. "They were formed before he came here. He came here to express them."[17] Even Röling later observed that Pal "knew from the very start that he would not find anyone guilty of anything."[18]

Mei Ruao grew to dislike Pal intensely, even though they had in many ways lived parallel lives. The Chinese and Indian judges were both brainy

self-made men from the rural hinterlands of their vast, developing countries; both had used education and the law to vault themselves into the
upper echelons; both had mastered English as the language of global
power; both had utilized the prevailing power structure—the Nationalist government for Mei, the British Empire for Pal—to propel themselves upward. Mei respectfully commented that his Indian colleague
was "knowledgeable in law and extremely hardworking" and "a diligent
reader who always carries a book in his hands." In a different setting, they
might have been friends.[19] Yet in Tokyo the two judges from major Asian
powers found themselves adversaries. Mei railed that Pal was the most
conservative legal thinker and the leader of the minority, often debating
intensely with the other judges. At one point, Mei churlishly described
him as burly, slow, and antisocial.[20] Mei reported to the Chinese government that the Indian judge was "conservative and stubborn," committed to writing a dissent: "He persistently refused to cooperate with the
majority."[21]

Neither Pal nor Röling realized that there were two stalwart members
of the court's majority who privately doubted that aggressive war was a
crime. Major General Myron Cramer, the second U.S. judge, had in 1944
approved a paper that denied that aggression was a crime.[22] And Webb
himself held much the same opinion in private.[23] That left the prospect
of as many as four judges razing the tribunal when it had barely gotten
under way.

Despite the Tokyo trial's reputation in Japan today as American-imposed
victors' justice, the court's majority was effectively dominated by the British Empire. Its three-person nucleus was the judges from Britain, Canada, and New Zealand. They banded together, united by shared English
common-law traditions, outrage at Japan's war, reverence toward the British Empire, and cultural outlook; they were also all furious at Webb.[24]
The British government feared that a botched verdict in Tokyo would
undo the achievement of the Nuremberg judgment. The Canadian government was indignant at Japan for its abuse of prisoners of war, urging
vigorous steps to democratize Japan.[25] New Zealand, as well as Australia,
was frightened about Japanese rearmament.[26] Behind the scenes, this bloc
superseded the official president of the court, cajoling and leading the
other judges.[27]

Led by Patrick, this British bloc became the reliable core of the court's
avenging majority, joined by Mei and Delfin Jaranilla of the Philippines,
and often by Major General Ivan Zaryanov of the Soviet Union. The U.S.

judge, who could have made himself *primus inter pares* because of the might of the United States, proved to be one of the least vocal and least influential—perhaps in part due to whatever doubts Cramer might privately hold. Certainly Patrick did not take him seriously, dismissively noting that he hardly ever spoke up in court or in chambers.[28]

The fractious judges at Tokyo, in a signed photograph, August 6, 1946. Front row: Lord Patrick (Britain), Major General Myron Cramer (the United States), Sir William Webb (Australia), Mei Ruao (China), Major General Ivan Zaryanov (the Soviet Union). Back row: Radhabinod Pal (India), Bert Röling (Holland), E. Stuart McDougall (Canada), Henri Bernard (France), Erima Harvey Northcroft (New Zealand), Delfin Jaranilla (the Philippines).

With Joseph Keenan having made a hash of the prosecution's argument for jurisdiction, the alarmed British, Canadian, and New Zealand judges tried to offer a more respectable explanation. Patrick was privately indignant at the wrangling—what he with Scottish flair called "a long 'collieshangie.'" He believed that the court's charter, based on that at Nuremberg, was justified by a series of antiwar pronouncements by governments beginning with the Treaty of Versailles and culminating in 1928 with the Kellogg-Briand Pact outlawing war.[29] The real reason for the "portentous institution" of the Tokyo court, he told the British government confidentially, was to establish both that planning or waging a war of aggression was a crime and that individual leaders should be held responsible for what had previously been considered acts of state.[30]

In private, Patrick was exceptionally candid about how much the court's legal jurisdiction rested on Allied power. "The Tribunal's powers are not derived from any Constitution or Statute, as the individual judge's powers are derived when he is sitting in his own territory," he lectured Webb. "The Tribunal's powers are derived from might, from the power to carry orders into effect, just as every judge's powers are." Public international law had long recognized the authority of a military commander to set up military tribunals, he noted, which is what General Douglas MacArthur had done in the charter. The judges could not override the charter laid down by the Allied governments, which declared aggression a crime: "it is nonsense to assert that the Allied Powers have conferred on the members of the Tribunal by implication the right to pronounce the actions of the Allied Powers null and void."[31]

Patrick and these two judges from British dominions started with a simple argument: having accepted appointments as judges under the charter, it would be "plain defiance" for judges to refuse to apply the law of that same charter.[32] As a scandalized Patrick secretly wrote to British officials, it was "rank dishonesty" for dissenters such as Pal to "accept a mandate, being minded to defeat its prime purpose." Without the charter's authority, he argued, the judges had "no jurisdiction to sit in Japan."[33] The New Zealand judge believed that any judge who disagreed with the charter should have declined to serve on the court—a volley lobbed directly at Pal and Röling.[34]

Next the British bloc had to answer whether the war crimes listed in the charter really were crimes under international law. If aggression was not already a war crime, could the Allied governments suddenly make it one by writing it into the court's charter? Here Patrick wavered. In private, he believed that before World War II, experts on international law had almost unanimously denied that there was individual criminal responsibility for wars of aggression. Perhaps the judges could simply rely on the terms of surrender to argue that Japan had accepted that aggression was a crime, but that justification would not apply to any subsequent war which did not end with similar particulars. He warned the British government that such a narrow ruling would have no value for the future, doing nothing to build up international law.[35]

Instead, Patrick and the Canadian and New Zealand judges argued that the charter was simply an expression of international law as it stood after World War I. Drawing a progressive, dynamic image of international law, they quoted the Nuremberg judgment: "The law of war is to be found not only in treaties but in the customs and practices of States which gradually obtain universal recognition. This law is not static but by continual adaptation follows the need of a changing world."[36]

Here they relied not just on treaties but on another core source of international law, known as customary international law.[37] Such law is made up of a general, consistent practice of states, which they carry out because of a sense of legal obligation—what Patrick confidently termed "practice crystallising into law."[38] Of course, the invocation of customary international law leads to thorny debates about what exactly state practice is and whether governments are acting under a sense of legal duty.[39] As is often the case, here custom conveniently followed what powerful states wanted.[40]

Before the twentieth century, the three Commonwealth judges conceded, it had been the sovereign right of states under international law to wage war, even wars of aggression. But after the catastrophe of World War I, they argued, aggression had been rendered unlawful by a series of interwar international agreements, although these were actually rather less definitive than the trio made them out to be. The League of Nations, which Japan had joined, rested on obligations not to resort to war. In the Treaty of Versailles, the Allies, including Japan, sought to prosecute Kaiser Wilhelm II of Germany for "a supreme offence against international morality and the sanctity of treaties." (The kaiser had fled to Holland, but as the judges correctly noted, if he had been nabbed, one of his five judges would have been Japanese.)[41] This trend of pinning individual criminal responsibility on leaders who waged an illegal war, they argued, reached its pinnacle in 1928 with the Kellogg-Briand Pact renouncing war as an instrument of national policy. For the British bloc of judges, this landmark pact—which Japan had joined—"clearly established that the criminality of aggressive war had obtained universal recognition." Aggressive war, they contended, was outlawed both by treaties and by custom; the Tokyo trial, far from imposing ex post facto law, was "merely declaratory of existing law." True, the Kellogg-Briand Pact and all the various other antiwar conventions and resolutions did not include criminal penalties, but the Commonwealth judges argued that these pacts would be meaningless or futile without criminal punishment of the offenders.

Compared to Nuremberg, there would be relatively little controversy at Tokyo about the charges for crimes against humanity. Although the defense lawyers claimed that MacArthur had exceeded his authority by including crimes against humanity in the charter, the British bloc of judges argued that such enormities, when carried out in the course of waging war, were simply conventional war crimes. It had long been illegal to attack civilian populations.[42] "The inclusion of crimes against humanity," Webb observed, was not "seriously questioned."[43]

As for the claim that the defendants could not bear individual criminal responsibility for acts done on behalf of the Japanese state, the trio of Commonwealth judges argued, "By a fiction of law only can a State or other juridical person commit crimes. Crimes are committed by individuals." There was no immunity for an act of state if that act itself was criminal. The judges pointed to the Treaty of Versailles' clauses charging the kaiser and other German officials as war criminals, the recent U.S. Supreme Court case upholding military commissions for German saboteurs, and the Nuremberg judgment, which held individuals accountable for war crimes.[44]

Finally, the British bloc of judges took on the argument that the Japanese defendants could not possibly get a fair trial from judges from the victorious Allied powers. They offered two rebuttals. First, in domestic trials, the state itself stood as the accuser, but its appointed judges were not to be challenged. It was standard practice for warring states to put enemy nationals on trial for breaking the laws of war. Second, almost every country had been involved in World War II. If all those states were disqualified as biased, then every war criminal would get off unpunished. While it was surely impossible to find any serious judge on the planet without well-formed opinions about the rights and wrongs of World War II, the three judges never confronted the meat of the defense argument: that they and their fellow judges were profoundly biased by their own patriotic loyalties and prejudices.[45]

"Judicial Murderers"

Even though nine judges—before the arrival of the Indian and Philippine members—had already unanimously agreed that they had jurisdiction, Webb as chief judge proved painfully unable to turn that unity into a communal explanation of their reasons why. Whatever the weaknesses of the British Commonwealth judges' paper, the pragmatic course for Webb would have been to pocket as much of it as could pass muster, improve the rest of it, and then draw up a majority opinion that embraced as many judges as possible. Yet instead of building on the arguments of the Commonwealth judges, he penned his own rival opinion, apparently with the hope of writing an enduring judgment that would resonate in history.[46] He botched the job, exploding the judges' dispute rather than settling it.

Unable to make up his own mind, which flitted from siding with the Japanese defense lawyers to invoking natural law to vindicate the prosecution, Webb struggled to patch together a single ruling that all the judges would have signed. Insecure in his own authority, he leaned on the Nuremberg tribunal's justification of its jurisdiction.[47] As he floundered, he left breathing space for ambitious, wayward, or pedantic judges who, as

Northcroft, the New Zealand judge, put it, "think this is an opportunity to write learned treatises on international law in defence of the Charter, but each upon different grounds."[48] While wavering in his own mind, Webb berated those who disagreed with him in theirs. "Meantime he antagonised every member of his Tribunal," Patrick wrote.[49]

Astonishingly, in private, Webb did not believe that aggressive war was actually a crime. Agreeing with Tojo Hideki's defense lawyer, Webb in an unreleased draft statement wrote that the Allies could not go beyond international law as it currently existed: "To claim that General MacArthur can, in effect, create new offences not known heretofore is to concede to him a power to raise himself, as it were, by his own shoe laces."[50] He found it impossible to believe that the various treaties confidently cited by the British bloc of judges really amounted to making aggression a crime. As Webb contended, the 1924 Geneva Protocol for the Pacific Settlement of International Disputes, which declared aggressive war to be an international crime, was a dud, opposed by Britain and never ratified by the requisite number of governments; the Kellogg-Briand Pact strenuously avoided any references to criminality, instead using the weaker language of renunciation and condemnation; Japan's acceptance of the Potsdam Declaration and its surrender on the USS *Missouri* did not suffice to make aggression a war crime.[51] Anticipating the blowback from his colleagues, he contended that dropping the aggression charges did not mean that the entire trial should be abandoned; it should be continued for conventional war crimes. But plowing forward as things were, he worried privately, the judges might "for all time be condemned by a large section of the world as judicial murderers."[52]

If Webb had stuck to these beliefs, the Tokyo trial might have entirely cracked up. How could General Headquarters possibly go forward if the chief judge himself thought that the court's core charges were not crimes at all, and that its executions for those counts would be nothing less than murder? How would the Allied governments respond to the prospect of dissents from the Australian, Indian, and Dutch judges, and probably more?

Yet Webb backed down. He clearly felt the weight of his role of president of the court and remained solicitous of MacArthur throughout the trial. For all his protestations of judicial independence, when the moment came to assert his own reading of the law even if it infuriated General Headquarters, he trimmed his sails.

As if trying to salve his conscience, Webb started out by assuring his fellow judges that the Allies could not "put the war criminals to death without trial. . . . That, I think, would amount to murder." The

Australian judge wrote soothingly that they could follow Nuremberg's interpretation of law, although with one big exception: "the doctrine of immunity of a head of state has no place here because the Emperor is not arraigned." Webb then offered some of his candid thinking, insisting that MacArthur could not "add to or modify international" law and that if the judges were to find that the Tokyo court's charter was not authorized by international law, they had a duty to disregard it: "We cannot bind ourselves to commit judicial murder." He denied that aggressive war had been a crime in the nineteenth and twentieth centuries; if making war was a crime, it must have become so since World War I. He bluntly noted that the Kellogg-Briand Pact never referred to war as a crime. And he mocked Keenan's argument that the horrors of war showed it to be criminal, since "war has always been horrible."

At this point, Webb sounded just about ready to dissent himself. Yet despite his own obvious skepticism, he flinched from the logical conclusion: telling his fellow judges that they should defy MacArthur and refuse to treat aggression as a war crime. Instead, drawing on papers provided to him by the Canadian judge, he claimed that the diplomatic correspondence leading to the Kellogg-Briand Pact showed that it was meant to confirm several prior antiwar agreements—including an unratified 1923 treaty, that League of Nations resolution in 1927, and a 1928 Pan-American Conference resolution—and therefore "we may safely hold that aggressive war is a crime, as contrary to the dictates of humanity."[53] The judges would, perhaps, become judicial murderers after all.

Having muddied the waters, Webb asked all the judges their opinion about the tribunal's jurisdiction.[54] The three Commonwealth judges sought frantically to salvage the leaking ship, with Northcroft of New Zealand urging Webb to make a swift, clear-cut judgment that argued simply that the court's jurisdiction came from the charter.[55]

The Canadian judge, E. Stuart McDougall, stoutly defended the tribunal's mandate and its charges for aggressive war. For him, aggression was criminalized in a variety of treaties and international agreements, offering what would become a standard litany: the arraignment of the kaiser in the Treaty of Versailles, the 1924 Geneva Protocol for the Pacific Settlement of International Disputes, a 1927 League of Nations resolution declaring aggression an international crime, a similar 1928 resolution by the Pan-American Conference, and the Kellogg-Briand Pact. While the Kellogg-Briand Pact had conspicuously failed to declare aggressive war a crime, the Canadian judge contended that an unlawful act that caused the deaths of human beings must face criminal judgment. Furthermore, he argued that aggression was criminalized by customary international law: "Nations of every race, creed and color from 1919 forward decried, outlawed, abhorred and declared criminal aggressive war. . . . The opinion or conscience of the civilized world could hardly have been more clearly seen."[56]

The only judge who thought that everything was fine was Zaryanov. Reliably punitive, indifferent to such bourgeois niceties as facts and law, the Soviet judge's rationales tended toward Bolshevik-inflected word salad.[57] The only Tokyo judge who would think to cite Joseph Stalin as a legal authority, he insisted that aggressive war was a crime since at least 1928. Yet he used a distinctive conception of aggression, carefully defining it to include Japan's border clashes with the Soviets but not the Soviet invasions of Poland, Finland, Lithuania, Latvia, or Estonia. He followed the party line laid down before Nuremberg by the Soviet jurist A. N. Trainin, an underling of Andrey Vyshinsky, that aggression was the most dangerous international crime, although "[i]t goes without saying that this does not refer to just wars, wars of liberation."[58] For Zaryanov, revolutionary wars were inherently defensive wars, waged in defense of peoples' rights. What mattered was not who started the war but what its goals were. When wars were aimed at defending national existence or the rights of the people, they could not be seen as aggressive; when wars were meant to enslave peoples or violate their inherent rights, they were aggressive.

Having redefined aggression, Zaryanov could readily go along with everything that the prosecution wanted, which was, after all, the standard role of the Stalinist judiciary. He accepted a long list of condemnations of aggression after World War I—the Treaty of Versailles, the Covenant of the League of Nations, the Kellogg-Briand Pact, and more—as showing that world public opinion had unanimously criminalized aggressive war. (Although he included a 1927 League of Nations resolution declaring aggression to be an international crime, he conveniently overlooked its 1939 resolution expelling the Soviet Union from the League for its invasion of Finland.)[59] He insisted on the "strict personal responsibility of the criminal leaders of state policy." He even swallowed the prosecution's argument that killing in an aggressive war was murder. Far from questioning the impartiality of the resentful victors to judge the vanquished, Zaryanov argued that the "moral readiness to inflict stern punishment" made those who suffered in the war against fascism ideally qualified to sit in judgment.[60]

"The Earliest Opportunity of Expressing My Dissent"

Appointed late to the Tokyo bench, Radhabinod Pal had not been there when the nine judges had unanimously announced that they had jurisdiction. "He initially felt that perhaps if he voiced his concerns, he might be able to make a difference," says his grandson Satyabrata Pal. "But when he realized that it was set in stone, he could only walk away or lay down in stone his dissenting opinion." Like many Bengalis, he may have resented how the British were dressing up their postwar retribution against the pro-Japanese Indian National Army in legal forms, most dramatically in the public trial of rebel officers at the Red Fort in Delhi—with Jawaharlal Nehru himself defending them in court.[61] As early as July 1946—one day after the independence of the Philippines, and just a few days after the United States carried out its first postwar nuclear test, at Bikini Atoll in the Marshall Islands—Pal wrote a watershed note, boldly telling Webb that he refused to accept aggression as an international crime and would not hold the defendants guilty for crimes when they had been acting as agents of the Japanese government.[62]

Pal flatly denied that aggressive war had been a crime in international law during Japan's conquests. Unlike his colleagues, he made no analysis of international treaties or custom, instead gesturing broadly at "the nature of the international law itself." The vaunted Kellogg-Briand Pact, he wrote, "could not change the international law so as to make war a crime, and failed to bring itself within the category of law as understood in the international system." Even if the Tokyo tribunal's charter made aggressive war a crime, he argued that such new law could not be applied retroactively "to render acts perfectly legal at their date illegal now." The court could only claim jurisdiction over the war that ended with Japan's recent surrender—that is, the Pacific War launched at Pearl Harbor, but not earlier invasions such as Manchuria.

The Indian judge warned that the Allied powers could not determine the court's verdict. Once the victors had chosen to place the fate of the accused in the hands of a tribunal, they gave up their advantages as the winners of the war, leaving "the whole matter to further investigation and decision." If the victors meddled with the outcome, a sham trial would be worse than summary executions, with results that "may not sit easily on the conscience of the civilized world."

Pal did not doubt that warfare was regulated by the conventional laws of armed conflict. But he argued that the acts of the defendants while acting as state officials could not be crimes under international law. That would mean acquitting all the defendants. Pal, announcing a dissent of epic scale, concluded with a thunderclap: "I am preparing a detailed judgment of my own on this point."[63]

Behind closed doors, the other judges reeled. Webb glumly noted "the greatest division of opinion among experts as to scope" of the law, "and even as to its existence."[64]

Infuriated, the British judge demanded that his Indian colleague resign—either not seeing or not minding how imperialistic he might sound. Patrick insisted that the judges' powers flowed from the court's charter, which clearly declared that it could charge individuals for crimes against peace. The tribunal had no competence to ask whether MacArthur had exceeded his mandate when he drew up the charter: "no Judge of this Tribunal has any power to pronounce an order that these acts are not crimes, or that there is no individual responsibility for these acts." A judge who could not accept that these were crimes bearing personal responsibility should never have joined the court in the first place. He raged against Pal:

> If any Judge, having accepted an appointment under the Charter, at any time finds himself unable to subscribe to the plain declaration in the Charter that these acts are crimes for which there shall be individual responsibility, he should tender his resignation to the Allied Powers, explain that he cannot execute their mandate, and leave them to take such action as they think right. If he continues to act, minded at the end of the trial to deny effect to the Charter's declaration and to defeat the Charter's expressed purpose, he commits a "fraud" upon the Charter and upon the Allied Powers.[65]

Undaunted, Pal retorted, "I took the earliest opportunity of expressing my dissent from the majority view." He insisted that the judges were open to interpret the charter, even holding that it did not define any crimes at all. While a conqueror nation could lawfully set up a war crimes tribunal, "such a conqueror is not competent to legislate on international law." Here Pal was saying no more than what Webb had already said: if aggression was not already an international crime, Douglas MacArthur could not make it one.

Pal politely flayed the British judge: "I do not agree that any Judge who would take a view of the Charter different from what my learned brother is taking would thereby commit a 'fraud' upon the Charter or upon the Allied Powers. I believe none of us can claim infallibility for his own view and unless we are absolutely sure of the correctness of a particular view we should not be intolerant of other possible views." Aware of how bad the British judge would look if he contrived to sack the Indian judge, he coolly dared Patrick to do his worst: "I do not know if it is my learned brother's view that it is also for the Tribunal to decide whether or not a Judge should tender his resignation and when should he do that. If not, his remarks in this respect would, I believe, be somewhat misplaced in a note for the Tribunal."[66]

The other judges balked at forcing Pal off the court. Soon after, Webb wrote that there was no need to say at this point if a judge who found the charter to be invalid should resign.[67]

Yet at the height of this clash with Patrick, Pal tried to resign in disgust. "He felt that he was not going to be able to deliver justice," says his grandson Satyabrata Pal. "He was just out on a limb on his own." Furthermore, as his son Pratip Bijoy Pal recalls, his beloved wife was gravely sick. The Indian judge asked MacArthur for transportation home, saying that he had been appointed for six months only and wanted to get back to private practice in Calcutta. Rather than seizing the chance to get rid of the independent-minded Pal, MacArthur felt that his departure would be bad for the trial and that it was "impracticable at this late date to replace him."[68] The British rulers of India agreed that it would be disastrous for him to quit.[69] The Raj ordered him to stay put.[70] After a few tense days, he agreed to stick it out through the end of the trial.[71]

Several weeks later, a stung Pal left Tokyo for a month to tend to his wife in Calcutta.[72] He arrived home just three months after a well-organized clash of Muslims against Hindus had left at least four thousand dead there. Shops and homes had been looted; harmless rickshaw drivers and shopkeepers were burned; one Muslim militia had trucks loaded with corpses stacked three feet high.[73] At a frightening, mournful time for the city that he adored, he lingered for so long that the British authorities in India suggested that perhaps he could stay home permanently without gutting the proceedings.[74] Pal replied that a temporary absence was allowed by the court's charter, but frostily added that a permanent withdrawal would be up to the government. He boldly offered the Raj the chance to sack him, telling them that "I have already submitted note of dissent from the rest of Tribunal" on the court's jurisdiction. "Differing from them I proposed substantially to uphold defence objection." If the crumbling British Empire wanted to fire him, he asked that it be done quickly.[75]

Having been told explicitly that Pal would side with the defense, the British decided to leave him on the bench anyway. His wife rallied enough that Pal could return to Tokyo, with MacArthur solicitously declaring himself delighted to hear she was recuperating.[76] Thoroughly alienated, anxious for his family and his country, Pal settled down in the seclusion of his rooms at the Imperial Hotel to write up his colossal dissent denying the authority of his own court.

Natural Law

If Pal and other skeptics could not accept that aggressive war was a crime under the Kellogg-Briand Pact or the court's charter, was there any other higher authority that could stand above? Were there alternative justifications for the court's jurisdiction over these defendants? The three leading answers ranged from the practical to the celestial.

First, the British judge had already gone for the simplest, positivist solution: the court's powers came from the charter drawn up by the Allied governments. Second, for a more abstract authority, the French judge pointed to customary international law, which he termed the product of "the universal conscience," coming before those principles were written down in treaties. He proposed a progressive, dynamic view of law as evolving along with international society. The world conscience's condemnation of aggression, he argued, would allow the tribunal to judge and execute the defendants even without such authorities as the Potsdam Declaration.[77] And third, seeking a higher authority still, Webb sent around another draft, this time introducing the ancient concept of natural law.[78]

Under the theory of natural law, international law rests on a universal human sense of right and wrong, or on a higher law of nature, which transcends particular cultures and countries.[79] For natural lawyers, law rests on moral reasoning.[80] This is obviously a controversial claim, and over the centuries wildly different policies have been justified by the law of nature, such as rejecting or endorsing colonial conquests.[81] The Tokyo charter would be lawful not merely because it had been decreed to be law but because it drew on moral authority.

In postwar Japan and Germany, natural law was meant to give a universal footing for the criminality of aggressive war and crimes against humanity. It would rule out rebuttals that Japanese culture was too different for Western legal judgment; as Cicero had written, natural law applied equally in Athens and Rome.[82] Furthermore, natural law was enticing for postwar Allied planners because it would allow the criminalization of acts that were legal under Nazi Germany's bloodstained laws. That was how the liberal German philosopher Karl Jaspers justified the Nuremberg trial: "in the sense of humanity, of human rights, and of natural law, and in the sense of freedom and democracy as understood by the western powers, there were already laws in existence by which deliberate crimes could be determined."[83]

There is a venerable Catholic tradition of natural law, which, drawing on St. Thomas Aquinas, bases earthly moral law on divine law.[84] The other judges were aware that, as Mei noted in his diary, Webb and his wife were "devout Catholic believers"—hinting that the Chinese judge believed Webb's faith might be informing his jurisprudence.[85] The Australian jurist grew close with a Jesuit priest at Sophia University, a Catholic institution in Tokyo, who believed that natural law could defend individual rights in Japan and hoped that the American occupation could turn the country Christian.[86] He apparently helped Webb with this draft, and to his gratitude would provide him with a vast treatise on the punishment of war crimes under natural law, heavily influenced by Catholic theologians.[87]

Whatever Webb might have believed at heart, none of his public and private pronouncements show any noticeable use of Catholic dogma. He did not want to rest the court's legitimacy on the charter, believing that the charter had to follow international law. Thus he looked to natural law as a higher authority, although not a divine one: "international law is based on the natural law; that is, on the mankind sense of right and wrong." Citing Hugo Grotius and a host of other authorities, he argued that unjust wars had always been unlawful.[88] That illegality of war had been dormant for centuries until reaffirmed by the Kellogg-Briand Pact, a treaty which he understood as not in itself international law but really an indication of the existence of the law against unjust war. Since international law was properly understood as a sublime law of nature manifested in international relations, he contended, aggressive war was surely a crime.[89]

This bold claim satisfied nobody. Although Webb was touchingly proud of his classical training in public international law for the Queensland bar, his draft was a resounding flop, not winning over Pal and prompting a breach even among the judges who were most in agreement with Webb.[90]

As Webb's paper made the rounds, Mei took the lead in adopting a tough line against the Japanese accused. Acutely aware that the court's decision could set a lasting historical precedent, he girded himself for a grand debate. In a forceful paper, his straightforward argument was similar to that of the British bloc: "I still believe, as I always did, that the jurisdiction of this Tribunal is clearly defined by the Charter, no more and no less." While some of the less intellectually self-confident judges preferred to hide behind Nuremberg's argument for its jurisdiction, Mei, wary of giving "the impression that we are a less competent court," instead wanted the two tribunals to work independently of each other. If the Asian and European courts wound up reaching similar conclusions about legal principles, "so much the better! For then those principles would have a 'double foundation,' being separately and independently upheld by both of the two greatest military tribunals the world has ever set up. Thus I am convinced that for the development of international law, and to strengthen the foundation of those of its principles in regard to war-crimes, we must not follow Nuremberg slavishly, at least not in appearance."

Although Mei privately believed that there was considerable substance to the complex claims of the Japanese defense lawyers, in front of his colleagues he was utterly confident in denying them. "I have never for a moment thought that the jurisdiction of our Tribunal as prescribed by the Charter is open to challenge," he wrote to the other judges. The judges were bound by the charter in totality, not least to try crimes against peace. The Allies had been entirely correct "in declaring through the Charter that aggressive war is a crime. . . . I am firmly convinced that the Charter is intrinsically sound and its provisions in regard to war-crimes are simply declaratory of principles of law already in existence, instead of creating new ones."[91]

In his academic writings, Mei had accepted natural law as an important part of Chinese jurisprudence.[92] Yet now he rejected Webb's reliance on natural law. He thought that the Australian judge had made a hash of the literature, muddling together such disparate authorities as Plato, Aristotle, medieval theologians, Jean-Jacques Rousseau, and twentieth-century scholars. Obviously enjoying the opportunity to flaunt his expertise in European sources, he donnishly wrote, "It would be absurd to say that the new Natural Law theory of such French advocates as Charmont or Saleilles is identical with that of such German Neo-Kantians, as for example, Stammler." Furthermore, since Mei believed that the tribunal's charter was enough to establish jurisdiction, throwing in "highly controversial" natural law would only generate unnecessary disputes.[93]

Mei's paper was crushing. Northcroft, who usually found Mei to be "a mild, almost passive" judge, was thrilled by the Chinese judge's "devastating criticism."[94] Almost unanimously, the other judges concluded that natural law could not be the basis for their authority.[95] Far from allaying doubts about imposing Western ideas upon the Japanese, Webb's invocation of a wholly foreign pantheon of European authorities could equally well have made the court seem even more alien. When McDougall, the Canadian judge, gently offered Webb some constructive suggestions in an attempt to unite the judges, the chief judge snarled at him, curtly refusing even to read his conciliatory paper—a slap that left the British bloc of judges lastingly shocked.[96] Patrick, drawing on Mei's erudite critique with undisguised pleasure, griped to the British government that Webb's paper "contained *twenty pages* of quotations from such writers as Aristotle, Polybius, St. Paul, Ambrose of Milan, St. Augustine, Isidor of Seville, Thomas Aquinas, Ayala, Molina, Suarez, Grotius, Vattel, Sylvester Maurus, Colonna, John Gerson, and a host of others."[97] Northcroft privately called it "an impossible document," cobbled together for Webb by young researchers: "It read like a student's not very good essay on international law."[98]

Mei was impeccably polite as he dismantled Webb's essay, fondly referring to the other judges as the "charming brothers." Although his superb English was better than that of several of his colleagues, he graciously declared himself "entirely unqualified and incompetent" to comment on the style of the drafts.[99] Despite that, Webb was furious at the Chinese judge for drubbing him in intellectual sparring.[100] Northcroft watched in shock as Webb "subjected the poor Chinaman to vulgar verbal abuse in Chambers before other judges."[101]

Trounced, Webb retreated from using natural law. Soon after Mei's critique, Webb wrote that if it was up to him he would prefer to cite natural law as expounded by Aristotle, Cicero, St. Augustine, and the rest, but would not: "An international law based on the unalterable natural law has a great appeal but I feel bound to follow the law as it has been declared by English courts."

Falling into line behind Patrick, the Australian chief judge now argued that Japan by surrendering had accepted the authority of MacArthur and the terms of the Potsdam Declaration. In a nod to Pal, he conceded that the charter had no power to create new crimes. But he now contended that aggressive war, legal for centuries, had been suddenly criminalized by the Kellogg-Briand Pact—a complete reversal from when he had believed that unjust wars had always been illegal and downplayed the significance of that pact. He ducked behind the Nuremberg judgment, which ruled, as he put it, that "practically the whole civilized world, including Japan, expressly agreed to stigmatize aggressive war in such terms and in such circumstances that it must have been intended to regard it as a legal crime." As to the objection of victors' justice, Webb believed that the judges should not be personally biased against the defendants—setting a low bar, which even so would not be cleared by Mei or Jaranilla, both bitter after their wartime ordeals at Japanese hands. The Australian chief judge declared himself in full agreement with Zaryanov that there was nothing wrong with judgment by Allied judges: "This is a military tribunal . . . which is invariably constituted of nationals of the victors."[102]

Zaryanov, of all people, remained Webb's most reliable ally. Backing up the Australian chief judge, he declared that he had no qualms about the criminality of aggression. Putting Soviet political imperatives front and center, he asserted that the court's true legal basis was the "historic justice of the victory of democratic states and freedom-loving nations over the forces of reaction and aggression in World War II." The task of the tribunal was to "consolidate this victory."[103] Grateful for the support, Webb—in contrast to his insolence toward the judges from China, Britain, and Canada—unctuously thanked the Soviet judge for his "scholarly and courteous criticism," which was "typical of your attitude throughout the trial."[104]

Webb gave up on unanimity. Wearily sending around a new draft that incorporated several suggestions from Zaryanov, he sought to capture the opinions of eight judges, some of whom disagreed among themselves.[105] He suggested including several clashing arguments from the majority— justifications based on Japan's surrender, or the general assent of civilized nations as demonstrated by agreements from the interwar years, or natural law—with a public warning that the judges did not all take the same viewpoints. He braced for trouble when outsiders discovered how bitterly divided the court was. "I do not know how the world regards a decision of a number of judges arrived at for different reasons," he wrote to the other judges. "However, that is a political consideration."[106]

THE NEXT DISSENTERS

Webb immediately lost half of his majority of eight. First the British bloc of judges decided to write their own opinion. Webb curtly declared that he would do likewise, producing a draft that retained natural law as a possible way of criminalizing aggression but also suggested that the Kellogg-Briand Pact had made war a crime.[107] Northcroft noted confidentially that he and Patrick got "short petulant letters" from Webb which demonstrated that he had not understood their views but did reject them.[108]

Next Röling, whom Webb had optimistically counted in his majority, made his debut as a court renegade. In a long paper, he shocked his fellow judges by denying that aggressive war was a crime. This necessitated a dissent from the court's verdict, since he could not convict men for something that he did not believe was a crime. "In this trial the fate of the accused is relatively of no importance," he wrote loftily. "What matters is the decision about international law."

The Dutch government tried to rein him in. As he later wrote, the commission in The Hague advised him that aggression was a recognized crime in international law. "I was accustomed to working as an independent judge," he recalled, "guided only by the law, without any interference from outside." He says that he threatened to resign, and was relieved when his government backed down.[109]

Instead of the epoch-making trial for aggression sought by his own government, Röling wanted to charge the Japanese leaders only for conventional war crimes and atrocities, albeit with greater blame for those crimes if they had cooperated in launching the war. Although the charter gave jurisdiction over the planning or waging of aggressive war, he argued that aggression could only be punished if it was already a crime under existing international law.[110] Thus "the lives of the prisoners are pawns in the interpretation of law and justice as it existed in the thirties."

After a long study of the interwar period, Röling concluded that nations still had a "sovereign right" to start a war. He rubbished the claim that aggressive war had suddenly become a crime in the years after World War I. Crimes against peace, as written into the Nuremberg charter by the Allies, had "appeared from nowhere." Even the famous Kellogg-Briand Pact "was merely the expression of a pacific mood," and had quickly been hobbled into irrelevance by governments who reserved the right to fight in self-defense, while deciding for themselves what counted as self-defense. Nor had the Kellogg-Briand Pact provided for individual criminal responsibility.

Further unnerving the other judges, the Dutch judge suggested that Japan had good reason to reject restrictions on its ability to make war. Although Japan had joined the Kellogg-Briand Pact, he wrote, its neighbors had not reciprocated with real concessions in their disputes. The Pact, he wrote, "seems a clever manoeuvre to perpetuate existing conditions not only by force, but also by virtue of quasi-justice. It would be an expression of power politics in disguise, a demonstration of 'justice' in the service of power instead of power being subservient to justice."

If treaties did not outlaw aggressive war, what about natural law? Ridiculing Webb with none of Mei's courteousness, Röling scoffed that natural law, if it was ever "more than a mere desideratum," was not a part of positive international law in the nineteenth and early twentieth centuries. "Nor do I feel I can quote Grotius, Gentili, and Vattel in the trial of Japanese aggression," he wrote, since their ideals had not been "living law" in their own eras of imperial violence. Repudiating his own country's conquests in Indonesia, the Dutch judge powerfully denounced European colonialism: "I hesitate to approach the Far East in our effort to determine the criminality of aggression with quotations from idealists and philosophers of the very period when our heroes and soldiers were conquering its territories in what could hardly be called a defensive war."

He recoiled at the prosecution's claim that the killings that began an aggressive war should be prosecuted as murders. Killings in war might be illegal or perhaps even criminal, but unless they were conventional war crimes, they were not murder.[111] If the Japanese had given their declaration of war a minute before hitting Pearl Harbor, he asked, was that essentially different from giving it an hour and a half afterward?

Röling thought that General Headquarters had every right to lock up threatening Japanese leaders; there was no real difference between preventing "a dangerous lunatic or a dangerous politician from doing harm." Yet he warned that "using war crimes trials for the purpose of eliminating undesirable elements would mean the mixing up of justice and expediency, and would frustrate both." He doubted that criminal punishment would deter future aggressors, since those making war either hoped to win or did not care what happened to themselves in defeat.

Unlike Pal, who argued that the defendants could not be charged for acts of state, Röling was prepared to find the accused guilty for all sorts of conventional war crimes, as well as crimes against humanity. He hoped that a trial solely for such cruelties would fulfill the Allied political goal of educating the Japanese public about the real causes of the war. Along the way it would have to fix blame for launching the war, with the proponents of starting a war held more blameworthy for the war crimes that followed. Since much of the fury among the Allied publics was over Axis atrocities, such a trial would satisfy the "desire for vengeance."

This was a dissent in everything but name, and previewed most of his minority opinion. Yet Röling seemed uncomfortable in his emerging role of rebel, appealing for unity. He suggested postponing these divisive debates about jurisdiction until the final judgment, hoping that harmony would emerge by then. He wrote that he preferred to keep minority viewpoints out of the public spotlight, as was the custom in Dutch courts. Still, he added that if one of the other judges insisted on a dissent—as Pal had already announced he would—then he would write a short one himself. The Tokyo trial was now certain to have two formal dissents.[112]

.   .   .

Webb muddled forward with minor revisions to his clunker of a draft, still including a section on natural law, petulantly saying that he had "recast my reasons without altering my views."[113] Counting noses, he reckoned that six of eleven judges thought that the Kellogg-Briand Pact had made aggressive war a crime.[114]

Yet the damage was already done. Jaranilla, desperate to avoid dissenting or diverging opinions that would lessen the impact of the court's final judgment, urged his bickering colleagues either to give a minimal decision based only on the authority of the charter—or simply stay mum about jurisdiction until the end of the trial. Better silence than cacophony.[115]

Zaryanov exhorted the judges to issue their ruling about jurisdiction swiftly. He remained more or less uninterested in the reasons why. Nearly all the judges, he somehow claimed, agreed on the principles, differing on "only argumentation and aspects of certain details." By issuing a decisive ruling soon, the court could box in the defense counsel before they even got started. He saw no need to let dissenters express their viewpoints; if Pal or Röling could not be persuaded, they could be hushed up.[116]

Myron Cramer, the U.S. judge, blanched at this. Supporting Jaranilla, he urged waiting until the final judgment to rule on jurisdiction. The members were too divided to issue a majority opinion. He fretted that if it became public how riven the judges were, then law journals and newspapers that were now keenly debating the merits of the Nuremberg judgment would turn critical of the Tokyo court itself.[117]

To lose two dissenters may be regarded as a misfortune; to lose three looks like carelessness. Yet now the French judge, Henri Bernard—a fifth member of Webb's ostensible majority of eight—warned that he too might dissent.

His was a more measured dispute. Unlike Pal, the French judge was comfortable that MacArthur had the right to set up a tribunal to prosecute aggression, satisfied that individuals could be held criminally responsible for acts of state, and even persuaded that crimes against peace and crimes against humanity were criminal under "natural and universal law." In the absence of a truly global court of justice, the Allies had "not only the right but the duty" to set up a war crimes tribunal. Instead, Bernard had a more doctrinal complaint: "it is useless to consider whether and to what extent breaches of treaties are a crime." He hoped that the majority might avoid that issue, but if not, he would write a dissent. This was a rupture that a more collegial group of judges or a more skillful chief judge might have avoided.[118]

These splits would never be fixed. Held together by the three British Commonwealth jurists, a majority of the feuding judges did manage to agree that they had jurisdiction, but were unable to provide any explanation for rejecting the defense motions to dismiss the trial.[119] Mei, who had once hoped that Pal would be the only dissenter, anxiously sought to avoid giving outsiders "the impression that the Tribunal is necessarily divided."[120] As New Zealand's judge wrote in despair, "this problem has become more difficult and the evil day has been postponed to the final judgment."[121]

The Tokyo court's struggle to justify its own legitimacy has remained a point of bitter protest among Japanese nationalists to this day. It is a fixation for Aso Taro, a populist stalwart of the ruling Liberal Democratic Party who became prime minister in 2008–9. As foreign minister in February 2006, under questioning by a Diet committee, Aso bluntly denounced Webb's "lack of a clear response" to the arguments from Kiyose Ichiro, Tojo's lawyer, questioning the court's validity.[122]

CHAPTER 17

The Defense Rises

A S THE TOKYO TRIAL wore on, the accused men in Sugamo Prison joked mordantly among themselves how fortunate it was that they had built such a nice jail. Even Marquis Kido Koichi, accustomed to surroundings that were literally palatial, declared himself comfortable enough in his small cell with three straw mats. They busied themselves with reading and writing, with many defendants churning out traditional Japanese poems. Tojo Hideki, who began to show up at services run by the Buddhist priest at the prison, mixed newfound spirituality with old defiance: "Even if the eternal truth shines on my face, I do not shrink."[1]

As the defense began its case in January 1947, Mei Ruao expected a fierce battle.[2] Since the judges had not yet explained their jurisdiction, the resolute defense lawyers, both Japanese and American, were bound to keep raising fundamental questions about whether aggression was a crime under international law and whether the court itself was lawful. Yet this came at a crisis moment outside the courtroom. After huge protests by labor unions and leftist organizers outside the Imperial Palace, General Douglas MacArthur announced that he would forbid a nationwide strike by government workers and public utility unions that threatened to topple the conservative, pro-American government of Yoshida Shigeru. As American troops went on alert, ready to enforce his edict, the unions backed down.[3] This marked a shift at General Headquarters, starting a retreat from its more radical liberalization plans.[4]

The defense counsel put forward several motions to dismiss the charges against the accused. In one joint motion, defense lawyers argued that their clients were facing vague charges that had not previously been defined as crimes, that the defendants' actions had really been those of a sovereign state, and that aggressive war was not a crime. Sir William Webb dismissively said, "All those points were put in May, last, and subsequently by learned counsel"—not mentioning that the judges still had not answered those points.[5] When some defense lawyers moved for a mistrial, Webb refused to hear such a motion until the whole trial was concluded. Despite the backstage squabbling among the judges, he loftily said that an "overwhelming majority" of the judges had already decided that they had jurisdiction "for reasons to be given later. Those reasons will be given in due course."

American defense lawyers pugnaciously filed a motion contending that without an act of Congress, MacArthur had no legal authority to create the Tokyo court. This offended Webb: "There is no need to publicly challenge the position of the Supreme Commander. . . . [Y]ou will do it as a respectful legal argument and not as a political harangue. This is not the floor of Congress or the floor of the Senate of the United States or of any other parliament." The legality of U.S. processes, the Australian chief judge said, was a question for the United States: "We are not a court of any of the particular countries concerned." An American defense lawyer shot back that they intended to go to the U.S. federal courts in Washington. Webb scornfully told him to do his best in Washington, Ottawa, or Moscow.[6]

A chorus of American lawyers rose with motions that their clients should walk free, on the grounds that even if all the prosecution's evidence went unchallenged, it would not prove their guilt beyond a reasonable doubt.[7] One American defense counsel argued that it was impossible to prove a conspiracy among bitterly feuding Japanese politicians who had flailed through seventeen different cabinets in the period covered by the indictment. Some of the army generals argued that the prosecution's evidence showed only that they had merely been carrying out orders from more senior officers.[8] General Matsui Iwane's lawyer said that his superiors had decided to attack Nanjing, and that there was no evidence to establish beyond a reasonable doubt that he had ordered or allowed the massacres of civilians and unarmed soldiers.[9]

Even Tojo joined in, ably represented by a Philadelphia defense lawyer who had been sent by the American Bar Association to ensure that the defendants got a fair trial.[10] Channeling his client's defiance, this lawyer insisted that there was not enough evidence to convict the former prime minister for aggressive war, and that the prosecution had not shown evidence that Tojo had "issued a single positive order" to any field officer or camp commander to commit or permit war crimes.[11]

Kido's skillful American lawyer argued that the prosecution's evidence actually vindicated his client. He deftly sampled from the lord keeper's diary to show him as pro-British, an opponent to the army over Manchuria, and a voice for diplomacy before Pearl Harbor.[12] The most powerful claim of innocence came from Togo Shigenori, the former foreign minister. His American counsel, Major Ben Bruce Blakeney, argued that his client had striven tenaciously for peace with the United States; Japan's attacks on the United States and the British Empire were "in spite of, certainly not because of, Togo's efforts."[13]

These defense motions offered the prosecutors a fresh opportunity to make their case in more pointed terms in their reply. They held a rather awkward advantage: their U.S. chief, Joseph Keenan, was sidelined in Washington for major surgery. Because of his blustery ineptitude and his open feud with Webb about the war guilt of the emperor, his absence was greeted with general relief among the judges and prosecutors.[14] While he was away, the British associate prosecutor, Arthur Comyns Carr, became the dominant face of the prosecution. He worked hand in glove with the acting chief prosecutor, Frank Tavenner, a U.S. federal prosecutor from Virginia, who proved to be icily efficient. Comyns Carr, delighted to see the back of Keenan, only feared that he would return or try to control things from Washington by cable.[15]

With undisguised relish, Comyns Carr gave a crisp, punchy synopsis of the evidence against each defendant. He scorned the defense contention that Japan had been acting in self-defense. To the contrary, he said, all the Allies—which would include the Soviet Union—had been provoked by various aggressive moves of Japan: "There is not the smallest evidence of an intention by any of them to attack Japan." Relying on the U.S. Supreme Court's ruling in *Yamashita*, he argued that Japan's top commanders could be held responsible either for ordering war crimes or for failing to take steps to restrain their troops from committing war crimes. Perhaps most effectively, he pointed out that Japan's senior leaders had often worked to change their country's policies, which implied that they could have found ways to avert war, either by swaying their colleagues, rallying public opinion, or resigning in protest. He said, "it is the duty of even a soldier or sailor, and equally certainly of a civilian, to disobey an order which he knows to be contrary to International Law."[16]

He condemned every suspect in turn, excoriating Tojo Hideki as the head of the alleged conspiracy, and General Matsui Iwane for his command role during the Nanjing massacre.[17] Hirota Koki, accused of taking advantage of the Marco Polo Bridge clash to invade China, had been "an aggressor from start to finish, and the contrast between his public and private words and acts shows that he was a particularly clever one." Comyns Carr said that Shigemitsu Mamoru, as foreign minister, had contemptuously "turned a deaf ear" to Allied protests about their prisoners of war, lying about the abuses and denying requests to visit the camps.[18]

Comyns Carr held Togo Shigenori, who had been disgusted by Nazi totalitarianism, responsible for building Japan's relationship with Germany. Togo was condemned for Pearl Harbor, wrongly accused of agreeing with bellicose decisions in crucial meetings where he had actually argued against war.[19] In a more knotty allegation, Togo was faulted for passing along Allied complaints about the abuse of prisoners of war but doing nothing to ensure that Japan honored its pledge to uphold the Geneva Convention. "Every one of the accused must have been aware of the horrible notoriety attached to the Japanese army by the outrages at Nanking and elsewhere in China," Comyns Carr declared, "and of the danger that this might recur." Their duty, he said, was to bring the abuses to the cabinet and to resign if no improvements were made.[20]

The most delicate case for the Allied prosecutors was Kido. Comyns Carr's brief presumed that the monarch was a figure whose decisions mattered, begging the question of why his top adviser should be on trial but not him. The lord keeper of the privy seal, said Comyns Carr, had dissuaded Emperor Hirohito from restraining the army and "from taking a firm line about anything for fear it should bring him into controversy." His diary "proves him an aggressor at heart." Before Pearl Harbor, instead of installing a peaceful prime minister, Kido had "procured Tojo's appointment as premier." Yet if that was a crime, then surely it was a crime committed by the emperor as well, who was the one who actually named a prime minister. Kido "knew very well of the plans for the surprise attack" on the United States, yet had neither spoken up nor resigned. During the war, Comyns Carr declared, "From start to finish it does not appear that he ever drew the attention of the Emperor . . . to the moral aspect either of the initiation of the Pacific War or of the manner in which it was conducted." Again, this suggested that the emperor could have done something to prevent the invasions and atrocities that his army was committing in his name.[21]

The Soviet judge, Major General Ivan Zaryanov, was enraged to see defense lawyers doing what defense lawyers do. He railed against the claim that Japan had fought in self-defense, decrying "[t]his absolutely inadmissible attempt to show that democratic powers were aggressors in World War II." By waging aggressive war, the Japanese defendants were "responsible for this gravest of crimes."[22]

Webb privately exhorted the other judges that "it is clear beyond reasonable doubt" that Japan had vastly expanded its Asian empire by waging aggressive wars, had brutalized civilians, and had fought with "the greatest barbarity and in contravention of practically every rule of warfare and in complete disregard of human rights, dignity, honour and feelings." Each of the defendants, he wrote, had played a leading role in these notorious campaigns. None of them had taken any real steps to prevent aggression or atrocities, which they must have known about: "It would be revolting to common sense to suggest that such persons were ignorant of facts so notorious."[23]

Despite the vigorous efforts of the defense lawyers, the judges would not dismiss the charges against any of the defendants—not even Togo and Shigemitsu, against whom the prosecution case was most obviously ramshackle. They quickly ruled that the trial could proceed.[24] In private, the prosecutors reckoned that they had presented enough evidence to hang seven or eight generals, including Tojo and Matsui, while Shigemitsu would probably be acquitted.[25]

Inequality of Arms

After Comyns Carr's oration, the exhausted defense counsel, straining to keep up with the voluminous facts and the complex law, asked for a month to prepare their case. Not disguising his irritation, Webb gave them two weeks.[26]

The defense was badly overmatched by the resources of the prosecution. The prosecutors had the might of Allied armies behind them, could gather evidence from Japan's conquered government, and had eleven Allied governments to provide staff, research, and legal expertise. The defense was a threadbare assortment of Japanese and American lawyers doing their best under impossible circumstances.

They pleaded repeatedly to Webb for more staff, translators, resources, and time.[27] Many of the underpaid Japanese lawyers had abandoned their regular professional work and were worried about their livelihoods; to their embarrassment, they had to beseech the court for more money. Their allowances were not sufficient to cover office expenses.[28] Although General Headquarters had assembled enough American lawyers to ensure that each defendant got at least one American counsel, it was hard to coordinate a group of roughly a hundred defense lawyers. While the prosecution formed a largely united front in court, the defense of one accused man could implicate another one, which meant that the defense lawyers were inevitably splintered among themselves.[29]

Most of the defense counsel were Japanese and the rest of them Americans, which meant that most of the lawyers were unfamiliar with the workings of a trial "conducted largely upon Anglo-Saxon principles," as New Zealand's judge described it.[30] One leading Japanese defense lawyer explained that Japan had an inquisitorial criminal system with judges cross-examining the accused, unlike the American-style or British-style adversarial proceedings under way at Ichigaya, where prosecution and defense clashed before an impartial judge.[31] (In fact, the judges in the Tokyo trial did often interject questions.)

Before the defense counsel could even open their case, the Soviet Union made a strenuous effort to silence them. Zaryanov, having curried favor with Webb during the fracas over jurisdiction, sought to have defense statements submitted to the judges in advance to be censored to prevent Japanese defense lawyers from "using the Tribunal as an open forum for the propaganda of fascist and militarist ideas and imperialist conceptions." When the other judges refused, next he asked that the defense submit its opening statement to the judges, meaning to prevent the Japanese counsel from any fresh attacks on the jurisdiction of the court or the illegality of aggression: "The aggressive war was planned, prepared, initiated and waged by definite individuals who are personally responsible for this gravest of crimes." Although the other judges blocked him, a mainstay of the majority was doing his utmost to quash the defense.[32]

It was against that dismal prologue that the defense lawyers took the floor for opening statements. This began badly. William Logan Jr., the American defense lawyer representing Kido, explained that the defendants found it impossible to agree on a common opening statement, disagreeing among themselves about "some of the various statements of facts, reasonings, philosophies, inferences and complicities." Several of the defendants set themselves apart from the entirety of the defense opening statement that was to come, while another took issue with bits of it.[33]

With that, Kiyose Ichiro, the gray-haired defense lawyer for Tojo and others, rose. The *Yomiuri* had once scorned Kiyose as an advocate of militarism and imperialism, thus making "a most ideal defense counsel for war criminal suspects."[34] From the bench, Mei disapproved of his pedantic bearing, weedy voice, and careless tailoring, but had to admit that he spoke calmly and cogently, with a modest manner.[35] An *Asahi Shimbun* reporter once described Kiyose as unshaven, short, in everyday clothes, but he knew English law and had a fighting spirit as he fired off objections.[36] He wore his erudition heavily, giving plummy orations in posh English.[37]

Kiyose delivered an extended oration that could serve as a master template for generations of subsequent nationalistic Japanese defenses of the country's wartime record. He presented Japan as using its might on behalf of fellow Asians trampled by Western colonialists. Encircled by a predatory West, Japan had no choice but to fight a justifiable war of self-defense. Since a crime ordinarily consists both of a criminal act and a criminal intention, if the defense could prove that the defendants have been motivated by innocent self-defense, they might have committed no crime. As Webb told the other judges, if the accused could "show that they held that view genuinely and reasonably, it *may* afford a defense, even though the Tribunal does not agree with their view."[38]

The defense faced an uphill climb. The classic standard for self-defense—articulated by Daniel Webster in 1841–42 and freshly reaffirmed in the Nuremberg judgment—was that a government must "show a necessity of self-defence, instant, overwhelming, leaving no choice of means, and no moment for deliberation." Furthermore, the defending government must do "nothing unreasonable or excessive; since the act justified by the necessity of self-defence, must be limited by that necessity, and kept clearly within it." It would be no easy task to demonstrate that Japan's recent wars would meet both of those requirements of necessity and proportionality.[39]

Although Webb insisted that the defense's opening statement concentrate on facts and evidence, not on arguments about the law itself, Kiyose carefully skirted that prohibition. He denied that individuals could be convicted as criminals for their political acts while "acting on behalf of the state in its sovereign capacity." He insisted that the killings at Pearl Harbor, as well as in Japan's initial attacks on Hong Kong and the Philippines, had not been murder but an ordinary wartime loss of life. He rejected the prosecution's charges of a criminal conspiracy as alien to Japanese law, declaring that "the doctrine of conspiracy, as has been developed in England and America as one entity, cannot be deemed to constitute international law." It was wrong "to apply a particular legal theory which has developed in a particular country with its peculiar historical background at this Tribunal as if it were a general principle of law of universal application."

Kiyose contended that Japan's system of cabinet government was incapable of conspiracy. Cabinet authority drew on Japan's history of rule by a consortium of senior statesmen, known as the *genro*. He was in good company in noting that the conspiracy charges built for Nuremberg did not fit the Japanese context well. As Webb himself privately told the Australian prime minister, "there is no one leader of all the accused like

Hitler or Goering. There were different leaders at different periods."[40] Japan had lacked an equivalent to both the Führer and the *Führerprinzip* of its German allies, instead going through seventeen cabinets in the years under scrutiny. As prime minister, Tojo had wielded more power than any single person in Japan for at least half a century, but his policies had relied on many other leaders. When pressed to resign in July 1944, he had quietly left office in a way unimaginable for Adolf Hitler. Awkwardly for the Allied prosecutors, only one Japanese leader had been in office for the entire period covered by the indictment: Hirohito.[41]

Kiyose argued that the Kellogg-Briand Pact did not stipulate that aggressive war is an international crime and could not deprive Japan of its right to self-defense. Furthermore, a state invoking self-defense had "the sole and absolute discretion to determine the valid existence of such right"—which meant that no outsiders could second-guess what a government did in the name of self-defense. This was the theoretical prelude to a protracted retelling of Japan's foreign policy as legitimate self-defense, the actions of a peaceful, victimized nation struggling to defend its independence and culture ever since the U.S. Navy squadron of Commodore Matthew Perry sailed into Tokyo Bay in 1853 to force the country open to foreigners.

For the first time in the Tokyo trial, Kiyose put racism front and center. The entire Japanese nation, he said, was devoted to the "abolition of racial discrimination." With Western empires dominating much of southern Asia and threatening to carve up China, Japan had a special duty to promote "the common development of all Asiatic races." Japan and China "are of the same race," using the same Confucian ethics and writing the same characters. He proudly pointed out that the Greater East Asia Conference in Tokyo in November 1943 had formally called for abolishing racial discrimination. Although many Japanese nationalists in this period saw themselves as representing a superior Yamato race, Kiyose dismissed "any alleged theory of Japanese racial superiority" as a fanciful invention of the prosecutors.

Having extolled Japan's opposition to racism, Kiyose was hard put to explain away its alliance with Nazi Germany. "Intentional violation of human decency as was alleged to have been committed against the Jews in Germany was never present in Japan," he said, in a muted reference to the Holocaust over two years after the liberation of Auschwitz. He averred that "there is no taint of racial superiority in Japan as is found in Germany," while insisting that "the Japanese Government had no intention to conquer the world in cooperation with Germany and Italy."[42]

THE EMPIRE STRIKES FIRST

Kiyose launched into an alternative history of Japanese imperialism, justifying its expansion at every stage as defensive.

Japan, he maintained, had a legitimate claim to special rights in Manchuria. With a large population overflowing its home islands, and emigration to the United States blocked by hateful nativism, Japan had nowhere else to send its swelling populace. He presented the renegade Kwantung Army as a small, plucky force encircled by menacing Chinese threatening its legal right to be in Manchuria. After the Mukden clash in September 1931, he said, "the Kwantung Army for its own self-defense and for the execution of its duty had to defeat the Chinese forces."

In the rest of China, Kiyose held that the hostile Chinese had provoked and insulted the Japanese beyond endurance. Although Japan wanted nothing more than neighborly concord and a common defense against Communism, he said, Chiang Kai-shek had connived with the Chinese Communists. He blamed the Chinese for escalating after the skirmish at the Marco Polo Bridge in July 1937, while peace-loving Japan pursued a "policy of non-aggravation." When Japan had marched three army divisions into north China in late August, that was "to safeguard her lawful interests." He lapsed into the passive voice to describe the massive invasion of China: "the hostilities, against Japan's desire, spread far and wide."

The atrocities in China were "admittedly most regrettable," he said, but "are believed to be unduly magnified and in some degree fabricated." Since Japan had sought racial friendship with the Chinese, Kiyose said, it was "quite unthinkable" that the defendants would have ordered or ignored such horrors. The charges against the accused were "without foundation," and the defense "shall leave no stone unturned to prove that none of the accused ever ordered, authorized or permitted such acts or deliberately and recklessly disregarded his legal duty."

Kiyose, who was fiercely anti-Communist, was disgusted by the charges of Japanese aggression against the Soviet Union: "these accusations are beyond the pale of this Tribunal." Japan, he said, had no intention of attacking the Soviet Union, and the two border battles raised by the Soviets had been amicably resolved. As proof that Japan had no aggressive intentions, he pointed to the treaty of neutrality it had signed with the Soviet Union in 1941. It was the Soviets who had committed aggression and violated that treaty in their August 1945 attack on Japan, with the decision to attack made at the Yalta conference—an accusation that implicated not just Joseph Stalin but Franklin Delano Roosevelt and Winston Churchill too.

Japan's alliance with Nazi Germany and Italy was presented as self-defense against Communist subversion. The Soviet Union was actively exporting revolution, threatening the Japanese Empire. Since the Communists had been plotting the destruction of both Germany and Japan, the Axis powers had been "obliged for their self-protection" to band together.[43]

The war against the United States, too, was put down to "the supreme necessity" of self-defense, with the Americans as the real aggressors. With the Japanese "unwittingly" bogged down in China, the United States had pressured and intimidated them by backing the Nationalist government in China. Joining with China, Britain, and Holland, the United States had put "an iron ring of encirclement" around Japan. After the United States misunderstood what Kiyose blandly called "Japan's peaceful sending of troops to French Indo-China," the subsequent American, British, and Dutch economic sanctions amounted to something close to violence: "The inalienable right to live was deprived from the Japanese people."

Togo Shigenori, the foreign minister who had pressed for meaningful concessions in Indochina and China to mollify the United States, had to sit silently as Kiyose ignored the possibility that Japan could have withdrawn from those occupied lands. The U.S. oil embargo, Kiyose said, hobbled Japan's innocuous war machine: "Japan's navy was thus to lose mobility after her oil in stock was exhausted; solution of the China Incident was made practically impossible; Japan's defense was emasculated." For Kiyose, the oil embargo amounted to an act of war. Although Japan had made "sincere efforts" for peace, after the Hull note it was "crystal clear that not one single factor contributing to a *casus belli* could be settled by pacific means." In the end Japan's government "was forced at last to resolve upon recourse to the right of self-defense."

Kiyose presented the bolt from the blue at Pearl Harbor not as a surprise attack but the product of an embarrassing bureaucratic snafu. Japan had tried to notify the United States with a note to be delivered twenty-five minutes before the raid began, Kiyose said, but the deciphering and typing in Washington took too long. Anyway, the Americans knew that a diplomatic rupture had come and had intercepted most of Japan's note, he said, so they could hardly have been surprised.

Kiyose accepted the legitimacy of the standard laws of warfare, but insisted that Japan had not carried out "terrorism and atrocities . . . of the same type that Germany committed." Japan had strictly sought to obey the rules of armed conflict, he said. He would only concede that "inhumane acts may have been committed" late in the war when Japanese troops ran short on food, lacked orders from their commanders, or faced "cruel guerrilla warfare by natives." None of the accused, he said, had ordered or permitted atrocities. Whatever war crimes against Allied prisoners or civilians might have happened were "incidental errors on the part of individuals," not national policy.

Wrapping up, Kiyose declared that truth "is not a matter of proving that one party is entirely right and the other absolutely wrong." He loftily urged the judges to find the deeper causes of modern wars, whether "due to racial prejudice or unequal distribution of natural resources or mere misunderstanding between governments." The real injustice, he suggested, was Western bigotry toward Asians and the unfairness that other countries had the natural resources that Japan needed.[44]

Americans were shocked by the boldness of Kiyose's opening statement. "All the hoary propaganda myths propagated by the Japanese war lords to justify their crimes are being heard again at the war crimes trial in Tokyo," editorialized *The New York Times*. "To present such a defense at this late date, and before an Allied tribunal, is an impertinence. The Nazis did not dare to equal it."[45]

Some Japanese citizens recoiled at Kiyose's contentions. During the invasion of Manchuria, Yokota Kisaburo, a future chief justice of Japan, had spoken up against threadbare claims of self-defense, arguing that a railway clash could not possibly justify the Kwantung Army's assaults on major Chinese cities.[46] One Tokyo man, carefully following the courtroom proceedings in Japanese newspapers, complained that the defense lawyers could shamelessly "talk black into white" and urged the "heaviest penalties" for the accused.[47]

Soon after Kiyose finished his statement in court, Tojo Hideki's younger brother, Tojo Tadao, forty-six years old, was swept up in a police raid of homeless people in an Osaka subway station. After suffering paralysis on one side of his body, he had lost his job and wound up on the streets. Such bleak stories were all too common in postwar Japan, yet the younger Tojo interpreted his tribulation as fitting punishment for the sins of his brother. "This life of a vagrant is only what might have been expected of one who shares the blood of the man who has plunged many to the rock bottom of life in apology to these people," he said.[48]

The judges' failure to explain their jurisdiction hung over the defense's opening. Although Webb had forbidden arguments about the law from the opening statements, another Japanese defense lawyer, Takayanagi Kenzo, rose after Kiyose to challenge the jurisdiction of the court.

Takayanagi, a prominent legal scholar who had argued that Japan needed to expand on the Asian continent, would later become president of Seikei University in Tokyo.[49] He had prepared a massive opening statement in which he questioned the use of conspiracy charges, the conceit that aggressive war was a crime, and the fixing of individual responsibility for acts of state. Yet no sooner had he begun than Webb shut him up, saying that all those issues were beyond the proper scope of a defense opening; he could save those points for his closing statement. Takayanagi objected that the prosecution had been allowed to make a full statement of its theory of the law in Joseph Keenan's opening statement, and pleaded that many of the defendants wanted to raise these fundamental legal questions in their defense. Webb refused and adjourned for the day.[50]

The next morning, Takayanagi tried again, saying that he had been unable to carve apart his statement overnight. He pleaded that he represented defendants who "think that the law of the Charter is a momentous element in the present trial: their life and death, their confinement or liberty depends in large measure upon its interpretation." Webb again would not hear him out. Zaryanov privately praised Webb for it.[51]

With Takayanagi muzzled, an American defense lawyer found an ingenious way to highlight the unfairness of a trial that only prosecuted one side. Major Ben Bruce Blakeney argued that the actions of other states demonstrated that they did not believe that starting a war was a crime. The Kellogg-Briand Pact, he said, had been breached so much that it was a dead letter. Like many of the judges, he sought to discern international law not just from treaties but from custom—except that in his version the actual practice of states did not reveal pacifism but a widespread willingness to attack other countries. Blakeney's legal argument, drawn from eminently respectable texts, allowed him to open an embarrassing examination of aggression by the Allied powers.[52]

His foremost examples of state practice were a Soviet incursion into Manchuria in 1929, the Soviet attack on Finland in 1939, the Soviet conquest of the Baltic states, and the Soviet occupation of Romania since 1944. He sought to cover a joint Soviet-British invasion of Iran in 1941 and the United States' moves to dominate Greenland, a Danish colony, after the German conquest of Denmark.[53] Most spectacularly, to show that the Allies had violated the laws of war, he proposed scrutinizing the United States for using atomic bombs on Japan.

The prosecutors fumed. As Blakeney offered into evidence the League of Nations' expulsion of the Soviet Union for invading Finland, Comyns Carr called the material "entirely irrelevant." When Webb pointed out that the court only had jurisdiction to try major Japanese war criminals, Blakeney parried that "a pact may fall into desuetude as the result of repeated violations." This, the judges agreed, was a major question worth discussing.[54]

After a tense weekend mulling it over, though, Webb's mind slammed shut. Behind closed doors, Zaryanov—who only operated under political guidance from Moscow—urged the other judges to stop the defense from using the courtroom for militaristic propaganda, lest they "turn it into the trial for the alleged aggression of Allied Powers against Japan." He complained that Kiyose's opening statement had not merely glorified "the criminal aggressive policy of militaristic and imperialistic cliques ruling Japan," but was "an attempt to launch an attack against Allied Powers, to show that war waged by Japan was defensive and caused by the aggression of the said Powers." After Blakeney's salvo against Soviet aggression, Zaryanov feared that the other judges might allow evidence about the Soviet invasions of Finland and Poland. If so, he threatened a time-wasting, embarrassing diversion as the Soviets would demonstrate that their conquest of Poland was "a legitimate act of self-defence."[55]

Webb returned to the bench determined not to allow Blakeney and the other defense lawyers to slug it out with the Soviets. The Australian chief judge noted that the Kellogg-Briand Pact had been joined by more than sixty countries; breaches by one or two states "do not destroy the law." Blakeney, arguing that international law is molded by the great powers, shot back that "five of the great powerful victor nations of the world among the prosecutor nations here" had violated the treaty. When Webb said that his court was not about to dig into the rights and wrongs of every war since the Kellogg-Briand Pact in 1928, Blakeney retorted that "it is going to look perilously like a double standard if the Tribunal finds these defendants guilty and finds other great nations to have been innocent in doing the same acts."

Comyns Carr, speaking for the Allied prosecution, took keen exception. He warned that the trial would become mired in controversial inquiries about Allied actions over which the court had no jurisdiction. It was no defense for someone accused of a crime to show that the prosecutor had also committed a crime. Comyns Carr observed that the Allied governments had still claimed to be upholding their Kellogg-Briand Pact commitments. All of Blakeney's incidents had come after Axis aggression unleashed World War II, he claimed, with the Allies moving defensively to occupy lands that the Germans would otherwise grab—a point which might possibly apply to Iran or Greenland but not to Poland and the Baltics, where the Soviet Union had secretly colluded with Nazi Germany in their conquests at the outbreak of World War II. The League of Nations had shown the continuing authority of the international law against aggression by condemning the Soviet Union for invading Finland—"rightly or wrongly," he added in prim deference to a seething Zaryanov.

Taking a fifteen-minute recess, the judges conferred on whether to accept the defense's evidence about Finland, Poland, Romania, Iran, and Greenland. Standing up for Zaryanov, Webb rebuked Comyns Carr for suggesting that the court could take judicial notice of the League of Nations' finding that the Soviet Union had attacked Finland. By a majority, the judges decided not to hear Blakeney's evidence about Allied aggression. "These are collateral and irrelevant issues," ruled Webb brusquely, giving no other explanation.

Blakeney was left to stubbornly offer his documents one by one—the League's condemnation of the Soviet invasion of Finland, Winston Churchill's speech explaining the British occupation of Iran—to be rejected, which worked merely as theatrics. He only managed to sneak in some press accounts about the Australian and Dutch occupation of Portuguese-colonized Timor in an unsuccessful attempt to keep it from falling to Japan.

Blakeney did succeed in forcing a rare debate in the Tokyo trial about the annihilation of Hiroshima and Nagasaki. To show that the Allies had disregarded the laws of warfare, he tried to introduce into evidence a much publicized recent *Harper's Magazine* article by Henry Stimson recounting the American decision to use atomic bombs, which had been reprinted widely in the Japanese press and almost certainly read by every person in the courtroom.[56] Yet Comyns Carr responded that what he blandly called the American "choice of weapons" had "no bearing upon any issue before this Tribunal." He said that "nobody has ever suggested that there is any law of war which forbade the use of such a weapon, and if there were it could . . . afford no excuse for the commission of offenses by the Japanese against prisoners of war."

This was feeble. While of course there were no specific laws on the books against an entirely new technology, the laws of war had long forbidden the indiscriminate slaughter of civilians.[57] The United States was a party to the 1907 Hague Convention IV on land warfare, which banned the use of projectiles or weapons calculated to cause unnecessary suffering, which Blakeney pointed to as "law prohibiting the use of certain types of weapons."[58] What would it matter, Webb asked starkly, if the atom bombs were war crimes? Blakeney, with no illusions about putting Stimson on trial, argued instead that the U.S. use of atomic bombs showed that the Hague Convention was obsolete, potentially exonerating his clients charged with conventional war crimes in land warfare. If both the Americans and the Japanese had violated the laws of land warfare, those laws had been substantially reinterpreted by states or were a dead letter.

Webb rejected Stimson's *Harper's* article. Not addressing the larger issues, he tersely said that while it might be arguable that the atom bombs justified Japanese abuse of American prisoners in the final few days of the war, that could not excuse Japanese crimes before Hiroshima.[59]

Thwarted, Blakeney tried a final gambit, this time arguing against the notion of individual criminal responsibility. Those treaties about the laws of war did not demand that anyone face an international trial as a war criminal. The Hague Convention IV on land warfare of 1907, for instance, stipulated only that those who violated its terms pay compensation, he contended. Cannily, he tried to introduce an official U.S. brief from after World War I in which Woodrow Wilson's secretary of state had argued that chiefs of state and kings were immune from prosecution.[60]

Fed up, Webb suggested that Blakeney's questioning of what counted as international law had to follow an important Supreme Court precedent from 1900 which said that international law was revealed in "the customs and usages of civilized nations."[61] Blakeney genially agreed and said that he was doing precisely that: showing that one of the most important world powers, the United States, had refused the principle of international criminal responsibility. Webb blew up, barking that the practice of states could not be found in the report by Wilson's secretary of state. Blakeney shot back that the man had been secretary of state.[62]

By a majority vote, the judges refused to allow the U.S. report.[63] Blakeney, having scored plenty of hits, was shut down for now.

While the trial had been slow going during the prosecution's case, it now became pure molasses. As defense lawyers began to present their case, there was often no clear plan to their counterargument. They seemed, as New Zealand's judge noted frostily, to be "just muddling along."[64]

For their first several days, the defense counsel read aloud a numbing stream of public documents such as the Japanese constitution or the Potsdam Declaration, rather than insider accounts of the deliberations of the Japanese government—the evidence that might have absolved their clients.[65] Often the defense gave evidence that was immaterial to the charges. Some of the witnesses were authors, academics, or junior functionaries who had not been in the high-level meetings where the crucial decisions were made. When a former vice minister in the Greater East Asia Ministry testified that Japan's puppet regimes in Manchuria and elsewhere had been independent states, Comyns Carr in cross-examination forced him to admit that Manchukuo and Thailand had had Japanese armies garrisoned there. The British associate prosecutor read aloud official Japanese cables that dictated the foreign policy of Manchukuo and the collaborator regime ruling over the Japanese-conquered parts of China.[66]

One defense witness, Major General Okada Kikusaburo, ran afoul of the court for a Japanese army habit: shouting. "There is no need to speak so loudly," said Webb, who had a tendency to yell himself. "You have a microphone in front of you."[67] Later, when Webb tried to cut him off during a long cross-examination about war plans, the witness barked, "I feel it is extremely regrettable that this most important question has been disallowed." "I think we will have to deal with this Japanese Major General," snapped Webb. "He is not addressing the Japanese Army now." The tribunal's marshal shouted, "Order in the court." Soon after, as a Japanese lawyer questioned the major general, Webb sighed, "The witness is utterly impossible." The major general yelled, "I am not impossible; I have not even said anything!" Again, the marshal called for order. The Japanese defense lawyer gave up and dismissed the major general, who stalked out of the courtroom.[68]

With their Japanese and American lawyers sitting in front of them, the accused listen during the defense phase of the trial, November 17, 1947. Togo Shigenori is in the back row on the far left; Marquis Kido Koichi is one row ahead, second from the right.

The prosecution was delighted at the shambles. Comyns Carr reported confidently to London that the defense was unable to establish a case. To speed up the proceedings, he cut back on cross-examination of defense witnesses, deeming them not worth the time.[69] After some particularly irrelevant testimony—from a Japanese doctor who had done relief work in Manchuria but knew nothing about the actions of the defendants—a prosecutor wearily said, "the prosecution has no questions." "I am not surprised," said Webb.[70]

As the trial grew haphazard and lurching, Webb did his irritable best to hurry along the defense lawyers. "We cannot tolerate these delays," he said. "This trial will never end at this rate."[71] After more dawdling, he declared, "I voice no suspicions, but if the defense wanted to prevent us from ever reaching a verdict this would be the way to do it."[72] He impatiently threw out defense evidence and snapped at defense counsel. As Marquis Kido Koichi later complained, "The attitude of the judges was lacking in fairness and evidence advantageous for the defendants was readily disallowed."[73]

An American defense lawyer, cut off one time too many, took "exception to the undue interference" by Webb. The Australian chief judge exploded, demanding that the lawyer withdraw the "offensive expression" and apologize, or be expelled for insulting the court. "I will not listen to another word from you until you do," he bellowed. The defense lawyer, who represented Hirota Koki, coolly refused, saying he had tried cases for twenty years and had said the same sort of thing in U.S. courts without trouble. The judges threw him out until he apologized. He calmly refused, walking out of the courtroom with a batch of documents tucked under his arm.

The Japanese defense lawyers, shocked, complained that they were under more restrictions than the prosecutors had been. Yet if the defense was so hobbled that it collapsed, then the trial would fall too. So Webb backtracked, saying that he was only objecting to the American lawyer's purported insult.[74]

After several months of backdoor efforts by the defense to bring back the banished lawyer, he returned to court. As he expressed his "profound regret," Webb cut him off three times, asking him to come back and abase himself again a few days later when all of the judges would be present. Stunned, the defense lawyer quit on the spot and asked the court to appoint another American to help Hirota. Webb cut him off for the last time: "There is no need for you to say any more." The defense lawyer stalked off to return to Washington.[75]

One day, Webb started the day's session with a stern reprimand from the judges to stop wasting time by giving "statements in the nature of propaganda." Not long after, Webb made a bigoted complaint against wordy affidavits from Japanese witnesses: "I know it is a Japanese weakness to express themselves at great length, and it is difficult to control it, but the indulgence of this weakness has a devastating effect on the paper and ink supply."[76] In private, Delfin Jaranilla, the Philippine judge, pressed his fellow judges to discipline unruly defense lawyers for contempt of court, even though such punishments were not found in its own charter.[77]

ISHIWARA'S WAR

The defense's first major historical task was rebutting accusations of aggression in Manchuria. Rather than challenging the prosecution evidence from internal Japanese cables and the testimony of three former prime ministers, the defense instead concentrated on vindicating Japan's colonial claims to Manchuria.

The Japanese people, the defense asserted, believed that they had a moral right to Manchuria as a lifeline against the threatening Soviet Union. Manchuria, an American defense lawyer noted with jarring candor, became "an indispensable source" of raw materials for Japan—a point which could equally well have been made by the prosecution. The Japanese residing in Manchuria, the defense said, were attacked by thieving bandits, with the Chinese government powerless to restore order.[78]

Relying on an official Japanese investigation, the defense accused Chinese troops of blowing up the South Manchuria Railway at Mukden. Yet the Japanese investigators, who arrived several days later, had no more compelling evidence for Chinese responsibility than the presence of the corpses of three Chinese men in army uniforms in the vicinity. On behalf of the judges, Webb asked if the Japanese investigators had checked the tags of the dead to identify them as Chinese soldiers, and was disgruntled when told that the Japanese had not.[79]

The defense presented the Kwantung Army's invasion of Manchuria as self-defense. Facing Chinese bandits and revolutionaries, the Kwantung Army had just ten thousand soldiers to defend some two hundred thousand Japanese and eight hundred thousand Koreans living along the South Manchuria Railway. The only way to protect them, the defense claimed, was to seize Chinese positions. Even marching as far as Harbin, according to the defense, Japanese troops were merely defending Japanese residents from Chinese bandits and terrorists.[80] These claims of self-defense were amplified by the first of the accused to testify, a haggard General Minami Jiro, who had then been army minister.[81] The judges did not hide their skepticism. "A nation may go to the rescue of its nationals in a foreign country," commented Webb. "It certainly is not the orthodox thing to invade a foreign country immediately."[82]

Muddying the defense's case, the Japanese military commanders called to testify proved to be distinctly belligerent in court. "If another battle should be caused in the future," warned one Japanese officer, "we will exterminate the Chinese unit of 10,000 strength to the last man and with no casualties on our side."[83] A Japanese general testified about getting orders to wage a "mountain 'Blitzkrieg'" in Manchuria, which would have made fine evidence for the prosecution.[84] In a blunder, a Kwantung Army colonel testifying for the defense admitted he had asked for approval from Itagaki Seishiro, then a colonel, now one of the Tokyo trial's defendants. After the bombing of the South Manchuria Railway, this witness said he duly charged ahead without finding out who was responsible for the explosion nor how much damage had been done. "I had no time to investigate the damages," he said. "You only had time to start a great war?" retorted Comyns Carr.[85]

One infamous defense witness was lucky not to be on trial himself: Lieutenant General Ishiwara Kanji of the Kwantung Army, a brainy and hawkish military thinker who had been one of the prime instigators of the conquest of Manchuria. A few weeks into the fighting, his friend Itagaki had privately said, "it's Ishiwara's war."[86] Nobody in the court knew how Ishiwara had managed to escape the Allied lists of war criminals, but he had opposed plans for an invasion of China and had become an adversary of Tojo Hideki, which might have complicated conspiracy charges. For several days, the New Zealand judge, Erima Harvey Northcroft, went mysteriously missing from court; it turned out that he had snuck away with a defense team to take an affidavit from an ailing Ishiwara near his farm in northern Japan. With Ishiwara near death, this would be his last big public statement.[87]

Ishiwara's hard-line account sounded almost familiar by now, contending that an outnumbered Kwantung Army had faced superior Chinese forces burning with anti-Japanese rage. "Our Kwantung Army was driven to the extreme limit of indignation," he testified, not denying his importance in the Manchurian clash. He admitted that the Japanese civilian government's policy was for its troops to hold back, but justified the Kwantung Army's disobedience "because the central authorities failed to understand the real situation in the field." He claimed that the crucial decision to attack after the railway bombing had been made by the Kwantung Army's commander in chief, a convenient person to blame since he had committed suicide soon after the end of the war. On Ishiwara's account, Itagaki had been following the intent of this dead man, who was obviously unavailable for questioning. At one point, when pressed by the prosecutors about his claims of self-defense, Ishiwara retorted, "Attack is a method of defense—is one method of defense."[88]

"Far Beyond the Breaking Point"

Midway through the clumsy Manchuria presentation, the defense buckled under the strain of its work. Outside of the courtroom, the defense pleaded for more translators and typewriters, stenographers and typists, for money to look after witnesses (bills were being footed by the relatives of the defendants or donations from the Japanese public), more American lawyers, and free military railway transport for Japanese lawyers so they could avoid having to commute for two or three hours on crowded trains and buses from the Tokyo suburbs or other cities.[89] Several of the judges privately wrote off the defense as inept, obstructionist, or glaringly political.[90]

Led by the indomitable Ben Bruce Blakeney, the defense lawyers met in chambers with the judges to plead for a week's recess for preparation. If not, they warned, there would be a breakdown. Some of the judges were annoyed, but Webb was shaken. Delaying the already overlong proceedings would annoy the Allied governments, but without a functioning defense, the trial would become a nullity. He solicitously expressed "profound regret" and "great apprehension" for the defense lawyers. When a prosecutor grumbled about the defense's dawdling, Webb retorted, "we should go on until there is a break down? Will that improve the situation?"[91]

Webb and the other judges granted the defense's request for a break, but with an unusual stipulation. Zaryanov, still enraged at the "vicious" defense counsel, persuaded Webb to insist that defense witnesses would give their initial testimony by written affidavits before being cross-examined and then reexamined.[92] This was meant to avoid time-wasting testimony, but it risked abuse if biased Allied judges unfairly threw out defense evidence. It was, the New Zealand judge admitted confidentially, "an unusual" measure, "but the trial is unusual."[93]

When the defense understandably objected, Webb blew up: "Words, just words." If the defense would not accept, he growled, they would not get their recess. An American defense lawyer pleaded that the additional burden of preparing affidavits "will place us far beyond the breaking point at which we are now." The judges did not relent, although they did grant the beleaguered defense lawyers their weeklong recess.[94]

In response to the defense's complaints about these affidavits, Webb and the American and Canadian judges formed a committee to investigate their slow pace.[95] As the Canadian judge, E. Stuart McDougall, reported grimly, the defense lawyers were poorly organized; only a handful spoke English; their clients had clashing interests; they did not get along. While the prosecution had had as many as two hundred translators, the defense had only seventy-two, of whom four or five were competent. To pay the bills, the Japanese defense lawyers were scrounging funding from their friends, the Japanese government, or even from the defendants; they were deep in debt to a local hotel that had put up witnesses. If the defense could not get their act together, the Canadian judge warned, they might drag out the trial for untold months—or, worse, declare that they could not go on, terminating without presenting all the relevant evidence.[96]

Soon after, the British judge, Lord Patrick, wrote confidentially that the defense was mired in an "extraordinary mess. . . . Personally I am convinced they will never be in anything but a mess." He jeered, "Their only system is to take every topic in the long history on which the prosecution have touched, and where the Prosecution has said 'Yes' to attempt to establish 'No,' or to make a most protracted and utterly fulsome apologium for Japan's acts."[97]

Northcroft, the New Zealand judge, confidentially told his government that much of the defense evidence was "utterly useless." The American lawyers were "not of good quality," dwelling on "time-wasting technicalities, rarely going to merits, and largely in delay and obstruction. . . . The Japanese counsel are absolutely hopeless. They have no notion at all of advocacy, and wade through masses of irrelevant and sentimental nonsense of no value to the Court, and of no help at all to their clients." Northcroft warned that the defense might dramatically abandon the trial, claiming they had been prevented from presenting their clients' case, thereby making any convictions "an act of grave injustice." He noted contemptuously that "the purpose of the Japanese defence counsel, in as far as they have formed any purpose, seems to be by way of vindication of Japan to the world instead of the exculpation of the accused before our Court."[98]

Zaryanov urged Webb to screen defense evidence, which might speed up the trial but at the cost of compromising its basic fairness. Rather than having the judges rule in open court about admitting evidence, he proposed that a new committee—made up of Webb, two judges, one prosecution lawyer, and one defense lawyer—should decide in advance which documents would be allowed, and another special committee would look over witnesses' affidavits before they testified in court. Such a committee could easily be skewed against the defense.[99] In addition, he proposed that an average of three days apiece would suffice for the individual defense of each of the accused. Whatever else could be said about Soviet purge trials, they were not slow.[100]

This tough Soviet proposal was blocked by the other judges after a contentious meeting.[101] Patrick indignantly pointed out that a Scottish court could not delegate its functions on any decision that could affect the merits of the case. When the defendants eventually had their sentences reviewed by General Douglas MacArthur, he warned, they would say that evidence had been rejected by a committee, rather than the whole tribunal, which could render the court "a fundamental nullity."[102] Webb was at first inclined to try out Zaryanov's committee, but gagged at a suggestion by the Soviet judge that the defense could only appeal to the whole tribunal if the committee judges could not agree. That, he said, would violate the charter and "the Supreme Commander might wholly disregard the Tribunal's verdict."[103] The defense was left to stagger on.

CHAPTER 18

A Very British Coup

B Y NOW THE BRITISH government feared that the Tokyo trial was collapsing. In a panic, the British secretly schemed to replace both the U.S. chief prosecutor and the Australian chief judge—a brazen assertion of state power over what was supposed to be an independent court.

The British associate prosecutor, Arthur Comyns Carr, warned direly that the prosecution was a shambles. He resentfully wrote to Sir Hartley Shawcross, Britain's attorney general and its adroit prosecutor at Nuremberg, "It is amazing that the Americans, who started this as their show and merely invited us to help in a subordinate capacity, should be content to let it go to pieces now."

Joseph Keenan, the American chief prosecutor, had suddenly bolted for Washington without telling anyone or leaving instructions, purportedly to consult with Harry Truman ("eyewash," Comyns Carr thought). Several other U.S. prosecution lawyers had departed, leaving the prosecution relying heavily on its weary Commonwealth lawyers. Comyns Carr glumly reported that he would be left with only a few competent Canadian, Australian, and British staffers: "Of the non-Anglo-Saxons," only a "young Dutchman" was of any use. Keenan, after staying off alcohol for months, had "been drinking heavily again for the last six weeks, with recent renewed semi-public exhibitions." Comyns Carr volunteered himself as chief prosecutor instead, but refused to "act as an inebriate home attendant for Keenan." The British associate prosecutor threw down the gauntlet: "I feel that the time has come when you will have to put your foot down with the Americans and say that unless they put the thing in order you will recall me."[1]

Alarmed, Shawcross urged Ernest Bevin, Britain's foreign secretary, to complain to the U.S. government about British "grave dissatisfaction" with Keenan in particular and the trial in general. Keenan "has become notorious not only for inefficiency but for almost constant insobriety." Shawcross cautioned that "it would be most unfortunate if the trial broke down or if large numbers of the defendants were acquitted."[2]

Britain's Labour government resolved to oust Keenan and replace him with their own man. Bevin, a headstrong working-class unionist, was both an outspoken foe of the Soviet Union and a keen imperialist—a leader of the Labour Party's postwar efforts to hold on to Britain's colonies.[3] Asserting British power with all the swagger of a global empire, Bevin defied the United States, agreeing that the only solution was to put Comyns Carr in charge, either as chief prosecutor or as acting chief prosecutor while Keenan stayed away indefinitely.[4] Knowing who really ran the show, Bevin took the matter up with General Douglas MacArthur first, not bothering with the White House or State Department unless they got no satisfaction from him.[5]

MacArthur stopped the British cold. He was not about to replace the pliant Keenan for someone British. For an hour and a quarter, he chewed out the senior British diplomat sent on this disastrous errand. The supreme commander, as this wretched British official reported back to Bevin, was "highly incensed" and "violently hostile" to their mutinous proposal. Scorching Comyns Carr as an ambitious reprobate, MacArthur called it a "dastardly act to stab a man in the back and make accusations against him when he was not present to answer them." He claimed that Keenan had not been drinking immoderately, and lauded him for the "monumental achievement" of getting prosecutors from eleven countries to function together. Quite falsely, MacArthur declared that he could not possibly be more pleased than he was with the functioning of the Tokyo trial. He denied that the prosecution was faltering, declaring its case to be "cast iron" and in many respects better than Nuremberg—a taunt sure to infuriate Shawcross.

"I entirely refuse to act as the British Government wishes me to in this case," MacArthur growled. If there was to be a new chief prosecutor, he said, that would be an American; he had already given the British Commonwealth its due by making Sir William Webb the chief judge. Once the Allied governments had appointed their prosecutors, he said, he could not tamper with them. He pointed out that Harry Truman had taken a personal interest in Keenan's appointment, and warned that there would be "unpleasant repercussions" if the British pushed this "unwelcome" matter. MacArthur put the British on notice: "I should like to warn you that if His Majesty's Government take this to the United States Government they will find themselves up against President Truman himself."

In a sop to the British, MacArthur pointed out that Keenan was in poor health, hospitalized in the United States, and was quite likely finished in Tokyo, unlikely to reappear. The British diplomat who had absorbed MacArthur's wrath urged Bevin to slink away.[6]

After MacArthur bared his teeth, all British bravado vanished. Bevin and Shawcross tiptoed away; Comyns Carr did not resign.[7] A month later, the British got word that Keenan was coming back to Tokyo after all, which they accepted with bad grace. "It is obvious that Keenan is a political crony of Truman's and that the latter would very much resent any suggestion that he should give his pal the sack," wrote a British official sourly. The British resolved to stick it out to the end "to look after our interests."[8]

DRAFTING

Bad as things were among the prosecutors, it was, if anything, worse between the judges. United only in resentment of Webb's leadership, the judges were careening toward not just dissents but possibly several resignations. To groans, Webb told the other judges that in case they could not ultimately agree on one opinion, he was going to work on the court's lead judgment, which was "my duty and privilege as President."[9] He planned to write a comprehensive account of the development of international law about aggression, trimming his discussion of natural law but not abandoning it.[10]

The dispirited, feuding judges in Tokyo began writing drafts of parts of their judgment as early as February 1947, hoping to deliver a prompt verdict when the trial finally ended. It is common for judges in big, sprawling cases to start drafting their judgment while a trial is still under way. While this could reflect closed minds, it would be impractical to wait until the proceedings were over to start some sketching, and seasoned judges can roughly anticipate some of how a trial will unfold.[11] Unlike in a standard criminal trial, the judges arrived in Tokyo knowing plenty about the events of World War II. As Webb explained at one point, about a piece of defense evidence, "we cannot help knowing these things. We read them before we came to Japan."[12]

To allow the judges to change their minds during the trial, Webb wanted to start with basic sections that would be required no matter what the verdicts were, such as an overview of the law and statements of the evidence in general. Because writing "a history involves conclusions,"

Webb noted, he saw these draft studies as a prelude for the harder task of finding the individual accused guilty or innocent beyond reasonable doubt. Each of the judges would handle two of the twenty-five remaining defendants, except for Webb, who would handle seven, and Radhabinod Pal, who would take no part in any of this. Webb sometimes made the trial feel like a foregone conclusion: "It is hoped to have the statement against each accused prepared before the accused begin to give evidence."[13]

Many of Webb's assignments were roughly predictable: Mei Ruao would take China, Major General Ivan Zaryanov would handle Japan's relations with the Axis, the influential New Zealander would handle the attacks on the United States and the British Empire, the French judge would cover French Indochina. For others, he was at first inclined to mix it up: the American judge would deal with Manchuria, the Filipino would cover Indonesia, and the Canadian would do the Soviet Union. Röling and Pal would be asked to deal with conventional war crimes, since those were the only offenses they were sure were actually criminal.[14]

The judges worked having heard out the Allied prosecution but not the other side. While the defense was still presenting its case on the invasion of China, Webb's assistant had drawn up a summary of Japan's militarization, its wars in Manchuria and the rest of China, and its Axis alliance.[15] Before the individual suspects got their chance to speak in their own defense, the U.S. judge drafted his preliminary findings of fact about Manchuria, and Webb circulated a study of the prosecution's case on China.[16]

Röling, despite his disputes with the other judges, urged a united judgment. It was impossible for all the judges to fathom all the evidence, and he complained that the Nuremberg judgment had "no logical line" and seemed made up of disparate sections pasted together. Yet he was driven more by idealism:

This trial is of a special importance for the whole world, not only for the facts proven, or the kind of judgment delivered. It is more or less the touchstone for the possibility of organized international justice. We have, if possible, to prove by our activity that representatives of eleven nations can come together and really can cooperate. If it is true that the future of the world depends partly on the possibility of the creation of international courts, then it is of the utmost importance that we prove the possibility of international judicial cooperation. We would not prove that by producing unnecessarily more than one judgment.[17]

The Dutch judge was fascinated by his task, relishing the revelations from secret meetings, government telegrams, and speeches. Yet he found himself "looking more for understanding than for judgment." Tasked with weighing the guilt of each accused, he instead saw "how individuals think to make history, and how they are in fact, by time and place chosen marionnets who fulfill a more or less necessary and predestined function."[18] He worried that the work was corrupting his soul. He wrote to a friend: "Whoso handles pitch shall foul his fingers!"[19]

"A SQUALID FARCE IN JAPAN"

The trio of British Commonwealth judges were disenchanted and despondent. By the spring of 1947, the unshowy judges from Canada and New Zealand had asked their governments to bring them home, while the British judge was seriously contemplating quitting.[20]

The British judge, who was from Scotland, vented his spleen in a blistering letter sent back home to a friend, Scotland's top judge in Edinburgh. Although Lord Patrick kept an arm's distance from the British government for the sake of appearances, he told his friend to circulate the letter as he saw fit, hinting with zero subtlety that "I only write it because I feel that people like the Lord Chancellor and the Attorney General should be prepared for the failure of the hopes which led to the appointment of this Tribunal. If you do not agree, put it in the fire."

No way was this letter going into the fire. As intended, Patrick's complaint was promptly sent on to the British lord chancellor and other senior officials in London, flaying Webb as "a quick-tempered turbulent bully . . . , resentful of the expression of any view differing from his own." Patrick scoffed at France's judge for suggesting that international law grew out of "le bon coeur," and derided the Philippines' judge as dependably vengeful but too stupid to understand how he was voting: "what his judgment will be like, or with what view he will concur no man can say." The Soviet judge wanted "a lot of fulminations inserted about the dastardly attack by the fascist nations against the sacred rights of democracy."

Patrick was especially appalled with the dissenters. He scorned Röling for arguing that aggression was not a crime while also voting that the court had jurisdiction: "In other words you keep poor devils on trial for their lives for eighteen months, although all the time you know you can never convict them." Patrick reported with horror that Pal had circulated an opinion that was well over two hundred pages long, arguing that aggressive war was not a crime and that there was no individual criminal responsibility for acts of state. Suspecting that Pal meant to publish his dissent as a book, Patrick rebuked his own government for inflicting the Indian judge on the court: "He has made his position quite clear since first he was appointed, so why the Government of India ever nominated him, and why Great Britain insisted on India being represented on this Tribunal—America objecting—it is difficult to see."[21] Patrick warned the senior British diplomat in Tokyo that Pal's draft had some "thinly concealed backslaps at Great Britain."[22]

Patrick anticipated catastrophe when the judges had to compose their final judgment. "Far from adding some weight to the Nurnberg judgment as a precedent in international law," he wrote, the Tokyo judgment "will cast doubts on its soundness. It is a deplorable situation." With considerable accuracy, he predicted what was to come:

> We shall have a little core which will be on the same lines as Nurnberg. The President [Webb] will sustain the Indictment upon a special ground of contract, useless as a precedent for the future, the Frenchman will sustain it as being in accord with his "bon coeur." Russia will sustain it because of Japan's dastardly attack on democracy. The Phillipines [*sic*] will sustain it on I know not what grounds. And Holland and India will deliver a detailed attack on the grounds of the Nurnberg judgment.

The British judge lambasted his own government for not vetting the judges properly. "Britain should never go into such an International Court again without much more careful screening of the calibre of the members," he wrote. "There are four members of this Tribunal whom no decent Lord Advocate would make Sheriff Substitute anywhere." He was especially glum about Webb: "A man appointed because of the length of the entry he has had inserted in 'Who's Who' can so antagonise the members of his court that the only purpose of the institution of the Tribunal is frustrated."

He considered resigning, but feared that if he did so, at least two other judges—presumably the Canadian and New Zealander—would press their governments to let them quit too. "The trial would be quite discredited," with a worrying impact on "world opinion and on the occupation of Japan."[23]

The British government was appalled. "It would be very amusing were it not so tragic," wrote a top British legal official. "It is indeed lamentable that these proceedings should undo much of the good of Nuremberg. . . . [T]he hopes with which we started this trial seem to have failed." He wished that Patrick was running the tribunal instead of Webb.[24]

Lord Patrick, the British judge, in his chambers at the Tokyo trial, August 6, 1946

Soon after, Erima Harvey Northcroft, a Supreme Court judge in New Zealand, sent an equally dire warning to his chief justice, intending that he pass it along to the prime minister. "I am in despair," Northcroft wrote. He excoriated Webb, who was "seldom wise or discreet in his utterances and much that he says and does can, and no doubt will[,] be used to create the impression that the trial has been an unjust one."[25]

The Australian chief judge had split the judges between himself and everyone else. "Eleven so different Judges required a President of exceptional ability and disposition," but Webb, "from the start, has preferred to 'walk alone.' He has behaved as a presiding Judge sitting with a jury, never as primus inter pares"—first among equals. Webb had been grossly offensive to him. While the other judges often ate together "as a judicial family" at the Imperial Hotel or at the Ichigaya courthouse, Webb had taken to snubbing the others, sometimes showily. Once he walked into the dining room at the former Army Ministry, saw the Canadian, New Zealand, and Soviet judges eating together, and rudely ignored them to sit down with a group of U.S. officials. It was impossible to talk business with him: "he regards any comment by anybody as criticism, to which he is acutely sensitive."

Northcroft warned, "The Tribunal, if it is to make a useful contribution to international law, must be entirely or substantially of one mind. The chance to secure that, I fear, has gone." Webb's dismissal of his colleagues and his "determination to be the author of a monumental judgment has produced chaos." He lamented that "everybody is working independently and I hate to think of the futility of persuading them to shed their pet theories and conclusions." Pal had already written a draft dissent of no less than two hundred and fifty pages, while another judge—apparently Röling—was at work on another tree-killing dissent. "I fear the result of this long trial will be futile and valueless or worse," Northcroft wrote morosely. "This Court will not speak with a clear voice upon any topic of law or fact. If a Court of this standing is seriously divided, and I feel sure it will be, then the modern advances in international law may suffer a serious setback. . . . Varying opinions from this Court including sharp dissent from Nuremberg must be disastrous."

Finding his position "intolerable," he begged his own government to let him resign and come home: "Discomfort and embarrassment I have accepted, and, of course, would continue to accept it if I thought I could advance the cause of international justice." He urged finding some way to suspend the tribunal's proceedings, in order to avoid a disastrous conclusion. Since he could not sway the court, "I feel entitled to ask for relief from the position in which I find myself."[26]

Throwing discretion to the winds, Northcroft told a senior British official in Tokyo that he was so disgusted with the court that he had asked his government to withdraw him.[27] Informing a British general in Tokyo that Pal and Röling might well dissent, he warned that the result of the trial might negate the good done at Nuremberg. If possible without losing face, he wanted "to cancel it altogether."[28]

THE EMPIRE STRIKES BACK

Patrick urged his government to act fast to save the Tokyo trial. He informed the top British diplomat in Tokyo that Webb's "autocratic methods and rude and eccentric manner" had torn the judges apart, leaving a "fundamental disagreement between Webb and Dominions judges" about the final judgment.[29] In another letter to Whitehall by way of Edinburgh, Patrick indirectly urged the British government to force Webb out as chief judge of the court. The Canadian and New Zealand governments, he warned, were forced to consider pulling out of the Tokyo tribunal. Would Webb be ousted, or would the other three be? He asked bluntly: "Are we to be withdrawn?"

Patrick wrote that the Australian chief judge had "often been offensive to many of us," recently rebuffing the stately Northcroft "in grossly offensive terms." (Patrick unpersuasively feigned indifference to such "vulgar personal squabbles," noting that Webb "is at times almost intolerable, but, as the Americans say, 'I can take it.'") If the British government let the judges muddle on, the final judgment and dissents would be mortifying.

What to do? If the British, Canadian, and New Zealand judges were allowed to stomp out of the Tokyo trial, that "would clear our countries of responsibility for the result of the Trial," but would still leave the precedents set at Nuremberg in peril. Instead, Patrick clearly preferred that the British government "ask Australia to withdraw the President, who sets us all by the ears." If Webb could be replaced by Northcroft as the chief judge, that antipodean shuffle would result in eight judges supporting the Nuremberg judgment. While Patrick obviously yearned to see Webb sent packing back to Queensland in disgrace, he politely told the British government that the question was above his pay grade: "The matter is one which concerns world politics and statesmanship."[30]

Patrick's note caused panic in the British government.[31] The shaken lord chancellor, a top British judicial official, vilified Webb for a "complete absence of any legal capacity" and mocked his natural law ruling (which the lord chancellor had not read) as "really a laughable document if it were not so serious." He concluded that it would probably be necessary to ask Webb to retire. The lord chancellor, who had signed the London agreement that had created the Nuremberg tribunal, concluded, "It is a tragic thing that a trial which went so well at Nuremberg is degenerating into a squalid farce in Japan."[32] He warned Shawcross, the attorney general, that "the tragic farce which is being played out in Japan" might "undo much of the good of Nuremberg."[33]

The British quickly ruled out the New Zealand judge's excitable suggestion of shutting down the trial.[34] Bevin notified the prime minister's office that it would be "disastrous to abandon the trial now." Doing so would "deal a shattering blow to European prestige," and would "proclaim to the world that Japanese militarism had been justified since we had tried to convict it but failed."[35]

Instead, the British secretly tried to whip the wayward Dutch judge into line. A senior British official alerted a Dutch counterpart that Röling was likely to dissent and challenge the Tokyo tribunal's charter. The Dutch official checked with the commission of jurists who were supposed to control Röling, who themselves were somewhat dubious about the validity of the charter but claimed to have heard nothing about his dissent. "It is to be hoped that the Dutch judge will conform when the time comes," the British official informed the Foreign Office.[36]

Shawcross gathered the lord chancellor, diplomats, and other mandarins at the House of Lords. After an anxious discussion, they decided to warn MacArthur about the impending dissents from the Indian and Dutch judges and the danger that the trial might break down altogether. They hoped, with MacArthur's help, to send to Tokyo an eminent, elderly British jurist—who had chaired an important Allied war crimes commission preceding Nuremberg—to discreetly urge the judges not to impugn the court's charter and to persuade Webb to change his tune. The lord chancellor suggested leaning on the Australian foreign minister to whip Webb into line.[37]

Patrick warned his government that this was a terrible plan. If that British jurist was sent to Tokyo, the other judges would deeply resent the attempt to interfere with their judgment and "Webb would blow off the handle." Such a frontal assault would destroy any chance of making the other judges see the light; better that Patrick do his best to persuade his fellow judges to uphold the Nuremberg principles, while privately keeping in close touch with the British government. And if MacArthur were to pressure Webb, that would only further harden his views. Anyway, after convening the tribunal, MacArthur had no further authority over it and could not tamper with it.[38] After the court reached its verdict, MacArthur would have to review it; it would be improper, Patrick warned—rediscovering his concern for judicial independence—for the supreme commander to be informed of any disputes among the judges, or for him to do anything to influence its deliberations.[39]

The senior British diplomat in Tokyo was gingerly instructed to "avoid giving the impression that we are accusing an Australian judge to the Americans," although that was precisely what the British were doing. He was ordered to warn MacArthur that the Tokyo judgment might thwart the Nuremberg judgment criminalizing aggressive war, and to explain that it was "absurd" that any of the judges should contemplate ruling that aggressive war was not a crime in international law.[40]

For the second time, MacArthur quickly put an end to a British plot. When the British diplomat approached MacArthur, he found that Webb's careful cultivation of the supreme commander had paid off. To be sure, MacArthur was depressed by the prolix courtroom proceedings, aware of the prospect that the Tokyo court might defeat its own objectives, and indignant at the "American shysters" serving as defense lawyers, whom he thought were taking full advantage of the peculiar international character of the tribunal and dragging the trial out. Yet rather than repudiating Webb, MacArthur said that it was a pity that the Australian chief judge had not been given supreme power over the other judges and lamented that he was sometimes outvoted by them.

MacArthur, keen on punishment for Pearl Harbor, took little interest in the advancement of international law. He expected that most of the accused would be convicted but not necessarily according to the Nuremberg judgment. Yet he emphatically declared that the defendants responsible for attacking Pearl Harbor must surely be guilty, since they had started the war without prior declarations while negotiations between American and Japanese diplomats were still going on.[41]

With that salvo from MacArthur, the British government scurried away from its machinations against Webb, Pal, and Röling. As a British diplomat informed the lord chancellor, "in view of the delicacy of General MacArthur's position vis-a-vis the Tribunal," there was "no useful purpose" in pestering him.[42] The lord chancellor glumly agreed. All that the British government could do was hope that Patrick would prevail over the other judges.[43]

Bevin, who had ably served as labor minister in Winston Churchill's wartime coalition government, worried that Nuremberg's legacy was at stake. Patrick would have to remain to win over those judges who were "considering questioning in their judgments that Nuremberg doctrine that waging an aggressive war is a crime. This is a serious matter, not only because of its effects on the Tokyo trial itself, but because it would weaken the force of the Nuremberg judgment." If Patrick was withdrawn, there might be "only a bare majority, if that, for the Nuremberg doctrine."[44]

Under pressure, the British and Canadian judges backed away from their threats to quit. The Canadian judge decided that doing so would be unpatriotic. Patrick, who had been hospitalized and keenly wished to get out of Japan for his own health, realized that this would be impossible.[45] When Scotland's top judge tried to bring him home to help the overburdened Scottish courts, Bevin snapped that this would be disastrous. It would then be impossible to hold back the Canadian and New Zealand judges as well, which could turn the trial into "a farce." There was, Bevin declared, no question of withdrawing the British judge from Tokyo before the bitter end.[46] He instructed the Canadians that "they must stick it out."[47] Patrick pledged himself to trying to lead Webb, Röling, and Pal back into line with the Nuremberg judgment.[48]

THE PLAGUE

Grim as the litany of war crimes before the judges was, the United States was secretly covering up what it knew about some of Japan's most shocking atrocities.

Hidden away outside the frigid northeastern city of Harbin in occupied Manchuria, the Japanese army had since 1936 operated a top secret unit for human experiments with bacteriological warfare. In its hellish work, Unit 731 had killed some two thousand Chinese and Manchurian prisoners, as well as launching attacks on several Chinese cities. The operation had been run by General Ishii Shiro, a microbiologist who had been captured by the Americans and remained in their custody. According to U.S. intelligence, Unit 731 had produced some four hundred kilograms of dried anthrax—which, if aerosolized properly and carefully spewed by airplane over a big city, could have killed hundreds of thousands, and perhaps even millions, of people.[49]

Japan had used its secret biological weapon against Chinese targets. In 1940 and 1941, with approval from Japan's army, Ishii's team flew a small airplane low over the Chinese cities of Quzhou, Ningbo, Jinhua, and Changde, spraying plague-ridden fleas and grains. Soon plague broke out in all the cities except Jinhua. In 1942, Ishii's teams used germ bombs and spray to support the conventional warfare of the Zhejiang-Jiangxi campaign. Some 250,000 Chinese civilians died in that onslaught, although it is not clear how many of them perished from the weapons of plague, cholera, and anthrax. Japan also set up a secret facility in occupied Singapore to do biowarfare experiments on humans, as well as centers in China and Burma.[50]

Both General Headquarters and the office of the U.S. Army chief of staff—by this time, General Dwight Eisenhower—knew a great deal about Unit 731's work.[51] Yet the Tokyo trial's prosecutors quietly avoided the issue. Ishii would not face trial at Tokyo nor the U.S. military courts at Yokohama. Nor would the Allied prosecutors pursue germ warfare charges against three generals already on trial in Tokyo who had supported Ishii's work: Umezu Yoshijiro, Araki Sadao, and Tojo Hideki himself, who had spent three years in Manchukuo and was familiar with the secret program.[52] To the contrary, the United States and the Soviet Union sought to learn more about the human experiments for their own military purposes.[53]

As the defense was getting under way in February 1947, the Soviet prosecutor at the Tokyo trial, Sergei Golunsky, asked the Americans for permission to interrogate Ishii and two Japanese colonels running the experiments. General Headquarters would not allow Ishii to be prosecuted, while some of its officials hoped that the Soviets would not get much out of him that the Americans had not already gleaned from their own interrogations. U.S. officials were skeptical that the Soviets would be interested in prosecuting Ishii's unit for crimes committed against Chinese, and as MacArthur's staffers noted with alarm, they had expressed an interest in the mass production of typhus and cholera bacteria, as well as typhus-bearing fleas.[54]

Wary of letting the Soviets learn about how to churn out typhus and cholera, the State and War Departments agreed only to a onetime interrogation strictly controlled by General Headquarters, grudgingly allowed as "an amiable gesture toward a friendly Government." The Japanese colonels, the U.S. government ordered, would first be questioned by U.S. interrogators. If they said anything noteworthy, they would be ordered not to repeat it to the Soviets, nor to mention that the Americans had interrogated them first.[55] In April 1947, the War Department dispatched Norbert Fell, a biological weapons expert at Camp Detrick in secluded rural Maryland, the U.S. Army's principal base for research on bioweapons—established in 1942 after reports of Japanese germ warfare in China.[56]

The U.S. government was eager to tap Ishii's sinister knowledge. U.S. military intelligence and Major General Alden Waitt, a specialist in chemical warfare, took a keen interest in his interrogation. The War Department instructed Fell to ask Ishii about who had been involved in the program, how the laboratory had operated, what diseases and organisms had been studied, and whether the Japanese planned to use the agents by dropping bombs or spraying them from planes.[57] As a colonel at General Headquarters wrote in a top secret note, there was "great intelligence value" to the United States in learning more about "[h]uman experiments," "[f]ield trials against Chinese," and strategic and tactical uses of biological weapons, as well as the likely possibility that the Japanese general staff had known about and authorized the program. The Japanese had done battlefield trials against the Chinese army on at least three occasions. This General Headquarters colonel hoped that lower-level Japanese in Unit 731, who were somehow seen as not liable for war crimes, could provide "most of the valuable technical BW [biological warfare] information as to results of human experiments."[58]

So far the captive officers of Unit 731 had talked out of a mixture of persuasion, fear of the Soviets, and hopes of ingratiating themselves with the Americans. Yet Ishii had admitted that he had superiors who had authorized his program and knew about it, as would be expected for a project of such size and sensitivity. Those higher-ranked Japanese officers, a colonel at General Headquarters noted, would want promises that they would not be prosecuted as war criminals before they would talk. (This colonel repeatedly wrote "war crimes" in quotation marks, downplaying the possibility of criminality or accountability.) Ishii tacitly confirmed that his unit had experimented on human beings, and offered to describe his program in detail if the United States would guarantee in writing immunity from charges of war crimes for himself, his superiors, and his subordinates. He added that he had extensive knowledge of biological weapons, including how to use them in the frigid climate of northern China—an unsubtle attempt to make himself useful for coming U.S. contests against the Soviet Union. Eager to learn more, General Headquarters wanted to assure the Japanese that their disclosures would be kept in intelligence channels, not to be used for evidence for war crimes trials.[59]

To find out if there was any evidence that might get in the way of immunity for Ishii and the others, the War Department urgently instructed the head of MacArthur's legal section, Colonel Alva Carpenter, and Frank Tavenner, then the U.S. acting chief prosecutor at the Tokyo trial, to relay whatever material the U.S. government had against them. Were Ishii and his confederates among the remaining major Japanese war criminals awaiting an international trial, and were any other Allies planning to charge them?[60] Carpenter reassuringly replied to the War Department that his files on these Japanese biowarriors held nothing more than anonymous letters, unconfirmed allegations, hearsay affidavits, and rumors—not enough evidence to support charges of war crimes. Neither Ishii nor his associates were on the list of fifty or so major Japanese war criminals awaiting trial, and no other Allied countries had charged them so far. Still, several generals who had been Ishii's superior officers were, including Tojo, who had been the Kwantung Army's chief of staff in 1937 and 1938.

Tavenner warned that the Soviet Union would probably launch its own trials for Unit 731. During their conquest of Manchuria, the Soviets had captured two of Ishii's subordinates, Major General Kawashima Kiyoshi and another officer, who were being held as presumed war crimes suspects. Kawashima's affidavit to Soviet investigators, which the Tokyo prosecutors had on file, revealed that they had been secretly researching viruses for warfare and conducting experiments, on orders from the Japanese general staff. Another affidavit, from a Chinese doctor, accused Japanese planes of scattering infected wheat grains on four Chinese cities in 1940, causing outbreaks of bubonic plague. Still, Tavenner explained that the Allied prosecutors had ruled out adding these crimes to the charges against Ishii's superiors on trial in Tokyo, due to insufficient evidence connecting Tojo and the others with Ishii's secretive project.[61]

The War Department quickly pronounced itself satisfied that the evidence at General Headquarters would not warrant putting Ishii and his group on trial as war criminals, but wanted to know whether the prosecutors at the Tokyo trial thought that any evidence showed that Ishii's operation had violated the rules of land warfare.[62] Of course, biological weapons violate the core principles of the laws of war: they cannot be aimed to avoid infecting civilians as well as soldiers, nor controlled to have a proportionate effect, and they are most likely to kill elderly people or children.[63] The Hague Convention IV on land warfare of 1907 forbade the use of poison and poisoned weapons, and in 1925, a League of Nations conference had created a Geneva Protocol prohibiting the use of chemical and biological weapons, which Japan had signed.[64] The fact that this top secret bioweapons facility was hidden away in remote Manchuria suggested that the Kwantung Army understood that its work was beyond the pale.

At the Tokyo tribunal, Tavenner and his prosecutors carefully reviewed the Unit 731 affidavits held by the Soviets. They concluded that Ishii's biological weapons group "did violate rules of land warfare," but wanted more corroboration and investigation before indicting him and his team for war crimes. Still, the Tokyo prosecutors knew in chilling detail about Japan's biological warfare against Chinese cities. In October 1940, in an experiment by Unit 731, Japanese airplanes had scattered infected wheat grain over the port city of Ningbo; two days later, the city suffered an outbreak of bubonic plague that left ninety-seven people dead. There was strong circumstantial evidence, the prosecutors noted, of "bacteria warfare" in three other cities. At one, Japanese planes had scattered rice and wheat grains mixed with fleas; a month later, bubonic plague erupted. In November 1941, at Changde, in Hunan province, a Japanese plane had dropped wheat and rice grains, paper, cotton wadding, and mysterious particles; these caused several cases of what seemed to be bubonic plague. For use against the Chinese army in 1940, Ishii's group had manufactured seventy kilograms of typhus, five kilograms of cholera, and five kilograms of plague-infected fleas. In 1942, Ishii had infected areas in central China with typhoid and bubonic plague bacilli, and in 1943 and 1944 he had overseen seven or eight experiments using anthrax and bubonic plague on Manchurians. By 1944, according to the prosecutors, Ishii's team had accumulated tons of materials to cultivate these lethal bacilli in "preparation of mass production of bacteria."

Such a vast, complex, and costly project would have almost certainly required approval from senior Japanese officials, not least for permission to bombard Chinese cities with biological weapons. Yet the U.S. prosecutors still claimed that they had not been able to prove links between the senior Japanese leaders on trial in Tokyo and the actions of the biowarfare group. Having decided to keep Unit 731 out of the Tokyo trial, the U.S. prosecutors' review of the Soviets' evidence made them worry that the Soviet prosecutor would try to cross-examine some of the witnesses and bring up some of this evidence.[65]

In the end, the Soviets chose to run their own show trial, which meant that they could keep the biowarriors in their custody while rebuking the United States. In December 1949, twelve Japanese officers would be swiftly convicted by a Soviet military tribunal in Khabarovsk, the largest Soviet city near Harbin.[66] In a Stalinist indictment raging against the "insane" anti-Soviet plotting of "imperialist Japan's ruling clique," these Japanese were accused of using "a criminal means of mass extermination of human beings." One after another, all twelve Japanese defendants either said "I plead guilty" or "I fully plead guilty." After just five days, the verdict treated the Soviet Union as the leading victim of Japan's biowarfare program, commenting that the Tokyo trial had already established the centrality of anti-Soviet aggression in Japanese policy. On top of that, the Soviet prosecutors sought to implicate General Umezu Yoshijiro and Emperor Hirohito himself, claiming that the creation of bacteriological warfare units had been done on secret royal instructions.[67]

In contrast to the Khabarovsk drama, Unit 731 would remain invisible throughout the Tokyo trial. Although a Soviet colonel handled the prosecution's cross-examination of the witnesses called on behalf of Umezu, he asked nothing about biological warfare.[68] Decades later, the failure to prosecute the Japanese involved in biowarfare is one of the gravest stains of the Tokyo trial. "Everything connected with it was kept from the tribunal," Bert Röling, the Dutch judge, complained bitterly years later. The cover-up, he said, had "severely damaged" the authority of the Tokyo trial.[69] Ishii got his Japanese army pension and lived out his days in comfort.[70]

CHAPTER 19

Denial at Nanjing

MEI RUAO STILL HAD exalted hopes for the Tokyo trial. He believed that the court could create new principles for international law that would establish a peaceful global order. The trial would teach the world that aggressive war was a crime and that individual war criminals should be punished for it. It would educate the Japanese masses, he explained to a leading Chinese newspaper, and help them to build a genuine democracy.[1]

Mei's patrons in the Nationalist government of China maintained a keen interest in the trial. China's foreign minister, Wang Shijie, visited the courtroom and met with the judges in Sir William Webb's chambers.[2] After having been insultingly berated by Webb in front of the other judges, Mei worked hard to charm him and win his sympathy about conditions in China. "He is a very pleasant chap," Webb wrote privately. "We are good friends."[3]

Yet as the Chinese judge sat in judgment in Tokyo, his country was collapsing beneath him. With no chance to recover from eight years of ruinous fighting against Japan, China plunged into civil war between Communist revolutionaries and the Nationalist government.[4] As Communist forces surged, Chinese army officers who had been proud to fight endlessly against the Japanese lacked the stomach to do so against fellow Chinese. Some Chinese soldiers despaired; some did not understand what the bloodshed was about; others succumbed to Communist appeals to lay down their arms.[5]

Chiang Kai-shek's government proved squabbling, blundering, and corrupt, losing battles while desperately using police repression to hold its own territory. From China, India's astute envoy, K. P. S. Menon, reported to Jawaharlal Nehru that "the prospects of defeated Japan appear to be far brighter than those of victorious China."[6] Bert Röling wrote privately that despite the great talents of the Chinese, there "is not a more corrupt and miserable people today. Their philosophy is one of harmony, and nowhere is more fighting." There were "nowhere so many wise men as in China and behaves no nation so stupid as a people."[7]

From Harry Truman on down, the U.S. government secretly braced for the collapse of Chiang's government.[8] Since the end of World War II, the United States had gotten dismal results from a policy of limited military assistance to the Chinese army and air force.[9] As secretary of state, General George Marshall—who had spent an exasperating year trying in vain to broker a deal between the Communists and Nationalists—wanted to withhold any U.S. military aid that would inflame the civil war.[10] Although U.S. officials still paid lip service to the dream of a multiparty democracy that drew in Chinese liberals who were disgusted with Chiang's rule, they were preoccupied with fear of an imminent victory by Mao Zedong's Communists.[11]

Most of the Truman administration saw Mao's revolution as part of a Soviet-inspired international Communist movement. By allowing Chinese Communists to take over Manchurian cities, the Soviet Union had signaled its disdain for the Nationalists.[12] As the Soviets established a hard-line Stalinist regime in northern Korea, many of Truman's senior officials feared that Manchuria too could become a Soviet satellite. The secretary of war argued that the United States could not accept the military collapse of China's Nationalist government, while a U.S. general sent by Truman on a fact-finding mission to China warned that a Communist takeover would be a disaster for the United States.[13] "The Soviet Union is proceeding, slowly and circumspectly, towards eventual domination of China," wrote U.S. military intelligence, warning that the Soviet Union was "an immense amoeba-like organism which surrounds and digests any object incapable of offering sufficient resistance."[14]

It was against that looming background of Chinese civil war that the defense counsel in the Tokyo trial turned to Japan's invasion, which had weakened the Chinese state and ravaged its society. An American defense lawyer undiplomatically observed that there were "in fact two states in China . . . making war on each other."

Webb upstaged the defense with a public tantrum that called into question his own impartiality more than any defense counsel could have done. He had been shown a preview of the opening statement by a young

Marine Corps lawyer, Lieutenant Aristides Lazarus. The U.S. lieutenant meant to say that a glance at the map showed why Japanese leaders
were afraid of the Soviet Union—referring to the invasion of Finland, the
dismemberment of Poland, and the annexation of Estonia, Latvia, and
Lithuania. To explain Japanese fears about the Chinese Communists,
he wanted to include an anti-Communist statement by Truman. Webb
exploded, "do not take advantage of the great tolerance displayed by this
Allied Court to indulge in what might be termed enemy propaganda."

The defense counsel retorted that it was hard to see the words of Harry
Truman as Japanese propaganda. Webb shot back that the defense lawyer had been permitted "to attack the great United States of America"
when it was relevant, as well as Britain and the Soviet Union, but "you
appear to take a sheer delight in insulting Allied countries." He barred
the American lawyer from uttering the unremarkable sentence about the
map, even though everyone in the courtroom had a pretty good mental
image of what the Soviet Union had done to its neighbors. Webb suffered
a patriotic explosion: "Through it all I remain a British judge, an Australian judge, and I will never be anything else. And I will not stand for
gratuitous insults to my country or any other country represented in this
Court. I have no higher loyalty than that to my own country. If American
counsel think they have a higher loyalty than their loyalty to their own
country, they are at liberty to indulge it."

This was jarring. Did the chief judge have no higher loyalty to justice
or the law? If he as chief judge was primarily an Australian patriot, what
kind of objectivity could the accused expect from him—or from the Chinese, Philippine, U.S., or Soviet judges?

It fell to the American defense lawyer to vindicate the integrity of the
court. He chided Webb that defending his client did not mean attacking
his own country, while denying any grudge against the Soviets: "I never
forget that we fought on the same side and that it may be due to the fact
that some Russian officers and soldiers fought as hard as they did that I,
today, am alive to appear in this courtroom." The Marine gave a basic
explanation of a fair trial that should have gone without saying: "You
must remember, please, sir, that much of this might be distasteful to us
personally; but, as attorneys appointed by the United States at the request
of this Tribunal to help defend these people, we have a high duty: We
must present all the evidence available. Please understand that, sir."[15]

With that awkward beginning, Lazarus launched into his case. In this
opening statement and the subsequent parade of Japanese military officers

and government officials called as witnesses, the defense contended that the Chinese had no one to blame but themselves for driving the Japanese into invading their country. Lazarus flatly said, "Japan did not attack China."

Japan, the defense held, had been defending itself against an existential threat from international Communism. "Japan had reason to fear, and in fact did fear, that the spread of Communism in China, and then in Japan itself meant Japan's destruction," said Lazarus. "The Chinese Communist Party was the armed vanguard of the world Communist movement." The Chinese Communists, covertly aided by the ruling Nationalists, had whipped up anti-Japanese hatred until it exploded into unlawful violence.

As the defense framed it, Japan had had every legal right to station troops in north China. In the clash at the Marco Polo Bridge on the fateful day of July 7, 1937, unoffending Japanese soldiers had been exercising their right to go on maneuvers when they were fired upon by Chinese forces. After insufferable Chinese provocations, the Japanese garrison had felt it had no alternative but to fight. While Japan had tried to keep the incident localized, the defense claimed, the Nationalist government had poured troops northward, forcing Japan to send three divisions to China: "China had expanded a series of local incidents into an armed conflict tantamount to war on a large scale." To explain the creation of puppet regimes, the defense said that since China was so impoverished and chaotic, Japan had supported authentic, autonomous governments to bring stability to the occupied areas. As for opium, the defense faulted the Chinese government for never managing to solve its national drug problem.

As the defense reached the Nanjing massacre, its claims turned more extreme, trying to deny what had happened. For all the flaws of the Chinese prosecution evidence, the defense's was noticeably weaker. The defense could only point to the orders given by Japanese commanders before their troops entered a Chinese city and to a relatively small number of courts-martial for offenses against civilians. But since these efforts clearly had not prevented a slew of atrocities, defense lawyers turned to outright denial.

Arguing the bad brief he had been handed, Lazarus told the court of "the exaggeration of stories of atrocities in some places, the non-existence of atrocities in others, and atrocities by Chinese which were charged to the Japanese." As a fallback position—what lawyers call arguing in the alternative—he argued that if there had been killings, they were justifiable. The dead Chinese, he declared in an assertion that was dubious as both fact and law, had been "bandits, irregulars, guerrillas, and others

who cannot claim the status of soldiers and whom international law pro-
nounces outlaws and beyond the protection accorded combatants."

All in all, the defense case tracked the official Japanese line during the
war: there had been a provocative attack by Chinese soldiers; Japan had
tried to localize it; then Japanese troops had had to act in self-defense;
throughout, Japanese troops had been respectful to the Chinese populace.[16] Lazarus summed it up, "the accused did not enter into any conspiracy, did not plan and initiate a war of aggression against China, did
not use opium to debauch its people and to raise funds for war, nor did
they foist upon China a puppet government."[17]

To answer accusations of aggression against China, the defense did not
introduce the evidence that would have been most compelling: records
of internal Japanese deliberations that proved no hostile intentions. Here
the defense benefited from the Japanese burning of evidence before the
Allied occupiers arrived. At one point, the defense pointed to a series of
documents that had been destroyed at the end of the war, including Japanese plans for military operations in China from 1937, leaving the court
relying on sworn testimony about what those documents had said. The
prosecution complained that Japanese officials had been ordered to burn
selectively, getting rid of the incriminating papers.[18]

Instead of secret documents, the defense produced a series of Japanese
military officers and government officials to give a familiar litany: Japan
was allowed to station troops at certain points in China; the Marco Polo
Bridge clash was started by the hateful Chinese; Japan had had no plans
to invade; the Japanese had charged deep into China only for self-defense;
and the collaborationist government of Wang Jingwei was legitimate, not
a Japanese puppet.

Japan's legal claim to post troops in China raised bad colonial memories
of the "unequal treaties" forced upon the Chinese. Around Beijing, that
right rested on an agreement imposed on China by the Western powers
and Japan after the Boxer Rebellion. To justify the incursion of Japanese
forces into Shanghai in 1932, the defense quoted from a Japanese government statement that it was only doing what "the leading countries"—that
is, the Western imperial powers who had enclaves in Shanghai and other
Chinese cities—had frequently done there to protect the Japanese residents and properties.[19]

The defense gave one emotional example of how Japanese nationals
had been at risk. In Tongzhou, on the outskirts of Beijing, after a clash

between Japanese and Chinese forces in late July 1937, scores of Japanese and Korean civilians were killed.[20] A retired Japanese lieutenant general testified to the horrible sight of butchered children and women after the massacre, some of them raped or violated with bayonets. These awful scenes, he said in terse and emotional testimony, would stay with him for the rest of his life. While detailed and gruesome eyewitness testimony from two other Japanese officers did not always line up precisely, the three accounts together gave a plausible overview of what one called a "picture-scroll of hell." In a pond red with blood, a witness saw six corpses: a whole family bound and stabbed to death. One witness had taken photographs of slaughtered civilians, which added credibility. The best that the prosecution could do was try to suggest that the killings might have been done by a Japanese collaborationist force in the area, not by Chinese government troops. Webb fixated on differences about timing: "At present the evidence given by these three witnesses is most contradictory and most unsatisfactory."[21]

Whatever confusion there might be about the Marco Polo Bridge fighting, the defense had a rather harder time condoning the massive ground assault that had followed. While Japan might perhaps be justified in taking proportional steps to protect its colonists, that hardly warranted a full-scale invasion. In testimony that backfired, a retired Japanese army lieutenant general, who had in 1937 been a war planner at the Army Ministry, said that on July 8 or 9, the Japanese government had adopted a policy of not enlarging the Marco Polo Bridge incident. Yet that policy, on his account, lasted all the way until July 11, when the government, he said, was "utterly compelled to send forces to North China to cope with anti-Japanese armed actions, planned by the Chinese side." He blamed the Chinese for continuing to fire on the Japanese, saying that after another clash on July 26, the Japanese government decided to mobilize troops from the homeland to north China "to carry out the duty of self-defense." Japan sent four divisions in July, seven more in August, and four more in September and October, for a total of fifteen divisions on foreign soil by October 1937. By 1938, that went up to twenty-three divisions. All of this, the retired lieutenant general said, was done for self-defense.[22]

It was same story of self-defense for Japan's second major assault on Shanghai, which had begun in August 1937 and continued for months. This was presented as a necessary response to the shooting of a Japanese navy lieutenant there. Despite combat involving colossal numbers of troops, a defense lawyer insisted that there was no "deliberate or systematic plan to conquer China." Arthur Comyns Carr, the British associate prosecutor, scoffed at this, noting that the armada of twenty-eight Japanese warships that had swiftly gathered in Shanghai harbor was "one of the most imposing displays of naval might Shanghai has ever seen."[23]

NEGATION AT NANJING

The defense took three approaches to accusations of atrocity at Nanjing and elsewhere. First, they contended that Japanese troops had orders to treat the Chinese population decently; the rare soldiers who did not had been punished. Second, they argued that any outrages were the fault of low-level officers, nothing to do with the defendants atop the chain of command.[24] And third, when all else failed, they simply denied that there had been any massacres or rapes at all.

A major serving under General Matsui Iwane emphatically denied seeing any signs of massacre in Nanjing. With the whole world watching, the troops had been under orders to keep strict discipline and avoid illegal acts. Still, Matsui had gotten a report about "some crimes connected with military discipline," and therefore, after marching into the city, had ordered his officers to be more strict in maintaining discipline. This major claimed that the many protests from the International Committee for the Nanking Safety Zone had not made it to Matsui, conceding only that the commander had learned of a "rumor" of vague "unlawful acts," which left him "quite uneasy."

Pressed by a prosecutor on cross-examination, this Japanese major admitted that Matsui had received reports from army officers, the Kempeitai, and foreign diplomats. According to him, Matsui had issued verbal instructions forbidding any illegal acts for the honor of the Japanese army. Such honorable conduct was all the more crucial, Matsui had allegedly noted, because the troops were led by Prince Asaka Yasuhiko, the uncle of Emperor Hirohito. While admitting there had been a few instances of rape, this major denied there had been any massacres at Nanjing, scorning international outcry as "a form of propaganda."[25]

A senior officer in Japan's military judiciary was a bit more forthcoming. He testified in an affidavit that "unlawful acts were committed by Japanese troops" in Nanjing, and that he had examined these cases and done enough to punish the offenders. He recalled that Matsui had gathered all his officers soon after taking the city, informing them about such cases and giving strict orders for severe military discipline. Yet he claimed that the offenses had been minimal: just four or five officers involved in the noteworthy cases, only a few murder cases, some plunder and rape,

Matsui Iwane, who had been the commander of Japanese troops at Nanjing during the massacre, while being held for trial in Tokyo, circa 1946

but few injuries. He had not dealt with "mass slaughter criminals." In the crucial months of December 1937 and January 1938, he had handled perhaps ten cases.

Under a blistering cross-examination from a U.S. prosecutor, the military judiciary officer retreated from his own affidavit. Realizing that he had shown that Matsui had known about war crimes in Nanjing, the officer now claimed that the commander had not been referring to specific incidents in Nanjing but had merely imprecisely mentioned past events elsewhere and pressed for stricter discipline. Scoffing at the assertion that there had been just a handful of cases, the U.S. prosecutor noted that the International Committee had reported four hundred and twenty-five groups of cases of Japanese war crimes, some of which contained more than thirty individual cases.

Did the Japanese officer know that at one time some one thousand five hundred refugees were marched out of the Safety Zone and shot, their bodies thrown into a pond? "I never heard of such a matter up to now," replied the officer. "I believe that it is possibly not true." Did you investigate the more than one thousand Chinese civilians taken to the banks of the Yangzi River and machine-gunned? "No," said the witness. Did you know about Chinese policemen taken out and shot? "I don't think there was any such incident." Did you advise Japanese troops that they could search out former Chinese soldiers who had thrown away their weapons and shoot them? "I don't think there was any such case." Did you not know this was being done systematically by Japanese officers? "I never heard about that matter."[26]

The defense had an easier time challenging the sparse prosecution evidence about killing, rape, and plunder in Changsha, in Hunan province. The defense provided a Japanese lieutenant general who testified he had followed orders to "love the people." The only atrocities, he said, were from U.S. warplanes that bombed civilian houses. He testified that he had ordered his men to obey "the fundamental rules of 'Do not commit crimes,' 'Do not plunder,' 'Do not burn houses,' and 'Do not kill,' based upon the principle of 'Love the people'"—an innocent version of Japan's "three alls" counterinsurgency campaign: kill all, burn all, loot all. The troops had followed the injunction of the emperor, he said, who had sent a letter to his younger brother, Prince Mikasa, who spent a year fighting in China: "As this war is a holy war, you must love the enemy."[27]

Decades later, the elderly Prince Mikasa—who became an outspoken pacifist after the war—would tell a thoroughly different story, revealing to the *Yomiuri Shimbun* that in 1944 he had condemned Japan's "policy of aggression" in China and had been revolted by the use of Chinese prisoners for bayonet practice to toughen up new recruits. "It was truly a horrible scene that can only be termed a massacre," he said. He dismissed Japanese questioning of the death toll in Nanjing: "If you kill prisoners in an atrocious manner, that is a massacre."[28]

A series of army officers sought to exonerate Field Marshal Hata Shunroku, who had succeeded Matsui as commander of Japanese forces in central China. His chief of staff, a lieutenant general with a massive handlebar mustache, gave an affidavit insisting that Hata had been a strict disciplinarian: "there was not a single case of violation of military discipline in Hankow, such as massacre, violence, plunder and etc." Although he admitted there had been tough fighting, he was "astounded" at "inconceivable testimony" that there had been a massacre.[29] Similarly, a Japanese lance corporal testified that his unit "never did anything which in any way incurred the enmity of the Chinese natives." Chinese women showed no fear of Japanese soldiers, he swore, and Chinese children grew so fond of them that they cried at their departure for the front. He had once met Hata, who had told him to "love the Chinese natives."[30]

The chief of the Japanese army's judicial affairs bureau, a former lieutenant general, testified that Hata had "paid extremely close attention to military discipline and morality." Yet he said that the army orders insisting on strict punishment had all been burned at the end of the war, leaving it unclear whether that was due to the Japanese cover-up or American firebombing. Webb and Comyns Carr skeptically asked why the Japanese government would have burned evidence that made it look good. In response, an American defense lawyer made a rare, stinging reference to the devastation all around them: "in traveling to and fro to this building every day I am sure we all see mute evidence of what happened to the buildings in which these documents were housed."

In a lacerating cross-examination, Comyns Carr dismissed Japanese military justice: "Is it permitted to the Kempeitai under Japanese law to torture a prisoner in order to make him confess?" When asked whether any officers had actually been punished for the Nanjing massacre, the witness chose denial: "I am even unfamiliar with the so-called Nanking case." While conceding that he had gotten reports about "the so-called Nanking outrages," he could not remember any officers being punished by courts-martial. When Comyns Carr pressed him about the numerous complaints of rape, the witness again could recall nothing. Yet the witness had in his affidavit admitted that the army had revised its penal code to make rape a military crime some five years after the mass rapes in Nanjing. Was that change not done, asked Comyns Carr, because the Japanese military knew there had been great numbers of rapes which had not been punished? Yes, the witness finally admitted, they had known of "numerous cases of rape in the field" in Nanjing and other parts of China, and the central authorities had issued orders to deal with such cases severely. Comyns Carr acidly asked why "it took you five years to make up your minds to alter the law?"[31]

Despite these vigorous efforts at denial, some of the defense testimony unintentionally revealed how the Japanese army had blurred the line between Chinese soldiers and civilians, allowing the slaughter of people who should have been protected by the laws of war.

A Japanese diplomat posted in Nanjing explained that the Japanese army there had seen Chinese male civilians as potential targets: "many [Chinese] military men audaciously took clothing from civilians (some civilians were murdered), and, putting it on instead of military uniform, entered the 'Safety Zone' disguised as civilians.... It was a matter of course that the Japanese Army for this reason held suspicions and doubts." Similarly, a Japanese diplomat who had served in Shanghai suggested that the most vulnerable Chinese civilians there had not been off-limits: "Even the few old men, women and children who remained in the occupied area acted as spies, sabotaged, or attacked Japanese soldiers in the dark.... Japanese soldiers at first tried to treat civilians with kindness, taking them as quite apart from military men. As a matter of fact, however, confronted with such an attitude on the part of the inhabitants there arose among the Japanese soldiers a feeling of hostility and an attitude of suspicious watchfulness."[32]

A Japanese lieutenant general testified that in villages under Chinese Communist control, "all the people" resisted the Japanese army. When Japanese troops entered these towns, "we could not distinguish underground soldiers from the villagers. In those areas we could not but fight the people in general." One of the judges—possibly Mei—lunged at that, asking Webb to press the witness on what exactly the Japanese troops had done. Realizing his blunder, the lieutenant general retreated, saying he had been incorrect to speak of fighting the people.[33]

In addition, some defense witnesses ended up helping to provide what the prosecution had struggled to establish: a clear link between the Nanjing massacre and a specific defendant. While seeking to absolve General Matsui Iwane, a Japanese diplomat based in Nanjing wound up possibly implicating Hirota Koki. This diplomat admitted that foreigners in Nanjing had sent reports to the Japanese consulate about atrocities, but dismissed them as mostly based on hearsay and said that the consulate did not have time to investigate them all. These reports had been sent, he said, to the army headquarters in Nanjing and to the Foreign Ministry in Tokyo, which informed the Army Ministry about them. Based on his own observations and discussions with foreigners in Nanjing, he had sent an overview to the Foreign Ministry and had reported directly to Hirota, then foreign minister, in January 1938. The prosecution, delighted by this linking of Hirota with the atrocities, did not bother to cross-examine, pointing instead to the evidence already gathered about rape and massacre there.[34]

A Foreign Ministry official provided further evidence that Hirota had known about the Nanjing massacre. He testified that Japan's consul general in Nanjing had quickly reported about atrocities once Japanese troops entered the city. Hirota, this defense witness said, had been alarmed and worried, urging him to do something quickly to stop these disgraceful deeds. This Foreign Ministry official said that Hirota had rebuked a senior Army Ministry official and demanded strict measures to stop the abuses immediately. The official testified that the atrocities had abated. This official remembered Hirota telling him that he had asked the army minister to take strict measures about the Nanjing massacre.

Comyns Carr pounced. The British associate prosecutor got this Foreign Ministry official to admit that he had received a whole series of reports from Nanjing, including many from the foreigners in the city, which showed the atrocities continuing. Pressed by Comyns Carr, the witness admitted that he had given all these reports to Hirota. The Foreign Ministry official testified that Hirota, on his own account, had only taken the matter up with the army minister once or twice, and had never discussed bringing it to the cabinet, although he had reports showing that the war crimes had not stopped.[35]

THE BOMBING WAR

The defense sought to absolve the defendants for Japan's aerial bombing campaign against China. While the prosecution had not emphasized it, this had been a watershed moment in the war: a sustained bombardment without any apparent end, a terror bombing which obliterated the line discriminating between military and civilian targets.

None of the defense lawyers seemed to realize that Mei had been in Chongqing during the period it was under Japanese bombardment. It is not clear which of the more than two hundred bombing raids the Chinese judge might have endured, nor which of the more than 9,500 Japanese aircraft he might have seen overhead, nor which of the 21,600 bombs he might have heard exploding.[36] Since his diary is incomplete, there is no record of what went through his mind as he sat quietly in court and listened to the defense counsel explain away the fragmentation and incendiary bombs raining down on terrified Chinese civilians.

In the end, the defense counsel might as well not have bothered. The United States, after its incineration of Japanese cities in 1944–45, had no intention of opening a discussion of the criminality of strategic bombing campaigns. Such amnesia was made easier because there was scant international law about aerial bombardment during World War II, before the adoption of the Geneva Conventions in 1949 and their Additional Protocols in 1977. Today states are legally obliged not to intentionally attack civilians, to be sure that any collateral damage to civilians is proportionate to the direct military advantage from blowing up a target, and take all feasible precautions to spare civilians from harm. But despite the fundamental principle that civilians should not be targeted, states during World War II faced only murky legal constraint—and in total war were not inclined to follow the rules anyway. In 1899, the first Hague peace conference had adopted a convention banning launching projectiles or explosives from balloons, but that lapsed after five years; there had been a serious attempt to negotiate a new Hague treaty on aerial bombardment based on rules drafted in 1922–23, which would have banned bombing meant to terrorize civilians, but it had come to naught.[37] States had little more to restrict them than the 1907 Hague Convention IV on land warfare, which prohibited bombarding undefended towns.[38] Invoking that Hague Convention, an interwar arbitration tribunal had condemned Germany for bombing Salonika during World War I.[39] Still, in the *American Journal of International Law* in 1929, a Harvard scholar noted "the still nebulous state of international air law."[40]

The commander of Japan's First Combined Air Corps testified that his airmen had strictly obeyed the laws of war: "At no time did we bomb any city or town indiscriminately without a military objective in view."[41] A Japanese fighter pilot said that his mission had been "the annihilation of the enemy air forces" in Shanghai and elsewhere, and that he and his underlings had been forbidden from attacking civilian houses or the buildings of non-Chinese foreigners.[42]

Nanjing had been heavily bombed before its fall in December 1937, which the defense sought to present as nothing more than routine warfare. In response to U.S. complaints about the bombing, the Japanese government had formally declared that Nanjing was a Chinese military stronghold that had to be bombed. A retired Japanese navy rear admiral testified that the Naval Air Corps under his command had notified Chinese noncombatants about the coming air raids and warned them to take refuge, as if that was a realistic option for the Chinese.

If Mei remembered the mangled civilians and scorched houses in Chongqing, that must have been vividly called to life as he heard the testimony of a senior Japanese officer who had helped lead the bombing of the city in 1940 and 1941. He claimed that the Japanese had carefully selected only military targets, using street maps to guide them. Believing that Chiang Kai-shek's headquarters were moving in the western part of town, they had launched air assaults there from between two thousand and three thousand meters altitude. While he did apologize for nearly hitting a U.S. gunboat in the harbor, he gave no mention that any Chinese civilians might have been harmed.[43]

A prominent Japanese legal adviser at the Navy Ministry explained that at the start of the China war, there was a "lack of recognized rules" and no treaties outlawing inhumane forms of aerial attack. In a pamphlet for naval officers written by this legal adviser, the officers had been left considerable latitude. Japanese bombers could not target noncombatants but were allowed to hit civilian factories making military supplies. If large armed forces were concentrated in a city or town, those could be bombed, with efforts taken to minimize the "unavoidable" danger to civilians. Since the pamphlet began by reminding the naval officers that the international rules were not fixed, it was not hard to see how tactical advantage could overwhelm such constraint.[44]

The defense did not mention that Japan had shifted course just a few months later. In military directives issued in December 1938 by the high command and approved by Hirohito, Japan had launched a terror bomb-ing campaign in central China, allowing attacks on political and strategic targets. While civilians had often been accidental victims of the bombs beforehand, these new directives made it obvious that the Chinese public would intentionally be bombarded. The goal was to cause such pervasive fear that the destabilized Nationalist government would have no option but submission.

By January 1939, Chongqing suffered the first strike on predominantly civilian neighborhoods. In May that year, Japanese bombers began to rain incendiaries and bombs on residential and commercial areas of the city, destroying a market district and a cinema complex. The city was mostly made of wood and bamboo, which proved ideal for firebombing. In another round of attacks launched in May 1940, Japanese bombers destroyed schools and civilian neighborhoods, expanding out into the suburbs and nearby towns. The bombing only declined in intensity in the middle of 1941 as Japan turned its attention toward the impending war with the United States.[45] If the courtroom had wanted a witness to what Chongqing had looked like in this period, there was one sitting on the bench.

THE EAST IS RED

The defense sought to portray China as a hotbed of Communist revo-lution, which had an eerie resonance in the courtroom as Mao's forces gained ground. Yet the judges refused to hear a key aspect of the Japa-nese case: self-defense against the threat of Communism. This fear was integral to the worldview of many of the defendants. Its exclusion was especially bizarre in the early Cold War, when the United States, Brit-ain, France, Holland, and their allies were conspicuously making policies driven by their own fears of the spread of Communism.

The defense sought to argue, as an American defense lawyer from Iowa put it, that "the Japanese were justified in their fears of the spread of communism and the interference with the peace of Asia." To the embarrassment of the Chinese delegation, the defense lawyers accused the Nationalists of collaborating with the Communists—particularly in the period when the rival parties had formed a shaky united front against the Japanese.

The prosecution leaped to block this line of argument. Comyns Carr declared it absurd to say that Japan could have been entitled to invade China in order to wipe out Communism. The question about the war, he said, was: "Who effectively began it? Or if it began in some trifling frontier incident, who effectively took advantage of that to create a large scale war?"

The judges deliberated briefly. The subject was obviously embarrassing for several of them: Mei, whose own government was slowly falling to Mao's revolutionaries; Major General Myron Cramer, the U.S. judge, whose country was rallying its allies for the dawning Cold War; and Major General Ivan Zaryanov, the Soviet judge, who disliked Japanese complaints about Soviet efforts to export the revolution. A majority of the judges sided with the prosecution, largely gutting this entire defense line of argument.

Webb announced that no evidence about the spread of Communism in China was relevant in the general defense. However, the court would accept evidence about specific Communist attacks on Japanese nationals in China, and the individual defendants would be allowed to testify about their own fears of Communism. While the defense lawyers spluttered, the judges rejected a slew of documents about Soviet influence and Communist organizing across China, including Japanese diplomatic cables and Edgar Snow's well-known book, *Red Star Over China*.[46] The defense did manage to sneak past an essay by Mao on guerrilla warfare—a rare mention of the Chinese rebel chief in the Tokyo trial.[47]

Nevertheless Communism hovered over the whole trial. It was impossible to tell the history of this period—nor to explain today's newspaper read over breakfast at the Imperial Hotel—without considering Communist revolutionaries in the Soviet Union, China, and beyond. At one point, a defense lawyer managed to assert in court that the Chinese Communist Party had become essentially "an independent Chinese-Soviet Government, acting in concert with the Nationalist Government."[48] A while later, an American defense lawyer tried again to sneak in a series of statements by the Chinese Communists. In a topsy-turvy moment, Comyns Carr came to the defense of the Chinese Communist Party, declaring that "not only a Chinese communist but any other Chinese was well entitled" to resist the Japanese aggressors. If the Nationalists had worked temporarily with the Communists to fend off the invasion, that was their business. Webb and the judges rejected the Communist statements as irrelevant to the trial.[49]

As the Japanese and American defense counsel poked away at this tender spot, the Soviet associate prosecutor jumped to his feet in protest again and again. One Japanese defense lawyer argued convincingly that the Chinese Communist Party was a significant military force and had clearly played a role in the war, and should not be excluded from the defense's account of recent history.[50] Soon after, an American defense lawyer sharply pointed out that it was hard to present evidence about Japan's entry into the Anti-Comintern Pact without discussing anti-Communism, and hinted that the "policy of the American government" shared that fear of Communism. Webb exploded: "This is not an American court. This court is international and non-political and I should not have to tell you that." As the American lawyer protested, Webb snapped, "This Court is not going to be dragged into the vortex of national politics of any kind. The debate is closed."[51]

While the Tokyo trial tried to pretend that the Chinese Communist Party did not exist, the rising Chinese Communists treated the Tokyo court with all the contempt due to a Nationalist project. They accused Chiang's government of incompetence and of conniving to exonerate the Japanese war criminals. They proposed kicking Mei off the tribunal and replacing him with a proper Communist representative of the Chinese people.

The *Liberation Daily* editorialized, "The strange show at the International Tribunal for the Far East symbolizes the Chiang Kai-shek government's forfeiture of national rights, humiliation of national pride, and corruption." The Nationalist reactionaries had given away Manchuria and colluded with Japanese war criminals to suppress the Chinese people; they had put up feeble resistance against the Japanese and collaborated with Japanese bandits; Chiang had adopted the "absurd principle" of not dwelling on past evils. The party organ warned that "Chinese fascist reactionaries still keep in contact with Japan's fascist remnants, treacherously collaborating with each other."[52]

Communist Party organs were appalled at the trial's due process, particularly the defense lawyers: "the atmosphere within the court is not like trials of war criminals but a dialogue between the Allied powers and Japanese war criminals."[53] One leading propagandist wrote, "Known by everyone in China, Doihara can arrogantly practice sophistry at the International Tribunal and use the courtroom as a podium to promote Japanese fascist militarism." This writer complained that Tojo Hideki was allowed to eat delicacies and read magazines in prison.[54] While the *People's Daily* covered the testimony of Chinese witnesses about atrocities in Nanjing and elsewhere, the Chinese Communist Party's senior leaders were conspicuously silent, not using the trial as an opportunity to castigate Japan.[55]

The Communists did use the trial to excoriate the United States for indulging "Japanese fascist war criminals instead of seriously punishing them," as the *Liberation Daily* put it.[56] The American reactionaries had joined with the Nationalist dictatorship to deprive the Chinese people of the fruits of their victory over Japan, unleashing a civil war against the Communists.[57] "With respect to the handling of Japanese war criminals, MacArthur cannot be more lenient," wrote a senior Communist Party propagandist.[58]

Most Chinese would have seen Tojo or Matsui as Japan's leading villains. Yet Chinese Communist propaganda was obsessed with "the Number One war criminal" Okamura Yasuji, the Japanese general who had led the bloody "three alls" campaign against areas thought to be sympathetic to the Communist armies.[59] Not only had he gone unpunished by the Tokyo trial, Chiang had hired him as a military adviser, after he had been conveniently exonerated in a swift review by a military war crimes tribunal run by the Nationalists.[60] "The entire Chinese nation experienced an immeasurable amount of suffering at his hands and is anxious to eat his flesh," said a People's Liberation Army spokesman. "[T]his Number One fascist war criminal, under the protection of American imperialists and their running dog Chiang Kai-shek, not only escaped trial and execution but also resides safely in Nanjing to assume the role of so-called 'liaison officer.'"[61] The official *Liberation Daily* raged that "Japanese war criminals are the Chinese people's irreconcilable enemies, but Chiang Kai-shek treated Japanese war criminals as good friends. . . . Of course, Okamura Yasuji's 'rich experience' in killing Chinese people is highly valued by Chiang Kai-shek and American imperialists."[62] When Okamura was eventually sent back to Japan, Mao himself demanded that he be turned over to the People's Liberation Army. He wrote that "the absurd measure taken by the traitorous Nationalist government and MacArthur's Headquarters in an attempt to safeguard the revival of Japanese aggressive force against China completely violates the Chinese people's will and cannot be recognized by the Chinese people."[63]

CONSTITUTION

As the trial wore on, Tojo remained vigilant in the courtroom, jotting down notes with "religious care," as the *Mainichi Shimbun* noted. Despite a bout of bronchial trouble, the *Mainichi* reported, he showed no signs of physical or spiritual weakness.[64] There was a group of mannerly defendants, who sat still throughout, including Marquis Kido Koichi and Hirota Koki. In contrast, General Itagaki Seishiro seemed uninterested in the proceedings; several army men were especially unruly; and General Minami Jiro, whose hearing was bad, napped in court.[65]

Shigemitsu Mamoru, the cerebral former foreign minister, was unshaven and unkempt, in a stained suit, his jowls sagging. One day he picked up an old copy of *Life* magazine, and suddenly jolted: he saw for the first time the famous picture of himself in morning coat and top hat signing Japan's surrender aboard the USS *Missouri*. "It's been such a long time," he muttered.[66]

In Sugamo Prison, the defendants squabbled, formed factions, reconciled, and fell out again. Bored and irritable, they idled away their time reading day-old newspapers or, for exercise, silently pacing up and down their eighteen feet of hallway. Shigemitsu devoted himself to Chinese thought, reading a new translation of *The Analects* of Confucius and a book on the ancient Chinese philosophers Laozi and Zhuangzi. Some of the accused played endless matches of Go, the classical board game of strategy, using paper instead of black-or-white game pieces. The main consolation of the accused came from family visits. Edith Togo, who attended court every day, was especially devoted to her ailing husband. Although Tojo Hideki had forbidden relatives from visiting him in his early months in jail, he had started to allow two daughters to come see him.[67]

The stately pace of the trial was outraced by the headlong transformation of Japanese society outside the courtroom. As K. P. S. Menon reported to Jawaharlal Nehru, the American occupiers were showing all "their youthfulness, buoyancy, naiveté, idealism and a touch of dollar imperialism." He wondered if the Japanese, whom he considered intensely nationalistic and still potentially aggressive, were sincere in their rapid changes: "There is something almost uncanny in the welcome which the people of Japan have given to their ex-enemies, their acquiescence in the drastic measures introduced by SCAP [Supreme Commander for the Allied Powers], and the homage, almost amounting to worship, which they pay MacArthur."[68]

As General Headquarters boasted, in two years the occupation had crushed the secret police, modernized a feudalistic government, freed thousands of political prisoners, scrapped the Army and Navy ministries, abolished State Shinto and emperor worship, advanced equality for women, and guaranteed new freedoms of speech, press, religion, and organization. A General Headquarters report noted condescendingly that the Japanese masses who had been "docile by training and terrorized by fear" were now assured freedom, and looked forward to taking "a dignified and helpful place . . . in a world community of peaceful democratic nations." In April 1947, Japan held nationwide elections at all levels of government, voting in almost a quarter of a million new elected officials, from the Diet in Tokyo all the way down to local assemblies and prefecture officials. The Japan Socialist Party made an impressive showing, proving itself a powerful competitor against the conservatives.[69]

On May 3—while the Tokyo trial was chewing over the bloody Japanese assault on Shanghai some ten years earlier—a progressive new constitution went into effect. The emperor lent his support to it as part of a national celebration, greeted by rousing cheers and joyous tears—an event shown widely on newsreels in movie theaters across the country.[70] The product of long wrangling between the Diet and General Headquarters, the constitution was transformational. It vested democratic power in the people, guaranteed "the fundamental human rights," declared equality before law, gave laborers the right to unionize and to work, protected freedom of speech and religion and assembly, banned torture, and created an independent judiciary. The emperor was downgraded to a symbolic figurehead. The most distinctive change was the constitution's Article 9, in which "the Japanese people forever renounce war as a sovereign right of the nation and the threat or use of force as means of settling international disputes"—language which General Headquarters drafters had drawn from the Kellogg-Briand Pact that featured so prominently in the Tokyo trial.[71]

MacArthur's staff talked less about the hard edge of this societal overhaul: scouring away the many people who had upheld the old order. By now the United States had arrested more than two thousand lower-level Japanese suspected of conventional war crimes or crimes against humanity, to be tried by the various Allied countries. The U.S. military courts moved much faster than the Tokyo trial, prosecuting and executing Japanese accused of war crimes against U.S. prisoners of war abused or killed in camps or aboard "hell ships," subjected to surgical experiments by the Japanese army medical corps, or tortured by the Kempeitai. Some of the Japanese officers hanged by the United States were quite senior, such as a Japanese navy vice admiral and rear admiral put to death at Guam.[72]

Even more sweeping was the ongoing purge. The Americans preferred it to be known that the Japanese government was carrying out the purge, although General Headquarters could and did review Japanese decisions. In January 1947, the Japanese government had issued an extension of MacArthur's purge directive, expanding it to cover all elected officials in national or local government, leaders of powerful companies and associations, and the media. By that July, the Japanese authorities had screened half a million cases and banned 1,681 individuals from public life.[73]

Soon after the new constitution went into effect, Webb grandly declared in court that "it is the purpose of the Supreme Commander and, indeed, of the Allied Powers that this trial, the evidence in this trial should get the widest publicity, and it is getting it." An American defense lawyer retorted, "As a matter of publicity, I suggest that in this atomic age this case has gone to the back page of the newspapers so long ago that it is forgotten."[74]

CHAPTER 20

Self-Defense at Pearl Harbor

I N MARCH 1947, HARRY TRUMAN stood at a wooden podium festooned with bulky microphones before a joint session of Congress. He delivered a somber speech announcing his Cold War doctrine of supporting "free peoples who are resisting attempted subjugation by armed minorities or by outside pressures"—aimed against Communist subversion and Soviet expansionism, although not European colonialism.[1] Three months later, George Marshall, the U.S. secretary of state, delivered his Harvard address announcing the European recovery program that would be known as the Marshall Plan, meant in large part to undercut Soviet influence in Europe.[2] As Marshall was speaking, the defense at the Tokyo trial turned to rebutting the accusations of the Soviet Union.

In the Tokyo courtroom's furious preview of the Cold War, the air was filled with a clash of American and Russian accents, gone topsy-turvy: the Russian voices speaking for the cause of the United States, the American defense counsel taking the Japanese side. The Japanese onlookers knew that the Soviets were still interning vast numbers of Japanese prisoners of war. With tempers flaring in Tokyo's steamy summer heat, the irate Soviet prosecutors, led by a Red Army major general and a colonel, fought the defense every step of the way. "I expected to hear the proofs and evidence," jeered Major General A. N. Vasiliev, a new Soviet associate prosecutor, "but I didn't hear anything beyond a long speech."

If the Soviets were expecting that the judges would collegially follow Major General Ivan Zaryanov, they were keenly disappointed. Again and again, the judges sided with the defense against the Soviet prosecutors, who did not hide their rancor.[3] Cut off once more by Sir William Webb, a Soviet major general spluttered, "You haven't heard my objection to the end. You haven't listened to my objection to the end. I was interrupted right in the middle of my objection and I couldn't give the grounds for my objection." "Well," snapped Webb, "there is a limit to the time we can spend on objections that patently must fail."[4]

Joseph Stalin's regime had grown impatient with the Tokyo trial. The Soviets officially hoped to use the trial to showcase the essence of Japanese imperialism, reeducate the Japanese people, and discourage any future aspirants to world domination—the latter a none too subtle slap at the United States.[5] Yet the plodding proceedings lacked the speed, decisiveness, and stage-managed theatrics of Soviet political trials.[6] The Soviets showed much more dissatisfaction with the Tokyo trial than they ever did at Nuremberg.[7] Sergei Golunsky, the first Soviet associate prosecutor, had returned to Moscow to an influential position in the Foreign Ministry. In the state-run media, he bitterly complained that while Nuremberg had rested on equal prerogatives of four Allied powers, the United States dominated in Tokyo. He was scandalized that the Japanese accused got American defense lawyers, paid for by the U.S. government, often in U.S. Army uniform, depicting Japan as a victim of foreign encirclement. He wrote, "Many of these American lawyers dish up the hackneyed arguments of Japanese wartime propaganda and are lavish in libellous attacks on the Soviet Union."

He criticized the failure to prosecute capitalistic chiefs of the *zaibatsu*, which he termed "the mainsprings of piratical aggression. Wherever the Japanese armies appeared, the giant monopoly octopuses stretched their tentacles." Golunsky complained that the indictment did not include the Japanese strike on Port Arthur in 1904, calling it "a prototype of the Japanese attack on Pearl Harbor." And he lambasted Japanese imperialism and anti-Communism, contending that Japan had sleeplessly plotted aggression and attacked the Soviet Union in two border clashes in 1938 and 1939. Rather than downplaying the Soviet violation of its neutrality treaty with Japan in the last days of World War II, Golunsky boasted that the Soviets had "declared war on the Japanese aggressors." The Soviet Union took full credit for ending the war, not even mentioning the atomic bombs: "It needed the devastating blow delivered by the Soviet army at the Japanese troops concentrated in Manchuria to make the overweening Japanese imperialists at last understand they had lost the war."[8]

The defense's main task was to explain as innocuous those two border battles from 1938 and 1939. Their best evidence was the fact that both clashes had been resolved without war. At Mukden and the Marco Polo Bridge, Japan had readily escalated a small crisis into a big war; here it conspicuously had not.

For the first clash, in the summer of 1938 at Lake Khasan, near the Soviet frontier with Japanese-controlled Manchuria, the defense brought forward the inveterately undependable Major General Tanaka Ryukichi, the former aide to Tojo Hideki who had previously testified for the prosecution. He was fat, witty, and contemptuous of many of the defendants; he expected to be assassinated for testifying.[9] He had commanded an artillery regiment nearby, part of Japan's army in Korea. Like other Japanese witnesses, he blamed the fighting on the Soviets grabbing a hill on the Manchurian side of the border. Even under fire, he said, the Japanese had taken care not to cross the border. More reliably, the defense introduced the diary of a Soviet diplomat, which showed that Shigemitsu Mamoru, as Japan's foreign minister, had tried to reach a cease-fire to resolve the fracas quickly.[10]

The next incident had been a Manchurian border battle in the spring and summer of 1939, when the Soviet client state of Outer Mongolia faced off with Japanese troops at the Khalkhin-Gol River. "Japan at that time was not capable of contemplating an attack against Soviet Russia," testified a Japanese lieutenant general, "so much so she did her utmost to avoid starting any trouble with Soviet Russia." A Soviet prosecutor, a uniformed Red Army colonel who had previously been on the Soviet team at Nuremberg, rankled at the accusation that it had been Soviet troops who violated the frontier.[11]

When Vasiliev airily referred to "the Japanese war criminals," Webb was taken aback at the flash of Stalinist candor. "You must not refer to the accused as Japanese war criminals," chided the Australian chief judge. "They have not yet been convicted." The Soviet prosecutor huffily shot back, "As far as I understand they were brought before this Tribunal as Japanese war criminals, major Japanese war criminals. Maybe I am mistaken, I don't know. But so far I was not mistaken." Disgusted, Webb retorted, "That is not so. And as far as we are concerned they are innocent until they are proved guilty." Although the Soviet prosecutor grudgingly said he agreed, he added, "the defense defend the interests of the Japanese war criminals, and, therefore, I call them this name."[12]

Plenty of evidence never made it to court. Whatever Foreign Ministry papers about those two border clashes had not been incinerated by U.S. firebombing, one Japanese archivist testified, had been burned at the end of the war.[13] The defense introduced a certificate stating that the intelligence telegrams of the Kwantung Army and the Japanese army in Korea about the Soviet Union's entry into the war had been burned at the end of World War II.[14]

The defense counsel had two built-in disadvantages. First, they were badly hamstrung by the decision by the judges against introducing general evidence about Japanese fears of Communism. No such restraints had been imposed on the prosecution in its discussions of Allied alarm at Japanese militarism or colonialism. This restriction made it all but impossible to talk sensibly about the agitated relationship between the Soviet Union and Japan.

Second, some of the Soviet case for Japanese aggression rested on statements that imprisoned Japanese officers had given to their Soviet captors, but these Japanese were conveniently unavailable to speak to anyone else—either dead, jailed, or sick. Major Ben Bruce Blakeney, the pugnacious American defense lawyer, provided a list of a dozen senior Japanese officers captured in Manchuria who had given evidence for the Soviet prosecution but could not be cross-examined because they were in Soviet custody or dead. Except for Zaryanov, the judges were uneasy at the prospect of allowing witness testimony that had not been challenged by the defense; the judges reluctantly allowed them to be entered as evidence, but Webb, speaking for many on the bench, said that he thought they had no value.[15] Blakeney protested that "whereas the prosecution, with the stupendous resources of the most powerful nations of the earth at their disposal, can at will pick and choose which witnesses they will produce, the defence have no such power."[16]

It would not be until months later that the Soviets finally complied with a court order to produce six witnesses to testify, including some captured Japanese.[17] Blakeney pressed the judges to strike from the record the testimony of some Japanese "witnesses imprisoned behind the Iron Curtain"—Winston Churchill's phrase, then only a little more than a year old. There was no point in trying to get honest testimony "from a man with a gun in his back," Blakeney said, and the affidavits were a "hodge-podge of opinion, conclusion, affirmative answers to flagrantly leading questions, hearsay upon hearsay." Vasiliev protested "such insolent attacks on the Soviet Union." Blakeney retorted, "Counsel's remarks are not only offensive but they are irrelevant." Leaping in, Webb asked all counsel to avoid "vituperation" toward any of the Allied powers.[18] In the end, to Vasiliev's chagrin, the judges disregarded the evidence of two witnesses in Soviet captivity and rejected affidavits by witnesses who were not produced for cross-examination.[19]

Blakeney complained that the Soviets were ignoring defense subpoenas for evidence. The Soviets had stiffed a request from General Douglas MacArthur to produce documents subpoenaed for the defense, such as captured Japanese military records and even copies of an issue of *Pravda*. Blakeney scoffed that "the newspaper *Pravda* . . . seemingly cannot be found in the U.S.S.R., although it is the official organ of the Communist Party and is reputed to have a considerable circulation in that country."[20]

RACING THE ENEMY

Moving away from two clashes resolved without war, the defense changed the subject to an actual war: the Soviet campaign against Japan in the last days of World War II, which the defense said violated the 1941 neutrality pact between the two countries.

Blakeney argued that Japan had meant to honor the neutrality pact, having rebuffed Nazi Germany's request that its Axis ally join in its invasion of the Soviet Union.[21] Blakeney introduced the Nuremberg testimony of Germany's foreign minister, Joachim von Ribbentrop: "I also tried to have Japan attack Russia, for in such a way I saw a quick ending of the war. Japan, however, did not do that. Rather I should say, she did neither the one thing we wanted nor the other, but she did do a third thing. She attacked the United States at Pearl Harbor."[22]

Vasiliev objected to Blakeney's evidence about the Soviet war against Japan. The Soviet Union, he said, had spurned Japan's plea for mediation and, acting as a loyal ally of the United States and Britain, "declared war against the Japanese aggressor." Blakeney retorted that the notion of imposing criminal responsibility for breaking an assurance was a novel one, whose validity as international law could be tested by seeing whether the Soviet Union had treated its own treaty commitments as binding. If the Soviet Union had attacked Japan at the request of the Allies, had the prosecuting nations really recognized a new principle of international law outlawing aggression? He scorned the Soviet prosecutor for claiming "that there can be no other opinion than that the acts of the U.S.S.R. and its allies, of which my own nation is one, are right and correct. This has not the sound of argument addressed to a Tribunal."

After the judges debated, they ruled out evidence about the Soviet onslaught on simple grounds: it was irrelevant since there were no charges against any of the defendants about it. But although Blakeney lost, he managed to sneak some exculpatory evidence into the trial record, such as desperate cables sent by Togo Shigenori, as foreign minister, pleading in vain for Soviet mediation to help end the war.

To show that the Soviet Union had committed aggression by violating the neutrality pact, Blakeney had lined up a sterling American witness: the chief of the U.S. military mission in Moscow in the last years of the war, a U.S. major general who had attended all the major Allied summits from Cairo to Yalta. This time the U.S. acting chief prosecutor, Frank

Tavenner, rose to challenge the defense in three hours of strenuous debate. (When Vasiliev approached the lectern, Webb sent him right back, saying he wanted only to hear from Tavenner.) If Japan had launched an aggressive war in the first place, Tavenner said, "it can be no defense to the accused that the Allied Powers sought or acquired the assistance of another power or powers to resist the aggressor." The Soviet violation of the neutrality pact was irrelevant and outside the tribunal's jurisdiction.[23]

In response, another American defense lawyer said it was the Soviets who had committed aggression against Japan, while Blakeney suggested dropping all Soviet charges from the indictment. After withdrawing to deliberate, this time a majority of the judges sided with the defense, allowing the U.S. major general's affidavit—revealing how both the Roosevelt and Truman administrations had urged the Soviet Union to enter the war, with the Soviets pledging to do so soon after Nazi Germany was defeated. He recalled hearing Stalin himself say "by our common front we shall win."[24]

The Soviet phase ended with another outburst by Webb in which he rejected much of the Soviet prosecution. He was set off by an American defense lawyer, Owen Cunningham, even more contentious than Blakeney, who said that "Asia then, and Asia today suffered and is suffering from Russian interference or communistic interference with the establishment and maintenance of peace." Webb in vain instructed Cunningham to stop trying to ignite political discussions. "How shallow, how hollow it all sounds when we know that the only hostility displayed by Japan toward Russia was in connection with border incidents," Webb lectured. "She did not declare war against Russia." This gutted much of the Soviet prosecution's case.

Webb launched into a political tirade of his own that again called into question his impartiality. He said that Japan "attacked the two great protagonists of democracy, America and Britain. She endeavored to destroy the only two nations in the world who could have combatted totalitarianism in any form." Another American lawyer leaped to his feet to protest. Japanese aggression had not yet been decided, he reminded the judges; the defense had not fully presented its case. Boiling over with frustration, Tavenner retorted, "I think it is time to inquire of defense counsel if they contend that the United States attacked Japan at Pearl Harbor."[25]

In Moscow, the Soviet rulers, already frosty toward the Tokyo trial, were enraged. *Red Star,* an official organ of the Soviet military, accused the United States of being in cahoots with the Japanese criminals. Since neither Hirohito nor any industrial or financial bosses were on trial, the court was prevented "from disclosing the real roots of Japanese imperialism." The defense counsel "preach the criminal ideology of their clients" to a wider world, assisted by American newspapers that reprinted their words, and by U.S. military officers and officials who testified for the defense. *Red Star* complained that the defense was "relying on contemporary statements of certain American circles regarding the need 'to halt the spread of Communism,' to justify the analogous desire on the part of the leaders of imperialist Japan."[26]

Another Soviet state journal bitterly complained that the Tokyo trial was dominated by Anglo-Saxon staffers and procedures, unlike Nuremberg, where the Soviet Union had been one of four Allied powers. This journal denounced Kiyose Ichiro, the leading Japanese defense lawyer, as a "militant fascist" who insolently gave a torrent of lies and calumny. The capitalistic American lawyers, it declared, were driven by the need to advertise their law firms and thus earn dollars.[27] Since the Soviet commissars could not dictate the unfolding of the Tokyo trial, they had no use for it.

Defense of Empire

On June 3, as the defense counsel in Tokyo was about to begin its presentation on Pearl Harbor, the news of an imminent Partition was broadcast on All India Radio. The undoing of British colonialism in its central possession made a singularly incongruous moment for the defense lawyers to deliver a justification of Japan's preservation of its own empire.

"Long years ago we made a tryst with destiny," intoned Jawaharlal Nehru, toward midnight on August 14–15, to the packed Constituent Assembly of what now became an independent India. "At the stroke of the midnight hour, when the world sleeps, India will awake to life and freedom." The grandeur of his oratory marked the emergence of history's largest democracy, a vast experiment in human liberation.[28] Yet even as he spoke, India's founding prime minister was privately mourning the escalating bloodshed as the subcontinent was sliced into India and Pakistan. Soon before delivering his speech, a friend in Lahore telephoned him to describe bodies lying in the alleys as enraged Muslims hunted down Hindus and Sikhs. Nehru wept as he put down the phone.[29]

India's independence came two years to the day after Japan's surrender. Especially in Punjab and Bengal, the home state of Radhabinod Pal, Partition would mean one of the bloodiest disasters of the twentieth century. After the worst violence, the corpses of Hindus and Muslims were strewn in the rivers, canals, and lanes of Pal's home city of Calcutta.[30] His beloved city would be flooded with more than three million refugees.

Like many Bengalis, he would later blame Partition on Britain's desire to divide and rule India.[31] All told, between half a million and a million people would die across India and Pakistan, and some twelve million traumatized people had to move from one country to the other. On a tour of one camp, a grief-shattered refugee would slap Nehru in the face, crying, "Give my mother back to me! Bring my sisters to me!"[32]

This historical backdrop of independence and Partition was keenly embarrassing for many parties at the Tokyo trial. The massacres were grim proof that, no matter what the Tokyo trial might be accomplishing, the end of World War II did not mean a law-governed peace for ordinary people in Asia. The chaotic collapse of the Raj was a reminder that Britain, under a postwar Labour government that embraced imperialism, was still holding on to its colossal empire in such places as Burma, Malaya, Hong Kong, Kenya, Nigeria, Southern Rhodesia (today Zimbabwe), Jamaica, Aden, Palestine, and Cyprus, among others.[33] France still sought to rule over Indochina, Algeria, Morocco, Madagascar, and many other lands; Holland was reasserting control over Indonesia and Suriname. For its part, the Truman administration was gingerly backing away from the more anticolonial attitude of Franklin Delano Roosevelt's administration in order to bolster its European allies in the early Cold War.[34] Truman's team hoped that a gradual decolonization would create newly independent pro-Western countries without too badly alienating its British, French, and Dutch partners, but found that Asians and Africans struggling against imperial domination were not inclined to wait.[35] As India and Pakistan proclaimed their postcolonial sovereignty, the defense's vehement arguments for the necessities of Japan's lost empire called an awkward attention to the other empires that were still standing.

Starting in June, the defense counsel turned to Japan's path to Pearl Harbor. They recounted an audacious blow for survival by a smaller empire encircled by the combined might of its American, British, Dutch, Chinese, and Filipino foes. As one American defense lawyer put it, "It was a case of the midget striking the giant in order to defend himself."[36]

This had been a desperate gambit, the defense conceded, potentially something close to national suicide. A Japanese admiral who had served as vice chief of the navy general staff testified chillingly about his prewar fears that incendiary bombs used against Japan's wooden houses would cause fiery conflagrations—a prediction whose accuracy was apparent outside the Tokyo courtroom.[37]

The defense began with the Axis, which the prosecution had already

The Allied judges listening to the defense counsel in the Army Ministry courtroom, March 30, 1948

shown to be a tottery partnership. Cunningham added that Japan had innocently allied with Nazi Germany "for the defensive and peaceful purpose of contributing to the world peace." Even though Germany had promptly declared war on the United States after Pearl Harbor, Cunningham fancifully claimed that had nothing to do with the Tripartite Pact.[38]

To the amusement of spectators, the defense did not bother to present any evidence about Italy, an "impotent and useless ally." The most macabre piece of defense evidence was the last declaration of Joachim von Ribbentrop, the Nazi foreign minister, from the day before he was hanged at Nuremberg. Although he obviously could not be cross-examined, the judges gave extra credence to a man who knew he was about to die. The convicted war criminal treated Japan as an unreliable ally, complaining that Japan had "done everything possible to keep out of the conflict with Soviet Russia." Pearl Harbor, he said, came as "a complete surprise" to him, hearing about it on the radio.[39]

With that, the court adjourned for a month. The exhausted defense lawyers, who had been working in offices that lacked air-conditioning in Tokyo's sultry summer, begged for a pause. Webb granted it grudgingly, noting publicly that a majority of the judges were bitterly opposed.[40] As he explained privately to MacArthur, he had only consented when it became clear that otherwise the defense would "come to a standstill."[41] Zaryanov was against it anyway, and Delfin Jaranilla was incensed, pressing to wrap up the trial before the Allies signed a formal peace treaty that would restore Japan's sovereignty.[42] "I am utterly indifferent as to what effect the doing of justice in this case has on the peace treaty," Webb reprimanded him. "I am absolutely impervious to such political considerations."[43]

By the time the court reconvened, Joseph Keenan, the U.S. chief prosecutor, had to general dismay returned from Washington.[44] Arthur Comyns Carr, who had gotten used to running the prosecution with Tavenner, threatened again to resign. Sir Hartley Shawcross was frustrated at the prospect of Keenan interfering with an outfit that was at last running smoothly.[45] Yet the British government dared do no more than quietly complain to the Americans, concluding that there was no way to prevent Keenan's return. Comyns Carr, miserable, promised not to quit unless the man proved "absolutely impossible."[46]

Better prepared after the adjournment, a Japanese defense lawyer declared that the defendants "did not wage a war of aggression but in reality were involved in a conflict of self-defense which jeopardized national existence." He candidly explained the need for raw materials that had driven Japan to imperial conquest: "even though Japan desperately needed oil and supplies for her civilian economy she was at the same time warned that if she moved south in quest of it, it meant war." Facing economic strangulation after seizing southern Indochina, Japan had made every effort to find a peaceful way to "escape the imminent danger of extinction as a power." The last straw for Japan, said the defense lawyer, was the "unyielding dictate" of Cordell Hull's note on November 26, 1941, which would have meant "literally her disappearance as a power militarily, industrially and commercially."

The strike at Pearl Harbor had been no surprise to the Americans, claimed the Japanese lawyer: "When on 1 December 1941 Japan, hope all but abandoned, decided on war, it was a decision long anticipated by the United States." True, the final Japanese note to the U.S. government was not delivered until after the attacks at Pearl Harbor and elsewhere in Asia were under way, but that was an unintentional bureaucratic blunder in Washington beyond the control of these defendants.

He concluded that Japan "was inevitably driven . . . to wage a war of self-preservation and in self defense." Yet on his own account, at best Japan could claim self-defense of a new empire, clashing with the European and U.S. empires already entrenched in Asia.[47] Unwilling to pull troops out of China, reluctant to budge from Indochina, Japan sought to maintain its imperial conquests, not merely protect its home islands.

An American defense lawyer from New York City, William Logan Jr., was even more forceful. He accused the Western powers of deliberate, premeditated military and economic pressure: "As an affirmative defense it will be shown that the situation became so increasingly oppressive and acute that, true to expectations and desires of the Western Powers that Japan strike the first blow, Japan ultimately was forced to make a decision to fight for her very existence." He blasted the United States for its bold support for China, which "literally meant the spilling of more Japanese blood on China soil." It was the United States' embargo, Logan asserted, joined promptly by Britain and Holland, that had really started the war, not Pearl Harbor: "From the Japanese point of view those embargoes and freezing orders assumed the gravity and proportions of the denial of a right to live."

In an explicit justification of Japan's imperialism, Logan explained that Japan had needed more land, some of which was found in Korea and Taiwan. Without expanding, Japan was entirely dependent for petroleum on the United States, the Netherlands East Indies, and British-controlled Burma. Its industrial potential was pathetically weak; at the time of Pearl Harbor, he noted, Japanese total annual production of iron and steel was less than what the Americans made in a month—which, he did not mention, was an excellent reason not to attack them.[48]

As the defense plunged into a numbing discussion of rice, steel, tariffs, and shipping, Webb made it clear in court that he was skeptical. Japan may have been provoked by U.S. economic sanctions, he noted, but that did not mean it was acting in self-defense: "acting under provocation and acting in self-defense are two distinct matters."[49]

While sparring with Logan, Webb startled the courtroom by implicating Hirohito for Pearl Harbor. He highlighted the devastating entry in Marquis Kido Koichi's diary for November 30, 1941—which the prosecution had studiously tried to overlook. "The Emperor then directed that the program be carried out," said Webb. That stark statement hung in the air: the emperor had *ordered* the attack on the United States.

When Logan said that the emperor had merely been playing his constitutional role, Webb replied: "If a cabinet advises a king to commit a crime, and the king directs that it be committed, there is no constitutional protection." Logan retorted that self-defense was a good defense to any crime. "They didn't want to go to war, your Honor," he said. "They knew that they couldn't win the war and the prosecution evidence so shows it and so does ours. They were driven to it." Unpersuaded, Webb blamed both the emperor and his advisers: "It still remains that the men who advised the commission of a crime, if it be one, are in no worse position than the man who directs the crime be committed." In open court, the chief judge essentially declared Hirohito just as guilty as Tojo.[50]

The defense's evidence made a powerful counterpoint to the prosecution's, but it had its weaknesses. It laid more culpability on the military defendants, with Blakeney saying that the army and navy had been "supreme and omnipotent."[51] In addition, the defense's case revealed how inflexible the Japanese government, driven by military hard-liners, had been about the crucial issue of pulling its soldiers out of China. Blakeney referred to "the Army's intransigence" over withdrawing from China.[52] The best proposal that Japan ever managed—one which was meant to be cheated on quietly—was that some of its army would be withdrawn two years after a peace agreement with China, whenever that might be, with troops remaining in north China for as long as necessary.[53] According to the defense's evidence, the Japanese government had told Hull in September 1941 that it had to maintain troops in parts of China for an unspecified amount of time in order to ward off foreigners and stamp out Chinese Communism: "[T]o defend the existence of Japan herself, the stationing of forces is indeed inevitable."[54]

The defense relied heavily on the insider diary of Prince Konoe Fumimaro, the more conciliatory prime minister who had been supplanted by Tojo Hideki soon before Pearl Harbor. While it put some of the defendants in a good light, it revealed an obstinate refusal by the army leaders, especially Tojo, to consider real concessions. As Konoe crisply explained in his diary, "it is clear to all that the outstanding problem is the withdrawal of troops." In October 1941, according to Konoe's diary, Tojo, as army minister, had flatly told him that it would be difficult for the army to accept pulling out. A few days later, Tojo had refused any concessions of withdrawing troops from China, calling that "the life of the Army." When Konoe beseeched him a few days later, Tojo had replied that weakness would only encourage the Americans to ask for more, while undermining the army's fighting spirit. He had pressed the cabinet to end talks with the Americans.

Even when the army's obduracy triggered the collapse of Konoe's government in mid-October, the former prime minister's cabinet had believed that diplomatic negotiations were not yet so hopeless as to trigger a Japanese attack. The real stumbling block was China: "Especially, if we could get our Army authorities to relax their position somewhat, with reference to the withdrawal of troops, we believe that there is a good possibility of reaching an agreement." But the army fervently believed that the posting of troops was the only tangible benefit of the China war, and feared that a withdrawal would sweep their ranks with defeatism.[55]

Bad as the defense evidence was for Tojo, it was more heartening for Togo Shigenori. A Foreign Ministry official testified that during the heated liaison conferences that October and November, the new foreign minister always insisted on successful negotiations, even as the army refused concessions in China. When the army pressed to open hostilities, Togo had vigorously refused, urging maximum exertions for peace almost until the end.[56] He had kept urging his own government for more flexibility while pressing the U.S. negotiators to accept his two final proposals.[57]

The defense pinned particular blame on the uncompromising Hull note, treating it as an ultimatum. Two days afterward, Hull had told a U.S. general that the negotiations with Japan were over, with scant chance of restarting, and U.S. military officials had braced for a possible war. The Roosevelt administration, Blakeney said, had "anticipated that the delivery of the note of November 26 would result in rupture of the negotiations and of peaceful relations."[58] The defense seized on a War Department message to the West Coast command the day after the Hull note: "If hostilities cannot repeat cannot be avoided the United States desires that Japan commit the first overt act." The problem for the defense, though, was that the message insisted that U.S. forces take no offensive action until Japan struck. Webb was unimpressed: "I am reminded that if Japan did not strike there was to be no war."[59]

The records of the December 1 imperial conference revealed the Japanese leaders seething with indignation and insult. As prime minister and army minister, Tojo Hideki had complained bitterly that the new U.S. demands would destroy Japan's prestige, make a resolution in China impossible, and endanger Japan's very existence. He had concluded, "Japan has no other way now than to wage war against the United States, Britain and the Netherlands in order to achieve a solution of the present critical situation and to secure its existence and self-defense."

While Togo Shigenori had fought hard against war in previous meetings, in this one he largely concurred. He complained that "the United States Government obstinately adhered to the doctrinarian principles to which it had traditionally submitted," including disapproval of the occupation of China, support for Chiang Kai-shek's government, and a demand "that Japan should give up the policy of force." He had been willing to accept some of the Hull note, but its "unreasonable" demands about China, Indochina, and the Axis were "utterly unacceptable." Japan would have to retreat completely from the Asian continent; the United States and Britain would dominate instead; Manchukuo would be imperiled; and Japan would face defeat in China. Togo told the imperial conference, "If we accepted the present proposal of the United States, Japan would be in an international position inferior even to that which it had held before the outbreak of the Manchurian incident, and its very existence would also be endangered."[60]

Having presented the Hull note as the last straw, the defense played down the personal appeal for peace that Roosevelt had sent directly to the emperor on December 6, 1941. The prosecution had emphasized that the United States was still seeking to talk at the highest levels. This telegram from Roosevelt—clearly the kind of note that ought to be delivered with maximum speed—had been bafflingly delayed for hours on its way to the U.S. embassy, which the defense tried to explain as merely an accident.[61] The defense drew a picture of the Japanese state as capable of executing a successful surprise attack on a well-fortified enemy stronghold thousands of miles away but unable to deliver its mail on time.

The surprise attack, Blakeney said, had been not a treacherous breach of the Hague Convention III of 1907 but simply a dreadful bureaucratic snafu. The prosecution had angrily pointed out that the fourteenth section of a long fourteen-part telegram to Roosevelt, in which Japan suspended the Washington negotiations, had been delayed on December 7 until after the Pearl Harbor attack was under way. In the defense version, Japan's leaders had meant to notify the United States but had been undone by a typing pool which will live in infamy.[62] The Japanese embassy had needed to get the message to the U.S. government by 1 p.m. on December 7, a Sunday afternoon. This message could not be entrusted to the usual typists, and there had been only one senior official in the Japanese embassy who could operate a typewriter halfway properly. His first draft was a mess, so he began redoing it around 11 a.m., and then had to retype a few pages. As the minutes ticked by in front of the typewriter, Japanese bombers and fighter planes were speeding toward Pearl Harbor. The Japanese embassy staffers finally finished typing around 1:50 p.m., and two senior officials raced to the State Department. They were kept waiting there for about twenty minutes, finally handing the pages to Hull at about 2:20 p.m.—an hour after the bombs had already started falling at Pearl Harbor.[63]

Anyway, Blakeney argued, the Roosevelt administration had secretly been intercepting Japanese diplomatic messages and knew that an attack was coming. The judges allowed the spectacular testimony of senior U.S. military officers about the most sensitive codebreaking—the MAGIC cryptanalysis program. A U.S. Army intelligence colonel then at the War Department revealed that the U.S. government had by December 3 intercepted orders to Japanese embassies to destroy their codes and documents, which presaged a break in diplomatic relations or war.

On December 6, according to his testimony, the United States had intercepted thirteen out of the fourteen parts of Japan's message by 10 p.m. The colonel had promptly sent this by locked pouch to Hull's office. He got the fourteenth part by 8:30 a.m. on December 7, which was immediately sent to the State Department. By 11:25 a.m., General George Marshall, the Army chief of staff, had read the full message, which included instructions to the Japanese embassy to deliver it to the U.S. government by 1 p.m. Marshall and his team had expected a Japanese attack somewhere by 1 p.m. By just before noon, Marshall had sent warnings to the Army and Navy in Hawaii, the Philippines, Panama, and other American outposts in the Pacific that the Japanese would be presenting an ultimatum by 1 p.m. and were under orders to destroy their code machines.[64] Still, Marshall's note told nothing more specific than to be on alert, and according to this colonel, his warning would probably not have arrived until about 12:30 p.m. or later. According to a major general who had been with Marshall that day, they had expected the Japanese to attack in Thailand and perhaps elsewhere.[65]

A U.S. Navy commander posted to the White House testified that on December 6, at around 9:30 p.m., some important papers had been brought to the White House. He later read in the newspapers that these had been thirteen out of fourteen parts of the final Japanese message. He had given them to Roosevelt, he said, and then stayed in the room as the president read them. After Roosevelt showed them to Harry Hopkins, his closest adviser on foreign policy, the president had "said in substance—I am not sure of the exact words, but in substance—'This means war.'"[66]

This evidence has fueled decades of speculation about whether Roosevelt misled the American public or even wanted a back door to war.[67] Still, even the strongest case made by the defense does not do much to support such dramatic conclusions. While the defense's version suggests that Roosevelt understood that Japan was about to do something big, the intercepts did not reveal how and where the blow would fall, which could have been anywhere across Asia or even the Panama Canal.[68] Webb pointed out that the fact that a senior U.S. official had "contemplated a possible surprise attack is not evidence of the legality of the attack or the justification for the attack."[69]

Even based on defense evidence, there was little question that the Japanese navy had wanted as much advantage of surprise as possible.[70] A Japanese Foreign Ministry official, called as a defense witness, admitted under cross-examination that the navy had believed that a surprise attack was a necessity.[71] Even granting the full rigmarole about typing, the Japanese notification about suspending talks would have reached the State Department just before the first explosion at Pearl Harbor, which was cutting it awfully close. Worse, the defense never managed to refute the prosecution's evidence that Japan had started the war unannounced on several other fronts earlier that same day, surprise attacks even if the typing had gone properly: attacking unannounced in Shanghai at 10:45 a.m., Washington time, in Malaya at 11:40 a.m., and in Thailand at 1:05 p.m.[72]

The defense's most shocking witnesses were several Japanese navy officers who had participated in the raid on Pearl Harbor.[73] These officers were meant to show the difficulty of carrying off a tactical surprise strike against the U.S. fleet, but had a wholly different impact in court. The affidavit of a bluff Japanese navy captain who had commanded an air attack unit, proud of the remarkable military achievement, drove home how crucial a thunderbolt blow had been to the Japanese war plan. Flabbergasted, Webb asked the defense what exactly they were trying to prove with this testimony: "We know the attack took place and that it was highly successful." The purpose, explained an American defense lawyer, was to show the Japanese navy's lack of preparation for war. "You do not prove that by showing it was a very successful operation," replied Webb.[74]

PRISONERS

The final task for the defense was to address war crimes against Allied civilians and prisoners of war. Here their argument was largely formalistic: Japanese officers had given appropriate orders, and therefore there could not have been abuse.

Witness after witness insisted that Japan had ordered that prisoners of war and civilians in its custody be treated decently. As one Japanese officer put it, "You must endeavor to make the people in the occupied areas know the superiority of the Japanese race and believe that they consider it the highest honor to be Japanese subjects sharing in the boundless benevolence of the Emperor." Another senior officer bluntly explained that the Japanese had "attained the status when they would be able to use white prisoners of war, and the result was that Japanese superiority could be demonstrated to the native population by the Japanese using prisoners of war before the eyes of these natives."[75]

For the most part the defense denied that any war crimes had taken place. A Japanese colonel testified that "there was absolutely no case of murder, atrocity and looting" by his infantry division in Hong Kong.[76] A Japanese vice admiral based in the Philippines testified that he had not even dreamed of the atrocities that had taken place in Manila, although he did mention that local women and children had harassed Japanese troops in that city—which suggested how the Japanese troops might have broadened their definitions of who could be targeted as a guerrilla. Again and again, the prosecution did not bother to cross-examine, instead frostily pointing out the eyewitness testimony already presented about atrocities at all these places.[77]

The difficulty for the defense was establishing that humane regulations had actually been followed. Where it could, the defense presented Red Cross reports that some of the prisoner of war camps had been acceptably run, but these were mostly from smaller camps in the early stages of the war.[78] After a laudatory affidavit from the British wife of a diplomat in Hong Kong, Webb asked, "Do you think you are going to meet the sweeping charges made against you by reading the individual experiences of a few people?" Speaking for some of the underwhelmed judges, he continued, "The defense case as I see it is just this: In ten thousand cases there may have been bad treatment but listen to this case of good treatment."[79]

On several occasions, defense witnesses gave evidence that showed bad treatment. A senior Japanese official under Tojo Hideki's command who had been at Bataan remembered seeing the corpses of prisoners of war lying by the side of the road after the march. He mentioned that the Japanese had been overwhelmed by the number of surrendering Americans and Filipinos, "so we had a very hard time escorting them to the camp." Worse, he admitted attacks on Filipino civilians as part of Japan's counterinsurgency campaign: "the Japanese Army . . . in the course of their fighting, suppressed guerrilla activities, and, while doing so, they may have suppressed the good native population in the same way they have engaged in the suppression of guerrilla activities, largely due to language difficulties, and so forth."[80]

A Japanese captain in charge of a prisoner of war camp at Rangoon gave an affidavit that noted outbreaks of beriberi, smallpox, and cholera, adding that weaker captives were often hospitalized.[81] Another Japanese officer, who had been in charge of five camps where more than four hundred prisoners had died, gave a disconcertingly honest answer when asked why he had taken away Red Cross supplies in camps where prisoners were dying: "That was lack of wisdom and virtue on my part." "You didn't expect that," said Webb to the crestfallen defense lawyer.[82]

The defense backfired by calling the lieutenant general who had been in charge of occupied Shanghai during the war. After he blandly testified about the need to treat prisoners well, Tavenner asked him if he had anything to do with the trial and execution of three of the Doolittle fliers. The lieutenant general had already been convicted by a postwar U.S. military commission and sentenced to five years of hard labor.[83] Caught off guard, an American defense lawyer objected that this was beyond the scope of the witness's testimony. "It is not and you know it," said Webb. "Objection overruled." The lieutenant general said that he had been ordered to put the Doolittle airmen on trial by his direct superior, one of the Tokyo defendants, Field Marshal Hata Shunroku. He recalled telling Hata that the sentence—death by firing squad—had been very heavy, and noted that Hata had been under orders, perhaps from Tojo Hideki himself. When Hata's lawyer jumped in to say that his client had had no choice but to obey orders from Tojo or other bosses in Tokyo, Webb snapped, "It is nonsense."[84]

As defense witnesses kept showing, the chain of command led straight to Tojo Hideki as army minister from 1940 to 1944. The army minister was in charge of prisoners of war held in Japan itself, including the annexed colonies of Korea and Taiwan; he was also responsible for the Kempeitai there.[85] A colonel working at the Army Ministry testified that prisoners of war came under the jurisdiction of the army minister, were put in camps established by the army minister, which were supervised by a commander designated by the army minister and run by a bureaucracy supervised by the army minister. He testified that the construction of the Burma–Thailand death railway had been a project of the army minister with the prisoners under Tojo's jurisdiction.[86] With defense witnesses like this, Tojo hardly needed prosecutors.

CHAPTER 21

The Emperor Waltz

F OR OVER A YEAR, Tojo Hideki, Marquis Kido Koichi, Togo Shigenori, and the other verbose defendants had been made to sit silently in court. Unaccustomed to such passivity, the former leaders of an empire chafed as their lawyers spoke for them in a general defense of Japan. (Only General Minami Jiro had given some testimony.) But starting on September 10, 1947, the final phase of the defense at last allowed each defendant to take the stand to vindicate himself individually.

Proceeding in alphabetical order from Araki to Umezu, this last phase would take months. It produced a fresh burst of public interest in the court's long rewind through World War II, allowing a chance to see some of the most powerful men in Japan give what could be their last public declarations. After the prosecution and defense completed their dueling *Rashomon* versions, now the trial splintered into twenty-five diverging accounts. These individual testimonials showed just how hard it was for the defense counsel to mount a common case that served all their remaining clients. Despite the prosecution's claim of a joint criminal conspiracy, the individual defendants pointed accusatory fingers in every direction: civilians versus military, army versus navy, all against all.[1] Only a few of them, on advice of their lawyers, chose not to testify. Many of the accused denied having had any real power, implicating other defendants in a long parade of self-exculpation.

One previously strutting general told a reporter, "I had no authority. I did nothing. I only obeyed orders."[2] General Muto Akira, who had been in both Nanjing and Manila as the massacres unfolded there, testified that he had known nothing about the slaughtering of Filipinos and averred that General Matsui Iwane had strictly enforced military discipline in Nanjing after hearing of cases of plunder and rape.[3] One former prime minister and foreign minister, Hirota Koki, decided his case was too precarious to risk taking the stand himself.[4]

With so many moving targets, the prosecution misfired repeatedly. Joseph Keenan, back from Washington, wrested control away from Arthur Comyns Carr and Frank Tavenner. As Comyns Carr recorded with dismay, Keenan assigned the case of one defendant to "a newly arrived and perfectly incompetent American," and took another case "away from a probably incompetent Filippino [sic], and given him to a certainly incompetent, though very pleasant American."[5] Comyns Carr privately told Sir Hartley Shawcross, Britain's attorney general, "it must be admitted that in XXN [cross-examination] most of the defendants have simply danced round the set of incompetence put up against them, with probably damaging propaganda effects."[6]

Not all the accused got off lightly. Major General Oshima Hiroshi, who as ambassador in Berlin had championed the Axis alliance, strained to downplay his enthusiasm for Nazi Germany. "I knew of the concentration camps but have never seen them," he said. "And also I heard rumors of maltreatment but I have never investigated the facts." He admitted that he had personally shown Adolf Hitler a military map of Singapore showing gun emplacements. Did Hitler ask how long it would take to conquer Singapore? "Yes, he did," Oshima replied, before defensively adding, "There should be nothing wrong in showing them a map in answer to their wish."[7]

General Matsui Iwane, accused for the Nanjing massacre, was too sick to make his own case to the court.[8] He only made a short appearance, otherwise letting his American lawyer and a series of Japanese officers speak for him. The one judge who would be most impressed by this testimony, Radhabinod Pal, did not actually hear it; he was home in Calcutta throughout, tending to his wife.

On the stand, the elderly Matsui looked wan, his eyes dull. He only spoke briefly.[9] In a statement read aloud by his American lawyer, he declared, "The two races of Chinese and Japanese ought to have cooperated with each other as brethren in the nature of things." He claimed that, sick in bed about a hundred and forty miles away from the battle, he had only heard about the fall of Nanjing from reports by the two Japanese army commanders there—one of whom was Prince Asaka Yasuhiko, the uncle of Emperor Hirohito. While conceding that it was possible that many Chinese civilians had been killed by bombs and bullets during the fighting, he heatedly denied "the slander" that the Japanese army staff had ordered or tolerated a massacre. "I had no desire to turn Nanking into a field of carnage," he testified to the court, "and I was most sorry when that happened."[10]

His American and Japanese lawyers argued that Matsui's militant pan-Asianism was a mere cultural divertissement, demonstrating his innocuous love for the Chinese he would soon be invading. They minimized his authority: as commander in chief he had no units under his direct command, and he had been relieved of his command of the Central China Area Army soon after the fall of Nanjing. Anyway, his American defense lawyer contended, there had been no atrocities in Nanjing.

A series of Japanese army officers who had served under Matsui all testified that Nanjing had been a scene of courtly chivalry. One said that he had seen only the corpses of Chinese soldiers and had never heard of any massacres. Then he added that it was "utterly impossible" to differentiate Chinese soldiers in plain clothes from civilians, and admitted to sometimes rounding up an entire village and holding them until the soldiers among them surrendered, to be turned over to the Kempeitai. Another Japanese officer testified that the only offense he had seen was a lieutenant who brought the elegant shoe of a Chinese woman back to his quarters to show it off to his soldiers, and was nearly court-martialed for plunder. "There is no such fact that organized rapes were committed by Japanese soldiers," said one colonel. "There were a few scattered offenses concerning discipline as I recall, but I know they were all punished in accordance with the laws."[11]

Not content merely to deny sexual violence, a senior Japanese army lawyer sought to blame the Chinese women for their own rape. Before the conquest of Nanjing, he said, Chinese women would often "take a suggestive attitude towards Japanese soldiers"; when accused of adultery by their jealous husbands, "they suddenly changed their attitude and asserted exaggeratedly that they had been raped." Having made this calumny, he offered no explanation how the otherwise debauched Chinese women had on this occasion managed to refrain from flinging themselves at the Japanese menfolk.[12]

Most revealingly, in the testimony in defense of General Itagaki Seishiro, whom Mei Ruao despised for his role in invading China, the Chinese prosecution produced a powerful piece of Japanese evidence about atrocities there. As army minister, Itagaki had tried to muzzle Japanese troops returning from China from telling their friends and family at home about what the army was really doing abroad, fearing that the truth would damage morale and undercut the war effort. A pugnacious Chinese prosecutor dramatically confronted a Japanese general, who had served as Itagaki's vice minister of the army, with a top secret Japanese

Army Ministry report about what Japanese soldiers back from China said about their own deeds.

The Japanese general admitted the authenticity of the Army Ministry report, which was labeled "Handle with Extreme Care to Prevent Leakage." The testaments of Japan's own soldiers revealed murder, pillage, and rape. "The plundering by our army in the battle area is beyond imagination," said one soldier. Another soldier said, "The thing I like best during the battle is plundering." One said, "In the front lines the superiors turn a blind eye to plundering and there were some who plundered to their heart's content." Yet another said that in half a year of battle "about the only things I learned are rape and burglary."

The troops admitted routine instances of rape: "we captured a family of four. We played with the daughter just as we would with a harlot. But as the parents insisted that the daughter be returned to them we killed them. We played with the daughter as before until the unit's departure and then killed her." One soldier said, "In the battlefield we think nothing of rape." Another soldier said, "One company commander gave instructions for raping as follows: 'In order that we won't have problems, either pay them money or kill them in some obscure place after you have finished.' If the army men who participated in the war were investigated individually they will probably be all guilty of murder, robbery or rape."

The army had used Chinese spies, said a Japanese soldier, but then killed them when they became unnecessary. One soldier said, "The prisoners of the Chinese Army were sometimes lined up in one line and killed to test the efficiency of the machine gun." At that, the Chinese prosecutor said icily, "I think that will be sufficient to cover the point of military discipline."[13]

The Emperor on Trial

The most delicate case was that of Marquis Kido Koichi. His testimony would be as close as the Tokyo trial came to a cross-examination of Emperor Hirohito himself, who was securely ensconced in the Imperial Palace about two miles and a world away from the Ichigaya courtroom. For all his preparations in his monologues, the emperor would never be interrogated, nor made to give testimony, nor turn over his papers.[14] Yet as the lord keeper of the privy seal, the emperor's top adviser, Kido had been at Hirohito's side at every major turning point. Sir William Webb privately told Australia's prime minister that Kido was one of the two most important suspects on trial, alongside Tojo Hideki.[15]

Like the emperor he served, Kido cut an unassuming figure. A small man, he was overshadowed by the beefy U.S. Army officer standing at attention to his left as he sat in the witness box. Dressed conservatively in suits and ties with a white shirt, he had round wire-rimmed glasses and a neatly cropped mustache; he was mostly bald beneath the bulky headphones used for translation. His voice was thin but steely, and he spoke with self-control. Under cross-examination, his nerves showed in his habit of stuffing both his hands into his jacket pockets, in his coughing, in the clenching of his jaws.

Kido did not deny how close he had been to his sovereign. "The Lord Keeper of the Privy Seal is answerable only to the Emperor and serves at His pleasure," he told the courtroom with discernible pride. "If at any stage the views of the Lord Keeper do not coincide with those of the Emperor, the Emperor would ask for his resignation." In many parts, his testimony amounted to a public airing of Hirohito's secret self-justifying monologues.

The marquis would need all his wiles. As Webb told General Douglas MacArthur privately, the prosecution's evidence implicated the emperor.[16] Kido's own diary recorded that a week before Pearl Harbor, the emperor had "ordered" Tojo "to act according to program."[17] Listening to Kido's testimony, Webb was privately convinced of the emperor's guilt. "The Emperor was the leader," he jotted in notes that would become his draft judgment. "The Emperor's authority was required for war. If he did not want war he should have withheld his authority and we must assume that if he had withheld it the war would not have taken place. He was the only man in Japan who could decide on peace or war." The emperor, Webb scrawled, could not excuse himself as a figurehead bound to approve his ministers' advice: "He was not a limited monarch." He coldly scribbled, "It is no answer to say that he might have been assassinated. More risks are run by all rulers."[18]

In open court, Webb had repeatedly made clear his annoyance—as well as that of some of the other judges—at Keenan's blatant maneuvering to avoid incriminating the emperor.[19] Mei was struck by Webb's "denunciation of Prosecutor Keenan, who was flushed with shame, over the question of the Emperor's responsibility."[20]

Keenan redoubled his efforts to clear the emperor. Soon before Kido took the stand, the U.S. chief prosecutor had told the press that a "thorough investigation convinced the prosecution that no evidence was available to support the charge that the Emperor participated in the conspiracy"—a remarkable claim to make before the emperor's top aide had even testified. Keenan blamed Japan's aggression on "a group of gangsters" that had seized control of the government: "They deceived

Hirohito and defrauded the Japanese people into believing the Emperor was with them in waging this aggressive warfare."[21] When Keenan used in court the same line about the defendants swindling the Japanese people into blaming the emperor, Webb shot back, "This is the first time in the lengthy trial that that has been suggested, and it is contrary to the prosecution's evidence."[22]

With Kido's testimony looming, MacArthur keenly needed to have the emperor exonerated. As noted by the Japanese diplomat who served as liaison between the "two big shots (General and Emperor)," Hirohito had become friendly with several top U.S. officials. The emperor had reached out to Brigadier General Bonner Fellers, probably his strongest advocate in MacArthur's inner circle, to express his deep appreciation for all that Fellers had done for him.[23]

Joseph Keenan, the U.S. chief prosecutor, walks alongside General Douglas MacArthur, Tokyo, circa 1945–47.

The continued importance of the throne was equally apparent to an influential Indian diplomat, K. P. S. Menon, who reported to Jawaharlal Nehru that "the Emperor is still regarded as the personification and essence of Japan, a symbol of continuity of 2,000 years of (semi-mythical) Japanese history." He worried that General Headquarters had "strengthened, rather than weakened, the position of the Emperor by investing it with a modern, instead of a medieval halo." At a dinner party given by Japanese friends, the Indian envoy was stunned when all the Japanese guests burst into a song about dying for the emperor: "I have but one wish: to be by my Emperor, alive or dead."[24]

. . .

Kido meant to absolve himself and the emperor by laying blame on the military, especially Tojo Hideki and the army. He later recalled the commotion among the army defendants when he submitted his affidavit.[25] Kido's self-exculpation emphasized his "constant clashes" with a dangerous army over fifteen years, undercutting the claims of other defendants that an innocuous Japan had been forced into a defensive war by the outrageous demands of the Hull note. It was only natural, he thought, that the army men would retaliate.[26] As an overexcitable Associated Press reporter wrote, "The atomic bomb explosions which devastated Hiroshima and Nagasaki could not have created more consternation among the Japanese leaders now in the prisoner's dock than Kido's testimony."[27]

Kido was delighted with the "marvelous" performance of his American lawyer, William Logan Jr., grateful to him for the rest of his life. "If I had had only Japanese attorneys, there probably would have been no hope for me," he later recalled. Working with Kido's second son, Logan spent more than a month preparing at the marquis' vacation home south of Tokyo: "he all but memorized nearly all of my voluminous diary."

The prosecution's plan was to set a fox to catch a fox, having the wily Comyns Carr go after the crafty Kido in the witness box—what promised to be a supremely artful match of wits. The marquis, unnerved, worried that his British adversary "was quite a scoundrel and the most unscrupulous of the prosecutors, and I . . . had been warned to be thoroughly on my guard." Kido and Logan bet everything on the marquis' own testimony. "This bombshell announcement drove Comyns Carr mad," Kido later crowed.[28]

But at the last moment, Keenan shoved Comyns Carr aside, perhaps to ensure that Hirohito got off lightly. The British government was outraged. As a senior British official notified Shawcross, this last-minute reshuffle was "discourteous" and "half-witted."[29] Keenan "has now started to display the cloven hoof," wrote an enraged Comyns Carr in a letter he decided was too rude to send. The U.S. chief prosecutor, fumed Comyns Carr, wanted to "prevent the British Commonwealth from figuring too prominently in the case," and continue his feud with Webb about the emperor's guilt.[30]

Comyns Carr wrote to a British official that "Keenan, although, or perhaps because he's apparently still on [the] wagon, has been playing merry hell with the case and the British Commonwealth contingent, and seems finally to have disgusted most of the Americans, though none of them has the guts to tell him so. What a life!"[31] He wrote to Shawcross, "I put my pride in my pocket and did about three times as much work in trying to teach Keenan how to X X [cross-examine] KIDO as I would have needed to do it myself, and to educate his entirely incompetent staff."[32]

Before Kido could begin his defense, Keenan stood up to object that Kido's affidavit was too long and argumentative. Kido believed that the U.S. chief prosecutor's complaint was really more about protecting the emperor. He later explained that Keenan had been surprised and greatly troubled by the affidavit's extensive description of Kido's relationship with the emperor: "It appears that Mr. Keenan may have been told by General MacArthur that it was the policy of the Allied countries that every effort should be made to avoid mention of the Emperor."[33]

The Power Broker

The witness box was exceptionally crowded when Kido was in it, joined by the invisible but palpable presence of the emperor. Kido claimed that his monarch had been an enlightened voice of peace but was incapable of constraining the army hard-liners.[34] In addition to the apparition of the emperor, there were really two Kidos on the stand: the Kido present on trial and the Kido past of his own diary. While the marquis emphasized that he had turned over the single most important piece of prosecution evidence voluntarily, he was nevertheless frustrated to find his diary entries frozen in time and hurled back at him.

Logan, a balding man with keen eyes behind round spectacles, read aloud his client's lengthy self-justifying affidavit. "My life had been devoted to fighting the militarists," the marquis declared. He singled out several fellow defendants from the army, bluntly condemning the coup plotting of Colonel Hashimoto Kingoro as a "curse on this country, inviting the misery of today." On one awkward bus ride back to Sugamo Prison, the army defendants glared at him. "Ordinarily, a scoundrel like this would be choked to death," said Hashimoto. "But we can't do a thing like that now."[35]

The prosecution's real accusation was that Kido had been an enabler of the extremists, a right-wing establishment figure who should have known how important it was to stand up to the army zealots. Here his defense did himself fewer favors. He said that he had opposed the insubordinate Kwantung Army's expansion into Manchuria; at the same time, he conceded that he had agreed that Japan would have to defend those Japanese living in Manchuria, afraid that they might be massacred by Chinese Communists. If he had not obliged, he had feared a military coup or revolution. After the capture of Manchuria, when the emperor was asked for an imperial rescript sanctioning Japan's withdrawal from the League of Nations, Hirohito had obliged, although privately instructing that the text should mention that it was regrettable that Japan had been forced to quit the League.

Kido recalled with horror the military revolt in February 1936, when he had been jolted from a deep sleep in a snowy predawn to be told that his predecessor as lord keeper had been assassinated at his house by soldiers. Hirohito himself had rebuked the army minister, ordering that the insurgents be brought under control as soon as possible. Yet after this terrifying episode, the emperor had little appetite for further confrontations with the military. The insurrection frightened civilian politicians into quiescence, reckoning that it might be safer to let the army blow off steam in foreign conquests rather than in power grabs at home. As Kido informed the court, out of fear of assassins, he and his family were already guarded by five policemen.[36]

Kido dodged blame for the Japanese invasion of China, the part of the general defense which he thought had gone off the worst.[37] The prosecution accused him of joining a conspiracy by entering the cabinet in October 1937, a few months after the full-scale war began. He bristled at the assertion that his votes as education minister made him guilty for everything that Japan had done until his stint in the cabinet ended in August 1939. Yet even the most exculpatory entries in his diary suggested that, while he had hoped that peace talks with Chiang Kai-shek would succeed, he balked at pressuring the army hard-liners about it. He had been in the cabinet meeting that made the crucial decision not to deal any more with the Nationalist government, but had not expressed any opinion.[38] Kido testified that he feared that army extremists would again revolt at home if Japan made peace in China, telling the prime minister that "it may be necessary to keep the safety valve ajar"—acknowledging the need to indulge the army's foreign adventures.[39]

Kido was indignant to find himself "aggressively pursued for responsibility concerning the Nanjing incident," which had occurred when he was education minister.[40] He maintained that he had not heard of the massacre until after the end of the war. "If I had heard about it at the time I would certainly have tried to do something about it," Kido testified, "even though it was not a matter of cabinet responsibility." It strained belief that the well-informed, gossipy Kido would have heard nothing. Nor did he mention that his diary showed that he had met in July 1943 with Prince Mikasa, Hirohito's younger brother, who as a soldier fighting in China had been shaken by atrocities there, and had told him about "the actual situation in China."[41]

"Nothing Ventured, Nothing Gained"

Kido had returned to the halls of power in a more rarefied role in May 1940, as the lord keeper of the privy seal. Called on by such top leaders as Tojo Hideki, he had a catbird seat as Japan careened toward war. Yet like the emperor he served, he presented his job at the pinnacle as almost ceremonial. His Imperial Palace duties, he emphasized, did not allow him to interfere in policymaking; he could only express his true opinions privately. Once the government had decided on a national policy, he said, he would counsel the emperor to approve it as a matter of constitutional principle.

After the Japanese seizure of southern French Indochina in July 1941 and the U.S. imposition of economic sanctions on Japan, when the chief of the navy general staff briefed the emperor about Japan's dwindling oil supplies, Kido had been "filled with trepidation by the Imperial anxiety about the danger of having to wage a desperate war." Yet he had reassured Hirohito that the navy's grim assessment was too simple and argued against backing out of the Tripartite Pact with Nazi Germany and Italy.[42]

In early August 1941, Kido had cautioned his boyhood friend Prince Konoe Fumimaro against hastily deciding on war against the United States. A few days later, he claimed that he had fortified the prime minister with arguments to sway the military, warning that securing oil by attacking the Netherlands East Indies would prompt a U.S. declaration of war. He urged resolve to bear ten years of hard struggle: "We could not do what we wanted on account of the lack of our national power."[43]

Kido emphasized that he had not been in the room for the crucial imperial conference on September 6 where Japan's leaders for the first time decided on war against the United States if there was no diplomatic solution reached by mid-October. Kido said that he had cautioned the prime minister that the deadline was dangerous. Yet when the emperor had told him that he wanted to ask questions at the imperial conference, the lord keeper had preferred that he let the president of the privy council handle the important queries, with the emperor pressing the military command to give diplomacy its chance. Kido reminded the courtroom how the emperor had recited a peace-minded poem composed by his grandfather the Meiji Emperor: "Over the four seas prevails universal fraternity,/ I think, Why turbulent waves wage so furiously."

In his affidavit, Kido had called the September 6 decision for war "poisonous" and a "cancer." His diary showed him urging a gloomy Konoe to reconsider the decision for war against the United States—but also advocating a fierce military assault against the Chinese strongholds of

Chongqing and Kunming in order to end the China war. Japan, he had said, would have to gird for ten or fifteen years of hard struggle. Undone by his diary, his affidavit had to inventively claim that he had only sought intensified war in China in order to better pursue peace with the United States.[44]

By mid-October, Kido testified, Hirohito had started pondering the imperial rescript declaring war that he might have to issue any day now. The monarch had resignedly said that his government should plan for the end of the war, using the Vatican as a channel for peace talks. The emperor had complained that his recent rescripts on pulling out of the League of Nations and allying with Nazi Germany had somehow been misunderstood by his people, although he thought he had emphasized the cause of world peace.[45]

After Konoe's cabinet collapsed in the face of military intransigence, Kido had confronted his most consequential decision: the choice of a new prime minister. Yet his diary showed that he had worked harder at protecting the throne than anything.

While many in the peace camp favored Prince Higashikuni Naruhiko, an army general who had married a daughter of the Meiji Emperor, Kido had feared having "a prince of the blood" bear responsibility for a possible war, which could spark a revolution against the monarchy.[46] He testified bluntly, "I thought the Imperial family might become the target of hatred by the people." Instead, Kido had urged the emperor to pick Tojo as prime minister—a man whom the marquis knew as an unyielding advocate of an immediate war. A career army man, the marquis claimed, might be able to yank the army back from war. The emperor approved, saying, "Nothing ventured, nothing gained."[47]

At this point, Kido's testimony careened off the rails. Keen to explain his amply documented advocacy for Tojo's premiership, he made the mistake of pointing out how much the incoming prime minister had deferred to the emperor. Kido testified in his affidavit, "Respect for Imperial wishes was common to all soldiers, but it was stronger in Tojo." Kido meant to show that a compliant Tojo would follow the emperor's instructions to reconsider the decision for war taken at the last imperial conference. Yet this assertion was a disaster for Kido's broader defense of the throne. If Kido had such confidence in the emperor's supremacy over his army, then why had he not made sure that Hirohito reined in Tojo and the generals from their conquests over the past decade? Why hadn't Hirohito instructed Tojo to avoid an unwinnable war?

Like many of the conservatives in history who have ushered rightist extremists into power, Kido may have fancied that Tojo would prove possible to control.[48] He boasted that the new prime minister "devoted his all to the negotiation with America in pursuance of Imperial wishes." In fact, the Tojo government's commitment to reversing Japan's rush to war lasted less than three weeks. While Togo Shigenori, the new foreign minister, fought loudly for painful concessions in China and Indochina that might avert a war, Kido remained a cipher. "I did not reveal my real intentions to anybody except two or three very close to me," he testified. "I consistently kept my silence."[49] After the date to attack was set, he got to work on an imperial rescript to declare war.

On the way to the office as the attack on Pearl Harbor was under way, Kido saw the rising sun above the Tokyo cityscape. As he wrote in his diary, he found it symbolic of Japan's destiny at war against "the two greatest powers in the world," the United States and Britain; he closed his eyes and prayed for the victory of Japan's planes. Later that morning, he had heard "the great news of our successful attack upon Hawaii." He had been most impressed by the self-possessed attitude of the emperor, who issued his fateful rescript declaring war.[50]

"THE EXCELLENT RESULTS WHICH WE ARE REPEATEDLY FAVORED WITH"

Kido's affidavit said little about his wartime deeds. Yet his diary shows that he was an integral part of the Imperial Palace as it did its bit. His own words show that he was exhilarated by his country's remarkable initial successes, using the throne to promote fervid wartime patriotism.[51] Rather than seizing those early victories to negotiate a way out of the war before the United States mobilized its industrial might, he showed scant inclination to confront the armed forces in their heady months of triumph.[52]

Kido did make much of one noteworthy instance when, in February 1942, he urged the emperor to make peace as soon as possible, having pummeled the Americans enough to make them return to the negotiating table on better terms. A few days later, Hirohito had told Tojo not to miss opportunities to end the war—probably the emperor's strongest warning to the armed forces during the war.[53] Yet his testimony did not mention that just a few days later, he had exulted that the swift conquest of Singapore was "courageous" and "truly inspiring."[54] The emperor had crowed, "Kido, it seems as though I harp on this matter often, but I say again that it is my sincere belief that the excellent results which we are repeatedly favored with are the results of our thoroughly thought out plans." Kido, according to his diary, had been unable to keep himself from weeping with joy.[55] A few weeks later, Kido had congratulated the emperor on the fall of the Netherlands East Indies, barely managing to get in his felicitations as the jubilant monarch chattered on.[56] He worked on imperial rescripts sanctifying battles in Burma and the Coral Sea.[57]

Kido ducked blame for war crimes against Allied prisoners of war by asserting that he had trusted the military—even though the rest of his affidavit cast himself as suspicious of them. After the fall of Hong Kong, his diary shows that he had been informed about loud British complaints about widespread atrocities there.[58] He claimed in his affidavit that he reported this information to Hirohito, who had asked Tojo to look into it. Kido testified that Tojo had assured him that there was no truth to the British allegations, which he had believed wholeheartedly.[59] At another point, Kido claimed that he had occasionally heard from the foreign minister about Allied protests, but had assumed that the army was working sincerely to improve its behavior. The well-informed courtier claimed that it was only during his own trial that he had heard detailed reports "to my great astonishment."

When the tide of the war had turned against Japan after the disastrous naval defeat at the battle of Midway in June 1942, a shaken Kido prudently decided that this time it would be better not to issue an imperial rescript.[60] By early 1944, Kido had despaired of the army's mirage of a "decisive battle" which would allow peace talks on terms favorable to Japan.[61] His mounting opposition to the war was driven in large part by his fear that it could lead to a Communist revolution. Yet he remained reluctant to make the hard concessions that might allow peace, emphasizing that Japan could not consider pulling troops out of China until the relationship between Chiang's government and the United States and Britain was severed.[62]

By the end of 1944, he could hear air raids over the capital, with as many as seventy B-29 bombers in the skies and antiaircraft guns roaring. On one occasion, Kido had gaped at B-29s flying in nine formations over the city, and saw for the first time one of them shot down by a Japanese fighter plane. He noted huge conflagrations around Tokyo from American firebombing.[63] His affidavit did not mention that in March 1945, he and the emperor had left the Imperial Palace to tour areas damaged by the war—in other words, to see the nearly sixteen square miles of ruin left by the devastating American firebombing of Tokyo a week earlier.[64] Wearing a military uniform, Hirohito had headed for areas near the Sumida River,

Marquis Kido Koichi, who as lord keeper of the privy seal was Emperor Hirohito's closest aide, testifies in his own defense, October 1947.

where some of the worst devastation had been. He had met with dazed survivors, and then retreated back into the Imperial Palace in the center of Tokyo. It is not clear what impression the tour left on the emperor, but an aide was troubled by the reproach visible on the faces of people digging through the rubble when they recognized the imperial motorcade.[65]

With a U.S. ground invasion of the Japanese home islands imminent, Kido had steered into place a new cabinet to pursue peace under the elderly Admiral Suzuki Kantaro. In an advisory meeting with senior statesmen on April 5, Kido had at last had an emotional confrontation with Tojo. As Kido noted in his affidavit, everyone had known to avoid speaking up for peace in front of Tojo since "any tactless remark might stimulate the Army to an unscrupulous countermeasure"—that is, he could arrange for them to get shot. While Tojo had proposed an army man as prime minister instead of Suzuki, Kido had warned that the Japanese nation was turning against the military and that "our homeland is about to turn into a battlefield."

Tojo had made an oblique but terrifying threat if he did not get his way. "There is a fear that the army may take on an aloof standing," he had declared, which would make the cabinet collapse. Taken aback, Kido had asked if there were signs of such a drastic step, which he thought meant a coup. "Can't say there is none," Tojo had snapped. Several of the senior statesmen were shaken at this explicit menace. Kido had admonished Tojo that if that happened, the Japanese people might abandon the war effort. With that, the stormy meeting had broken up. At last, Kido and the emperor had chosen the way of peace.[66]

.   .   .

Kido's affidavit highlighted the emperor's peace initiative in June and July 1945. Clearly shaken by the firebombing of Tokyo and other cities, Kido had noted with "awe and trepidation" that there was no alternative but to ask the emperor to act. On June 22, the emperor had at last instructed his senior leaders to move toward ending the war. When the chief of the army general staff had pushed back, the emperor had warned that they should not miss their chance, and the chief had duly fallen into line—an impressive demonstration of royal power.[67]

The choice of a Soviet channel for the failed peace feeler may have included a racial motivation. As Kido noted in a diary passage prudently not read in the courtroom, the best way to "avoid being isolated and attacked by nations as a colored race" was by "secretly cooperating with Soviet Russia and China, which are essentially Oriental in their stand against the Anglo-Saxons—the U.S.A. and Great Britain."[68]

The courtroom listened with fascination to Kido's version of the end of the war. Soon after the obliteration of Nagasaki, Kido testified, he had urged Hirohito to broadcast by radio an imperial rescript ending the war. After the climactic late-night imperial conference on August 9–10, the emperor had told Kido that while the army vigorously sought a decisive battle on the Japanese homeland, he had questioned how they could possibly win the war. The emperor had said that "I could not bear the sight of our loyal troops being disarmed, or those responsible for the war being punished, especially since they were unswerving in their devotion and unalloyed in their loyalty to me. But I think that now is the time to bear the unbearable." The monarch had choked back his tears and approved peace. When Kido saw him afterward, Hirohito had tears in his eyes, and the lord keeper had been so overwhelmed that he could not lift his head.[69]

Kido's account of the war ended as it had begun: with him fearing a military coup. After 3 a.m. in the early hours of August 15, a palace official rushed to the lord keeper's room to tell him that the Imperial Guard was in revolt, ransacking the palace looking for the phonograph recording of the emperor reading his rescript ending World War II. Jolted awake, Kido hid himself in the quarters of the court physician, but then raced back to his room to tear up all the important classified documents and throw them into his toilet. He holed up in the underground vault room for the rest of the night, not emerging until early morning when a palace functionary came to tell him that a top army general had taken control of the mutineers.

Kido testified that the insurgents had been seen scouring the palace for him. At around 4:30 a.m., seven or eight men—armed with grenades, handguns, and swords—had raided his burned home in the Akasaka district, southwest of the Imperial Palace, injuring one of the policemen assigned to protect him. The gang, Kido said in his affidavit, had brought a dagger on a ceremonial tray for him to commit ritual suicide; if he had not, they would have killed him themselves. The foiled assassins later went to a Tokyo hilltop and blew themselves up with hand grenades.

When the surrender message was broadcast at noon that day, Kido's diary noted that he was overwhelmed with tears. As Kido framed it, that ended both the war and his fight against the militarists. He presented himself as a near-martyr for peace, having risked his neck during the February 1936 coup, in the run-up to Pearl Harbor, and in bringing the war to an end. "I was opposed to the Pacific war from beginning to end," he claimed. "I had never supported it in any positive way."[70]

"We Are Not Trying the Emperor"

After Kido's American lawyer finished reading his lengthy statement, everyone pounced. First the marquis was barraged with peeved inquiries from other defense lawyers. Kido nervously stated that he was not specifying particular individuals as militarists, although he did name General Itagaki Seishiro as one of the bad batch. When pressed by Tojo Hideki's defense lawyer, Kiyose Ichiro, Kido even disavowed his own finest hour: the stormy meeting in which Tojo had perhaps threatened a putsch. Kido allowed Tojo just enough cover to claim that he had not really meant a coup.[71]

Next up, Joseph Keenan rose to cross-examine for the prosecution. His goal was to spare the emperor but hook his underling. The result, as the discarded Comyns Carr privately informed his government, was a disaster. Comyns Carr secretly warned that the testimony of the Japanese defendants had quite conclusively proved Hirohito's guilt.[72]

Keenan spoke sonorously, with an elaborately plummy vocabulary that drove the court's Japanese translators to distraction. His hand on his earpiece, he often sounded like he was on the brink of either losing his train of thought or losing his temper. When he accused Kido of trying to save his own skin, the marquis bristled, his eyes blinking keenly behind his round glasses, his jaw jutting.

As Kido later noted with relief, Keenan had not studied his case sufficiently: "much of his cross-examination was off the mark. . . . I, the defendant, was better prepared, and Prosecutor Carr, watching from the side, hammered the desk in frustration."[73] Again and again, other prosecutors had to leap up to show papers to guide Keenan at his lectern, pointing out what he ought to be covering. Comyns Carr, whom Keenan had asked to help, could only endure brief spells of the spectacle.[74]

Keenan's questioning was meandering and haphazard. He made a churlish point of calling his mark "Mr. Kido," while the marquis retreated into a chilly hush whenever possible. The judges, passing notes to each other, were dismayed. Webb repeatedly rebuked Keenan, at one point condescendingly telling him, "The simpler you make your questions, the better."[75]

Keenan managed to home in on two points: the role of the emperor in the attack on the United States and Kido's complicity in the China war.

At the outset, the Japanese lord keeper and the U.S. prosecutor waltzed together to spare the emperor. Kido explained that since the Meiji era, emperors did not veto the decisions of their governments. Lest anyone miss the upshot, Keenan asked, "are you intending to say that if the cabinet agreed upon war the Emperor of Japan would have no actual power to prevent it?" "Yes," Kido agreed, "the Emperor has no power to prevent it." Then Keenan blamed the army for Hirohito's rescript declaring war, calling it "a fraud upon the people of Japan to make them believe that it was the act of their Emperor when in truth and in fact he couldn't do anything else regardless of his real wishes and desires and his feelings for the best interests of Japan." Webb recoiled. "Mr. Chief of Counsel," he chided, "we are not trying the Emperor."

Keenan and Kido's concord ended fast when the U.S. chief prosecutor tried to blame the Pacific War on the lord keeper, portraying him as a master string-puller in Japanese politics. Keenan accused Kido of dissuading the emperor from asking skeptical questions at the important imperial conference of September 6. Logan shot back that Keenan should hold his concluding summation to the end of the trial.

Keenan confronted a diary entry that was particularly awkward for Hirohito. Soon before Pearl Harbor, Kido had recorded that the emperor urged that Nazi Germany be discouraged from making a separate peace with the Allies, insisting that it help Japan in the war against the United States.[76] That implicated Hirohito in the alleged conspiracy to wage aggressive war, encouraging Nazi Germany's declaration of war against the United States. In a bewildering move, Keenan accused the lord keeper of fabricating that incriminating entry in an attempt "to escape your own responsibility by transferring it to the Emperor of Japan."

This was a disastrous salvo. By calling into question the marquis' fidelity as a diarist, the U.S. chief prosecutor was trashing his own team's best evidence. General Headquarters was relying on other bits of Kido's diary to absolve the emperor. If Kido had slanted his diary against the emperor he revered, would he not have done worse against his rivals in the army? Impugning Kido's diary was the defense's job, not the prosecution's.

Keenan found it hard to nail the lord keeper without nailing the emperor too. He asked Kido why he had not told the emperor to refuse to sign an imperial rescript for war. Kido tensely replied that the emperor could not veto a cabinet decision. Trying to show the emperor's wish for peace, he added that Hirohito had pressed his underlings to reconsider the war decision of the September 6 imperial conference. Webb, convinced that the emperor was guilty, pounced: "Where did he get that authority?" It was a tough point: if the emperor had the power to ask his subordinates to revise policy, could he not have done more to prevent war?

Kido admitted that the emperor's move had gone beyond earlier practices, but continued to insist that when "the incident of the eighth of December broke out," the emperor could not veto the decision for war. Keenan jumped in to derail a damaging line of questioning. "And is the attack upon Pearl Harbor to go down in your history as another incident?" he asked in a patriotic huff, referring to Japan's labeling of the wars in Manchuria and China as incidents. This vacuously ended the questioning about whether the palace could have done more to stop the war.[77]

Keenan did rather better in trying to implicate Kido in the 1937 invasion of China, when the grandee had been education minister and later welfare minister. He asked if he had known that more than a million Japanese troops had stormed into China. "Such matters were never brought up for discussion at a cabinet meeting," Kido replied politely. Keenan confronted the lord keeper with his own diary, in which he had blamed the army minister for sending an army of one million six hundred thousand troops abroad. Kido insisted that he had nothing to do with troop deployments in China.[78]

Keenan contended that Kido must have known about the Nanjing massacre. Soon after the fall of Nanjing, Kido had answered a question in the Diet about foreign outrage at the behavior of Japanese troops in Nanjing and Shanghai. Despite that, Kido denied knowing anything about the atrocities in Nanjing. "You and the others have engaged in a conspiracy of silence," Keenan said. "No, that is entirely not so," Kido insisted. "We had not at any time been informed of such an incident." Yet Kido was rattled enough to admit that "the Japanese were apt to hold a sense of superiority vis-a-vis the Chinese people and hold the Chinese people in contempt"—a rare moment of candor about Japanese prejudices.[79]

Keenan challenged Kido with fresh evidence. During the defense presentation, the prosecution discovered another insider source: the recollections of Prince Saionji Kinmochi, a venerable former prime minister who had been one of Japan's most influential elder statesmen. These had been written out as a memoir of over three thousand pages by his aide, Baron Harada Kumao, and then edited by Prince Saionji. Because the Saionji-Harada memoirs ended after the prince's death in 1940, they were mostly useful about the China war and the Axis alliance. Translated into English by U.S. military intelligence, the memoirs ran to forty volumes, which further slowed down an already laggard trial. The defense tried to deny its accuracy, which was no small task given its bulk.[80]

Kido found himself snared by someone else's habit of punctilious diary-keeping. He took the line that Baron Harada was a longtime friend but a lousy diarist. Again and again, Kido said he had no recollection of the conversations recorded in the pages.[81]

The prosecution used the Saionji-Harada memoirs to charge that Kido's record on China was distinctly bellicose. Keenan accused him of going along when the Japanese government had refused to deal with Chiang Kai-shek's government. In December 1937, the marquis had attended a cabinet meeting which laid out a harsh China policy, including a massive Japanese military commitment in north China. Kido admitted that he had concurred, but contended that as education minister he had "no special interests in these policies."

Harada's memoirs quoted Kido as questioning efforts for peace in early 1938, saying, "it is impossible after our Japanese troops have killed 700,000 to 800,000 soldiers of the Chinese Army to look grave and say 'Let us shake hands' and truly mean it." Kido had continued, "is Japan a victorious nation or a defeated one?" In court, Kido said that he did not recall saying that and that it did not reflect his views. Keenan asked sharply, "Well, you as a champion of peace with China, what kind of a battle did you put up at that critical moment to attain your end for which you entered the cabinet?"[82]

Keenan made a final attempt to convict Kido for Pearl Harbor. According to Harada's notes, Kido had once told him that the emperor was a peaceable liberal, urging making it "appear as if we understood the Army a little more." Taken aback in court, Kido stopped short of flatly denying the quotes, but said that he had no memory of saying these words and that they did not match with his beliefs. "I do not recognize much accuracy in the writings of Harada," he said.

In another passage, Harada had noted that Kido had told him that the emperor "has no sympathy for the ideas of the right wing. It is very troubling because he is too orthodox." Kido insisted that there must be some misunderstanding. Doubting the Saionji-Harada memoirs, he said that the elderly and unwell Harada had dozed off during their conversations. Keenan snapped, "Do you think, Mr. Kido that was because he was tired, or tired [of] listening to the things you were saying?"[83]

The questioning turned heated about Tojo Hideki, whose selection as prime minister before Pearl Harbor had to be pinned on Kido rather than Hirohito. Tojo himself listened impassively. Suggesting less aggressive candidates, Keenan jeered, "You could not have found a much more belligerent individual in the entire Empire of Japan than Tojo on the 15th of October 1941, could you?" Kido replied, "I don't think that criticism is just."[84]

Keenan skeptically asked whether the emperor could change Tojo's hard-line views. Kido replied, "What I felt in regard to Tojo was if the Emperor told him to do something he would faithfully obey." This was a bad misstep: that implied that the emperor could have ordered Tojo to call off the war. Keenan lunged in to shift the blame onto Kido, asking, "didn't you well realize that when you helped Tojo reach the position of Prime Minister in the middle of October 1941 you were placing within his hands the decision as to whether or not there would be war or peace with the Western powers?" "No," said Kido flatly, not about to implicate himself quite so easily.

Webb jumped in: "This morning you told us, if I apprehended rightly, that the Emperor could instruct his ministers on the outline of foreign policy." Kido explained that the emperor would give his opinion and the cabinet would study those views. Reversing himself, Kido said that Tojo, rather than faithfully obeying the monarch, would merely consider the emperor's views.[85]

When it was all over, it was apparent who had lost the most. The outfoxed Keenan had publicly humiliated himself at some length. Kido's testimony had gone badly for Hirohito and worse for Tojo and the army hard-liners.

An appalled Comyns Carr reported to Shawcross that Keenan and his staffers had "made a complete and utter mess of it."[86] In a letter he decided was too harsh to mail, Comyns Carr wrote that the case was "in danger of being finally reduced to a laughing stock, if it wasn't already," hoping that nobody was reading the transcripts being mailed to London.[87] A senior British official jokingly suggested getting Keenan investigated by the House Un-American Activities Committee, "although from my experience of American lawyers, they would find nothing un-American about his behaviour."[88]

To offset the embarrassment of Kido's testimony, the emperor set out to consolidate his authority with his people and to demonstrate his importance to General Headquarters. On November 15, 1947, soon after Kido wrapped up his testimony, Hirohito paid his fifth visit to MacArthur. There is no record of what they discussed. Yet the mere fact of the meeting was a demonstration of Allied dominance, which, as a senior British diplomat noted, was itself a reeducation to the Japanese people.[89]

Earlier that year the emperor had resumed making national tours across the country, which were so triumphal that they alarmed officials at General Headquarters. Now wearing Western-style suits instead of military regalia, he had drawn huge crowds of cheering loyalists, many yelling *"Banzai!"* and thousands of them waving a banned flag of the rising sun.[90] Hirohito, visibly uncomfortable mixing with his people, doggedly learned how to smile and ask questions.

After Kido's testimony, the emperor launched a seventeen-day tour across four southern prefectures on Honshu. Its highlight was a short speech at a partially rebuilt Hiroshima on December 7, where the emperor marked the sixth anniversary of Pearl Harbor with a promise that his country would never again pursue warlike policies.[91] He was greeted by kneeling war orphans in black robes and scarred mothers holding scarred children, who recounted their terrible ordeals as he murmured sympathetically. His lip trembling, he bowed and returned to his car, as the crowd roared and people shouted *"Banzai!"*[92] When he climbed to a platform to speak at the center of the blast radius, a crowd of forty thousand burst into the national anthem. People wept with emotion. "I cannot but feel very sorry for the disaster that this city suffered," the emperor said, standing alone near the exposed steel skeleton of the prefectural government building. Yet he used the calamity to call for reconstruction and world peace, without any hint of reprimand to the Americans: "we must construct a peaceful Japan, keeping this deep disaster deep in our memory."

The speech was a sensation. The cheering was so loud that Australian military police had to help their Japanese counterparts to restore order on the packed plaza.[93] The *London Daily Herald* reported unhappily that the emperor was greeted with "fanatical enthusiasm," carping that "Emperor worshipping is back where it started."[94] Soon after, General Headquarters would ban the imperial tours, fearing that they were bolstering the power of the throne too much.[95] As an appalled Menon wrote to Nehru,

"Recently, when the Emperor visited Hiroshima, the joy of Hiroshimans knew no bounds; they did not have the faintest suspicion that he was responsible for their atomic misfortune."[96]

After the humiliation of Kido's testimony, the emperor craved the kind of respectability that could only be conferred by crowned heads. Early in 1948, at MacArthur's urging, Hirohito secretly wooed King George VI by granting an audience to a visiting British lord. In a cold and gloomy building at the Imperial Palace, for over two and a half hours, Hirohito expressed what the lord called "pathetic admiration" for the British monarchy, claiming that was his prototype for Japan. Hirohito said that he had always deplored the war and begged that his greetings be passed along to Buckingham Palace. Regretting the suffering inflicted by the Japanese, he politely asked if the destruction in Malaya had not been too great. The British lord tactfully replied that Hirohito's surrender order had come through before the British had to flatten Singapore. He was, the British lord concluded, "pathetically anxious to show his genuine and profound regret for Japan's outrageous part in the late war."[97]

The pleas did reach Buckingham Palace, but King George VI would say nothing publicly. He secretly allowed the top British diplomat in Tokyo to tell the emperor orally that his message had been sent to Buckingham Palace, and that he was authorized to express the thanks of the king and queen to the emperor and empress for their kind thought. Thus do kings talk to each other when they are not talking to each other.[98]

KANGAROO COURT

During the individual testimonies, Sir William Webb kept a secret: he was planning to wing home to Australia for several months, returning to his Tokyo duties later. Australia's prime minister and attorney general were badgering him about his long absence from the short-staffed High Court, where he had not yet been sworn in as its seventh justice.[99] Webb was lonely in Tokyo and his wife had been seriously ill.[100]

The other judges, who also had things to do back home, seethed. How could the trial possibly be fair if the chief judge skived off? Yet Lord Patrick, the British judge who had schemed to oust Webb, was privately gratified to find his wish coming true after all. He reckoned that the New Zealand judge, Erima Harvey Northcroft, under traditions of seniority, would become president. Under the resulting supremacy of the British bloc of judges, Patrick hoped for, as a British diplomat put it, "a verdict on all fours with that of Nuremberg," with only the Indian and Dutch judges dissenting.[101]

When MacArthur found out, he scolded Australia's prime minister, Ben Chifley, that it would be "an international calamity to have the presiding magistrate relieved at this late date from his seat on the tribunal."[102] MacArthur showed his message to Webb beforehand, who declared himself "profoundly moved."[103] Trying to win back MacArthur, Webb showed him all his secret correspondence with his government.[104]

The Australian judge starchily told Chifley that, while he would do as he was told, "I do know that this Tokyo trial is one of the greatest in all history; and the only question is whether the Australian people, as represented by their government, desire me to take a full or a limited part in it."[105] This time, the Australian government defied MacArthur, telling Webb to get to Sydney by early November.[106] He stayed in Tokyo for Kido's defense, flying back in time to hear out Tojo Hideki and Togo Shigenori. Webb knew that he would miss the individual cases of twelve out of the twenty-five remaining defendants, wondering if it was proper to vote on their guilt or innocence based only on documents.[107] Chifley, while not wanting Australia to lose stature by having Webb quit the tribunal altogether, proved untroubled by compromising the trial's fairness by having its presiding judge vanish for more than a month.[108]

In the middle of the testimony about General Matsui Iwane, Webb made his bombshell announcement: "I am returning to Australia." There was a gasp across the courtroom.[109] While some thought for a frantic moment that he was quitting altogether, he added softly that he would be back in December.

Owen Cunningham, the brash American defense lawyer, was on his feet immediately with a motion to object. It was the right of the defendants to have the judges present at all stages: "It is the duty of Australia to accede to the Allied Powers and make their sacrifice." Webb shot back, "It is not for you to tell Australia what her duty is, nor for me to listen to you." When Webb explained that British precedent covered his departure, Cunningham snapped, "Well, being an Irish-American, your Honor, that doesn't bind me."

Visibly annoyed, Webb dismissed the motion.[110] He soared home in style, aboard a four-engine B-24 Liberator heavy bomber that he had browbeaten the Australian government into providing for him. Conspiratorial rumors swirled around the court about why he had suddenly departed.[111]

MacArthur decided that New Zealand was too insignificant as a power for the job of acting president. He offered it to Patrick. In poor health, the elderly British judge had no stomach for reframing the judgment to match Nuremberg only to have Webb quash his work upon his return.

He refused without first checking with the British government, which was crestfallen to lose the plum. MacArthur was dumbfounded, grumbling that the British judge should have "risked sudden death in court rather than turn down the appointment." Finally the supreme commander named the U.S. judge, Major General Myron Cramer. He too at first declined, claiming he was too old and lacked the necessary experience, but MacArthur browbeat him into accepting.[112]

The British government considered reprimanding the Australian government but prudently decided against it.[113] In private, Patrick scorned Webb's "running away" as "the gravest blot that had yet stained the honour of the Court." Despite missing many weeks of crucial testimony, the Australian would participate in the verdicts and sentences. This was, Patrick fumed, against all decency and contrary to every British legal concept; Webb ought to resign.[114]

CHAPTER 22

"The Great Sorrow of My Life"

TOGO SHIGENORI, LOCKED UP at Sugamo Prison, still remembered the shining stars on a frosty night. Late at night on December 8, 1941, soon before the attack on Pearl Harbor, he had retired from a reverential audience with Emperor Hirohito at 3:15 a.m., Tokyo time. As foreign minister, he had read aloud to the emperor a personal telegram from Franklin Delano Roosevelt and advised him to disregard it as insufficient. Gazing upon the monarch, who was dressed in a naval uniform, Togo had been deeply moved by the royal countenance, in which he saw "his noble feeling of brotherhood with all peoples" as well as "his unflinching attitude" at the coming war. Solemnly retreating, Togo had been ushered by a court official down the long corridors, tranquil and serene, of the hushed Imperial Palace in the deep of night. He had emerged at the carriage entrance of the imposing Sakashita Gate, where he gazed up at the brilliant stars. He had felt bathed in a sacred spirit.

Driving out of the palace in silence, he had heard only the crunch of gravel beneath his car's wheels, with no sound from the unaware people sleeping in the doomed capital. When he had arrived back at his ministerial residence at 4:30 a.m., the telephone had rung: the Navy Ministry informed him that the Imperial Japanese Navy had successfully attacked the U.S. fleet. He had accepted the news with composure. He later wrote that he had done everything he could for peace and believed that heaven knew that his heart was true to Japan and mankind. His deeds, he wrote in prison, "must find approval in the ultimate judgment of Heaven."[1]

He would not find it below. At the Tokyo trial, Togo was beset on all sides: by prosecutors who lumped him in with his bellicose rivals, by judges who did not have his full record, and by defendants who feared that he might spare himself by getting them hanged. In his testimony, the former foreign minister presented himself as a tragic figure: a patriot who had served his country as it had lurched into catastrophe, an isolated man of peace who had warned against disaster but failed.

"Whenever he was convinced that there was some logic, he never backed away," recalls Togo's grandson, the diplomat Togo Kazuhiko. "He never shouted but he kept on saying the same thing." In a note in his appointment diary in Sugamo Prison, Togo Shigenori wrote that he did not think it would be reasonable to punish him, but if that punishment would help advance the happiness of humankind, "I will be happy to be the sacrifice."[2]

He had entered Sugamo suffering from anemia and chest pains from coronary heart disease, which regularly kept him out of court.[3] His wife, Edith Togo, warned the Allied authorities that his pulse had sometimes stopped. He had suffered from "the strain of responsibility" trying to end the war, and now from the pressure of the trial and the lack of air-conditioning in jail. "He has not done anything wrong and does not deserve to be tortured," she wrote in despair. "On the contrary he always worked in such a way that wars of any kind should be prevented."[4] In response, Sir William Webb merely told a colonel at General Headquarters that he assumed that Togo was getting proper medical attention.[5]

An ailing Togo Shigenori, the foreign minister who struggled against attacking the United States, in detention in Tokyo, circa 1946

Ill as he was, Togo's defense lawyer, Major Ben Bruce Blakeney, decided to put his client front and center. "Our grandfather immediately knew Ben Bruce Blakeney's value," says Togo Kazuhiko. "He is not going to play down, he's not going to play up. He'll testify vis-à-vis history. From that perspective he has nothing to fear."

When Togo Shigenori took the stand on December 17, 1947, his daughter hopefully thought he seemed lively. At last he could speak for himself.[6] With headphones on for English translation, he listened attentively as he sparred. He was polite but combative, at one point laughing sarcastically.[7] He wore an impeccable three-piece suit with peak lapels, a dark tie, and round spectacles. The clothes announced him as a cosmopolitan and sophisticated civilian, in contrast to the army men around him. But he was wan from his ongoing struggle with heart disease; his hair was gray; at times, his voice was tremulous. His wife and daughter watched in stricken sympathy.[8]

His life's work—as presented in his affidavit, read aloud in court by Blakeney—was that of a dogged advocate of peace. He had been a professional diplomat, not a leader of any military faction or party. Although he had been a member of the Imperial Rule Assistance Association, a notorious political organization meant to supplant political parties in order to unify Japan for its imperial conquests, he had taken so little interest in it that he claimed he could not remember when he had joined.[9] Far from being part of a clique around Tojo Hideki, he had barely known the prime minister: "We never had more than this bowing acquaintance; I knew nothing, before entering his cabinet, of his personality or outlook and he, I suppose, nothing of mine."

He had been opposed to most of the decisions made by more belligerent politicians: quitting the League of Nations, allying with Nazi Germany, invading China, advancing into Southeast Asia.[10] Although he had served as ambassador to Nazi Germany from October 1937 to October 1938, that had been a disaster: disgusted by Adolf Hitler's tyranny, he had quickly become unpopular with Joachim von Ribbentrop and other Nazi leaders. He had recoiled at the Tripartite Pact, believing it would only alienate the United States and Britain.

Having long dreamed of becoming ambassador in Moscow, he resented being accused of fomenting conflict with the Soviet Union. As ambassador starting in 1938, he had laid the groundwork for the nonaggression pact with the Soviet Union and made progress resolving border disputes between the Soviet Union and Manchukuo. Despite the Soviet prosecutors' claims that he had been embroiled in the 1939 clash at the Khalkhin-Gol River, he testified that he had nothing to do with it, only finding out about the fighting from Soviet complaints and then working with the Soviets to resolve the incident without a war.[11]

TOGO CONTRA MUNDUM

Before Togo testified, the bench could have been left in the dark about his advocacy for peace by the prosecution's incomplete evidence about the crucial meetings resolving on war against the United States and the British Empire. By the time Togo finished his testimony, the judges had no such excuse.

Togo had become foreign minister in Tojo Hideki's new cabinet on October 18, 1941. "I did not enter the Tojo Cabinet to strive for domination of the world," he testified, "which I had never dreamed of, nor for the annihilation of America and Britain nor their expulsion from East Asia." He had always opposed southward expansion, which would ignite conflict with Britain and Holland, and probably the United States as well. He had warned Tojo that if the army would not budge on stationing troops in China, the negotiations with the United States would collapse. He had only agreed to join the cabinet after being assured by Tojo that the army would show genuine flexibility about its forces in China and other crucial negotiating issues.

Yet when he arrived at the Foreign Ministry, he found himself thoroughly boxed in by prior decisions. He had, he testified, known nothing of the imperial conference on July 2 which had approved an advance against Indochina and Thailand. He had only vaguely known about the imperial conference on September 6 deciding on war with the United States if there was not diplomatic progress soon. Reviewing the Washington talks, he was appalled to find them stalemated by fundamental differences, which had only gotten worse since the Japanese move into southern Indochina and the U.S. imposition of economic sanctions. He was taken aback by the military's "unceasing acceleration" of preparations for an attack and its obstinacy toward the negotiations. Still, he hoped that progress was possible: "there remained only one large point of contention—the stationing of troops in China—between the United States and Japan."

In seven grueling weeks of liaison conference meetings which were dominated by the army and navy, he said candidly, "debate often developed into heated argument." He pressed for a breakthrough in the negotiations with the United States rather than rushing into conflict, urging the overconfident army to make concessions on maintaining troops in China.

Having "consistently opposed the China Incident from its beginning," he was keen to settle that conflict anyway.[12] When one of the judges asked him how it could be a war of self-defense when Japanese troops were fighting in the heart of China, he easily replied, "Oh, with regard to that it was my belief that that was going too far."[13]

From the start, though, most of the liaison conference opposed withdrawing soldiers, with the army fiercely insisting on keeping Japanese troops in parts of China indefinitely. To his surprise, the navy was scarcely less resistant than the army. As he truthfully said, "I had to fight unceasingly."

He struggled to get the army to agree to keep soldiers out of Shanghai and other points, and had to threaten to resign to get the army to agree to accept time limits for keeping soldiers in China. He asked for five years, to no avail; he then floated eight or ten years; others suggested fifty or ninety-nine years; they finally settled on twenty-five years. This was so outrageous that his proposal to the United States listed it only as "a necessary period," hoping that if the Americans were receptive, he might be able to lower it. He also had to threaten to resign over the stationing of soldiers in Indochina, eventually prevailing on the military to accept that upon reaching an agreement with the United States they would pull all troops out of southern Indochina.

He called attention to a crucial meeting that had not been part of the prosecution's evidence: the all-night liaison conference that began on November 1. He testified that he had "insisted with all possible force on avoiding war" at almost any cost. In fact, he had had his limits, such as refusing to allow the United States a voice on China, but his affidavit was truthful about the ferocity of his advocacy against war. The military had "retorted with the utmost vehemence that Japan must fight sooner or later," before the petroleum ran out. He was not reassured by confident military boasts, knowing how long and difficult a war against the United States and Britain would be.

The liaison conference had agreed to make Togo's two final proposals to the United States, and if those were rejected, to go to war. Late that night, he testified, he considered resigning. Without access to military secrets, he was in no position to refute the generals and admirals about how a war might unfold. Hirota Koki, a mentor of his, urged him not to quit, since that would just bring in a more hawkish foreign minister. At last he notified Tojo Hideki that he would stay on.

His hopes, he said, had been crushed when he got Cordell Hull's tough note on November 26. Here he was in accord with the other defendants: the United States had given "what we viewed as an ultimatum" with maximal demands. Tojo Hideki had seen absolutely no hope in continued diplomacy; Marquis Kido Koichi had privately told Togo that accepting the Hull note might spark a civil war among the Japanese. The price of peace, Togo recounted, was "total surrender by Japan to the American position." Japan would have to "abandon all the gains from her years of sacrifice," and to "surrender her international position as a power in the Far East. That surrender, as we saw it, would have amounted to national suicide. The only other way to face this challenge and defend ourselves was war."

Togo testified that after the Hull note he had again considered resigning, but had decided to stay on to "work for every last chance to avoid war" or, if that failed, do what he could to end it as fast as possible. Going into the imperial conference on December 1 that decided when to start the war, he had believed that "[t]he very existence of the Japanese nation was at stake, and I was compelled to agree that we must wage war, whatever the prospects, unless America would reconsider." He had told the imperial conference of the failure of the negotiations, while Tojo Hideki had explained the circumstances compelling them to fight: "There was then unanimous agreement on the necessity of going to war."

He had kept the negotiations going, he said, on the faint hope that the Americans would relent. He had not known about the delay in delivering Roosevelt's personal telegram to the emperor and had had nothing to do with that: "For continuing the negotiations in the only way that I could see open I am now charged with deceit and perfidy, with having kept up a pretence only to gain time to cloak the military preparations which were going forward." He declared, "I did not dream that the Japanese Navy would ever attack the American fleet in Pearl Harbor," guessing that the Philippines and Malaya would be Japan's first targets instead.

He blamed the surprise attack squarely on the navy. He claimed to have argued for notifying the United States before a strike, only to be told by the chief of the navy general staff that "the Navy wished to carry out a surprise attack." The vice chief of the navy general staff said that the negotiations should be kept going so that "the war be started with the maximum possible effectiveness." He had rejected this as "highly improper" and a blot on "our national honor." The top navy man retorted that if they were going to war, they must win. "I was disgusted by the Navy's position," Togo told the court. The navy relented and proposed delivering notice of the end of the negotiations at the very last moment: 1 p.m. on December 7, Washington time. His back to the wall, Togo had accepted the position that an hour's advance warning was legally enough: "My feeling was that after a hard struggle I had succeeded in stopping the Navy's demand, but had stopped it at the ultimate limit of international law."[14]

Having worked on the Kellogg-Briand Pact as a young diplomat in Washington, he believed it did not override a country's right to fight a war of self-defense. Although Japan had not given a formal declaration of war, he maintained that a notice of termination of negotiations would suffice to put Japan in compliance with international law. Since the Japanese regarded the Hull note as an ultimatum that demanded capitulation or war, Japan's rejection of that ultimatum was "in effect a declaration of war."

Only after the war began, he claimed, would he find out that the navy had meant to strike Pearl Harbor about twenty minutes after the note breaking off negotiations was delivered to the United States. He had been dismayed to find out from American radio broadcasts that the note had not been delivered in time. This was the result of "mismanagement in Washington," he said, not negligence or intention. Yet that claim was undercut by his own admission that Japan had not notified Britain it was under attack either, on the lame argument that notification to the United States should suffice. Togo testified that a few days into the war, the vice chief of the naval general staff had told him, "I am sorry for you; we cut it too fine." When Togo chided Tojo Hideki for the "great propaganda value" the surprise attack had for their enemies, the prime minister had asked, "I wonder how such a delay could have taken place? Can it be that the United States itself delayed the delivery?"

Togo Shigenori refused to take blame for what he saw as the navy's treachery. He scornfully noted, "Since the end of the war—or, more precisely, since the beginning of this trial—the Navy has taken the line that nothing was ever further from their intention than to mount a 'surprise attack' against the United States." His own testimony contradicted that, and the court would have to decide who was telling the truth: "I have fought throughout my life for what I thought was right, and now at the end of it I am determined, for the sake of history as well as the purposes of this Tribunal, to the best of my ability and recollection to tell the full truth as it is known to me, neither attempting to evade responsibility which is mine nor accepting that which others would transfer to me."[15]

Togo said that the cabinet had been "somewhat intoxicated by the initial victories of the war." Tojo Hideki, he said, had believed the war could last ten to twenty years, and that the sluggish Americans could not begin a counteroffensive before 1944. In contrast, Togo had been convinced that

Japan could not overcome the combined industrial and military power of the United States and the British Empire.

He blamed the army for the abuse of Allied prisoners. Although he had taken seriously his commitment on Japan's behalf to treat Allied prisoners of war according to the Geneva Convention of 1929, all the real power lay with the Army Ministry. The Foreign Ministry had been an impotent channel for fielding the complaints from the Allied governments. As for Japan's cruelty across Asia, he had wanted to help other Asian countries achieve peaceful prosperity, not annexing or exploiting them, nor "any policy of exerting control over those countries by force." His disputes with Tojo Hideki over the insulting domination inherent in the creation of the new Greater East Asia Ministry, he said, had ultimately led to his resignation from the cabinet in September 1942. He condemned "the idea of a New Order in East Asia or a Greater East Asia Co-prosperity Sphere, which originated in such concepts as those of bloc-economy and *Lebensraum*."

Togo had returned as foreign minister in April 1945 with "only one purpose: ending the war." After the defeat of Nazi Germany, he had reported to the emperor that with Allied air raids intensifying, they should promptly quit the war. Soon after, he had pressed to request Soviet mediation to get out of the war without an unconditional surrender, although he had suspected the Soviets had already cut a secret deal with the United States and Britain to attack Japan. After Marquis Kido Koichi told him that the emperor wanted peace and Soviet mediation, he had launched a peace initiative.

When the Potsdam Declaration was issued, he had told the other Japanese leaders that it "offered in effect a peace on terms," with terrible consequences if it was rejected. After Hiroshima and the Soviet entry into the war, he recounted the pivotal late-night meeting on August 9–10 that produced a surrender. In the presence of the emperor, he had "strongly urged" accepting the Potsdam Declaration "without any condition excepting that of the preservation of the fundamental structure of the state." With the army minister and the army and navy chiefs still trying to impose more conditions, the debate was ended only by Hirohito: "Finally the Emperor expressed accord with my views and the wish that the Potsdam Declaration be accepted to relieve the sufferings of mankind and to save the country from ruin."

Togo concluded that he had "exerted every possible effort" to avoid the Pacific War. "At last I was driven into a position where, as I saw it, conditions no longer permitted me to oppose war, and I failed," he said. "It is the great sorrow of my life that I was not successful in preventing war in 1941, but it is a matter of some consolation for me that I was able by my efforts to contribute to lessening the suffering of mankind by ending it in 1945."[16]

Having denounced many of his fellow defendants in shattering terms, before his cross-examination by the prosecution, Togo faced harsh questioning from defense lawyers for the army and navy defendants.[17]

The admirals bristled at Togo's accusation that they had wanted a sneak attack. None of the other accused who had been at the liaison conferences remembered hearing the vice chief of the naval general staff insist on a surprise attack, said a defense lawyer: "Are you prepared to say that these men are actually lying now?" Togo retorted, "Well, I do not have much confidence in the memory of these men." He added, "it is possible that they would would forget some things that are unfavorable to them."

To the court's shock, he accused Admiral Shimada Shigetaro, one of the defendants, of trying to threaten him into silence—recalling the assassination of civilian politicians who dared to speak up against the military. Togo said that the admiral had urged him not to "say anything about the fact that the Navy desired to carry out the surprise attack," adding "something in the nature of a threat, saying if I said so, it would not be worth my while." There was a hubbub in the courtroom.[18]

Togo testified that he remembered other occasions when "the Navy side requested me not to speak of the Navy's desire for conducting a surprise attack." He said that navy leaders had told him that they had wanted to attack without notice but had not wanted him to reveal that. Here he candidly stated the obvious: a successful strike on Pearl Harbor could not be carried out without the element of surprise.[19]

While denouncing the army and navy, Togo covered for Hirohito as best he could, claiming that the emperor had told of him of his wish for peace several months before Pearl Harbor.[20] He slipped up by politely saying that "it is unthinkable for a Japanese to deceive the Emperor." While meant to be respectful, that implicated the emperor in everything that his underlings had done.[21] When asked provocatively by one of the judges if the emperor had violated the Japanese constitution by deciding upon surrender without the unanimous consent of his split government, Togo stoutly defended his monarch: "because the question was one requiring most urgent action and there was no time to await any unanimity of opinions within the government, or to await the formation of a new cabinet, rather than do that, I think, his majesty the Emperor gave his heroic decision at that time."[22]

No such courtesy was extended to the slippery Kido, whom Togo eyed with obvious distaste. He was not about to let the lord keeper hide behind the emperor. He angrily complained that Kido had not told him that the emperor had wanted peace in 1942. In response, a defense lawyer suggested that if Kido had revealed such sensitive information to Togo, and if Togo had turned out really to be a militarist, then Kido would not have been around for long.

"I don't believe there is anybody who believes that I am more of a militarist than Kido," Togo shot back.

"You don't like him, do you, Mr. Togo?" asked the defense lawyer.

"No, I am a friend of his," Togo replied politely, smiling, as the Japanese in the courtroom burst out laughing. The marshal had to pound on his desk for silence.[23]

Naming Names

Joseph Keenan strode to the lectern, with his fellow prosecutors cringing as he did. Arthur Comyns Carr, the British associate prosecutor, reported confidentially to Sir Hartley Shawcross, the Nuremberg prosecutor who was then serving as British attorney general, that Keenan, having botched the cross-examination of Kido, "has taken over Togo . . . in a similar manner and with equally disastrous results."[24]

Togo was subjected to several days of condescension by Keenan, a man whose spine was made of considerably more malleable stuff. The U.S. chief prosecutor accused Togo of dishonesty and duplicity, even outright lying. He admonished Togo to avoid diplomatic talk and "weasel words," unsubtly rebuking the former foreign minister for his mere profession. Yet their back-and-forth would produce one of the most sensational exchanges in the whole trial, with Togo directly accusing Tojo Hideki and two other defendants by name.

Keenan got off to a rocky start by spending hours badgering Togo about the late-night message from Roosevelt to Hirohito in the hours before Pearl Harbor, trying to show that the foreign minister had deviously sabotaged a last chance for peace. Given what Togo had just told the court about his exertions for peace, this was among the least plausible accusations against him. Yet Keenan proposed that Togo, who could read some of the English text without a translator, had deceitfully omitted some of Roosevelt's note as he explained it to both the emperor and the prime minister. Togo explained that since Roosevelt's message called for Japan to withdraw troops from Indochina without major reciprocal concessions from the United States, Tojo Hideki had reacted by saying that nothing more could be done. As for the emperor, Togo calmly insisted that he had read Roosevelt's telegram aloud word for word to him.

Keenan tried to show that Togo and Tojo had nefariously settled on the emperor's noncommittal reply to Roosevelt, implying that they had scuppered a more conciliatory response. Keenan blustered, "Are you indicating that the Emperor of Japan was a mere figurehead and obtaining his consent was nothing more than a rubber stamp to be put on by you, and that the Emperor's consent to the conclusions reached was of so little significance it wasn't even worthwhile bothering one of boys around the place . . . to find Kido?"

Togo, who would neither implicate nor deprecate his monarch, could say little. Keenan seemed to be fishing to get Togo to exonerate the emperor of war responsibility by declaring him a powerless figurehead, or at least to declare admiringly how dedicated the emperor was to peace. Either would serve General Headquarters' purposes. The reality was that Togo had been far more outspoken for peace than the emperor or Kido, yet unlike the monarch did not enjoy the privilege of being protected by General Headquarters.

Choosing a minimal response, Togo politely said that he had told the emperor that both Tojo Hideki and Kido Koichi had agreed with him: Roosevelt's note was not enough.

"Those are weasel words, Mr. Togo," snapped Keenan.

"No, I am not using what you said, weasel words," retorted Togo. "I am telling you the facts as they occurred."[25]

The U.S. chief prosecutor insinuated that Togo had entered Tojo Hideki's cabinet in bad faith: "Did you not realize, when you joined the Tojo Cabinet, that in all probability you were joining what would be a war cabinet?" Togo replied, "My feeling in joining that cabinet was that I was joining a war prevention cabinet."

Keenan asked repeatedly what he had known of the imperial conference on September 6, 1941—before Togo joined the cabinet—that had decided on war if a diplomatic resolution was not secured soon. Togo replied that that was a paramount state secret, although he had gathered from his Foreign Ministry friends that the army had taken a hard line and that the negotiations would have to be settled by mid-October. This proved only that Togo, like every well-informed functionary in Tokyo, had known that there was a looming danger of war, not that he had sought it.

Keenan asked why Togo had joined the cabinet if he opposed the war in China. Togo conceded that he had known that Tojo Hideki had been adamant that troops not be withdrawn from China. "In October of 1941 you didn't regard General Tojo as being one of the outstanding pacifists of Japan, did you?" asked Keenan. He scoffed, "as the late Will Rogers from America expressed it, all you knew was what you read in the newspapers." "Well," said Togo, baffled, "I don't know what Will Rogers said or did not say."

Keenan lectured him that China's sovereignty and territorial integrity had been trampled by Japan's invading armies and its aerial bombardment of cities and villages. Togo conceded those were not "normal actions," but said their justifiability would depend on whether the China war was one of self-defense. What about invading Manchuria? Not all of Japan's actions could be justified, Togo dodged, but it was hard to say that one side was entirely wrong and the other entirely right.

Keenan scored his only successes on Japan's alliance with Nazi Germany, where Togo could sound evasive. Togo said that although he had opposed joining the Axis, by the time he became foreign minister a year later the alliance was an established fact. He denounced Nazi Germany as "a dictatorial totalitarian state," but equivocally said that the Tripartite Pact could not be evil if it had prevented war—that is, by deterring the United States.

He admitted that he had known that life was becoming "very difficult" for Jews in Nazi Germany as ambassador there, yet when asked if he had known they were being put in concentration camps, he replied, "I didn't know too much about these concentration camps." A little later, he said that he was not well acquainted with the Nazi regime. Keenan skeptically asked, "Did you not know that, in 1941, in October, the regime of Hitler in Germany, in his own country, had been one of terror, force and oppression?" Togo replied, "It was a dictatorial rule, so I did consider that in some points there was oppression." When Keenan asked if he had favored Hitler's call for a new order in Europe and Asia, Togo cagily said he could not say what Hitler's new order actually meant. Keenan snapped that surely Hitler and Benito Mussolini had amply demonstrated what they meant.[26]

Keenan was at his worst where it mattered most: Togo's record as foreign minister. The U.S. prosecutor asked almost nothing about Togo's efforts to end the war in 1945, essentially conceding the defendant's version of events. Nor did Keenan mount an effective challenge to Togo's testimony about his struggle to avoid war in 1941. He barely touched the records of

Togo's advocacy, which showed him as working harder than anyone in the Japanese cabinet to preserve the peace.[27]

While Togo, like other civilians in the government, had not known that Pearl Harbor was the target until after it was struck, Keenan asserted that he had been "completely and thoroughly in on the deal." In fact, as a diplomat on especially poisonous terms with the military, it was inconceivable that he would have been entrusted with the most sensitive operational secrets.[28]

Keenan asked Togo if he agreed with the conclusions of the imperial conference on November 5, which had resolved to attack the United States and Britain unless there was a diplomatic breakthrough soon. Since the prosecution's evidence only had the conclusions of that conclave, not its debates, Keenan was apparently unaware that Togo had still been pressing to avoid war, although this time with much of the wind out of his sails. He had warned against getting Japan encircled by a vast coalition of the United States, the British and Dutch Empires, and China, and had successfully urged making his two final diplomatic proposals to the United States. When Keenan contended that those two last proposals to the United States had practically been ultimatums, Togo flatly denied that. Togo had to concede that he had agreed to the imperial conference's conclusions, but could only hint at the roiling internal debates beforehand: "before that agreement all sorts of things transpired."[29]

Keenan pressed Togo about the brawling seventeen-hour liaison conference that started on November 1, although once again the prosecutor lacked a proper record of how Togo had sparred with the military. Togo said vaguely that if negotiations failed, some wanted to go to war while others preferred patience. Keenan, whose own diction was noticeably more flowery than Togo's, pressed him for "an abandonment of the polished verbiage of diplomacy." Which of the defendants wanted war if the talks failed? "Name them," said Keenan, "and all of them." Looking back at the rows of defendants, he jabbed a finger at their faces, moving from left to right.

The court hushed. Togo was being asked to blame the war directly on his former colleagues. Some of them looked disconcerted. Togo paused for a moment, and then replied clearly, "Tojo, Shimada and Suzuki."[30]

To their faces, under oath, Togo directly implicated Tojo Hideki, as well as Admiral Shimada Shigetaro and General Suzuki Teiichi. Keenan tried to snare a few more necks. He asked about another general: "Will you answer that question and, for the moment, abandon the purple verbiage of diplomacy?" Togo replied that he did not remember that general saying anything in this meeting, nor a civilian functionary and an admiral. Even so, he might have just convicted three of his fellow defendants.[31]

Winding up on a far-fetched note, Keenan tried to claim that if Togo as foreign minister had refused to agree to war, Tojo Hideki's cabinet could not have lawfully gone forward. This was true in the formal sense that cabinet decisions had to be unanimous, and that a minister, by breaking with the will of the government on the most important of questions, would have brought down the government. In reality, of course, it would most likely have meant a cabinet reshuffle that brought in a more pliable foreign minister. Togo replied that he had often wondered whether resigning from the cabinet could have helped, but by late October had concluded that it would not matter. Exploding, the U.S. prosecutor said that he could not get a direct answer out of the witness, and asked Webb to help him.

"Could you not have stopped war by voting against it in the cabinet?" asked Webb. Togo said that while cabinet decisions had to be unanimous, after the Hull note, "it was the feeling in Japan that Japan was being forced to choose between war and suicide." He could not have changed the situation by quitting. "I can say legally speaking that if I had opposed I could have prevented war, but under the actual situation prevailing at that time I should like to state clearly that I cannot conceive that I could have prevented war merely by my resignation."

Keenan did not really wrap up, instead giving up his hectoring midway through a question. "Unless the Chief of Counsel desires to receive more answers from me, I have no intentions of continuing," said an exasperated Togo. Getting in one last insult, Keenan said, "We have finally reached an agreement upon one point."[32]

Togo was relieved. Despite the froth of Keenan's cross-examination, he had got onto the record much of his advocacy against the Pacific War. "My personal part of the trial had ended," he wrote privately. "There are many things which I could not say enough, but by my affidavit and cross-examination over five days, I could explain generally. I don't want to be an arrogant person who wants to show one's properness to the world. I just want to be a right person in front of the gods."[33]

CHAPTER 23

Tojo Takes the Stand

Hundreds of Japanese began lining up at the gates of the Army Ministry at 6 a.m. on December 26, 1947, waiting for Tojo Hideki to testify for his life. The balcony reserved for Japanese spectators was crammed to overflowing to see the most famous defendant. Photographers and newsreel cameramen strained for a view of the former prime minister.[1] "The stage is being set for one of the most dramatic soliloquies in history," wrote an American reporter for *Star and Stripes,* crudely calling him "the foremost figure among the once arrogant, saber wearing little brown-skinned generals of the conquest-minded Japanese army."[2]

Sixty-three years old, convinced that he would soon be hanged, Tojo looked pallid and weary. Yet at a time of intrusive press censorship by General Headquarters, he and his Japanese defense lawyer spoke more freely in the courtroom about the war than almost any other Japanese. He gave an unflinching vindication of Imperial Japan's policies. "Tojo testified with the cold assurance of a conquering samurai," wrote *Life* magazine.[3] *Time* magazine went with the same cliché, reporting that Tojo walked to the stand with "the unearthly smugness of the samurai."[4]

His country occupied, its empire dissolved, its armies disbanded, its people impoverished, its cities reduced to ashes, Tojo only admitted minor errors in judgment. He took responsibility for Japan's defeat but insisted that he had been right to take on the United States, the British Empire, and the Dutch Empire simultaneously in a necessary war of self-defense. He expressed scant remorse for all those who had suffered and died in the war, although he did regret losing it. Proudly wearing his army uniform, shorn of medals, he had tied a piece of string around his right middle finger as a reminder to curb his quick temper.[5]

Tojo's combative testimony sent shockwaves through Japan. Having won the war, the Allies now handed a microphone to their chief antagonist and his skillful defense lawyer to justify his actions to the Japanese people. This was the price of the Allied commitment to a fair trial: allowing the unmuzzled former Japanese prime minister a final chance to rationalize the war, thereby undermining the legitimacy of the occupation. Although Tojo's stature among Japanese had plummeted, his performance was a sensation, with scalpers selling tickets at twice the price of an expensive kabuki drama or five times the cost of an American movie.[6]

The result was, as a *New York Herald Tribune* reporter put it, "one of the most expensive propaganda failures ever charged to American taxpayers."[7] For days, Tojo would wipe the floor with Joseph Keenan. As an American reporter noted, it was a contest of wit, double talk, and sarcasm between the "florid-faced prosecutor and hard-jawed ex-dictator." Even *Life* magazine, reliably partisan for the Chinese, admitted that Keenan's cross-examination failed to put a dent in the former prime minister's apologia: "Tojo's defiance was a summons to the old codes of Shinto nationalism." Heartened by Tojo's bravado, the other defendants watched "a trial that could have been a salutary and valuable lesson in democratic procedure turn into an abysmal flop."[8]

The Allies knew how badly it had gone. In private, Arthur Comyns Carr, the British associate prosecutor, was grudgingly impressed. He told the British attorney general, "Tojo's evidence is really a plea of guilty but a very fine performance, accepting responsibility for everything and seeking to justify it."[9] After watching Tojo testify, a top Indian diplomat, K. P. S. Menon, reported to Jawaharlal Nehru that "the firm, unrepentant and almost defiant manner in which he justified Pearl Harbour and the measures he took to wage a 'defensive war' was most impressive. And in Japanese eyes Tojo, who some time ago was derided for his inability even to commit suicide properly, became a hero overnight."[10]

Even liberal Japanese admitted that Tojo, widely reviled after the surrender, had burnished his legend. Japanese reporters covering the trial concluded that both Tojo and his imperialist policies still drew respect from a substantial proportion of Japanese. Yet there were signs that the war-weary Japanese were growing inured to Tojo. "We should seriously criticize what we have done," warned a Japanese journalist. "There can be no such foolish thing as a revival of General Tojo's popularity."[11] When a Japanese publisher rushed out an edition of Tojo's affidavit, priced to move, thinking they had a best-seller on their hands, it sold just five thousand copies. Soon after, a Japanese translation of Keenan's closing summation, priced even cheaper, would sell fifty thousand copies in two months. "The Japanese generally think why should they pay sixty yen for the defense of the soldiers who ruined the country," said Tojo's publisher ruefully. "They would rather spend the sixty yen for a box of cigarettes."[12]

Keenan had no excuse to be surprised, since Tojo had previewed his themes under Allied interrogation. Far from blaming other Japanese officials, he had seemed vaguely insulted at any insinuation from Allied interrogators that he, as prime minister and army minister, had not been in charge. When asked if he was primarily responsible for the attack on Pearl Harbor and British targets, he had crisply replied, "Yes, I am responsible."[13] To him, though, what he had done was no crime. "Strategically, Japan was on the defense; tactically, she was on the offense," he had told his interrogators. "Japan was surrounded by much greater forces than she herself possessed. The big picture was that of defense. In actual fighting, she attacked."[14]

Tojo was ably represented in court by his lawyer Kiyose Ichiro, who read aloud a fiery statement that "the attacks were unavoidably instituted by Japan in self-defense and for self-existence." Whatever the Allied evidence of atrocities against interned civilians or prisoners of war, Kiyose said that his client "gave neither orders for, tolerated, nor connived at any inhuman acts."

With that, Tojo took the witness box, dressed as usual in his simple boxy uniform. As his other counsel, George Francis Blewett, read aloud his two-hundred-fifty-page affidavit, Tojo spoke in the voice of an American.

At every major turning point, Tojo accepted political responsibility while denying any criminal guilt. The China war was the fault of Communists and the anti-Japanese policy of China, exacerbated by U.S. and British support for the Nationalists. He conspicuously failed to accept the legitimacy of Chiang Kai-shek's government, while readily admitting the authenticity of a pungent piece of prosecution evidence: a note he had written in June 1937, as chief of staff of the Kwantung Army, in which he had urged striking a blow against China. He combatively explained that with an anti-Japanese movement sweeping across China, it was necessary for the Kwantung Army "to deal a blow to the Nanking regime."

Tojo saw no reason to apologize for the Axis alliance. He testified that Japan had no territorial ambitions, nor any wish to dominate any part of the world. As army minister, he claimed to have supported the Tripartite Pact to balance against American and British support for the Nationalist government in China. Yet his own testimony showed that, joining the cabinet soon after the fall of France, he clearly saw how Nazi Germany's victories in Europe allowed Japan to march into northern French Indochina.

Tojo said that he had never intended to attack the Soviet Union and had taken care that border incidents were resolved. He informed the court that Japan had conscientiously kept to its Soviet neutrality pact, implying that the Soviets had been the real aggressors in their August 1945 offensive against Japan.[15]

His affidavit pugnaciously treated Pearl Harbor as unavoidable self-defense by Japan. He made clear how rapidly the negotiations with the United States had soured after April 1941. Japan would not abandon its Axis alliance, while pressing the United States to end its aid to China. By May, Tojo recalled, the talks were deadlocked; by June, the United States had "adopted an unfriendly attitude."

He explained that Japan had seized southern Indochina to get access to vital supplies and to cut off support from the United States and Britain to China. (Much the same logic applied for Thailand, he said, which Japan would conquer in December 1941.) Indochina, he argued, was crucial for the American and British encirclement of Japan; those hostile powers might decide to attack at any moment. When the United States, Britain, and Holland imposed an economic embargo in response to the seizure of southern Indochina in July, he avowed that Japan's very existence was threatened without petroleum from the Netherlands East Indies. The navy and the air force would be put out of action, dealing "a fatal blow" to Japan's national defense. After two years, the navy would be unable to move: "our national power was losing its force day by day."

Although he said that the Washington negotiations were now a matter of life and death for Japan, his testimony showed that he had stuck with a hard line on China, as well as opposing pulling troops out of Indochina so long as the Chinese war dragged on. It was out of the question, he said, for Japan to accept a withdrawal under pressure from foreign powers.

He admitted candidly that in the imperial conference of September 6, the leaders had decided to go to war with the United States, Britain, and Holland if Japan's demands were not met by mid-October. Despite that, he added a dubious claim that Japan did not make up its mind to go to war until later, in the imperial conference on December 1. He averred that the September 6 decision was required for self-preservation, pointing to the buildup of encircling American, British, and Dutch forces: "the United States was exerting itself feverishly in military expansion."

Remarkably, Tojo clearly understood that Japan had little chance of winning the war it was about to start. It was a "dire necessity that Japan avoid war with America and Britain on top of the China Incident," since "we could not be too hopeful of winning against the two greatest powers in the world." At best, he meant to hold off their combined might while snapping up resources from an expanded Japanese Empire, hoping to translate a military stalemate into a negotiated settlement on terms preferable to what he was rejecting. As he explained, "Japan had no alternative but to advance to the Pacific and Indian Oceans, holding important strategical points, occupying regions for military resources and repulsing enemy attacks to the best of our ability and spirit to the last ditch."

Although the September 6 imperial conference had decided on war only if diplomacy failed, Tojo's affidavit showed that he had thought the negotiations were hopeless. Japan had made "almost unbearable" concessions already but the United States did not budge. Although he knew that troops in China were the core issue, he refused to annul four years of army sacrifices under American duress. Warning against the growing power of the Chinese Communists, he predicted darkly that a pullout would lead to "the China Incident II and the China Incident III."

Refuting the image of himself as power-hungry, he said that he had never dreamed of becoming prime minister. He had been astonished when, summoned to the Imperial Palace, Emperor Hirohito had given him the imperial mandate to form a government, and had considered declining the job. The emperor had charged him to reconsider the imperial conference of September 6, walking back from the decision for war. If the military refused to do so, Tojo said, he had preferred that a member of the royal family take over as prime minister instead, allowing the emperor's authority to press the armed forces into line.

He testified that Togo Shigenori had only accepted the Foreign Ministry after being assured that the new cabinet would do its utmost for peace negotiations. Yet Tojo's affidavit gave no indications that he as prime minister had reconsidered diplomacy. Without petroleum, he insisted, Japan could not wait long for American hearts to soften; patience would mean self-annihilation.

Breezing past Togo Shigenori's fervent opposition to war at the November 1 liaison conference and the November 5 imperial conference, Tojo instead cast the emperor as the foremost voice for peace. On November 2, Tojo recalled, while he and the chiefs of the army and navy general staffs were briefing the emperor, "I could see from the expression of His Majesty that he was suffering from a painful sense of distress arising from his peace loving faith." After listening gravely, the monarch had asked,

"Is there no way left but to determine, against our wishes, to wage war against America and Britain in case our effort in America-Japan talks should fail to break the deadlock[?] . . . If the state of affairs is just as you have stated now there will be no alternative but to proceed in the preparations for operations, but I still do hope that you will further adopt every possible means to tide over the difficulties in the America-Japan negotiations." Tojo reverentially added, "I still remember quite vividly, even today, that we were awe-stricken by these words."

Tojo understated how much the imperial conference on November 5 had driven for war. In an affidavit packed with detail about such matters as Australian conscription and Indian textile imports, Tojo professed to have no memory of the particulars of this pivotal debate, overlooking Togo Shigenori's loud warnings. He only said that the military encirclement of Japan by the Americans, British, Chinese, and Dutch—known as the ABCD powers—was growing tighter, so that "only a tiny spark was wanted to set off a giant conflagration."

Although Tojo's affidavit showed that he had seen diplomacy as stone dead long before the Hull note on November 26, he fixated on it as an intolerable outrage that left no choice but war. Japan, he said, could not unconditionally withdraw from China and Indochina, nor turn its back on Manchukuo and the collaborator regime in China, nor abandon the Axis. "We were all dumbfounded at the severity of the U.S. proposition," he testified. "The United States seemed to have already decided upon war against Japan. Putting it bluntly, Japan might be attacked by the United States at any moment." He claimed that he later learned that the United States and Britain had decided on war against Japan, although the United States was intent on having Japan commit "the first overt act."[16]

A few days later, he recalled, the emperor had summoned him to the Imperial Palace, where he anxiously told the prime minister that his younger brother, Prince Takamatsu, a navy officer, had explained that the navy wanted to avoid war. Tojo assured the emperor that there was no alternative left but a war of self-defense, with the military leadership convinced they would be victorious. According to Tojo, this sufficiently allayed the emperor's concerns to allow him to convene the final prewar imperial conference on December 1.

Having downplayed the bellicose imperial conference of November 5, Tojo presented the one on December 1 as truly decisive, rather than just fixing the date for a war that he had long seen as inevitable. This allowed him to depict Japan as peace-loving until the eleventh hour and to emphasize the impact of the Hull note. Chillingly, his affidavit noted that the chief of the army general staff had conceded that in a long war there could be mass air raids on the Japanese home islands—the reality of which was manifest in the ruins of the city beyond the courtroom.

While Tojo gave scant credit to Togo Shigenori for his diplomacy, he did blame the foreign minister for failing to deliver the final note breaking off negotiations to the United States before the bombs started falling at Pearl Harbor. If the contents of the note had not been a proper legal declaration of war, Tojo lumped that on Togo too: the cabinet, he said, relied entirely on the Foreign Ministry to work according to international law. Tojo had learned to his "great regret" that the note had been delivered too late.

Except for the navy minister and himself—informed in his role as army minister, not prime minister—nobody in the cabinet had known that the plan was to hit Pearl Harbor. Yet in a dramatic flourish, Tojo asserted that "the United States had full knowledge of our attack prior to its actual launching." This meant that the delay in delivering the note would not have mattered. He essentially accused the Roosevelt administration of conniving at the death of its own sailors in Hawaii. When he was notified at 4:30 a.m. on December 8 that the strike on Pearl Harbor had succeeded, Tojo recalled, "I was enthusiastic and grateful for this miraculous success."[17]

Tojo bent over backward to exonerate the emperor at every stage. This was particularly confounding since during the war, he had given all credit to the emperor; after the fall of Singapore, for instance, he had told the Diet that "[t]hese brilliant victories are solely due to the august virtue of His Majesty the Emperor."[18] Now he gave Hirohito credit only for the good bits. The emperor, Tojo testified, had repeatedly admonished him to be sure that the United States was notified before the opening of hostilities.[19] The emperor had wanted the Doolittle fighters spared, he said, and had firmly wished that Japan should always be on the friendliest terms with the United States and Britain. To absolve Hirohito of possible responsibility for war crimes, he noted that the emperor had stressed the necessity of strict military discipline.[20] Even the imperial rescript after Pearl Harbor was, on Tojo's account, merely aimed at the Japanese people and not a declaration of war under international law. Although the government had drafted the rescript, Tojo said, the emperor had added the line that "It has been truly unavoidable and far from our wishes that our Empire has now been brought to cross swords with America and Britain."

Tojo testified that "the full responsibility for the decision of 1 December 1941 for war is that of the Cabinet Ministers and members of the High Command, and absolutely not the responsibility of the Emperor." Even the emperor's crucial task of selecting a prime minister, he explained, was dictated by the advice of the council of elder statemen. Hirohito would occasionally make suggestions or express his own wishes through Marquis Kido Koichi, but the emperor would not veto any final decisions made by his cabinet or military commanders: "I recall no instance where the Emperor refused to accept the persuasion of these political counsellors and military advisers."[21]

Turning from aggression to conventional war crimes, Tojo seemed rather more offended by the idea that his subordinates were undisciplined than by the atrocities they had committed. Affronted to be accused, he barely defended himself: "I have nothing whatever to say on this point other than to state frankly that at no time during my entire career did I ever contemplate the commission of a criminal act."

Yet his power as prime minister and army minister spoke against him. He testified that he had been "politically responsible" for laws about punishing prisoners of war, although not conceding any criminal guilt. As army minister, he had established Japan's camps for prisoners of war and had been in charge of interned enemy civilians in war zones. Yet he evasively said that before the prisoners reached the camps, they were the responsibility of the chief of the army general staff, not the army minister. This allowed him to duck blame for, in his own examples, the Bataan death march, abuses of Allied prisoners on the Malay Peninsula, and the deaths on the "hell ships." (He had become chief of the army general staff too from February to July 1944.)

Rather than addressing specific war crimes, Tojo pointed to a list of army regulations that clearly had not prevented massive abuses. He explained that "the Japanese conception regarding prisoners of war differs from that of Europeans and Americans." Japan had rejected the Geneva Convention's rules because "from ancient times the Japanese have deemed it most degrading to be taken prisoner, and all combatants have been instructed to choose death rather than be captured as a P.O.W." Anyway, with so many prisoners over so much territory from "many different races," with supplies scarce, it had been impossible for Japan to apply the Geneva Convention precisely.

In the one specific atrocity that he did consider, Tojo stoutly defended the Burma–Thailand death railway. "I agreed to the employment of prisoners of war," he testified, who fell under his authority as army minister. Although he blamed the chief of the army general staff for directing the construction work, he conceded that as army minister "I held the administrative responsibility as supervising authority over the P.O.W.'s."

The Hague Convention IV on land warfare of 1907 banned the use of prisoners of war for tasks connected with the operation of the war, as well as forbidding excessive work.[22] Yet he insisted that "there was not ever the faintest thought in our minds that this type of employment would ever be challenged as prohibitive under international standards." The project was vital for Japan, the area was far from the front lines, and it was "not an uncommonly unhealthy" spot. He testified that Japanese soldiers had worked there too and been treated equally with the Allied prisoners of war—a contention that flew in the face of the testimony of numerous Australians. Admitting that he had heard of "deficiencies" in sanitation and the treatment of the prisoners, he said that he had sacked an officer and sent another to improve conditions, and that one company commander had faced a court-martial.

Tojo accused the United States of war crimes in bombarding Japanese cities, but in doing so inadvertently blew apart much of the defense's argument. Denouncing the Doolittle bombing raid on Tokyo and other Japanese cities, he said that atrocities against a civilian population were war crimes under established international law. Japan had created a new law to punish enemy airmen in August 1942, which Tojo treated not as something novel but merely a compilation of extant international laws and regulations. (In fact, the Army Ministry's legal department had concluded that it would be illegal to execute the Doolittle prisoners, only to be instructed that "the execution would take place regardless of the legality.") While all eight of the captured U.S. airmen had been sentenced to death, Tojo noted that he had reported to the emperor and got five of the sentences commuted.

Here Tojo blundered in at least three ways. First, he placed Hirohito in the chain of command: if the emperor could pardon five U.S. prisoners, why could he not have saved the other three who were executed by officers evidently under his authority?[23] Second, he highlighted that the Doolittle fliers had been hastily tried under a law created after their bombing raids—the same kind of ex post facto justice that the Japanese defendants were complaining about in the Tokyo trial. If a Japanese court could convict and execute the Doolittle airmen with a law not in effect at the time they committed their war crimes, why couldn't the Allies do the same to Tojo? Third, the same legal principles that Tojo embraced would also outlaw Japan's bombing of Chongqing and other Chinese cities, contrary to the ambiguity that Japanese military lawyers had at first tried to use to justify their own aerial bombardment. If it was a war crime to bomb civilians, that should apply equally regardless of whether they were Japanese or Chinese.[24]

·   ·   ·

Tojo was unrepentant about how Japan had treated its Asian neighbors. He vouched that he could never imagine that Japan's benevolent policies toward what he called Greater East Asia could "be construed as the planning of conquest, the domination of the world, or of aggression." Japan had sought to bring independence to Asian nations that "groaned under the oppression of western powers."

He took aim at Western racism against Asians, although denying that Japan had meant to "drive the white race from their fruitful field in East Asia." Liberation for Asians, he said, was a cherished Japanese goal since Japan had tried and failed to write racial equality into the Covenant of the League of Nations after World War I. He complained that Australia in 1901 and the United States in 1924 had imposed restrictions on Japanese immigration.

The Greater East Asia Co-Prosperity Sphere was based on an Eastern "moral and spiritual foundation," replacing a depraved Western-influenced order "which sacrifices other races and other countries for their own benefit and prosperity." Japan meant to win over the locals by respecting their "racial traits, customs and habits." Trumpeting the superiority of Eastern spirituality over Western materialism, he advocated his own version of the *mission civilisatrice*: "From ancient times there has been a superior culture in Greater East Asia which is a form of spiritual culture marked by sublimity and profoundness. We thought if we spread this culture all over the world, after a long process of fostering and refining, that it would tend to counteract the shortcomings of the material culture, and greatly contribute to the general welfare of all mankind."[25]

Reminding the courtroom of India's recent independence, Tojo's affidavit pointed out that "our Empire gave full support" to the movement for "the freedom, independence and prosperity of India under the leadership of Chandra Bose." He quoted from Bose's speech at the Greater East Asia Conference in Tokyo in November 1943 cheering on the "liberated nations" helped by Japan. Still, it was hard to disguise the exploitative side of Japan's reign. While Tojo pointed triumphantly to Japan's recognition of Burma and the Philippines, he had to admit that the Japanese army and navy had insisted on keeping the Netherlands East Indies under their own military administration for the time being—necessary, as he did not say, to secure Indonesian oil for the war effort.

Tojo concluded fierily. He said "the fruitless and devastating war that broke out on December 8, 1941, was absolutely provoked by the [A]llied powers to force America into the European conflict," accusing China and

European colonial powers in Asia of dragging the United States into the war. Despite the lost war, he insisted Japan had had no choice: "I believe firmly and will contend to the last that it was a war of self-defense and in no manner a violation of presently acknowledged international law."

He directly questioned the lawfulness of the Tokyo court: "Never at any time did I ever conceive that the waging of this war would or could be challenged by the victors as an international crime or that regularly constituted public officials of the vanquished nation would be charged individually as criminals under any recognized international law or under alleged violations of treaties between nations." While denying all legal guilt as a war criminal, he as prime minister accepted responsibility for Japan's defeat: "The responsibility in that sense I am not only willing but sincerely desire to accept fully."[26]

The press ran long excerpts from Tojo's affidavit verbatim, which allowed him to address the Japanese public directly with a message that defied the Allied occupiers. Breaking through General Headquarters' censorship, all six of the major Japanese daily newspapers devoted almost all of their front pages to his exoneration of the emperor and his claims of national self-defense, although they carefully put "self-defense" in quotation marks.

The *Mainichi Shimbun*, the only newspaper to run an editorial about Tojo's statement, challenged him sharply. Under the headline "We Apologize to the World," the editors wrote that Japan's wars had been unjustifiable aggression, while urging the country to "continue to repent and reflect upon its misdeeds of the past." Since Tojo took responsibility for the defeat but not for wrongdoing, "the Japanese people's verdict on him must necessarily be cold and stern."[27]

The Japanese public was fascinated by Tojo's statement. The exoneration of the emperor came as a relief to many.[28] As one Japanese newspaper reported, most Japanese had never much respected Tojo and still did not, but their impressions of their wartime prime minister were considerably improved because he had absolved the emperor and had accepted blame himself. "I hate Tojo when I think of the cause which plunged Japan into her present plight," said one policeman. "I hate Tojo for his sin of leading the nation to defeat but I don't hate him as a human being," said a journalist. A university student appreciated Tojo's statement but hoped that he would die to take responsibility for the death of millions of people. A former soldier who had lost a brother at Okinawa said that Tojo was not alone to blame for the war, and hoped he would not be executed. On the whole, as some Japanese newspaper editors concluded, most young men still believed that the war had been forced upon Japan. While intellectuals were critical of Tojo and even of the emperor, ordinary Japanese expressed more sympathy than hatred for their former prime minister.[29]

"The Defendants . . . Have Proved the Guilt of the Emperor Pretty Conclusively"

Under cross-examination, Tojo's star turn became the talk of Tokyo. Giving crisp, sardonic answers that often drew laughter from the crowd, Tojo proved to be one witness the impatient Sir William Webb saw no reason to reprimand. At one point the laughter from both non-Japanese and Japanese spectators was so raucous that the marshal of the court had to rap for order.[30] When asked if it was unusual for a potential minister to ask for conditions before joining the cabinet, Tojo wryly replied, "Well, I couldn't quite reply to that question because I had only one experience in forming a cabinet."[31] One day he had special visitors in the spectators' gallery: General Douglas MacArthur's wife and his nine-year-old son, Arthur MacArthur. "Arthur wanted to see Tojo," his mother explained.[32]

Yet early on Tojo slipped up catastrophically, doing the last thing he wanted to: incriminating the emperor. While an American defense counsel representing Marquis Kido Koichi was fishing for evidence that his client had sought peace, Tojo stuck to his script of defending the monarch. Did Tojo knew of any instance where Kido had acted contrary to the emperor's wishes for peace? "In so far as I know there was no such instance whatsoever," Tojo replied primly. But then the general rashly added a flourish: "And I further wish to add that there is no Japanese subject who would go against the will of His Majesty; more particularly, among high officials of the Japanese government or of Japan."

It took a moment for Tojo's statement to sink in. Webb broke in: "Well, you know the implications from that reply." A stunned hush fell as everyone else caught up with the chief judge. Since no Japanese official would ever go against the will of the emperor, then the emperor must have *wanted* the war. Tojo had just testified under oath that the Japanese government had gone to war in accord with the will of the emperor.

This was a disaster not just for Hirohito, Tojo, and the defense but also for the prosecution and General Headquarters, who were straining to spare the emperor. The American defense counsel stood frozen at the lectern, unsure what to do next, before finally sitting down mutely. Other defense lawyers shot wondering looks at each other. At last Webb called another defense lawyer to the stand, but the damage was done.

Webb had previously let it be known that he did not accept Joseph Keenan's exonerations of the emperor. Now he had Tojo Hideki's own word to confirm his opinion. Through the end of the trial, he would condemn Hirohito by using Tojo's spectacular statement as proof that the Japanese would have carried out their beloved emperor's will without question.[33]

After this fiasco, a mortified Tojo strained to get back to his intended line. He testified that the navy had never advocated an attack on the United States or Britain without first giving lawful notice, and that the emperor, too, had made clear to him that he wanted proper forewarning given. A defense lawyer asked for a clarification which would implicate Hirohito: so advocating war without notice would have been against the emperor's wishes? Keenan quickly objected, in a head-snapping display: the U.S. chief prosecutor cutting off a question about the guilt of the Japanese emperor. Webb grudgingly upheld the objection.[34]

The importance of Tojo's gaffe was obvious. As Comyns Carr confidentially explained to Sir Hartley Shawcross, the British attorney general, "the defendants if they have done nothing else, have proved the guilt of the Emperor pretty conclusively, which, in view of the decision not to prosecute him, we had been trying to keep in the background, and K[eenan] has been going out of his way, quite unsuccessfully to disprove. Of course, they have all been parading their loyalty to him, but that is the practical effect of their evidence."[35]

"Tojo Had a Good Morning Hanging Keenan"

Keenan rose to begin his cross-examination. He meant it to be the defining clash of the entire trial: the U.S. chief prosecutor against the foremost Japanese warlord.

It was a debacle. The judges were obviously appalled, the prosecutors dismayed. Comyns Carr wrote to Shawcross, "The results are best summarised by a girl from the British embassy who was in court this morning and said, 'Tojo had a good morning hanging Keenan.'"[36]

Keenan was distracted by his long-running vendetta with Webb, which had become so public that *Life* magazine wrote that it nullified much of the court's effectiveness as a model of Western justice. Webb kept dragging the emperor into the proceedings, making Keenan look useless in

MacArthur's eyes. At one point, when Keenan stumbled into comparing the authority of the Japanese emperor and the president of the United States, Webb flushed red, leaned forward, and shouted: "Go immediately to something else!" Tojo sneered and several other defendants smiled.[37]

Tojo Hideki giving his defiant testimony in the old Army Ministry courtroom, January 1948

Keenan had meant to have most of the cross-examination handled by an assistant he had brought over from Washington, whom Comyns Carr called "an American of moderate competence."[38] This aide had spent a year specializing on Tojo and then put in five weeks of intensive preparation for the big day. But in court Keenan asked to split the task between himself and his aide, "which is against the rules here, as he well knew," Comyns Carr privately wrote. Keenan prevailed upon the defense lawyers not to complain about the breach of procedure, and Webb obligingly said the rules could be waived so long as it did not set a precedent. But some of the judges wanted to know the reason. Since Keenan could not very well say that his aide was better at this than him, he instead said that he as chief prosecutor was awfully busy. A majority of the judges, who were busy too, voted against divvying up the questioning. Startled, Keenan bit the bullet and said that he would do the whole cross-examination himself. His aide "walked out of court and left him to it," never to return, wrote Comyns Carr. "The whole thing is a farce."[39]

Keenan began with coarse contempt: "Accused Tojo, I shall not address you as General because, of course, you know there is no longer any Japanese Army." His first question was whether Tojo's testimony was meant to convince the court of his innocence or was meant to be a fresh dose of "imperialistic, militaristic propaganda to the people of Japan."

Keenan asked if Tojo believed that every nation had the right to determine its own form of government, a question that reminded many in the courtroom about Western imperialism. Had anyone given Tojo the right to determine what way of life should be imposed upon the people of Greater East Asia? "You mean to me?" replied Tojo, his eyebrows jumping in surprise. He took the easy opportunity to pose as an anticolonialist: "No, I got such rights from nowhere."

Keenan more successfully turned to a staple of American war rhetoric: linking Tojo with Adolf Hitler. Was Tojo, as army minister, for or against the Tripartite Pact? "Under the situation prevailing at that time I was in favor of it." Had Tojo not understood the horrors of Hitler's New Order in Europe? Tojo replied that he had only known "the general status, outline of the Hitlerian new order," but had not studied it. "I did not know what Hitler himself thought of what it meant," Tojo said absurdly. Keenan asked, "Is your memory becoming faint about that now, Tojo, because you are ashamed of the alliance?" Tojo took the bait. "No," he shot back, "I do not entertain any such cowardly views."

Having refused to renounce the Axis, Tojo was readily tarred with the Nazi record around the time of the Tripartite Pact. Had he approved of Hitler breaking his promises in marching into Belgium and Holland? "I have no knowledge as to whether Germany renounced its promise vis-à-vis Holland and Belgium, or whether if such promises were broken whether they were justified or not. I think future history will judge that." Had Tojo heard of the Munich agreement? "I heard the name," said Tojo, "but I do not know the contents." Was Tojo really claiming that he did not know about the notorious Munich deal? "Well, whether it is in front of this Tribunal or in the presence of God I am telling the truth."

Since Tojo had built his exculpation on self-defense, Keenan asked whether Nazi Germany had also been acting in self-defense. Rather than drawing a bright line between Japan's claims of self-defense and Nazi Germany's invasions, Tojo equivocated. Was Hitler's conquest of Czechoslovakia self-defense? "Whether that was self-defense or not I say that future history will be the best judge of that." What about Hitler's invasion of Norway? "I have never said that it was in self-defense. I am telling you that I am in no position to judge whether or not it was an act of self-defense." Keenan scornfully said Tojo did not know much about Hitler or Germany's recent actions, despite approving the Tripartite Pact as a cabinet member.

Had he known about Nazi purges and the concentration camps? Tojo replied limply that he did not know about the concentration camps: "What I knew prior to the Tripartite Pact was the persecution of the Jews." By his own account, oppressing Jews was no reason not to ally with Nazi Germany. Tojo had sullied two of his core arguments: that he had acted in self-defense and that he had stood against racial discrimination.

Having found his feet on the Axis, Keenan crashed back to earth as he turned to China. Ill-prepared, he gave a largely irrelevant series of questions which at best called attention to the fact that the war in China had been awful, but did nothing to link Tojo specifically with its horrors.

Tojo did not disguise his loathing for Puyi, the puppet Qing emperor who had testified for the prosecution. When Keenan asked if he had heard his testimony in this courtroom, Tojo coolly replied, "I did. I didn't believe it, of course." When Keenan asked if Puyi had been treated as a royal when he visited Japan, Tojo replied that he had been royally treated "from the bottom of our hearts, but he betrayed our confidence before this Tribunal." This brought loud laughter in the courtroom, forcing the marshal to rap to restore order.[40] Had Tojo known he was undependable before this trial? "No, I trusted him," Tojo said. "I trust him more than anyone else. It must have been my lack of insight."[41]

Tojo worked hard to downplay the China war. "Japan has never invaded Manchuria," he claimed, before suggesting that Japan had been justified in marching troops into other parts of China as well.[42] When Keenan read from a published Japanese army report that over two million Chinese had been killed from July 1937 to June 1941, Tojo jumped in to claim this horrifying statistic was just battlefield bluster: "The commanders at the front are very fond of reporting their own exploits, and, therefore, they are apt to report the number of casualties inflicted on the enemy and of booty taken in exaggerated figures." When Keenan read that this military report listed Japanese deaths at just over one hundred thousand, Tojo reversed gears and insisted that the Japanese had lost far more: some one million two hundred thousand, including Japanese residents in China who had been massacred. Soon after, Tojo, looking directly at Keenan, said that Chinese leaders who incited against the Japanese and massacred innocent Japanese residents in China had "constituted one of the great causes of the war."[43]

Would Tojo agree that wars are crimes against the people? "I don't agree with your statement that war is a crime," said Tojo, who was not going to be snared so easily, "but I do agree with you so far as to say that wars have an unfortunate effect upon the people, and that unfortunate effect is the same for the victor as for the vanquished."

"I Did What Was Right and True"

As the days wore on, the judges grew irritated and impatient. Tojo, having taken the measure of his courtroom adversary, was flush with confidence. Keenan kept missing opportunities to delve into the records of high-level conferences that showed Tojo's own complicity. Rather than a disciplined inquiry about specific incidents, Keenan hopscotched around from topic to topic, hoping that Tojo would slip up and say something revealing.

Keenan slowly became aware that he was being trounced. "I would like to get a word in edgewise occasionally, Mr. Tojo," he said as the defendant made another long answer. At another point, Keenan fumed, "I am doing the questioning and you are doing the answering. Do you understand?" "I understand," Tojo replied politely.[44] Trying to cast Tojo as a dictator, Keenan asked his opinion about democratic Diet elections like those that had recently happened under Allied occupation. Tojo had a blistering retort: "Well, having been incarcerated at Sugamo Prison, I do not know what the United States has done recently in Japan."[45]

When Keenan asked him how Japan could possibly have felt threatened by the American fleet at Hawaii, Tojo cannily replied, "threat is a subjective thing. That was felt by Japan and I felt it." He pointed to U.S. and British support for China, deepening coordination between the United States, Britain, and Holland, and increasing Allied armed forces in the Philippines, Malaya, Burma, and the Netherlands East Indies. When Keenan said that the U.S. buildup was defensive, Tojo replied, "Well, the United States is free to think what it thought, but as far as Japan was concerned, we considered these acts as threats against us."

Trashing the prosecution's evidence, Tojo questioned the reliability of the Saionji-Harada memoirs, saying that Baron Harada Kumao was "just a sort of a high class information broker." He took issue with several points where Harada's version showed Japan as more aggressive toward the United States than the official records from the liaison conference. As Keenan read from the Saionji-Harada memoirs' version of a meeting, he asked, "do you still contend that this document is an exhibition of the miscellaneous gatherings of some high-class information broker?" "Naturally," replied Tojo.

As Keenan meandered, the scale of the missed opportunity became apparent. In an exchange about French Indochina, Tojo's fidelity to the

Axis was on embarrassing display: "I was well aware of the fact that the Vichy Government was operating under German occupation, but I considered the Vichy Government as the legitimate government of France." Then he equated Nazi Germany's occupation of France with the American occupation of Japan: "It is just as the present Japanese Government, operating under the American Government, is the legitimate government of Japan."[46]

On several occasions, Tojo let slip his condescending view of other Asian peoples. In a discussion of Greater East Asia, Tojo said that the term "does not in any way suggest the idea of slavery or a status of slavery." Keenan, who had not mentioned slavery, shot back, "I don't know, Mr. Tojo, what put the idea of slavery into your mind." When asked what countries counted as part of Greater East Asia, Tojo gave a vague reply that suggested that the malleable concept was driven by political convenience. Burma did not count, nor Australia; the Philippines was only added after Pearl Harbor. At first it included Japan's main targets for expansion: Manchuria, China, Indochina, Thailand, and Indonesia. What about Malaya? "Oh, I forgot," Tojo said. "The Malays are also included." Keenan sarcastically asked, "How about India, a little country like India?" "Well, India is pretty big," Tojo replied, but not part of Greater East Asia.[47]

In one notable exchange, Tojo tarred the emperor with knowledge about Pearl Harbor. Although he had met with Hirohito several times in the first seven days of December to discuss the war that was about to begin, he claimed that he had not talked to the emperor about the strike coming at Pearl Harbor, since the government had no responsibility to tell the monarch about operations. But with obvious reluctance, he made a damning revelation: "I believe they"—the military high command—"did tell the Emperor the general outline of this plan beforehand." The plan to attack Pearl Harbor? "Yes."

Despite that moment of incrimination, Keenan and Tojo mostly worked together to absolve the emperor. A few days after Tojo had disastrously testified that no Japanese would have defied the will of the emperor, prosecutor and defendant made an elaborately choreographed effort to undo the shambles. The theatrics began as Keenan noted that Hirohito had many times expressed to Tojo that he was a man of peace and did not want war. Was it the will of Emperor Hirohito that war was instituted? Tojo obligingly took the blame: "It might have been against the Emperor's will, but it is a fact that because of my advice and because of the advice given by the High Command the Emperor consented, though reluctantly, to the war." He declared, "The Emperor's love for and desire for peace remained the same right up to the very moment when hostilities commenced, and even during the war his feelings remained the same."

By now Tojo was hard-faced, strained from eight days of defending his policy and his emperor. Although he never lost his composure, he stumbled more over his words, looked at the ceiling, and sometimes raised his voice with bombast. On January 7, 1948, the last day of Tojo's testimony, Keenan went for a big finish. He asked Tojo if he, as prime minister of Japan, had committed any legal or moral wrong. "I feel that I committed no wrong," replied Tojo in a rasping voice. "I feel that I did what was right and true." Keenan asked if Tojo was acquitted by the court, would he feel at liberty "to go out and do the same thing over again?" Tojo's American defense lawyer objected, and Webb sided with the defense—bringing the cross-examination to an inglorious finish. With a confident air, Tojo ambled back to his seat with the other defendants.[48]

The damage was unmistakable. *Time* wrote that Tojo spoke "for millions of Japanese." One Japanese said, "I used to think that Tojo should be hanged. Now I don't know. If we had won we would have tried the Americans." Another predicted that when the Americans left Japan, the first to be enshrined as a divine spirit would be Tojo.[49]

The Dutch judge, Bert Röling, recalled that Tojo "restored his dignity in the eyes of the Japanese people."[50] In its *People's Daily,* the Chinese Communist Party reviled Tojo's "absurd and arrogant" claims of self-defense and his excuses for the emperor: "MacArthur's protection and indulgence is the real reason why war criminals such as Tojo dare to be so arrogant."[51]

Life magazine ran a scathing story about Tojo's success in court, mocking Keenan and Webb for feuding publicly over the guilt of the emperor.[52] Webb darkly suspected that Keenan—who was friends with the magazine's publisher, Henry Luce, and had brought him to visit the court—had planted the *Life* piece. Embarrassed, Webb wrote to both MacArthur and the chief justice of Australia's High Court to deny the contents of the article, especially the true parts.[53] "The Tribunal has never bogged down," he lied to MacArthur. "I have never had any feud with the Chief of Counsel or any other Counsel. . . . I have always been polite to the Chief of Counsel and all other Counsel. . . . I have never shouted in Court."

Even less plausibly, Webb assured MacArthur that he was not out to get the emperor. True, he admitted, he thought "there was a prima facie case against the Emperor," and he had pointed out to Keenan that "the Prosecution's evidence implicated the Emperor." Yet despite that, the chief judge insisted that he had never questioned any witness to show that the emperor was guilty or responsible for the war. He had even told Keenan once or twice that "the question whether the Emperor was guilty or not was irrelevant as he was not on trial." He claimed that he had told the Australian government that the emperor's fate had to be decided at the highest level and that he had told the Australian foreign minister in writing that "if the Emperor were indicted I would not take part in his trial." None of this really disguised Webb's belief that the emperor was guilty, although it did suggest a willingness to punt that question to his political superiors.[54]

In private, the British government was appalled by Tojo's triumph. "Things in the trial have gone from bad to worse," Comyns Carr reported to his government, "and I must again make it clear that the set up being what it is, I can accept no responsibility whatever for them."[55] Shawcross was ready to give up on the whole Tokyo trial. "The whole thing has been most disastrous," he wrote, "and but for Comyns Carr, I think the proceedings might well have collapsed in complete fiasco." Keenan was "at all times hopelessly incompetent, and at most times also completely intoxicated."[56] The British lord chancellor lamented, "All one can say is that the sooner this thing is ended the better for everyone."[57]

PART III

NEMESIS

CHAPTER 24

Mr. X

GENERAL DOUGLAS MACARTHUR VIEWED himself as Julius Caesar occupying Gaul. George Kennan, on his way from Washington to Tokyo, was just as grandiosely classical: he saw MacArthur as the Byzantine military commander Belisarius during the ancient occupation of Italy, with himself as an itinerant Byzantine daring to visit, "enjoying his hospitality, and listening to his complaints about the inept and ignorant interference he had to endure from the imperial court at Constantinople."[1]

While the Tokyo trial was wrapping up, the Truman administration was taking a hard look at its Japan policy. With tensions escalating fast with the Soviet Union, officials in Washington realized how strategically useful an anti-Communist Japan could be. Maybe Japan was the prize after all, not China. While the United States drafted plans for a formal peace treaty with Japan that would end the occupation, General Headquarters was already retreating from its bold policies for democratization.[2] American officials were gripped by doubts about purging and prosecuting Japanese conservatives and reactionaries who could be used to build an anti-Soviet stronghold.[3]

George Kennan, who had never set foot in Japan, helped to build a consensus in the Truman administration that the Cold War necessitated a new realpolitik-minded strategy there—what became known as the "reverse course." A scholar-diplomat renowned as the mastermind of the Cold War policy of containment of the Soviet Union, he would confront MacArthur and emerge as the most influential advocate of a softer American approach to Japan.[4] "I turned our whole occupation policy," he later boasted.[5]

Kennan was brilliant, gloomy, and verbose; he was thin, tall, and balding, with expressive blue eyes. A historian, a Russianist, and a seasoned diplomat, he had served at the U.S. embassies in Moscow and then Berlin, where he and the embassy staff had been interned by Nazi Germany for five months after Pearl Harbor.[6] He was preoccupied not just with Soviet power but American decadence, privately favoring an elite American aristocracy that froze out minorities and immigrants.[7] In his diary, he brooded about "more or less inferior races."[8] A committed advocate of realpolitik, he came to believe that the biggest fault in U.S. foreign policy was what he called "the legalistic-moralistic approach to international problems."[9]

Kennan had gained an oddly anonymous fame for the grand strategy of containment, laid out confidentially in his Long Telegram to the State Department in 1946 and then publicly in a *Foreign Affairs* article in July 1947—cryptically signed "X" to conceal that the author was the State Department's director of policy planning.[10] In the "X" article, he argued for "a long-term, patient but firm and vigilant containment of Russian expansive tendencies," allowing time for the decaying Soviet system to mellow or collapse. Containment, he wrote, would require "the adroit and vigilant application of counter-force at a series of constantly shifting geographical and political points, corresponding to the shifts and manoeuvres of Soviet policy."[11]

In Asia, Kennan saw containment as almost entirely about the defense of Japan. Japan and West Germany, the industrial powerhouses of Asia and Europe, were, he later wrote, "the theaters of our greatest dangers, our greatest responsibilities, and our greatest possibilities." While a sturdy Japan would make an essential rampart against Soviet expansion, he fretted that the ongoing liberalization of Japan meant trashing parts of the economy, inviting Communist subversion, and endangering the country's stability. He was contemptuous of directives from MacArthur which reflected "the love for pretentious generality, the evangelical liberalism, the self-righteous punitive enthusiasm, the pro-Soviet illusions, and the unreal hopes for great-power collaboration in the postwar period"—vices which were all combined in the Tokyo tribunal.[12]

Kennan followed in the conservative footsteps of Henry Stimson and Joseph Grew, who were quietly advising him.[13] Like them, he disliked lawyerly moralism, doubted the United States' ability to reshape Japanese society, and believed that Japan was more useful to the United States than a collapsing China. Bemused by the American fascination with China, he saw it as peripheral to the United States' security; he wanted to wrest free of obligations to the Nationalists in a civil war, accepting that China might fall under Communist rule or Soviet domination. Instead, as he urged George Marshall, now the secretary of state, the United States must retain "effective control" of Japan and the Philippines to keep them in friendly hands, which would suffice to ward off serious regional threats to U.S. national security. The Philippines should only be granted independence in a way that assured it would be a pro-American bulwark.[14]

Wary of moral preening in general, Kennan disliked war crimes trials in particular. After his years in Moscow, he recoiled at the language of purges.[15] Instead of trials at Nuremberg, he had preferred to execute captured Nazi leaders immediately. For him, a war crimes tribunal could only be justifiable if it repudiated "mass crimes of every sort," particularly those committed by the Soviets. He later wrote that accepting a Soviet judge at Nuremberg—despite the well-known horrors of the Russian Revolution, collectivization, and the 1930s purges, as well as wartime atrocities against Poland and the Baltics—"was to make a mockery of the only purpose the trials could conceivably serve, and to assume, by association, a share of the responsibility for those Stalinist crimes themselves."[16]

Grimly surveying instability in China, India, Indonesia, and Indochina, Kennan feared that Japan too would plunge into chaos as soon as the Americans departed. Despite a growing consensus in Washington, nobody from Harry Truman on down dared to confront MacArthur about rethinking the occupation.[17] Kennan had advised Marshall that a senior State Department official (himself, obviously) should trek to Japan to get the supreme commander into line.[18] Early in February 1948, the secretary of state told Kennan to pack his bags.[19]

The meetings would be awkward in the extreme. Truman continued to stew about MacArthur, noting in his diary that he had gleefully discussed "MacArthur and his superiority complex" with Dwight Eisenhower. The president worried that "MacArthur expects to make a Roman Triumphal return to the U.S. a short time before the Republican Convention meets in Philadelphia," a prospect so dire that he privately encouraged Eisenhower to run for president as the Democratic nominee, with Truman as his vice presidential candidate. The president wrote that "my family & myself would be happy outside this great white jail, known as the White House."[20]

MacArthur was no more keen on the Truman team. He had, as Kennan later wrote, "a violent prejudice against the State Department," so much that arranging the trip felt like opening up diplomatic relations with a hostile foreign government. Marshall steered clear of anything to do with MacArthur, sick of his showboating. The War Department was daunted by the supreme commander, Kennan noted, doing nothing more than sending along a general to watch the fun: "I think they licked their lips as they watched a civilian David prepare to call upon this military Goliath."[21]

General Headquarters was already facing hard questions from Washington about sidelining the leaders of Japan's wartime economy. If Japan was to be self-sufficient, the army secretary declared publicly, it needed a centralized industrial sector—which meant rethinking MacArthur's efforts to undercut the *zaibatsu*, the powerful family-run cartels that had dominated Japan's economy.[22] The purge had been extended to leading businessmen; in the winter of 1947–48, MacArthur had followed up with two Diet laws aimed at melting the lingering economic power of the dissolved *zaibatsu*.[23] MacArthur insisted that these Japanese laws—which froze family members out of their old *zaibatsu* for ten years—were needed to undercut "the powerful octopus of monopolistic financial, industrial and commercial combines" standing in the way of capitalism and democracy. He urged his skeptical superiors to avoid "the softening of Allied policy" and "the coddling of war guilty and their associates." If the *zaibatsu* were not busted by the Allied occupation, he warned, the irate Japanese people would probably launch a violent revolution.[24]

Kennan was coming to Tokyo to press for precisely that kind of softening of U.S. policy. MacArthur planned to overload his uninvited guest with everything that Kennan didn't know that he didn't know. From the moment the diplomat landed, he would be hustled through a grueling series of meetings with Americans. Rather than exploring Japanese society beyond MacArthur's offices at the Dai-Ichi Building, his schedule provided two hours to sightsee in Tokyo. On the last day, when Kennan should be ready to collapse, his schedule allowed an optional two-hour visit to the Tokyo trial.[25] "I'll have him briefed until it comes out of his ears," MacArthur growled.

"These Are Political Trials"

These were not the days of nonstop transpacific air travel. Kennan, forty-four years old, took off from Seattle and arrived about thirty turbulent hours later, after refueling in Anchorage and then making a terrifying stop for more fuel on a tiny island in the North Pacific. He spent the bumpy flight gazing out the window, writing poetry, and trying to relax with an old book about tsarist prisons in Siberia.[26] For the last two thousand miles, the heating conked out. By the time he landed in a snowstorm at Haneda Airport in Tokyo, around 4 a.m. on March 1, he was jet-lagged, exhausted, and frozen.

Kennan recorded no impressions of the bombed-out city or its people. He was packed off to the Imperial Hotel, where the judges of the Tokyo trial were sleeping early on a Monday morning. But reporters kept calling and waking him up. By the time he got to MacArthur's residence for a pitilessly scheduled lunch, he had not slept for about forty-eight hours. Hunched in groggy misery, Kennan sat motionless as a well-rested MacArthur orated for some two hours, pounding the table with a single vertical finger for emphasis. Seated between Kennan and the general sent along by the War Department, MacArthur spoke only to the latter, offering his back to the State Department's man. His lecture sounded to an enervated Kennan like the standard spiel that MacArthur gave to visitors.

MacArthur opined that the only successful historical example of a military occupation was Julius Caesar ruling the barbarian provinces. The American Caesar's own occupation, he vowed, would bring democracy and Christianity to the Japanese, filling the political and spiritual void left by their military defeat. The Japanese, "the most advanced of the Oriental peoples," were tasting freedom for the first time and would not go back to slavery. To Kennan's consternation, MacArthur insisted that the Japanese Communists were no menace, with just four seats in the Diet. The Japanese would never accept Communist domination, unless they were conquered by military force, in which case they were by nature an obedient people. Anyway, MacArthur explained, although "the Russians were Orientals under the skin," they "could not pass as Orientals among the other Oriental peoples, and therefore could not exercise great influence in the Far East." Starting in Japan, he proposed, Americans had a historic opportunity to introduce Christianity and democracy throughout Asia, where the next thousand years of human history would be determined.[27]

After that, MacArthur politely shooed Kennan off. The next day, General Headquarters functionaries barraged the jet-lagged diplomat with numbing briefings at the Dai-Ichi Building.[28] Frustrated and humiliated, he sat down at his desk at the Imperial Hotel, pulled out a sheet of the same letterhead that the Tokyo trial's judges often used, and beseeched the supreme commander for a personal, substantial meeting. "I am entirely at your disposal," he wrote. Meanwhile, to demonstrate that he was no Washington squish, Kennan made a point of giving anti-Soviet lectures to MacArthur's staff.[29]

The mixture of threat and flattery did the trick. Three days later, MacArthur hosted Kennan alone for a candid evening discussion. Beforehand, the diplomat sent over a paper arguing that the United States needed to secure a demilitarized Japan from Soviet invasion or Communist subversion. Many in Washington, Kennan wrote, believed that "the keynote of occupational policy, from here on out, should lie in the achievement of maximum *stability* of Japanese society, in order that Japan may best be able to stand on her own feet when the protecting hand is withdrawn."

That evening, a garrulous MacArthur bluntly explained his worries about Japan's security. Obviously anticipating a Communist takeover of China, he insisted that an amphibious force could never be allowed to strike at the United States from an Asian port. Like Kennan, he thought that Okinawa would make a crucial American base, which, along with the Philippines, would free the United States from maintaining bases on Japan's home islands.

He and Kennan agreed on plenty: the occupation could not last; economic recovery was a top priority; the Soviets were up to no good; the United States would need a defensive perimeter of bases in Asia.[30] Yet MacArthur defended the project of democratization. He argued that many Japanese wanted it; the experience of defeat had had a profound effect on their psychology. The article in the new constitution that renounced war was a Japanese initiative, he claimed, reflecting a national recoil against militarism. As for the purge, the supreme commander said that it was no loss to get rid of the *zaibatsu* chiefs, elderly incompetents equivalent to "the most effete New York club men." The real brains of Japan, he said, were in the military, and he regretted that he had been ordered to eliminate them from public life.

Kennan urged a simple, nonpunitive peace treaty with Japan; he argued vehemently against reparations. He growled that the Russians could not understand sophisticated legal agreements; their concepts of something like property "were as primitive as those of a crow." When he suggested bypassing the Far Eastern Commission, MacArthur, who loathed it as a seedbed of Soviet influence, slapped his thigh in approval. Kennan left confident that they had had a meeting of the minds.[31]

From then on, the trip went more smoothly. MacArthur provided a private railway car to let Kennan tour in comfort. His limited forays around the country served to confirm what he had already believed about Japan. His most visceral reaction, though, was revulsion at the "peculiarly American brand of Philistinism" in the occupation, gorging on luxury in a strange land, impervious to the miseries of the defeated Japanese in their ruined country. He recoiled to find all the drunken fakery, hypocrisy, and "monotony of American social life" transplanted to Japan. Singling out American officers' wives for amassing lacquer tables and butlers and ski trips to Hokkaido, he wondered if this was what the war had been for. Setting off for a week in Okinawa and the Philippines, he wrote privately, "the shrill cackling of these gatherings still rings in my ears."[32]

On Kennan's return to Tokyo, the supreme commander hosted him for a third meeting at his office before he left Asia. This time they argued about whether Japan should be rearmed, as Kennan was considering. MacArthur was unalterably opposed: that would enrage Asian countries who were still terrified of Japan. Without its empire, even a rearmed Japan could at best become a fifth-rate military power, "a tempting morsel, to be gobbled up by Soviet Russia at her pleasure." The Americans would look ridiculous after having put so much effort into disarmament, and the Japanese themselves had sincerely renounced war and had no desire to go backward.[33]

Kennan was already in a foul mood when, on March 10, he evidently spent two hours at the Tokyo trial during its morning session. Although General Headquarters hoped he would be impressed, he was disgusted by the lawyerly spectacle. "These are political trials," he later wrote.[34]

That day, four American defense lawyers were making their concluding arguments. If Kennan was on schedule, he would have heard William Logan Jr., the astute American defense counsel representing Marquis Kido Koichi. A balding lawyer in a conservative suit, Logan would have blended in at the State Department, but he spent most of that day arguing that Japan had been provoked by the United States into a war of self-defense. He contended that economic blockades were an act of war, almost as destructive as bombs. Japan, he noted, had not meddled with the Western Hemisphere; it was the imperialist Western powers who had forced themselves upon the far side of the globe.[35]

This was standard stuff for the Tokyo trial, but Kennan was stunned. Noting the parades of witnesses, the vast amounts of documentary evidence, and exhaustive hearings, he wrote, "the War Crimes Trials have been hailed as the ultimate in international justice." He conceded that "the trials have been *procedurally* thoroughly correct, according to our concepts of justice, and that at no time in history have conquerors conferred upon the vanquished such elaborate opportunities for the public defense and for vindication of their military acts." Yet he was convinced that "these trials are working increasing injury to the Allied cause in Japan."[36]

He condemned the trials not for their unfairness but for their fairness. As he argued afterward, "It is a rule with peoples, as with individuals, that punishment, if it is to have any exemplary effect, must be swift and incisive and must follow immediately on the heels of the offense." (This was a page out of Niccolò Machiavelli, who argued that cruelties should be inflicted in a single stroke.)[37] These "interminable trials," Kennan wrote, had long ceased to do anything but spark public "sympathy for these fellow Japanese who are forced to sit through these endless and humiliating ordeals which have so little to do with anything that anyone in Japan can understand."

Kennan, given his horror at Soviet participation at Nuremberg, might have recoiled at the Soviet judge at Tokyo. Yet he wrote nothing about the sight of Major General Ivan Zaryanov in his Red Army uniform. Instead, his objection was not against political trials as such but that the politics were being poorly managed. The lawyers had been selected for their legal qualifications, but war crimes trials required "persons deeply versed in the history and practice of international relations." He scorned the counsel serving both the prosecution and defense: "The medium in which these people are working is politics, and international politics at that—not law."

Above all, he was scandalized by the American defense lawyers. "The spectacle of American lawyers defending the policies of past Japanese Governments, in order to improve the defense of their clients, is absolutely preposterous in its impact on the Japanese," he wrote. "It undermines the whole effect of the trials." He warned that the Japanese could not understand what a defense lawyer was, apparently unaware that Japanese criminal trials already had them.[38] Therefore he argued that the Japanese would conclude that "the rightness or wrongness of Japan's policies prior to the war was not a matter of conviction among the Americans but a moot legal point, on which Americans themselves are divided and which could be settled only by two years of abstruse judicial procedure."[39]

REVERSE COURSE

Kennan flew back to Washington in relief and triumph. Convinced that the liberalizing reforms in Japan had gone too far and needed to be stopped, he threw himself into transforming the Truman administration's policy.[40]

He did not believe that the occupiers could make the Japanese over like Americans. All they were doing, he thought, was tearing apart the fabric of Japanese society, giving the Soviets an opportunity to infiltrate the country. The tens of thousands of militarists purged from the army, police, industry, and bureaucracy would become, he predicted, an underground cluster to be exploited by the Communists. Some of the young officers at General Headquarters, he complained, were outdoing the Soviets in their enthusiasm for uprooting traditional structures.[41]

The strain of the journey, and perhaps MacArthur-induced stress, set off an ulcer which left him bedridden. He spent two days writing a long report, and then checked himself into Bethesda Naval Hospital for two weeks.[42]

In the report, he argued that freedom and democracy were alien to Japanese society. "The reforms cut deeply into almost every phase of Japanese life," he wrote. "Founded as they are on western models, they cannot fail to produce considerable bewilderment and confusion in the public mind." Energetic reform would undermine the stability of Japanese society, at least in the short term. Regarding Imperial Japan's atrocities and aggression, he preferred to look forward. As he sportingly wrote, the forthcoming peace treaty "should constitute, in essence, an encouraging pat on the back to the Japanese for the future, rather than another reminder of their bad behavior in the past."[43]

He cautioned that General Headquarters' reforms "are based almost exclusively on western models or on western ideas" that did not apply to Japanese conditions, and that these foreign transplants would "unseat older institutions which corresponded to specific Japanese needs, without replacing them with anything that can be easily or practically absorbed by Japanese society." (Japan, influenced by such synthesizing philosophers as Nishi Amane, had in fact been drawing on Western models long before the occupation, from French laws adopted in the Meiji era to a 1922 code of criminal procedure modeled on German law.)[44] The Soviet Union and China, he thought, preferred sweeping social reform because they favored "a situation in which the Japanese society is kept weak and unstable, while we pay the costs."

To build up Japan as an anti-Soviet bastion, Kennan wanted to dispose of "the punitive aspects of Allied policy" promptly. The purge reminded him of Soviet oppression: "The indiscriminate purging of whole categories of officials" bore a "sickening resemblance to the concepts of certain totalitarian governments." It had sidelined hundreds of thousands of the best-educated leaders, some supporters of the United States, and many people "whose only crime was to serve their country in time of war." The initial purge decree, which had targeted active supporters of militarism, was so ill-defined that it could allow "stark political expediency."

Although war crimes trials sought to separate the innocent from the guilty, Kennan was disgusted by them as well. After his two hours at the Tokyo trial, he reported with distaste about the proceedings.

While urging a gentler approach toward rightists, he exhorted cracking down on leftists. He proposed establishing an "effective central intelligence authority" along the lines of the FBI, which Japan currently lacked. While admitting that such an agency could "easily develop into a political police along Russian or Nazi lines," and that launching one probably violated Allied agreements against reviving Japan's secret police, he argued that Japan could not withstand Communist pressure without it. Worried that Japan's regular police forces were small and needed more pistols, he urged beefing up the forces of domestic repression to withstand "strong communist pressures in the direction of provocation, mystification and disorder."

Despite MacArthur's blandishments, Kennan urged the Truman administration to rein in the occupation. He thought that General Headquarters was too big and too domineering, not allowing the Japanese to take control of their own lives. He warned that breaking up the *zaibatsu* would hurt industrial production, and complained that labor reforms ("generous even by western standards") were unsustainable. Still, in a liberal flourish at odds with much of what he had previously written, he wanted to loosen censorship, arguing that "a tightly muzzled public opinion" would not withstand the Communist threat.[45]

Kennan was disquieted by the success of MacArthur's demilitarization of Japan, which necessitated the ongoing protection of large numbers of U.S. troops. So long as the Soviets remained a menace, he believed, the United States would either have to keep armed forces in Japan or "permit Japan to re-arm to the extent that it would no longer constitute an open invitation to military aggression." If the United States kept troops indefinitely, that would mean giving up on a formal peace treaty that returned sovereignty to Japan, since it would be "psychologically unsound" to keep Allied armies in central Japan afterward. (This was a prescient warning about the perennial tensions around U.S. military bases in today's Japan.)[46] Instead he preferred to use the outlying southwestern island of Okinawa to base U.S. troops, although the Ryukyu "islanders are clearly not fit for independence." Kennan was obviously tempted to rearm Japan, even though MacArthur strongly felt that would be dangerous, an idea whose mere mention would shock and alienate the other Allies.[47]

Some U.S. officials were uncomfortable with Kennan's campaign. A senior State Department official argued that there would be no real stability in Japan without democratic liberty and political rights; without them, the Japanese would turn to either fascism or Communism.[48] Yet

Kennan immediately won over the secretary of state. In a cabinet meeting, Marshall called his report "a very closely reasoned and persuasive document," and pressed to get it on Truman's desk.[49]

In June, Kennan's Policy Planning Staff circulated its top secret recommendations for Japan policy to Truman, MacArthur, Marshall, and the rest of the national security team. In this important paper—whose final version would be tagged by the White House bureaucracy with the nondescript moniker of NSC 13/2—the United States would turn away from democratization and concentrate instead on building up Japan as an anti-Communist industrial powerhouse.[50]

In his proposal, Kennan's north star was containing "the Soviet Union's policy of aggressive Communist expansion." Rather than bogging down in claims about restitution and war crimes, Kennan had his eyes fixed on the dawning Cold War. Although he cautioned correctly that the Soviet Union would stand in the way of a formal peace treaty that would end the occupation—the Soviets would ultimately boycott the Treaty of San Francisco when it was signed in 1951—he wanted that treaty to be "as nonpunitive as possible." Having demilitarized Japan, the United States would have to keep troops there until a peace treaty was signed, but the number should be cut to a minimum, and they should be kept as far away from the Japanese populace as possible.

Kennan urged an end to the democratization measures, insisting instead that the primary U.S. objective in Japan should be economic recovery. There should be no more reform edicts or legislation, and General Headquarters should "relax pressure steadily but unobtrusively" about the directives already in place. Nor should there be any more punishment of those who had driven Japan to war. General Headquarters should tell the Japanese government that there would be no further extension of the purge, and that some of those on the lists should be allowed back into government, business, or the media. Consistent with Kennan's dismay at the Tokyo trial, a draft urged "an early conclusion of the war crimes trials of [Class] 'A' suspects"—wrapping up the Tokyo trial and dispensing with a second round of international trials. Kennan proposed an early end to investigations into Japanese accused of conventional war crimes or crimes against humanity, "with a view to releasing those whose cases we do not intend to prosecute. Trials of the others should be instituted and concluded at the earliest possible date."[51]

At the newly established National Security Council at the White House, the military was prominently represented, which proved to be a boon for Kennan. Unlike some State Department proposals, this one got limited pushback from the Army Department—which wanted to go even further in scrapping reparations and getting rid of the Far Eastern Commission. The only real opposition came from MacArthur. While prudently agreeing to much of the paper, he complained about cutting back U.S. forces in Japan and warned that the other Allies would be outraged at bolstering the Japanese police.[52]

Kennan presented the paper in October at a White House meeting of the National Security Council, attended by such mandarins as James Forrestal, the secretary of defense, and Robert Lovett, the undersecretary of state. There was little debate, which indicated how much Cold War fears had already swept through the Truman administration. After the State Department locked horns with the military over reparations, that section was taken out. With that, his policy was accepted and sent on to the president, and the group turned their attention to the danger that the Soviets might interrupt the Berlin Airlift.[53] On November 5, Truman signed off on the new policy.[54]

MacArthur, having lost in Washington, did his best to stall in Tokyo. He tried to keep up the purge of militarists, and groused that as Allied supreme commander, he took his orders from the Allies, not from the National Security Council. That earned him a reprimand from both the State and Army Departments, instructing him to move forward with NSC 13/2. Knowing which way the wind was blowing in the early Cold War, even MacArthur had to trim his sails.[55]

After his victory in Washington, Kennan worked at persuading other Allied governments. He had little difficulty winning over Britain. Long disillusioned with the Tokyo trial, the British firmly agreed that the war crimes trials and the purge were "ill-conceived, psychologically unsound," and ought to be wrapped up as soon as possible. The British, too, wanted the occupation to butt out of Japan's political life.[56] After a visit to Japan, an influential Indian diplomat, K. P. S. Menon, shrewdly reported to Jawaharlal Nehru that the United States had grown disenchanted with China, which could not ward off Communism even on its own territory, and was instead "fastening its hopes on Japan" as "a bulwark against Communism."[57]

Kennan was euphoric. He reveled at achieving a major change in occupation policy. It was, he later recalled, "the most significant constructive contribution I was ever able to make in government," aside from his role in the Marshall Plan. "On no other occasion, with that one exception, did I ever make recommendations of such scope and import; and on no other occasion did my recommendations meet with such wide, indeed almost complete, acceptance."[58]

In reality, the implementation would move gradually, with MacArthur stalling where he could. Still, alongside the retention of the emperor, the "reverse course" would prove crucial in renewing the legitimacy of conservatives in postwar Japan. Emboldened by the emphasis on economic recovery, right-wing politicians and businessmen could launch a comeback surprisingly soon after having chaperoned their country to unprecedented disaster. On top of that, Kennan's calls for a crackdown on Communists helped initiate a new purge in late 1948—this time aiming at suspected leftists. This "Red purge" drove thousands of trade unionists, teachers, and civil servants out of their jobs; it would reach its zenith in 1950, as the Korean War began, when General Headquarters pressed Japanese political leaders to sack tens of thousands of suspected Communists from government positions or outside jobs. The "Red purge" continued after Japan regained its sovereignty in 1952, with the CIA coming to secretly fund and back the main conservative party, the Liberal Democratic Party, as the best bet to ward off the leftists.[59] Meanwhile right-wing war criminals and militarists were increasingly allowed to slip away from punishment. Japan had fully entered the Cold War era.[60]

CHAPTER 25

Days of Judgment

Tojo Hideki, as he awaited the judges' deliberations, was ready to die for Japan. "My attitude of mind is tranquil," he said in a statement to Japanese reporters in January 1948. Equating his courtroom travail with combat, he said, "I believe that I have testified in the same attitude of mind as the war dead enshrined at the Yasukuni Shrine"—the Shinto memorial in Tokyo to those who died in Japan's modern wars—"and the people who had suffered because of the war." Rather than starting its history in 1928, he said that the Tokyo court's judgment should go back three hundred years or at least to the Opium Wars, thereby treating British imperialism as a root cause of World War II. He proposed that the victorious Allies should be investigated too.[1]

In contrast, Togo Shigenori tried to stay serene. The former foreign minister wrote in Sugamo Prison, "it is a blessing beyond estimation that this most dreadful of wars has been brought to a close, ending our country's agony and saving millions of lives; with that my life's work is done, it does not matter what befalls me."[2]

Neither defiant nor tranquil, Emperor Hirohito braced himself for the judgment in considerably more comfortable surroundings at the Imperial Palace. Surely he would have to take some responsibility when many of his ministers and generals were convicted. There was a wave of speculation in Japan that Hirohito would abdicate when the judgment was handed down, leaving his teenage son Akihito to revive the monarchy.[3] After a meeting with the emperor, Ashida Hitoshi, a politician who briefly served as prime minister, reckoned from the monarch's intonation and attitude that he was considering standing down.[4] The chief justice of Japan told the *Asahi Shimbun* that "the Emperor should have reproached himself for the war, which was brought about by a lack of sagacity." It was not just liberals who were keen to see him off; some of the most conservative devotees of the emperor system thought that the monarchy would be more secure without his stigma.[5]

The American and British occupiers remained convinced that losing the emperor would be a disaster.[6] General Douglas MacArthur was thoroughly sick of the Tokyo trial, telling Sir William Webb and others that he would have preferred "a much smaller number of accused on a few major charges."[7] While General Headquarters could not overtly influence the Tokyo judgment, MacArthur's inner circle secretly encouraged Hirohito to tough it out, no matter what happened to his underlings.

Brigadier General Bonner Fellers, MacArthur's confidant and a fervent advocate of the monarchy, discreetly reached out through a palace official to the emperor. Quitting would not give the monarch peace of mind, Fellers warned, and his "abdication would be considered a victory for all Communists and especially the Russians." It "would be a blow to the MacArthur occupation as the General's success has made the very best use of the Emperor's prestige and personal leadership." As a new Japan "merged spiritually with Democratic America," it needed "the stabilizing influence which only the Sire can give."

Worse, quitting would be taken as an admission of war guilt: "His abdication, especially if it coincided with the announcement of war crimes punishments, would, in the eyes of the world, identify the Sire as one of the Military clique. . . . Abdication would fix the Sire's place in history as one who sympathized with the war criminals and, as a jesture [*sic*] of his sympathy for them, gave up his throne."[8]

SUMMATIONS

After an exceptionally long trial, the prosecution and defense staggered into their closing arguments. Arthur Comyns Carr, the disgruntled British associate prosecutor, had hoped to deliver the concluding address for the prosecution. When shoved aside by Joseph Keenan yet again, he tried to ensure that his bumbling chief could not do too much damage in his final courtroom act. "The evidence is there whatever they say," he wrote to Sir Hartley Shawcross, the British attorney general, "and it is all going into the final speech in what I think is a really good analysis, mostly prepared by our able little American Jew named Horwitz."[9] A senior British official cringed at the prospect of Keenan's "large masses of verbiage both illiterate and irrelevant," while dismissively adding, "not that the Philippine, French, Chinese or Dutch prosecutors are likely to add to the dignity of international law."[10]

As Keenan rose, most of the accused watched carefully, occasionally glancing at the judges to see if they appeared swayed. Although Tojo kept his headphones on to hear the translation, he studiously ignored Keenan, writing steadily in a notebook without looking up.

Keenan used his closing argument to demand that the accused be hanged. In domestic law, he said, murder was punishable by death; the same must be true for international leaders. "It literally required atomic bombs to jolt them from their seats of authority," he said. He insisted that the evidence showed a carefully planned conspiracy, rather than accident and improvisation. From Manchuria to Pearl Harbor, none of Japan's conquests could be considered self-defense. Linking aggression with crimes against humanity, he argued that all of the accused knew that a war would "inevitably reach non-combatants, men, women and children in every village, in every city." To the last, he tried to exonerate the emperor, carefully noting that Hirohito had decided to end the war after Hiroshima, and arguing that the warlords might "make a divinity or a figurehead of their ruler as the occasion required for their evil purposes."[11]

Keenan left the meat of the summations to Comyns Carr, Frank Tavenner, Xiang Zhejun, Pedro Lopez, and other prosecutors.[12] The Soviet associate prosecutor demanded the harshest punishment on behalf of "millions and millions of victims of the barbaric aggression of the Japanese militarists." With the Cold War hanging over the court, he rebuked the United States: "Your sentence should be a threatening warning to all those who would like to kindle the fire of a new war."[13]

By now Webb and Keenan could barely stand the sight of each other, with Webb still nettled by the U.S. chief prosecutor's attempts to protect the emperor. On his feet, Keenan complained that Webb's court had been "extremely zealous" in safeguarding the right of the Japanese defendants to a fair trial. He groused that the judges had "shown great patience in permitting the vituperative and insolent comments about the Hull note," saying that without Franklin Delano Roosevelt and his secretary of state this trial might never have happened. Showily taking offense, Webb interrupted him. Leaning far over the bench, he snapped that he had been praised for "protecting the Allied Powers against any insult." He intoned, "Australians will always revere and protect the memory of President Roosevelt." This fresh declaration of patriotic bias from the chief judge again called into question how the accused could get a fair hearing from him.[14]

The defense summation was as lofty as Keenan's, invoking every authority from Winston Churchill to the ancient Chinese classic *Yi Jing*. Takayanagi Kenzo argued that unless aggression was proved to be an international crime, punishing the accused was "nothing but lawless violence." He cautioned that U.S., British, and Soviet leaders should be judged by the same legal standards. Strikingly, he pointed out that unlike Germany, Japan had surrendered without being overrun by Allied troops, limiting the demands that the victors could impose on their defeated enemies. By accepting the Potsdam Declaration, the Japanese had agreed to be prosecuted only for standard war crimes, not such newfangled offenses as criminal conspiracy, crimes against peace, murder at the start of a war, or crimes against humanity.[15]

Encircled by menacing enemies, the defense contended, Japan had had no choice but to fight for its survival. One of the American defense lawyers argued that the first blow of the conflict was not Pearl Harbor but the "economic war" imposed on Japan by a U.S. embargo so devastating that it threatened Japan's existence. "These men are Japanese," he said. "They are not Americans or members of the great British Commonwealth of Nations—nor Dutch, nor Russian, nor French. They were Japanese and their decision was one of life or death for their country." He asked each of the judges to put himself in their position: "Would you, could you as patriots, have made any other decision?"[16]

At last on April 16, Webb adjourned the Tokyo trial.[17] Camera bulbs popped. General Headquarters pressed a Japanese publisher into issuing a translation of Keenan's summation, priced cheaply to reach a wide audience.[18] *The New York Times* editorialized that the Tokyo trial could give new authority to international law against aggression. Expressing a commonplace calumny among Americans, the *Times* cautioned that the Japanese defendants had followed the tenets of their "civilization which could still invest with the highest religious standards a 'holy war' of conquest and which regarded massacre and cruelty as natural, and under certain circumstances even laudable."[19]

With the case now in the hands of the judges, most of the U.S. officers serving as defense lawyers were ordered to return home. Aghast, the defense counsel petitioned MacArthur to let these Americans stay until the trial was actually over—once the verdicts were concluded, reviewed by the supreme commander, and possibly appealed. Both the United States Constitution and the new Japanese constitution guaranteed defendants the right of counsel at all times, and, as the American defense lawyers noted, the Allies, by setting up an impartial court for the accused, had bound "themselves to extend to them what we regard as the inalienable rights of man." Such a premature dismissal, the defense lawyers warned, would prove correct those critics who claimed "that the whole proceeding has been but a false front, a sham and a fraud, that we know no real desire that our justice shall fall alike on friend and enemy."[20] A few days later, General Headquarters announced that it would keep the defense lawyers on until the judgment was announced.[21]

THE WORKING MAJORITY

The bickering judges settled down to the mammoth task of writing their concluding judgment, confronting trial transcripts twice as long as those of Nuremberg.[22] The enormous drafts were patched together from the particular national grievances of the eleven countries. Mei Ruao reported in embarrassment to his mentor Sun Ke, now the powerful president of the Legislative Yuan, about the slow pace.[23] "I am like a bookworm," he wrote, "moving through hundreds of thousands of pages of court records, which pile up like a mountain."[24]

"The writing of the judgment is a colossal task," worried Webb, "as there are eleven judges, each with strong views."[25] Watching the cherry blossoms return, he thought it was lunacy that he had been in Japan for so many springs.[26] He privately admitted himself heartily sick of the country.[27] Bert Röling may have been the only judge who had warmed to the place, as he spent his weekends "at Kobe with friends, saw the pearl fishing at Mikimoto's palace, and said hello to the gods at Ise."[28]

No matter how badly the court still needed to justify its fundamental legitimacy, the Australian chief judge was in no mood to go through another punishing debate about jurisdiction.[29] As he admitted privately to Quincy Wright, an American law professor who had been a legal adviser at Nuremberg, "we shall not have a lengthy judgment on the law," although "we shall have a lot to say about the evidence."[30] Instead of making a bold statement about natural law, he was intent on corralling the votes for a respectable majority. He mended fences with Mei and sought to charm his fellow Commonwealth judges.[31] He accepted that the law utilized in the final judgment would bear little resemblance to his earlier ambitions.[32] His own draft judgment had only one reference to natural law, inserted at the request of the French judge.[33] "I think we are all too tired to quarrel," he wrote.[34]

Webb had to fend off his own prime minister, Ben Chifley, who wanted him to take another break to return to Australia's High Court for cases about his Labour government's nationalization of private banks.[35] Webb refused.[36] If the prime minister insisted, he would return but would resign from the Tokyo tribunal.[37] He wrote a draft of a menacing letter from

MacArthur for him, warning that a second absence would undermine Webb's authority so much that "he should seriously consider resigning as President."[38] To MacArthur's relief, the Australian prime minister backed down.[39]

Previewing his draft judgment for MacArthur, Webb lamely explained that the judges had already upheld the legitimacy of the tribunal back in May 1946: "All we have to do now is give our reasons." Webb suggested that he would largely parrot the Nuremberg judgment.[40] The Allied judges in Nuremberg had held simply that their authority came from their charter, that that charter—which was identical on the crucial points to the Tokyo court's charter—was a valid expression of international law as it existed at the time, that aggressive war had been made criminal by the Kellogg-Briand Pact, and that individuals could be held responsible. As he limply told MacArthur, "Somehow or other I get the impression that the Nuremberg Tribunal stated the law very well and that it is going to be difficult to amplify what they said to any considerable extent."[41]

Webb, Mei, and the British Commonwealth bloc of judges cobbled together a working majority. The U.S. judge would obviously be reliable, and Delfin Jaranilla would be an obliging vote for whatever General Headquarters wanted. The Philippine judge privately fawned on MacArthur and reminded him that he had been in the U.S. Army at Bataan.[42]

Leading the British bloc, Lord Patrick was determined to uphold the Nuremberg judgment. Often too ill to work, the British judge was bolstered by the Canadian and New Zealand judges.[43] This faction feared that a splintered verdict could undercut whatever progress for world legal order had been achieved at Nuremberg.

While Patrick was confident that a majority of the judges was persuaded that aggressive war was a crime, he feared that several of them would flinch at the assertion that conspiracy was too. The distinctively American and British concept of conspiracy was baffling to European judges, especially Henri Bernard of France and Röling of Holland; Webb, although trained in English law, was wary too. Although Nuremberg had ruled that merely conspiring to commit aggression was in itself a crime, several judges balked at convicting defendants only for conspiring about a crime which was never actually committed, such as plotting a murder but never killing anyone. Patrick admitted that most European legal systems only recognized conspiracy in regard to particularly heinous offenses such as treason; ordinarily it was no crime in itself to plan a crime but never enact it. Still, he hoped that since the conspiracies had actually been carried out, all eleven legal systems among the judges could comfortably include them.[44]

The British judge was so dedicated to the Nuremberg precedents that he threatened to dissent if the Tokyo judgment deviated from them. Yet the New Zealand judge, Erima Harvey Northcroft, usually a stalwart ally for Patrick, was uncomfortable convicting defendants for merely conspiring to wage aggressive war.[45] The British judge blew up at him. If the conspiracy itself was not treated as criminal, the British judge warned that he would dissent—which would have made him the fourth to do so. Rattled, Northcroft backed down.[46]

Webb was unpersuaded. If conspiracy was not a crime already, he told the other judges, then the Tokyo court's charter could not suddenly make it into a crime. Perhaps Nuremberg, which billed itself as an act of sovereign authorities wielding the legislative power of Germany in the absence of a German government, could make new law; but MacArthur, in framing the Tokyo charter, had never pretended to be a legislative authority for Japan, but merely an agent of the Allied powers.[47] Yet despite his misgivings, Webb ruled that the majority should go ahead writing the judgment their way. Although Bernard wanted a debate about conspiracy, Webb refused to convene a meeting to discuss the matter, letting the British perspective stand.[48]

If Webb did not buy Patrick's legal arguments, he certainly understood the power of the British bloc. Swallowing his pride, he set up a drafting committee: himself and the British and Canadian judges. Although the judges divided up the massive case among themselves, the British bloc had firmly seized control of expounding the law and facts of the Tokyo judgment.[49] The final member of the British bloc, Northcroft, was assigned the crucial task of drawing up a study of the outbreak of the Pacific War.[50] "We get along very well," Webb claimed.[51]

Sobered by his drubbing in previous judicial debates, Webb accepted that his solo draft, hundreds of pages long, would not become the basis of the historic judgment. Instead he would have to content himself with a brief concurring opinion about the law and the facts.[52] The other judges winced when Webb announced this. The prospect of a split decision loomed: one majority version led by the British bloc, one from Webb, and as many as three dissents from Pal, Röling, and perhaps Bernard too.[53]

Mei drove for a short, conclusive, stern judgment.[54] "Simplicity and forcefulness are always preferred," he instructed Webb.[55] Taking control of the sections on Japan's invasion of China, he briskly completed his draft while slower judges were just getting under way on their portions.[56] He secretly took his instructions directly from China's scholarly foreign minister, Wang Shijie, at one point assuring him that he knew "about the Executive Yuan's opinions on the individual responsibilities of war criminals and will act accordingly." Writing of himself formally in the third person, Mei cabled that it was his "obligation to make the last attempt, with his limited ability, at the victory of this unprecedented struggle for justice in international law on behalf of our nation."[57]

In a bizarre attempt to prepare Chinese public opinion for the judgment, Mei wrote a Chinese newspaper article profiling the eleven judges, which he published under someone else's name. It gives a score-settling sense of his likes and pungent dislikes among his colleagues: the blustery Australian, the hard-drinking American, the formidable and aloof Briton, the beefy and mistrusted Soviet, the argumentative Dutchman, the contentious and antisocial Indian, and of course the renowned Mei. Although he was in fact working closely with China's government, he praised the court's judicial independence. On China's behalf, he hoped that the judges could "prevent the pests of mankind and enemies of peace from escaping the sacred international law's righteous punishment, as well as to warn future fanatics. . . . Your decision will have a decisive impact on world history."[58]

Earlier Mei had insisted that the Tokyo judges should defend their jurisdiction with their own arguments, rather than echoing Nuremberg's exposition.[59] Yet now he settled for the simplest version. The court's jurisdiction, he reiterated, came from its charter, which was an expression of current international law. He dismissed Pal's and Röling's objections that the charter violated international law as "purely hypothetical and academic."[60]

Despite his resentment of British colonialism, Mei had to align himself with the British Commonwealth bloc of judges. For years, Mei had urged the judges to avoid parochial rulings from British and American law, which he feared would mar the tribunal's international character.[61] Yet now he gritted his teeth and went along with Patrick's decidedly British argument about conspiracy, despite the "peculiarities of the Anglo-American doctrine of Conspiracy." While the Chinese criminal code had no punishment for planning to commit ordinary crimes, he explained, it did for particularly nefarious ones, such as treason, rebellion, murder, and kidnapping. Since aggressive war was a crime far more heinous than murder or treason, he concluded that conspiracy charges for aggression would fit with Chinese conceptions of criminal law.[62]

Mei awkwardly got support from the Soviet imperium too. Despite the novelty of the charges of crimes against humanity in China, Major General Ivan Zaryanov argued that the atrocities against Chinese and Filipino citizens must be treated as worse than conventional war crimes. (The judges could not use the newly minted crime of genocide, which Röling dismissively called "this terrible term of 'genocide,'" because it was not in the charter.)[63] As defined in the charter, crimes against humanity meant murder, extermination, enslavement, and persecution of a group on political or racial grounds. While racist intentions are notoriously hard to prove in court, Zaryanov confidently asserted that the enormities in Shanghai and Nanjing were the result of Japanese bigotry toward the Chinese—resting that claim entirely on Marquis Kido Koichi's admission under cross-examination that "the Japanese were apt to hold a sense of superiority vis-a-vis the Chinese people and hold the Chinese people in contempt."[64]

While Mei labored, it was increasingly obvious that he represented a government that was about to be killed. As the Indian military attaché in China bluntly observed, it was a disastrous period for the tottering Nationalist government, with the Communists scoring humiliating victories throughout Manchuria and in Henan province, Jinan in the east, and recapturing Yan'an. Demoralized Nationalist soldiers surrendered in vast numbers; untold thousands of government troops mutinied or defected over to the Communist side; impoverished citizens in Changchun and Mukden subsisted on leaves or weeds. Communist forces drove toward central China, threatening Shanghai and Nanjing, and cutting off Beijing for days. The Indian attaché wrote, "Militarily the defeat of the KMT [Kuomintang] is complete and not even the Americans can save the old regime."[65]

While the judges typed away on their drafts, the Soviets were blockading West Berlin from western Germany, prompting an American and British airlift of food and supplies.[66] "The Japanese are putting the place together again," wrote Webb anxiously. "I hope they won't be burned out in another raid. It isn't a very bright world."[67]

Early in this Berlin crisis, an official Soviet newspaper insisted that the Tokyo verdict be "a most severe condemnation" of Japanese war criminals, enshrining "the aggression against the USSR as part of the conspiracy against the world and humanity." Reflecting Zaryanov's frustrations, the newspaper complained about insolent American defense lawyers unchecked by the judges. It was "the baneful influence of Wall Street" that explained why U.S. Army officers "took it upon themselves to be defense counselors, ignoring professional honor and the elementary rules of decency, to save the worst enemies of progressive humanity."

Shifting its reproach to the Western democracies, this state mouthpiece demanded that the Tokyo court issue "a stern warning to those who, blinded by the grandiose idea of world domination, would have a desire to accomplish something similar to what was done by the defendants." Japanese monopolies such as Mitsubishi and Mitsui, the real drivers of imperialism, had been spared by the representatives of Wall Street, who "could not allow the well justified punishment of those, who are so close to them in spirit, whom they need for converting defeated Japan into a new base for aggression."[68]

As the Soviet Union turned hostile toward the Western powers, Webb assiduously wooed Zaryanov, who remained a reliable part of the majority. The Soviet judge made clear the price of his cooperation: that the Soviet Union be treated as a main victim of Japanese belligerence. He barred any discussion of the Soviet Union's 1941 neutrality pact with Japan, lest that raise awkward questions about the Soviet violation of it. Racing the accused to the gallows, he gave detailed suggestions for how to stream-line the judgment, many of which would make it into the final version. "I submit that it is high time all argument on the Charter be stopped," he exhorted. "The Charter is an indisputable source of International Law." Rather than rejecting conspiracy charges as distinctively American or British, he contended that all national legal systems made illegal a con-spiracy to commit crimes against state security—which fit neatly with his Bolshevik approach to political trials.

Zaryanov had no doubts that aggressive war—as defined by Stalin-ist authority—was the supreme international crime, urging Webb not to bog down in debates about the meaning of the Kellogg-Briand Pact. While Pal and Röling insisted that the charter could not violate existing international law, Zaryanov wanted the judgment to proclaim that the Allied victors could establish new principles of international law. The declarations of the Allied conferences at Potsdam, Cairo, and Moscow were international law; the Tokyo charter was both an embodiment of international law and a new source of international law. International law, in short, was whatever the Allies said it was.[69]

Webb accepted the necessity of using Zaryanov, who had reliably backed him in the fracas over jurisdiction. The Australian chief judge consulted closely with him and pressed the other judges to incorporate his "valuable suggestions." This scandalized several judges, and even Webb balked at the Bolshevik conception of criminal guilt: "The General takes the view that guilt must be determined objectively; but I think the other judges take a different view."[70] Yet the Soviet judge won the prize he needed, being assigned by the majority to pen a draft about Japan's warmongering against the Soviet Union. In a draft heavy with Stalinist jargon, he chuntered that aggression was "an inseparable part of the over-all conspiracy of the Japanese imperialistic clique against peace-loving peoples."[71] Whatever the majority's misgivings about Soviet totalitarian jurisprudence, they made ample use of its man in Tokyo.[72]

Silencing Dissent

Without the courtroom hubbub, the judges were left in hushed solitude to write. With only the seven majority judges and a few assistants coming to work, Mei did not like the quiet: "Now the tribunal seems deserted, and the scene is depressing. . . . The length of the trials is beyond expectation. It is disappointing, but we can do nothing about it. One will find it hard to understand without being here."[73]

The working majority of seven represented Britain, Canada, New Zealand, China, the Philippines, the United States, and the Soviet Union. The United States judge, Major General Myron Cramer, became chair of the majority drafting committee.[74] Mei assured the Chinese Foreign Ministry that they were working separately in cooperative spirits, while rashly downplaying how divided the judges really were. He told the Chinese government that Webb's opinion was barely different from the majority and still hoped that the Dutch and French judges would rejoin the fold too. He had only written off one vote: "Pal, the Indian judge, is stubborn and conservative. He has a strong personality and has said that he would absolutely not cooperate. He is writing a personal letter of dissent whose length may reach 1,000 pages."[75]

Two days later, Röling secretly pleaded to the Dutch foreign minister for permission to give a public dissent, lest he give the impression that he agreed with dangerous arguments that went against international law. He could not accept that the Kellogg-Briand Pact and some League of Nations resolutions had made aggressive war a crime, instead treating crimes against peace as a purely political offense which should not be the sole basis for hanging anyone.[76] He complained that evidence about Communist activity in China had been excluded, even though anti-Communist motives were now driving Western foreign policies. He argued that "the land of Grotius" should not endorse gross legal errors, and that the expression of dissenting opinions would show the Japanese that the judges had not been controlled by their governments.[77]

Bert Röling, the dissenting Dutch judge, in his chambers at the Tokyo trial, September 6, 1947

The French judge abandoned the majority. Even though he accepted the illegality of aggressive war and embraced unfamiliar Anglo-American notions of conspiracy without a hint of Gallic complaint, Henri Bernard was exasperated that there were few meetings for the judges to debate together.[78] He complained that the majority's drafts only used facts unfavorable to the accused.[79] Moreover, since the accused argued they had been acting in self-defense against aggressive adversaries, the real evidence to exonerate them would be found in the files of the Allied governments.[80] Bernard warned that it was immoral and dangerous to place too much weight on treaties such as the Kellogg-Briand Pact. Even if their country had not accepted responsibilities under a treaty, those who violated customary international law or fundamental norms were criminals under what he called "universal law."[81]

Mei was livid. On Manchuria alone, he sent a blistering fifteen-page note to Bernard accusing him of sloppy misquotation, downplaying the belligerence of the Japanese army, and worse. "I am surprised at the way you quote," he snapped. He called Bernard's reasoning "quite beyond my comprehension" and accused him of "a glaring mistake" about basic facts. He particularly resented a comment by Bernard that Chinese emperors, generals, and presidents were not heads of a democratic state—aimed mostly at Henry Puyi, but also encompassing Chiang Kai-shek. "I simply cannot understand how you can bring this question into the present discussion," Mei wrote with palpable fury. "Nor can I believe that your knowledge of Chinese history and culture warrants you to make generalizations of this kind."[82]

Unable to persuade the dissenters, the majority moved to muzzle them. General Headquarters planned to translate only the majority judgment into Japanese, although other opinions would be part of the record. While translation was onerous and brought the risk of leaks, it is still striking that the judges did not demand that all their opinions be laid before the Japanese people. Although dissents might be translated later, they would be shrouded from the Japanese people at the crucial moment when the Tokyo trial concluded.[83]

Röling and Bernard were stunned when they discovered from a newspaper that translation of the final judgment was about to start.[84] In a formal protest, Röling complained that the judgment was being translated even before the judges knew what was in it.[85] Webb merely assured Röling and Bernard that the judgment would be sent out for translation when a majority of all eleven members had agreed upon the text. In his only sop to Bernard, Webb agreed to have meetings to discuss the case of each accused.[86] The majority did not seem to grasp how badly its failure to win over these dissenters would undermine their final judgment.

"THE EVIDENCE WE PROVIDED IS MISERABLY INSUFFICIENT"

Mei set a pace to spur the other judges. While the controversial sections about Pearl Harbor and the Soviet Union were still under construction, the Chinese judge had finished on Manchuria and a long study of aggression against China, which was swiftly approved by the other judges.[87] As he proudly informed the Chinese foreign minister, his paper "contains detailed accounts of why Japan invaded us and the rights and wrongs, as well as conclusions to our advantage." His draft would "leave no room for future historians to give a far-fetched interpretation or distort truth."[88]

At the same time, Mei was privately distraught about his coverage of Japanese atrocities in China. "The evidence for this section is very weak," he secretly cautioned his government. "In the indictment, although our charges account for about half of the items in the atrocity section, the evidence we provided is miserably insufficient. Besides the Rape of Nanjing, we have almost no evidence for Hankou, Changsha, Guangzhou, Hengyang, Guilin, and Liuzhou." He strained to produce a verdict that did "not embarrass the prosecutors and our country too much."[89]

The Chinese foreign minister warned him that Chinese people were criticizing the tribunal's delay in announcing its verdicts.[90] Mei defensively replied that he understood that the Chinese people "have the greatest expectations for the Tokyo trial. . . . A speedy end is what we desire, and victory is what we strive for." He vowed to do his best "to make our country gain something out of this struggle for justice in international law and not to greatly disappoint the Chinese people with the result of such a lengthy process."[91] He pledged that the judgment would compile a comprehensive history of international relations in Asia, which he hoped would be "an everlasting contribution of great value."[92]

Despite his personal misgivings, Mei's drafts quickly won the approval of the majority. Webb assured him, "I take the view that Japan's wars were notoriously aggressive in China and elsewhere."[93] He condemned Japan for the intentional killing of civilians in the bombing of Nanjing and Guangzhou (Canton), deliberately committing atrocities in numerous Chinese cities, as well as weakening Chinese society by promoting opium. He estimated that as many as three hundred thousand Chinese had been killed at Nanjing in the first six weeks of Japanese conquest, as well as twenty thousand cases of rape.[94]

Webb held that all Japanese cabinet ministers had a duty to prevent the Nanjing atrocities, and could be convicted for crimes of omission if they had not brought down the government over it. He had no hesitation convicting General Matsui Iwane for the Nanjing massacre: "He was on the spot when these frightful excesses were committed; he must have known they were being committed; he had the duty above all others to prevent them; and he took no real steps to prevent them." Unlike the majority, he also wanted to convict Matsui for crimes against peace, since Japanese generals in China must have known they were fighting in a criminal war of aggression.[95]

Mei's handiwork only ran into trouble with two of the dissenters. Röling was most persuaded about Nanjing, where the Chinese evidence was strongest, concluding that there had been mass killing, mass rape, arson, and looting. He condemned Japanese troops for rounding up and killing defenseless Chinese soldiers who had thrown away their weapons. He contemptuously rejected the defense witnesses who had claimed to have seen no atrocities in Nanjing: "I think it not necessary to deal with them. They just should have looked."

Röling scorched Matsui, noting that his anodyne calls for restraint and minimal punishments of bloodstained officers had not fulfilled his duty as a commander to prevent war crimes at Nanjing. In addition, he singled out Emperor Hirohito's uncle by marriage, Prince Asaka Yasuhiko, an unindicted general, as "the directly responsible Army Commander," while noting that it would have been embarrassing for Japan's government to punish a royal.

Beyond Nanjing, though, Röling probed at the weaknesses in China's evidence. In Hankou, he pointed out, the Chinese prosecutors had relied on a single witness to the execution of captured Chinese soldiers, while the defense produced a dozen witnesses testifying that Japanese behavior had been irreproachable. In Changsha, the Chinese prosecution offered a single affidavit from a witness alleging murder, rape, and arson. He concluded that the charges in Hankou, Changsha, and three other cities were not proven.[96]

Radhabinod Pal went further still. He would be the only judge who questioned the evidence of atrocities all over China, including at Nanjing. He doubted the accounts of carnage in Hankou, Changsha, Guangzhou, and elsewhere. Strikingly, he even claimed there were propagandistic exaggerations and distortions in the eyewitness evidence of massacre and rape at Nanjing. The Indian judge dismissed not just the weak evidence but the strong stuff too.[97]

RED VERSUS EXPERT

The most acrimonious backroom fight was about the Soviet sections, with Röling clashing openly with the Soviet judge. Mei alerted the Chinese government that the judges were stalemated over the Soviet charges of aggression.[98] For over a month, the committee reviewing that section deadlocked over what Mei called "so many complex and tricky problems."[99]

Röling, appalled by the Soviets' blustery presence in the courtroom, complained to the judges that the Soviet Union was promoting dangerous Communist revolutions around the globe.[100] Several of the other judges were fed up with the Soviets too, with Bernard concluding that the Soviet Union had threatened Japan in Manchuria.[101] As he fought, the young Dutch judge was left "spiritually even more deep down," he wrote privately. "I think life pretty difficult and unpleasant at this moment. The work does not go as it should go."[102]

Zaryanov sparked the fight by accusing Röling of downplaying the mass crimes of the Japanese army as resulting from a mere lack of control.[103] Röling responded with a broadside against Soviet claims to have been a principal victim of Japanese aggression. In July—as the Truman administration was debating George Kennan's proposals for the new Cold War approach to Japan—the Dutch judge startled his colleagues with a sixty-five-page paper trashing the majority's draft judgment finding that Japan had waged aggressive war against the Soviet Union. He upbraided the Soviets about how important it was that the court disprove widespread suspicions that a tribunal of the victors would be arbitrary and lawless.

The Tokyo court, he contended, had no jurisdiction over the two border battles between Japan and the Soviet Union in 1938 and 1939; authority drawn from the surrender terms of the Potsdam Declaration could hardly cover these previous clashes. In the second battle in Mongolia, the prosecution had accepted the Soviet client state of Outer Mongolia as an independent country, which meant that any aggression was not against the Soviet Union. Furthermore, Röling contended that the documentary record showed that Japan had dreaded a Soviet attack. Preoccupied with the United States and the British Empire, Japan had at most vaguely hoped to tackle the Soviet Union someday if the tide of war allowed. He was dismayed that the majority judgment claimed that there was no evidence of Soviet aggressive intentions against Japan—an unnecessary whitewash inserted by the Soviets.[104]

Dispensing with the collegial courtesies among the judges, Zaryanov denounced "the vicious character" of Röling's critique and his "clearly unfounded" opinions. He called the Dutch judge dishonest and unfair, an apologist for German and Japanese aggression, full of falsehoods. Reading Zaryanov's letter with shock, Röling underlined the rudest bits, irately jotting "No" in the margins.

Zaryanov insisted that Japan had incessantly plotted anti-Soviet aggression. Relying on the Stalinist redefinition of aggression so that Soviet conquests did not qualify, he complained that "Justice Roling ignores the principal distinction between the aggressive nations and those which fought aggression during World War II, a distinction that was the original prerequisite for the establishment of the Tribunal and the legal foundation of its jurisdiction."[105] If the judges did not accept the two border clashes as part of Japan's overall plan of conspiracy, he rumbled, they would also have to renounce prosecutions for Manchuria, China, and other conquests preceding Pearl Harbor. (In large letters, Röling wrote "NO" in the margin.) At one point, Zaryanov contemptuously wrote that an argument by his Dutch colleague "aimed at a complete justification of Germany's aggression against the Soviet Union." ("NO," wrote Röling in the margin.) Zaryanov wrote that Röling grossly distorted reality by parroting Japanese "slanderous fascist propaganda," concluding that "the conspiracy against the U.S.S.R. was only an integral part of a far wider conspiracy."[106]

Dubious and furious as Zaryanov's arguments were, they were good enough for Webb, who did not waver from his endorsement of the Soviet position. As he told the other judges, "conspiracy was executed in the border wars," even if only in plotting aggressive war without actually waging it.[107] Following the Soviet party line, the Australian chief judge concluded that "Japan continually prepared for war and performed acts of aggression against the U.S.S.R."[108]

"THE EMPEROR WAS THE LEADER"

Despite having lost control of the writing of the court's judgment, Webb encouraged the majority to believe that he might join them in the end.[109] He felt "great anxiety" while the other judges worked, fretting that several "are very much concerned about matters affecting their own countries."[110]

Webb made his last attempt to sway the majority on September 17, submitting a final draft of his massive opinion.[111] As he boasted to the Australian government, his paper covered over six hundred and fifty foolscap pages, while the Nuremberg judgment had been less than three hundred pages. Done with his task, he was so keen to return to Australia that he offered to resign as president of the court, although agreeing to stay if MacArthur wanted.[112]

His draft gave the majority what it wanted most: finding all twenty-five of the individual defendants guilty, including the peace-minded Togo Shigenori. On international law, too, he mostly satisfied the majority. Following the Nuremberg judgment, he held that the court's jurisdiction came from the charter and Japan's surrender under the Potsdam Declaration. Still, he repeatedly proposed natural law as an authority behind the charter: "The Charter . . . does not violate International Law or the Natural Law, but gives effect to it."[113]

Most dramatically, Webb pressed to tar Hirohito with war guilt, while noting that "the Prosecution made it clear that the Emperor would not be indicted." The prosecution's own evidence showed his leading role in starting the Pacific War, as well as revealing the "power which he possessed to end the war as well as to begin it." Webb marked Tojo Hideki's slipup under cross-examination: "According to Tojo the Japanese so loved the Emperor that they would have carried out his wishes without question."

Webb returned to a stern formulation he had first jotted down in October 1947: "The Emperor was the leader. He was the only man in Japan who could decide on peace or war." He shrugged off the risk of assassination: "No ruler can commit the crime of launching aggressive war and then validly claim to be excused for so doing because his life would have been in danger if he did not commit it." With feigned deference, Webb added that he did not mean to suggest that Hirohito should have been prosecuted; that was a question which the Allied governments had decided. He only meant to consider the immunity of the emperor when sentencing his minions: if the monarch was spared, how could the judges fairly punish his underlings?[114]

Outside of his written opinion, Webb stubbornly objected to the majority's efforts to whitewash Hirohito out of the judgment. After reading a draft about Pearl Harbor by the U.S. judge, Webb chastised Cramer for "the complete absence of any reference to the part played by the Emperor in starting and ending the war." He added, "I think that if the judgment plays down his part to this extent it will lead to devastating criticism."[115] Later he complained that a subsequent draft failed to implicate the emperor for colluding with Nazi Germany, and that it omitted a damning entry from Kido's diary "showing the part played by the Emperor in starting the war"—a reference to how, on November 30, 1941, the emperor had "ordered" Tojo Hideki "to act according to program."[116]

Still, Webb was willing to go only so far in defying the Americans. Although he told Cramer that "there was a *prima facie* case against the Emperor," he claimed to have advised the Australian government before coming to Tokyo that that case should be dealt with at top political levels—a belief he had relayed to MacArthur as well. He gingerly wrote, "I realize this is a delicate business."[117]

THE GREAT DISSENTER

Isolated from his cherished family for more than two years, Radhabinod Pal wrote with great intelligence and passion. He was racked with worry as he finished his dissent. Mei, again scorning Pal's "strong personality" and "conservative" orientation, warned the Chinese government that the Indian judge was fixated on his dissent and refused to work with the majority.[118]

Pal had had less opportunity to have his mind changed by the courtroom drama than his fellow judges: he was away from court far more than any of them, either typing away at the Imperial Hotel or back in Calcutta on several trips to tend to his ailing wife. The British judge, showing no sympathy for a devoted husband, considered Pal's months away from court as a grave blot on the proceedings.[119] The Indian judge had started missing sessions during the prosecution's China phase and was absent for much of its testimony about Pearl Harbor.[120] With his wife sick again, he had missed almost two months of the testimonies of individual defendants, including that about General Matsui Iwane.[121] Yet his absences from the trial put him more in touch with Asian realities than any of the judges. He came home to a newly independent India, straining with the burdens of self-rule: relieving poverty, coping with vast flows of refugees after the slaughters of Partition, upholding a democratic government. His old adversary from Calcutta University, Syama Prasad Mookerjee, was now industries minister.[122]

On the one occasion that he did speak publicly during the trial, Pal was as cheerful about the Allied occupation as the most Pollyannaish General Headquarters official. "I thought I would find the Japanese people sullen and smarting under a feeling of national humiliation for their defeat," Pal told a leading Bengali newspaper while in Calcutta. "But shortly after my arrival in Japan I realised that I was completely wrong. I found that the Japanese, a very disciplined people as they are, had accepted their defeat in a very placid, rational and realistic spirit." He applauded MacArthur's efforts to build a peaceful and free society. "The Japanese do not feel the pinch of alien military occupation," he said, praising "the sympathetic and statesmanlike policy followed in Japan by General MacArthur and this policy." MacArthur himself was "an extremely genial and likeable person," hardworking, efficient, and informal.

Pal only hinted at his profound disagreements with the Tokyo trial, briefly mentioning questions about whether preparing for or waging an aggressive war was a crime. The defendants, facing their trial in a "truly sportsmanlike spirit," seemed to have confidence in the fairness and impartiality of the tribunal—a sunny assessment that was quite wrong for many of the accused, not least Tojo. The trial had sparked keen interest in Japan, particularly among the intelligentsia. In addition to the legal value of the trial, he said, it would have useful lessons for developing countries such as India, showing that Japan developed its industries swiftly—not exactly what the prosecution had meant to take away from its history of Japan's militarization.[123]

Pal was close-lipped about his dissent. According to Webb, Pal claimed that he had never told anyone outside of the court about it.[124] Yet secretly, Pal was repeatedly in touch with Indian officialdom. Two years before the verdicts, he had notified the British authorities in India that he had dissented about the tribunal's jurisdiction, taking the side of the defense.[125] He consulted once or twice on legal points with the Indian ambassador in Washington, telling him that the Dutch and French judges had agreed with him but then had backed off, perhaps under secret instructions from their governments.[126] After a chance encounter with a senior Indian diplomat visiting Tokyo, Pal decided to write to him exposing the innermost workings of the court, as well as to send along his dissenting opinion months before it would be made public—all of which he must have known would be passed along to the Indian government. He explained the factions among the judges, exposed who was in the seven-member majority, revealed that the French and Dutch judges were dissenting and that Webb was writing a separate opinion, and outlined his own dissent.[127] As the verdict approached, he provided his dissent to the

Indian political representative in Tokyo, whom he had repeatedly briefed about the machinations of the court.[128]

Pal took a summer trip back to India as his colleagues toiled on the judgment, arriving in the months of turmoil after the assassination of Mahatma Gandhi. The word was widely out in Tokyo that Pal had written a long dissenting opinion.[129] He returned to Japan in early September, but after less than two weeks his wife became critically ill with pericarditis, in piercing pain. He immediately flew back to Calcutta, leaving word that unless she recovered or died, he could not return for the imminent reading of the judgment.[130]

After a stressful journey via Manila, a careworn Pal found his wife somewhat improved but still in a precarious condition.[131] "I am so so," he admitted to Webb. Pal politely asked him to give him two weeks' notice before the judgment so that he could rush back to Tokyo. The Australian chief judge brusquely told him to leave by October 20 if he wished, but without any encouragement to return—or even the decency of expressing concern for his wife.[132]

"I desire to read out my judgment in open court," he beseeched Webb. "In my country judgments are always read out in open court."[133] Some of his fellow judges had warned Pal that such an oration, which would take days, would never be allowed. Months before, Mei had told the Chinese government that the judges had already decided not to read any dissents.[134] Aware that his fellow judges would muzzle him, and knowing that a Soviet dissent against the acquittals at Nuremberg had not been read aloud, Pal requested that Webb at least state in court that there were separate and dissenting opinions which would become part of the official record.[135]

Although Pal did not want to leave his wife's bedside, he keenly felt his duty to speak up for his principles. "I may just think of taking a risk," he wrote to Röling, his one real friend on the court, days before Webb's deadline.[136] In the end he decided to make the long journey from Calcutta to Tokyo with faint hopes of voicing his dissent from the bench. Soon before leaving home, he sent an anguished telegram to Webb that his wife's condition was worsening.[137]

Röling alone heartened Pal. "I would never forget the days I could associate with you in Tokyo," the Indian judge fondly wrote from Calcutta. "I am sincerely glad to learn that you have made up your mind to give a short dissenting opinion. I have always felt that justice demands this. We are not there to minister to the worst prejudices of the world public and even at the risk of wounding such public opinion we are not to sacrifice our own convictions."[138]

THE MACHINERY OF DEATH

On November 2, with Mount Fuji again capped with snow, the judges gathered to decide the guilt of the individual defendants.[139] While there was little question that Tojo Hideki and the chief militarists would be convicted, some of the others provoked consternation. Röling wanted to acquit three foreign ministers: Togo Shigenori, Shigemitsu Mamoru, and Hirota Koki, who had risen to prime minister. He would later say that Shigemitsu should never even have been indicted, blaming that overreach on the Soviets and Chinese.[140]

Unswayed, Webb wanted to convict Shigemitsu for "malicious and cowardly aggression" and for neglecting his duties as foreign minister to help Allied prisoners of war, although admitting that other parts of his record were clean.[141] He was set to convict Togo Shigenori too, not only for voting for war immediately before Pearl Harbor but for encroachments on China, for joining Tojo's bellicose cabinet (despite his hopes to sway it), for doing nothing to change that government's attitude (overlooking his dogged efforts to do so), and for being "grossly neglectful" of his duty to protect Allied prisoners. Togo should have forced a cabinet crisis or appealed to the emperor, Webb argued.[142]

Marquis Kido Koichi's vigorous defense did him little good with the judges. Webb blistered the emperor's top man as a strong supporter of the war in China, avoiding peace there rather than accept anything but unyielding Japanese terms, not halting the abuse of Allied prisoners of war, and installing the bellicose Tojo Hideki as prime minister. He only grudgingly stopped short of convicting Kido for starting the war against the United States.[143]

It became clear that although some of the defendants would be cleared on certain charges, not a single defendant would be acquitted outright, as several had been at Nuremberg. As Webb wrote, "I am open to conviction in all cases."[144]

The final sparring among the judges was about sentencing. The judges were sharply divided about which defendants should be killed. The U.S. and Chinese judges strongly supported executions, backed up by the British Commonwealth bloc and Delfin Jaranilla.[145] When some of the judges balked at some death sentences and suggested postponing the sentencing, Mei urged a decisive conclusion: "We must not discredit ourselves by leaving the sentence undecided."[146]

Others were queasy. Bernard doubted the validity of the proceedings and was therefore against the death penalty.[147] Pal could not hang men he thought were not guilty. An anguished Röling wrote, "Now I am hard at work again, and except for the one or two hours on the horse in the early morning, I sit at my desk wondering whether someone has to be hanged or to be shot, which is in the long run a rather depressing activity. To be frank I would rather wonder about other things in life, but, to speak with old Thackeray, 'I can't but accept the world as I find it, including a rope's end, as long as it is in fashion.' I hate it though."[148]

Webb, who had never before sentenced anyone to die, was agonized. Turning to Nuremberg for guidance, he found that the Nazis executed for aggression had also been convicted of war crimes and crimes against humanity, suggesting that the Nuremberg judges were wary of hanging men for crimes against peace alone. Following that standard, he concluded that no Japanese defendants should be sentenced to death for preparing or waging aggressive war unless they were also found guilty of grave war crimes or crimes against humanity.[149]

The U.S. judge, usually one of the quieter members, was appalled to hear that Webb apparently wanted to spare several defendants from the rope, perhaps even sending them into exile outside Japan. In an argument that was not about law at all, Cramer warned that a dozen Japanese leaders could wreak great harm once the American occupying forces were gone. He argued that nearly every country in the world allowed the execution of convicted murderers: "Do you mean to say . . . that they should not be executed when the result of their acts has been not one murder but many thousands of murders? . . . It is a matter of *justice,* plain and simple." Cramer was galled by Webb's feeling that the death penalty was vindictive. "If carrying out the law is vindictive, why have laws?" wrote the U.S. judge. "You invite criminals to run amuck, killing, torturing, bayonetting and beheading whomever they choose but you do not punish them according to the law clearly applicable to such acts, as that would be 'vindictive.'" Executing the war criminals would "make sure that they will never again be a menace to humanity and the laws of God, and that their just punishment may deter others from perpetrating similar crimes. To my mind if we find certain of these defendants guilty as charged it would be a travesty on justice if we did not give them the death penalty."[150]

While courteous to Cramer in a manner not always shown to representatives of less powerful countries, Webb replied that the defendants would probably prefer a swift death to protracted banishment, and insisted that judges often disagreed about sentencing. In the end, he refused on principle to vote for executions.[151]

More surprisingly, Zaryanov was instructed to oppose executions too, since the Soviet Union had recently outlawed the death penalty, in a rare Stalinist bid for international respectability during the drafting of the

Universal Declaration of Human Rights. In reality, Soviet state security courts were still secretly allowed to execute people for counterrevolutionary crimes; mass death continued as usual across the Gulag; and the death penalty would soon be formally reintroduced for political crimes.[152]

All told, the result was that Tojo Hideki and five others would be sent to the gallows on a vote of seven to four. According to a judge who leaked anonymously to the press, Hirota Koki, the former prime minister and foreign minister, was sentenced to die based on a single vote, six to five. And four other men narrowly missed being executed, including Kido, the emperor's top adviser.[153]

WALKING AWAY

As the judges finished writing their judgment, there were many more major Japanese leaders who might have faced war crimes trials, such as Prince Asaka Yasuhiko or Kishi Nobusuke, who had been an important chief in occupied Manchuria, a member of the Pearl Harbor cabinet, and a wartime vice minister of munitions.[154] There were some fifty additional senior Japanese suspects still under arrest as Class A war criminals—those accused of aggression—some of whom had been waiting in jail for almost two years for a second round of international trials for major perpetrators. Yet the Allies, looking forward to a formal peace treaty that would restore Japan's sovereignty, were keen to wind down the punishment of Japanese war criminals.

MacArthur, who had never wanted a sprawling international trial in the first place, secretly scorned the Tokyo trial as "cumbersome, slow, costly, and generally unsatisfactory." He urged his superiors in Washington not to go through a second round of international trials. Keeping people locked up in Sugamo for so long without trial was "contrary to any accepted concept of justice" and reflected poorly on the occupation. He suggested putting the remaining senior Japanese suspects on trial before U.S. courts for conventional war crimes and for crimes against humanity, which would avoid a repetition of the ponderous Tokyo trial.[155]

The British government was equally unenthusiastic. "Keenan persists in asserting that there is to be a second major trial—presumably all-American," wrote Comyns Carr privately. "Anyway, don't ask me to take part in it."[156] The British government quickly agreed that it wanted nothing to do with a second big trial of Class A war criminals.[157] The British political representative coolly notified the State Department that if the Americans went through with it, they would be on their own.[158]

The U.S. prosecutors in Tokyo scoured the files of all the remaining

Class A suspects incarcerated in Sugamo Prison or elsewhere, figuring out what war crimes they could be charged with.[159] The prosecutors hoped that most of them could be relegated to Class B or Class C—that is, charged for conventional war crimes or for crimes against humanity—allowing the United States to wrap up major trials for aggression with the Tokyo judgment.[160] Together with General Headquarters lawyers, they winnowed a list of forty-eight Class A suspects down to sixteen or nineteen, with the others to face trial by U.S. military commissions for Class B or Class C war crimes.[161] There were three Class A suspects under house arrest, and sixteen others stuck in Sugamo Prison awaiting trial, including Kishi.[162]

Renewing his objections, MacArthur warned that the prolonged detention of these unindicted Class A suspects was becoming "an international scandal," insisting that the Tokyo court could not possibly be used for a second round of high-level trials.[163] Falling into line, Keenan endorsed the end of major war crimes trials. Since he was the official responsible for indicting Class A war criminals, his word was essentially final. None of the remaining Class A suspects, he wrote, counted as major war criminals, and an international trial of them would be "a sharp anticlimax" to the Tokyo trial: "it is strongly recommended that no further Class A trials be held." He wanted a few suspects put on trial for Class B or C war crimes, and the rest of them freed.[164]

By early 1948, the United States gave up on any further international trials. Unless the United States put the suspects in front of its own military commissions, or another government requested them for trial, they would all be released.[165] None of the Allies showed any interest in Class B or C proceedings for them, except for one Japanese general whom China might prosecute.[166]

General Headquarters concluded that it could not make war crimes charges stick for eight of the suspects in custody, including the general in China's sights; they would be freed after the Tokyo court issued its verdict. The U.S. government expected to put eleven suspects on trial for conventional war crimes or crimes against humanity, including Kishi.[167]

Such plans soon faded. In late July, in a meeting of the Far Eastern Commission, New Zealand formally proposed the end of the war crimes project. New Zealand's government argued that more trials would only produce backlash among the Japanese. There should be no further trials of Class A war criminals, which would take so long that they would become "farcical." There would be no investigations of Class B or C suspects after the end of 1948, and all Class B or C trials would be wrapped up by the end of June 1949.[168] The United States concurred. The secretary of the army told MacArthur that "it has been my desire for some time that all war crimes trials be concluded at earliest practical date, because I do not believe that public opinion will or should support long continuing war crimes trials."[169] General Headquarters signed off on the end of Class A war crimes trials, meaning that there would be no sequel to the Tokyo trial.[170]

At the same time that the Tokyo trial delivered its verdicts, the Far Eastern Commission voted to finish up all trials as proposed.[171] In the end, only one Japanese admiral and one lieutenant general who had been held as Class A suspects would be indicted by MacArthur for Class B and Class C war crimes.[172] On December 24, 1948, the day after the hangings for the Tokyo trial, all nineteen remaining unindicted Class A suspects would be released, with several of them returning to public life.[173] Kodama Yoshio, a shadowy extremist who got rich in occupied China, would become a backroom power broker in the dominant Liberal Democratic Party, still complaining bitterly about one-sided war crimes trials by the victors.[174] The most prominent Class A suspect freed that Christmas Eve would be Kishi Nobusuke, who had had been commerce and industry minister in Tojo Hideki's cabinet; he went on to become prime minister in 1957. In his Sugamo Prison diary, Kishi decried the Tokyo trial as a "farce."[175]

CHAPTER 26

"Blowing Up a Ton of Dynamite"

DAYS BEFORE THE TOKYO court handed down its judgment, General Douglas MacArthur fretted that anything could happen. Emperor Hirohito, distraught at the verdicts, might abdicate or worse. Under the strain of having his generals and ministers sentenced to death, MacArthur worried aloud that the emperor might kill himself.

MacArthur's top political adviser agreed about the risk of suicide, "as the Emperor is both Oriental and Japanese." Disgusted at the imminent lawyerly hash, MacArthur fumed that the judgment of the Tokyo trial "is like blowing up a ton of dynamite—one cannot possibly foresee what might happen."

The supreme commander vowed to do everything he could to prevent an abdication. He decided that he would call on the emperor immediately after the judgment was announced to tell him that resigning would be "ridiculous and preposterous," a disservice to the Japanese people. The political adviser agreed, saying that this was the U.S. government's view too. The fall of the emperor, he said, would only promote Communism and chaos in Japan.[1]

The day before the verdict, Hirohito unsubtly informed Harry Truman—who had just won a surprise reelection over Thomas Dewey—that he wanted the closest and most cordial relationship with the United States. That oral message was sent by Joseph Keenan, stalwart to the end in his protection of the emperor. The U.S. chief prosecutor explained to reporters that the emperor was a constitutional monarch—a way of insulating him from war guilt—seeking to bring democracy to his people.[2]

General Headquarters and the tribunal painstakingly choreographed the public announcement of the judgment. While grandees across Tokyo clamored for seats to watch the climactic moments, MacArthur decided that he would not attend, although his wife and son would.[3]

It was an official objective of General Headquarters to drive home to the Japanese people the facts of their defeat, their war guilt, and the militarists' responsibility for their suffering. Helped by the Tokyo court, General Headquarters ran a formal War Guilt Information Program, aiming to put out the Allied line through Japanese newspapers, books, magazines, radio, and film. To steer Japanese reporters on deadline, General Headquarters wrote up summaries of the judgment, allowing the occupiers to emphasize the crucial points for public consumption.[4] As a General Headquarters staffer noted, Japanese press coverage at this pivotal hour would shape "their permanent impression of the guilt of the defendants and of the Japanese nation, as well as the nature of the Allied victory and the quality of Allied justice."[5]

The Tokyo court meticulously modeled its judgment day after Nuremberg: floodlights, radio chains, verdicts translated in advance for the local reporters.[6] Working with the Allied authorities, the court added twenty-five telephones in the Japanese press rooms, laid in individual IBM lines from the courtroom for each of the leading fifteen Japanese newspapers to get the text of the judgment as Sir William Webb read it aloud, allowed for newsreels and radio broadcasts, and built a new telephone booth for a pool report shared with the entire Japanese press.[7] Even the death sentences were based on Nuremberg's, with the U.S. military carefully planning how to carry out whatever hangings were ordered.[8]

The judges were equally obsessed with theatrics. To maximize television coverage in the United States, Webb met beforehand with the NBC correspondent, assuring him that the judges wanted the world to know their judgment.[9] The judges treated all their decisions of law and findings of fact as top secret; their Japanese translators were kept incommunicado under military surveillance in a separate building while they worked.[10] Although the four Allied judges at Nuremberg had taken turns reading their judgment aloud, Webb would read the entire judgment himself—an ego-soothing consolation prize from the majority, whose words he would be reciting.[11] Delfin Jaranilla, the Philippine judge, nervously wanted spectators to be searched for firearms and weapons. Fearing angry outbursts from the defendants, he persuaded the judges that the accused should be forbidden to make statements before or after sentencing.[12]

Yet outside critics of the Tokyo trial could not be stifled. At an American Bar Association meeting in Seattle, Owen Cunningham, an outspoken American defense lawyer who had clashed with Webb, gave a speech decrying the "major evils" of the Tokyo trial to a posh crowd including senators, members of Congress, the judge advocate general of the United States, and senior judges. "The object of the trial was vengeance, vindication and propaganda," he said. He argued that the Tokyo charter was bad law, the proceedings were stacked against the accused, and some of the judges were biased, singling out Jaranilla as a survivor of the Bataan death march and Webb for running an Australian investigation of war crimes.[13] Stung, some of judges wanted to book Cunningham for contempt of court.[14] Webb balked at that, but barred him from any proceedings in the last weeks of the court's existence.[15] When Cunningham pointed out that freedom of speech still reigned in the United States, the irate judges notified him that he could only watch the judgment from the spectators' gallery.[16] Such petty vindictiveness tanked whatever lofty impression of justice the judges were trying to make.

JUDGMENT

Under the blazing glare of banks of floodlights, the Tokyo trial convened on November 4, 1948, for its last order of business: the reading of the judgment and verdicts. The cavernous Ichigaya courtroom was packed and hushed, brilliantly lit for the Allied and Japanese photographers who were taking stills and motion pictures.

Promptly at 9:30 a.m., the judges filed in, somber in black robes, except for the U.S. and Soviet judges in military uniforms.[17] The prisoners were marched in to take their seats. The twenty-five remaining defendants sat in anger, frustration, exhaustion, and terror. They looked dark-eyed and pallid. While Tojo Hideki, sitting stiffly, fully expected to be sentenced to death, many others were hoping to escape the gallows.[18] One American reporter crudely told his readers that the group "belies the common belief of Occidentals that all Japanese look alike. Some of them have long faces, others are round-heads; some are clean-shaven, others have beards, and others have little mustaches in the Charlie Chaplin fashion." General Doihara Kenji was "a little fellow of insignificant appearance with a face like that of a frightened rabbit." Shigemitsu Mamoru "looks like a worried professor in a small college—scribbling notes and rumpling his hair now and then."[19]

Webb carried a huge sheaf of paper. He leaned forward and in a clear, strong voice began to read the judgment written by his majority colleagues. He would go on for seven long days.

Embarrassingly, he had to begin by vindicating the court's jurisdiction, a foundational question which the court had left hanging for two and a half years. After all the rancorous debates among the judges, the majority settled on the lowest common denominator. There were no invocations of natural law, universal conscience, or any other higher authorities. The court "derives its jurisdiction from the Charter," Webb read simply. The tribunal had been created by MacArthur under proper authority given him by the Allied governments. Still, the majority judges agreed that the Allies were bound by the limits of existing international law, accepting the arguments made by Radhabinod Pal and Bert Röling.

Making their own ruling all the more threadbare, the Tokyo judges declared themselves "in complete accord" with the Nuremberg court's explanation of its jurisdiction, which they quoted at length on three points. Rather than admitting that they were cribbing from Nuremberg as a presentable way out of their own brawls over jurisdiction, the majority instead claimed it was better to echo Nuremberg than risk allowing conflicting interpretations by providing their own reasoning.

First, the Tokyo judges quoted the Nuremberg judgment to claim that the Tokyo court was not making new international law but merely upholding the law as it was: "The Charter is not an arbitrary exercise of power on the part of the victorious nations but is the expression of international law existing at the time of its creation." This was meant to silence defense arguments that the Allies had no right to suddenly make aggressive war a crime. According to Nuremberg, the Kellogg-Briand Pact had criminalized war in 1928. Having signed that pact, Japan had violated it by launching an aggressive war: "those who plan and wage such a war, with its inevitable and terrible consequences, are committing a crime in so doing."

Second, the Tokyo majority judges quoted Nuremberg to address the cardinal legal principle that no one should be held guilty for an act that was not a crime when it was committed—known in lawyerly Latin as *nullum crimen sine lege*.[20] The Nuremberg judgment had accepted this dictum as a principle of justice but held that it did not apply to German invaders since "the attacker must know that he is doing wrong, and so far from it being unjust to punish him, it would be unjust if his wrong were allowed to go unpunished." The same argument fit for Japanese aggressors.

Finally, the Tokyo court quoted Nuremberg's famous position that defendants acting under superior orders were not freed from criminal responsibility, although such orders could be considered in mitigation of punishment. That principle was written into the similar charters of both the Asian and European international military tribunals. The real test, the Nuremberg judgment asserted, was not the existence of a superior order to commit a war crime but "whether moral choice was in fact possible."

Stepping out from under the protective umbrella of Nuremberg, the Tokyo judges rejected the defense's claim that when Japan accepted the Potsdam Declaration's pledge of justice for war crimes, it had only meant that for conventional war crimes. "Aggressive war was a crime at international law long prior to the date of the Declaration of Potsdam," Webb said. Nor did the majority accept the defense's claim that the Japanese government had surrendered without understanding that those responsible for the war would be prosecuted. Twisting the knife, the judges quoted the emperor himself from Marquis Kido Koichi's diary: "I could not bear the sight . . . of those responsible for the war being punished . . . but I think now is the time to bear the unbearable."

To make clear that the court's condemnations would not rest on fanciful legal theories, the judgment emphasized Japan's treaty commitments throughout. By joining the League of Nations, Japan had pledged to respect the territorial integrity of China and other League member states. Under the Nine-Power Treaty of 1922, Japan was obligated to respect the administrative and territorial independence of China, and to resolve disputes through diplomacy or mediation. Under the Hague Convention IV of 1907 on land warfare, signed and ratified by Japan, Japan had pledged to treat prisoners of war humanely and not to work them excessively, not to use poison weapons, and not to destroy hospitals or religious sites. Japan's duties were further amplified in the Geneva Convention of 1929 on prisoners of war, which Japan had signed and pledged to follow *mutatis mutandis,* although it had not ratified it.

Most importantly, by joining the Kellogg-Briand Pact, Japan had pledged to renounce war and settle disputes only through peaceful means. While the judges agreed that the pact would not prevent a state facing imminent attack from defending itself, they did not allow the state resorting to war to make the final determination of whether it was justified in doing so—an interpretation of the treaty that would essentially nullify it, since any aggressor state could claim it had acted in self-defense. "Japan had claimed a place among the civilized communities of the world and had voluntarily incurred the above obligations designed to further the cause of peace, to outlaw aggressive war, and to mitigate the horrors of war," the majority wrote. "It is against that background of rights and obligations that the actings of the accused must be viewed and judged."

The Tokyo judges concluded, "The challenge to the jurisdiction of the Tribunal wholly fails."[21]

A CONSPIRACY SO IMMENSE

Webb spent the bulk of his seven-day recital delivering a long account of Japanese aggression, singling out the role of each of the accused. After all the *Rashomon*-like tellings and retellings of Asia's recent history by the prosecution, defense, and individual defendants, this was meant to be the definitive chronicle. To those listening as Webb recited in court, the judgment was less a legal brief than a lengthy, discursive, and highly opinionated history of Japan's recent wars. Each time that Webb named one of the defendants as part of this overarching conspiracy for aggression, his chances of survival sank.

One powerful former army minister flushed when his name was mentioned; another, who usually sat ramrod straight, stiffened further. Kido Koichi, implicated as a member of the cabinet during the invasion of China, put his head between his arms on his desk. Tojo, wearing the drab remnants of his military uniform, dozed, making a show of indifference to the snapping of his neck.[22] He expected nothing else. One day he met with his wife during a court recess to turn over a small bundle of his belongings, including a cigarette case. "I now feel bright," he told her. "There is nothing to worry me."[23]

Although the majority judges aimed to speak in unison, they had produced a document with all the unity of a bag full of cats. It lurched from one section to another, with noticeable shifts in tenor and occasional contradictions in argument. And while aspiring to be definitive, the judgment complained that its chronicle was "handicapped by the absence" of official Japanese army, navy, and government documents. Instead, the majority relied heavily on Kido's diaries and the Saionji-Harada memoirs. Some of the crucial government evidence had been destroyed by the Japanese as a cover-up, and other documentation had been incinerated by American firebombing; the majority wondered why such important papers had not been removed to safety before the bombs hit, as if safe places had been easy to find.[24]

On almost every point of interpretation, the historical sections favored the prosecution. The judgment resoundingly rejected claims that Japan had been acting in self-defense. It gave no weight to the defendants' assertions that Japan had been fighting against illegitimate European and American empires in Asia. To keep Major General Ivan Zaryanov on side, the majority had to agree that the Japanese defendants had had no reason to be afraid of the Soviet Union—although outside the courtroom, the United States and its European allies were themselves making Cold War policies driven by fear of Soviet power.

Japanese observers had expected that as many as half a dozen defendants might be acquitted, particularly the civilian politicians and diplomats; the best bets for acquittal were two foreign ministers, Togo Shigenori and Shigemitsu, followed by Hirota Koki, who had been foreign minister and prime minister.[25] Those hopes were quickly dashed as Webb read methodically. The acceptance of the Saionji-Harada memoirs was a tough blow for the defense, which had disparaged it as unreliable hearsay. The lawyers for the defense, the majority judgment said frostily, were often "contesting the seemingly incontestable," and the defense witnesses had given "prolix equivocations and evasions, which only arouse distrust."[26] Several of the defendants told their lawyers that they were surprised and disappointed that the court was discounting their claims to have acted in self-defense and to prevent the spread of Communism in Asia. The verdicts would be harsh.[27]

The judgment recounted the rise to supremacy of the Japanese military. As the military gained the upper hand, it embarked on foreign wars, bulldozing past the hesitancy of civilian cabinets while its extremists threatened coups and assassinations.

The judgment gave a stern assessment of Japanese encroachments on Manchuria. Using Mei Ruao's words, the majority declared that "Japan had secured concessions from China in the days of her weakness; the resurgent nationalism of China resented the losses which the decadent Empire of China had been unable to avoid."[28] The judgment squarely blamed Japanese army officers for secretly planning the clash at Mukden (Shenyang) in September 1931 as a pretext to invade Manchuria, noting with disdain the army minister's claim that it was "an act of righteous self-defence."

Singling out several army officers in the dock, the judgment condemned the army for a "war of conquest in Manchuria," despite the hesitation of the civilian cabinet. Deflating pretentions that Manchukuo had been a legitimate state, the majority noted that two colonels on trial had enthroned Puyi as a puppet emperor of "a totalitarian State" under their control. Japan's democratic-minded prime minister, Inukai Tsuyoshi, had dared to oppose the recognition of Manchukuo and seek peace with Chiang Kai-shek. After he was assassinated by naval officers, the frightened cabinet fell into line behind the military.[29]

The judgment condemned Japan's pattern of provoking "incidents" as pretexts for further expansion in China, pointing to a 1932 battle in Shanghai as following the example set at Mukden. Japan, determined to show its military might to overawe the Chinese, had used force out of all proportion to whatever danger there was to Japanese citizens and property in Shanghai. The Japanese bombed a central industrial neighborhood in the city and massacred Chinese civilians.[30] Several army defendants were blamed for chipping away at northern China, setting up autonomous governments in Inner Mongolia and five provinces of north China in 1935.

Anyone who defied the army risked assassination or insurrection—a prospect which became more terrifying after February 1936, when a group of young army officers revolted against the government. With the army ascendant, Hirota Koki became prime minister in March 1936; his cabinet was stuffed with militarists and nationalists, including several of the defendants. Although he only lasted as prime minister until February 1937, the judgment excoriated his cabinet for drawing up a secret policy aiming to dominate East Asia and extend its influence southward: "the Army's scheme for a new order in East Asia became the settled policy of the Japanese government."

CHINA

Mei Ruao reported proudly to the Chinese foreign minister, Wang Shijie, that the judgment "contains detailed descriptions and clear conclusions about the prewar dictatorship of Japanese militarists, their preparation for war, and their gradual practice of aggression." He had drafted the huge section on Japan's aggressive war against China, which thrums with his elegant, authoritative English. It made up two hundred and fifty pages out of some four hundred pages on Japan's aggressions. Mei "personally took comfort in the fact that the rights and wrongs will be revealed to the whole world and to future generations."[31]

He admitted that he disagreed with some aspects of the judgment but was not about to undermine the verdicts by dissenting. Even while Webb was reading the judgment aloud in court, Mei somehow still thought that it was possible that Röling, Henri Bernard, and Webb could be kept from issuing their fractious opinions. Although Pal had already submitted his dissent, Mei reassured the Chinese government that it would not be read in court.[32]

Mei had good reason to feel triumphant. The judgment followed the Chinese line throughout, with only a few swerves. It gave a detailed condemnation of Japan's aggression, from Manchuria to encroachments on northern China to the full-scale invasion that began in July 1937. Having glared at Tojo Hideki, Doihara Kenji, and Itagaki Seishiro on the first day of the trial, the Chinese judge now ended it by excoriating them, as well as Hirota and several generals.[33]

Soon before the crisis month of July 1937, the judgment noted, Tojo, then the chief of staff of the Kwantung Army, had argued that the time was ripe to "deliver a blow" against the Nationalist Chinese government.[34] As Mei had hoped, his fellow majority judges blamed the Marco Polo Bridge clash squarely on the Japanese army as the culmination of its plotting to control northern China. On July 7, the judgment noted, some Japanese troops had held unusual maneuvers on the outskirts of Beijing, and then demanded to enter the nearby Chinese fortress of Wanping to find a missing Japanese soldier. The Japanese opened fire, according to the majority judges. The judgment faulted the Japanese for then issuing an ultimatum that the Chinese in the fortress surrender or face bombardment. This led to a battle that ended with the Japanese, having found their missing soldier, agreeing to a truce after three days. But instead of de-escalating, more Japanese troops poured in, while Japanese soldiers again opened fire in sporadic clashes. The cabinet declared that Japan would take all necessary measures to get troops to the area: "Although the Army had chosen the time and place for the attack, war with China was a foreseen consequence of Japanese national policy." Japan issued a new ultimatum, which led to large-scale fighting in Beijing in late July.

Beginning a massive conquest, Japan marched in troops while its air force bombed Nanjing and other Chinese cities. Mei carefully included the aerial bombardment of Chongqing, although without mentioning that he had been living there in that period.[35] The judges dismissed the notion that Japan had acted in self-defense, concluding instead that it meant to "secure a steady footing of her Empire on the continent."[36] As the judgment noted, the Chinese army alone recorded having 3.2 million men killed, wounded, or missing; the Chinese government had not managed to tally its civilian deaths, but they must have been colossal.[37]

For what the majority judges bluntly called "the Rape of Nanking," they singled out General Matsui Iwane, commander in chief of Japan's Central China Expeditionary Forces, as well as General Muto Akira, his vice chief of staff. Soon before the slaughter there, Matsui issued a chilling statement that "the devil-defying sharp bayonets were just on the point of being unsheathed to develop their divine influence." Although his army was a newly formed grouping, the judgment noted, it was composed of experienced troops. Matsui made a personal triumphant entry a few days after the city fell on December 13, 1937, during the height of the slaughter.[38]

The judgment castigated Japan for trafficking opium and narcotics in order to finance its operations and to weaken the Chinese people: "Wherever the Japanese Army went in China, Korean and Japanese drug peddlers followed closely upon its heels." Some of Japan's leading corporations were involved, with the Mitsubishi and Mitsui companies buying large quantities of Iranian opium and distributing it in China.[39]

The judgment heaped blame for the China quagmire on an assortment of army men, with particular odium for Tojo, who then was vice minister of the army. Although the cabinet agreed that the war should be wrapped up fast, a powerful army faction led by Tojo was determined to conquer China, rejecting peace talks with its Nationalist government. Yet some civilians stood condemned too. Kido Koichi, as welfare minister, was denounced as "a staunch supporter of Japanese domination in China": supporting a new offensive that captured Hankou, backing a decision to break all ties with Chiang Kai-shek, and insisting that Chinese resistance must be crushed before a peace settlement.[40] Hirota Koki, as foreign minister, was pilloried as a shameful enabler of the army, torpedoing any compromise that might have brought peace.[41]

In a triumph for Mei, the judgment put China at the center of Japan's plotting—drawing a direct line from aggression in Manchuria ultimately to Pearl Harbor. "The basic causes of the Pacific War are to be found in the conquest of China," the court held. Western opposition to Japan's aggression in China drove Japan to more war preparations, particularly securing oil, petroleum, and raw materials; that drive for self-sufficiency "demanded . . . an advance to the south." This formulation welded the cause of China to that of the United States.[42]

THE GREAT PATRIOTIC WAR

Ivan Zaryanov had reason to be satisfied too. The tone and content of the judgment lurched when the Soviet judge's influence became apparent, sounding like Webb was suddenly reading from a completely different document. Seeking to displace China as the preeminent victim, Zaryanov described the Soviet Union as Japan's "proximate enemy, whose growing strength was a constant challenge to the Japanese goal of supremacy in East Asia." He even made the judgment laud the notorious nonaggression pact between Adolf Hitler and Joseph Stalin in August 1939—which secretly carved up Poland and allowed the Soviet takeover of the Baltic states—for temporarily freeing the Soviet Union from anxiety about its western flank.

While Zaryanov offered considerable evidence that Japanese leaders believed war with the Soviets was impending, he strained to prove that, as the judgment asserted, the Japanese meant to start it. Often the evidence could equally well show that the Japanese were preparing against a looming Soviet assault.

The Soviet judge belabored the two battles near Manchuria. For the clash at Lake Khasan in July and August 1938, Zaryanov got his colleagues to accept that this had been an attack deliberately planned by General Itagaki Seishiro as army minister, authorized by senior ministers. Although Japan was sobered after taking a drubbing at Lake Khasan, the judgment insisted that Japan's army meant to attack the Soviet Union as soon as practicable. In the spring and summer of 1939, the judgment concluded, the Kwantung Army attacked Soviet troops at the Manchurian border, challenging the Soviet client state of Outer Mongolia. After another lost battle, Togo Shigenori, then ambassador in Moscow, helped reach a settlement within a few days.

In April 1941, the judgment had to note, Japan had signed a neutrality pact with the Soviet Union, and had not joined in Nazi Germany's invasion of the Soviet Union that June. Although the judgment showed that some of the most ferocious Japanese militarists fretted that they were not strong enough to battle both in Southeast Asia and against the Soviet Union, it nevertheless unequivocally concluded that Japan had planned aggression against the Soviet Union—ignoring that when fighting did at last come, in August 1945, it was started by the Soviets.[43] In a trial that was meant to prohibit aggression and the violation of treaties, the majority had essentially absolved the Soviet Union of tearing up its own neutrality pact with Japan.[44]

THE AXIS

The judgment returned to safer ground as it turned to the Axis pact. The majority judges understood that Japan had been driven toward an alliance with Nazi Germany primarily to offset the threat of their common foes. Yet the judges treated Germany and Japan as birds of a feather, both bent upon wars of conquest, despite considerable evidence that Japan's foreign policy lacked the ideological imperative of Hitler's drive for *Lebensraum*.

Remarkably, the judgment held that Japan's cabinet had left the Axis alliance up to the military, acting through the fervently pro-Nazi military attaché in Berlin, Major General Oshima Hiroshi, now one of the defendants. Joachim von Ribbentrop, Nazi Germany's foreign minister, had bypassed Togo Shigenori, then ambassador in Berlin, to work with Oshima. Indeed, the judgment could not show any enthusiasm on Togo's part for allying with Hitler's Germany. To the contrary, it noted that Ribbentrop was disappointed that Togo would not promise the Third Reich any special favors in China. After Ribbentrop grew indignant, eventually securing a privileged position in occupied China, Togo was sacked and replaced as ambassador by Oshima.

Far from showing a hell-bent rush toward allying with Nazi Germany, the judgment gave a protracted account of Japanese ambivalence. Ribbentrop insisted on a general military alliance against all comers, but Japan's cabinet, wary of being dragged into a European war against Britain and France whenever Hitler ignited it, preferred a partnership directed only against the Soviet Union. In an unusually direct intervention in politics, Emperor Hirohito supported an exclusively anti-Soviet treaty, not a broader one, as the army wanted. Itagaki, then army minister, falsely told the emperor that the foreign minister had come to favor a general military alliance; when Hirohito discovered the deceit, the judgment noted, "he taxed Itagaki with deliberate falsehood and severely rebuked him." Kido, shaken, said that the army was going to destroy the nation.

As the judgment emphasized, Shigemitsu Mamoru, then the ambassador in London, was one of the few officials who strenuously argued for better relations with Britain and the United States. Expecting that the Western powers would eventually win World War II, he had been a lonely voice against a southward thrust into Southeast Asia. He hoped that peace in China, secured by generous concessions by Japan, would remove any American or European excuses to intervene.

Dismissing Shigemitsu's temperate advice, the army pressed to conclude an alliance with Nazi Germany, hoping this would daunt the United States into continued neutrality. After two imperial conferences, the Tripartite Pact was unanimously accepted, announced in September 1940 with an imperial rescript that somehow managed to declare that an alliance with Hitler and Benito Mussolini would be an instrument of peace. Japan recognized the leadership of Germany and Italy in establishing a new order in Europe, while Germany and Italy did the same for Japan's establishment of a new order in Asia. A few days before, Kido, now lord keeper of the privy seal, had told the emperor that the alliance would eventually spell confrontation with Britain and the United States. The judgment held that the emperor had said that he would never give his consent to the alliance but had been tricked by Kido.

The judgment presented the Axis pact as a necessary prelude for Japan's expansion into Southeast Asia, as well as possible war with the United States if it got in the way of those conquests. The Tripartite Pact, far from being defensive, was "a compact made between aggressor nations for the furtherance of their aggressive purposes."[45]

PEARL HARBOR

The tone of the judgment lurched again as it came to the outbreak of the Pacific War, resting heavily on a study by Erima Harvey Northcroft, the New Zealand judge—a mainstay of the British bloc of judges.[46] Reading his words, Webb now spoke in a crisp and authoritative mode. Thanks to Mei, the judgment framed the war in China as a crucial issue snarling the negotiations between Japan and the United States. And under Zaryanov's influence, the judgment claimed that Japan only turned to Southeast Asia after getting thumped by the Soviets in two border clashes and being scared off by the infamous Hitler-Stalin pact: "As the door of opportunity closed in the North the Southern gates began to open."

Nazi victories in Europe emboldened Japan to challenge the European empires ruling over Southeast Asia. The judgment treated the stationing of troops and establishment of airbases in northern French Indochina, accepted by the feeble Vichy authorities, as tantamount to an invasion. By October 1940, according to the judgment, Japan's government was determined to take the Netherlands East Indies, Singapore, and Malaya. Japan would take advantage of independence movements among "the natives" in Indochina, Burma, and Malaya to help its advance. Unable to get Winston Churchill's government to accept Japan's claims on Southeast Asia, the Japanese leadership planned to seize Singapore by sudden force.

Under Mei's influence, the judgment framed the protracted Washington negotiations as fundamentally deadlocked over Japan's refusal to give up its political, economic, and military dominance of China. By the summer of 1941, according to the majority judges, Japan turned to final preparations for war against the United States and the British and Dutch Empires. Japanese leaders hoped that after a successful surprise attack, the United States would grow weary of a prolonged, bloody war and negotiate a peace which accepted Japan's supremacy over the lands it had seized.[47]

Under the apparent influence of the British bloc of judges, the judgment puzzlingly declared that Japan's appetite for southern Indochina was really due to its planned attacks on Singapore and the East Indies and had "nothing to do" with China—having apparently forgotten Mei's insistence elsewhere that Japan's designs on Indochina had everything to do with China. On July 2, an imperial conference resolved on a southward advance. If Vichy France did not acquiesce, Tojo and several other defendants resolved to use force to get their way in Indochina. After Vichy knuckled under, Japanese troops took over southern Indochina.

Although the Washington negotiations had not been promising, the seizure of southern Indochina brought relations with the United States to a perilous new low. On July 25, Franklin Delano Roosevelt issued his directive freezing all Japanese assets in the United States. Here the judgment treated the emperor as a voice for peace, fretting to Kido about having to wage a desperate war. The monarch peppered his military chiefs and his anxious prime minister, Prince Konoe Fumimaro, about military strategy, with the navy nervous about running out of oil.

On September 6, an imperial conference—attended by Tojo as army minister, among other defendants—made the crucial decision to advance into Southeast Asia, while offering a last chance for negotiations with the United States and Britain. As presented by the judges, Japan's terms were stiff to the verge of outrageousness: the United States and Britain should stop interfering with Japan's efforts to win the China war, halt military and economic aid to China's Nationalist government, accept Japan's foothold in Indochina, stop strengthening their military positions in Asia, end their embargoes, and help Japan obtain raw materials. In return, Japan would not make any more Asian conquests, and would withdraw its troops from Indochina once peace had been established—meaning, not least, whenever the China war somehow ended. These Japanese demands were miles away from the United States' stated principles of respecting China's territorial integrity and domestic sovereignty. If there was not a diplomatic deal by October, Japan would go to war.

The judgment squarely blamed Japan for the failure of the peace talks: refusing to withdraw from China and Indochina, as well as sticking to the Axis alliance. The majority judges pronounced that the United States and Britain were perfectly entitled to give aid to "the legitimate government of China which had long been the victim of Japan's aggression."

Kido worried about the rush to war, suggesting waiting until Japan was better prepared—meaning, according to the judgment, the military defeat of China.[48] In another part of the judgment drafted by Mei, the tribunal recorded that Kido had wanted to prepare for military action to complete the war in China that could last for ten or fifteen years, and to use all of Japan's military might against Kunming and Chongqing. At Mei's behest, the judgment emphasized how Tojo, as army minister, had driven the cabinet to agree that Japan must not waver on its policy of stationing troops in China.[49]

The judgment faulted Tojo's obstinacy for toppling Konoe's cabinet, urging the government to make up its mind for war. Even when Konoe told him point-blank that there was no hope of a deal with the Americans so long as Japan insisted on keeping troops in China, he declared that he could not agree to pull the soldiers out, even if he had to resign from the cabinet. The next day, Konoe told his old friend Kido that he could not continue as prime minister because of his disagreement with Tojo. By now, Tojo was so angry that he refused to talk any longer to the prime minister—never mind the Americans—because he could not control his rage.

Here the judgment brought the hammer down on Kido for his efforts to install Tojo as prime minister. When the group of senior statesmen suggested a royal prince or a more moderate army general, Kido opposed both and instead favored Tojo. Hirota Koki, too, was singled out for supporting Tojo. For all Kido's energetic self-justifications in the witness box, the most he won from the judgment was an acknowledgment that, on his advice, the emperor had issued special instructions to Tojo, as his new prime minister, to reconsider the war decision of September 6.

True to MacArthur's original vision of a swift trial for the Pearl Harbor cabinet, the judges implicated by name a long list of the defendants who had been Tojo's ministers, advisers, or senior military chiefs, including Togo Shigenori as foreign minister. While the judges painstakingly listed the numerous defendants who had been involved in a flurry of liaison conferences held to reexamine the prospects for war, they did not understand how the discussions had unfolded. Ignoring Togo's detailed testimony, the judges made no mention of his struggle for peace. The judgment quoted mostly from Togo's correspondence with the ambassador to the United States, which of course made no mention of his loud fights with the army. Instead the judgment recounted Togo's instructions to the ambassador that Japan would not yield on its demand to keep troops in China.

As diplomacy flickered out, the judges were obviously unimpressed with Togo's final two diplomatic proposals. The judgment scorned his first proposal to the United States as a demand to "condone the invasion of China and to leave that country in servitude to Japan." Cordell Hull, the U.S. secretary of state, scorned the absence of specifics about a withdrawal of troops from Japan; after that, the judgment held, "Togo began final preparations for the attack." Finally Togo sent the Americans a second proposal, his last fallback—an attempt to rewind to before the seizure of southern Indochina and the U.S. oil embargo. Japan offered to pull out of southern Indochina and then, after either a peace treaty with Chiang Kai-shek or an equitable peace in the Pacific, from northern Indochina; in return, the United States was asked to provide oil to Japan and cut a deal for Japan to secure natural resources in the East Indies. Dismissing Togo's "so-called concessions," the judgment essentially endorsed the U.S. government's view that this proposal was insincere: the troops withdrawn from southern Indochina would just go to northern Indochina, ready to march back anytime. The judges underwrote the Roosevelt administration's stance that accepting this proposal meant condoning Japanese aggression, abandoning American principles, and betraying China.

According to the judgment, diplomacy had expired by the time that Japan got the tough terms of the Hull note on November 26. That morning, a Japanese carrier task force sailed toward Pearl Harbor, just in case. Following the prosecution's line to the letter, the judges treated Hull as merely reiterating his original principles of territorial integrity and sovereignty. Yet the specifics of his terms were clearly tough: withdrawing troops from China and Indochina, ending all support to the collaborationist government in China, entering an Asian nonaggression deal that would nullify the Tripartite Pact. The Hull note, the majority wrote, "brought the leaders of Japan sharply face to face with reality." They "had never been prepared . . . to surrender the booty of the past and to abandon the booty in prospect."

The judges condemned Japan for trickery in keeping the moribund talks going as "a screen" to cover the strike on Pearl Harbor. As they noted, Japan attacked Hong Kong before a declaration of war against Britain, and Japanese warships were shelling beaches in Malaya over an hour before the time when the Japanese ambassador was supposed to be breaking the bad news to Hull. Yet to American consternation, the judges refused to weigh in on whether these surprise attacks constituted a war crime. The Hague Convention III of 1907 demanded either a reasoned declaration of war or an explicit warning before starting hostilities. Yet that convention, the judges noted, did not specify how much advance notice was required, generating disputes among international lawyers. Since the Japanese defendants were guilty of the graver crime of aggressive war, the judges wrote, it was unnecessary to grapple with ancillary charges about providing advance warning.

Crucially, the judgment squarely rejected Japanese claims of self-defense. The judges held that the Allies had been entirely justified in imposing economic sanctions to dissuade Japan from aggression in China and elsewhere. Upholding the sovereignty of empires, the tribunal concluded that Japan's leaders had committed unprovoked acts of aggression first against France (meaning its possession of Indochina), and then the United States (at Hawaii and Guam, as well as the Philippines), Britain (meaning the British Empire in Hong Kong, Singapore, and Malaya), and Holland (meaning the Netherlands East Indies) in order to cut off those Western powers' aid to China and for southern expansion. Japan was also held to have waged aggressive war against Australia as a part of the British Commonwealth. In deference to U.S. imperial claims, the judges held that the attack on the Philippines was really part of the war of aggression against the United States. The defendants' pleas of self-defense, the majority concluded, were "merely a repetition of Japanese propaganda."[50]

As Webb read on, Emperor Hirohito was in the odd position of not being indicted yet also being in essence acquitted. Over and over, the judgment held that the military hard-liners had deceived a peace-loving emperor into approving their handiwork.[51]

Four days before the clash at Mukden in September 1931, the emperor had in vain warned the army minister that these schemes must stop. Next Hirohito, according to the judgment, had supported a soothing statement from the civilian government denying that Japan had any territorial aims in Manchuria, to the indignation of the army.[52] The judgment criticized General Itagaki Seishiro for falsely informing Hirohito that the navy and the Foreign Ministry approved of a plan to attack the Soviet Union at Lake Khasan, thus apparently securing the emperor's consent for that.[53] With scant evidence, the judgment held that the emperor had been tricked by Kido into consenting to the Tripartite Pact.[54]

The judgment presented the emperor as anxious about war against the United States, pressing the army and navy chiefs of staff about war strategy.[55] The majority did so even though the Australian and French judges had been struck by a signal piece of the prosecution's evidence: the entry in Kido's diary on November 30, 1941, in which Hirohito, after being reassured by the navy, "ordered" Tojo "to act according to program."[56] Although the prosecutors turned a blind eye to it, this was apparently a direct order by the emperor to his prime minister to proceed with the attack on the United States. Remarkably, it was never mentioned in the detailed judgment.

In the end, the judgment spared Hirohito of war guilt, but only by painting him as a chump repeatedly gulled by the army, his ministers, and his own lord keeper. If the imperial neck had been spared, the majority judges had nevertheless written him into history as one of its greatest saps.

ATROCITIES

The crime of aggression so dominated the Tokyo trial that it was only around noon on the sixth of seven days of reading that Webb got to conventional war crimes and crimes against humanity. It was, he said, "not practicable" to fully cover the mass of oral and documentary evidence. After a largely antiseptic recounting of Japan's foreign policy,

Webb recited an unbearable litany of horrors to a shuddering audience, from the death marches to summary executions to lethal forced labor in tropical heat.

The judges concluded that the Japanese army's and navy's use of torture, murder, and rape had been a matter of systematic policy. Although the military bureaucracy for prisoners of war had not performed its protective duties, it nevertheless provided a chain of command to condemn defendants who had served as army vice minister or chiefs of the army's bureau in charge of prisoners of war and civilian detainees. Sanctioning abuses, Tojo told chiefs of the prisoner camps, "In Japan we have our own ideology concerning prisoners of war." The detailed testimony of witnesses showed "atrocities committed in all theaters of war on a scale so vast, yet following so common a pattern in all theaters, that only one conclusion is possible—the atrocities were either secretly ordered or wilfully permitted." In the European theater, some 4 percent of American and British prisoners of war had died in German or Italian captivity; in the Pacific, it was 27 percent, with 35,756 perishing.

In a section that was unbearable to hear, Webb described massacres of prisoners of war, civilian detainees, medical staffs, and ordinary civilians. This carnage was, the judges held, the result of orders by commissioned officers, in some cases from admirals and generals, with officers present to oversee the crimes. "When killing Filipinos," the navy ordered late in the war, "assemble them together in one place as far as possible thereby saving ammunition and labor." The judges pointed to Japanese battle reports and Japanese soldiers' diaries to show that the killings had been well known to superior authorities. In one prison camp in Formosa (Taiwan), the chief of staff of a Japanese military police unit had ordered, "Whether they are destroyed individually or in groups, or however it is done, with mass bombing, poisonous smoke, poison, drowning, decapitation, or what, dispose of them as the situation dictates. In any case, it is the aim not to allow the escape of a single one, to annihilate them all, and not to leave any traces."

In Burma, Indonesia, and the Philippines, the judgment concluded that "massacres were freely committed as a means of terrorizing the civilian population and subjecting them to the domination of the Japanese." The judges offered a horrifyingly long list of slaughters of prisoners of war in Hong Kong, Malaya, Thailand, Sumatra, Java, Timor, New Guinea, Indochina, and the Philippines, as well as one case of Soviets being killed in Manchuria. The judgment pointed to killings at hospitals in Java, Singapore, and Malaya as evidence of contempt for the laws of war, citing the prosecution's horrific testimony about the bayoneting of the sick or wounded in their beds at St. Stephen's College Hospital in Hong Kong and the rape and murder of nurses.

From Burma to Sumatra, the judgment concluded, prisoners of war and civilian detainees were killed en masse because they were too starved or sick to be of further use. In Saigon and Hainan Island, laborers were massacred to impose discipline or for minor offenses such as using a radio. Toward the end of the war, prisoners of war and civilians in China, Borneo, and Timor were slaughtered to prevent them from being liberated by Allied forces. The judgment drew at length on the most gruesome evidence from the Philippine prosecutors, recounting how people in Manila were set on fire with gasoline, and women raped and mutilated, sometimes bayoneted with their babies in their arms.

The judgment treated the Bataan death march as a precedent for what became a widespread practice. Recounting the horrors, the judges estimated as many as eight thousand dead—a death toll that is more than twice as high as the standard historical estimate today. While the judgment made no conclusions about who had ordered the Bataan march, it condemned Tojo for not taking steps to prevent a repetition. By his own admission, Tojo, as prime minister, was well aware of the incident. Yet he had explained that field commanders should be left "considerable autonomy," which the judges took as license to other Japanese officers to repeat such forced marches elsewhere. The judgment pointed to subsequent death marches in Timor and in New Guinea, where ailing Indian prisoners who could not keep up were shot, and a notorious forced march of Australian prisoners from the Sandakan camp in Borneo through a hundred miles of mud, mountains, and jungle, with those who faltered being shot or bayoneted.

In his Queensland accent, Webb read about the death railway from Thailand to Burma, which was infamous in Australia. The judges concluded that, under Tojo's advice, Japan had decided to use Allied prisoners of war to build a railroad from Bangkok to help communications with Japanese troops fighting in Burma. Out of forty-six thousand prisoners, sixteen thousand died over the course of eighteen months. Although the judgment was overwhelmingly concerned with the suffering of Allied citizens, it did briefly note that conditions were even worse for the Burmese, Malays, Chinese, Indians, and Javanese building the railway: out of one hundred and fifty thousand of them, at least sixty thousand died.

The judges could not find orders implicating Tojo or other senior leaders for the Burma–Thailand railway. Instead they condemned him for knowing about conditions there yet doing nothing more than court-martialing a company commander—which amounted, the judges held, to condoning the enormities. While the army knew in some detail what was happening along the line, and the Foreign Ministry fielded repeated Allied protests, Japanese military imperatives were paramount. As the judgment quoted Tojo: "International Law should be interpreted from the viewpoint of executing the war according to our own opinions."[57]

The inherent one-sidedness of the judgment was painfully apparent when it came to the Japanese execution of captured American bomber crews. To the American people, this was a well-publicized war crime; to the Japanese command, it was a fitting punishment for Americans who had themselves committed a war crime. Wholly taking the American side of that argument, the judgment dodged the hard question of why aerial bombardment of Japanese cities should not be reckoned a war crime. Here the incomplete nature of international law favored the United States: the established laws of war forbade killing prisoners of war but had not yet outlawed aerial bombardment, in large part because the Americans preferred it that way.

After the shock of the Doolittle raid, Tojo, as prime minister, ordered a new law that retroactively imposed the death penalty on enemy aviators bombing Japan, Manchukuo, or occupied areas of China. While the Japanese could be faulted for adding a law retroactively, they had reason to complain that the bombs had hit ordinary civilians, not military objectives—a violation of the bedrock legal principle requiring discrimination between civilian and military targets. In response, the judges pointed out that Japan had regularly carried out indiscriminate aerial bombardment to terrorize Chinese civilians. While true, this only begged the question: if the judges condemned the Japanese for doing it to the Chinese, why not condemn the Americans for doing it to the Japanese?

The judgment noted, accurately, that the eight captured Doolittle fliers were abused, starved, and tortured. It called their trials, which lasted an hour, "a mere mockery," with the Kempeitai secretly ready to falsify evidence if necessary. It was true that Tojo and other senior Japanese commanders had been involved in sealing the fates of the Doolittle airmen. Yet although Lieutenant Colonel James Doolittle had ordered his men to avoid civilian targets, the best evidence to date gives reason to think that they killed some civilians, including an infant and a thirteen-year-old schoolboy, by strafing an elementary school in Tokyo and bombing homes in Yokohama.[58]

The judgment condemned the executions of captured airmen as Allied bombing intensified in 1944–45, without going beyond their remit to ponder why the Japanese objected to the firebombing of their cities. The majority judges complained that Allied fliers were routinely tortured and mistreated before being swiftly executed, and that their court-martial, if it happened at all, was a mere formality. Yet the judges made the perplexing choice to include a firebombing raid on Tokyo in May 1945, complaining that sixty-two Allied airmen had been left in inflammable wooden buildings at a prison, while hundreds of Japanese jailers and Japanese prisoners had sheltered in more durable buildings. All sixty-two Allied prisoners died in the firebombing, while none of the Japanese did. While it was fair to note the deaths of those airmen, the judgment made no mention of the masses of civilians in Tokyo who perished in their own wooden houses.

In some of the most wrenching passages of the judgment, the majority condemned the systematic use of torture. "Methods of torture were employed in all areas so uniformly as to indicate policy both in training and execution," the judges ruled, noting that these techniques were used all over Japan's possessions—in China, Formosa, Indochina, Malaya, Burma, Thailand, Borneo, Sumatra, Java, Timor, and the Philippines, as well as in the Japan home islands. In order to show that these were elaborate techniques that must have been taught, the judgment recounted the tortures in grisly detail: the "water treatment," where a victim had water forced down the mouth and nostrils until blacking out; burning with cigarettes, candles, hot irons, or scalding water, used on the most sensitive parts of the body, such as ears, belly, genitals, or breasts; forcing a victim to kneel with a pole inserted behind the knee joints, in order to cause intense pain as the knee joints separated; suspending a victim to pull joints from their sockets; forcing victims to kneel on sharp blocks for hours on end.

Sometimes the abuse served a strategic goal, such as parading frail, malnourished British and American prisoners through the streets of colonized Korean cities as a way of demonstrating the power of the Japanese Empire over white men. The same was done in Formosa and Burma. Yet often the cruelty served no apparent purpose. Japanese medical officers had in some cases conducted vivisections. Soldiers had mutilated and dismembered prisoners, slicing off limbs or genitals. And the judgment recorded several incidents of cannibalism, not out of necessity but by choice, sometimes as a festive occasion for officers ranked as high as general or rear admiral.

Although the Kempeitai were the most notorious torturers, the judgment also castigated the army, navy, camp guards, and Kempeitai-trained local police. Since the Kempeitai were run by the Army Ministry, the judges concluded that their actions reflected the ministry's policy. A Japanese army division fighting in Burma issued a pamphlet of instructions for interrogating prisoners of war, listing torture by kicking and beating as a clumsy but necessary option.

Several of the defendants had, as military commanders, administered prison camps, including General Doihara Kenji in Singapore and General Itagaki Seishiro in Korea. Higher up the chain of command, the judgment fixed blame on Tojo and other leading army officers. While much of the incriminating paperwork had been burned at the end of the war, some damning orders had survived. Tojo had commanded "strict discipline," although specifying not to break international law. Itagaki had informed Tojo about his plans to jail American and British prisoners in Korea to stamp out "any ideas of worship of Europe and America which the greater part of Korea still retains at bottom."

Despite repeated Allied protests, the judges held that Japan's government had condoned the abuse by neglecting to punish the guilty, or giving trifling punishments such as a reprimand for repeatedly lynching prisoners. The powerless Foreign Ministry would process the complaints from the Allied governments, the military affairs bureau would consider them, and then the foreign minister would send a response. The judgment castigated Togo Shigenori and Shigemitsu Mamoru, as foreign ministers, for falsely assuring the Allies that their prisoners were being treated well. Shigemitsu had repeatedly rebuffed Swiss requests to inspect the prisoner of war camps, and had told the British government that their prisoners on the Burma–Thailand railway were getting adequate medical care while they were dying by the thousands from cholera and malaria.[59]

The section about atrocities in China was prominently placed before those about abuses of Allied prisoners of war. Yet it was far shorter and concentrated heavily on Nanjing—a reflection of the comparative paucity of Chinese evidence.

Under Mei's influence, the judgment condemned Japan for fighting a race war to terrorize the inferior Chinese into submission. Since Japan officially claimed that the conflict was merely an "incident" where the laws of war did not apply, Chinese prisoners were systematically treated as bandits to be wiped out, intentionally deprived of their rights as lawful combatants. The judges ruled that the conflict was indeed an international war "fought to punish the people of China for their refusal to acknowledge the superiority and leadership of the Japanese race and to cooperate with Japan." As a senior commander in China wrote to Itagaki, then the army minister, Japanese aerial bombardment should "terrorize the enemy forces and civilians, and so develop among them an anti-war, pacifist tendency." One defendant told the Diet that he hoped the Chinese understood Japan's intentions: "As for those who fail to understand, we have no other alternative than to exterminate them."

Chinese captives were tortured, massacred, coerced into the armies of Japanese puppet regimes, or put to forced labor. In Manchuria, Kwantung Army troops in pursuit of defeated Chinese volunteer troops went on a killing rampage in several villages. More than two thousand seven hundred civilians were killed, which the Kwantung Army explained as part of a "program of exterminating 'bandits.'" The Kwantung Army's chief of staff told the army vice minister, "Racial struggle between Japanese and Chinese is to be expected. Therefore, we must never hesitate to wield military power in case of necessity."

The judgment treated the Nanjing massacre as the worst instance of a systematic policy. The bloodbath was not an overreaction by frightened Japanese soldiers; by the time the Japanese entered the city, nearly all the Chinese soldiers had fled, or ditched their weapons and uniforms to seek refuge in the International Safety Zone. Japanese troops, many of them drunk, "roamed over the city murdering, raping, looting and burning." The streets and alleys were littered with the Chinese dead. The judgment declared that at least twelve thousand noncombatant Chinese men, women, and children were killed in the first two or three days.

Murder, arson, and rape went on for at least six weeks. Chinese civilian men, treated as soldiers who had shed their uniforms, faced "organized and wholesale murder" with the apparent approval of the Japanese commanders. The Japanese rounded up groups of Chinese civilians, bound their hands behind their backs, marched them outside the city walls, and then killed them with machine guns or bayonets. (The judgment was clear that they were civilians.) The Japanese troops killed more than twenty thousand Chinese men of military age this way. They were no kinder to actual Chinese soldiers who surrendered, machine-gunning more than thirty thousand to death along the banks of the Yangzi River. Although many of Nanjing's residents fled, the Japanese forces captured their refugee camps, starving and torturing the refugees to death, or killing them with machine guns or bayonets.

Many women were sadistically raped, including young girls and the elderly. Afterward, the victims were often killed and their corpses mutilated. If the victims resisted, or their family tried to protect them, they were frequently killed for it. The judges declared that there had been approximately twenty thousand rapes during the first month of Japanese occupation.

The city's burial societies had counted more than one hundred and fifty-five thousand bodies buried, most of them with their hands tied behind their backs. Other corpses had been burned or dumped into the river. All told, the judgment estimated that more than two hundred thousand civilians and prisoners of war were murdered in and around Nanjing in the first six weeks under Japanese occupation.

The judges could not point to specific orders by Japanese political leaders or military chiefs to murder and rape, but ruled that the atrocities were known up the chain of command. The foreigners running the International Safety Zone complained incessantly to the Japanese army and embassy; the diplomatic corps and the press, as well as the Japanese embassy, sent out reports of horrors. Some of these official accounts went to Hirota Koki as foreign minister, as well as the vice minister of the army; they were discussed at liaison conferences, which were usually attended by the prime minister, the army and navy ministers, and the chiefs of the army and navy general staffs. One defendant, then governor general of Korea, admitted reading about the atrocities in the press.

There were only two defendants slated for the Nanjing atrocities: General Matsui Iwane and Muto Akira, then a colonel serving under him. There was no mention of Prince Asaka Yasuhiko, the emperor's uncle by marriage, the lieutenant general in command during the fall of Nanjing while Matsui was sidelined with illness. Rather than condemning Matsui and Muto for directly ordering mass killing or rape, the judgment hammered them for failing to stop the enormities. Matsui had entered the city in triumph and remained for nearly a week while the killing was raging, and Muto had joined him. Both Matsui and Muto admitted they had heard of the atrocities, yet took no effective action to stop them. Embarrassed by the bad press coverage, the Japanese government recalled Matsui and dozens of his officers, but did not punish them. The judgment cited Matsui's prideful statement that he was replaced not because of the massacres by his troops but because he considered his work done and wished to retire.

The judgment declared that Japan's onslaughts upon Shanghai, Hankou, Suzhou, and elsewhere showed that Japan was pursuing "settled policy" to bring China's Nationalist government to heel. Yet except for Nanjing, as Mei had privately feared, there was relatively little Chinese evidence for the judges to use. The judgment did not mention that it was relying on the testimony of one sole witness to conclude that Japanese troops in Hankou had marched hundreds of Chinese prisoners into the river and shot them. Nor did the judgment note that a single witness was used to prove that Japanese forces in Changsha had murdered, raped, and burned. The judges spoke with an authority that Mei himself did not feel.

Still, there was little real doubt about what the judgment termed "large-scale atrocities" in the Chinese interior. The most devastating evidence came from loose-lipped Japanese soldiers returning home, who had told stories about their macabre deeds there or showed off stolen loot. This became so widespread after the capture of Hankou that the Army Ministry had to issue orders that troops returning to Japan should keep their mouths shut, lest they undercut public support for the army. According to a damning Army Ministry document, a company commander in China gave directions for carrying out rape: "In order that we will not have problems, either pay them money or kill them in some obscure place after you have finished." A soldier described capturing a Chinese family: "We played with the daughter as we would with a harlot. But as the parents insisted that the daughter be returned to them we killed them. We played with the daughter as before until the unit's departure and then killed her."

One returning soldier said, "The prisoners taken from the Chinese Army were sometimes lined up in one line and killed to test the efficiency of the machine gun." Another said, "in the half year of battle, about the only things I learned are rape and burglary." A soldier said, "The thing I like best during the battle is plundering. In the front lines the superiors turn a blind eye to plundering and there were some who plundered to their heart's content." One soldier saw the army's deeds as ordinary crimes: "If the army men who participated in the war were investigated individually, they would probably all be guilty of murder, robbery or rape."[60]

CHAPTER 27

Judgment at Tokyo

I<small>T WAS A TRAGICALLY</small> beautiful autumn day with a clear blue sky, but the fateful day had come," wrote an *Asahi Shimbun* columnist on November 12, 1948, the final day of the Tokyo trial. Hours earlier, crowds of Japanese citizens had assembled outside the barbed wire enclosure surrounding the old Army Ministry.[1] "The day for reaping the results of the eighteen-year history of aggression had come. . . . It is a people's sadness beyond mourning that swells in the heart."[2]

Before getting on the bus from Sugamo Prison to the Army Ministry courtroom, all the defendants had been carefully inspected for poison capsules or other ways of committing suicide.[3]

"I am prepared to meet my Maker," Tojo Hideki greeted his American defense lawyer. "If the verdict is against me, I shall not ask for my life, and I do not want you to ask MacArthur for my life." Expecting to die, he had sent his wife a lock of his hair and a long fingernail clipping, and composed a traditional poem for the Buddhist priest at Sugamo Prison: "Looking up, I hear reverently the voice of Buddha calling me from the limitless clean sky."[4]

After the lunch break, Sir William Webb, sitting in front of the banked flags of the Allied powers, at last delivered his findings of guilt or innocence for each of the accused. The spectators' gallery was packed with the wives and daughters of Allied personnel, as well as high-ranking Allied military officers sporting colorful ribbons and medals. The klieg lights were dazzling.[5] General Matsui Iwane seemed to be under great strain, twisting his hands.[6] One American reporter spitefully wrote that Marquis Kido Koichi, slumped in his chair, wore "the expression of a dyspeptic Mickey Mouse," while a Japanese general's "long, Mongol face" was "an inscrutable mask." In a faded army jacket, Tojo sat still, often with his eyes closed.[7]

The judges had streamlined the indictment, cutting out several of the prosecution's original fifty-five counts. They held that only conspiracy to commit aggression was in itself a crime, but not conspiracy to carry out crimes against humanity or war crimes. At the urging of the British bloc of judges, the judgment agreed that conspiring to plan for or prepare for aggression was criminal, but then said that it was not necessary to convict any of the defendants for such planning alone. They rebuffed the prosecution's argument that killing at the start of an unlawful war in December 1941—at Pearl Harbor, Hong Kong, and Davao in the Philippines, in the sinking of a British gunboat in Shanghai, and in the first big battle in Malaya—was nothing more than murder. That contention, which had originated with General Douglas MacArthur, could potentially be extended to say that there were murders not just at the beginning of the war but throughout it, condemning every soldier who killed in a war of aggression as a murderer. So the judges warily stepped back, declaring that there was "no good purpose" in murder counts which would fall away if the war itself was shown to be a lawful one.[8] The judges insisted that a count of aggression against the Philippines should be treated as aggression against the United States, a point which was both pedantic and colonialist.

Foreshadowing the outcome, Webb began with findings that went almost entirely against the defendants. After all the backroom wrangling about conspiracy charges, the judgment ruled that there had indeed been a conspiracy to dominate Asia, although not the entire world alongside Nazi Germany and Italy. Furthermore, the court found that the prosecution had proved the existence of a criminal conspiracy to wage wars of aggression: "no more grave crimes can be conceived of than a conspiracy to wage a war of aggression or the waging of a war of aggression, for the conspiracy threatens the security of the peoples of the world, and the waging disrupts it." Next, the judgment ruled that it had been proved that wars of aggression had been waged against China, the United States, the British Commonwealth, Holland, France, Thailand, and the Soviet Union in those two border clashes.

The grim-faced accused men sat silently.[9] Webb summoned forward each of the accused in alphabetical order, from Araki Sadao to Umezu Yoshijiro, to pronounce them guilty or not. They would be called back later to hear their sentences.

If the accused had any remaining hopes, they were extinguished with the first verdicts. A score of army and navy men were swiftly convicted. While the majority judges did find several defendants not guilty on some of the counts, all twenty-five of the accused would be convicted on at least some charges. Unlike at Nuremberg, where three senior German defendants were cleared, there were no outright acquittals.

Webb declared that General Doihara Kenji, whom Mei Ruao had glared down at the opening of the trial, was deeply involved in starting and waging a war of aggression against China. "We find him to be guilty," Webb intoned, of preparing and executing wars against China, the United States, the British Commonwealth, Holland, and the Soviet Union. As commander of the Seventh Area Army in Borneo, Sumatra, Java, and Malaya, he was convicted of war crimes for not providing adequate food and medicine to Allied prisoners of war.

Field Marshal Hata Shunroku was pronounced guilty as a former army minister and a commander of Japanese forces in China. While the tribunal could not convict him for direct orders to commit war crimes in China, it did so for command responsibility: either he knew about the atrocities his troops were committing and did nothing to prevent them, or he was so indifferent that he did not find out whether his underlings were obeying orders for the humane treatment of prisoners of war and civilians. He was convicted of waging aggressive war against China, the United States, the British Commonwealth, and Holland, although not the Soviet Union.

That acquittal on Soviet charges would be repeated over and over. Major General Ivan Zaryanov and the Soviet prosecutors proved disastrously incapable of winning over non-Soviet judges. With two separate charges of aggression for the border clashes, the Soviets managed to secure just five convictions, while nineteen counts were ruled not guilty. No other country had such a lopsided ratio. The Soviet prosecution even managed to get Tojo acquitted on one count, the only time he was ruled not guilty.

Baron Hiranuma Kiichiro was the first civilian up. As president of the privy council, prime minister, and home minister, he was held to be a member of the conspiracy, actively supporting the aggressive plans of the militarists. At a meeting of senior statesmen advising the emperor soon before Pearl Harbor, the reactionary aristocrat had argued that war was inevitable, which was enough to get him convicted for waging aggressive war against the United States. He was further found guilty of waging war against China, the British Commonwealth, Holland, and the Soviet Union, although not France. For lack of evidence, he was not guilty on two counts of war crimes.

Next came another former powerful civilian, Hirota Koki. As prime minister in 1936, the judges rebuked him for adopting a dangerous policy of domination. As foreign minister during the invasion of China in 1937, he was held responsible for pressing to subjugate the country and topple the Nationalist government. While Hirota's defense counsel had portrayed him as a diplomat seeking peace, the judges concluded that he was never willing to give up the gains Japan had made, and consistently agreed to use force if diplomacy did not realize Japan's demands. Still, the tribunal held that he had advised against the Pacific War in 1941, and thus he had not been proved guilty of aggression against the United States, the British Commonwealth, and Holland. Nor was there proof of aggression against the Soviet Union or France.

The judges found no evidence that Hirota had ordered or permitted the abuse of Allied prisoners of war, but convicted him of war crimes for the Nanjing massacre. As foreign minister at the time, he was condemned for not insisting to the cabinet that the atrocities be stopped, relying on empty assurances from the army. "His inaction amounted to criminal negligence," Webb said.

The judges hammered General Itagaki Seishiro, another of Mei's prime suspects, who was found guilty of planning and waging wars of aggression against China, the United States, the British Commonwealth, Holland, and the Soviet Union. He was held to have engineered the Mukden clash in September 1931, and then led the creation of the puppet state of Manchukuo. As army minister during the China war, he participated in meetings that decided to destroy the Nationalist government in China and create a puppet regime there. He had backed an unrestricted military alliance with Nazi Germany and Italy.

For a few of the war's final months, Itagaki held a command headquartered in Singapore with responsibility for Java, Sumatra, Malaya, and Borneo. Only the prison camps in Singapore were under his direct control, but he was in charge of supplying food and medical needs for the rest. "During this period the conditions in these camps were unspeakably bad," Webb declared, with grossly inadequate food, medicine, and hospitals. The judges rejected Itagaki's claim that Allied attacks on Japanese shipping made it hard to supply these far-flung areas, holding him "responsible for the deaths or sufferings of thousands of people whose adequate maintenance was his duty." The judges convicted him of ordering or permitting war crimes against Allied prisoners of war and civilian detainees.

.   .   .

Marquis Kido Koichi looked fretful as his verdict was read.[10] Despite the efforts of General Headquarters and the prosecution to suggest he had tricked his monarch, holding him guilty would be as close as the Tokyo trial would come to convicting the emperor of Japan.

The judges firmly rejected Kido's presentation of himself as a staunch foe of the militarists. To make it easier to convict him but not the emperor, the judges threw the book at him for his actions before becoming lord keeper of the privy seal in June 1940. As education minister and home minister in 1937–39, Webb pronounced, he "adopted the views of the conspirators and devoted himself wholeheartedly to their policy." Although Kido was found not guilty for the conquest of Indochina and the border clashes with the Soviet Union, he was convicted for aggression against China. He had zealously supported the China war, seeking military and political domination there, resisting efforts to make peace. Yet although he had been in the cabinet during the Nanjing massacre, the judges modestly held there was not enough evidence to convict him for failing to prevent them.

The judges treaded gingerly around Kido's role at the Imperial Palace, but found that he had used his sway to promote the domination of China and all of Asia: "As Lord Keeper of the Privy Seal, Kido was in a specially advantageous position to advance the conspiracy." Although he had some hesitations before Pearl Harbor, the court held him "largely instrumental" in installing Tojo as prime minister, while the judges studiously ignored the possibility that the emperor could have overruled his lord keeper and picked a less belligerent prime minister. Implicitly admitting that the emperor could have done more to stop the war, the judges blamed Kido for the monarch's quiescence: "He refrained from advising the Emperor to take any stand against war either at the last or earlier when it might have been more effective."

The best news for the Imperial Palace was that the judges held that the lord keeper could not be held responsible for war crimes against Allied prisoners and civilians after Pearl Harbor. This implied that there was nothing that Kido, and perhaps by extension the emperor, could have done to rein in the military from these crimes. Yet for empowering Tojo and not resisting the rush to war in 1941, Kido was found guilty of aggression against the United States, the British Commonwealth, and Holland—which made it conceivable that the emperor himself might have been judged guilty too.

·   ·   ·

General Matsui Iwane was the most prominent defendant on trial for atrocities at Nanjing. Yet the judges dismissively depicted him as a second-tier warlord, sufficiently out of the loop to be acquitted of being part of the conspiracy and found not guilty of aggression against the United States, the British Commonwealth, Holland, and the Soviet Union. To Mei's chagrin, he was even acquitted of aggression against China. His tours of duty there in 1937–38 were not held in themselves as the waging of aggressive war. Nor had the prosecution given sufficient evidence that he had known of the criminal character of the war in China—although it was a little hard to see how he could really have believed Japan was merely engaged in self-defense there.

In December 1937, he had been commander in chief of the Central China Area Army as it seized Nanjing. The court concluded that over six or seven weeks, more than a hundred thousand people were killed there, and thousands of women were raped. Despite Japanese denials, the court ruled that "the contrary evidence of neutral witnesses of different nationalities and undoubted responsibility is overwhelming." Matsui made a triumphal entry into Nanjing a few days after it fell, and admitted hearing of wrongdoing of his army from the Kempeitai and consular officials; daily reports of the atrocities had been made by foreigners in the city to Japanese diplomats, who had passed them to the Japanese government in Tokyo. "The Tribunal is satisfied that Matsui knew what was happening," Webb said.

"He was in command of the Army responsible for these happenings," Webb announced. "He knew of them. He had the power, as he had the duty, to control his troops and to protect the unfortunate citizens of Nanking. He must be held criminally responsible for his failure to discharge this duty." Yet the court did not have sufficient evidence to convict Matsui of ordering or permitting the atrocities. He was only found guilty on a single count, for failing to prevent war crimes at Nanjing.

The other senior army officer accused for Nanjing was Muto Akira, then a colonel serving as vice chief of staff under Matsui. Like his superior officer, he was portrayed as peripheral to the major decisions, and cleanly acquitted for aggression against France and the Soviet Union. Only when he became chief of the military affairs bureau in 1939 was he deemed a leading part of the conspiracy, making him guilty for aggression against the United States, the British Commonwealth, and Holland. The judges convicted him of aggression against China, apparently for contributing to the war effort in his powerful post.

As for Nanjing, the judges concluded, "We have no doubt that Muto knew, as Matsui knew, that atrocities were being committed over a period of many weeks." Yet they ruled that Muto in his subordinate position could do nothing to stop the slaughter—a baffling conclusion, predicated on the notion that a vice chief of staff was powerless. Mei was distraught. If this logic was to be taken seriously, it would gut the doctrine of command responsibility, placing guilt only at the very most senior ranks.

Acquitted for the Nanjing massacre, Muto was undone by his subsequent promotions. Commanding troops in northern Sumatra, he was held responsible for the starvation, torture, and murder of Allied prisoners of war, and for the massacre of civilians. Late in the war, as chief of staff to General Yamashita Tomoyuki in the Philippines, the judges held that Muto was in a position "very different from that which he held during the so-called 'Rape of Nanking.' He was now in a position to influence policy." As such, the judges held him responsible for a campaign of massacre and torture against Filipino civilians. He was found guilty of ordering and permitting war crimes, and of failing to take adequate steps to prevent war crimes in the Philippines.

The knottiest cases were three civilian ministers who had claims to be innocent.

Kaya Okinori, as finance minister, was the first defendant who—as proved by secret army records that the judges had not seen—had actively opposed the attack on the United States in 1941. While he was acquitted on war crimes for lack of evidence, he was condemned for formulating aggressive policies and for making economic and financial preparations for war. Although Kaya had not been as resolutely against war with the United States as Togo Shigenori, the judges might have ruled differently had they had the full records of the liaison conference where he had begged for more negotiations, warning that victory was impossible and that Japan's centuries of national existence were at risk. With no apparent sense that they were judging on an incomplete record, the majority found him guilty of waging aggressive war first against China, and then the United States, the British Commonwealth, and Holland in 1941.

Shigemitsu Mamoru, a former foreign minister with influential friends in Western countries, was one of the least blameworthy men on trial. Since he had not testified on his own behalf, his record was left unclear. Still, the judges easily acquitted him of being part of the conspiracy; they knew that he had repeatedly opposed the militarists' policies. He had never gone beyond the proper functions as ambassador to the Soviet Union, Britain, and China. Yet as foreign minister in 1943–45, the judges concluded that he was fully aware that Japan was waging a war of aggression. Paradoxically, his own antiwar efforts were held against him. He knew full well, the judges held, that the conspirators had caused the war, having argued against their bellicose policies; yet he had nevertheless "played a principal part in waging that war." For that he was found guilty of aggression against China, the United States, the British Commonwealth, Holland, and France, although not the Soviet Union.

As foreign minister he had received a steady stream of protests from the Allies about crimes against their prisoners of war, which the Foreign Ministry merely processed for the domineering military. Shigemitsu must have been suspicious that prisoners were being abused, the judges held. Despite his responsibility as a cabinet member, he "took no adequate steps to have the matter investigated. . . . He should have pressed the matter, if necessary to the point of resigning." This argument was perplexing: was is not possible that a minister could be working against war crimes even short of resigning in protest? What allowances did the judges make for the difficulty of effective civilian protest against the army in a highly militarized wartime climate? Moreover, the majority judges' argument would have sounded rather more convincing if they had not just acquitted Muto Akira for war crimes at Nanjing without making any such demands that he too should have resigned in protest.

While the tribunal acquitted Shigemitsu of ordering or permitting war crimes, he was found guilty of failing to prevent war crimes. But then the majority judges, in a fit of bad conscience, added a fretful note in mitigation of his sentence—the only time they did so. Webb announced, "we take into account that Shigemitsu was in no way involved in the formulation of the conspiracy; that he waged no war of aggression until he became Foreign Minister in April 1943, by which time his country was deeply involved in a war . . . ; and in the matter of war crimes that the military completely controlled Japan while he was Foreign Minister so that it would have required great resolution for any Japanese to condemn them."

As Togo Shigenori awaited his fate, his mind was on educating his young grandsons: "I think the basic thing is that in childhood they have an ambition to be a great man, but also that we educate them to be always honest and take a way of fairness."[11] The verdict upon him was the most glaring injustice of the Tokyo trial. Following MacArthur's original vision of a speedy trial for the Pearl Harbor cabinet, the judgment said that his "principal association" with war crimes was his few months serving as foreign minister in Tojo Hideki's cabinet.

The judges did not have the records of internal debates in the liaison conferences and imperial conferences in the autumn of 1941 that showed Togo's anguished opposition to the war. Yet they did have considerable evidence of his antiwar labors from his own detailed and persuasive testimony—an extraordinary performance which the majority judges ignored. Even Tojo Hideki had corroborated Togo's sworn statement that the foreign minister had only joined the cabinet to try to prevent the war. "From the date of his first appointment until the outbreak of the Pacific War he participated in the planning and preparing for the war," Webb pronounced, with no modesty about how wrong he was. "He attended Cabinet meetings and conferences and concurred in all decisions adopted." This was simply false: only at the end had Togo, despairing, gone along with the choice for war. He was, for all intents and purposes, being condemned for being in the room.

As with Shigemitsu, Togo was condemned for failing to quit the cabinet. Webb declared, "when the negotiations failed and war became inevitable, rather than resign in protest he continued in office and supported the war. To do anything else he said would have been cowardly." For the court, the only one of his deeds that counted was his concurrence with war at the last moment—something for which he could reasonably be faulted, but only as part of a complete record. In fact, he had testified about threatening to resign on at least two occasions in 1941, trying to get the army to show some flexibility over withdrawing troops from China and Indochina. He had nearly quit after the fiery liaison conference of November 1, according to his testimony, agreeing to stay on as foreign minister for fear that he would be replaced with someone more bellicose. Making him out as a petty hypocrite, the judges complained that he had resigned in September 1942 over a cabinet squabble. Despite such a conspicuously short stint as foreign minister, the judges were unswayed by his own explanation that he had quit over the domination of the new Greater East Asia Ministry—an expression of dismay at the violent path Japan was following during the war.

Togo did get acquitted on several charges. The judges cleared him of aggression against the Soviet Union, saying he had done nothing worse than sign an agreement setting a borderline to help resolve the 1939 battle. Like Shigemitsu, Togo was accused of war crimes for his role as foreign minister in processing Allied protests. Here the judges went easier on him than Shigemitsu. They accepted that in the months after Pearl Harbor he had tried to uphold the observance of the laws of war. He had passed on the Allied complaints and in several cases there had been some action to improve conditions. By the time he resigned in 1942, the tribunal ruled, the war crimes committed by Japanese troops were not so notorious that he must have known about them. When he returned as foreign minister in the spring of 1945, Allied protests had accumulated, which he passed on to the proper military authorities. The judges concluded that there was not sufficient proof of Togo's neglect of his duty to prevent war crimes.

The balance was harsh. While Togo was acquitted of conventional war crimes, he was found guilty of being part of the conspiracy, and of aggression against China, the United States, the British Commonwealth, and Holland. Unlike Shigemitsu, the judges said nothing in mitigation. Standing almost alone before Pearl Harbor, Togo had in fact heatedly told the military to "give up the idea of going to war." Now in blind judgment, he was convicted along with those same militarists as part of a common conspiracy for aggression.

Tojo Hideki, the most famous name, was second to last. At sixty-three, he was as defiant as ever. Soon before, he had told his American defense lawyer, "At the beginning of the trial I was worried that the responsibility of the Emperor might be questioned. I feel at rest now that the doubt has been cleared. From the beginning I was ready to take the entire responsibility for the war, but regrettably others were brought into the trial." Thanking his lawyer for a vigorous defense, he said, "I can only say it is a victor's trial."[12]

Tojo stared over Webb's head.[13] The verdict on him was as stern as it was unsurprising. "He bears major responsibility for Japan's criminal attacks on her neighbors," the Australian judge declared.

He was ruled a principal in the conspiracy since 1937, when he had become chief of staff of the Kwantung Army. He planned and prepared to attack the Soviet Union, setting up Manchuria as a base for that. He urged further assaults on China. As vice minister of the army, he mobilized Japanese society for war and opposed a compromise peace with China. Next he became army minister in 1940: "thereafter his history is largely the history of the successive steps by which the conspirators planned and waged wars of aggression against Japan's neighbors. . . . He advocated and furthered the aims of the conspiracy with ability, resolution and persistency."

Becoming prime minister from October 1941, as well as army minister, he consistently supported keeping troops in China, plundering the country for Japan's benefit, and crushing the Nationalist government. In the negotiations with the Americans before Pearl Harbor, he resolutely insisted on terms that would preserve "the fruits of her aggression against China" and bring about Japan's domination of Asia. The judges roundly rejected his claims to have acted in legitimate self-defense. "The importance of the leading part he played in securing the decision to go to war in support of that policy cannot be over-estimated," Webb intoned. While he was not guilty for the 1939 clash with the Soviet Union, when he was out of office, the tribunal found him guilty as part of the conspiracy and guilty of aggression after aggression: against China, the United States, the British Commonwealth, Holland, and France.

While most defendants were found guilty of failing to take adequate steps to prevent war crimes, the judges did not bother to rule on that count. Instead they convicted Tojo for the uglier charge of ordering, authorizing, or permitting war crimes. He was held responsible for ordering that prisoners who did not work should not eat, which led to suffering and death among the sick and the wounded who were forced to work. He had been head of the Army Ministry, responsible for caring for Allied prisoners of war and civilian captives with food, shelter, medicine, and hospitals. He had also been head of the Home Ministry, with similar duties toward Allied civilians detained in Japan. Above all, he had been head of the government, with all the responsibility that implied.

"The barbarous treatment of prisoners and internees was well known to Tojo," Webb declared. "He took no adequate steps to punish offenders and to prevent the commission of similar offences in the future." He was in meetings where the high death rates in prison camps were discussed, and he was responsible for covering up information about the real conditions in those camps from the outside world. Tojo knew about and did not disapprove of the "shocking attitude" that the China conflict was not recognized as a war, a policy that systematically deprived Chinese captives of the rights due to prisoners of war.

The judges found that he had recommended using prisoners of war to construct the Burma–Thailand railway but made no adequate arrangements to house and feed them, nor to care for those who got sick in the tropical climate. He sent an officer to investigate the camps along the line, but did nothing more than prosecute one company commander. Webb declared, "The shocking condition of the prisoners in 1944, when Tojo's Cabinet fell, and the enormous number of prisoners who had died from lack of food and medicines is conclusive proof that Tojo took no proper steps to care for them."

Tojo had known that many prisoners had died on the Bataan death march but did not call for a report, nor punish any Japanese officers. On a visit to the Philippines afterward, he made perfunctory inquiries but took no action. His explanation, the judges noted with scorn, was that Japanese commanders in the field were not subject to specific orders from Tokyo.

As the head of government, Tojo had knowingly and willfully refused to carry out Japan's duty to enforce the conduct of the laws of war. "The Tribunal finds Tojo guilty," Webb said, for ordering or allowing war crimes.

After he finished reading the verdicts, Webb for the first time officially revealed the disarray among the judges. "The Member for India dissents from the majority Judgment and has filed a statement of his reasons for such dissent," he said. The French and Dutch judges too, he said, had written dissents.

This was a bombshell. Having just convicted all the defendants, the court now revealed that three of its members doubted the judgment.

With Radhabinod Pal's dissent an open secret around the court, all of the Japanese defendants petitioned that each of the dissenting opinions be read aloud. The judges swiftly dismissed the plea. All the dissents and opinions would be filed into the record, Webb said, but not aired in open court.[14] The dissents were available to the supreme commander, the defense lawyers, and others who wanted them, and they would eventually be published. While the press quickly reported the gist of the dissenting opinions, they had less impact than the judgment itself.[15]

Adding to the confusion, Webb announced that the majority could not even agree with itself. The Philippine judge had filed a separate opinion concurring with his fellow majority judges. And disconcertingly, Webb gave a final kick of frustration at the majority judges who had privately defied him. He said that he generally agreed with the majority about the facts and was not dissenting, but wanted to add his own "brief statement of my reasons for upholding the Charter and the jurisdiction of the Tribunal and of some general considerations that influenced me in deciding on the sentences."

At 3:30 p.m., Webb, his hands clasped together, adjourned for a break before reading the sentences.[16]

WHO BY ROPE

There was an excruciating pause. The convicted men endured fifteen minutes of profound dread.

The judges filed back in for the last time. One by one, each accused was marched into the stilled auditorium alone to hear his fate, led by a U.S. lieutenant colonel who had overseen them at Sugamo Prison. A half dozen U.S. military policemen stood behind the newly convicted war criminals.[17] "Each one stood pinned to the courtroom by thousands of eyes—some friendly and sympathetic, the majority stern and uncom-promising," wrote MacArthur's political adviser.[18] After being sentenced by Webb, who spoke softly but firmly, each man would be marched out alone. None of them protested or tried to blurt out a last speech. "The images of the defendants, earphones on and standing like clay figures, overflowed with intensity," reported the *Asahi Shimbun*. "Particularly notable was the fact that the defendants who received severe sentences simply nodded to the court and exited the courtroom without saying a word."[19]

The first of them, General Araki Sadao, got life imprisonment. Then a ghastly hush fell as the court meted out death for the first time. Webb intoned, "Accused Doihara Kenji, on the Counts of the Indictment on which you have been convicted, the International Military Tribunal for the Far East sentences you to death by hanging." The condemned general calmly removed his headphones, bowed to the court, and walked out.

A host of army and navy men got imprisonment for life. They stood at attention and bowed. One of them, the elderly General Minami Jiro, a former army minister, fumbled with his headphones, seemingly bewil-dered and uncomprehending.[20]

Baron Hiranuma Kiichiro, the first civilian politician to be sentenced, also got life imprisonment. So did another former prime minister, a min-ister, and the ambassador to Italy. Kaya Okinori, the finance minister who had argued against attacking the United States, got life in prison.

"What struck me most was the dignified bearing of the accused," reported the Indian political representative in Tokyo. "It was somewhat pathetic to see some of the older men tottering and hobbling to the dock to receive their sentences. None of them appeared to be moved by the sentence, presumably because they were all prepared for it."[21]

Hirota Koki was not. He had reason to hope to survive. Some noto-rious military men had avoided the rope. Gray and quiet, the former prime minister closed his eyes when Webb announced his fate: "Accused Hirota Koki, on the Counts of the Indictment on which you have been convicted, the International Military Tribunal for the Far East sentences you to death by hanging." The doomed man, visibly stunned, turned to lock eyes with his weeping family in the gallery. He would be the only civilian to go to the gallows. Surprised Japanese reporters murmured, "Harsh! Harsh!"[22]

General Itagaki Seishiro would hang. He removed his headphones and paused gravely for a moment. The same fate was given to General Kimura Heitaro, a vice minister of the army and commander of Japanese forces in Burma.

Marquis Kido Koichi, the top adviser to the emperor of Japan, bowed to the court. He was sentenced to prison for life.

General Matsui Iwane, convicted for failing to prevent war crimes at Nanjing, was sentenced to death by hanging.

So was General Muto Akira, who had been the main target of the Philippine prosecutors.

Shigemitsu Mamoru, pressing his hands on the bench, found out what the judges meant by mitigation. He got the lightest sentence of anyone, seven years imprisonment starting from when he had been arraigned.

Togo Shigenori was sentenced to twenty years in prison. This was the second-lightest punishment. Yet at sixty-six years old with heart disease, he was unlikely to see the end of those two decades. His wife, Edith Togo, fainted when told his sentence, then lamented loudly that the trial had been unfair.[23]

The hush deepened as Tojo Hideki filed in and bowed to the judges. He put on his headphones. Japanese spectators leaned forward. The American military police stiffened. Tojo and everyone else knew what was coming. Two of his sons watched from the gallery. In a clear, firm voice, Webb declared, "Accused Tojo Hideki, on the Counts of the Indictment on which you have been convicted, the International Military Tribunal for the Far East sentences you to death by hanging." Tojo, resigned, gave a bow to the court. He was the seventh war criminal sentenced to die. "He was merely a brown, bald, shabby little man," crowed the Associated

Tojo Hideki listens to Sir William Webb sentence him to death, November 12, 1948.

Press. Outside the Ichigaya courtroom, when told the sentence, his wife and daughter wept beneath a tree.[24]

The last defendant, General Umezu Yoshijiro—who had signed the surrender aboard the USS *Missouri*—got life in jail. He was already slowly dying of advanced colorectal cancer.[25] That made a total of sixteen sentences of life imprisonment.

As Webb at last fell silent, there was chaos in the courtroom. Reporters raced to the telephones. Families of the convicted men sat in shock.

At 4:12 p.m., the Tokyo trial adjourned.[26]

The World Reacts

Nine of the convicted men, including four sentenced to die, handed poems in classical form to their defense lawyers after the sentencing. These were published in the Japanese press. "My conscience is as clear as the sun and moon," declared Kaya Okinori. Baron Hiranuma Kiichiro had law on his mind: "The rule of law, the rule of form are at an end/ And yet, remains a rule of truth and the nation is at peace."

Some condemned men were wistful. Matsui invoked the familiar symbol of eternal Japan: "Whether a cloud, whether a peak, I cannot tell./ The clear sky from a distance is a mist/ And yet, behind that pallid mist/ There soars unchanging an eternal peak/ And with the dawning of the light,/ I know it is Mount Fuji." Hirota, surprised to be dying, chose an image often used to symbolize the loss of young soldiers: "In spring, men like cherry blossoms fall,/ In fall, men like sparkling dews, purge themselves."

Tojo, too, went with that metaphor in his haiku: "Oh, look, see how the cherry blossoms fall mutely."[27] In a letter that he wanted made public, he said that he deserved his death sentence and was sorry that the judges had not allowed him to shoulder sole responsibility. It was a great comfort to him that the emperor was not involved. His death sentence, he felt, did not absolve him of responsibility for the wartime hardships of his countrymen. Although determinedly unremorseful about Pearl Harbor, Tojo admitted that atrocities against Allied prisoners of war were "utterly deplorable," accepting responsibility for failing to drive home to Japanese troops the kindness of the emperor. Still, he claimed that only a small part of the army had committed war crimes, and neither the Japanese nation nor the army as a whole was responsible for them.

Matsui, sentenced to hang for his command role during the Nanjing massacre, privately blamed his divisional commanders. In so doing, he suggested how the slaughter had resulted from the shared cruelty of senior army officers. The Nanjing incident, he told a Buddhist priest at Sugamo, was "a terrible disgrace." After his triumphal march into Nanjing, he claimed, he had asked for memorial services for the Chinese dead as well, only to be scorned by his senior officers as he wept tears of rage. He had told his top officers, including Prince Asaka, that "after all our efforts to enhance the Imperial prestige, everything had been lost in one moment through the brutalities of the soldiers." His officers, he said, laughed at him. One of his division commanders asked, "What's wrong about it?"[28]

Emperor Hirohito and the empress listened to the sentencing on the radio. The Imperial Palace only let it be known that he sighed and looked mournful.[29]

Tojo's defense lawyer, Kiyose Ichiro, told the *Asahi Shimbun*, "Tojo's mind is eased very much by the verdict, knowing he has given no additional trouble to the Emperor."[30] In fact, with Hirohito's wartime counselors found guilty as war criminals, including his own lord keeper and his handpicked prime ministers, his throne hung in the balance. The rumors of abdication became a frenzy. It was fortunate for the imperial family that nobody outside of Sugamo Prison knew that the condemned Matsui was blaming the unindicted Prince Asaka for the Nanjing massacre.[31] Despite all this pressure to step down, in private, an Imperial Palace adviser reached out to a senior U.S. diplomat in Tokyo to say that on the day of the sentencing, the emperor had written to MacArthur to say that he had definitely decided not to abdicate.[32]

Harry Truman congratulated the prosecution for having "contributed immeasurably to the cause of humanity and the further development of international law," while MacArthur praised "a high standard of justice which has exemplified to the Japanese people the moral concepts which underlie our own traditional judicial processes."[33] Joseph Keenan publicly pronounced the trial "another milestone in the quest of mankind for peace," although he found the judgment too lenient.[34] Yet many citizens in the Allied countries were frustrated by the verdicts.

Mei Ruao publicly hailed the judgment as a "great historical document," declaring that "as a member of the majority judges from the very beginning to the end, I shall defend the majority judgment also from beginning to end." Yet he publicly broke with the majority on one crucial point, telling the Chinese press that the emperor should be tried as a major war criminal. Despite "plenty of evidence" to implicate Hirohito, he had been spared as a "matter of political consideration."[35]

At the invitation of the *Asahi Shimbun*, Mei wrote a generous open letter to the Japanese people, saying that they had not known about the atrocities in China, and hoping that the verdict would help to build peaceful cooperation between China and Japan.[36] In private, though, he was mortified by the acquittal of Matsui for aggression against China and Muto for atrocities in Nanjing, as well as the jail sentences given to some men whom China's government had hoped to hang. "The only soothing fact is that the most hated and heinous war criminals who have hurt us the most are on the list for heavy penalties," he wrote to the Chinese foreign minister, Wang Shijie. "You understand why, and there is no need to say much about that."[37]

Some Chinese newspapers demanded that Hirohito be punished too.[38] Having been hounded by his government about the Chinese people's rage, Mei humbly wrote that he did not "know if domestic public opinion is satisfied or dissatisfied." Questioning himself, he thought that having done his best, he "may not feel guilty in front of the people."[39]

Seizing a chance to embarrass the Nationalists, the Chinese Communist Party immediately declared itself "absolutely unsatisfied with the results of the trials." The *People's Daily* wrote that "because of America's protection, indulgence, and encouragement, the solemn International Military Tribunal for the Far East turned into a podium for war culprits such as Tojo to promote militarism."[40] In another article, the *People's Daily* scorned the jail sentences, while complaining that the judgment whitewashed Hirohito's responsibility for the war: "The Chinese people are satisfied with the sentences of the seven war criminals including Tojo, but cannot be satisfied with the other results of the trial."[41]

In the Philippines, despite satisfaction that Muto was sentenced to hang, anti-Japanese fury ran high. The *Bagong Buhay*, a Manila newspaper, warned that the Japanese were fundamentally a militaristic nation and would once again try to conquer their weaker neighbors. The *Manila Chronicle* challenged Tojo's complaint about a "trial by conquerors" by editorializing that the "conquerors were not America, Russia or China" but "freedom, justice and humanity."[42]

The British largely applauded the verdict, seen as a necessary continuation of Nuremberg.[43] The Tokyo trial, editorialized the left-wing *Manchester Guardian*, "has lacked Nuremberg's brutal decisiveness." It "has made legal history, but in quavering hesitant fashion." While pointing out that the victors were "forgetting such minor matters as the atom bombs' victims," it warned that sparing Hirohito "had a lamentable effect upon the legal fabric of the case. It is no good laying down a principle that crimes against peace mean—for the conquered—death, if one starts to discriminate."[44]

In Australia, the newspapers cried that the verdicts did not go far enough. "The Jap has not a soul to think in terms of decency," editorialized one newspaper with undisguised bigotry. "He is still as much a part of the jungle as the dank rot which infests a jungle."[45] Another wrote that the Japanese were pagans who believed that their own divine race was naturally superior, and could only be judged by "their own lower code."[46] *The Sydney Morning Herald* declared that the evidence was even more shocking and conclusive than expected.[47] Yet like Webb, many Australians fumed that the emperor—"this little man who declared war," as a Sydney tabloid columnist called him—had been spared. "Hard-boiled Americans admit that to hang Tojo and let Hirohito go free is screwy, but they argue that Hirohito is doing a vital job for America."[48]

The American press was dissatisfied. *The New York Times,* among the most upbeat, praised the documentation of Japanese aggression as a warning for the future. While bluffly assuring its readers that the legal problems in the case had been solved, it cautioned that the moral impact of the trial was lessened by the omission of the emperor from prosecution and the inclusion of a Soviet judge, whose country was pursuing the same policies the court was condemning. It praised "a law which strips away the protection of sovereignty in the case of aggressive war and makes such a war both an international and personal crime."[49] More dourly, *Time* magazine wrote, "After three years of war trials, . . . the world is no farther along than it was in 1945 to an understanding of whether these proceedings represent justice or victor's vengeance."[50]

EMBRACING DEFEAT

Large crowds gathered in central Tokyo around the special four-page extra editions rushed out by the big newspapers, with many Japanese copying down the sentences in their notebooks. Some said the penalties were entirely proper; others anxiously said that they could not express what they really thought. At the Diet, legislators gathered around the radio to hear the punishments, before silently filing into the assembly room. The speaker let out a loud sigh but refused to comment.[51]

The Tokyo trial's verdicts received considerable support and muted opposition from the Japanese public, according to the careful soundings taken confidentially by General Headquarters. Given that this was a foreign court hanging and jailing famous Japanese, the Allies were pleasantly surprised by the Japanese national response.

To gauge Japanese public opinion under censorship, General Headquarters routinely opened and read the private letters that Japanese wrote to each other. This snooping found a split Japanese verdict on the verdicts: 39 percent of the mail opposed them, with 34 percent approving, and 27 percent not giving a clear opinion either way—unsurprised by the verdict but confused about the moral and legal foundations for the court's conclusions. For the Allied occupiers, this came as a relief.

There were few bitter denunciations. The bulk of the Japanese critics felt sorry for the convicted war criminals and their families, or recoiled to see old men going to the gallows. Only a few ardent nationalists still called them heroes. The judgment had improved the reputation of the Tokyo trial even to the skeptics; although previously there had often been letters saying that the court was driven by revenge, now only a handful wrote that "might is right."

Many Japanese praised the trial's fairness, impressed by its openness and the performance of the defense. "Every effort has been made to ensure justice," wrote one. Younger Japanese saw the trial as marking "the end of the era of militarism in Japan." The lower-income Japanese praising the judgment took it personally, with one writing that "the wicked men who caused us all this suffering deserve to be punished." The parents and widows of killed soldiers were especially emotional; one wrote that "now, at last, they can rest in peace." Most of the supporters saw the verdict as justice, saying that the war criminals set to hang "are only reaping the just consequences of their evil deeds." Strikingly, more than one-third of those Japanese who supported the verdicts expressed a sense of national guilt, rather than leaving all the blame on their wartime leaders. One letter writer insisted that "the responsibility for the war rests not only with Tojo, but with all the nation. We blindly obeyed."[52]

In addition to rifling through other people's mail, the American occupiers tracked Japanese public sentiment through Counter Intelligence Corps field detachments in all prefectures.[53] Out of fifty-three localities (which mostly corresponded to Japan's prefectures), the Counter Intelligence Corps found a total of twenty-six in approval of the Tokyo trial's judgment—almost half—while there was opposition in thirteen. In twelve localities, people were indifferent. Among those approving of the verdicts were demobilized soldiers, leftists, Communists, and Koreans. In five localities, the general public felt that "the entire nation is guilty"; in four localities, people believed that the emperor was guilty, although in one of those they were nevertheless relieved that he had been spared.

The opposition to the court was mostly right-wing, including former army officers and some educated people. Some of them blamed the Chinese for the death sentences. In six localities, the sentences were seen as too severe, with more death sentences than expected. There was overt anti-American sentiment only in Ishikawa Prefecture, mostly from veterans. In four localities, there were signature campaigns asking to reduce the sentences, although people were afraid of reprisals for doing so. According to the Counter Intelligence Corps, some Japanese complained that the Tokyo trial was dictatorial.[54]

Similar patterns came up in street interviews by reporters and in General Headquarters' unscientific soundings of elite Japanese opinion, with considerable support for the judgment among liberals and leftists.[55] "The verdicts were fair," said Ozaki Yukio, a famously independent-minded constitutionalist who had been in the Diet for many decades.[56] Against the death penalty on principle, he made an exception for the seven war criminals bound for the gallows. Tokuda Kyuichi, the secretary general of the Japanese Communist Party, who had spent eighteen years in jail before being freed by the Allies, reckoned the trial a success, although wishing that the sentences had been tougher. Kato Shizue, a Diet member and a leading feminist, said, "Intelligent Japanese long ago decided that the punishment of the war criminals was inevitable, and they think the verdicts were just."[57]

More warily, the British political representative warned that there was active Japanese sympathy with the war criminals. He noted some support for Shigemitsu Mamoru and Hirota Koki, although not for Kido, who was seen as having deceived the emperor. Most Japanese, he reported, thought that the emperor was guilty but still did not want him to abdicate. Even among the younger generation, he saw little real resentment of the war criminals except for their failure. He warned that when Japanese liberals framed the judgment as a condemnation of the whole Japanese people, that would in time generate sympathy for the war criminals. Some Japanese admitted that "the tacit condemnation of the whole people embraces the Emperor himself. Tojo's view that the decisions of the court represent 'victor's justice' is probably echoed in many minds but finds little open expression."[58]

The Japanese press covered the judgment with fascination. While India's political representative in Japan noted that the media was uniformly in

favor of the convictions and sentences, he astutely warned that no newspaper could dare to defy General Headquarters by publishing criticism.
He reported that in private Japanese officials believed that there was no
conspiracy to wage war and the convicted men were not directly responsible for crimes against humanity. While they accepted that the China
war could be seen as Japanese aggression, they saw the war against the
United States and the British Empire as self-defense.[59]

Japanese editorials, operating under Allied censorship, urged a national
reckoning with war guilt. "We must not allow ourselves to think that
the sentences meted out to a few individuals absolve the Japanese people
but must realize that we were all on trial and have all been found guilty,"
exhorted the liberal *Mainichi Shimbun*. The conservative *Yomiuri Shimbun*
praised the establishment of aggression as an international crime and
denounced any sympathy for the war criminals as the promotion of fascism. "We fear that with the passage of time much of our united hate for
our militarists has faded and some misguided people even regard them
as heroes being punished for the misdeeds of the nation," cautioned a
Yomiuri editorial. "This is, of course, absurd and what we must reflect
upon is why, as a people, we were so easily misled and controlled by these
criminals." The *Jiji Shimpo* editorialized that it was hard to imagine a
more fair judgment, only regretting that the Japanese people had not had
the chance to try the war criminals themselves. While one *Jiji Shimpo*
article doubted that it was "right for judges from victor nations to convict
the defeated on the basis of ex-post facto law," it also praised the "rectitude
and thoroughness" of the trial.[60]

The liberal *Asahi Shimbun*, with a circulation of three and a half million, led the embrace of the verdicts. As its managing editor privately
wrote to Webb, "We Japanese do not take the trials as judgements only
on Hideki Tojo and twenty-four defendants, but as the bitterest criticism
to Japan and all Japanese. Consequently we cannot help being deeply
impressed by the final decision." Praising the tribunal's intensive study of
Japan's real history, he declared, "Through the lessons from the trial we
are just now standing at the start-line for a new life."[61]

A prominent *Asahi* columnist, embracing a popular "hatred for war,"
pointed out the broader responsibility of citizens who had supported the
convicted war criminals, as well as proposing Japanese national trials
for fanatical young officers who had driven the country "to fascism and
war."[62] Another *Asahi* writer, scorning Tojo for arguing fine points of
international law, wrote that the Japanese "have learned much through
the entire process of the trial. . . . We, in our present restricted daily lives,

have realized a great windfall simply by being able to see through this window the actions of people representing eleven countries, and hear the footsteps of the world."[63] Another columnist called for more Japanese attention to "crimes of cruelty," urging its readers to remember the Nanjing horrors: "If the same events had taken place in Tokyo or Osaka, and our beloved relatives and friends had met with the same fate, our blood would surely have boiled."[64]

CHAPTER 28

Dissensus

"T HE TEAM WORK HAS been admirable," Sir William Webb brazenly informed Australia's prime minister. "After two and one-half
years of strenuous labor and much difference about important matters of
opinion we part eleven good friends." This glossed past three dissents, one
of them revolutionary, and two separate opinions—one of them written
by himself—as well as the sour feelings left by his bullying ways.[1]

The immediate consequence of this explosion of dissents and separate
opinions was a hasty scramble by the American defense lawyers to try to
save their clients. They asked General Douglas MacArthur for copies of
the dissents, which indicated that "a substantial minority of the Tribunal
was excluded from participation in the making up of the judgment and
verdict." They had been tipped off that most of the death sentences had
been approved with only six votes out of eleven judges and that none had
gotten more than seven votes.[2] General Headquarters replied only with
assurances from Webb that all the verdicts and sentences had received a
majority of the full court, meaning six out of eleven judges.[3]

More profoundly, these clashing viewpoints certainly demonstrated
that the judges had considerable independence. Yet they blighted the
credibility of the majority judgment. As the British bloc of judges had
feared, the discord in Tokyo even called the Nuremberg judgment into
question. Bert Röling's dissent was well reasoned and damaging. To the
consternation of General Headquarters, two opinions directly targeted
Emperor Hirohito, permanently tarnishing his name. Most importantly,
Radhabinod Pal's sweeping dissent—more than one thousand two hundred pages long—was a profound statement of an entirely different view
of global justice and World War II.

However legitimate on the merits, this quarreling undermined the impact of the Tokyo judgment.[4] Why should Japanese heed a verdict that could not satisfy so many of the judges themselves?

TARGETING THE EMPEROR

Webb's separate opinion grabbed the headlines for blasting Hirohito as in essence a leading war criminal who had escaped justice. He stated bluntly that the monarch had been spared for political reasons.[5] Mei Ruao made much the same points to the Chinese press.[6]

Joseph Keenan, after feuding with Webb throughout the trial over the emperor, casually admitted to reporters that there had been an Allied political decision to spare Hirohito. He claimed that he had wanted to haul the monarch into a court as a witness, if only to tell his side, but had been overruled by MacArthur. "The evidence showed the Emperor to be a weak character, in our own Occidental concept," said Keenan, "but always on the side of peace."[7]

MacArthur fumed privately that Webb was pandering to Australian public rage against the emperor, but decided that issuing a rebuttal would only add fuel to the fire.[8] The British government, too, was stunned that Webb was questioning the fairness of his own trial.[9] The Foreign Office drew up a memorandum arguing that the emperor was merely a constitutional figurehead who could not be held guilty.[10] "On general political grounds," wrote a Foreign Office functionary confidentially, "I feel sure that we should wish to resist any campaign to indict the Emperor as a war criminal."[11]

In his opinion, Webb bluntly wrote that the prosecution's own evidence had shown the "outstanding part" of the emperor in both starting and halting the war, with his authority "proved beyond question when he ended the war." Although toned down from earlier drafts, this was a final hard slap at General Headquarters for protecting the emperor. "The Emperor's authority was required for war," he wrote. "If he did not want war he should have withheld his authority."

He breezily dismissed the emperor's peril of getting assassinated, saying that was no excuse for committing the crime of launching aggressive war. Webb accepted that the emperor was always for peace but had taken his ministers' advice for war, probably against his own better judgment. Still, the emperor could not hide behind his advisers; he had chosen his actions. Even if he had only been a constitutional monarch, he "would not be excused for committing a crime at International Law on the advice of his Ministers." Since those advisers and ministers had just been convicted as war criminals, Webb implied that Hirohito would have been found guilty too.

"I do not suggest the Emperor should have been prosecuted," he added impeccably. "That is beyond my province. His immunity was, no doubt, decided upon in the best interests of all the Allied Powers." Instead, Webb argued that the tribunal should consider the immunity granted to the emperor to lighten the punishment of his convicted underlings, especially those sentenced to die. A court of British judges would surely "take into account, if it could, that the leader in the crime, although available for trial, had been granted immunity."

The rest of Webb's opinion was replete with legal score-settling with the majority who had spurned his views on jurisdiction. While he had written a full judgment of his own, he junked almost all of it because, he said, the majority agreed with him on most matters.

In a faint echo of his previous advocacy for natural law, he argued that international law could be "supplemented by rules of justice and general principles of law. . . . The natural law of nations is equal in importance to positive or voluntary." He cited a leading British jurist who contended that *modern International Law came and was received in the name of the law of nature.*" Yet he argued that the court's authority came not from natural law but from the charter, as well as Japan's acceptance of the terms of the Potsdam Declaration.

Although confident that aggressive war was a crime, he drew the line at charges for conspiracy for crimes that were never carried out. The court "has no authority to create a crime of naked conspiracy based on the Anglo-American concept," he wrote. Doing so would be "nothing short of judicial legislation."

Although Webb had convicted all twenty-five suspects, and said that he would have convicted two more for conventional war crimes, he remained leery of executions. He doubted that the death penalty would deter future criminals and worried that "[i]t may prove revolting to hang or shoot such old men." He argued that no war criminals should be sentenced to death for aggression alone, but also for committing war crimes and crimes against humanity. Undercutting his own argument that aggressive war was already criminal, he pointed out that the Nuremberg judges "took into account the fact that aggressive war not universally regarded as a justiciable crime" as they handed down their sentences.[12]

"Universal Conscience"

Several of Webb's most important themes were echoed by Henri Bernard of France. Yet his dissent was embarrassing because some of it was avoidable—the product of long months of needless estrangement from the majority, who had missed the chance to allay his concerns. Mei publicly scorned his opinion as "utterly incomprehensible."[13]

Most sensationally, Bernard also targeted Hirohito. He wrote that the prosecutors had chosen their targets wrongly, which was "particularly apparent and regrettable in regard to Emperor Hirohito whom the trial revealed could have been counted among the suspects." If there had been a criminal conspiracy, "it had a principal author who escaped all prosecution," with Bernard calling the defendants mere accomplices to the emperor. While the prosecution had downplayed it and the majority ignored it, Bernard quoted in full the damning entry from Marquis Kido Koichi's diary in which the emperor "ordered" Tojo "to act according to program" in attacking the United States.[14]

Even more boldly than Webb, Bernard justified the Tokyo trial on natural law. He argued that "natural and universal law" was the foundation of law and civil society, existing "outside and above nations." Individual criminal responsibility, he contended, was "inscribed in natural law." Since there was currently no universal authority to judge crimes against universal law, those states with actual power could set up courts—such as the Tokyo tribunal—to prosecute those who had violated natural law. Aggressive war "is and always has been a crime in the eyes of reason and universal conscience,—expressions of natural law upon which an international tribunal can and must base itself."

In many ways, Bernard was sympathetic to the majority, even largely accepting the Anglo-American notion of conspiracy. His real objections were mostly about deficiencies in procedure, which he thought might be grave enough to nullify the whole trial. He warned that the majority was really enacting a new version of international law, not just enforcing the law as it existed. He complained that the majority cavalierly took it for granted that army or navy commanders could always issue orders that would prevent conventional war crimes during the chaos of wartime; he would only convict officers who really were able to curb their subordinates.

His core objection was that, in practice, the accused had not been given the essential principles of a fair defense. The defendants had no opportunity to defend themselves before being indicted. The opinions of the dissenting judges had been quashed: there had not been oral deliberations among all eleven judges, and the judgment had been drafted by the majority. These procedural deficiencies left him uncertain about the guilt of the convicted suspects. "A verdict reached by a Tribunal after a defective procedure cannot be a valid one," he concluded.[15]

A DUTCH DISSENT

Throughout the trial, Bert Röling had stood out as one of the most principled judges, challenging judicial overreach, European colonialism, and Soviet expansionism.[16] In a thoughtful and wide-ranging dissent, he slipped his own government's leash. After letting the Dutch foreign minister read about his dissent in the newspapers, Röling secretly assured him that he regretted going public with his minority opinion. He had wanted to voice his disagreements only in private with the other judges. But since Pal and others insisted on making public dissents, Röling explained, his own silence would have seemed like an endorsement of the majority judgment.[17]

Röling's opinion, although ostentatiously scholarly, aimed at an audience of one: MacArthur. Since the supreme commander could review the penalties, Röling hoped to persuade him to spare five defendants. He thought that four civilians—Hirota Koki, Kido Koichi, Shigemitsu Mamoru, and Togo Shigenori—should be acquitted, and that Field Marshal Hata Shunroku had not been proven guilty beyond a reasonable doubt.

Most importantly, Röling doubted that aggressive war was really a crime. While he agreed that the court was bound by its charter, the charter itself must be limited by international law: "victorious powers have no authority to create new international crimes, but are bound by the provisions of existing international law." One by one, Röling knocked down the antiwar treaties and resolutions that were held to have made aggressive war a crime. Japan had quit the League of Nations. Two interwar treaties criminalizing aggressive war—the draft Treaty of Mutual Assistance of 1923 and the 1924 Geneva Protocol for the Pacific Settlement of International Disputes—never became law. The League had passed a 1927 resolution calling aggressive war "an international crime," but had specified no penalties; Röling said it was like constructing a roof before building the house. A 1928 resolution of the Pan-American Conference had declared aggression an international crime, but that could hardly apply to faraway Japan. Even the vaunted Kellogg-Briand Pact did not mention criminality nor individual responsibility. Worse, many of the signatories—including the United States, Japan, Britain, and France—

had specified that they retained their right of self-defense, and they themselves would judge whether they were fighting in self-defense.

While some jurists had treated the Kellogg-Briand Pact as evidence of a new custom in international law, he rejected that: customary international law only counted if it was shown in state behavior, yet the actual way that governments had dealt with each other since 1928 hardly demonstrated such a transformation. The idea of individual criminal guilt for aggression, he wrote, did not solidify in U.S. policy until as late as June 1945. Perhaps the awfulness of World War II and the horror of the atomic bomb might compel governments to take new legal steps to criminalize war, but they had not done so yet.

On the verge of outright denying that aggression was a crime, Röling balked. Victorious states in a just war, he believed, were allowed to detain leaders who threatened postwar order, as was done to Napoléon Bonaparte without the bother of a trial; it could hardly be against international law that the Allies had afforded the Japanese warlords a proper trial before punishing them.[18] He proposed that crimes against peace were rather like "political crimes in domestic law, where the decisive element is the danger rather than the guilt, where the criminal is considered an enemy rather than a villain, and where the punishment emphasizes the political measure rather than the judicial retribution." Since the dominant principle was the danger posed by bellicose leaders, their punishment should aim only at security.

Under this fresh understanding of crimes against peace, he concluded that nobody should be executed only for crimes against peace. In practice, this would only have saved Hirota's life; he supported hanging Tojo Hideki and the five other condemned military men for conventional war crimes only. Lest he be considered soft, he added that two more admirals and one general sentenced to life imprisonment for war crimes should die too.

Pal was frustrated that Röling shrank from the full implications of denying that aggression was an international crime.[19] He privately told the top Indian diplomat in Japan that Röling had initially agreed with him but seemed to have been pressured out of it by the Dutch government.[20]

Yet the rest of Röling's spirited dissent hardly suggested a judge cowed by his home government. Although representing the Dutch Empire as it fought to reconquer Indonesia, he emphasized Japan's anticolonial policies. He saw Japanese pan-Asianism not as a mode of warfare but an alternative to it. By luring colonized people "into the Japanese orbit by the fascinating slogan of 'Asia for the Asiatics,'" Japan could gain decisive influence across Asia without war. Ultimately, though, he decided that

Japan was insincerely exploiting these liberation slogans. After deciding on war against the Dutch Empire, he noted, Japan had quietly shelved its rhetoric about liberating the Indonesians, wanting them dependent on Japan. Japan sought "the birth of an empire so vast and mighty that it might have dominated the rest of the world."

Röling continued his feud with the Soviet Union with gusto. If the charter rested on the Potsdam Declaration and the Japanese surrender, he slyly argued, then the court had jurisdiction only over the Pacific War, not the two "border clashes"—he doubted that they counted as wars—with the Soviet Union in 1938 and 1939. Japan, he wrote, had not wanted war in either battle. Röling depicted Japan's leaders as fearful of the Soviet Union, which could acquit defendants for aggression: if they were motivated by self-defense, they might lack the requisite criminal intention. He argued that Japan had been quite sincere in signing its 1941 nonaggression pact with the Soviet Union—thereby implicitly blaming the Soviets for violating that treaty by entering the war in August 1945.

Röling filled out his dissent with doctrinal qualms. Like many judges who were neither British nor American, he was left cold by the conspiracy charges. A conspiracy to plan a war that never actually came would be outside the court's jurisdiction. With Togo Shigenori in mind, he fretted about condemning "every single member of the government, who votes for war after having entered the government with the purpose of maintaining peace."

Furthermore, he worried about the thorny problem of commanders charged only for failing to prevent their troops from committing war crimes. The majority had followed the stern precedent laid down by the Supreme Court in *Yamashita*, holding that a military commander could be charged personally for failing to take appropriate measures within his power in order to prevent war crimes by his troops, but Röling—a dissenter who liked other dissenters—was impressed with the minority opinions by Justices Wiley Rutledge and Frank Murphy. He proposed his own standard: a commander had to know, or should have known, about the war crimes; had to take all possible steps to prevent war crimes; and had to have a particular responsibility for thwarting war crimes. There was a division of labor in government, he wrote, complaining that the majority went too far in assuming that every member of a government—he obviously was thinking of Shigemitsu Mamoru—bore responsibility for stopping atrocities committed on the front lines.

On top of these legal contentions, Röling doubted that some of the civilian defendants, in danger of assassination, had planned and waged wars of aggression. He argued that Japan had sometimes been provoked by Chiang Kai-shek. He contended that Japan had tried to localize the Marco Polo Bridge clash and that it was at least possible that it was China, not Japan, that was looking for a chance to launch a war.

At last, Röling voted to acquit five defendants. Field Marshal Hata Shunroku, he wrote, had been a professional soldier, loyally carrying out policy set by his government—an assertion that would have been more plausible if Hata had not been army minister, formulating policy rather than just carrying it out.[21] Although the general had been convicted for failing to prevent widespread atrocities by his troops in China, Röling poked at the paucity of Chinese evidence, which he found insufficient for a conviction beyond reasonable doubt. Years later, when he found out about Unit 731 and Japan's biowarfare program, he would wonder if he had been wrong about Hata.[22]

Röling contended that Hirota Koki, sentenced to hang, should walk free. As prime minister, he had sought to squeeze the Western powers out of Asia, but without war. As foreign minister, he had undermined and bullied China, but those were not international crimes. After the Japanese military provoked the clash at the Marco Polo Bridge, Hirota had tried to resolve the mess without war, according to Röling. Although the majority had convicted him for failing to demand an end to atrocities at Nanjing and elsewhere in China, Röling contended that the foreign minister had done enough by complaining to the army minister about Nanjing. While there were plenty of other atrocities in China, the Chinese prosecutors had not given evidence implicating Hirota in them.

Kido Koichi was a slippery case; Röling often found it hard to tell whether he had really "worked for peace or war." He conceded that Kido had made "fatal errors in judgment," but in a criminal case, the lord keeper got the benefit of the doubt. So did the emperor, whom Röling believed could express his opinion but had no choice but to accept the policies decided upon by his government. Röling defended the decision to install Tojo Hideki as prime minister, arguing that only a strong figure respected by the army could have chosen peace with the United States without igniting a civil war. He was unpersuaded that the emperor could have prevented the war, nor that Kido should have counseled him to do so: "From the limited power of the Emperor follows the limited power of his advisor."

Shigemitsu Mamoru, according to Röling, was a diplomat striving for peace. Röling accepted that he had only joined the cabinet in 1943 to try to halt the war. As foreign minister, he had been powerless to do more than pass along Allied complaints about their abused prisoners to the Army Ministry, and thus should be acquitted for allowing war crimes.

Finally Röling cleared Togo Shigenori. Unlike the majority, the Dutch judge accepted that the foreign minister had pressed for serious concessions before Pearl Harbor, particularly withdrawing troops from China, and there was no evidence he had deceived the Americans in the Washington negotiations. It was no crime to become foreign minister to prevent a war, nor to stay on to work for peace. Togo had provided enough evidence of his desire for peace that he should not be convicted of criminal aggression. Far from committing an international crime, Röling wrote, Togo had "fulfilled an international duty."[23]

"INEVITABLE INCIDENTS OF BATTLE"

Infuriated by this cacophony of dissent, Delfin Jaranilla of the Philippines upheld the American cause to the last. Priding himself as a veteran of the U.S. Army at Bataan, he privately hailed the United States as "the greatest Republic of the world."[24] Writing a concurring opinion, his complaint with the judgment was that it was not harsh enough. Written with phrase after phrase underlined for emphasis, his opinion read rather like he was shouting. "[I]f any criticism should be made at all against this Tribunal," he wrote, "it is only that the Tribunal has acted with so much leniency in favor of the accused."

Most strikingly, Jaranilla heatedly justified the use of atomic bombs, endorsing the White House position. To give him credit, he directly took on a grave problem which had lurked in the background of the entire trial: did not Hiroshima and Nagasaki eliminate any American moral pretensions to sit in judgment? Yet his legal argument was that many kinds of weapons killed civilians while hitting military targets. Such deaths were "inevitable incidents of battle," treating the atomic bomb merely as a firearm or artillery "only on a large scale." This was bilge. Atomic bombs dropped on cities do not accidentally kill civilians while aiming at soldiers; city-killing weapons are too disproportionately lethal and too indiscriminate for that.

In addition, he justified the atomic bombings on essentially strategic grounds—a dubious move in a legal opinion. If Japan had produced atom bombs, he asserted, it would have used them too. He argued, "If a means is justified by an end, the use of the atomic bomb was justified, for it brought Japan to her knees and ended the horrible war." Quoting at length from Henry Stimson's *Harper's* article arguing that the atomic bombs were the least abhorrent option, Jaranilla weighed not just the toll on Americans and Japanese, but on Asians. Before its defeat, Japan's "claws were still stretched out to Java, Singapore, the Philippines, Manchuria and others."

At every turn, Jaranilla took the toughest possible view. He protested that some of the penalties were "too lenient, not exemplary and deterrent, and not commensurate with the gravity of the offense. . . . Our action may be construed as weakness and failure." Unlike the majority, he believed that the evidence had proved that Japan, alongside Nazi Germany and Italy, had meant to dominate the whole world. He argued that there could be a criminal conspiracy to commit crimes against humanity, war crimes, or even murder. While upholding the court's jurisdiction, he was unfazed about retroactively punishing the defendants for actions that might not have been criminal at the time: "Japan and her leaders were perfectly conscious that they were embarking on a war of conquest and hate, in defiant violation of her commitments and of international law."

Finally, Jaranilla laced into Pal with undisguised bitterness. The Indian judge, he wrote, could not question the legitimacy of a court he had voluntarily joined. By consenting to be a judge under the charter, Pal had "unconditionally accepted" the validity of that charter's definitions of crimes against peace and individual criminal responsibility. If the charter itself was bad law, as Pal held, then his appointment was invalid, and "it follows that he has no valid powers at all, that all his acts are invalid, that his rendering any opinion at all is without any legal authority." By dissenting so completely, Pal had essentially declared himself not to be a judge at all, and there was no reason anybody should listen to him.[25] Jaranilla's concurring opinion revealed a prescient fear: that many people in Japan and across Asia would heed the Indian judge's rejection of the Tokyo judgment.

CHAPTER 29

"I Am Wholly Dissenting"

R ADHABINOD PAL'S TITANIC DISSENT is regularly romanticized by Japanese nationalists today as reflecting the authentic opinion of India, and more broadly of grateful Asians. Yet in private, from Jawaharlal Nehru on down, the government of a newly independent India was aghast about Pal's opinion.

As Pal worked, he had quietly passed along chunks of his dissent to the Indian government, where it was circulated to the legal advisers, the Ministry of External Affairs, and the Ministry of Defence. His main contact was K. P. S. Menon, now the foreign secretary (the top diplomat in the civil service), who had met and charmed Pal on a visit to Japan during the trial. Half a year before the verdicts, it was old news for Menon to receive "more instalments of Justice Pal's monumental judgment."[1]

As the judgment was being drafted, Pal provided India's government with an inside look at the judges' secretive deliberations. Although Menon discreetly called it "purely a personal letter arising out of my accidental meeting with him in Japan," he promptly shared it with the rest of the government.[2] "We are now going to have at least four different sets of judgments," Pal explained. He revealed who was in the majority of seven writing the judgment and gave the gist of the dissents coming from the Dutch and French judges, as well as Sir William Webb's separate opinion. Pal outlined his vast dissent in six succinct points. First, the court's charter did not define war crimes. Second, even if it did, those definitions were *ultra vires*—beyond its powers. Third, "Aggressive war is not crime in international law." Fourth, "We are not here to see whether the victor nations would take any political measures"—a rejection of Bert Röling's dissent. Fifth, there had been no overall conspiracy established.

And sixth, there was difficulty in defining aggressive war. "I am wholly dissenting," he wrote.[3]

Forewarned, India's government braced for disaster.[4] Nehru himself, India's founding prime minister, had long loathed Japanese militarism; he was appalled by Pal's opinion.[5] Although in later years the prime minister would emerge as a leader of the Non-Aligned Movement, here he still felt the need to reassure the United States and Britain. Menon, a confidant of Nehru, was disgusted: "Not content with holding that Tojo and Co. are not guilty, the learned Judge has chosen to justify Japan's actions and to condemn those who, after all, were our wartime allies. In fact, from a casual reading of his judgment, I felt that it was a monumental justification of Japan's conduct during the last three decades."[6]

Despite its dismay, Nehru's government decided not to try to muzzle its judge in Tokyo. After checking with the Defence Ministry and the ambassador to the United States, Menon wrote, "All of us agreed that, however extreme the view taken by Justice Pal in the War Crimes Tribunal might be, and however unfortunate the language in which he has couched his views, it would not be expedient for the Government of India to interfere with his judgment." Ordering him to rewrite his dissent "would be contrary to our best judicial traditions under which the executive does not interfere with the judiciary." Pal had never formally consulted with his government, nor received orders. India's government had not given him advice or instructions, nor fettered his individual judgment: "The views he has expressed are his own and not those of the Government of India." After consulting with Menon, Nehru personally signed off on this approach.[7]

After reading more of the dissent, Menon and the Ministry of External Affairs feared that the United States and other countries would be so outraged that India would have to declare publicly that Pal's views did not reflect those of India's government.[8] He anxiously informed India's diplomats in Tokyo, Washington, and London that "Justice Pal has taken an extreme view, wholly dissenting from the views of his colleagues," adding that "some of the passages in his judgment amount almost to a justification of Japan's conduct during the war."[9]

India's outspoken high commissioner in London, V. K. Krishna Menon—a grand figure who would go on to become defense minister and ambassador to the United Nations—immediately set up a meeting with Britain's foreign secretary, Ernest Bevin, to make it clear that Pal did not speak for India's government. The high commissioner wanted to "dissociate ourselves from the views of Justice Pal which is not shared by us," fearing that it would alienate China, the United States, the Soviet

Union, Australia, and Britain.[10] It was especially awkward to raise this with Bevin, a leading Labour Party imperialist.[11] As the British recorded, the Indian diplomat told Bevin that the Indian judge "exonerated Japan from any guilt for the Second World War or for crimes committed by Japanese forces." While Pal was writing up his denunciation of European colonialism, his own government had already secretly gone to the British to disavow him.[12]

The British, although grateful to Nehru's government for being so helpful, were stunned by what Pal had in store.[13] One senior Foreign Office mandarin fumed at "Justice Pal's obiter dicta on Japanese war-innocence," while Arthur Comyns Carr described Pal as "an agreeable & sincere individual who unfortunately has a bee in his bonnet about 'Asia for the Asiatics.'" A Foreign Office diplomat sneered, "We can perhaps sympathise with his dislike of War Crimes trials, but his version of events leading up to Japan's entry into the war is dangerously false."[14]

At first the British discreetly encouraged India to renounce Pal's coming dissent.[15] But then Lord Patrick, the British judge, warned that it would be highly improper for governments to comment on a matter before a court.[16] After mulling it over, the British government asked the Indian government not to repudiate Pal. It would be inappropriate to say anything about a court's proceedings, and an official Indian condemnation would only give more publicity to the dissent.[17] So long as Pal's opinion did not attract too much attention in Japan, a British Foreign Office official wrote, "silence seems to be best rejoinder."[18]

Pal had spoken repeatedly about his dissent to the top Indian diplomat in Japan, who now relayed the judge's self-justification back to Nehru's anxious government. As Pal pointed out, India's newborn government could hardly be held responsible for a dissent that had been in the works while the country was still part of the British Empire. He had alerted his intention to dissent to the other judges over a year before India's independence. He could hardly have been ordered to dissent by an Indian government that did not yet exist.

Pal had a few defenders in India's government. The Indian ambassador in Washington pointed out that he had a sterling reputation for integrity, independence, and legal knowledge.[19] India's top official in Japan did not want to repudiate him. While Allied politicians and many lawyers would "bitterly criticise his judgement," this Indian diplomat wrote, Pal would win acclaim from those international lawyers who doubted Nuremberg's case that aggression was a crime. Any official disavowal would "only disclose an unnecessary nervousness on the part of the Government which will certainly not enhance our prestige." Presciently, this Indian diplomat saw how popular Pal's dissent might become among Japanese: "A public statement of the type contemplated will not please anybody and its only effect will be to destroy the good impression that the judgement may create in Japan."[20]

THE JUDGMENT OF PAL

Pal's dissent has taken on mythic stature in Japan, despite the best efforts of the Tokyo judges and American censors to muzzle him.[21] It became celebrated by Japanese conservatives and nationalists, eventually reaching into mainstream consciousness. "He made a fair comment and a fair judgment," says Shindo Yoshitaka, a right-wing Liberal Democratic Party lawmaker and former minister, the grandson of the famous Japanese commander at Iwo Jima. Pal pointedly called his dissent a judgment, and it has become widely seen among Japanese as the true, enduring moral judgment of the Tokyo trial.

His remarkable dissent is more often invoked than actually read. It is usually described in Japan today as a legalistic treatise, scholarly in its disputations, never excusing historical abuses. In fact, it is something altogether richer and stranger, both more profound and more political. It grows out of a distinctive philosophical view of international relations as a realpolitik struggle where the weak suffer at the hands of the strong, a bleak realist vision that leaves little room for moralistic judgments. It is the only Tokyo judgment that explicitly treats both racism and imperialism as major themes in world politics.[22] Pal alone dared to question the Allies' motives: "Formalized vengeance can bring only an ephemeral satisfaction, with every probability of ultimate regret." He perceptively warned against unconscious biases and revenge, cautioning against "keeping the hatefire burning."

More than that, Pal's vast dissent is an overtly political document.[23] The bulk of it is a contrarian exoneration of Japanese expansion. "It is not natural to squander the victory," he wrote in a revealing passage about Japan's imperial conquests. "It is criminal to squander the victory so as to thus to frustrate the very war aim."[24] Contrary to what Japanese rightists like to claim, it does indeed do gymnastic apologetics for Imperial Japan's misdeeds, downplaying atrocities in China and the Philippines.[25]

Certainly the dissenting Pal cut a very different profile from his relative quiescence in Calcutta under the Raj. He went from quietly working under imperial authority to loudly denouncing it. He even upturned his

view of law itself: while his early academic writings on Hindu jurisprudence sometimes derived law from human reason, now he took a narrowly
positivist reading of international law.

Since his family will not allow access to whatever papers he left, it is
not clear what exactly sparked this shift. Most obviously, with the British
gone, he could at last speak his mind freely. His dissent clearly shows that
he was deeply shaken by Hiroshima and Nagasaki, sternly writing that
American arguments for "these inhuman blasts" were not much different
from how Kaiser Wilhelm II had justified Germany's cruel military tactics during World War I.[26] Beyond that, there are several other possible
causes. Like millions in the colonized world, he obviously dreaded the
resurgence of European imperialism; the postwar struggle for an enduring independence in Indonesia, Vietnam, Burma, Singapore, Hong Kong,
and elsewhere was just beginning.[27] The most searing wartime event in
Bengal, the terrible famine, is not mentioned in the dissent, but it is
quite possible that that calamity soured him on British rule. He must
have been encouraged by the victorious freedom struggle in India, which
made it easier to criticize European colonialism, as well as destroying
any career advantages from deferring to the departing British. He could
have been stirred by popular appeals by Nehru, whom he quoted at one
point in the dissent and later spoke of with deep admiration.[28] There
is nothing in the dissent to suggest that he, like many Bengalis in this
period, admired Subhas Chandra Bose in particular. He could have been
radicalized by the bloodshed of Partition, which was especially violent
in Calcutta. And seeing the bombed-out ruins of Tokyo all around him
could have reminded him of Allied hypocrisy.

His grandson Satyabrata Pal says that the judge was driven not by
anticolonial wrath but by a hatred of hypocrisy: "Like Indians of his
generation, Dadu spent much of his life hoping that the West, whose
laws and civilisation he had studied and admired, would actually practise
what it preached."[29]

"I sincerely regret my inability to concur in the judgment and decision
of my learned brothers," Radhabinod Pal began. It was because of the
gravity of the case, he explained, that he felt the need to explain himself
at such length.

He started with the law, rebutting the claim that the defendants could
not get an impartial trial from judges of the victorious Allied countries. In
a passage ahead of his time, he cautioned that judges might have a "bias
created by racial or political factors," which "may indeed operate even

unconsciously." Despite that, though, he argued that his colleagues should be evaluated on their moral integrity, putting his faith in the judges' reluctance to accept anything that comported with their unconscious wishes: "In spite of all such obstacles it is human justice with which the accused must rest content."

Yet after that, he turned his fire on the majority. Their judgment rested its jurisdiction on the charter, as well as invoking the Potsdam Declaration, but Pal was having none of that. The Potsdam Declaration, like other Allied declarations, were merely announcements of the Allied powers with no legal value. True, Japan had surrendered, but that did not mean that the vanquished were legally wholly at the mercy of the victor. Neither the Potsdam Declaration nor Japan's surrender entitled the Allies to redefine past actions as crimes, and any trial based on that "will only be a sham employment of legal process for the satisfaction of a thirst for revenge."

Furthermore, if the Tokyo trial rested on the Potsdam Declaration's surrender terms, that could only apply to the Pacific War and not to earlier wars such as the "Manchuria incident" (as Pal termed it in the euphemistic Japanese fashion), nor Japan's incursions into northern China, nor the two border battles with the Soviet Union. He conceded that the China war should be included, but also wrote at one point that the charge of aggression in China was not part of the USS *Missouri* surrender and that therefore all the accused should be acquitted for it.

As for the charter, Pal believed the same thing he had written as early as July 1946: it could not create new crimes. The charter could only ask for judgment on crimes that already existed in international law at the time the acts were committed, which for him meant only conventional war crimes.[30] Crucially, Pal did not believe that aggressive war had been criminalized. He held a stark realpolitik view of "the system of Power Politics prevailing in international life," with sovereign states acting coldly to preserve their security and stature.[31] International law did little to change that system; war remained an act of statecraft.[32]

Even the vaunted Kellogg-Briand Pact "FAILED TO MAKE VIOLATION OF ITS TERMS AN INTERNATIONAL CRIME." More profoundly, for Pal, the Kellogg-Briand Pact was so weakly written that it wasn't even really law. It allowed for wars of self-defense, and he claimed that it let each state determine for itself whether its wars should be counted as self-defense. Therefore the only wars it outlawed were those which a government admitted it had intended as aggression—in other words, none of them. This took "the Pact out of the category of law." As a result, "war in international life remained, as before, outside the province of law."

The violation of treaties, he held, was not a crime. The prosecution had invoked not just treaties but also customary international law that made aggression a crime, but Pal scoffed that a bunch of pronouncements did not make new customary law. Anyway, a novel customary law that renounced war would crash up against the more fundamental law of the sovereign right of each state to wage war. "In my opinion, no category of war became illegal or criminal either by the Pact of Paris or as a result of the same," he wrote. "Nor did any customary law develop making any war criminal."

The majority judgment had not bothered with natural law, and even Webb had largely abandoned it, but Pal trashed it anyway. If there was a natural law, he wrote, it was a fundamental principle of right and wrong, but too lofty to apply to specifics. It could not be accepted as positive law. Nor was there an existing international community that agreed upon what natural law was.[33]

Pal was especially tough on Soviet theories outlawing aggressive war. He scorned Soviet jurists such as A. N. Trainin, who had been invoked by Major General Ivan Zaryanov for conjuring up a crime against peace from the progressive character of international law. The Indian judge scoffed at Soviet claims that since the Moscow Declaration in 1943, which pledged to punish the major Axis war criminals, a new international society had somehow come into being. If there was any widening sense of a common humanity, Pal wrote, he had not noticed it among the powerful nations. Here he powerfully evoked colonialism: since "domination of one nation by another continued to be regarded by the so-called international community only as a domestic question for the master nation, I cannot see how such a community can even pretend that its basis is humanity."[34]

While the majority had truckled to Zaryanov, Pal castigated the hypocrisy of the Soviet Union, pointing out its aggressions against Poland and the Baltic states.[35] The Soviets had launched "a war against already defeated Japan" in August 1945, which Pal could not consider as self-defense. He did not even want to bring up the Soviet invasion of Finland, he added politely, thereby bringing up the Soviet invasion of Finland.[36]

Pal was equally withering on Western colonialism. If the domination of one nation by another was an international crime, he forcefully wrote, then many of the powerful nations would be criminal. "The entire international community would be a community of criminal races," he argued. More searchingly, he questioned whether the attacks on colonial possessions could properly be defined as aggression. He wrote that "the so-called Western interests in the Eastern Hemisphere" were based on how past generations of colonialists had turned military violence into riches.[37]

Next Pal denied that any individuals could be held criminally responsible for aggressive war. He accepted that victor nations could punish enemy war criminals, but not for acts of state—and all the deeds in the indictment were in his opinion acts of state. While the majority viewed the defendants as having run an outlaw regime, Pal saw them as merely "working their own constitution" in a legitimate and sovereign government.

Pal doubted that individual criminal punishment would serve any social purpose—neither as prevention, reform, deterrent, or retribution. So long as persons would only face trial if they lost a war, those trials could not prevent or deter crime. All that a trial could offer was retribution, which he saw as revenge. "The mere feeling of vengeance is not of any ethical value," he wrote.

He was more impressed by the *"ingenious"* argument that fixing blame on individuals would avoid imposing collective guilt on a whole nation: "By the trial and punishment of those few persons who were really responsible for the war, the world will know that the defeated nation like all other nations was equally sinned against by these warlords." Still, that goal could equally well be accomplished by a commission of inquiry about war guilt, rather than a criminal trial that strained the law.[38]

In his final salvo about the law of the case, Pal argued that the accused simply had not received a fair trial. Under any circumstances, it would be painfully difficult to discern if a particular Japanese action had been intended as aggressive. The charter "PRACTICALLY DISCARDED ALL THE PROCEDURAL RULES" of national courts, and there was an "almost hopeless confusion" around the rules for establishing conspiracy. Pal was guardedly skeptical about the accuracy of Marquis Kido Koichi's diary and wholly dismissive of the prosecution's late introduction of the insider Saionji-Harada memoirs. The court allowed too much hearsay. And under the high-handed Webb, it had idiosyncratically refused to hear evidence about such crucial matters as the threat of Communism in China, Soviet aggression against Finland and the Baltic states, and the U.S. decision to use atomic bombs.[39]

THE CHINA WAR AS SELF-DEFENSE

As Pal turned from the law to the facts of the case, his dissent became more rebellious. Seeking to explain Japan's actions as something other than aggression, he portrayed a vulnerable, overpopulated country beset by enemies: Nationalists and Communists in China, the arrogant United States, the racist British Empire, the predatory Soviet Union. He repeatedly complained of the hypocrisy of Western imperialists, arguing that Japan was doing nothing worse than mimicking them. He justified Japanese colonial annexations of Formosa (Taiwan) and Korea. He offered a case for Japan's self-defense and its appropriate national interests in Asia, meaning to introduce a reasonable doubt about the aggressive intentions of the defendants.

He rejected the notion that the accused had formed a huge conspiracy to wage aggressive war: "the whole story of the over-all conspiracy is a preposterous one." Such a doctrine, he wrote, would bring "unprecedented risk and responsibility on the part of those who might be called upon to work the machinery of their own national governments." He chided his fellow judges, "We must avoid all eagerness to accept as real anything that may lie in the direction of our unconscious wishes."[40] His dissent became a mirror image of the prosecution's use of conspiracy: while the prosecutors used conspiracy as an easy way to convict, Pal used the absence of conspiracy as an easy way to acquit.

Reasonably enough, Pal saw a series of disparate decisions by different Japanese cabinets over some seventeen years, not a coherent conspiracy: "Unlike Hitler, no one in Japan was in a continuous position of control."[41] Going further, Pal accepted the army's participation in politics without fuss. He saw nothing untoward about military censorship, propaganda, and curtailment of civil liberties; that happened in every country engaged in modern warfare.[42] Apparently unaware of how Imperial Japan had silenced, intimidated, and jailed its critics, he wrote that public opinion had been molded "in a perfectly legitimate manner" but never stifled, leaving the Japanese "complete freedom in respect of their own creeds, beliefs and behaviour."

Scathing about European colonialism, Pal was nonchalant about the Japanese variety. He voiced no objections to Japan's seizure of Formosa and Korea—particularly odd since there was no need to weigh in on conquests which happened well before the period under indictment. After Japan's victory over Russia in 1905, which let Japan grab Korea as a protectorate, Pal wrote that it was "natural" for the Japanese to keep the spoils of war. Accepting Japan's annexation of Korea in 1910, he approvingly quoted a historian who argued that the Japanese had a better claim to Korea than the British to India, the French to Indochina, the Dutch to Indonesia, or the Americans to the Philippines.[43]

Starting with Manchuria, Pal gave a counter-history which turned the judgment on its head: treating Japan's conquests as self-defense and denying a conspiracy for aggression. Japan's position as a great power was precarious, "with Nationalist China, Soviet Russia, and the race-conscious English-speaking peoples of the Pacific closing in on her."

Japan, he asserted, dreaded a Soviet onslaught through Manchuria, and Japanese there suffered from banditry, civil unrest, and Communist subversion. Citing the League of Nations' report on Manchuria, he claimed, "Fundamental among the interests of Japan in Manchuria is the STRATEGIC IMPORTANCE OF THIS TERRITORY TO HER SELF-DEFENSE AND NATIONAL DEFENSE." Noting that today "the whole world is reverberating with expressions of terror of communistic development," Japan's actions in Manchuria could be explained by its own fears of Communism.

Going further, he suggested that Japan, like Western imperial powers encroaching on China, had a legitimate interest in Manchuria—a vast space for an overpopulated Japan to colonize. As an apparent precedent, he pointed to Japan's annexation of Korea. If Western empires could legally impose themselves on China, so could the Japanese: "the majority of the interests claimed by the Western Prosecuting Powers in the Eastern Hemisphere including China were acquired by such aggressive methods."

He treated the Mukden clash of September 1931 as possible self-defense by Japanese troops; the railway explosion might have been the handiwork of the Chinese, according to Pal. As for Japan's subsequent conquest of Manchuria, he argued that Japanese troops had good reason to be there. "The position of the Japanese forces was not that of a force having violated a national frontier," he wrote. Far from committing aggression, they were merely restoring order there, since the League had no peacekeeping forces of its own.[44]

Pal took much the same approach to Japan's march into the rest of China: proposing that Japan had acted in self-defense, while denying that its actions could be ascribed to a conspiracy. He wrote that "Japan had acquired some 'interest' in China which Japan felt was very vital for her existence. Almost every great power acquired similar interests within the territories of the Eastern Hemisphere and, it seems, every such power considered that interest to be very vital." Japan's invasion of China, for Pal, was little different from what Western colonial powers had done: "As a program of aggrandisement of a nation we do not like, we may deny to it the terms like 'manifest destiny', 'the protection of vital interests', 'national honour' or a term coined on the footing of 'the whiteman's burden', and may give it the name of 'aggressive aggrandisement' pure and simple. Even then we do not come to the conspiracy as alleged in the indictment."

For Pal, Japan had a legitimate concern about China's ongoing civil war and its fear of Communism there—a point that carried a particular punch on the eve of Mao Zedong's victory. Since there was a "WORLD TERROR" of Soviet-backed revolution, why should the Japanese not fear Communist advances in China? Communism in China, Pal argued, was not merely an ideology but a rival government with its own army, law, and territory. Since the Nationalists increasingly could not rule their own country, he argued that a government's protracted inability to maintain domestic order (China) would legitimately allow a foreign power (Japan) to take steps to look after the life and property of its own citizens living there.[45]

Yet Pal said barely anything about the Japanese assault on China in 1937. He gave no account of the Marco Polo Bridge clash, nor of the subsequent surge of Japanese troops into China. At one point, he blamed China's Nationalist government for causing Japan's attack: "at the end of 1936 Chiang Kai-shek and the Kuomintang united with the Chinese Communists against Japan. It was this unification, which in July 1937, precipitated the present Japanese war against China." While he made a tenable case that Japan had reasons to worry about the civil war and Communism in China, he gave no reason why that concern was appropriately expressed by a massive ground invasion.[46]

"PROTECTING THEIR RACE"

In the most penetrating and distinctive pages of his dissent, Pal was the sole judge to confront directly the impact of racism. In his newly independent India, many were keenly concerned with racial equality both in their own multiethnic country and abroad, startling U.S. diplomats with popular outrage at Jim Crow segregation and racial discrimination in the United States.[47] Tellingly, the only other judge who considered racism at any length was Mei Ruao, another anticolonialist from Asia, under whose influence the judgment condemned Japan's attack on China as a racist war.

Pal emphasized how Western racism had alienated Japan, driving it toward war. He argued that Japan's own inculcation of a sense of supremacy among its people was, while deplorable, a defensive measure against Western bigotry. Having explained Japanese imperialism as a defensive reaction to Western imperialism, he now justified Japanese racism as a response to Western racism.

Throughout the dissent, Pal was conscious of how racism had excluded the Japanese and wounded their psyches. English-speaking Protestants, he suggested, had justified their colonial conquests from Latin America to India by a sense of racial superiority over supposedly primitive peoples.

Citing the British historian Arnold Toynbee, he contended that Western imperialists saw themselves as a biblical chosen people doing God's will in subjugating the Canaanites. (Ironically, here Pal struck an antisemitic note in his own discussion of bigotry.)

During the drafting of the League of Nations' Covenant, Pal noted, Japan's delegates in Paris had sought to wipe away centuries of white supremacy, hoping for a more egalitarian world that did not treat non-white peoples as naturally inferior. They introduced a clause that all League member states would treat foreigners equally without discrimination on race or nationality. Yet the Japanese had been foiled by the British Empire—in particular, by William Morris Hughes, Australia's prime minister, who, according to a history that Pal quoted, "constituted himself Champion of the cause of White Supremacy."[48] The Indian judge lamented, "Neither the League nor any other international organization ever could get rid of this race-feeling."

Pal warned against "the movement on the part of the white nations on the Pacific rim to exclude Asiatics on economic and racial grounds," as well as cultural and biological arguments for blocking Asian immigrants. An overpopulated Japan, he noted, was told it could not send its citizens to white countries, nor China, nor Siberia. He condemned the United States laws which had barred immigrants from Asia, calling one such act "an overt political humiliation" for Japan.[49] The exclusion of Japanese immigrants created a festering sense of inferiority: "The white nations did not show any consideration for the national sensibilities of the excluded nations including the Japanese."

The prosecution, he wrote, had complained about aggressive educational policies "designed to create in every youthful mind a feeling of RACIAL SUPERIORITY." Yet such racial supremacy was "a failing common to all nations. Every nation is under a delusion that its race is superior to all others, and, so long as racial difference will be maintained in international life, this delusion is indeed a defensive weapon." Furthermore, the leaders of a nation might believe in good faith that a sense of superiority could "protect the nation from the evil effects of any inferiority complex, and that the western racial behaviour necessitates this feeling as a measure of self-protection."[50]

Elsewhere in his dissent, he came close to accepting a possible war crime in order to discredit white supremacy. In 1942, the Japanese army had paraded British and American prisoners of war through the streets in Korea, hoping this would drive home to the colonized Koreans the power of the Japanese Empire. Although such public humiliation of prisoners was against the 1929 Geneva Convention, Pal wrote that the

Koreans' "faith in white supremacy" was such that the Japanese "simply believed that the very fact that white soldiers could be taken prisoner would demolish that myth. I do not see why this should be looked upon as an insult or exposition to public curiosity."[51]

Pal understood that racism still ran deep in world politics. He rightly scorned present-day politicians who argued that segregation was necessary to avoid "Mongrelization," while movingly hoping that World War II "has succeeded in killing this race-feeling and in humbling every mind so as to make it capable of thinking in racial equality." His consideration of racism was a crucial perspective that was conspicuously lacking in the majority judgment.

Yet throughout his dissent, Pal was oddly blasé about Japan's alliance with the quintessential racist power, Nazi Germany. Passionate elsewhere, he turned conspicuously abstract about Adolf Hitler. In Pal's realpolitik theory of international relations, he argued that alliances grew out of shared threats, not domestic affinity or ideological uniformity: Japan and Nazi Germany were pushed together by a common fear of Communism. Pal never asked how an alliance with a regime as bloody and aggressive as Hitler's Germany, already at war in Europe, could really be considered defensive. Despite his keen eye for racism in politics, he said next to nothing about Nazi racial obsessions.[52]

In the end, Pal believed that the Japanese defendants had considered their own fostering of prejudice "to be a *necessary measure of protection* for their race." He concluded, "I cannot condemn those of the Japanese leaders who might have thought of protecting their race by inculcating their racial superiority in the youthful mind."[53]

PEARL HARBOR AS SELF-DEFENSE

Giving an alternative history of Pearl Harbor, Pal depicted a peaceful Japan forced into war by the United States. "The evidence convinces me that Japan tried her utmost to avoid any clash with America," he wrote. "There is clear indication that Japan did not start with any design of the Pacific war which ultimately happened."

By supporting China after Japan's invasion, he argued, the United States had made itself a belligerent against Japan. He saw American political and military support of China as steps just short of war. American economic sanctions against Japan for its invasion of China, he believed, were in essence an act of war: "THE EMPLOYMENT OF A BOYCOTT AGAINST A COUNTRY ENGAGED IN WAR AMOUNTS TO A DIRECT PARTICIPATION IN THE CONFLICT."[54]

Pal saw nothing untoward in Japan's march into Indochina, since aid to China was flowing through there. Yet he objected to the U.S. economic sanctions and oil embargo on Japan for taking southern Indochina: "This was declaration of economic war." He argued that the sanctions violated the Kellogg-Briand Pact, as well as the Nine-Power Treaty and other pacts.

These Allied economic sanctions drove Japan to negotiations with the Netherlands East Indies to secure oil—or, if that failed, to an invasion. In its drive for raw materials, he contended, Japan was no different from the Western powers except for the misfortune of a late start on imperialism. He pinned the real blame on the United States, claiming that U.S. military and political leaders unanimously believed "that these economic sanctions against Japan would drive Japan to the very steps which Japan as a matter of fact pursued."[55]

He was untroubled by Tojo Hideki's ascension to prime minister. Tojo could have controlled the army, Pal wrote, and there was reason to believe that "he did not advocate waging war immediately with America." Clearing him of criminal intentions, he pronounced that Tojo held an honest opinion that Japan's very existence as a nation was in grave danger. He contended that Tojo, "to the best of his ability as a statesman, continued the diplomatic move, but ultimately failed in coming to any honourable settlement with the U.S." He declared that "people occupying Tojo's position should be capable of coming to a decision and should have the courage of his conviction. What followed, did so as a matter of course."[56]

Pal argued that the Washington talks had foundered on American intransigence. His best evidence of Japanese compromise, though, was its proposal that after a peace deal in China its troops would remain there for some twenty-five years—although Tojo himself privately admitted that meant close to forever. "Twenty-five years might have been a reasonable period in the circumstances or it might have been unreasonable, but that is not the question before us," Pal shrugged.

In contrast, he saw the Hull note as all but a declaration of war. Cordell Hull, he asserted without evidence, had already decided to break off negotiations. Pal wrote that "the note amounted to the maximum terms of an American policy for the whole Orient." He quoted an American critic writing that even Monaco or Luxembourg would have taken up arms against the United States after getting such a note.[57]

Since the United States had already launched an economic war, Pal suggested, Pearl Harbor was merely an escalation of a conflict already under way: "After the embargo of July 1941 the only question was when and where Japan would strike the blow that precipitated war." He argued,

"The evidence does not entitle us to characterize the Japanese attack as a sudden, unexpected, treacherous act committed while relations between the two countries were peaceful." Japan was not really starting a war: "justly or unjustly, rightly or wrongly, the Allied Nations had already participated in the conflict by these actions and any hostile measures taken against them by Japan THEREAFTER would not be 'aggressive.'"[58]

"Distortion and Exaggeration"

In Japan today, Pal's right-wing admirers routinely declare that he never sought to deny Japanese atrocities. This is simply false. To the contrary, he was avowedly skeptical about the evidence of the slaughter of civilians in China and the Philippines. He doubted not just some of the evidence that Mei privately considered weak but also some of the best stuff, particularly credible eyewitness accounts of killing and rape at Nanjing. In later years, Pal would deny some of the facts of the Holocaust.

He cautioned against demonizing wartime enemies. "Stories of war crimes generate passion and desire for vengeance," Pal wrote, pointing to World War I propaganda. He doubted the veracity of the jingoistic wartime press, engaged in a "vile competition" to whip up public fury. He argued that "a sort of unconscious processes were going on" in the minds of those who sought to prosecute defeated warlords. "The result might be a partial distortion of reality. There would always be some eagerness to accept as real anything that lies in the direction of the unconscious wishes."

While Pal admitted that the accounts of Japanese atrocities were similar across Asia, for him this was not necessarily evidence of a systematic policy. It was equally possible that these patterns were the product of "some common source shaping the allegations and evidence"—apparently meaning Allied propaganda. Even eyewitnesses were not to be trusted: "we cannot always believe men who saw 'something happen' even when they saw with their own two eyes." Although Japan's techniques of torture were alike far and wide, he refused to believe any government would formulate such methods.

Returning to his theme of Western racism, he speculated that the Japanese capture of vast numbers of Allied prisoners was a humiliation that had to be avenged by demonizing the Japanese. The Japanese victories "indicated a result of the fight which, as every white nation felt, completely undermined the myth of white supremacy. A certain amount of propaganda against the non-white enemy might have been thought of to repair the loss."

Of course, Chinese accounts of mass atrocities could hardly be dismissed as the revenge of humiliated white supremacists. Yet Pal assiduously doubted the evidence about the massacre and abuse of Chinese civilians. Without mentioning that the Japanese army had burned its documentation, he wrote that there was "absolutely no evidence on the record to show that there was any order, authorization or permission" to slaughter civilians and disarmed soldiers in Nanjing, Guangzhou, Hankou, Changsha, and several other Chinese cities. There was "absolutely no evidence of this alleged atrocity" in Guangzhou; he was not convinced there had been any atrocities in Hankou or Guangdong province; the evidence about enormities in Changsha was unsatisfactory; he was not convinced by accounts of rape and killing in two cities in Guangxi; he discounted "stray cases" elsewhere in China.[59]

Pal's prime example of an overhyped atrocity story was the Nanjing massacre itself. It was impossible, he wrote, to avoid "some suspicion of distortion and exaggeration." Although he did write that "even making allowance for everything that can be said against the evidence, there is no doubt that the conduct of Japanese soldiers at Nanking was atrocious," he spent page after page trying to call into question the horrors there.

He sowed doubt about rape in particular. Seeking to discredit the witnesses more broadly, he concentrated on debunking two eyewitnesses in particular: Hsu Zhuanying, a Nanjing railway official, and Reverend John Magee, an American Episcopal minister. Pal complained that Hsu and Magee "accepted every story told to them and viewed every case as a case of rape." It was, he wrote, "difficult to read this evidence without feeling that there has been distortions and exaggerations."

Pal did not explain exactly why these firsthand accounts under oath were implausible or falsified. He was unconvinced by Magee's eyewitness testimony about catching a Japanese soldier in the act of raping a Chinese woman, which to him merely suggested "instances of misbehaviour" by Japanese troops which the witnesses "unhesitatingly assert . . . as cases of rape." Hsu had testified to seeing numerous rapes and hearing about more, yet Pal asserted doubts about one instance when Hsu said he had personally seen a Japanese soldier raping a woman in a bathroom, and another when Hsu and other Chinese had found a naked Japanese man sleeping and brought him to the police as a suspected rapist. Impugning the motivations of the witnesses, Pal noted that these were "accounts of events witnessed only by excited or prejudiced observers."

Pal's doubts became almost epistemological. The witnesses, he asserted, could only have seen the events fleetingly. How were they so sure what they had seen? "In many cases, their conviction was induced only by excitability which perhaps served to arouse credulity in them and acted as a persuasive interpreter of probabilities and possibilities. All the irrelevancies of rumours and canny guesses became hidden under a predisposition to believe the worst, created perhaps by the emotions normal to the victims of injury."[60]

Pal discounted eyewitnesses to the massacre in Nanjing, as well as in Hankou and Changsha. He favored the testimony of the Japanese commander at Changsha over that of a homeless Chinese refugee who had fled the shootings. One Nanjing man testified that he had personally seen some forty people being taken away and machine-gunned to death by Japanese troops; a few days later he had seen a group of young men being bayoneted. "This seems to me a somewhat strange witness," Pal wrote. "The Japanese seem to have taken such a special fancy to him as to take him to various places to witness their various misdeeds and yet spare him unharmed." Apparently this witness lacked credibility because he had not been killed.

Judges have a duty to be skeptical of all testimony. It is always hard to get courtroom-ready evidence about rape, where often only a victim and a rapist were present during the crime, or for massacres, where the best witnesses are dead. It is true that people who have been subjected to crimes against humanity are often hostile to those who committed them. Such problems are endemic to all modern war crimes prosecutions. Yet Pal glided smoothly from asking questions about specific incidents to refusing to accept a vast mass of persuasive evidence. Confronted with these gruesome facts, he wished them away.

Pal conceded that, even "making every possible allowance for propaganda and exaggeration," there was still overwhelming evidence of Japanese atrocities against civilians and prisoners of war. Yet he concluded that not a single defendant could be held responsible for ordering or allowing these enormities. The Allies' desire for vengeance, he wrote, should be quenched by the prosecutions they had already mounted for numerous lower-ranked perpetrators.

None of the defendants bore guilt for the Nanjing massacre, according to Pal: "I do not see why, from this evidence, we should be driven to the conclusion that such atrocities were the results of the policy of the Japanese Government." He all but commended General Matsui Iwane for his conduct at Nanjing, contending that the Japanese commander had issued impeccable orders and had gallantly ordered compliance when he learned that "notwithstanding his strict warning, there were breaches of military discipline and morality." While Pal had to concede that such measures had been ineffective, he pronounced them sincere.

He was skeptical of testimony about war crimes against civilians in the Philippines, Burma, Indochina, Malaya, Singapore, and Indonesia. In Burma, he wrote, "At the worst these are all stray instances of cruelty"; in Borneo, "One would expect much better evidence"; in Timor, he saw only "stray cases." He was no more moved when the victims were Indians who had been jailed, beaten, or forced into brothels.

In the Philippines, he was confronted with a vast body of gruesome evidence of torture, beheading, rape, mutilation, and bayoneting of civilians. "The devilish and fiendish character of the alleged atrocities cannot be denied," he acknowledged. "However unsatisfactory the evidence may be, it cannot be denied that many of these fiendish things were perpetrated." Still, he saw no need to punish any top leaders. The men who had committed these crimes had already been prosecuted by lower-level Allied courts; the Tokyo defendants "had no apparent hand in the perpetration of these atrocious deeds."

Pal wrote that "the rape of Manila is likened to the rape of Nanking," meaning to discredit it. He shrugged off the slaughter and mass rape in Manila as "stray instances" that would be committed by any army. He threw the dictionary at the prosecution: "There is no evidence, testimonial or circumstantial, concomitant, prospectant, restrospectant, which would in any way lead to the inference that the government in any way permitted the commission of such offenses." He acquitted sixteen political and military leaders, including Tojo, of having either ordered or allowed war crimes: "War is hell. Perhaps it has been truly said that if the members of the government can be tried and punished for happenings like this, it would make peace also a hell."

Having downplayed Japanese enormities from China to the Philippines, Pal found his voice only for the slaughtered civilians of Hiroshima and Nagasaki. If there was anything in the Pacific War that approached Kaiser Wilhelm II's ruthless methods of warfare during World War I, he wrote, "it is the decision coming from the allied powers to use the ATOM BOMB. Future generations will judge this dire decision." He asked "whether it has become legitimate by such indiscriminate slaughter to win the victory by breaking the will of the whole nation to continue to fight." He sternly compared the Americans who decided to use the atomic bombs to the Nazis: "if any indiscriminate destruction of civilian life and property is still illegitimate in warfare, then, in the Pacific war, this decision to use the atom bomb is the only near approach to the directives of the German Emperor during the first world war and of the Nazi leaders during the second world war. Nothing like this could be traced to the credit of the present accused."[61]

"An Isolated Instance of Cruelty"

Pal was less skeptical about Japanese abuse of prisoners of war, repeatedly writing that their behavior had been "inhuman" and saying that it had been right to punish the war criminals in lower-level Allied courts. Yet again he managed to acquit every single senior defendant. The sergeants and captains could hang; the generals and ministers should walk free.

Having begun by attacking the novel crime of aggressive war, Pal finished by sidestepping the most conventional of war crimes. Although the proper treatment of prisoners of war was well established in the laws of war, he wrote that there was no law to apply. Japan had not ratified the Geneva Convention and he argued that the Hague Convention on land warfare only applied if all its signatories had ratified it; since Italy and Bulgaria had not, the whole thing was junk.

Pal explained the abuse of prisoners of war as the accidental result of Japan having to cope with overwhelming numbers of surrendering enemy troops. Rather than faulting Japan for breaking the laws of war, he suggested that those laws had to be updated so that they were not a permanent obstacle to achieving military goals. The United States, he noted, had not been willing to give up the military advantages of the atom bomb because of the indiscriminate damage it inflicted on civilians. Why should not Japan similarly mold international law to suit its battlefield imperatives?

In addition, he treated the abuse of prisoners of war as a matter of profound Japanese custom. There was, he wrote, a fundamental difference between Japanese and Western views of shame in war. The Japanese fought to the death, a psychological trait that he said ran deep in their national life, while its dissolute enemies would prudently quit fighting. Quoting an anthropologist, he asserted that the Japanese believed that Western prisoners "were disgraced by the mere fact of surrender."

Despite considerable evidence of common methods of torture and abuse across Asia, he wrote that "no such similarity of pattern has been established as would entitle us to hold that all these inhuman treatments were the result of the government policy or directive." The Allies had formally protested these war crimes against their prisoners, but Pal saw no reason for the Japanese defendants to see these complaints as anything more than enemy propaganda, meant to make people "swallow the most bizarre fairy tales." There was no obligation, he argued, for a minister to resign from a wartime cabinet as an act of opposition to war crimes. Alternatively, when prisoners had been abused—jammed into "hell ships" or forced to labor in the war effort, for instance—he shrugged that these were acts of state, for which none of the accused could be held criminally responsible.

The Bataan death march was "really an atrocious brutality," he wrote, and this time he did not question the testimony of survivors. Yet he did not see how any of the accused could be held responsible for it—not even Tojo, who had been prime minister and army minister. "It is an isolated instance of cruelty," Pal wrote. "I cannot connect any of the present accused with this incident."

Nor did Pal convict any of the accused for the Burma–Thailand railway. He did not doubt that vast numbers of prisoners had died along the line, but pinned the horrors on "the overzealousness of the local officers." He blamed a general, a lieutenant colonel, and a corporal, but concluded that officers at that rank had already been dealt with by Australian, Dutch, and U.S. tribunals. The railway was a major strategic initiative meant to open up a front against India and choke off Chinese supply lines, obviously the stuff of high-level deliberations, yet Pal saw no reason to think that the top men of Japan "should have even foreseen such brutalities." Nor did he convict anyone for using prisoners of war for military work. He did hold that Tojo was fully responsible for putting Allied prisoners to work on the railway, but wrote that "this violation of the rules regarding the labour of prisoners of war is a mere act of state. It is not criminal *per se* and I would not make him criminally liable for it."

The execution of Allied bomber crews gave Pal a chance to turn the tables on the Allies. He saw the airmen in essence as war criminals, although the law had not caught up with conscience. If the Allies wanted to set up war crimes tribunals that could make new law, he argued, then so could the Japanese. Overlooking how shoddy the Japanese trials had been, he denied that any senior Japanese leaders could be faulted for allowing the torture and summary executions of Allied bomber crews. All the same, he made a powerful case that indiscriminate aerial bombardment of civilians ought to be a war crime, filling a gaping hole in the laws of war. In one of the rare instances during the Tokyo trial when the bombing of cities—a defining feature of the war—was explicitly addressed, he highlighted the Japanese public's fury at the firebombing of Tokyo, Nagoya, Osaka, Kobe, and other cities. That rage reached its zenith after Hiroshima and Nagasaki. Pal wrote that "the real horror of air warfare is not the possibility of a few airmen being captured and ruthlessly killed, but the havoc which can be wrought by the indiscriminate launching of bombs and projectiles. The conscience of mankind revolts not so much against the punishment meted out to the ruthless bomber as against his ruthless form of bombing."[62]

Pal concluded his dissent resoundingly: *"I would hold that each and every-one of the accused must be found not guilty of each and every one of the charges in the indictment and should be acquitted of all those charges."* Having weighed Nanjing, Pearl Harbor, Bataan, Manila, and all the rest, he found not a single defendant guilty on a single count.

He turned against his friend and fellow dissenter Bert Röling, who had argued for punishing the accused for public order, invoking the example of Napoléon Bonaparte's peremptory exile at St. Helena. Since the victors after the Napoleonic Wars had not bothered with a trial, Pal sensibly questioned how this nonprecedent could be used to build international law. Furthermore, while Napoléon or Hitler were tyrannical usurpers, Pal insisted that the Japanese leaders were entitled to the prerogatives of legitimate rulers of a sovereign state. *"The constitution of Japan was fully working,"* he wrote, notwithstanding the assassinations and coup attempts by army extremists.

Haunted by Hiroshima and Nagasaki, he recoiled at the early days of the Cold War. Quoting from a *New York Times* editorial about the atomic bomb, he wrote, "The real question arising in a genuinely anxious mind is, 'can mankind grow up quickly enough to win the race between civilization and disaster?'" He warned that the vengeful punishment of defeated leaders would only distract the public from thinking about the fundamentals of peace and world union.

He declared the trial a mockery of justice. The Tokyo court looked like it was made "only for the attainment of an objective which was essentially political though cloaked by a juridical appearance. It has been said that A VICTOR CAN DISPENSE TO THE VANQUISHED EVERYTHING FROM MERCY TO VINDICTIVENESS; BUT THE ONLY THING THE VICTOR CANNOT GIVE TO THE VANQUISHED IS JUSTICE." There was blame to be assigned to the Allies, not just their defeated Japanese foes. Instead of Allied vengeance, he called for mercy: "The name of Justice should not be allowed to be invoked only for the prolongation of the pursuit of vindictive retaliation. The world is really in need of generous magnanimity and understanding charity."

In an opinion remarkable for its forceful discussion of racism, he ended by admiringly quoting a famous white supremacist. He gave the last word to Jefferson Davis, defeated in the Civil War, who is most commonly admired by American bigots. The Confederate leader's words are today attributed to Pal in a stone monument to him at the Yasukuni war shrine in Tokyo: "It is very likely that *'When time shall have softened passion and prejudice, when Reason shall have stripped the mask from misrepresentation, then justice, holding evenly her scales, will require much of past censure and praise to change places.'"*[63]

"Wild and Sweeping Statements"

Jawaharlal Nehru was horrified by Pal's dissent.[64] "In this judgment wild and sweeping statements have been made with many of which we do not agree at all," he wrote privately.[65] When an old friend of Nehru proposed officially publishing the dissent as a landmark in international law, the prime minister refused, personally signing off on a reply stating that Pal had been on the Tokyo court only in his capacity as a judge, not representing India's government.[66]

Major Indian newspapers made the dissent front-page news for a day but mostly did not follow up.[67] Many of them were as scathing as Nehru. *The Times of India* editorialized that Pal's dissent had "no relation whatever to the facts of recent Japanese history," while scorning how "Mr. Justice Pal explains away the doctrine of aggressive racial superiority which the Japanese themselves preached and practised and which brought such suffering and humiliation most of all to fellow-Asiatics in China, the Philippines, Korea, Burma and Siam."[68] The *Times of India*'s legal correspondent wrote that Pal should have refused to join a tribunal that he thought was illegitimate, and roundly condemned his dissent: "Mr. Justice Pal has done very dubious service to the cause of international justice by insisting that a callous and brutal disregard of human rights and decencies, and of the rules and customs of civilised warfare, shall go unpunished so long as an ideal machinery of international justice is not set up."[69] Yet some Indians rallied to Pal. After a Calcutta newspaper published serial extracts from his dissent, one prominent Indian barrister scoffed that "there was nothing judicial about the Tokio tribunal," merely "crude and ineffective attempts at clothing the sword with something like a wig."[70]

British officials were stung. "It is indeed astonishing that Mr. Justice Pal should have sat through a trial of such length while rejecting the very principles upon which it was based," snarled a British Foreign Office official. "His resignation would doubtless have been welcome to his colleagues on the Tribunal. His judgement will now be welcome to General Tojo and many of the Japanese."[71] The Canadian judge complained that Pal had come to Japan with the fixed intention of torpedoing any judgment that convicted the accused. The top British diplomat in Japan speculated—falsely—that Pal might have been prompted by Nehru's government to dissent in order to win favor among the Japanese.[72]

The immediate response in Japan was quieter than Nehru's government had feared, with the Japanese press under censorship largely supporting the majority judgment.[73] Although General Headquarters kept Pal's dissent from being published during the occupation, its gist quickly made it into Japanese and American newspapers.[74] While the full impact was muffled, it did impress some nationalists. "This is a courageous shout of the colored races against the white race!" enthused a lieutenant commander in Japan's navy who enterprisingly got ahold of a copy.[75]

Awkwardly, Pal's dissent went down well with the convicted Japanese at Sugamo Prison. "His words cover all we might want to say about such matters," said Matsui Iwane. "A typical Indian, he views things from a philosophical standpoint." After spending three days reading Pal's dissent, Itagaki Seishiro declared himself "deeply impressed," incongruously adding how much he admired Mahatma Gandhi.[76]

When Pal returned to India, he grabbed headlines again. He told a reporter that it was highly improper to suggest, as Webb had, that the emperor should have been put on trial: "The Emperor was not on trial before us and we have absolutely no material which will entitle us to say whether he is guilty or not." He noted that the defendants in court had been respectful throughout, accepting their convictions without any show of defiance. The Japanese, he said, were a disciplined nation that would rise again. Having learned the futility of war, they would succeed in economic and industrial reconstruction.[77]

Pal's dissent ruffled the most feathers in Australia.[78] One reporter wrote that he "attacked the white races in the Pacific, particularly Australia," and accused him of a "racial, rather than juridical, finding."[79] "Between lines of his judgment runs an under-current of instinctive ingrained Indian hostility to the old-model British Raj," wrote a Sydney columnist. "This, consciously or unconsciously, predisposes him in favor of fellow-Oriental enemies of the white West." In a somewhat less crude passage, that columnist quoted an attorney at the Tokyo court urging all Australians to read Pal's dissent carefully: "It will enrage most of them. But, whether they like it or not, it is the voice of Asia—a new intelligent Asia. And, whether they want to or not, they or their sons will have to listen to it—more loudly and more ominously—in years to come."[80]

With screaming front-page headlines of "Blames Us for Jap War Plans," the Australian press castigated Pal for accurately denouncing William

Morris Hughes as a white supremacist who had blocked Japanese efforts to enshrine racial equality in the League of Nations covenant.[81] Proving the Indian judge's point, Hughes replied that open immigration among League members would have meant that Australia "would have been flooded by Japanese—every one a trained soldier—and when the 1939–45 war broke out they would have swarmed into Australia overnight. Yes, I opposed the racial equality clause. Had I not done so I would have been a traitor to Australia."[82]

After a few jittery weeks, the Indian government concluded it would be better to ride out the storm without comment, while privately making sure that the British government knew of its disapproval of Pal's dissent.[83] Nehru's team was particularly relieved that despite widespread Chinese fury at Japanese war criminals, the Chinese press did not engage with Pal's dissent.[84] "It is comforting to think that Justice Pal's judgment has not evoked as much criticism as we expected," K. P. S. Menon wrote. "However it was just as well that it was not read out or published at length."[85] A frustrated Nehru secretly wrote, "In view of suspicion that Government of India had inspired Pal's judgment, we have had to inform Governments concerned informally that we are in no way responsible for it."[86]

CHAPTER 30

Equal Justice Under Law

FOUR NEW GALLOWS WERE built at Sugamo Prison, ready to be used any moment. With a news blackout from the jail, rumors flew around Tokyo that Tojo Hideki and the other six condemned men were already dead.[1]

After the death penalties were decreed, the doomed war criminals were moved into small, adjacent single cells in the same block at Sugamo. This block had more than fifty cells, but the seven men were the only ones held there. In their barred cells, the prisoners were watched constantly by a squad of eight guards. Every fifteen minutes, a medical aid man on suicide watch checked to see that they were still breathing and had not found a way to slit an artery.

The seven convicted men spent these macabre last days writing, reading, and playing cards. They got a supply of Japanese cigarettes, which had to be lit by a guard. They were allowed visits from their immediate family once a month. To make sure that their family members did not commit suicide, Japanese plainclothes police watched their houses.[2]

Meanwhile their defense counsel did everything they could to spare their clients from the rope. Their first hope, not a bright one, was General Douglas MacArthur. Under the Tokyo tribunal's charter, the Allied supreme commander was to review the sentences; while he could not reverse the guilty verdicts, he could lessen the penalties. MacArthur was not obviously inclined to mercy, as shown in the vengeful hanging of General Yamashita Tomoyuki, but some Japanese hoped that the incipient Cold War would change his calculations. Lieutenant General Robert Eichelberger, a confidant of MacArthur, had recently speculated that in a future war against the Soviet Union, Japan would side with the United States.[3]

All twenty-five convicted Japanese leaders made formal appeals to MacArthur to review their sentences. Major Ben Bruce Blakeney filed an eloquent plea on behalf of his client Togo Shigenori, noting that three judges had dissented and the Dutch judge had acquitted him. "Americans in time to come are unlikely to be proud of this verdict," he wrote.[4]

From Rome, Pope Pius XII urged Harry Truman to show "Christ-like mercy" by commuting the death sentences, particularly for Hirota Koki.[5] A fervent anti-Communist, the pope also called for clemency for Nazi war criminals in the early Cold War.[6] Truman refused him, leaving the matter up to MacArthur.[7]

MacArthur asked the Allied governments to share their views.[8] His desk was piled high with trial papers, as well as some ten thousand petitions signed by at least a hundred thousand Japanese. He was most troubled by the cases of Hirota and Shigemitsu Mamoru. A growing number of British grandees, led by the well-connected former cabinet secretary Maurice, Lord Hankey, beseeched him for clemency for Shigemitsu, calling him a true friend of Britain who had striven for peace.[9] Joseph Keenan tried to influence MacArthur by telling reporters that the prosecutors were "ashamed" of Shigemitsu's seven-year sentence, letting slip that he was only charged at the insistence of the Soviets.[10]

The Indian political representative in Tokyo secretly cautioned that the court had been bitterly divided, that the Australian and French judges opposed the death penalty, and that the death sentences were imposed by a bare majority. He suggested asking that the death sentences for Tojo and the six others be commuted to life imprisonment.[11] Jawaharlal Nehru's government agreed. In general, wrote K. P. S. Menon, now the foreign secretary, India opposed the death penalty, and there was such discord among the judges that executions would be improper.[12] Privately, Indian officials worried that Indian public opinion was sympathetic to the Japanese, with newspaper editorials and influential legislators pressing Nehru to get the sentences reduced.[13]

Still, Nehru would only go so far for the Japanese warlords he reviled. When the governor of Bengal, the volatile home state of Radhabinod Pal, suggested asking MacArthur for mercy, the prime minister slapped him down. After consulting with others in government, Nehru bluntly wrote, "We are unanimously of opinion that you should not (repeat NOT) send any telegram to General MacArthur." He warned that "any such move on our part would associate us with Justice Pal's dissenting judgment in

Tokyo trials. . . . Any statement sent by you might well create great difficulties for us without doing much good to anyone else."[14]

On November 22, 1948, MacArthur consulted with representatives of the eleven Allied countries in his office at the Dai-Ichi Building. Without any judges to hold back state power, it was all over in half an hour.

The British Foreign Office, while thinking the trial had been "a sorry affair," believed it had been fair, and was not about to undermine its political and moral impact in Japan by second-guessing its sentences.[15] Arthur Comyns Carr, back in London, urged the British government to stand by Shigemitsu's sentence, expressing surprise that the former foreign minister had been acquitted for aggressive war.[16] The British political representative in Tokyo personally hoped that MacArthur would show mercy to Shigemitsu but would not take the initiative.[17] The British government, authorized to speak on behalf of New Zealand as well, had its political representative support the sentences.[18]

"I have no changes to recommend," said the U.S. representative loudly.[19] The Chinese delegate would not tinker with the decision of a majority of judges after a long, fair trial. New Zealand, Canada, and the Philippines followed suit. Although the Soviet Union had officially outlawed the death penalty, the Soviet delegate accepted all the sentences.[20] Sir William Webb had opposed the death sentences, but the Australian government snubbed him by leaving it up to MacArthur to decide. Two diplomats showed their personal discomfort, though. The French delegate said that his government agreed with the sentences but left MacArthur a voluminous document with his personal recommendation that the death penalties should be commuted to life imprisonment.[21] The Canadian representative sent MacArthur a personal letter asking him to slash the jail terms for Togo and Shigemitsu.[22]

Only the Dutch and Indian delegates spoke against the sentences, following the dissents of their judges. The Dutch representative wanted to spare the neck of Hirota—whom Bert Röling had voted to acquit—and lock him up for life instead, as well as reducing the jail terms of two foreign ministers, Togo and Shigemitsu, and two army men, Field Marshal Hata Shunroku and General Umezu Yoshijiro. (Except for Umezu, these tracked Röling's dissent.) Togo's intentions were "fundamentally peaceful" with no criminal intent.

The Indian delegate proposed that all seven war criminals sentenced to death, including Tojo Hideki, should get life imprisonment instead. Noting that countries were increasingly abolishing capital punishment, the Indian official warned presciently against fixing into international law a precedent for this extreme penalty. In some countries, he added, it took a unanimous jury to give the death penalty; since several of the Tokyo judges opposed the death sentences, the defendants ought to get the benefit of the doubt. MacArthur briefly sparred with the Indian representative, and then asked if anyone had anything else to say. No one did.[23]

On November 24, the supreme commander announced on the radio that all of the sentences would stand. His political adviser recalled that he had never seen his boss in such deep emotion.[24] "No duty I have ever been called upon to perform in a long public service replete with many bitter, lonely and forlorn assignments and responsibilities is so utterly repugnant to me as that of reviewing the sentences of the Japanese War Criminal defendants adjudged by the International Military Tribunal for the Far East," he declared. The orotund prose clearly came straight from MacArthur himself: "No human decision is infallible but I can conceive of no judicial process where greater safeguard was made to evolve justice." He added a prayer for the worldwide repudiation of war, while urging all Japanese to pray on the execution day "that the world keep the peace lest the human race perish."[25]

Emperor Hirohito seized on MacArthur's ruling as a chance to dispel the latest abdication rumors. He met with Keenan—the U.S. chief prosecutor who had absolved him—at the palace grounds, where the emperor expressed his hopes for world peace and Japanese democracy, saying nothing about the Tokyo trial or its death sentences.[26] A front-page editorial in the *Yomiuri Shimbun*, which was widely seen as either dictated or inspired by the Imperial Palace, declared that the monarch believed that he could better contribute to reconstructing a peaceful country by staying on the throne. He felt, the *Yomiuri* wrote, that he could do more to make amends for his war responsibility by not abdicating.[27]

The censored Japanese press accepted MacArthur's decision quietly—in part because no one dared to criticize the supreme commander directly. The *Asahi Shimbun* editorialized of the "perfection both in reason and sentiment" of his announcement.[28] In private, many Japanese civilian officials remained sympathetic to Hirota. "Time will help all those who are in prison while nothing can help those condemned to death," the governor of Hiroshima Prefecture told a British official.[29]

At Sugamo Prison, Doihara Kenji said that he would not begrudge the Chinese if they took satisfaction in his execution, while complaining that crimes were being committed in the name of democracy.[30] Shivering in the first cold snap of autumn, Hirota's grown son and two daughters went to Sugamo Prison to bid farewell to their father, held in a cramped solitary cell. He smiled with composure at the news of MacArthur's decision.[31] After they left, he was despondent, saying that everything ended in blankness.[32]

MacArthur personally ordered the commanding general of the U.S. Eighth Army to carry out the hangings soon.[33] Even the Indian government—still embarrassed by Pal's dissent—decided not to press its case against the death penalties, refusing to raise the issue among the Allies in the Far Eastern Commission.[34] Reporters began a "death watch," awaiting news of the executions at any minute.[35]

"A GRAND INQUEST"

The defense lawyers cast about for a power superior to MacArthur. With nowhere else to go, they decided to pit the Supreme Court against the supreme commander.

The American defense lawyers had been mulling this last-ditch option for almost two years. At the start of the defense case, they had announced in court that they planned to challenge the legitimacy of the Tokyo trial in the United States federal courts in Washington. Annoyed at the impertinence, Webb had retorted, "It is a matter of sheer indifference to us whether you go to the federal court in Washington or to the federal court in Ottawa or to the federal court in Moscow or any other court. One has as much right to review as the other."[36] The Soviet judge, Major General Ivan Zaryanov, had roared with laughter.[37]

Immediately after MacArthur upheld the sentences, American lawyers for Hirota and Doihara—both sentenced to death—filed a motion for leave to seek a writ of habeas corpus, as well as a motion for a stay of execution. So did lawyers for others facing jail terms, including Marquis Kido Koichi.[38] These motions named as respondents the U.S. secretary of defense, the secretary of the army, the commanding general of the Eighth Army, and MacArthur himself.[39] This was a terribly long shot, even if the Court had recently split in some cases about German war criminals, with several justices unsuccessfully seeking a hearing about the Court's jurisdiction.[40] The motions challenged the convictions and sentences, and implicitly the legitimacy of the Tokyo court itself.

In his hasty petitions, Hirota's lawyer rehashed his client's declarations of innocence. Hirota had had nothing to do with the Pacific War; he had done nothing wrong during "the so-called 'Rape of Nanking'"; the trial had been unfair. Even so, three of the Tokyo judges had voted to acquit him, and five had opposed the death penalty. The rushed lawyers strained to raise constitutional claims: only Congress could define and punish offenses against the law of nations; the executive branch could not punish the Japanese in a way that violated the Constitution's ban on Congress passing ex post facto law; MacArthur had had no authority from Congress or the president to create the Tokyo tribunal. Still, the petitions did little to establish that the Supreme Court—which generally hears cases that were decided in lower U.S. courts first—had appellate jurisdiction over Hirota and the rest. Without jurisdiction, all the other objections were pointless.[41]

The army secretary ordered MacArthur to stay the executions until the Supreme Court acted.[42] Although grudgingly promising to act with "appropriate discretion," MacArthur jeered that "that Court has no more jurisdiction in the premises than does the High Court of England or China or France or Russia, or any other of the Allied nations, none of which have the power of unilateral action."[43] The supreme commander duly announced that he would postpone the hangings until the Court had decided.[44] When Tojo Hideki, meeting with his family for what could be the last time, heard about the delay, he said that he wanted to get it over with as early as possible. He was trying to avoid catching a cold, his wife said, the better "to die in a manly, warrior's way."[45]

At the Supreme Court, Justice Robert Jackson was keeping his head down.

He was a brilliant orator and an ambitious political operator, himself a former attorney general and solicitor general.[46] In his powerful dissent recoiling at the Court's validation of "the principle of racial discrimination in criminal procedure" in *Korematsu*, he had worried about how wartime exigencies could distort the Constitution, as well as sympathizing with the deported and detained Japanese Americans: "here is an attempt to make an otherwise innocent act a crime merely because this prisoner is the son of parents as to whom he had no choice, and belongs to a race from which there is no way to resign."[47]

He had only recently returned to the Court after a sensational tour as the United States' chief prosecutor at Nuremberg.[48] That had drawn him worldwide acclaim, but the unprecedented stint had provoked grumbling among the other justices. His relationships with them were so strained that he had not been sure he would return.[49] "Jackson is away conducting his high-grade lynching party in Nuremberg," Harlan Fiske Stone, then the chief justice, had written. "I don't mind what he does to the Nazis, but I hate to see the pretense that he is running a court and proceeding according to common law. This is a little too sanctimonious a fraud to meet my old-fashioned ideas."[50]

Jackson obviously had to recuse himself from voting on whether to hear the habeas corpus petitions. He was too embroiled with the war crimes trials to touch this case.

Yet the Court deadlocked in conference.[51] Ultimately, four justices voted they had no jurisdiction and four wanted to hear arguments. Leading the latter were Frank Murphy and Wiley Rutledge, anxious about the quashing of civil liberties in wartime, whose earlier bitter dissents in *Yamashita* indicated enduring concerns about American war crimes trials.[52] They were joined by Hugo Black and the famously liberal William O. Douglas. These four publicly announced their votes.[53]

Rutledge saw "serious challenges" to the Tokyo tribunal, which in turn raised "grave questions" about the Supreme Court's jurisdiction, suggesting it might indeed be able to step in. These cases were different in important ways from the Court's previous encounters with accused Japanese war criminals, General Yamashita Tomoyuki and Lieutenant General Homma Masaharu: they had been combatants fighting against the United States, while Hirota had served in civilian positions and had left government before Pearl Harbor. Rutledge wrote, "In the *Yamashita* and *Homma* cases determined, as I thought, that enemy belligerents have none of our constitutional protections, it does not follow that they held enemy civilians to occupy the same denuded status." Nor had the Court yet decided that enemy civilians who had no access to a lower U.S. court should have no remedy for harmful decisions made by a U.S. military tribunal. These "are not for me either self-evident or frivolous matters," he wrote.[54]

With the Court split, Jackson faced "a choice between evils," as he explained in an agonized but silver-tongued statement. On the one hand, if he did nothing, the resulting executions would always be stained "in Oriental memory" as punishments that "half of this Court tells the world are on so doubtful a legal foundation that they favor some kind of provisional relief and fuller review." The four votes against "would for all time be capitalized in the Orient, if not elsewhere, to impeach the good faith and to discredit the justice of this country."

On the other hand, if he asserted jurisdiction, that would likewise embarrass the United States before Asians: "On American initiative, under direction of the President as Commander-in-Chief, this country invited our Pacific allies, on foreign soil, to coöperate in conducting a grand inquest into the alleged crimes, including the war guilt, of these defendants." The Tokyo trial, he wrote, appeared as an international enterprise carried out under the president's war powers and control of foreign affairs: "For this Court now to call up these cases for judicial review under exclusively American law can only be regarded as a warning to our associates in the trials that no commitment of the President or of the military authorities, even in such matters as these, has finality or validity under our form of government until it has the approval of this Court." The great issue at stake, he thought, was not the outcome of the war crimes trial but whether the slow-moving judiciary could review the president's conduct of foreign policy.

Jackson, savvy and well connected in the Democratic Party, must have known that hearing the case would infuriate Truman. While the president had championed the Nuremberg trial, he had no patience for showboating judges. As Truman once wrote privately, "when you have an organization of dissenters it won't work. They all want to be Holmeses and Brandeises and you can't run the Court that way."[55]

Despite that, Jackson reluctantly stepped in to clear up the mess made by his divided colleagues. He wanly had to assert that his own prominent involvement—he had negotiated for the United States in drafting the Nuremberg charter, which the Tokyo charter largely copied—was somehow not disqualifying, any more than a justice ruling on a law he had helped to make in an earlier career in Congress. He voted to hear arguments about the condemned Hirota and Doihara in what he called "a tentative assertion of jurisdiction," hoping that a fuller hearing would swing enough votes to deliver a more united affirmation of the Tokyo trial's legitimacy. If he let the Japanese be executed now, he reasoned, their partisans would always point to the divided Court to accuse the United States of doing injustice. He hoped that a clear majority would emerge that would not require him to vote again.[56]

On December 6, Chief Justice Fred Vinson announced that the Court would hear arguments about the defense lawyers' motions for leave to file petitions for writs of habeas corpus. Oral arguments would be held in ten days.[57]

In Japan, radio stations broke into their regular broadcasts to announce the thunderbolt, while the newspapers rushed out early-morning extras. The Japanese were startled, amazed, and confused by this latest display of Allied indecision about its own war crimes tribunal.[58]

"Tonight Japan's sense of war guilt has been virtually erased," declared a CBS correspondent. "The Supreme Court session appears to have undermined the whole moral value of the 2 ½ year trial." Some Japanese reckoned that Americans were not sure that justice had been done and that Tojo Hideki was probably right after all. The Court, CBS reported, had left Tojo as a bigger hero now than he had been before he lost the battle for Saipan.[59]

To many Japanese, it looked like the guilt of the convicted men was not clearly established and that the Tokyo trial itself might be illegal.[60] The *Asahi Shimbun*, while lauding the Court for seeking perfect justice, warned that its intervention could allow Japanese to minimize the crimes of the convicted men.[61] "Most Japanese were simply bewildered by the legal mumbo jumbo of the inscrutable Occidentals," sniffed *Time* magazine. "Many an American felt the same way."[62] As an Indian diplomat reported, Japanese were buzzing that perhaps the Supreme Court would reduce the severe sentences of the Tokyo tribunal. Some Japanese murmured that the American government hoped to spare Tojo and the others in order to use them to fend off the Soviet Union.[63] Others said that since there was so much doubt in Allied minds about the guilt of the offenders, perhaps Japan's war policies were partly justifiable.[64]

Other defense lawyers scrambled to file motions in Washington. Two more condemned generals petitioned for their lives, as well as Shigemitsu Mamoru and one general facing lifetime imprisonment. Tojo Hideki refused to ask for American mercy.[65]

The news quickly reached Sugamo Prison. Tojo thought that the Court was dragging things out to torment the doomed men. "I don't like this dillydallying," he snapped.[66] "It appears that the American Supreme Court has taken up our case," said Matsui Iwane, sentenced to death for the Nanjing massacre. "It's all the same thing, though. In my opinion, the quicker it's over the better." Having steeled himself to hang, he grumbled to a Buddhist priest, it would be "quite difficult" if the Court reduced his sentence to life imprisonment.[67]

MacArthur accepted the affront with bad grace. An army man who shrugged off orders from the president could hardly appreciate being bossed around by five justices. While complaining that the Court was driven by internal political reasons, he had General Headquarters announce that the seven death sentences would be put off until it had ruled. If the Court were to serve a writ of habeas corpus, he grumbled, he would ignore it and let the Far Eastern Commission handle it. In private, he was confident that the Court would swiftly reject the motions, since he claimed that he had created the court not as a U.S. officer but as an international official acting on behalf of eleven states.[68]

The Truman administration was aghast. The Court's action embarrassingly insinuated that the Tokyo court had not been an international tribunal at all but really a blunt American instrument. At the Justice Department, the solicitor general—the official who handled the administration's litigation at the Supreme Court—pressed the State Department into swiftly issuing a statement that the Tokyo court really was an international court.[69] In addition, the State Department's legal advisers secretly asked the Allies, assembled in the Far Eastern Commission, to declare formally that the Tokyo tribunal had been an international court properly established under Allied authority. Since it would be too embarrassing for the U.S. delegation to introduce the proposal, they furtively fished around for another Allied country to do so.[70]

Jackson had written hopefully, "Our allies are more likely to understand and to forgive any assertion of excess jurisdiction against this background than our enemies would be to understand or condone any excess of scruple about jurisdiction to grant them a hearing."[71] In fact, the other Allies were furious. Soviet state media immediately declared that the Supreme Court had acted unlawfully.[72] This intervention, *Pravda* wrote, served to "annul with a flourish of the pen all the work of the tribunal," showing that American policy was really directed by monopolist "merchants of death."[73] "It was the last thing I expected," said the dissenting Röling.[74] Startled, the British and Dutch missions in Tokyo groused privately that the Supreme Court was clearly without jurisdiction, and had trashed the legal standing of the Tokyo court by implying that it was merely an American creation.[75]

Many Chinese rankled at the prospect that an American court would wipe away a judgment about Chinese suffering.[76] "I am utterly amazed by the Supreme Court's decision," an irate Mei Ruao told reporters. The Court was "committing a great mistake and creating a dangerous precedent." The Tokyo tribunal's jurisdiction, he said, came from eleven Allied nations, not from the United States alone. If one national court could wipe away a decision of an international tribunal, it would wreck future cooperation and mutual trust. "It is a great testing case in history and will have repercussions in future international dealings and mutual good faith," he warned.[77] At the same time, the Chinese Communist Party took full advantage of the chance to embarrass both the Americans and the Nationalists. "MacArthur and the American judiciary are carrying out a shameless plot to delay execution and modify the original verdicts," wrote the *People's Daily*.[78]

Only the Indian government, while dumbfounded, was vaguely relieved: if the Supreme Court wiped out the Tokyo judgment, that would vindicate Pal's dissent.[79] Still, Nehru's top officials lined up against the

Court's action.[80] Menon agreed that the Tokyo tribunal was an international one, although established in a "peculiar" way, and was mostly anxious that the Supreme Court's intervention "should not become a precedent for the future." Although Menon noted that there was considerable public feeling in India against the death penalties, India's government maintained its silence.[81]

Despite the State Department's request, the British government shuddered at the notion of a formal Allied statement trying to shut up the Supreme Court. Britain initially instructed India, Australia, Canada, and New Zealand that any attempt to influence the Court would be unwise.[82] Still, when the U.S. solicitor general formally asked the Far Eastern Commission whether the Tokyo court had been international or American, the Allies had to say something.[83] The mortified British told the Commonwealth governments to allow an Allied statement that the Tokyo court had been an "international court, appointed and acting under international authority."[84] Rushed by the Truman administration, the Allies got their statement out just before the Court heard arguments.[85]

Hirota's defense lawyer scrambled to find the constitutional arguments and case law that might sway the Supreme Court. All too often, his brief instead fell back on general principles, quotations from the *Federalist Papers,* or loud exhortations. It would be "truly catastrophic" if no U.S. courts could issue a writ of habeas corpus for prisoners outside the territorial jurisdiction of the United States. MacArthur and other army officers were not beyond the reach of U.S. courts if they did unlawful and unconstitutional deeds, since "the Constitution of the United States follows the flag into the military occupied territory of Japan."[86]

In a lengthy brief, the Truman administration's formidable legal machine swatted such rhetoric away. Most importantly, the solicitor general of the United States argued that, unlike an ordinary case that had started out in lower U.S. courts, the decisions in Tokyo came from an international court which was simply beyond the Supreme Court's jurisdiction. Therefore there was no need to address the petitioners' various complaints about violations of the Constitution and international law. Even if the Supreme Court did somehow have appellate jurisdiction, no lower U.S. court could issue a writ of habeas corpus, since the Japanese petitioners were "foreigners in a foreign land" with no rights under the Constitution. They lived in a country governed not by the United States alone but by the Allies—a formalistic denial of who actually called the shots at General Headquarters. The president of the United States, argued his solicitor general, had "great powers" over foreign policy as commander in chief. He was not limited by U.S. domestic law against ex post facto law. American courts "should so act as not to embarrass the executive arm in its conduct of foreign affairs."[87]

"THEY HAVE NO RIGHTS OF ANY KIND"

On December 10, the United Nations General Assembly adopted the Universal Declaration of Human Rights, and the next day unanimously affirmed the principles of the Nuremberg charter and judgment.[88] Five days later, the Supreme Court assembled for oral arguments.

Jackson uncomfortably joined his colleagues. The chamber was packed with spectators, including Joseph Keenan. Over two days of fierce debate, the Court was badly divided.[89]

William Logan Jr., the brash Tokyo defense lawyer speaking for the Japanese petitioners, was bombarded by skeptical questions from every justice except William O. Douglas. He argued that the power of the Tokyo court flowed from the executive authority of the United States, not from any treaty. When Logan said that there was "no other court to which we could go," Chief Justice Fred Vinson, aware that eleven countries made up the Tokyo tribunal, cut him off: "May there not be ten others?" Soon after, Vinson told Logan that while the Supreme Court had original jurisdiction over international affairs, that was limited to cases about ambassadors and ministers, and those in which a state was a party. "In which of these does this case fall?" asked the chief justice of the United States. "None of them," admitted Logan, arguing instead that the Constitution should be elastic enough to let the Court get involved. The president and U.S. military authorities, he said, had created new definitions of international crimes without congressional approval, usurping the legislative branch's power to do that.

Justice Felix Frankfurter scathingly asked question after question. He interrupted Logan to say that "something may be illegal and yet international, and so be something over which this Court has no jurisdiction." The Tokyo court was an international organization no matter how it was created: "It is a matter of no moment whether we initiated it or Great Britain or Iran."

Speaking for the Truman administration, the solicitor general argued that the convicted Japanese war criminals had no rights under the Constitution: "Supreme dominion over Japan is held not by the United States or any single nation, but internationally and jointly by a group of powers." He declared the executive branch's "deep concern at any such threat to our power to engage in international activities."[90]

On the second day of oral argument, Douglas, who had voted for hearings, pounced when the solicitor general said that MacArthur ultimately took his orders from the Far Eastern Commission, not the United States courts. "That is a rather startling statement," said Douglas. "Why cannot General MacArthur release these Japanese when he, as their jailer, is an American citizen? So far as he acts as an American, can't he be controlled by American courts?" The solicitor general flatly replied, "Your processes can't reach him, as Supreme Commander. In that capacity he is not acting under any American law or under the U.S. Constitution."

The Japanese petitioners' lawyers recoiled at that. "So long as there was American participation in this trial, to the extent of that participation the safeguards of the Constitution must apply," said George Yamaoka, a Japanese American attorney from New York City. "No American officer can act in contravention of those safeguards." Another lawyer for the Japanese said, "We are not asking you to review what the international tribunal did. We are asking review of what an American citizen and an Army officer did."

Summing up, the solicitor general scolded, "What we are faced with is an effort by enemies of this country to use processes of this court to get rights for themselves that never belonged to them and never could be granted. These motions are filed on behalf of the conspirators who planned the destruction of this government and were responsible for dropping the bombs on Pearl Harbor. Now at this late date they have the audacity and temerity to appear before this court." Justice Hugo Black, who had voted for this hearing, interrupted him to ask about the Court's jurisdiction over the Tokyo tribunal. "They have no rights of any kind in any court of this country," retorted the solicitor general. "There is no reason why the Supreme Court should attempt to interfere."[91]

The Supreme Court moves fast on motions for leave to file for habeas corpus. Three days later, the chief justice read aloud its ruling in *Hirota v. MacArthur, General of the Army, et al.*, covering all the Japanese who had petitioned. Having roiled the Japanese occupation, creating a possible historic opportunity to assert judicial principles over the punishment of enemy war criminals of the highest rank, the justices of the Supreme Court now wanted no part of it.

In a show of unity, the Court issued a short, simple *per curiam* opinion—an unsigned judgment on behalf of the whole body. Their previous deadlock had vanished. Five justices joined in, including Black, who had voted to hear oral arguments. Douglas, who had done the same, would write a concurring opinion several months later. Even though Wiley Rutledge became convinced that the Tokyo court had been an international one after all, he said that he would announce his vote later—but died of an apparent cerebral hemorrhage at the age of fifty-five before doing so.[92] Only an emotional Frank Murphy dissented, although ill health kept him from writing the scorching opinion he had in mind. He too would die unexpectedly: just seven months later, fifty-nine years old, he suffered a fatal coronary occlusion.[93]

With a robust majority of six justices voting to let the executions proceed, Jackson could with relief sit this round out.[94]

"We are satisfied that the tribunal sentencing these petitioners is not a tribunal of the United States," the Court declared tersely. "The military tribunal sentencing these petitioners has been set up by General MacArthur as the agent of the Allied Powers." Therefore "the courts of the United States have no power or authority to review, to affirm, set aside or annul the judgments and sentences imposed." The petitions for permission to file petitions for writs of habeas corpus were denied.[95]

MacArthur could do as he pleased. Hirota Koki and all the rest would hang.

The Court's curt opinion barely explained its reasoning. Put in the worst light, it allowed the wartime executive to do whatever it wanted. In the best light, it was a minimalist statement of the Court's own constitutional limits. The Supreme Court could only serve as an appellate court for cases coming up from lower U.S. courts, which might include the U.S. military commission that had doomed Yamashita, but not such an outlandish international creation as the Tokyo tribunal. Yet if that modest position was the right answer, then why had half the Court not been able to accept it at first?

There were plenty of other lingering questions. Could a U.S. general really act without judicial restraint so long as he claimed to be an Allied official? Would international tribunals always be beyond the reach of U.S. courts, even when Americans were creating and molding them? Would U.S. courts really defer to an international court that was punishing American citizens, rather than hated foreigners? How had the justices accepted the claim that MacArthur, who had for years scorned and defied the squabbling Far Eastern Commission, was nothing but its instrument? Why had the justices cast such doubt on the Tokyo judgment only to do nothing about it in the end? Truman, MacArthur, and all of Japan could only wonder.

In private, several of the justices had considered a broader critique of the Tokyo trial. Jackson had barely bothered with the question of whether the Supreme Court had appellate jurisdiction, seeing grander issues at stake. Rutledge had deep doubts about the Tokyo tribunal's legitimacy. Murphy's law clerks prodded him to write a sweeping dissent criticizing Truman's war crimes policy, arguing that the Court could declare that the president had to follow some minimum standards of due process, such as a ban on ex post facto charges. There was a risk that the high courts of other Allied countries would rule that the convictions were valid, which a Murphy clerk accepted coolly: "if the Aussies want to take the petitioners out and shoot them, let them go ahead."[96] Yet all these questions were silenced in the Court's brusque *per curiam* ruling.

Only the progressive Douglas—one of three justices who had voted to hear oral arguments but then sided with the Truman administration—offered a proper explanation, giving a blistering critique of the Tokyo trial. Since it took him several months to write it, though, it had scant political impact in Japan. Arching an eyebrow at "the 'crimes' which came within the jurisdiction of the tribunal" and "various so-called war crimes against humanity," he signaled his skepticism about the legality of those charges. His paper was clearly written as a dissent but then repurposed as a concurring opinion. On at least three points, he trashed the Court's ruling, even though he had voted for it.

First, he insisted that U.S. courts had the authority to issue writs of habeas corpus regardless of where in the world a person was detained. "Today Japanese war lords appeal to the Court for application of American standards of justice," he wrote. "Tomorrow or next year an American citizen may stand condemned in Germany or Japan by a military court or commission." It would be "grave and startling" if U.S. courts could not reach them. If MacArthur was holding Japanese prisoners illegally, the writ of habeas corpus could free them, even if he was acting on behalf not just of the United States but also the Allies.

Second, it hardly mattered if the Tokyo tribunal was an international body. The Court's opinion, he wrote, "leaves practically no room for judicial scrutiny of this new type of military tribunal which is evolving. It leaves the power of those tribunals absolute." By declaring itself powerless to challenge international courts, the Supreme Court was sacrificing principle. "I cannot believe that we would adhere to that formula if these petitioners were American citizens," he bluntly wrote.

Third, Douglas recoiled at the solicitor general's claim that the Court had no authority over MacArthur. "If an American General holds a prisoner, our process can reach him wherever he is," he wrote. "To that extent at least, the Constitution follows the flag. It is no defense for him to say that he acts for the Allied Powers. He is an American citizen who is performing functions for our government." Although the Tokyo court was international, what mattered was that "the chain of command from the United States to the Supreme Commander is unbroken."

Only on one point did Douglas side with the rest of the Court: that the president could do what he wanted to defeated wartime enemies.[97] That was enough to get him back on side. In a dazzling zigzag conclusion, he argued that Harry Truman was right because Radhabinod Pal was right. Since the Tokyo tribunal was not a real court, U.S. courts had no say over it.

The president of the United States, Douglas conceded, was the "sole organ" of foreign policy, especially during war. (Since a 1936 case, the executive branch has routinely pressed this "sole organ" language, although the Court has never adopted it as doctrine.)[98] War crimes prosecutions were part of the conduct of war. Truman could have done as he pleased with the Japanese war criminals, just like the victorious European powers banishing Napoléon Bonaparte without trial after Waterloo. Quoting admiringly from Pal's dissent, Douglas saw the Tokyo court as fundamentally a political creature set up by the supreme commander: establishing its charter, setting its procedure, describing "the 'crimes' that came within the jurisdiction of the tribunal"—the quotation marks indicating that he, like Pal, did not see them as crimes at all.

"The Tokyo Tribunal acted as an instrument of military power of the Executive Branch of government," wrote Douglas. "It took its law from its creator and did not act as a free and independent tribunal to adjudge the rights of petitioners under international law. As Justice Pal said, it did not therefore sit as a judicial tribunal. It was solely an instrument of political power." As such, there was no constitutional objection to Truman's political action: "the capture and control of those who were responsible for the Pearl Harbor incident was a political question on which the President as Commander-in-Chief . . . had the final say." Douglas, in short, upheld the president's authority to set up a bogus noncourt.[99]

Whatever the legal merits, the Court had inflicted a political fiasco upon the Allied occupation of Japan. It had called into question the Tokyo judgment but then left it in place. In its ultimate acquiescence to wartime executive power, its actions confirmed what Oliver Wendell Holmes Jr., who had stepped down from the Supreme Court not long after Japan invaded Manchuria, had once written with clear-eyed realism: "The felt necessities of the time, the prevalent moral and political theories, even the prejudices which judges share with their fellow-men, have had a good deal more to do than the syllogism in determining the rules by which men should be governed."[100]

As the days passed, more and more Japanese had dared to hope that the Supreme Court would overturn the verdicts. So the Court's blunt ruling was met with weak-kneed relief among the Allied missions in Tokyo.[101]

At Sugamo Prison, the convicted men were not surprised. Hirota said, "The matter had been decided by the Allied Powers already." "That's considerate, isn't it," jeered Itagaki Seishiro. "I am grateful that America was thinking about us until the end."[102]

This time Japanese newspapers did not rush out extra editions. Many Japanese received the news with a cynical shrug, not surprised to see the Court fall into line. If it had not, some Japanese opined, the United States would have lost all its Allied friends. Japanese liberals were alarmed that the Supreme Court had given credence to claims that the Tokyo trial had acted illegally, which in the future might be used by right-wing factions to make Tojo and other war criminals into martyrs.[103]

Nothing now stood between the seven condemned Japanese and the gallows.

CHAPTER 31

One Minute After Midnight

THE TIME HAD COME for Tojo Hideki and the six other condemned men to die.

Detailed planning for the executions had begun months earlier, based closely on Nuremberg.[1] Hanging was meant as a humiliating death, deny-ing the military men the honor of a firing squad. To prevent posthumous memorials to the dead men, the bodies would be cremated and disposed of, not returned to their families.[2] Unlike at Nuremberg, there would be no photographs of the executions.[3] The U.S. military was convinced that the grisly images of the dead Nazi leaders had been a terrible mistake, and General Douglas MacArthur told an aide that photographs "would violate all sense of decency."[4]

Nor would any reporters be allowed to attend, to the outrage of the Tokyo press corps. Although the army secretary had wanted to permit a few reporters, MacArthur had furiously shot that down: "The press exploitation of the sordid details of such executions . . . as was permit-ted at Nuremberg, is in my opinion repulsive to all standards of human decency and could well destroy the very purposes which such trials and punishments serve."[5] General Headquarters would simply release a terse notice when it was over, skipping any "gruesome or sensational details."[6] The executions, done by the U.S. Eighth Army, would be witnessed by doctors and prison staff. MacArthur invited the Allied powers to send official representatives to watch and then certify that the sentences had been carried out: William Sebald, a U.S. diplomat and MacArthur's political adviser; Patrick Shaw, an Australian official representing the British Commonwealth; General Shang Zhen, a Chinese battlefield commander; and Lieutenant General Kuzma Derevyanko, the Soviet officer who had signed the USS *Missouri* surrender.[7]

After being sentenced, the condemned war criminals began seeing a Buddhist priest at Sugamo Prison daily. When the priest asked Tojo—clad in a grubby, ill-fitting purple gown over work clothes—why he had shot himself, the former prime minister explained that he had spent his life instructing his subordinates to choose death rather than be captured. He was glad, though, that he had not succeeded, both because he had found religion and because "I was able to clear up certain points during the trial."

The priest told reporters that Tojo was a changed man, embracing Buddhism, his mind serene.[8] After a lifetime dedicated to violence, the general took on a Buddhist name, which prompted ridicule from Japanese newspapers; one wrote that the name should mean "Atonement in the nether world for sins committed in this." According to the Buddhist priest, the career army man spent his last days in ascetic spiritual contemplation, expounding that world peace would only be possible when humans lost their avarice, or trying to imagine a celestial Buddha enthroned above a great solar system. Tojo studied an elementary Buddhist book on the holy scriptures into which he had pasted a picture of Emperor Hirohito clipped from a newspaper. He told his wife that he wanted to carry the volume with him to the gallows, which made the Sugamo authorities worried that he would somehow use it to commit suicide. The jailers were especially strict about his own propensity to kill himself, he said wryly.[9]

Tojo, as well as several others, left clippings of his hair and fingernails to be placed in his family shrine as ancestor tokens for veneration. He spent his last days composing poems, writing long letters to his defense lawyers, and drafting a testament titled "To the World," containing his last political and military opinions, which reportedly echoed his testimony defending the attack on Pearl Harbor.[10]

Most of the other condemned men claimed to face their demise with resignation. There was some bickering among them, blaming the others for talking too much during the trial or for ducking responsibility.[11] Matsui Iwane still claimed that he was innocent.[12] Doihara Kenji rankled at the disgrace of being branded a war criminal but declared himself grateful that his death might prove helpful. He sent a classical poem to his children: "Born like a bubble of foam and to fade like the dew on the grass, my precious being."

As the country waited, some Japanese warned against a creeping tendency to sympathize with men facing their doom. "People are easily moved by death before their very eyes," wrote a prominent *Asahi Shimbun* editorialist, urging its readers not to forget what Tojo and the others had wrought. "Tens of thousands, hundreds of thousands of children, fathers, and husbands lost their lives day after day on the battlefield, and innocent, good mothers, wives, and children followed them, charred beside the meager air-raid shelters of their homes. A trial in the hearts of these dead would surely have been much more severe than the Tokyo court."[13]

Promptly after the Supreme Court ruled, on December 21, 1948, at 9 p.m., the seven men were filed into the prison chaplain's office two at a time. Tojo was brought in alone. They were told that they would be executed at one minute after midnight on December 23.

The men were ashen and grim. Hirota Koki was glassy-eyed.[14] Tojo had feared that they would be jolted awake and then immediately killed; he had things to write. He nodded repeatedly, bowed and said in English "okay, okay" several times. He made several last requests. His jailers could do nothing to get money to the families of the convicted men, and would not allow him sleeping pills—apparently out of fear of suicide. But they did allow him time with the Buddhist priest, a simple Japanese meal, and some sake.

Tojo said that there was a bright light in his cell day and night, and that it was a wonder he hadn't had a nervous breakdown. "I am able to offer myself as a sacrifice to peace and become one stone in the foundation for the rebuilding of Japan," he said. "I can die in peace of mind because no trouble was brought upon the Emperor." He was old and decrepit, he said, and could not go on living much longer anyway; he looked forward to being absorbed into the soil of Japan. He had composed a flurry of farewell poems. One was patriotic: "Though I depart/ Would that I might return to this land of mine,/ For there remains so much to do/ For my country." Another was reflective: "Not a cloud is there to cross/ And darken the mind./ And with a full heart/ I hurry on my journey West."

MacArthur told the four Allied representatives to come to Sugamo to witness the hangings.[15] Shang turned pale. Shaw had a whiskey. The Chinese and Soviet officials, not on speaking terms, insisted on riding in separate cars.[16]

It was a cold, bleak winter's day. Muto Akira was the only one who admitted to waves of terror, but said that the others felt it too.[17] The men spent their last day visiting with the Buddhist priest, writing letters and poems, and saying farewell to each other. As a final dinner, they got rice, miso soup, broiled fish, and meat, as well as bread and jam. They ate little.

In the priest's telling, the condemned men consecrated their fleeting hours to spiritual purification. Yet this account shows how consumed with worldly statecraft they were even as the minutes ticked away. Hirota Koki asked about the news from China, and when told that the Communists were winning, said that "what we most feared has come to pass." Matsui complained that impetuous young army officers had brought Japan to its present state and speculated that the Chinese Communists were more moderate than their Soviet comrades. Doihara said that things in China had failed, but hoped that they would be made better by his death. Itagaki Seishiro, too, remained obsessed with China, saying that he prayed for the prosperity of China and Korea, and hoped that in the afterlife he would be able to pursue a unified Asia.

Hirota, too depressed to leave letters or farewell poems, said that he wanted to go to death in silence. Nobody else did. Itagaki said resentfully, "As for the Declaration of Potsdam, I consider that we are sacrifices on the Altar of a Lasting Peace." Muto was indignant that the Tokyo trial's prosecutors had accused Japanese troops of bayoneting babies in the Philippines. In a letter to his wife, Matsui wrote, "It happens that I have come to be sacrificed for the Nanking Incident." Since so many had already died under his command in China—soldiers and civilians, Japanese and Chinese—it was only proper, he wrote, that he follow them himself. He accepted some responsibility for the China war and pledged to make "full apology for everything," while bitterly mourning "the betrayal and disgrace of a defeated Japan."[18]

About twenty minutes before midnight on December 22, guards came to the cells of Doihara Kenji, Matsui Iwane, Muto Akira, and Tojo Hideki. Two American guards accompanied each handcuffed man. They were simply dressed in U.S. Army work clothes and Japanese laced shoes.

The four condemned war criminals were taken to a cell being used as a makeshift shrine, which the Buddhist priest had fitted with candlesticks, an incense burner, wine, chocolate and biscuits, cups and water. Since they could not all fit in, they had to pray in the hall. There for seven minutes they received improvised Buddhist last rites with incense. They bowed their heads and closed their eyes. The priest offered cookies but the old men had taken out their dentures; only Matsui munched a soft biscuit. They drank wine from full paper cups with their manacled hands. Tojo was pleased that, as requested, he had gotten at least one drink.

One of the four said, *"Banzai"*—a battle cry, short for "Long live his Majesty the Emperor." The army men decided to shout it in defiance. "Matsui-san, if you please," said Tojo, asking the eldest man to lead them.

Tojo and the other generals bellowed in unison, *"Banzai! Banzai! Banzai!"* Then they yelled the imperial slogan *"Dai Nippon!"*—Great Japan.[19]

The shouts of *"Banzai!"* were so loud that Sebald heard them ricocheting through the hush. To him they were a farewell to the emperor and a symbol of defiance.

The men said goodbye to each other. The Buddhist priest thought they were happy. A steel door opened. Flanked by two American soldiers, followed by the Buddhist priest and the U.S. Army chaplain at Sugamo, the condemned men were marched across a cold, dark courtyard to the brightly lit death chamber. Tojo and some of the others chanted the name of Amida Buddha, a traditional way of seeking tranquility and salvation.

As they entered, each man—first Doihara, then Matsui, then Tojo, and finally Muto—was individually identified directly in front of Sebald, Shaw, Shang, and Derevyanko, as well as doctors and prison staffers.

The condemned men continued saying Buddhist prayers. In their shapeless salvage clothing, they struck Sebald as "very old, helpless, pitiful, and tragic. They seemed to shuffle as they walked, and each face was a vacant stare as it passed me."

Then they were marched up thirteen steps to the gallows platform. They walked their last steps without assistance. Tojo and the others continued to chant.

The American executioners put black hoods over their heads. They fitted ropes to necks.

The chief executioner saluted the commander of the execution detail and said that the four men were prepared. "Proceed!" yelled someone. At 12:01 a.m. on December 23, the hangman gave a signal and all four trapdoors crashed open. Sebald thought the traps sounded like a rifle volley.

The Buddhist priest had assured Tojo that they would die instantaneously as their spinal cords were severed. In fact, it took Doihara six minutes to die. An American senior medical officer listened for heart sounds with a stethoscope. "I declare this man dead," he said. Muto was pronounced dead after ten minutes and Matsui after eleven minutes. Tojo died after nine minutes. Their trousers were fouled from involuntary discharges of urine and feces.

Immediately afterward, a second group—Itagaki Seishiro, Hirota Koki, and Kimura Heitaro—was marched to the improvised chapel. They had heard the chants of *"Banzai!"* Hirota edged over to the Buddhist priest and asked earnestly if they had had a *manzai*—his regional way of pronouncing *banzai,* which in the priest's dialect meant a gossipy party. The priest, missing the point, said no. The men lit incense and listened to a reading.

Afterward, Hirota asked again about the *banzai,* and this time the priest got it. A civilian unaccustomed to war cries, he turned to Itagaki and told the general, "You'd better lead us." Together the three of them yelled, *"Banzai! Banzai! Banzai!"*

The priest put wine cups to their lips and they drank. They walked across the courtyard to the bright lights of the death house. According to the priest, they were calm and composed. "There was the same shuffling walk, the same quiet, unidentifiable mumbling, the same hopelessness," remembered Sebald. As Hirota passed, he turned his head and looked directly into Sebald's eyes, seeming to appeal for sympathy and understanding.

They were led up the gallows and hooded. At 12:20 a.m., the trapdoors crashed open again.

"I pronounce this man dead," said the American medical officer. Itagaki died after twelve minutes. Hirota died after fourteen minutes. Kimura died after fifteen minutes.[20]

Sebald was humbled. He recalled, "These men, who had wielded such enormous power and influence, died secretly and alone, surrounded by former enemies." He and the other shaken witnesses downed whiskey straight.[21]

Outside a light rain drizzled. With maximum secrecy, under heavy guard, the seven corpses were driven away from Sugamo Prison by military vehicles from the United States Eighth Army. At 7:45 a.m., the wooden coffins—apparently American-made, larger than those usually used in Japan—arrived at a drab square stucco building, the municipal crematorium in the bombed-out ruins of Yokohama. Wood and coal flames in seven rusty ovens began to burn the bodies at 8:10 a.m. Under an hour and a half later, they were all reduced to ashes. These were put into U.S. Army regulation boxes, five inches wide and two inches deep.

Tojo had asked that his remains, and those of the other six, be turned over to their families for Buddhist funerals.[22] Led by Tojo's wife, the families of the condemned men had petitioned MacArthur to let them say prayers over the dead bodies or at least their ashes. General Headquarters refused, fearing that even the private enshrinement of Tojo's ashes could encourage defiance, with him exalted in death as a *kami,* a Shinto divine spirit. Instead the remains were taken away by seven American military jeeps, rumored to be bound for an American cemetery. Sentries there with bayonets fixed warded away reporters. In fact, to be sure that burial sites could never become memorials in the future, the ashes of all seven executed war criminals were secretly dumped out over some thirty miles of the Pacific by a U.S. Eighth Army airplane.[23]

"Well, it's all over," said a Japanese worker at the crematorium. "It is just what we expected for Tojo."[24]

A New Japan

MacArthur had asked for a day of prayer: Shinto shrines, Buddhist temples, and Christian churches were packed. The ancient Senso-ji in Tokyo, known as the Asakusa Kannon Temple, was overflowing, with priests intoning prayers for peace while the bell tolled. The speaker of the Diet's lower chamber urged the nation to find "a burning desire for peace in the solemn reality of the executions." The Imperial Palace let it be known that Emperor Hirohito, on hearing the news from the grand chamberlain, had joined the people in offering a silent prayer for peace.[25] The executions happened to have occurred on the birthday of Crown Prince Akihito, which later generations of Japanese hard-liners have taken as a show of spite.[26]

For the most part, the families of the executed men accepted the news with composure. Doihara's widow said that her husband had completely accepted a life of religion; Itagaki's widow declared that her husband had been fully prepared to meet his death; Matsui's widow, having listened all night to the radio, voiced only relief.

Only Tojo's family was less resigned. His second son told a reporter that his mother had gathered his children and told them, "From now on you are fatherless. But don't think your father died. He shall still be living with us." His lead defense lawyer, Kiyose Ichiro—who would become speaker of the lower house of the Diet—voiced defiance on his dead client's behalf: "The question of whether the carrying out [of] this trial was right or wrong will be judged by future history."

On the streets, the mood was calm. Older Japanese seemed sobered but did not want to talk to reporters. Younger people were indifferent. Indian diplomats reported that the hangings caused little excitement among the Japanese. "In Japanese eyes failure is the worst of crimes and Tojo himself had admitted that his only crime was that he failed in his mission," wrote the Indian political representative in Tokyo. "No wonder therefore that the topranking leaders of militaristic Japan passed away unsung, unwept and almost unnoticed."[27]

Japanese newspapers mostly editorialized that the seven hanged men had gotten what they deserved and merited no compassion, while adding that the nation should assume moral and spiritual responsibility for the war.[28] "They are now dead," wrote the *Mainichi Shimbun.* "Let us pray for their souls as we do for all who have died. The best prayer would be one calling for the elimination of war and the establishment of peace throughout the world." The hanged war criminals were not the only ones responsible for the war, the newspaper noted, warning that "ennobling the executed as having been sacrificed on behalf of the Japanese people affirms a wrongful war." While doubting some of the law of the Tokyo trial and pointing to Radhabinod Pal's dissent, the *Mainichi* concluded that "[t]he executions of Japan's war leaders must become a symbol of the rejection of war for the entire world."[29]

The liberal *Asahi Shimbun,* usually critical of the militarists, was the only major newspaper to suggest it was appropriate to offer condolences to the families. Its columnist was troubled: "we cannot help but feel a bitter jarring in our chests, like a rumbling in the earth." But the writer quickly turned to praising pacifism, arguing that Japan could never defend itself in a future atomic war.[30]

Major Ben Bruce Blakeney, the American defense lawyer, was disgusted. He wrote to Bert Röling, "this morning brought the execution of the seven defendants, who, some say, were murdered by you and your colleagues."[31]

Mei Ruao declared that the executions were a "source of satisfaction and comfort to those [who] suffered from Japanese aggression, particularly the Chinese who suffered the most." Although admitting that thousands of Japanese war criminals had gotten away without punishment, he still saw the Nuremberg and Tokyo trials as establishing the important principles that aggression was an international crime and that those individuals who committed it should be held personally responsible. The hangings showed that aggression was not a "path to glory but a road to the gallows."[32]

PAROLE

The day after the hangings, General Headquarters announced that the nineteen remaining Class A war crimes suspects were to be freed after being held in Sugamo Prison or under house arrest for up to three years and a few months. General Headquarters lawyers noted that the precedents set by the Tokyo court in acquitting some defendants on several counts would make it almost impossible to convict these remaining suspects for aggression. This, General Headquarters stated, marked the end of trials of major war criminals in Japan.[33]

The Chinese Communist Party, which had been pleased to see Tojo hang, was enraged.[34] "Many murderers who directly massacred Chinese people and culprits of the aggression against China were among the arbitrarily freed," wrote the *People's Daily*. "The blood of millions of Chinese victims during the war against Japan cannot go down the drain, and millions of widows and orphans must be avenged."[35]

Not long ago, the United States had taken the lead in prosecuting over a thousand lower-level criminals, followed closely by Australia and Britain, and distantly trailed by China. The U.S. military commissions in Yokohama and Manila had handled high-profile cases such as a Japanese major general and colonel sentenced to death for the Bataan death march.[36] These courts were unforgiving: the U.S. and British trials convicted more than 90 percent of their defendants, while the Chinese courts found 75 percent guilty. The Americans executed 19 percent of their defendants and sentenced 21 percent to more than twenty-five years in jail—a rate topped only by China, which executed a quarter of its accused.

That was then. Now the Allies hoped to be entirely finished with these proceedings by the end of 1948. The British, who held trials in Hong Kong and Singapore, were the first to wrap up. The United States was starting to commute punishments, with the War Department exhorting General Headquarters to finish the lower-level war crimes trials by the end of the summer.[37] Under the Cold War policy pressed by George Kennan, the United States was wrapping up or undoing its purges—a prospect which alarmed MacArthur, who feared that Japanese extremists would in time take revenge on those Japanese who had worked with the American occupiers.[38]

MacArthur, never keen on war crimes trials, showed just how disenchanted he was with them in his first and only meeting with Harry Truman. In October 1950, the two men had an awkward encounter on Wake Island, with the president struggling to keep his commander under control during the Korean War. When asked about Korean war criminals, MacArthur replied sharply that he would try them swiftly with military commissions. "Don't touch the war criminals," he told Truman. "It doesn't work. The Nurnberg trials and Tokyo trials were no deterrent."[39]

As the Allies finalized a formal peace treaty to end the occupation, they understood that a sovereign Japanese government would soon face considerable agitation for parole or sweeping reductions of sentences for war criminals. Hundreds of thousands of Japanese signed petitions for clemency, while a mainstream Japanese magazine, complaining that the Tokyo verdict was "plainly a disregard of International Law," urged springing the Class A war criminals from jail.[40] Led by the United States, the weary Allies adopted a conspicuous leniency on the war criminals—a predictable result of Kennan's shift to building up Japan as a Cold War stronghold.[41]

The peace treaty, signed in San Francisco on September 8, 1951, went into force on April 28, 1952—restoring Japan as a sovereign country. Japan committed itself to the United Nations Charter and the Universal Declaration of Human Rights. In the San Francisco treaty, Japan formally accepted the judgments of the Tokyo trial as well as other Allied war crimes courts, and committed to carry out the sentences on Japanese citizens. An independent Japan was still under some limitations: it could only grant clemency, reduce sentences, or parole imprisoned war criminals with the agreement of whichever Allied government imposed those sentences. For those convicted by the Tokyo trial, Japan could only reduce their jail terms if a majority of the eleven Allied governments agreed.[42]

General Headquarters turned over the task of imprisoning Japanese war criminals to the new Japanese government.[43] Truman created a parole board for hundreds of imprisoned Japanese who had been convicted by U.S. military commissions. Knowing that Japan's new government would seek to free large numbers of them, the Truman administration wanted to settle the question on judicial grounds rather than political pressure. It was clear to everyone that the era of clemency had arrived.[44]

After the Tokyo trial, Edith Togo worked tirelessly for the release of her husband, Togo Shigenori, from prison.[45] She found an ally in Röling, who had voted to acquit him. "It is wonderful to think that there were some judges who had wisdom in their judgment," she wrote to the Dutch judge. "I hope that someday the people of the world will come to an understanding for what my husband has done for them and thereafter restore his honor in the eyes of the world, which is more precious to him than anything else."[46] She enterprisingly secured a letter from Princess Takamatsu, who had married one of Emperor Hirohito's brothers, declaring Togo a diplomat dedicated to peace.[47]

Röling and Edith Togo joined forces with an odd coalition: Joseph Grew, the former U.S. ambassador to Japan; Lord Hankey, a posh British former cabinet secretary and member of Neville Chamberlain's war cabinet who had written a book attacking war crimes trials for Germans and Japanese; and Blakeney, the defense lawyer.[48] Although they wanted to set free several convicted men, including Marquis Kido Koichi, Röling preferred to start with Shigemitsu Mamoru, who was hoping to return to public service and diplomacy.[49] He wrote to MacArthur urging parole for the former foreign minister.[50]

Shigemitsu was freed by a parole board in November 1950.[51] "I had read your 'dissenting opinion' well and admired so much your understanding of the case," he wrote gratefully to Röling from his home in Kamakura. "As for the trial, I was rather glad that my whole work has come out substantially to the public through it, even under the hard judicial" scrutiny.[52] Röling hoped that he would soon return to making Japanese foreign policy.[53] Sure enough, after being de-purged, he returned to public life as a stalwart of conservative political parties. In 1954 he would again become Japan's foreign minister.[54]

After the end of the occupation in 1952, a sovereign Japan moved speedily to release the remaining convicted Class A war criminals still in jail. Often their release was explained on grounds of ill health. This almost certainly was not the whole reason, but it was a convenient rationale for these old men, particularly for the first five who were set free; one former prime minister died in Sugamo Prison in 1950. Baron Hiranuma Kiichiro was paroled early in 1952; Field Marshal Hata Shunroku in 1954; and Kido, Kaya Okinori, and several others in 1955. In April 1958, Japan announced that the final ten surviving parolees were unconditionally released.[55]

Togo Shigenori had not been so lucky. In Sugamo Prison, he wasted away from heart disease, pernicious anemia, and bouts of gallbladder illness, while slowly going blind from cataracts.[56] "I genuinely hoped to construct an eternal peace of the world," he wrote in a letter to his family. He worked on a memoir to record his own story. He consoled himself with Meiji-era classics and translated European books in Sugamo's library, and with letters from his family. As he wrote to them, he wished that he could be a sparrow on the eaves of the family home in an upscale Tokyo neighborhood. He missed his wife, daughter, and young grandsons: "Receiving good letters from the children, I would sleep sound in a cold cement room."[57]

Prince Takamatsu pressed for Togo's release. Years later, Emperor Hirohito would praise him: "Foreign Minister Togo, his attitude was always the same, at the end of the war, and at the beginning of the war."[58] In despair, Edith Togo urged Röling to get her "sick, meritorious husband" out of Sugamo Prison immediately. It was "unthinkable," she wrote, that "the man who terminated the war should now go on to stay in prison for another 3 years."[59]

Before dawn on July 23, 1950, she was jolted awake by the telephone call she had been dreading: her husband had died three minutes ago, alone in a prison hospital. She nearly committed suicide from grief. Later she wrote that "since that day I had lost my soul, my faith in God, my wish to live."[60]

CHAPTER 32

A Silent Prayer

IN THE DECADES AFTER his dissent, Radhabinod Pal became an icon for Japanese nationalists, romanticizing the war as being about liberating colonized Asians from Western imperialism. As his grandson Satyabrata Pal puts it, his grandfather and postwar Japan "were thrown together into something like an arranged Hindu marriage: he did not have a choice and went in sight unseen, accepting it as a social responsibility. It defined him from then on, and it became a relationship for life. Love certainly did develop from time-to-time in such marriages, as it did in Dadu's with Japan."[1]

He returned after the Tokyo verdict to Calcutta, where his beloved wife died in April 1949, according to his granddaughter Ruby Pal. Bereft, he was comforted by his large family and "millions of grandchildren," as his urbane grandson Satyabrata Pal affectionately puts it. Soon after her death, the Indian judge sent a heartfelt letter to General Douglas MacArthur thanking him for always helping him to fly home to see her. "I feel I have no strength left in me that can sustain me after this at this hour of my life," Pal confided to MacArthur. "How much I wish I could have been non-attached and could have been blessed with a glimpse into what the philosophers characterize as the real nature of ultimate reality."[2]

As a celebrated lawyer at home in an independent India, Pal argued that there was no real global community under the rule of international law, warning that weaker states risked exploitation by unscrupulous big powers.[3] He grew more vociferous in his criticism of Western imperialism and the United States in the early Cold War. Delivering the prestigious Tagore Law Lectures at Calcutta University in 1951, Pal was horrified at France and Holland for fighting to reimpose their colonial rule over

Indochina and Indonesia, denouncing the deployment of British troops to help the Dutch try to pound Java into submission.[4] After the Indonesians appealed to Harry Truman, he recounted, "Washington promptly asked the British if they would not please *remove the American insignia* and the initials 'USA' from their fighting gear. Neither did that *stalwart action* in the spirit of the Atlantic Charter halt the war in Java!" The postwar world, he pronounced, seemed about the same as it was before World War II: a subjugated people would get freedom only if they were strong enough to fight for it.[5]

When the Korean War broke out, he blamed the United States. Under Japanese rule, he said, Korea had functioned as a single unit; now the country was cut in half and paralyzed. "I do not know if even after all this the conventional picture of the American in Asia as 'the picture of a well-meaning blunderer' can still persist," he said. "I do not know how the myth could grow that the American role in Asia had been 'the role of distinterested benevolence.'" Despite his past praise of MacArthur and the tenderness of his recent letter to him, he publicly excoriated him: "M[a]cArthur wanted war."[6]

His realpolitik-minded skepticism about international morality, which in many ways echoed the thinking of George Kennan, only deepened. "I cannot think of anything more atrocious and criminal than this use of atom bomb," he said. "But those who were perpetrators of this atrocity still go unpunished and untried simply because they belong to victor nations. This is how law, even when recognized as such, operates in international life!"[7]

His beliefs could lead him into dark corners. In those Calcutta University lectures, he was as skeptical of Nuremberg as he had been about the Tokyo trial. Six years after the worldwide screening of newsreels showing the realities of the Nazi death camps, Pal shockingly doubted the facts of the Holocaust—in much the same way as he had questioned the Nanjing massacre. After recounting some of the atrocities against the Jews, Pal warned his audience against the dangers of Allied war propaganda. Nuremberg's findings about Auschwitz and the murder of six million Jews, he said, "reminds me of the story given out during the First World War about the use of dead bodies by the Germans. The story will remain recorded in history as the classic lie of war propaganda." Repeating verbatim lines from his dissent used to discount Japanese atrocities, he called into question the facts of the Holocaust:

Since the First World War there has been such a demand for the trial and conviction of defeated warlords, that a sort of unconscious processes were going on in the mind of every one who devoted his interest and energies to get these persons punished. These processes in most cases remain unobserved by the conscious part of the personality and are influenced only indirectly and remotely by it. The result might be a partial distortion of reality. There would always be some eagerness to accept as real anything that lies in the direction of the unconscious wishes.

He doubted the reliability of the testimony of Holocaust survivors, reusing phrases from his dissent discrediting eyewitnesses to the Nanjing massacre, while disputing Nuremberg's documentation of the extermination of the Jews: "Let us hope that this past history of propaganda was kept in view while considering the evidence on these points. . . . Let us hope that the witnesses to these facts did not come with conviction induced only by excitability serving to arouse credulity in them and acting as a persuasive interpreter of probabilities and possibilities."[8]

Pal was appointed to the United Nations International Law Commission in 1952, where he eventually became chairman, urging that international law catch up with the "fundamental human needs" of newly independent postcolonial countries.[9] Yet not quite ready to ease into retirement, in 1953 he ran for a seat representing southeast Calcutta in Parliament. (Ironically enough, the seat had been vacated by the death of his old enemy from his days at Calcutta University, the Hindu nationalist firebrand Syama Prasad Mookerjee.) With a redoubtable public reputation, Pal probably would have fared better running as an independent, but—despite Jawaharlal Nehru's wariness about him—the ruling Congress Party enlisted him as their candidate. This allowed the local Communists to run a campaign against Congress in general, accusing him of selling out by joining it. "Congress is to blame if Dr Pal is defeated," wrote the influential Bombay-based *Economic Weekly*. After a lackluster campaign, he was trounced by the Communist candidate, a crusading blind lawyer named Sadhan Gupta, who would have a long career as one of India's leading leftists.[10] "He lost in that election because he never went canvassing," recalls his son Pratip Bijoy Pal with fond exasperation. "He never gave any speeches."

BIG IN JAPAN

Thwarted at home, neglected by Nehru's government, Pal's thoughts turned again to Japan. "He came to love Japan," says Satyabrata Pal. "He had a deep sense of admiration for these people."

His most ardent promoter in Japan was Tanaka Masaaki, a fervent admirer of General Matsui Iwane, who was convicted and hanged by Pal's colleagues for the Nanjing massacre. An industrious denier of Japanese atrocities, Tanaka later wrote a shoddy book titled *What Really Happened in Nanking*.[11] After he edited the published wartime diary of Matsui, he was caught doctoring it, making several hundred alterations.[12] He once suggested that Chinese may get pleasure from sexual assaults while Japanese "have never found such acts amusing."[13]

Tanaka says that he secured a Japanese copy of Pal's dissent from Kiyose Ichiro, Tojo Hideki's defense lawyer. Under General Headquarters' censorship, Japanese newspapers had only published a brief mention of the dissent. "It was like I was possessed; I was consumed with the desire to obtain Justice Pal's opinion and publish it to sound an alarm bell for the Japanese people, who were being crushed by a postwar sense of guilt," Tanaka wrote. He wrote to Pal asking to publish his dissent; the Indian jurist agreed, according to Tanaka, saying that a judicial opinion is a public document but admonishing him not to willfully alter it.

Tanaka prepared a partial edition of the dissent with his own commentary, secretly printing the book so that it would be ready in bookstores on the day the Allied occupation ended in April 1952. It hit the shelves as *Japan Is Innocent*—a title that implied a far more thorough exoneration than Pal's complex dissent actually delivered.[14] It did so alongside another condensed version of the dissent, also with a misleading title: *Refuting the History of the War: Japan Was Innocent*.[15] As Tanaka later boasted, his edition "drew a sensational response from the public, and became a bestseller." Pal refused any royalties for Tanaka's book, saying that his dissent was a public record.[16] The Indian judge drew the attention of an elderly nationalist publisher, Shimonaka Yasaburo, who had testified for the defense at the Tokyo trial about Matsui's love for China. According to Tanaka, he invited Pal to Japan, funding and organizing a monthlong visit.[17]

Pal clearly had reservations about being used as a tool for these Japanese extremists. He complained that only a partial version of his dissent had been published, urging the subsequent publication of the whole thing.[18] He initially canceled the trip after getting a letter from a famous Japanese urging him not to cause trouble with the Americans, saying that he did not want his presence to be unwelcome for even a single Japanese. Then he decided to go through with it.[19]

Almost four years after the Tokyo judgment, he returned to a sovereign Japan for a sensational tour in October and November 1952.[20] Silver-haired and handsome at sixty-six, impeccably dressed in a spring jacket or three-piece suits, he was elated to be back in Japan. On arrival at Haneda

Airport in Tokyo, he told reporters that his verdict had "caused a stir," but his mind was unchanged: "I strongly believe that my way of thinking is how the whole world thinks now."[21] While condemning the "inhumane blows dealt on Hiroshima and Nagasaki," he declared himself "a great admirer of Japan's national character. Japan is truly a trustworthy nation." He praised Japanese loyalty, dignity, and resilience: "Even defeat could not rob the Japanese of their morality."[22]

At a freewheeling press conference back at the Imperial Hotel in Tokyo, he endorsed a standard Japanese imperialist explanation of the war: "We cannot deny Japan was wrong in provoking a war, but we must recognize that at least she had one problem—her ever increasing population."[23] He condemned the San Francisco peace treaty as "unnecessarily harsh" while complaining that too many Japanese were embracing as generous a treaty they had been forced to accept. (Nehru had refused to sign the San Francisco treaty, signaling India's detachment from the United States in the Cold War.)[24] If a war was unjustified, he said, then all soldiers who fought in it were war criminals—a gratuitous reference to the murder charges that had formed no part of the final Tokyo judgment. Yet both the Nuremberg and Tokyo courts were "confused" about whether a war was just and who decided that. Japan, he said, should dissolve MacArthur's decisions, try Japanese war criminals under Japanese sovereignty, and release them.[25]

When Pal faced criticism for his vehement press conference, he explained that he did not mean to criticize the other judges but the tribunal itself. As a result of the war, the truth was lost. He contended that before the war, Japan had sought to feed its growing population by peaceful means and had only turned to "other policies" when stymied by a monopolistic American and British economic world order that excluded developing countries. He said that the Allies should have held a commission to examine Japan's grievances: "The Allied Powers should not have established the Far Eastern Military Tribunal. But because they went ahead and did so, they lost a chance for peace."[26]

For a month, he gave forthright talks in numerous cities across the country. He had tea with Japan's foreign minister at his Foreign Ministry offices.[27] At famed Tokyo University, he told a crowd of five hundred students that Japan should not rearm but instead learn from Mahatma Gandhi's creed of nonviolent resistance to British colonialism. In a new nuclear era that risked a fatal Third World War, he advised, Japan would be better off staying demilitarized and not taking sides in the Cold War.[28] He said that Japan's former leaders had strengthened Japan's defenses, but the West had understood that as aggression—endorsing at least in part claims that Japan's war had been in self-defense. He warned that while "the light of the West guides us all," that "light may one day become a fire."[29] At an Indian-influenced Buddhist shrine in Tokyo, he prayed for the soul of his late wife, clasping his hands in devotion.[30] He was joined there by Edith Togo, the widow of Togo Shigenori.[31]

Pal spoke even more sharply when reporters were not around. He pointedly called his minority opinion a judgment, an aggrandizement that has become standard in Japan today. In a closed-door speech at the Tokyo Bar Association attended by the chief justice of Japan's Supreme Court, he contended that the Tokyo court's charter, imposed by "the war victors," went against international law. To applause, he encouraged a newly sovereign Japan to make its own decisions about releasing war criminals from Sugamo Prison. When a survivor of the atomic bombs asked him whether it was a crime to harm innocent civilians, Pal replied that atom bombs meant only "barbarous destruction" despite high-minded explanations for their use. He said that "bringing about peace with a hydrogen bomb or an atom bomb is absolutely unthinkable."[32]

For much of this trip, he became an instrument of the far right. Guided by Shimonaka and Tanaka, he conducted a kind of book tour promoting his own recently published dissent. His welcoming committee included Kiyose Ichiro, the defense lawyer for Tojo Hideki.[33] Dressed somberly in a dark suit, he went to the Yasukuni Shrine to pray for the Japanese war dead.[34] He laid flowers on the grave of Rashbehari Bose, the Bengali revolutionary who had helped found the Greater Asia Association in Japan.[35]

On arriving, he had announced that he meant to visit with the families of Class A war criminals. Some of his Japanese friends cautioned him that this would be exploited by far-right political parties and get him in trouble. Explaining that he had not written his dissent to win the good opinion of the Japanese people, he decided to go ahead even if it offended the Japanese.[36]

He visited Tojo's family at their home.[37] Most dramatically, he met with the surviving men who had sat before him accused as Class A war criminals. First was Okawa Shumei, the militant putschist and propagandist who had been ruled insane after slapping Tojo's head, who called on the Indian jurist at the Imperial Hotel. In an amiable hourlong chat, Pal quoted from the Bengali sage Rabindranath Tagore to urge the Japanese people to return to a simple spiritual life. Rather than learning from Europe and the United States, he advised, Japan should study the two hundred years of British oppression that India had survived. Afterward Okawa said that Pal was "truly a person of integrity."[38]

In another session at the Imperial Hotel, Pal discussed the Tokyo trial with Shigemitsu Mamoru, now paroled and leading the Reform Party, who expressed his "deepest gratitude and respect" to the one judge who had "argued for Japan's innocence." When the former foreign minister urged more efforts to release the remaining war criminals, Pal replied, "The war criminals held at Sugamo should be released under Japan's restored sovereignty as soon as possible, a just cause for which I too will do the utmost."[39]

With an enduring revulsion for the atomic bombings, he went to Hiroshima for a conference on world government.[40] Pal prayed silently at the new cenotaph for victims of the atomic bomb, which has a delicately nonjudgmental inscription: "Rest in peace for we shall not repeat the error." Reading that, he wondered what error the Japanese were pledging to avoid. He said that he agreed that if Japan were to rearm itself, that would be a desecration of the souls of the victims. Yet he fumed at the dodge of American responsibility. Gathered here are the souls of atom bomb victims, he said, and it is clear that the ones who used the atom bomb were not the Japanese. He declared that the hands of those who dropped the bomb had yet to be cleansed.[41]

He gave a speech at a Hiroshima primary school near a domed industrial building that was the only structure left standing near the hypocenter of the atomic blast, and today is famous as the Hiroshima Peace Memorial. He declared that "experiments by big powers with arms have failed miserably and the world must start a new experiment for world peace." He got loud applause for expressing "deep sympathy" for the pain suffered by the Japanese during and after the war.[42] He announced that it was the responsibility of the West that nationalist conflicts in Asia had not yet been resolved. Soon before a group of atom bomb victims displayed their scarred faces to a hushed crowd, Pal thundered, "What excuses were given at the time of the bombing of Hiroshima and Nagasaki? Why did they have to be bombed?"[43]

He asked why the United States had dropped the atom bombs when Japan had already made a peace proposal through the Soviet Union. The Allies, he said, should have realized that Japan would be defeated; he accused them of using the bombs on Japan as an experiment. "While I have heard various excuses from the country that dropped the bombs, I have yet to hear any words of true confession," he said. "The hands that dropped the bombs have yet to be purified." Then he toughened his accusation, declaring that racism lay at the heart of the attitude that had used the atomic bombs. The race problem, he said, was fundamental and deep-rooted; he pointed to the defeat of the racial equality clause for the League of Nations, as well as to apartheid South Africa.[44]

The next day, he gave a fifty-minute speech in Hiroshima warning about Western aggression against Asia. A group of local girls, painfully scarred from the atomic blast, came onstage and read a message of peace.[45]

Finally, six hours before flying out of Haneda Airport on November 11, Pal made his most sensational gesture: a visit to convicted war criminals in Sugamo Prison. He walked around the various cells and the infirmary, shaking hands with the men behind bars. The meeting was "deeply moving," reported the *Mainichi Shimbun*. With a respectful attitude, Pal greeted the prisoners with his palms pressed together, eliciting applause. He spent about forty minutes in a conference room with all twelve remaining convicted Class A war criminals. That included Marquis Kido Koichi; Kaya Okinori, the finance minister who had argued against Pearl Harbor; Field Marshal Hata Shunroku, who had bloodily commanded Japanese forces in China; General Araki Sadao, a hard-liner who had supported the secret biowarfare of Unit 731; and Lieutenant General Oshima Hiroshi, the pro-Nazi ambassador in Berlin, a lifelong admirer of Adolf Hitler.[46] Meeting with thirty Class B and Class C prisoners, convicted of war crimes and crimes against humanity, Pal said that he would "continue to push for their release." There were many more convicts who wanted to meet with him, so some three hundred war criminals were allowed to wave goodbye.[47]

Since many of these meetings were not open to the press, the activist Tanaka Masaaki has been able to promote his own versions of what happened. Yet given his track record, his accounts cannot be trusted. Tanaka's tales are best understood as the imagined Pal that Japanese rightists wish for, rather than the actual Pal. The accounts of Pal's speeches in the mainstream Japanese press are noticeably less inflammatory than those given by Tanaka. Sometimes Tanaka's own versions of Pal's words contradict each other. (Pal would continue to work with Tanaka, which suggests that when he exaggerated the Indian jurist's words, he did so subtly enough that it was not immediately apparent, or perhaps was simply shrouded in translation.) In a best-selling book about Pal published in 1963, Tanaka would distort the Indian judge's dissent to omit its condemnations of Japanese war crimes.[48] In a 1995 book, he would claim that Pal told Japanese reporters that they had a "masochistic view of history"—a distinctive stock phrase of Japanese nationalists that is unlikely to have tripped from Pal's lips. He purports that Pal told him that the impact of the Tokyo trial was more severe than the damage from the atom bombs—a quote that is entirely at odds with Pal's deep revulsion at real atomic devastation.[49]

Pal retained his outrage at Western racism until his last days. During a 1959 talk in Calcutta calling for the abolition of military force, he warned, "The possibility that the man of colour may eventually bring the white man's ascendancy to an end and may even establish an ascendancy of his own haunts the white mind like a nightmare."[50] And in a wide-ranging 1961 speech in Geneva, he complained that a billion Asians were condemned to "degrading poverty and primitive backwardness" resulting from Western plunder of the wealth of the East.[51] In a 1963 lecture in Calcutta about the Universal Declaration of Human Rights, he lauded its commitment to secure racial equality against the "dangerous weapon" of what he called "[r]ace-feeling." He repeated from his dissent the story of Japanese delegates seeking to enshrine racial equality into the League of Nations, only to be thwarted by the British Empire; he even reused the quote about William Morris Hughes as the "champion of the cause of White Supremacy."[52]

At the age of eighty, an ailing Pal made a last visit to Japan in October 1966, to promote a new edition of his dissent. By now conservatives had been in power for long enough that it was not shocking to hear Japanese critics denounce the Tokyo trial as an American tool to brainwash their people.[53] On this trip he was so firmly ensconced as a fixture of powerful Japanese rightists that he was hosted by Kishi Nobusuke, the former Class A suspect who, after being released by the Americans from Sugamo Prison without being tried, had gone on to become foreign minister and then prime minister, as well as Kiyose Ichiro, the defense lawyer for Tojo who had later been speaker of Japan's House of Representatives.[54] Pal and Kishi became friends, according to his grandchildren Satyabrata Pal and Ruby Pal.

At Haneda Airport, Pal walked slowly down the ramp. He still had a full head of hair, now gray, and wore the same smart suits, but his face was gaunt with age. He vigorously shook hands with Kiyose and other defense lawyers from the Tokyo trial. He was, he said, very happy to see the Japanese people one last time before he died. "The war was not something that occurred as a matter of the responsibility of a single country; all of the countries that participated in the war bear responsibility for it," he announced. "Despite that all of the other judges found Japan guilty, I did not. I still believe that my opinion represents the truth."[55]

He was greeted enthusiastically, particularly among nationalists, who held him up as an authentic Asian voice who appreciated wartime Japan. The Japanese government's chief cabinet secretary honored him with the Grand Cordon of the Order of the Sacred Treasure, while the vice governor of Tokyo presented him with the key to the city.[56] One law professor wrote in the conservative *Yomiuri Shimbun* that "the Indian nation decided there was no better person than Dr. Pal to represent Asian peoples and stand up against the impending attack of the victorious Western nations upon a defeated Japan," unaware that Pal had actually been appointed by the British.[57] Another *Yomiuri* writer praised "his sense of justice and courage as a legal scholar working for peace."[58] The liberal *Asahi Shimbun*, too, praised him for decrying the atomic bomb and hailed him as a follower of Gandhi.[59]

Back at the Imperial Hotel for the last time, he was hosted for a lunch by Kishi and Kiyose, where he was struck with abdominal pain. He clutched his stomach through a ceremony receiving an honorary doctorate from Nihon University. He was scheduled to give a major speech in central Tokyo, sponsored by the *Yomiuri*, titled "World Peace and International Law: A View of the Pacific War." Kiyose introduced him to a crowd of hundreds, but Pal was too ill to come out. The crowd waited patiently for over an hour and a half, until he unexpectedly appeared at the back of the hall. Clad in a black suit, supported on both sides by assistants, he made his way up the aisle with his hands pressed together before his chest as if in prayer. Reaching the stage, he bowed deeply to the rapt audience. He was unable to speak. He later said he was overcome not with illness but with emotion. He wept, and many in the crowd burst into tears too. After a long moment of silence, Kiyose embraced him and told the crowd that Pal needed to rest. As he walked out, the audience applauded thunderously, some of them praying and accompanying him to his car. "Silence had moved people's hearts far more effectively than an eloquent speech could have," reported the *Yomiuri Shimbun*.[60]

He had to cancel his planned visits to Hiroshima and Nagasaki.[61] At one point, he wrote "I love Japan" on a photograph, recalls his granddaughter Ruby Pal. At a farewell reception in Tokyo hosted by Shimonaka and others, his hands pressed together, he said that he had always "felt the deep affection of the Japanese people" while visiting. His doctor had warned him not to come, but "I thought that if I died in responding to the affection of the Japanese people, I could die with peace of mind." The Tokyo trial, he said, had "a tendency for evidence advantageous to Japan to be hidden and for disadvantageous evidence to be presented. My only desire is that Japanese come together in their own way and, without surrendering to a sense of guilt, rise up for the benefit of the world. The whole world is watching."[62]

After Pal's death in 1967, he has largely been forgotten in India but lionized in Japan. "While my grandfather was alive, every Japanese prime minister visiting India would come to Calcutta to meet him," claims Satyabrata Pal.

In 1974, he and his Japanese patron were honored with the Pal-Shimonaka Memorial Hall in Hakone, where many of his belongings are kept. Japan's prime minister, Miki Takeo, wrote that Pal was "the personification and unflinching champion of the cause of law who had exemplified the cardinal principle of justice and peace, neither obsequious to the victor nor disdainful to the vanquished."[63] In 1997 some of his children went to Kyoto for a ceremony establishing a memorial for the Indian judge at a shrine there, according to his granddaughter Ruby Pal.

The Yasukuni war shrine in Tokyo, which had long since become a centerpiece for right-wing nationalists, added a handsome stone monument to Pal on its grounds. At the unveiling ceremony, the chief priest spoke the lingo of rightist nationalists: "It is my earnest wish that the drift of masochism will end."[64] Since 1959, Yasukuni has enshrined almost a thousand dead Class B and Class C war criminals; in 1978, it added fourteen Class A war criminals, including Tojo Hideki and the other six

Japanese pay their respects at the memorial to Radhabinod Pal at the Yasukuni Shrine, Tokyo, August 15, 2015.

who were hanged, as well as those who died of natural causes while in custody. The monolith for Pal fixes his stature in a rightist pantheon. It has a prime location near a statue of a kamikaze pilot and the polemical Yushukan museum, and is an easy stroll to a monument to the Kempeitai. It shows Pal in judicial robes with his arms sternly crossed, and bears the concluding lines of his dissent, wrongly attributed to him instead of Jefferson Davis. Admirers leave fresh flowers there.

In August 2007, Abe Shinzo, Japan's taboo-breaking rightist prime minister—and the grandson of Kishi Nobusuke—visited India as part of a concerted effort to build alliances with Asia's other democracies.[65] He risked controversy to make a side trip to Kolkata (previously known as Calcutta) to meet one of Pal's elderly sons. In an inflammatory move, Abe visited a museum to the rebel Subhas Chandra Bose, which features a photograph of him shaking hands with Adolf Hitler in Berlin. "Many Japanese have been moved deeply by such persons of strong will and action of the independence of India like Subhas Chandra Bose," the Japanese prime minister said. "Even to this day, many Japanese revere Radhabinod Pal."[66] In Delhi, Abe told the Indian Parliament: "Justice Pal is highly respected even today by many Japanese for the noble spirit of courage he exhibited during the International Military Tribunal for the Far East."[67] South Korea's biggest newspaper, the *Chosun Ilbo*, was disgusted at Abe: "He will travel all the way to India to embrace the descendants of a judge hailed as a hero by Japanese militarists for claiming innocence for Class A war criminals."[68]

In 2013, India's president, Pranab Mukherjee, hosting Emperor Akihito in Delhi, paid tribute to Pal—something which may not have gone down well with the pacifistic emperor.[69] In an NHK miniseries about the Tokyo trial, Pal was played by the excellent and globally famous Bollywood movie star Irrfan Khan.

Pal's name is routinely invoked by Indian leaders visiting Japan, as well as India's Ministry of External Affairs and even the navy. Manmohan Singh, as India's prime minister, praised Pal's "principled judgement" in a speech to the Diet in Tokyo.[70] Although Pal was an ardent foe of one of the originators of Hindu chauvinist politics, Syama Prasad Mookerjee, today he has been embraced by hard-line Hindu nationalists. In a speech in Japan in 2019, Narendra Modi, India's strongman prime minister, listed Pal alongside such legendary Indian friends of Japan as Rabindranath Tagore and Subhas Chandra Bose.[71]

Pal has become a fixture in Japanese popular culture. He features prominently in a shocking 1998 movie, *Pride: The Fateful Moment*, which extolls Tojo Hideki for a postwar generation of Japanese. While reviling the Tokyo trial as a vengeful sham, *Pride* uses a soulful Pal character to suggest that Tojo was really fighting to liberate all of Asia from Western colonialism.[72] A prominent right-wing writer and manga artist, Kobayashi Yoshinori, drew Pal into his 1998 manga polemic *On War*, which contends that Japan fought a just war of self-defense and liberation. "All defendants are not guilty!" says Pal in the manga.[73] Glossing over Pal's rich complexities—the anticolonialist who made his career through the Raj, the champion of Asians who became so at odds with the Chinese that he doubted the Nanjing massacre, the tolerant friend of minorities in India who questioned the facts of the Holocaust, the principled opponent of racism who quoted Jefferson Davis—the Japanese right wing has at last literally reduced him to a cartoon.

His grandson Satyabrata Pal remembers a more decorous tribute. Throughout his long career as an Indian diplomat and ambassador, Japanese officials would do a double take when they heard his surname: " 'Pal? Are you related to the judge?' Irrespective of the Japanese's rank, he would take two steps back and bow to the waist. He wasn't bowing to me, he was bowing to the judge."

CHAPTER 33

The Inescapable Purge
of Comrade Mei

WHILE MEI RUAO SAT in the Tokyo courtroom in November 1948 listening to the reading of the judgment he had labored to make, Chinese Communist forces were closing in on the capital of Nanjing. Terrified at the advance, some people in the city fled, while others turned to looting and mob violence. Americans and other foreigners were evacuating. The police were losing control of the situation or deserting.[1]

The U.S. ambassador in Nanjing secretly warned that the "early fall [of] present Nationalist Government is inevitable." When Mao Zedong's revolutionaries seized power, he wrote, "We shall have to make the best of a bad situation and save what we can from the wreckage."[2] Though Chiang Kai-shek had vowed to fight to his dying breath, the U.S. ambassador warned—in a cable passed directly to Harry Truman—that the bulk of the Chinese people and virtually all government officials were resigned to a Communist victory. The ambassador urged an orderly transfer of power, fearing a hasty flight of Chiang and his entourage into exile.[3]

A few days later, while Sir William Webb was still reading the Tokyo judgment aloud, Chiang sent a frantic appeal to Truman for more military aid and for American military advisers—unaware that U.S. officials in China had already concluded that the situation was so dire that there were no military steps with which Chiang could salvage it. "The Communist forces in Central China are now within striking distance of Shanghai and Nanking," wrote the falling Chinese potentate. "If we fail to stem the tide, China may be lost to the cause of democracy."[4]

The same day that General Douglas MacArthur confirmed the Tokyo sentences, the director of the newly established CIA informed Truman that Communist forces could wipe out the remaining Nationalist pockets of resistance, which would "effectively destroy the Nationalist military machine and open the door to Nanking." The only question was whether it would take weeks or months.[5] The Truman administration grew noticeably frosty to the frantic entreaties from Chiang and his inner circle for military assistance and political support.[6]

Chinese Nationalist officials turned to talking about fighting on from Taiwan.[7]

Mei grieved for his country's ordeal. Throughout the Tokyo trial, he had been embarrassed by newspaper headlines about Chinese poverty, turmoil, and civil war. "For someone situated abroad," he once wrote in his diary, "it felt especially painful to see your own nation disappointing."[8]

After the trial, Chiang's crumbling government offered Mei a lofty position as justice minister. He faced the most agonizing political decision of his life. Should he follow his Nationalist patrons into exile on Taiwan, or return to the mainland and throw in his lot with the Communists?

Since most of his diaries were destroyed in the Cultural Revolution—a fact which in itself indicates both what he chose and how it went—it is difficult to say how he decided.[9] Of course, his extended family was on the mainland and a life in Taiwan would be unfamiliar. The judge, says his son Mei Xiaoao, had a Confucian sense of responsibility to his parents, and would have been uncomfortable leaving them behind to go to Taiwan. Furthermore, Chiang's dictatorial government was embarking on four decades of martial law. Most notoriously, starting in February 1947, mainland Nationalist troops crushed a Taiwanese uprising, with at least eighteen thousand people killed. Many progressive Chinese were disgusted by the subsequent "white terror" unleashed against the regime's domestic critics beginning in 1949, with more than a thousand people executed and tens of thousands arrested before that repressive era at last came to an end by 1992.[10] As Mei's daughter Mei Xiaokan says, "I heard he didn't want to board a sinking ship. He was disappointed about the corrupt KMT [Nationalist] government."

Like many intellectuals at the time, he was drawn by the Communists' claims to work for the poor and build a more fair and democratic society.[11] "At that time, the Communists were quite a new hope for people," says his daughter. "I guess he believed they would make China a better country." His son says, "He has hope in the Chinese Communist Party's governance."

Mei chose the new revolution. Evading the Nationalists, he instead went to Hong Kong in June 1949, where he was reunited with his wife.

There he was contacted by the Communist Party's representative in Hong Kong, the leading diplomat and future foreign minister Qiao Guanhua, asking him to work for them. He held press conferences expressing his admiration for the Communist Party. In December, soon after Mao's proclamation of the People's Republic of China, he sailed north for Beijing.

On his arrival, he attended a ceremony where he was publicly praised by no less than Zhou Enlai, the premier and foreign minister. "We know that he worked at the International Military Tribunal for the Far East for nearly three years and issued serious and righteous sentences to major criminals who invaded our country," said Zhou. "He did a great thing for the people and added glory to our nation. People of the entire country should thank him."

At first, Mei was treated well enough. He was appointed as a Foreign Ministry adviser and later became a member of the People's Congress. He moved his family into a courtyard home where he could sing Beijing opera, draw cartoons on the frosted windows, buy toy swords for his son, and teach his daughter to sing children's folk songs from his rural hometown. Under Zhou, one of the founding revolutionaries of the People's Republic, the Foreign Ministry was somewhat insulated from the radical changes sweeping the government and society.[12] Mei's well-educated colleagues were pleasant; old specialists could still research problems of international law or world politics, which suited his academic leanings. He worked on a manuscript about the Tokyo trial.[13]

Mei reinvented himself as a loyal Communist. Forsaking his hard-won formal Chinese and elegant English, he trained himself to produce the stock jargon of Maoist propaganda, as required of any successful cadre. His political views, as revealed in his diary, were revised.

He had long adored the United States. Yet just two years after leaving Tokyo, he wrote a blistering article: "Because of the American imperialists' single-handed domination over Japan and their ambition to rule the world, not only did a free and democratic new Japan fail to emerge, but the old Japan characterized by fascist rule of terror is coming back at an accelerating pace." Although Mei had actually believed that the American promotion of democratization was too generous, he now dismissed it as merely cosmetic. American imperialists and monopoly capitalists, he wrote, were rebuilding Japan as their colony in order to attack Asia. Mei, who had been awestruck by MacArthur in the flesh, now condemned him (a "white emperor") for brutalizing the Japanese Communist Party, promoting reactionary rule, and empowering the *zaibatsu*. Only on one point did his true opinions emerge: criticizing MacArthur for releasing and paroling Japanese war criminals.[14] He endorsed a Soviet proposal to put the emperor on trial for Japanese biowarfare: "Only the American imperialists are trying to defend Hirohito and other war criminals."[15]

During the Korean War, with Chinese and American troops in pitched combat, Mei implausibly accused the Americans of sending warplanes to spread germ warfare against northeastern China—playing his part in an almost certainly false propaganda campaign by North Korea, China, and the Soviet Union.[16] In 1952, Mao's regime used his credentials from the Tokyo trial to condemn the Americans as genocidal war criminals worse than Imperial Japan. In an open letter to his fellow Tokyo judges, Mei wrote, "The severity of this crime is worse than that of any atrocity we heard at Nuremberg and the International Military Tribunal for the Far East!" After conducting an ersatz official investigation, he offered to be a witness if there was ever an international tribunal for the American war criminals. Invoking the Nanjing massacre and the Bataan death march, he declared that "the evilness of the American invaders' germ warfare against peaceful Chinese people exceeds that of the Japanese war criminals' atrocities."[17]

Despite such efforts, Mei simply did not fit in Mao's new regime.[18] After all, he was a bourgeois, English-speaking, American-educated lawyer who had worked for the Nationalists. He was expected to renounce his worldview, report on the evolution of his political thinking, join in a never-ending series of political movements, and learn Russian. He grew nervous and frustrated.

He had a first brush with peril during the Anti-Rightist Campaign in 1957. Like countless others, he made the mistake of taking Mao at his word when he welcomed the "blooming of a hundred flowers," a risky invitation to criticize the regime. The Party later said it had managed to "lure the snake out of its hole." Afterward, more than half a million people—including intellectuals, artists, and writers—were suddenly branded as rightists and sent off to work in the countryside or a labor camp. Many of them were, like Mei, solid supporters of the Chinese Communist Party.[19]

His criticisms were mild enough. At a seminar of senior experts at the Foreign Ministry, Mei decorously said that the Communist Party's leadership was unquestionable and its achievements were apparent. Yet he suggested that the Party should give real power to the People's Congress. Soon before the Soviet Union fell out of favor, he said, "Revering the Soviet Union as deities and regarding the words of Soviet experts as golden rules are acts of dogmatism and xenomania."[20]

For that, he was branded as a rightist. He got off lightly compared to many others: the attacks on him stayed mostly inside the government, and

his name did not appear on the terrifying blacklists of supposed reactionaries published in the state press. His salary and benefits were cut but he
managed to keep his job. As Mei's children later wrote, he was "treated
unfairly" in the Anti-Rightist Campaign, yet he remained as patriotic as
ever, conscientiously and diligently reflecting upon himself.[21]

"You Cannot Apologize Every Day, Can You?"

Mei's harsh opinions about Japanese war crimes proved to be a distinct
political liability in the People's Republic.

The Communist Party held itself up as the only leader of the war
against the Japanese, accusing the Nationalists of cowardice, humiliating defeat, or treasonous collaboration with the invaders. Communist
propagandists had paid little attention to the Tokyo trial, a Nationalist
initiative, while it was ongoing.[22] Although the Communists accused
the Nationalists of neglecting the punishment of Japanese evildoers, they
were more interested in besmirching Chiang and his retinue than in pursuing anything so bourgeois as war crimes trials.[23] Mei, as a functionary in the Nationalist war effort, had been disdainfully described by the
People's Daily as "Judge Mei Ruao, whom bandit Chiang sent to Tokyo to
attend the International Military Tribunal for the Far East."[24]

Then in the early Cold War, the issue of Japanese war criminals
became a way of excoriating the Americans. "It is American imperialists,
not Japan, who helped Chiang Kai-shek fight the civil war," explained
Mao. "Consequently, the target of our hatred has moved away from Japan
and onto American imperialism."[25] Zhou Enlai accused the United States
of reviving Japanese militarism and coddling the war criminals, while
Japan's conservative rulers were denounced as running dogs of American
imperialism. When MacArthur allowed an early release of some Japanese
war criminals, Zhou reprimanded him for violating "the solemn and just
decisions of the International Military Tribunal for the Far East to punish Japanese war criminals."[26] Emperor Hirohito, who had made himself
so useful to the United States, was reviled as a leading war criminal,
with a renewed push in 1950 to charge him for germ warfare.[27] Early
in the Korean War, Zhou complained that the American occupiers had
released many important war criminals, seeking to "completely make
Japan an American colony and use Japan as America's tool to invade
Asian nations."[28]

Yet China's official attitude toward Japan softened dramatically as it
sought to lure it away from the United States, pursuing a normalization of

relations that would be achieved in 1972. The Japanese were portrayed as fellow victims of Western imperialism.[29] "The Chinese people no longer resent Japan as much as before and, instead, have adopted a friendly attitude," Mao told Burma's president in 1954.[30] Zhou emphasized two thousand years of friendship between China and Japan, interrupted briefly by a regrettable conflict which was now over.[31] "We are your friends," Mao told visiting Japanese legislators in 1955. "You clearly see the Chinese people treat you not as enemies but as friends. . . . [W]e must think of every means possible to make America withdraw its hands." He added an astonishingly conciliatory statement that no Chinese Communist cadre could say today: "You have apologized. You cannot apologize every day, can you? It is not good for a nation to sulk."[32]

Since the issue of repatriating some remaining Japanese war criminals got in the way of normalization, China adopted a decidedly lenient treatment of them.[33] "This issue could be resolved as quickly as possible after the normalization of diplomatic relations," Mao candidly told those Japanese politicians. "The reason is very simple: we do not need to keep these war criminals. What benefits can come out of keeping these war criminals?"[34] Not long after, in April 1956, the Chinese authorities decided on a generous policy toward just over a thousand Japanese soldiers they held as war criminals. Almost all of them were immediately released without prosecution and sent home to Japan; they were low-ranking, their crimes were seen as relatively light, and they were said to be contrite. In Shenyang and Taiyuan, a special military tribunal put forty-five more senior accused war criminals on trial, most notably a lieutenant general and the former head of a ministry in Manchukuo. They got sentences ranging from eight to twenty years; except for one who died in detention, they were all released, some ahead of schedule, by March 1964.

The Chinese Communist Party publicly crowed that the Japanese war criminals under their control had been reeducated, repenting and becoming friends of the new China. This emphasis on indoctrination rather than punishment was meant to cure a downtrodden, colonized China of its "distorted servile attitude to foreign things and the sense of national inferiority," as a Communist Party history put it.[35]

In private, Zhou drove to resolve the issue of war criminals quickly in order to achieve normalization, even when that meant defying Chinese public opinion. He reminded a group of Japanese visitors of just how far the Communists were going in freeing all those Japanese soldiers: "All of them have committed serious crimes. It will be difficult to explain to the Chinese people if none of the Japanese war criminals receives a sentence."[36] He once angrily reminded a visiting Japanese Socialist politician,

"It was Japan that waged the war of aggression, it was the Japanese who invaded the Chinese, and a lot more Chinese people died than Japanese people did." But then he reassuringly added, "In general, we let bygones be bygones."[37]

Even Henry Puyi, the notorious Qing emperor of Manchukuo who had testified at the Tokyo trial, was released on amnesty in December 1959. In a subsequent meeting with Puyi, Zhou assured him, "We feel no hatred against the Japanese people at all, and the Japanese people were also a victim to militarism."[38] By the early 1960s, Mao went so far as to see the bright side of Japan's invasion. He told a visiting Japanese legislator, "Precisely because the Japanese imperial army occupied over half of China, the Chinese people had no other choice but to wake up, pick up their weapons, and establish many anti-Japanese bases, thereby creating the conditions for victory in the War of Liberation. Therefore Japanese warlords and monopolistic capital did a good thing. If I need to say thanks, I would rather thank Japanese warlords."[39]

In this period the Chinese Communist Party insisted that it was only a small clique of wicked Japanese imperialists who had caused the war, casting the Japanese masses as hoodwinked, innocent victims. To avoid whipping up national hatred of the Japanese, Chinese textbooks and movies avoided depictions of Imperial Japan's wartime atrocities. When a group of historians in Nanjing researched the massacre there, they were unable to publish their work until 1979, and even then only as an internal publication. Ironically, much of Mao's approach to war guilt lined up with that of Japanese conservatives: fixing all the blame on a few bad apples, downplaying the Nanjing massacre, looking to the future.[40]

In 1962, Mei dared to challenge that party line. He had become frustrated by Japanese publications about the atomic bombs, praising the Japanese scholarship but arguing that more people had died at Nanjing than at Hiroshima and Nagasaki combined. Criticizing other Chinese historians for misinterpretation, he enterprisingly managed to get a bold article published in a government journal, in which he excoriated Japanese leaders and troops for the Nanjing massacre. At a time when the Chinese Communist Party was downplaying the realities of Japan's wartime record, Mei harshly wrote, "The Nanjing Massacre was no doubt the most striking atrocity committed by Japanese troops during the Second World War, its cruelty being comparable to the Holocaust at Auschwitz, although different from the latter in nature and in its means." Demonstrating a noticeable ignorance about the Holocaust, he suggested that Nanjing was actually worse than Auschwitz: instead of being quickly gassed, he wrote, the Chinese victims were first insulted, robbed, beaten, mutilated, tortured, or raped before being killed.

Mei extolled the Tokyo trial, praising the reliability of its evidence, particularly about mass rape, and lauding its judgment for showing that "the cruelty and brutality of the Japanese troops in Nanking were indeed unprecedented in the history of modern war." Although the judgment had reckoned that the death toll there was about two hundred thousand, he called that a "prudent and conservative" estimate and argued that the total was most likely around three hundred and fifty thousand. He scorched General Matsui Iwane as the leading criminal of Nanjing: "His sentence to death by hanging was a demonstration of justice and a form of small solace for the Chinese people, although it does not make us forget this unprecedented tragedy in Chinese history."

In some ways Mei toed the official line: blaming the cowardice and incompetence of Chiang Kai-shek and his troops for the fall of Nanjing. Yet his article directly challenged Maoist orthodoxies. He urged laggard historians to interview survivors before it was too late. "I am not a revanchist," he wrote defensively. "Neither do I intend to ascribe the debt of blood owed to us by the Japanese imperialists to the Japanese people. I believe, however, that to forget the suffering of the past is to be vulnerable to tragedy in the future."[41]

This article was a disaster for Mei. A year later, Zhou Enlai told a Japanese former prime minister that the Chinese government was overcoming "a small group of people who find the discussion of friendship with Japan unacceptable because of Japan's long aggression against China."[42] Mei was accused of stirring up national hatred and revenge against the Japanese. Some Communist critics even said that his discussion of a humiliating Chinese defeat implied a hidden admiration for the prowess of Japanese troops.[43]

"I Am Only a Tattered and Out-of-Date Dictionary"

Mei's timing was terrible: his combative article came out only a few years before the start of the Cultural Revolution.

In 1966, an elderly Mao unleashed what he called a "great revolution that touched people's souls." Fearing that the revolution had lost its way, worried that the Soviet Union had gone soft, he meant to transform the Chinese into "Communist new men" liberated from their feudal selfishness. The Cultural Revolution would build a totalitarian society, relying on an all-powerful ruler with no rule of law.[44] The result was a mass political campaign to get rid of the power of bureaucracy, intellectuals, and professionals. With radical Communist Party cadres and fanatical young Red Guards suddenly allowed to attack upward, the party-state essentially collapsed. The youth were encouraged to attack their parents and teachers, to force their elders to do groveling self-criticism, to trash religious and historical sites, to burn books and antiques, and to destroy "the four olds": old ideas, old customs, old culture, and old habits. China plunged into a bloody decade of chaos and street violence.[45]

This utopia left little room for bookish lawyers with fond memories of student days at Stanford and Chicago. Early in the Cultural Revolution, Mei was denounced as a "reactionary academic authority"—a term for intellectuals or scholars vilified by the radicals.[46] The Foreign Ministry was no longer protected. "The Red Guards came to our home," says his daughter Mei Xiaokan. "They searched everything to see if we had any anti-revolutionary things." Fortunately these Red Guards were not so furious, not the ones inclined to whip people with their belts. Even so, Mei found himself accused of such iniquities as "being a reactionary who glorifies the Americans and the Japanese," "vainly hoping to recover his former authority," and "opposing Sino-Japanese friendship." Because he had warned in his article about the Nanjing massacre not to forget past suffering, he was denounced for "slandering the party as being forgetful."

Trying to defend himself, he claimed—demonstrably falsely—that he had no special skills or knowledge, no decent pieces of published work. He said that "over the years I've been the most enthusiastic person in revealing America and Japan's collusion to revive militarism." He reminded his youthful accusers that the Nationalists saw him as a wanted criminal: "If I really regained my authority, I would probably get executed before all of you young comrades!" He knew that his scholarly achievements were irrelevant to the killing and upheaval all around him: "In reality I am only a tattered and out-of-date dictionary."

None of this saved him. While he was apparently not physically beaten, he was forced to perform self-criticism, endlessly denouncing his own reactionary and bourgeois tendencies and promising to remake himself as a better Communist. Compared to countless others with a Nationalist past, he could have faced a harsher fate, but that was cold comfort. Instead of writing his book on the Tokyo trial, he had to compose investigative reports about other people who had also fallen afoul of the revolution. The materials he had assembled for his book about the Tokyo trial—journals, notes, cards, newspaper clippings—were confiscated and never found again; the book was never finished.[47] He was put to forced labor, meant both to make him understand the working classes and to humiliate him: a Stanford-educated lawyer cleaning offices and scrubbing toilets.

Mei despaired. He was rocked by terrible news of old colleagues being killed and old friends committing suicide. He grew profoundly sad. He smoked too much: it was the one thing he liked that he could still do. At one point, he wrote to the government asking them to investigate and punish arson at a British government office, which could only have made things worse for him. "We had seen so many people being beaten to death," says Mei Xiaokan. "Some people in our neighborhood killed themselves. We had people jumping from their apartments."

Under the cumulative strain, suffering from hypertension and heart disease, his health deteriorated. He was too sick to write. On April 23, 1973, he died at the age of sixty-nine.[48]

AFTERLIFE

After Mao died and the Cultural Revolution came to an end, Mei Ruao was forgotten, written out of Chinese history.

Like many of his generation, his reputation was rehabilitated in the reform era under Deng Xiaoping. The new ruler launched an initiative to improve relations with Japan, opening a brief honeymoon between the two countries. In October 1978, he became the first Chinese leader to visit Japan after more than two thousand years of contact. As they signed a treaty of peace and friendship, he impulsively hugged the startled Japanese prime minister. He had a two-hour lunch with Hirohito at the Imperial Palace. Although no records were kept, Deng said that bygones should be bygones, and the emperor referred to the "unfortunate happening," which the Chinese side chose to take as an indirect apology.[49]

Under Deng as paramount leader, Chinese elites went through a searing introspection about what had gone wrong during the chaos of the Cultural Revolution. That repudiation of the Cultural Revolution made it possible to revive Mei's reputation. After being officially labeled a rightist for some two decades, in 1979 Foreign Ministry officials found his family and showed them documents saying that he had been cleared. "I think it's fair," says his son Mei Xiaoao. "It shows that the Chinese government had admitted the mistake made in the Cultural Revolution."

In 1985, Mei was reintroduced to the Chinese public in a long three-part magazine profile, heralding his restored status as a luminary of the People's Republic. This was part of a nationalistic rediscovery of the war against Japan: the same year, a large memorial museum was built in Nanjing for the victims of the massacre there. The magazine profile presented heroic episodes from his adventure in Tokyo that have become famous in China. Although Mei's labor at the trial actually mostly consisted of writing intricate memoranda and cajoling the other judges, here he leapt out as a man of action: brandishing a ceremonial sword while vowing vengeance on the war criminals, demanding a prime seat next to Webb, insisting that the judgment include a section about Japanese atrocities. According to this version, Mei resolved that if General Matsui Iwane and General Doihara Kenji did not get the death penalty, then he "must commit suicide by jumping into the sea to apologize to the Chinese people. . . . Mei Ruao was so anxious that his hair turned gray. While his personal dignity and life was a small matter, the debt of blood for millions of fellow Chinese people must be repaid."

The article treated Mei as every inch a Communist, emphasizing how he had broken with the Nationalists. It duly denied any World War II glory to them: "Chiang Kai-shek's government had no interest in sending people to collect evidence of the Japanese military's atrocities; instead, it was fully committed to provoking a civil war and eliminating the Chinese Communist Party." Yet in keeping with the reform spirit of the Deng era, the magazine rehabilitated the judge for his modest criticism of the Party before the Anti-Rightist Campaign: "From today's perspective, his words were undoubtedly right. However, he suffered unfair treatment at that point in time."

The article regretted that for "historical reasons"—meaning the Cultural Revolution—young Chinese knew almost nothing about the Chinese judge who had wielded such power at the Tokyo trial. It celebrated the establishment of a museum to commemorate the Nanjing massacre and efforts to document it. "We would like to use this to let rest in comfort Mei Ruao—the Chinese judge at the Tokyo tribunal."[50]

Since then, Mei's legend has grown. His devoted children have tenderly looked after his legacy, getting his works published posthumously. The local government in Nanchang set up a small museum about him. Newspapers publish admiring stories about his achievements at the Tokyo trial, sometimes hinting at his persecution during the Cultural Revolution.[51] His prestigious alma mater, Tsinghua University, named a law school chair after him. "His story is well known today," says Feng Xiang, the Mei Ruao Professor in Law at Tsinghua, a soft-spoken legal theorist. "People recognize his name."

Deng's rapprochement with Japan proved short-lived, in part due to recurrent squabbles over wartime memory. Starting with a heated row about nationalistic Japanese textbooks in 1982, China began the kind of loud protests against Japan that are familiar today.[52] To the benefit of Mei's reputation, China's own textbooks and media began to give some credit to the Nationalists for their stubborn fight against the Japanese imperialist aggressors, making Japanese war crimes a central theme. After the Tiananmen Square massacre in June 1989, the beleaguered Communist Party intensified its memorialization of China's national humiliation, exemplified by the Nanjing massacre.[53] Starting in 1991, the authorities pushed a campaign of "patriotic education" that vilified the Japanese, as well as Western imperialism, breaking from the Mao-era habit of ducking the subject of the war: too humiliating, too strategically inconvenient, too apt to show the Nationalists as heroes.[54]

The Communists have realized that nurturing popular hatred of Japan can be useful at home, justifying the Party's iron grip on power. It may sometimes strengthen their bargaining position in international disputes, showing that their own hands are tied or that the ruling Communists are actually easier to deal with than the enraged masses. Yet such indulgence of popular rage must be handled carefully: enough to bolster the Party, but not so much that it gets out of hand.[55] In 2005 and 2013, China's rulers tried to both ride and manage waves of protests and riots against the Japanese that threatened to spin out of state control.[56]

The tension between China and Japan boils well beyond a standard realpolitik wariness between two rival countries. Since the 1980s, Chinese officials have viewed Japan with a visceral dread and loathing out of all proportion to the actual threat posed by a largely disarmed, peaceful, smaller nation. New generations of postwar Chinese leadership find it hard to believe that Japanese pacifism is genuine, nor that Japan will continue to accept its status as a demilitarized power. Chinese military and civilian analysts have long feared that Japan's dominant Liberal Democratic Party really means first to become an economic superpower and then become a major military power too.[57]

Chinese television and movies are saturated with stories about China's heroic war against the bloodthirsty Japanese.[58] In 2006, to mark the seventy-fifth anniversary of Japan's invasion of Manchuria, a big-budget Chinese film called *The Tokyo Trial* was released in major theater chains, telling the story with Mei as the central character. Xinhua, the Chinese official news agency, praised its box office success despite competition from a junky Hollywood superhero movie, *X-Men: The Last Stand*.[59] The part of Mei was played by a dashing Hong Kong action-movie star, Damian Lau, who usually plays assassins, swordsmen, or cops. "Mei Ruao is a person with a strong sense of ethics and national pride," said Lau in a story for Chinese state radio. "I tried to master his inner world through these aspects. I really respect him." Another star in the film, Ken Chu, a Taiwanese actor and member of a boy band, said, "Maybe this movie is not an entertaining film, but it's a movie that all Chinese should watch because it retells historical facts all Chinese should know."[60]

Mei's children are bemused by the action-hero version of their scholarly father. "Before the movie, many people in China didn't know about the Tokyo tribunal and now they know," says Mei Xiaoao. "So that's good. But it has many defects in the details, like how the court actually worked, how those terms of law are being used." The nationalistic exaltation of Mei has grown so omnipresent that it took considerable courage for a dissident in Sichuan, scornfully reviewing the movie, to criticize him for "a perspective dominated by hatred, bitterness, punishment, and revenge."[61]

In recent years, as the Chinese Communist Party has embraced a fiercely xenophobic nationalism, Mei has found a new estimation as an anti-Japanese champion, with glowing profiles in official publications.[62] "He is very famous," says a senior Chinese Foreign Ministry official who voices the party line. "He is regarded as a patriot, an eminent scholar who has upheld historical justice." To parry right-wing Japanese polemicists, the authorities had Shanghai Jiaotong University set up a major research center to study the Tokyo trial.[63] The Chinese Communist Party, disdainful of the Tokyo trial at the time, now celebrates it as an act of historic justice—thereby rebuking Japan's conservative governments.[64] The *People's Daily* argued that the trial was not Allied victors' justice but a trial for all human beings.[65] "The Tokyo trial was peaceful, civilized, and righteous," declared a People's Liberation Army newspaper.[66]

Under Xi Jinping, the Chinese government has escalated the preoccupation with history, especially a heroic version of World War II, seen as essential to its claim on power. The authorities persistently remind their people of China's long victimhood while working to conflate the nation with the party, so that criticism of the Communists is treated as an attack on the Chinese people.[67] As a core feature of his reign, the powerful Xi decries "historical nihilism," a Communist slogan which means allowing enemies to dwell on ugly episodes in history. He warns that the Soviet Communist Party fell in large part because it discredited Soviet history and besmirched Joseph Stalin's achievements, "creating historical nihilism and confused thinking." As Xi exhorted in a major speech urging an ideological struggle, "The crucial point of historical nihilism is to fundamentally negate the leading position of Marxism, the inevitability that China would take the socialist path, and the leadership of the CCP."

Therefore Communists must zealously put forward a glorious chronicle of the past that enhances their infallible aura; China has criminalized public criticism of revolutionary history.[68] In November 2021, Xi had the Communist Party's central committee push through a landmark historical resolution—something previously only done by Mao Zedong in 1945 and Deng Xiaoping in 1981—that celebrated his nationalistic view of history and national security.[69]

The Chinese People's War of Resistance Against Japanese Aggression, as the war is called in China, is essential to Xi's fight against historical nihilism. Rather than yielding the spotlight to the Nationalist government for leading the war, let alone discussing the uncomfortable fact that many Chinese collaborated with the Japanese, he has urged cadres and scholars to exalt the Communists' central role in combating the Japanese invaders.[70] Although Chinese historians and school textbooks used to treat the war as beginning at the Marco Polo Bridge in July 1937, Xi had them rewind the start date to the invasion of Manchuria in September 1931, treating it as a "fourteen-year War of Resistance."[71] Since taking power, he has established two official days of commemoration for the war: September 3 is Victory Day of the Chinese People's War of Resistance Against Japanese Aggression, marking Japan's surrender, and December 13 is National Memorial Day, mourning the Nanjing massacre.[72] To celebrate the seventieth anniversary of Japan's surrender in September 2015, he held a massive military parade in Tiananmen Square, featuring tanks and long-range strategic missiles.[73] His remembrances of the war combine themes of Chinese victimhood and Chinese greatness. Victory over Japan, Xi told the parade audience, was the "first complete victory won by China in its resistance against foreign aggression in modern times," at last putting "an end to the national humiliation of China" inflicted by foreign imperialists.[74]

Xi has made Japanese war crimes a major theme of his rhetoric.[75] In 2014, the paramount leader somberly presided over the national government's first official day of remembrance of the Nanjing massacre, expanding on previous commemorations by city and local governments. Wearing a white flower on his lapel, he fixed war guilt on a small circle of militarists but acclaimed the verdicts of the Tokyo trial and China's own military tribunal against "a group of Japanese war criminals whose hands were full of Chinese people's fresh blood to legal and righteous trials and severe punishments. They are permanently nailed to the historical pillar of shame"— a Chinese expression meaning that the guilt will never be forgotten.[76] In another talk that year, aiming at Abe Shinzo and other rightists, he raged that "some Japanese political organizations and political figures still deny

Xi Jinping, China's paramount leader, meets with elderly survivors of the Nanjing massacre after attending an official ceremony marking the eightieth anniversary of the atrocities, Nanjing, December 13, 2017.

the Japanese military's barbaric crime of aggression, still stubbornly pay homage to the souls of war criminals whose hands were tainted with fresh blood, still make statements beautifying the war of aggression and colonial dominance, and still challenge the conscience of mankind."[77]

During a fiery speech at the Marco Polo Bridge on July 7, 2017—which a well-connected Chinese official says was meant to respond to Abe's historical provocations—Xi declared, "The Chinese people who have made heavy sacrifices will unyieldingly defend the history written with our blood and lives. The Chinese people and people in all other countries will absolutely not allow anyone to reject, distort, or even beautify the history of aggression."[78] In an online summit in April 2022, European Union leaders invoked the horrors of World War II as a justification for speaking up for human rights in Ukraine, Xinjiang, and elsewhere; Xi replied with a lecture about European colonialism and bigotry. He emphasized that the Nanjing massacre had left Chinese with a strong feeling about human rights, and about foreigners with double standards too.[79]

Of course, the Chinese Communist Party has brought death to more Chinese than were ever killed by the Japanese invaders. There is no prospect of a real historical accounting within China for Mao's purges, the untold millions of deaths in the terror-famine of the Great Leap Forward, or the violent convulsions of the Cultural Revolution, nor for more recent enormities such as the internment camps for more than a million Uyghurs and other Turkic Muslims. Yet the Chinese state, eliding its own record, keeps up an incessant drumbeat about history.

Although Chinese leaders regard the United States as the most menacing foreign power, China's official embrace of the Tokyo trial has unleashed waves of populist hatred against the Japanese. While it is hard to get reliable soundings of Chinese public opinion under authoritarianism, there is little doubt about a deep popular loathing for Japan, with widespread remembrance of war crimes and scant credence given to more recent acts of repentance.[80] After CCTV News posted about the Tokyo trial on Weibo, a leading social media site, one commenter asked, "When will the Japanese people disappear from the earth like dinosaurs?" "The globe is warming up and sea level rising," replied another netizen. "Japan, the little island, will be underwater soon."[81] When the Chinese Youth League posted about the Tokyo trial, it got comments ranging from "Trial of justice!" to "All little Japanese should die. Why didn't the Americans drop more nuclear bombs?"[82]

Such sentiments are easily found in conversations around China. People have learned about the Nanjing massacre from textbooks and watching state television, and some even mention the biowarfare Unit 731. "They have not apologized enough," says a hipster architect. "The emperor is the mastermind." Although some younger people have a warm impression of Japan, enjoying its pop culture and envying its freedom, more typical is a thoughtful retired People's Liberation Army officer with a crew cut who remembers the Nanjing massacre as "a scar." China's weakness invited Japanese aggression, he says, adding, "We cannot easily be bullied by other nations now." In a Beijing hutong, a grizzled middle-aged worker, his face worn and weathered, says, "There should be a giant earthquake that sinks all of Japan." After his friends laugh with approval, he says, "All Japanese people are bad. They haven't changed." Leaning in, he adds, "They are like Jews. They should be eliminated from the earth. There should be an extermination of the Japanese like what the Germans did to the Jews." Seeing that he has crossed a line, he clarifies that he doesn't mean that for Jews, only for Japanese.

In an editorial in 2017, the *People's Daily* blasted Japanese right-wingers who rejected history, emphasizing "the historical truth of Japan's aggression against China, as symbolized by the Nanjing massacre." The state newspaper, which had in 1948 taunted Mei as the instrument of "bandit" Chiang Kai-shek, now treated him with respect and admiration. Like the lavish museum and memorial to the massacre in Nanjing, the newspaper even approvingly quoted the very words that had got him in such trouble during the Cultural Revolution about the need not "to forget the suffering of the past."[83]

Martyrs of Showa

G ROWING UP, I WAS told, 'Be proud at least within the family,'" remembers Tojo Hidetoshi. His parents had never told him about his lineage until he was about ten years old. One day his mother had taken the boy to a movie theater to see a long, somber documentary about the Tokyo trial. When General Tojo Hideki appeared in the courtroom on-screen, his mother abruptly whispered to the stunned child that that was his great-grandfather.

Tojo Hidetoshi, arriving on a sweltering summer day seventy years after the war in a bright office space in Tokyo's hectic Shibuya ward, has none of his great-grandfather's military swagger. An entrepreneur who promotes pride in Japanese culture, he was forty-two years old, friendly and relaxed, his face framed by sideburns and stylishly shaggy hair. Sporting a slouchy textured jacket over a gray V-neck T-shirt, with a modish chin-beard, he looks like the kind of layabout junior army officers would have roughed up during the war.

It was excruciating growing up with a family name that was synonymous with disastrous, discredited militarism. Immediately after the war, he recalls, his grandfather could not get a job, so his grandmother had to work instead to support the family. According to his aunt, the family feared assassins, at one point hiding out in a horse stable. Teachers had shunned his father and other students had mocked him. Even as an adult, his otherwise stern father once broke down in tears, sobbing over the taunting he had endured at school as a child. "Maybe most Japanese see the Tojo family as an enemy," he says.

When the word got out at school after that shocking day at the movies, the little boy was relentlessly teased, just as his father had been. Every time one teacher called on him, his classmates would pipe up, "Tojo's great-grandson, Tojo Hidetoshi!" He tried to avoid his ancestry. "I developed a kind of a complex," he says. "I would take world history instead of Japanese history to escape from my identity." When he grew up, he moved to Hong Kong for four years and remains pained by Chinese hostility toward his great-grandfather. Yet when he told his Hong Kong friends his secret, he was relieved to be told that that heritage had nothing to do with him: "So the complex I have has alleviated."

While some members of his family are fiery defenders of Japan's wartime record, he oscillates between reflection and occasional apologetics.[1] "I believe the responsibility of starting the war lies with my great-grandfather," he says. "But it is my great-grandfather's claim that under international law, he was innocent. I believe that what Japan has done is not much different from what Europe and America did during the war." Remembering how many people suffered and died in Hiroshima, Nagasaki, and the firebombing of Tokyo, he thinks it unfair to single out Japan alone. Still, he concludes, "It was his responsibility for making people lose so many lives in war."

Without hesitation he admits that Japanese did "terrible things in the war," pointing to camps for prisoners of war. "I believe that we should be remorseful about what Japan has done." Yet when asked about the Nanjing massacre, he hedges: "I believe the definition of a massacre is unclear. Back then, the Guomindang and the Communist Party were engaging in guerrilla warfare. It could be considered that the people killed in Nanjing were civil soldiers, not professional soldiers. That is one view held in Japan." He warns that the Chinese government is using propaganda as a tool: "If we accept every detail, including about the comfort women, the problematic parts get overblown."

He is more forthright in disputing the justice of the Tokyo trial: "The judges were all from Allied powers. On that point, it lacked some fairness." War was not illegal then, he says. Asked if he has heard of Radhabinod Pal, he cracks up laughing at the stupid question. "I know Judge Pal as much as every Japanese person. Every person wants to hold on to the facts that Judge Pal had claimed." Repeating the right-wing canard that Pal was the only judge versed in international law, he adds, "When Judge Pal said that it was kind of a joke, I agree."

In recent years, he says, the burden of being a Tojo has lightened, as rightist politicians have grown bolder. "Until ten years ago," he says, "it was the biggest taboo of postwar Japan. No one discussed my great-grandfather." The postwar generation, he says, was schooled to believe that the war was terrible and that Japan did a terrible thing, blaming Tojo Hideki. That began to change, he says, after 2001, when Koizumi Junichiro, a conservative prime minister, began a series of showy visits to the Yasukuni Shrine in Tokyo, which consecrates the country's wartime dead but also Tojo and thirteen other Class A war criminals who were executed or died in custody during or after the Tokyo trial, as well as many more Class B and C war criminals.[2]

"After Prime Minister Koizumi visited the Yasukuni Shrine," he says, "and the whole Yasukuni issue was brought to light, my great-grandfather was also discussed in public." He adds, "some people who learned about my great-grandfather from the internet, they've started to believe he wasn't such a terrible person, not as terrible as they had imagined."

The Japan of Tojo Hidetoshi is a radically different country from that of his great-grandfather. He and his gentle, prosperous, liberal nation would both be unrecognizable—if not outright repulsive—to his strutting great-grandfather. The Japanese people have thoroughly remade their society with profound national commitments to freedom and peace. Yet it is not hard to find lenient opinions here about the legacy of Tojo Hidetoshi's great-grandfather: that Japan was forced into fighting out of inevitable self-defense, that the war was really meant to liberate Asian nations from Western colonialism, that the wartime leaders might have made mistakes but did not commit crimes, that the Americans who incinerated Hiroshima and Nagasaki are in no position to judge.

It is hardly surprising that new generations of Japanese would grow weary of decades of subordination to the United States, nor unusual that they would contemplate their own defenses against an increasingly powerful China and a nuclear-armed Stalinist regime in North Korea. Yet Japanese conservatives have gone well beyond that, spending decades stirring a peculiar brew of self-determination and resentment. The revisionists hope that a remilitarized Japan will find a fresh purpose in national pride. Hiroshima and Nagasaki are presented as nuclear martyrdoms that came out of the blue, casting the war essentially as a story of Japanese victimhood. Quick to point out the suffering of their citizenry, they are frequently impatient with reminders about the Japanese Empire's record in Nanjing or Manila, or reflections about aggression at the Marco Polo Bridge or Pearl Harbor. They believe that Japan has apologized more than enough; their neighbors—even the free people of a democratic South Korea—are exploiting wartime memory as an extortion racket.[3] And they reject what they call "the Tokyo trial view of history" for condemning their empire, denying Japan a glorious past that could inspire new patriotic generations.[4]

The right-wing campaign against the Tokyo trial began the very day after Tojo Hideki and six other senior war criminals were hanged. On December 24, 1948, General Headquarters set free the remaining Class A suspects in Sugamo Prison. One of those going free that Christmas Eve was Kishi Nobusuke, a sharp-witted potentate in Japanese-run Manchuria who had gone on to serve in Tojo's cabinet at the time of Pearl Harbor. A consummate insider with a haughty manner, he had a thin face with a weak chin. "My wish is to explain for posterity the just war that is known by a different name," he wrote in a poem while in jail. Enduringly proud of what he had achieved in occupied Manchuria, as late as 1965 he would boast, "With the ideals of ethnic harmony and the paradise of the Kingly Way shining bright, a scientific, conscientious, and bold experiment was carried out there. It was a correct and 'unique' way to make a modern state. . . . At that time, Manchukuo was the hope of East Asia."[5] From Sugamo, he was delivered by a U.S. jeep directly to the official residence of Japan's chief cabinet secretary, who was his younger brother; still in his grubby prison uniform, he was already close to the apex of power.

The Americans had made a sloppy mistake by throwing all the suspected war criminals together. Along with Class B and C prisoners—those convicted for conventional war crimes and crimes against humanity, respectively—who were released or paroled in subsequent years, the Class A suspects had forged bonds with each other in prison and would later comprise a nucleus of opposition to the Allied brand of justice. Some of these military or colonial officers banded together to press for a sweeping amnesty for war criminals.[6]

Kishi, like a sizable number of rightists, watched in revulsion as postwar Japan adopted its pacifist constitution and signed a peace treaty at San Francisco that officially accepted the Tokyo trial's judgment and the verdicts of other Allied war crimes trials.[7] As he reentered politics through right-wing parties, he worked assiduously to discredit the Tokyo trial, declaring it "something with no basis whatsoever in legal theory and unworthy of being considered a trial."[8] As he later recalled, "even if we were responsible to the Japanese people and the emperor for having lost the war, we had no responsibility to America." Had he gone on trial for aggression, he said, he would have told future generations that "we were forced into a corner and had to fight." He dismissed the trial as victors' justice: "winners punish losers."[9] And he contended that Pal's dissent revealed "the essence of the Tokyo trial," praising "its resistance to the popular mood and dogged pursuit of reason."[10]

Many in the new Japan wanted to reenter world politics as a responsible, peaceful country, undergoing considerable soul-searching about how their society had plunged into such a disastrous, unwinnable war.[11] Prominent Japanese legal experts—including Yokota Kisaburo and Dando Shigemitsu, both of whom would become justices on Japan's Supreme Court—argued that the Tokyo trial was legitimate and worthwhile.[12] Soldiers returning from China spread the word of what the Japanese army had done there, and Japanese writers published searing exposés about the Nanjing massacre and the biowarfare of Unit 731.[13]

Yet the grievance-fueled faction proved industrious and relentless in the newly sovereign Japan. The enduring presence of Emperor Hirohito on the throne, albeit reduced to a ceremonial capacity, symbolized continuity with the old Imperial Japan. By 1958, all remaining Class B and C war criminals were released. Despite the San Francisco peace treaty, the war criminals were seen by some Japanese as having committed no offense under Japan's domestic laws—stigmatizing Allied justice as a foreign imposition rather than the international verdict of a global conscience. To counteract pacifist voices calling for contrition, nationalistic writers sought to justify Japan's colonial expansion—most notably Hayashi Fusao, who from 1963 to 1965 wrote a series of articles in a prominent literary magazine defending the war as a necessary response to Western imperialism, highlighting Pal's dissent.[14]

The Cold War put the wind in the sails of the rightists, who had always been fierce anti-Communists. After the Communist revolution in China in 1949 and the outbreak of war in Korea, the United States was more worried about purging Japan's leftists than its rightists. The ruling conservatives, many of them more centrist than Kishi, found it convenient to restrict blame for the war to a small clique of misguided militarists—a line that aligned with that of General Headquarters and the Chinese Communists under Mao Zedong. Driven by right-wing oversight, Japanese textbooks indoctrinated the next generation with this distinctive viewpoint, as well as overlooking the empire's repression of Asian nations.[15]

In a remarkable ascent from Sugamo Prison, Kishi became prime minister in 1957. He yearned in vain to revise the pacifist constitution, thereby "eradicating completely the consequences of Japan's defeat and of the American Occupation," allowing the Japanese to rediscover their national pride and "finally to move out of the postwar era."[16] As he toured Asia to restore his country's stature, he made some effective apologies, despite

Kishi Nobusuke (second from left), released as a suspected Class A war criminal, as prime minister of Japan, on a vacation. He holds hands with his little grandson, Abe Shinzo (left), wearing a New York Yankees baseball cap, who is a future prime minister himself. Abe Shintaro, Kishi's son-in-law and Abe Shinzo's father, a future foreign minister, is second from the right. Hakone, July 7, 1957.

a vagueness about exactly what fell deeds Imperial Japan had committed.[17] In Burma, he expressed "deep regret" for "the vexation we caused," while in Australia he voiced "our heartfelt sorrow for what occurred in the war."[18]

With secret advice from the CIA, he helped to unite two big conservative parties into what has become the dominant Liberal Democratic Party. The CIA, impressed with Kishi's anti-Communist fervor, began covertly funding the Liberal Democratic Party with millions of dollars.[19] Despite having signed the declaration of war against the United States, he now saw the superpower as vital to restoring Japan's status as an anti-Communist power, albeit wanting to make the relationship less humiliatingly one-sided. Defying a public with no appetite for remilitarization, he rammed through the ratification of a revised U.S.-Japan Security Treaty, which would continue to allow U.S. military bases on Japanese land.

His efforts sparked massive demonstrations that ultimately encompassed as many as a third of the Japanese. At the height of the unrest, the speaker of the House of Representatives—who was Kiyose Ichiro, Tojo Hideki's skillful defense lawyer at the Tokyo trial—called the police into the Diet to haul out Socialist legislators holding a sit-in. Kiyose pressed through the ratification of the treaty in a chamber whose opposition seats were empty. The hardball tactics of Kishi and Kiyose brought gigantic crowds to the Diet, where a female Tokyo University student was trampled to death, and the police beat enraged protesters unconscious and bloody. This mayhem drove Kishi to announce his resignation in June 1960. Still, his premiership had done much to establish the theme that the pacifistic constitution had been imposed upon Japan by foreigners, infantilizing the country and impinging on its sovereignty.[20]

In 1965, Japan worked with the South Korean strongman Park Chung-hee, who had first come to power in a military coup in 1961, to sign a normalization treaty to resolve issues from the colonial past, although leaving out their old territorial dispute over the two little islets and sundry rocks called Dokdo by Koreans or Takeshima by Japanese.[21] The deal, which included a Japanese lump-sum payment for claims but not a statement of repentance in the treaty (during the negotiations Japan's foreign minister vaguely called the past "most regrettable"), sparked nationwide demonstrations against Park. As Kishi explained, "Fortunately, South Korea is under a military regime where Park Chung Hee and a handful of leaders can decide things on their own."[22]

DIVINE SPIRITS

The physical and spiritual flashpoint for the rejection of the Tokyo trial is the Yasukuni Shrine—a serene, beautiful, tree-lined haven in Tokyo's central Chiyoda ward. Founded in the Meiji era in 1869, the Shinto institution is consecrated to some two and a half million Japanese who died mostly fighting the nation's wars since the late nineteenth century, particularly in World War II. It maintains registers of their names, exalted souls who are sanctified by solemn ritual and enshrined here as *kami*, divine spirits. Soldiers and kamikaze suicide pilots went to their deaths saying "See you at Yasukuni!" During the war, the shrine was an official state institution under the Army, Navy, and Home ministries.

When General Headquarters abolished State Shinto as the national religion and the emperor abnegated his divinity, Yasukuni reinvented itself as a private religious institution, although one with a continued entanglement with the state. Hirohito visited there numerous times in the years after the war.[23] Winning out over more innocuous sites—such as the Chidorigafuchi National Cemetery, a nearby official cemetery in Tokyo holding the remains of unknown Japanese who died abroad during

World War II—Yasukuni has won a semiofficial stature as the national war memorial.[24]

Soon after Japan regained its sovereignty in April 1952, relatives of dead war criminals began pressing to have them enshrined at Yasukuni. The Health and Welfare Ministry, which had a key bureau dominated by veterans, proposed names of the fallen to the shrine. In April 1959, after years of reticence, Yasukuni enshrined a first batch of Class B and C war criminals. Three more batches followed, so that by October 1967, there were 984 Class B and C war criminals honored there as *kami*.[25]

In 1978, Yasukuni's governing council named a zealous new head priest, Matsudaira Nagayoshi, who had been a military officer during the war. As he later said, "Even before I became the Head Priest, I had thought that Japan would never recover its spirit until it countered the historical view created by the Tokyo War Crimes Trials that 'everything about Japan was bad.'"[26] Acting in secret on October 17, 1978, he conducted the rites to deify all fourteen dead Class A war criminals at Yasukuni—the *kami* of General Tojo Hideki and the six other men hanged, several of them widely reviled in China, particularly General Matsui Iwane, who had been convicted for failing to prevent the atrocities at Nanjing. Also enshrined were two Class A suspects who had died of natural causes during the trial, including the fiercely pro-Nazi foreign minister Matsuoka Yosuke, and five men who had died of illness in custody after being convicted.

Whatever one thinks of the Tokyo trial, the only one of these with any real claim to decency was Togo Shigenori. The shrine equates elderly chieftains who were hanged after being convicted in a long trial with young soldiers who were killed fighting a war they had not chosen: all of them divine spirits who gave their lives for the nation. Yasukuni treats the Tokyo trial as the final battle of World War II.

After the Japanese press enterprisingly broke the news, many Japanese recoiled. Emperor Hirohito, according to records of two Imperial Household staffers that were later discovered, was shocked and blamed the head priest. Although Matsudaira meant to honor what the shrine calls the "Martyrs of Showa," the Showa Emperor himself never again visited. Nor has any subsequent emperor.[27]

Japanese prime ministers and senior officials kept on praying at Yasukuni, even now that the shrine had made an implicit rejection of the Tokyo verdicts.[28] The first several times that Japanese prime ministers visited after the enshrinement of the Class A war criminals, the Chinese government largely maintained a diplomatic quiet. That ended when Nakasone Yasuhiro, a nationalistic prime minister who had blamed the

Tokyo trial for promoting "a self-torturing belief that our country was to blame for everything," made an official visit on August 15, 1985—the fortieth anniversary of Japan's surrender. (As a young lieutenant on Borneo during the Pacific War, Nakasone had organized a military "comfort station" for his unruly men, as he later recalled in a memoir.)[29] The official *People's Daily* barked that Japan was obfuscating "the war of aggression launched by the Japanese militarists," which "hurts the feelings of Chinese people and Asian people." After backlash from the Japanese public, subsequent prime ministers called a temporary halt to these visits.[30]

On a chilly gray day in December 1970, the chancellor of West Germany, Willy Brandt, went to the grounds of the ghetto in central Warsaw. He had just signed a treaty accepting the German-Polish border, renouncing German territorial claims on the Polish east. Somberly dressed in a dark overcoat, his expression was mournful as he stood before the Warsaw Ghetto Heroes Monument to the Jews who had fought and died there. He laid a wreath of white flowers and adjusted it. Then as he later explained, he did what people do when words fail. He sank to his knees on the wet granite, his head bowed.

His grand gesture got mixed reviews at home. For rightists and older Germans, the chancellor had sold out German territories and abased himself before a foreign audience in a Communist country. For younger Germans, though, the impromptu deed by Brandt—who had resisted Adolf Hitler's regime before becoming the postwar Federal Republic's first Social Democratic chancellor—marked a break with the baleful past. Some 48 percent of Germans thought the kneeling was overdone, while 41 percent praised it. Of course, Brandt had a strategic agenda: he wanted wider international recognition of the Federal Republic and a finalization of demands for reparations. Yet his obvious emotional sincerity defused the warnings by Soviet and Polish propagandists that if the Communists ruling over Central Europe faltered, the unrepentant Nazis would charge back. Both morally and strategically, Brandt's gesture was a triumph.[31]

Japanese leaders have apologized scores of times for the country's wartime deeds since 1952, but there has never really been a Japanese equivalent to Brandt's *Warschauer Kniefall*.[32] While the Federal Republic of Germany has moved on from relatively lukewarm early gestures to achieving a more profound reconciliation with its European neighbors, Israel, and the Jewish people, that kind of concord has eluded Japan in its own region. Although Japanese public debates tended to scrutinize West Germany's experience as a possible template, official Japanese repentance is often more formalistic or tepid, even grudging—"Japan clears its throat these days for a small, dry cough of remorse about its conduct during World War II," Nicholas Kristof of *The New York Times* once reported from Tokyo.[33] But it is probably more important that Japanese rightists keep undercutting the genuine statements of contrition, suggesting that these pronouncements were really transactional.[34]

Some of the finest attempts at repentance came from Emperor Akihito, who made conscientious, contrite reflection on the war a major theme of his reign. After taking the throne in January 1989, he went beyond his late father Hirohito's more pallid words about the "unfortunate" or "regrettable" past. He expressed "deep regret" to Koreans, and then, as the first Japanese emperor ever to visit China, declared at a 1991 state dinner in the Great Hall of the People in Beijing, "there was an unfortunate period in which my country inflicted great suffering on the people of China. About this I feel deep sadness."[35] On trips to Indonesia, the Philippines, Malaysia, Vietnam, Thailand, and Singapore, he paid tribute to Imperial Japan's victims and promised that his country had embraced peace. For the seventieth anniversary of the end of the war, he spoke of "feelings of deep remorse." While many Asians wished he had gone further and plenty of Japanese conservatives thought he had gone too far, Akihito's efforts helped to rehabilitate Japan's reputation across Asia.[36] After his abdication in 2019, his son Emperor Naruhito, sophisticated and Oxford-educated, has emphasized the tragedy of the war.[37]

With the end of the Cold War, as Japan moved to play a bigger role on the world stage, its government made a renewed effort at reconciliation. In 1993, Kono Yohei, the chief cabinet secretary, expressed the government's "sincere apologies and remorse" for Japanese "coercion" of so-called comfort women, many of them Koreans, "who suffered immeasurable pain and incurable physical and psychological wounds." That apology was buttressed by Japanese government donations to a special fund for former "comfort women," which totaled some 4.8 billion yen from 1995 to 2007.[38] On the fiftieth anniversary of Japan's surrender on August 15, 1995, Murayama Tomiichi—a rare prime minister from the Socialist Party who was less beholden to right-wing shibboleths—bluntly condemned Japan's "colonial rule and aggression," which had "caused tremendous damage and suffering" to Asian nations. In this impressive renunciation of colonialism, endorsed by a cabinet packed with Liberal Democratic Party ministers, he accepted "these irrefutable facts of history"—a hard slap at denialists about such enormities as the Nanjing massacre—and expressed "my feelings of deep remorse and state my heartfelt apology."[39] Although some rightists in the Liberal Democratic Party bristle at Murayama's apology, subsequent prime ministers have reaffirmed it.

In the Philippines, where postwar resentments ran especially high, Japan has tried a noticeably more generous script than that used for Korea or China. In 1956, to secure the normalization of diplomatic relations, Japan signed a reparations agreement to pay $550 million in goods and services to the Philippines, as well as giving a development loan of $250 million.[40] On a 1983 visit to the Philippines, Nakasone Yasuhiro, a conservative Japanese prime minister, said that "our country deeply regrets and repents having caused your country and people such trouble in the past war"—an unusually fulsome apology for him. When Corazon Aquino, as president of the Philippines, made a state visit to Japan in 1986, a Philippine government press aide claimed that Hirohito had privately apologized to her for the pain caused during the war, while she reportedly told him to forget about it. Although many Filipinos remained irate over wartime sexual coercion, in 1993 Japan's foreign minister said, "From the bottom of my heart I would like to apologize to those Filipino women who underwent indescribable hardships as so-called comfort women."[41] Emperor Akihito himself made a specific reference to civilians who perished in the battle of Manila before a 2016 visit to the Philippines, where he expressed contrition, although stopping short of an apology.[42]

Japan's image among Filipinos has been bolstered by a range of pro-Japanese leaders from Ferdinand Marcos to Benigno Aquino III to Rodrigo Duterte. Today Japan's relationship with the Philippines is buttressed by investment and official development assistance, a high-profile free trade agreement, a common ally in the United States, and defense deals meant to ward off a shared threat from China.[43] (Both Japan and the Philippines could be frontline countries in a war over Taiwan.) All told, young generations in the Philippines have largely moved past the chilling stories told by their elders: in a 2014 poll, 80 percent of Filipinos had a positive view of Japan, while 93 percent were worried about territorial disputes with China.[44]

Yet these admirable Japanese efforts for reconciliation have been undercut by the nationalists who poke and provoke the neighbors. In 1986, Matsudaira reopened the handsome military history museum at Yasukuni, called the Yushukan, decked out with hard-line exhibits justifying the Pacific War and rejecting the Tokyo trial.[45] Soon after Murayama's bold statement in 1995, conservatives got organized to campaign for more patriotic textbooks, while a caucus of Diet members pressed for ghoulish historical reevaluations of the Nanjing massacre and the sexual coercion of Korean women.[46]

In 2001, a flamboyant outsider politician, Koizumi Junichiro, out-flanked a more temperate rival with an opportunistic promise to the pow-erful Japan War-Bereaved Families Association that as prime minister he would return to the suspended habit of praying at Yasukuni. (One prime minister, Hashimoto Ryutaro, had gone in 1996, calling it a private visit.) China's president, Hu Jintao, bluntly warned him that visiting Yasukuni would imply a return to militarism. Koizumi plowed ahead anyway in August 2001, two days before the emotionally charged date of August 15. Despite punctilious Japanese stipulations that he accepted the results of the Tokyo trial and was not visiting for the sake of the Class A war crimi-nals, the Chinese Foreign Ministry bellowed that the visit demonstrated an absence of remorse for Japanese aggression. Twenty South Korean men sliced off the tips of their little fingers in protest.[47]

To offset the affront, he went to the Marco Polo Bridge outside Beijing to make a "heartfelt apology," becoming the first Japanese prime minister to lay a wreath at a nearby memorial hall. Days later he went to Seoul, where, hounded by angrily vocal protesters, he made a similar state-ment at a monument to Koreans tortured to death by Imperial Japan.[48] Yet Koizumi visited Yasukuni every year as prime minister between 2001 and 2006, each time prompting brickbats from China and South Korea. It did little to mend fences when he repeated much of the language of the Murayama apology in 2005 at a summit in Indonesia and again on the sixtieth anniversary of the end of World War II in August 2005.[49] A year later, dressed up in a formal black coat, he visited Yasukuni on August 15, 2006. No prime minister had gone on that solemn day for more than twenty years.[50]

SADISTIC HISTORY

No Japanese leader did more to revise his country's attitude toward the war—and restore its stature as a power—than Kishi Nobusuke's reverent grandson, Abe Shinzo, the country's longest-serving modern prime min-ister. Following his grandfather's vision, he insisted publicly that Japan had to "depart from the postwar regime," overcoming the humiliation of defeat and American occupation.[51] Teased at school as the descendant of a war criminal, since childhood his outlook was deeply influenced by his beloved grandfather's bitterness at the three years and three months he spent languishing in American custody.[52] As he later wrote, "Some people used to point to my grandfather as a 'Class-A war criminal suspect,' and I felt strong repulsion."[53]

In two tours in power, he framed his project as normalizing Japan:

to allow it to ward off mounting threats from China and North Korea like any other country, shore up the economy, and strengthen its vital alliance with the United States, which is Japan's sole treaty ally.[54] Abe whittled away at Japan's prohibition on self-defense, beefing up the military and the intelligence services, although without realizing the family dream of revising the pacifist constitution. He drove through security bills that allowed the Self-Defense Forces to provide logistical support for operations abroad that are approved by the United Nations. In a historic move, his government reinterpreted Article 9 of the Constitution to allow for the use of force not just to defend against an armed attack on Japan but also, under certain conditions, to ward off an armed attack against a friendly foreign country that threatened Japan's survival.[55] He stood up to North Korea, appalled by its abductions of Japanese citizens. He successfully launched the self-styled Quad alignment of maritime democracies—Australia, India, Japan, and the United States—to protect a free Indo-Pacific against Chinese domination.[56]

At the same time, Abe flung himself into the crusade against what Japan's fervent new conservatives call a "masochistic" attitude toward World War II. As a young politician, he took full advantage of his lineage as a prime minister's grandson to drive his ascendance, with his early writings celebrating Kishi's achievements. Complaining that the pacifist constitution had been forced upon Japan by the United States, he attacked the Kono statement and tried to leave the facts about the wartime sexual coercion of Korean women out of textbooks.[57] When he rose to become chief cabinet secretary to Koizumi, he tried to distinguish Japan's wartime actions from those of Nazi crimes that killed German citizens, noted that Japan had no role in judging the defendants at the Tokyo trial, and questioned whether the Japanese government should express determinations about historical events.[58]

In Abe's first brief stint as prime minister in 2006–7, he sought to deny official Japanese responsibility for the sexual subjugation of Korean women, claiming that "there is no evidence to prove there was coercion"—essentially calling the elderly Korean survivors a pack of liars.[59] He pointedly undercut the Tokyo trial, arguing that the Class A convicts were not criminals under Japanese law: "I think that the very act of calling such people criminals is strange." He told the Diet that the Japanese had had to accept the judgment of the Tokyo trial and Allied war crimes tribunals under the San Francisco peace treaty in order to regain their independence, but there was no reason now to brand those convicted as criminals. He misleadingly claimed that nobody had been prosecuted for crimes against humanity; in fact, those charges had been lumped into conventional war crimes in the Tokyo judgment, with numerous convictions. When pressed by a Diet member about whether Tojo Hideki bore responsibility for the war, he said that politicians should be humble about making historical judgments.[60]

Abe was a more canny, careful politician after returning to power in a landslide election in 2012. Just before taking power he visited Kishi's tomb, saying that he hoped to fulfill his grandfather's wish of recovering Japan's independence.[61] His long premiership was an exhausting series of provocations. He told a Diet committee that Japan's wartime actions were determined to be criminal not by the Japanese but by the Tokyo trial: "the Allied powers, in other words, through the judgment of victors made this determination."[62] This accusation of victors' justice provoked indignation from China, with one writer in the Communist Party's jingoistic organ, the *Global Times,* extolling the trial: "The international community should collaboratively preserve the postwar international order founded upon the Tokyo trial."[63] In December 2013, despite pressure from the Obama administration, Abe visited Yasukuni, which prompted the usual Chinese denunciations and one unusual one: the Chinese ambassador in London wrote that "If militarism is like the haunting Voldemort of Japan, the Yasukuni shrine in Tokyo is a kind of horcrux."[64]

Abe Shinzo (center), prime minister of Japan, wearing formal dress, walks behind a Shinto priest as he visits the Yasukuni Shrine, which honors fourteen Class A war criminals, Tokyo, December 26, 2013.

Abe's left-wing opponents feared he was floating a possible reversal of Japan's formal apologies. In 2014, a government panel created by him trashed the Kono apology, issuing a report suggesting that the statement was not based wholly on historical evidence but the product of South Korean pressure.[65] Then in 2015, his Liberal Democratic Party set up a historical panel to evaluate the Tokyo trial and the Allied occupation, as well as the Nanjing massacre and the coercion of Korean women.[66] This was run by Inada Tomomi, a hard-line politician who had rubbished the Tokyo trial as "lacking legal grounds," questioned details of the Nanjing massacre, and complained that Japanese textbooks taught "a one-sided view of history." Abe later named her as the country's second female defense minister.[67]

Abe could be more forthcoming about history when he courted his maritime partners, above all the United States. He movingly repented in Washington at a joint session of Congress—although conspicuously failing to directly mention the "comfort women"—and on a dramatic trip to Pearl Harbor with Barack Obama.[68] In a landmark address to the Australian Parliament in Canberra, he gave "sincere condolences" for the Australian war dead, singling out Japan's notorious Sandakan camp in Borneo.[69] On a high-profile visit to India, for once his historical obsessions aligned with his diplomacy: he visited Pal's family, praising the dissenting judge as well as the pro-Axis rebel Subhas Chandra Bose.

In 2015 Abe and Park Geun-hye, South Korea's first female president, made a stab at improving relations. Their fellowship had a macabre intergenerational resonance: Park's father, the general and military dictator Park Chung-hee, had been a second lieutenant in the Japanese army in Japanese-controlled Manchuria, and later developed close ties to Abe's grandfather Kishi.[70] Abe and Park cut a "final and irreversible resolution" for the tens of thousands of Korean women forced into prostitution for Japanese troops at wartime brothels. Japan agreed to give a billion yen (about $8.3 million at the time) to a foundation to be set up by South Korea to support Korean women survivors, while the foreign minister, Kishida Fumio—who is today prime minister—made an apology in Abe's name.[71]

Yet after Abe's nettling, the deal smacked of opportunism. Japanese rightists groused that their country had already apologized enough, while South Koreans hollered that their president was breaking faith with these elderly women as a geopolitical quid pro quo. A majority of South Koreans wanted the agreement undone.[72] After Park was impeached and convicted for corruption, her successor, Moon Jae-in, lambasted her deal and dissolved the foundation. When South Koreans pressed Abe for more apologies, he refused.[73] Today South Koreans remain utterly unreconciled toward Japan.[74] At the worst moments, 98 percent of these democratic citizens said that Japan has not apologized enough for its wartime deeds—more even than among Chinese strong-armed under dictatorship.[75] There is a surreal quality to the decades of buttoned-down parleys and bland, carefully parsed statements layered on top of this seething resentment among so many South Koreans.

Today it is understandable that many Japanese fear that no atonement will ever be enough for the Chinese Communist Party, which has made Japan-bashing part of its strategy for domestic survival. How can even the loudest Japanese apology be heard over the relentless din of the Communist propaganda apparatus? What contrition could be made that would not invite fresh demands for groveling, costly reparations, or giving up the contested Senkaku (to Japanese) or Diaoyu (to Chinese) islands in the East China Sea? Who can take seriously the moral dudgeon of a high-tech authoritarian state with an appalling record on human rights? Yet real apology is not made in order to get something but out of a genuine compulsion to remember and to repent. The more that Japanese argue that there is no point apologizing to China, the easier it is for Chinese popular hostility to thrive—and to escalate.

Abe's premiership ended in 2020 when ulcerative colitis left him too ill to govern; he was murdered in July 2022 by an assassin whose political motives were unrelated to nationalism. It has taken decades for revisionist views of wartime history to reach the Japanese mainstream, but they are firmly ensconced now. Two-thirds of Japanese believe either that their country has apologized enough or that no apology is necessary.[76] While Kishi and Abe sought the reemergence of Japan as a regional power, right-wing historical revanchism gets in the way of the statecraft that might allow that. Faced with mounting threats from China and North Korea, and startled by the Russian mauling of Ukraine, an officially pacifist Japan has begun its biggest military buildup since World War II.[77] Yet it does so while remaining shackled to narratives about its wartime past that are morally odious and historically dubious.

THE VICTORS

Throughout the Tokyo trial, the Allies repeatedly asserted that these new principles of international law would apply to themselves as well. Yet in the decades since the judgments at Nuremberg and Tokyo, the United States, the Soviet Union, and the European colonial powers have proved distinctly unwilling to abide by the ideals that they loftily imposed upon the defeated. Nor have they shown an inclination to commemorate and atone for their own sins.[78]

There has been an incomplete but noticeable decline in major international wars since 1945, perhaps driven in part by the norms against aggression propounded at Nuremberg and Tokyo, but also due to such unromantic factors as the balance of power and Cold War nuclear deterrence.[79] Today a great many Japanese believe that war is an international crime, while the governments of the old Allies readily accept the recourse to war as a tool of statecraft. The high hopes encouraged at Nuremberg and Tokyo were undercut in the immediately following decades by the willingness of the various victors to engage in a panorama of war crimes and aggressions of their own: the Soviet Union's invasions of Hungary, Czechoslovakia, and Poland; the British Empire's crackdowns in Kenya, Malaya, and Yemen; France's record of torture and repression in Algeria; the United States' aerial and ground devastation of Vietnam and its violation of Cambodian neutrality; China's invasion of Vietnam in support of the Khmer Rouge.[80] Bert Röling would later fault the Soviet Union for intervening in Hungary, Czechoslovakia, Poland, and Afghanistan, and the United States for intervening in Guatemala, Cuba, the Dominican Republic, Vietnam, Grenada, and Nicaragua.[81] After the invasion of Iraq in 2003, the United States under George W. Bush and Donald Trump emerged as the most powerful adversary of the International Criminal Court, a permanent war crimes tribunal in The Hague.

This is not to suggest any lazy moral equivalences, as some Japanese rightists like to do, meant to excuse Imperial Japan's most horrific actions. The point is that a moral or legal code must be a living thing.[82] If it is never applied to new cases, then its authority is vitiated. Agonized about war crimes in Vietnam, Telford Taylor, the U.S. chief prosecutor in the second round of trials at Nuremberg, asked if the American people were able to "examine their own conduct under the same principles that they applied to the Germans and Japanese at the Nuremberg and other war crimes trials?"[83]

As for shows of contrition after imperialism, France has never come to terms with—let alone apologized for—its colonial rule of Algeria and the bloody 1954–62 war it waged there, which remains a topic almost as sensitive as collaboration with the Nazis.[84] Even Emmanuel Macron, who before becoming president called the colonization of Algeria a "crime against humanity" and admits that torture was widely used by French forces, still rules out an apology.[85] Although more than a hundred thousand people died in the Dutch fight to hold on to Indonesia from 1945 to 1949, the Dutch government gave apologies or compensation for specific incidents but did not issue a general apology until 2013.[86]

The British government has not managed to apologize for the 1919 massacre at the Jallianwala Bagh public gardens in Amritsar. In 1997 Queen Elizabeth II did lay a wreath and give half a minute of silent homage to the hundreds of Indians gunned down there by British troops, but British officials privately explained that an admission of guilt for the massacre would open them up to dozens of claims from other former colonies.[87] In 2013, David Cameron became the first serving British prime minister to visit Jallianwala Bagh, which he termed a "deeply shameful event" but added, "I don't think the right thing is to reach back into history and to seek out things you can apologize for."[88] Not until 2013—after elderly Kenyan plaintiffs sued for recompense in the British courts and reached a landmark settlement—did the British foreign secretary, William Hague, express regret in the House of Commons for the torture and abuse of Kenyans during the brutal crushing of the Mau Mau insurgency in 1952–60.[89]

The most jarring commemorations of the Tokyo trial come from Vladimir Putin, who makes the punishment of war crimes a core theme of his incessant commemoration of World War II. He is not the type to follow the lead of Mikhail Gorbachev, who offered condolences for the Soviet abuse of Japanese prisoners, nor Boris Yeltsin, who in 1993 made an apology in Japan for the Soviet detention of more than six hundred thousand Japanese civilian and military prisoners for years after the war, many of them perishing in labor camps.[90] Putin was raised on stark tales from his father—a combat veteran with a limp from having his legs blasted by a German grenade—about the siege of Leningrad, where Putin's two-year-old brother died.

He promotes a valiant, untarnished Russian history that edits out the Molotov-Ribbentrop Pact, the seizure of the Baltics and eastern Poland in secret cooperation with Nazi Germany, and mass rape in the capture of Berlin. He has upheld the annexation of Estonia, Latvia, and Lithuania—the fruit of the pact with Adolf Hitler—as defensive, legal, and consensual.[91] For him the Great Patriotic War remains a victory of the "entire Soviet people," uniting all the fifteen republics of the old Soviet Union, including such wayward bits as Georgia and Ukraine.[92]

Putin valorizes the Soviet Union's opposition to Japanese aggression and militarism, which is useful for keeping Japan on the defensive as it seeks a formal peace treaty.[93] During a 2015 squabble with Japan about four contested islands grabbed by the Soviet Union at the end of World War II, his longtime foreign minister, Sergei Lavrov, complained that "Japan is the only country that calls into question the outcome of the Second World War, no one else does."[94] Putin accuses the West of appeasing the Japanese militarists and faults the League of Nations for failing to prevent Japanese aggression against China, although he is predictably silent about the League's condemnation of Soviet aggression against Finland. In a major speech on the seventy-fifth anniversary of the Soviet victory, he justified the Molotov-Ribbentrop Pact as necessary due to "a real threat of war on two fronts—with Germany in the west and with Japan in the east, where intense fighting on the Khalkhin Gol River was already underway." He exalted the Soviet Union for declaring war on Japan in August 1945 and defeating the Kwantung Army.[95] In 2014, he went to Mongolia to commemorate the seventy-fifth anniversary of the Soviet clash with Japanese forces there in 1939, declaring the battle at the Khalkhin-Gol River a famous victory that kept Japanese militarists from entering the wider war for more than two years.[96]

Putin routinely professes his reverence for Nuremberg and, less frequently, the Tokyo trial.[97] "We constantly refer to the lessons of the Nuremberg Trials," he told an academic conference in 2020. "It is the duty of the entire international community to safeguard the Nuremberg Trials' decisions, because they concern the principles that underlie the values of the post-war world order and the norms of international law."[98] He used Nuremberg to emphasize the victimhood of Russians, not the extermination of the Jews. In 2021, he sent a message to a conference in Khabarovsk about the Soviet military tribunal held there in 1949 for Japanese officers in the secret biowarfare program, declaring that that show trial had "passed a legal, moral and ethical judgment on those who unleashed World War II and were guilty of terrible crimes against humanity—just as the Nuremberg and Tokyo trials did."[99]

Nuremberg and Tokyo appeal to the Russian autocrat's legalistic side; he frequently emphasizes a tradition of conservative Russian legal thought, while highlighting the United Nations Charter and postwar international law as a defense against a unipolar world dominated by an aggressive United States.[100] Equally important, he heavy-handedly uses Nuremberg to implicate Ukrainians, Latvians, and other disfavored nations for a purported glorification of Nazi collaborators.[101] As he told a Serbian newspaper, "Regrettably, in some European countries the Nazi virus 'vaccine' created at the Nuremberg Tribunal is losing its effect."[102]

Putin's sharpest defense of the Tokyo trial bolstered his alignment with China. In September 2015, before visiting Beijing for Xi Jinping's celebration of the seventieth anniversary of Japan's defeat, Putin cast China alongside the Soviet Union as the two countries that had borne the brunt of German and Japanese aggression. "Today, both in Europe and in Asia, we witness the attempts to falsify the history of World War II, to promote loose and distorted interpretations of the events that are not based on facts," he told China's state news agency, aiming at Japan under Abe. "Efforts by certain countries to glorify and exonerate war criminals and their henchmen are an outrageous flouting of the Nuremberg and Tokyo trials. This is an outright insult to the memory of millions who fell in the war."[103]

Putin was doggedly proclaiming his devotion to Nuremberg while Russia invaded Georgia in 2008, annexed Crimea from Ukraine in 2014, and sponsored a separatist war in eastern Ukraine, in prelude to its current brutal war of aggression in Ukraine. Casting himself as the true champion of the postwar legal order, he uses a barrage of quasi-legal verbiage to justify his aggressions: he is defending Russians abroad, he is rescuing civilian populations beset by Ukrainian neo-Nazis, he is reclaiming Crimea which is really part of Russia, he is upholding the right to self-determination of tiny nations inside Ukraine.[104] His sponsorship of puppet regimes in Abkhazia, South Ossetia, Transnistria, Donetsk, and Luhansk is right out of Imperial Japan's playbook in Manchukuo and north China. He insists upon historical truth while whitewashing Soviet history; he exalts the postwar legal order while his troops march across international borders; he decries crimes against humanity as he systematically kills civilians in Chechnya, Syria, and Ukraine. Although Putin seems to be more a modern Russian imperialist than a Stalinist ideologue, the Soviet prosecutors at Tokyo would have found much to admire in his rhetorical handiwork.[105]

The Tokyo trial, an obsession across East Asia, is almost entirely absent from American political discourse. In a rare presidential mention of the controversies around Japan's capitulation, Obama in 2009 cautioned that discussing victory in Afghanistan "invokes this notion of Emperor Hirohito coming down and signing a surrender to MacArthur"—showing that even a well-informed, historically minded president did not understand that Hirohito had actually been protected from such a humiliation by the Truman administration.[106] The only major American figure to highlight Japanese war crimes prosecutions in recent decades was John McCain, the Republican presidential nominee in 2008, who on the campaign trail stated that waterboarding must be torture, since Japanese had been convicted and executed for inflicting it upon American prisoners of war.[107] This marked him as an outlier in his own party, as Trump yearns to use tortures "a hell of a lot worse than waterboarding."[108]

The United States has belatedly begun a reckoning for slavery and

Jim Crow and their ongoing legacy, as well as a growing awareness of the enduring scourge of anti-Asian bigotry.[109] In 1988, Ronald Reagan signed into law a civil liberties act that gave a national apology and offered payments to the surviving Japanese Americans interned during World War II, and in 1993 Bill Clinton put out a letter of apology.[110] Yet the broader American popular approach toward World War II is marked by triumphalism, historical ignorance, and a lack of self-examination. World War II was a just war forced upon the Allies by Axis aggression, but that does not mean that the Americans could do no wrong in fighting it.

There is no prospect of a U.S. apology for the firebombing of Tokyo and scores of other Japanese cities, not least because few Americans have any awareness that such a thing happened. No U.S. president has seriously considered visiting the somber memorial at Yokoamicho Park in Tokyo where the remains of more than a hundred thousand bombing victims are interred. Yet even for the atomic bombs, whose horrors have been well known since John Hersey's vivid reporting from Hiroshima in *The New Yorker* in August 1946, the United States has dug in on the position that the atomic bombs helped bring the war to an end and therefore there is no need for official remorse—even for the civilians and children who were scorched to death, as well as Koreans who had been put to forced labor in both cities.

The pattern was set by Harry Truman, who, although privately troubled by the atomic bombs at the time, for decades afterward insisted that he had saved half a million American lives. "I never lost any sleep over that decision," he said—a folksy phrase that clanged in the ears of Japanese survivors.[111] His successors argued that the atomic bombings were a necessity, with George H. W. Bush, who was lucky to have survived the war, saying, "No apology is required, and it will not be asked of this president, I can guarantee you. I was fighting over there!" In 1995, the Smithsonian Institution canceled an exhibition of the *Enola Gay*, the B-29 that bombed Hiroshima, which was to have a well-researched but sternly critical exhibit script that included graphic accounts of the killing of Japanese civilians. Newt Gingrich, the Republican speaker of the House of Representatives, said that Americans were "sick and tired of being told by some cultural elite that they ought to be ashamed of their country."[112] Clinton said that "the United States owes no apology to Japan for having dropped the atomic bombs on Hiroshima and Nagasaki."[113] Although strong American support for Truman's use of atomic bombs has slowly declined over the years, three-quarters of Americans still believe that the United States should not apologize for doing so.[114]

Obama, in a 2009 speech in Prague calling for a world without nuclear weapons, said that the United States, as "the only nuclear power to have used a nuclear weapon," had a moral responsibility to pursue disarmament. In May 2016, accompanied by Abe, he became the first sitting U.S. president to visit Hiroshima. (Trump, then the presumptive Republican presidential nominee, who has reviled Japan since the 1980s, tweeted that Obama should discuss "the sneak attack on Pearl Harbor.")[115] "I don't know if I'd second-guess Truman's decision to drop the bomb," Obama told an aide as they flew into the city. "But there's something about the way we did it." He warmly greeted a group of *hibakusha*, atomic bomb survivors, embracing a tearful old man.[116] Although Obama neither apologized nor criticized Truman in his speech to a receptive, solemn crowd of Japanese, he emphasized the terror of the bombing as well as a common humanity: "Those who died, they are like us."[117]

War Without Mercy

There is one neuralgic subject that hints at how the Tokyo trial could have usefully done more: racism. In the early Cold War, a renewed struggle against racial segregation, lynching, and disenfranchisement in the United States rose in parallel to mounting demands overseas for racial equality in colonized lands in Asia and Africa.[118] With the United States today engaged in soul-searching about racial discrimination at home, it is worthwhile to remember the ways in which World War II in the Pacific was shot through with bigotry and hatred. The subject of racism was a potent undercurrent throughout the Tokyo trial; its courtroom proceedings offered an underutilized window for understanding how prejudices can influence the conduct of foreign policy and war.[119]

Given the discrimination of the period, the Tokyo trial went off with surprisingly few overtly bigoted remarks. In a memorandum to the other judges, Röling once noted that a Japanese proclamation was written "in a swollen Oriental style."[120] When General Minami Jiro under cross-examination said "Yes" in answer to a question, Webb asked, "What does he mean? Sometimes the Japanese 'yes' means 'no,' I understand."[121] On one occasion when confronted with a baldly racist remark, some of the main actors behaved rather decently. "I have thirty years of experience in oriental question and answer," said a U.S. interpreter, Major M. L. Moore, being pressed about Chinese translations, "and it is an established fact that an oriental, when pressed, will dodge the issue." Webb immediately lashed him for the slur, pointing out that the U.S. major could not even speak Chinese. "You said a thing which you should not have said," the Australian chief judge growled. "It is quite beyond your province to comment on the nature of evidence given by orientals; and I ask you to withdraw that comment." Although the U.S. interpreter apologized, Xiang Zhejun, the Chinese associate prosecutor, was incensed: "I think it is quite a gratuitous charge against the oriental people. I disagree with his understanding of the oriental mind." Next Joseph Keenan jumped in to say that it compromised the ideal of a fair trial to have an allegedly impartial translator "who carries the notion that Orientals have the invariable habit of dodging the issue." Speaking for the judges, Webb concluded, "I think I can safely say on behalf of every Member of the Court that we do not share Major Moore's view."[122]

Yet questions of racism lurked throughout the trial. The racial optics of the court were always jarring: a group of mostly white men sitting in judgment over Asians. The Asian judges were the most aware of this: Radhabinod Pal was the only judge to make racism a major theme of his opinion, while Mei Ruao stewed privately about British white supremacism.[123] Still, in their own ways, both the defense and the prosecution put forward contrasting narratives of racism that ran throughout the proceedings.

The defense counsel fretted that Western prejudices against the Japanese would spill over into the courtroom. Such bigotry had been only too apparent, manifested in U.S. immigration policy, which had barred Chinese workers in 1882 before moving on to shut out Koreans and Japanese.[124] Soon before Pearl Harbor, no less an authority on American racism than W. E. B. Du Bois, who came to admire Japan as a colored nation resisting white colonialism, diagnosed a profound American anxiety about "above all—Japan! Japan is about to conquer the world for the yellow race and then she'll be ready to swallow America."[125] To get into a White House press conference, a Chinese reporter pinned a hand-lettered note to his lapel: "CHINESE REPORTER *NOT JAPANESE PLEASE*." During the war, *Life* magazine labeled a photograph of Tojo's face with his purportedly representative racial features: "earthy yellow complexion, less frequent epicanthic fold, flatter nose, sometimes rosy cheeks, heavy beard, massive cheek and jawbone." Henry Luce's influential magazine explained that "Peasant Jap is squat Mongoloid" and that Tojo "betrays aboriginal antecedents in a squat, long-torsoed build, a broader, more massively boned head and face, flat, often pug nose, yellow-ocher skin and heavier beard."[126]

Since only Japanese were on trial, the defense had few ways to probe the impact of that kind of anti-Japanese racism on the making of U.S. policy. Still, in his opening address in court, Kiyose Ichiro declared that Japan was dedicated to uprooting racial discrimination, skillfully playing to a Japanese domestic audience that resented such prejudices.[127] If Prince Konoe Fumimaro, the Japanese prime minister who invaded China in 1937, had not committed suicide before being arrested, his defense at the Tokyo trial would almost certainly have featured his long-standing repugnance for Western "racial discrimination against the yellow race."[128] As a young man attending the Paris Peace Conference after World War I, he had been repelled by American and British racism, fearing that the League of Nations was really meant to uphold an Anglo-Saxon economic imperialism. When Japan, on the victorious side, failed to get its allies to include clauses of racial equality in the League covenant, he blamed that on white supremacy—a point echoed by Pal in his dissent.[129]

Some Japanese expansionists had envisioned their rule as that of a benevolent mentor instilling racial harmony, pointing to their puppet state in Manchuria as a model of multiracial fellowship among Mongols, Manchus, Han Chinese, Koreans, and Japanese.[130] One former commander of the Kwantung Army explained that Japan meant to build a utopia of "racial harmony" among the varied peoples in Manchukuo.[131] As the defense pointed out, the Greater East Asia Co-Prosperity Sphere was officially dedicated to "the removal of all discrimination based on racial prejudice."[132] Despite that, some of the defense evidence revealed a less tolerant racial vision. One wartime prime minister told the Diet in 1940 that "the Japanese race is surely a divine race," arguing for expanding southward "because we possess Indonesian blood."[133]

Röling did not consider such racism in his own dissent, but later—possibly influenced by his friend Pal—contended that Western discrimination against Asians might have been one of the roots of the Pacific War, as well as arguing that American soldiers had been indoctrinated to see the Japanese as subhuman: "The bombing of the Japanese cities, followed by the atomic bombing of Hiroshima and Nagasaki, was made possible by precisely that feeling that it was not human beings they were cremating by the hundreds of thousands."[134] Although the atomic bomb was first developed with Nazi Germany in mind, Röling's contention has some echoes of the widespread belief in Japan that the weapon was used as a racist scientific experiment.[135]

For its part, the prosecution presented evidence of various strands of prejudice in Japanese imperialism. This echoed similar points made by the Allies during the war. As the Chinese finance minister had warned in 1935, "Japan wants to bring about a race war—yellow men against white men—and to dominate a great union of the billion people of Asia."[136] In a BBC broadcast in 1942, George Orwell had pointed to the Japanese subjugation of Koreans, Taiwanese, and Chinese: "To those who say that the cause of Japan is the cause of Asia as against the European races, the best answer is: Why then do the Japanese constantly make war against other races who are Asiatics no less than themselves?"[137] In familiar narratives of Japanese guards brutalizing Allied prisoners, it is too often forgotten that most of the Allied troops who surrendered to the Japanese were not white.[138]

As the Tokyo trial showed, a fast-growing Japanese Empire struggled to cope with the diversity of the Asian peoples it had conquered.[139] In February 1932, Matsuoka Yosuke, a future foreign minister and Tokyo defendant, had explained to Emperor Hirohito that according to principles of biology, it was hard for close races—namely, Japanese and Chinese—to have friendly relations.[140] In June 1933, as army minister, Araki Sadao gave a celebrated speech, which was made into a movie: "It is the holy mission of Japan, the Yamato race, to establish peace in the Orient with its ideals and power."[141]

After the invasion of China in July 1937, some Japanese commanders feared a race war between Japanese and Chinese, warning that the Chinese public had a "very deep and keen racial consciousness and anti-Japanese feeling."[142] As a senior Japanese officer in China testified as a defense witness at the Tokyo trial, "we considered that if we opened war against China, it would grow into a racial conflict and that the conflict might be a prolonged war."[143]

Decades after the trial, there is a greater awareness of how racism fueled the Pacific War, led by the work of the historian John Dower.[144] It is only through that prism that one can make sense of the fact that, in a fateful meeting of top Japanese leaders a month before Pearl Harbor, the president of the privy council had warned that "hatred of the yellow race" might unite "the white race" in Britain, Nazi Germany, and the United States against an isolated Japan.[145] Similarly, in January 1944, Marquis Kido Koichi urged that "we should carefully avoid being isolated and attacked by nations as a colored race," hoping to cooperate secretly with the Soviet Union and China because they were "essentially Oriental in their stand against the Anglo-Saxons—the U.S.A. and Great Britain."[146]

For anyone inclined to introspection, the trial proceedings offer hard lessons about how racism has manifested in international relations. Togo Kazuhiko, the diplomat and grandson of Togo Shigenori, explains that in Japanese eyes, "The war against—let me use the racial expression—whites was a war fought on an equal basis." He adds, "With Asians, we were perpetrators; with whites, we were equals; with Soviets, we were victims. This is the underlying psychology." In a time of reflection about racism, the Tokyo trial offers telling evidence about bigotry as a driver of empire and war.

The Unmasterable Past

Seventy years after the end of the war, August 15, 2015, is a muggy late-summer day in Tokyo. Tucked away from the city's tumult on serene leafy grounds, the Yasukuni Shrine is a sheltering sanctuary. Without the din of traffic and trains, crickets drone in the claggy humidity. There is a long pedestrian avenue leading to the main shrine: a magnificent, imposing Shinto wooden temple with simple lines, ornate decorations close up, and sweeping metal eaves and peaked roofs.

By 8 a.m., an orderly crowd is forming, processing down the avenue toward the shrine to pay their respects to the war dead. A huge drum booms repeatedly. Solemn and dignified, people pause on the avenue at a wooden torii, a gate which usually marks the entry to a Shinto shrine, and bow deeply toward the big shrine. Two hours later, the place is packed, with thousands of visitors in tidy lines streaming toward the shrine under a scorching sun. They are overwhelmingly bourgeois, well dressed, and grave, with a prayer tour group from Hiroshima Prefecture and a group of veterans' families from Aomori Prefecture wearing mourning black. Most say they have come out of a mixture of patriotism, familial duty toward a fallen veteran, or curiosity. There are a few elderly men in military uniforms, as well as some right-wing cosplayers: a young man dressed up as a World War II pilot looks more self-conscious than frightening. More daunting are some groups of tough-looking men in dark blue military-style uniforms, marching behind a huge Japanese flag in what they mean to be fearsome military formation.

The police, taking no chances, arrive early in the morning in big blue Isuzu buses with metal gates shielding the windows. Row after row of policemen march just outside the grounds, blue uniforms layered with riot-control vests, some of them carrying wicked-looking white truncheons the length of a sword. They have barred *gaisensha*, the big sound trucks tricked out with loudspeakers to blast political messages, although there are still plenty of them parked around the perimeter, sporting massive rising sun flags.

It is no accident that this place attracts zealots. The Yushukan, the military museum, ostentatiously showcases the lethal machines of war: a Zero fighter; a *kaiten* suicide torpedo, a colossal black tube of steel to rupture the hulls of American warships; and a hulking black steam locomotive, which had chugged along the Burma–Thailand death railway, built by Australian prisoners of war and Asian laborers who were routinely beaten or worked to death. Its didactic exhibits tell how the United States supported Chiang Kai-shek's government and imposed an oil embargo which triggered war. Below a large panel about Pal's dissent, there are somber portraits of the seven Class A war criminals who were hanged. The gift shop sells books extolling Pal and denying the Nanjing massacre.

On the way to the nearby subway station, the sidewalk is jammed with a cacophonous array of irate activists from the right and far right. "Japan is not a criminal nation!" bellows one campaigner under the watchful eyes of stone-faced policemen at a barricade. "Japan freed the peoples of Asia and Africa! We will defend Yasukuni!" There are T-shirts for sale with slurs against Chinese, petitions to revise the pacifist constitution, radicals of various kinds (one elderly man has a sign reading, "Koreans tell lies without scruple as they breathe in and out"), and campaigners denying the Nanjing massacre and bashing the Tokyo trial. When leftist activists show up, someone shouts, "Get away from me, you traitor!"

The Tokyo trial is never far out of mind at Yasukuni. There are fresh flowers at the handsome stone monument to Pal, just outside the Zero fighter in the Yushukan. One of the Indian judge's admirers is Hada Natsuko, a bright-eyed, cheerful thirty-year-old editor and translator dressed for the occasion in an elegant white kimono, who says, "I personally do not agree with the Tokyo trial." She explains that when we die, we become *kami*, forgiven for all that we did in our lives. What about the Class A war criminals? "I think they have as much right as anyone else to become gods, to be worshipped," she says. Sugiyama Kazuyuki, a sixty-two-year-old retired civil servant, dismisses the court's verdict on Tojo and other Class A war criminals: "I don't think they're war criminals. But even if they were, we have to consecrate and thank them."

Although the extremists and loudmouths at Yasukuni invariably draw more attention, there is elsewhere another Japan with a wiser, more humane approach to history.[147] Utsumi Keiko, who as a teenager survived an American firebombing of Yokohama in 1945, is a warm, dignified grandmother, retired as a nurse and midwife, impeccably dressed in a beige linen blazer at a senior citizens office in the sweltering Tokyo summer heat. "It was like the sound of rain," she recalls, "the sound of firebombs dropping." She remembers huddling in a bomb shelter all night, terrified, as wooden homes all around burned and collapsed. When she emerged into a scorched wasteland the next morning, she saw the dead: "they were all black, all burned." Despite being instructed to hate the occupying Americans when they arrived, she did not; she recalls her relief when she realized that they were not there to enslave the men and rape the women. She wonders why a small country like Japan started a war against big countries like the United States and Britain. Although she is glad that Hirohito was not prosecuted, she says she had heard about the army doing terrible things, and thinks it unavoidable that they would be tried as war criminals.

Hada Reiko, who was nine years old when she survived the atomic bombing of Nagasaki, is a cheerful woman with a winning grin, her eyes crinkling behind purple half-rimmed glasses. Her girlhood memories of that day—an otherworldly flash, the blast of the shockwave, a completely red sky, naked and scorched people dying—are still fresh. Yet in her old age she is reflective, refusing to hate any Americans, except for Truman. "I feel this war was wrong, the way we fought was wrong," she says. "Before the atomic bomb was dropped, it was a war of aggression." She adds, "Japan is a victim in the context of the atomic bomb, but it was also an aggressor in the context of the wider war."

Hada remembers radio and newspaper stories about the Tokyo trial while it was happening, but was too young to understand it; only when she entered high school did she start to grasp what it meant, helped by hearing stories from her father and brother—who had been in a kamikaze unit and was lucky to return—about the trial. "As I grew up, I felt that the war leaders in Japan should repent on the fact that they prolonged the war," she says. "I feel that the war was wrong, and that they should not have delayed surrender." Although she thinks that the United States should apologize for the atomic bombings, she believes that Japan's own apologies have been inadequate, pointing to the counterexample—well known in Japan—of Richard von Weizsäcker, who as West Germany's president in 1985 rebuked elderly Germans for claiming not to have known about the Holocaust.[148] On a bright summer day in a rebuilt Nagasaki, despite memories that could easily drive her to hate and resentment, her vision looks higher. Putting conscience over nationalism in a way that is more and more rare, she concludes with simple clarity, "Even though we're all Japanese people, I think the war leaders were wrong."

Notes

Note on Sources

This book is based on archival research and interviews in Tokyo, Hiroshima, Nagasaki, Beijing, Nanjing, Hong Kong, Taipei, Seoul, Delhi, Kolkata, London, Edinburgh, Paris, The Hague, Canberra, Washington, Norfolk, and Independence, Missouri.

The main source of the book is documentary evidence, many thousands of pages gathered from eighteen archives in seven nations. Thousands of pages of Chinese and Japanese documents were carefully translated into English and reviewed for substance and tone; sometimes two translators would do versions of the same paper to be sure that no nuances were lost. Unless otherwise noted, translations from Chinese and Japanese are by my researchers, and translations from French are my own. The objective was to work in Chinese archives, as well as Japanese records, in the same way that I would in archives where I read and spoke the language. This meant that some documents were laboriously translated but not used in the book, although they did inform my understanding. The project aimed to follow Robert Caro's imperative: "Turn every page."

There were distinctive difficulties throughout: the relevant papers of the Republic of China are largely written in calligraphy, not the simplified characters used in mainland China today; in Taiwan's otherwise splendidly efficient archives, papers about Chiang Kai-shek cannot be photocopied and had to be copied out by hand; and many Chinese participants in these events would have burned their diaries and records during the Cultural Revolution in order to avoid persecution. Yet the greatest challenge was the sheer bulk of documentation about World War II and the early Cold War, which took years and years to get through.

Although I could not have known the main historical figures in this book, some of their families generously shared their personal recollections in interviews held in China, Japan, and India. To better understand the historical legacy of the events in this book, I did interviews with people across Asia, including Japanese and Allied veterans of the war, and survivors of Hiroshima, Nagasaki, and the American firebombing campaign. I interviewed government officials and activists in China, Japan, the United States, Britain, and other countries. Quotations without endnotes from people in the present day are from my reporting in Japan, China, India, and South Korea. The book is enriched throughout by those Japanese, Chinese, Koreans, Indians, and others who were kind enough to share their thoughts and feelings with an outsider.

In addition to the original archival research and reporting, this book benefits from the work of previous generations of scholars of international relations. Nobody writes about World War II and the Cold War without the benefit of an excellent and dauntingly large literature. This book pays tribute in the traditional way—citation in the endnotes—but I am indebted to the superb work of these scholars.

For Chinese, Japanese, and Korean names, this book follows their usage in putting fammily names first, followed by given names: Togo Shigenori, not Shigenori Togo. The only exception is in the endnotes: when Japanese authors publishing in English have put their surname last, this book cites their work as it was published, so that it can be readily found in library catalogues.

The book uses Hepburn romanization for Japanese words and names, without the macrons used to indicate long vowels. For Chinese words and names, the book uses pinyin transliterations, without diacritics for tones: Mao Zedong, not Mao Tse-tung. The exceptions are when an older Wade-Giles or other romanization has gained widespread acceptance, such as Chiang Kai-shek, Manchukuo, or the Kwantung Army. In 1928, the Nationalists changed the name of Beijing to Beiping, which was then reversed by the victorious Communists in 1949; to minimize confusion, this book simply uses Beijing throughout. When quoting from official courtroom transcripts, the book retains the Wade-Giles transliterations used at the time rather than tampering with the original text.

Key to Citations

National Archives of Australia, Canberra: NAA
    War Cabinet papers
        International Military Tribunal for the Far East papers

Australian War Memorial, Canberra: AWM
    Private Records Collection
        Papers of Sir William Webb
        Manuscripts of Australian soldiers

British National Archives, Kew, London: BNA
    Prime Minister's Office papers: PREM
    Cabinet Office papers: CAB
    Foreign Office papers: FO
    Foreign and Commonwealth Office papers: FCO
    Dominions Office and Commonwealth Relations Office papers: DO
    Lord Chancellor's Office papers: LCO

British Library, London: BL
    India Office Records: IOR
        Public and Judicial Department Records 1795–1950: L/P&J
        Private Papers (European Manuscripts): Mss Eur
    Endangered Archives Programme: EAP

National Records of Scotland, Edinburgh: NRS
Private Office papers

Academia Historica, Taipei, Taiwan: Guoshiguan
Chiang Kai-shek collections
Foreign Ministry papers
Judicial Yuan papers

Ministère des Affaires Étrangères, Archives diplomatiques, La Courneuve, Paris: MAE
Secrétariat des Nations-Unies et Organisations internationales: NUOI
Série Asie-Océanie, sous-série Indochine
Série Asie-Océanie, sous-série Japon

Bibliothèque de documentation internationale contemporaine, Nanterre, France: BDIC
Fonds du juge Henri Bernard

Nationaal Archief, The Hague: NL-HaNA
B. V. A. Röling papers

National Archives of India, New Delhi: NAI
External Affairs Department, Government of India, British Empire: EAD
Ministry of External Affairs, Republic of India: MEA

Radhabinod Pal family papers, Kolkata, India

United States National Archives II, College Park, Maryland: NARA
Record Group (RG) 24: Bureau of Naval Personnel records
RG 43: records of international conferences
RG 59: State Department records
RG 84: records of State Department foreign posts
RG 107: Office of the Secretary of War records
RG 218: Joint Chiefs of Staff records
RG 331: World War II Allied operational and occupation headquarters records

Harry S. Truman Library and Museum, Independence, Missouri: HSTL
PSF: President's Secretary's Files
CF: Confidential File
OF: Official File
NAP: Staff Member and Office Files, Naval Aide to the President Files
SIR: Samuel I. Rosenman papers

MacArthur Memorial Archives, Norfolk, Virginia: MMA
Record Group (RG) 5: Supreme Commander for the Allied Powers papers
RG 9: radiograms
RG 10: MacArthur correspondence
RG 32: oral history collection
RG 44, RG 44a: Bonner F. Fellers papers

Yale University libraries, New Haven, Connecticut
  Henry L. Stimson Diaries
  John G. Magee family papers, Yale Divinity Library

Harvard Law School Library, Cambridge, Massachusetts: HLS
  Justice Felix Frankfurter papers

International Military Tribunal for the Far East digital collection, University of Virginia:
  UVA

Bentley Historical Library, University of Michigan, Ann Arbor: UM
  Justice Frank Murphy papers

The State Department's official *Foreign Relations of the United States* series: cited as *FRUS*.

R. John Pritchard, ed., *The Tokyo Major War Crimes Trial: The Transcripts of the Court Proceedings of the International Military Tribunal for the Far East* (Lewiston, N.Y.: Edwin Mellen Press, 1998), 124 volumes: cited as *IMTFE Transcripts*.

Introduction

1. Associated Press, "Tojo Sees Time Vindicating Japan; Calls MacArthur a Clean Fighter," *New York Times*, 11 September 1945, pp. 1–2.
2. George E. Jones, "M'Arthur Seizing 40 for War Crimes; Tojo Shoots Himself to Avoid Arrest, But Is Kept Alive by American Doctor," *New York Times*, 12 September 1945, pp. 1–2. "Snafu Suicide," *Life*, 24 September 1945, pp. 36–37. Associated Press, "Tojo Feels Better; He Talks of Plight," *New York Times*, 14 September 1945, p. 8.
3. John W. Dower, *War Without Mercy: Race and Power in the Pacific War* (New York: Pantheon, 1986), pp. 40–41.
4. Barrett Tillman, *Whirlwind: The Air War Against Japan, 1942–1945* (New York: Simon & Schuster, 2010), pp. 149, 152. "51 Square Miles Burned Out in Six B-29 Attacks on Tokyo," *New York Times*, 30 May 1945. James M. Scott, *Black Snow: Curtis LeMay, the Firebombing of Tokyo, and the Road to the Atomic Bomb* (New York: W. W. Norton, 2022), pp. 219–22.
5. William J. Sebald with Russell Brines, *With MacArthur in Japan: A Personal History of the Occupation* (New York: W. W. Norton, 1965), pp. 39–40.
6. Jones, "M'Arthur Seizing 40 for War Crimes."
7. AWM, Webb papers, 3DRL/2481, series 1, wallet 10, Röling to Webb, 17 February 1947.
8. Guoshiguan, Foreign Ministry files, IMTFE Major Cases (Part II), Mei to Webb, 8 December 1946, 020-010117-0027-0104a to 020-010117-0027-0115a.
9. Ian W. Toll, *Twilight of the Gods: War in the Western Pacific, 1944–1945* (New York: W. W. Norton, 2020), pp. 438–68. James M. Scott, *Rampage: MacArthur, Yamashita, and the Battle of Manila* (New York: W. W. Norton, 2018).
10. Sarah Kovner, *Prisoners of the Empire: Inside Japanese POW Camps* (Cambridge, Mass.: Harvard University Press, 2020), p. 1.

11. Rana Mitter, *Forgotten Ally: China's World War II, 1937–1945* (Boston: Houghton Mifflin Harcourt, 2013), p. 139. See Dara Kay Cohen, *Rape During Civil War* (Ithaca, N.Y.: Cornell University Press, 2016).

12. Kovner, *Prisoners of the Empire*, p. 94.

13. NARA, RG 59, Office of Chinese Affairs, 250/46/4/01, box 2, War crimes and war criminals; RG 59, Legal Adviser, Japanese War Criminals, 250/49/25/06, box 28, Sato Kesakichi case.

14. Dower, *War Without Mercy*, p. 12.

15. AWM, Webb papers, 3DRL/2481, series 4, wallet 20, Webb memo, 2 August 1946.

16. Kurosawa Akira's classic film was released in 1950, not long after the Tokyo trial concluded.

17. *IMTFE Transcripts*, 11 December 1946, pp. 12575–76.

18. *IMTFE Transcripts*, 10 January 1947, pp. 15031–42.

19. James Bradley, *Flyboys: A True Story of Courage* (Boston: Little, Brown, 2003).

20. NL-HaNA, 2.21.273, folder 27, Röling to Patricia, 27 August 1946.

21. Oona A. Hathaway et al., "What Is a War Crime?," *Yale Journal of International Law*, vol. 44, no. 1 (Winter 2019), pp. 53–114.

22. Kathryn Sikkink, *The Justice Cascade: How Human Rights Prosecutions Are Changing World Politics* (New York: W. W. Norton, 2011), pp. 5–20, 96–98.

23. MMA, RG-5, box 107, folder 2, Sebald to Benninghoff, 29 October 1948.

24. Mei to Wang, 1 June 1948, Mei Xiaoao and Mei Xiaokan, eds., *Mei Ruao Dongjing shenpan wengao* [The Tokyo Trial Manuscripts of Mei Ruao] (Shanghai: Shanghai Jiaotong University Press, 2013), pp. 9–10.

25. AWM, Webb papers, 3DRL/2481, series 1, wallet 10, Röling to Webb, 17 February 1947.

26. The leading Japanese account, an excellent book by Higurashi Yoshinobu, draws extensively on American, British, and Australian documents. Higurashi Yoshinobu, *Tokyo saiban no kokusai kankei: Kokusai seiji ni okeru kenryoku to kihan* [International Relations of the Tokyo Trial: Power and Norms in International Politics] (Tokyo: Bokutakusha, 2002), pp. 2–23. My book also benefited from the important scholarship of Awaya Kentaro, Fujita Hisakazu, Onuma Yasuaki, Yoshimi Yoshiaki, Yoshida Yutaka, and others. Among the rich studies in English, see John W. Dower, *Embracing Defeat: Japan in the Wake of World War II* (New York: W. W. Norton, 1999), pp. 443–84; David Cohen and Yuma Totani, *The Tokyo War Crimes Tribunal: Law, History, and Jurisprudence* (Cambridge: Cambridge University Press, 2018); Neil Boister and Robert Cryer, *The Tokyo International Military Tribunal: A Reappraisal* (Oxford: Oxford University Press, 2008); Yuma Totani, *The Tokyo War Crimes Trial: The Pursuit of Justice in the Wake of World War II* (Cambridge, Mass.: Harvard University Press, 2008); Yuki Tanaka, Tim McCormack, and Gerry Simpson, eds., *Beyond Victor's Justice? The Tokyo War Crimes Trial Revisited* (Leiden: Martinus Nijhoff, 2010); Arnold C. Brackman, *The Other Nuremberg: The Untold Story of the Tokyo War Crime Trials* (London: Collins, 1989); Timothy P. Maga, *Judgment at Tokyo: The Japanese War Crimes Trials* (Lexington: University Press of Kentucky, 2001); Kerstin von Lingen, ed., *Transcultural Justice at the Tokyo Tribunal: The Allied Struggle for Justice, 1946–48* (Leiden: Brill, 2018); and Richard Minear, *Victor's Justice: The Tokyo War Crimes Trial* (Princeton: Princeton University Press, 1971).

27. On writing international history, see David Armitage, *Foundations of Modern International Thought* (Cambridge: Cambridge University Press, 2013), pp. 17–32; Erez

Manela, "International Society as a Historical Subject," *Diplomatic History,* vol. 44, no. 2 (April 2020), pp. 184–209; Lynn Hunt, *Writing History in the Global Era* (New York: W. W. Norton, 2014); Charles S. Maier, "Marking Time," in Michael Kammen, ed., *The Past Before Us: Contemporary Historical Writing in the United States* (Ithaca, N.Y.: Cornell University Press, 1980), pp. 355–87; Akira Iriye, "Internationalizing International History," in Thomas Bender, ed., *Rethinking American History in a Global Age* (Berkeley: University of California Press, 2002), pp. 47–62; and Odd Arne Westad, "The New International History of the Cold War," *Diplomatic History,* vol. 24, no. 4 (2000), pp. 551–65.

28. Christopher Hemmer and Peter J. Katzenstein, "Why Is There No NATO in Asia?," *International Organization,* vol. 56, no. 3 (June 2002), pp. 575–607.

29. Caroline Elkins, *Legacy of Violence: A History of the British Empire* (New York: Alfred A. Knopf, 2022). Odd Arne Westad, *The Cold War: A World History* (New York: Basic Books, 2017), pp. 129–32. Tim Harper, *Underground Asia: Global Revolutionaries and the Assault on Empire* (Cambridge, Mass.: Harvard University Press, 2021). Christopher Bayly and Tim Harper, *Forgotten Armies: The Fall of British Asia, 1941–1945* (Cambridge, Mass.: Belknap Press of Harvard University Press, 2006) and *Forgotten Wars: Freedom and Revolution in Southeast Asia* (Cambridge, Mass.: Belknap Press of Harvard University Press, 2010). William Dalrymple, *The Anarchy: The Relentless Rise of the East India Company* (London: Bloomsbury, 2019).

30. Theodore H. White and Annalee Jacoby, *Thunder Out of China* (New York: William Sloane Associates, 1946), p. xiii.

31. MMA, RG-5, box 115, folder 15, IMTFE proclamation, 19 January 1946.

32. Telford Taylor, *Nuremberg and Vietnam: An American Tragedy* (Chicago: Quadrangle, 1970), p. 82.

33. Brackman, *Other Nuremberg,* p. 428. On non-Western origins of modern human rights, see Kathryn Sikkink, *Evidence for Hope: Making Human Rights Work in the 21st Century* (Princeton: Princeton University Press, 2017), pp. 55–93.

34. BDIC, fonds du Bernard, Fᵒ Δ res 0874/10, Bernard to judges, 10 May 1948. O-Gon Kwon, "Forgotten Victims, Forgotten Defendants," in Tanaka, McCormack, and Simpson, eds., *Beyond Victor's Justice?,* pp. 227–39.

35. Richard Rhodes, "The General and World War III," *The New Yorker,* 19 June 1995, p. 48.

36. Stimson Diaries, vol. 51, 6 June 1945.

37. Ian Buruma, *The Wages of Guilt: Memories of War in Germany and Japan* (New York: Farrar, Straus & Giroux, 1994)—a superb, definitive comparison of historical memory in the old Axis.

38. Yinan He, *The Search for Reconciliation: Sino-Japanese and German-Polish Relations Since World War II* (Cambridge: Cambridge University Press, 2009).

39. See, for instance, Karin Laub, "AfD Chief: Nazi Era a 'Speck of Bird Poop,'" Associated Press, 2 June 2018.

40. Tony Judt, *Postwar: A History of Europe Since 1945* (London: Penguin, 2005). On macrohistorical comparisons, see Theda Skocpol and Margaret Somers, "The Uses of Comparative History in Macrosocial Inquiry," *Comparative Studies in Society and History,* vol. 2 (1980), pp. 174–97; and Dietrich Rueschemeyer and John D. Stephens, "Comparing Historical Sequences," *Comparative Social Research,* vol. 16 (1997), pp. 55–72.

41. Ayse Zarakol, *After Defeat: How the East Learned to Live with the West* (Cambridge: Cambridge University Press, 2011), pp. 160–200.

42. Victor D. Cha, *Alignment Despite Antagonism: The United States-Korea-Japan Security Triangle* (Stanford, Calif.: Stanford University Press, 1999). David C. Kang, "Between Balancing and Bandwagoning," *Journal of East Asian Studies,* vol. 9, no. 1 (January–April 2009), pp. 1–28.

43. Austin Ramzy, "Xi Condemns Efforts to Play Down Japan's Wartime Aggression," *New York Times,* 7 July 2014.

44. Bruce Stokes, "Hostile Neighbors," Pew Research Center, 13 September 2016.

45. Beth Simmons, *Mobilizing for Human Rights: International Law in Domestic Politics* (Cambridge: Cambridge University Press, 2009). Thomas Risse and Kathryn Sikkink, "The Socialization of International Human Rights Norms into Domestic Practices," in Thomas Risse, Stephen C. Ropp, and Kathryn Sikkink, eds., *The Power of Human Rights: International Norms and Domestic Change* (Cambridge: Cambridge University Press, 1999), pp. 1–38.

46. Putin interview, Xinhua and TASS, 1 September 2015, http://en.kremlin.ru/events /president/news/50207.

47. Buruma, *Wages of Guilt,* pp. 160–68. Ian Buruma, *Inventing Japan, 1853–1964* (New York: Modern Library, 2003), p. 147. Watanabe Shoichi, *"Tokyo saiban" o saibansuru* [The "Tokyo Trial" on Trial] (Tokyo: Chichi Shuppansha, 2007) and *Paru hanketsusho no shinjitsu* [The Truth of Pal's Judgment] (Tokyo: PHP Kenkyujo, 2008). Sato Kazuo, *Sekai ga sabaku Tokyo saiban* [The Tokyo Trial as Judged by Intellectuals] (Tokyo: Kokusai Kikaku, 1996). Kobori Keiichiro, *Tokyo saiban Nihon no benmei* [Japan's Defense at the Tokyo Trial] (Tokyo: Kodansha, 1995).

48. Kishi Nobusuke, *Kishi Nobusuke kaikoroku: Hoshu godo to Anpo kaitei* [Memoirs of Kishi Nobusuke: The Conservative Consolidation and Security Treaty Revision] (Tokyo: Kosaido Publishing, 1983), p. 18.

49. Jun Uchida, *Brokers of Empire: Japanese Settler Colonialism in Korea, 1876–1945* (Cambridge, Mass.: Harvard University Press, 2011).

50. Rana Mitter, *China's Good War: How World War II Is Shaping a New Nationalism* (Cambridge, Mass.: Belknap Press of Harvard University Press, 2020), pp. 212–49. See Thomas J. Christensen, *Worse Than a Monolith: Alliance Politics and Problems of Coercive Diplomacy in Asia* (Princeton: Princeton University Press, 2011), pp. 231–59; Jessica Chen Weiss, *Powerful Patriots: Nationalist Protest in China's Foreign Relations* (Oxford: Oxford University Press, 2014); and He, *Search for Reconciliation.*

51. Xinhua, "Xi Jinping's Speech at the Commemoration of the 69th Anniversary of the Victory of the Chinese People's War of Resistance Against Japanese Aggression and the World Anti-Fascist War," *People's Daily,* 4 September 2014, p. 2.

52. Elizabeth D. Samet, *Looking for the Good War: American Amnesia and the Violent Pursuit of Happiness* (New York: Farrar, Straus & Giroux, 2021). Steven Levitsky and Daniel Ziblatt, *How Democracies Die* (New York: Crown, 2018). Peter Baker and Susan B. Glasser, *The Divider: Trump in the White House, 2017–2021* (New York: Doubleday, 2022). Gideon Rachman, *The Age of the Strongman: How the Cult of the Leader Threatens Democracy Around the World* (London: Bodley Head, 2022).

53. *IMTFE Transcripts,* 4 November 1948, p. 48426.

54. Dower, *Embracing Defeat,* pp. 22, 87–120. Kovner, *Prisoners of the Empire,* p. 157.

55. Stimson Diaries, vol. 50, 11 January 1945.

56. Robert A. Pape, "Why Japan Surrendered," *International Security*, vol. 18, no. 2 (Autumn 1993), pp. 154–201.

57. See Marc Gallicchio, *Unconditional: The Japanese Surrender in World War II* (Oxford: Oxford University Press, 2020), pp. 38–70. In defense of Hirohito, see Dominic Lieven, *In the Shadow of the Gods: The Emperor in World History* (London: Allen Lane, 2022), pp. 426–27. For an excellent account of the ideology of the emperor system, see Carol Gluck, *Japan's Modern Myths: Ideology in the Late Meiji Period* (Princeton: Princeton University Press, 1985).

58. On historical legacies, see Paul Pierson, *Politics in Time: History, Institutions, and Social Analysis* (Princeton: Princeton University Press, 2004); Paul Pierson, "Increasing Returns, Path Dependence, and the Study of Politics," *American Political Science Review*, vol. 94 (2001), pp. 251–67; Kathleen Thelen and James Mahoney, eds., *Advances in Comparative Historical Analysis* (New York: Cambridge University Press, 2015); and Kathleen Thelen and Sven Steinmo, "Historical Institutionalism in Comparative Politics," in Kathleen Thelen et al., eds., *Structuring Politics: Historical Institutionalism in Comparative Analysis* (New York: Cambridge University Press, 1992).

59. Herbert P. Bix, *Hirohito and the Making of Modern Japan* (New York: HarperCollins, 2000), p. 618. Franziska Seraphim, *War Memory and Social Politics in Japan, 1945–2005* (Cambridge, Mass.: Harvard University Press, 2006), pp. 6, 273–74.

60. Buruma, *Wages of Guilt*, pp. 62–63, 296.

61. Buruma, *Wages of Guilt*, pp. 172–76.

62. Odd Arne Westad, *Cold War and Revolution: Soviet-American Rivalry and the Origins of the Chinese Civil War, 1944–1946* (New York: Columbia University Press, 1993). See David Armitage, *Civil Wars: A History in Ideas* (New York: Alfred A. Knopf, 2017), pp. 196–231.

63. See Paul Thomas Chamberlin, *The Cold War's Killing Fields: Rethinking the Long Peace* (New York: Harper, 2018).

64. Norbert Frei, *Adenauer's Germany and the Nazi Past: The Politics of Amnesty and Integration*, trans. Joel Golb (New York: Columbia University Press, 2002). Marie-Bénédicte Vincent, *La dénazification des fonctionnaires en Allemagne de l'Ouest: Épuration et réintégration* (Paris: Éditions CNRS, 2022). Frederick Taylor, *Exorcising Hitler: The Occupation and Denazification of Germany* (London: Bloomsbury, 2011).

65. Yamamuro Shin'ichi, *Manchuria Under Japanese Domination*, trans. Joshua A. Fogel (Philadelphia: University of Pennsylvania Press, 2006), pp. 4–5, 178, 182–90.

66. Justin McCurry, "Japanese Election Victory Hands Shinzo Abe a Chance for Redemption," *Guardian*, 16 December 2012.

67. See Jeremy A. Yellen, *The Greater East Asia Co-Prosperity Sphere: When Total Empire Met Total War* (Ithaca, N.Y.: Cornell University Press, 2019), pp. 159–60.

68. See Manjari Chatterjee Miller, *Wronged by Empire: Post-Imperial Ideology and Foreign Policy in India and China* (Stanford, Calif.: Stanford University Press, 2013).

69. See Antony Anghie, *Imperialism, Sovereignty and the Making of International Law* (Cambridge: Cambridge University Press, 2004).

70. Dower, *War Without Mercy*, pp. 6–7. Richard Overy, *Blood and Ruins: The Great Imperial War, 1931–1945* (London: Allen Lane, 2021).

71. Ronald H. Spector, *A Continent Erupts: Decolonization, Civil War, and Massacre in Postwar Asia, 1945–1955* (New York: W. W. Norton, 2022), p. 2.

72. B. V. A. Röling, *The Tokyo Trial and Beyond: Reflections of a Peacemonger,* ed. Antonio Cassese (Cambridge: Polity, 1993), p. 37.

73. G. John Ikenberry, *After Victory: Institutions, Strategic Restraint, and the Rebuilding of Order After Major Wars* (Princeton: Princeton University Press, 2001), pp. 3–79, 163–214, and *A World Safe for Democracy: Liberal Internationalism and the Crises of Global Order* (New Haven: Yale University Press, 2020). Elizabeth Borgwardt, *A New Deal for the World: America's Vision for Human Rights* (Cambridge, Mass.: Belknap Press of Harvard University Press, 2005). For important critical perspectives on U.S. dominance, see Stephen Wertheim, *Tomorrow, the World: The Birth of U.S. Global Supremacy* (Cambridge, Mass.: Belknap Press of Harvard University Press, 2020); and Alexander Cooley and Daniel Nexon, *Exit from Hegemony: The Unraveling of the American Global Order* (Oxford: Oxford University Press, 2020).

74. See Priya Satia, *Time's Monster: History, Conscience, and Britain's Empire* (Cambridge, Mass.: Harvard University Press, 2020).

75. See W. G. Beasley, *Japanese Imperialism, 1894–1945* (Oxford: Clarendon, 1987), pp. 1–54, 175–250; Jack Snyder, *Myths of Empire: Domestic Politics and International Ambition* (Ithaca, N.Y.: Cornell University Press, 1991), pp. 112–52; Ramon H. Myers and Mark R. Peattie, eds., *The Japanese Colonial Empire, 1895–1945* (Princeton: Princeton University Press, 1984); Mark R. Peattie, Peter Duus, and Ramon H. Myers, *The Japanese Informal Empire in China, 1895–1937* (Princeton: Princeton University Press, 2014); Liao Ping-hui and David Der-wei Wang, eds., *Taiwan Under Japanese Colonial Rule, 1895–1945: History, Culture, Memory* (New York: Columbia University Press, 2006); Gi Wook Shin and Michael Robinson, eds., *Colonial Modernity in Korea* (Cambridge, Mass.: Harvard University Press, 1999); and Carter J. Eckert, *Korea, Old and New: A History* (Cambridge, Mass.: Harvard University Press, 1990).

76. NAI, MEA file no. 489, CJK/49, Nehru to Katju, 29 November 1948.

77. Erez Manela, *The Wilsonian Moment: Self-Determination and the International Origins of Anticolonial Nationalism* (Oxford: Oxford University Press, 2007). Robert O. Keohane, *After Hegemony: Cooperation and Discord in the World Political Economy* (Princeton: Princeton University Press, 1984). Celeste Wallander, "Institutional Assets and Adaptability," *International Organization,* vol. 54, no. 4 (2000), pp. 705–35.

78. Atul Kohli, *Imperialism and the Developing World: How Britain and the United States Shaped the Global Periphery* (Oxford: Oxford University Press, 2020).

79. John King Fairbank, *The United States and China* (Cambridge, Mass.: Harvard University Press, 1983), pp. 158–70. Pär Kristoffer Cassel, *Grounds of Judgment: Extraterritoriality and Imperial Power in Nineteenth-Century China and Japan* (Oxford: Oxford University Press, 2012). Teemu Ruskola, *Legal Orientalism: China, the United States, and Modern Law* (Cambridge, Mass.: Harvard University Press, 2013).

80. See Daniel Immerwahr, *How to Hide an Empire: A History of the Greater United States* (New York: Farrar, Straus & Giroux, 2019); Gerald L. Neuman and Tomiko Brown-Nagin, eds., *Reconsidering the Insular Cases: The Past and Future of the American Empire* (Cambridge, Mass.: Harvard University Press, 2015); Anders Stephanson, *Manifest Destiny: American Expansion and the Empire of Right* (New York: Hill & Wang, 1995); Kal Raustiala, *Does the Constitution Follow the Flag? The Evolution of Territoriality in American Law* (Oxford: Oxford University Press, 2009); Julian Go and Anne L. Foster, eds., *The American Colonial State in the Philippines: Global Perspectives* (Durham,

N.C.: Duke University Press, 2003); Amy Kaplan and Donald Pease, eds., *Cultures of United States Imperialism* (Durham, N.C.: Duke University Press, 1993); Stephen Wertheim, "Reluctant Liberator," *Presidential Studies Quarterly*, vol. 39, no. 3 (2009), pp. 494–518; Juan R. Torruella, "Ruling America's Colonies: The *Insular Cases*," *Yale Law and Policy Review*, vol. 32 (2013), pp. 57–95; H. W. Brands, *Bound to Empire: The United States and the Philippines* (Oxford: Oxford University Press, 1992); and Christopher Capozzola, *Bound by War: How the United States and the Philippines Built America's First Pacific Century* (New York: Basic Books, 2020). For classic studies of U.S. imperialism, see, variously, Ernest R. May, *American Imperialism: A Speculative Essay* (New York: Atheneum, 1968); William Appleman Williams, *The Tragedy of American Diplomacy* (New York: W. W. Norton, 1988); Walter LaFeber, *The American Search for Opportunity, 1865–1913* (Cambridge: Cambridge University Press, 2013); A. G. Hopkins, *American Empire: A Global History* (Princeton: Princeton University Press, 2018); and Andrew Bacevich, *American Empire: The Realities and Consequences of U.S. Diplomacy* (Cambridge, Mass.: Harvard University Press, 2002).

81. John Fabian Witt, *Lincoln's Code: The Laws of War in American History* (New York: Free Press, 2012), pp. 353–57.

82. Daniel Immerwahr, "The Greater United States," *Diplomatic History*, vol. 40, no. 3 (June 2016), pp. 376–77.

83. Immerwahr, *How to Hide an Empire*, pp. 3–20, 215–390.

84. W. E. B. Du Bois, "Of Mr. Booker T. Washington and Others," *The Souls of Black Folk: Essays and Sketches* (Amherst: University of Massachusetts Press, 2018), p. 51.

85. Dower, *War Without Mercy*, p. 11.

86. Radhabinod Pal, *International Military Tribunal for the Far East: Dissentient Judgment of Justice R. B. Pal* (Calcutta: Sanyal, 1953), pp. 315–20.

87. Frank White, "Tojo on Trial," *Far East Stars and Stripes Weekly Review*, 2 November 1947, p. 6.

88. Franklin D. Roosevelt, "Shall We Trust Japan?," *Asia*, vol. 23, no. 7 (July 1923), pp. 475–78, 526–28. See Greg Robinson, *By Order of the President: FDR and the Internment of Japanese Americans* (Cambridge, Mass.: Harvard University Press, 2003), pp. 37–38.

89. Dower, *War Without Mercy*. Gerald Horne, *Race War: White Supremacy and the Japanese Attack on the British Empire* (New York: New York University Press, 2004).

90. Potsdam Declaration, 26 July 1945, Winston S. Churchill, *The Second World War: Triumph and Tragedy* (Cambridge, Mass.: Houghton Mifflin, 1953), pp. 642–44.

91. See, for instance, Lydia N. Yu-Jose, *Japan Views the Philippines, 1900–1944* (Manila: Ateneo de Manila University Press, 1999).

92. Dower, *War Without Mercy*, pp. 8–10, 262–90.

93. Mei Ruao, *Dongjing da shenpan: Yuandong guoji junshi fating Zhongguo faguan Mei Ruao riji* [The Great Tokyo Trial: Diary of Mei Ruao, Chinese Judge at the International Military Tribunal for the Far East] (Nanchang: Jiangxi Education Press, 2005), 12 May 1946, p. 153.

94. Pal, *Dissentient Judgment*, p. 7.

95. "President's Address on the Radio," *New York Times*, 9 May 1945, p. 6.

96. Witt, *Lincoln's Code*, pp. 128–29. Oona Hathaway and Scott J. Shapiro, *The Internationalists: How a Radical Plan to Outlaw War Remade the World* (New York: Simon & Schuster, 2018). Jeremy Waldron, "Deep Morality and the Laws of War," in Helen Frowe and Seth Lazar, eds., *The Oxford Handbook of Ethics of War* (Oxford: Oxford

University Press, 2018), pp. 80–98. Jens David Ohlin, "Justice After War," in Frowe and Lazar, eds., *Oxford Handbook of Ethics of War,* pp. 519–37. Jens David Ohlin, *The Assault on International Law* (Oxford: Oxford University Press, 2015).

97. "Japan's War Criminals," *New York Times,* 26 January 1947, p. E8.

98. Eva Bellin, "The Iraqi Intervention and Democracy in Comparative Historical Perspective," *Political Science Quarterly,* vol. 119, no. 4 (2004–5), pp. 596–608. Alexander B. Downes, *Catastrophic Success: Why Foreign-Imposed Regime Change Goes Wrong* (Ithaca, N.Y.: Cornell University Press, 2021).

99. Richard A. Primus, *The American Language of Rights* (Cambridge: Cambridge University Press, 1999), pp. 194–96. Westad, *Cold War,* pp. 135–36.

100. John Lewis Gaddis, *The United States and the End of the Cold War: Implications, Reconsiderations, Provocations* (Oxford: Oxford University Press, 1992), pp. 48–50. On early American attempts to establish the laws of war, see Witt, *Lincoln's Code.* For a cautionary note, see Jack L. Goldsmith, "Liberal Democracy and Cosmopolitan Duty," *Stanford Law Review,* vol. 55 (2003), pp. 1667–96.

101. Truman speech at Rio de Janeiro conference, 2 September 1947, *Public Papers of the Presidents: Harry S. Truman, 1947* (Washington, D.C.: U.S. Government Printing Office, 1963), p. 429.

102. Togo Shigenori, *The Cause of Japan,* trans. Togo Fumihiko and Ben Bruce Blakeney (New York: Simon & Schuster, 1956), p. 264.

103. Samuel P. Huntington, *The Third Wave: Democratization in the Late Twentieth Century* (Norman: University of Oklahoma Press, 1991).

104. Dower, *War Without Mercy,* p. ix.

105. Nuremberg judgment, 1 October 1946, *The Trial of German Major War Criminals: Proceedings of the International Military Tribunal Sitting at Nuremberg, Germany* (London: His Majesty's Stationery Office, 1946–51), vol. 22, p. 447. Gabriella Blum, "The Crime and Punishment of States," *Yale Journal of International Law,* vol. 38 (2013), pp. 57–122.

106. Taylor, *Nuremberg and Vietnam,* pp. 86–87.

107. Dower, *Embracing Defeat,* p. 444.

108. George H. Gallup, ed., *The Gallup Poll: Public Opinion, 1935–1971* (New York: Random House, 1972), vol. 1, 20 December 1944, pp. 477–78.

109. NARA, RG 218, Leahy records, box 8, Japan military government 1946, MacArthur to War Department and Joint Chiefs, 31 October 1945.

110. NARA, RG 218, Leahy records, box 8, Japan military government 1946, Joint Chiefs to MacArthur, 10 November 1945.

111. Röling, *Tokyo Trial and Beyond,* p. 54.

112. Mark V. Tushnet, ed., *Arguing* Marbury v. Madison (Stanford, Calif.: Stanford University Press, 2005), p. 171.

113. John Locke, "The Second Treatise: An Essay Concerning the True Original, Extent, and End of Civil Government," *Two Treatises of Government,* ed. Peter Laslett (Cambridge: Cambridge University Press, 1989; orig. 1689), ch. II, §13, p. 276.

114. Madison, *Federalist* no. 10, in James Madison, Alexander Hamilton, and John Jay, *The Federalist Papers,* ed. Isaac Kramnick (London: Penguin Classics, 1987; orig. 1788), p. 124. Noah Feldman, *The Three Lives of James Madison: Genius, Partisan, President* (New York: Random House, 2017), pp. 180–83.

115. *In re Yamashita,* 327 U.S. 1 (1946).

116. *Hirota v. MacArthur, General of the Army, et al.,* 338 U.S. 197 (1948).

117. On standards of self-defense, see Michael W. Doyle, *Striking First: Preemption and Prevention in International Conflict* (Princeton: Princeton University Press, 2008); and Witt, *Lincoln's Code*, pp. 111–13.

118. Hathaway and Shapiro, *Internationalists*. Oona Hathaway and Scott J. Shapiro, "Outcasting: Enforcement in Domestic and International Law," *Yale Law Journal*, vol. 252 (2011), pp. 252–349.

119. Samuel Moyn, *Humane: How the United States Abandoned Peace and Reinvented War* (New York: Farrar, Straus & Giroux, 2021).

120. Judith N. Shklar, *Legalism: Law, Morals, and Political Trials* (Cambridge, Mass.: Harvard University Press, 1986), pp. 143–90. In a brilliant book, Shklar's bracing critique of the Tokyo trial itself is hampered by her insistence that the Japanese only understand situational ethics that are "inherently unlegalistic," and her incorrect assertion that the Tokyo judgment rested on natural law. Onuma Yasuaki, *Tokyo saiban kara sengo sekinin no shiso e* [From the Tokyo Trial to Postwar Responsibility] (Tokyo: Yushindo, 1985), pp. 174–78.

121. Anne Applebaum, *Iron Curtain: The Crushing of Eastern Europe, 1944–1956* (New York: Doubleday, 2012), pp. 3–246.

122. See Taylor, *Nuremberg and Vietnam*.

123. Gardiner Harris, "In Hiroshima, Summoning Better Angels," *New York Times*, 28 May 2016, p. A1.

124. Robert H. Jackson, *The Case Against the Nazi War Criminals: Opening Statement for the United States of America* (New York: Alfred A. Knopf, 1946), pp. 1–11.

1. Nuremberg to Tokyo

1. MMA, RG-135, box 17, Boyce manuscript. For Japanese views of Bataan, see Sarah Kovner, *Prisoners of the Empire: Inside Japanese POW Camps* (Cambridge, Mass.: Harvard University Press, 2020), pp. 74–84.

2. John W. Dower, *War Without Mercy: Race and Power in the Pacific War* (New York: Pantheon, 1986), pp. 33–36.

3. NARA, RG 107, 390/8/32/06, Stimson "safe file," box 8, Hull statement, 7 December 1941.

4. Franklin Delano Roosevelt, *Fireside Chats* (New York: Penguin, 1995), 9 December 1941, p. 73.

5. NARA, RG 107, 390/8/32/06, Stimson "safe file," box 8, Marshall to Stimson, 8 October 1945. NARA, RG 107, 390/8/32/06, Stimson "safe file," box 8, FDR to Stimson, 9 September 1943. This supports my hypothesis that even liberal states will refrain from war crimes prosecutions when that would put their soldiers at risk (*Stay the Hand of Vengeance: The Politics of War Crimes Tribunals* [Princeton: Princeton University Press, 2000], pp. 29–30).

6. FDR statement, 21 April 1943, *The Department of State Bulletin* (Washington, D.C.: U.S. Government Printing Office, 1943), vol. 8, no. 200 (24 April 1932), p. 337. See Cordell Hull, *The Memoirs of Cordell Hull* (New York: Macmillan, 1948), vol. 2, p. 1589.

7. Michel Paradis, *Last Mission to Tokyo: The Extraordinary Story of the Doolittle Raiders and Their Final Fight for Justice* (New York: Simon & Schuster, 2020). James M. Scott, *Target Tokyo: Jimmy Doolittle and the Raid That Avenged Pearl Harbor* (New York: W. W. Norton, 2015).

8. NARA, RG 107, 390/8/32/06, Stimson "safe file," box 8, Marshall to Stimson, 8 October 1945.

9. Samuel Moyn, *Humane: How the United States Abandoned Peace and Reinvented War* (New York: Farrar, Straus & Giroux, 2021), pp. 122–37.

10. Buckner to Adele Buckner, 8 April 1945, *Seven Stars: The Okinawa Battle Diaries of Simon Bolivar Buckner, Jr., and Joseph Stilwell*, ed. Nicholas Evan Sarantakes (College Station: Texas A&M University Press, 2004), p. 35.

11. U.S. Senate, Subcommittee of the Committee on Armed Services, *Malmedy Massacre Investigation* (Washington, D.C.: U.S. Government Printing Office, 1949). James J. Weingartner, *Crossroads of Death: The Story of the Malmedy Massacre and Trial* (Berkeley: University of California Press, 1973). Stimson Diaries, vol. 49, 31 December 1944.

12. George H. Gallup, ed., *The Gallup Poll: Public Opinion, 1935–1971* (New York: Random House, 1972), vol. 1, 1 July 1942, p. 339. In addition, 6 percent said Hitler would not be alive, 2 percent wanted to be lenient in punishment, 2 percent said it was not our affair, and 13 percent gave no opinion.

13. *Gallup Poll,* vol. 1, 1 October 1944, p. 463.

14. W. H. Auden and Christopher Isherwood, *Journey to a War* (London: Faber & Faber, 1939), p. 195.

15. *Gallup Poll,* vol. 1, 20 December 1944, pp. 477–78.

16. Stimson Diaries, vol. 47, 23 June 1944; vol. 48, 11 September 1944, 3 October 1944. NARA, RG 107, box 15, 390/8/32/07, Stimson top secret file, White House correspondence, FDR to Stimson, 26 August 1944.

17. John Lewis Gaddis, *The United States and the Origins of the Cold War, 1941–1947* (New York: Columbia University Press, 1972), p. 119.

18. John W. Dower, *Embracing Defeat: Japan in the Wake of World War II* (New York: W. W. Norton, 1999), pp. 444–45. See Henry Morgenthau Jr., *Morgenthau Diary—Germany* (Washington, D.C.: U.S. Government Printing Office, 1967), vol. 1, p. 526.

19. Stimson Diaries, vol. 51, 10 May 1945.

20. Godfrey Hodgson, *The Colonel: The Life and Wars of Henry Stimson, 1867–1950* (New York: Alfred A. Knopf, 1990).

21. Hodgson, *Colonel,* pp. 172, 219.

22. Stimson Diaries, vol. 50, Stimson notes, 3 January 1945. Henry L. Stimson and McGeorge Bundy, *On Active Service in Peace and War* (New York: Harper & Brothers, 1947), pp. 220–63, 588–91.

23. Stimson Diaries, vol. 51, 12 April 1945.

24. Martin Gilbert, *Auschwitz and the Allies* (London: Holt, Rinehart & Winston, 1981), pp. 299–322. David S. Wyman, *The Abandonment of the Jews: America and the Holocaust, 1941–1945* (New York: Pantheon, 1984), pp. 288–307.

25. Wyman, *Abandonment of the Jews,* pp. 210, 262, 305. Michael Beschloss, *The Conquerors: Roosevelt, Truman and the Destruction of Hitler's Germany, 1941–1945* (New York: Simon & Schuster, 2002), p. 88.

26. Hodgson, *Colonel,* pp. 217, 251–60. Dower, *War Without Mercy,* p. 80.

27. NARA, RG 107, 390/8/32/06, Stimson "safe file," box 8, Stimson to Marshall, 8 October 1943.

28. NARA, RG 107, 390/8/32/06, Stimson "safe file," box 8, White memorandum, 23 May 1944. Sandra Wilson, Robert Cribb, Beatrice Trefault, and Dean Aszkielo-

wicz, *Japanese War Criminals: The Politics of Justice After the Second World War* (New York: Columbia University Press, 2017), p. 16.

29. Stimson Diaries, vol. 47, 24 May 1944.

30. Stimson Diaries, vol. 48, Stimson notes for FDR, 25 August 1944.

31. Stimson Diaries, vol. 48, 4 September 1944.

32. Morgenthau to Truman, 29 May 1945, Henry Morgenthau Jr., *Morgenthau Diary—Germany* (Washington, D.C.: U.S. Government Printing Office, 1967), vol. 2, pp. 1544–45.

33. Post-Surrender Germany program, 4 September 1944, *Morgenthau Diary*, vol. 1, pp. 508–9.

34. *Morgenthau Diary*, 4 September 1944, vol. 1, p. 486.

35. Stimson Diaries, vol. 48, Stimson notes for FDR, 25 August 1944. Nuremberg's charter declares "the fact that the defendant acted pursuant to an order of his Government or of a superior shall not free him from responsibility, but may be considered in mitigation of punishment." Even before Nuremberg, there was an established American doctrine that soldiers are not bound by illegal orders. See *U.S. v. Otto Ohlendorf et al.* (Einsatzgruppen case), U.S. Military Tribunal, Nuremberg, 8–9 April 1948, *International Law Studies*, vol. 60 (1979), pp. 408–21; "Command Responsibility for War Crimes," *Yale Law Journal*, vol. 82 (1973), pp. 1274–1304; and Gary D. Solis, "Obedience to Orders," *Journal of International Criminal Justice*, vol. 2 (2004), pp. 988–98.

36. Bohlen minutes, Soviet embassy dinner, 29 November 1943, *FRUS: The Conferences at Cairo and Tehran 1943* (Washington, D.C.: U.S. Government Printing Office, 1961), p. 554. Winston S. Churchill, *The Second World War* (London: Cassell, 1952), vol. 5, p. 330.

37. Stimson Diaries, vol. 47, 15 June 1944. See Stimson Diaries, vol. 48, FDR-Stimson conversation, 8 June 1944.

38. Stimson Diaries, vol. 48, 25 August 1944. Stimson Diaries, vol. 48, Stimson notes for FDR, 25 August 1944.

39. Stimson Diaries, vol. 48, 26 August–3 September 1944.

40. Stimson Diaries, vol. 48, Stimson memo, 5 September 1944.

41. Stimson Diaries, vol. 48, 5 September 1944.

42. Stimson Diaries, vol. 48, FDR-Stimson memcon, 25 August 1944.

43. Stimson Diaries, vol. 48, 6 September 1944.

44. Stimson Diaries, vol. 48, 5 September 1944. Stimson Diaries, vol. 48, 4 and 7 September 1944.

45. H. N. Hirsch, *The Enigma of Felix Frankfurter* (New York: Basic Books, 1981), pp. 24–31.

46. Frankfurter to FDR, 28 January 1933, Max Freedman, ed., *Roosevelt and Frankfurter: Their Correspondence, 1928–1945* (Boston: Little, Brown, 1967), p. 105.

47. *Takao Ozawa v. United States*, 260 U.S. 178 (1922).

48. *Hirabayashi v. United States*, 320 U.S. 81, 100-1 (1943). Noah Feldman, *Scorpions: The Battles and Triumphs of FDR's Great Supreme Court Justices* (New York: Twelve, 2010), pp. 235–42. William H. Rehnquist, *All the Laws but One: Civil Liberties in Wartime* (New York: Alfred A. Knopf, 1998), pp. 192–200.

49. Lorraine K. Bannai, *Enduring Conviction: Fred Korematsu and His Quest for Justice* (Seattle: University of Washington Press, 2015).

50. *Korematsu v. United States*, 323 U.S. 214, 223 (1944). See Rehnquist, *All the Laws but One*, pp. 200–11. Stephen Breyer, *Making Our Democracy Work: A Judge's View* (New

York: Alfred A. Knopf, 2010), pp. 172–93. Mark Tushnet, "Defending *Korematsu?*," in Mark Tushnet, ed., *The Constitution in Wartime: Beyond Alarm and Complacency* (Durham, N.C.: Duke University Press, 2005), pp. 124–40.

51. "Justice Black, Champion of Civil Liberties for 34 Years on Court, Dies at 85," *New York Times*, 26 September 1971, p. 76.

52. *Ex parte Quirin et al.*, 317 U.S. 1 (1942). See, for instance, *Hamdi et al. v. Rumsfeld, Secretary of Defense, et al.*, 542 U.S. 507 (2004).

53. Leonard Baker, *Brandeis and Frankfurter: A Dual Biography* (New York: Harper & Row, 1984), pp. 396–97. See Jack Goldsmith, "Justice Jackson's Unpublished Opinion in *Ex parte Quirin*," *Green Bag*, vol. 9, no. 3 (Spring 2006), pp. 223–31.

54. Stimson Diaries, vol. 48, 7 September 1944.

55. Stimson Diaries, vol. 48, Stimson to FDR, 7 and 9 September 1944.

56. Stimson Diaries, vol. 48, 9 September 1944.

57. Stimson Diaries, vol. 50, 29 March 1945.

58. Stimson Diaries, vol. 48, 14 September 1944.

59. Stimson Diaries, vol. 48, 16–19 September 1944.

60. NARA, RG 107, box 15, 390/8/32/07, Stimson top secret file, White House correspondence, Stimson to FDR, 15 September 1944.

61. Stimson Diaries, vol. 48, 20 September 1944.

62. "Morgenthau Plan on Germany Splits Cabinet Committee," *New York Times*, 24 September 1944, pp. 1, 8.

63. Stimson Diaries, vol. 49, 4 November 1944. In an April 1945 poll, 13 percent of Americans wanted to pastoralize Germany, while 56 percent preferred keeping close supervision over German industry. (Gallup, ed., *Gallup Poll*, vol. 1, p. 499.)

64. Stimson Diaries, vol. 48, 27 September–1 October 1944. Gaddis, *United States and the Origins of the Cold War*, pp. 120–21.

65. Stimson Diaries, vol. 48, 27 September–1 October 1944.

66. Stimson Diaries, vol. 48, 3 October 1944.

67. Stimson Diaries, vol. 50, 29 March 1945.

68. Stimson Diaries, vol. 52, 2 July 1945.

69. Stimson Diaries, vol. 48, 25 October 1944; vol. 50, 21 January 1945.

70. Stimson-Cramer conversation, 5 September 1944, in Bradley F. Smith, *The American Road to Nuremberg: The Documentary Record, 1944–1945* (Stanford, Calif.: Hoover Institution Press, 1982), pp. 25–27.

71. Abraham S. Goldstein, "Conspiracy to Defraud the United States," *Yale Law Journal*, vol. 68, no. 3 (January 1959), pp. 405–63. Philip E. Johnson, "The Unnecessary Crime of Conspiracy," *California Law Review*, vol. 61, no. 5 (September 1973), pp. 1137–88. In defense of conspiracy charges, see Neal Kumar Katyal, "Conspiracy Theory," *Yale Law Journal*, vol. 112, no. 6 (April 2003), pp. 1307–98.

72. Stimson Diaries, vol. 48, 25 October 1944. Dower, *Embracing Defeat*, p. 463.

73. Herbert Wechsler, *Principles, Politics, and Fundamental Law* (Cambridge, Mass.: Harvard University Press, 1961), p. 145. Telford Taylor, *Nuremberg and Vietnam: An American Tragedy* (Chicago: Quadrangle, 1970), p. 84.

74. See Philippe Sands, *East West Street: On the Origins of Genocide and Crimes Against Humanity* (London: Weidenfeld & Nicolson, 2016), pp. 270–302.

75. Michael Walzer, *Just and Unjust Wars: A Moral Argument with Historical Illustrations* (New York: Basic Books, 1977). Richard Tuck, *The Rights of War and Peace: Political*

Thought and the International Order from Grotius to Kant (Oxford: Oxford University Press, 1999). Yoram Dinstein, *War, Aggression, and Self-Defense* (Cambridge: Cambridge University Press, 2005). Benjamin B. Ferencz, *Defining International Aggression, the Search for World Peace: A Documentary History and Analysis* (Dobbs Ferry, N.Y.: Oceana, 1975), 2 vols. Carrie McDougall, *The Crime of Aggression Under the Rome Statute of the International Criminal Court* (Cambridge: Cambridge University Press, 2013). Tom Dannenbaum, *The Crime of Aggression, Humanity, and the Soldier* (Cambridge: Cambridge University Press, 2018). Noah Weisbord, *The Crime of Aggression: The Quest for Justice in an Age of Drones, Cyberattacks, Insurgents, and Autocrats* (Princeton: Princeton University Press, 2019).

76. FDR to Stettinius, 3 January 1945, Smith, ed., *American Road to Nuremberg*, p. 92. General Treaty for Renunciation of War as an Instrument of National Policy, August 27, 1928, 94 L.N.T.S. 57. Sheldon Glueck, *Nuremberg Trial and Aggressive War* (New York: Alfred A. Knopf, 1946). Oona Hathaway and Scott J. Shapiro, *The Internationalists: How a Radical Plan to Outlaw War Remade the World* (New York: Simon & Schuster, 2017). Telford Taylor, *The Anatomy of the Nuremberg Trials: A Personal Memoir* (New York: Alfred A. Knopf, 1992), p. 44.

77. Stimson Diaries, vol. 48, 27 October 1944. See Stimson Diaries, vol. 49, 7 November 1944.

78. Stimson Diaries, vol. 51, 12 April 1945.

2. Unconditional Surrender

1. Truman diary, 12 April 1945, *Off the Record: The Private Papers of Harry S. Truman*, ed. Robert H. Ferrell (New York: Harper & Row, 1980), pp. 14–15.

2. David McCullough, *Truman* (New York: Simon & Schuster, 1992), pp. 327, 800.

3. Truman to Martha Ellen and Mary Jane Truman, 11 April 1945, *Off the Record*, pp. 13–14.

4. Truman diary, 12 April 1945, *Off the Record*, pp. 15–16.

5. Arthur S. Krock, "President Roosevelt Is Dead," *New York Times*, 13 April 1945, p. A1.

6. Truman diary, 12 April 1945, *Off the Record*, pp. 15–16.

7. Stimson Diaries, vol. 50, 23 January 1945; vol. 49, 12 December 1944; vol. 47, 11 June 1944.

8. Stimson Diaries, vol. 51, 12 April 1945.

9. Stimson Diaries, vol. 51, 12–15 April 1945.

10. Stimson Diaries, vol. 51, 12 April 1945.

11. Krock, "President Roosevelt Is Dead."

12. Hiromichi Yahara, *The Battle for Okinawa*, trans. Roger Pineau and Masatoshi Uehara (New York: John Wiley & Sons, 1995), p. 45.

13. Truman diary, 13 April 1945, *Off the Record*, pp. 16–18.

14. Truman diary, 14 April 1945, *Off the Record*, pp. 18–19.

15. Stimson Diaries, vol. 51, 12 April 1945.

16. Stimson Diaries, vol. 51, 15 April 1945.

17. Truman diary, 15 April 1945, *Off the Record*, pp. 19–20.

18. Truman to Southern, 13 May 1945, *Off the Record*, p. 23.

19. Truman diary, 15 April 1945, *Off the Record*, p. 19n2.

20. Truman diary, 1 June 1945, *Off the Record*, pp. 39–41.

21. Truman to Bess Truman, 13 September 1946, *Dear Bess: The Letters from Harry to Bess Truman, 1910–1959*, ed. Robert H. Ferrell (New York: W. W. Norton, 1983), p. 536. Truman to Bess Truman, 9 September 1946, *Dear Bess*, p. 535.

22. Truman diary, 1 June 1945, *Off the Record*, pp. 39–41.

23. Truman diary, 20 September 1945, *Off the Record*, p. 67.

24. Truman to Bess Truman, 14 December 1918, 31 July 1939, *Dear Bess*, pp. 286, 416.

25. Truman to Bess Truman, 27 September 1942, *Dear Bess*, p. 490. Truman to Bess Truman, 1 September 1918, *Dear Bess*, pp. 270–71.

26. Truman to Bess Truman, 6 October 1918, 8 October 1918, *Dear Bess*, pp. 272–74.

27. Truman to Bess Truman, 1 November 1918, *Dear Bess*, pp. 277–78.

28. Truman to Bess Truman, 30 April 1942, *Dear Bess*, p. 474. His italics.

29. Robert Dallek, *Franklin D. Roosevelt and American Foreign Policy, 1932–1945* (Oxford: Oxford University Press, 1995), pp. 373–76. David M. Kennedy, *Freedom from Fear: The American People in Depression and War, 1929–1945* (Oxford: Oxford University Press, 1999), p. 588. James MacGregor Burns, *Roosevelt: The Soldier of Freedom* (New York: Harcourt Brace Jovanovich, 1970), p. 323. Tsuyoshi Hasegawa, *Racing the Enemy: Stalin, Truman, and the Surrender of Japan* (Cambridge, Mass.: Harvard University Press, 2005), pp. 21–23.

30. Stimson Diaries, vol. 51, 16 April 1945.

31. Truman address to joint session of Congress, 16 April 1945, *Public Papers of the Presidents of the United States: Harry S. Truman, 1945* (Washington, D.C.: U.S. Government Printing Office, 1961), pp. 1–5.

32. HSTL, OF, box 1144, Truman to Booth, 25 May 1945.

33. HSTL, OF, box 1144, Truman statement, 16 March 1946.

34. HSTL, OF, box 1144, Truman to Drake, 11 January 1946. HSTL, OF, box 1144, Truman to Vaughan, 11 January 1946.

35. Truman press conference, 2 May 1945, *Public Papers*, pp. 32–39. Truman press conference, 7 June 1945, *Public Papers*, pp. 105–12. HSTL, PSF, box 197, Japanese Surrender, Truman radio address, 9 August 1945.

36. Truman memorandum, 12 May 1945, *Off the Record*, p. 22.

37. Truman statement, 1 September 1945, *Public Papers*, p. 253.

38. Truman press conference, 3 October 1946, *Public Papers of the Presidents of the United States: Harry S. Truman, 1946* (Washington, D.C.: U.S. Government Printing Office, 1962), pp. 439–42.

39. Truman diary, 17 June 1945, *Off the Record*, p. 46.

40. Truman appointment sheet, 5 September 1945, *Off the Record*, p. 64.

41. Truman appointment sheet, 16 May 1945, *Off the Record*, p. 25.

42. Stimson Diaries, vol. 51, 25 April 1945.

43. Stimson Diaries, vol. 52, 3 July 1945, pp. 12–13.

44. HSTL, OF, box 1145, Truman to Smith, 4 May 1946.

45. HSTL, OF, box 1144, Truman statement, 25 February 1946.

46. HSTL, OF, box 1144, Truman to Biddle, 12 November 1946.

47. Truman speech at Rio de Janeiro conference, 2 September 1947, *Public Papers of the Presidents: Harry S. Truman, 1947* (Washington, D.C.: U.S. Government Printing Office, 1963), p. 429.

48. John Lewis Gaddis, *The United States and the End of the Cold War: Implications, Reconsiderations, Provocations* (Oxford: Oxford University Press, 1992), pp. 48–50.

49. Max Hastings, *Retribution: The Battle for Japan, 1944–45* (New York: Alfred A. Knopf, 2008), p. 371.

50. Hastings, *Retribution*, p. 369. Robert Leckie, *Okinawa: The Last Battle of World War II* (New York: Viking, 1995), p. 3.

51. Yahara, *Battle for Okinawa*, pp. 24–25, 46, 49, 209.

52. E. B. Sledge, *With the Old Breed at Peleliu and Okinawa* (Annapolis, Md.: Naval Institute Press, 1981), pp. 164–65. Buckner diary, 26 March 1945, *Seven Stars: The Okinawa Battle Diaries of Simon Bolivar Buckner, Jr., and Joseph Stilwell*, ed. Nicholas Evan Sarantakes (College Station: Texas A&M University Press, 2004), pp. 26–27.

53. Sledge, *With the Old Breed*, p. 179.

54. Sledge, *With the Old Breed*, pp. 188, 192.

55. Yahara, *Battle for Okinawa*, pp. 61, 87.

56. Hastings, *Retribution*, p. 377. See William Manchester, "The Bloodiest Battle of All," *New York Times Magazine*, 14 June 1987.

57. Yahara, *Battle for Okinawa*, p. 106. Hastings, *Retribution*, pp. 373–74. See Ruth Ann Keyso, *Women of Okinawa: Nine Voices from a Garrison Island* (Ithaca, N.Y.: Cornell University Press, 2000), pp. 3–53.

58. Buckner to Adele Buckner, 8 April 1945, *Seven Stars*, p. 35.

59. Yahara, *Battle for Okinawa*, p. 109.

60. Sledge, *With the Old Breed*, p. 260.

61. Hastings, *Retribution*, p. 402.

62. Yahara, *Battle for Okinawa*, pp. 137, 46.

63. Truman to Eleanor Roosevelt, 10 May 1945, *Off the Record*, pp. 20–22.

64. NARA, RG 107, box 15, Stimson top secret file, White House correspondence, Stimson to Truman, 24 April 1945. Stimson Diaries, vol. 51, 25 April 1945; Stimson Diaries, vol. 51, Truman-Stimson memcon, 25 April 1945.

65. Stimson Diaries, vol. 51, 10 May 1945.

66. Henry L. Stimson and McGeorge Bundy, *On Active Service in Peace and War* (New York: Harper & Brothers, 1947), p. 617.

67. Truman press conference, 2 May 1945, *Public Papers*, pp. 32–39.

68. Truman to Eleanor Roosevelt, 10 May 1945, *Off the Record*, pp. 20–22.

69. NAI, EAD file no. 6-W/45, Indian military intelligence memorandum, 28 February 1945.

70. Yahara, *Battle for Okinawa*, p. 47.

71. Truman V-E Day broadcast, 8 May 1945, *Public Papers*, pp. 48–49. HSTL, PSF, box 197, German Surrender, April–May 1945. See Odd Arne Westad, *Empire and Righteous Nation: 600 Years of China-Korea Relations* (Cambridge, Mass.: Harvard University Press, 2021).

72. Truman V-E Day press conference, 8 May 1945, *Public Papers*, pp. 43–48. See HSTL, PSF, box 197, Truman proclamation, 8 May 1945.

73. Truman V-E Day press conference, 8 May 1945, *Public Papers*, pp. 43–48. HSTL, PSF, box 197, Truman statement, 8 May 1945. Italics in original at HSTL.

74. Truman V-E Day press conference, 8 May 1945, *Public Papers*, pp. 43–48.

75. Churchill speech, 13 May 1945, Winston S. Churchill, *The Second World War: Triumph and Tragedy* (Cambridge, Mass.: Houghton Mifflin, 1953), p. 550.

76. Stimson Diaries, vol. 50, 11 March 1945. See Oona A. Hathaway and Scott J. Shapiro,

The Internationalists: How a Radical Plan to Outlaw War Remade the World (New York: Simon & Schuster, 2017), pp. 131–57.

77. Henry L. Stimson, *The Far Eastern Crisis: Recollections and Observations* (New York: Harper & Brothers, 1936). Stimson Diaries, vol. 51, 17 June 1945, and vol. 47, 23 June 1944. Stimson and Bundy, *On Active Service in Peace and War,* pp. 220–63.

78. Stimson, *Far Eastern Crisis,* pp. xi, 241–54.

79. Stimson Diaries, vol. 50, 11 January 1945.

80. Stimson Diaries, vol. 50, Stimson notes for talk to combined staffs, 3 January 1945.

81. Stimson Diaries, vol. 49, 7–8 November 1944; vol. 50, 8 January 1945.

82. Stimson Diaries, vol. 51, 15 May 1945.

83. Stimson Diaries, vol. 51, 16 May 1945.

84. Stimson Diaries, vol. 51, 1 June 1945.

85. Robert H. Ferrell, ed., *Truman in the White House: The Diary of Eben A. Ayers* (Columbia: University of Missouri Press, 1991), pp. 27–28.

86. Truman-Hoover memcon, 28 May 1945, https://www.trumanlibrary.org/hoover/exile .htm. See Hasegawa, *Racing the Enemy,* p. 98; and Dale M. Hellegers, *We, the Japanese People: World War II and the Origins of the Japanese Constitution* (Stanford, Calif.: Stanford University Press, 2001), vol. 1, p. 96.

87. Stimson Diaries, vol. 51, 11 June 1945. NARA, RG 107, 390/8/32/06, Stimson "safe file," box 8, Truman to Stimson, 9 June 1945.

88. NARA, RG 107, 390/8/32/06, Stimson "safe file," box 8, Hoover to Truman, 30 May 1945.

89. Herbert P. Bix, *Hirohito and the Making of Modern Japan* (New York: HarperCollins, 2000), p. 492.

90. Joseph C. Grew, *Report from Tokyo: A Message to the American People* (New York: Simon & Schuster, 1942), p. 16.

91. Joseph C. Grew, *Ten Years in Japan* (New York: Simon & Schuster, 1944), pp. 14–15, 204.

92. Grew, *Ten Years in Japan,* pp. 69, 101, 122–25, 141, 236, 339, 347, 354, 409, 443, 462.

93. Truman-Grew memcon, 28 May 1945, *FRUS: The British Commonwealth: The Far East,* vol. 6 (Washington, D.C.: U.S. Government Printing Office, 1969), pp. 545–47.

94. Truman-Grew memcon, 28 May 1945, *FRUS: The British Commonwealth: The Far East,* vol. 6, p. 547.

95. Stimson Diaries, vol. 51, 29 May 1945. See Truman-Grew memcon, 29 May 1945, *FRUS: The British Commonwealth: The Far East,* vol. 6, pp. 548–49; and Grew to Byrnes, 7 August 1945, Joseph C. Grew, *Turbulent Era: A Diplomatic Record of Forty Years, 1904–1945* (Boston: Houghton Mifflin, 1952), vol. 2, pp. 1438–40.

96. Truman appointment sheet, 17 May 1945, *Off the Record,* p. 27.

97. Truman diary, 27 May 1945, *Off the Record,* pp. 37–38.

98. Truman to Congress, 1 June 1945, *Public Papers,* pp. 83–98.

99. Stilwell memo, 17 July 1945, *Seven Stars,* pp. 96–97.

100. Stimson Diaries, vol. 51, Stimson to Truman, 16 May 1945.

101. Robert A. Pape, "Why Japan Surrendered," *International Security,* vol. 18, no. 2 (Autumn 1993), p. 163. Sheldon Garon, "Food Insecurity in Wartime Japan," in Hartmut Berghoff, Jan Logemann, and Felix Römer, eds., *The Consumer on the Home Front: Second World War Civilian Consumption in Comparative Perspective* (Oxford:

Oxford University Press, 2017), p. 50. James M. Scott, *Black Snow: Curtis LeMay, the Firebombing of Tokyo, and the Road to the Atomic Bomb* (New York: W. W. Norton, 2022). David Feldman and Cary Karacas, "A Cartographic Fade to Black," *Journal of Historical Geography*, vol. 38, no. 3 (2012), pp. 306–28. Saotome Katsumoto and Richard Sams, "Saotome Katsumoto and the Firebombing of Tokyo," *Asia-Pacific Journal*, vol. 13, no. 1 (March 2015), pp. 1–32. NARA, RG 107, 390/8/32/06, Stimson "safe file," box 8, Arnold to Stimson, 2 June 1945. Sheldon Garon, "On the Transnational Destruction of Cities," *Past & Present*, no. 247 (May 2020), pp. 235–71.

102. Richard B. Frank, *Downfall: The End of the Imperial Japanese Empire* (New York: Random House, 1999), pp. 74–75. Hasegawa, *Racing the Enemy*, p. 80.

103. Frank, *Downfall*, p. 149. Sheldon Garon, "On the Transnational Destruction of Cities," *Past & Present*, no. 247 (May 2020), pp. 235–71.

104. Nosaka Akiyuki, "A Grave of Fireflies," trans. James R. Abrams, *Japan Quarterly*, vol. 25, no. 4 (October 1978), pp. 445–63.

105. Hastings, *Retribution*, pp. 436–37.

106. *Reports of General MacArthur: Japanese Operations in the Southwest Pacific Area* (Washington, D.C.: U.S. Government Printing Office, 1966), vol. 2, part 2, pp. 613–14.

107. Frank, *Downfall*, p. 334. Including Hiroshima and Nagasaki, the United States' reckoning of the total death toll is 330,000 and the Japanese is 323,495. For an updated survey, see Saotome Katsumoto's multivolume study, *Nihon no kushu* [Air Raid in Japan] (Tokyo: Sanseido, 1981).

108. Dunn to Stettinius, 6 March 1945, *FRUS: The British Commonwealth: The Far East*, vol. 6, pp. 470–71. Grässli to Byrnes, 30 July 1945, *FRUS: The British Commonwealth: The Far East*, vol. 6, pp. 471–72.

109. Stimson Diaries, vol. 51, 1 June 1945.

110. NARA, RG 107, 390/8/32/06, Stimson "safe file," box 8, Stimson to Arnold, 11 June 1945. NARA, RG 107, 390/8/32/06, Stimson "safe file," box 8, Eaker to Stimson, 11 June 1945.

111. NARA, RG 107, 390/8/32/06, Stimson "safe file," box 8, Arnold to Stimson, 2 June 1945.

112. Stimson Diaries, vol. 52, Stimson to Spaatz, 1 September 1945.

113. Stimson Diaries, vol. 51, 6 June 1945.

114. Fredrik Logevall, *JFK: Coming of Age in the American Century, 1917–1956* (New York: Random House, 2020), pp. 359–61.

115. HSTL, NAP, box 12, Hopkins-Stalin Conference, Hopkins to Truman, 29 May 1945. HSTL, NAP, box 12, Hopkins-Stalin Conference, Hopkins-Stalin memcon, 28 May 1945, 8 p.m. U.S. Department of State, *FRUS: The Conference of Berlin* (Washington, D.C.: U.S. Government Printing Office, 1960), vol. 1, p. 861.

116. Stimson Diaries, vol. 49, 10 November 1944.

117. John Lewis Gaddis, *The Cold War: A New History* (New York: Penguin, 2005), p. 24. Jay Taylor, *The Generalissimo: Chiang Kai-shek and the Struggle for Modern China* (Cambridge, Mass.: Belknap Press of Harvard University Press, 2009), p. 301.

118. Churchill to Truman, 12 May 1945, Churchill, *Triumph and Tragedy*, p. 573. Churchill to Halifax, 14 May 1945, Churchill, *Triumph and Tragedy*, p. 576.

119. Anne Applebaum, *Iron Curtain: The Crushing of Eastern Europe, 1944–1956* (New York: Doubleday, 2012), pp. 192–96. Stimson Diaries, vol. 51, 10 May 1945.

120. Truman to Bess Truman, 30 December 1941, *Dear Bess*, p. 471. Truman to Eleanor Roosevelt, 10 May 1945, *Off the Record*, pp. 20–22.

121. Truman diary, 13 June 1945, *Off the Record*, p. 45. Truman appointment sheet, 19 and 22 May 1945, *Off the Record*, pp. 31, 35. Truman diary, 7 and 13 June 1945, *Off the Record*, pp. 44–45. HSTL, NAP, box 12, Hopkins-Stalin Conference, Hopkins-Stalin memcon, 26 May 1945, 8 p.m. HSTL, NAP, box 12, Hopkins-Stalin Conference, Hopkins to Truman, 28 May 1945. HSTL, NAP, box 12, Hopkins-Stalin Conference, Hopkins to Truman, 1 June 1945. HSTL, NAP, box 12, Hopkins-Stalin Conference, Hopkins to Truman, 3 June 1945. HSTL, NAP, box 12, Hopkins-Stalin Conference, Churchill to Truman, 4 June 1945.

122. Truman diary, 7 June 1945, *Off the Record*, p. 44.

123. Truman appointment sheet, 19 May 1945, *Off the Record*, p. 31.

124. HSTL, NAP, box 12, Hopkins-Stalin Conference, Hopkins-Stalin memcon, 28 May 1945, 8 p.m. HSTL, NAP, box 12, Hopkins-Stalin Conference, Hopkins to Truman, 30 May 1945.

125. Truman to Bess Truman, 12 June 1945, *Dear Bess*, pp. 515–16.

126. Truman diary, 1 June 1945, *Off the Record*, p. 39. See Truman statement, 21 May 1945, *Public Papers*, pp. 59–61.

127. Truman diary, 17 June 1945, *Off the Record*, p. 47.

128. Logevall, *JFK*, p. 363.

129. Truman to Congress, 1 June 1945, *Public Papers*, pp. 83–98.

130. Konoe memorial, 14 February 1945, John W. Dower, *Empire and Aftermath: Yoshida Shigeru and the Japanese Experience, 1878–1954* (Cambridge, Mass.: Harvard University Press, 1988), pp. 260–64.

131. HSTL, NAP, box 12, Japan Surrender, Joint Chiefs to MacArthur and Nimitz, 14 June 1945.

132. Frank, *Downfall*, pp. 85–86, 188–90.

133. Stimson Diaries, vol. 50, 11 January 1945.

134. Truman address to Congress, 1 June 1945, *Public Papers*, pp. 83–98.

135. HSTL, PSF, box 197, Truman speech to Congress, 1 June 1945.

136. NARA, RG 107, 390/8/32/06, Stimson "safe file," box 8, Grew to Truman, 13 June 1945.

137. NARA, RG 107, 390/8/32/06, Stimson "safe file," box 8, Grew to Rosenman, 16 June 1945.

138. Truman-Grew memcon, 18 June 1945, 9:30 a.m., *FRUS: Berlin*, vol. 1, pp. 177–78.

139. Richard Frank estimates, at the low end, between 32,969 and 38,683 American combat deaths in a Kyushu invasion which took ninety days (*Downfall*, p. 194).

140. Gerhard L. Weinberg, *A World at Arms: A Global History of World War II* (Cambridge: Cambridge University Press, 1994), p. 894.

141. Harry S. Truman, *Memoirs: Year of Decisions* (Garden City, N.Y.: Doubleday, 1955), vol. 1, p. 417.

142. Hastings, *Retribution*, p. 441.

143. White House meeting, 18 June 1945, *FRUS: Berlin*, vol. 1, pp. 903–10. Both Fleet Admiral Ernest King and General Henry Arnold had reservations about the invasion (Hastings, *Retribution*, pp. 447–48), but Arnold was not at this meeting, and King spoke up for invasion.

144. Stimson Diaries, vol. 51, 18 June 1945.

145. William D. Leahy, *I Was There: The Personal Story of the Chief of Staff to Presidents Roosevelt and Truman Based on His Notes and Diaries Made at the Time* (New York: Whittlesey House, 1950), pp. 384–85.

146. White House meeting, 18 June 1945, *FRUS: Berlin*, vol. 1, pp. 903–10. See HSTL, PSF, box 174, Atomic Bomb, White House notes, 8 March 1947.

147. Truman to Bess Truman, 19 June 1945, *Dear Bess*, p. 516.

3. *"Prompt and Utter Destruction"*

1. Tsuyoshi Hasegawa, *Racing the Enemy: Stalin, Truman, and the Surrender of Japan* (Cambridge, Mass.: Harvard University Press, 2005), pp. 45–46. Max Hastings, *Retribution: The Battle for Japan, 1944–45* (New York: Alfred A. Knopf, 2008), p. 403. For a discussion of possible justifications of the destruction of Hiroshima, see Gabriella Blum, "The Laws of War and the 'Lesser Evil,'" *Yale Journal of International Law*, vol. 35 (2010), pp. 24–31.

2. Stimson Diaries, vol. 51, 19 June 1945. See Stimson Diaries, vol. 52, 31 July 1945. Hastings, *Retribution*, 442.

3. Stimson Diaries, vol. 51, 19 June 1945.

4. Stimson Diaries, vol. 52, 4 July 1945.

5. Truman press conference, 21 June 1945, *Public Papers of the Presidents of the United States: Harry S. Truman, 1945* (Washington, D.C.: U.S. Government Printing Office, 1961), pp. 131–37.

6. *FRUS: The Conference of Berlin 1945* (Washington, D.C.: U.S. Government Printing Office, 1960), vol. 1, Combined Chiefs of Staff war plan, 29 June 1945, pp. 910–11.

7. Richard B. Frank, *Downfall: The End of the Imperial Japanese Empire* (New York: Random House, 1999), pp. 188–90, 204. Hastings, *Retribution*, p. 513. Frank estimates that 380,000 Japanese civilians could easily have perished in an invasion of Kyushu, as well as a quarter of a million Japanese soldiers. At a minimum, he reckons approximately 580,000 to 630,000 Japanese deaths (Frank, *Downfall*, p. 194).

8. Stimson Diaries, vol. 51, 26–30 June 1945.

9. *FRUS: Berlin*, vol. 1, Stimson-Grew-Forrestal meeting, 26 June 1945, pp. 887–88.

10. Stimson Diaries, vol. 51, 26–30 June 1945.

11. Stimson Diaries, vol. 52, 2 July 1945.

12. NARA, RG 107, box 15, 390/8/32/07, Stimson top secret file, Stimson to Truman, 2 July 1945. NARA, RG 107, 390/8/32/06, Stimson "safe file," box 8, Stimson to Truman, 2 July 1945. HSTL, NAP, box 4, Berlin Conference, Stimson to Truman, 2 July 1945.

13. HSTL, PSF, box 197, Japanese Surrender, Ayers note, 7 November 1951. Hal Brands, "The Emperor's New Clothes," *The Historian*, vol. 68, no. 1 (2006), pp. 4–5.

14. George H. Gallup, ed., *The Gallup Poll: Public Opinion, 1935–1971* (New York: Random House, 1972), vol. 1, pp. 511–12. In a private State Department poll in June, 36 percent of Americans wanted to kill, torture, or starve the emperor, with 17 percent pushing to try him as a war criminal, and just 3 percent seeking to use him as a puppet. (Katherine E. McKinney, Scott D. Sagan, and Allen S. Weiner, "Why the Atomic Bombing of Hiroshima Would Be Illegal Today," *Bulletin of the Atomic Scientists*, vol. 76, no. 4 [2020], p. 159.)

15. Stimson Diaries, vol. 52, 2–3 July 1945.

16. *FRUS: Berlin*, vol. 1, draft proclamation, 2 July 1945, pp. 893–94. *FRUS: Berlin*, vol. 1, draft proclamation, 6 July 1945, pp. 897–99.

17. *FRUS: The Conference of Berlin 1945* (Washington, D.C.: U.S. Government Printing Office, 1960), vol. 2, Grew to Byrnes, 19 July 1945, pp. 1270–71.

18. Cordell Hull, *The Memoirs of Cordell Hull* (New York: Macmillan, 1948), vol. 2, pp. 1590–93.

19. Stimson Diaries, vol. 52, 10 August 1945.

20. Robert Dallek, *Franklin D. Roosevelt: A Political Life* (New York: Viking, 2017), p. 383.

21. Dean Acheson, *Present at the Creation: My Years in the State Department* (New York: W. W. Norton, 1969), pp. 112–13.

22. *FRUS: Berlin*, vol. 1, MacLeish to Byrnes, 6 July 1945, pp. 895–97.

23. *FRUS: Berlin*, vol. 1, State Department meeting, 7 July 1945, pp. 900–901.

24. *FRUS: Berlin*, vol. 1, MacLeish to Byrnes, 6 July 1945, pp. 895–97. See *FRUS: Berlin*, vol. 1, State Department meeting, 7 July 1945, pp. 900–901.

25. Truman to Bess Truman, 21 December 1946, *Dear Bess: The Letters from Harry to Bess Truman, 1910–1959*, ed. Robert H. Ferrell (New York: W. W. Norton, 1983), p. 541. Truman diary, 7 July 1945, *Off the Record: The Private Papers of Harry S. Truman*, ed. Robert H. Ferrell (New York: Harper & Row, 1980), p. 49.

26. James F. Byrnes, *Speaking Frankly* (New York: Harper & Brothers, 1947), pp. 85–86.

27. Hull, *Memoirs*, vol. 2, p. 1594.

28. *FRUS: Berlin*, vol. 2, Hull to Byrnes, July 1945, p. 1267. See *FRUS: Berlin*, vol. 2, Hull-Grew memcon, 17 July 1945, p. 1268.

29. *FRUS: Berlin*, vol. 2, Stimson diary, 24 July 1945, p. 1272. See Marc Gallicchio, *Unconditional: The Japanese Surrender in World War II* (Oxford: Oxford University Press, 2020), pp. 38–70.

30. William D. Leahy, *I Was There: The Personal Story of the Chief of Staff to Presidents Roosevelt and Truman Based on His Notes and Diaries Made at the Time* (New York: Whittlesey House, 1950), pp. 418–19.

31. Leahy, *I Was There*, p. 419.

32. *FRUS: Berlin*, vol. 2, Leahy to Truman, 18 July 1945, pp. 1268–69.

33. Fredrik Logevall, *JFK: Coming of Age in the American Century, 1917–1956* (New York: Random House, 2020), p. 403.

34. Truman diary, 9 July 1945, *Off the Record*, p. 49.

35. Truman diary, 7 July 1945, *Off the Record*, pp. 48–49.

36. Byrnes, *Speaking Frankly*, p. 68.

37. Truman diary, 16 July 1945, *Off the Record*, pp. 50–52.

38. Truman diary, 16 July 1945, *Off the Record*, pp. 50–52.

39. Hasegawa, *Racing the Enemy*, p. 132.

40. Truman diary, 18 July 1945, *Off the Record*, pp. 53–54.

41. Truman to Bess Truman, 18 July 1945, *Dear Bess*, p. 519.

42. Truman diary, 16 July 1945, *Off the Record*, pp. 50–52.

43. Truman to Acheson (unsent), 15 March 1957, *Off the Record*, pp. 348–49.

44. Winston S. Churchill, *The Second World War: Triumph and Tragedy* (Cambridge, Mass.: Houghton Mifflin, 1953), p. 609. Truman diary, 25 July 1945, *Off the Record*, pp. 55–56.

45. Anne Applebaum, *Iron Curtain: The Crushing of Eastern Europe, 1944–1956* (New York: Doubleday, 2012), pp. 64–115. Truman diary, 26 July 1945, *Off the Record*, pp. 56–57.

46. HSTL, NAP, box 4, Berlin Conference, Berlin conference report, 2 August 1945.

47. Stimson Diaries, vol. 52, 23 July 1945.

48. Truman diary, 17 July 1945, *Off the Record*, pp. 50–52. See Stimson Diaries, vol. 52, 23 July 1945, and Stalin-Stimson conference, 25 July 1945; *FRUS: Berlin*, vol. 2, Sato to Togo, 21 July 1945, 5 p.m., p. 1259; and *FRUS: Berlin*, vol. 2, Joint Chiefs proposal, 21 July 1945, p. 1325.
49. Truman to Bess Truman, 18 July 1945, *Dear Bess*, p. 519.
50. *FRUS: Berlin*, vol. 1, Cairo Declaration briefing, 1945, pp. 926–27. *FRUS: Berlin*, vol. 2, Stimson diary, 23 July 1945, p. 1324.
51. *FRUS: Berlin*, vol. 1, Dooman memorandum, 15 July 1945, pp. 933–35.
52. *FRUS: Berlin*, vol. 2, Groves to Stimson, 18 July 1945, pp. 1361–68. The light of eighty suns was visible at six miles away. B. Cameron Reed, *The Physics of the Manhattan Project* (Berlin: Springer, 2011), pp. 116–17. Nelson Eby et al., "Trinitite," *Geology Today*, vol. 26, no. 5 (September–October 2010), pp. 180–85.
53. Stimson Diaries, vol. 52, 18 July 1945.
54. Stimson Diaries, vol. 52, 21 July 1945.
55. Churchill, *Triumph and Tragedy*, pp. 637–41. *FRUS: Berlin*, vol. 2, Harrison to Stimson, 17 July 1945, pp. 1360–61.
56. *FRUS: Berlin*, vol. 1, combined policy committee meeting, 4 July 1945, pp. 941–42.
57. *FRUS: Berlin*, vol. 2, Stimson diary, 23 July 1945, p. 1324.
58. Truman diary, 18 July 1945, *Off the Record*, pp. 50–52.
59. *FRUS: Berlin*, vol. 1, combined policy committee meeting, 4 July 1945, pp. 941–42.
60. Churchill, *Triumph and Tragedy*, pp. 628–29.
61. *FRUS: Berlin*, vol. 1, combined policy committee meeting, 4 July 1945, pp. 941–42.
62. Hugh Sebag-Montefiore, *Dunkirk: Fight to the Last Man* (Cambridge, Mass.: Harvard University Press, 2006). Churchill, *Triumph and Tragedy*, pp. 628–29, 637–41.
63. His official biography is Hagiwara Nobutoshi, *Togo Shigenori: Denki to kaisetsu* [Togo Shigenori: Biography and Commentary] (Tokyo: Hara Shobo, 2005).
64. John W. Dower, *War Without Mercy: Race and Power in the Pacific War* (New York: Pantheon, 1986), pp. 262–90.
65. Togo Shigehiko, *Sofu, Togo Shigenori no shogai* [Life of Grandfather Togo Shigenori] (Tokyo: Bungei Shunju, 1993), pp. 9–18, 157–60, 172–74, 181–82.
66. Togo Shigenori, *The Cause of Japan*, trans. Togo Fumihiko and Ben Bruce Blakeney (New York: Simon & Schuster, 1956), pp. 263–66.
67. Togo, *Cause of Japan*, pp. 1–42, 46–56, 138, 100–101. Eri Hotta, *Japan 1941: Countdown to Infamy* (New York: Alfred A. Knopf, 2013), p. 216.
68. Hasegawa, *Racing the Enemy*, p. 106.
69. Kido Koichi, *The Diary of Marquis Kido, 1931–45* (Frederick, Md.: University Publications of America, 1984), 22 June 1945, pp. 437–38. HSTL, PSF, box 197, U.S. Strategic Bombing Survey, "Japan's Struggle to End the War," 1 July 1946. HSTL, PSF, box 159, *ONI Review*, June 1946, Sakomizu interrogation. HSTL, PSF, box 174, Atomic Bomb, U.S. Strategic Bombing Survey report, "The Effects of the Atomic Bombings of Hiroshima and Nagasaki," 19 June 1946.
70. Daikichi Irokawa, *The Age of Hirohito: In Search of Modern Japan*, trans. Mikio Hane and John K. Urda (New York: Free Press, 1995).
71. *FRUS: Berlin*, vol. 1, Togo to Sato, 11 July 1945, 7 p.m., pp. 874–75.
72. James F. Byrnes, *All in One Lifetime* (New York: Harper & Brothers, 1958), pp. 292, 297.

73. *FRUS: Berlin*, vol. 1, Togo to Sato, 11 July 1945, 3 p.m., pp. 874–75.

74. Konoe memorial, 14 February 1945, John W. Dower, *Empire and Aftermath: Yoshida Shigeru and the Japanese Experience, 1878–1954* (Cambridge, Mass.: Harvard University Press, 1988), pp. 260–64.

75. *FRUS: Berlin*, vol. 1, Togo to Sato, 12 July 1945, 8:50 p.m., pp. 875–76.

76. *FRUS: Berlin*, vol. 1, Sato to Togo, 15 July 1945, pp. 882–83. Applebaum, *Iron Curtain*, pp. 19–22.

77. *FRUS: Berlin*, vol. 2, Sato to Togo, 21 July 1945, 5 p.m., p. 1259.

78. *FRUS: Berlin*, vol. 1, Sato to Togo, 12 July 1945, pp. 877–78. See Byrnes, *All in One Lifetime*, p. 308; *FRUS: Berlin*, vol. 1, Sato to Togo, 19 July 1945, p. 1251; Frank, *Downfall*, p. 230; and Hastings, *Retribution*, pp. 467–68.

79. Truman diary, 18 July 1945, *Off the Record*, pp. 50–52. Churchill, *Triumph and Tragedy*, p. 641. *FRUS: Berlin*, vol. 1, p. 873; Byrnes, *All in One Lifetime*, p. 308.

80. *FRUS: Berlin*, vol. 2, Stimson to Truman, 16 July 1945, pp. 1265–67.

81. Churchill, *Triumph and Tragedy*, pp. 641–42. Hastings, *Retribution*, p. 447.

82. Byrnes, *All in One Lifetime*, pp. 290, 297. Byrnes, *Speaking Frankly*, p. 205.

83. *FRUS: Berlin*, vol. 2, Lozovsky to Sato, 18 July 1945, p. 1251. Truman diary, 18 July 1945, *Off the Record*, pp. 50–52.

84. Byrnes, *All in One Lifetime*, p. 308.

85. *FRUS: Berlin*, vol. 2, Togo to Sato, 17 July 1945, p. 1249.

86. *FRUS: Berlin*, vol. 2, Sato to Togo, 20 July 1945, pp. 1252–57.

87. Byrnes, *All in One Lifetime*, p. 308.

88. Truman diary, 18 July 1945, *Off the Record*, pp. 50–52.

89. Truman diary, 20 July 1945, *Off the Record*, p. 55.

90. HSTL, NAP, box 12, Japan Surrender, Hurley to Truman, 25 July 1945.

91. Rana Mitter, *Forgotten Ally: China's World War II, 1937–1945* (Boston: Houghton Mifflin Harcourt, 2013), p. 353.

92. HSTL, NAP, box 4, Berlin Conference, draft proclamation, July 1945.

93. HSTL, NAP, box 12, Japan Surrender, Truman to Hurley, 24 July 1945.

94. HSTL, NAP, box 12, Japan Surrender, Truman to Hurley, 25 July 1945.

95. HSTL, NAP, box 12, Japan Surrender, Hurley to Truman, 26 July 1945. HSTL, NAP, box 12, Japan Surrender, Tyree to Bowen, 26 July 1945. HSTL, NAP, box 12, Japan Surrender, Hurley to Byrnes, 26 July 1945.

96. HSTL, NAP, box 4, Berlin Conference, draft proclamation adding China, July 1945.

97. Stimson Diaries, vol. 52, 17 July 1945.

98. Stimson Diaries, vol. 52, 24 July 1945, 10 August 1945. Henry L. Stimson, "The Decision to Use the Atomic Bomb," *Harper's*, February 1947, p. 104. Joseph C. Grew, *Turbulent Era: A Diplomatic Record of Forty Years, 1904–1945* (Boston: Houghton Mifflin, 1952), vol. 2, pp. 1425–28.

99. Henry L. Stimson and McGeorge Bundy, *On Active Service in Peace and War* (New York: Harper & Brothers, 1947), p. 629. Grew, *Turbulent Era*, vol. 2, pp. 1425–28.

100. Byrnes, *All in One Lifetime*, p. 300. Leahy, *I Was There*, p. 429.

101. David Holloway, *Stalin and the Bomb: The Soviet Union and Atomic Energy, 1939–1956* (New Haven: Yale University Press, 1994), pp. 116–18. Richard Reeves, *Dark Sun: The Making of the Hydrogen Bomb* (New York: Simon & Schuster, 1995), pp. 175–77. Hasegawa, *Racing the Enemy*, pp. 154–55.

102. Truman diary, 25 July 1945, *Off the Record*, pp. 55–56.

103. D. Clayton James, *The Years of MacArthur: 1941–1945* (Boston: Houghton Mifflin, 1975), vol. 2, p. 775. Frank, *Downfall*, p. 34.

104. Dwight D. Eisenhower, *Crusade in Europe* (New York: Doubleday, 1948), pp. 488–89.

105. Alfred D. Chandler Jr. and Louis Galambos, eds., *The Papers of Dwight David Eisenhower* (Baltimore: Johns Hopkins University Press, 1978), vol. 6, p. 205.

106. Omar N. Bradley with Clay Blair, *A General's Life: An Autobiography* (New York: Simon & Schuster, 1983), p. 444.

107. NARA, RG 107, 390/8/32/06, Stimson "safe file," box 8, Stimson to Arnold, 11 June 1945. Stimson Diaries, vol. 52, 22 July 1945.

108. Stimson Diaries, vol. 52, 24 July 1945.

109. McKinney, Sagan, and Weiner, "Why the Atomic Bombing of Hiroshima Would Be Illegal Today," p. 158.

110. Gallup, ed., *Gallup Poll*, vol. 1, pp. 521–22.

111. Truman diary, 25 July 1945, *Off the Record*, pp. 55–56.

112. *FRUS: Berlin*, vol. 2, Togo to Sato, 25 July 1945, 7 p.m., pp. 1260–62.

113. Frank, *Downfall*, p. 338.

114. Leahy, *I Was There*, pp. 418–19.

115. James, *Years of MacArthur*, vol. 2, p. 775.

116. NAI, EAD file no. 6-W/45, Pethick-Lawrence to Mountbatten, no. 443, 11 August 1945.

117. HSTL, NAP, box 12, Japan Surrender, Ross to Ayers, 26 July 1945. HSTL, NAP, box 12, Japan Surrender, Ayers to Ross, 27 July 1945.

118. Potsdam Declaration, 26 July 1945, Churchill, *Triumph and Tragedy*, pp. 642–44.

4. Atomic Fire

1. Dean Acheson, *Present at the Creation: My Years in the State Department* (New York: W. W. Norton, 1969), p. 113.

2. Cordell Hull, *The Memoirs of Cordell Hull* (New York: Macmillan, 1948), vol. 2, pp. 1594–95.

3. HSTL, NAP, box 12, Japan Surrender, Bowen to Vardaman, 29 July 1945.

4. Tsuyoshi Hasegawa, *Racing the Enemy: Stalin, Truman, and the Surrender of Japan* (Cambridge, Mass.: Belknap Press of Harvard University Press, 2005), pp. 165–67. HSTL, PSF, box 197, U.S. Strategic Bombing Survey, "Japan's Struggle to End the War," 1 July 1946.

5. Koichi Kido, *The Diary of Marquis Kido, 1931–45* (Frederick, Md.: University Publications of America, 1984), 5 April 1945, pp. 426–27.

6. Robert J. C. Butow, *Japan's Decision to Surrender* (Stanford, Calif.: Stanford University Press, 1954), p. 62. Joseph C. Grew, *Ten Years in Japan* (New York: Simon & Schuster, 1944), p. 176. See *Kido Diary*, 18 June 1944, p. 395.

7. *FRUS: The Conference of Berlin 1945* (Washington, D.C.: U.S. Government Printing Office, 1960), vol. 2, Suzuki press conference, 28 July 1945, p. 1293. Sadao Asada, "The Shock of the Atomic Bomb and Japan's Decision to Surrender," *Pacific Historical Review*, vol. 67, no. 4 (1998), pp. 502–3. See Butow, *Japan's Decision to Surrender*, pp. 145–49; Herbert P. Bix, "Japan's Delayed Surrender," *Diplomatic History*, vol. 19,

no. 2 (Spring 1995), p. 208; and for a more skeptical view, Hasegawa, *Racing the Enemy*, p. 168.

8. This account draws on a vast literature by Gar Alperovitz, Sadao Asada, Barton Bernstein, Kai Bird, Herbert Bix, John W. Dower, Herbert Feis, Michael D. Gordin, Lawrence Lifschultz, Sean L. Malloy, Wilson D. Miscamble, Martin Sherwin, and others.

9. Richard F. Haynes, *The Awesome Power: Harry S. Truman as Commander in Chief* (Baton Rouge: Louisiana State University Press, 1973), p. 40. See Harry S. Truman, *Memoirs: Year of Decisions* (Garden City, N.Y.: Doubleday, 1955), vol. 1, p. 421.

10. MMA, RG-108, Siemes account, "Atomic Bombing on Hiroshima," 1945.

11. HSTL, PSF, box 174, Atomic Bomb, Edwards to Leahy, 6 August 1945.

12. HSTL, PSF, box 174, Atomic Bomb, U.S. Strategic Bombing Survey report, "The Effects of the Atomic Bombings of Hiroshima and Nagasaki," 19 June 1946.

13. MMA, RG-108, Siemes, "Atomic Bombing on Hiroshima," 1945.

14. HSTL, PSF, box 174, Atomic Bomb, *The Effects of the Atomic Bombs at Hiroshima and Nagasaki: Report of the British Mission to Japan* (London: His Majesty's Stationery Office, 1946), p. 12.

15. Inokuchi Takeshi talk, *hibakusha* event, Hiroshima, 6 August 2015. MMA, RG-108, Siemes, "Atomic Bombing on Hiroshima," 1945.

16. Alex Wellerstein, *Restricted Data: The History of Nuclear Secrecy in the United States* (Chicago: University of Chicago Press, 2021), p. 122. See Gar Alperovitz, *The Decision to Use the Atomic Bomb* (New York: Alfred A. Knopf, 1995), pp. 521–23; and Lynn Eden, *Whole World on Fire: Organizations, Knowledge, and Nuclear Weapons Devastation* (Ithaca, N.Y.: Cornell University Press, 2004).

17. HSTL, PSF, box 174, Atomic Bomb, U.S. Strategic Bombing Survey report, "The Effects of the Atomic Bombings of Hiroshima and Nagasaki," 19 June 1946.

18. Hasegawa, *Racing the Enemy*, p. 180.

19. Katherine E. McKinney, Scott D. Sagan, and Allen S. Weiner, "Why the Atomic Bombing of Hiroshima Would Be Illegal Today," *Bulletin of the Atomic Scientists*, vol. 76, no. 4 (2020), p. 157.

20. HSTL, PSF, box 174, Atomic Bomb, Stimson to Truman, 6 August 1945. See HSTL, PSF, box 174, Atomic Bomb, Edwards to Leahy, 6 August 1945; Stimson Diaries, vol. 52, 6 August 1945.

21. Truman diary, 5 August 1945, *Off the Record: The Private Papers of Harry S. Truman*, ed. Robert H. Ferrell (New York: Harper & Row, 1980), pp. 59–60.

22. William D. Leahy, *I Was There: The Personal Story of the Chief of Staff to Presidents Roosevelt and Truman Based on His Notes and Diaries Made at the Time* (New York: Whittlesey House, 1950), p. 430.

23. Truman, *Memoirs*, vol. 1, p. 421.

24. *FRUS: Berlin*, vol. 2, Truman statement, 6 August 1945, pp. 1376–78.

25. *FRUS: Berlin*, vol. 2, Truman statement, 6 August 1945, pp. 1376–78. HSTL, PSF, box 195, Hiroshima statement, 6 August 1945. See HSTL, box 197, Japanese Surrender, Truman radio address, 9 August 1945.

26. Truman, *Memoirs*, vol. 1, p. 420. Alex Wellerstein suggests that Stimson confused Truman into seeing Hiroshima as more of a military target in order to contrast it with Kyoto, which was spared.

27. McKinney, Sagan, and Weiner, "Why the Atomic Bombing of Hiroshima Would Be Illegal Today," pp. 158–59.

28. Leahy, *I Was There*, p. 433.

29. Ian Buruma, *The Wages of Guilt: Memories of War in Germany and Japan* (New York: Farrar, Straus & Giroux, 1994), p. 106. HSTL, PSF, box 174, Atomic Bomb, U.S. Strategic Bombing Survey report, "The Effects of the Atomic Bombings of Hiroshima and Nagasaki," 19 June 1946.

30. Swiss legation to Byrnes, 11 August 1945, *FRUS: The British Commonwealth: The Far East*, vol. 6 (Washington, D.C.: U.S. Government Printing Office, 1969), pp. 472–73.

31. Butow, *Japan's Decision to Surrender*, p. 152.

32. John Lewis Gaddis, *The Cold War: A New History* (New York: Penguin, 2005), p. 25. See Michael D. Gordin, *Five Days in August: How World War II Became a Nuclear War* (Princeton: Princeton University Press, 2007).

33. Leahy, *I Was There*, p. 441.

34. Truman news conference, 8 August 1945, *Public Papers of the Presidents of the United States: Harry S. Truman, 1945* (Washington, D.C.: U.S. Government Printing Office, 1961), p. 200.

35. HSTL, NAP, box 12, Japan Surrender, Harriman to Byrnes, 11 August 1945. See NAI, EAD file no. 6-W/45, military intelligence memorandum, 28 February 1945.

36. Hasegawa, *Racing the Enemy*, pp. 189–91. See essays by Barton J. Bernstein, Richard B. Frank, Sumio Hatano, Tsuyoshi Hasegawa, and David Holloway in Tsuyoshi Hasegawa, ed., *The End of the Pacific War: Reappraisals* (Stanford, Calif.: Stanford University Press, 2007).

37. Hasegawa, *Racing the Enemy*, pp. 197–201. Hasegawa's outstanding book is unmatched in its triangular perspective from Washington, Moscow, and Tokyo.

38. Stimson Diaries, vol. 52, Truman-Stimson meeting, 8 August 1945, 10:45 a.m.

39. Truman to Russell, 9 August 1945, Dennis Merrill, ed., *Documentary History of the Truman Presidency: The Decision to Drop the Atomic Bomb on Japan* (Bethesda, Md.: University Publications of America, 1995), vol. 1, pp. 210–12.

40. HSTL, PSF, box 197, Japanese Surrender, Truman radio address, 9 August 1945.

41. Wellerstein, *Restricted Data*. William J. Broad, "The Truth Behind the News," *New York Times*, 10 August 2021, p. D1.

42. William L. Laurence, "Atomic Bombing of Nagasaki Told by Flight Member," *New York Times*, 9 September 1945, pp. A1, A35. HSTL, PSF, box 174, Atomic Bomb, War Department press release, 9 September 1945.

43. HSTL, PSF, box 174, Atomic Bomb, U.S. Strategic Bombing Survey report, "The Effects of the Atomic Bombings of Hiroshima and Nagasaki," 19 June 1946.

44. Laurence, "Atomic Bombing of Nagasaki Told by Flight Member." HSTL, PSF, box 174, Atomic Bomb, War Department press release, 9 September 1945.

45. HSTL, PSF, box 174, Atomic Bomb, U.S. Strategic Bombing Survey report, "The Effects of the Atomic Bombings of Hiroshima and Nagasaki," 19 June 1946.

46. Hasegawa, *Racing the Enemy*, pp. 122, 203–4, 207, 212.

47. For an outstanding account of the *kokutai*, see Carol Gluck, *Japan's Modern Myths: Ideology in the Late Meiji Period* (Princeton: Princeton University Press, 1985), pp. 144–46, 282–84.

48. Hoshina Zenshiro, *Daitoa senso hishi: Hoshina Zenshiro kaiso-roku* [Secret History of the Greater East Asia War: Memoir of Hoshina Zenshiro] (Tokyo: Hara-shobu,

1975), pp. 139–49. See HSTL, PSF, box 197, United States Strategic Bombing Survey, "Japan's Struggle to End the War," 1 July 1946; HSTL, PSF, box 159, *ONI Review*, June 1946, Sakomizu interrogation; MMA, RG-5, box 73, folder 2, Kase paper, 31 May 1946; Butow, *Japan's Decision to Surrender*, pp. 159–65; Hasegawa, *Racing the Enemy*, pp. 203–14; and Richard B. Frank, *Downfall: The End of the Imperial Japanese Empire* (New York: Random House, 1999), p. 290.

49. Butow, *Japan's Decision to Surrender*, pp. 168–75. Hasegawa, *Racing the Enemy*, pp. 210–11. Frank, *Downfall*, p. 293.

50. Hoshina, *Daitoa senso hishi*, pp. 139–49. See Togo Shigenori, *The Cause of Japan*, trans. Togo Fumihiko and Ben Bruce Blakeney (New York: Simon & Schuster, 1956), pp. 318–39; *Kido Diary*, 7 April 1945, pp. 424–25, 443, and 10 August 1945, p. 445; Butow, *Japan's Decision to Surrender*, pp. 166–78; HSTL, PSF, box 197, United States Strategic Bombing Survey, "Japan's Struggle to End the War," 1 July 1946; HSTL, PSF, box 159, *ONI Review*, June 1946, Sakomizu interrogation; and MMA, RG-5, box 73, folder 2, Kase paper, 31 May 1946.

51. Truman diary, 10 August 1945, *Off the Record*, pp. 60–62.

52. HSTL, NAP, box 12, Japan Surrender, Domei broadcast, 11 August 1945, 11:41 p.m. HSTL, PSF, box 197, Japanese Surrender, Swiss government note, 10 August 1945.

53. HSTL, NAP, box 12, Japan Surrender, Domei broadcast, 10 August 1945, 7:33 a.m. HSTL, PSF, box 197, Japanese Surrender, Swiss government note, 10 August 1945.

54. Stimson Diaries, vol. 52, 10 August 1945. James F. Byrnes, *All in One Lifetime* (New York: Harper & Brothers, 1958), p. 305. James F. Byrnes, *Speaking Frankly* (New York: Harper & Brothers, 1947), p. 209.

55. Stimson Diaries, vol. 52, 10 August 1945.

56. Leahy, *I Was There*, p. 434. HSTL, PSF, box 197, Japanese Surrender, Ayers note, 7 November 1951.

57. Byrnes, *All in One Lifetime*, p. 305.

58. Hasegawa, *Racing the Enemy*, p. 220.

59. Stimson Diaries, vol. 52, 10 August 1945.

60. HSTL, NAP, box 12, Japan Surrender, Byrnes to Bevin, 10 August 1945. HSTL, PSF, box 197, Japanese Surrender, Byrnes to Grassli, 11 August 1945. NARA, RG 107, 390/8/32/06, Stimson "safe file," box 8, "Byrnes answer to Jap," 11 August 1945.

61. Byrnes, *All in One Lifetime*, p. 305.

62. Stimson Diaries, vol. 52, 10 August 1945.

63. Truman diary, 10 August 1945, *Off the Record*, pp. 60–62.

64. Stimson Diaries, vol. 52, 10 August 1945.

65. Truman to Cavert, 11 August 1945, *Documentary History of the Truman Presidency*, vol. 1, p. 213.

66. David McCullough, *Truman* (New York: Simon & Schuster, 1992), p. 460.

67. HSTL, NAP, box 12, Japan Surrender, Byrnes to Bevin, 10 August 1945. HSTL, NAP, box 12, Japan Surrender, Byrnes to Hurley, 10 August 1945.

68. Andrew Adonis, *Ernest Bevin: Labour's Churchill* (London: Biteback, 2020), pp. 244–45.

69. HSTL, NAP, box 12, Japan Surrender, Winant to Byrnes, 11 August 1945. NAI, EAD file no. 6-W/45, Pethick-Lawrence to Mountbatten, no. 443, 11 August 1945. Byrnes, *All in One Lifetime*, p. 305. Stimson Diaries, vol. 52, 11 August 1945.

70. BNA, DO 35/1979, "Australian Views on Peace Terms," *Times*, 14 August 1945. BNA, DO 35/1979, Evatt to Attlee, 12 August 1945, 4 p.m.

71. BNA, DO 35/1979, Dixon note, 14 August 1945.

72. BNA, DO 35/1979, Dominions Office to Australia, 17 August 1945.

73. Chiang diary, 11 August 1945, in Wang Zhenghua, ed., *Jiang Zhongzheng zongtong dangan: Shilue gaoben* [The Chiang Kai-shek Collections: Chronological Events] (Taipei: Academia Historica, 2011), vol. 62, pp. 74–78. HSTL, NAP, box 12, Japan Surrender, Chiang to Truman, in Hurley to Truman, 11 August 1945.

74. Byrnes, *All in One Lifetime*, p. 305. HSTL, NAP, box 12, Japan Surrender, Harriman to Byrnes, 11 August 1945.

75. HSTL, NAP, box 12, Japan Surrender, Byrnes to Harriman, 10 August 1945. HSTL, NAP, box 12, Japan Surrender, Harriman to Byrnes, 11 August 1945.

76. HSTL, NAP, box 12, Japan Surrender, Byrnes to Attlee, 11 August 1945. HSTL, NAP, box 12, Japan Surrender, Byrnes to Chiang, 11 August 1945. HSTL, NAP, box 12, Japan Surrender, Winant to Byrnes, 11 August 1945.

77. HSTL, NAP, box 12, Japan Surrender, Hurley to Byrnes, 11 August 1945.

78. Barton J. Bernstein, "The Atomic Bombings Reconsidered," *Foreign Affairs*, vol. 74, no. 1 (January–February 1995), p. 148.

79. Truman diary, 11 August 1945, *Off the Record*, p. 62.

80. Hasegawa, *Racing the Enemy*, p. 221.

81. *Kido Diary*, 12 and 13 August 1945, pp. 447–48. Butow, *Japan's Decision to Surrender*, pp. 192–200. Hasegawa, *Racing the Enemy*, pp. 227–33.

82. Frank, *Downfall*, p. 87.

83. Butow, *Japan's Decision to Surrender*, pp. 198–99.

84. Hasegawa, *Racing the Enemy*, p. 238.

85. HSTL, NAP, box 12, Japan Surrender, Arnold to Spaatz, 11 August 1945.

86. *Kido Diary*, 14 August 1945, p. 448. Butow, *Japan's Decision to Surrender*, pp. 205–7. Hasegawa, *Racing the Enemy*, pp. 238–42. Frank, *Downfall*, pp. 314–15. Bix, "Japan's Delayed Surrender," pp. 218–23.

87. *Kido Diary*, 14 August 1945, pp. 448–49.

88. HSTL, PSF, box 197, U.S. Strategic Bombing Survey, "Japan's Struggle to End the War," 1 July 1946. HSTL, PSF, box 159, *ONI Review*, June 1946, Sakomizu interrogation. Butow, *Japan's Decision to Surrender*, pp. 205–8. Hasegawa, *Racing the Enemy*, pp. 238–40. Frank, *Downfall*, pp. 314–15.

89. Max Hastings, *Retribution: The Battle for Japan, 1944–45* (New York: Alfred A. Knopf, 2008), pp. 512–13. Frank, *Downfall*, pp. 317–20.

90. *Kido Diary*, 15 August 1945, pp. 449–50. Butow, *Japan's Decision to Surrender*, pp. 211–20. Hasegawa, *Racing the Enemy*, pp. 241–48. Frank, *Downfall*, pp. 317–20. See Samuel Eliot Morison, "Why Japan Surrendered," *The Atlantic*, October 1960, pp. 41–47.

91. Byrnes, *All in One Lifetime*, p. 306.

92. HSTL, PSF, box 159, Japan, Togo to Allies, 14 August 1945. HSTL, PSF, box 197, Japanese Surrender, Grassli to Byrnes, 14 August 1945. HSTL, NAP, box 12, Japan Surrender, Marshall to MacArthur, 14 August 1945.

93. HSTL, PSF, box 197, Japanese Surrender, Ayers note, 7 November 1951. Leahy, *I Was There*, pp. 436–37. McCullough, *Truman*, p. 462.

94. HSTL, NAP, box 12, Japan Surrender, Truman to Attlee, Stalin, and Chiang, 14 August 1945.

95. HSTL, NAP, box 12, Japan Surrender, Marshall to MacArthur, 14 August 1945.

96. Barbara W. Tuchman, *Stilwell and the American Experience in China, 1911–45* (New York: Grove, 1985), p. 521.

97. NARA, RG 107, 390/8/32/06, Stimson "safe file," box 8, Stimson to Byrnes, 11 August 1945.

98. Stimson Diaries, vol. 52, 14 August 1945 (12 August–3 September 1945).

99. Stimson Diaries, vol. 52, 4–5 September 1945.

100. Butow, *Japan's Decision to Surrender*, pp. 1–5. Hasegawa, *Racing the Enemy*, pp. 248–49. HSTL, PSF, box 159, Japan, Sebald summary of radio intelligence, 15 August 1945.

101. Imperial Rescript, 15 August 1945, in Butow, *Japan's Decision to Surrender*, p. 248.

102. Butow, *Japan's Decision to Surrender*, p. 5.

103. NARA, RG 218, Leahy papers, box 9, Bissell to Leahy, 12 August 1945.

104. HSTL, NAP, box 12, Japan Surrender, Marshall to Stimson, 16 August 1945.

105. MMA, RG-9, box 160, folder W.O. August–September 1945, Marshall to MacArthur, 12 August 1945. HSTL, NAP, box 12, Japan Surrender, Truman directive to MacArthur, 13 August 1945.

106. HSTL, PSF, box 159, Japan, Togo to Allies (via Switzerland), 16 August 1945, 9:30 a.m.

107. HSTL, NAP, box 13, Japan Surrender, Lincoln to Marshall, 17 August 1945.

108. HSTL, PSF, box 159, Japan, State Department news digest, 15 August 1945.

109. HSTL, PSF, box 159, Japan, CINCPAC order 150842/139, 16 August 1945.

110. HSTL, NAP, box 12, Japan Surrender, Stalin to Truman, 16 August 1945.

111. HSTL, NAP, box 13, Japan Surrender, Truman to Stalin, 18 August 1945.

112. HSTL, NAP, box 13, Japan Surrender, Stalin to Truman, 22 August 1945.

113. HSTL, NAP, box 13, Japan Surrender, MacArthur to War Department, 17 August 1945. HSTL, NAP, box 13, Japan Surrender, Deane to Stimson, 18 August 1945.

114. HSTL, NAP, box 13, Japan Surrender, Harriman to Truman and Byrnes, 29 August 1945.

115. William F. Nimmo, *Behind a Curtain of Silence: Japanese in Soviet Custody* (New York: Greenwood, 1998), pp. 115–17. Frank, *Downfall*, p. 326. See Dower, *War Without Mercy*, pp. 298–99.

116. Hasegawa, *Racing the Enemy*, pp. 195, 253–58.

117. NARA, RG 218, Leahy papers, box 8, MacArthur correspondence file, MacArthur to Marshall, 2 November 1945. On widespread Red Army rape in Germany at the same time, see Antony Beevor, *Berlin: The Downfall, 1945* (London: Viking, 2002).

118. Barbara Demick, *Nothing to Envy: Ordinary Lives in North Korea* (New York: Spiegel & Grau, 2009), pp. 21–23. Victor Cha, *The Impossible State: North Korea Past and Future* (New York: HarperCollins, 2012), pp. 20–34.

119. HSTL, PSF, box 197, Japanese Surrender, Korea surrender, 9 September 1945. HSTL, PSF, box 197, Japanese Surrender, Philippines surrender, 3 September 1945. HSTL, PSF, box 197, Japanese Surrender, Singapore surrender, 12 September 1945. HSTL, NAP, box 13, Japanese Surrender, Marshall to MacArthur, 12 August 1945. NARA, RG 218, box 8, Leahy files, Japanese General Headquarters to MacArthur, 24 August 1945. See NARA, RG 107, 390/8/32/06, Stimson "safe file," box 8, van Slyck memorandum, August 1945; and Joseph C. Grew, *Turbulent Era: A Diplomatic Record of Forty Years, 1904–1945* (Boston: Houghton Mifflin, 1952), vol. 2, p. 1406.

120. Hastings, *Retribution*, p. 509. NARA, RG 218, box 8, Leahy files, MacArthur to Marshall, 3 August 1945.

121. NARA, RG 218, Leahy papers, box 9, Bissell to Leahy, 12 August 1945.

122. Hastings, *Retribution*, pp. 516–17.

123. NARA, RG 218, Leahy papers, box 9, Bissell to Leahy, 12 August 1945. NARA, RG 218, Leahy papers, box 8, Japanese General Headquarters to MacArthur, 23 August 1945.

124. NARA, RG 218, Leahy papers, box 9, Nimitz to Ultra channel, 16 August 1945.

125. Frank, *Downfall*, p. 329.

126. HSTL, NAP, box 13, Japanese Surrender, Wedemeyer to Stimson, 27 August 1945.

127. *Kido Diary*, 20–21 August 1945, p. 451.

128. Chiang victory message, 15 August 1945, in Chinese News Service, *Contemporary China*, vol. 5, no. 7 (20 August 1945).

129. Christopher Bayly and Tim Harper, *Forgotten Wars: The End of Britain's Asian Empire* (London: Allen Lane, 2007).

130. *FRUS: The British Commonwealth: The Far East*, vol. 6, Acheson to Robertson, 5 October 1945.

131. Charles de Gaulle, *Mémoires de guerre: Le salut, 1944–1946* (Paris: Libraire Plon, 1959), vol. 3, pp. 550–53. *FRUS: Diplomatic Papers, 1945: Europe* (Washington, D.C.: U.S. Government Printing Office, 1968), vol. 4, Truman–de Gaulle memcon, 22 August 1945, pp. 708–11.

132. Charles de Gaulle, *The War Memoirs of Charles de Gaulle: Salvation, 1944–1946*, trans. Richard Howard (New York: Simon & Schuster, 1960), vol. 3, pp. 256–64.

133. AWM, Webb papers, 3DRL/2481, series 4, wallet 2, van Mook broadcast, September 1947. Adrian Vickers, *A History of Modern Indonesia* (Cambridge: Cambridge University Press, 2005), pp. 97–101.

134. MMA, RG-9, box 160, folder W.O. August–September 1945, Marshall to MacArthur, 12 August 1945.

135. Christopher Bayly and Tim Harper, *Forgotten Armies: The Fall of British Asia, 1941–1945* (London: Allen Lane, 2004), pp. 457–58.

136. HSTL, NAP, box 13, Japanese Surrender, Mountbatten to Leahy, 31 August 1945.

137. NAI, EAD file no. 6-W/45, Dening to Sterndale-Bennett, 31 August 1945.

5. Supreme Commander

1. D. Clayton James, *The Years of MacArthur: 1941–1945* (Boston: Houghton Mifflin, 1975), vol. 2, p. 55.

2. HSTL, NAP, box 13, Japanese Surrender, Marshall to MacArthur, 12 August 1945. HSTL, PSF, box 159, Joint Chiefs to MacArthur, 24 September 1945.

3. Douglas MacArthur, *Reminiscences* (New York: McGraw-Hill, 1964), pp. 269–71.

4. Sarah Kovner, *Prisoners of the Empire: Inside Japanese POW Camps* (Cambridge, Mass.: Harvard University Press, 2020), pp. 70–71.

5. James, *Years of MacArthur*, vol. 2, pp. 15, 23–35, 46–67.

6. Fredrik Logevall, *JFK: Coming of Age in the American Century, 1917–1956* (New York: Random House, 2020), p. 334.

7. James, *Years of MacArthur*, vol. 2, pp. 68–81, 93–109, 126–27.

8. Max Hastings, *Retribution: The Battle for Japan, 1944–45* (New York: Alfred A. Knopf, 2008), p. 27.

9. MMA, RG-44a, box 2, folder 7, Fellers note, 11 February 1966.

10. Hastings, *Retribution,* pp. 123–27, 224. MacArthur, *Reminiscences,* pp. 216–17.
11. Hastings, *Retribution,* p. 539. MMA, RG-9, box 160, folder W.O. August–September 1945, MacArthur to Marshall, 2 September 1945. HSTL, NAP, box 13, Japanese Surrender, Harriman to Truman and Byrnes, 29 August 1945.
12. MMA, RG-9, box 160, folder W.O. August–September 1945, Marshall to MacArthur, 12 August 1945. John W. Dower, *Embracing Defeat: Japan in the Wake of World War II* (New York: W. W. Norton, 1999), pp. 40–44.
13. Stilwell diary, 2 September 1945, *Seven Stars: The Okinawa Battle Diaries of Simon Bolivar Buckner, Jr., and Joseph Stilwell,* ed. Nicholas Evan Sarantakes (College Station: Texas A&M University Press, 2004), p. 111.
14. Theodore H. White and Annalee Jacoby, *Thunder Out of China* (New York: William Sloane Associates, 1946), p. xii.
15. Kaze Toshikazu, *Journey to the* Missouri (New Haven: Yale University Press, 1950), p. 4.
16. HSTL, NAP, box 12, Japan Surrender, Truman to Joint Chiefs, 13 August 1945.
17. Stilwell diary, 2 September 1945, *Seven Stars,* p. 111.
18. White and Jacoby, *Thunder Out of China,* p. xi.
19. Kaze, *Journey to the* Missouri, p. 8.
20. Stilwell diary, 2 September 1945, *Seven Stars,* p. 111.
21. Koichi Kido, *The Diary of Marquis Kido, 1931–45* (Frederick, Md.: University Publications of America, 1984), 23 August 1945, p. 452.
22. HSTL, NAP, box 12, Japan Surrender, Instrument of Surrender, 2 September 1945.
23. HSTL, NAP, box 12, Japan Surrender, Japan Surrender Documents, 2 September 1945.
24. Stilwell diary, 2 September 1945, *Seven Stars,* p. 111.
25. HSTL, NAP, box 13, Japanese Surrender, Harriman to Truman and Byrnes, 29 August 1945.
26. Kaze, *Journey to the* Missouri, pp. 6–8.
27. MacArthur, *Reminiscences,* p. 278.
28. Stilwell diary, 2 September 1945, *Seven Stars,* p. 112.
29. MacArthur, *Reminiscences,* pp. 271–72.
30. HSTL, NAP, box 12, Japan Surrender, Japan Surrender Documents, 2 September 1945.
31. Stilwell diary, 2 September 1945, *Seven Stars,* p. 112.
32. Kaze, *Journey to the* Missouri, p. 10. Hastings, *Retribution,* p. 540.
33. HSTL, PSF, box 197, Japanese Surrender, Truman speech, 1 September 1945.
34. *Kido Diary,* 21 August 1945, p. 451.
35. HSTL, NAP, box 12, Japan Surrender, Japan Surrender Documents, Hirohito notes, 1–2 September 1945. *Kido Diary,* 1 September 1945, p. 454.
36. HSTL, NAP, box 12, Japan Surrender, Instrument of Surrender, 2 September 1945.
37. *Kido Diary,* 2 September 1945, p. 454.
38. MMA, RG-5, box 73, folder 2, Kase paper, 31 May 1946.
39. William Manchester, *American Caesar: Douglas MacArthur, 1880–1964* (Boston: Little, Brown, 1978), pp. 3–11. Hastings, *Retribution,* p. 545.
40. Manchester, *American Caesar,* pp. 149–52.
41. Stimson Diaries, vol. 50, 30 March 1945.
42. Truman diary, 1 June 1945, *Off the Record: The Private Papers of Harry S. Truman,* ed.

Robert H. Ferrell (New York: Harper & Row, 1980), pp. 40–41; 23 October 1945, p. 72.

43. Truman diary, 17 June 1945, *Off the Record*, p. 47.
44. Truman diary, 10 August 1945, *Off the Record*, p. 60.
45. MMA, RG-9, box 160, folder W.O. August–September 1945, MacArthur to Marshall, 3 September 1945.
46. HSTL, PSF, box 159, MacArthur talks, 14–17 October 1945, in Locke to Truman, 19 October 1945.
47. HSTL, PSF, box 159, Compton to Truman, 4 October 1945.
48. John W. Dower, *Empire and Aftermath: Yoshida Shigeru and the Japanese Experience, 1878–1954* (Cambridge, Mass.: Harvard University Press, 1988), p. 264.
49. James, *Years of MacArthur*, vol. 2, p. 775.
50. HSTL, PSF, box 159, MacArthur talks, 14–17 October 1945, in Locke to Truman, 19 October 1945.
51. NARA, RG 218, Leahy papers, box 9, Japan Surrender, MacArthur to Marshall, 4 September 1945.
52. HSTL, PSF, box 159, Compton to Truman, 4 October 1945.
53. Truman to Martha Ellen Truman and Mary Jane Truman, 23 October 1945, *Off the Record*, pp. 71–72. Truman diary, 26 September 1946, *Off the Record*, pp. 98–99.
54. HSTL, NAP, box 13, Japanese Surrender, Marshall to MacArthur, 17 August 1945. MacArthur, *Reminiscences*, p. 291.
55. NARA, RG 218, Leahy papers, box 8, MacArthur correspondence file, MacArthur to Joint Chiefs, 25 September 1945. HSTL, PSF, box 159, U.S. Initial Post-Surrender Policy for Japan, SWNCC 150/4, 22 September 1945. MMA, RG-5, U.S. Initial Post-Surrender Policy for Japan, 22 September 1945. NARA, RG 218, Leahy papers, box 8, MacArthur correspondence file, Chifley to MacArthur, 21 September 1945.
56. NARA, RG 218, Leahy papers, box 9, Japan Surrender, MacArthur to Marshall, 19 September 1945.
57. John Lewis Gaddis, *The Cold War: A New History* (New York: Penguin, 2005), pp. 24–25.
58. HSTL, PSF, box 159, Japan, SWNCC and Joint Chiefs to Truman, 13 August 1945.
59. HSTL, PSF, box 159, MacArthur talks, 14–17 October 1945, in Locke to Truman, 19 October 1945.
60. MacArthur, *Reminiscences*, p. 285.
61. HSTL, PSF, box 159, MacArthur talks, 14–17 October 1945, in Locke to Truman, 19 October 1945.
62. *Kido Diary*, 27 August 1945, p. 452.
63. Barak Kushner, *Men to Devils, Devils to Men: Japanese War Crimes and Chinese Justice* (Cambridge, Mass.: Harvard University Press, 2015), p. 84. NARA, RG 218, Leahy papers, box 9, Japan Surrender, MacArthur to Marshall, 27 September 1945. NARA, RG 218, Leahy papers, box 9, Japan Surrender, MacArthur to Marshall, 9 October 1945.
64. HSTL, PSF, box 159, Japan, SWNCC and Joint Chiefs to Truman, 13 August 1945.
65. Cordell Hull, *The Memoirs of Cordell Hull* (New York: Macmillan, 1948), vol. 2, p. 1590.
66. *FRUS: The Conference of Berlin 1945* (Washington, D.C.: U.S. Government Printing Office, 1960), vol. 1, military briefing, n.d., pp. 924–26.

67. Stimson Diaries, vol. 52, 17 September 1945. NARA, RG 218, Leahy papers, box 9, Japan Surrender, MacArthur to Marshall, 27 September 1945.

68. NARA, RG 218, Leahy papers, box 9, Japan Surrender, MacArthur to Marshall, 4 September 1945.

69. "Social-Economic Overturn in Japan Declared State Department Policy," *New York Times*, 20 September 1945, pp. A1, A3. Truman press conference, 18 September 1945, *Public Papers of the Presidents of the United States: Harry S. Truman, 1945* (Washington, D.C.: U.S. Government Printing Office, 1961), p. 326.

70. NARA, RG 218, Leahy papers, box 9, Japan Surrender, Marshall to MacArthur, 17 September 1945. NARA, RG 218, Leahy papers, box 9, Japan Surrender, MacArthur to Marshall, 18 September 1945.

71. Truman statement, 19 September 1945, *Public Papers*, pp. 327–28.

72. HSTL, PSF, box 174, Atomic Bomb, U.S. Strategic Bombing Survey report, "The Effects of the Atomic Bombings of Hiroshima and Nagasaki," 19 June 1946.

73. A. Frank Reel, *The Case of General Yamashita* (Chicago: University of Chicago Press, 1949), p. 74.

74. Stilwell diary, 1 September 1945, *Seven Stars*, pp. 110–11.

75. MacArthur, *Reminiscences*, p. 280.

76. HSTL, PSF, box 159, Compton to Truman, 4 October 1945.

77. Herbert P. Bix, *Hirohito and the Making of Modern Japan* (New York: HarperCollins, 2000), p. 539.

78. *Kido Diary*, 4 September 1945, p. 455.

79. HSTL, PSF, box 159, MacArthur talks, 14–17 October 1945, in Locke to Truman, 19 October 1945.

80. MacArthur, *Reminiscences*, pp. 280–81.

81. MacArthur, *Reminiscences*, p. 283.

82. NARA, RG 107, 390/8/32/06, Stimson "safe file," box 8, van Slyck memorandum, August 1945.

83. Stilwell diary, 1 September 1945, *Seven Stars*, p. 111.

84. Edwin O. Reischauer, *My Life Between Japan and America* (New York: Harper & Row, 1986), pp. 104–5.

85. MMA, RG-9, box 160, Marshall to MacArthur, 6 September 1945.

86. HSTL, PSF, box 159, U.S. Initial Post-Surrender Policy for Japan, SWNCC 150/4, 22 September 1945. MMA, RG-9, box 160, Marshall to MacArthur, 6 September 1945.

87. MMA, RG-5, box 2, folder 1, U.S. Sixth Army, Status of Demobilization of Kempei Tai, 25 October 1945.

88. HSTL, PSF, box 159, U.S. Initial Post-Surrender Policy for Japan, SWNCC 150/4, 22 September 1945.

89. MMA, RG-9, box 160, Marshall to MacArthur, 6 September 1945.

90. MacArthur, *Reminiscences*, p. 285.

91. MMA, RG-5, box 1, folder 2, Japanese Reaction to U.S. Occupation, October 1945.

92. MacArthur, *Reminiscences*, pp. 279–80.

93. MacArthur, *Reminiscences*, pp. 284–86.

94. Reischauer, *My Life Between Japan and America*, p. 105.

95. *FRUS: The Conference of Berlin 1945* (Washington, D.C.: U.S. Government Printing Office, 1960), vol. 2, Stimson to Truman, 16 July 1945, pp. 1322–23.

96. NARA, RG 218, box 8, MacArthur communications file, Joint Chiefs to MacArthur, 6 September 1945.

97. MMA, RG-9, box 160, Marshall to MacArthur, 6 September 1945. HSTL, PSF, box 159, U.S. Initial Post-Surrender Policy for Japan, 22 September 1945.

98. MMA, RG-9, box 160, folder W.O. August–September 1945, Marshall to MacArthur, 11 August 1945. Edwin O. Reischauer, *The Japanese* (Cambridge, Mass.: Belknap Press of Harvard University Press, 1978), p. 85.

99. Joseph C. Grew, *Turbulent Era: A Diplomatic Record of Forty Years, 1904–1945* (Boston: Houghton Mifflin, 1952), vol. 2, pp. 1412–13.

100. HSTL, PSF, box 159, Compton to Truman, 4 October 1945.

101. MacArthur, *Reminiscences,* pp. 279–82.

102. Hirohito to Akihito, 9 September 1945, "Showa tenno no dokuhaku hachijikan" [The Showa Emperor's Eight-Hour Monologue], *Bungei Shunju,* December 1990, p. 122.

103. Robert Trumbull, "Hirohito Promises Japan a Recovery," *New York Times,* 5 September 1945, pp. A1, A3. *Kido Diary,* 1 September 1945, p. 454.

104. MMA, RG-5, box 1, folder 2, Japanese Reaction to U.S. Occupation, October 1945.

105. "Showa tenno no dokuhaku hachijikan" [The Showa Emperor's Eight-Hour Monologue], *Bungei Shunju,* December 1990, p. 141.

106. Bix, *Hirohito,* pp. 536–37.

107. Frank L. Kluckhohn, "Japan's Premier Explains Defeat," *New York Times,* 6 September 1945, pp. A1, A3. *Kido Diary,* 15–16 August 1945, pp. 449–50. MMA, RG-5, box 1, folder 2, Japanese Reaction to U.S. Occupation, October 1945.

108. Herbert P. Bix, "The Showa Emperor's 'Monologue' and the Problem of War Responsibility," *Journal of Japanese Studies,* vol. 18, no. 2 (Summer 1992), p. 303.

109. MMA, RG-9, box 160, Marshall to MacArthur, 6 September 1945. HSTL, PSF, box 159, U.S. Initial Post-Surrender Policy for Japan, 22 September 1945.

110. MacArthur, *Reminiscences,* pp. 282–83.

111. Truman to Bess Truman, 21 January 1919, *Dear Bess: The Letters from Harry to Bess Truman, 1910–1959,* ed. Robert H. Ferrell (New York: W. W. Norton, 1983), p. 293.

112. Truman diary, 7 June 1945, *Off the Record,* p. 44.

113. Truman to Acheson (unsent), 15 March 1957, *Off the Record,* pp. 348–49.

114. NARA, RG 107, 390/8/32/06, Stimson "safe file," box 8, van Slyck memorandum, August 1945.

115. Grew, *Turbulent Era,* vol. 2, pp. 1409–19.

116. Grew to Harriman, 9 September 1945, Grew, *Turbulent Era,* vol. 2, pp. 1440–41.

117. BNA, FO 371/54126, MacDermot to Bevin, "Report on Allied Occupation Problems and Policy in Japan," 29 November 1945.

118. MacArthur, *Reminiscences,* pp. 283–84.

119. HSTL, PSF, box 159, MacArthur talks, 14–17 October 1945, in Locke to Truman, 19 October 1945.

120. Manchester, *American Caesar,* p. 4. John Lewis Gaddis, *George F. Kennan: An American Life* (New York: Penguin, 2011), p. 301.

121. MacArthur, *Reminiscences,* pp. 282–84.

122. HSTL, PSF, box 159, U.S. Initial Post-Surrender Policy for Japan, 22 September 1945; MMA, RG-5, U.S. Initial Post-Surrender Policy for Japan, 22 September 1945. Eto Jun, *Closed Linguistic Space: Censorship by the Occupation Forces and Postwar Japan* (Tokyo: Japan Publishing Industry Foundation for Culture, 2020).

123. MMA, RG-9, box 160, Marshall to MacArthur, 22 August 1945.

124. MacArthur, *Reminiscences*, pp. 282–89.

6. Apprehensions

1. *IMTFE Transcripts*, 13 May 1947, p. 22010. Richard B. Frank, *Downfall: The End of the Imperial Japanese Empire* (New York: Random House, 1999), p. 88.

2. *IMTFE Transcripts*, 22 May 1947, pp. 22761–62. HSTL, PSF, box 159, Japan, Sebald summary of radio intelligence, 15 August 1945.

3. Yukiko Koshiro, *Imperial Eclipse: Japan's Strategic Thinking About Continental Asia Before August 1945* (Ithaca, N.Y.: Cornell University Press, 2013), p. 4.

4. *IMTFE Transcripts*, 16 October 1947, p. 31195. Kido Koichi, *The Diary of Marquis Kido, 1931–45* (Frederick, Md.: University Publications of America, 1984), 15 August 1945, p. 449.

5. Frank, *Downfall*, p. 329.

6. *IMTFE Transcripts*, 9 January 1947, pp. 14701–6.

7. Michel Paradis, *Last Mission to Tokyo: The Extraordinary Story of the Doolittle Raiders and Their Final Fight for Justice* (New York: Simon & Schuster, 2020), p. 29.

8. HSTL, NAP, box 13, Japan Surrender, Wedemeyer to Stimson, 27 August 1945.

9. Daqing Yang, "Convergence or Divergence?," *American Historical Review*, vol. 104, no. 3 (June 1999), p. 863.

10. MMA, RG-9, box 159, War Crimes, Myers to War Department, 6 May 1947.

11. Jeanne Guillemin, *Hidden Atrocities: Japanese Germ Warfare and American Obstruction of Justice at the Tokyo Trial* (New York: Columbia University Press, 2017), pp. xviii–xix.

12. *IMTFE Transcripts*, 22 May 1947, pp. 22760–61.

13. Herbert P. Bix, *Hirohito and the Making of Modern Japan* (New York: HarperCollins, 2000), p. 448.

14. Paradis, *Last Mission to Tokyo*, pp. 31–32.

15. NARA, RG 84, Tokyo political adviser 1945, box 2, Allen to Imperial Japanese Government, 22 November 1945.

16. HSTL, NAP, box 13, Japanese Surrender, Halsey to MacArthur, 29 August 1945.

17. NAI, EAD file no. 6-W/45, Dening to Bevin, 14 September 1945.

18. HSTL, NAP, box 13, Japanese Surrender, Wedemeyer to Stimson, 31 August 1945.

19. "Out of Japan's Prisons," *New York Times*, 2 September 1945, p. 52.

20. HSTL, NAP, box 13, Japanese Surrender, Halsey to Nimitz, 30 August 1945.

21. United Press, "Still 'Too Many Nips Left,' Halsey Quoted as Saying," *New York Times*, 25 September 1945, p. 2.

22. Truman speech, 27 October 1945, *Public Papers of the Presidents of the United States: Harry S. Truman, 1945* (Washington, D.C.: U.S. Government Printing Office, 1961), p. 430.

23. MMA, RG-9, box 160, War Department to MacArthur, 6 September 1945.

24. Yinan He, *The Search for Reconciliation: Sino-Japanese and German-Polish Relations Since World War II* (Cambridge: Cambridge University Press, 2009), pp. 122–33.

25. MMA, RG-9, box 160, War Department to MacArthur, 6 September 1945.

26. *Kido Diary*, 30 August 1945, p. 454.

27. *IMTFE Transcripts*, 14 October 1947, pp. 30719–22.

28. *IMTFE Transcripts*, 15 October 1947, p. 30892.

29. HSTL, PSF, box 197, United States Strategic Bombing Survey, "Japan's Struggle to End the War," 1 July 1946, p. 3.

30. *Kido Diary*, 1 June 1940, pp. 236–37. Robert J. C. Butow, *Japan's Decision to Surrender* (Stanford, Calif.: Stanford University Press, 1954), pp. 12–13.

31. *Kido Diary*, 12 December 1942, p. 345.

32. *Kido Diary*, 29 August 1945, p. 453.

33. "Arrest of Ex-Premier Tojo Is Ordered by M'Arthur," *New York Times*, 11 September 1945, p. 1.

34. Frank L. Kluckhohn, "M'Arthur Seizing 40 for War Crimes," *New York Times*, 12 September 1945, pp. 1, 3. "Roster of 40 Ordered Arrested as War Criminals by MacArthur," *New York Times*, 12 September 1945, p. 3. MMA, RG-5, box 2, folder 1, War Criminals List, Supplement 1, September 1945.

35. "Jap War Criminals Await Trial," *Life*, 12 November 1945, pp. 29–33.

36. Kluckhohn, "M'Arthur Seizing 40 for War Crimes," pp. 1, 3. "Roster of 40 Ordered Arrested as War Criminals by MacArthur." MMA, RG-5, box 2, folder 1, War Criminals List, Supplement 1, September 1945.

37. UVA, Morgan papers, box 11, Edith Togo to Morgan, 6 April 1945.

38. MMA, RG-9, box 24, Sugamo liaison section, 20 May 1946. MMA, RG-9, box 24, Bunker to Carpenter, 16 May 1946. MMA, RG-9, box 160, GHQ to Joint Chiefs, War Department folder, 21 May 1946. Shinsho Hanayama, *The Way of Deliverance: Three Years with the Condemned Japanese War Criminals*, trans. Hideo Suzuki, Eiichi Noda, and James K. Sasaki (New York: Charles Scribner's Sons, 1950), pp. 114–20.

39. John L. Ginn, *Sugamo Prison, Tokyo* (Jefferson, N.C.: McFarland, 1992), pp. 1–2. "Sugamo," *Far East Stars and Stripes Review*, 31 August 1947, p. 7.

40. NARA, RG 218, box 8, MacArthur communications file, War Department to MacArthur, 14 September 1945. MMA, RG-9, box 159, War Crimes folder, War Department to MacArthur, 15 September 1945.

41. MMA, RG-9, box 159, War Crimes folder, War Department to MacArthur, 22 September 1945.

42. MMA, RG-5, box 2, folder 1, War Criminals List, Supplement 1, September 1945. MMA, RG-5, box 2, folder 1, Apprehension of War Criminals, 9 October 1945. NARA, RG 84, Tokyo political adviser papers, box 2, MacArthur to Eichelberger, 6 October 1945.

43. Bix, *Hirohito*, p. 581.

44. *Kido Diary*, 12 September 1945, p. 456.

45. MMA, RG-9, box 159, War Crimes folder, MacArthur to War Department, 23 September 1945. Yoshitake Oka, *Konoe Fumimaro: A Political Biography*, trans. Shumpei Okamoto and Patricia Murray (Tokyo: University of Tokyo Press, 1983), pp. 181–94.

46. MMA, RG-9, box 159, War Crimes folder, MacArthur to Marshall, 24 September 1945. This confirms my argument that liberal states will shelve the prosecution of war crimes in order to protect their own soldiers (*Stay the Hand of Vengeance: The Politics of War Crimes Tribunals* [Princeton: Princeton University Press, 2000], pp. 29–30, 277–78).

47. NARA, RG 218, Leahy papers, box 8, MacArthur correspondence file, Joint Chiefs to MacArthur, 11 September 1945. MMA, RG-9, box 159, War Crimes folder, Joint Chiefs to MacArthur, 12 September 1945.

48. NARA, RG 84, Tokyo political adviser papers, box 2, Atcheson to Byrnes, War Criminals List, 5 October 1945.

49. NARA, RG 84, Tokyo political adviser papers, box 2, Marshall to Atcheson, 7 November 1945.

50. MMA, RG-9, box 159, War Crimes folder, army regulations, 24 September 1945.

51. Truman radio address, 2 September 1945, *Public Papers,* p. 258.

52. MMA, RG-9, box 159, War Crimes folder, War Department to MacArthur, 22 September 1945.

53. MMA, RG-5, box 2, folder 1, War Criminals List, Supplement 1, September 1945.

54. MMA, RG-9, box 159, War Crimes folder, War Department to MacArthur, 22 September 1945.

55. MMA, RG-44a, box 4, folder 23, interview statements, n.d. Frank L. Kluckhohn, "Hirohito in Interview Puts Blame on Tojo in Sneak Raid," *New York Times,* 25 September 1945, pp. A1–A2.

56. *Kido Diary,* 26 September 1945, p. 458.

57. Samuel P. Huntington, *The Third Wave: Democratization in the Late Twentieth Century* (Norman: University of Oklahoma Press, 1991), pp. 211–31. Tina Rosenberg, *The Haunted Land: Facing Europe's Ghosts After Communism* (New York: Vintage, 1996), pp. 397–407. Jack Snyder and Leslie Vinjamuri, "Trials and Errors," *International Security,* vol. 28, no. 3 (Winter 2003–4), pp. 5–44; Jack Snyder, *Human Rights for Pragmatists: Social Power in Modern Times* (Princeton: Princeton University Press, 2022), pp. 91–104.

58. Douglas MacArthur, *Reminiscences* (New York: McGraw-Hill, 1964), p. 287.

59. Bix, *Hirohito,* p. 542.

60. Faubion Bowers, "The Day the General Blinked," *New York Times,* 30 September 1988, p. A35.

61. Kojima Noboru, "Tenno to Amerika to Taiheiyo senso," *Bungei Shunju,* November 1975, pp. 115–19.

62. For a convincingly skeptical reading of MacArthur's version, see John W. Dower, *Embracing Defeat: Japan in the Wake of World War II* (New York: W. W. Norton, 1999), pp. 296–97.

63. MacArthur, *Reminiscences,* pp. 287–88.

64. Kojima, "Tenno to Amerika to Taiheiyo senso."

65. Faubion Bowers, "The Day the General Blinked," *New York Times,* 30 September 1988, p. A35.

66. "Ex-God Descends," *Life,* 22 October 1945, p. 40.

67. Bix, *Hirohito,* pp. 550–51.

68. MMA, RG-44a, box 2, folder 20, Fellers to MacArthur, 4 October 1945. "The Emperor Goes Calling," *New York Times,* 28 September 1945, p. 20.

69. *Kido Diary,* 29 September 1945, pp. 458–59.

70. MMA, RG-44a, box 1, folder 1, Anderton to MacArthur, 1 October 1945.

71. MMA, RG-5, box 2, folder 2, Fellers to MacArthur, 2 October 1945.

72. MMA, RG-44a, box 2, folder 20, Fellers to MacArthur, 4 October 1945.

73. Truman press conference, 18 October 1945, *Public Papers,* pp. 399–400.

74. Bix, *Hirohito,* pp. 583–84.

75. Dower, *Embracing Defeat,* p. 81.

76. Monica Braw, *The Atomic Bomb Suppressed: American Censorship in Occupied Japan* (London: Routlege, 1991), pp. 29–32.

77. For a clear-eyed look at the controversies around the term State Shinto, see Helen Hardacre, *Shinto: A History* (Oxford: Oxford University Press, 2017), pp. 355–57.

78. Yoshio Kodama, *I Was Defeated,* trans. Taro Fukuda (Tokyo: Radiopress, 1959), p. 200.

79. Associated Press, "Abolition of Peers Proposed," *New York Times,* 2 December 1945.

80. MMA, RG-4, box 22, folder 2, GHQ press review, 23 December 1945. See MMA, RG-4, box 22, folder 2, GHQ press review, 24 December 1945.

81. MMA, RG-5, box 1, folder 2, Japanese Reaction to U.S. Occupation, October 1945.

82. NARA, RG 84, Tokyo political adviser papers, box 10, Atcheson to MacArthur, 8 October 1945.

83. NARA, RG 218, Leahy papers, box 8, MacArthur correspondence file, Joint Chiefs to MacArthur, 3 November 1945. Dower, *Embracing Defeat,* p. 81.

84. "Break-Up of Trusts Ordered by Tokyo," *New York Times,* 6 November 1945, p. 5. MMA, RG-9, box 161, folder DA, MacArthur to Draper, 9 January 1948.

85. MMA, RG-5, box 1, folder 2, Japanese Reaction to U.S. Occupation, October 1945.

86. Dower, *Embracing Defeat,* p. 82.

87. MMA, RG-5, box 2, folder 1, Masaki to Fellers, 12 November 1945.

88. MMA, RG-5, box 1, folder 2, Japanese Reaction to U.S. Occupation, October 1945.

89. "Jap War Criminals Await Trial," *Life,* 12 November 1945, pp. 29–33.

90. MacArthur, *Reminiscences,* pp. 135–36, 145–46.

91. MMA, RG-9, box 159, War Crimes folder, MacArthur to Marshall, 7 October 1945.

92. Ronald H. Spector, *Eagle Against the Sun: The American War with Japan* (New York: Vintage, 1985), pp. 527–28.

93. Frank Reel, *The Case of General Yamashita* (Chicago: University of Chicago Press, 1949), pp. 50–51.

94. A. J. Barker, *Yamashita* (New York: Ballantine, 1973). Allan A. Ryan, *Yamashita's Ghost: War Crimes, MacArthur's Justice, and Command Accountability* (Lawrence: University Press of Kansas, 2012), pp. 10–11, 17. Roberta Wohlstetter, *Pearl Harbor: Warning and Decision* (Stanford, Calif.: Stanford University Press, 1962), pp. 398–99. Masanobu Tsuji, *Singapore: The Japanese Version,* trans. Margaret E. Lake (Sydney: Ure Smith, 1960), pp. 34–41. John W. Dower, *War Without Mercy: Race and Power in the Pacific War* (New York: Pantheon, 1986), p. 84.

95. Richard Connaughton, John Pimlott, and Duncan Anderson, *The Battle for Manila* (London: Bloomsbury, 1995). James M. Scott, *Rampage: MacArthur, Yamashita, and the Battle of Manila* (New York: W. W. Norton, 2018). Daniel Immerwahr, "The Greater United States," *Diplomatic History,* vol. 40, no. 3 (June 2016), pp. 387–88. Spector, *Eagle Against the Sun,* pp. 523–24.

96. MMA, RG-44a, box 2, Fellers memorandum, 2 May 1945.

97. MMA, RG-5, MacArthur to Marshall, 5 September 1945.

98. MMA, RG-9, box 159, War Crimes folder, army regulations, 24 September 1945.

99. MacArthur, *Reminiscences,* p. 296.

100. Ryan, *Yamashita's Ghost,* pp. 61–64.

101. Reel, *Case of General Yamashita,* p. 13.

102. D. Clayton James, *The Years of MacArthur: Triumph and Disaster, 1945–1964* (Boston: Houghton Mifflin, 1985), vol. 3, p. 94.

103. MMA, RG-9, box 159, War Crimes folder, MacArthur to Osmena, 9 October 1945.

MMA, RG-9, box 159, War Crimes folder, Montelibano to MacArthur, 27 October 1945. MMA, RG-9, box 159, War Crimes folder, Marshall to Whitlock, 27 October 1945.

104. Ryan, *Yamashita's Ghost*, pp. 71–82. George F. Guy, "The Defense of Yamashita," *Wyoming Law Journal*, vol. 4 (1950), pp. 153–58.

105. Ryan, *Yamashita's Ghost*, pp. 75–89. Guy, "Defense of Yamashita," pp. 162–63.

106. Ryan, *Yamashita's Ghost*, pp. 115–19, 122, 154.

107. Robert Trumbull, "Girl, 11, Stirs Yamashita Hearing by Story of Stabs, Parents' Slaying," *New York Times*, 6 November 1945, pp. A1, A5.

108. Ryan, *Yamashita's Ghost*, pp. 75–89, 172–73. Guy, "Defense of Yamashita," pp. 165–66.

109. Reel, *Case of General Yamashita*, pp. 12–26. Ryan, *Yamashita's Ghost*, pp. 205–12.

110. Ryan, *Yamashita's Ghost*, p. 241.

111. Ryan, *Yamashita's Ghost*, p. 222.

112. Robert Trumbull, "Yamashita Trial Sets Precedents," *New York Times*, 11 November 1945, p. E5.

113. Guy, "Defense of Yamashita," p. 158.

114. Ryan, *Yamashita's Ghost*, p. 249.

115. "'Yamashita Will Die,'" *Newsweek*, 17 December 1945, p. 51. Robert Trumbull, "Yamashita Is Found Guilty," *New York Times*, 7 December 1945, pp. 1, 3.

116. MMA, RG-9, box 159, War Crimes folder, Marshall to Whitlock, 14 November 1945.

117. Guy, "Defense of Yamashita," p. 172.

118. MMA, RG-9, box 159, War Crimes folder, Judge Advocate General to MacArthur, 9 December 1945. MMA, RG-9, box 159, War Crimes folder, MacArthur to Manila command, 8 December 1945. Reel, *Case of General Yamashita*, pp. 210–13. Ryan, *Yamashita's Ghost*, pp. 273–76.

119. Felix Frankfurter, *The Public and Its Government* (New Haven: Yale University Press, 1930), pp. 46–48.

120. Alpheus Thomas Mason, *Harlan Fiske Stone: Pillar of the Law* (New York: Viking, 1956), p. 651.

121. *Ex parte Quirin*, 317 U.S. 1 (1942).

122. MMA, RG-9, box 159, War Crimes folder, Judge Advocate General to MacArthur, 22 December 1945. Reel, *Case of General Yamashita*, pp. 210–13. Ryan, *Yamashita's Ghost*, pp. 273–76.

123. Reel, *Case of General Yamashita*, pp. 210–14.

124. *In re Yamashita*, 327 U.S. 1, 11–13, 23 (1946).

125. *In re Yamashita*, 327 U.S. 1, 15–17 (1946).

126. John M. Ferren, *Salt of the Earth, Conscience of the Court: The Story of Justice Wiley Rutledge* (Chapel Hill: University of North Carolina Press, 2004), pp. 304–5.

127. Ferren, *Salt of the Earth*, p. 303.

128. Geneva Convention Relative to the Treatment of Prisoners of War, July 27, 1929, Art. 63, 47 Stat. 2021, T.I.A.S. no. 846, 27 *A.J.I.L.* Supp. 59.

129. *In re Yamashita*, 327 U.S. 1, 41–82 (1946). Mason, *Harlan Fiske Stone*, p. 667.

130. Ferren, *Salt of the Earth*, p. 320. See Edward S. Corwin, *Total War and the Constitution* (New York: Alfred A. Knopf, 1947), p. 121.

131. J. Woodford Howard Jr., *Mr. Justice Murphy: A Political Biography* (Princeton: Princeton University Press, 1968), pp. 370–72.

132. *In re Yamashita*, 327 U.S. 1, 26–41 (1946).

133. MMA, RG-9, box 159, War Crimes folder, MacArthur to Styer, 5 February 1946.

134. Ryan, *Yamashita's Ghost,* pp. 265, 282.

135. MMA, RG-9, box 159, War Crimes folder, MacArthur to Styer, 9 February 1946. HSTL, OF, box 1144, Connelly to Wyzanski, 21 February 1946. Reel, *Case of General Yamashita,* pp. 237–39.

136. Guy, "Defense of Yamashita," p. 179. Reel, *Case of General Yamashita,* p. 239. "Yamashita Hanged Near Los Banos Where Americans Were Tortured," *New York Times,* 23 February 1946, pp. 1, 4.

137. *Homma v. Patterson, Secretary of War, et al.* and *Homma v. Styer, Commanding General, et al.,* 327 U.S. 757, 759–61 (1946).

138. "Homma Executed by Firing Squad as Punishment for 'Death March,'" *New York Times,* 3 April 1946, pp. 1, 10. Max Hastings, *Retribution: The Battle for Japan, 1944–45* (New York: Alfred A. Knopf, 2008), pp. 546–47.

139. Guénaël Mettraux, *The Law of Command Responsibility* (Oxford: Oxford University Press, 2009), pp. 5–8.

140. MMA, RG-9, box 159, War Crimes folder, Marshall to MacArthur, 7 October 1945. MMA, RG-9, box 159, War Crimes folder, MacArthur to Marshall, 7 October 1945.

141. MMA, RG-9, box 159, War Crimes folder, Marshall to Sutherland, 8 October 1945.

142. NARA, RG 84, Tokyo political adviser papers, box 2, Atcheson to MacArthur, 6 November 1945.

143. NARA, RG 84, Tokyo political adviser papers, box 2, Marshall to Atcheson, 7 November 1945.

144. NARA, RG 84, Tokyo political adviser papers, box 2, Allen to Imperial Japanese Government, 16, 20, 21, 23 November 1945. NARA, RG 84, Tokyo political adviser papers, box 2, Atcheson to Byrnes, 11 December 1945.

145. MMA, RG-9, box 159, War Crimes folder, MacArthur to Whitlock, 12 November 1945.

146. MMA, RG-9, box 159, War Crimes folder, Joint Chiefs to MacArthur, 25 April 1946. NAI, EAD file no. 27-W/46, Bevin to Halifax, 4 January 1946.

147. AWM, Webb papers, 3DRL/2481, series 1, wallet 1, U.S. Eighth Army, rules of procedure, 5 February 1946. See MMA, RG-9, box 159, War Crimes folder, Carpenter to Royall, 9 November 1948.

148. Kyodo-AP, "5 Japanese Given Supreme Penalty," *Nippon Times,* 2 March 1946, p. 1.

149. Kyodo-AP, "Thought Police Head Sentenced to Death," *Nippon Times,* 14 March 1946, p. 1.

150. Kyodo-AP, "Beheading U.S. Flier Enacted at Tribunal," *Nippon Times,* 11 April 1946, p. 1.

151. NARA, RG 84, Tokyo political adviser papers, box 2, Atcheson to MacArthur, 12 November 1945. NARA, RG 84, Tokyo political adviser papers, box 2, "Major Japanese War Criminals," first list, 12 November 1945. NARA, RG 84, Tokyo political adviser papers, box 2, Atcheson to Byrnes, 13 November 1945. NARA, RG 84, Tokyo political adviser papers, box 2, Atcheson to MacArthur, 14 November 1945.

152. NARA, RG 84, Tokyo political adviser papers, box 2, "Major War Criminals," second list, 14 November 1945; third list, 27 November 1945; fourth list, 27 November 1945. NARA, RG 84, Tokyo political adviser papers, box 2, Allen to Imperial Japanese Government, 17 November 1945. "Arrest of 11 Chiefs Ordered in Japan," *New York Times,* 19 November 1945, p. 2.

153. "Honjo Kills Himself, Balks Tokyo Arrest," *New York Times,* 20 November 1945, p. 1. "Araki and Kuzuu Put in Tokyo Jail," *New York Times,* 23 November 1945, p. 3.

154. Robert H. Jackson, *The Case Against the Nazi War Criminals: Opening Statement for the United States of America* (New York: Alfred A. Knopf, 1946), p. xi.

155. Jackson, *Case Against the Nazi War Criminals,* p. 90.

156. *Kido Diary,* 6 November 1945, p. 463.

157. Bix, *Hirohito,* p. 552. *Kido Diary,* 23 October 1945, p. 461.

158. NARA, RG 84, Tokyo political adviser papers, box 2, Atcheson to MacArthur, 14 November 1945.

159. Konoe memorial, 14 February 1945, John W. Dower, *Empire and Aftermath: Yoshida Shigeru and the Japanese Experience, 1878–1954* (Cambridge, Mass.: Harvard University Press, 1988), pp. 260–64. MMA, RG-9, box 159, War Crimes folder, *New York Herald Tribune* editorial, 31 October 1945, in Byrnes to Atcheson, 3 November 1945.

160. MMA, RG-9, box 159, War Crimes folder, Joint Chiefs to MacArthur, 30 November 1945. See NARA, RG 218, box 8, Leahy files, Joint Chiefs to MacArthur, 29 November 1945.

161. NARA, RG 84, Tokyo political adviser 1945, box 2, Allen to Imperial Japanese Government, 1 December 1945.

162. Hardacre, *Shinto,* p. 452.

163. "Imperial Prince Gives Up in Japan," *New York Times,* 13 December 1945, p. 19. Herbert P. Bix, "The Showa Emperor's 'Monologue' and the Problem of War Responsibility," *Journal of Japanese Studies,* vol. 18, no. 2 (Summer 1992), p. 318. Oka, *Konoe Fumimaro,* p. 189.

164. *Kido Diary,* 18 October 1945, p. 460.

165. *Kido Diary,* 29 November, 2 December 1945, p. 465.

166. NARA, RG 84, Tokyo political adviser 1945, box 2, Allen to Imperial Japanese Government, 6 December 1945.

167. *Kido Diary,* 4–6 December 1945, pp. 465–66.

168. Kido Koichi, *Kido Koichi nikki: Tokyo saiban-ki* [Kido Koichi Diary: The Tokyo Trial Period] (Tokyo: University of Tokyo Press, 1980), pp. 450–51.

169. Arnold C. Brackman, *The Other Nuremberg: The Untold Story of the Tokyo War Crime Trials* (London: Collins, 1989), p. 55.

170. *IMTFE Transcripts,* 14 October 1947, pp. 30716–18.

171. Frank White, "Tojo on Trial," *Far East Stars and Stripes Weekly Review,* 2 November 1947, p. 6.

172. NARA, RG 84, Tokyo political adviser 1945, box 2, Atcheson to Byrnes, 18 December 1945.

173. *Kido Diary,* 15 October 1941, pp. 312–13.

174. Oka, *Konoe Fumimaro,* pp. 181–94.

175. NARA, RG 84, Tokyo political adviser 1945, box 2, Atcheson to Byrnes, 18 December 1945.

176. Oka, *Konoe Fumimaro,* pp. 194–97.

177. NARA, RG 84, Tokyo political adviser 1945, box 10, folder 711.6, Atcheson to Byrnes, 7 January 1946, attached Konoe note, n.d. (16 December 1945).

178. MMA, RG-9, box 159, War Crimes folder, MacArthur to Marshall, 7 October 1945.

179. Jackson, *Case Against the Nazi War Criminals,* pp. x–xi. MMA, RG-9, box 159, War Crimes folder, Patterson to MacArthur, 18 November 1945.

180. MMA, RG-9, box 159, War Crimes folder, Marshall to MacArthur, 11 October 1945. See NARA, RG 218, Leahy papers, box 8, MacArthur correspondence file, Marshall to MacArthur, 2 November 1945.

181. MMA, RG-9, box 159, War Crimes folder, McCloy to Cutter, 25 October 1945.

182. MMA, RG-9, box 159, War Crimes folder, MacArthur to Marshall, 31 October 1945.

183. MMA, RG-9, box 159, War Crimes folder, War Department to MacArthur, 22 September 1945.

184. MMA, RG-9, box 159, War Crimes folder, Byrnes to MacArthur, 25 October 1945.

185. MMA, RG-10, box 21, Fellers correspondence, Fellers to MacArthur, 27 October 1945.

186. MMA, RG-9, box 159, War Crimes folder, MacArthur to Marshall, 31 October 1945.

187. HSTL, OF, box 1145, McGrath to Truman, 23 November 1945. HSTL, OF, box 1144, Clark to Truman, 29 October 1945. HSTL, OF, box 1145, Latta to McGrath, 29 November 1945. HSTL, OF, box 1145, Truman executive order, 29 November 1945. HSTL, OF, box 1145, Truman to Keenan, 18 July 1946.

188. "The Prosecution Rests," *Time,* 3 February 1947, p. 25.

189. BNA, FO 371/69834, Gascoigne to Bevin, 1 December 1948.

190. See David M. Crowe, "MacArthur, Keenan and the American Quest for Justice at the IMTFE," in Kerstin von Lingen, ed., *Transcultural Justice at the Tokyo Tribunal: The Allied Struggle for Justice, 1946–48* (Leiden: Brill, 2018), pp. 65–83.

191. MMA, RG-9, box 159, War Crimes folder, Patterson to MacArthur, 2 November 1945.

192. MMA, RG-9, box 159, War Crimes folder, Marshall to MacArthur, 11 November 1945. On these trials, see Sandra Wilson, Robert Cribb, Beatrice Trefault, and Dean Aszkielowicz, *Japanese War Criminals: The Politics of Justice After the Second World War* (New York: Columbia University Press, 2017).

193. MMA, RG-9, box 159, War Crimes folder, MacArthur to Marshall, 12 November 1945.

194. MMA, RG-9, box 159, War Crimes folder, Patterson to MacArthur, 14 November 1945.

195. MMA, RG-9, box 159, War Crimes folder, Patterson to MacArthur, 17 November 1945.

196. MMA, RG-9, box 159, War Crimes folder, MacArthur to Patterson, 17 November 1945.

197. MMA, RG-5, box 2, folder O.C., McCloy to MacArthur, 19 November 1945. His emphasis.

198. MMA, RG-9, box 159, War Crimes folder, MacArthur to Patterson, 17 November 1945. MMA, RG-9, box 159, War Crimes folder, Patterson to MacArthur, 18 November 1945.

199. MMA, RG-5, box 32, folder 1, MacArthur to Keenan, 26 December 1945.

200. MMA, RG-5, box 2, folder 3, official correspondence file, Keenan to MacArthur, 11 March 1946.

201. MMA, RG-5, box 32, Keenan file, Keenan to MacArthur, 3 September 1946.

202. MMA, RG-5, box 63, folder 2, Bunker to MacArthur, 11 October 1947.

203. MMA, RG-9, box 159, War Crimes folder, Keenan to MacArthur, 22 December 1945. MMA, RG-9, box 159, War Crimes folder, MacArthur to Eisenhower, 9 December 1945.

204. MMA, RG-9, box 159, War Crimes folder, Joint Chiefs to MacArthur, 20 December

1945. NARA, RG 218, box 8, Leahy files, Joint Chiefs to MacArthur, 19 December 1945. MMA, RG-9, box 159, War Crimes folder, Keenan to MacArthur, 22 December 1945. MMA, RG-9, box 159, War Crimes folder, MacArthur to Eisenhower, 22 December 1945.

7. *"When the Emperor Violates the Law"*

1. Mei Ruao: 梅汝璈. Guoshiguan, Foreign Ministry files, IMTFE trials 1945–46, Wei to Foreign Ministry, 22 October 1945, 020-010117-0029-0006a. MMA, RG-9, box 159, War Crimes folder, Marshall to MacArthur, 1 October 1945.

2. Guoshiguan, Foreign Ministry files, United Nations War Crimes Commission file, Gu Weijun call, 24 June 1944, 020-010117-0021-0025a.

3. MMA, RG-9, box 159, War Crimes folder, Marshall to MacArthur, 1 October 1945. MMA, RG-9, box 159, War Crimes fiolder, Fair to Marshall, 21 September 1945.

4. Mei Xiaoao interview by author, Beijing, 24 May 2016. Mei Xiaoao and Mei Xiaokan, eds., *Mei Ruao Dongjing shenpan wengao* [The Tokyo Trial Manuscripts of Mei Ruao] (Shanghai: Shanghai Jiaotong University Press, 2013), pp. 1–2. AWM, Webb papers, 3DRL/2481, series 1, wallet 2, judges' biographies, 23 October 1946.

5. Madeline Y. Hsu, *The Good Immigrants: How the Yellow Peril Became the Model Minority* (Princeton: Princeton University Press, 2015). Rana Mitter, *Forgotten Ally: China's World War II, 1937–1945* (Boston: Houghton Mifflin Harcourt, 2013), p. 51. Mae Ngai, *The Chinese Question: The Gold Rushes and Global Politics* (New York: W. W. Norton, 2021).

6. Mei Ruao, *Dongjing da shenpan: Yuandong guoji junshi fating Zhongguo faguan Mei Ruao riji* [The Great Tokyo Trial: Diary of Mei Ruao, Chinese Judge at the International Military Tribunal for the Far East] (Nanchang: Jiangxi Education Press, 2005), 20 March 1945, pp. 27–28; 30 March 1946, p. 47; 10 April 1946, p. 77; 14 April 1946, p. 91; 10 May 1946, p. 150.

7. Mei Xiaokan interview, Beijing, 24 May 2016. Mei and Mei, eds., *Mei Ruao Dongjing shenpan wengao,* p. 2. AWM, Webb papers, 3DRL/2481, series 1, wallet 2, judges' biographies, 23 October 1946.

8. Mei, *Dongjing da shenpan,* 14 April 1946, p. 90.

9. Mei and Mei, eds., *Mei Ruao Dongjing shenpan wengao,* pp. 2–3. Academia Historica (Guoshiguan), Xindian district, New Taipei City, Mei Ruao personnel questionnaire, no. 34138.

10. H. L. A. Hart, "Positivism and the Separation of Law and Morals," *Harvard Law Review,* vol. 71, no. 4 (February 1958), pp. 593–629. Lon L. Fuller, "Positivism and Fidelity to Law—A Reply to Professor Hart," *Harvard Law Review,* vol. 71, no. 4 (February 1958), pp. 630–72.

11. Mencius, "Emperor Hui of Liang Book Two," *The Four Chinese Classics,* trans. David Hinton (Berkeley: Counterpoint, 2013), II.8, p. 415.

12. NARA, RG 43, Far Eastern Commission, box 70, Far Eastern Section press summary, 14 November 1948.

13. Ju-ao Mei (Mei Ruao), "China and the Rule of Law," *Pacific Affairs,* vol. 5, no. 10 (October 1932), pp. 683–72. As was conventional then, he used Wade-Giles romanization.

14. Guoshiguan, "War Criminals," October 1945, 020-010117-0041-0075x.

15. Jay Taylor, *The Generalissimo: Chiang Kai-shek and the Struggle for Modern China* (Cambridge, Mass.: Belknap Press of Harvard University Press, 2009), p. 161.

16. Mitter, *Forgotten Ally*, p. 5.

17. Richard Bernstein, *China 1945: Mao's Revolution and America's Fateful Choice* (New York: Alfred A. Knopf, 2014), pp. 65–66.

18. Guoshiguan, Xindian, Mei Ruao personnel questionnaire, no. 34138.

19. "From Day to Day," *North-China Daily News*, 8 January 1935, p. 6. Guoshiguan, Xindian, Mei Ruao personnel questionnaire, no. 34138. AWM, Webb papers, 3DRL/2481, series 1, wallet 2, judges' biographies, 23 October 1946.

20. Mei Ju-ao (Mei Ruao), "On the Eve of Constitutional Government in China," *T'ien Hsia Monthly*, vol. 2, no. 5 (May 1936), pp. 443–53.

21. Mitter, *Forgotten Ally*, pp. 79–97.

22. Martha Gellhorn, *The Face of War* (New York: Simon & Schuster, 1959), p. 76.

23. Mitter, *Forgotten Ally*, p. 87. Erwin Wickert, ed., *The Good Man of Nanking: The Diaries of John Rabe*, trans. John E. Woods (New York: Alfred A. Knopf, 1998), p. 18.

24. Barbara W. Tuchman, *Stilwell and the American Experience in China, 1911–45* (New York: Grove, 1985), p. 169. Mitter, *Forgotten Ally*, pp. 98–108.

25. W. H. Auden and Christopher Isherwood, *Journey to a War* (New York: Paragon House, 1990), p. 240.

26. Mitter, *Forgotten Ally*, pp. 126–33. *Diaries of John Rabe*, 10 December 1937, pp. 57, 59.

27. For a powerful argument that soldiers should not always be legitimate targets, see Gabriella Blum, "The Dispensable Lives of Soldiers," *Journal of Legal Analysis*, vol. 2, no. 1 (Spring 2010), pp. 115–70. The 1907 Hague Convention IV makes it forbidden "[t]o kill or wound an enemy who, having laid down his arms, or having no longer means of defence, has surrendered at discretion" (Hague Convention [No. IV] Respecting the Laws and Customs of War on Land, Oct. 18, 1907, Art. 23, 36 Stat. 2277, T.I.A.S. 539). The crucial Common Article 3 of the 1949 Geneva Conventions, for non-international armed conflicts, mandates humane treatment for "[p]ersons taking no active part in the hostilities, including members of armed forces who have laid down their arms and those placed hors de combat by sickness, wounds, detention, or any other cause" (Geneva Convention for the Amelioration of the Condition of the Wounded and Sick in Armed Forces in the Field, Aug. 12, 1949, Art. 3, 75 U.N.T.S. 31; Geneva Convention Relative to the Treatment of Prisoners of War, Aug. 12, 1949, Art. 3, 75 U.N.T.S. 135). The importance of Common Article 3—fundamental principles at the heart of the laws of war—gives additional weight to those provisions, widely seen as applying to all armed conflicts. As the 1952 commentary to the Geneva Convention by the International Committee of the Red Cross notes, "It is only the soldier who is himself seeking to kill who may be killed. The abandonment of all aggressiveness should put an end to aggression" (Blum, "Dispensable Lives of Soldiers," p. 126). Ryan Goodman musters a powerful legal argument that soldiers should not be killed when it is unnecessary and that recent international law gives considerable support to the principle that defenseless soldiers should be considered hors de combat ("The Power to Kill or Capture Enemy Combatants," *European Journal of International Law*, vol. 24, no. 3 [2013], pp. 819–53).

28. Mark Eykholt, "Aggression, Victimization, and Chinese Historiography of the Nanjing Massacre," in Joshua A. Fogel, ed., *The Nanjing Massacre in History and Historiography* (Berkeley: University of California Press, 2000), pp. 11–69. See Yuki Tanaka, *Hidden Horrors: Japanese War Crimes in World War II* (Boulder, Colo.: Westview, 1996).

29. *Diaries of John Rabe,* 13 December 1937, pp. 66–67; 15 December 1937, p. 71; 16 December 1937, p. 75; 24 December 1937, p. 92.

30. *Diaries of John Rabe,* 17 December 1937, p. 77; 31 January 1938, pp. 165–66.

31. Central News Agency, "Rikou zai Nanjing shouxing" [Japanese Bandits' Savage Actions in Nanjing], *Xinhua Ribao [Xinhua Daily],* 9 March 1938, p. 2. See Central News Agency, "Rikou zai Nanjing shouxing" [Japanese Bandits' Savage Actions in Nanjing], *Xinhua Ribao [Xinhua Daily],* 11 March 1938, p. 4.

32. *Diaries of John Rabe,* 6 February 1938, p. 178; 21 December 1937, p. 85; 2 February 1938, p. 170.

33. Mitter, *Forgotten Ally,* pp. 124–44. Eykholt, "Aggression, Victimization, and Chinese Historiography of the Nanjing Massacre," pp. 11–69.

34. Sarah Kovner, *Prisoners of the Empire: Inside Japanese POW Camps* (Cambridge, Mass.: Harvard University Press, 2020), pp. 210–11.

35. Bernstein, *China 1945,* p. 78.

36. Jeremy A. Yellen, *The Greater East Asia Co-Prosperity Sphere: When Total Empire Met Total War* (Ithaca, N.Y.: Cornell University Press, 2019), pp. 2–3.

37. Herbert P. Bix, *Hirohito and the Making of Modern Japan* (New York: HarperCollins, 2000), pp. 365–67. Taylor, *Generalissimo,* p. 173.

38. *President Chiang Kai-shek's Selected Speeches and Messages, 1937–1945* (Taipei: China Cultural Service, 1945), 13 August 1938 speech, p. 65. *Chiang Kai-shek's Selected Speeches and Messages, 1937–1945,* 13 August 1940 speech, p. 143.

39. Chinese Ministry of Information, *The Collected Wartime Messages of Generalissimo Chiang Kai-shek, 1937–1945* (New York: John Day, 1946), vol. 2, 9 October 1937 speech, p. 45.

40. Diana Lary, *The Chinese People at War: Human Suffering and Social Transformation, 1937–1945* (Cambridge: Cambridge University Press, 2010).

41. Mitter, *Forgotten Ally,* pp. 157–64. Taylor, *Generalissimo,* pp. 154–55.

42. Theodore H. White and Annalee Jacoby, *Thunder Out of China* (New York: William Sloane Associates, 1946), pp. 169–72.

43. Mitter, *Forgotten Ally,* pp. 263–74.

44. Alan Brinkley, *The Publisher: Henry Luce and His American Century* (New York: Alfred A. Knopf, 2010), pp. 3–25, 282. "Chiang Kai-shek . . . and His Real Enemy, Japan," *Life,* 28 December 1936, pp. 54–55.

45. T. Christopher Jespersen, *American Images of China, 1931–1949* (Stanford, Calif.: Stanford University Press, 1996), pp. 77–78.

46. Auden and Isherwood, *Journey to a War,* p. 253.

47. Mei, *Dongjing da shenpan,* 20 March 1946, p. 30.

48. White and Jacoby, *Thunder Out of China,* pp. 11–16. Mitter, *Forgotten Ally,* pp. 1–5, 176–78, 259–60. Hans van de Ven, *China at War: Triumph and Tragedy in the Emergence of the New China* (Cambridge, Mass.: Harvard University Press, 2018), pp. 123–26. Edna Tow, "The Great Bombing of Chongqing and the Anti-Japanese War, 1937–1945," in Mark Peattie, Edward Drea, and Hans van de Ven, eds., *The Battle for China: Essays on the Military History of the Sino-Japanese War of 1937–1945* (Stanford, Calif.: Stanford University Press, 2011), pp. 256–57.

49. White and Jacoby, *Thunder Out of China,* pp. 14–16.

50. "How to Tell Japs from the Chinese," *Life,* 22 December 1941, pp. 81–82.

51. HSTL, PSF, box 151, Elsey memo for Truman, 3 September 1945.

52. Mitter, *Forgotten Ally*, p. 6. Taylor, *Generalissimo*, p. 189.

53. Fredrik Logevall, *Embers of War: The Fall of an Empire and the Making of America's Vietnam* (New York: Random House, 2012), pp. 53–54. Rana Mitter, "An Uneasy Engagement," in Rosemary Foot, John Gaddis, and Andrew Hurrell, eds., *Order and Justice in International Relations* (Oxford: Oxford University Press, 2003), pp. 207–35. Liu Xiaoyuan, *A Partnership for Disorder: China, the United States and Their Policies for the Postwar Disposition of the Japanese Empire, 1941–1945* (Cambridge: Cambridge University Press, 1996).

54. HSTL, NAP, box 12, Hopkins-Stalin Conference, Hopkins-Stalin memcon, 28 May 1945, 8 p.m.

55. Mitter, *Forgotten Ally*, p. 298.

56. Mitter, *Forgotten Ally*, pp. 306–11. Cordell Hull, *The Memoirs of Cordell Hull* (New York: Macmillan, 1948), vol. 2, pp. 1583–84.

57. Gordon H. Chang, "China and the Pursuit of America's Destiny," *Journal of Asian American Studies*, vol. 15, no. 2 (June 2012), pp. 145–69.

58. Mitter, *Forgotten Ally*, pp. 306–11.

59. *Chiang Kai-shek's Selected Speeches and Messages, 1937–1945*, 1 January 1944, pp. 234–35. Hull, *Memoirs*, vol. 2, pp. 1583–84. Taylor, *Generalissimo*, pp. 247–49, 254.

60. *Chiang Kai-shek's Selected Speeches and Messages, 1937–1945*, 1 January 1944, pp. 233–34.

61. Chiang Kai-shek, *China's Destiny and Chinese Economic Theory*, ed. Philip Jaffe (London: Dennis Dobson, 1947), p. 142. Chiang Kai-shek, *Before Final Victory: Speeches by Generalissimo Chiang Kai-shek, 1943–1944* (New York: Chinese News Service, 1944), 26 February 1943 speech, pp. 13–15.

62. Srinath Raghavan, *India's War: World War II and the Making of Modern South Asia* (New York: Basic Books, 2016), pp. 1–6, 12, 20–22, 209, 224, 227, 270–72. Mitter, *Forgotten Ally*, pp. 246–49.

63. Taylor, *Generalissimo*, pp. 195–96.

64. Mitter, *Forgotten Ally*, pp. 318–19.

65. Richard B. Frank, *Downfall: The End of the Imperial Japanese Empire* (New York: Random House, 1999), pp. 163, 359.

66. Odd Arne Westad, *Decisive Encounters: The Chinese Civil War, 1946–1950* (Stanford, Calif.: Stanford University Press, 2003).

67. Chiang Kai-shek, *Declaration to Kuomintang Members, April 1927* (Shanghai: Commercial Press, 1927), pp. 7–8, 11.

68. Chiang Kai-shek, "The Cause and Cure of Rural Decadence," 14 June 1935, in Chiang Kai-shek and Wang Ching-wei, *China's Leaders and Their Policies: Messages to the Chinese People* (Shanghai: China United Press, 1935), pp. 35–36.

69. *Chiang Kai-shek's Selected Speeches and Messages, 1937–1945*, 6 March 1941 speech, pp. 179–88. Taylor, *Generalissimo*, pp. 169–70.

70. Taylor, *Generalissimo*, p. 171.

71. Mitter, *Forgotten Ally*, pp. 188–89, 194–95.

72. Zhu De, *Zhu De xuanji* [Selected Works of Zhu De] (Beijing: People's Publishing House, 1983).

73. Central News Agency, "Dijun baoxing yiban" [A Glimpse into the Enemy's Atrocities], *Xinhua Ribao* [*Xinhua Daily*], 27 January 1938, p. 2. Central News Agency, "Kongbu de Nanjing cheng" [Terrifying Nanjing City], *Xinhua Ribao* [*Xinhua Daily*], 23 January 1938, p. 2.

74. Popular Press, "Sharen jingsai" [Killing Competition], *Xinhua Ribao [Xinhua Daily]*, 25 January 1938, p. 2. See Barak Kushner, *Men to Devils, Devils to Men: Japanese War Crimes and Chinese Justice* (Cambridge, Mass.: Harvard University Press, 2015), pp. 166–74. Kushner's book is a landmark study on Nationalist postwar policy. Daqing Yang, "Convergence or Divergence?," *American Historical Review,* vol. 104, no. 3 (June 1999), p. 844.

75. Zhu De and Peng Dehuai, "Dijun baoxing" [The Enemy's Atrocities], *Xinhua Ribao [Xinhua Daily]*, 14 March 1938, p. 2.

76. Peng Dehuai, *Memoirs of a Chinese Marshal*, trans. Zheng Longpu (Beijing: Foreign Languages Press, 1981), pp. 416–20.

77. Mitter, *Forgotten Ally*, pp. 188–89, 194–95.

78. Taylor, *Generalissimo*, p. 241.

79. Bernstein, *China 1945*, p. 38.

80. Westad, *Decisive Encounters*, pp. 8–9.

81. Brinkley, *Publisher*, pp. 293–300.

82. Auden and Isherwood, *Journey to a War*, p. 8.

83. Gellhorn, *Face of War*, pp. 76–77.

84. Sun Yat-sen, *The Three Principles of the People*, trans. Frank W. Price (Taipei: China Publishing, 1927), p. 58. Elizabeth J. Perry, "Chinese Conceptions of 'Rights': From Mencius to Mao—and Now," *Perspectives on Politics*, vol. 6, no. 1 (March 2008), pp. 37–50.

85. Guoshiguan, Judicial Yuan files, Mei speech, "Understanding of the May 5 Draft Constitution," April 1944, 015-020100-0005-0001a to 015-020100-0005-0018x.

86. Chiang, *China's Destiny*, pp. 100, 209–10.

87. Andrew J. Nathan, *Chinese Democracy* (New York: Alfred A. Knopf, 1985), pp. 67, 110, 132.

88. Mei, "On the Eve of Constitutional Government in China," *T'ien Hsia Monthly*, vol. 2, no. 5 (May 1936), p. 443.

89. Guoshiguan, Judicial Yuan files, Mei speech, "Understanding of the May 5 Draft Constitution," April 1944, 015-020100-0005-0001a to 015-020100-0005-0018x. The phrase is a popularization of a line by Robert Lowe in a British parliamentary debate over education in 1867 (David William Sylvester, *Robert Lowe and Education* [Cambridge: Cambridge University Press, 2011], p. 118).

90. Westad, *Decisive Encounters*, pp. 7, 28–32. Taylor, *Generalissimo*, pp. 307–8. *Chiang Kai-shek's Selected Speeches and Messages, 1937–1945*, 3 September 1945 speech, pp. 271–79.

91. *Chiang Kai-shek's Selected Speeches and Messages, 1937–1945*, 7 July 1940, p. 127.

92. *Chiang Kai-shek's Selected Speeches and Messages, 1937–1945*, 1 January 1944, p. 235.

93. Guoshiguan, Foreign Ministry files, war criminals file 1945–46, arrest and trial guideline, n.d., 020-010117-0041-0009x to 020-010117-0041-0016x. Guoshiguan, Foreign Ministry files, war criminals file 1945–46, code of conduct for trying war criminals, n.d., 020-010117-0041-0024x to 020-010117-0041-0026x. Guoshiguan, Foreign Ministry files, war criminals file 1945–46, War Criminals, n.d., 020-010117-0041-0075x to 020-010117-0041-0114x. Guoshiguan, Foreign Ministry files, war criminals file 1945–46, Detailed Rules Regarding How to Try War Criminals, n.d., 020-010117-0041-0199x to 020-010117-0041-0200a.

94. Kushner, *Men to Devils*, pp. 159–64.

95. Yang, "Convergence or Divergence?," p. 844.

96. Guoshiguan, Foreign Ministry files, war criminals file 1945–46, War Criminals, n.d., 020-010117-0041-0075x to 020-010117-0041-0114x. Guoshiguan, Foreign Ministry files, war criminals file 1945–46, martial law bureau note, 5 July 1946, 020-010117-0041-0171x. Guoshiguan, Foreign Ministry files, war criminals file 1945–46, Revised Proposal for Ways to Try War Criminals, n.d., 020-010117-0041-0209x to 020-010117-0041-0215a.

97. Kushner, *Men to Devils*, pp. 8–9, 29–30. As Kushner notes, the totals do not always add up, so these numbers are an approximation of cases in several places.

98. Katie Stallard, *Dancing on Bones: History and Power in China, Russia and North Korea* (Oxford: Oxford University Press, 2022), p. 25.

99. Kushner, *Men to Devils*, pp. 95–99.

100. Zhu De, "Lun fangri youji zhanzheng" [On Anti-Japanese Guerrilla Warfare], *Zhu De xuanji*, pp. 49–50.

101. Peng, *Memoirs of a Chinese Marshal*, pp. 407–8.

102. Stuart R. Schram, ed., *Mao's Road to Power: Revolutionary Writings, 1912–1949* (Armonk, N.Y.: M. E. Sharpe, 1992), vol. 6, p. 369. See Michael Walzer, *Just and Unjust Wars: A Moral Argument with Historical Illustrations* (New York: Basic Books, 1977), pp. 225–26.

103. Zhu De and Peng Dehuai, "Di jiang fang dujun tusha wo minzhong" [The Enemy Will Release Poisonous Bacteria to Massacre Our Civilians], *Xinhua Ribao [Xinhua Daily]*, 29 March 1938, p. 2. MMA, RG-9, box 159, War Crimes, Myers to War Department, 6 May 1947.

104. Mao Zedong, "Yi ziligengsheng weizhu tongshi bufangsong zhengqu waiyuan" [Rely Mainly on Our Own Efforts and Simultaneously Do Not Relax Pursuit of External Assistance], *Mao Zedong waijiao wenxuan* [Selected Works of Mao Zedong on Diplomacy] (Beijing: Zhongyang Wenxian Publishing House, 1994), p. 15.

105. Mao Zedong, "Lun lianhe zhengfu" [On Coalition Government], 24 April 1945, *Mao Zedong xuanji* [Selected Works of Mao Zedong] (Beijing: People's Publishing House, 1991), pp. 1029–100. Peng, *Memoirs of a Chinese Marshal*, pp. 422–23.

106. *Zhou Enlai nian pu, 1898–1949* [Chronicle of Zhou Enlai, 1898–1949] (Beijing: Zhongyang Wenxian Publishing House, 1989), p. 578.

107. Roderick MacFarquhar, *The Origins of the Cultural Revolution: The Great Leap Forward, 1958–1960* (New York: Columbia University Press, 1983), vol. 2, pp. 193–223. Roderick MacFarquhar, *The Origins of the Cultural Revolution: The Coming of the Cataclysm, 1961–1966* (New York: Columbia University Press), vol. 3, pp. 5, 14–16, 148, 163–64. Lu Yi, "Peng Dehuai tan qianxian qingkuang" [Peng Dehuai Discusses the Current Situation at the Front Line], *Xinhua Ribao [Xinhua Daily]*, 20 January 1938, p. 2. As is often the case in Maoist agitprop, it is not clear whether these words are from Peng Dehuai or the *Xinhua* writer.

108. "Yancheng zhanzheng zuifan" [Seriously Punish War Criminals], *Xinhua Ribao [Xinhua Daily]*, 5 November 1943, p. 2.

109. "Dui dongfang de zhanzhengfan zenme ban" [How Should War Criminals in the East Be Dealt With], *Xinhua Ribao [Xinhua Daily]*, 4 June 1945, p. 2.

110. Lin, "Riben de zhanzheng zuifan (1)" [Japan's War Criminals (1)], *Xinhua Ribao [Xinhua Daily]*, 14 August 1945, p. 3. Lin, "Riben de zhanzheng zuifan (2)" [Japan's War Criminals (2)], *Xinhua Ribao [Xinhua Daily]*, 16 August 1945, p. 3.

111. "Zhanling le Riben yihou" [After Japan Is Occupied], *Xinhua Ribao [Xinhua Daily]*, 1 September 1945, p. 2.

112. Lin, "Riben de zhanzheng zuifan (1)" [Japan's War Criminals (1)], *Xinhua Ribao [Xinhua Daily]*, 14 August 1945, p. 3. See Mao Zedong, "Dui Nanjing maiguo zhengfu shifang Riben qinhua zhanfan Zhonggong zhongyang fabiao yanzheng shengming" [CCP Central Committee Issues a Formal Statement About the Traitorous Nanjing Government's Release of Japanese War Criminals], *Renmin Ribao [People's Daily]*, 6 February 1949, p. 1.

113. Tobias S. Harris, *The Iconoclast: Shinzo Abe and the New Japan* (London: Hurst, 2020), p. 11.

114. "Riben de caifa junxu zibenjia—tamen doushi ying shou chengban de zhanzheng zuifan" [Japanese *Zaibatsus* and Military Supply Capitalists—All of Them Are War Criminals Who Deserve to Be Punished], *Xinhua Ribao [Xinhua Daily]*, 21 September 1945, p. 3.

115. "Zai lun guanzhi riben—Riben minzhuhua de tujing" [Talk Again About Control over Japan—Pathway to Japan's Democratization], *Xinhua Ribao [Xinhua Daily]*, 21 September 1945, p. 2.

116. "Daibu zhanfan yu guanzhi Riben" [The Arrest of War Criminals and Control over Japan], *Xinhua Ribao [Xinhua Daily]*, 15 September 1945, p. 2.

117. Guoshiguan, Foreign Ministry files, IMTFE trials 1945–46, Ministry of Military Command to Foreign Ministry, 3 November 1945, 020-010117-0029-0026x. Guoshiguan, Foreign Ministry files, IMTFE trials 1945–46, Ministry of Military Command to Foreign Ministry, 4 November 1945, 020-010117-0029-0027x to 020-010117-0029-0028x. Guoshiguan, Foreign Ministry files, IMTFE trials 1945–46, Lu profile, 1945, 020-010117-0029-0029a.

118. Guoshiguan, Foreign Ministry files, IMTFE trials 1945–46, Ministry of Military Command to Foreign Ministry, 12 February 1946, 020-010117-0029-0032x.

119. Guoshiguan, Foreign Ministry files, IMTFE trials 1945–46, Foreign Ministry to Ministry of Military Command, 15 February 1945, 020-010117-0029-0034x to 020-010117-0029-0035x. Guoshiguan, Foreign Ministry files, IMTFE trials 1945–46, Foreign Ministry to Wei, 15 February 1945, 020-010117-0029-0036x. Guoshiguan, Foreign Ministry files, IMTFE trials 1945–46, Ministry of Judicial Administration to Foreign Ministry, 15 November 1945, 020-010117-0029-0045x to 020-010117-0029-0046x.

120. Guoshiguan, Foreign Ministry files, IMTFE trials 1945–46, Wei memo, 22 December 1945, 020-010117-0029-0117a to 020-010117-0029-0118a. "Hsiang Che-chun (LL.B. 1925)," *GW Law International and Comparative Law Perspectives* (Autumn 2009), pp. 6–7. "Yale Forms Polity Federation," *Harvard Crimson*, 14 May 1914. Guoshiguan, Foreign Ministry files, IMTFE trials 1945–46, Xiang to Wang and Xie, December 1945 or January 1946, 020-010117-0029-0121a. Guoshiguan, Foreign Ministry files, IMTFE trials 1945–46, Wang to Wei, 3 January 1946, 020-010117-0029-0123x.

121. Guoshiguan, Foreign Ministry files, IMTFE trials 1945–46, Foreign Ministry to Ministry of Military Command, 15 February 1945, 020-010117-0029-0034x to 020-010117-0029-0035x. Guoshiguan, Foreign Ministry files, IMTFE trials 1945–46, Foreign Ministry to Wei, 15 February 1945, 020-010117-0029-0036x. Guoshiguan, Foreign Ministry files, IMTFE trials 1945–46, Ministry of Judicial

Administration to Foreign Ministry, 15 November 1945, 020-010117-0029-0045x to 020-010117-0029-0046x.

122. Guoshiguan, Foreign Ministry files, IMTFE trials 1945–46, Luo to Wu, January 1946, 020-010117-0029-0134a. Guoshiguan, Foreign Ministry files, IMTFE trials 1945–46, Lin Dingping to Foreign Ministry, n.d., 020-010117-0029-0069a.

123. Guoshiguan, Foreign Ministry files, IMTFE trials 1945–46, Foreign Ministry to Chiang Kai-shek, 29 November 1945, 020-010117-0029-0072x to 020-010117-0029-0073x; Foreign Ministry to Ministry of Judicial Administration and Ministry of Military Command, 18 December 1945, 020-010117-0029-0088x to 020-010117-0029-0089x; Chiang Kai-shek to Wang, 8 December 1945, 020-010117-0029-0094a; Executive Yuan to Foreign Ministry, 1945, 020-010117-0029-0098x; Foreign Ministry to Wei, 8 January 1946, 020-010117-0029-0131x; Guoshiguan, Foreign Ministry files, IMTFE trials 1945–46, Luo to Wu, January 1946, 020-010117-0029-0134a.

124. Wolfgang Saxon, "V. K. Wellington Koo Dies," *New York Times,* 16 November 1985. Guoshiguan, Foreign Ministry files, IMTFE trials 1945–46, Koo to Foreign Ministry, 19 November 1945, 020-010117-0029-0048 to 020-010117-0029-0052a.

125. Guoshiguan, Foreign Ministry files, IMTFE trials 1945–46, Xiang to Wang and Xie, December 1945 or January 1946, 020-010117-0029-0121a. Guoshiguan, Foreign Ministry files, IMTFE trials 1945–46, Wang to Wei, 3 January 1946, 020-010117-0029-0123x. Guoshiguan, Foreign Ministry files, IMTFE trials 1945–46, Chen to vice minister, 8 February 1946, 020-010117-0029-0143a.

126. Guoshiguan, Foreign Ministry files, IMTFE trials 1945–46, Gan to Mei, 29 December 1945, 020-010117-0029-0116x.

127. Mei, *Dongjing da shenpan,* 3 May 1946, p. 130.

128. Guoshiguan, Foreign Ministry files, IMTFE trials 1945–46, Chen to Wang, 16 March 1946, 020-010117-0029-0252a to 020-010117-0029-0253a; Foreign Ministry to Wei, 22 March 1946, 020-010117-0029-0254x; Wei to Foreign Ministry, 4 April 1946, 020-010117-0029-0256a.

129. Mei, *Dongjing da shenpan,* 3 May 1946, p. 130.

8. The God That Failed

1. Odd Arne Westad, *The Cold War: A World History* (New York: Basic Books, 2017), p. 134.

2. Helen Hardacre, *Shinto: A History* (Oxford: Oxford University Press, 2017), p. 449. Donald Keene, *Emperor of Japan: Meiji and His World, 1852–1912* (New York: Columbia University Press, 2002), pp. 138–43.

3. MMA, RG-5, box 2, folder 3, Imperial Rescript, 1 January 1946. Lindesay Parrott, "Hirohito Disclaims Divinity," *New York Times,* 1 January 1946, pp. 1, 15.

4. "Showa tenno no dokuhaku hachijikan" [The Showa Emperor's Eight-Hour Monologue], *Bungei shunju,* December 1990, p. 104. John W. Dower, *Embracing Defeat: Japan in the Wake of World War II* (New York: W. W. Norton, 1999), pp. 315–16. Herbert P. Bix, "The Showa Emperor's 'Monologue' and the Problem of War Responsibility," *Journal of Japanese Studies,* vol. 18, no. 2 (Summer 1992), pp. 320–21.

5. Lindesay Parrott, "Japanese Stunned by Hirohito's Move to Abjure Divinity," *New York Times,* 2 January 1946, pp. 1, 3.

6. Helen Hardacre, *Shinto and the State, 1868–1988* (Princeton: Princeton University Press, 1989), pp. 23–26, 90–92.

7. BNA, FO 371/57430, Australian First List of Major Japanese War Criminals, January 1946. Herbert P. Bix, *Hirohito and the Making of Modern Japan* (New York: HarperCollins, 2000), p. 560. Edwin O. Reischauer, *My Life Between Japan and America* (New York: Harper & Row, 1986), p. 107.

8. Hal Brands, "The Emperor's New Clothes," *The Historian*, vol. 68, no. 1 (2006), pp. 9–28.

9. Miyoshi Tatsuji, "Natsukashi Nihon (4)" [Japan in Nostalgia (4)], *Shincho*, vol. 43, no. 6 (June 1946), pp. 50–56.

10. MMA, RG-9, box 160, War Department to MacArthur, 6 September 1945. "Removal and Exclusion of Undesirable Personnel for Public Office," GHQ directive, 4 January 1946, Atcheson to Byrnes, 5 January 1946, *FRUS: The Far East* (Washington, D.C.: U.S. Government Printing Office, 1971), vol. 8, pp. 94–95.

11. Kennan observations, PPS/28/2, 25 March 1948, *The State Department Policy Planning Staff Papers 1948* (New York: Garland, 1983), vol. 2, pp. 227–28.

12. Shigeru Yoshida, *The Yoshida Memoirs: The Story of Japan in Crisis*, trans. Kenichi Yoshida (London: Heinemann, 1961), pp. 147–60.

13. Lindesay Parrott, "M'Arthur Guidance Nearly Complete," *New York Times*, 22 December 1945, p. 1.

14. MMA, RG-5, box 115, folder 15, IMTFE proclamation, 19 January 1946.

15. NARA, RG 84, Tokyo political adviser papers, box 2, Atcheson to Minter, 22 November 1945. NAI, EAD file no. 27-W/46, Pethick-Lawrence to Bajpai, 23 January 1946.

16. NAI, EAD file no. 27-W/46, Bajpai to Wavell, 6 January 1946. MMA, RG-9, box 159, War Crimes folder, Byrnes to Atcheson, 7 January 1946. MMA, RG-9, box 159, War Crimes folder, JAG to Keenan, 27 January 1946.

17. NARA, RG 84, Tokyo political adviser 1945, box 2, Robertson to Atcheson, 6 December 1945. MMA, RG-9, box 159, War Crimes folder, Marshall to MacArthur, 24 November 1945.

18. Guoshiguan, Foreign Ministry files, War Criminals Policies 1946–48, "Record of the War Criminal Handling Committee's Meeting on Policies Regarding How to Deal with War Criminals," 25 October 1946, 020-010117-0039-0017a to 020-010117-0039-0028a.

19. BNA, FO 371/57430, Australian First List of Major Japanese War Criminals, January 1946. MMA, RG-9, box 159, War Crimes folder, Eisenhower to MacArthur, 22 January 1946. NARA, RG 84, Tokyo political adviser papers, box 10, Atcheson to MacArthur, 29 December 1945.

20. BNA, FO 371/57430, Australian First List of Major Japanese War Criminals, January 1946.

21. NARA, RG 84, box 10, Atcheson to MacArthur, 29 December 1945.

22. MMA, RG-9, box 159, War Crimes folder, MacArthur to Eisenhower, 24 January 1946.

23. MMA, RG-9, box 159, War Crimes folder, Eisenhower to MacArthur, 8 February 1946.

24. Brands, "The Emperor's New Clothes," pp. 1–8.

25. "Prince Suggested That Hirohito Quit," *New York Times*, 4 March 1946, p. 6. Bix, *Hirohito*, p. 605.

26. "Hirohito Plans Two More Trips," *New York Times*, 25 March 1946, p. 4.

27. "Showa tenno no dokuhaku hachijikan," p. 98. Bix, *Hirohito*, pp. 2, 589–92.

28. Mariko Terasaki Miller, "On the Discovery of This Record and Its Publication," *Bungei Shunju*, December 1990, pp. 96–97.

29. "Showa tenno no dokuhaku hachijikan," pp. 99–100. Bix, *Hirohito*, pp. 589–92.

30. Bix, *Hirohito*, p. 3.

31. MMA, RG-44a, box 4, folder 23, Terasaki "A" version, 1946.

32. "Showa tenno no dokuhaku hachijikan," p. 124.

33. See Chow Tse-tsung, *The May 4th Movement: Intellectual Revolution in Modern China* (Cambridge, Mass.: Harvard University Press, 1960).

34. "Showa tenno no dokuhaku hachijikan," pp. 100–101.

35. "Showa tenno no dokuhaku hachijikan," p. 104.

36. "Showa tenno no dokuhaku hachijikan," pp. 105–10, 113–14. Charles D. Sheldon, "Japanese Aggression and the Emperor, 1931–1941, from Contemporary Diaries," *Modern Asian Studies*, vol. 10, no. 1 (1976), pp. 27–28.

37. "Showa tenno no dokuhaku hachijikan," pp. 110–14.

38. "Showa tenno no dokuhaku hachijikan," pp. 114–19.

39. "Showa tenno no dokuhaku hachijikan," pp. 114–19.

40. "Showa tenno no dokuhaku hachijikan," pp. 119–29.

41. Daikichi Irokawa, *The Age of Hirohito: In Search of Modern Japan*, trans. Mikiso Hane and John K. Urda (New York: Free Press, 1995).

42. "Showa tenno no dokuhaku hachijikan," pp. 129–38.

43. "Showa tenno no dokuhaku hachijikan," pp. 138–45.

44. Michel Paradis, *Last Mission to Tokyo: The Extraordinary Story of the Doolittle Raiders and Their Final Fight for Justice* (New York: Simon & Schuster, 2020), p. 328.

45. Mei Ruao, *Dongjing da shenpan: Yuandong guoji junshi fating Zhongguo faguan Mei Ruao riji* [The Great Tokyo Trial: Diary of Mei Ruao, Chinese Judge at the International Military Tribunal for the Far East] (Nanchang: Jiangxi Education Press, 2005), 8 April 1946, p. 74.

46. MMA, RG-9, box 159, War Crimes folder, Joint Chiefs to MacArthur, 25 April 1946. See NARA, RG 218, Leahy papers, box 8, MacArthur correspondence file, Joint Chiefs to MacArthur, 23 April 1946.

9. The Imperial Hotel

1. Mei Ruao, *Dongjing da shenpan: Yuandong guoji junshi fating Zhongguo faguan Mei Ruao riji* [The Great Tokyo Trial: Diary of Mei Ruao, Chinese Judge at the International Military Tribunal for the Far East] (Nanchang: Jiangxi Education Press, 2005), 20 March 1946, pp. 30–31.

2. Mei, *Dongjing da shenpan*, 20–22 March 1946, pp. 31–36. See Sheldon Glueck, *War Criminals: Their Prosecution and Punishment* (New York: Alfred A. Knopf, 1944).

3. Mei, *Dongjing da shenpan*, 4 April 1946, p. 62.

4. Mei, *Dongjing da shenpan*, 15 and 28 April 1946, pp. 95, 118.

5. Mei, *Dongjing da shenpan*, 11 April 1946, pp. 81–82; 20 April 1946, p. 103.

6. Mei, *Dongjing da shenpan*, 10 April 1946, p. 79.

7. Mei Ruao, "A Vote on the Right to Life," March 1948, Mei Xiaoao and Mei Xiaokan, eds., *Mei Ruao Dongjing shenpan wengao* [The Tokyo Trial Manuscripts of Mei Ruao] (Shanghai: Shanghai Jiaotong University Press, 2013), pp. 393–400. MMA, RG-9, box 159, War Crimes folder, Byrnes to Atcheson, 8 January 1946. AWM, Webb papers, 3DRL/2481, series 1, wallet 2, judges' biographies, 23 October 1946. See Neil Boister, "New Zealand's Approach to International Criminal Law from Versailles to Tokyo," in Kerstin von Lingen, ed., *Transcultural Justice at the Tokyo Tribunal: The Allied Struggle for Justice, 1946–48* (Leiden: Brill, 2018), pp. 182–201.

8. MMA, RG-9, box 159, War Crimes folder, Eisenhower to MacArthur, 11 January 1946. MMA, RG-9, box 159, War Crimes folder, Acheson to Atcheson, 11 January 1946.

9. AWM, Webb papers, 3DRL/2481, series 1, wallet 2, judges' biographies, 23 October 1946. MMA, RG-9, box 159, War Crimes folder, War Department to Keenan, 18 January 1946.

10. AWM, Webb papers, 3DRL/2481, series 4, wallet 2, Webb to Mayer, 20 October 1947. H. A. Weld, "Webb, Sir William Flood (1887–1972)," in John Ritchie and Diane Langmore, eds., *Australian Dictionary of Biography* (Melbourne: Melbourne University Press, 2002).

11. MMA, RG-5, box 60, Webb folder, MacArthur to Webb, 7 July 1943. MMA, RG-5, box 60, Webb to MacArthur, 7 September 1945.

12. MMA, RG-5, box 60, Webb folder, MacArthur to Webb, 5 March 1946. See Adam Wakeling, *Stern Justice: The Forgotten Story of Australia, Japan, and the Pacific War Crimes Trials* (Sydney: Viking, 2018), pp. 97–98; and Narrelle Morris, "Sir William Webb and Beyond," in von Lingen, ed., *Transcultural Justice at the Tokyo Tribunal*, pp. 44–64.

13. NAI, EAD file no. 27-W/46, Pethick-Lawrence to Bajpai, 19 January 1946.

14. BNA, FO 371/69834, Gascoigne to Bevin, 1 December 1948.

15. NAI, EAD file no. 27-W/46, Pethick-Lawrence to Bajpai, 19 January 1946. See A. S. Comyns Carr et al., *National Insurance* (London: Macmillan, 1912).

16. B. V. A. Röling introduction, in C. Hosoya et al., eds., *The Tokyo War Crimes Tribunal: An International Symposium* (Tokyo: Kodansha, 1986), p. 16. On Comyns Carr, see Kerstin von Lingen, "Managing Justice," in von Lingen, ed., *Transcultural Justice at the Tokyo Tribunal*, pp. 101–12.

17. Mei, *Dongjing da shenpan*, 12 May 1946, p. 153.

18. MMA, RG-9, box 159, War Crimes folder, Acheson to Atcheson, 24 January 1946. MMA, RG-9, box 159, War Crimes folder, Byrnes to MacArthur, 30 January 1946. B. V. A. Röling, *The Tokyo Trial and Beyond: Reflections of a Peacemonger*, ed. Antonio Cassese (Cambridge: Polity, 1993), pp. 19–20. B. V. A. Röling, *International Law in an Expanded World* (Amsterdam: Djambatan, 1960). Jan Klabbers, "Principled Pragmatist?," in Frédéric Mégret and Immi Tallgren, eds., *The Dawn of a Discipline: International Criminal Justice and Its Early Exponents* (Cambridge: Cambridge University Press, 2020), pp. 205–29.

19. Mei, "Vote on the Right to Life," pp. 393–400.

20. NL-HaNA, 2.21.273, folder 27, Röling to Hentig, 28 August 1947.

21. NL-HaNA, 2.21.273, folder 27, Röling to Nisbet, 22 July 1946.

22. AWM, Webb papers, 3DRL/2481, series 1, wallet 2, judges' biographies, 23 October 1946.

23. AWM, Webb papers, 3DRL/2481, series 4, wallet 4, Bernard to Webb, 23 August 1946. Mei, "Vote on the Right to Life," pp. 393–400.

24. MMA, RG-9, box 159, War Crimes folder, MacArthur to Eisenhower, 18 January 1946.

25. MMA, RG-9, box 159, War Crimes folder, Green to Keenan, 20 January 1946. See Yuki Takatori, "The Forgotten Judge at the Tokyo War Crimes Trial," *Massachusetts Historical Review*, vol. 10 (2008), pp. 115–41. Truman press conferences, 6 and 2 September 1945, *Public Papers of the Presidents of the United States: Harry S. Truman, 1945* (Washington, D.C.: U.S. Government Printing Office, 1961), pp. 312, 315, 317. Telford Taylor, *The Anatomy of the Nuremberg Trials: A Personal Memoir* (New York: Alfred A. Knopf, 1992), pp. 94–95.

26. MMA, RG-9, box 159, War Crimes folder, Keenan to Clark, 21 January 1946. MMA, RG-9, box 159, War Crimes folder, Keenan to Green, 21 January 1946.

27. MMA, RG-9, box 159, War Crimes folder, Eisenhower to MacArthur, 5 February 1946.

28. MMA, RG-5, box 60, Webb and Northcroft folders, Webb to MacArthur, 27 February 1946.

29. MMA, RG-5, box 2, folder 3, Webb to MacArthur, 5 March 1946.

30. MMA, RG-5, box 2, folder 3, Webb to MacArthur, 6 March 1946.

31. MMA, RG-5, box 2, folder 3, Webb to MacArthur, 8 March 1946.

32. Mei, *Dongjing da shenpan*, 11 April 1946, p. 81; 15 April 1946, p. 94.

33. Mei, *Dongjing da shenpan*, 23 March 1946, p. 40.

34. Mei, *Dongjing da shenpan*, 20 March 1946, pp. 27–29.

35. Mei, *Dongjing da shenpan*, 29 March 1946, pp. 43–44.

36. Mei, *Dongjing da shenpan*, 3 April 1946, p. 60.

37. Mei, *Dongjing da shenpan*, 11 April 1946, p. 80.

38. Mei, *Dongjing da shenpan*, 29 March 1946, pp. 43–44; 8 April 1946, p. 74; 23 April 1946, p. 108.

39. AWM, Webb papers, 3DRL/2481, series 1, wallet 1, judges' conference, 3 May 1946.

40. Kennan to Byrnes, 22 February 1946, *FRUS 1946: Eastern Europe; The Soviet Union* (Washington, D.C.: U.S. Government Printing Office, 1969), vol. 6, pp. 696–709.

41. Churchill speech, 5 March 1946, in James W. Muller, ed., *Churchill's "Iron Curtain" Speech Fifty Years Later* (Columbia: University of Missouri Press, 1999), pp. 1–13. Westad, *Cold War*, pp. 89–90. John Lewis Gaddis, *The United States and the Origins of the Cold War, 1941–1947* (New York: Columbia University Press, 1972), pp. 306–9.

42. Westad, *Cold War*, pp. 90–91. Gaddis, *United States and the Origins of the Cold War*, pp. 296–304.

43. Truman to Byrnes (unsent), 5 January 1946, *Off the Record: The Private Papers of Harry S. Truman*, ed. Robert H. Ferrell (New York: Harper & Row, 1980), pp. 79–80.

44. Truman press conference, 20 December 1945, *Public Papers*, p. 565. Douglas MacArthur, *Reminiscences* (New York: McGraw-Hill, 1964), pp. 291–93. Mei, *Dongjing da shenpan*, 5–6 April 1946, pp. 66, 68.

45. Kennan to Byrnes, 22 February 1946, *FRUS 1946*, vol. 6, pp. 696–709. The definitive account of the Soviet role at Nuremberg is Francine Hirsch, *Soviet Judgment at Nuremberg: A New History of the International Military Tribunal After World War II* (Oxford: Oxford University Press, 2020).

46. NARA, RG 84, Tokyo political adviser 1945, box 10, Byrnes to Keenan, 10 February 1946. NARA, RG 84, Tokyo political adviser 1945, box 10, Keenan to Byrnes, 11 February 1946. NARA, RG 84, Tokyo political adviser 1945, box 10, Bishop to Byrnes, 9 February 1946.

47. Mei, *Dongjing da shenpan*, 14 April 1946, p. 89. MMA, RG-5, box 1, folder 2, Soviet delegation, December 1946.

48. Valentyna Polunina, "The Soviets at Tokyo," in von Lingen, ed., *Transcultural Justice at the Tokyo Tribunal*, p. 129.

49. Francine Hirsch, "The Soviets at Nuremberg," *American Historical Review*, vol. 113, no. 3 (June 2008), pp. 710–13.

50. AWM, Webb papers, 3DRL/2481, series 1, wallet 3, Zaryanov biography, n.d. Michael David-Fox, *Revolution of the Mind: Higher Learning Among the Bolsheviks, 1918–1929* (Ithaca, N.Y.: Cornell University Press, 1997), pp. 133–91.

51. AWM, Webb papers, 3DRL/2481, series 1, wallet 3, Zaryanov biography, n.d. MMA, RG-9, box 159, War Crimes folder, Green to Keenan, 20 January 1946. RG-9, box 159, War Crimes folder, Byrnes to MacArthur, 30 January 1946. See Judith N. Shklar, *Legalism: Law, Morals, and Political Trials* (Cambridge, Mass.: Harvard University Press, 1986), pp. 143–50; and Jan T. Gross, "A Note on the Nature of Soviet Totalitarianism," *Soviet Studies*, vol. 34, no. 3 (July 1982), pp. 374–76.

52. David Remnick, *Lenin's Tomb: The Last Days of the Soviet Empire* (New York: Random House, 1993), p. 506.

53. *Report of Robert H. Jackson, United States Representative to the International Conference on Military Trials, London, 1945* (Washington, D.C.: U.S. Government Printing Office, 1949), pp. v–vi, 303.

54. Mei, *Dongjing da shenpan*, 15 April 1946, p. 93.

55. "Prosecution on Task of Proving Charge," *Nippon Times*, 25 June 1946, p. 2.

56. Mei, "Vote on the Right to Life," pp. 396–97.

57. Mei, *Dongjing da shenpan*, 21 March 1946, p. 35.

58. Mei, *Dongjing da shenpan*, 3 April 1946, p. 59.

59. Mei, *Dongjing da shenpan*, 21 April 1946, p. 104.

60. Mei, *Dongjing da shenpan*, 5–6 and 22 April 1946, pp. 66, 68, 107.

61. Mei, *Dongjing da shenpan*, 4 April 1946, pp. 62–63.

62. Mei, *Dongjing da shenpan*, 3 April 1946, p. 60; 1 April 1946, p. 55.

63. Mei, *Dongjing da shenpan*, 14 April and 1 May 1946, pp. 90, 125.

64. Mei, *Dongjing da shenpan*, 22 March 1946, pp. 36–37, 41.

65. Mei, *Dongjing da shenpan*, 21 March 1946, p. 35.

66. Mei, *Dongjing da shenpan*, 6 April 1946, p. 70.

67. Mei, *Dongjing da shenpan*, 5 April 1946, p. 65.

68. Mei, *Dongjing da shenpan*, 9 April 1946, p. 75.

69. Mei, *Dongjing da shenpan*, 13 April 1946, p. 87.

70. Mei, *Dongjing da shenpan*, 3 April 1946, pp. 60–61.

71. Mei, *Dongjing da shenpan*, 29 March 1946, p. 42.

72. NL-HaNA, 2.21.27, folder 27, Eichelberger note, 12 March 1946.

73. Mei, *Dongjing da shenpan*, 30 March 1946, pp. 47–51.

74. MMA, RG-5, box 60, Webb folder, charter amendments, MacArthur to Webb, 23 April 1946.

75. "Kiyose, Shiobara Set to Defend Gen. Tojo," *Nippon Times,* 10 March 1946, p. 2. Takayanagi Kenzo, "International Military Tribunal," *Nippon Times,* 30–31 March 1946, p. 4; 1 April 1946, p. 4.

76. MMA, RG-5, box 43, Northcroft folder, MacArthur to Northcroft, 19 March 1946. UVA, Williams Papers, box 1, folder 1, Ohta to Dell, 15 March 1946. UVA, Williams Papers, box 1, folder 1, Northcroft to MacArthur, 15 March 1946. MMA, RG-9, box 159, War Crimes folder, MacArthur to JAG, 1 April 1946.

77. Kido Koichi, *Kido Koichi nikki: Tokyo saiban-ki* [Kido Koichi Diary: The Tokyo Trial Period] (Tokyo: University of Tokyo Press, 1980), p. 447.

78. Lindesay Parrott, "Shidehara Blocks War Guilt Board," *New York Times,* 2 December 1945.

79. NAI, EAD file no. 27-W/46, Fox to Bevin, 8 and 15 February 1946.

80. NARA, RG 218, box 8, Leahy files, Joint Chiefs to MacArthur, 18 December 1945.

81. NAI, EAD file no. 27-W/46, Fox to Bevin, 8 February 1946.

82. AWM, Webb papers, 3DRL/2481, series 4, wallet 7, Yokota Kisaburo, "Illegal Warfare Presupposes Murder," *Mainichi Shimbun,* 6 June 1946.

83. BNA, FO 371/54126, MacDermot to Bevin, "Report on Allied Occupation Problems and Policy in Japan," 29 November 1945.

84. NAI, EAD file no. 27-W/46, Bevin to Fox, 15 February 1946.

85. NAI, EAD file no. 27-W/46, Sansom to Bevin, 23 February 1946.

86. NAI, EAD file no. 27-W/46, Bevin to Fox, 28 February 1946.

87. Mei, *Dongjing da shenpan,* 8 April 1946, p. 73.

88. NARA, RG 218, Leahy papers, box 8, MacArthur correspondence file, Bishop to Byrnes, 10 April 1946.

89. NARA, RG 218, Leahy papers, box 8, MacArthur correspondence file, Far Eastern Commission to MacArthur, 26 March 1946.

90. MMA, RG-9, box 160, W.O. folder, Harriman to Byrnes, 30 October 1946 (in Byrnes to Atcheson, 2 November 1946). NARA, RG 218, Leahy papers, box 8, MacArthur correspondence file, Bishop to Byrnes, 10 April 1946.

91. Mei, *Dongjing da shenpan,* 8 May 1946, p. 146; 10 April 1946, p. 77.

92. Lindesay Parrott, "Moderates Ahead in Japan," *New York Times,* 12 April 1946, pp. 1, 15.

93. Ian Buruma, *Inventing Japan, 1853–1964* (New York: Modern Library, 2003), pp. 139–40.

94. MMA, RG-9, box 160, War Department folder, Baker to Parks, 23 April 1946.

95. MMA, RG-9, box 160, W.O. folder, Harriman to Byrnes, 30 October 1946 (in Byrnes to Atcheson, 2 November 1946).

96. Westad, *Cold War,* pp. 134–35.

97. NARA, RG 218, Leahy papers, box 8, MacArthur correspondence file, Bishop to Byrnes, 10 April 1946. On the relations between the Japanese Communist Party and the Soviet Union, see Tatiana Linkhoeva, *Revolution Goes East: Imperial Japan and Soviet Communism* (Ithaca, N.Y.: Cornell University Press, 2020), pp. 159–84; and David Wolff, "Japan and Stalin's Policy Toward Northeast Asia After World War II," *Journal of Cold War Studies,* vol. 15, no. 2 (Spring 2013), pp. 4–29.

98. MMA, RG-9, box 160, War Department folder, Baker to Parks, 23 April 1946.

99. Mei, *Dongjing da shenpan,* 5 April 1946, p. 65.

100. Mei, *Dongjing da shenpan,* 11 April 1946, p. 80.

101. Mei, *Dongjing da shenpan*, 14 April 1946, p. 89.

102. NL-HaNA, 2.21.27, folder 27, Chamberlin to Röling, 8 March 1946.

103. Mei, *Dongjing da shenpan*, 12 April 1946, pp. 83–86.

104. Mei, *Dongjing da shenpan*, 12 April 1946, pp. 83–86; 13 April 1946, p. 87.

105. Mei, *Dongjing da shenpan*, 10 and 12 April 1946, pp. 77, 83. NAI, EAD file no. 27-W/46, Fox to Bevin, 15 February 1946.

106. UVA, Tavenner papers, box 1, Horwitz memorandum, "Conferences Before the Emperor (Gozenkai)," 7 March 1946. UVA, Morgan papers, box 1, IPS executive committee meeting, 18 March 1946.

107. Solis Horwitz, "The Tokyo Trial," *International Conciliation*, vol. 28 (1950), pp. 495–96.

108. Mark R. Peattie, *Ishiwara Kanji and Japan's Confrontation with the West* (Princeton: Princeton University Press, 1975). Takehiko Yoshihashi, *Conspiracy at Mukden: The Rise of the Japanese Military* (New Haven: Yale University Press, 1963). Michael A. Barnhart, *Japan Prepares for Total War: The Search for Economic Security, 1919–1941* (Ithaca, N.Y.: Cornell University Press, 1987). Nicholas D. Anderson, "Inadvertent Expansion in World Politics," Ph.D. diss., Yale University, 2021.

109. Indictment, 29 April 1945, Neil Boister and Robert Cryer, eds., *Documents on the Tokyo International Military Tribunal: Charter, Indictment and Judgments* (Oxford: Oxford University Press, 2008), appendix A, section 6, p. 39. Herbert P. Bix, *Hirohito and the Making of Modern Japan* (New York: HarperCollins, 2000), pp. 592–94.

110. UVA, Morgan papers, box 1, IPS executive committee meeting, 18 March 1946. MMA, RG-9, box 159, War Crimes, Marshall to MacArthur, 24 November 1945.

111. Richard Minear, *Victors' Justice: The Tokyo War Crimes Trial* (Princeton: Princeton University Press, 1971), p. 104.

112. B. V. A. Röling introduction, in C. Hosoya et al., eds., *The Tokyo War Crimes Tribunal: An International Symposium* (Tokyo: Kodansha, 1986), p. 19. William J. Sebald, *With MacArthur in Japan: A Personal History of the Occupation* (New York: W. W. Norton, 1965), p. 166. Arnold C. Brackman, *The Other Nuremberg: The Untold Story of the Tokyo War Crime Trials* (London: Collins, 1989), p. 91.

113. Horwitz, "Tokyo Trial," p. 496.

114. AWM, Webb papers, 3DRL/2481, series 4, wallet 20, Webb memo, 2 August 1946.

115. NAI, EAD file no. 27-W/46, Muir to Wavell, 27 February 1946.

116. BNA, FO 371/57424, Comyns Carr to War Crimes Section, 26 February 1946.

117. Mei, *Dongjing da shenpan*, 26 April 1946, p. 114.

118. "Keenan Submits 55-Count Document to Military Tribunal on Monday," *Nippon Times*, 30 April 1946, pp. 1–2. Mei, *Dongjing da shenpan*, 29 April 1946, pp. 119–20.

119. Indictment, 29 April 1945, Boister and Cryer, eds., *Documents on the Tokyo International Military Tribunal*, pp. 16–17. AWM, Webb papers, 3DRL/2481, series 1, wallet 5, indictment, 29 April 1945.

120. David Cohen and Yuma Totani, *The Tokyo War Crimes Tribunal: Law, History, and Jurisprudence* (Cambridge: Cambridge University Press, 2018), pp. 72–79, 92–93.

121. Indictment, 29 April 1945, Boister and Cryer, eds., *Documents on the Tokyo International Military Tribunal*, appendix A, pp. 18–19, 34–46.

122. On the U.S. role in the Hague conferences of 1899 and 1907, see John Fabian Witt, *Lincoln's Code: The Laws of War in American History* (New York: Free Press, 2012), pp. 348–62. Indictment, 29 April 1945, Boister and Cryer, eds., *Documents on the Tokyo International Military Tribunal*, appendix B, pp. 46–55.

123. See Philippe Sands, *East West Street: On the Origins of Genocide and Crimes Against Humanity* (London: Weidenfeld & Nicolson, 2016); Geoffrey Robertson, *Crimes Against Humanity: The Struggle for Global Justice* (New York: New Press, 2012); and M. Cherif Bassiouni, *Crimes Against Humanity: Historical Evolution and Contemporary Application* (Cambridge: Cambridge University Press, 2011).

124. Paul Whitcomb Williams, "Legitimate Targets in Aërial Bombardment," *American Journal of International Law*, vol. 23, no. 3 (1929), pp. 570–81. Katherine E. McKinney, Scott D. Sagan, and Allen S. Weiner, "Why the Atomic Bombing of Hiroshima Would Be Illegal Today," *Bulletin of the Atomic Scientists*, vol. 76, no. 4 (2020), pp. 157–65. Indictment, 29 April 1945, Boister and Cryer, eds., *Documents on the Tokyo International Military Tribunal*, pp. 16–17.

125. *IMTFE Transcripts*, 14 May 1946, p. 259.

126. Indictment, 29 April 1945, Boister and Cryer, eds., *Documents on the Tokyo International Military Tribunal*, pp. 27–31. For an argument for greater legal protection of soldiers at war, see Gabriella Blum, "The Dispensable Lives of Soldiers," *Journal of Legal Analysis*, vol. 2, no. 1 (Spring 2010), pp. 115–70.

127. Yuma Totani, *The Tokyo War Crimes Trial: The Pursuit of Justice in the Wake of World War II* (Cambridge, Mass.: Harvard University Press, 2008), p. 13.

128. Yoshimi Yoshiaki, *Comfort Women: Sexual Slavery in the Japanese Military During World War II*, trans. Suzanne O'Brien (New York: Columbia University Press, 2000).

129. Jeanne Guillemin, *Hidden Atrocities: Japanese Germ Warfare and American Obstruction of Justice at the Tokyo Trial* (New York: Columbia University Press, 2017).

130. AWM, Webb papers, 3DRL/2481, series 4, wallet 7, "Comments on the Indictment by Individual Japanese," *Jiji Shimpo*, 30 April 1946.

131. AWM, Webb papers, 3DRL/2481, series 4, wallet 7, "We Learn from the Indictment," *Yomiuri-Hochi*, 30 April 1946.

132. AWM, Webb papers, 3DRL/2481, series 4, wallet 7, *Yomiuri-Hochi*, 30 April 1946.

133. AWM, Webb papers, 3DRL/2481, series 4, wallet 7, "Comments on the Indictment by Individual Japanese," *Jiji Shimpo*, 30 April 1946.

134. "The Japanese Criminals," *New York Times*, 30 April 1946, p. 20.

135. Mei, *Dongjing da shenpan*, 2 May 1946, pp. 126–28.

10. The Anatomy of the Tokyo Trial

1. Mei Ruao, *Dongjing da shenpan: Yuandong guoji junshi fating Zhongguo faguan Mei Ruao riji* [The Great Tokyo Trial: Diary of Mei Ruao, Chinese Judge at the International Military Tribunal for the Far East] (Nanchang: Jiangxi Education Press, 2005), 3 May 1946, p. 133.

2. "Setting for Coming Big Trials Is Completed," *Nippon Times*, 23 March 1946, p. 3.

3. Author's visit to Ichigaya, August 2015.

4. Mei, *Dongjing da shenpan*, 23 March 1946, p. 39.

5. *IMTFE Transcripts*, 8 August 1946, p. 3471.

6. "Setting for Coming Big Trials Is Completed," *Nippon Times*, 23 March 1946, p. 3.

7. "Tribunal Members Not Yet in Tokyo Delay Trial Plan," *Nippon Times*, 17 March 1946, pp. 1–2.

8. "Setting for Coming Big Trials Is Completed," *Nippon Times*, 23 March 1946, p. 3.

9. Mei, *Dongjing da shenpan*, April 1946, p. 100.

10. "War Crimes," *Time*, 20 May 1946, p. 26.

11. Arnold C. Brackman, *The Other Nuremberg: The Untold Story of the Tokyo War Crime Trials* (London: Collins, 1989), p. 98.

12. AWM, Webb papers, 3DRL/2481, series 4, wallet 7, "Momentary Tension of the Accused Toward the American Defense Counsels," *Tokyo Shimbun*, 15 May 1946.

13. William J. Sebald, *With MacArthur in Japan: A Personal History of the Occupation* (New York: W. W. Norton, 1965), p. 153.

14. Brackman, *Other Nuremberg*, p. 101.

15. Lindesay Parrott, "Tojo Faces Court as a War Criminal," *New York Times*, 3 May 1946, pp. 1, 10.

16. Mei, *Dongjing da shenpan*, 17 April 1946, p. 99.

17. Mei Ruao, "A Vote on the Right to Life," March 1948, Mei Xiaoao and Mei Xiaokan, eds., *Mei Ruao Dongjing shenpan wengao* [The Tokyo Trial Manuscripts of Mei Ruao] (Shanghai: Shanghai Jiaotong University Press, 2013), pp. 393–400. See He Qinhua, "The Legal Bases and Present Significance of the Tokyo Trial," in Cheng Zhaoqi et al., *The Tokyo Trial: Recollections and Perspectives from China* (Cambridge: Cambridge University Press, 2016), pp. 228–30.

18. Mei, *Dongjing da shenpan*, 29 April 1946, p. 120.

19. AWM, Webb papers, 3DRL/2481, series 4, wallet 20, Webb to judges, 1 May 1946.

20. AWM, Webb papers, 3DRL/2481, series 4, wallet 7, "President Webb Read a Statement in a Gentle Tone," *Asahi Shimbun*, 4 May 1946.

21. "Men Visiting War Trials in Tokyo Feel Accused Guilty, Women Not So Interested," *Nippon Times*, 25 June 1946, p. 2. There is an exhausting sexism to this article.

22. AWM, Webb papers, 3DRL/2481, series 4, wallet 11, trial procedure, 2 May 1946.

23. *IMTFE Transcripts*, 3 May 1946, pp. 21–23. AWM, Webb papers, 3DRL/2481, series 4, wallet 11, Webb draft speech, 2 May 1946.

24. Mei, *Dongjing da shenpan*, 3 May 1946, pp. 130–34.

25. NL-HaNA, 2.21.273, folder 27, Röling to Nisbet, 6 May 1946.

26. AWM, Webb papers, 3DRL/2481, series 4, wallet 7, "President Webb Read a Statement in a Gentle Tone," *Asahi Shimbun*, 4 May 1946.

27. Lindesay Parrott, "Tokyo Defendant Removed at Trial," *New York Times*, 4 May 1946, p. 9.

28. "Tokyo Trial in Recess," *New York Times*, 5 May 1946, p. 27.

29. "War Crimes," *Time*, 20 May 1946, p. 26.

30. Mei, *Dongjing da shenpan*, 3 May 1946, pp. 130–34.

31. Mei, *Dongjing da shenpan*, 4 May 1946, pp. 136–37.

32. AWM, Webb papers, 3DRL/2481, series 4, wallet 7, Ryusahuro Shikiba, "Psychology of War Criminals," *Asahi Shimbun*, 20 May 1946.

33. *IMTFE Transcripts*, 6 May 1946, pp. 100–104. Mei, *Dongjing da shenpan*, 6 May 1946, pp. 142–43.

34. "Tojo's Wife, Harried by War Guilt Stigma, Retires in Shame to Simple Country Life," *Nippon Times*, 6 April 1946, p. 3.

35. Mei, *Dongjing da shenpan*, 7 May 1946, p. 145.

36. AWM, Webb papers, 3DRL/2481, series 4, wallet 7, "Legal Significance of the International Tribunal," *Jiji Shimpo*, 6 May 1946.

37. AWM, Webb papers, 3DRL/2481, series 4, wallet 7, Ryusahuro Shikiba, "Psychology of War Criminals," *Asahi Shimbun*, 20 May 1946.

38. AWM, Webb papers, 3DRL/2481, series 1, wallet 3, biographies of Japanese counsel, n.d. Mei, *Dongjing da shenpan*, 6 May 1946, p. 141.

39. *IMTFE Transcripts*, 4 May 1946, p. 74.

40. AWM, Webb papers, 3DRL/2481, series 1, wallet 2, Coleman to MacArthur, 8 May 1946.

41. MMA, RG-5, box 1, folder 2, Coleman to MacArthur, 31 May 1946. MMA, RG-5, box 1, folder 2, Levin et al. to MacArthur, 31 May 1946. MMA, RG-5, box 1, folder 2, MacArthur to Coleman, 2 June 1946. Mei, *Dongjing da shenpan*, 9–10 May 1946, pp. 148–51.

42. MMA, RG-9, box 159, War Crimes folder, Webb to MacArthur, 11 July 1946. MMA, RG-9, box 159, War Crimes folder, Carpenter note, 17 July 1946. MMA, RG-9, box 159, War Crimes folder, MacArthur to Webb, 19 July 1946. MMA, RG-9, box 159, War Crimes folder, Webb to MacArthur, 24 July 1946.

43. "Tojo Plans His Defense," *New York Times*, 2 May 1946, p. 4.

44. "Tojo Reported Busy Writing His Own Arguments," *Nippon Times*, 11 June 1946, p. 1.

45. *IMTFE Transcripts*, 6 May 1946, pp. 93–97. AWM, Webb papers, 3DRL/2481, series 4, wallet 7, "Kiyose Challenges the President," *Jiji Shimpo*, 7 May 1946.

46. Mei, *Dongjing da shenpan*, 6 May 1946, pp. 141–42.

47. AWM, Webb papers, 3DRL/2481, series 1, wallet 7, Jurisdiction opinion by members for Britain, Canada, and New Zealand, May 1946. *IMTFE Transcripts*, 13 May 1946, pp. 118–36. Parrott, "Tokyo Defendant Removed at Trial."

48. Guoshiguan, Foreign Ministry files, IMTFE Major Cases (Part II), Mei to Webb, 8 December 1946, 020-010117-0027-0104a to 020-010117-0027-0115a.

49. Lindesay Parrott, "Allies to Defend Tokyo Trial Right," *New York Times*, 8 May 1946, p. 12.

50. Mei, *Dongjing da shenpan*, 8 May 1946, p. 147.

51. AWM, Webb papers, 3DRL/2481, series 1, wallet 7, Jurisdiction opinion by members for Britain, Canada, and New Zealand, May 1946.

52. *IMTFE Transcripts*, 13 May 1946, p. 123.

53. AWM, Webb papers, 3DRL/2481, series 4, wallet 7, Kiyose Ichiro, "The Jurisdiction of the Tribunal," *Jiji Shimpo*, 6 June 1946.

54. *IMTFE Transcripts*, 13–14 May 1946, pp. 118–36, 195–232, 198, 212, 281, 214–15. AWM, Webb papers, 3DRL/2481, series 1, wallet 7, Jurisdiction opinion by members for Britain, Canada, and New Zealand, May 1946.

55. Brackman, *Other Nuremberg*, pp. 110–11.

56. AWM, Webb papers, 3DRL/2481, series 1, wallet 10, Röling to Webb, 23 January 1947.

57. AWM, Webb papers, 3DRL/2481, series 4, wallet 20, Webb second draft, 12 June 1946.

58. Brackman, *Other Nuremberg*, p. 108.

59. *IMTFE Transcripts*, 13 May 1946, pp. 137–38, 152–58.

60. Mei, *Dongjing da shenpan*, 13 May 1946, p. 155. Guoshiguan, Foreign Ministry files, IMTFE trials 1946–47, Zhu note, 22 May 1946, 020-010117-0030-0023x.

61. *IMTFE Transcripts*, 13 May 1946, pp. 137–45. "Japanese Assails War Crimes Basis," *New York Times*, 13 May 1946, p. 16.

62. *IMTFE Transcripts*, 13–14 May 1946, pp. 146–58, 236–38.

63. *IMTFE Transcripts*, 14 May 1946, p. 205.

64. Mei, *Dongjing da shenpan*, 13 May 1946, pp. 155–56.

65. AWM, Webb papers, 3DRL/2481, series 4, wallet 20, Webb second draft, 12 June 1946.

66. AWM, Webb papers, 3DRL/2481, series 4, wallet 7, "Civilized Way of Trial," *Yomiuri Shimbun*, 15 May 1946.

67. AWM, Webb papers, 3DRL/2481, series 4, wallet 7, "Advocate of Militarism," *Yomiuri Shimbun*, 27 May 1946.

68. AWM, Webb papers, 3DRL/2481, series 4, wallet 4, Bernard to judges, 16 May 1946.

69. AWM, Webb papers, 3DRL/2481, series 4, wallet 6, judges' meeting, 16 May 1946.

70. *IMTFE Transcripts*, 17 May 1946, pp. 318–19. Guoshiguan, Foreign Ministry files, IMTFE Major Cases (Part II), Mei to Webb, 8 December 1946, 020-010117-0027-0104a to 020-010117-0027-0115a.

71. Yoshiro Matsui, "The Social Science of International Law," *Japanese Annual of International Law*, no. 45 (2002), pp. 3–6, 21.

72. AWM, Webb papers, 3DRL/2481, series 4, wallet 7, Yokota Kisaburo, "Illegal Warfare Presupposes Murder," *Mainichi Shimbun*, 6 June 1946. See Yokota Kisaburo, *Kokusaiho* [International Law] (Tokyo: Iwanami Shoten, 1941), 2 vols.; *Kokusai saiban no honshitu* [The Essence of International Trials] (Tokyo: Iwanami Shoten, 1941); and "Political Questions and Judicial Review," in Dan Fenno Henderson, ed., *The Constitution of Japan: Its First Twenty Years, 1947–67* (Seattle: University of Washington Press, 1968), pp. 141–66.

73. Yokota Kisaburo, *Senso hanzai ron* [On War Crimes] (Tokyo: Yuhikaku, 1947). Urs Matthias Zachmann, "Yokoto Kisaburo," in Frédéric Mégret and Immi Tallgren, eds., *The Dawn of a Discipline: International Criminal Justice and Its Early Exponents* (Cambridge: Cambridge University Press, 2020), pp. 335–57.

74. AWM, Webb papers, 3DRL/2481, series 1, wallet 6, judges' meeting, 15 May 1946.

75. "War Trials in Tokyo Will Open on June 3," *New York Times*, 7 May 1946, p. 3.

76. MMA, RG-9, box 159, War Crimes folder, Clark to MacArthur, 25 June 1946. MMA, RG-9, box 159, War Crimes folder, MacArthur to Clark, 30 June 1946. MMA, RG-9, box 159, War Crimes folder, Higgins to MacArthur, 21 June 1946.

77. MMA, RG-9, box 160, War Crimes folder, MacArthur to Eisenhower and Clark, 21 June 1946.

78. AWM, Webb papers, 3DRL/2481, series 1, wallet 3, Cramer biography.

79. Cramer to McCloy, 22 November 1944, Bradley F. Smith, *The American Road to Nuremberg: The Documentary Record, 1944–1945* (Stanford, Calif.: Hoover Institution Press, 1982), pp. 58–61.

80. MMA, RG-9, box 159, War Crimes folder, MacArthur to State Department, 6 July 1945.

81. Mei, "Vote on the Right to Life," pp. 393–400.

82. Bradley F. Smith, *The Road to Nuremberg* (New York: Basic Books, 1981), pp. 103–5.

83. MMA, RG-9, box 159, War Crimes folder, State Department to Cramer, 2 September 1946.

84. *IMTFE Transcripts*, 22 July 1946, pp. 2342–61.

85. AWM, Webb papers, 3DRL/2481, series 4, wallet 7, "Examination of Mental Condition of Shumei Okawa," *Yomiuri*, 8 May 1946.

86. "Okawa Ordered Hospitalized," *Nippon Times,* 11 June 1946, p. 1.
87. Frank Emery, "Insane Dr. Okawa Says He Waited 9 Years to Slap Tojo's Bald Head," *Nippon Times,* 27 June 1947, p. 3.
88. "Physicians Doubtful Hospitalized Okawa Will Be Able to Attend War Trials Again," *Nippon Times,* 1 July 1946, p. 2. *IMTFE Transcripts,* 9 April 1947, pp. 19,637–38.
89. "Yosuke Matsuoka Dies in Tokyo at 66," *New York Times,* 27 June 1946, p. 21. See Ian Buruma, *Inventing Japan, 1853–1964* (New York: Modern Library, 2003), pp. 87–88; and Oona Hathaway and Scott J. Shapiro, *The Internationalists: How a Radical Plan to Outlaw War Remade the World* (New York: Simon & Schuster, 2018), p. 156.
90. "Keenan Fires Opening Broadside in Fight to Convict War Leaders," *Nippon Times,* 5 June 1946, p. 1.
91. Advertisement, *Nippon Times,* 22 June 1946, p. 2.
92. AWM, Webb papers, 3DRL/2481, series 4, wallet 7, "Cruelties Committed by the Japanese," *Jiji Shimpo,* 5 June 1946.
93. *IMTFE Transcripts,* 4 June 1946, pp. 383–455.
94. AWM, Webb papers, 3DRL/2481, series 4, wallet 7, "Cruelties Committed by the Japanese," *Jiji Shimpo,* 5 June 1946.
95. AWM, Webb papers, 3DRL/2481, series 4, wallet 7, "Earphone Swiftly Delivers the Translations of Keenan's Address," *Yomiuri Shimbun,* 5 June 1946.
96. AWM, Webb papers, 3DRL/2481, series 4, wallet 7, "Field of 'Battle of Civilization,'" *Asahi Shimbun,* 5 June 1946.
97. AWM, Webb papers, 3DRL/2481, series 4, wallet 7, "Earphone Swiftly Delivers the Translations of Keenan's Address," *Yomiuri Shimbun,* 5 June 1946.
98. Jiji, "State and Individual Responsiblity," *Nippon Times,* 9 June 1946, p. 4.
99. John W. Dower, *War Without Mercy: Race and Power in the Pacific War* (New York: Pantheon, 1986), pp. 33–39, 41–52.
100. AWM, Webb papers, 3DRL/2481, series 4, wallet 7, "Cruelties Committed by the Japanese," *Jiji Shimpo,* 5 June 1946.
101. "Men Visiting War Trials in Tokyo Feel Accused Guilty, Women Not So Interested."
102. "Tribunal's Probe into Wartime Education Hailed by Imperial University Students," *Nippon Times,* 2 July 1946, p. 2.
103. "No Hirohito Trial, Says Keenan," *New York Times,* 18 June 1946, pp. 1, 13. "Keenan Opposes Trial of Emperor," *Nippon Times,* 19 June 1946, pp. 1–2.
104. John W. Dower, *Embracing Defeat: Japan in the Wake of World War II* (New York: W. W. Norton, 1999), p. 467.
105. Guoshiguan, Foreign Ministry files, IMTFE trials 1946–47, Xiang to Wang, 21 June 1946, 020-010117-0030-0115a.
106. MMA, RG-5, box 60, Webb folder, Webb to Chifley, 1947.
107. "FEC Also Opposed," *Nippon Times,* 19 June 1946, p. 2.
108. Mei, *Dongjing da shenpan,* 7 May 1946, p. 145.
109. James Brooke, "A Japanese Witness to History Adroitly Survived It," *New York Times,* 8 November 2003, p. A4. "Sumako Kase, the Wife of Japanese Diplomat," *New York Times,* 31 October 1982, p. 44. MMA, RG-5, box 73, folder 2, Kase paper, 31 May 1946.
110. HSTL, PSF, box 159, *ONI Review,* June 1946, Sakomizu interrogation.
111. Koichi Kido, *The Diary of Marquis Kido, 1931–45* (Frederick, Md.: University Publications of America, 1984), 10 November 1945, p. 463. See Strobe Talbott, *The Master of*

the Game: Paul Nitze and the Nuclear Peace (New York: Alfred A. Knopf, 1988); Fred Kaplan, *The Wizards of Armageddon* (New York: Simon & Schuster, 1983), pp. 136–41; and Nicholas Thompson, *The Hawk and the Dove: Paul Nitze, George Kennan, and the History of the Cold War* (New York: Henry Holt, 2009), p. 45.

112. MMA, RG-9, box 159, War Crimes folder, Eisenhower to MacArthur, 27 December 1945. MMA, RG-9, box 159, War Crimes folder, MacArthur to Eisenhower, 27 December 1945.

113. Herbert P. Bix, *Hirohito and the Making of Modern Japan* (New York: HarperCollins, 2000), pp. 583–84.

114. Talbott, *Master of the Game,* pp. 37–38. Thompson, *Hawk and the Dove,* pp. 45–47. HSTL, PSF, box 197, United States Strategic Bombing Survey, "Japan's Struggle to End the War," 1 July 1946. HSTL, PSF, box 174, Atomic Bomb, U.S. Strategic Bombing Survey report, "The Effects of the Atomic Bombings of Hiroshima and Nagasaki," 19 June 1946.

115. See Herbert P. Bix, "The Showa Emperor's 'Monologue' and the Problem of War Responsibility," *Journal of Japanese Studies*, vol. 18, no. 2 (Summer 1992), pp. 300–302.

116. James F. Byrnes, *Speaking Frankly* (New York: Harper & Brothers, 1947), p. 204.

117. NARA, RG 107, 390/8/32/06, Stimson "safe file," box 8, van Slyck memorandum, August 1945.

11. "Asia for the Asiatics"

1. AWM, Webb papers, 3DRL/2481, series 1, wallet 2, judges' biographies, 23 October 1946.

2. Author's interviews with Pal family, Kolkata and Uttar Pradesh. Satyabrata Pal, "My Grandfather and Japan," *India & Japan,* pamphlet on file with author. Ashis Nandy, "The Other Within," *The Savage Freud and Other Essays on Possible and Retrievable Selves* (Princeton: Princeton University Press, 1995), pp. 66–70.

3. Thomas Babington Macaulay, "Warren Hastings," *Edinburgh Review,* no. 74 (October 1841), pp. 172–73. See Andrew Sartori, *Bengal in Global Concept History: Culturalism in the Age of Capital* (Chicago: University of Chicago Press, 2008).

4. Tim Harper, *Underground Asia: Global Revolutionaries and the Assault on Empire* (London: Allen Lane, 2020), pp. 98–102.

5. BL, IOR, Mss Eur, Photo 048/1, Casey diary, 19 February 1944.

6. "Paru hakase—Kyo no mondai" [Dr. Pal—Today's Question], *Asahi Shimbun,* 6 October 1966, p. 1. See Higurashi Yoshinobu, *Tokyo saiban no kokusai kankei: Kokusai seiji ni okeru kenryoku to kihan* [International Relations of the Tokyo Trial: Power and Norms in International Politics] (Tokyo: Bokutakusha, 2002), pp. 443–54.

7. John Appleman, *Military Tribunals and International Crimes* (Indianapolis: Bobbs-Merrill, 1954). Elizabeth S. Kopelman, "Ideology and International Law," *New York University Journal of International Law and Politics,* vol. 23, no. 2 (Winter 1991), pp. 435, 439.

8. Radhabinod Pal, "The International Law in a Changing World," *All India Reporter,* vol. 48, part 575, November 1961, p. 98.

9. William Dalrymple, *The Last Mughal: The Fall of a Dynasty: Delhi, 1857* (London: Bloomsbury, 2006). Kim A. Wagner, *Amritsar, 1919: An Empire of Fear and the Making of a Massacre* (New Haven: Yale University Press, 2018).

10. AWM, Webb papers, 3DRL/2481, series 1, wallet 2, judges' biographies, 23 October 1946.

11. Radhabinod Pal, *The History of Hindu Law in the Vedic Age and in Post-Vedic Times Down to the Institutes of Manu* (Calcutta: University of Calcutta, 1958), pp. iii, 86–89. See Milinda Banerjee, "Sovereignty as a Motor of Global Conceptual Travel," *Modern Intellectual History*, vol. 12, no. 2 (2020), pp. 499–503.

12. Mithi Mukherjee suggests that sometimes British imperial governance was restrained by a supranational belief in natural law that was used to criticize arbitrary abuses of power by the empire (*India in the Shadows of Empire: A Legal and Political History, 1774–1950* [Oxford: Oxford University Press, 2010]). For a searing critique of British liberal imperialism, see Caroline Elkins, *Legacy of Violence: A History of the British Empire* (New York: Alfred A. Knopf, 2022).

13. Pal, *History of Hindu Law*, pp. iii–vii, 259–60, 330, 355. I am grateful to Gyan Prakash for this insight. See Nandy, "The Other Within," pp. 72–76; and Milinda Banerjee, "India's 'Subaltern Elites' and the Tokyo Trial," in Kerstin von Lingen, ed., *Transcultural Justice at the Tokyo Tribunal: The Allied Struggle for Justice, 1946–48* (Leiden: Brill, 2018), pp. 270–83.

14. AWM, Webb papers, 3DRL/2481, series 1, wallet 2, judges' biographies, 23 October 1946.

15. Radhabinod Pal and Balai Lal Pal, *The Law of Income Tax in British India, Being Act XI of 1922 as Amended by Act VII of 1939, with Explanatory Notes and Commentaries* (Calcutta: Eastern Law House, 1940).

16. Pal, *History of Hindu Law*, pp. v, 5–6.

17. Christopher Bayly and Tim Harper, *Forgotten Armies: The Fall of British Asia, 1941–1945* (London: Allen Lane, 2004), pp. 1–8, 313–16. Harper, *Underground Asia*, pp. 33–44, 103. Ezra Vogel, *China and Japan: Facing History* (Cambridge, Mass.: Harvard University Press, 2019).

18. Edwin O. Reischauer, *The Japanese* (Cambridge, Mass.: Belknap Press of Harvard University Press, 1978), pp. 78–85. Ian Buruma, *Inventing Japan, 1853–1964* (New York: Modern Library, 2003).

19. W. G. Beasley, *Japanese Imperialism, 1894–1945* (Oxford: Oxford University Press, 1987), pp. 42–54.

20. Nandy, "The Other Within," p. 65.

21. Sunil Khilnani, *Incarnations: India in Fifty Lives* (New York: Farrar, Straus & Giroux, 2016), p. 31.

22. Ramachandra Guha, *Gandhi Before India* (New York: Alfred A. Knopf, 2014), pp. 281–82. See Karuna Mantena, "Another Realism," *American Political Science Review*, vol. 106, no. 2 (May 2012), pp. 455–70.

23. Amartya Sen, *The Argumentative Indian: Writings on Indian History, Culture and Identity* (New York: Farrar, Straus & Giroux, 2005), pp. 109–10.

24. Eri Hotta, "Rash Behari Bose," in Sven Saaler and Christopher W. A. Szpilman, eds., *Pan-Asianism: A Documentary History* (Lanham, Md.: Rowman & Littlefield, 2011), vol. 1, pp. 231–40. He was no relation to Subhas Chandra Bose. Lizzie Collingham, *Curry: A Tale of Cooks and Conquerors* (Oxford: Oxford University Press, 2006), pp. 252–53.

25. Eri Hotta, *Pan-Asianism and Japan's War, 1931–1945* (New York: Palgrave Macmillan, 2007), pp. 32–37, 60–62. Edwin O. Reischauer, *Japan: Past and Present* (New York: Alfred A. Knopf, 1946), pp. 167–69.

26. Torsten Weber, "The Greater Asia Association and Matsui Iwane, 1933," in Sven Saaler and Christopher W. A. Szpilman, eds., *Pan-Asianism: A Documentary History* (Lanham, Md.: Rowman & Littlefield, 2011), vol. 2, pp. 137–42.

27. Hallett Abend, *My Life in China, 1926–1941* (New York: Harcourt, Brace, 1943), pp. 278–79.

28. "The Reasons for the Founding of the Greater Asia Association," 1 March 1933, in Saaler and Szpilman, eds., *Pan-Asianism*, vol. 2, pp. 142–44.

29. Matsui, "Greater Asianism," May 1933, in Saaler and Szpilman, eds., *Pan-Asianism*, vol. 2, pp. 144–47.

30. Konoe radio address, 3 November 1938, in Saaler and Szpilman, eds., *Pan-Asianism*, vol. 2, pp. 167–72.

31. Krishna Dutta and Andrew Robinson, *Rabindranath Tagore: The Myriad-Minded Man* (London: Bloomsbury, 1995), pp. 200, 203. Khilnani, *Incarnations*, p. 238.

32. Tagore to Noguchi, 1 September 1938, Krishna Dutta and Andrew Robinson, eds., *Rabindranath Tagore: An Anthology* (New York: St. Martin's Griffin, 1997), pp. 191–95. Khilnani, *Incarnations*, p. 243.

33. Lee Kuan Yew, *The Singapore Story: Memoirs of Lee Kuan Yew* (Singapore: Times Editions, 1998), pp. 45–47. See Fredrik Logevall, *JFK: Coming of Age in the American Century, 1917–1956* (New York: Random House, 2020), pp. 315–16.

34. Lee, *Singapore Story*, pp. 47–50.

35. Akira Iriye, *Power and Culture: The Japanese-American War, 1941–1945* (Cambridge, Mass.: Harvard University Press, 1981), pp. 64–74.

36. Kido Koichi, *The Diary of Marquis Kido, 1931–45* (Frederick, Md.: University Publications of America, 1984), 6 May 1942, p. 332.

37. Tsuji Masanobu, *Singapore: The Japanese Version*, trans. Margaret E. Lake (Sydney: Ure Smith, 1960), p. 270.

38. Tsuji, *Singapore*, p. xvii. See Jeremy A. Yellen, *The Greater East Asia Co-Prosperity Sphere: When Total Empire Met Total War* (Ithaca, N.Y.: Cornell University Press, 2019).

39. Ian Buruma and Avishai Margalit, *Occidentalism: The West in the Eyes of Its Enemies* (New York: Penguin, 2004), pp. 2–7, 143–44.

40. John W. Dower, *War Without Mercy: Race and Power in the Pacific War* (New York: Pantheon, 1986), p. 6.

41. Josef Silverstein, ed., *The Political Legacy of Aung San* (Ithaca, N.Y.: Cornell University Press, 1993), pp. 19–22.

42. Yellen, *Greater East Asia Co-Prosperity Sphere*, pp. 105–12, 116–24.

43. Sarah Kovner, *Prisoners of the Empire: Inside Japanese POW Camps* (Cambridge, Mass.: Harvard University Press, 2020), pp. 87–90.

44. Fredrik Logevall, *Embers of War: The Fall of an Empire and the Making of America's Vietnam* (New York: Random House, 2012), p. 37.

45. Rana Mitter, *Forgotten Ally: China's World War II, 1937–1945* (Boston: Houghton Mifflin Harcourt, 2013), pp. 38–40, 218–22. On Chinese collaboration, see Rana Mitter, *The Manchurian Myth: Nationalism, Resistance, and Collaboration in Modern China* (Berkeley: University of California Press, 2000); and David Barrett and Larry Shyu, eds., *Chinese Collaboration with Japan, 1932–1945: The Limits of Accommodation* (Stanford, Calif.: Stanford University Press, 2001).

46. Barak Kushner, *The Thought War: Japanese Imperial Propaganda* (Honolulu: University of Hawaii Press, 2006).

47. MMA, RG-44, box 2, folder 6, PWB File no. 3, "Under the Heel of Japan," 1942.

48. W. J. West, ed., *Orwell, the War Broadcasts* (London: British Broadcasting Corporation, 1985), 25 July 1942, p. 121.

49. Bayly and Harper, *Forgotten Armies*, pp. 72–85.

50. Sugata Bose, *His Majesty's Opponent: Subhas Chandra Bose and India's Struggle Against Empire* (Cambridge, Mass.: Belknap Press of Harvard University Press, 2011), p. 222.

51. Hotta, *Pan-Asianism and Japan's War*, pp. 213–14, 226–37.

52. Dower, *War Without Mercy*, p. 8.

53. "Read This Alone—And the War Can Be Won," 1941, in Tsuji, *Singapore*, pp. 300–311.

54. *Kido Diary*, 29 May 1943, pp. 360–61.

55. *IMTFE Transcripts*, 5 December 1946, Hashimoto, "The Greater East Asia Sphere Under Imperial Influence," 5 January 1942, p. 12022.

56. Teresa Watanabe, "Hirohito's Brother Assailed Japan's WWII 'Aggression,'" *Los Angeles Times*, 7 July 1994.

57. *IMTFE Transcripts*, 26 September 1946, Hitler-Matsuoka conference, 27 March 1941, pp. 6485–98.

58. *IMTFE Transcripts*, 25 September 1946, Matsuoka to Ott, 27 September 1940, p. 6402.

59. Mark Mazower, *Hitler's Empire: How the Nazis Ruled Europe* (New York: Penguin, 2008), pp. 105–6.

60. *Kido Diary*, 15 February 1943, p. 352.

61. Geoffrey B. Robinson, *The Killing Season: A History of the Indonesian Massacres, 1965–66* (Princeton: Princeton University Press, 2018), pp. 31–32.

62. Adrian Vickers, *A History of Modern Indonesia* (Cambridge: Cambridge University Press, 2005), pp. 88–95.

63. Lee, *Singapore Story*, pp. 49–50, 53, 57–59.

64. Sukarno, *Sukarno: An Autobiography: As Told to Cindy Adams* (Indianapolis: Bobbs-Merrill, 1965), pp. 168–69, 173–74.

65. Ba Maw, *Breakthrough in Burma: Memoirs of a Revolution* (New Haven: Yale University Press, 1968), pp. 175–86.

66. Dower, *War Without Mercy*, p. 7.

67. *President Chiang Kai-shek's Selected Speeches and Messages, 1937–1945* (Taipei: China Cultural Service, 1945), 1 January 1944, p. 236.

68. Mary Ann Glendon, *A World Made New: Eleanor Roosevelt and the Universal Declaration of Human Rights* (New York: Random House, 2001), pp. 10–11. Elizabeth Borgwardt, *A New Deal for the World: America's Vision for Human Rights* (Cambridge, Mass.: Belknap Press of Harvard University Press, 2005), pp. 14–45, 303–304.

69. Cordell Hull, *The Memoirs of Cordell Hull* (New York: Macmillan, 1948), vol. 2, pp. 1595–98. Logevall, *Embers of War*, pp. 48–51.

70. Logevall, *JFK*, p. 360.

71. FDR Presidential Library and Museum, FDR press conference #992, 23 February 1945, at http://www.fdrlibrary.marist.edu/_resources/images/pc/pc0169.pdf.

72. Elliott Roosevelt, *As He Saw It* (New York: Duell, Sloan & Pearce, 1946), pp. 115–16.

73. BL, IOR, L/P&J/5/149, Herbert to Linlithgow, 21 May 1942. BL, IOR, L/P&J/5/150, Bengal political report, December 1943.

74. BL, IOR, L/P&J/5/149, Bengal political reports, January, February, and April 1942.

75. BL, IOR, L/P&J/5/149, Bengal political reports, February and March 1942. BL, IOR, L/P&J/5/149, Bengal press adviser's report, January 1942.

76. BL, IOR, L/P&J/5/149, Bengal provincial press reports, January and November 1942. See BL, IOR, Mss Eur, Photo 048/3, Casey diary, 9 November 1944.

77. BL, IOR, L/P&J/5/149, Herbert to Linlithgow, 22 March 1942. See David Armitage, *The Ideological Origins of the British Empire* (Cambridge: Cambridge University Press, 2000), pp. 11–13, 125–45.

78. BL, IOR, L/P&J/5/149, Bengal provincial press report, January 1942.

79. Srinath Raghavan, *India's War: World War II and the Making of Modern South Asia* (New York: Basic Books, 2016), pp. 7–12, 270.

80. S. Mitra, ed., *Indian Law Reports: Calcutta Series, 1941* (Alipore: Bengal Government Press, 1941), vol. 1, p. 3.

81. S. Mitra, ed., *Indian Law Reports: Calcutta Series, 1942* (Alipore: Bengal Government Press, 1942), vol. 1, *Budh Karan Chaukhani v. Thakur Prasad Shah,* pp. 30–48. S. Mitra, ed., *Indian Law Reports: Calcutta Series, 1943* (Alipore: Bengal Government Press, 1943), vol. 1, *Syed Shah Majubal Islam v. Commissioner of Wakfs,* pp. 457–68. S. Mitra, ed., *Indian Law Reports: Calcutta Series, 1942,* vol. 1, *Naresh Chandra Das v. Emperor,* pp. 436–80.

82. S. Mitra, ed., *Indian Law Reports: Calcutta Series, 1941,* vol. 1, *Tarit Bhusan Ray v. Sree Sree Iswar Sridhar Salgram Sila Thakur,* pp. 477–79, 495–533.

83. BL, IOR, L/P&J/5/151, Total Deaths in Bengal, September 1944.

84. As the economists Jean Drèze and Amartya Sen have shown, democratic India has not had any major famines since independence (*Hunger and Public Action* [Oxford: Clarendon, 1989], pp. 122–33, 211–15, 221–25).

85. BL, IOR, L/P&J/5/150, Bengal political report, December 1943.

86. Amartya Sen, *Poverty and Famines: An Essay on Entitlement and Deprivation* (Oxford: Oxford University Press, 1981), pp. 52–85. Raghavan, *India's War,* pp. 349–51. Yasmin Khan, *The Raj at War: A People's History of World War II* (London: Bodley Head, 2015), pp. 202–16. Madhusree Mukerjee, *Churchill's Secret War: The British Empire and the Ravaging of India During World War II* (New York: Basic Books, 2010), pp. 137–50, 191–212.

87. S. Mitra, ed., *Indian Law Reports: Calcutta Series, 1943,* vol. 2, *Ram Tarak Singha v. Salgram Singha,* pp. 192–203.

88. Bose, *His Majesty's Opponent,* pp. 11326–27. "Netaji Bose Played Major Role in Freeing India from Colonialism," Press Trust of India, 23 January 2017.

89. "Netaji Is a Much Respected Name in Our Country, Says Premier Shinzo Abe," *The Hindu,* 24 August 2007.

90. Bose address, November 1944, in Subhas Chandra Bose, *Chalo Delhi: Writings and Speeches, 1943–1945,* eds. Sisir K. Bose and Sugata Bose (Kolkata: Netaji Research Bureau, 2007), vol. 12, pp. 285–301.

91. Raghavan, *India's War,* pp. 278–80.

92. BL, IOR, L/P&J/5/149, Bengal political report, July 1942. Bose broadcast, 1 May 1942, Subhas Chandra Bose, *Azad Hind: Writings and Speeches, 1941–1943,* eds. Sisir K. Bose and Sugata Bose (Kolkata: Netaji Research Bureau, 2002), vol. 11, pp. 98–99. Bose to Third Reich, 9 April and 3 May 1941, Bose, *Azad Hind,* vol. 11, pp. 38–49, 50–52. Bose to Ribbentrop, *Azad Hind,* vol. 11, 63–64.

93. BL, IOR, L/P&J/5/149, Bengal political report, April 1942.

94. Tojo speech, 16 February 1942, T. R. Sareen, ed., *Select Documents on Indian National Army* (Delhi: Agam Prakashan, 1988), pp. 8–10. Bose broadcast, 6 April 1942, Bose, *Azad Hind,* vol. 11, pp. 87–88.

95. Raghavan, *India's War*, p. 253. Sarvepalli Gopal, *Jawaharlal Nehru: A Biography* (London: Jonathan Cape, 1975), vol. 1, pp. 288–89. Elkins, *Legacy of Violence*, pp. 279–87.

96. Saul Friedländer, *Nazi Germany and the Jews, 1939–1945: The Years of Extermination* (New York: HarperCollins, 2007), pp. 139, 160–61, 251–55, 298, 331–36. See Bose, *His Majesty's Opponent*, p. 221.

97. Bose broadcast, 17 June 1942, Bose, *Azad Hind*, vol. 11, p. 120. His italics.

98. Bose broadcast, 1 May 1942, Bose, *Azad Hind*, vol. 11, pp. 94–99.

99. Adolf Hitler, *Mein Kampf*, trans. Ralph Manheim (Boston: Houghton Mifflin, 1962), pp. 656–59.

100. Hitler-Bose conference, 29 May 1942, Bose, *Azad Hind*, vol. 11, pp. 102–8.

101. Bose, *His Majesty's Opponent*, pp. 240–47.

102. Bose, *Chalo Delhi*, vol. 12, p. 43. Raghavan, *India's War*, p. 290.

103. Raghavan, *India's War*, pp. 283–89.

104. Bose address to Tojo, 6 July 1943, Bose, *Chalo Delhi*, vol. 12, pp. 49–50.

105. Bose address, 21 October 1943, Bose, *Chalo Delhi*, vol. 12, pp. 108–20.

106. Bose address, 23 October 1943, Bose, *Chalo Delhi*, vol. 12, pp. 128–38.

107. Bose, *Chalo Delhi*, vol. 12, pp. 146–53. Mitter, *Forgotten Ally*, pp. 304–6.

108. Bose statements, 21 August 1944, 24 April 1945, *Chalo Delhi*, vol. 12, pp. 264–65, 317–18. Bose, *His Majesty's Opponent*, pp. 266–88. Fergal Keane, *Road of Bones: The Siege of Kohima 1944* (London: HarperPress, 2010). Bayly and Harper, *Forgotten Armies*, pp. 370–92.

109. Bose broadcast, 15 August 1945, *Chalo Delhi*, vol. 12, pp. 407–8.

110. Bose, *His Majesty's Opponent*, pp. 300–303. Khilnani, *Incarnations*, pp. 280–88.

111. BL, IOR, L/P&J/5/153, Bengal political report, January 1946.

112. Ramachandra Guha, "Soldiers of the Nation," *Telegraph* (Kolkata), 23 January 2021.

113. B. V. A. Röling, *The Tokyo Trial and Beyond: Reflections of a Peacemonger*, ed. Antonio Cassese (Cambridge: Polity, 1993), p. 28.

114. Leonard A. Gordon, *Brothers Against the Raj: A Biography of Indian Nationalists Sarat and Subhas Chandra Bose* (New York: Columbia University Press, 1990). BL, IOR, Mss Eur, Photo 048/1, Casey diary, 19 February 1944.

115. BL, IOR, Mss Eur, Photo 048/4, Casey diary, 14 and 24 November 1945.

116. BL, IOR, Mss Eur, Photo 048/1, Casey diary, 31 March, 14 May, and 7 July 1944.

117. BL, IOR, Mss Eur, Photo 048/4, Casey diary, 28 January 1946.

118. BL, IOR, Mss Eur, Photo 048/4, Casey diary, 7 and 13 July 1945. Bz, IOR, L/P&J/5/152, Casey to Wavell, 19 July 1945. BL, IOR, L/P&J/5/152, Casey speech, 14 July 1945. "Youth's Growing Responsibilities," *Amrita Bazar Patrika*, 15 July 1945, p. 5. "No Superficial Tinkering," *Amrita Bazar Patrika*, 15 July 1945, p. 5.

119. Joya Chatterji, *Bengal Divided: Hindu Communalism and Partition, 1932–1947* (Cambridge: Cambridge University Press, 1994), pp. 220–65. Modi speech, 6 July 2012, at https://www.narendramodi.in/cm-and-p-a-sangma-celebrate-azad-hind-fauz -foundation-day-4580. See Christophe Jaffrelot, *Les nationalistes hindous: Idéologie, implantation et mobilisation des années 1920 aux années 1990* (Paris: Presses de la Fondation nationale des sciences politiques, 1993).

120. Myron Weiner, *Party Politics in India: The Development of a Multi-Party System* (Princeton: Princeton University Press, 1957), pp. 177–98.

121. BL, IOR, Mss Eur, Photo 048/4, Casey diary, 7 July 1945.

122. BL, IOR, L/P&J/5/152, Casey to Wavell, 19 July 1945.

123. BL, IOR, L/P&J/5/152, Bengal provincial press report, September 1945.

124. BL, IOR, L/P&J/5/152, Bengal provincial press report, early August 1945.

125. NAI, EAD file no. 27-W/46, Fowle to Bevin, 13 February 1946. Nisid Hajari, *Midnight's Furies: The Deadly Legacy of India's Partition* (Boston: Houghton Mifflin Harcourt, 2015), pp. 1–5.

126. NAI, EAD file no. 27-W/46, Muir note, 6 January 1946. NAI, EAD file no. 27-W/46, Muir to Bajpai, 4 March 1946.

127. NAI, EAD file no. 27-W/46, Pethick-Lawrence to Auchinleck, 17 November 1945. NAI, EAD file no. 27-W/46, Auchinleck to Pethick-Lawrence, 1 December 1945.

128. NAI, EAD file no. 27-W/46, Muir note, 15 January 1946. NAI, EAD file no. 27-W/46, Bevin to Bajpai, 17 January 1946.

129. NAI, EAD file no. 27-W/46, Muir note, 21 November 1945. NAI, EAD file no. 27-W/46, Duke note, 23 November 1945. NAI, EAD file no. 27-W/46, Muir note, 6 January 1946.

130. Yasmin Khan, *The Great Partition: The Making of India and Pakistan* (New Haven: Yale University Press, 2007), p. 17.

131. NAI, EAD file no. 27-W/46, Bajpai to Muir, 24 January 1946. For an excellent sketch of Bajpai, see Banerjee, "India's 'Subaltern Elites' and the Tokyo Trial," pp. 264–70.

132. NAI, EAD file no. 27-W/46, Bevin to Halifax, 14 December 1945. NAI, EAD file no. 27-W/46, Muir to Pethick-Lawrence, 12 January 1946.

133. NAI, EAD file no. 27-W/46, Bajpai to Byrnes, 4 January 1946. Bajpai to Byrnes, 4 January 1946, *FRUS 1946: The Far East* (Washington, D.C.: U.S. Government Printing Office, 1971), vol. 8, p. 383.

134. NAI, EAD file no. 27-W/46, Bajpai to Wavell, 6 January 1946.

135. Grew to Bajpai, 23 January 1946, *FRUS 1946: The Far East*, vol. 8, pp. 393–94. NAI, EAD file no. 27-W/46, Burnett note, 25 January 1946.

136. NAI, EAD file no. 27-W/46, Bajpai to Bevin, 10 January 1946. See NAI, EAD file no. 27-W/46, Bajpai to Wavell, 6 January 1946.

137. NAI, EAD file no. 27-W/46, Halifax to Muir, 7 March 1946.

138. Valentyna Polunina, "From Tokyo to Khabarovsk," in Kerstin von Lingen, ed., *War Crimes Trials in the Wake of Decolonization and Cold War in Asia, 1945–1956: Justice in Time of Turmoil* (London: Palgrave Macmillan, 2016), p. 244.

139. NAI, EAD file no. 27-W/46, Bajpai to Muir, 24 January 1946.

140. NAI, EAD file no. 27-W/46, Bajpai to Halifax, 7 February 1946. NAI, EAD file no. 27-W/46, Dominions Office to Canada, Australia, New Zealand, and South Africa, 12 February 1946.

141. NAI, EAD file no. 27-W/46, Delhi to Halifax, 28 January 1946.

142. MMA, RG-9, box 159, War Crimes folder, Marshall to MacArthur, 16 March 1946.

143. MMA, RG-9, box 159, War Crimes folder, Marshall to MacArthur, 6 April 1946. NAI, EAD file no. 27-W/46, Bajpai to Muir, 29 March 1946.

144. NAI, EAD file no. 27-W/46, Halifax to Bevin, 23 March 1946.

145. MMA, RG-5, box 60, Webb folder, Webb to MacArthur, 24 April 1946. AWM, Webb papers, 3DRL/2481, series 1, wallet 1, revised IMTFE charter, 26 April 1946. MMA, RG-9, box 159, War Crimes folder, MacArthur to Marshall, 16 March 1946.

146. NAI, EAD file no. 27-W/46, Menon and Lal notes, 31 December 1946. NAI, EAD file no. 27-W/46, Wavell to Bajpai, 8 January 1946.

147. NAI, EAD file no. 27-W/46, Bajpai to Auchinleck, 19 April 1946. NAI, EAD file no.

27-W/46, Delhi external affairs to Bajpai, 11 April 1946. NAI, EAD file no. 27-W/46, Bajpai to Auchinleck, 19 April 1946.

148. NAI, EAD file no. 27-W/46, Bajpai to Auchinleck, 18 and 19 April 1946.

149. NAI, EAD file no. 27-W/46, Muir to High Courts, 23 April 1946.

150. NAI, EAD file no. 27-W/46, Lahore High Court to Muir, 25 April 1946. The judge was Muhammad Munir.

151. NAI, EAD file no. 27-W/46, Muir to Pal, 27 April 1946. NAI, EAD file no. 27-W/46, Muir to Bajpai, 27 April 1946.

152. MMA, RG-5, box 115, IMTFE folder, Pal appointment, 16 May 1946.

153. NAI, EAD file no. 27-W/46, Muir to Pal, 27 April 1946. NAI, EAD file no. 27-W/46, Muir to Bajpai, 27 April 1946. NAI, EAD file no. 27-W/46, Muir to GHQ, 6 May 1946.

154. NAI, EAD file no. 27-W/46, Muir to Pethick-Lawrence, 20 June 1946.

155. *IMTFE Transcripts,* 17 May 1946, pp. 318–19.

156. MMA, RG-9, box 159, War Crimes folder, Commonwealth judges to MacArthur, 28 June 1946.

157. "Asia's Voice Spoke to Us," *Sunday Sun* (Sydney), 21 November 1948, p. 23.

12. The First Conquest

1. MMA, RG-5, box 30, Jaranilla folder, Jaranilla to MacArthur, 6 March 1948. AWM, Webb papers, 3DRL/2481, series 1, wallet 2, judges' biographies, 23 October 1946.

2. Charles G. Roland, *Long Day's Journey into Night: Prisoners of War in Hong Kong and Japan* (Waterloo, Ont.: Wilfred Laurier Press, 2001), pp. xiv–xv.

3. "The Bench and Bar in News," *The Lawyers Journal* (Manila), 28 February 1951, pp. 103–4.

4. Rodolfo P. Gumabong, "The 'Hellish March,'" *Philippines Free Press,* 8 April 1961, pp. 20–22. George M. Man, "Mann to Man," *Ukiah Republican Press,* 26 January 1949, p. 2.

5. "Filipino Named on Tribunal," *Nippon Times,* 6 June 1946, p. 1.

6. Douglas MacArthur, *Reminiscences* (New York: McGraw-Hill, 1964), pp. 235–37. Stanley Karnow, *In Our Image: America's Empire in the Philippines* (New York: Random House, 1989), pp. 306–7, 326–28. Theodore Friend, *The Blue-Eyed Enemy: Japan Against the West in Java and Luzon, 1942–1945* (Princeton: Princeton University Press, 1988), pp. 199–200, 243–44.

7. Gumabong, "The 'Hellish March.'"

8. AWM, Webb papers, 3DRL/2481, series 1, wallet 2, judges' biographies, 23 October 1946.

9. "Students in Debate," *Sunday Star* (Washington, D.C.), 24 March 1907, p. 14.

10. "The Bench and Bar in News," *Lawyers Journal* (Manila), 28 February 1951, pp. 103–4.

11. AWM, Webb papers, 3DRL/2481, series 1, wallet 2, judges' biographies, 23 October 1946. David Boguslav, "Osmena Inducts New Cabinet at Manila," *Christian Science Monitor,* 10 March 1945, p. 7.

12. Christopher Capozzola, *Bound by War: How the United States and the Philippines Built America's First Pacific Century* (New York: W. W. Norton, 2020).

13. MMA, RG-5, box 30, Jaranilla folder, Jaranilla to MacArthur, 1 July 1947.

14. MMA, RG-5, box 30, Jaranilla folder, Jaranilla to MacArthur, 25 June 1946.

15. "Jaranilla Hails Work of Tokyo Tribunal," Associated Press, 6 January 1946.

16. AWM, Webb papers, 3DRL/2481, series 4, wallet 4, Jaranilla to Webb, 6 August 1946.

17. AWM, Webb papers, 3DRL/2481, series 1, wallet 1, Jaranilla to judges, 12 March 1947.

18. Mei Ruao, "A Vote on the Right to Life," March 1948, Mei Xiaoao and Mei Xiaokan, eds., *Mei Ruao Dongjing shenpan wengao* [The Tokyo Trial Manuscripts of Mei Ruao] (Shanghai: Shanghai Jiaotong University Press, 2013), pp. 393–400.

19. Mei, "Vote on the Right to Life."

20. B. V. A. Röling, *The Tokyo Trial and Beyond: Reflections of a Peacemonger,* ed. Antonio Cassese (Cambridge: Polity, 1993), p. 28.

21. BNA, LCO 2/2992, Patrick to Cooper, 1947.

22. "Defense Asks for Disqualification of P.I. Judge," *Nippon Times,* 12 June 1946, p. 1.

23. *IMTFE Transcripts,* 13 June 1946, pp. 490–91. See Hitoshi Nagai, "Burdened by the 'Shadow of War,'" in Kerstin von Lingen, ed., *Transcultural Justice at the Tokyo Tribunal: The Allied Struggle for Justice, 1946–48* (Leiden: Brill, 2018), pp. 202–20.

24. MMA, RG-5, box 30, Jaranilla folder, Jaranilla to MacArthur, 1 July 1947.

25. *IMTFE Transcripts,* 13 June 1946, pp. 510–11. "Prosecution Offers Historic Documents in Launching Case," *Nippon Times,* 14 June 1946, pp. 1–2.

26. "Defense Asks for Disqualification of P.I. Judge," *Nippon Times,* 12 June 1946, p. 1.

27. Jeremy A. Yellen, *The Greater East Asia Co-Prosperity Sphere: When Total Empire Met Total War* (Ithaca, N.Y.: Cornell University Press, 2019), pp. 15–16. Jack Snyder, *Myths of Empire: Domestic Politics and International Ambition* (Ithaca, N.Y.: Cornell University Press, 1991), pp. 121–25. Mark R. Peattie, *Ishiwara Kanji and Japan's Confrontation with the West* (Princeton: Princeton University Press, 1975), pp. 21–25. Takehiko Yoshihashi, *Conspiracy at Mukden: The Rise of the Japanese Military* (New Haven: Yale University Press, 1963). Michael A. Barnhart, *Japan Prepares for Total War: The Search for Economic Security, 1919–1941* (Ithaca, N.Y.: Cornell University Press, 1987), pp. 27–29.

28. Stephen Kotkin, *Stalin: Waiting for Hitler, 1929–1941* (New York: Penguin, 2017), p. 88. Louise Young, *Japan's Total Empire: Manchuria and the Culture of Wartime Imperialism* (Berkeley: University of California Press, 1998), p. 106.

29. Rana Mitter, *Forgotten Ally: China's World War II, 1937–1945* (Boston: Houghton Mifflin Harcourt, 2013), pp. 56–65. Young, *Japan's Total Empire,* pp. 21–52. Ramon H. Myers and Mark R. Peattie, eds., *The Japanese Colonial Empire, 1895–1945* (Princeton: Princeton University Press, 1984).

30. *IMTFE Transcripts,* 4 June 1946, pp. 436–41, 465–67.

31. *IMTFE Transcripts,* 14 May 1946, pp. 272–77.

32. BDIC, fonds du Bernard, F° Δ res 0874/10, Bernard to judges, 10 May 1948.

33. W. G. Beasley, *Japanese Imperialism, 1894–1945* (Oxford: Clarendon, 1987), pp. 1–54, 175–250. Snyder, *Myths of Empire,* pp. 112–52.

34. Guoshiguan, Foreign Ministry files, postwar Japan file, Japan policy draft outline, 020-010122-0010-0057a to 020-010122-0010-0074a.

35. Guoshiguan, Foreign Ministry files, Japan demilitarization file, Wang to Marshall, 17 May 1946, 020-010122-0009-0095a.

36. Guoshiguan, Foreign Ministry files, Japan demilitarization file, draft disarmament treaty, 6 March 1946, 020-010122-0009-0107a to 020-010122-0009-0125a. Guoshiguan, Foreign Ministry files, Japan demilitarization file, Chinese draft terms, 1946, 020-010122-0009-0162x to 020-010122-0009-0168x.

37. Guoshiguan, Foreign Ministry files, Japan demilitarization file, Tang paper, n.d., 020-010122-0009-0223a to 020-010122-0009-0236a.

38. Guoshiguan, Foreign Ministry files, postwar Japan file, Guo note, 28 March 1945, 020-010122-0010-0035a. Guoshiguan, Foreign Ministry files, postwar Japan file, Supreme National Defense Council, "How to Deal with Japan," 16 January 1946, 020-010122-0010-0034a to 020-010122-0010-0038x.

39. Guoshiguan, Foreign Ministry files, Japan demilitarization file, Tang paper, n.d., 020-010122-0009-0223a to 020-010122-0009-0236a. See Anja Bihler, "On a 'Sacred Mission,'" in von Lingen, ed., *Transcultural Justice at the Tokyo Tribunal*, pp. 84–102.

40. Guoshiguan, Foreign Ministry files, IMTFE trials 1946–47, Yang note, n.d. (May or June 1946), 020-010117-0030-0076a to 020-010117-0030-0077a.

41. Guoshiguan, Foreign Ministry files, East Asia-Pacific bureau, political team resolutions, n.d. 1947, 020-019902-0027-0002a to 020-019902-0027-0005x. Guoshiguan, Foreign Ministry files, Japan demilitarization file, defense ministry opinions, n.d., 020-010122-0009-0171a.

42. Guoshiguan, Foreign Ministry files, postwar Japan file, Japan policy draft outline, 020-010122-0010-0057a to 020-010122-0010-0074a.

43. This calculation uses the February 1947 exhange rate, fixed at 12,000 yuan to one U.S. dollar. S. H. Steinberg, ed., *The Statesman's Year-Book: Statistical and Historical Annual of the States of the World for the Year 1947* (London: Macmillan, 1947), p. 781. Harold James, *International Monetary Cooperation Since Bretton Woods* (New York: Oxford University Press, 1996), pp. 67–69.

44. Guoshiguan, Foreign Ministry files, IMTFE trials 1945–46, Chen to Foreign Ministry, 26 February 1946, 020-010117-0029-0155x. Guoshiguan, compensation memo, 020-010117-0029-0156x to 020-010117-0029-0161x.

45. Guoshiguan, Foreign Ministry files, East Asia-Pacific bureau, political team resolutions, 1947, 020-019902-0027-0002a to 020-019902-0027-0005x.

46. Guoshiguan, Foreign Ministry files, Hirohito and War Crimes file, Lin paper, Hirohito's Responsibilities for War Crimes, 1948, 020-010122-0001-0005x to 020-010122-0001-0011a.

47. Guoshiguan, Foreign Ministry files, postwar Japan file, Japan policy draft outline, 020-010122-0010-0057a to 020-010122-0010-0074a.

48. Guoshiguan, Foreign Ministry files, East Asia-Pacific bureau, political team resolutions, 1947, 020-019902-0027-0002a to 020-019902-0027-0005x.

49. BNA, FO 371/57430, Australian First List of Major Japanese War Criminals, January 1946. Guoshiguan, Foreign Ministry files, United Nations War Crimes Commission file, note to Zhu, 23 March 1944, 020-010117-0021-0125x. Guoshiguan, Foreign Ministry files, United Nations War Crimes Commission file, notes to Washington, London, and Moscow embassies, 25 March 1944, 020-010117-0021-0126x.

50. NARA, RG 84, Tokyo political adviser 1945, box 2, Robertson to Atcheson, 6 December 1945. MMA, RG-9, box 159, War Crimes folder, Marshall to MacArthur, 24 November 1945.

51. Guoshiguan, Foreign Ministry files, postwar Japan file, Supreme National Defense Council, "How to Deal with Japan," 16 January 1946, 020-010122-0010-0034a to 020-010122-0010-0038x.

52. Guoshiguan, Foreign Ministry files, Japan demilitarization file, Tang paper, n.d., 020-010122-0009-0223a to 020-010122-0009-0236a.

53. Guoshiguan, Foreign Ministry files, postwar Japan file, Japan policy draft outline, 020-010122-0010-0057a to 020-010122-0010-0074a; Guoshiguan, Foreign Ministry files, postwar Japan file, Zhang to Chiang, 13 August 1946, 020-010122-0010-0052a to 020-010122-0010-0056a. Guoshiguan, Foreign Ministry files, Japan public opinion file, Shang note, 11 September 1947, 020-010107-0016-0022a to 020-010107-0016-0029a. See Guoshiguan, Foreign Ministry files, Japan public opinion file, Katayama to Chiang, 16 October 1946, 020-010107-0016-0014x to 020-010107-0016-0015a.

54. Guoshiguan, Foreign Ministry files, postwar Japan file, Japan policy draft outline, 020-010122-0010-0057a to 020-010122-0010-0074a.

55. Guoshiguan, Foreign Ministry files, postwar Japan file, Zhang to Chiang, 13 August 1946, 020-010122-0010-0052a to 020-010122-0010-0056a.

56. Guoshiguan, Foreign Ministry files, IMTFE trials 1946–47, Yang note, n.d. (May or June 1946), 020-010117-0030-0076a to 020-010117-0030-0077a.

57. Guoshiguan, Foreign Ministry files, postwar Japan file, Li note, 1945, 020-010122-0010-0042x to 020-010122-0010-0043x.

58. Guoshiguan, Foreign Ministry files, postwar Japan file, Li note, 23 December 1945, 020-010122-0010-0044x to 020-010122-0010-0047x.

59. See Ian Buruma, *Inventing Japan, 1853–1964* (New York: Modern Library, 2003), pp. 90–92.

60. AWM, Webb papers, 3DRL/2481, series 4, wallet 7, "Court Memoranda," *Jiji Shimpo*, 27 June 1946.

61. *IMTFE Transcripts*, 25 June 1946, p. 1332.

62. Arnold C. Brackman, *The Other Nuremberg: The Untold Story of the Tokyo War Crime Trials* (London: Collins, 1989), pp. 144–45.

63. Akira Iriye, *Power and Culture: The Japanese-American War, 1941–1945* (Cambridge, Mass.: Harvard University Press, 1981), p. 65.

64. *Taiheiyo senso e no michi: Kaisen gaiko shi* [The Road to the Pacific War: A Diplomatic History of the Origins of the War], in James William Morley, ed., *Japan Erupts: The London Naval Conference and the Manchurian Incident, 1928–1932* (New York: Columbia University Press, 1984), pp. 182–84, 208–10, 245–46, 258, 332. See Shidehara Kijuro, *Gaiko gojunen* [Fifty Years of Foreign Relations] (Tokyo: Yomiuri Shimbunsha, 1951).

65. *IMTFE Transcripts*, 25 June 1946, pp. 1318–25, 1335–38, 1340–41, 1392.

66. AWM, Webb papers, 3DRL/2481, series 4, wallet 7, "Court Memoranda," *Jiji Shimpo*, 27 June 1946. *IMTFE Transcripts*, 25 June 1946, p. 1393.

67. "Emperor Desired Manchu War End, Tribunal Is Told," *Nippon Times*, 29 June 1946, pp. 1–2.

68. *IMTFE Transcripts*, 28 June 1946, pp. 1553–73.

69. *IMTFE Transcripts*, 28 June 1946, p. 1591.

70. Yoshitake Oka, *Five Political Leaders of Modern Japan*, trans. Andrew Fraser and Patricia Murray (Tokyo: University of Tokyo Press, 1986), pp. 172–73.

71. *IMTFE Transcripts*, 27 June 1946, pp. 1515–16. The son was Inukai Takeru, who used the English first name Ken.

72. *IMTFE Transcripts*, 27 June 1946, pp. 1526–49.

73. *IMTFE Transcripts*, 8 April 1947, pp. 19554–55. Herbert P. Bix, *Hirohito and the Making of Modern Japan* (New York: HarperCollins, 2000), pp. 246–47.

74. *IMTFE Transcripts*, 5 July 1946, p. 1938.

75. *IMTFE Transcripts,* 2 July 1946, pp. 1819–25.

76. *IMTFE Transcripts,* 2 July 1946, pp. 1830–32.

77. "A 'Dead Man' Speaks," *Life,* 26 January 1948, pp. 87–90.

78. "Showa tenno no dokuhaku hachijikan" [The Showa Emperor's Eight-Hour Monologue], *Bungei Shunju,* December 1990, p. 124.

79. Bix, *Hirohito,* p. 366.

80. *IMTFE Transcripts,* testimony for 5, 8, and 9 July 1946. "Tanaka Reveals He Tried to Oust Tojo During War," *Nippon Times,* 9 July 1946, pp. 1–2. AWM, Webb papers, 3DRL/2481, series 4, wallet 7, "Summarized Proceedings," *Asahi Shimbun,* 6 July 1946.

81. *IMTFE Transcripts,* 28 June 1946, pp. 1596–97.

82. *IMTFE Transcripts,* 5 July 1946, p. 1938.

83. UVA, Tavenner papers, box 24, IPS document no. 1767, Analysis of Documentary Evidence, 3 June 1946.

84. *IMTFE Transcripts,* 30 July 1946, pp. 2719–28.

85. "Showa tenno no dokuhaku hachijikan," p. 101.

86. Puyi, *From Emperor to Citizen: The Autobiography of Aisin-Gioro Pu Yi,* trans. W. J. F. Jenner (Beijing: Foreign Languages Press, 1965), vol. 2, pp. 268–69.

87. *IMTFE Transcripts,* 31 July 1946, pp. 2847–96. Victor Alexander George Robert Bulwer-Lytton, Earl of Lytton, *Report of the Commission of Enquiry of the League of Nations: Signed at Peiping, September 4, 1932* (Nanjing: Waichiaopu, 1932).

88. Oona Hathaway and Scott J. Shapiro, *The Internationalists: How a Radical Plan to Outlaw War Remade the World* (New York: Simon & Schuster, 2018), pp. 156–57. Rana Mitter, *The Manchurian Myth: Nationalism, Resistance, and Collaboration in Modern China* (Berkeley: University of California Press, 2000).

89. HSTL, PSF, box 151/9, China 1946 folder, Truman to Wallace, 25 January 1946.

90. Srinath Raghavan, *The Most Dangerous Place: A History of the United States in South Asia* (London: Allen Lane, 2018), p. 119.

91. Truman to Bess Truman, 28 December 1945, *Off the Record: The Private Papers of Harry S. Truman,* ed. Robert H. Ferrell (New York: Harper & Row, 1980), pp. 75–76.

92. Truman memorandum, November 1945, *Off the Record,* p. 74.

93. Truman statement, 10 October 1945, *Public Papers of the Presidents of the United States: Harry S. Truman, 1945* (Washington, D.C.: U.S. Government Printing Office, 1961), p. 394.

94. Daniel Kurtz-Phelan, *The China Mission: George Marshall's Unfinished War, 1945–1947* (New York: W. W. Norton, 2018).

95. Truman statement, 15 December 1945, *Public Papers,* pp. 543–45.

96. MMA, RG-5, C-in-C's personal file, MacArthur to Marshall, 30 November 1945.

97. Truman to Bess Truman, 19 September 1946, *Dear Bess: The Letters from Harry to Bess Truman, 1910–1959,* ed. Robert H. Ferrell (New York: W. W. Norton, 1983), p. 538.

98. Odd Arne Westad, *Decisive Encounters: The Chinese Civil War, 1946–1950* (Stanford, Calif.: Stanford University Press, 2003), pp. 6–13.

99. Mei Ruao, *Dongjing da shenpan: Yuandong guoji junshi fating Zhongguo faguan Mei Ruao riji* [The Great Tokyo Trial: Diary of Mei Ruao, Chinese Judge at the International Military Tribunal for the Far East] (Nanchang: Jiangxi Education Press, 2005), 11 April 1946, p. 80.

100. Mei, *Dongjing da shenpan,* 4 May 1946, p. 139.

101. Mei, *Dongjing da shenpan,* 8 May 1946, p. 146.

102. Mei, *Dongjing da shenpan*, 12 May 1946, p. 154.

103. K. P. S. Menon, *Many Worlds: An Autobiography* (Oxford: Oxford University Press, 1965), p. 248.

104. Russell Brines, "Japan's Scarecrow War Crime Suspects Now Sleek, Assured," *Nippon Times*, 31 July 1946, p. 1.

105. AWM, Webb papers, 3DRL/2481, series 4, wallet 7, "Momentary Tension of the Accused Toward the American Defense Counsels," *Tokyo Shimbun*, 15 May 1946.

106. AWM, Webb papers, 3DRL/2481, series 4, wallet 7, Ryusahuro Shikiba, "Psychology of War Criminals," *Asahi Shimbun*, 20 May 1946.

107. "Defendant Kimura Sees Son in War Court," *Nippon Times*, 18 August 1946, p. 2.

108. *IMTFE Transcripts*, 27 June 1946, p. 1521.

109. "Prosecution on Task of Proving Charge," *Nippon Times*, 25 June 1946, p. 2.

110. *IMTFE Transcripts*, 11 March 1947, p. 18153.

111. *IMTFE Transcripts*, 25 June 1946, p. 1320.

112. *IMTFE Transcripts*, 19 August 1947, p. 26223.

113. Röling, *The Tokyo Trial and Beyond*, p. 52.

114. BNA, LCO 2/2992, Northcroft to O'Leary, 18 March 1947.

115. AWM, Webb papers, 3DRL/2481, series 4, wallet 4, Webb to Patrick, 10 May 1946.

116. AWM, Webb papers, 3DRL/2481, series 4, wallet 4, Patrick to Webb, 8 May 1946.

117. AWM, Webb papers, 3DRL/2481, series 4, wallet 9, Mueller to Webb, 22 July 1946.

118. Mei, *Dongjing da shenpan*, 21 April 1946, p. 105.

119. AWM, Webb papers, 3DRL/2481, series 4, wallet 4, Patrick to Webb, 8 May 1946.

120. Mei, *Dongjing da shenpan*, 2 April 1946, p. 56.

121. Mei, *Dongjing da shenpan*, 13 May 1946, p. 156.

122. *IMTFE Transcripts*, 15 July 1946, p. 2294.

123. AWM, Webb papers, 3DRL/2481, series 4, wallet 11, Webb to Walbridge, 1 May 1946.

124. NL-HaNA, 2.21.273, folder 27, Röling to Nisbet, 22 July 1946.

125. NL-HaNA, 2.21.273, folder 27, Röling to Nisbet, 6 May 1946.

126. NL-HaNA, 2.21.273, folder 27, Röling to Nisbet, 6 May 1946.

127. Mei, *Dongjing da shenpan*, 22 April 1946, p. 106.

128. NL-HaNA, 2.21.273, folder 27, "The BCOF Prayer," 1946.

129. Danielle Elisseeff, *Puyi: Le dernier empereur de Chine* (Paris: Perrin, 2014).

130. NL-HaNA 2.21.273, folder 27, Röling to Patricia Daly, 27 August 1946.

131. Guoshiguan, Foreign Ministry files, IMTFE trials 1946–47, Zhu to Wang, 13 July 1946, 020-010117-0030-0119a. Guoshiguan, Foreign Ministry files, IMTFE trials 1946–47, Tokyo delegation to Foreign Ministry, 30 July 1946, 020-010117-0030-0121a; Foreign Ministry to Tokyo delegation, 13 August 1946, 020-010117-0030-0122x.

132. "Pu Yi Expected in Tokyo to Testify at War Crimes Trials Under Russian Custody," *Nippon Times*, 8 August 1946, p. 1.

133. "Pu Yi Here to Testify at Trials," *Nippon Times*, 11 August 1946, p. 1.

134. Reginald F. Johnston, *Twilight in the Forbidden City* (London: Victor Gollancz, 1934), pp. 231–40.

135. Puyi, *From Emperor to Citizen*, vol. 2, pp. 327–29.

136. Puyi, *From Emperor to Citizen*, vol. 2, pp. 280–83, 297–301.

137. Puyi, *From Emperor to Citizen*, vol. 2, pp. 253–58, 273–76, 292–93, 304–7. "Pu Yi Expected in Tokyo to Testify at War Crimes Trials Under Russian Custody."

138. Puyi, *From Emperor to Citizen*, vol. 2, pp. 314–28. Elisseeff, *Puyi*, pp. 232–35.

139. Puyi, *From Emperor to Citizen,* vol. 2, pp. 283–84, 287.

140. *IMTFE Transcripts,* 23 August 1946, p. 4204.

141. Puyi, *From Emperor to Citizen,* vol. 2, pp. 327–29. See Li Shuxian with Wang Qing-xiang, *My Husband Puyi,* trans. Ni Nan (Beijing: China Intercontinental Press, 2016).

142. *IMTFE Transcripts,* 27 August 1946, 4324–26.

143. *IMTFE Transcripts,* 16 August 1946, pp. 3945–71.

144. *IMTFE Transcripts,* 19 August 1946, pp. 3974–4002.

145. *IMTFE Transcripts,* 20 August 1946, pp. 4049–50.

146. AWM, Webb papers, 3DRL/2481, series 1, wallet 10, Röling to Webb, 26 August 1946.

147. Puyi, *From Emperor to Citizen,* vol. 2, p. 329.

148. *IMTFE Transcripts,* 19 August 1946, pp. 3974–4002.

149. Helen Hardacre, *Shinto: A History* (Oxford: Oxford University Press, 2017), pp. 431–40.

150. *IMTFE Transcripts,* 19 August 1946, pp. 4002–25.

151. Ben Bruce Blakeney, "Pu Yi," *Life,* 16 July 1945, p. 78.

152. *IMTFE Transcripts,* 20 August 1946, pp. 4055–79; 21 August 1946, pp. 4082–141; 22 August 1946, pp. 4144–48; 23 August 1946, pp. 4211–17. "Pu Yi Tells Court He Became Ruler to Oust Japanese," *Nippon Times,* 20 August 1946, pp. 1–2.

153. HLS, Keenan Papers, Keenan to Puyi, 27 August 1946.

154. Guoshiguan, Foreign Ministry files, IMTFE trials 1946–47, Xiang to Foreign Ministry, 27 August 1946, 020-010117-0030-0124a to 020-010117-0030-0125a.

155. MMA, RG-9, box 159, War Crimes folder, Acheson to Atcheson, 10 July 1946; War Department to MacArthur, 31 July 1946; Atcheson to Byrnes, 1 August 1946.

156. "PI Prosecutors Want Laurel and Vargas as Witnesses but Other Nations Object," *Nippon Times,* 28 August 1946, p. 1.

157. Guoshiguan, Foreign Ministry files, IMTFE trials 1946–47, Xiang to Foreign Ministry, 27 August 1946, 020-010117-0030-0124a to 020-010117-0030-0125a. Guoshiguan, Foreign Ministry files, IMTFE trials 1946–47, Wang to Gan and Liu, 14 August 1946, 020-010117-0030-0126a; Gan and Liu to Wang, 19 August 1946, 020-010117-0030-0127x.

158. Puyi, *From Emperor to Citizen,* vol. 2, pp. 325–28, 333–40.

159. China Fushun War Criminals Management Center, *Place of New Life of Japanese War Criminals* (Beijing: China Intercontinental Press, 2015), p. 49.

160. Puyi, *From Emperor to Citizen,* vol. 2, pp. 340–472, 440, 466–67.

13. The Rape of Nanjing

1. Philippe Sands, *East West Street: On the Origins of Genocide and Crimes Against Humanity* (London: Weidenfeld & Nicolson, 2016), pp. 114–15.

2. Guoshiguan, Foreign Ministry files, IMTFE trials 1946–47, Sutton to Wang, 23 April 1946, 020-010117-0030-0048a.

3. Guoshiguan, Foreign Ministry files, IMTFE trials 1945–46, Chiang to Soong, March 1946, 020-010117-0029-0238a; Executive Yuan administrative order, 25 March 1946, 020-010117-0029-0237a.

4. Guoshiguan, Foreign Ministry files, IMTFE trials 1945–46, Chiang to Soong, March 1946, 020-010117-0029-0238a; Executive Yuan administrative order, 25 March 1946, 020-010117-0029-0237a.

5. Guoshiguan, Foreign Ministry files, IMTFE trials 1945–46, Xiang to Wang, 21 March 1946, 020-010117-0029-0206a; Xiang to Xu and Wang, 23 March 1946, 020-010117-0029-0239a. Guoshiguan, Foreign Ministry files, IMTFE trials 1945–46, Xiang to Wang, 9 March 1946, 020-010117-0029-0204a. Guoshiguan, Foreign Ministry files, IMTFE trials 1945–46, Liu to Foreign Ministry, 9 March 1946, 020-010117-0029-0202a.

6. Guoshiguan, Foreign Ministry files, IMTFE trials 1945–46, Xiang to Wang, 25 March 1946, 020-010117-0029-0205a; Xiang to Wang, 21 March 1946, 020-010117-0029-0206a.

7. MMA, RG-5, box 2, folder 4, Madame Chiang interview, 28 March 1946.

8. Guoshiguan, Foreign Ministry files, IMTFE trials 1945–46, Wang and Yang to Lu and Wang, 25 March 1946, 020-010117-0029-0209x; Foreign Ministry to Xiang, March 1946, 020-010117-0029-0214a; Xiang note, 6 April 1946, 020-010117-0029-0215x. Guoshiguan, Foreign Ministry files, IMTFE trials 1945–46, Lu and Wang memo, March 1946, 020-010117-0029-0216a to 020-010117-0029-0217a.

9. Guoshiguan, Foreign Ministry files, IMTFE trials 1945–46, Xiang request to Ministry of Military Command, Ministry of Judicial Administration, Ministry of Military Affairs, Ministry of Internal Affairs, Executive Yuan's Compensation Survey Committee, Central Bureau of Investigation and Statistics, Bureau of Investigation and Statistics, and Research Institute of International Relations, 20 February 1946, 020-010117-0029-0151x. Guoshiguan, Foreign Ministry files, IMTFE trials 1945–46, Caraway to Wang, 19 February 1946, Xiang note, 020-010117-0029-0167x.

10. Guoshiguan, Foreign Ministry files, IMTFE trials 1945–46, Xiang to Ministry of Judicial Administration, 4 March 1946, 020-010117-0029-0182x. Guoshiguan, Foreign Ministry files, IMTFE trials 1945–46, Foreign Ministry to consulates, 5 March 1946, 020-010117-0029-0184x.

11. Guoshiguan, Foreign Ministry files, IMTFE trials 1945–46, Huang to Wang, 8 March 1946, 020-010117-0029-0219a.

12. Guoshiguan, Foreign Ministry files, IMTFE trials 1945–46, Yang to Ye, 30 March 1946, 020-010117-0029-0241a; Ye to Yang, 3 April 1946, 020-010117-0029-0242a to 020-010117-0029-0245a. Guoshiguan, Foreign Ministry files, IMTFE trials 1946–47, Zhu note, 22 May 1946, 020-010117-0030-0020a.

13. Guoshiguan, Foreign Ministry files, IMTFE trials 1945–46, Chai note, 17 May 1946, 020-010117-0029-0265x; Yang note, n.d., 020-010117-0029-0264a; Yang Jueyong to Yang Yunzhu, n.d., 020-010117-0029-0263a.

14. Guoshiguan, Foreign Ministry files, IMTFE trials 1945–46, Yuan to Foreign Ministry, 1946, 020-010117-0029-0191a; Foreign Ministry to Ministry of Judicial Administration, 10 April 1946, 020-010117-0029-0193x; Yuan to Foreign Ministry, 4 April 1946, 020-010117-0029-0195a. Guoshiguan, Foreign Ministry files, IMTFE trials 1945–46, Sun to Foreign Ministry, 25 May 1946, 020-010117-0029-0200a; Foreign Ministry to Sun, 1 August 1946, 020-010117-0029-0201a.

15. Guoshiguan, Foreign Ministry files, IMTFE trials 1945–46, Zhang to Foreign Ministry, 29 March 1946, 020-010117-0029-0197a to 020-010117-0029-0198a.

16. Guoshiguan, Foreign Ministry files, IMTFE trials 1945–46, Xie to Xiang, 21 February 1946, 020-010117-0029-0152x to 020-010117-0029-0153x. Guoshiguan, Foreign Ministry files, IMTFE trials 1945–46, Luo documents, n.d., 020-010117-0029-0162a. Guoshiguan, Foreign Ministry files, IMTFE trials 1945–46, Executive Yuan to Foreign Ministry, 28 February 1946, 020-010117-0029-0168x.

17. Guoshiguan, Foreign Ministry files, IMTFE trials 1945–46, Chen to Foreign Ministry, 26 February 1946, 020-010117-0029-0155x. Guoshiguan, Foreign Ministry files, IMTFE trials 1945–46, Executive Yuan to Foreign Ministry, 28 February 1946, 020-010117-0029-0168x. Guoshiguan, Foreign Ministry files, IMTFE trials 1945–46, Zhang letter, 6 March 1946, 020-010117-0029-0171x. Guoshiguan, Foreign Ministry files, IMTFE trials 1945–46, Xie to Foreign Ministry, 10 March 1946, 020-010117-0029-0183x. Guoshiguan, Foreign Ministry files, IMTFE trials 1945–46, Guo to Foreign Ministry, 12 March 1946, 020-010117-0029-0186a.

18. Guoshiguan, Foreign Ministry files, IMTFE trials 1946–47, Yang note, May or June 1946, 020-010117-0030-0076a to 020-010117-0030-0077a.

19. Guoshiguan, Foreign Ministry files, IMTFE trials 1946–47, notes on Yang report, 1946, 020-010117-0030-0079x.

20. Guoshiguan, Foreign Ministry files, IMTFE trials 1946–47, Xiang to Foreign Ministry, 10 June 1946, 020-010117-0030-0035a to 020-010117-0030-0036a. See Guoshiguan, Foreign Ministry files, IMTFE trials 1946–47, Defense Ministry to Foreign Ministry, 10 June 1946, 020-010117-0030-0053x.

21. Guoshiguan, Foreign Ministry files, IMTFE trials 1946–47, Qin to Military Command Ministry, June 1946, "The Facts of the July 7 Incident," n.d., 020-010117-0030-0055a to 020-010117-0030-0069a.

22. Herbert P. Bix, *Hirohito and the Making of Modern Japan* (New York: HarperCollins, 2000), pp. 594–95. Yuma Totani, *The Tokyo War Crimes Trial: The Pursuit of Justice in the Wake of World War II* (Cambridge, Mass.: Harvard University Press, 2008), p. 188.

23. Guoshiguan, Foreign Ministry files, IMTFE trials 1946–47, Yang note, n.d. (May or June 1946), 020-010117-0030-0076a to 020-010117-0030-0077a.

24. AWM, Webb papers, 3DRL/2481, series 4, wallet 13, International Prosecution Section memo, 27 June 1946. There was also a translator, Henry Chiu.

25. Cheng Zhaoqi, *A History of War Crimes Trials in Post 1945 Asia-Pacific,* trans. Jun He and Fangbin Yang (Singapore: Palgrave Macmillan, 2019), pp. 312, 318–24.

26. Kyodo-AP, "Nanking Rape Witnesses Fly to Tokyo to Testify at War Crimes Trials," *Nippon Times,* 10 June 1946, p. 1.

27. Mei Ruao, "A Vote on the Right to Life," March 1948, Mei Xiaoao and Mei Xiaokan, eds., *Mei Ruao Dongjing shenpan wengao* [The Tokyo Trial Manuscripts of Mei Ruao] (Shanghai: Shanghai Jiaotong University Press, 2013), p. 393.

28. Mei Ruao, *Dongjing da shenpan: Yuandong guoji junshi fating Zhongguo faguan Mei Ruao riji* [The Great Tokyo Trial: Diary of Mei Ruao, Chinese Judge at the International Military Tribunal for the Far East] (Nanchang: Jiangxi Education Press, 2005), 4 May 1946, p. 138; 8 April 1946, p. 74.

29. AWM, Webb papers, 3DRL/2481, series 4, wallet 19, Northcroft to judges, 3 December 1946.

30. HSTL, NAP, box 13, Japan Surrender, Wedemeyer to Stimson, 27 August 1945. Yukiko Koshiro, *Imperial Eclipse: Japan's Strategic Thinking About Continental Asia Before August 1945* (Ithaca, N.Y.: Cornell University Press, 2013), p. 4.

31. Ono Kenji, "Massacres Near Mufushan," in Bob Tadashi Wakabayashi, ed., *The Nanking Atrocity, 1937–38: Complicating the Picture* (New York: Berghahn Books, 2009), pp. 70–85.

32. Sun Zhaiwei, ed., *Nanjing datusha* [The Nanjing Massacre] (Beijing: Beijing Publishing House, 1997), pp. 623–37.

33. Daqing Yang, "Convergence or Divergence?," *American Historical Review*, vol. 104, no. 3 (June 1999), pp. 855–57. Kasahara Tokushi, *Nankin jiken* [The Nanjing Incident] (Tokyo: Iwanami Shoten, 1997).

34. Odd Arne Westad, *Restless Empire: China and the World Since 1750* (New York: Basic Books, 2012), p. 261.

35. "Showa tenno no dokuhaku hachijikan" [The Showa Emperor's Eight-Hour Mono-logue], *Bungei Shunju*, December 1990, pp. 132–33.

36. Benjamin Lai, *Shanghai and Nanjing 1937: Massacre on the Yangtze* (New York: Osprey, 2017), pp. 15–16, 79, 89.

37. *IMTFE Transcripts*, 8 August 1946, pp. 3460–61. See AWM, Webb papers, 3DRL/2481, series 2, wallet 1, Webb judgment, p. 236, 17 September 1948, pp. 436–37.

38. Asaka was the commander of the Shanghai Expeditionary Army. Irokawa Daikichi, *Aru Showa shi: Jibunshi no kokoromi* [A Certain History of the Showa Period: An Attempt at Self-History] (Tokyo: Chuo Koronsha, 1975), pp. 64–69. Wakabayashi, ed., *Nanking Atrocity*, p. 11. Ono, "Massacres Near Mufushan," in Wakabayashi, ed., *Nanking Atrocity*, pp. 70–85.

39. Guoshiguan, Foreign Ministry files, IMTFE trials 1946–47, Xiang to Foreign Min-istry, 10 June 1946, 020-010117-0030-0035a to 020-010117-0030-0036a. Guoshiguan, Foreign Ministry files, IMTFE trials 1946–47, Qin to Military Command Minis-try, June 1946, "The Facts of the July 7 Incident," n.d., 020-010117-0030-0055a to 020-010117-0030-0069a.

40. *IMTFE Transcripts*, 22 July 1946, p. 2334. Guoshiguan, Foreign Ministry files, IMTFE trials 1946–47, Defense Ministry note, June 1946, 020-010117-0030-0054x.

41. *IMTFE Transcripts*, 7 August 1946, pp. 3355–64.

42. *IMTFE Transcripts*, 22 July 1946, pp. 2318–34.

43. *IMTFE Transcripts*, 22 July 1946, pp. 2318–34. For Qin's prepared testimony, see Guoshiguan, Foreign Ministry files, IMTFE trials 1946–47, Qin to Military Command Ministry, June 1946, "The Facts of the July 7 Incident," n.d., 020-010117-0030-0055a to 020-010117-0030-0069a.

44. *IMTFE Transcripts*, 24 July 1946, pp. 2435–40.

45. *IMTFE Transcripts*, 23 July 1946, p. 2412.

46. "Nankin no gyakusatsu jiken hakujitsuka ni bei ishi shogen" [Nanjing Massacre Under the Light of Day, U.S. Doctor Testifies], *Yomiuri Shimbun*, 26 July 1946, p. 3.

47. *Liberation Daily* editorial, "Yuandong guoji fating shang de guaiju" [A Strange Show at the International Tribunal for the Far East], *Renmin Ribao [People's Daily]*, 2 August 1946, p. 1.

48. Rana Mitter, *Forgotten Ally: China's World War II, 1937–1945* (Boston: Houghton Miff-lin Harcourt, 2013), pp. 79–97. Mitter's book is a superb, pathbreaking account.

49. *IMTFE Transcripts*, 8 August 1947, p. 3487.

50. *IMTFE Transcripts*, 8 August 1947, pp. 3563–64.

51. *IMTFE Transcripts*, 9 August 1947, pp. 3584–99.

52. *IMTFE Transcripts*, 5 May 1947, pp. 21423–45.

53. *IMTFE Transcripts*, 13 May 1947, pp. 22034–35.

54. *IMTFE Transcripts*, 9 August 1946, pp. 3641–51.

55. *IMTFE Transcripts*, 13 May 1947, pp. 22026–27.

56. "Nankin no gyakusatsu jiken hakujitsuka ni bei ishi shogen" [Nanjing Massacre Under the Light of Day, U.S. Doctor Testifies], *Yomiuri Shimbun*, 26 July 1946, p. 3.

57. NL-HaNA, 2.21.273, folder 27, Röling to Patricia Daly, 27 August 1946.

58. Hallett Abend, *My Life in China, 1926–1941* (New York: Harcourt, Brace, 1943), p. 270.

59. AWM, Webb papers, 3DRL/2481, series 4, wallet 11, Rubin memorandum, 15 January 1947.

60. Russell Brines, "Japan's Scarecrow War Crime Suspects Now Sleek, Assured," *Nippon Times,* 31 July 1946, p. 1.

61. "Nankin no gyakusatsu jiken hakujitsuka ni bei ishi shogen" [Nanjing Massacre Under the Light of Day, U.S. Doctor Testifies], *Yomiuri Shimbun,* 26 July 1946, p. 3.

62. *IMTFE Transcripts,* 8 August 1946, pp. 3436–40.

63. See Martha Lund Smalley, ed., *American Missionary Eyewitnesses to the Nanking Massacre, 1937–1938* (New Haven: Yale Divinity School Library, 1997); and Suping Lu, *They Were in Nanjing: The Nanjing Massacre Witnessed by American and British Nationals* (Hong Kong: Hong Kong University Press, 2004).

64. *IMTFE Transcripts,* 25 July 1946, pp. 2527–39.

65. Wilson letter, 18 December 1937, in Timothy Brook, ed., *Documents on the Rape of Nanking* (Ann Arbor: University of Michigan Press, 1999), p. 214.

66. *IMTFE Transcripts,* 29 July 1946, pp. 2624–48.

67. *IMTFE Transcripts,* 29 July 1946, pp. 2661–62.

68. Arnold C. Brackman, *The Other Nuremberg: The Untold Story of the Tokyo War Crime Trials* (London: Collins, 1989), pp. 194–95.

69. "Women Attend Trial to Hear Rape Stories," *Nippon Times,* 31 July 1946, p. 2.

70. Zhang Kaiyuan, ed., *Eyewitnesses to Massacre: American Missionaries Bear Witness to Japanese Atrocities in Nanjing* (Armonk, N.Y.: M. E. Sharpe, 2001).

71. Yale Divinity Library, Magee papers, RG 242, series IV, Nanking documentation.

72. *IMTFE Transcripts,* 15 August 1946, pp. 3893–916. *IMTFE Transcripts,* 16 August 1946, p. 3929.

73. *IMTFE Transcripts,* 26 July 1946, pp. 2556–97. In Wade-Giles transliteration, his name is Hsu Chuan-ying.

74. *IMTFE Transcripts,* 26 July 1946, pp. 2600–2606.

75. *IMTFE Transcripts,* 26 July 1946, pp. 2609–15. In Wade-Giles transliteration, his name was given as Chen Fu-pao.

76. *IMTFE Transcripts,* 29 August 1946, pp. 4451–54.

77. *IMTFE Transcripts,* 29 August 1946, pp. 4483–90.

78. *IMTFE Transcripts,* 29 August 1946, pp. 4464–66, 4498–99. See Suping Lu, ed., *Terror in Minnie Vautrin's Nanjing: Diaries and Correspondence, 1937–38* (Urbana: University of Illinois Press, 2008); and Hua-ling Hu and Zhang Lian-hong, eds., *The Undaunted Women of Nanking: The Wartime Diaries of Minnie Vautrin and Tsen Shui-fang* (Carbondale: Southern Illinois University Press, 2010).

79. *IMTFE Transcripts,* 29 August 1946, pp. 4536–48.

80. *IMTFE Transcripts,* 29 August 1946, pp. 4456–58.

81. *IMTFE Transcripts,* 29 August 1946, pp. 4508–36.

82. *IMTFE Transcripts,* 30 January 1947, pp. 16820–21.

83. *IMTFE Transcripts,* 8 August 1946, pp. 3510–13.

84. *IMTFE Transcripts,* 8 August 1946, pp. 3453–65.

85. *IMTFE Transcripts,* 8 August 1946, pp. 3552–59.

86. *IMTFE Transcripts,* 30 August 1946, pp. 4604–5.

87. *IMTFE Transcripts,* 12 August 1946, pp. 3769–70.

88. *IMTFE Transcripts,* 30 August 1946, pp. 4614–28, 4645.

89. *IMTFE Transcripts,* 3 September 1946, pp. 4660–63.

90. *IMTFE Transcripts,* 30 August 1946, pp. 4607–14.

91. Julia Lovell, *The Opium War: Drugs, Dreams, and the Making of Modern China* (New York: Overlook Press, 2014). Mao Haijian, *The Qing Empire and the Opium War: The Collapse of the Heavenly Dynasty* (Cambridge: Cambridge University Press, 2016). Stephen R. Platt, *Imperial Twilight: The Opium War and the End of China's Last Golden Age* (New York: Alfred A. Knopf, 2018). Chang Hsin-pao, *Commissioner Lin and the Opium War* (Cambridge, Mass.: Harvard University Press, 1964). Jonathan D. Spence, *The Search for Modern China* (New York: W. W. Norton, 1990), pp. 147–64.

92. *IMTFE Transcripts,* 20 August 1946, pp. 4040–43.

93. *IMTFE Transcripts,* 28 August 1946, pp. 4407–23.

94. *IMTFE Transcripts,* 26 July 1946, pp. 2547–48.

95. Lewis S. C. Smythe, *War Damage in the Nanking Area, December 1937 to March 1938* (Shanghai: Mercury Press, 1938).

96. *IMTFE Transcripts,* 9 August 1946, pp. 3655–74.

97. "Nankin no gyakusatsu jiken hakujitsuka ni bei ishi shogen" [Nanjing Massacre Under the Light of Day, U.S. Doctor Testifies], *Yomiuri Shimbun,* 26 July 1946, p. 3.

98. "Chugokujin ni shai" [Gratitude to the Chinese], *Yomiuri Shimbun,* 31 July 1946, p. 1. See "Meiso" [The Sunlit Window], *Yomiuri Shimbun,* 25 July 1946, p. 1.

99. Lindesay Parrott, "Tokyo Reporters Assess Tojo Trial," *New York Times,* 18 July 1948, p. 30.

100. "Women Attend Trial to Hear Rape Stories," *Nippon Times,* 31 July 1946, p. 2.

101. "Chugokujin ni shai" [Gratitude to the Chinese], *Yomiuri Shimbun,* 31 July 1946, p. 1.

102. "Chugokujin ni shai" [Gratitude to the Chinese], *Yomiuri Shimbun,* 31 July 1946, p. 1.

103. Diana Lary, "Father and the Republic," *Journal of Chinese Military History,* vol. 2 (2013), pp. 78–79. See Bai Xianyong, *Fuqin yu Minguo* [Father and the Republic] (Taipei: Shibao Wenhua, 2012).

104. Guoshiguan, Foreign Ministry files, IMTFE trials 1946–47, Yang note, May or June 1946, 020-010117-0030-0076a to 020-010117-0030-0077a.

105. Guoshiguan, Foreign Ministry files, War Criminals Policies 1946–48, "Record of the War Criminal Handling Committee's Meeting on Policies Regarding How to Deal with War Criminals," 25 October 1946, 020-010117-0039-0017a to 020-010117-0039-0028a.

106. Guoshiguan, Foreign Ministry files, IMTFE trials 1946–47, Yang note, May or June 1946, 020-010117-0030-0076a to 020-010117-0030-0077a.

14. Remember Pearl Harbor

1. Fredrik Logevall, *JFK: Coming of Age in the American Century, 1917–1956* (New York: Random House, 2020), p. 302.

2. HSTL, OF, box 1145, Keenan to Truman, 1 August 1946. HSTL, OF, box 1145, Connelly to Keenan, 8 August 1946.

3. "A Lesson in History," *Nippon Times,* 6 July 1946.

4. *IMTFE Transcripts,* 4 November 1946, pp. 9328–34.

5. Eberhard Jäckel, *Hitler's World View: A Blueprint for Power,* trans. Herbert Arnold

(Cambridge, Mass.: Harvard University Press, 1981), pp. 27–66. Timothy Snyder, *Bloodlands: Europe Between Hitler and Stalin* (New York: Basic Books, 2010).

6. Richard Overy, *Blood and Ruins: The Great Imperial War, 1931–1945* (London: Allen Lane, 2021).

7. Herbert P. Bix, *Hirohito and the Making of Modern Japan* (New York: HarperCollins, 2000), pp. 410–11.

8. Jack Snyder, *Myths of Empire: Domestic Politics and International Ambition* (Ithaca, N.Y.: Cornell University Press, 1991), pp. 129–30.

9. Scott D. Sagan, "The Origins of the Pacific War," *Journal of Interdisciplinary History,* vol. 18, no. 4 (Spring 1988), pp. 916–17.

10. Logevall, *JFK,* p. 302.

11. Sagan, "Origins of the Pacific War," pp. 913, 917–20. See Ian W. Toll, *Twilight of the Gods: War in the Western Pacific, 1944–1945* (New York: W. W. Norton, 2020), pp. 768–75.

12. Telford Taylor, *The Anatomy of the Nuremberg Trials: A Personal Memoir* (New York: Alfred A. Knopf, 1992), pp. 610–11.

13. Ian Buruma, *The Wages of Guilt: Memories of War in Germany and Japan* (New York: Farrar, Straus & Giroux, 1994), p. 9.

14. Richard J. Evans, *The Third Reich in Power* (London: Allen Lane, 2005), p. 604.

15. *IMTFE Transcripts,* 23 September 1946, pp. 6026–28, Himmler memorandum, 31 January 1939.

16. Jeremy A. Yellen, *The Greater East Asia Co-Prosperity Sphere: When Total Empire Met Total War* (Ithaca, N.Y.: Cornell University Press, 2019), pp. 26–45.

17. Ian Kershaw, *Hitler, 1936–45: Nemesis* (New York: W. W. Norton, 2000), p. 27.

18. Adolf Hitler, *Mein Kampf,* trans. Ralph Manheim (Boston: Houghton Mifflin, 1962), pp. 290–91, 638–40.

19. Richard J. Evans, *The Third Reich at War* (New York: Penguin, 2009), p. 112. Stephen Kotkin, *Stalin: Waiting for Hitler, 1929–1941* (New York: Penguin, 2017), p. 582. William L. Shirer, *The Rise and Fall of the Third Reich: A History of Nazi Germany* (New York: Simon & Schuster, 1960), p. 125.

20. *IMTFE Transcripts,* 25 September 1946, pp. 6351–78.

21. *IMTFE Transcripts,* 25 September 1946, Japan privy council meeting, 26 September 1940, pp. 6379–90.

22. *IMTFE Transcripts,* 25 September 1946, Hirohito rescript, 27 September 1940, pp. 6394–95.

23. *IMTFE Transcripts,* 25 September 1946, pp. 6405–11.

24. *IMTFE Transcripts,* 26 September 1946, Hitler-Matsuoka conference, 27 March 1941, pp. 6485–98.

25. *IMTFE Transcripts,* 23 September 1946, Hiranuma to Hitler, 4 May 1939, pp. 6103–7.

26. *IMTFE Transcripts,* 23 September 1946, Hitler-Terauchi talk, 25 September 1939, pp. 6133–37.

27. *IMTFE Transcripts,* 13 November 1946, Tojo interrogation, 28 January 1946, p. 10306.

28. *IMTFE Transcripts,* 25 September 1946, pp. 6351–78.

29. *IMTFE Transcripts,* 26 September 1946, pp. 6444–52.

30. *IMTFE Transcripts,* 26 September 1946, Ribbentrop-Matsuoka conversation, 29 March 1941, pp. 6522–32.

31. *IMTFE Transcripts,* 26 September 1946, Hitler directive, 3 March 1941, pp. 6469–73.

32. *IMTFE Transcripts*, 26 September 1946, Hitler-Matsuoka conference, 27 March 1941, pp. 6485–98.

33. *IMTFE Transcripts*, 26 September 1946, Hitler-Matsuoka conference, 4 April 1941, pp. 6537–45.

34. *IMTFE Transcripts*, 26 September 1946, Ribbentrop note, 28 June 1941, pp. 6562–65.

35. *IMTFE Transcripts*, 19 September 1946, pp. 5872–76. *IMTFE Transcripts*, 26 September 1946, imperial conference resolution, 2 July 1941, pp. 6566–69.

36. *IMTFE Transcripts*, 19 September 1946, pp. 5852–92.

37. *IMTFE Transcripts*, 27 September 1946, pp. 6657–61.

38. *IMTFE Transcripts*, 27 September 1946, Axis declaration, 11 December 1941, pp. 6668–70.

39. *IMTFE Transcripts*, 27 September 1946, Hitler-Oshima talk, 14 December 1941, pp. 6670–80.

40. *IMTFE Transcripts*, 12 November 1946, Kido diary, 7 August 1941, pp. 10198–201. *IMTFE Transcripts*, 8 November 1946, Kido diary, 22 June 1941, pp. 10021–23.

41. Kershaw, *Hitler, 1936–45: Nemesis*, pp. 504–5.

42. *IMTFE Transcripts*, 30 September 1946, pp. 6715–17. Telford Taylor, *Munich: The Price of Peace* (New York: Vintage, 1980), pp. 207–12.

43. Fredrik Logevall, *Embers of War: The Fall of an Empire and the Making of America's Vietnam* (New York: Random House, 2012), pp. 24–25, 43–66, 89–91.

44. Ernest R. May, *Strange Victory: Hitler's Conquest of France* (New York: Hill & Wang, 2000), p. 5. *IMTFE Transcripts*, 6 November 1946, pp. 9691–93.

45. MAE, NUOI, carton 99, French evidence, Kido diary, 14 September 1940.

46. Logevall, *Embers of War*, pp. 27–41. *IMTFE Transcripts*, 30 September 1946, pp. 6708–28.

47. AWM, Webb papers, 3DRL/2481, series 4, wallet 13, Keenan to Webb, 3 October 1946. AWM, Webb papers, 3DRL/2481, series 4, wallet 4, Chu to Mei, 16 July 1946; Mei to Webb, 17 July 1946.

48. MAE, NUOI, carton 99, Bernard to Bidault, 11 October 1946. MAE, NUOI, carton 99, Bernard to Webb, 6 September 1946. AWM, Webb papers, 3DRL/2481, series 4, wallet 4, Bernard to Webb, 30 September 1946.

49. MAE, NUOI, carton 99, Bernard to Webb, 9 September 1946.

50. *IMTFE Transcripts*, 1 October 1946, pp. 6746–63. "French Prosecutor Stalls Proceedings of Tokyo Tribunal," *Nippon Times*, 2 October 1946, pp. 1–2.

51. *IMTFE Transcripts*, 2 October 1946, pp. 6787–91. MAE, NUOI, carton 99, Keenan to Onéto, 8 October 1946.

52. *IMTFE Transcripts*, 3 December 1946, pp. 11632–34.

53. *IMTFE Transcripts*, 4 December 1946, pp. 11784–85.

54. Benedict Anderson, ed., *Violence and the State in Suharto's Indonesia* (Ithaca, N.Y.: Cornell Southeast Asia Program, 2001), p. 11. Geoffrey B. Robinson, *The Killing Season: A History of the Indonesian Massacres, 1965–66* (Princeton: Princeton University Press, 2018), pp. 31–32.

55. *IMTFE Transcripts*, 3 December 1946, pp. 11635–68.

56. Robinson, *Killing Season*, p. 33.

57. Kotkin, *Stalin*, p. 729.

58. Anne Applebaum, *Iron Curtain: The Crushing of Eastern Europe, 1944–1956* (New York: Doubleday, 2012), pp. 7–10, 24, 89, 94, 124, 251–52. Anne Applebaum, *Red Famine:*

Stalin's War on Ukraine (New York: Doubleday, 2017). Robert Conquest, *The Harvest of Sorrow: Soviet Collectivization and the Terror-Famine* (Oxford: Oxford University Press, 1986).

59. MMA, RG-9, box 160, Cooley to Byrnes, 26 August 1946.
60. BNA, FO 262/2046, Moscow embassy to Bevin, 13 October 1946.
61. BNA, FO 371/66553, Moscow embassy to Bevin, 17 May 1947. "Long Absent Soviet Judge Quits World Court Post," *New York Times*, 31 July 1953, p. 4.
62. Anne Applebaum, *Gulag: A History* (New York: Random House, 2003), pp. xxxiii–xl. Snyder, *Bloodlands*, p. 27. See Applebaum, *Red Famine*, p. 99.
63. Kotkin, *Stalin*, pp. 535–39.
64. Kotkin, *Stalin*, pp. 644–45, 650–51, 667–70. Robert Conquest, *The Great Terror: A Reassessment* (Oxford: Oxford University Press, 1990), p. 452.
65. *IMTFE Transcripts*, 8 October 1946, pp. 7285–95.
66. MMA, RG-9, box 160, W.O. folder, Harriman to Byrnes, 30 October 1946 (in Byrnes to Atcheson, 2 November 1946).
67. *IMTFE Transcripts*, 1 November 1946, pp. 9265–76.
68. *IMTFE Transcripts*, 4 November 1946, pp. 9424–26.
69. *IMTFE Transcripts*, 8 November 1946, p. 9996.
70. *IMTFE Transcripts*, 1 November 1946, p. 9284.
71. *IMTFE Transcripts*, 1 November 1946, pp. 9288–95.
72. *IMTFE Transcripts*, 7 November 1946, pp. 9891–978.
73. *IMTFE Transcripts*, 12 November 1946, imperial conference, 2 July 1941, pp. 10145–48; Kido diary, 2 July 1941, pp. 10144–45.
74. Nobutaka Ike, ed., *Japan's Decision for War: Records of the 1941 Policy Conferences* (Stanford, Calif.: Stanford University Press, 1967), imperial conference, 2 July 1941, pp. 77–90.
75. Eri Hotta, *Japan 1941: Countdown to Infamy* (New York: Alfred A. Knopf, 2013), p. 269.
76. *IMTFE Transcripts*, 1 November 1946, pp. 9288–95.
77. *IMTFE Transcripts*, 12 November 1946, imperial conference, 6 September 1941, pp. 10216–18.
78. Ike, ed., *Japan's Decision for War*, imperial conference, 6 September 1941, pp. 133–63, 151n36.
79. *IMTFE Transcripts*, 12 November 1946, pp. 10251–71.
80. *IMTFE Transcripts*, 13 November 1946, pp. 10285–88.
81. *IMTFE Transcripts*, 12 November 1946, pp. 10251–71.
82. *IMTFE Transcripts*, 13 November 1946, pp. 10291–95. "Showa tenno no dokuhaku hachijikan" [The Showa Emperor's Eight-Hour Monologue], *Bungei Shunju*, December 1990, pp. 117–18.
83. Hotta, *Japan 1941*, pp. 215–16.
84. *IMTFE Transcripts*, 12 November 1946, pp. 10272–75.
85. *IMTFE Transcripts*, 13 November 1946, pp. 10289–90.
86. Togo Shigenori, *The Cause of Japan*, trans. Togo Fumihiko and Ben Bruce Blakeney (New York: Simon & Schuster, 1956), pp. 126–27.
87. Togo, *Cause of Japan*, pp. 1–42, 46–57, 100–101, 138. Hotta, *Japan 1941*, p. 216.
88. Ike, ed., *Japan's Decision for War*, liaison conference, 30 October 1941, pp. 196–99.
89. *IMTFE Transcripts*, 13 November 1946, pp. 10331–32. Togo, *Cause of Japan*, pp. 145–46.

90. *IMTFE Transcripts,* 13 November 1946, pp. 10333–40.

91. Ike, ed., *Japan's Decision for War,* imperial conference, 5 November 1941, pp. 208–39.

92. Ike, ed., *Japan's Decision for War,* liaison conference, 30 October 1941, p. 198.

93. Langford memorandum, 25 October 1941, *FRUS: The Far East, 1941* (Washington, D.C.: U.S. Government Printing Office, 1956), vol. 4, pp. 544–52.

94. Hotta, *Japan 1941,* pp. 236–38.

95. *IMTFE Transcripts,* 13 November 1946, pp. 10323–28. Togo, *Cause of Japan,* pp. 160–65.

96. Togo, *Cause of Japan,* p. 167.

97. *IMTFE Transcripts,* 13 November 1946, pp. 10389–90.

98. Togo, *Cause of Japan,* pp. 118–19, 197.

99. *IMTFE Transcripts,* 13 November 1946, Kido diary, 26 November 1941, p. 10429.

100. Robert Dallek, *Franklin D. Roosevelt and American Foreign Policy, 1932–1945* (Oxford: Oxford University Press, 1995), pp. 299–306.

101. *IMTFE Transcripts,* 19 November 1946, pp. 10819–23.

102. *IMTFE Transcripts,* 14 November 1946, pp. 10442–43.

103. Togo, *Cause of Japan,* pp. 170–89. Hotta, *Japan 1941,* pp. 270–71.

104. Hotta, *Japan 1941,* pp. 261–76.

105. *IMTFE Transcripts,* 14 November 1946, p. 10468. Koichi Kido, *The Diary of Marquis Kido, 1931–45* (Frederick, Md.: University Publications of America, 1984), 30 November 1941, p. 321.

106. *IMTFE Transcripts,* 14 November 1946, imperial conference resolution, 1 December 1941, pp. 10518–23.

107. Ike, ed., *Japan's Decision for War,* imperial conference, 1 December 1941, pp. 262–83.

108. *IMTFE Transcripts,* 19 November 1946, pp. 10825–29. FDR to Hirohito, 6 December 1941, U.S. Department of State, *Peace and War: United States Foreign Policy, 1931–1941* (Washington, D.C.: U.S. Government Printing Office, 1943), pp. 828–30.

109. Dallek, *Roosevelt and American Foreign Policy,* p. 309.

110. *IMTFE Transcripts,* 1 November 1946, pp. 9295–326.

111. Dallek, *Roosevelt and American Foreign Policy,* p. 309.

112. Togo, *Cause of Japan,* pp. 217–21.

113. Roberta Wohlstetter, *Pearl Harbor: Warning and Decision* (Stanford, Calif.: Stanford University Press, 1962), pp. 273, 382.

114. Wohlstetter, *Pearl Harbor,* pp. 339–43.

115. Hague Convention (No. III) Relative to the Opening of Hostilities, Oct. 18, 1907, Art. 1, 36 Stat. 2259, T.S. 538. Japan ratified this convention on December 13, 1911. *IMTFE Transcripts,* 14 November 1946, pp. 10537, 10547. *IMTFE Transcripts,* 15 November 1946, pp. 10627–29.

116. Togo, *Cause of Japan,* pp. 198–213.

117. *IMTFE Transcripts,* 15 November 1946, pp. 10623–24. Togo, *Cause of Japan,* pp. 197–200.

118. *IMTFE Transcripts,* 18 November 1946, Hirohito rescript, 8 December 1941, pp. 10686–89.

15. The Narrow Road to the Deep North

1. AWM photograph 019418, September 1945, https://www.awm.gov.au/collection /C324544.

2. AWM, Colin Brien oral history, 25 February 1983, https://www.awm.gov.au /collection/C1006600.

3. *IMTFE Transcripts*, 16 December 1946, pp. 12883–92. "Tojo and 11 Others Held Responsible for POW Brutality," *Nippon Times,* 17 December 1946, p. 1.

4. *IMTFE Transcripts*, 12 November 1948, pp. 49759–60.

5. Hague Convention (No. IV) Respecting the Laws and Customs of War on Land, Oct. 18, 1907, 36 Stat. 2277, T.I.A.S. 539.

6. Cordell Hull, *The Memoirs of Cordell Hull* (New York: Macmillan, 1948), vol. 2, p. 1589. *IMTFE Transcripts,* 16 December 1946, pp. 12856–59. Aiko Utsumi, "Prisoners of War in the Pacific War," in Gavan McCormack and Hank Nelson, eds., *The Burma-Thailand Railway: Memory and History* (St. Leonards, Australia: Allen & Unwin, 1993), p. 69.

7. *IMTFE Transcripts,* 7 January 1947, pp. 14477–84.

8. Sarah Kovner, *Prisoners of the Empire: Inside Japanese POW Camps* (Cambridge, Mass.: Harvard University Press, 2020). Kovner's book, which makes a vital contribution by studying Japanese sources, makes a convincing case that there was nothing inherent about Japanese culture that caused this abuse.

9. Paul H. Kratoska, "Labor Mobilization in Japan and the Japanese Empire," in Paul H. Kratoska, ed., *Asian Labor in the Wartime Japanese Empire: Unknown Histories* (London: M. E. Sharpe, 2005), pp. 3–7. Michel Paradis, *Last Mission to Tokyo: The Extraordinary Story of the Doolittle Raiders and Their Final Fight for Justice* (New York: Simon & Schuster, 2020), pp. 194–95.

10. Kovner, *Prisoners of the Empire,* p. 5. Utsumi, "Prisoners of War in the Pacific War," pp. 69–73.

11. AWM, Webb papers, 3DRL/2481, series 4, wallet 19, Northcroft to judges, 3 and 4 December 1946.

12. David Cohen and Yuma Totani, *The Tokyo War Crimes Tribunal: Law, History, and Jurisprudence* (Cambridge: Cambridge University Press, 2018), pp. 204–8.

13. Kovner, *Prisoners of the Empire,* pp. 210–11.

14. BNA, FO 371/66551, Reed to Garner, 6 January 1947.

15. *IMTFE Transcripts,* 10 September 1946, pp. 5351–62.

16. *IMTFE Transcripts,* 12 September 1946, p. 5489.

17. *IMTFE Transcripts,* 13 September 1946, p. 5544.

18. Kovner, *Prisoners of the Empire,* p. 56.

19. Utsumi, "Prisoners of War," p. 75.

20. Yoshinori Murai, "Asian Forced Labour *(Romusha)* on the Burma-Thailand Railway," in McCormack and Nelson, eds., *Burma-Thailand Railway,* pp. 61–62. E. Bruce Reynolds, "The Abuse of Labor Along the Thailand-Burma Railway," in Kratoska, ed., *Asian Labor in the Wartime Japanese Empire,* p. 329. Another estimate found about ten thousand Allied deaths and thirty thousand Asian laborer deaths (*IMTFE Transcripts,* 13 September 1946, p. 5568).

21. Christopher Bayly and Tim Harper, *Forgotten Armies: The Fall of British Asia, 1941– 1945* (London: Allen Lane, 2004), pp. 405–8.

22. *IMTFE Transcripts,* 12 September 1946, pp. 5433–97.

23. *IMTFE Transcripts,* 27 November 1946, pp. 11403–55.

24. *IMTFE Transcripts,* 29 November 1946, pp. 11529–34; 2 December 1946, pp. 11536– 610; 3 December 1946, pp. 11612–28.

25. Kovner, *Prisoners of the Empire*, p. 210.

26. Charles G. Roland, "Massacre and Rape in Hong Kong," *Journal of Contemporary History*, vol. 32, no. 1 (1997), pp. 50–57. *IMTFE Transcripts*, 18 December 1946, pp. 13112–25, 13147, 13162–65.

27. Tim Barlass, "Australian Nurse Was Ordered to Keep War Crimes Secret," *Sydney Morning Herald*, 8 April 2019.

28. *IMTFE Transcripts*, 20 December 1946, pp. 13454–76. Gary Nunn, "The WW2 Massacre and a 'Truth Too Awful to Speak,'" BBC News, 18 April 2019.

29. *IMTFE Transcripts*, 2 January 1947, pp. 14075–80.

30. Geneva Convention Relative to the Treatment of Prisoners of War, July 27, 1929, Art. 2, 47 Stat. 2021, T.I.A.S. no. 846, 27 *A.J.I.L.* Supp. 59.

31. *IMTFE Transcripts*, 7 January 1947, pp. 14475, 14492–529.

32. *IMTFE Transcripts*, 10 January 1947, p. 15046.

33. *IMTFE Transcripts*, 8 August 1946, pp. 3517–30. See Hallett Abend, *My Life in China, 1926–1941* (New York: Harcourt, Brace, 1943), pp. 272–73.

34. Paradis, *Last Mission to Tokyo*, pp. 51, 60, 68, 106–7, 244.

35. *IMTFE Transcripts*, 11 December 1946, pp. 12605–9.

36. *IMTFE Transcripts*, 12 December 1946, pp. 12640–67.

37. *IMTFE Transcripts*, 11 December 1946, pp. 12578–91, 12610–26.

38. *IMTFE Transcripts*, 11 December 1946, pp. 12576–77. See Gordon L. Rottman, *Japanese Army in World War II: The South Pacific and New Guinea, 1942–43* (London: Bloomsbury, 2005), pp. 82–87.

39. *IMTFE Transcripts*, 13 January 1947, pp. 15031–42. See NARA, RG 24, Bureau of Naval Personnel records, Casualty Branch, Japanese War Crimes Involving POWs, box 1.

40. Gerald M. Boyd, "Bush Confers with Other Leaders After Funeral," *New York Times*, 25 February 1989, p. A7.

41. Jon Meacham, *Destiny and Power: The American Odyssey of George Herbert Walker Bush* (New York: Random House, 2015), pp. 59–66. Joe Hyams, *Flight of the Avenger: George Bush at War* (San Diego: Harcourt Brace Jovanovich, 1991), pp. 107–8. James Bradley, *Flyboys: A True Story of Courage* (Boston: Little, Brown, 2003), p. 333.

42. Paradis, *Last Mission to Tokyo*, pp. 285–87.

43. *IMTFE Transcripts*, 3 January 1947, pp. 14205–22.

44. *IMTFE Transcripts*, 8 January 1947, p. 14625.

45. *IMTFE Transcripts*, 3 January 1947, pp. 14205–37.

46. BNA, FO 371/66551, Gascoigne to Bevin, 9 January 1947.

47. Arnold C. Brackman, *The Other Nuremberg: The Untold Story of the Tokyo War Crime Trials* (London: Collins, 1989), p. 265.

48. MMA, RG-9, box 159, War Crimes folder, Hanley to Draper, 1 December 1947.

49. MMA, RG-9, box 159, War Crimes folder, Patterson to MacArthur, 23 October 1946.

50. Frank White, "Prosecution Acts in Surprise Move to Speed Up Trial," *Nippon Times*, 13 September 1947, p. 1.

51. MMA, RG-5, box 30, Jaranilla file, Jaranilla to Wheeler, 22 December 1946.

52. Kovner, *Prisoners of the Empire*, p. 94.

53. *IMTFE Transcripts*, 10 December 1946, pp. 12345–61.

54. See Kovner, *Prisoners of the Empire*, pp. 67–95.

55. *IMTFE Transcripts*, 11 December 1946, p. 12488. See Terada Takefumi, "Christianity

and the Japanese Occupation," in Ikehata Setsuho and Lydia N. Yu Jose, *Philippines-Japan Relations* (Manila: Ateneo de Manila University Press, 2003), pp. 223–60.

56. James M. Scott, *Rampage: MacArthur, Yamashita, and the Battle of Manila* (New York: W. W. Norton, 2018).

57. *IMTFE Transcripts*, 10 December 1946, pp. 12362–90.

58. Stuart Creighton Miller, *Benevolent Assimilation: The American Conquest of the Philippines, 1899–1903* (New Haven: Yale University Press, 1982), pp. 247–52.

59. *IMTFE Transcripts*, 10 December 1946, pp. 12345–61.

60. *IMTFE Transcripts*, 10 December 1946, pp. 12393–401.

61. "P.I. Prosecutor Describes Japanese Orgy in Manila," *Nippon Times*, 12 December 1946, pp. 1–2.

62. *IMTFE Transcripts*, 11 December 1946, pp. 12484–89, 12494–96, 12510–12, 12520–36.

63. *IMTFE Transcripts*, 11 December 1946, pp. 12567–76.

64. *IMTFE Transcripts*, 23 December 1946, p. 13491.

65. *IMTFE Transcripts*, 26 December 1946, pp. 13658–84.

66. *IMTFE Transcripts*, 15 January 1947, pp. 15293–304.

67. *IMTFE Transcripts*, 16 January 1947, pp. 15307–472.

68. *IMTFE Transcripts*, 17 December 1946, pp. 13087–94.

69. *IMTFE Transcripts*, 18 December 1946, pp. 13108–11.

70. *IMTFE Transcripts*, 7 January 1947, pp. 14540–42.

71. *IMTFE Transcripts*, 3 January 1947, pp. 14262–68.

72. *IMTFE Transcripts*, 11 September 1946, pp. 5365–432.

73. *IMTFE Transcripts*, 16 December 1946, pp. 12859–76. Brackman, *Other Nuremberg*, p. 285.

74. *IMTFE Transcripts*, 12 September 1946, p. 5491. Kovner, *Prisoners of the Empire*, pp. 6, 85.

75. *IMTFE Transcripts*, 8 January 1947, pp. 14662–65.

76. *IMTFE Transcripts*, 16 December 1946, pp. 12859–76.

77. *IMTFE Transcripts*, 3 January 1947, pp. 14270–81.

78. "Ex-Admiral Nagano, War Crime Suspect, Dies of Pneumonia," *Nippon Times*, 7 January 1947, p. 1. *IMTFE Transcripts*, 6 January 1947, pp. 14306–7.

79. *IMTFE Transcripts*, 3 January 1947, pp. 14295–96.

80. Togo Shigenori, *The Cause of Japan*, trans. Togo Fumihiko and Ben Bruce Blakeney (New York: Simon & Schuster, 1956), pp. 233–36.

81. *IMTFE Transcripts*, 9 January 1947, pp. 14736–45.

82. Brackman, *Other Nuremberg*, p. 285.

83. *IMTFE Transcripts*, 12 September 1946, pp. 5492–93; 13 September 1946, pp. 5919–26.

84. *IMTFE Transcripts*, 9 January 1947, pp. 14736–45, 14792.

85. *IMTFE Transcripts*, 3 January 1947, pp. 14285–94. "A 'Dead Man' Speaks," *Life*, 26 January 1948, pp. 87–90.

86. *IMTFE Transcripts*, 3 January 1947, pp. 14285–94.

87. *IMTFE Transcripts*, 6 January 1947, pp. 14318–26, 14339–41.

88. *IMTFE Transcripts*, 7 January 1947, pp. 14484–97.

89. *IMTFE Transcripts*, 7 January 1947, pp. 14530–38.

90. *IMTFE Transcripts*, 7 January 1947, pp. 14424–30.

91. *IMTFE Transcripts*, 8 January 1947, pp. 14558–91.

92. *IMTFE Transcripts*, 8 January 1947, pp. 14575–97.

93. *IMTFE Transcripts*, 30 December 1947, pp. 36421–22.

94. UVA, Tavenner papers, Tojo affidavit, defense document 3000, pp. 196–97.

95. Paradis, *Last Mission to Tokyo*, pp. 206–11, 333.

96. *IMTFE Transcripts*, 8 January 1947, pp. 14597–606.

97. *IMTFE Transcripts*, 24 January 1947, p. 16259.

16. Eleven Angry Men

1. Mei Ruao, "A Vote on the Right to Life," March 1948, Mei Xiaoao and Mei Xiaokan, eds., *Mei Ruao Dongjing shenpan wengao* [The Tokyo Trial Manuscripts of Mei Ruao] (Shanghai: Shanghai Jiaotong University Press, 2013), pp. 393–400.

2. BDIC, fonds du Bernard, F° Δ res 0874/15, party invitations.

3. NL-HaNA, 2.21.273, folder 27, Röling to Hentig, 28 August 1947.

4. NL-HaNA, 2.21.273, folder 27, Röling to Nisbet, 22 July 1946; Röling to Daly, 27 August 1946; Röling to Nisbet, 6 May 1946.

5. NL-HaNA, 2.21.273, folder 27, Röling to Nisbet, 22 July 1946; Röling to Daly, 27 August 1946.

6. B. V. A. Röling, *The Tokyo Trial and Beyond: Reflections of a Peacemonger*, ed. Antonio Cassese (Cambridge: Polity, 1993), pp. 21–22.

7. NL-HaNA, 2.21.27, folder 27, Röling to Nisbet, 12 November 1947.

8. NL-HaNA, 2.21.27, folder 27, Röling to Daly, 27 August 1946.

9. *IMTFE Transcripts*, 17 May 1946, pp. 318–19.

10. AWM, Webb papers, 3DRL/2481, wallet 7, Zaryanov to judges, 3 March 1947.

11. BNA, LCO 2/2992, Patrick to Cooper, 1947.

12. BNA, LCO 2/2992, Northcroft to O'Leary, 18 March 1947.

13. BNA, FO 371/66553, note to Sargent, 21 May 1947.

14. AWM, Webb papers, 3DRL/2481, series 1, wallet 10, Röling to Webb, 23 January 1947.

15. NL-HaNA, 2.21.273, folder 27, Röling to Schick, 6 November 1947.

16. NL-HaNA, 2.21.273, folder 27, Röling to Patricia Daly, 27 August 1946.

17. BNA, LCO 2/2992, Patrick to Cooper, 29 March 1947.

18. Röling, *Tokyo Trial and Beyond*, p. 29.

19. See Manjari Chatterjee Miller, *Wronged by Empire: Post-Imperial Ideology and Foreign Policy in India and China* (Stanford, Calif.: Stanford University Press, 2013).

20. Mei, "Vote on the Right to Life," pp. 393–400.

21. Guoshiguan, Foreign Ministry files, Major Cases of the International Military Tribunal for the Far East (Part II), Mei to Wang, 20 August 1948, 020-010117-0027-0041a to 010117-0027-0043a.

22. Bradley F. Smith, *The Road to Nuremberg* (New York: Basic Books, 1981), pp. 103–5.

23. AWM, Webb papers, 3DRL/2481, series 4, wallet 20, Webb second draft, 12 June 1946.

24. AWM, Webb papers, 3DRL/2481, series 4, wallet 4, Patrick to Webb, 8 May 1946.

25. Kennan memcon, 3 June 1948, *FRUS 1948* (Washington, D.C.: U.S. Government Printing Office, 1974), vol. 6, pp. 801–7.

26. Kennan-Dening memcon, 28 May 1948, *FRUS 1948*, vol. 6, pp. 788–94.

27. See Yuki Takatori, "'America's' War Crimes Trial?," *Journal of Imperial and Commonwealth History*, vol. 35, no. 4 (2007), pp. 549–68.

28. BNA, FO 371/66552, Gascoigne to Bevin, 1 May 1947.

29. Jack Goldsmith and Eric Posner argue that self-interested states make use of treaties because they reflect bargaining and reduce ambiguity, as well as requiring domestic ratification processes that can provide information that improves cooperation and coordination. *The Limits of International Law* (Oxford: Oxford University Press, 2005), pp. 10–14, 83–106.

30. BNA, LCO 2/2992, Patrick to Cooper, 1947.

31. AWM, Webb papers, 3DRL/2481, series 1, wallet 9, Patrick to Webb, 1 July 1946.

32. AWM, Webb papers, 3DRL/2481, series 1, wallet 7, Jurisdiction opinion by members for Britain, Canada, and New Zealand, May 1946.

33. BNA, LCO 2/2992, Patrick to Cooper, 1947.

34. BNA, LCO 2/2992, Northcroft to O'Leary, 18 March 1947.

35. BNA, LCO 2/2992, Patrick to Cooper, 1947.

36. AWM, Webb papers, 3DRL/2481, series 1, wallet 7, Jurisdiction opinion by members for Britain, Canada, and New Zealand, May 1946. This has echoes of Oliver Wendell Holmes's famous 1881 statement: "The life of the law has not been logic: it has been experience." Oliver Wendell Holmes Jr., *The Common Law* (Boston: Little, Brown, 1923), p. 1. See John Fabian Witt, *Lincoln's Code: The Laws of War in American History* (New York: Free Press, 2012), p. 369.

37. See Statute of the International Court of Justice, June 26, 1945, Art. 38(1)(b), 59 Stat. 1055, 1060. *Restatement (Third) of the Foreign Relations Law of the United States* § 102(2) (1987).

38. BNA, LCO 2/2992, Patrick to Cooper, 1947. See David A. Strauss, *The Living Constitution* (Oxford: Oxford University Press, 2010).

39. *The Paquete Habana*, 175 U.S. 677 (1900). Ian Brownlie, *Principles of Public International Law* (Oxford: Clarendon, 1990), pp. 7–9. Martti Koskenniemi, *From Apology to Utopia: The Structure of International Legal Argument* (Cambridge: Cambridge University Press, 2006), pp. 388–473. Bruno Simma and Philip Alston, "The Sources of Human Rights Law," *Australian Year Book of International Law*, vol. 12 (1992), pp. 88–100.

40. Jack L. Goldsmith and Eric A. Posner, "A Theory of Customary International Law," *University of Chicago Law Review*, vol. 66, no. 4 (Autumn 1999), pp. 1113–77; "Further Thoughts on Customary International Law," *Michigan Journal of International Law*, vol. 23 (2001), pp. 191–200; and *The Limits of International Law*, pp. 23–78. Witt, *Lincoln's Code*, pp. 368–70.

41. Gary J. Bass, *Stay the Hand of Vengeance: The Politics of War Crimes Tribunals* (Princeton: Princeton University Press, 2000), pp. 76, 58–105.

42. AWM, Webb papers, 3DRL/2481, series 1, wallet 7, Jurisdiction opinion by members for Britain, Canada, and New Zealand, May 1946.

43. See AWM, Webb papers, 3DRL/2481, series 4, wallet 20, Webb revised judgment, 20 January 1947.

44. *Ex parte Quirin*, 317 U.S. 1, 27–28, 30–31 (1942).

45. AWM, Webb papers, 3DRL/2481, series 1, wallet 7, Jurisdiction opinion by members for Britain, Canada, and New Zealand, May 1946.

46. BNA, LCO 2/2992, Northcroft to O'Leary, 18 March 1947.

47. AWM, Webb papers, 3DRL/2481, series 4, wallet 20, Webb memo, 2 August 1946.

48. BNA, LCO 2/2992, Northcroft to O'Leary, 18 March 1947.

49. BNA, LCO 2/2992, Patrick to Cooper, 1947.

50. AWM, Webb papers, 3DRL/2481, series 4, wallet 20, Webb first draft, 12 June 1946.

51. See Manley O. Hudson, *Synopsis of the Geneva Protocol for the Pacific Settlement of International Disputes* (New York: League of Nations Non-Partisan Association, 1924); John F. Williams, "The Geneva Protocol of 1924 for the Pacific Settlement of International Disputes," *Journal of the British Institute of International Affairs*, vol. 3, no. 6 (November 1924), pp. 288–304.

52. AWM, Webb papers, 3DRL/2481, series 4, wallet 20, Webb second draft, 12 June 1946.

53. AWM, Webb papers, 3DRL/2481, series 4, wallet 20, Webb to judges, 12 June 1946. BDIC, fonds du Bernard, F° Δ res 0874/10, Webb to judges, 12 June 1946.

54. AWM, Webb papers, 3DRL/2481, series 4, wallet 20, Webb to judges, 27 June 1946.

55. BDIC, fonds du Bernard, F° Δ res 0874/10, Northcroft to Webb, 1 July 1946.

56. BDIC, fonds du Bernard, F° Δ res 0874/10, McDougall to Webb, 2 July 1946.

57. BDIC, fonds du Bernard, F° Δ res 0874/10, Zaryanov to Webb, July 1946.

58. A. N. Trainin, *Hitlerite Responsibility Under Criminal Law*, ed. A. J. Vishinsky, trans. Andrew Rothstein (London: Hutchinson, 1945), p. 37.

59. Ingeborg Plettenberg, "The Soviet Union and the League of Nations," in *The League of Nations in Retrospect* (Berlin: Walter de Gruyter, 1983), pp. 171–72.

60. BDIC, fonds du Bernard, F° Δ res 0874/10, Zaryanov to Webb, August 1946.

61. Christopher Bayly and Tim Harper, *Forgotten Wars: The End of Britain's Asian Empire* (London: Allen Lane, 2007), pp. 86–91. Sarvepalli Gopal, *Jawaharlal Nehru: A Biography* (London: Jonathan Cape, 1975), vol. 1, pp. 307–8.

62. Serhii Plokhy, *Atoms and Ashes: From Bikini Atoll to Fukushima* (London: Allen Lane, 2022), pp. 1–42.

63. BDIC, fonds du Bernard, F° Δ res 0874/10, Pal to Webb, 5 July 1946.

64. AWM, Webb papers, 3DRL/2481, series 4, wallet 20, Webb memo, 2 August 1946.

65. BDIC, fonds du Bernard, F° Δ res 0874/10, Patrick to Webb, 11 October 1946.

66. BDIC, fonds du Bernard, F° Δ res 0874/10, Pal to Webb, 17 October 1946.

67. AWM, Webb papers, 3DRL/2481, series 4, wallet 20, Webb to judges, 14 January 1947.

68. MMA, RG-9, box 159, War Crimes folder, MacArthur to Joint Chiefs, 1 October 1946.

69. MMA, RG-9, box 159, War Crimes folder, Joint Chiefs to MacArthur, 19 October 1946. NAI, EAD file no. 306-FEA/46, Dune note, 9 October 1946.

70. NAI, EAD file no. 306-FEA/46, War Department to Jain, 12 October 1946. MMA, RG-5, box 60, Webb folder, Webb to MacArthur, 11 October 1946.

71. NAI, EAD file no. 306-FEA/46, Jain to Wavell, 14 October 1946.

72. MMA, RG-5, box 45, Pal folder, Pal to MacArthur, 7 November 1946.

73. Yasmin Khan, *The Great Partition: The Making of India and Pakistan* (New Haven: Yale University Press, 2007), pp. 63–67. Sugata Bose, *Agrarian Bengal: Economy, Social Structure and Politics, 1919–1947* (Cambridge: Cambridge University Press, 2009).

74. NAI, EAD file no. 306-FEA/46, Wavell to Pal, 18 November 1946.

75. NAI, EAD file no. 306-FEA/46, Pal to Wavell, 20 November 1946.

76. NAI, EAD file no. 306-FEA/46, Wavell to air booking center, 21 November 1946. MMA, RG-5, box 45, Pal folder, MacArthur to Pal, 7 November 1946. See MMA, RG-5, box 45, Pal folder, Pal to MacArthur, 12 November 1946.

77. BDIC, fonds du Bernard, F° Δ res 0874/10, Bernard to Webb, 10 October 1946.

78. AWM, Webb papers, 3DRL/2481, series 4, wallet 20, Webb to judges, 27 November 1946.

79. H. L. A. Hart, "Are There Any Natural Rights?," *Philosophical Review*, vol. 64, no. 2 (April 1955), pp. 175–91. Lon L. Fuller, "Positivism and Fidelity to Law," *Harvard Law Review*, vol. 71, no. 4 (February 1958), pp. 630–72. A. P. d'Entrèves, *Natural Law: A Historical Survey* (New York: Harper & Row, 1965). Anver M. Emon, Matthew Levering, and David Novak, *Natural Law: A Jewish, Christian, and Islamic Trialogue* (Oxford: Oxford University Press, 2014).

80. For a brilliant treatment of these issues, see Scott J. Shapiro, *Legality* (Cambridge, Mass.: Belknap Press of Harvard University Press, 2011), pp. 27–32, 42–50, 250–54, 389–92.

81. Richard Tuck, *The Rights of War and Peace: Political Thought and the International Order from Grotius to Kant* (Oxford: Oxford University Press, 1999), pp. 2–8, 73–74, 84–89, 99–108, 170–81.

82. Marcus Tullius Cicero, *The Republic: Cicero XVI*, trans. C. W. Keyes (Cambridge, Mass.: Loeb Classical Library, Harvard University Press, 1928), III.33.xxii, p. 211.

83. Karl Jaspers, "The Significance of the Nürnberg Trials for Germany and the World," *Notre Dame Law Review*, vol. 50 (1947), p. 155.

84. St. Thomas Aquinas, *The Treatise on Law: Summa Theologiae, I-II, QQ. 90-97*, trans. R. J. Henle (South Bend, Ind.: University of Notre Dame Press, 1993). D. J. O'Connor, *Aquinas and Natural Law* (London: Macmillan, 1967).

85. Mei, "Vote on the Right to Life," p. 395.

86. AWM, Webb papers, 3DRL/2481, series 1, wallet 13, Webb to Herzog, 20 October 1947. Peter J. Herzog, "Political Theories in the Japanese Constitution," *Monumenta Nipponica*, vol. 7 (1951), pp. 1–23.

87. AWM, Webb papers, 3DRL/2481, series 4, wallet 20, Webb to judges, 27 November 1946. AWM, Webb papers, 3DRL/2481, series 1, wallet 13, Peter J. Herzog, "The Punishment of War Crimes and the Law of Nature." AWM, Webb papers, 3DRL/2481, series 1, wallet 13, Webb to Herzog, 20 October 1947.

88. See Hersch Lauterpacht, "The Grotian Tradition in International Law," *British Year Book of International Law*, vol. 23 (1946), pp. 1–53.

89. AWM, Webb papers, 3DRL/2481, series 4, wallet 20, Webb memorandum, 5 August 1946.

90. AWM, Webb papers, 3DRL/2481, series 4, wallet 20, Webb to judges, 27 November 1946.

91. Guoshiguan, Foreign Ministry files, IMTFE Major Cases (Part II), Mei to Webb, 8 December 1946, 020-010117-0027-0104a to 020-010117-0027-0115a. Mei Ruao, *Dongjing da shenpan: Yuandong guoji junshi fating Zhongguo faguan Mei Ruao riji* [The Great Tokyo Trial: Diary of Mei Ruao, Chinese Judge at the International Military Tribunal for the Far East] (Nanchang: Jiangxi Education Press, 2005), 8 May 1946, p. 147.

92. Ju-ao Mei (Mei Ruao), "China and the Rule of Law," *Pacific Affairs*, vol. 5, no. 10 (October 1932), pp. 683–72.

93. Guoshiguan, Foreign Ministry files, IMTFE Major Cases (Part II), Mei to Webb, 8 December 1946, 020-010117-0027-0104a to 020-010117-0027-0115a.

94. BNA, LCO 2/2992, Northcroft to O'Leary, 18 March 1947.

95. BDIC, fonds du Bernard, F° Δ res 0874/10, Zaryanov to Webb, 3 January 1947.

96. AWM, Webb papers, 3DRL/2481, series 1, wallet 9, McDougall to Webb, 23 Decem-

ber 1946. AWM, Webb papers, 3DRL/2481, series 1, wallet 9, Webb to McDougall, 26 December 1946.

97. BNA, LCO 2/2992, Patrick to Cooper, 1947.

98. BNA, LCO 2/2992, Northcroft to O'Leary, 18 March 1947.

99. Guoshiguan, Foreign Ministry files, IMTFE Major Cases (Part II), Mei to Webb, 8 December 1946, 020-010117-0027-0104a to 020-010117-0027-0115a.

100. AWM, Webb papers, 3DRL/2481, series 4, wallet 20, 11 December 1946.

101. BNA, LCO 2/2992, Northcroft to O'Leary, 18 March 1947.

102. BDIC, fonds du Bernard, F° Δ res 0874/10, Webb to judges, 20 December 1946.

103. BDIC, fonds du Bernard, F° Δ res 0874/10, Zaryanov to Webb, 3 January 1947.

104. AWM, Webb papers, 3DRL/2481, series 4, wallet 12, Webb to Zaryanov, 22 January 1947.

105. AWM, Webb papers, 3DRL/2481, series 4, wallet 12, Webb to Zaryanov, 22 January 1947.

106. BDIC, fonds du Bernard, F° Δ res 0874/10, Webb to judges, 10 January 1947. AWM, Webb papers, 3DRL/2481, series 4, wallet 20, Webb to judges, 14 January 1947.

107. AWM, Webb papers, 3DRL/2481, series 4, wallet 20, Webb revised judgment, 20 January 1947.

108. BNA, LCO 2/2992, Northcroft to O'Leary, 18 March 1947.

109. Röling, *Tokyo Trial and Beyond*, p. 61.

110. See AWM, Webb papers, 3DRL/2481, series 1, wallet 1, IMTFE Charter, Sec. 2, Art. 5.

111. See Gabriella Blum, "The Dispensable Lives of Soldiers," *Journal of Legal Analysis*, vol. 2, no. 1 (Spring 2010), pp. 115–70. See Ryan Goodman, "Controlling the Recourse to War by Modifying *Jus in Bello*," *Yearbook of International Humanitarian Law*, vol. 12 (December 2009), pp. 53–84.

112. NL-HaNA 2.21.273, folder 11, Röling to Webb, 23 January 1947. AWM, Webb papers, 3DRL/2481, series 1, wallet 10, Röling to Webb, 23 January 1947. See Lisette Schouten, "In the Footsteps of Grotius," in Kerstin von Lingen, ed., *Transcultural Justice at the Tokyo Tribunal: The Allied Struggle for Justice, 1946–48* (Leiden: Brill, 2018), pp. 242–61.

113. AWM, Webb papers, 3DRL/2481, series 4, wallet 20, Webb to judges, 23 January 1947 and Webb jurisdiction judgment, 23 January 1947.

114. AWM, Webb papers, 3DRL/2481, series 4, wallet 4, Webb to Jaranilla, 23 January 1947.

115. BDIC, fonds du Bernard, F° Δ res 0874/10, Jaranilla to judges, 22 January 1947.

116. BDIC, fonds du Bernard, F° Δ res 0874/10, Zaryanov to judges, 28 January 1947.

117. AWM, Webb papers, 3DRL/2481, series 1, wallet 9, Cramer to Webb, 29 January 1947.

118. BDIC, fonds du Bernard, F° Δ res 0874/10, Bernard to Webb, 30 January 1947.

119. BNA, LCO 2/2992, Patrick to Cooper, 1947.

120. Guoshiguan, Foreign Ministry files, IMTFE Major Cases (Part II), Mei to Webb, 8 December 1946, 020-010117-0027-0104a to 020-010117-0027-0115a.

121. BNA, LCO 2/2992, Northcroft to O'Leary, 18 March 1947.

122. Aso statement, 164th session of the Diet, House of Representatives budget committee meeting, 16 February 2006, https://www.shugiin.go.jp/internet/itdb_kaigirokua.nsf /html/kaigirokua/001816420060216013.htm.

17. The Defense Rises

1. Shinsho Hanayama, *The Way of Deliverance: Three Years with the Condemned Japanese War Criminals,* trans. Hideo Suzuki, Eiichi Noda, and James K. Sasaki (New York: Charles Scribner's Sons, 1950), pp. 29–32.
2. "Aim of Tokyo War Crimes Trial Told," *North-China Daily News,* 12 January 1947, p. 3.
3. Lindesay Parrott, "Unions Call Off Japanese Strike," *New York Times,* 1 February 1947, p. 6.
4. Nick Kapur, *Japan at the Crossroads: Conflict and Compromise After Anpo* (Cambridge, Mass.: Harvard University Press, 2018), pp. 9–10.
5. *IMTFE Transcripts,* 28 January 1947, pp. 16662–76.
6. *IMTFE Transcripts,* 27 January 1947, pp. 16261–71. A. C. Brackman, "Mistrial Rejected as Defense Phase of Hearing Starts," *Nippon Times,* 28 January 1947, pp. 1–2.
7. *IMTFE Transcripts,* 24 December 1946, p. 13577.
8. *IMTFE Transcripts,* 27 January 1947, pp. 16277–91, 16303–77.
9. *IMTFE Transcripts,* 28 January 1947, pp. 16444–53.
10. Frank White, "Tojo on Trial," *Far East Stars and Stripes Weekly Review,* 2 November 1947, p. 6.
11. *IMTFE Transcripts,* 28 January 1947, pp. 16628–35.
12. *IMTFE Transcripts,* 27 January 1947, pp. 16385–408.
13. *IMTFE Transcripts,* 28 January 1947, pp. 16594–628.
14. "A 'Dead Man' Speaks," *Life,* 26 January 1948, pp. 87–90.
15. BNA, FO 371/66552, Gascoigne to Bevin, 27 February 1947. "F. S. Tavenner Jr., House Panel Aide," *New York Times,* 22 October 1964, p. 35.
16. *IMTFE Transcripts,* 30 January 1947, pp. 16768–801.
17. *IMTFE Transcripts,* 31 January 1947, pp. 16950–58.
18. *IMTFE Transcripts,* 30 January 1947, pp. 16819–25, 16856–62, 16895–900.
19. *IMTFE Transcripts,* 31 January 1947, pp. 16939–49.
20. *IMTFE Transcripts,* 30 January 1947, pp. 16768–801.
21. *IMTFE Transcripts,* 30 January 1947, pp. 16846–55.
22. BDIC, fonds du Bernard, F° Δ res 0874/10, Zaryanov to Webb, 31 January 1947.
23. BDIC, fonds du Bernard, F° Δ res 0874/10, Webb to judges, 2 February 1947.
24. *IMTFE Transcripts,* 3 February 1947, p. 16997.
25. Arnold C. Brackman, *The Other Nuremberg: The Untold Story of the Tokyo War Crime Trials* (London: Collins, 1989), pp. 306–7.
26. *IMTFE Transcripts,* 30 December 1946, pp. 13878–92, 13924.
27. AWM, Webb papers, 3DRL/2481, series 4, wallet 16, Mattice to Webb, 20 September 1946.
28. AWM, Webb papers, 3DRL/2481, series 4, wallet 16, Japanese defense counsel note, 27 July 1947.
29. AWM, Webb papers, 3DRL/2481, series 4, wallet 16, list of accused and American counsel, 21 January 1947. AWM, Webb papers, 3DRL/2481, series 4, wallet 4, Jaranilla to Webb, 6 August 1946. AWM, Webb papers, 3DRL/2481, series 4, wallet 4, Northcroft to Webb, 6 August 1946.
30. BNA, LCO 2/2992, Northcroft to O'Leary, 28 March 1947.

31. AWM, Webb papers, 3DRL/2481, series 4, wallet 7, Kiyose, "Inquisitorial System and Litigious System," *Jiji Shimpo*, 4 June 1946.

32. AWM, Webb papers, 3DRL/2481, series 4, wallet 12, Zaryanov to Webb, 20 February 1947.

33. *IMTFE Transcripts*, 24 February 1947, pp. 17004–10.

34. AWM, Webb papers, 3DRL/2481, series 4, wallet 7, "Ichiro Kiyose," *Yomiuri*, 25 May 1946.

35. Mei Ruao, *Dongjing da shenpan: Yuandong guoji junshi fating Zhongguo faguan Mei Ruao riji* [The Great Tokyo Trial: Diary of Mei Ruao, Chinese Judge at the International Military Tribunal for the Far East] (Nanchang: Jiangxi Education Press, 2005), 6 May 1946, p. 141.

36. AWM, Webb papers, 3DRL/2481, series 4, wallet 7, "President Webb Read a Statement in a Gentle Tone," *Asahi Shimbun*, 4 May 1946.

37. *IMTFE Transcripts*, 24 February 1947, p. 17048.

38. AWM, Webb papers, 3DRL/2481, series 1, wallet 9, Webb to Röling, 17 March 1947.

39. Nuremberg judgment, 1 October 1946, *The Trial of German Major War Criminals: Proceedings of the International Military Tribunal Sitting at Nuremberg, Germany* (London: His Majesty's Stationery Office, 1946–51), vol. 22, p. 435. Webster to Fox, 24 April 1841, Arnold McNair, *International Law Opinions: Selected and Annotated* (Cambridge: Cambridge University Press, 1956), vol. 2, p. 222.

40. MMA, RG-5, box 60, Webb folder, Webb to Chifley, 1947.

41. Edwin O. Reischauer, *The Japanese* (Cambridge, Mass.: Belknap Press of Harvard University Press, 1978), pp. 239–40.

42. *IMTFE Transcripts*, 24 February 1947, pp. 17088–103.

43. *IMTFE Transcripts*, 24 February 1947, pp. 17011–29, 17032–87.

44. *IMTFE Transcripts*, 24 February 1947, pp. 17088–103.

45. "Tojo's Defense," *New York Times*, 26 February 1947, p. 24.

46. Hatsue Shinohara, *U.S. International Lawyers in the Interwar Years: A Forgotten Crusade* (Cambridge: Cambridge University Press, 2012), pp. 105, 113.

47. AWM, Webb papers, 3DRL/2481, series 4, wallet 6, Imai to Webb, 18 March 1947.

48. "Tojo's Brother Found Living in Osaka Subway," *Nippon Times*, 27 February 1947, p. 3.

49. Kenzo Takayanagi, "A Japanese View of the Struggle in the Far East," *International Affairs*, vol. 18, no. 1 (January–February 1939), pp. 29–55. See Kenzo Takayanagi, "Some Reminiscences of Japan's Commission on the Constitution," *Washington Law Review*, vol. 43 (1968), pp. 961–78.

50. *IMTFE Transcripts*, 24 February 1947, pp. 17107–12.

51. AWM, Webb papers, 3DRL/2481, series 1, wallet 7, Zaryanov to judges, 3 March 1947.

52. *IMTFE Transcripts*, 28 February 1947, pp. 17594–603.

53. See Winston S. Churchill, *The Second World War: The Grand Alliance* (Boston: Houghton Mifflin, 1950), vol. 3, pp. 476–500.

54. *IMTFE Transcripts*, 28 February 1947, pp. 17594–603. On desuetude, see Thomas M. Franck, "Who Killed Article 2(4)?," *American Journal of International Law*, vol. 64, no. 5 (October 1970), pp. 809–37; and Michael J. Glennon, *Limits of Law, Prerogatives of Power: Interventionism After Kosovo* (New York: Palgrave Macmillan, 2001), pp. 60–64. Blakeney's sources were William Edward Hall, *Treatise on International Law*, ed.

A. Pearce Higgins (Oxford: Clarendon, 1924), 8th ed., pp. 5–8; and Lassa Oppenheim, *International Law: A Treatise* (London: Longmans, Green, 1928), 4th ed., vol. 1, p. 24.

55. AWM, Webb papers, 3DRL/2481, wallet 7, Zaryanov to judges, 3 March 1947.

56. Henry L. Stimson, "The Decision to Use the Atomic Bomb," *Harper's Magazine*, February 1947, pp. 97–107.

57. Nina Tannenwald, *The Nuclear Taboo: The United States and the Non-Use of Nuclear Weapons Since 1945* (Cambridge: Cambridge University Press, 2009), pp. 73–114. St. Petersburg Declaration Renouncing the Use, in Time of War, of Explosive Projectiles Under 400 Grammes Weight, Dec. 11, 1868, 138 Consol. T.S. 297, 298.

58. Hague Convention (No. IV) Respecting the Laws and Customs of War on Land, Arts. 22 and 23(e), Oct. 18, 1907, 36 Stat. 2277, T.I.A.S. 539.

59. *IMTFE Transcripts*, 3 March 1947, pp. 17605–62.

60. Gary J. Bass, *Stay the Hand of Vengeance: The Politics of War Crimes Tribunals* (Princeton: Princeton University Press, 2000), pp. 92–104.

61. *The Paquete Habana*, 175 U.S. 677 (1900).

62. *IMTFE Transcripts*, 3 March 1947, pp. 17662–77.

63. *IMTFE Transcripts*, 4 March 1947, pp. 17682–83.

64. BNA, LCO 2/2992, Northcroft to O'Leary, 28 March 1947.

65. *IMTFE Transcripts*, 25 February 1947, pp. 17142–84.

66. *IMTFE Transcripts*, 7 March 1947, pp. 17924–45.

67. *IMTFE Transcripts*, 12 March 1947, pp. 18271–86.

68. *IMTFE Transcripts*, 13 March 1947, pp. 18335–41.

69. BNA, FO 371/66552, Gascoigne to Bevin, 17 April 1947.

70. *IMTFE Transcripts*, 2 April 1947, p. 19234.

71. *IMTFE Transcripts*, 8 April 1947, p. 19542.

72. *IMTFE Transcripts*, 12 June 1947, p. 24251.

73. Kido Koichi, *Kido Koichi nikki: Tokyo saiban-ki* [Kido Koichi Diary: The Tokyo Trial Period] (Tokyo: University of Tokyo Press, 1980), p. 447.

74. *IMTFE Transcripts*, 5 March 1947, pp. 17774–77. "Defense Attorney Is Ousted by Webb at Military Trial," *Nippon Times*, 6 March 1947, pp. 1–2.

75. *IMTFE Transcripts*, 5 September 1947, pp. 27726–28. Frank White, "Attorney Smith Bares Withdrawal as Counsel for Ex-Premier Hirota," *Nippon Times*, 7 September 1947, p. 1.

76. *IMTFE Transcripts*, 8 May 1947, pp. 21720–72, 21745.

77. AWM, Webb papers, 3DRL/2481, series 4, wallet 4, Jaranilla to judges, 13 June 1947.

78. *IMTFE Transcripts*, 18 March 1947, pp. 18630–38.

79. *IMTFE Transcripts*, 9 April 1947, pp. 19620–28, 19657–58.

80. *IMTFE Transcripts*, 19 March 1947, pp. 18641–60.

81. *IMTFE Transcripts*, 15 April 1947, pp. 19982–83.

82. *IMTFE Transcripts*, 20 March 1947, p. 18808.

83. *IMTFE Transcripts*, 8 April 1947, p. 19485.

84. *IMTFE Transcripts*, 8 April 1947, p. 19500.

85. *IMTFE Transcripts*, 3 April 1947, pp. 19275–313.

86. Mark R. Peattie, *Ishiwara Kanji and Japan's Confrontation with the West* (Princeton: Princeton University Press, 1975), pp. 122–23.

87. "Ailing Ishihara's Testimony Likely to Have Big Effect on Tokyo Trial," *Nippon Times*, 3 May 1947, p. 1.

88. *IMTFE Transcripts*, 14 May 1947, pp. 22094–133; 15 May 1947, 22135–53. The transcripts spell his name as Ishihara. Frank White, "Ishihara Recounts Origin of 'Incident,'" *Nippon Times,* 16 May 1947, pp. 1–2.

89. AWM, Webb papers, 3DRL/2481, series 4, wallet 16, Hargadon to Webb, 31 March 1947.

90. BNA, LCO 2/2992, Northcroft to O'Leary, 28 March 1947.

91. AWM, Webb papers, 3DRL/2481, series 4, wallet 19, Northcroft to Webb, 2 October 1946. *IMTFE Transcripts*, 24 March 1947, pp. 18956–64.

92. AWM, Webb papers, 3DRL/2481, series 4, wallet 12, Zaryanov to Webb, 20 March 1947; Webb to Zaryanov, 21 March 1947.

93. BNA, LCO 2/2992, Northcroft to O'Leary, 28 March 1947.

94. *IMTFE Transcripts*, 25 March 1947, pp. 19091–101.

95. BNA, LCO 2/2992, Northcroft to O'Leary, 28 March 1947.

96. BNA, LCO 2/2992, McDougall to judges, 27 March 1947.

97. BNA, LCO 2/2992, Patrick to Cooper, 29 March 1947.

98. BNA, LCO 2/2992, Northcroft to O'Leary, 28 March 1947.

99. AWM, Webb papers, 3DRL/2481, series 4, wallet 20, Webb to judges, 6 May 1947.

100. AWM, Webb papers, 3DRL/2481, series 4, wallet 12, Zaryanov to Webb, 2 May 1947.

101. AWM, Webb papers, 3DRL/2481, series 4, wallet 20, Webb to judges, 5 May 1947. *IMTFE Transcripts*, 8 May 1947, pp. 21720–22.

102. AWM, Webb papers, 3DRL/2481, series 4, wallet 12, Patrick to judges, 6 May 1947.

103. AWM, Webb papers, 3DRL/2481, series 4, wallet 20, Webb to judges, 6 May 1947.

18. A Very British Coup

1. BNA, FO 371/66551, Comyns Carr to Shawcross, 17 December 1946. See BNA, FO 371/66551, Garner note, 22 January 1947.

2. BNA, FO 371/66551, Shawcross to Bevin, 14 January 1947.

3. Caroline Elkins, *Legacy of Violence: A History of the British Empire* (New York: Alfred A. Knopf, 2022), pp. 369–71. Andrew Adonis, *Ernest Bevin: Labour's Churchill* (London: Biteback, 2020), pp. 238–45.

4. BNA, FO 371/66551, Bevin to Gascoigne, 23 January 1947.

5. BNA, FO 371/66551, Bevin to Shawcross, 24 January 1947. BNA, FO 371/66551, Garner note, 22 January 1947.

6. BNA, FO 371/66551, Gascoigne to Bevin, 26 January 1947, telegrams 112 and 113.

7. BNA, FO 371/66553, Gascoigne to Bevin, 15 June 1947.

8. BNA, FO 371/66551, Garner to Reed, 11 February 1947.

9. AWM, Webb papers, 3DRL/2481, series 4, wallet 20, Webb to judges, 19 February 1947.

10. AWM, Webb papers, 3DRL/2481, series 1, wallet 20, Webb to McDougall and Röling, 21 February 1947. AWM, Webb papers, 3DRL/2481, series 1, wallet 20, Webb form of judgment, 21 February 1947.

11. See Birke Häcker and Wolfgang Ernst, eds., *Collective Judging in Comparative Perspective: Counting Votes and Weighing Opinions* (Cambridge: Intersentia, 2020); and Andrew J. Wistrich, Jeffrey J. Rachlinski, and Chris Guthrie, "Heart Versus Head," *Texas Law Review,* vol. 93 (2015).

12. *IMTFE Transcripts*, 18 August 1947, p. 26104.

13. AWM, Webb papers, 3DRL/2481, series 4, wallet 20, Webb to judges, 17 and 19 February 1947.

14. AWM, Webb papers, 3DRL/2481, series 1, wallet 20, Webb scheme of study, 21 February 1947.

15. AWM, Webb papers, 3DRL/2481, series 4, wallet 20, Webb to judges, 5 May 1947.

16. AWM, Webb papers, 3DRL/2481, series 4, wallet 4, Jaranilla to judges, 26 August 1947. AWM, Webb papers, 3DRL/2481, series 4, wallet 20, Webb to judges, 3 September 1947.

17. AWM, Webb papers, 3DRL/2481, series 1, wallet 10, Röling to Webb, 17 February 1947.

18. NL-HaNA, 2.21.273, folder 27, Röling to Henting, 28 August 1947.

19. NL-HaNA, 2.21.273, folder 27, Röling to Nisbet, 12 November 1947.

20. BNA, LCO 2/2992, Cooper to Jowitt, 17 April 1947.

21. BNA, LCO 2/2992, Patrick to Cooper, 1947. See BNA, LCO 2/2992, Normand to Jowitt, 5 February 1947, and BNA, LCO 2/2992, Jowitt to Normand, 6 February 1947.

22. BNA, LCO 2/2992, Gascoigne to Bevin, 26 April 1947.

23. BNA, LCO 2/2992, Patrick to Cooper, 1947.

24. BNA, LCO 2/2992, Jowitt to Normand, 6 February 1947.

25. BNA, LCO 2/2992, Northcroft to O'Leary, 28 March 1947.

26. BNA, LCO 2/2992, Northcroft to O'Leary, 18 March 1947.

27. BNA, FO 371/66553, Gascoigne to Dening, 23 April 1947.

28. BNA, FO 371/66553, Gairdner to Gascoigne, 23 April 1947.

29. BNA, LCO 2/2992, Gascoigne to Bevin, 26 April 1947.

30. BNA, LCO 2/2992, Patrick to Cooper, 29 March 1947.

31. BNA, LCO 2/2992, Cooper to Jowitt, 17 April 1947. BNA, LCO 2/2992, Sargent note, 18 April 1947. BNA, LCO 2/2992, Gascoigne to Bevin, 26 April 1947.

32. AWM, Webb papers, series 1, wallet 15, Prosecution and Punishment of the Major War Criminals of the European Axis, 8 August 1945. BNA, LCO 2/2992, Jowitt to Addison, 18 April 1947. The lord chancellor was William Jowitt. See BNA, LCO 2/2992, Jowitt private secretary to Cooper, 18 April 1947.

33. BNA, LCO 2/2992, Jowitt to Shawcross, 8 May 1947.

34. BNA, FO 371/66553, Gascoigne to Bevin, 20 May 1947.

35. BNA, FO 371/66553, Henniker to Addis, 22 May 1947.

36. BNA, FO 371/66553, note to Sargent, 21 May 1947.

37. BNA, LCO 2/2992, lord chancellor's meeting, 14 May 1947.

38. BNA, FO 371/66553, Gascoigne to Bevin, 20 May 1947; BNA, LCO 2/2992, Gascoigne to Bevin, 20 May 1947.

39. BNA, FO 371/66553, Gascoigne to Bevin, 19 May 1947. BNA, LCO 2/2992, Gascoigne to Bevin, 21 May 1947.

40. BNA, LCO 2/2992, Bevin to Gascoigne, 17 May 1947.

41. BNA, FO 371/66553, Gascoigne to Bevin, 15 May 1947.

42. BNA, LCO 2/2992, Sargent to Jowitt, 30 May 1947.

43. BNA, FO 371/66553, Jowitt to Sargent, 3 June 1947. BNA, FO 371/66553, Foreign Office to Gascoigne, 12 June 1947. BNA, LCO 2/2992, Jowitt to Cooper, 24 June 1947.

44. BNA, LCO 2/2992, Bevin to Westwood, 24 July 1947.

45. BNA, LCO 2/2992, Gascoigne to Bevin, 26 April 1947.

46. BNA, FO 371/66553, Westwood to Bevin, 8 July 1947. NRS, HH 36/94, Cooper to Westwood, 19 July 1947. NRS, HH 36/94, Westwood to Cooper, 31 July 1947.

47. BNA, FO 371/66553, Bevin to Westwood, 24 July 1947.

48. BNA, LCO 2/2992, Jowitt to Cooper, 24 June 1947. BNA, LCO 2/2992, Cooper to Jowitt, 26 June 1947. BNA, LCO 2/2992, Gascoigne to Bevin, 21 September 1947.

49. MMA, RG-9, box 159, War Crimes folder, Myers to War Department, 6 May 1947. See U.S. Congress, Office of Technology Assessment, *Proliferation of Weapons of Mass Destruction: Assessing the Risk* (Washington, D.C.: U.S. Government Printing Office, August 1993), report OTA-ISC-559, pp. 52–55.

50. Jeanne Guillemin, *Hidden Atrocities: Japanese Germ Warfare and American Obstruction of Justice at the Tokyo Trial* (New York: Columbia University Press, 2017), pp. xi–xix.

51. Guillemin, *Hidden Atrocities*, pp. 192–204.

52. Guillemin, *Hidden Atrocities*, p. xii.

53. MMA, RG-9, box 159, War Crimes folder, MacArthur to Eisenhower, 7 February 1947. See Peter Williams and David Wallace, *Unit 731: Japan's Secret Biological Warfare in World War II* (New York: Free Press, 1989); Daniel Barenblatt, *A Plague Upon Humanity: The Secret Genocide of Axis Japan's Germ Warfare Operation* (New York: HarperCollins, 2004); Hal Gold, *Unit 731: Testimony* (Tokyo: Yenbooks, 1996); and Nicholas D. Kristof, "Japan Confronting Gruesome War Atrocity," *New York Times*, 17 March 1995, pp. A1, A12. For the Chinese Communist Party version, see Yan Yuanjun, *Japan's Bacteriological Warfare in China* (Beijing: Foreign Languages Press, 2016).

54. MMA, RG-9, box 159, War Crimes folder, MacArthur to Eisenhower, 7 February 1947.

55. MMA, RG-9, box 159, War Crimes folder, Joint Chiefs of Staff to MacArthur, 21 March 1947.

56. MMA, RG-9, box 159, War Crimes folder, War Department Office of Plans and Operations (WDGPO) to MacArthur, 2 April 1947. See Stephen Kinzer, "The Secret History of Fort Detrick," *Politico*, 15 September 2019.

57. MMA, RG-9, box 159, War Crimes folder, War Department chemical corps to Fell, 15 May 1947.

58. MMA, RG-9, box 159, War Crimes folder, Myers to War Department, 6 May 1947. MMA, RG-9, box 159, War Crimes folder, GHQ memo, 6 May 1947.

59. MMA, RG-9, box 159, War Crimes folder, Myers to War Department, 6 May 1947. MMA, RG-9, box 159, War Crimes folder, GHQ memo, 6 May 1947.

60. MMA, RG-9, box 159, War Crimes folder, War Department to Carpenter, 3 June 1947.

61. MMA, RG-9, box 159, War Crimes folder, Carpenter to War Department, 6 June 1947.

62. MMA, RG-9, box 159, War Crimes folder, War Department to Carpenter, 22 June 1947.

63. Paul G. Cassell, "Establishing Violations of International Law," *Stanford Law Review*, vol. 35, no. 2 (January 1983), pp. 259–96.

64. Hague Convention (No. IV) Respecting the Laws and Customs of War on Land, Oct. 18, 1907, Art. 23(a), 36 Stat. 2277, T.I.A.S. 539. Protocol for the Prohibition of the Use in War of Asphyxiating, Poisonous or Other Gases, and of Bacteriological Methods of Warfare, June 17, 1925, 26 U.S.T. 571, 94 L.N.T.S. 65. Bernard J. Brungs, "The Status of Biological Warfare in International Law," *Military Law Review*,

vol. 24 (1964), pp. 47–51. For a more skeptical view, see Jack M. Beard, "The Shortcomings of Indeterminacy in Arms Control Regimes," *American Journal of International Law,* vol. 101, no. 2 (April 2007), pp. 271–321.

65. MMA, RG-9, box 159, War Crimes folder, Carpenter to War Department, 27 June 1947.

66. Guillemin, *Hidden Atrocities,* pp. 308–17.

67. *Materials on the Trial of Former Servicemen of the Japanese Army Charged with Manufacturing and Employing Bacteriological Weapons* (Moscow: Foreign Languages Publishing House, 1950), pp. 5–535. George W. Christopher et al., "Biological Warfare," *Journal of the American Medical Association,* vol. 278, no. 5 (6 August 1997), pp. 412–17. See Valentyna Polunina, "The Khabarovsk Trial," in Kirsten Sellars, ed., *Trials for International Crimes in Asia* (Cambridge: Cambridge University Press, 2015); and Valentyna Polunina, "From Tokyo to Khabarovsk," in Kerstin von Lingen, ed., *War Crimes Trials in the Wake of Decolonization and Cold War in Asia, 1945–1956: Justice in Time of Turmoil* (London: Palgrave Macmillan, 2016), pp. 239–60.

68. *IMTFE Transcripts,* 7–8 January 1948, pp. 36839–961.

69. B. V. A. Röling introduction, in C. Hosoya et al., eds., *The Tokyo War Crimes Tribunal: An International Symposium* (Tokyo: Kodansha, 1986), p. 18.

70. Guillemin, *Hidden Atrocities,* pp. 321–22.

19. Denial at Nanjing

1. "Aim of Tokyo War Crimes Trial Told," *North-China Daily News,* 12 January 1947, p. 3.

2. AWM, Webb papers, 3DRL/2481, series 4, wallet 20, Webb to judges, 24 October 1947. In the Wade-Giles transliteration used at the time, he was Wang Shih-chieh.

3. AWM, Webb papers, 3DRL/2481, series 4, wallet 4, Webb to Wootton, 22 October 1947.

4. Odd Arne Westad, *Decisive Encounters: The Chinese Civil War, 1946–1950* (Stanford, Calif.: Stanford University Press, 2003).

5. HSTL, PSF, box 151, Acheson to Truman, March 1947. HSTL, PSF, box 151, Stuart to Marshall, 12 and 21 March 1947.

6. NAI, MEA file no. 6-FEA/48, Menon to Nehru, January 1948. See K. P. S. Menon, *Many Worlds: An Autobiography* (Oxford: Oxford University Press, 1965), pp. 223–43.

7. NL-HaNA, 2.21.27, folder 27, Röling to Nisbet, 12 November 1947.

8. HSTL, PSF, box 151, Marshall to Truman, 29 July 1947. HSTL, PSF, box 151, Wedemeyer to Forrestal, 29 July and 8 August 1947. HSTL, PSF, box 151, Wedemeyer to Marshall, 18 August 1947.

9. HSTL, PSF, box 151, Patterson to Marshall, 26 February 1947. Odd Arne Westad, *Cold War and Revolution: Soviet-American Rivalry and the Origins of the Chinese Civil War, 1944–1946* (New York: Columbia University Press, 1993), pp. 162–64.

10. Daniel Kurtz-Phelan, *The China Mission: George Marshall's Unfinished War, 1945–1947* (New York: W. W. Norton, 2018). HSTL, PSF, box 151, Marshall to Forrestal, 11 February 1947.

11. HSTL, PSF, box 151, Marshall to Truman, September 1947. HSTL, PSF, box 151, Wedemeyer, *Report to the President on China-Korea, September 1947.*

12. Westad, *Cold War and Revolution,* pp. 165–70.

13. HSTL, PSF, box 151, Patterson to Marshall, 26 February 1947. HSTL, PSF, box 151, Marshall to Truman, September 1947. HSTL, PSF, box 151, Wedemeyer, *Report to the President on China-Korea, September 1947.*

14. HSTL, PSF, box 151, U.S. naval intelligence report, 12 September 1947.

15. *IMTFE Transcripts,* 22 April 1947, pp. 20476–84.

16. *IMTFE Transcripts,* 25 April 1947, pp. 20875–79.

17. *IMTFE Transcripts,* 22 April 1947, pp. 20484–505, 20510–14.

18. *IMTFE Transcripts,* 13 May 1947, pp. 21961–73, 21984, 21996, 22006–11.

19. *IMTFE Transcripts,* 8 April 1947, pp. 19559–63.

20. A. T. Steele, "Chinese Routed by Japanese in District 100 Miles Wide," *New York Times,* 31 July 1937, pp. 1–2. A. T. Steele, "Puppets of Tokyo Now Rule Peiping," *New York Times,* 1 August 1937, p. 31.

21. *IMTFE Transcripts,* 25 April 1947, pp. 20831–59. "Killing of Japanese by Chinese Debated," *Nippon Times,* 26 April 1947, pp. 1–2.

22. *IMTFE Transcripts,* 23 April 1947, pp. 20669–703.

23. *IMTFE Transcripts,* 2 May 1947, pp. 21282–336, 21305.

24. *IMTFE Transcripts,* 8 May 1947, p. 21813.

25. *IMTFE Transcripts,* 12 May 1947, pp. 21885–931; 13 May 1947, pp. 21934–48.

26. *IMTFE Transcripts,* 6 May 1947, pp. 21561–81.

27. *IMTFE Transcripts,* 8 May 1947, pp. 21796–80.

28. Teresa Watanabe, "Hirohito's Brother Assailed Japan's World War II 'Aggression,'" *Los Angeles Times,* 7 July 1994. See Reiji Yoshida, "Prince Mikasa, a China War Veteran Who Spanned Three Reigns, Dies at 100," *Japan Times,* 27 October 2016; and "Prince Mikasa of Japan, 100, Brother of Emperor Hirohito," *New York Times,* 30 October 2016, p. A24.

29. *IMTFE Transcripts,* 7 May 1947, pp. 21695–718.

30. *IMTFE Transcripts,* 8 May 1947, pp. 21808–11.

31. *IMTFE Transcripts,* 7 May 1947, pp. 21651–88.

32. *IMTFE Transcripts,* 5 May 1947, pp. 21445–67.

33. *IMTFE Transcripts,* 7 May 1947, pp. 21695–718.

34. *IMTFE Transcripts,* 5 May 1947, pp. 21445–67.

35. *IMTFE Transcripts,* 3 October 1947, pp. 29969–97.

36. Edna Tow, "The Great Bombing of Chongqing and the Anti-Japanese War, 1937–1945," in Mark Peattie, Edward Drea, and Hans van de Ven, eds., *The Battle for China: Essays on the Military History of the Sino-Japanese War of 1937–1945* (Stanford, Calif.: Stanford University Press, 2011), pp. 256–82. See Richard Overy, *The Bombing War: Europe, 1939–1945* (London: Allen Lane, 2013).

37. Paul Whitcomb Williams, "Legitimate Targets in Aërial Bombardment," *American Journal of International Law,* vol. 23, no. 3 (1929), pp. 570–81. Katherine E. McKinney, Scott D. Sagan, and Allen S. Weiner, "Why the Atomic Bombing of Hiroshima Would Be Illegal Today," *Bulletin of the Atomic Scientists,* vol. 76, no. 4 (2020), pp. 157–65.

38. Hague Convention (No. IV) Respecting the Laws and Customs of War on Land, Oct. 18, 1907, Art. 25, 36 Stat. 2277, T.I.A.S. 539.

39. Charles Rousseau, *Le droit des conflits armés* (Paris: Éditions Pedone, 1983), p. 360.

40. Williams, "Legitimate Targets in Aërial Bombardment."

41. *IMTFE Transcripts,* 2 May 1947, pp. 21373–76.

42. *IMTFE Transcripts,* 5 May 1947, pp. 21398–402.

43. *IMTFE Transcripts,* 5 May 1947, pp. 21383–91, 21477–85.

44. *IMTFE Transcripts,* 6 May 1947, pp. 21507–36.

45. Edna Tow, "The Great Bombing of Chongqing and the Anti-Japanese War, 1937–1945," in Peattie, Drea, and van de Ven, eds., *Battle for China,* pp. 258–63.

46. *IMTFE Transcripts,* 29 April 1947, pp. 21068–81. *IMTFE Transcripts,* 30 April 1947, p. 21115.

47. *IMTFE Transcripts,* 21 May 1947, p. 22675.

48. *IMTFE Transcripts,* 21 May 1947, pp. 22672–73.

49. *IMTFE Transcripts,* 9 September 1947, pp. 28035–49.

50. *IMTFE Transcripts,* 16 May 1947, pp. 22437–39.

51. *IMTFE Transcripts,* 19 May 1947, pp. 22448–51.

52. *Liberation Daily* editorial, "Yuandong guoji fating shang de guaiju" [A Strange Show at the International Tribunal for the Far East], *Renmin Ribao [People's Daily],* 2 August 1946, p. 1.

53. Xinhua News Agency, "Fating qingxing youru erxi" [Situation in the Courtroom Looks Like Children's Play], *Renmin Ribao [People's Daily],* 27 July 1946, p. 1.

54. Moye, "Maike'ase shi zenyang guanzhi Riben de?" [How Does MacArthur Manage Japan?], *Renmin Ribao [People's Daily],* 11 August 1946, p. 1.

55. Xinhua News Agency, "Riben diguo zhuyi tusha Nanjing xuezhang" [Japanese Imperialists' Blood Debt from the Massacre in Nanjing], *Renmin Ribao [People's Daily],* 1 August 1946, p. 1. Xinhua News Agency, "Qian Jinda jiaoshou Bader zhengming Rijun zai Nanjing canbao kongqian" [Former Professor at Jinling University Bates Testified About the Japanese Military's Unprecedented Brutality in Nanjing], *Renmin Ribao [People's Daily],* 2 August 1946, p. 1.

56. *Liberation Daily* editorial, "Yuandong guoji fating shang de guaiju" [A Strange Show at the International Tribunal for the Far East], *Renmin Ribao [People's Daily],* 2 August 1946, p. 1.

57. "Riben touxiang yizhounian" [First Anniversary of Japan's Surrender], *Renmin Ribao [People's Daily],* 17 August 1946, p. 1.

58. Moye, "Maike'ase shi zenyang guanzhi Riben de?" [How Does MacArthur Manage Japan?], *Renmin Ribao [People's Daily],* 11 August 1946, p. 1.

59. "Zhongguo Gongchandang zhongyang weiyuanhui 'qiqi' jinianri fabu dui shiju kouhao" [The CCP's Central Committee Published Slogans About Current Affairs on the "July 7" Anniversary], *Renmin Ribao [People's Daily],* 7 July 1947, p. 1. Xinhua News Agency, "Jiang Jieshi youru guoti" [Chiang Kai-shek Humiliates the Nation], *Renmin Ribao [People's Daily],* 4 August 1946, p. 1. Xinhua News Agency, "Gangcun chong Jiang junshi guwen" [Okamura Assumes the Role of Chiang's Military Adviser], *Renmin Ribao [People's Daily],* 3 December 1946, p. 1. Xinhua News Agency, "Yan'an juxing 'shuangshier' jinianhui" [Yan'an Held "December 12" Memorial Meeting], *Renmin Ribao [People's Daily],* 16 December 1946, p. 1.

60. Herbert P. Bix, *Hirohito and the Making of Modern Japan* (New York: HarperCollins, 2000), pp. 594–95. *Liberation Daily* editorial, "Yuandong guoji fating shang de guaiju" [A Strange Show at the International Tribunal for the Far East], *Renmin Ribao [People's Daily],* 2 August 1946, p. 1. "Jiu Nanjing weizhengfu 'hetan' yinmou ji shifang Riben zhanfan Gangcun Ningci Zhonggong fayanren biaoshi yanzheng yijian" [The CCP's Spokesperson Issues a Serious and Formal Statement on the Nanjing Puppet Govern-

ment's Fake "Peace Talk" and Release of Japanese War Criminal Okamura Yasuji], *Renmin Ribao [People's Daily]*, 29 January 1949, p. 1.

61. Xinhua News Agency, "Gangcun Ningci dao Xuzhou zhijie zhihui Jiang jun zuozhan" [Okamura Yasuji Sent to Xuzhou to Take Direct Command of Chiang's Army in Combat], *Renmin Ribao [People's Daily]*, 16 June 1947, p. 1.

62. *Liberation Daily* editorial, "Zhanfan de pengyou" [War Criminals' Friend], *Renmin Ribao [People's Daily]*, 10 December 1946, p. 1.

63. Mao Zedong, "Dui Nanjing maiguo zhengfu shifang Riben qinhua zhanfan Zhong-gong zhongyang fabiao yanzheng shengming" [CCP Central Committee Issues a Formal Statement About the Traitorous Nanjing Government's Release of Japanese War Criminals], *Renmin Ribao [People's Daily]*, 6 February 1949, p. 1. See "Gangcun Ningci ranman Zhongguo renmin xianxue" [Okamura Yasuji Is Fully Tainted with the Chinese People's Fresh Blood], *Renmin Ribao [People's Daily]*, 6 February 1949, p. 1.

64. "Top War Criminals in Prison for Year," *Nippon Times*, 9 May 1947, p. 3. This reprints the *Mainichi Shimbun* story.

65. "Life in Prison Is Soft, Dull," *Life*, 26 January 1948, p. 90.

66. "War Crimes," *Time*, 5 January 1948, pp. 24–25.

67. "Top War Criminals in Prison for Year," *Nippon Times*, 9 May 1947, p. 3. See Kawabata Yasunari, *The Master of Go*, trans. Edward G. Seidensticker (New York: Alfred A. Knopf, 1972).

68. NAI, MEA file no. 6-FEA/48, Menon to Nehru, January 1948.

69. MMA, RG-5, box 75, folder 13, GHQ, "Two Years of Occupation," August 1947. Allan B. Cole, George O. Totten, and Cecil H. Uyehara, *Socialist Parties in Postwar Japan* (New Haven: Yale University Press, 1966).

70. "He Holds Japan Together," *Nippon Times*, 8 January 1947.

71. MMA, RG-5, box 75, folder 13, GHQ, "Two Years of Occupation," August 1947. Koseki Shoichi, *The Birth of Japan's Postwar Constitution*, trans. Ray A. Moore (London: Routledge, 2018).

72. MMA, RG-9, box 159, War Crimes folder, Joint Chiefs to MacArthur, 23 July 1947.

73. MMA, RG-5, box 75, folder 13, GHQ, "Two Years of Occupation," August 1947.

74. *IMTFE Transcripts*, 20 May 1947, pp. 22563–65.

20. Self-Defense at Pearl Harbor

1. Truman speech, 12 March 1947, in Jussi Hanhimäki and Odd Arne Westad, eds., *The Cold War: A History in Documents and Eyewitness Accounts* (Oxford: Oxford University Press, 2004), pp. 115–18.

2. Benn Steil, *The Marshall Plan: Dawn of the Cold War* (New York: Simon & Schuster, 2019). For a critical view, see Michael Cox and Caroline Kennedy-Pipe, "The Tragedy of American Diplomacy?," *Journal of Cold War Studies*, vol. 7, no. 1 (2005), pp. 97–134.

3. *IMTFE Transcripts*, 21 May 1947, pp. 22691–95. Ian Mutsu, "Tribunal Overrules Soviet Prosecutor," *Nippon Times*, 27 May 1947, p. 1. Sidney B. Whipple, "Soviet Prosecutor Overruled by Webb," *Nippon Times*, 4 June 1947, p. 1. Frank White, "Tribunal Over-rules Protest by Russian," *Nippon Times*, 5 June 1947, p. 1.

4. *IMTFE Transcripts*, 28 May 1947, pp. 23149–50.

5. BNA, FO 371/66553, "Japanese Criminals and Their Protectors," *Red Star*, 8 July 1947.

6. See Adam B. Ulam, *Stalin: The Man and His Era* (Boston: Beacon Press, 1989),

p. 413. Václav Havel, "The Trial," *Open Letters: Selected Writings, 1965-1990* (New York: Alfred A. Knopf, 1991), pp. 104–5.

7. BNA, FO 371/66553, Moscow embassy to Bevin, 17 May 1947.

8. BNA, FO 371/66553, Sergei Golunsky, "Trial of the Japanese War Criminals," *New Times*, no. 18, 1947, pp. 6–10.

9. "War Crimes," *Time*, 5 January 1948, pp. 24–25.

10. *IMTFE Transcripts*, 21 May 1947, pp. 22715–38; 22 May 1947, pp. 22740–58, 22825–36.

11. *IMTFE Transcripts*, 20 May 1947, pp. 22576–648.

12. *IMTFE Transcripts*, 22 May 1947, pp. 22971–75.

13. *IMTFE Transcripts*, 22 May 1947, pp. 22760–78.

14. *IMTFE Transcripts*, 20 May 1947, p. 22575.

15. *IMTFE Transcripts*, 28 May 1947, pp. 23152–70.

16. *IMTFE Transcripts*, 2 June 1947, p. 23346.

17. *IMTFE Transcripts*, 16 October 1947, pp. 31211–15.

18. *IMTFE Transcripts*, 9 June 1947, pp. 23788–829.

19. *IMTFE Transcripts*, 17 June 1947, pp. 24517–18, 24560–72.

20. *IMTFE Transcripts*, 28 May 1947, pp. 23172–77.

21. *IMTFE Transcripts*, 29 May 1947, pp. 23289–99.

22. *IMTFE Transcripts*, 4 June 1947, pp. 23557–58.

23. *IMTFE Transcripts*, 4 June 1947, pp. 23565–15.

24. *IMTFE Transcripts*, 5 June 1947, pp. 23617–44.

25. *IMTFE Transcripts*, 6 June 1947, pp. 23764–74; 9 June 1947, pp. 23776–82.

26. BNA, FO 371/66553, "Japanese Criminals and Their Protectors," *Red Star*, 8 July 1947.

27. BNA, FO 371/66554, Moscow embassy to Foreign Office, 5 August 1947. BNA, FO 371/66554, "The International Trial in Tokio" summary, *Soviet State and Law*, no. 3, 1947.

28. Sunil Khilnani, *The Idea of India* (New York: Farrar, Straus & Giroux, 1999), p. 4.

29. Nisid Hajari, *Midnight's Furies: The Deadly Legacy of India's Partition* (Boston: Houghton Mifflin Harcourt, 2015), pp. 133–34. Philip Ziegler, *Mountbatten* (New York: Alfred A. Knopf, 1985), pp. 422–24.

30. BNA, WO 216/662, Eastern Command report, 24 August 1946.

31. "Paru hakase oi ni kataru!" [Wide-Ranging Discussion with Dr. Pal], *Bungei Shunju*, vol. 30, no. 17 (December 1952), pp. 100–108.

32. Yasmin Khan, *The Great Partition: The Making of India and Pakistan* (New Haven: Yale University Press, 2007), pp. 1–10, 63–67, 189. Patrick French, *Liberty or Death: India's Journey to Independence and Division* (London: HarperCollins, 1997).

33. Caroline Elkins, *Legacy of Violence: A History of the British Empire* (New York: Alfred A. Knopf, 2022), p. 370. On British atrocities, see Caroline Elkins, *Imperial Reckoning: The Untold Story of Britain's Gulag in Kenya* (New York: Henry Holt, 2005). On empire and decolonization, see, variously, David Armitage, "Greater Britain," *American Historical Review*, vol. 104, no. 2 (April 1999), pp. 427–45; Partha Chatterjee, *The Black Hole of Empire: History of a Global Practice* (Princeton: Princeton University Press, 2012); Timothy Harper, *The End of Empire and the Making of Malaya* (Cambridge: Cambridge University Press, 1999); and William Roger Louis, *Imperialism at Bay: The United States and the Decolonization of the British Empire, 1941–1945* (Oxford: Oxford University Press, 1987).

34. Elkins, *Legacy of Violence*, p. 372.

35. Thomas Borstelmann, *The Cold War and the Color Line: American Race Relations in the Global Arena* (Cambridge, Mass.: Harvard University Press, 2001), pp. 67–74.

36. *IMTFE Transcripts,* 21 August 1947, p. 26411.

37. *IMTFE Transcripts,* 25 August 1947, pp. 26672–73.

38. *IMTFE Transcripts,* 12 June 1947, pp. 24165–77.

39. *IMTFE Transcripts,* 19 June 1947, pp. 24736–46.

40. *IMTFE Transcripts,* 10 June 1947, pp. 23874–83. Sidney B. Whipple, "Tribunal Approves Request for Recess," *Nippon Times,* 12 June 1947, p. 1.

41. AWM, Webb papers, 3DRL/2481, series 4, wallet 3, Webb to MacArthur, 12 June 1947.

42. AWM, Webb papers, 3DRL/2481, series 4, wallet 4, Webb to Jaranilla, 12 June 1947. AWM, Webb papers, 3DRL/2481, series 4, wallet 4, Jaranilla to judges, 11 June 1947.

43. AWM, Webb papers, 3DRL/2481, series 4, wallet 4, Webb to Jaranilla, 12 June 1947.

44. Frank White, "Class 'A' Suspects to Be Tried Soon, Keenan Declares," *Nippon Times,* 13 August 1947, p. 1.

45. BNA, FO 371/66553, Sargent to Shawcross, 19 July 1947.

46. BNA, FO 371/66553, Gascoigne to Bevin, 15 June 1947.

47. W. G. Beasley, *Japanese Imperialism, 1894–1945* (Oxford: Oxford University Press, 1991).

48. *IMTFE Transcripts,* 4 August 1947, pp. 24778–95.

49. *IMTFE Transcripts,* 8 August 1947, p. 25335.

50. *IMTFE Transcripts,* 5 August 1947, pp. 24881–84.

51. *IMTFE Transcripts,* 13 August 1947, pp. 25647–62.

52. *IMTFE Transcripts,* 13 August 1947, pp. 25647–62.

53. *IMTFE Transcripts,* 18 August 1947, p. 26077.

54. *IMTFE Transcripts,* 14 August 1947, pp. 25827–30.

55. *IMTFE Transcripts,* 14 August 1947, pp. 25817, 25860–73.

56. *IMTFE Transcripts,* 15 August 1947, pp. 25920–25, 25951–52.

57. *IMTFE Transcripts,* 15 August 1947, pp. 25961–64, 25966–74.

58. *IMTFE Transcripts,* 13 August 1947, pp. 25624–62.

59. *IMTFE Transcripts,* 12 August 1947, pp. 25614–17; 13 August 1947, pp. 25619–741.

60. *IMTFE Transcripts,* 18 August 1947, pp. 26072–95.

61. *IMTFE Transcripts,* 18 August 1947, pp. 26166–79. See FDR to Hirohito, 6 December 1941, U.S. Department of State, *Peace and War: United States Foreign Policy, 1931–1941* (Washington, D.C.: U.S. Government Printing Office, 1943), pp. 828–30.

62. *IMTFE Transcripts,* 13 August 1947, pp. 25647–62.

63. *IMTFE Transcripts,* 19 August 1947, pp. 26207–15.

64. *IMTFE Transcripts,* 20 August 1947, pp. 26352–57.

65. *IMTFE Transcripts,* 19 August 1947, pp. 26238–51, 26275–84.

66. *IMTFE Transcripts,* 19 August 1947, pp. 26254–56.

67. See Charles Beard, *President Roosevelt and the Coming of the War, 1941: A Study in Appearances and Realities* (New Haven: Yale University Press, 1948); and Charles C. Tansill, *Back Door to War: The Roosevelt Foreign Policy, 1933–1941* (Chicago: Regnery, 1952). For critiques, see Robert H. Ferrell, "Pearl Harbor and the Revisionists," *The Historian,* vol. 17, no. 2 (Spring 1955), pp. 215–33; and R. J. C. Butow, "How Roosevelt Attacked Japan at Pearl Harbor," *Prologue,* vol. 28, no. 3 (Autumn 1996).

68. Robert E. Sherwood, *Roosevelt and Hopkins: An Intimate History* (New York: Harper, 1950), pp. 427–29.

69. *IMTFE Transcripts,* 12 August 1947, pp. 25516–17.
70. *IMTFE Transcripts,* 19 August 1947, pp. 26286–304; 20 August 1947, pp. 26305–48.
71. *IMTFE Transcripts,* 18 August 1947, pp. 26134–45.
72. Frank White, "Slow Typing Blamed for Delay in Presenting Final Note to U.S.," *Nippon Times,* 20 August 1947, p. 1.
73. *IMTFE Transcripts,* 26 August 1947, pp. 26768–69.
74. *IMTFE Transcripts,* 25 August 1947, pp. 26732–42.
75. *IMTFE Transcripts,* 29 August 1947, pp. 27182–90, 27201–10, 27235.
76. *IMTFE Transcripts,* 4 September 1947, pp. 27519–27.
77. *IMTFE Transcripts,* 2 September 1947, pp. 27324–34.
78. *IMTFE Transcripts,* 29 August 1947, pp. 27169–76.
79. *IMTFE Transcripts,* 3 September 1947, pp. 27473–75.
80. *IMTFE Transcripts,* 5 September 1947, pp. 27761–85.
81. *IMTFE Transcripts,* 4 September 1947, pp. 27565–73-D.
82. *IMTFE Transcripts,* 29 August 1947, pp. 27211–28.
83. Michel Paradis, *Last Mission to Tokyo: The Extraordinary Story of the Doolittle Raiders and Their Final Fight for Justice* (New York: Simon & Schuster, 2020), pp. 324–27.
84. *IMTFE Transcripts,* 3 September 1947, pp. 27443–70.
85. *IMTFE Transcripts,* 29 August 1947, pp. 27139–42.
86. *IMTFE Transcripts,* 5 September 1947, pp. 27693–722. Frank White, "Death of Britishers Said Caused by Tojo," *Nippon Times,* 6 September 1947, p. 1.

21. The Emperor Waltz

1. *IMTFE Transcripts,* 21 August 1947, pp. 26398–412.
2. Russell Brines, "Stale Propaganda He Originated Used by Araki in Fight for Life," *Nippon Times,* 12 September 1947, pp. 1–2. Frank White, "Gen. Araki on Stand at Tokyo Tribunal," *Nippon Times,* 11 September 1947, pp. 1–2. *IMTFE Transcripts,* 10 September 1947, p. 28170.
3. *IMTFE Transcripts,* 13 November 1947, pp. 33080–168.
4. *IMTFE Transcripts,* 10 September 1947, pp. 28108–22. Ian Mutsu, "A-Class War Suspects Expected to Take Stand Individually Soon," *Nippon Times,* 8 September 1947, pp. 1–2.
5. BNA, LCO 2/2992, Comyns Carr to Shawcross (unsent), 6 October 1947.
6. BNA, LCO 2/2992, Comyns Carr to Shawcross, 2 January 1948.
7. *IMTFE Transcripts,* 28 November 1947, pp. 34111–99.
8. *IMTFE Transcripts,* 5 November 1947, p. 32432.
9. Arnold C. Brackman, *The Other Nuremberg: The Untold Story of the Tokyo War Crime Trials* (London: Collins, 1989), p. 381.
10. *IMTFE Transcripts,* 24 November 1947, p. 33812–80.
11. *IMTFE Transcripts,* 6 November 1947, pp. 32578–658.
12. *IMTFE Transcripts,* 7 November 1947, pp. 32672–77.
13. *IMTFE Transcripts,* 6 October 1947, pp. 30125–35.
14. Herbert P. Bix, *Hirohito and the Making of Modern Japan* (New York: HarperCollins, 2000), pp. 596–97.
15. MMA, RG-5, box 60, Webb folder, Webb to Chifley, 1947.
16. MMA, RG-5, box 60, Webb folder, Webb to MacArthur, 11 February 1948.

17. *IMTFE Transcripts*, 14 November 1946, Kido diary, 30 November 1941, p. 10468. Koichi Kido, *The Diary of Marquis Kido, 1931–45* (Frederick, Md.: University Publications of America, 1984), 30 November 1941, p. 321.

18. AWM, Webb papers, 3DRL/2481, series 4, wallet 4, "The Emperor was the leader," October 1947.

19. "Sir William Webb on Protecting Allies from Insult," *North-China Daily News*, 12 February 1948, p. 2. "A 'Dead Man' Speaks," *Life*, 26 January 1948, pp. 87–90.

20. Mei Ruao, "A Vote on the Right to Life," March 1948, in Mei Xiaoao and Mei Xiaokan, eds., *Mei Ruao Dongjing shenpan wengao* [The Tokyo Trial Manuscripts of Mei Ruao] (Shanghai: Shanghai Jiaotong University Press, 2013), pp. 393–400.

21. "Finds No Hirohito Guilt," *New York Times*, 26 September 1947, p. 13.

22. *IMTFE Transcripts*, 25 September 1947, pp. 29304–5.

23. MMA, RG-44a, box 4, folder 23, Terasaki folder, Terasaki to Fellers, 19 December 1947.

24. NAI, MEA file no. 6-FEA/48, Menon to Nehru, January 1948. See K. P. S. Menon, *Many Worlds: An Autobiography* (Oxford: Oxford University Press, 1965), pp. 244–49.

25. Frank White, "Tojo on Trial," *Far East Stars and Stripes Weekly Review*, 2 November 1947, p. 6.

26. Kido Koichi, *Kido Koichi nikki: Tokyo saiban-ki* [Kido Koichi Diary: The Tokyo Trial Period] (Tokyo: University of Tokyo Press, 1980), p. 447. BNA, LCO 2/2992, Comyns Carr to Shawcross, 2 January 1948.

27. Frank White, "Tojo on Trial," *Far East Stars and Stripes Weekly Review*, 2 November 1947, p. 6.

28. Kido, *Kido Koichi nikki: Tokyo saiban-ki*, p. 447.

29. BNA, LCO 2/2992, Reed to Shawcross, 11 November 1947.

30. BNA, LCO 2/2992, Comyns Carr to Shawcross (unsent), 6 October 1947.

31. BNA, LCO 2/2992, Comyns Carr to Reed, 21 October 1947.

32. BNA, LCO 2/2992, Comyns Carr to Shawcross, 21 October 1947.

33. Kido, *Kido Koichi nikki: Tokyo saiban-ki*, p. 451.

34. *IMTFE Transcripts*, 15 October 1947, p. 30910.

35. Brackman, *Other Nuremberg*, p. 369.

36. *IMTFE Transcripts*, 15 October 1947, pp. 30947–48.

37. Kido, *Kido Koichi nikki: Tokyo saiban-ki*, p. 449.

38. *IMTFE Transcripts*, 14 October 1947, pp. 30711–878.

39. *IMTFE Transcripts*, 14 October 1947, pp. 30711–878.

40. Kido, *Kido Koichi nikki: Tokyo saiban-ki*, p. 449.

41. *Kido Diary*, 24 July 1943, p. 363.

42. *IMTFE Transcripts*, 22 October 1947, pp. 31552–53.

43. *IMTFE Transcripts*, 12 November 1946, Kido diary, 7 August 1941, pp. 10198–201.

44. *Kido Diary*, 12 October 1941, pp. 310–11.

45. *Kido Diary*, 13 October 1941, pp. 311–12.

46. *Kido Diary*, 15 and 16 October 1941, pp. 312–14.

47. *Kido Diary*, 17 and 20 October 1941, pp. 314–15.

48. See Steven Levitsky and Daniel Ziblatt, *How Democracies Die* (New York: Crown, 2018); and Robert O. Paxton, *The Anatomy of Fascism* (New York: Alfred A. Knopf, 2004).

49. *IMTFE Transcripts*, 16 October 1947, pp. 31179–228.

50. *Kido Diary,* 8 December 1941, pp. 322–23.

51. *Kido Diary,* 10 December 1941, p. 323; 14–15 December 1941, p. 324; 30 December 1941, p. 325.

52. See Fred Iklé, *Every War Must End* (New York: Columbia University Press, 1971); Gideon Rose, *How Wars End: Why We Always Fight the Last Battle* (New York: Simon & Schuster, 2011); H. E. Goemans, *War and Punishment: The Causes of War Termination and the First World War* (Princeton: Princeton University Press, 2000).

53. *IMTFE Transcripts,* 15 October 1947, pp. 30879–31062.

54. *Kido Diary,* 15 February 1942, pp. 328–29.

55. *Kido Diary,* 16 February 1942, p. 329.

56. *Kido Diary,* 9 March 1942, p. 330.

57. *Kido Diary,* 7 and 11 May 1942, pp. 332–33.

58. *Kido Diary,* 13 March 1942, p. 331.

59. *IMTFE Transcripts,* 15 October 1947, pp. 30879–31062.

60. *Kido Diary,* 11 June 1942, p. 336.

61. *Kido Diary,* 5 February 1944, p. 378.

62. *Kido Diary,* 23 September 1943, pp. 368–69.

63. *Kido Diary,* 7, 24, and 30 November 1944, 27 December 1944, pp. 401, 403.

64. *Kido Diary,* 16 February and 18 March 1945, pp. 407, 410. Motoko Rich, "This Survivor of the Firebombing of Tokyo Won't Let Us Forget," *New York Times,* 6 September 2020, p. F6.

65. *Kido Diary,* 18 March 1945, p. 410. Bix, *Hirohito,* p. 491. Richard B. Frank, *Downfall: The End of the Imperial Japanese Empire* (New York: Random House, 1999), pp. 18–19.

66. *IMTFE Transcripts,* 16 October 1947, pp. 31122–43. See *Kido Diary,* 5 April 1945, pp. 417–28.

67. *IMTFE Transcripts,* 16 October 1947, pp. 31143–228.

68. *Kido Diary,* 6 January 1944, pp. 373–75.

69. *IMTFE Transcripts,* 16 October 1947, pp. 31177–79.

70. *IMTFE Transcripts,* 16 October 1947, pp. 31179–228.

71. *IMTFE Transcripts,* 17 October 1947, pp. 31229–92.

72. BNA, LCO 2/2992, Comyns Carr to Shawcross, 2 January 1948.

73. Kido, *Kido Koichi nikki: Tokyo saiban-ki,* pp. 447–49. BNA, LCO 2/2992, Comyns Carr to Shawcross, 2 January 1948.

74. BNA, LCO 2/2992, Comyns Carr to Reed, 21 October 1947.

75. *IMTFE Transcripts,* 22 October 1947, p. 31524.

76. *Kido Diary,* 13 October 1941, pp. 311–12.

77. *IMTFE Transcripts,* 18 October 1947, pp. 31313–96.

78. *IMTFE Transcripts,* 18 October 1947, pp. 31313–96.

79. *IMTFE Transcripts,* 22 October 1947, pp. 31483–561.

80. BNA, LCO 2/2992, Comyns Carr to Shawcross, 2 January 1948. "The Saionji-Harada Memoirs," Military Intelligence Section of the U.S. Far East Command, at Donovan Research Library, Armor School Research Library, Fort Benning, Georgia. AWM, Webb papers, 3DRL/2481, series 4, wallet 5, Webb to Bailey, 22 October 1947.

81. *IMTFE Transcripts,* 23 October 1947, pp. 31562–614.

82. *IMTFE Transcripts,* 21 October 1947, pp. 31397–482.

83. *IMTFE Transcripts,* 22 October 1947, pp. 31483–561.

84. *IMTFE Transcripts,* 23 October 1947, pp. 31562–614.

85. *IMTFE Transcripts,* 23 October 1947, pp. 31562–614.

86. BNA, LCO 2/2992, Comyns Carr to Reed, 21 October 1947.

87. BNA, LCO 2/2992, Comyns Carr to Shawcross (unsent), 6 October 1947.

88. BNA, LCO 2/2992, Reed to Shawcross, 11 November 1947.

89. BNA, FO 371/69837, Gascoigne to Bevin, 20 December 1947.

90. Bix, *Hirohito,* pp. 624–28.

91. "He Holds Japan Together," *Nippon Times,* 8 January 1947.

92. Bix, *Hirohito,* pp. 628–31.

93. Arthur M. Goul, "Emperor Breaks Precedent with Speech at A-Bomb Site," *Nippon Times,* 8 December 1947. United Press, "Hirohito Rules Out New 'Pearl Harbor,'" *New York Times,* 8 December 1947, p. 1.

94. BNA, FO 371/69837, Gascoigne to Bevin, 20 December 1947.

95. Bix, *Hirohito,* p. 631.

96. NAI, MEA file no. 6-FEA/48, Menon to Nehru, January 1948. Menon, *Many Worlds,* p. 249.

97. BNA, FO 371/69912, Killearn-Hirohito conversation, 25 January 1948.

98. BNA, FO 371/69912, Henniker to Lascelles, 12 February 1948. BNA, FO 371/69912, Lascelles to Henniker, 13 February 1948. BNA, FO 371/69912, Gascoigne to Bevin, 31 March 1948.

99. MMA, RG-5, box 60, Webb folder, Evatt to MacArthur, 1947. AWM, Webb papers, 3DRL/2481, series 4, wallet 5, Webb to Evatt, 29 September 1947.

100. MMA, RG-5, box 60, Webb folder, Webb to Chifley, 1947. MMA, RG-5, box 60, Webb folder, Webb to Chifley, 17 October 1947.

101. BNA, LCO 2/2992, Gascoigne to Bevin, 9 October 1947.

102. AWM, Webb papers, 3DRL/2481, series 4, wallet 5, MacArthur to Chifley, 7 October 1947.

103. MMA, RG-5, box 60, Webb folder, Webb to MacArthur, 7 October 1947.

104. AWM, Webb papers, 3DRL/2481, series 4, wallet 5, Webb to MacArthur, 17 October 1947. MMA, RG-5, box 60, Webb folder, Webb to MacArthur, 26 October 1947.

105. AWM, Webb papers, 3DRL/2481, series 4, wallet 5, Webb to Chifley, 17 October 1947.

106. AWM, Webb papers, 3DRL/2481, series 4, wallet 5, Webb to MacArthur, 6 October 1947.

107. MMA, RG-5, box 60, Webb folder, Webb to MacArthur, 13 October 1947.

108. AWM, Webb papers, 3DRL/2481, series 4, wallet 5, Chifley to Webb, 16 October 1947. MMA, RG-5, box 60, Webb folder, Chifley to Webb, 24 October 1947.

109. Brackman, *Other Nuremberg,* p. 375.

110. *IMTFE Transcripts,* 7 November 1947, pp. 32661–72.

111. AWM, Webb papers, 3DRL/2481, series 4, wallet 5, Webb to MacArthur, 6 November 1947.

112. BNA, LCO 2/2992, Gascoigne to Bevin, 10 November 1947. BNA, LCO 2/2992, Gascoigne to Bevin, 11 November 1947.

113. BNA, LCO 2/2992, Gascoigne to Bevin, 27 November 1947.

114. BNA, LCO 2/2992, Gascoigne to Bevin, 10 November 1947. *IMTFE Transcripts,* 10 November 1947, pp. 32774–76.

22. "The Great Sorrow of My Life"

1. Togo Shigenori, *The Cause of Japan*, trans. Togo Fumihiko and Ben Bruce Blakeney (New York: Simon & Schuster, 1956), pp. 223–24.
2. Togo Shigehiko, *Sofu, Togo Shigenori no shogai* [Life of Grandfather Togo Shigenori] (Tokyo: Bungei Shunju, 1993), p. 450.
3. AWM, Webb papers, 3DRL/2481, series 4, wallet 11, Hayden note, 25 July 1946.
4. AWM, Webb papers, 3DRL/2481, series 4, wallet 11, Edith Togo to Morgan, 8 June 1945 (actually 1946).
5. AWM, Webb papers, 3DRL/2481, series 4, wallet 11, Webb to Walbridge, 12 June 1946.
6. Togo, *Sofu, Togo Shigenori no shogai*, pp. 430–36.
7. Frank White, "Togo Admits Facts Kept from Throne," *Nippon Times*, 20 December 1947, pp. 1–2. United Press, "Tojo, Togo Drafted Reply for Emperor," *Nippon Times*, 23 December 1947, pp. 1–2.
8. Arnold C. Brackman, *The Other Nuremberg: The Untold Story of the Tokyo War Crime Trials* (London: Collins, 1989), p. 384.
9. See Supreme Commander for the Allied Powers, *Political Reorientation of Japan: September 1945 to September 1948* (Washington, D.C.: U.S. Government Printing Office, 1949), vol. 1, pp. 340–41.
10. *IMTFE Transcripts*, 18 December 1947, pp. 35746–50.
11. *IMTFE Transcripts*, 17 December 1947, pp. 35617–52. *IMTFE Transcripts*, 18 December 1947, pp. 35653–73.
12. *IMTFE Transcripts*, 18 December 1947, pp. 35746–51.
13. *IMTFE Transcripts*, 26 December 1947, p. 36134.
14. *IMTFE Transcripts*, 19 December 1947, pp. 25850–52. *IMTFE Transcripts*, 18 December 1947, pp. 35752–91.
15. *IMTFE Transcripts*, 18 December 1947, pp. 35665–739.
16. *IMTFE Transcripts*, 18 December 1947, pp. 35752–91.
17. MMA, RG-5, box 60, Webb folder, Australian mission to MacArthur, 8 December 1947.
18. Brackman, *Other Nuremberg*, p. 387.
19. *IMTFE Transcripts*, 19 December 1947, pp. 35830–60.
20. *IMTFE Transcripts*, 18 December 1947, p. 35740.
21. *IMTFE Transcripts*, 23 December 1947, p. 36032.
22. *IMTFE Transcripts*, 26 December 1947, p. 36139.
23. *IMTFE Transcripts*, 18 December 1947, pp. 35799–810. White, "Togo Admits Facts Kept from Throne."
24. BNA, LCO 2/2992, Comyns Carr to Shawcross, 2 January 1948.
25. *IMTFE Transcripts*, 22 December 1947, pp. 35889–968.
26. *IMTFE Transcripts*, 23 December 1947, pp. 35969–36048.
27. *IMTFE Transcripts*, 23 December 1947, pp. 35969–36048.
28. *IMTFE Transcripts*, 22 December 1947, pp. 35889–968.
29. *IMTFE Transcripts*, 23 December 1947, pp. 35969–36048.
30. "Keenan kenji no irei no jinmon" [Prosecutor Keenan's Unconventional Questioning], *Asahi Shimbun*, 25 December 1947, p. 1.

31. *IMTFE Transcripts*, 24 December 1947, pp. 36049–86.

32. *IMTFE Transcripts*, 26 December 1947, pp. 36093–115.

33. Togo, *Sofu, Togo Shigenori no shogai*, pp. 430–36.

23. Tojo Takes the Stand

1. United Press, "Tribunal Packed for Tojo Phase," *Nippon Times*, 27 December 1947, p. 1.

2. Frank White, "Tojo on Trial," *Far East Stars and Stripes Weekly Review*, 2 November 1947, p. 6.

3. "A 'Dead Man' Speaks," *Life*, 26 January 1948, pp. 87–90.

4. "War Crimes," *Time*, 5 January 1948, pp. 24–25.

5. "War Crimes," *Time*, 5 January 1948, pp. 24–25.

6. Russell Brines, "Tojo Better Drawing Card than Lamour, Scalpers Find," *Nippon Times*, 7 January 1948, p. 1.

7. Frank L. White, "We Made Tojo a Hero," *New York Herald Tribune*, 1 August 1948, pp. SM5, 12.

8. "A 'Dead Man' Speaks," *Life*, 26 January 1948, pp. 87–90.

9. BNA, LCO 2/2992, Comyns Carr to Shawcross, 2 January 1948.

10. NAI, MEA file no. 6-FEA/48, Menon to Nehru, January 1948.

11. Lindesay Parrott, "Tokyo Reporters Assess Tojo Trial," *New York Times*, 18 July 1948, p. 30.

12. "Testimony of Tojo Is Commercial Flop," *New York Times*, 18 February 1948, p. 12. "Tojo Outsold as Author by U.S. Prosecutor in Battle of Books from War Crimes Trial," *New York Times*, 25 May 1948, p. 16.

13. *IMTFE Transcripts*, 18 November 1946, Tojo interrogation, 7 February 1946, p. 10706.

14. *IMTFE Transcripts*, 28 August 1947, Tojo interrogation, 11 March 1946, pp. 27060–65.

15. *IMTFE Transcripts*, 29 December 1947, pp. 36196–218, 36255–65.

16. *IMTFE Transcripts*, 29 December 1947, pp. 36218–362.

17. *IMTFE Transcripts*, 30 December 1947, pp. 36364–98, 36407–10.

18. Tojo speech, 16 February 1942, T. R. Sareen, ed., *Select Documents on Indian National Army* (Delhi: Agam Prakashan, 1988), pp. 8–10.

19. *IMTFE Transcripts*, 6 January 1948, pp. 36799–800.

20. *IMTFE Transcripts*, 29 December 1947, pp. 36204–5.

21. *IMTFE Transcripts*, 30 December 1947, pp. 36405–7, 36364–83.

22. Hague Convention (No. IV) Respecting the Laws and Customs of War on Land, Oct. 18, 1907, Art. 6, 36 Stat. 2277, T.I.A.S. 539.

23. Michel Paradis, *Last Mission to Tokyo: The Extraordinary Story of the Doolittle Raiders and Their Final Fight for Justice* (New York: Simon & Schuster, 2020), pp. 55, 67, 169, 196.

24. *IMTFE Transcripts*, 30 December 1947, pp. 36364–83, 36412–25.

25. See Jeremy A. Yellen, *The Greater East Asia Co-Prosperity Sphere: When Total Empire Met Total War* (Ithaca, N.Y.: Cornell University Press, 2019).

26. *IMTFE Transcripts*, 30 December 1947, pp. 36364–83, 36426–88.

27. "How Japanese Newspapers Played Up Tojo Affidavit," *Nippon Times*, 28 December 1947, pp. 1–2.

28. "He Holds Japan Together," *Nippon Times,* 8 January 1947.

29. "Tojo's Stock Rises but He Is Not Likely to Become a Martyr," *Nippon Times,* 3 January 1948, pp. 1–2.

30. Peter Kalischer, "Bald Headed, Sardonic Tojo Still Plays Up to Gallery," *Nippon Times,* 1 January 1948, p. 1.

31. *IMTFE Transcripts,* 30 December 1947, p. 36523.

32. Frank White, "Keenan Grills Tojo on East Asia Sphere and Causes of War," *Nippon Times,* 1 January 1948, pp. 1–2.

33. AWM, Webb papers, 3DRL/2481, series 2, wallet 1, Webb judgment, p. 236, 17 September 1948.

34. *IMTFE Transcripts,* 31 December 1947, pp. 36518–33. White, "Keenan Grills Tojo on East Asia Sphere and Causes of War."

35. BNA, LCO 2/2992, Comyns Carr to Shawcross, 2 January 1948.

36. BNA, LCO 2/2992, Comyns Carr to Shawcross, 2 January 1948.

37. *IMTFE Transcripts,* 6 January 1948, pp. 36782–84. "A 'Dead Man' Speaks," *Life,* 26 January 1948, pp. 87–90.

38. LCO 2/2992, Comyns Carr to Reed, 21 October 1947.

39. BNA, LCO 2/2992, Comyns Carr to Shawcross, 2 January 1948.

40. Frank White, "Tojo Says Emperor Did Not Want War."

41. *IMTFE Transcripts,* 6 January 1948, pp. 36728–804. Russell Brines, "Tojo Loses Grip as Grilling Ends," *Nippon Times,* 8 January 1948, p. 1.

42. *IMTFE Transcripts,* 31 December 1947, pp. 36521–40. White, "Keenan Grills Tojo on East Asia Sphere and Causes of War."

43. *IMTFE Transcripts,* 2 January 1948, pp. 36556–73. Frank White, "War Is Not a Crime, Tojo Holds at Trial," *Nippon Times,* 3 January 1948, pp. 1–2.

44. *IMTFE Transcripts,* 5 January 1948, pp. 36642–727.

45. *IMTFE Transcripts,* 2 January 1948, pp. 36557–640.

46. *IMTFE Transcripts,* 6 January 1948, pp. 36728–804. Brines, "Tojo Loses Grip as Grilling Ends."

47. *IMTFE Transcripts,* 2 January 1948, pp. 36557–640. On Japanese expansionism and Tojo's views on Japan's rule over the region, see Yellen, *Greater East Asia Co-Prosperity Sphere.*

48. *IMTFE Transcripts,* 6 January 1948, pp. 36728–804. Brines, "Tojo Loses Grip as Grilling Ends."

49. "War Crimes," *Time,* 5 January 1948, pp. 24–25.

50. B. V. A. Röling, *The Tokyo Trial and Beyond: Reflections of a Peacemonger,* ed. Antonio Cassese (Cambridge: Polity, 1993), p. 34.

51. Xinhua News Agency, "Meidi baobi Riben zhanfan" [American Imperialists Protect Japanese War Criminals], *Renmin Ribao [People's Daily],* 21 January 1948, p. 2.

52. "A 'Dead Man' Speaks," *Life,* 26 January 1948, pp. 87–90.

53. AWM, Webb papers, 3DRL/2481, series 4, wallet 8, Webb to Latham, 12 February 1948.

54. AWM, Webb papers, 3DRL/2481, series 4, wallet 3, Webb to MacArthur, 11 February 1948. MMA, RG-5, box 60, Webb folder, Webb to MacArthur, 11 February 1948.

55. BNA, LCO 2/2992, Comyns Carr to Shawcross, 2 January 1948.

56. BNA, LCO 2/2992, Shawcross to Jowitt, 23 January 1948.

57. BNA, LCO 2/2992, Jowitt to Shawcross, 29 January 1948.

24. Mr. X

1. George F. Kennan, *Memoirs, 1925–1950* (Boston: Little, Brown, 1967), vol. 1, p. 371.

2. Nick Kapur, *Japan at the Crossroads: Conflict and Compromise After Anpo* (Cambridge, Mass.: Harvard University Press, 2018), pp. 9–10.

3. Odd Arne Westad, *The Cold War: A World History* (New York: Basic Books, 2017), pp. 134–38. John Lewis Gaddis, *Strategies of Containment: A Critical Appraisal of American National Security Policy During the Cold War* (Oxford: Oxford University Press, 2005), pp. 24–52. Michael Schaller, *The American Occupation of Japan: The Origins of the Cold War in Asia* (Oxford: Oxford University Press, 1985), pp. 90–92.

4. John W. Dower, "A Rejoinder," *Pacific Historical Review*, vol. 57, no. 2 (May 1988), p. 207.

5. John Lewis Gaddis, *George F. Kennan: An American Life* (New York: Penguin, 2011), p. 303.

6. Gaddis, *Kennan*, pp. 147–54, 212.

7. Walter Isaacson and Evan Thomas, *The Wise Men: Six Friends and the World They Made* (New York: Simon & Schuster, 1986), pp. 171–73.

8. Gaddis, *Kennan*, pp. 67–69, 109, 113.

9. George F. Kennan, "Diplomacy in the Modern World," *American Diplomacy* (Chicago: University of Chicago Press, 1984), pp. 91–103. For other excellent studies of Kennan, see Barton Gellman, *Contending with Kennan: Toward a Philosophy of American Power* (New York: Praeger, 1984); Nicholas Thompson, *The Hawk and the Dove: Paul Nitze, George Kennan, and the History of the Cold War* (New York: Henry Holt, 2009); Walter L. Hixson, *George F. Kennan: Cold War Iconoclast* (New York: Columbia University Press, 1989); David Mayers, *George Kennan and the Dilemmas of U.S. Foreign Policy* (New York: Oxford University Press, 1988); Wilson D. Miscamble, *George F. Kennan and the Making of American Foreign Policy, 1947–1950* (Princeton: Princeton University Press, 1992); and Anders Stephanson, *Kennan and the Art of Foreign Policy* (Cambridge, Mass.: Harvard University Press, 1989).

10. Gaddis, *Kennan*, pp. 251, 258–59, 272–75.

11. X (George F. Kennan), "The Sources of Soviet Conduct," *Foreign Affairs*, vol. 25, no. 4 (July 1947), pp. 566–82. For a brilliant interpretation of the "X" article, see Gaddis, *Kennan*, pp. 259–62, 694.

12. Kennan, *Memoirs*, vol. 1, pp. 368–72. Gaddis, *Strategies of Containment*, pp. 35–49. Paul J. Heer, *Mr. X and the Pacific: George F. Kennan and American Policy in East Asia* (Ithaca, N.Y.: Cornell University Press, 2018), pp. 50–51, 214–35.

13. Kennan to Marshall, PPS/10, 14 October 1947, *The State Department Policy Planning Staff Papers 1947* (New York: Garland, 1983), vol. 1, pp. 108–14.

14. Kennan, *Memoirs*, vol. 1, p. 381. Heer, *Mr. X and the Pacific*, pp. 215–16.

15. Kennan to Hull, 19 October 1944, *FRUS: Diplomatic Papers, 1944* (Washington, D.C.: U.S. Government Printing Office, 1966), vol. 4, p. 1209.

16. Kennan, *Memoirs*, vol. 1, pp. 260–61. See Anne Applebaum, *Gulag: A History* (New York: Random House, 2003), p. 568.

17. Gaddis, *Kennan*, p. 300.

18. Kennan to Marshall, PPS/10, 14 October 1947, *Policy Planning Staff Papers 1947*, vol. 1, pp. 108–14.

19. Heer, *Mr. X and the Pacific*, p. 63.

20. HSTL, Truman diary, 25 July 1947.

21. Kennan, *Memoirs*, vol. 1, pp. 382–91.

22. Heer, *Mr. X and the Pacific*, pp. 60, 85–88.

23. HSTL, PSF, box 178, NSC files, Army recommendations for NSC 13/1, 29 September 1948.

24. MMA, RG-9, box 161, folder DA, MacArthur to Draper, 9 January 1948.

25. MMA, RG-5, box 32, Kennan folder, Kennan visit memorandum, 27 February 1948.

26. Heer, *Mr. X and the Pacific*, p. 66.

27. MacArthur memcon, PPS/28/2, 1 March 1948, *The State Department Policy Planning Staff Papers 1948* (New York: Garland, 1983), vol. 2, pp. 184–86.

28. Kennan, *Memoirs*, vol. 1, pp. 382–91.

29. MMA, RG-5, box 32, Kennan folder, Kennan to MacArthur, 2 March 1948. Kennan, *Memoirs*, vol. 1, pp. 384–85.

30. Gaddis, *Strategies of Containment*, p. 76.

31. MacArthur-Kennan memcon, PPS/28/2, 5 March 1948, *Policy Planning Staff Papers 1948*, vol. 2, pp. 186–97. Kennan, *Memoirs*, vol. 1, pp. 385–86. See BNA, FO 371/69912, Gascoigne to Bevin, 6 February 1948.

32. Heer, *Mr. X and the Pacific*, p. 70.

33. MacArthur-Kennan memcon, PPS/28/2, 21 March 1948, *Policy Planning Staff Papers 1948*, vol. 2, pp. 196–203.

34. Kennan memorandum, PPS/28/2, 25 March 1948, *Policy Planning Staff Papers 1948*, vol. 2, pp. 203–43.

35. *IMTFE Transcripts*, 10 March 1948, pp. 43046–233.

36. Kennan memorandum, PPS/28/2, 25 March 1948, *Policy Planning Staff Papers 1948*, vol. 2, pp. 203–43.

37. Niccolò Machiavelli, *The Prince*, trans. Harvey C. Mansfield Jr. (Chicago: University of Chicago Press, 1985), ch. VIII, pp. 34–38.

38. Minoru Shikita and Shinichi Tsuchiya, *Crime and Criminal Policy in Japan: Analysis and Evaluation of the Showa Era, 1926–1988* (New York: Springer-Verlag, 1992), pp. 102–4.

39. Kennan memorandum, PPS/28/2, 25 March 1948, *Policy Planning Staff Papers 1948*, vol. 2, pp. 203–43.

40. Kennan to Lovett, 23 March 1948, *FRUS 1948* (Washington, D.C.: U.S. Government Printing Office, 1974), vol. 6, pp. 689–90. Kennan-Dening memcon, 28 May 1948, *FRUS 1948*, vol. 6, pp. 788–94. HSTL, PSF, box 178, NSC files, NSC meeting on NSC 13/1, 30 September 1948.

41. Kennan memcon, 3 June 1948, *FRUS 1948*, vol. 6, pp. 801–7.

42. Gaddis, *Kennan*, p. 307.

43. Kennan memorandum, PPS/28/2, 25 March 1948, *Policy Planning Staff Papers 1948*, vol. 2, pp. 203–43.

44. Richard H. Minear, "Nishi Amane and the Reception of Western Law in Japan," *Monumenta Nipponica*, vol. 28, no. 2 (Summer 1973), pp. 151–75. J. E. de Becker, "Law System of Japan," *Georgetown Law Journal*, vol. 10, no. 3 (April 1922), pp. 1–22.

45. Kennan memorandum, PPS/28/2, 25 March 1948, *Policy Planning Staff Papers 1948*, vol. 2, pp. 203–43.

46. Alexander Cooley, *Base Politics: Democratic Change and the U.S. Military Overseas*

(Ithaca, N.Y.: Cornell University Press, 2008). Andrew Yeo, *Activists, Alliances, and Anti-U.S. Base Protests* (Cambridge: Cambridge University Press, 2011).

47. Kennan memorandum, PPS/28/2, 25 March 1948, *Policy Planning Staff Papers 1948*, vol. 2, pp. 203–43.
48. Saltzman to Butterworth, 9 April 1948, *FRUS 1948*, vol. 6, pp. 727–36.
49. Heer, *Mr. X and the Pacific*, p. 78. Butler to Lovett, 26 May 1948, *FRUS 1948*, vol. 6, pp. 775–76. Lovett to Royall, 28 October 1948, *FRUS 1948*, vol. 6, pp. 1035–40.
50. MMA, RG-9, box 156, War Department Plans and Operations Division chief of staff to MacArthur, 8 June 1948.
51. HSTL, PSF, box 178, NSC files, State Department recommendations on U.S. policy toward Japan, 2 June 1948. HSTL, PSF, box 178, NSC files, State Department recommendations on U.S. policy toward Japan, 24 September 1948. This paper, with slight modications, would become NSC 13/2.
52. Heer, *Mr. X and the Pacific*, pp. 76–79.
53. HSTL, PSF, box 178, NSC files, NSC meeting, 7 October 1948. NSC 13/2, *FRUS 1948*, vol. 6, pp. 857–62. Heer, *Mr. X and the Pacific*, pp. 79–80.
54. HSTL, PSF, box 178, NSC files, Souers to Truman, 27 October 1948. HSTL, PSF, box 178, NSC files, Truman note, 5 November 1948.
55. Heer, *Mr. X and the Pacific*, pp. 80–88.
56. Kennan-Dening memcon, 28 May 1948, *FRUS 1948*, vol. 6, pp. 788–94.
57. NAI, MEA file no. 6-FEA/48, Menon to Nehru, January 1948.
58. Kennan, *Memoirs*, vol. 1, p. 393.
59. Kapur, *Japan at the Crossroads*, pp. 9–11.
60. Westad, *Cold War*, pp. 136–37.

25. Days of Judgment

1. AWM, Webb papers, 3DRL/2481, series 4, wallet 7, Tojo statement, 8 January 1948.
2. Togo Shigenori, *The Cause of Japan*, trans. Togo Fumihiko and Ben Bruce Blakeney (New York: Simon & Schuster, 1956), p. 339.
3. "Spots on the Symbol," *Time*, 7 June 1948, p. 37.
4. MMA, RG-5, box 107, folder 2, Sebald to Benninghoff, 26 October 1948.
5. Lindesay Parrott, "Hirohito's Reign Seen Nearing End," *New York Times*, 25 May 1948, p. 16.
6. BNA, FO 371/69837, Gascoigne to MacDermot, 26 June 1948.
7. AWM, Webb papers, 3DRL/2481, series 4, wallet 2, Webb to Higgins, 6 October 1948.
8. MMA, RG-44a, box 4, folder 23, Terasaki file, Fellers to Terasaki, 8 July 1948.
9. BNA, LCO 2/2992, Comyns Carr to Shawcross, 2 January 1948.
10. BNA, LCO 2/2992, Reed to Shawcross, 11 November 1947.
11. *IMTFE Transcripts*, 11 February 1948, pp. 38948–39120.
12. *IMTFE Transcripts*, 11–27 February 1948, pp. 38989–41710; 1–2 March 1948, pp. 41711–42076.
13. *IMTFE Transcripts*, 18 February 1948, pp. 39884–40087.
14. *IMTFE Transcripts*, 11 February 1948, pp. 38951–53. "Sir William Webb on Protecting Allies from Insult," *North-China Daily News*, 12 February 1948, p. 2.

15. *IMTFE Transcripts*, 2–29 March 1948, pp. 42076–45556; 1–15 April 1948, pp. 46202–48109.

16. *IMTFE Transcripts*, 10 March 1948, pp. 43161–62.

17. *IMTFE Transcripts*, 16 April 1948, p. 48412.

18. "Tojo Outsold as Author by U.S. Prosecutor in Battle of Books from War Crimes Trial," *New York Times*, 25 May 1948, p. 16.

19. "The Tokyo Trial," *New York Times*, 12 February 1948, p. 22.

20. MMA, RG-5, box 115, folder 15, Japanese defense counsel to MacArthur, 20 May 1948; U.S. defense attorneys to MacArthur, 23 May 1948.

21. "Tokyo Counsel Kept On," *New York Times*, 27 May 1948, p. 13.

22. AWM, Webb papers, 3DRL/2481, series 4, wallet 2, Webb to Allan, 24 March 1948.

23. Mei to Sun and Wang, 8 May 1948, Mei Xiaoao and Mei Xiaokan, eds., *Mei Ruao Dongjing shenpan wengao* [The Tokyo Trial Manuscripts of Mei Ruao] (Shanghai: Shanghai Jiaotong University Press, 2013), p. 7.

24. Fang Jinyu, "Zhongguo faguan Mei Ruao" [Chinese Judge Mei Ruao], *Liaowang Zhoukan [Outlook Weekly]*, December 1985, p. 46.

25. AWM, Webb papers, 3DRL/2481, series 4, wallet 8, Webb to Latham, 1 April 1948.

26. AWM, Webb papers, 3DRL/2481, series 4, wallet 2, Webb to Rex, 31 March 1948.

27. AWM, Webb papers, 3DRL/2481, series 4, wallet 2, Webb to Byrne, 17 August 1948.

28. NL-HaNA, 2.21.27, folder 27, Röling to Delphine, 25 June 1948.

29. AWM, Webb papers, 3DRL/2481, series 4, wallet 10, Shaw to Burton, January 1948.

30. AWM, Webb papers, 3DRL/2481, series 4, wallet 4, Webb to Wright, 26 January 1948.

31. AWM, Webb papers, 3DRL/2481, series 4, wallet 19, Webb to judges, 17 May 1948. AWM, Webb papers, 3DRL/2481, series 4, wallet 4, Webb to Mei, 28 June 1948. AWM, Webb papers, 3DRL/2481, series 4, wallet 4, Webb to Wootton, 22 October 1947. AWM, Webb papers, 3DRL/2481, series 4, wallet 20, Webb to Patrick, McDougall, and Northcroft, 24 September 1947.

32. AWM, Webb papers, 3DRL/2481, series 4, wallet 2, Webb to Renner, 14 July 1948.

33. AWM, Webb papers, 3DRL/2481, series 4, wallet 4, Webb to Jaranilla, 14 May 1948.

34. AWM, Webb papers, 3DRL/2481, series 4, wallet 2, Webb to Higgins, 9 March 1948.

35. MMA, RG-5, box 107, Chifley to MacArthur, 25 January 1948. AWM, Webb papers, 3DRL/2481, series 4, wallet 10, Bailey to Webb, 9 January 1948. MMA, RG-5, box 60, Webb folder, Webb to Latham, 18 December 1947.

36. AWM, Webb papers, 3DRL/2481, series 4, wallet 10, Webb to Shaw, 21 January 1948.

37. AWM, Webb papers, 3DRL/2481, series 4, wallet 10, Webb to Latham, 27 January 1948.

38. MMA, RG-5, box 107, Webb to MacArthur, 26 January 1948. MMA, RG-5, box 107, MacArthur to Chifley, 27 January 1948.

39. AWM, Webb papers, 3DRL/2481, series 4, wallet 10, MacArthur to Chifley, 30 January 1948. AWM, Webb papers, 3DRL/2481, series 4, wallet 8, Webb to Latham, 2 February 1948.

40. Webb praised Quincy Wright's article "The Law of the Nuremberg Trial," *American Journal of International Law*, vol. 41, no. 1 (January 1947), pp. 38–72.

41. AWM, Webb papers, 3DRL/2481, series 4, wallet 3, Webb to MacArthur, 12 February 1948. MMA, RG-5 box 60, Webb folder, Webb to MacArthur, 12 February 1948.

42. MMA, RG-5, box 30, Jaranilla folder, Jaranilla to MacArthur, 24 December 1947, 1 February and 6 March 1948. See James Burnham Sedgwick, "Building Blocs," in Kerstin von Lingen, ed., *Transcultural Justice at the Tokyo Tribunal: The Allied Struggle for Justice, 1946–48* (Leiden: Brill, 2018), pp. 29–43.

43. AWM, Webb papers, 3DRL/2481, series 4, wallet 4, Webb to Jaranilla, 14 May 1948.

44. BDIC, fonds du Bernard, F° Δ res 0874/10, Patrick to judges, 30 January 1948.

45. AWM, Webb papers, 3DRL/2481, series 4, wallet 19, Northcroft memo, 18 August 1948.

46. AWM, Webb papers, 3DRL/2481, series 4, wallet 19, Northcroft to Webb, 18 August 1948.

47. AWM, Webb papers, 3DRL/2481, series 4, wallet 12, Webb to Zaryanov, 26 March 1948.

48. AWM, Webb papers, 3DRL/2481, series 4, wallet 19, Webb to judges, 24 March 1948. BDIC, fonds du Bernard, F° Δ res 0874/10, Webb to judges, 24 March 1948.

49. AWM, Webb papers, 3DRL/2481, series 4, wallet 19, Webb to Patrick and McDougall, 16 February 1948.

50. AWM, Webb papers, 3DRL/2481, series 4, wallet 19, Northcroft to Webb, 20 January 1948.

51. AWM, Webb papers, 3DRL/2481, series 4, wallet 8, Webb to Latham, 12 February 1948.

52. AWM, Webb papers, 3DRL/2481, series 4, wallet 2, Webb to Rex, 31 March 1948. For an incisive analysis of Webb's draft judgment, see David Cohen and Yuma Totani, *The Tokyo War Crimes Tribunal: Law, History, and Jurisprudence* (Cambridge: Cambridge University Press, 2018), pp. 305–38.

53. AWM, Webb papers, 3DRL/2481, series 4, wallet 19, Webb to judges, 24 March 1948. BDIC, fonds du Bernard, F° Δ res 0874/10, Webb to judges, 24 March 1948.

54. Guoshiguan, Foreign Ministry files, IMTFE Major Cases (Part II), Mei to Webb, 8 December 1946, 020-010117-0027-0104a to 020-010117-0027-0115a.

55. AWM, Webb papers, 3DRL/2481, series 4, wallet 2, Mei to Webb, 11 March 1948.

56. Mei to Sun and Wang, 8 May 1948, Mei and Mei, eds., *Mei Ruao Dongjing shenpan wengao*, p. 7.

57. Mei to Wang, 24 April 1948, Mei and Mei, eds., *Mei Ruao Dongjing shenpan wengao*, p. 6.

58. Mei Ruao, "A Vote on the Right to Life," March 1948, Mei and Mei, eds., *Mei Ruao Dongjing shenpan wengao*, pp. 393–400.

59. Guoshiguan, Foreign Ministry files, IMTFE Major Cases (Part II), Mei to Webb, 8 December 1946, 020-010117-0027-0104a to 020-010117-0027-0115a.

60. AWM, Webb papers, 3DRL/2481, series 4, wallet 2, Mei to Webb, 11 March 1948.

61. Guoshiguan, Foreign Ministry files, IMTFE Major Cases (Part II), Mei to Webb, 8 December 1946, 020-010117-0027-0104a to 020-010117-0027-0115a.

62. AWM, Webb papers, 3DRL/2481, series 4, wallet 2, Mei to Webb, 11 March 1948.

63. NL-HaNA, 2.21.27, folder 27, Röling to Graven, 28 June 1948. On the concept of genocide, see Philippe Sands, *East West Street: On the Origins of Genocide and Crimes Against Humanity* (London: Weidenfeld & Nicolson, 2016) and Samantha Power, *"A Problem from Hell": America and the Age of Genocide* (New York: Basic Books, 2002), pp. 37–73.

64. AWM, Webb papers, 3DRL/2481, series 4, wallet 5, Zaryanov to Webb, 18 March 1948. *IMTFE Transcripts,* 22 October 1947, p. 31522.

65. NAI, MEA file no. 616-CJK/49, Thakar report, 15 January 1949.

66. Odd Arne Westad, *The Cold War: A World History* (New York: Basic Books, 2017), pp. 116–17. MMA, RG-9, box 109, Civil Affairs Division chief of staff to Office of Military Government in Germany, 16 September 1948.

67. AWM, Webb papers, 3DRL/2481, series 4, wallet 2, Webb to Higgins, 16 August 1948.

68. AWM, Webb papers, 3DRL/2481, series 4, wallet 4, *Novosti Dnya [News of the Day]*, 2 July 1948.

69. AWM, Webb papers, 3DRL/2481, series 4, wallet 5, Zaryanov to Webb, 18 and 31 March 1948.

70. AWM, Webb papers, 3DRL/2481, series 4, wallet 12, Webb to judges, 22 and 24 March 1948.

71. AWM, Webb papers, 3DRL/2481, series 4, wallet 12, Zaryanov draft, 2 April 1948.

72. AWM, Webb papers, 3DRL/2481, series 4, wallet 12, Webb to Zaryanov, 26 March 1948.

73. Mei to Wang, 14 June 1948, Mei and Mei, eds., *Mei Ruao Dongjing shenpan wengao,* pp. 12–13.

74. BDIC, fonds du Bernard, F° Δ res 0874/10, Cramer to judges, 7 June 1948.

75. Mei to Wang, 1 June 1948, Mei and Mei, eds., *Mei Ruao Dongjing shenpan wengao,* pp. 9–10.

76. See AWM, Webb papers, 3DRL/2481, series 1, wallet 10, Röling to Webb, 5 February 1948.

77. NL-HaNA, 2.21.273, folder 27, Röling to Van Boetzelaer van Oosterhout, 3 June 1948.

78. AWM, Webb papers, 3DRL/2481, series 4, wallet 4, Bernard to judges, 7 October 1948. *FRUS 1948: The Far East and Australasia* (Washington, D.C.: U.S. Government Printing Office, 1974), vol. 6, Sebald to Marshall, 23 November 1948, p. 906.

79. BDIC, fonds du Bernard, F° Δ res 0874/10, Bernard to judges, "Deliberations," 28 April 1948.

80. BDIC, fonds du Bernard, F° Δ res 0874/10, Bernard to judges, "Remarks," 28 April 1948.

81. BDIC, fonds du Bernard, F° Δ res 0874/10, Bernard to judges, 10 May 1948.

82. Guoshiguan, Foreign Ministry files, IMTFE Major Cases (Part II), Mei to Bernard, 15 July 1948, 020-010117-0027-0181a to 020-010117-0027-0195a.

83. AWM, Webb papers, 3DRL/2481, series 4, wallet 19, Webb to judges, 4 May 1948. See AWM, Webb papers, 3DRL/2481, series 4, wallet 19, Webb to judges, 6 May 1948; AWM, Webb papers, 3DRL/2481, series 4, wallet 15, Webb to judges, 28 July 1948.

84. AWM, Webb papers, 3DRL/2481, series 4, wallet 15, Bernard to Webb, 29 July 1948.

85. AWM, Webb papers, 3DRL/2481, series 4, wallet 15, Röling to judges, 29 July 1948.

86. AWM, Webb papers, 3DRL/2481, series 4, wallet 15, Webb to judges, 28 July 1948.

87. BDIC, fonds du Bernard, F° Δ res 0874/10, Cramer to judges, 7 June 1948. Mei to Wang, 2 July 1948, Mei and Mei, eds., *Mei Ruao Dongjing shenpan wengao,* p. 14.

88. Mei to Wang, 1 June 1948, Mei and Mei, eds., *Mei Ruao Dongjing shenpan wengao,* pp. 9–10.

89. Mei to Wang, 1 June 1948, Mei and Mei, eds., *Mei Ruao Dongjing shenpan wengao,* pp. 9–10.

90. Wang to Mei, 9 July 1948, Mei and Mei, eds., *Mei Ruao Dongjing shenpan wengao,* p. 16.

91. Mei to Wang, 23 July 1948, Mei and Mei, eds., *Mei Ruao Dongjing shenpan wengao,* pp. 17–18.

92. Mei to Wang, 20 August 1948, Mei and Mei, eds., *Mei Ruao Dongjing shenpan wengao,* pp. 19–20.

93. AWM, Webb papers, 3DRL/2481, series 4, wallet 4, Webb to Mei, 12 July 1948.

94. AWM, Webb papers, 3DRL/2481, series 2, wallet 1, Webb draft judgment, 17 September 1948.

95. AWM, Webb papers, 3DRL/2481, series 4, wallet 19, Webb to judges, 1 November 1948.

96. AWM, Webb papers, 3DRL/2481, series 1, wallet 10, Röling to Webb, 5 February 1948.

97. Radhabinod Pal, *International Military Tribunal for the Far East: Dissentient Judgment of Justice R. B. Pal* (Calcutta: Sanyal, 1953), pp. 605–12, 620–36.

98. Mei to Wang, 14 June 1948, Mei and Mei, eds., *Mei Ruao Dongjing shenpan wengao,* p. 12.

99. Mei to Wang, 2 July 1948, Mei and Mei, eds., *Mei Ruao Dongjing shenpan wengao,* p. 14.

100. NL-HaNA, 2.21.27, folder 11, Röling to judges, 28 July 1948.

101. BDIC, fonds du Bernard, F° Δ res 0874/10, Bernard to judges, 10 May 1948.

102. NL-HaNA, 2.21.27, folder 27, Röling to Delphine, 25 June 1948.

103. AWM, Webb papers, 3DRL/2481, series 4, wallet 12, Zaryanov to Webb, 24 March 1948.

104. NL-HaNA, 2.21.27, folder 11, Röling to judges, 28 July 1948.

105. See BDIC, fonds du Bernard, F° Δ res 0874/10, Zaryanov to Webb, August 1946.

106. NL-HaNA, 2.21.27, folder 23, Zaryanov to judges, 21 August 1948.

107. AWM, Webb papers, 3DRL/2481, series 4, wallet 19, Webb to judges, 13 September 1948.

108. AWM, Webb papers, 3DRL/2481, series 2, wallet 1, Webb judgment, 17 September 1948, p. 236.

109. AWM, Webb papers, 3DRL/2481, series 4, wallet 19, Webb to judges, 20 May 1948.

110. AWM, Webb papers, 3DRL/2481, series 4, wallet 8, Webb to Latham, 16 June 1948.

111. AWM, Webb papers, 3DRL/2481, series 2, wallet 1, Webb judgment, 17 September 1948.

112. AWM, Webb papers, 3DRL/2481, series 1, wallet 9, Webb to Cramer, 8 July 1948. AWM, Webb papers, 3DRL/2481, series 4, wallet 7, Webb to Latham, 30 September 1948. MMA, RG-5, Webb folder, Webb to MacArthur, 30 September 1948. AWM, Webb papers, 3DRL/2481, series 4, wallet 8, Webb to Latham, 1 October 1948.

113. AWM, Webb papers, 3DRL/2481, series 2, wallet 1, Webb judgment, 17 September 1948, pp. 236, 272–74. See AWM, Webb papers, 3DRL/2481, series 1, wallet 9, Webb to Cramer, McDougall, and Northcroft, 18 August 1948.

114. AWM, Webb papers, 3DRL/2481, series 2, wallet 1, Webb judgment, 17 September 1948, pp. 236, 272–74.

115. AWM, Webb papers, 3DRL/2481, series 4, wallet 5, Webb to Cramer, 15 September 1948.

116. AWM, Webb papers, 3DRL/2481, series 1, wallet 9, 4 October 1948. See *IMTFE Transcripts*, 14 November 1946, Kido diary, 30 November 1941, p. 10468.

117. AWM, Webb papers, 3DRL/2481, series 4, wallet 5, Webb to Cramer, 15 September 1948.

118. Mei to Wang, 20 August 1948, Mei and Mei, eds., *Mei Ruao Dongjing shenpan wengao*, pp. 19–20.

119. BNA, LCO 2/2992, Gascoigne to Bevin, 10 November 1947.

120. *IMTFE Transcripts*, 9 August 1946, p. 3569. *IMTFE Transcripts*, 15 November 1946, p. 10578.

121. AWM, Webb papers, 3DRL/2481, series 4, wallet 3, Webb to MacArthur, 30 September 1947.

122. "Reform Bad Men but Not Kill or Turn Them Out," *Amrita Bazar Patrika*, 22 December 1947, p. 1.

123. BL, EAP 262/1/1/6155, "How the Japanese Are Faring Under Military Occupation," *Amrita Bazar Patrika*, 28 November 1947, p. 5.

124. AWM, Webb papers, 3DRL/2481, series 4, wallet 2, Webb to Higgins, 6 October 1948.

125. NAI, EAD file no. 306-FEA/46, Pal to Defence Department, 19 November 1946.

126. NAI, MEA file no. 489-CJK/49, Rama Rau to Menon, 4 August 1948.

127. NAI, MEA file no. 489-CJK/49, Pal to Menon, 4 May 1948.

128. NAI, MEA file no. 489-CJK/49, Chakravarty to Menon, 29 July 1948.

129. AWM, Webb papers, 3DRL/2481, series 3, wallet 2, Cunningham speech, 7 September 1948.

130. AWM, Webb papers, 3DRL/2481, series 4, wallet 19, UP story, 23 September 1948.

131. NL-HaNA, 2.21.27, folder 27, Pal to Röling, 11 October 1948.

132. AWM, Webb papers, 3DRL/2481, series 4, wallet 19, Pal to Webb, 27 September 1948.

133. AWM, Webb papers, 3DRL/2481, series 4, wallet 19, Pal to Webb, 1 November 1948.

134. Mei to Wang, 20 August 1948, Mei and Mei, eds., *Mei Ruao Dongjing shenpan wengao*, pp. 19–20.

135. AWM, Webb papers, 3DRL/2481, series 4, wallet 19, Webb to judges, 1 November 1948.

136. NL-HaNA, 2.21.27, folder 27, Pal to Röling, 11 October 1948.

137. AWM, Webb papers, 3DRL, 2481, series 4, wallet 19, Pal to Webb, November 1948.

138. NL-HaNA, 2.21.27, folder 27, Pal to Röling, 11 October 1948.

139. AWM, Webb papers, 3DRL/2481, series 4, wallet 2, Webb to Harrison, 11 October 1948. AWM, Webb papers, 3DRL/2481, series 4, wallet 19, Webb to judges, 1 November 1948.

140. B. V. A. Röling, *The Tokyo Trial and Beyond: Reflections of a Peacemonger*, ed. Antonio Cassese (Cambridge: Polity, 1993), pp. 58–59.

141. AWM, Webb papers, 3DRL/2481, series 3, wallet 1, Shigemitsu guilt, 1948.

142. AWM, Webb papers, 3DRL/2481, series 3, wallet 1, Togo guilt, 1948.

143. AWM, Webb papers, 3DRL/2481, series 2, wallet 1, Webb judgment, 17 September 1948, p. 236, especially pp. 272–74.

144. AWM, Webb papers, 3DRL/2481, series 1, wallet 9, Webb to Cramer, 17 June 1948.

145. NAI, MEA file no. 489-CJK/49, Chakravarty to Menon, 13 and 16 November 1948.

146. AWM, Webb papers, 3DRL/2481, series 4, wallet 4, Mei to Webb, 3 November 1948.

147. NAI, MEA file no. 489-CJK/49, Chakravarty to Menon, 13 and 16 November 1948.

148. NL-HaNA, 2.21.27, folder 27, Röling to Delphine, 25 June 1948.

149. AWM, Webb papers, 3DRL/2481, series 2, wallet 1, Webb judgment, 17 September 1948, p. 236. Telford Taylor, *The Anatomy of the Nuremberg Trials: A Personal Memoir* (Boston: Little, Brown, 1992), pp. 559–70. See Jens David Ohlin, "Applying the Death Penalty to Crimes of Genocide," *American Journal of International Law*, vol. 99, no. 4 (October 2005), pp. 747–77.

150. AWM, Webb papers, 3DRL/2481, series 1, wallet 9, Cramer to Webb, 15 June 1948.

151. AWM, Webb papers, 3DRL/2481, series 1, wallet 9, Webb to Cramer, 17 June 1948.

152. Matthew Light and Nikolai Kovalev, "Russia, the Death Penalty, and Europe," *Post-Soviet Affairs*, vol. 29, no. 6 (2013), p. 539. Anne Applebaum, *Gulag: A History* (New York: Random House, 2003), pp. 100–112, 334–43, 411–15, 578–86. Peter H. Solomon Jr., *Soviet Criminal Justice Under Stalin* (Cambridge: Cambridge University Press, 1996), p. 412.

153. Frank L. White, "4 Japs Escaped Hanging by Close Vote, Judge Says," *St. Louis Post-Dispatch*, 9 December 1948, p. 10. The others who were nearly hanged were Araki Sadao, Oshima Hiroshi, and Shimada Shigetaro.

154. Tobias S. Harris, *The Iconoclast: Shinzo Abe and the New Japan* (London: Hurst, 2020), p. 11.

155. MMA, RG-9, box 159, War Crimes folder, MacArthur to Joint Chiefs, 12 May 1947.

156. LCO 2/2992, Comyns Carr to Shawcross (unsent), 6 October 1947.

157. BNA, FO 371/66554, Comyns Carr to Shawcross, 13 August 1947. BNA, FO 371/66553, Sargent to Shawcross, 2 July 1947.

158. BNA, FO 371/66553, Foreign Office to Gascoigne, 16 July 1947.

159. MMA, RG-9, box 159, War Crimes folder, Keenan to Tavenner, 19 June 1947. MMA, RG-9, box 159, War Crimes, Tavenner to Keenan, 19 June 1947.

160. MMA, RG-9, box 159, War Crimes folder, Goulsby to War Department, 30 September 1947.

161. MMA, RG-9, box 159, War Crimes folder, MacArthur to Draper, 13 October 1947. MMA, RG-9, box 159, War Crimes folder, Draper to MacArthur, 23 October 1947.

162. MMA, RG-9, box 159, War Crimes folder, Keenan to Army Department, 13 January 1948.

163. MMA, RG-9, box 159, War Crimes folder, MacArthur to War Department, 13 October 1947.

164. MMA, RG-9, box 159, War Crimes folder, Keenan to Army Department, 13 January 1948. See Keenan to Johnson, 16 July 1948, *FRUS 1948*, vol. 6, pp. 831–33.

165. MMA, RG-9, box 159, War Crimes folder, War Department to MacArthur, 1 February 1948. MMA, RG-9, box 159, War Crimes folder, Carpenter to Army Department, 6 February 1948.

166. MMA, RG-9, box 159, War Crimes folder, Carpenter to MacArthur, 8 March 1948.

167. MMA, RG-9, box 159, War Crimes folder, Carpenter to Army Department, 18 May 1948.

168. BNA, LCO 2/2992, New Zealand proposal FEC-314, Far Eastern Commission, 29 July 1948.

169. MMA, RG-9, box 159, War Crimes folder, Royall to MacArthur, 18 September 1948.

170. MMA, RG-9, box 159, War Crimes folder, Levy to Army Department, 3 September 1948.

171. BNA, FO 371/69833, New Zealand and United States amendments, 2 November 1948.

BNA, FO 371/69834, Graves to Scarlett, 18 November 1948. BNA, FO 371/69834, Clarke to Graves, 4 December 1948.

172. Sebald to Marshall, 29 October 1948, *FRUS 1948,* vol. 6, pp. 880–82.

173. Sebald to Marshall, 24 December 1948, *FRUS 1948,* vol. 6, pp. 936–37.

174. MMA, RG-9, box 159, War Crimes folder, Carpenter to Army Department, 18 May 1948. Yoshio Kodama, *I Was Defeated,* trans. Taro Fukuda (Tokyo: Radiopress, 1959), pp. vii–ix. Ian Buruma, *Inventing Japan, 1853–1964* (New York: Modern Library, 2003), p. 139. Wolfgang Saxon, "Yoshio Kodama; Was Rightist," *New York Times,* 18 January 1984, p. D23.

175. Herbert P. Bix, *Hirohito and the Making of Modern Japan* (New York: HarperCollins, 2000), p. 612.

26. *"Blowing Up a Ton of Dynamite"*

1. MMA, RG-5, box 107, folder 2, Sebald to Benninghoff, 29 October 1948. See William J. Sebald, *With MacArthur in Japan: A Personal History of the Occupation* (New York: W. W. Norton, 1965), pp. 162–63.

2. "Emperor Sends Message to American President," *Nippon Times,* 4 December 1948.

3. AWM, Webb papers, 3DRL/2481, series 4, wallet 2, Webb to Robertson, 19 July 1948.

4. AWM, Webb papers, 3DRL/2481, series 4, wallet 17, Cramer to Webb, 9 August 1948; Webb to judges, 9 August 1948; Mei to Webb, 10 August 1948; Webb to GHQ, 20 September 1948.

5. AWM, Webb papers, 3DRL/2481, series 4, wallet 17, Nugent to Almond, 4 August 1948.

6. MMA, RG-9, box 159, War Crimes folder, Parks note, 28 February 1948.

7. AWM, Webb papers, 3DRL/2481, series 4, wallet 17, Nugent to Almond, 4 August 1948.

8. MMA, RG-9, box 159, War Crimes folder, Parks note, 5 March 1948.

9. AWM, Webb papers, 3DRL/2481, series 4, wallet 16, Webb-Folster conversation, 26 February 1948.

10. AWM, Webb papers, 3DRL/2481, series 4, wallet 11, Webb to general secretary, 19 May 1948.

11. AWM, Webb papers, 3DRL/2481, series 4, wallet 11, Australian External Affairs Ministry to Tokyo mission, 22 July 1948.

12. AWM, Webb papers, 3DRL/2481, series 4, wallet 4, Jaranilla to judges, 17 May 1948. AWM, Webb papers, 3DRL/2481, series 4, wallet 11, Webb to general secretary, 19 May 1948.

13. AWM, Webb papers, 3DRL/2481, series 3, wallet 2, Cunningham speech, 7 September 1948.

14. AWM, Webb papers, 3DRL/2481, series 4, wallet 11, McDougall to Webb, 13 October 1948.

15. AWM, Webb papers, 3DRL/2481, series 4, wallet 11, Webb to McDougall, 14 October 1948. AWM, Webb papers, 3DRL/2481, series 3, wallet 2, Walbridge to Cunningham, 13 October 1948.

16. AWM, Webb papers, 3DRL/2481, series 3, wallet 2, Cunningham to Walbridge, 15 October 1948. AWM, Webb papers, 3DRL/2481, series 3, wallet 2, Walbridge to Cunningham, 29 October 1948.

17. Miles W. Vaughan, "Court Scene Described," *Nippon Times*, 5 November 1948, pp. 1–2.
18. "Judge Begins Reading of Tojo Verdict," *Washington Post*, 4 November 1948, p. 19.
19. Vaughan, "Court Scene Described."
20. Beth Van Schaack, "Crimen Sine Lege," *Georgetown Law Journal*, vol. 97 (2008), pp. 119–92. Trevor W. Morrison, "Fair Warning and the Retroactive Judicial Expansion of Federal Criminal Statutes," *Southern California Law Review*, vol. 74 (2001).
21. *IMTFE Transcripts*, 4 November 1948, pp. 48435–42.
22. Lindesay Parrott, "Tojo Dozes in Dock," *New York Times*, 5 November 1948, p. 8.
23. "War Suspects Compose Poems," *Nippon Times*, 7 November 1948, p. 3.
24. *IMTFE Transcripts*, 4 November 1948, p. 48433.
25. Lindesay Parrott, "Japanese Predict 25 Guilty Verdicts," *New York Times*, 6 November 1948, p. 6.
26. *IMTFE Transcripts*, 4 November 1948, pp. 48429, 48432.
27. Ian Mutsu, "Heavy Punishment Seen for Tojo and War Makers," *Nippon Times*, 6 November 1948, pp. 1–2. Frank White, "Tribunal's Stand on Issue of Guilt Stuns Prisoners," *Nippon Times*, 7 November 1948, pp. 1–2.
28. *IMTFE Transcripts*, 8 November 1948, p. 49009.
29. *IMTFE Transcripts*, 4 November 1948, pp. 48454–626; 8 November 1948, pp. 49007–88; 9 November 1948, pp. 49092–132.
30. *IMTFE Transcripts*, 8 November 1948, pp. 49088–106.
31. Mei to Wang, 10 November 1948, Mei Xiaoao and Mei Xiaokan, eds., *Mei Ruao Dongjing shenpan wengao* [The Tokyo Trial Manuscripts of Mei Ruao] (Shanghai: Shanghai Jiaotong University Press, 2013), p. 24.
32. Mei to Wang, 11 November 1948, Mei and Mei, eds., *Mei Ruao Dongjing shenpan wengao*, p. 26.
33. *IMTFE Transcripts*, 9 November 1948, pp. 49092–286.
34. *IMTFE Transcripts*, 4 November 1948, pp. 48626–74.
35. *IMTFE Transcripts*, 10 November 1948, p. 49303.
36. *IMTFE Transcripts*, 4 November 1948, pp. 48626–74; 9 November 1948, pp. 49207–496.
37. *IMTFE Transcripts*, 10 November 1948, p. 49309.
38. *IMTFE Transcripts*, 9 November 1948, pp. 49238–40.
39. *IMTFE Transcripts*, 9 November 1948, pp. 49159–64; 10 November 1948, pp. 49322–26.
40. *IMTFE Transcripts*, 5 November 1948, pp. 48675–880; 9 November 1948, pp. 49092–286; 10 November 1948, pp. 49287–304.
41. *IMTFE Transcripts*, 9 November 1948, p. 49246.
42. *IMTFE Transcripts*, 4 November 1948, p. 48634; 5 November 1948, pp. 48806–8.
43. *IMTFE Transcripts*, 8 November 1948, pp. 48881–49091; 10 November 1948, pp. 49,327–405.
44. "Japan's Guilt," *South China Morning Post*, 10 November 1948, p. 3.
45. *IMTFE Transcripts*, 8 November 1948, pp. 48881–49091.
46. AWM, Webb papers, 3DRL/2481, series 4, wallet 19, Northcroft to Webb, 20 January 1948.
47. *IMTFE Transcripts*, 10 November 1948, pp. 49303–9, 49405–96.
48. *IMTFE Transcripts*, 11 November 1948, pp. 49497–698.
49. *IMTFE Transcripts*, 10 November 1948, pp. 49303–9.

50. *IMTFE Transcripts,* 11 November 1948, pp. 49497–592.

51. "Japan's Guilt," *South China Morning Post,* 9 November 1948, p. 9.

52. *IMTFE Transcripts,* 4 November 1948, pp. 48524–25, 48528; 8 November 1948, pp. 49058–59.

53. *IMTFE Transcripts,* 5 November 1948, pp. 48731–32.

54. *IMTFE Transcripts,* 8 November 1948, pp. 48999–49000.

55. *IMTFE Transcripts,* 11 November 1948, pp. 49517–18.

56. *IMTFE Transcripts,* 14 November 1946, Kido diary, 30 November 1941, p. 10468. Koichi Kido, *The Diary of Marquis Kido, 1931–45* (Frederick, Md.: University Publications of America, 1984), 30 November 1941, p. 321.

57. *IMTFE Transcripts,* 11 November 1948, pp. 49592–95, 49621–98.

58. Michel Paradis, *Last Mission to Tokyo: The Extraordinary Story of the Doolittle Raiders and Their Final Fight for Justice* (New York: Simon & Schuster, 2020), pp. 333–34. James M. Scott, *Target Tokyo: Jimmy Doolittle and the Raid That Avenged Pearl Harbor* (New York: W. W. Norton, 2015).

59. *IMTFE Transcripts,* 11 November 1948, pp. 49621–98; 12 November 1948, pp. 49698–761.

60. *IMTFE Transcripts,* 11 November 1948, pp. 49592–620. The judgment's quotations from this Army Ministry document have some minor differences in phrasing from the same evidence as presented by the prosecution in October 1947.

27. Judgment at Tokyo

1. "Tojo and Six Other Japanese to Be Hanged," *Daily Advertiser* (Australia), 13 November 1948, p. 1.

2. "Tensei Jingo" [Vox Populi], *Asahi Shimbun,* 13 November 1948, p. 1.

3. "Precautions Against Suicide," *Daily Advertiser* (Australia), 13 November 1948, p. 1.

4. "War Crimes," *Time,* 22 November 1948, pp. 31–32. "Ask No Clemency of MacArthur, Tojo Tells Lawyer," *Daily Boston Globe,* 12 November 1948, p. 23. Shinsho Hanayama, *The Way of Deliverance: Three Years with the Condemned Japanese War Criminals,* trans. Hideo Suzuki, Eiichi Noda, and James K. Sasaki (New York: Charles Scribner's Sons, 1950), p. 128.

5. Allen Raymond, "Tojo, 6 Others Doomed to Die," *New York Herald Tribune,* 13 November 1948, p. 3.

6. "Tojo and Six Other Japanese to Be Hanged," *Daily Advertiser* (Australia), 13 November 1948, p. 1.

7. Miles W. Vaughn, "Air of Unreality on Last Trial Day," *Nippon Times,* 13 November 1948, p. 3.

8. *IMTFE Transcripts,* 4 November 1948, pp. 48442–53. For a classic argument on the moral equality of soldiers, see Michael Walzer, *Just and Unjust Wars: A Moral Argument with Historical Illustrations* (New York: Basic Books, 1977), pp. 34–41. For critiques, see Jeff McMahan, "Innocence, Self-Defense and Killing in War," *Journal of Political Philosophy,* vol. 2, no. 3 (September 1994), pp. 193–221, and "The Ethics of Killing in War," *Ethics,* vol. 114 (July 2004), pp. 693–733; and Gabriella Blum, "The Dispensable Lives of Soldiers," *Journal of Legal Analysis,* vol. 2, no. 1 (Spring 2010), pp. 115–70.

9. "Tojo, 24 Other Jap Leaders Convicted in War Crime Trial," *San Francisco Examiner,* 12 November 1948, p. 1.

10. "Tojo, 24 Other Jap Leaders Convicted in War Crime Trial," *San Francisco Examiner,* 12 November 1948, p. 1.

11. Togo Shigehiko, *Sofu, Togo Shigenori no shogai* [Life of Grandfather Togo Shigenori] (Tokyo: Bungei Shunju, 1993), pp. 9–18.

12. Tamotsu Murayama, "'I Do Not Want Clemency,' Tojo Tells His Attorney," *Nippon Times,* 13 November 1948, p. 1.

13. "Tojo, 24 Other Jap Leaders Convicted in War Crime Trial," *San Francisco Examiner,* 12 November 1948, p. 1.

14. AWM, Webb papers, 3DRL/2481, series 3, wallet 23, IMTFE paper 1737, 12 November 1948. Earnest Hoberecht, "Dissenting View Hinted in Motion to Tribunal," *Nippon Times,* 9 November 1948, pp. 1–2.

15. Allen Raymond, "5 Tokyo Judges Dissent," *New York Herald Tribune,* 14 November 1948, p. 27.

16. *IMTFE Transcripts,* 12 November 1948, pp. 49762–853.

17. "Tojo Condemned by Court to Hang," *New York Times,* 12 November 1948, p. 1.

18. William J. Sebald, *With MacArthur in Japan: A Personal History of the Occupation* (New York: W. W. Norton, 1965), pp. 165–66.

19. "Sabakareta 'Nihon-koku'" [Japanese Nation Tried], *Asahi Shimbun,* 13 November 1948, p. 1.

20. Allen Raymond, "Tojo, 6 Others Doomed to Die," *New York Herald Tribune,* 13 November 1948, p. 3.

21. NAI, MEA file no. 489-CJK/49, Chakravarty to Menon, 16 November 1948.

22. "War Crimes," *Time,* 22 November 1948, pp. 31–32.

23. Raymond, "Tojo, 6 Others Doomed to Die."

24. "War Crimes," *Time,* 22 November 1948, pp. 31–32. Raymond, "Tojo, 6 Others Doomed to Die." Associated Press, "Tojo, 6 Others Face Gallows," *Spokesman-Review* (Spokane), 13 November 1948, p. 12. "Tojo Must Hang for War Guilt," *Minneapolis Star,* 12 November 1948, p. 1.

25. AWM, Webb papers, 3DRL/2481, series 4, wallet 16, Larson report, 30 July 1948.

26. *IMTFE Transcripts,* 12 November 1948, pp. 49854–58.

27. "Doomed Men Pen Poems," *Nippon Times,* 14 November 1948, pp. 1–2. "War Crimes," *Time,* 22 November 1948, pp. 31–32. Raymond, "5 Tokyo Judges Dissent."

28. Hanayama, *Way of Deliverance,* pp. 185–87, 199–201.

29. Raymond, "5 Tokyo Judges Dissent."

30. Lindesay Parrott, "Dooming of Tojo Impresses Japan," *New York Times,* 13 November 1948, pp. 1, 9.

31. Hanayama, *Way of Deliverance,* p. 186.

32. Sebald to Marshall, 18 November 1948, *FRUS 1948: The Far East and Australasia* (Washington, D.C.: U.S. Government Printing Office, 1974), vol. 6, p. 896. Sebald, *With MacArthur in Japan,* pp. 164–65.

33. HSTL, OF, box 1145, Truman to Keenan, 2 December 1948. MMA, RG-5, box 32, folder 1, MacArthur to Keenan, 26 November 1948.

34. Raymond, "Tojo, 6 Others Doomed to Die."

35. NARA, RG 43, box 70, *Central News* dispatch, 14 November 1948.

36. Fang Jinyu, "Zhongguo faguan Mei Ruao" [Chinese Judge Mei Ruao], *Liaowang Zhoukan [Outlook Weekly],* December 1985, p. 46.

37. Mei to Wang, 16 November 1948, Mei Xiaoao and Mei Xiaokan, eds., *Mei Ruao*

Dongjing shenpan wengao [The Tokyo Trial Manuscripts of Mei Ruao] (Shanghai: Shanghai Jiaotong University Press, 2013), pp. 28–29.

38. NAI, MEA file no. 489-CJK/49, Nanjing press report, November 1948.
39. Mei to Wang, 16 November 1948, Mei and Mei, eds., *Mei Ruao Dongjing shenpan wengao*, pp. 28–29.
40. Xinhua News Agency, "Guomindang maiguo zhengfu zhuisui Meidi bihu zhanfan" [Traitorous Nationalist Government Follows American Imperialists in Protecting War Criminals], *Renmin Ribao [People's Daily]*, 23 November 1948, p. 2.
41. "Meidi baobi Riben zhanfan Zhongguo renmin jiwei fenkai" [Chinese People Feel Extremely Indignant About American Imperialists' Protection of Japanese War Criminals], *Renmin Ribao [People's Daily]*, 30 November 1948, p. 3.
42. Nagai Hitoshi, "The Tokyo War Crimes Trial," in Ikehata Setsuho and Lydia N. Yu Jose, *Philippines-Japan Relations* (Manila: Ateneo de Manila University Press, 2003), pp. 282–84.
43. "Tokyo Trial Findings," *Times* (London), 13 November 1948.
44. "Tokio Sentences," *Manchester Guardian*, 13 November 1948.
45. "The Tokio Trial," *Western Grazier* (Wilcannia), 19 November 1948, p. 2.
46. D. G. M. Jackson, "Hirohito—War Criminal," *Southern Cross* (Adelaide), 19 November 1948, p. 3.
47. NAI, MEA file no. 489-CJK/49, Canberra press report, December 1948.
48. Massey Stanley, "We've Got Rid of Tojo, But . . ." *Daily Telegraph* (Sydney), 18 November 1948, p. 8.
49. "Japan Guilty," *New York Times*, 5 November 1948, p. 24.
50. "For Posterity," *Time*, 20 December 1948, pp. 25–26.
51. "Judgment Regarded Just by the Average Japanese," *Nippon Times*, 13 November 1948, p. 1.
52. MMA, RG-6, box 15, folder 46, personal letters, 18 November 1948.
53. *Reports of General MacArthur: MacArthur in Japan: The Occupation: Military Phase* (Washington, D.C.: U.S. Government Printing Office, 1966), vol. 1 supplement, pp. 241–43.
54. MMA, RG-6, box 15, folder 46, CIC summary, 18 November 1948.
55. MMA, RG-6, box 15, folder 46, individual opinions, 18 November 1948.
56. Ozaki Yuko, *The Autobiography of Ozaki Yukio: The Struggle for Constitutional Government in Japan*, trans. Fujiko Hara (Princeton: Princeton University Press, 2001).
57. MMA, RG-6, box 15, folder 46, individual opinions, 18 November 1948.
58. BNA, FO 371/69833, Gascoigne to Bevin, 17 November 1948. NAI, MEA file no. 489, CJK/49, Gascoigne to Bevin, 1 December 1948.
59. NAI, MEA file no. 489-CJK/49, Chakravarty to Menon, 16 November 1948.
60. BNA, FO 371/69833, Gascoigne to Bevin, 17 November 1948. "Judgment Regarded Just by the Average Japanese," *Nippon Times*, 13 November 1948, p. 1.
61. AWM, Webb papers, 3DRL/2481, series 4, wallet 7, Takano to Webb, 10 November 1948.
62. "Tensei Jingo" [Vox Populi], *Asahi Shimbun*, 13 November 1948, p. 1.
63. "Sabakareta 'Nihon-koku'" [Japanese Nation Tried], *Asahi Shimbun*, 13 November 1948, p. 1.
64. "Tensei Jingo" [Vox Populi], *Asahi Shimbun*, 19 November 1948, p. 1.

28. Dissensus

1. AWM, Webb papers, 3DRL/2481, series 4, wallet 7, Webb to Chifley, 16 November 1948.
2. MMA, RG-5, box 115, folder 15, defense lawyers to MacArthur, 13 November 1948.
3. MMA, RG-5, box 115, folder 15, Bunker to Blakeney and Furness, 15 November 1948.
4. BNA, FO 371/69834, Tokyo mission to Foreign Office, 13 December 1948.
5. Allen Raymond, "5 Tokyo Judges Dissent," *New York Herald Tribune*, 14 November 1948, p. 27.
6. NARA, RG 43, box 70, *Central News* dispatch, 14 November 1948.
7. Earnest Hoberecht, "Keenan Is Held Ashamed of Shigemitsu Sentence," *Nippon Times*, 21 November 1948, pp. 1–2.
8. William J. Sebald, *With MacArthur in Japan: A Personal History of the Occupation* (New York: W. W. Norton, 1965), pp. 164–65. MMA, RG-9, box 160, War Crimes folder, Lovett to MacArthur, 21 November 1948.
9. BNA, FO 371/69833, Scott minute, 15 November 1948.
10. BNA, FO 371/69834, Milward memorandum, 15 November 1948.
11. BNA, FO 371/69834, Cheke minute, 16 November 1948.
12. Webb judgment, 1 November 1948, Neil Boister and Robert Cryer, eds., *Documents on the Tokyo International Military Tribunal: Charter, Indictment and Judgments* (Oxford: Oxford University Press, 2008), pp. 630–39.
13. NARA, RG 43, box 70, *Central News* dispatch, 14 November 1948.
14. *IMTFE Transcripts*, 14 November 1946, Kido diary, 30 November 1941, p. 10468. Koichi Kido, *The Diary of Marquis Kido, 1931–45* (Frederick, Md.: University Publications of America, 1984), 30 November 1941, p. 321.
15. Bernard dissent, 12 November 1948, Boister and Cryer, eds., *Documents on the Tokyo International Military Tribunal*, pp. 662–77.
16. Robert Cryer, "Röling in Tokyo," *Journal of International Criminal Justice*, vol. 8 (2010), pp. 1109–26.
17. NL-HaNA, 2.21.273, folder 27, Röling to Stikker, 24 November 1948.
18. Gary J. Bass, *Stay the Hand of Vengeance: The Politics of War Crimes Tribunals* (Princeton: Princeton University Press, 2000), pp. 37–57.
19. NAI, MEA file no. 489-CJK/49, Pal to Menon, 5 May 1948.
20. NAI, MEA file no. 489-CJK/49, Chakravarty to Menon, 29 July 1948.
21. B. V. A. Röling, *The Tokyo Trial and Beyond: Reflections of a Peacemonger*, ed. Antonio Cassese (Cambridge: Polity, 1993), p. 32.
22. B. V. A. Röling introduction, in C. Hosoya et al., eds., *The Tokyo War Crimes Tribunal: An International Symposium* (Tokyo: Kodansha, 1986), p. 19.
23. Röling dissent, Boister and Cryer, eds., *Documents on the Tokyo International Military Tribunal*, pp. 679–807.
24. MMA, RG-5, box 30, Jaranilla folder, Jaranilla to MacArthur, 6 and 30 March 1948.
25. Jaranilla concurring opinion, 1 November 1948, Boister and Cryer, eds., *Documents on the Tokyo International Military Tribunal*, pp. 642–59.

29. "I Am Wholly Dissenting"

1. NAI, MEA file no. 489-CJK/49, Menon note, 15 June 1948.
2. NAI, MEA file no. 489-CJK/49, Menon note, 20 July 1948; Chakravarty to Menon, 30 June 1948.
3. NAI, MEA file no. 489-CJK/49, Pal to Menon, 5 May 1948.
4. NAI, MEA file no. 489-CJK/49, diplomat official note, 18 June 1948.
5. NAI, MEA file no. 489-CJK/49, Nehru to Katju, 29 November 1948.
6. NAI, MEA file no. 489-CJK/49, Menon note, 24 August 1948.
7. NAI, MEA file no. 489-CJK/49, Menon note, 22 July 1948.
8. NAI, MEA file no. 489-CJK/49, Menon notes, 20 July and 24 August 1948.
9. NAI, MEA file no. 489-CJK/49, Menon to Krishna Menon and Rama Rau, 22 July 1948.
10. NAI, MEA file no. 489-CJK/49, Krishna Menon to Menon, 4 August 1948. BNA, DO 35/2938, Gascoigne to Bevin, 3 September 1948.
11. Caroline Elkins, *Legacy of Violence: A History of the British Empire* (New York: Alfred A. Knopf, 2022), pp. 369–71. Andrew Adonis, *Ernest Bevin: Labour's Churchill* (London: Biteback, 2020), pp. 238–45.
12. BNA, DO 35/2938, James to Tomlinson, 5 August 1948.
13. BNA, DO 35/2938, Gascoigne to Bevin, 7 September 1948.
14. BNA, DO 35/2938, Tomlinson to James, 20 August 1948. BNA, DO 35/2938, Foreign Office minutes, 7–30 August and 27 September 1948.
15. BNA, DO 35/2938, James to Tomlinson, 5 August 1948.
16. BNA, DO 35/2938, Gascoigne to Bevin, 7 September 1948.
17. BNA, DO 35/2938, Noel to Menon, 2 October 1948.
18. BNA, DO 35/2938, Tomlinson to James, 20 August 1948.
19. NAI, MEA file no. 489-CJK/49, Rama Rau to Menon, 4 August 1948.
20. NAI, MEA file no. 489-CJK/49, Chakravarty to Menon, 29 July 1948.
21. Akira Nakamura preface, Radhabinod Pal, *International Military Tribunal for the Far East: Dissentient Judgment of Justice Pal* (Tokyo: Koshuko-Kankokai, 1999), pp. iii–vii.
22. United Press, "'Race Feeling Drove Japs to War'—Indian Judge," *Argus* (Melbourne), 23 November 1948, p. 4.
23. See Latha Varadarajan, "The Trials of Imperialism," *European Journal of International Relations,* vol. 21, no. 4 (2015), pp. 793–815. Adil Hasan Khan, "Inheriting a Tragic Ethos," *AJIL Unbound,* vol. 110 (2016), pp. 25–30.
24. Radhabinod Pal, *International Military Tribunal for the Far East: Dissentient Judgment of Justice R. B. Pal* (Calcutta: Sanyal, 1953), p. 445. All subsequent quotations from Pal's dissent are from this edition.
25. David Cohen and Yuma Totani write that "Pal's opinion . . . should not be taken seriously as jurisprudence," calling it "a political tract that bends and twists both international law and the evidence before the court to reach a conclusion determined by presupposition and ideology rather than by a competent and impartial evaluation of the evidence." *The Tokyo War Crimes Tribunal: Law, History, and Jurisprudence* (Cambridge: Cambridge University Press, 2018), p. 259; see pp. 431–95.
26. Pal, *Dissentient Judgment,* pp. 63–64.
27. Christopher Bayly and Tim Harper, *Forgotten Wars: The End of Britain's Asian Empire* (London: Allen Lane, 2007).

28. "Paru hakase oi ni kataru!" [Wide-Ranging Discussion with Dr. Pal], *Bungei Shunju*, vol. 30, no. 17 (December 1952), pp. 100–108.

29. Satyabrata Pal, "My Grandfather and Japan," *India & Japan*, pamphlet on file with author.

30. Pal, *Dissentient Judgment*, pp. 1–32, 577–82.

31. Pal, *Dissentient Judgment*, pp. 124, 212.

32. Pal, *Dissentient Judgment*, p. 569.

33. Pal, *Dissentient Judgment*, pp. 32–77. See Radhabinod Pal, "International Law," *Indian Law Review*, vol. 3, no. 1 (1949), pp. 31–41.

34. Pal, *Dissentient Judgment*, pp. 32–77, 133–35.

35. Pal, *Dissentient Judgment*, pp. 431–61.

36. Pal, *Dissentient Judgment*, pp. 93–99, 116–18.

37. Pal, *Dissentient Judgment*, pp. 71–105, 134–45. See Arnold J. Toynbee, *War and Civilization* (New York: Oxford University Press, 1950), p. 145. See Arnold J. Toynbee, *A Study of History* (Oxford: Oxford University Press, 1935), vol. 6, p. 180.

38. Pal, *Dissentient Judgment*, pp. 1–31, 71–105.

39. Pal, *Dissentient Judgment*, pp. 139–73, 227–28.

40. Pal, *Dissentient Judgment*, pp. 177–93, 560–62.

41. Pal, *Dissentient Judgment*, pp. 347–82, 560–62.

42. Pal, *Dissentient Judgment*, pp. 342–44.

43. Pal, *Dissentient Judgment*, pp. 437–48.

44. Pal, *Dissentient Judgment*, pp. 193–264, 273–75.

45. Pal, *Dissentient Judgment*, p. 471.

46. Pal, *Dissentient Judgment*, pp. 267–314, 548.

47. See Mary L. Dudziak, *Cold War Civil Rights: Race and the Image of American Democracy* (Princeton: Princeton University Press, 2000), pp. 32–34, 42, 104–5.

48. See Margaret Macmillan, *Paris 1919: Six Months That Changed the World* (New York: Random House, 2001), pp. 316–21. Paul Gordon Lauren, "Diplomacy and Racial Equality at the Paris Peace Conference," *Diplomatic History*, vol. 2, no. 3 (Summer 1978), pp. 257–78.

49. Pal, *Dissentient Judgment*, p. 252.

50. Pal, *Dissentient Judgment*, pp. 315–20.

51. Gordon Risius and Michael A. Meyer, "The Protection of Prisoners of War Against Insults and Public Curiosity," *International Review of the Red Cross*, vol. 33, no. 295 (August 1993), pp. 288–99. Pal, *Dissentient Judgment*, pp. 639–93.

52. Pal, *Dissentient Judgment*, pp. 411–28. For a realist approach, see A. J. P. Taylor, *The Origins of the Second World War* (London: Hamilton, 1961).

53. Pal, *Dissentient Judgment*, pp. 315–20.

54. Pal, *Dissentient Judgment*, p. 129.

55. Pal, *Dissentient Judgment*, pp. 465–554.

56. Pal, *Dissentient Judgment*, pp. 375–82.

57. Albert Jay Nock, *Memoirs of a Superfluous Man* (New York: Harper & Brothers, 1943), p. 249.

58. Pal, *Dissentient Judgment*, pp. 465–554.

59. Pal, *Dissentient Judgment*, pp. 610–11.

60. Pal, *Dissentient Judgment*, pp. 599–609.

61. Pal, *Dissentient Judgment*, pp. 599–635.

62. Pal, *Dissentient Judgment,* pp. 639–93.

63. Pal, *Dissentient Judgment,* pp. 697–701.

64. NAI, MEA file no. 489-CJK/49, P. A. Menon note, 15 November 1948.

65. NAI, MEA file no. 489-CJK/49, Nehru to Katju, 29 November 1948.

66. NAI, MEA file no. 489-CJK/49, Dalvi to Nehru, 16 November 1948. NAI, MEA file no. 489-CJK/49, Menon note, 8 December 1948.

67. NAI, MEA file no. 489-CJK/49, news cuttings, 11–12 November 1948; Pandya note, 15 November 1948. "Hirohito 'Leader in Crime,'" *Times of India,* 13 November 1948, pp. 1–7. "Tojo Sentenced to Death," *Indian Express,* 13 November 1948, p. 1.

68. "Judgment at Last," *Times of India,* 16 November 1948, p. 6.

69. "Are War Crimes Trials Just?," *Times of India,* 21 November 1948, p. 8.

70. K. K. Basu, "Tokio Trials," *Indian Law Review,* vol. 3, no. 1 (1949), pp. 25–30.

71. BNA, FO 371/69833, Scott minute, 15 November 1948.

72. BNA, DO 35/2938, Gascoigne to Deming, 25 November 1948.

73. NAI, MEA file no. 489-CJK/49, Chakravarty to Menon, 16 November 1948.

74. L. R. Miglani, "Full Acquittal on All Charges Is Asked by Pal," *Nippon Times,* 13 November 1948, pp. 1–2.

75. Kei Ushimura, "Pal's 'Dissentient Judgment' Reconsidered," *Japan Review,* no. 19 (2007), p. 220.

76. Shinsho Hanayama, *The Way of Deliverance: Three Years with the Condemned Japanese War Criminals,* trans. Hideo Suzuki, Eiichi Noda, and James K. Sasaki (New York: Charles Scribner's Sons, 1950), pp. 186–87, 242–43.

77. BNA, DO 35/2938, Reuters, 16 November 1948.

78. NAI, MEA file no. 489-CJK/49, Canberra press report, December 1948.

79. Massey Stanley, "We've Got Rid of Tojo, But . . . ," *Daily Telegraph* (Sydney), 18 November 1948, p. 8.

80. "Asia's Voice Spoke to Us," *Sunday Sun* (Sydney), 21 November 1948, p. 23.

81. "Blames Us for Jap War Plans," *Courier-Mail* (Brisbane), 15 November 1948, p. 1. "Judge Attacks Hughes at Jap Trials," *Daily Telegraph* (Sydney), 15 November 1948, p. 4.

82. "Mr. Hughes Replies to Indian," *Advertiser* (Adelaide), 15 November 1948, p. 1.

83. NAI, MEA file no. 489-CJK/49, MEA notes, 2 December 1948; P. A. Menon note, 6 December 1948; Menon to Rama Rau, 13 December 1948.

84. NAI, MEA file no. 489-CJK/49, Nanjing press report, November 1948.

85. NAI, MEA file no. 489-CJK/49, Menon to Patel, 4 December 1948.

86. NAI, MEA file no. 489, CJK/49, Nehru to Katju, 29 November 1948.

30. Equal Justice Under Law

1. Lindesay Parrott, "M'Arthur Affirms Secrecy over Tojo," *New York Times,* 28 November 1948, p. 32.

2. "News Curb Applied over Tojo Hanging," *New York Times,* 27 November 1948, p. 7. "4 Members of Allied Council Witness Execution," *Nippon Times,* 24 December 1948, pp. 1–2. Shinsho Hanayama, *The Way of Deliverance: Three Years with the Condemned Japanese War Criminals,* trans. Hideo Suzuki, Eiichi Noda, and James K. Sasaki (New York: Charles Scribner's Sons, 1950), p. 180.

3. Lindesay Parrott, "Dooming of Tojo Impresses Japan," *New York Times*, 13 November 1948, pp. 1, 9.

4. HSTL, OF, box 1144, Blakeney appeal, 19 November 1948.

5. HSTL, OF, box 1144, Cicognani to Truman, 20 November 1948.

6. David I. Kertzer, *The Pope at War: The Secret History of Pius XII, Mussolini, and Hitler* (New York: Random House, 2022). Susan Zuccotti, *Under His Very Windows: The Vatican and the Holocaust in Italy* (New Haven: Yale University Press, 2000). Suzanne Brown-Fleming, "Granting Absolution," *Kirchliche Zeitgeschichte*, vol. 19, no. 2 (2006), pp. 359–67. Saul Friedlander, *Pius XII and the Third Reich: A Documentation*, trans. Charles Fullman (New York: Alfred A. Knopf, 1966).

7. HSTL, OF, box 1144, Vaughan to Royall, 3 December 1948.

8. BNA, FO 371/69833, Gascoigne to Bevin, 12 November 1948. "Tojo and 24 Others File Appeals with MacArthur," *New York Times*, 20 November 1948, p. 4. Howard Handleman, "SCAP's Decision on Trial Review Expected Today," *Nippon Times*, 24 November 1948, pp. 1–2.

9. MMA, RG-9, box 150, War Crimes folder, U.S. Army Ground Intelligence Division to MacArthur, 19 November 1948.

10. Earnest Hoberecht, "Keenan Is Held Ashamed of Shigemitsu Sentence," *Nippon Times,* 21 November 1948, pp. 1–2.

11. NAI, MEA file no. 489-CJK/49, Chakravarty to Menon, 13 November 1948.

12. See Kamandaki, *The Essence of Politics*, trans. Jesse Roth Knutson (Cambridge, Mass.: Harvard University Press, Murty Classical Library of India, 2021), p. 197. NAI, MEA file no. 489-CJK/49, Menon to Chakravarty, 15 November 1948. See NAI, MEA file no. 489-CJK/49, Bhadkamkar note, 30 November 1948.

13. NAI, MEA file no. 489-CJK/49, Bhadkamkar note, 3 December 1948. NAI, MEA file no. 489-CJK/49, Govind Das note, 30 November 1948. MMA, RG-9, box 161, W.D. folder, Atcheson to Marshall, 24 June 1947.

14. NAI, MEA file no. 489, CJK/49, Nehru to Katju, 29 November 1948.

15. BNA, FO 371/69833, Foreign Office minutes, 12–15 November 1948. BNA, FO 371/69833, Sargent to Shawcross, 17 November 1948. BNA, FO 371/69833, Cheke notes, 19 November 1948.

16. BNA, FO 371/69833, Cheke notes, 16 November 1948.

17. BNA, FO 371/69833, Gascoigne to Bevin, 13 November 1948. BNA, FO 371/69833, Gascoigne to Bevin, 19 November 1948.

18. BNA, FO 371/69833, Gascoigne to Bevin, 22 November 1948.

19. William J. Sebald, *With MacArthur in Japan: A Personal History of the Occupation* (New York: W. W. Norton, 1965), pp. 168–69.

20. BNA, FO 371/69833, Gascoigne to Bevin, 12 November 1948. Associated Press, "MacArthur Plans to Rule This Week in Tojo Cases," *New York Times*, 22 November 1948, p. 10. Frank L. White, "SCAP to Render Final Judgment During the Week," *Nippon Times*, 23 November 1948, p. 1.

21. BNA, FO 371/69833, Gascoigne to Bevin, 22 November 1948.

22. MMA, RG-5, box 108, folder 3, Norman to MacArthur, 23 November 1948.

23. MMA, RG-5, box 115, folder 15, memorandum for record, 23 November 1948, and 1973 Bunker notes. NAI, MEA file no. 489, CJK/49, Chakravarty to Menon, 23 November 1948. NAI, MEA file no. 489, CJK/49, Gascoigne to Bevin, 1 December 1948.

BNA, FO 371/69833, Gascoigne to Bevin, 22 November 1948. Sebald to Marshall, 22 November 1948, *FRUS 1948: The Far East and Australasia* (Washington, D.C.: U.S. Government Printing Office, 1974), vol. 6, pp. 897–98.

24. Sebald, *With MacArthur in Japan*, p. 170.

25. MMA, RG-9, box 160, War Crimes folder, MacArthur review, 24 November 1948. BNA, FO 371/69833, Gascoigne to Bevin, 24 November 1948. "MacArthur Upholds Tribunal Sentences," *Nippon Times*, 25 November 1948, p. 1.

26. Duane Hennessy, "Keenan Talks with Emperor," *Nippon Times*, 26 November 1948, pp. 1–2.

27. Lindesay Parrott, "Hirohito Expected to Keep His Throne," *New York Times*, 25 November 1948, p. 27.

28. BNA, FO 371/69834, Gascoigne to Bevin, 27 November 1948.

29. BNA, FO 371/69834, Gascoigne to Bevin, 27 November 1948.

30. Hanayama, *Way of Deliverance*, pp. 133–27.

31. "Hirota Says 'Sayonara' to Members of Family," *Nippon Times*, 30 November 1948, pp. 1–2.

32. Hanayama, *Way of Deliverance*, pp. 140–48.

33. Duane Hennessy, "Families Not to Be Given Bodies of Condemned Men," *Nippon Times*, 25 November 1948, pp. 1–2.

34. NAI, MEA file no. 489-CJK/49, Menon to Rama Rau, 13 December 1948.

35. "Hirota Says 'Sayonara' to Members of Family," *Nippon Times*, 30 November 1948, pp. 1–2.

36. *IMTFE Transcripts*, 27 January 1947, p. 16268.

37. A. C. Brackman, "Mistrial Rejected as Defense Phase of Hearing Starts," *Nippon Times*, 28 January 1947, pp. 1–2.

38. "Appeals Papers Awaited," *New York Times*, 25 November 1948, p. 27. "Supreme Court Gets 5 Appeals," *Nippon Times*, 4 December 1948, p. 1.

39. HLS, Felix Frankfurter Papers, Part I, U.S. Supreme Court, Miscellaneous case dockets, October Term 1948, folder 001755-037-0080, no. 239 (Hirota), 240 (Doihara), 248 (Kido), 29 November 1948. "Hirota, Dohihara Appeal to U.S. Supreme Court," *Nippon Times*, 1 December 1948, pp. 1–2.

40. *Milch v. United States*, 332 U.S. 789 (1947). *Brandt v. United States*, 333 U.S. 836 (1948).

41. *Koki Hirota, Petitioner, v. General of the Army Douglas MacArthur et al.*, 338 U.S. 197 (1949). Petition, 29 November 1948, *Making of Modern Law: Supreme Court Records and Briefs, 1832–1978* digital resource. U.S. Constitution, Art. I, § 8; Art. I, § 9.

42. MMA, RG-9, box 160, War Crimes folder, Royall to MacArthur, 25 and 29 November 1948.

43. MMA, RG-9, box 160, War Crimes folder, MacArthur to Royall, 26 November 1948.

44. United Press, "Hanging to Await Court's Decision on Two Appeals," *Nippon Times*, 1 December 1948, p. 1.

45. "Tojo Sees His Family Again, Perhaps for the Last Time," *Nippon Times*, 3 December 1948, pp. 1–2.

46. Robert H. Jackson, *The Struggle for Judicial Supremacy: A Study of a Crisis in American Power Politics* (New York: Alfred A. Knopf, 1941). Robert H. Jackson, *That Man: An Insider's Portrait of Franklin D. Roosevelt*, ed. John Q. Barrett (Oxford: Oxford University Press, 2003).

47. *Korematsu v. United States*, 323 U.S. 214, 243, 246 (1944). Noah Feldman, *Scorpions: The Battles and Triumphs of FDR's Great Supreme Court Justices* (New York: Twelve, 2010), pp. 249–53. Eugene V. Rostow, "The Japanese American Cases—A Disaster," *Yale Law Journal*, vol. 54, no. 3 (June 1945), pp. 489–533.

48. Robert H. Jackson, *The Nürnberg Case* (New York: Alfred A. Knopf, 1947).

49. Feldman, *Scorpions*, pp. 196–200, 274–93, 285–302, 328–34, 350–51.

50. Alpheus Thomas Mason, *Harlan Fiske Stone: Pillar of the Law* (New York: Viking, 1956), p. 716.

51. HLS, Felix Frankfurter Papers, Part I, U.S. Supreme Court, Miscellaneous case dockets, October Term 1948, folder 001755-037-0080, no. 239, 29 November 1948. MMA, RG-9, box 160, War Crimes folder, Green to MacArthur, 7 December 1948.

52. Wiley B. Rutledge, "Symposium on Constitutional Rights in Wartime," *Iowa Law Review*, vol. 29, no. 3 (March 1944), pp. 379–82, and "Some Premises of Peace," *American Bar Association Journal*, vol. 29, no. 11 (November 1943), pp. 623–28.

53. HLS, Felix Frankfurter Papers, Part I, U.S. Supreme Court, Miscellaneous case dockets, October Term 1948, folder 001755-037-0080, no. 239, 29 November 1948. Associate Justices Hugo Black, William O. Douglas, Frank Murphy, and Wiley Rutledge wanted to hear the case; Associate Justices Harold Burton, Felix Frankfurter, Stanley Reed, and Chief Justice Fred Vinson were against.

54. UM, Frank Murphy Papers, Supreme Court case files, box 74, *Hirota* file, Rutledge note, 6 December 1948.

55. Truman to Bess Truman, 11 June 1946, *Dear Bess: The Letters from Harry to Bess Truman, 1910–1959*, ed. Robert H. Ferrell (New York: W. W. Norton, 1983), p. 525.

56. Decisions Per Curiam and Orders, 335 U.S. 801, 876–81 (1948). William W. Bishop Jr., "Judicial Decisions," *American Journal of International Law*, vol. 43, no. 1 (January 1949), pp. 170–72. See BNA, FO 371/69834, Franks to Bevin, 7 December 1948; "For Posterity," *Time*, 20 December 1948, pp. 25–26; Clinton Rossiter, *The Supreme Court and the Commander in Chief* (Ithaca, N.Y.: Cornell University Press, 1951), pp. 116–20; and Glendon Schubert, *Dispassionate Justice: A Synthesis of the Judicial Opinions of Robert H. Jackson* (New York: Bobbs-Merrill, 1969), pp. 306–11.

57. HLS, Felix Frankfurter Papers, Part III, correspondence, folder 001757-014-0230, court orders, 6 December 1948. "U.S. Court Decides to Review Hirota, Dohihara Appeals," *Nippon Times*, 8 December 1948, pp. 1–2.

58. "Japanese Amazed by Court Decision," *Nippon Times*, 8 December 1948, p. 1.

59. HLS, Felix Frankfurter Papers, Part III, folder 001757-014-0230, CBS broadcast, 7 December 1948.

60. BNA, FO 371/69834, Tokyo mission to Foreign Office, 13 December 1948.

61. BNA, FO 371/69834, Gascoigne to Bevin, 8 December 1948.

62. "For Posterity," *Time*, 20 December 1948, pp. 25–26.

63. NAI, MEA file no. 489-CJK/49, Chakravarty to Menon, 14 December 1948.

64. BNA, FO 371/69834, Gascoigne to Bevin, 8 December 1948.

65. BNA, FO 371/69834, Gascoigne to Bevin, 8 December 1948. "Four More Appeals Filed with U.S. Supreme Court," *Nippon Times*, 12 December 1948, p. 1. Kimura Heitaro and Muto Akira were condemned to death, and Umezu Yoshijiro faced life in jail.

66. Hanayama, *Way of Deliverance*, pp. 214, 219.

67. Hanayama, *Way of Deliverance*, pp. 183–84.

68. BNA, FO 371/69834, Gascoigne to Foreign Office, 2 December 1948. BNA, FO 371/69834, Gascoigne to Bevin, 8 December 1948.

69. BNA, FO 371/69834, Franks to Bevin, 13 December 1948. Lovett to Perlman, 14 December 1948, *FRUS 1948*, vol. 6, pp. 925–28.

70. BNA, FO 371/69834, Franks to Bevin, 10 December 1948.

71. Decisions Per Curiam and Orders, 335 U.S. 801, 876–81 (1948).

72. BNA, FO 371/69834, press clippings, TASS, 14 December 1948.

73. BNA, FO 371/69834, Peterson to Bevin, 22 December 1948.

74. BNA, FO 371/69834, Gascoigne to Bevin, 8 December 1948. Howard Handleman, "Court's Power over Executive Acts Is Involved," *Nippon Times*, 8 December 1948, pp. 1–2.

75. NAI, MEA file no. 489-CJK/49, Chakravarty to Menon, 14 December 1948.

76. Lindesay Parrott, "High Court Ruling Puzzles Japanese," *New York Times*, 8 December 1948, p. 21.

77. NARA, RG 43, box 70, Agence France Presse, 6 December 1948.

78. Xinhua News Agency, "Meidi tuoyan chujue Ri zhanfan jing mieshi guoji fating zunyan" [American Imperialists Delay Execution of War Criminals in Defiance of the International Tribunal's Authority], *Renmin Ribao [People's Daily]*, 14 December 1948, p. 3.

79. NAI, MEA file no. 489-CJK/49, Chakravarty to Menon, 14 December 1948.

80. NAI, MEA file no. 489-CJK/49, Rama Rau to Menon, 11 December 1948.

81. NAI, MEA file no. 489-CJK/49, Menon to Rama Rau, 13 December 1948.

82. BNA, FO 371/69834, Bevin to Franks, 11 December 1948.

83. BNA, FO 371/69834, Franks to Bevin, 13 December 1948.

84. BNA, FO 371/69834, Britain to Canada, Australia, New Zealand, and India, 16 December 1948.

85. BNA, FO 371/69834, Graves to Scarlett, 17 December 1948.

86. *Koki Hirota, Petitioner, v. General of the Army Douglas MacArthur et al.*, 338 U.S. 197 (1949). Petitioner's Brief (on Petition), 16 December 1948, *Making of Modern Law: Supreme Court Records and Briefs, 1832–1978* digital resource.

87. *Koki Hirota, Petitioner, v. General of the Army Douglas MacArthur et al.*, 338 U.S. 197 (1949). Brief in Opposition (on Petition), 15 December 1948, *Making of Modern Law: Supreme Court Records and Briefs, 1832–1978* digital resource.

88. Res. 95(I), U.N. GAOR, 1st Sess., 188 U.N. Doc. A/64/Add. 1 (1948).

89. UM, Frank Murphy Papers, Supreme Court case files, box 74, *Hirota* file, hearing notes, December 1948.

90. Lewis Wood, "Plea on Japanese Excites High Court," *New York Times*, 17 December 1948, p. 9. "Right to Review Tribunal Action Argued in Court," *Nippon Times*, 18 December 1948, pp. 1–2.

91. Lewis Wood, "Tojo Hearings End in Supreme Court," *New York Times*, 18 December 1948, p. 5. "Power of Court over MacArthur Discussed in U.S.," *Nippon Times*, 19 December 1948, pp. 1–2.

92. John M. Ferren, *Salt of the Earth, Conscience of the Court: The Story of Justice Wiley Rutledge* (Chapel Hill: University of North Carolina Press, 2004), pp. 410–16.

93. J. Woodford Howard Jr., *Mr. Justice Murphy: A Political Biography* (Princeton: Princeton University Press, 1968), pp. 379–80, 466–67.

94. "Supreme Court Spurns Appeals in 6 to 1 Decision," *Nippon Times*, 22 December 1948, pp. 1–2.

95. *Hirota v. MacArthur, General of the Army, et al.*, 338 U.S. 197, 197–99 (1948). MMA, RG-9, box 160, War Crimes folder, Green to MacArthur, 21 December 1948. Lewis Wood, "Supreme Court Denies Plea of Japanese War Criminals," *New York Times*, 21 December 1948, pp. 1, 4.

96. UM, Frank Murphy Papers, Supreme Court case files, box 74, *Hirota* file, Toland to Murphy, November–December 1948. See UM, Frank Murphy Papers, Supreme Court case files, box 74, *Hirota* file, "The Japanese Cases" memo, 16 December 1948; Dykema to Murphy, November–December 1948.

97. As Jack Goldsmith and Eric Posner note, U.S. courts almost invariably defer to the executive's view of customary international law, and the executive and legislative branches decide whether the United States will comply with it. *The Limits of International Law* (Oxford: Oxford University Press, 2005), pp. 77–78.

98. *United States v. Curtiss-Wright Export Corp.*, 299 U.S. 304 (1936).

99. *Hirota v. MacArthur, General of the Army, et al.*, 338 U.S. 197, 199–215 (1948).

100. Oliver Wendell Holmes Jr., *The Common Law* (Boston: Little, Brown, 1923), p. 1.

101. NAI, MEA file no. 489-CJK/49, Chakravarty to Menon, 28 December 1948.

102. Hanayama, *Way of Deliverance*, pp. 230, 244.

103. Lindesay Parrott, "Japan Apathetic on Court's Ruling," *New York Times*, 22 December 1948, p. 9.

31. One Minute After Midnight

1. MMA, RG-9, box 159, War Crimes folder, Parks note, 5 March 1948.

2. Duane Hennessy, "Families Not to Be Given Bodies of Condemned Men," *Nippon Times*, 25 November 1948, pp. 1–2.

3. "MacArthur Upholds Tribunal Sentences," *Nippon Times*, 25 November 1948, p. 1. Hennessy, "Families Not to Be Given Bodies of Condemned Men." United Press, "New Protest Filed," *Nippon Times*, 28 November 1948, p. 2.

4. "News Curb Applied over Tojo Hanging," *New York Times*, 27 November 1948, p. 7. William J. Sebald, *With MacArthur in Japan: A Personal History of the Occupation* (New York: W. W. Norton, 1965), p. 169.

5. MMA, RG-9, box 160, War Crimes folder, MacArthur to Royall, 26 November 1948; Royall to MacArthur, 27 November 1948.

6. MMA, RG-9, box 160, War Crimes folder, Echols to Army Department, 29 November 1948. Hennessy, "Families Not to Be Given Bodies of Condemned Men." United Press, "New Protest Filed," *Nippon Times*, 28 November 1948, p. 2.

7. Sebald, *With MacArthur in Japan*, p. 172.

8. Leslie Nakashima, "Tojo Called Changed Man," *Nippon Times*, 5 December 1948, p. 1.

9. Shinsho Hanayama, *The Way of Deliverance: Three Years with the Condemned Japanese War Criminals*, trans. Hideo Suzuki, Eiichi Noda, and James K. Sasaki (New York: Charles Scribner's Sons, 1950), pp. 202–13. "Tojo and Hirota Left Memorials," *New York Times*, 23 December 1948, p. 7. On Buddhist forgiveness, see Peter Harvey, *An Introduction to Buddhist Ethics: Foundations, Values and Issues* (Cambridge: Cambridge University Press, 2000), pp. 246–48.

10. "Tojo and Hirota Left Memorials," *New York Times*, 23 December 1948, p. 7. Hanayama, *Way of Deliverance*, pp. 221–24.

11. "News Curb Applied over Tojo Hanging," *New York Times*, 27 November 1948, p. 7.

12. "No Wills Left by Seven Men Condemned to Be Hanged," *Nippon Times*, 25 November 1948, p. 1.

13. "Tensei Jingo" [Vox Populi], *Asahi Shimbun*, 13 November 1948, p. 1.

14. Arnold C. Brackman, *The Other Nuremberg: The Untold Story of the Tokyo War Crime Trials* (London: Collins, 1989), p. 449.

15. MMA, RG-5, box 115, folder 15, MacArthur to Sebald, Shang, Shaw, and Derevyanko, 22 December 1948.

16. Sebald, *With MacArthur in Japan*, p. 172.

17. Hanayama, *Way of Deliverance*, p. 195.

18. Hanayama, *Way of Deliverance*, pp. 188, 225–29.

19. "Tojo Shouts 'Banzai' to Hirohito at Death," *San Francisco Examiner*, 24 December 1948, p. 4.

20. BNA, FO 371/69834, Gascoigne to Bevin, 23 December 1948. MMA, RG-9, box 160, War Crimes folder, Echols press release, 23 December 1948. Lindesay Parrott, "Tojo and 6 Others Hanged by Allies as War Criminals," *New York Times*, 23 December 1948, pp. 1, 6. "4 Members of Allied Council Witness Execution," *Nippon Times*, 24 December 1948, pp. 1–2. Hanayama, *Way of Deliverance*, pp. 220, 225–76. Sebald, *With MacArthur in Japan*, pp. 173–75. Brackman, *Other Nuremberg*, pp. 448–53.

21. Sebald, *With MacArthur in Japan*, p. 174.

22. "News Curb Applied over Tojo Hanging," *New York Times*, 27 November 1948, p. 7.

23. Livia Albeck-Ripka and Hikari Hida, "Tojo's Ashes Were Scattered at Sea," *New York Times*, 17 June 2021, p. A10.

24. NAI, MEA file no. 489-CJK/49, Chakravarty to Menon, 28 December 1948. Lindesay Parrott, "M'Arthur Affirms Secrecy over Tojo," *New York Times*, 28 November 1948, p. 32. Lindesay Parrott, "Tojo and 6 Others Hanged by Allies as War Criminals," *New York Times*, 23 December 1948, pp. 1, 6. Ian Mutsu, "Cremation Started at 8:10 and Finished by 9:30 A.M.," *Nippon Times*, 24 December 1948, pp. 1–2. Hanayama, *Way of Deliverance*, pp. 210–11.

25. "Buddhists Here Pray for Peace," *Nippon Times*, 24 December 1948, p. 1.

26. See, for instance, Tanaka Masaaki, *Paru hakushi no kotoba: Tokyo saiban-go rainichi sa reta toki no episodo* [Dr. Pal's Words: Episodes from Dr. Pal's Visit to Japan Following the Tokyo Trial] (Tokyo: Shimonaka Kinen Zaidan [Shimonaka Memorial Foundation], 1995), p. 19.

27. NAI, MEA file no. 489-CJK/49, Chakravarty to Menon, 28 December 1948. "Tojo and 6 Others Hanged Early Thursday Morning," *Nippon Times*, 24 December 1948, p. 1. "Public Receives Hangings Calmly," *Nippon Times*, 24 December 1948, pp. 1–2.

28. "Public Receives Hangings Calmly," *Nippon Times*, 24 December 1948, pp. 1–2.

29. "Kono shokei wo igi arashimeyo" [Make These Executions Meaningful], *Mainichi Shimbun*, 23 December 1948, p. 1.

30. "Tensei Jingo" [Vox Populi], *Asahi Shimbun*, 24 December 1948, morning edition, p. 1.

31. NL-HaNA, 2.21.27, folder 27, Blakeney to Röling, 23 December 1948.

32. NARA, RG 43, box 70, *Central News* dispatch, 22 December 1948.

33. BNA, FO 371/69834, Gascoigne to Bevin, 28 December 1948.

34. Xinhua News Agency, "Fandui Meiguo shifang Riben qinhua zhanfan" [Oppose

America's Release of Japanese War Criminals Who Invaded China], *Renmin Ribao [People's Daily]*, 5 January 1949, p. 1.

35. Xinhua News Agency, "Fandui Meiguo shifang Riben qinhua zhanfan" [Oppose America's Release of Japanese War Criminals Who Invaded China], *Renmin Ribao [People's Daily]*, 5 January 1949, p. 1.

36. Sebald to Marshall, 18 October 1948, *FRUS 1948: The Far East and Australasia* (Washington, D.C.: U.S. Government Printing Office, 1974), vol. 6, pp. 872–73.

37. Sebald to Marshall, 3 June 1948, *FRUS 1948*, vol. 6, pp. 807–9. MMA, RG-9, box 159, War Crimes folder, War Department to GHQ, 20 June 1948.

38. MMA, RG-9, box 156, Army G-3 chief of staff to MacArthur, 2 December 1948.

39. *FRUS 1950: Korea* (Washington, D.C.: U.S. Government Printing Office, 1976), vol. 7, Bradley notes on Wake Island conference, 15 October 1950, p. 954.

40. BNA, DO 35/2939, Tokyo embassy to Foreign Office, 17 November 1951.

41. BNA, DO 35/2939, Tokyo embassy to Foreign Office, 3 April 1952.

42. Treaty of Peace, *American Journal of International Law*, vol. 46, no. 3, supplement (July 1952), Art. 11, pp. 71–86.

43. BNA, DO 35/2939, Dening note, 11 February 1952.

44. HSTL, OF, box 1145, Bruce to Truman, 22 August 1952. HSTL, OF, box 1145, Hopkins to Acheson, 5 September 1952. HSTL, OF, box 1145, Truman executive order, 4 September 1952. Sandra Wilson, Robert Cribb, Beatrice Trefault, and Dean Aszkielowicz, *Japanese War Criminals: The Politics of Justice After the Second World War* (New York: Columbia University Press, 2017), pp. 153–269.

45. NL-HaNA, 2.21.27, folder 27, Edith Togo to Röling, 10 May 1950.

46. NL-HaNA, 2.21.27, folder 27, Edith Togo to Röling, 14 December 1948.

47. NL-HaNA, 2.21.27, folder 27, Takamatsu to Edith Togo, 18 November 1948.

48. Maurice Hankey, *Politics, Trials and Errors* (Chicago: Regnery, 1950). NL-HaNA, 2.21.27, folder 27, Hankey to Röling, 17 February 1950, 17 May 1950. NL-HaNA, 2.21.27, folder 27, Blakeney to Röling, 20 April 1950.

49. NL-HaNA, 2.21.27, folder 27, Röling to Hankey, 23 January 1950.

50. NL-HaNA, 2.21.27, folder 27, Röling to MacArthur, 5 May 1950.

51. NL-HaNA, 2.21.27, folder 28, Röling to Blakeney, 14 November 1950.

52. NL-HaNA, 2.21.27, folder 28, Shigemitsu to Röling, 20 January 1951.

53. NL-HaNA, 2.21.27, folder 28, Röling to Hankey, 14 November 1950.

54. NL-HaNA, 2.21.27, folder 28, Shigemitsu to Hankey, 19 March 1952. Shigemitsu Mamoru, *Major Foreign Policy Speeches* (Tokyo: Ministry of Foreign Affairs, 1955).

55. Richard H. Minear, *Victors' Justice: The Tokyo War Crimes Trial* (Princeton: Princeton University Press, 1971), pp. 174–75. Wilson, Cribb, Trefault, and Aszkielowicz, *Japanese War Criminals*, pp. 224–36.

56. NL-HaNA, 2.21.27, folder 27, Blakeney to Röling, 20 April 1950. NL-HaNA, 2.21.27, folder 27, Edith Togo to Röling, 24 May 1950.

57. Togo Shigehiko, *Sofu, Togo Shigenori no shogai* [Life of Grandfather Togo Shigenori] (Tokyo: Bungei Shunju, 1993), pp. 9–18, 458–73.

58. Togo, *Sofu, Togo Shigenori no shogai*, p. 494.

59. NL-HaNA, 2.21.27, folder 27, Edith Togo to Röling, 26 March 1950.

60. NL-HaNA, 2.21.27, folder 28, Edith Togo to Röling, 16 April 1952.

32. A Silent Prayer

1. Satyabrata Pal, "My Grandfather and Japan," *India & Japan,* pamphlet on file with author.

2. MMA, RG-5, box 45, Pal folder, Pal to MacArthur, 26 April 1949.

3. Radhabinod Pal, "International Law," *Indian Law Review,* vol. 3, no. 1 (1949), pp. 31–41.

4. Fredrik Logevall, *Embers of War: The Fall of an Empire and the Makings of America's Vietnam* (New York: Random House, 2012), p. 55.

5. Radhabinod Pal, *Crimes in International Relations* (Calcutta: University of Calcutta, 1955), pp. 51–52. His italics.

6. Pal, *Crimes in International Relations,* pp. 47–49.

7. Pal, *Crimes in International Relations,* p. 382.

8. Pal, *Crimes in International Relations,* pp. 130–31.

9. Radhabinod Pal, "Future Role of the International Law Commission in the Changing World," *United Nations Review,* vol. 9, no. 9 (September 1962), pp. 29–34, 43–44. See Rohini Sen and Rashmi Raman, "Retelling Radha Binod Pal," in Frédéric Mégret and Immi Tallgren, eds., *The Dawn of a Discipline: International Criminal Justice and Its Early Exponents* (Cambridge: Cambridge University Press, 2020), pp. 242–44.

10. "South-east Calcutta," *Economic Weekly,* vol. 5, no. 48 (28 November 1953), pp. 1309–10.

11. Tanaka Masaaki, *What Really Happened in Nanking: The Refutation of a Common Myth* (Tokyo: Sekai Shuppan, 2000). Ian Buruma, *The Wages of Guilt: Memories of War in Germany and Japan* (New York: Farrar, Straus & Giroux, 1994), pp. 118–22.

12. Daqing Yang, "Convergence or Divergence?," *American Historical Review,* vol. 104, no. 3 (June 1999), p. 845.

13. Timothy Brook, "The Tokyo Judgment and the Rape of Nanking," *Journal of Asian Studies,* vol. 60, no. 3 (August 2001), p. 674.

14. Radhabinod Pal, *Nihon muzairon: Shinri no sabaki: Kyokuto kokusai gunji saiban ni okeru Indo Paru hanji no hanketsubun* [Japan Is Innocent: Judgment of Truth: Judge Pal's Judgment in the International Military Tribunal for the Far East], ed. Tanaka Masaaki (Tokyo: Taiheiyo Shuppansha, 1952). Brook, "The Tokyo Judgment and the Rape of Nanking," p. 677.

15. Yoshimatsu Masakatsu, *Senshi o yaburu: Nihon wa muzainari* [Refuting the History of the War: Japan Was Innocent] (Tokyo: Nihon Shoseki, 1952). Kei Ushimura, "Pal's 'Dissentient Judgment' Reconsidered," *Japan Review,* no. 19 (2007), pp. 215–23.

16. "Bukkyo kyotokaigi: Paru hakase rainichi toridome" [World Buddhist Congress: Dr. Pal's Visit to Japan Canceled], *Mainichi Shimbun,* 25 September 1952, p. 3.

17. Tanaka Masaaki, *Paru hakushi no kotoba: Tokyo saiban-go rainichi sa reta toki no episodo* [Dr. Pal's Words: Episodes from Dr. Pal's Visit to Japan Following the Tokyo Trial] (Tokyo: Shimonaka Kinen Zaidan [Shimonaka Memorial Foundation], 1995), pp. 13–18.

18. Tanaka, *Paru hakushi no kotoba,* pp. 41–42.

19. "Paru hakase mo rainichi" [Dr. Pal Also Coming to Japan], *Yomiuri Shimbun,* 9 October 1952, p. 3. "Bukkyo kyotokaigi: Paru hakase rainichi toridome" [World Buddhist Congress: Dr. Pal's Visit to Japan Canceled], *Mainichi Shimbun,* 25 September 1952,

p. 3. "Paru hakase rainichi kimaru" [Dr. Pal Japan Visit Set], *Asahi Shimbun*, 9 October 1952, p. 3.

20. "Ex-IMT Justice Here from India," *Nippon Times*, 16 October 1952, p. 3.

21. "'Senhan muzai wo imamo kakushin'" ["'Still Convinced of War Innocence'"], *Asahi Shimbun*, 16 October 1952, p. 3.

22. "Shinrai dekiru Nihon" [A Trustworthy Japan], *Mainichi Shimbun*, 16 October 1952, p. 3.

23. "Noted Judge Raps Japanese Party," *Nippon Times*, 17 October 1952, p. 3.

24. Purnendra Jain, "Japan's Development Assistance to India," *Japan Forum*, vol. 33, no. 2 (2021), pp. 240–60.

25. "Senhan, Nihon de sabake" [Judge the War Criminals in Japan], *Asahi Shimbun*, 17 October 1952, p. 3.

26. "Paru hakase oi ni kataru!" [Wide-Ranging Discussion with Dr. Pal], *Bungei Shunju*, vol. 30, no. 17 (December 1952), pp. 100–108.

27. "Paru hakase wo kakomu ocha no kai" [Tea Party with Dr. Pal], *Asahi Shimbun*, 28 October 1952, p. 3.

28. Natsuno Torao, "Nihon ni chokugen suru Paru hakase" [Dr. Pal Speaking Plainly to Japan], *Jinbutsu Orai*, vol. 1, no. 12 (December 1952), pp. 71–74. "Justice Pal Urges Nonviolence Stand," *Nippon Times*, 26 October 1952, p. 1.

29. "'Ganji ni manabe'" ["'Learn from Gandhi'"], *Asahi Shimbun*, 26 October 1952, p. 7. My account does not rely on Tanaka's version of this speech: Radhabinod Pal, *Heiwa no sengen* [A Declaration of Peace], ed. Tanaka Masaaki, 25 October 1952 speech (Tokyo: Shogakukan, 2008), pp. 119–29.

30. "Pal at Memorial Rites," *Nippon Times*, 27 October 1952, p. 2.

31. "Paru hakase fujin no hoyo" [Buddhist Memorial Service for Dr. Pal's Wife], *Asahi Shimbun*, 27 October 1952, p. 3.

32. "Paru Hakase koenkai kiroku" [Record of Dr. Pal's Speech], 29 October 1952, *Jiyu to Seigi [The Liberty and Justice]*, vol. 4, no. 1 (1 January 1953), pp. 44–46. The chief justice of Japan was Tanaka Kotaro.

33. "Judge Pal Is Guest of Welcome C'tee," *Nippon Times*, 21 October 1952, p. 3.

34. "Dr. Pal at Shrine," *Nippon Times*, 22 October 1952, p. 3.

35. "Paru hakase ga hanataba" [Dr. Pal Lays Flowers], *Asahi Shimbun*, 26 October 1952, p. 2.

36. Natsuno, "Nihon ni chokugen suru Paru hakase" [Dr. Pal Speaking Plainly to Japan], pp. 71–74.

37. "Senhan shakuho de kondan" [Meeting on the Release of War Criminals], *Asahi Shimbun*, 22 October 1952, p. 3.

38. "Okawa Shumei hakase Paru hakase to kandan" [A Pleasant Talk Between Dr. Okawa Shumei and Dr. Pal], *Mainichi Shimbun*, 25 October 1952, p. 7.

39. "Senhan shakuho de kondan" [Meeting on the Release of War Criminals], *Asahi Shimbun*, 22 October 1952, p. 3. "Sugamo senhan sokyu shakuho ni doryoku" [Working Toward the Speedy Release of Sugamo War Criminals], *Yomiuri Shimbun*, 22 October 1952, p. 7.

40. "ACWF to Meet in Hiroshima," *Nippon Times*, 29 October 1952, p. 3.

41. Pal speech, 2 November 1952, Asian Congress for World Federation, *Nijunen no ayumi* [Twenty Years of History], on file with author, p. 144. See "Paru-shi koenryo nado

kifu" [Mr. Pal Donates His Fees for Speaking and Other Activities], *Asahi Shimbun*, 18 October 1966, p. 14.

42. Kiyoaki Murata, "800 Attend World Meet at Hiroshima," *Nippon Times*, 4 November 1952, p. 1.

43. "'Hibaku musume' ni kando Paru hakase senso no higeki kyocho" [Moved by "Nuclear Girls," Dr. Pal Stresses Tragedy of War], *Mainichi Shimbun*, 4 November 1952, p. 3.

44. Pal speech, 4 November 1952, Asian Congress for World Federation, *Nijunen no ayumi* [Twenty Years of History], on file with author, p. 146.

45. Kiyoaki Murata, "Pal Speaks at Hiroshima," *Nippon Times*, 5 November 1952, p. 3.

46. Masuda Tsuyoshi, "Unearthed Tapes Explain a Piece of World War II History," NHK World, 22 December 2020.

47. "Paru hakase, Sugamo homon" [Dr. Pal, Visit to Sugamo], *Asahi Shimbun*, 12 November 1952, p. 7. "Paru hakase, sakuya" [Dr. Pal Returned Home Yesterday], *Mainichi Shimbun*, 12 November 1952, p. 3.

48. Nakajima Takeshi, "The Tokyo Tribunal, Justice Pal and the Revisionist Distortion of History," *Asia-Pacific Journal*, vol. 9, issue 44, no. 3 (31 October 2011), pp. 1–20.

49. Tanaka, *Paru hakushi no kotoba*, p. 23.

50. Radha Binod Pal, "Renunciation of Force in Inter-state Relations," *India Quarterly*, vol. 16, no. 4 (1960), pp. 349–57.

51. Radhabinod Pal, "The International Law in a Changing World," *All India Reporter*, vol. 48 (October–November 1961), pp. 91–102.

52. Radhabinod Pal et al., *Lectures on Universal Declaration of Human Rights* (Calcutta: Federal Hall Society, 1965), pp. 3–21.

53. Chugo Koito, "From the Japanese Magazines," *Nippon Times*, 2 March 1966, p. 12.

54. "Kyo rainichi suru moto kyokuto kokusai gunji saibansho anji Rada Binoddo Paru" [Radhabinod Pal, Former Justice at the International Military Tribunal for the Far East, Arriving in Japan Today], *Yomiuri Shimbun*, 1 October 1966, p. 3. "War Crimes Judge Here for Visit," *Nippon Times*, 3 October 1966, p. 3.

55. "Paru hakase ga rainichi" [Dr. Pal Arrives in Japan], *Yomiuri Shimbun*, 2 October 1966, p. 14.

56. "Paru hakase ni kun it-to" [First Class Order to Be Presented to Dr. Pal], *Yomiuri Shimbun*, 5 October 1966, p. 14. "Reception Held for Indian Judge," *Nippon Times*, 5 October 1966, p. 3.

57. Ichimata Masao, "Paru hakase wo mukaeru" [Welcoming Dr. Pal], *Yomiuri Shimbun*, 30 September 1966, p. 7.

58. "Kyo rainichi suru moto kyokuto kokusai gunji saibansho hanji Rada Binoddo Paru" [Radhabinod Pal, Former Justice at the International Military Tribunal for the Far East, Arriving in Japan Today], *Yomiuri Shimbun*, 1 October 1966, p. 3.

59. "Paru hakase: Kyo no mondai" [Dr. Pal: Today's Question], *Asahi Shimbun*, 6 October 1966, p. 1.

60. "Heiwa no inori, byoku wo koete" [A Prayer for Peace, Going Beyond the Pain of Illness], *Yomiuri Shimbun*, 4 October 1966, p. 15. "Henshu techo" [Editorial Notebook], *Yomiuri Shimbun*, 5 October 1966, p. 1. "Paru hakase kyo Kyoto e" [Dr. Pal to Visit Kyoto Today], *Yomiuri Shimbun*, 7 October 1966, p. 14.

61. "'Atarashii kuni ga dekita yo': Paru hakase ga saigo no kisha kaiken" ["As if a New

Country Has Been Created": Dr. Pal's Last Press Conference], *Asahi Shimbun,* 11 October 1966, p. 10.

62. "'Nihon de shinde mo yoi'" ["Would Be Happy to Die in Japan"], *Asahi Shimbun,* 13 October 1966, p. 7.

63. Pal family papers, Kolkata, "Pal-Shimonaka Memorial Hall" pamphlet, p. 3.

64. Nakajima Takeshi, "Justice Pal (India)," in Yuki Tanaka, Tim McCormack, and Gerry Simpson, eds., *Beyond Victor's Justice? The Tokyo War Crimes Trial Revisited* (Leiden: Martinus Nijhoff, 2011), p. 143.

65. Michael J. Green, *Line of Advantage: Japan's Grand Strategy in the Era of Abe Shinzo* (New York: Columbia University Press, 2022), pp. 127–29.

66. Elizabeth Roche, "Abe Praises Indians Who Backed Japan in WWII," Agence France-Presse, 23 August 2007.

67. Norimitsu Onishi, "Decades After War Trials, Japan Still Honors a Dissenting Judge," *New York Times,* 31 August 2007.

68. George Nishiyama, "Abe Risks Ire by Meeting Son of Indian Judge," Reuters, 23 August 2007.

69. "Mukherjee Hosts Banquet for Japanese Royals," Asian News International, 3 December 2013.

70. Archis Mohan, "Prime Minister Shinzo Abe's visit," Indian Ministry of External Affairs paper, 22 January 2014, http://www.mea.gov.in/in-focus-article.htm?22762 /Prime+Minister+Shinzo+Abes+visit+pinnacle+of+IndiaJapan+relations.

71. "Japan Can Help India Become USD 5 Trillion Economy," *Business Standard,* 27 June 2019.

72. Michael J. Green, "Can Tojo Inspire Modern Japan?," *SAIS Review,* vol. 19, no. 2 (1999), pp. 243–50. Charles W. Nuckolls, "The Banal Nationalism of Japanese Cinema," *Journal of Popular Culture,* vol. 39, no. 5 (2006), pp. 817–37.

73. Nakajima, "Justice Pal (India)," p. 144. See Kobayashi Yoshinori, *Senso ron* [On War] (Tokyo: Gentosha, 1998).

33. The Inescapable Purge of Comrade Mei

1. HSTL, PSF, box 152, Lovett to Clifford, 12 November 1948. HSTL, PSF, box 152, Stuart to Marshall, 12 November 1948.

2. HSTL, PSF, box 152, Stuart to Marshall, 6 November 1948. See HSTL, PSF, box 152, Army intelligence division estimate on China, August 1948.

3. HSTL, PSF, box 152, Stuart cable summarized for Truman, 10 November 1948. Odd Arne Westad, *Cold War and Revolution: Soviet-American Rivalry and the Origins of the Chinese Civil War, 1944–1946* (New York: Columbia University Press, 1993), pp. 165–78.

4. HSTL, PSF, box 152, Chiang (via Koo) to Truman, 9 November 1948. See HSTL, PSF, box 152, Chiang (via Koo) to Truman, 5 April 1948.

5. HSTL, PSF, box 152, Hillenkoetter to Truman, 24 November 1948.

6. HSTL, PSF, box 152, Marshall memcon, 3 December 1948. HSTL, PSF, box 152, Hillenkoetter memo, 10 December 1948. HSTL, PSF, box 152, Hillenkoetter memo, 15 December 1948.

7. HSTL, PSF, box 152, Marshall memcon, 3 December 1948.

8. Mei Ruao, *Dongjing da shenpan: Yuandong guoji junshi fating Zhongguo faguan Mei Ruao riji* [The Great Tokyo Trial: Diary of Mei Ruao, Chinese Judge at the International Military Tribunal for the Far East] (Nanchang: Jiangxi Education Press, 2005), 9 April 1946, p. 75.

9. Mei Ju-ao (Mei Ruao), *The Tokyo Trial Diaries of Mei Ju-ao* (Singapore: Shanghai Jiaotong University Press and Palgrave Pivot, 2019), editor's note, p. v.

10. Lai Tse-han, Ramon H. Myers, and Wei Wou, *A Tragic Beginning: The Taiwan Uprising of February 28, 1947* (Stanford, Calif.: Stanford University Press, 1991). George H. Kerr, *Formosa Betrayed* (Boston: Houghton Mifflin, 1965). Nicholas D. Kristof, "The Horror of 2-28," *New York Times*, 3 April 1992, p. A4.

11. Richard Bernstein, *China 1945: Mao's Revolution and America's Fateful Choice* (New York: Alfred A. Knopf, 2014), pp. 35–36.

12. Peter Martin, *China's Civilian Army: The Inside Story of China's Quest for Global Power* (Oxford: Oxford University Press, 2021), pp. 96–113.

13. Mei Xiaoao and Mei Xiaokan preface in Mei Xiaoao and Mei Xiaokan, eds., *Mei Ruao Dongjing shenpan wengao* [The Tokyo Trial Manuscripts of Mei Ruao] (Shanghai: Shanghai Jiaotong University Press, 2013), p. 6. Fang Jinyu, "Zhongguo faguan Mei Ruao" [Chinese Judge Mei Ruao], *Liaowang Zhoukan [Outlook Weekly]*, December 1985, p. 48.

14. Mei Ruao, "Riben de qiantu—wei jinian Riben touxiang wu zhounian er zuo" [The Future of Japan—In Commemoration of the Fifth Anniversary of Japan's Surrender], *Shijie Zhishi [World Affairs]*, no. 9 (1950), pp. 5–7. "Mei Attacks SCAP's Releasing Criminals," New China News Agency, 14 March 1950, Foreign Broadcast Information Service.

15. "Dr. Mei Gives Support to USSR Proposal," New China News Agency, 10 February 1950, Foreign Broadcast Information Service.

16. Kathryn Weathersby, "Deceiving the Deceivers," and Milton Leitenberg, "New Russian Evidence on the Korean War Biological Warfare Allegations," *Cold War International History Project Bulletin*, no. 11 (winter 1998), pp. 176–84, 185–99. W. Seth Carus, "The History of Biological Weapons Use," *Health Security*, vol. 13, no. 4 (2015), pp. 239–43. A few Chinese historians, such as Qi Dexue, still contend that China had credible evidence (Shu Guang Zhang, *Mao's Military Romanticism: China and the Korean War, 1950–1953* [Lawrence: University Press of Kansas, 1995], p. 7).

17. "Mei Ruao zhihan qian yuandong guoji junshi fating geguo faguan konggao Meijun zai wodongbei sanbu xijun zuixing" [Mei Ruao Wrote to Former Judges at the International Military Tribunal for the Far East Accusing the American Military of Spreading Germs in Our Northeast], *Renmin Ribao [People's Daily]*, 9 April 1952. See Guoshiguan, Foreign Ministry files, Hirohito and War Crimes, "Mei Ruao on Trying Emperor Hirohito," n.d., 020-010122-0001-0017a to 020-010122-0001-0018a; Jia Xiaoming, "Dui Meijun xijunzhan de diaocha gongzuo" [Investigation into the American Military's Germ Warfare], *Renmin Zhengxie Bao [People's Political Consultation Newspaper]*, 1 June 2014; and Wei Ding, *Cong Yalujiang dao sanbaxian* [From the Yalu River to the 38th Parallel] (Beijing: Jiefangjun chubanshe, 2010).

18. Frank Dikötter, *The Tragedy of Liberation: A History of the Chinese Revolution, 1945–1957* (New York: Bloomsbury, 2014).

19. Philip P. Pan, *Out of Mao's Shadow: The Struggle for the Soul of a New China* (New York: Simon & Schuster, 2008), pp. 40–46. Kenneth Lieberthal, *Governing China: From*

Revolution Through Reform (New York: W. W. Norton, 2004), pp. 66–69. Ning Wang, "Victims and Perpetrators," *Twentieth-Century China*, vol. 45, no. 2 (May 2020), pp. 188–208.

20. Fang Jinyu, "Zhongguo faguan Mei Ruao" [Chinese Judge Mei Ruao], *Liaowang Zhoukan [Outlook Weekly]*, December 1985, p. 48. Mei and Mei preface, *Mei Ruao Dongjing shenpan wengao*, p. 8.

21. Mei and Mei preface, *Mei Ruao Dongjing shenpan wengao*, pp. 4–7.

22. Central News Agency, "Ri zhanzheng zuifan kaishi shenxun" [Trial of Japanese War Criminals Begins], *Xinhua Ribao [Xinhua Daily]*, 4 May 1946, p. 3.

23. "Zhanfan de pengyou" [War Criminals' Friend], *Renmin Ribao [People's Daily]*, 10 December 1946, p. 1. "Ri zhanfan mingdan yibu yi fabiao" [List of Japanese War Criminals Has Been Partially Released], *Xinhua Ribao [Xinhua Daily]*, 6 January 1946, pp. 2. Xinhua News Agency, "Zhonggong zai dongbei de duiri zhengce yancheng zhanfan moshou diwei zangwu" [The CCP's Policy Toward Japanese People in the Northeast: Seriously Punish War Criminals and Confiscate Property Stolen by the Enemy and Puppet Forces], *Xinhua Ribao [Xinhua Daily]*, 18 May 1946, p. 2.

24. Xinhua News Agency, "Jiangfei zonrong Riben zhanfan" [Bandit Chiang Indulges Japanese War Criminals], *Renmin Ribao [People's Daily]*, 29 May 1948, p. 2.

25. Mao Zedong, "Mei diguozhuyi shi Zhong Ri liangguo renmin de gongtong diren" [American Imperialism Is the Chinese and Japanese People's Common Enemy], 21 June 1960, *Mao Zedong waijiao wenxuan* [Selected Works of Mao Zedong on Diplomacy] (Beijing: Zhongyang Wenxian Publishing House, 1994), pp. 436–43.

26. Xinhua News Agency, "Zhou Enlai buzhang wuyue shiwuri fabiao shengming" [Minister Zhou Enlai Issues a Statement on May 15], *Renmin Ribao [People's Daily]*, 16 May 1950, p. 1.

27. Guoshiguan, Foreign Ministry files, Hirohito and War Crimes, Li to Shi, 8 February 1950, 020-010122-0001-0013a to 020-010122-0001-0015a.

28. Xinhua News Agency, "Zhou Enlai waizhang fabiao shengming" [Foreign Minister Zhou Enlai Issues a Statement], *Renmin Ribao [People's Daily]*, 5 December 1950, p. 1. See Zhou Enlai, "Guanyu Mei Ying dui Ri heyue caoan ji jiujinshan huiyi de shengming" [Statement Regarding America and Britain's Draft Peace Treaty with Japan and the San Francisco Conference], 15 August 1951, *Zhou Enlai waijiao wenxuan* [Selected Works of Zhou Enlai on Diplomacy] (Beijing: Zhongyang Wenxian Publishing House, 1990), pp. 38–46.

29. Mao Zedong, "Heping gongchu wuxiang yuanze ying tuiguang dao suoyou guojia guanxi zhong qu" [The Five Principles of Peaceful Coexistence Should Be Spread to All International Relations], 19 October 1954, *Mao Zedong waijiao wenxuan*, pp. 163–76.

30. Mao Zedong, "Heping gongchu wuxiang yuanze shi yige changqi de fangzhen" [The Five Principles of Peaceful Coexistence Is a Long-Term Policy], 1 December 1954, *Mao Zedong waijiao wenxuan*, pp. 177–96.

31. *Zhou Enlai nian pu, 1949–1976* [Chronicle of Zhou Enlai, 1949–1976] (Beijing: Zhongyang Wenxian Publishing House, 1997), vol. 1, 9 June 1955, p. 487.

32. Mao Zedong, "Zhong Ri guanxi he shijiedazhan wenti" [Sino-Japanese Relations and the Question of World War], 15 October 1955, *Mao Zedong waijiao wenxuan*, pp. 219–27.

33. Sandra Wilson, Robert Cribb, Beatrice Trefault, and Dean Aszkielowicz, *Japanese*

War Criminals: The Politics of Justice After the Second World War (New York: Columbia University Press, 2017), pp. 237–38.

34. Mao Zedong, "Zhong Ri guanxi he shijiedazhan wenti" [Sino-Japanese Relations and the Question of World War], 15 October 1955, *Mao Zedong waijiao wenxuan,* pp. 219–27.

35. Chinese People's Political Consultative Conference, ed., *Huiyi gaizao zhanfan* [Recollections About the Transformation of War Criminals] (Beijing: China Culture and History Press, 2013), pp. 1–4.

36. *Zhou Enlai nian pu,* vol. 1, 28 June 1956, p. 606.

37. *Zhou Enlai nian pu,* vol. 2, 25 August 1957, p. 71.

38. Zhou Enlai, "Jiejian Cuo'e Hao, Pu Jie, Pu Yi deng ren de tanhua" [Talk During Meeting with Saga Hiro, Pu Jie, and Pu Yi], 10 June 1961, *Zhou Enlai xuanji xiajuan* [Selected Works of Zhou Enlai] (Beijing: People's Publishing House, 1980), vol. 2, pp. 316–22.

39. Mao Zedong, "Riben renmin douzheng de yingxiang shi hen shenyuan de" [The Impact of the Japanese People's Struggle Is Very Deep and Far], 14 January 1961, *Mao Zedong waijiao wenxuan,* pp. 455–62.

40. He Yinan, "National Mythmaking and the Problems of History in Sino-Japanese Relations," in Lam Peng Er, ed., *Japan's Relations with China: Facing a Rising Power* (London: Routledge, 2006), pp. 73–75. Daqing Yang, "Convergence or Divergence?," *American Historical Review,* vol. 104, no. 3 (June 1999), p. 858.

41. Mei Ruao, "About Tani Hisao, Matsui Iwane and the Nanjing Massacre," Mei and Mei, eds., *Mei Ruao Dongjing shenpan wengao,* pp. 401–19.

42. Zhou Enlai, "Yi jilei jianjin de fangshi tuijin Zhong Ri bangjiao" [Advance Sino-Japanese Relations in a Cumulative and Gradual Manner], 9 October 1963, *Zhou Enlai waijiao wenxuan,* pp. 340–48.

43. Yang, "Convergence or Divergence?," p. 858.

44. Roderick MacFarquhar, *The Origins of the Cultural Revolution: The Coming of the Cataclysm, 1961–1966* (Oxford: Oxford University Press, 1997), vol. 3, pp. 466–73. Roderick MacFarquhar and Michael Schoenhals, *Mao's Last Revolution* (Cambridge, Mass.: Belknap Press of Harvard University Press, 2006). Yang Jisheng, *The World Turned Upside Down: A History of the Cultural Revolution,* trans. Stacy Mosher and Guo Jian (New York: Farrar, Straus & Giroux, 2021), pp. 72–76.

45. MacFarquhar, *Origins of the Cultural Revolution,* vols. 1–3. Frank Dikötter, *The Cultural Revolution: A People's History, 1962–1976* (London: Bloomsbury, 2016). Andrew G. Walder, *Agents of Disorder: Inside China's Cultural Revolution* (Cambridge, Mass.: Harvard University Press, 2019).

46. Anne Thurston, *Enemies of the People: The Ordeal of the Intellectuals in China's Great Cultural Revolution* (New York: Alfred A. Knopf, 1987).

47. He Qinhua, "The Legal Bases and Present Significance of the Tokyo Trial," in Cheng Zhaoqi et al., *The Tokyo Trial: Recollections and Perspectives from China* (Cambridge: Cambridge University Press, 2016), pp. 226–41.

48. Mei and Mei preface, *Mei Ruao Dongjing shenpan wengao,* pp. 7–8.

49. Ezra F. Vogel, *Deng Xiaoping and the Transformation of China* (Cambridge, Mass.: Harvard University Press, 2011), pp. 249–65, 294–310.

50. Fang, "Zhongguo faguan Mei Ruao" [Chinese Judge Mei Ruao], pp. 39–48.

51. Wu Tingting and Jiang Yuting, "Dongjing shenpan zhihou, sanming zhongguo faguan de mingyun zouxiang" [Lives of the Three Chinese Judges After the Tokyo Trial], *Xiaoxiang Chenbao [Xiaoxiang Morning News]*, 12 November 2016.

52. Yinan He, *The Search for Reconciliation: Sino-Japanese and German-Polish Relations Since World War II* (Cambridge: Cambridge University Press, 2009), pp. 1–11, 174–233.

53. William A. Callahan, "History, Identity, and Security," *Critical Asian Studies*, vol. 38, no. 2 (2006), pp. 179–208.

54. Howard W. French, *Everything Under the Heavens: How the Past Helps Shape China's Push for Global Power* (New York: Alfred A. Knopf, 2017), pp. 201–2. Zheng Wang, *Never Forget National Humiliation: Historical Memory in Chinese Politics and Foreign Relations* (New York: Columbia University Press, 2012), pp. 96–108.

55. Jessica Chen Weiss, *Powerful Patriots: Nationalist Protest in China's Foreign Relations* (Oxford: Oxford University Press, 2014). James Reilly, *Strong Society, Smart State: The Rise of Public Opinion in China's Japan Policy* (New York: Columbia University Press, 2011). Joseph Kahn, "China Is Pushing and Scripting Anti-Japanese Protests," *New York Times*, 15 April 2005, p. A1.

56. Joseph Kahn, "China Is Pushing and Scripting Anti-Japanese Protests," *New York Times*, 15 April 2005, p. A1. Jeremy L. Wallace and Jessica Chen Weiss, "The Political Geography of Nationalist Protest in China," *China Quarterly*, vol. 222 (June 2015), pp. 403–29.

57. Allen S. Whiting, *China Eyes Japan* (Berkeley: University of California Press, 1989). Thomas J. Christensen, "Chinese Realpolitik," *Foreign Affairs* (September–October 1996), pp. 40–45.

58. French, *Everything Under the Heavens*, p. 21.

59. "Tokyo Trial Film Enjoys Big Success," Xinhua, 19 September 2006.

60. "*Tokyo Trial:* A Movie No Chinese Should Miss," China Radio International, 11 September 2006.

61. Wang Yi, "Xianzai shi zhengjiu de rizi—dianying *Dongjing Shenpan* he *Riben Chenmo*" [Now Is the Time of Salvation—*Tokyo Trial* and *Japan Sinks*], *Nanfang Renwu Zhoukan [Southern People Weekly]*, 15 September 2006.

62. Wang, *Never Forget National Humiliation*. Weiss, *Powerful Patriots*. Reilly, *Strong Society, Smart State*. For warnings about government xenophobia along with a less alarmist view of Chinese popular sentiments, see Alastair Iain Johnston, "Is Chinese Nationalism Rising?," *International Security*, vol. 41, no. 3 (Winter 2016–17), pp. 7–43. Huang Ying and Ji Xiran, "Fuqin wei Zhongguoren yingde zuiyan" [Father Earned Dignity for the Chinese People], *Huanqiu Renwu [Global People]*, August 2014, pp. 56–59.

63. Cheng et al., *Tokyo Trial*.

64. Zhong Sheng (pen name), "Dongjing shenpan de yiyi burong yiwang" [The Meaning of the Tokyo Trial Should Not Be Forgotten], *Renmin Ribao [People's Daily]*, 14 November 2016. Cao Jijun, Yan Weiqi, and Wei Na, "Women weishenme yao huiwang Dongjing shenpan?" [Why Do We Need to Revisit the Tokyo Trial?], *Guangming Ribao [Guangming Daily]*, 14 November 2016, p. 4. Chen Zhiyan, "Henduo nian lai, Zhongguoren wangque le Dongjing shenpan" [For a Long Time, the Chinese People Forgot About the Tokyo Trial], *Nanfang Zhoumo [Southern Weekly]*, 16 May 2016.

65. Gao Shihua, "Dongjing shenpan shi zhengyi de shenpan (ji nian kangri zhanzheng

shengli 70 zhounian)" [The Tokyo Trial Is a Just Trial (in Commemoration of the 70th Anniversary of the Victory of the Anti-Japanese Resistance)], *Renmin Ribao [People's Daily]*, 3 August 2015.

66. Wu Zhendong and Wu Xia, "Dongjing shenpan shi yichang zhengyi dui xie'e de dashenpan" [The Tokyo Trial Is a Great Trial of Justice Versus Evil], Xinhua, 13 November 2016.

67. Tony Saich, *From Rebel to Ruler: One Hundred Years of the Chinese Communist Party* (Cambridge, Mass.: Belknap Press of Harvard University Press, 2021).

68. Glenn Tiffert, "30 Years After Tiananmen," *Journal of Democracy,* vol. 30, no. 2 (April 2019), pp. 38–49.

69. Minxin Pei, "A Tale of Three Resolutions," *China Leadership Monitor,* no. 71 (Spring 2022). "China's Xi Jinping Cements His Status with Historic Resolution," BBC, 11 November 2021.

70. See Timothy Brook, *Collaboration: Japanese Agents and Local Elites in Wartime China* (Cambridge, Mass.: Harvard University Press, 2005).

71. Katie Stallard, *Dancing on Bones: History and Power in China, Russia and North Korea* (Oxford: Oxford University Press, 2022), pp. 186–202.

72. Suisheng Zhao, "The Patriotic Education Campaign in Xi Jinping's China," *China Leadership Monitor,* no. 75 (Spring 2023).

73. Vincent K. L. Chang, "Recalling Victory, Recounting Greatness," *China Quarterly,* vol. 248 (December 2021), pp. 1152–73.

74. Chris Buckley, "Parade Gives Chinese Leader a Platform to Show Grip on Power," *New York Times,* 4 September 2015, p. A4.

75. Xi Jinping, *The Governance of China* (Beijing: Foreign Languages Press, 2017), vol. 2, pp. 484–86.

76. "Xi Jinping's Speech at the State Commemoration for Victims of the Nanjing Massacre," Xinhuanet, 13 December 2014.

77. Xinhua News Agency, "Xi Jinping's Speech at the Commemoration of the 69th Anniversary of the Victory of the Chinese People's War of Resistance Against Japanese Aggression and the World Anti-Fascist War," *Renmin Ribao [People's Daily]*, 4 September 2014, p. 2.

78. "Xi Jinping's Speech at Lugou Bridge in Commemoration of 'July 7 Incident,'" Xinhuanet, 7 July 2017.

79. "China Sees No Universal Values," *The Economist,* 16 April 2022.

80. He, *Search for Reconciliation*, pp. 262–63.

81. Weibo, 2 May 2017.

82. Weibo, 3 November 2017.

83. "*Renmin Ribao:* Chedi qingsuan yiqie qitu danhua, waiqu, mosha lishi de yanxing" [*People's Daily*: Thoroughly Eradicate All Acts and Speeches Intended to Whitewash, Skew or Obliterate History], *Pengpai Xinwen [Pengpai News]*, 14 December 2017.

Epilogue: Martyrs of Showa

1. See Nicholas D. Kristof, "A Tojo Battles History, for Grandpa and for Japan," *New York Times,* 22 April 1999, p. A4.

2. Akiko Takenaka, *Yasukuni Shrine: History, Memory, and Japan's Unending Postwar* (Honolulu: University of Hawai'i Press, 2015).

3. Ian Buruma, *The Wages of Guilt: Memories of War in Germany and Japan* (New York: Farrar, Straus & Giroux, 1994), pp. 97–109, 112–35, 294.

4. Helen Hardacre, *Shinto: A History* (Oxford: Oxford University Press, 2017), pp. 466–67. Ian Buruma, *Inventing Japan, 1853–1964* (New York: Modern Library, 2003), p. 147. Joseph Coleman, "Japan's Revisionists Rail Against 'Masochistic' View of History," Associated Press, 4 August 1997.

5. John Delury, "The Kishi Effect," *Asian Perspective*, vol. 39, no. 3 (July–September 2015), pp. 441–60.

6. Keyao Pan, "Networking for War Criminal Amnesty," *Asia-Pacific Journal*, vol. 18, 1 April 2020, pp. 1–12.

7. Tobias S. Harris, *The Iconoclast: Shinzo Abe and the New Japan* (London: Hurst, 2020), pp. 3, 11–14.

8. Kishi Nobusuke, *Kishi Nobusuke kaikoroku: Hoshu godo to Anpo kaitei* [Memoirs of Kishi Nobusuke: The Conservative Consolidation and Security Treaty Revision] (Tokyo: Kosaido Publishing, 1983), p. 18. See Hara Yoshihisa, *Kishi Nobusuke* (Tokyo: Iwanami Shoten, 1995), pp. 121–25.

9. Kishi Nobusuke, Yatsugi Kazuo, and Ito Takashi, *Kishi Nobusuke no kaiso* [Reminiscences of Kishi Nobusuke] (Tokyo: Bungei Shunju, 1981), p. 88. See Kase Hideaki, ed., *Kishi Nobusuke no saigo no kaiso: Sono shogai to rokuju-nen Anpo* [Final Reminiscences of Kishi Nobusuke: His Life and the Security Treaty Revision of 1960] (Tokyo: Bensei, 2016), pp. 42–43.

10. Kishi, *Kishi Nobusuke kaikoroku*, p. 21.

11. Franziska Seraphim, *War Memory and Social Politics in Japan, 1945–2005* (Cambridge, Mass.: Harvard University Press, 2006), pp. 14–25.

12. Yuma Totani, *The Tokyo War Crimes Trial: The Pursuit of Justice in the Wake of World War II* (Cambridge, Mass.: Harvard University Press, 2008), pp. 190–217.

13. Togo Kazuhiko, "Development of Japan's Historical Memory," *Asian Perspective*, vol. 35 (2011), pp. 337–60.

14. Hayashi Fusao, *Daitoa senso koteiron* [Affirmation of the Greater East Asia War] (Tokyo: Bancho Shobo, 1965).

15. Yinan He, *The Search for Reconciliation: Sino-Japanese and German-Polish Relations Since World War II* (Cambridge: Cambridge University Press, 2009), pp. 122–33. Gi-Wook Shin and Daniel Sneider, eds., *History Textbooks and the Wars in Asia: Divided Memories* (London: Routledge, 2011).

16. Nobusuke Kishi, "Political Movements in Japan," *Foreign Affairs*, vol. 44, no. 1 (October 1965), p. 93.

17. "The Kishi Mission," *New York Times*, 9 December 1957, p. 34.

18. Fujita Yukihisa, "Prime Minister Kishi's Diplomacy of Reconciliation," *Japan Echo*, August 2006, pp. 24–28.

19. Tim Weiner, Stephen Engelberg, and James Sterngold, "C.I.A. Spent Millions to Support Japanese Right in 50's and 60's," *New York Times*, 9 October 1994, pp. A1, A14. Harris, *Iconoclast*, pp. 19–20. See Odd Arne Westad, *The Cold War: A World History* (New York: Basic Books, 2017), pp. 401–2.

20. Nick Kapur, *Japan at the Crossroads: Conflict and Compromise After Anpo* (Cambridge, Mass.: Harvard University Press, 2018), pp. 1–34. Buruma, *Wages of Guilt*, pp. 61–62. Eri Hotta, "Contesting Peace," *World Policy Journal*, vol. 33, no. 3 (Autumn 2016), pp. 12–20.

21. Shigeru Oda, "The Normalization of Relations Between Japan and the Republic of Korea," *American Journal of International Law*, vol. 61, no. 1 (January 1967), pp. 35–56.

22. Delury, "Kishi Effect," p. 451. Jung-Hoon Lee, "Normalization of Relations with Japan," Byung-kook Kim and Ezra F. Vogel, eds., *The Park Chung Hee Era: The Transformation of South Korea* (Cambridge, Mass.: Harvard University Press, 2011), pp. 430–56. Robert Trumbull, "Tokyo and Seoul Move Toward Tie," *New York Times*, 21 February 1965, p. 5.

23. Buruma, *Wages of Guilt*, p. 64. Seraphim, *War Memory*, p. 239.

24. Shaun O'Dwyer, "The Yasukuni Shrine and the Competing Patriotic Pasts of East Asia," *History & Memory*, vol. 22, no. 2 (Autumn 2010), pp. 147–77. Seraphim, *War Memory*, pp. 226–57. Richard Flanagan, *The Narrow Road to the Deep North* (New York: Alfred A. Knopf, 2014), pp. 23–24.

25. Totani, *Tokyo War Crimes Trial*, pp. 232–35.

26. Sheila A. Smith, *Intimate Rivals: Japanese Domestic Politics and a Rising China* (New York: Columbia University Press, 2015), pp. 73–75.

27. "Hirohito Quit Yasukuni Shrine Visits over Concerns About War Criminals," *International Herald Tribune*, 26 April 2007.

28. Seraphim, *War Memory*, pp. 245–46.

29. C. Sarah Soh, *The Comfort Women: Sexual Violence and Postcolonial Memory in Korea and Japan* (Chicago: University of Chicago Press, 2020), p. 118.

30. Hardacre, *Shinto*, pp. 456–58, 460–70. Higurashi Yoshinobu, "Yasukuni and the Enshrinement of War Criminals," *Nippon*, 24 November 2013. Akiko Takenaka, "Enshrinement Politics," *Asia-Pacific Journal*, vol. 5, no. 6 (4 June 2007), pp. 1–9. He, *Search for Reconciliation*, pp. 209–10.

31. Adam Michnik, *The Trouble with History: Morality, Revolution, and Counterrevolution* (New Haven: Yale University Press, 2014), pp. 3–16. Charles S. Maier, *The Unmasterable Past: History, Holocaust, and German National Identity* (Cambridge, Mass.: Harvard University Press, 1988).

32. Buruma, *Wages of Guilt*, p. 9.

33. Seraphim, *War Memory*, pp. 263–70. Nicholas D. Kristof, "Why a Nation of Apologizers Makes One Large Exception," *New York Times*, 12 June 1995, p. A1.

34. See Jennifer Lind, *Sorry States: Apologies in International Politics* (Ithaca, N.Y.: Cornell University Press, 2008). Lind's book argues that international reconciliation can be possible even without apologies, while warning that contrition can spark a conservative backlash. In contrast, Melissa Nobles argues that apologies matter because they shape the meaning of membership in a political community, as well as that some political elites support rights for a victimized group or wish to express a sense of guilt (*The Politics of Official Apologies* [Cambridge: Cambridge University Press, 2010], pp. ix–xi).

35. Howard W. French, *Everything Under the Heavens: How the Past Helps Shape China's Push for Global Power* (New York: Alfred A. Knopf, 2017), pp. 191–92. David E. Sanger, "Japan's Emperor Tells China Only of His 'Sadness' on War," *New York Times*, 24 October 1992, p. A1.

36. Motoko Rich, "The Long Shadows of a Failed War," *New York Times*, 29 April 2019, p. A6.

37. Linda Seig, "Japan's Akihito Pushed Imperial Boundaries to Reach Out to Asia," Reuters, 12 August 2018.

38. Asian Women's Fund, https://www.mofa.go.jp/files/100173322.pdf.

39. Murayama statement, 15 August 1995, http://www.mofa.go.jp/announce/press/pm/murayama/9508.html.

40. Eufronio M. Alip, *Philippine-Japanese Relations* (Manila: Alip & Sons, 1959), pp. 85–90.

41. Nakano Satoshi, "The Politics of Mourning," in Ikehata Setsuho and Lydia N. Yu Jose, *Philippines-Japan Relations* (Manila: Ateneo de Manila University Press, 2003), pp. 337–43. Corazon Aquino's father-in-law, Benigno Aquino Sr., was a prominent wartime collaborator with the Japanese.

42. AFP, "Japan's Akihito in Philippines to Honor War Dead," *Taipei Times,* 27 January 2016, p. 6.

43. Lydia N. Yu Jose, ed., *The Past, Love, Money and Much More: Philippines-Japan Relations Since the End of the Second World War* (Manila: Japanese Studies Program, Ateneo de Manila University, 2008).

44. "Global Opposition to U.S. Surveillance and Drones, but Limited Harm to America's Image," Pew Research Center, 14 July 2014, pp. 37–39.

45. Hardacre, *Shinto,* p. 467.

46. Harris, *Iconoclast,* p. 47.

47. "Anger as Koizumi Visits War Shrine," CNN, 13 August 2001.

48. Michael J. Green, *Line of Advantage: Japan's Grand Strategy in the Era of Abe Shinzo* (New York: Columbia University Press, 2022), p. 51. Seraphim, *War Memory,* p. 282. John Gittings, "Japan's PM Offers Apology to China," *Guardian,* 8 October 2001. Sohn Jie-Ae, "Koizumi: 'Heartfelt Remorse' for Korean Suffering," CNN, 15 October 2001.

49. Koizumi statement, 15 August 2005, https://www.mofa.go.jp/announce/announce/2005/8/0815.html.

50. Smith, *Intimate Rivals,* pp. 82–86.

51. Hotta, "Contesting Peace," p. 19.

52. "Tracking the Samurai," *The Economist,* 16 July 2022, p. 86.

53. Reiji Yoshida, "Formed in Childhood, Roots of Abe's Conservatism Go Deep," *Japan Times,* 26 December 2012.

54. Richard J. Samuels, *Securing Japan: Tokyo's Grand Strategy and the Future of East Asia* (Ithaca, N.Y.: Cornell University Press, 2008).

55. Government of Japan, Japan's Legislation for Peace and Security, March 2016, https://www.mofa.go.jp/files/000143304.pdf. Japanese cabinet decision, 1 July 2014, https://www.cas.go.jp/jp/gaiyou/jimu/pdf/anpohosei_eng.pdf.

56. Green, *Line of Advantage,* pp. 77–161. Hotta, "Contesting Peace," p. 18.

57. Harris, *Iconoclast,* pp. 47–58.

58. 164th session of the Diet, House of Representatives budget committee meeting, 10 February 2006, https://www.shugiin.go.jp/internet/itdb_kaigirokua.nsf/html/kaigirokua/001816420060210009.htm.

59. Harris, *Iconoclast,* p. 133.

60. 165th session of the Diet, House of Representatives budget committee meeting, 6 October 2006, https://www.shugiin.go.jp/internet/itdb_kaigirokua.nsf/html/kaigirokua/001816520061006003.htm.

61. Delury, "Kishi Effect," p. 455.

62. Abe statement, 183rd session of the Diet, House of Representatives budget committee meeting, 12 March 2013, https://www.shugiin.go.jp/internet/itdb_kaigirokua

.nsf/html/kaigirokua/001818320130312012.htm. Julian Ryall, "Japan PM Dismisses WWII War Crimes Trials as 'Victors' Justice,'" *Telegraph,* 14 March 2013.

63. Zhou Yongsheng, "Dongjing shenpan de zhengyixing burong Anbei tiaozhan" [The Righteousness of the Tokyo Trial Cannot Be Challenged by Abe], *Huanqiu Shibao Pinglun [Global Times Opinion],* 14 March 2013.

64. Liu Xiaoming, "China and Britain Won the War Together," *Telegraph* (London), 1 January 2014.

65. Shannon Tiezzi, "Japanese Report on the Kono Statement Draws Ire from Seoul, Beijing," *Diplomat,* 24 June 2014.

66. "LDP to Set Up Panel to Review Tokyo War Crimes Verdicts and GHQ Policies," *Asahi Shimbun,* 12 November 2015.

67. Inada statement, 178th session of the Diet, House of Representatives budget committee meeting, 26 September 2011, https://www.shugiin.go.jp/internet/itdb_kaigirokua .nsf/html/kaigirokua/001817820110926001.htm. Kana Inagaki, "Japan's Prime Minister in Waiting," *Financial Times,* 8 September 2016.

68. Sabrina Siddiqui, "Japan's PM Apologises for US War Dead—But Fails to Mention 'Comfort Women,'" *Guardian,* 29 April 2015. "Shinzo Abe at Pearl Harbor," *New York Times,* 27 December 2016. Motoko Rich, "Japan Leader's Pearl Harbor Visit, Called a First, Turns Out to Be a Fourth," *New York Times,* 27 December 2016, p. A4.

69. Daniel Hurst, "Japan's PM Offers 'Sincere Condolences' for Horrors of Second World War," *Guardian,* 7 July 2014.

70. Delury, "Kishi Effect," pp. 441–60.

71. "Japan Officially Apologizes, Offers Funds," *Korea Herald,* 28 December 2015. Jennifer Lind, "Why Shinzo Abe Thought Japan Had to Change," *Foreign Affairs,* 12 July 2022.

72. Ankit Panda, "The 'Final and Irreversible' 2015 Japan–South Korea Comfort Women Deal Unravels," *Diplomat,* 9 January 2017.

73. Tomohiro Osaki, "Abe Rejects Seoul's New Call for Apology on 'Comfort Women' Issue," *Japan Times,* 12 January 2018.

74. Sheila Jager and Rana Mitter, eds., *Ruptured Histories: War, Memory, and the Post–Cold War in Asia* (Cambridge, Mass.: Harvard University Press, 2007). Gi-Wook Shin and Daniel Sneider, *Divergent Memories: Opinion Leaders and the Asia-Pacific War* (Stanford, Calif.: Stanford Univesity Press, 2016).

75. "Japanese Public's Mood Rebounding, Abe Highly Popular," Pew Research Center, 11 July 2013.

76. "Japanese Public's Mood Rebounding, Abe Highly Popular," Pew Research Center, 11 July 2013.

77. "Stronger, Faster," *The Economist,* 20 January 2023.

78. See Richard Overy, *Blood and Ruins: The Great Imperial War, 1931–1945* (London: Allen Lane, 2021). Nobles, *Politics of Official Apologies,* p. ix.

79. John Lewis Gaddis, *The Long Peace: Inquiries into the History of the Cold War* (Oxford: Oxford University Press, 1989). Nils Petter Gleditsch, "The Decline of War," *International Studies Review,* vol. 15, no. 3 (September 2013), pp. 397–99. See, variously, Oona Hathaway and Scott J. Shapiro, *The Internationalists: How a Radical Plan to Outlaw War Remade the World* (New York: Simon & Schuster, 2018); Joshua Goldstein, *Winning the War on War: The Decline of Armed Conflict Worldwide* (New York: Dutton, 2011); Steven Pinker, *The Better Angels of Our Nature: Why Violence Has Declined* (New

York: Penguin, 2011); and, for a skeptical view, Bear F. Braumoeller, *Only the Dead: The Persistence of War in the Modern Age* (Oxford: Oxford University Press, 2019).

80. Caroline Elkins, *Legacy of Violence: A History of the British Empire* (New York: Alfred A. Knopf, 2022).

81. B. V. A. Röling introduction, in C. Hosoya et al., eds., *The Tokyo War Crimes Tribunal: An International Symposium* (Tokyo: Kodansha, 1986), p. 22.

82. Kathryn Sikkink, *The Justice Cascade: How Human Rights Prosecutions Are Changing World Politics* (New York: W. W. Norton, 2011), pp. 5–20, 96–98; Kathryn Sikkink, *Evidence for Hope: Making Human Rights Work in the 21st Century* (Princeton: Princeton University Press, 2017), pp. 207–11.

83. Telford Taylor, *Nuremberg and Vietnam: An American Tragedy* (Chicago: Quadrangle, 1970), p. 13. For a critique of Taylor for ducking the charges of aggression, see Samuel Moyn, *Humane: How the United States Abandoned Peace and Reinvented War* (New York: Farrar, Straus & Giroux, 2021), pp. 161–63, 184–91.

84. Alastair Horne, *A Savage War of Peace: Algeria, 1954–1962* (New York: New York Review Books, 2006), pp. 11–20, 543–49. Tony Judt, *The Burden of Responsibility: Blum, Camus, Aron, and the French Twentieth Century* (Chicago: University of Chicago Press, 1998), pp. 165–68.

85. "En Algérie, Macron qualifie la colonisation de « crime contre l'humanité », tollé à droite," *Le Monde*, 15 February 2017. Roger Cohen, "Not Suicide, an Assassination, Macron Says," *New York Times*, 5 March 2021, p. A13.

86. "Netherlands Apology for Indonesia 1940s Killings," BBC News, 12 September 2013. Toby Sterling and Anthony Deutsch, "Dutch Apologize for Violence in Indonesian War of Independence," Reuters, 17 February 2022.

87. John F. Burns, "In India, Queen Bows Her Head over a Massacre in 1919," *New York Times*, 15 October 1997, p. A6.

88. Nicholas Watt, "David Cameron Defends Lack of Apology for British Massacre at Amritsar," *Guardian*, 20 February 2013. Kai Schultz, "100 Years After Massacre, India Awaits an Apology," *New York Times*, 14 April 2019, p. A8. See Sathnam Sanghera, *Empireland: How Imperialism Has Shaped Modern Britain* (London: Viking, 2021).

89. Elkins, *Legacy of Violence*, pp. 641–59.

90. Richard Boudreaux and Teresa Watanabe, "Yeltsin Apologizes to Japan for Abuse of WWII Prisoners," *Los Angeles Times*, 13 October 1993. On Gorbachev and Soviet ideological abuses of history, see David Remnick, *Lenin's Tomb: The Last Days of the Soviet Empire* (New York: Random House, 1993), pp. 36–51.

91. Vladimir Putin, *75th Anniversary of the Great Victory: Shared Responsibility to History and Our Future* (Moscow: Izvestia Publishing House, 2020), pp. 9–20.

92. Steven Lee Myers, *The New Tsar: The Rise and Reign of Vladimir Putin* (New York: Alfred A. Knopf, 2015), pp. 7–12, 279–80.

93. Harris, *Iconoclast*, pp. 301–4.

94. Kyodo, "Only Japan Is Challenging Results of World War II, Lavrov Says of Islands Dispute," *Japan Times*, 20 May 2015.

95. Putin, *75th Anniversary of the Great Victory*, pp. 9, 11–12, 14, 36.

96. Putin speech on Khalkhin-Gol anniversary, 3 September 2014, http://en.kremlin.ru /events/president/news/46553.

97. Putin in *Le Figaro*, 7 May 2005, http://en.kremlin.ru/events/president/transcripts

/22949. Putin statement, 3 July 2007, http://en.kremlin.ru/events/president/news /41019. Putin speech on Holocaust and siege of Leningrad, 29 January 2018, http:// en.kremlin.ru/events/president/news/56740. Putin greetings, 3 September 2020, http://en.kremlin.ru/events/president/news/63997. Putin video address to U.N. General Assembly, 22 September 2020, http://en.kremlin.ru/events/president/news/64074. Putin statement on Nuremberg and siege of Leningrad, 23 September 2021, http:// en.kremlin.ru/events/president/news/66757.

98. Putin speech at Nuremberg Lessons forum, 20 November 2020, http://en.kremlin.ru /events/president/news/64447.

99. Putin greetings to Khabarovsk forum, 6 September 2021, http://en.kremlin.ru/events /president/news/66618.

100. Putin speech at Munich security conference, 10 February 2007, http://en.kremlin.ru /events/president/transcripts/24034. See Masha Lipman, "How Putin Plays with the Law," *The New Yorker*, 19 March 2014.

101. Putin, *75th Anniversary of the Great Victory*, pp. 37–38.

102. Putin interview with *Politika*, 15 October 2014, http://en.kremlin.ru/events/president /news/46806.

103. Putin interview, Xinhua and TASS, 1 September 2015, http://en.kremlin.ru/events /president/news/50207.

104. Noah Weisbord, *The Crime of Aggression: The Quest for Justice in an Age of Drones, Cyberattacks, Insurgents, and Autocrats* (Princeton: Princeton University Press, 2019), pp. 21–44.

105. See Stephen Kotkin, "Russia's Perpetual Geopolitics," *Foreign Affairs*, May–June 2016.

106. ABC News, Obama interview transcript, 23 July 2009.

107. "McCain: Japanese Hanged for Waterboarding," CBS News, 29 November 2007.

108. Adam Serwer, "The War-Crimes President," *The Atlantic*, 27 November 2019.

109. Nobles, *Politics of Official Apologies*, pp. xii, 104–7, 132–35.

110. Leslie Hatamiya, *Righting a Wrong: Japanese Americans and the Passage of the Civil Liberties Act of 1988* (Stanford, Calif.: Stanford University Press, 1994).

111. See G. E. M. Anscombe, "Mr Truman's Degree," *The Collected Philosophical Papers of G. E. M. Anscombe* (Oxford: Blackwell, 1981), vol. 3, pp. 62–71.

112. Richard H. Kohn, "History and the Culture Wars," *Journal of American History*, vol. 82, no. 3 (December 1995), pp. 1036–63.

113. Asada Sadao, "The Mushroom Cloud and National Psyches," *Journal of American-East Asian Relations*, vol. 4, no. 2 (Summer 1995), pp. 95–116.

114. Bruce Stokes, "70 Years After Hiroshima, Opinions Have Shifted on Use of Atomic Bomb," Pew Research Center, 4 August 2015.

115. John Hudson and Josh Dawsey, "'I Remember Pearl Harbor,'" *Washington Post*, 28 August 2018.

116. Isamu Gari, "Obama in Hiroshima 5 Years On," *Mainichi*, 27 May 2021.

117. Ben Rhodes, *The World as It Is: A Memoir of the Obama White House* (New York: Random House, 2018), pp. 372–80.

118. W. E. B. Du Bois, "Introduction," in *An Appeal to the World: A Statement of the Denial of Human Rights to Minorities in the Case of Citizens of Negro Descent in the United States of America and an Appeal to the United Nations for Redress* (New York: National Association for the Advancement of Colored People, 1947), pp. 1–14. Thomas Borstelmann, *The Cold War and the Color Line: American Race Relations in the Global Arena*

(Cambridge, Mass.: Harvard University Press, 2001), pp. 45–84. Mary L. Dudziak, *Cold War Civil Rights: Race and the Image of American Democracy* (Princeton: Princeton University Press, 2000). Keisha N. Blain, "Civil Rights International," *Foreign Affairs*, September–October 2020.

119. See Gary J. Bass, "The Cost of Presidential Racism," *New York Times*, 4 September 2020, p. A27; and *The Blood Telegram: Nixon, Kissinger, and a Forgotten Genocide* (New York: Alfred A. Knopf, 2013), pp. 5–12, 143–45, 155, 214.

120. NL-HaNA, 2.21.27, folder 11, Röling to judges, 27 July 1948.

121. *IMTFE Transcripts*, 14 April 1947, p. 19844.

122. *IMTFE Transcripts*, 26 August 1946, pp. 4300–4302.

123. Mei Ruao, *Dongjing da shenpan: Yuandong guoji junshi fating Zhongguo faguan Mei Ruao riji* [The Great Tokyo Trial: Diary of Mei Ruao, Chinese Judge at the International Military Tribunal for the Far East] (Nanchang: Jiangxi Education Press, 2005), 12 May 1946, p. 153.

124. Mae Ngai, *The Chinese Question: The Gold Rushes and Global Politics* (New York: W. W. Norton, 2021). Erika Lee, *At America's Gates: Chinese Immigration During the Exclusion Era, 1882–1943* (Chapel Hill: University of North Carolina Press, 2003).

125. W. E. B. Du Bois, *Dusk of Dawn: An Essay Toward an Autobiography of a Race Concept*, ed. Henry Louis Gates Jr. (Oxford: Oxford University Press, 2007; orig. 1940), pp. 27, 79, 116, 161. W. E. B. Du Bois, *Color and Democracy: Colonies and Peace* (New York: Harcourt, Brace, 1945), pp. 5–7. Reginald Kearney, "The Pro-Japanese Utterances of W. E. B. Du Bois," *Contributions in Black Studies*, vol. 13 (1995), pp. 201–7.

126. "How to Tell Japs from the Chinese," *Life*, 22 December 1941, pp. 81–82.

127. See Yukiko Koshiro, *Trans-Pacific Racisms and the U.S. Occupation of Japan* (New York: Columbia University Press, 1999); Christopher Thorne, *The Far Eastern War: States and Societies, 1941–1945* (London: Unwin, 1986); and Gerald Horne, *Race War: White Supremacy and the Japanese Attack on the British Empire* (New York: New York University Press, 2003).

128. Eri Hotta, "Konoe Fumimaro," in Sven Saaler and Christopher W. A. Szpilman, eds., *Pan-Asianism: A Documentary History* (Lanham, Md.: Rowman & Littlefield, 2011), vol. 1, pp. 311–17.

129. Eri Hotta, *Japan 1941: Countdown to Infamy* (New York: Alfred A. Knopf, 2013), pp. 34–37. See Steven Ward, "Race, Status, and Japanese Revisionism in the Early 1930s," *Security Studies*, vol. 22, no. 4 (Autumn 2013), pp. 607–39.

130. See, for instance, *IMTFE Transcripts*, 17 April 1947, pp. 20110–11, 20120–21, 20173–74.

131. *IMTFE Transcripts*, 17 April 1947, pp. 20110–24.

132. *IMTFE Transcripts*, 17 December 1947, pp. 35579–81.

133. *IMTFE Transcripts*, 4 November 1947, Koiso speech in 1940, pp. 32422–25.

134. B. V. A. Röling, *The Tokyo Trial and Beyond: Reflections of a Peacemonger*, ed. Antonio Cassese (Cambridge: Polity, 1993), pp. 24–25.

135. Gerhard L. Weinberg, *A World at Arms: A Global History of World War II* (Cambridge: Cambridge University Press, 1994), pp. 570–73. Buruma, *Wages of Guilt*, p. 98.

136. Hallett Abend, *My Life in China, 1926–1941* (New York: Harcourt, Brace, 1943), p. 279.

137. W. J. West, ed., *Orwell, the War Broadcasts* (London: British Broadcasting Corporation, 1985), 4 April 1942, p. 75.

138. Sarah Kovner, *Prisoners of the Empire: Inside Japanese POW Camps* (Cambridge, Mass.: Harvard University Press, 2020), p. 10.

139. Yukiko Koshiro, "East Asia's 'Melting-Pot,'" in Walter Demel and Rotem Kowner, eds., *Race and Racism in Modern East Asia: Western and Eastern Constructions* (Leiden: Brill, 2012).

140. *IMTFE Transcripts,* 14 October 1947, pp. 30759–60.

141. *IMTFE Transcripts,* 9 November 1948, p. 49134.

142. *IMTFE Transcripts,* 9 August 1946, p. 3668. See *IMTFE Transcripts,* 28 August 1947, pp. 21976–77.

143. *IMTFE Transcripts,* 23 April 1947, p. 20633.

144. John W. Dower, *War Without Mercy: Race and Power in the Pacific War* (New York: Pantheon, 1986).

145. Nobutaka Ike, *Japan's Decision for War: Records of the 1941 Policy Conferences* (Stanford, Calif.: Stanford University Press, 1967), imperial conference, 5 November 1941, pp. 236–37.

146. Kido Koichi, *The Diary of Marquis Kido, 1931–45* (Frederick, Md.: University Publications of America, 1984), 6 January 1944, pp. 373–75.

147. Kenzaburo Oe, *Hiroshima Notes,* trans. David L. Swain and Toshi Yonezawa (New York: Grove, 1981).

148. Seraphim, *War Memory,* p. 264. James M. Markham, "'All of Us Must Accept the Past,' the German President Tells M.P.'s," *New York Times,* 9 May 1985, p. A20.

Acknowledgments

It took the support of many kind people to get through a decade of difficult work.

At Knopf, my friend and editor Andrew Miller was an undaunted enthusiast even as the pages and years accumulated. His peerless editing and historical judgment illuminated the book throughout. Thanks to Reagan Arthur for her support. Chip Kidd, the best jacket designer in the business, once again made a stunning cover. Thanks to Nicholas Latimer and Kathryn Zuckerman. Tiara Sharma smoothly guided the manuscript through production, while Fred Chase did a meticulous copyedit. Ravi Mirchandani's smarts and commitment kept me going. And I miss the calm wisdom of the late Sonny Mehta, a grand literary gentleman with a profound understanding of India.

Tina Bennett unwaveringly championed this project through the years. This book could not have been written without her singular brainpower, advocacy, and friendship.

At William Morris Endeavor, Jay Mandel was gracious and helpful, while Laura Bonner, Matilda Forbes Watson, Elizabeth Sheinkman, and Raffaella De Angelis did a wonderful job with global editions.

I was lucky to be guided by a series of exceptional Japan experts. Christina Davis and Shel Garon read chunks of the manuscript and gave insightful comments. David Leheny deserves extra thanks for assisting me with conducting research in Japan, as well as carefully reading all the sections about the country. Carol Gluck, Helen Hardacre, Kiichi Fujiwara, and Sheila Smith shared their vast knowledge of Japanese history. Lee Taniguchi in Tokyo, my primary translator of Japanese documents, has for years provided superb, careful, and literary work. Romeo Marcantuoni at Waseda University did fine Japanese translations and helped me find some Japanese materials.

Thanks to Dom Ziegler, Shel Garon, Miyatake Chika, and Wakabayashi Haruko for their help while researching in Japan. Kawamura Taeko helped arrange interviews, and Nakamura Yuriko translated for me in Tokyo, Hiroshima, and Nagasaki. My thanks to Shiramizu Hiromi at the Tokyo Bar Association and Kawaguchi Miki at the World Federalist Movement of Japan for assisting in unearthing lost speeches by Radhabinod Pal.

I mourn two of my earliest mentors about Japan. One of the foremost Japanese scholars of international law in general and the Tokyo trial in particular, the late Onuma Yasuaki, taught me much both in his books and in delightful conversations in Tokyo. My friend Jim Frederick guided me on my first trip to Japan long ago, sharing his warmth for the country. An extraordinary writer and thinker, he left us much too young.

In India, my thanks to Satyabrata Pal, Madhumita Roy, and members of Radhabinod Pal's family in Delhi, Uttar Pradesh, and Kolkata for sharing memories of the judge. In Delhi, thanks to Sanjukta Talukdar, Ashok Kumar, Jagmohan Singh and his team, and the splendid staff of the National Archives of India. In Kolkata, the late Krishna Bose generously showed me around the Netaji Research Bureau, providing rich insights about India during World War II. She is another great soul lost to us.

In Beijing, Gady Epstein, John Parker, Phil Pan, Tini Tran, and Ed Wong provided encouragement and *jiaozi*. Sha Hanting helped me do interviews in Beijing and Nanjing. My thanks to Mei Xiaoao and Mei Xiaokan for sharing their memories of their father, Mei Ruao. Needless to say, my portrait and analysis of him is my own interpretation.

In Taipei, thanks to Serena Chi-ting Chuang and Yi-Lin Lou, the excellent research assistants who made it possible for me to work in the archives of the Republic of China. At the earthquake-proof Academia Historica in Taipei, thanks to Chen Li-zhen, Hayley S. Y. Chen, and the able staff in both the Zhongzheng district and Xindian branches. For help with working in Taiwan, thanks to Evan Osnos, Barbara Demick, Monique Chu, and Debby Wu, as well as Chen Yung-fa and Wu Chin-en at the Academia Sinica. Barak Kushner provided good company and historical understanding while toiling together in the Taipei archives, plus street food and drinks.

Thanks to three grand China experts for wonderful comments on the China chapters: Alastair Iain Johnston, who taught me in grad school and ever since; Rana Mitter, the leading historian of China's experience in

World War II; and Ed Wong, a great foreign correspondent. Thanks to Tom Christensen, Mary Gallagher, Eric Thun, and Lucas Tse for sharing their knowledge of modern China. Yanchuan Liu, a talented graduate student at Princeton and later the University of California, was my main translator in Chinese sources, doing a terrific job over many years. I owe a particular debt to the late Roderick MacFarquhar, a wise and generous scholar of modern China.

Christopher Capozzola, Kent Eaton, and Megan Thomas helped with research about the Philippines. James Zobel, supreme commander of the MacArthur Memorial Archives, generously helped with his holdings. Paul Bollerman translated Bert Röling's letters from Dutch. Rob Lothman tempered justice with Murphy. Princeton's librarians Ellen Ambrosone, Nancy Pressman-Levy, and Joshua Seufert gathered books and documents across Asia.

Thanks to Gabby Blum and John Goldberg for hosting a rewarding workshop on the project at Harvard Law School. Kal Raustiala provided astute comments on international law and jurisdiction. As he has done for decades, Richard Primus shared his outstanding erudition on constitutional law. Jesse Furman explained how judges actually judge. For counsel on legal and normative questions, thanks to Chris Achen, Susan Farbstein, Noah Feldman, Jack Goldsmith, Oona Hathaway, Stan Katz, Steve Macedo, Kim Lane Scheppele, Scott Shapiro, Annie Stilz, and John Witt. For wisdom on international relations and global history, thanks to David Armitage, Martha Finnemore, Michael Hiscox, the late Stanley Hoffmann, Peter Katzenstein, Steve Kotkin, Fred Logevall, Kathryn Sikkink, Jack Snyder, Michael Walzer, and Keren Yarhi-Milo.

For helpful comments on colonialism and pan-Asianism, particular thanks to Eri Hotta, and to Jeremy Adelman, David Bell, Tom Conlan, Divya Cherian, Michael Laffan, Pratap Bhanu Mehta, Gyan Prakash, and Natasha Wheatley. Princeton's history department and its Shelby Cullom Davis Center held a reading seminar on empire that helped improve the project at an early stage, while the Center for International Security and Cooperation at Stanford hosted an engaging seminar on the manuscript. Nick Anderson provided guidance on Manchuria and Ayumi Teraoka did the same on postwar Japan. David Schwimmer did discerning editing. Atul Kohli, my wise teacher on South Asia, has provided invaluable comments on India and imperialism for two books in a row.

Scott Sagan gave trenchant advice on the atomic bombings and the end of the war. Rory MacFarquhar provided sources and understanding on the Soviet Union and present-day Russia. Rafaela Dancygier pondered comparisons with postwar Germany. Harold James tracked down Chinese exchange rates. Chris Chyba shared an astrophysicist's knowledge of atomic weapons and biowarfare. Sophie Gee explained Australian politics and culture. And Alison Wakoff Loren answered horrifying medical questions.

Peter Baker, who apparently covered the Truman White House as well, read the entire manuscript and provided a crucial road map forward. Mike Grunwald read lots and urged me onward.

For letting me try out some of these ideas, thanks to Jamie Ryerson, Pamela Paul, and Laura Secor at *The New York Times,* and to Henry Finder, David Rohde, and Clare Sestanovich at *The New Yorker.* Barry Gewen, my artful editor at *The New York Times Book Review* for more than two decades, built a friendship based on our political disagreements. My thanks to my old friends Daniel Franklin, Yvonne Ryan, and Ann Wroe at *The Economist,* as well as Ed Carr, the late Peter David, and suitably anonymous others.

At Princeton, thanks to bosses Ceci Rouse, Amaney Jamal, Miguel Centeno, and Alan Patten. The University Center for Human Values and the Bobst Center for Peace and Justice provided funding for translations, while the Ogasawara Fund paid for Japanese translation and travel to Japan. The University Committee on Research in the Humanities and Social Sciences funded top-notch student research assistants: Cathy Siyao Chen, Yip Man Hui, and Tianku Lu translated Chinese documents; Koji Kawamoto, Fumika Mizuno, Kouta Ohyama, and Shun Yamaya did Japanese translations; and Katherine Hosie, Tom Koenig, Ashwin Mahadevan, and Aliya Somani helped gather documentation. And Rita Alpaugh's cheery competence repeatedly saves me from my own ineptitude.

All Souls College at Oxford provided a serene place to write frantically. I learned from Diwakar Acharya, Charlie Blackford, Santanu Das, Wolfgang Ernst, Cécile Fabre, David Gellner, Stathis Kalyvas, Sir Noel Malcolm, Louise Richardson, Sir John Vickers, Gary Walsh, and Lucia Zedner.

This project started out in Brooklyn, supported by a much-missed crew: Harry Feder, Philip Gourevitch, Hallie Levin, Larissa MacFarquhar, George Packer, David Rohde, Laura Secor, Amy Davidson Sorkin, and Alex Star. Anthony Appiah and Henry Finder shared ducklings and afikomans. My deep thanks to indispensable friends for sustaining me throughout: Nurith Aizenman, Peter Baker, Peter Canellos, Mike Dorff, Ariela Dubler, Jason Furman, Jesse Furman, Susan Glasser, Jon Gross, Rebecca Musher Gross, Mike Grunwald, Sarah Cahn Handelsman, Jed

Kolko, Jack Levy, Alison Wakoff Loren, Rebecca Noonan Murray, Richard Primus, Daisy Ridley, and Mark Wiedman.

Special thanks and love to my amazing parents, Arthur and Karen Bass. Fatherhood has been a new lesson in just how much I owe to them. My brother, Warren, provided not just fraternity but my delightful nieces, Abigail and Emma. I remember with love and admiration my grandparents: Gert and Nate, Joe and Bess. Jon, Suzanne, and Daniel Glenn have brought warmth and joy into our larger family.

My beloved wife, Katherine Glenn Bass, is in all seasons a heaven-sent partner and a fantastic mother to our little girl. She enjoyed a decade of a husband whose mind was somewhere in the late 1940s; she brought me back with love, care, and timely baking.

I began this book years before my daughter, Miriam, was born; now she is seven years old. As she grows, she remains the most miraculously sweet, wise, loving, smart, brave, silly, cheerful, beautiful, and funny person. She provided giggles and cuddles, inspiration and joy, laughter and love. This book is for you, my darling precious child, with all the love in my heart. May you only know peace.

Index

Illustration Credits

A Note About the Author

GARY J. BASS is the author, most recently, of *The Blood Telegram: Nixon, Kissinger, and a Forgotten Genocide,* which was a finalist for the Pulitzer Prize in general nonfiction and won the Arthur Ross Book Award from the Council on Foreign Relations, the Bernard Schwartz Book Award from the Asia Society, the Lionel Gelber Prize, and the Cundill Prize in Historical Literature, among other awards. He is a professor of politics and international affairs at Princeton University. His previous books are *Freedom's Battle: The Origins of Humanitarian Intervention* and *Stay the Hand of Vengeance: The Politics of War Crimes Tribunals.* He has written articles for *Ethics, International Security, Philosophy & Public Affairs, The Yale Journal of International Law,* and other scholarly journals. A former reporter for *The Economist,* he often writes for *The New York Times* and has also written for *The New Yorker, The Washington Post, The Atlantic, Foreign Affairs,* and other publications.

A Note on the Type

This book was set in a modern adaptation of a type designed by William Caslon (1692–1766). The Caslon face, an artistic, easily read type, has enjoyed more than two centuries of popularity in the English-speaking world. This version, with its even balance and honest letterforms, was designed by Carol Twombly for the Adobe Corporation and released in 1990.

Composed by North Market Street Graphics
Lancaster, Pennsylvania

Printed and bound by LSC Communications
Crawfordsville, Indiana

Designed by Michael Collica